HOLT

ELEMENTS OF LITERATURE®

Sixth Course

ESSENTIALS OF BRITISH AND WORLD LITERATURE

HOLT, RINEHART AND WINSTON

A Harcourt Education Company

Orlando • **Austin** • New York • San Diego • London

Cover
Photo Credits: (Inset) *Houses of Parliament from Westminster Bridge,* 1906 by André Derain (1880–1954). Oil on canvas. 73.6 x 92 cm. © The Cleveland Museum of Art, Leonard C. Hanna, Jr. Fund, 1983.67. © 2005 Artists Rights Society (ARS), New York/ADAGP, Paris. (Background) Big Ben. © Jon Bower/Alamy.

Acknowledgments appear on pages 1255–1257, which are an extension of the copyright page.

Printed in the United States of America

ISBN 0-03-079379-3

1 2 3 4 048 10 09 08 07 06

Language Arts Standards

The following chart lists Pennsylvania's Academic Standards for Reading, Writing, and Speaking and Listening. These standards describe what you are expected to learn and do as a Pennsylvania high school student. The standards are divided into eight categories. Each standard appears in a yellow box. Below each standard, you will find either an explanation or a more detailed list of the standard's content. To the right of each standard is a specific example of how *Elements of Literature* helps you meet that standard.

1.1. LEARNING TO READ INDEPENDENTLY

1.1.11.A. Locate various texts, media and traditional resources for assigned and independent projects before reading.

This textbook presents information on locating various kinds of texts in a library, on the Internet, or through community resources. You will find strategies for identifying appropriate texts for a specific school purpose or for your own enjoyment and information. You'll get practice in locating traditional resources by using the card catalog and the *Readers' Guide to Periodical Literature,* as well as practice using almanacs, media sources, and electronic resources such as the Internet.

EXAMPLE: Locating Texts for Different Purposes

You will find suggestions for independent reading of fiction and nonfiction at the end of each collection.

For information on library, Internet, and community resources, see the Writing Workshop "Reporting Literary Research" on pages 240–259. Note especially the chart on page 242.

The Media Workshop "Analyzing and Using Media" on pages 1344–1351 contains ideas for finding print and electronic media sources.

1.1.11.B. Analyze the structure of informational materials explaining how authors used these to achieve their purposes.

To master this standard, you will learn about the ways authors help you locate and comprehend information. You will practice identifying organizational structures such as logical order and order of importance. You'll also analyze features of print material (titles, subtitles, headings, tables of contents, indices) as well as graphic organizers such as charts and diagrams.

EXAMPLE: Analyzing Structure

The feature "Noting Patterns of Organization" on page 637 introduces you to patterns of organization in a persuasive argument. Boxed questions throughout the selection that follows help you analyze its structure.

The Writer's Handbook explains several organizational patterns. See especially pages 1387–1388 for charts showing types of order and strategies for connecting ideas. The Writer's Handbook also helps you analyze design elements. See "Designing Your Writing," pages 1391–1394.

Academic Standards

1.1.11.C. Use knowledge of root words and words from literary works to recognize and understand the meaning of new words during reading. Use these words accurately in speaking and writing.

You will find clues to the meaning of a word by studying its root, the part that establishes its core meaning. You'll also look at the words surrounding an unfamiliar word for context clues that help you guess its meaning.

EXAMPLE: Learning New Words

Root: The Latin root *-tract-* means "pull" or "drag." You find this root in the words *contract, detract,* and *traction.* For a list of Greek and Latin roots, see pages 1375–1376.

Context: Many exercises in this textbook give you practice in determining the meaning of a new word from its context. "Using Context Clues" on page 792 explains and gives you practice with restatement, comparison, contrast, and synonym clues.

1.1.11.D. Identify, describe, evaluate and synthesize the essential ideas in text. Assess those reading strategies that were most effective in learning from a variety of texts.

Finding essential ideas and evaluating them require reading skills such as predicting, questioning, visualizing, retelling, and finding implicitly stated main ideas.

EXAMPLE: Focusing on What's Important

In Reading Matters (pages 1363–1376), you'll find tips for improving your comprehension, especially when the text is difficult to read. After each reading strategy is introduced, you'll find a Reading Up Close feature that gives you additional help and practice. See, for example, "Question the Text" on page 1367 with the Reading Up Close on pages 1367–1368.

1.1.11.E. Establish a reading vocabulary by identifying and correctly using new words acquired through the study of their relationships to other words. Use a dictionary or related reference.

You will expand your vocabulary by recognizing new words; seeking connections between those words and other, related words; and using reference sources such as dictionaries.

EXAMPLE: Building Vocabulary

Several types of Vocabulary Development exercises help you master this standard. One type shows you how to compare pairs of words that are related in the same way. For example, see "Analyzing Word Analogies" on page 1297. Another type shows you how to use a dictionary to make an etymology (word history) map of words related to each other (see page 613).

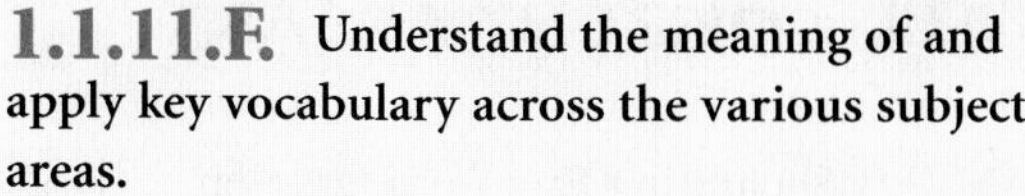

1.1.11.F. Understand the meaning of and apply key vocabulary across the various subject areas.

Many subjects have their own key words, such as *isosceles* in math and *polymorphous* in science. Applying a knowledge of word derivations is one way to figure out what words mean.

EXAMPLE: Learning Key Vocabulary

Key words in subject areas often have their origins in other languages. Turn to "Scientific and Mathematical Words Derived from Greek and Latin" on pages 413–414 for a lesson that shows you how words are built from Greek and Latin roots and affixes.

Also see "The Etymology of Political Science and Historical Terms" on page 1124.

1.1.11.G. Demonstrate after reading understanding and interpretation of both fiction and nonfiction text, including public documents.

This standard includes (1) Make, and support with evidence, assertions about texts. (2) Compare and contrast texts using themes, settings, characters and ideas. (3) Make extensions to related ideas, topics or information. (4) Assess the validity of the document based on context. (5) Analyze the positions, arguments and evidence in public documents. (6) Evaluate the author's strategies. (7) Critique public documents to identify strategies common in public discourse.

EXAMPLE: Demonstrating Understanding

Several collections include Political Points of View features that ask you to examine texts that explore an important issue. On pages 1306–1328, for example, you will compare ideas about human rights across the following: Ha Jin's short story "Saboteur," the Preamble to the United Nations' Universal Declaration of Human Rights, an excerpt from Desmond Tutu's speech "The Question of South Africa," and an excerpt from Aung San Suu Kyi's speech "Towards a True Refuge."

For help with the critiquing of public documents, see "Persuasive Documents," pages 1379–1380.

1.1.11.H. Demonstrate fluency and comprehension in reading.

This standard includes (1) Read familiar materials aloud with accuracy. (2) Self-correct mistakes. (3) Use appropriate rhythm, flow, meter and pronunciation. (4) Read a variety of genres and types of text. (5) Demonstrate comprehension.

EXAMPLE: Reading Fluently

"Improving Your Reading Rate" (pages 1373–1374) shows you how to figure your reading speed and change it to fit your purpose for reading.

The Listening and Speaking Workshop "Reciting Literature" (pages 550–551) guides you through preparing and performing the recitation of a literary work. Listening and Speaking assignments as well as Reading Skills lessons throughout the book give you opportunities to read different kinds of text.

1.2. READING CRITICALLY IN ALL CONTENT AREAS

1.2.11.A. Read and understand essential content of informational texts and documents in all academic areas.

This standard includes (1) Differentiate fact from opinion across a variety of texts by using complete and accurate information, coherent arguments and points of view. (2) Distinguish between essential and nonessential information across a variety of sources, identifying the use of proper references or authorities and propaganda techniques where present. (3) Use teacher and student established criteria for making decisions and drawing conclusions. (4) Evaluate text organization and content to determine the author's purpose and effectiveness according to the author's theses, accuracy, thoroughness, logic and reasoning.

EXAMPLE: Separating Fact from Opinion

The following examples are from "I Believe in a British Empire" on page 1135, paragraph 3.

Fact: "Here in the United Kingdom there are some forty millions of us."

Opinion: "Now is the time when we can mold that Empire and when we and those who live with us can decide its future destinies."

For more about facts, opinions, logical fallacies, and propaganda techniques, see "Presenting and Analyzing Speeches," pages 1352–1353.

The boxed questions throughout the excerpt from *The Education of Women* (pages 647–649) help you analyze the author's main ideas and argument as well as identify point of view and bias.

1.2.11.B. Use and understand a variety of media and evaluate the quality of material produced.

This standard includes (1) Select appropriate electronic media for research and evaluate the quality of the information received. (2) Explain how the techniques used in electronic media modify traditional forms of discourse for different purposes. (3) Use, design and develop a media project to demonstrate understanding (e.g., a major writer or literary period or movement).

EXAMPLE: Using and Understanding Media

The Media Workshop "Analyzing and Using Media" (pages 1344–1351) gives you practice interpreting, analyzing, and using the techniques of mass media. You will select a contemporary culture or country that interests you, choose one or more pieces of literature that reflect that culture or country, and organize a multimedia presentation of text, images, and sounds. Finally, after rehearsing and soliciting feedback, you will deliver your presentation.

1.2.11.C. Produce work in at least one literary genre that follows the conventions of the genre.

This standard requires you to create a short story, poem, play, or essay that follows the rules of that particular type of writing.

EXAMPLE: Producing Your Own Work

The Mini-Workshop "Writing a Short Story" (pages 1249–1250) gives step-by-step instruction for writing a story that follows the conventions of the genre. The Writing Workshop "Writing a Reflective Essay" (pages 856–863) guides you through writing one kind of essay.

1.3. READING, ANALYZING AND INTERPRETING LITERATURE

1.3.11.A. Read and understand works of literature.

A major goal of Pennsylvania's standards is that you learn to read literary works and to comprehend them.

EXAMPLE: Reading and Understanding

The introduction to each literary period places the literature in its historical and cultural context. For example, see "The Renaissance 1485–1660" by C. F. Main on pages 274–290. Response and Analysis pages throughout the textbook help you understand what you have read and extend the ideas in your own life.

1.3.11.B. Analyze the relationships, uses and effectiveness of literary elements used by one or more authors in similar genres including characterization, setting, plot, theme, point of view, tone and style.

You will evaluate characterization, analyze setting, recognize the building blocks of plot, and look at how authors use theme, point of view, tone, and style to evoke emotions and create meaning.

EXAMPLE: Analyzing Literary Elements

Each Before You Read page introduces you to a literary element that will be the focus of a particular selection. Following the selection you will find Response and Analysis questions that ask you to apply your knowledge of the element. For example, see page 343 on tone in John Donne's "Meditation 17." The use of tone by several other authors is analyzed throughout the textbook. See, for example, questions on tone (page 612) in Alexander Pope's "The Rape of the Lock."

1.3.11.C. Analyze the effectiveness, in terms of literary quality, of the author's use of literary devices.

This standard includes (1) Sound techniques (e.g., rhyme, rhythm, meter, alliteration). (2) Figurative language (e.g., personification, simile, metaphor, hyperbole, irony, satire). (3) Literary structures (e.g., foreshadowing, flashbacks, progressive and digressive time).

EXAMPLE: Analyzing Literary Devices

See the Before You Read (page 580) on verbal irony introducing Jonathan Swift's "A Modest Proposal." Note also the boxed questions on irony and satire throughout the selection.

To examine the effectiveness of literary devices in two versions of Psalm 23, the writing activity on page 377 asks you to begin by organizing details graphically. You will list the main ideas, imagery, sound effects, and syntax of each version on a chart. Then, you will write an essay giving your opinion about which version of the psalm is more effective in terms of literary quality.

Academic Standards

1.3.11.D. Analyze and evaluate in poetry the appropriateness of diction and figurative language (e.g., irony, understatement, overstatement, paradox).

The textbook gives you more than eighty poems to analyze, evaluate, and enjoy. Many of the poems focus on diction (word choice) and various kinds of figurative language.

EXAMPLE: Analyzing Diction and Figurative Language

W. H. Auden's diction is the focus of the Before You Read (page 1264) introducing "Musée des Beaux Arts."

Paradox—a seeming contradiction that is actually true—is illustrated in John Donne's "Death Be Not Proud" (page 349). This sonnet also contains one of the best-known examples of personification.

1.3.11.E. Analyze how a scriptwriter's use of words creates tone and mood, and how choice of words advances the theme or purpose of the work.

This standard emphasizes the influence of word choice on tone (the writer's attitude towards a subject, a character, or the audience) and mood (the atmosphere or feeling that a work evokes).

EXAMPLE: Paraphrasing Shakespeare

The writing assignment that follows four excerpts from Shakespeare's plays (pages 328–334) asks you to paraphrase one excerpt. Paraphrasing helps you understand how a playwright uses words to create tone and mood. Here's an example:

Hamlet: "To be, or not to be—that is the question."

Paraphrase: Should I keep living, or should I die? That's the question I need to answer.

1.3.11.F. Read and respond to nonfiction and fiction including poetry and drama.

To address this standard, you will read different types of texts for different purposes. You will read and respond to fiction (such as poems, short stories, and novels) for enjoyment and to learn about the elements of literature. You will read nonfiction works (such as essays, newspaper and magazine articles, and public documents) and learn reading strategies that will help you take information and ideas from texts.

EXAMPLE: Responding to Texts

Poetry: Poems by Robert Herrick and Andrew Marvell (pages 299–304) portray England in the late 1500s as an ideal, pastoral place of innocent pleasure and happiness.

Nonfiction: "Give Us This Day Our Daily Bread" (pages 305–306) is a related informational piece that describes the difficult lives of most English youths in the time of Herrick and Marlowe.

The Response and Analysis page following the selections asks you to respond to all three works.

1.4. TYPES OF WRITING

1.4.11.A. Write short stories, poems and plays.

This standard includes (1) Apply varying organizational methods. (2) Use relevant illustrations. (3) Utilize dialogue. (4) Apply literary conflict. (5) Include varying characteristics (e.g., from limerick to epic, from whimsical to dramatic). (6) Include literary elements. (7) Use literary devices.

EXAMPLE: Writing Stories, Poems, and Plays

The Mini-Workshop on pages 1249–1250 guides you through the process of writing a short story.

Several writing assignments throughout the textbook suggest that you write various kinds of poems and dialogue. On page 1168, for example, you are asked to write a poem describing your own ideal place of peace.

1.4.11.B. Write complex informational pieces (e.g., research papers, analyses, evaluations, essays).

This standard includes (1) Include a variety of methods to develop the main idea. (2) Use precise language and specific detail. (3) Include cause and effect. (4) Use relevant graphics (e.g., maps, charts, graphs, tables, illustrations, photographs). (5) Use primary and secondary sources.

EXAMPLE: Writing for a Variety of Purposes

The six Writing Workshops and three Mini-Workshops walk you through such tasks as writing essays, a research report, and a literary analysis. On the Response and Analysis pages following the selections (see page 165, for example) you'll find at least one writing assignment.

See "Designing Your Writing" (pages 1391–1394) for information on using graphics.

1.4.11.C. Write persuasive pieces.

This standard includes (1) Include a clearly stated position or opinion. (2) Include convincing, elaborated and properly cited evidence. (3) Develop reader interest. (4) Anticipate and counter reader concerns and arguments. (5) Include a variety of methods to advance the argument or position.

EXAMPLE: Writing Persuasive Essays

A Mini-Workshop "Writing a Persuasive Essay" (pages 1101–1102) takes you step-by-step through the process of writing a good persuasive essay. On page 1408, you will find guidelines for writing a persuasive composition in response to a testing prompt.

1.4.11.D. Maintain a written record of activities, course work, experience, honors and interests.

Keeping a journal can become a valuable resource that you will turn to many times as you grow older.

EXAMPLE: Keeping Track

"Writing a Reflective Essay" (pages 856–863) will help you record a meaningful personal experience. Also, several writing activities in this textbook ask you to create journal entries (pages 818, 1204, and 1317).

1.4.11.E. **Write a personal resume.**

A résumé summarizes your education and work experience to help a potential employer decide whether to hire you.

EXAMPLE: Writing a Résumé

For a useful résumé model, see pages 1380–1382.

1.5. QUALITY OF WRITING

1.5.11.A. **Write with a sharp, distinct focus.**

This standard includes (1) Identify topic, task and audience. (2) Establish and maintain a single point of view.

EXAMPLE: Writing with a Focus

The Writing Workshops and Mini-Workshops will help you consider focus in the prewriting stage of the writing process. See, for example, "Consider Audience and Purpose" (page 97).

1.5.11.B. **Write using well-developed content appropriate for the topic.**

This standard includes (1) Gather, determine validity and reliability of, analyze and organize information. (2) Employ the most effective format for purpose and audience. (3) Write fully developed paragraphs that have details and information specific to the topic and relevant to the focus.

EXAMPLE: Developing Content

Pages 1383–1388 of the Writer's Handbook review the writing process and give examples of a paragraph's main idea as well as types of supporting sentences (sensory details, facts and statistics, examples, and several other kinds of evidence). Also see "Designing Your Writing" (pages 1391–1394) for ideas on format and design.

1.5.11.C. **Write with controlled and/or subtle organization.**

This standard includes (1) Sustain a logical order throughout the piece. (2) Include an effective introduction and conclusion.

EXAMPLE: Keeping Order

For guidelines on the different ways to order and connect ideas (including a list of transitions), see pages 1387–1388 of the Writer's Handbook.

1.5.11.D. **Write with a command of the stylistic aspects of composition.**

This standard includes (1) Use different types and lengths of sentences. (2) Use precise language.

EXAMPLE: Improving Your Style

The Language Handbook will give you ideas for improving your writing style (pages 1450–1453). In addition, Grammar Links throughout the textbook give you practice in varying your sentences. See page 1078, for example.

1.5.11.E. Revise writing to improve style, word choice, sentence variety and subtlety of meaning after rethinking how questions of purpose, audience and genre have been addressed.

There are many ways to express the same idea. When you pay attention to subtleties—fine distinctions in language—you look for the best way.

EXAMPLE: Improving Words and Sentences

See "The Writer's Language" on pages 1389–1390 of the Writer's Handbook, for style techniques.

Each Writing Workshop includes an annotated Writer's Model and a rubric with evaluation questions, tips, and revision techniques to help you improve your first draft. There is also a feature called Style Guidelines in every Writing Workshop.

1.5.11.F. Edit writing using the conventions of language.

This standard includes (1) Spell all words correctly. (2) Use capital letters correctly. (3) Punctuate correctly. (4) Use nouns, pronouns, verbs, adjectives, adverbs, conjunctions, prepositions and interjections properly. (5) Use complete sentences (simple, compound, complex, declarative, interrogative, exclamatory and imperative).

EXAMPLE: Obeying Language Rules

The Language Handbook (pages 1436–1472) serves as a reference for all aspects of spelling, capitalization, punctuation, grammar, and sentence structure. There you'll find plenty of instruction, examples, and practice exercises. Be sure to consult the Handbook for help in writing your essays, especially when you're at the revising and publishing stages. In addition, see the "Questions for Proofreading" and "Symbols for Revising and Proofreading" charts on page 1384.

1.5.11.G. Present and/or defend written work for publication when appropriate.

You may want to keep some of your writing just for your own eyes, but there will be times when you'll want or be required to share your work with a wider audience.

EXAMPLE: Publishing Your Work

All of the Writing Workshops contain suggestions of where and how to share, present, or publish various kinds of writing. For example, see "Distribution Rights" on page 103 for ideas on sharing a descriptive essay.

1.6. SPEAKING AND LISTENING

1.6.11.A. Listen to others.

This standard includes (1) Ask clarifying questions. (2) Synthesize information, ideas and opinions to determine relevancy. (3) Take notes.

EXAMPLE: Analyzing Others

The Listening and Speaking Workshop "Presenting and Analyzing Speeches" (pages 1352–1355) shows you how to analyze rhetorical devices as well as how to evaluate delivery.

Academic Standards

1.6.11.B. Listen to selections of literature.

This standard includes (1) Relate them to previous knowledge. (2) Predict solutions to identified problems. (3) Summarize and reflect on what has been heard. (4) Identify and define new words and concepts. (5) Analyze and synthesize the selections relating them to other selections heard or read.

EXAMPLE: Listening to Literature

You can listen to many of the textbook's fiction and nonfiction selections on audio recordings.

One feature of the *Elements of Literature* Internet site gives you video and sound clips of famous speeches with tips for analyzing the elements that make speeches great.

1.6.11.C. Speak using skills appropriate to formal speech situations.

This standard includes (1) Use a variety of sentence structures to add interest to a presentation. (2) Pace the presentation according to audience and purpose. (3) Adjust stress, volume and inflection.

EXAMPLE: Speaking Skillfully

The Listening and Speaking Workshops identify and give you practice in using speaking skills in formal presentations. See, for example, "Performance Techniques" (page 261), "Deliver Your Recitation" (page 551), and "Delivery Techniques" (pages 693 and 865).

1.6.11.D. Contribute to discussions.

This standard includes (1) Ask relevant, clarifying questions. (2) Respond with relevant information or opinions to questions asked. (3) Listen to and acknowledge the contributions of others. (4) Adjust tone and involvement to encourage equitable participation. (5) Facilitate total group participation. (6) Introduce relevant, facilitating information, ideas and opinions to enrich the discussion. (7) Paraphrase and summarize as needed.

EXAMPLE: Participating in Class Discussion

For practice in class discussions, see the Thinking Critically and Extending and Evaluating questions on the Response and Analysis pages and the Analyzing Political Points of View questions. Also see the Talk About feature at the end of the introduction to each historical period. The feature gives you the chance to discuss with others your views on the Think About questions asked at the beginning of the introduction.

1.6.11.E. Participate in small and large group discussions and presentations.

This standard includes (1) Initiate everyday conversation. (2) Select and present an oral reading on an assigned topic. (3) Conduct interviews. (4) Participate in a formal interview. (5) Organize and participate in informal debate. (6) Use evaluation guides to evaluate group discussion.

EXAMPLE: Speaking with Others

Several Listening and Speaking exercises give you opportunities to practice the skills required to work successfully as a member of a team. You'll work in small groups for peer revising (commenting on each others' essays), dramatic readings, and other projects. See, for example, page 791.

1.6.11.F. **Use media for learning purposes.**

This standard includes (1) Use various forms of media to elicit information, to make a student presentation and to complete class assignments and projects. (2) Evaluate the role of media in focusing attention and forming opinions. (3) Create a multimedia presentation for display or transmission that demonstrates an understanding of a specific topic or issue or teaches others about it.

EXAMPLE: Using Media

You'll find help using film and video in the Media Workshop "Analyzing and Using Media" (pages 1344–1351). See especially the charts "Media Literacy Concepts," "Media Strategies," "Using Media," and "Organizing a Multimedia Presentation."

Media tutorials are also available on the *Elements of Literature* Internet site (go.hrw.com).

1.7. CHARACTERISTICS AND FUNCTIONS OF THE ENGLISH LANGUAGE

1.7.11.A. **Describe the influence of historical events on the English language.**

Knowing the origins and meanings of commonly used English words as well as prefixes, suffixes, and roots from other languages will help broaden your vocabulary.

EXAMPLE: History of English

The Vocabulary Development feature "Anglo-Saxon Legacy: Words and Word Parts" (page 53) deals with the many words and word parts that the Anglo-Saxons contributed to English.

1.7.11.B. **Analyze when differences in language are a source of negative or positive stereotypes among groups.**

Dialect, slang, and jargon are varieties of informal speech that may identify a person either positively or negatively as a member of a group.

EXAMPLE: Distinguishing Among Formal, Informal, Standard, and Nonstandard English

The "Glossary of Usage" on pages 1467–1472 of the Language Handbook defines and explains words and expressions that are standard, nonstandard, formal, or informal usage.

1.7.11.C. **Explain and evaluate the role and influence of the English language within and across countries.**

Many words come into English from other parts of the world, and English words find their way into other languages.

EXAMPLE: Understanding the Role and Influence of the English Language

The Vocabulary Development feature "Distinguishing Multiple Meanings of Words" (page 190) explains how words with the same spelling pick up different meanings over time. The Reading Skill "Reading Archaic Words" (page 762) tells you about words no longer in common use.

1.8. RESEARCH

1.8.11.A. Select and refine a topic for research.

When writing, you should first find a subject that interests you and might interest others. Then, you can ask questions and track down answers to narrow your research topic to fit your target audience.

EXAMPLE: Selecting a Research Topic

The Prewriting section of the Writing Workshop "Reporting Literary Research" (pages 240–259) focuses on choosing and narrowing a topic; considering purpose, audience, and tone; and making a research plan.

1.8.11.B. Locate information using appropriate sources and strategies.

This standard includes (1) Determine valid resources for researching the topic, including primary and secondary sources. (2) Evaluate the importance and quality of the sources. (3) Select sources appropriate to the breadth and depth of the research (e.g., dictionaries, thesauruses, other reference materials, interviews, observations, computer databases). (4) Use tables of contents, indices, key words, cross-references and appendices. (5) Use traditional and electronic search tools.

EXAMPLE: Locating Information

The "Information Resources" chart (page 242) tells you where to find various kinds of information in your library and in your community, from traditional sources like a card catalog to electronic search tools. "Get an Overview and Find Sources" (pages 242–243) explains why it's important to balance and evaluate primary and secondary sources, including sources you find on the Internet.

1.8.11.C. Organize, summarize and present the main ideas from research.

This standard includes (1) Take notes relevant to the research topic. (2) Develop a thesis statement based on research. (3) Anticipate readers' problems or misunderstandings. (4) Give precise, formal credit for others' ideas, images or information using a standard method of documentation. (5) Use formatting techniques (e.g., headings, graphics) to aid reader understanding.

EXAMPLE: Researching and Writing

On pages 243–256, you will find guidelines for preparing source cards, taking notes, analyzing your information, writing a thesis statement, developing an outline, documenting sources, giving credit by footnoting, and listing works cited.

See "Designing Your Writing" (pages 1391–1394) in the Writer's Handbook for tips on how to use the design elements (fonts, headings, graphics) available on a computer to make your paper visually appealing and easier to understand.

Taking the PSSA

You probably have been taking national and statewide **standardized tests** throughout your school career. These tests become increasingly important as you approach graduation and think about applying to college.

Pennsylvania currently requires high school students to take the **Pennsylvania System of School Assessment** (PSSA) to measure mastery of the skills and knowledge described in the **Academic Standards.** The PSSA covers both reading and writing.

The PSSA in reading consists of reading passages followed by two types of questions: **multiple-choice questions** that require you to use critical-thinking processes to determine the correct answers, and **open-ended questions** that require you to write a response in which you analyze and make critical judgments about the reading passage.

When you take the PSSA writing test, you will be given prompts that direct you to write persuasive and informational essays. You will also answer multiple-choice editing and revising questions.

In addition to the PSSA, you take many other tests. At the end of the school year, for instance, your science teacher may give you a test that includes multiple-choice items and questions that require written answers. Before you graduate from high school, you may take national tests like the SAT and ACT. The following pages provide hints for improving your scores on the PSSA in reading and writing, as well as on other tests.

TIPS FOR TAKING MULTIPLE-CHOICE TESTS

Multiple-choice questions are the most common type of assessment you will find on standardized tests. Teachers and other education professionals suggest the following tips for success:

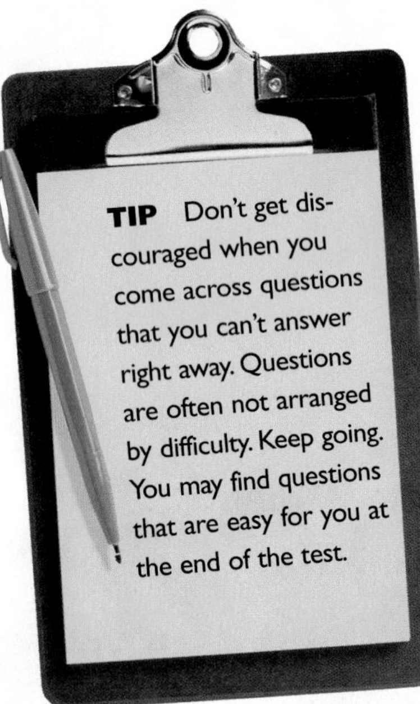

TIP Don't get discouraged when you come across questions that you can't answer right away. Questions are often not arranged by difficulty. Keep going. You may find questions that are easy for you at the end of the test.

TIP 1 **Keep track of the time.** Before you start, skim the test to see how many questions and passages there are so you can get a rough idea of how long you can spend on each. Mark the questions you're unsure of, and return to them later. Check often to see whether you need to work faster.

TIP 2 **Read everything carefully.** Stay focused and alert as you read, and don't skip anything. Pay special attention to *all* of these:

- the **reading passage**
- the **directions** that tell you what to do
- the **entire question,** including all four answer choices. If the question is complicated, circle **key words.**

TIP 3 **There are no trick questions.** Don't waste time wondering what a question *really* means. *Do* look closely for words that limit the choices that could be correct. Look for words such as *not* and *except,* which require you to choose an answer that is opposite or false in some way. Remember that *never* and *always* signal a choice that applies in no or all situations.

TIP 4 **Trust yourself.** Read the entire question at least three times. See whether you can predict what the answer will be. Then, read the choices. Don't make up your mind until you have read all four. Eliminate choices that you know are wrong. Then, make your best guess about the choices that are left. Always have a good reason for changing an answer.

TIP 5 **Go back to those hard questions.** The right answer didn't jump out at you? Read the entire question with each different answer, as if the other choices didn't exist. Which sentence makes the most sense?

TIP 6 **Mark each answer carefully.** After you've answered each question, double-check to make sure you selected the letter that goes with that answer. If you have an answer form, match every question's number to the same number on the form.

TIP 7 **Review the test.** If you have time, go back to make sure you have answered every question. Be sure you haven't marked two answers for the same question. Erase any stray pencil marks.

Taking the Reading Test

The PSSA in reading presents **fiction and nonfiction reading passages,** followed by **multiple-choice questions.** All of the multiple-choice questions have only one correct response. The questions measure your understanding of the passage's structure, content, purpose, and vocabulary. In each session, you will also be given an **open-ended question** for which you will write a response in which you will analyze and make critical judgments about the passage. (For more about open-ended questions, see page PA25.) All multiple-choice questions and open-ended questions in the PSSA reading test are aligned with Pennsylvania's statewide **Academic Standards** for reading. The questions assess your knowledge and mastery of the reading standards content at all grade levels.

In the section that follows, you will find a sample informational passage with questions like the ones you'll see in Pennsylvania's state assessment. After each question are tips to guide you to the correct answer. These questions have been grouped by specific reading skills. On the actual test, questions may not be grouped by reading skills, and some reading skills may have more questions than others.

The following article is about life in Europe in the year 999. Below are two items of background information to prepare you for the article.

- **Some people interpreted the Biblical book of Revelation to mean that the world would end at the millennium, in 1000 years, amid disease, war, famine, and death.**
- **Among those who interpret the Bible literally, this writing, known as the *apocalypse*, caused some concern even in 1999, on the eve of the second millennium.**

Read the following article to find out how the people of Europe lived in the final months of 999, and what they thought of the idea that the end of the world was near.

Life in 999: A Grim Struggle

by Howard G. Chua-Eoan

Today's world is measured in light-years and Mach speed and sheathed in silicon and alloy. In the world of 999, on the eve of the first millennium, time moved at the speed of an oxcart or, more often, of a sturdy pair of legs, and the West was built largely on wood. Europe was a collection of untamed forests, countless mile upon mile of trees and brush and brier, dark and inhospitable. Medieval chroniclers used the word *desert* to describe their arboreal world, a place on the cusp of civilization where werewolves and bogeymen still lunged out of the shadows and bandits and marauders maintained their lairs.

Yet the forests, deep and dangerous as they were, also defined existence. Wood kindled forges and kept alive the hearths of the mud-and-thatch huts of the serfs. Peasants fattened their hogs on forest acorns (pork was crucial to basic subsistence in the cold of winter), and wild berries helped supplement the meager diet. In a world without sugar, honey from forest swarms provided the only sweetness for food or drink. The pleasures of the serfs were few and simple: earthy lovemaking and occasional dances and fests.

Feudal lords ruled over western Europe, taking their share of the harvests of primitive agriculture and making the forests their private hunting grounds. Poaching was not simply theft (usually punishable by imprisonment) but a sin against the social order. Without the indulgence of the nobility, the peasants could not even acquire salt, the indispensable ingredient of preserving meat and flavoring [in] a culinary culture that possessed few spices. Though a true money economy did not exist, salt could be bought with poorly circulated coin, which the lord hoarded in his castle and dispensed to the poor only as alms.

It was in the lord's castle too that peasants and their flocks sought refuge from wolf packs and barbarian invaders. In 999, however, castles, like most other buildings in Europe, were made of timber, far from the granite bastions that litter today's imagined Middle Ages. The peasants, meanwhile, were relegated to their simple huts, where everyone—including the animals—slept around the hearth. Straw was scattered on the floors to collect scraps as well as human and animal waste. Housecleaning consisted of sweeping out the straw.

Illness and disease remained in constant residence. Tuberculosis was endemic, and so were scabrous skin diseases of every kind: abscesses, cankers, scrofula, tumors, eczema, and erysipelas. In a throwback to biblical times, lepers constituted a class of pariahs living on the outskirts of villages and cities. Constant famine, rotten flour, and vitamin deficiencies afflicted huge segments of society with blindness, goiter, paralysis, and bone malformations that created hunchbacks and cripples. A man was lucky to survive thirty, and fifty was a ripe old age. Most women, many of them succumbing to the ravages of childbirth, lived less than thirty years. There was no time for what is now considered childhood; children of every class had to grow up immediately and be useful as soon as possible. Emperors were leading armies in their teens. John XI became Pope at the age of twenty-one.

While the general population was growing faster than it had in the previous five centuries, there was still a shortage of people to cultivate the fields, clear the woodlands, and work the mills. Local taxes were levied on youths who did not marry upon coming of age. Abortion was considered homicide, and a woman who terminated a pregnancy was expelled from the church.

The nobility spent its waking hours battling foes to preserve its prerogatives, the clergy chanting prayers for the salvation of souls, the serfs laboring to feed and clothe everyone. Night, lit only by burning logs or the rare taper, was always filled with danger and terror. The seasons came and went, punctuated chiefly by the occurrence of plentiful church holidays. The calendar year began at different times for different regions; only later would Europe settle on the Feast of Christ's Circumcision, January 1, as the year's beginning.

Thus there was little panic, not even much interest, as the millennium approached in the final months of 999. For what terrors could the apocalypse hold for a continent that was already shrouded in darkness? Rather Europe—illiterate, diseased, and hungry—seemed grimly resigned to desperation and impoverishment. It was one of the planet's most unpromising corners, the Third World of its age.

February, *from Grimani Breviary* (prayer book) (detail).
Biblioteca Marciana, Venice. © Scala/Art Resource, NY

Some of the questions you encounter will measure your **comprehension** (understanding) and **interpretation** of the text. Other questions may ask you how the author uses **structure** (organization) to achieve a purpose. You may be asked to identify and evaluate **essential** ideas as well as to identify and correctly use **new words.**

1. The article is organized primarily by

A types of struggles.
B most to least dangerous diseases.
C types of food.
D past to future time.

EXPLANATION: To answer this question correctly, you must look at the whole article (including the title). Since little is said about the future, you can eliminate D. Dangerous diseases (B) and types of food (C) are mentioned in a couple of paragraphs, but when you examine the main idea of each paragraph, you see that most of them tell about a struggle or problem that the people faced (for example, unfair laws). **The correct answer is A.**

2. The first millennium was

A a golden age.
B a million dollars worth of gold.
C the first 100 days.
D the year 1000.

EXPLANATION: A *millennium* can mean a "golden age, a peaceful, prosperous time." That meaning is obviously not the correct one here when you look at the **context,** the surrounding words: "In the world of 999, on the eve of the first *millennium* . . . ." You can tell that millennium has something to do with time. Since 1000, not 100, follows 999, you know that **D is the correct answer.**

3. In 999, Europeans of every class had no

A work.
B rulers.
C childhood.
D religion.

EXPLANATION: This question and the next one test your ability to understand information that you read on your own. To make the correct choice, focus on taking time to read every word. There was plenty of work (A), and no shortage of feudal lords (B). The article suggests that religious holidays were important (D), and it states that there was no time for what we consider childhood. **C is the correct answer.**

4. According to the article, the forests were

A legal hunting grounds for rich and poor.
B places of refuge for the peasants.
C untamed wilderness.
D burned to clear the land.

EXPLANATION: A and B are contradicted by details in the article. D could be true but is not mentioned in the article. C is an important idea that is stated in several different ways. **The correct answer is C.**

Some of the questions you encounter will ask you to **differentiate** (separate) **facts** from **opinions.** You may also be asked to distinguish between **essential** and **nonessential** information. Some critical reading questions require you to **make inferences** (educated guesses), to **draw conclusions,** and to analyze and evaluate the author's **purpose, effectiveness,** and **reasoning.**

5. Which of the following is a fact?

A The serfs' pleasures were nothing compared to their daily hardships.
B At the age of 21, John XI became Pope.
C In 999, people were lucky to survive beyond the age of 30.
D Europe was the Third World of its age.

EXPLANATION: To eliminate the opinion choices, look for words and phrases that make judgments or signal beliefs (such as *were nothing compared to, lucky to survive,* and *Third World of its age*). Don't make the mistake of thinking that a statement of opinion is a fact because you happen to agree with it! Answer B is a fact that can be verified, or checked. **The correct answer is B.**

6. The most important thing feudal lords provided for the peasants was

A food on church holidays.
B protection from barbarian invaders.
C a money and banking system.
D simple huts close to the castle.

EXPLANATION: The article mentions church holidays (A), money (C), and simple huts (D), but it is clear that the lords did not provide any of them (except a few coins as alms). **The correct answer is B.**

7. From the information in this passage, you can logically conclude that

A the peasants were lazy.
B overpopulation was a big problem.
C the clergy and the lords could have helped the peasants more.
D there were places outside Europe where conditions were better.

EXPLANATION: The key word here is *logically.* A conclusion should be based on information in the reading passage. There is no evidence that either A or B is correct. While C could be true, it's not mentioned in the passage. The details in the article build to the conclusion stated in the final paragraph. **The correct answer is D.**

8. The author's primary purpose is

A to inform you about difficulties of life in Europe at a certain point in history.
B to persuade you that the peasants were ready to rise up against the lords.
C to interest you in European history.
D to describe the setting for a story about medieval Europe.

EXPLANATION: The author does not explicitly try to persuade you of anything, so you can eliminate B. The article is nonfiction, not a made-up story, so you can rule out D. The article may interest you in history (C), but most of the details discuss daily life. **The correct answer is A.**

Some of the questions you encounter will require you to understand **literature,** both **fiction** and **nonfiction.** You may find questions about **literary elements** such as **point of view, tone, style,** and **diction** (word choice). Other questions may ask you about **literary devices** such as **sound techniques, figurative language,** and **literary structures** (for example, **foreshadowing** and **flashbacks**).

9. The article alludes to the *apocalypse,* a Biblical writing that some believe describes the end of the world at the millennium. According to the author, why does Europe in 999 have no fear of the apocalypse?

A The clergy told the people that, when the world ended, they would go to Heaven.

B People were already suffering the ills that were supposed to come at the world's end.

C They didn't believe the world would end.

D They were too busy to worry.

EXPLANATION: Choices A, C, and D cannot be concluded from evidence in the article. The correct answer is stated in the final paragraph of the article. **B is the correct answer.**

10. The author's point of view on the lives of the peasants is

A humorous.

B gloomy.

C hopeful.

D mocking.

EXPLANATION: In fiction, point of view is the vantage point (first or third person) from which an author tells a story. In an informational article, the author's point of view is his or her attitude or opinion about the subject. A and D can be ruled out, because the author does not joke about the peasants. The author sympathizes with the peasants, but is not hopeful (C) about their future. **The correct answer is B.**

11. Which of the following choices contains personification?

A "the West was built largely on wood"

B "time moved at the speed of an oxcart"

C "Local taxes were levied on youths"

D "Night, lit only by burning logs"

EXPLANATION: A, C, and D do not contain any type of figurative language, so you can eliminate them. In B, the author speaks of time as if it were human, with a human's ability to move either quickly or slowly. **The correct answer is B.**

12. Which group of words from the text *best* describes life in 999?

A pleasures/simple/civilization

B arboreal/earthy/subsistence

C clergy/lords/peasants

D dangerous/primitive/disease

EXPLANATION: The words in all four choices come from the text, but only one group contains three words that all describe what medieval life was like. **D is the correct answer.**

Some of the questions you encounter may deal with **word origins** as well as **word variations.** The answers to some questions may depend on your knowledge of how historical events influenced and changed the English language. You may also find questions about language as a source of negative or positive stereotypes, and the influence of language across and within countries.

13. Which of the following words came into English most recently?

A alms
B millennium
C serf
D Mach

EXPLANATION: *Alms* (A), *millennium* (B), and *serf* (C) come from Old English or Latin. *Mach* is short for *Mach number,* the ratio of the speed of an object, such as an airplane, to the speed of sound. The word *Mach* honors the nineteenth-century physicist who introduced this ratio. **The correct answer is D.**

14. As it was used by medieval writers, the best definition of the word *desert* is

A leave without permission.
B a dry region.
C a wilderness.
D a deserved reward or punishment.

EXPLANATION: *Desert* is a multiple-meaning word. As a verb, it means to "leave without permission" (A). As a noun, with the accent on the second syllable, it means "a deserved reward or punishment" (D). As a noun, with the accent on the first syllable, it can mean either B or C. Because the article refers to the forest as *desert,* you can figure out that the meaning here is "a wilderness." **The correct answer is C.**

15. The word *malformation* comes from the Latin *mal* and *formatio* meaning

A male + handsome.
B busy + enclosed.
C faulty + structure.
D bent + part.

EXPLANATION: *Malformation* means "faulty structure." It is most often used to describe an irregular body part. Familiar words, such as *formal* and *formula*, come from *formatio.* Two of the many words beginning with *mal-* are *malfunction* and *malignant.* **The correct answer is C.**

16. The word *endemic* comes from the Greek word *endemia,* meaning "in the people." We use the word *endemic* to mean

A constantly present.
B rapidly spreading.
C usually fatal.
D affecting the skin.

EXPLANATION: The meaning of the Greek *endemia* clearly has nothing to do with C or D. *Endemic* sounds like—but does not share the meaning of—*epidemic*, which means "rapidly spreading among people" (B). The context ("Illness and disease remained in constant residence") confirms that *endemic* means "constantly present in people." **The correct answer is A.**

Some of the questions you encounter will test your understanding of the **research process,** especially how to locate information in print and nonprint resources. Test questions to assess these skills may require you to choose the most appropriate **research source** from four possible sources. You may be asked questions about **selecting** and **locating information, taking** and **organizing notes, crediting** the ideas of others, and using **formatting** techniques.

17. To begin researching the Middle Ages, the *best* source to consult is

A an encyclopedia.
B a newspaper.
C the Internet.
D a dictionary.

EXPLANATION: A newspaper (B) tells about current events. The Internet (C) would list thousands of sources on the Middle Ages that you would have to sift through before finding the information you want. A dictionary (D) merely defines the Middle Ages. To quickly get an overview of the Middle Ages, you would look it up in the encyclopedia. **A is the correct answer.**

18. In a book about the Middle Ages, information on the millennium would most likely be in which chapter?

A "Lords and Serfs"
B "The End of the World"
C "Chronicles and Chroniclers"
D "A Peasant's Life"

EXPLANATION: A, C, and D have nothing to do with the millennium. You would find information dealing with people's concerns about the year 1000 in "The End of the World." **B is the correct answer.**

19. The author's research notes for this article would include the main idea that

A bandits hid in the forests.
B feudal lords controlled the salt supply.
C famine caused many illnesses.
D due to illness and disease, life was short.

EXPLANATION: A and B are details included in the article, but neither is a main or important idea. C is a detail that supports the main idea stated in choice D. **The correct answer is D.**

20. If you used this article as one of your sources in a report about the first millennium, which statement would require a formal citation?

A Medieval forests were dangerous places.
B Western Europe was ruled by feudal lords.
C Disease was common in 999.
D Europe was "the Third World of its age."

EXPLANATION: You don't need to cite statements containing information that is common knowledge, such as A, B, and C. You do need to cite any direct quotation you use, or any idea that appears to be original with the author. **The correct answer is D.**

RESPONDING TO AN OPEN-ENDED QUESTION

In each session of the PSSA in reading, you will respond to an **open-ended question** that is aligned with the Pennsylvania Academic Standards for reading. The open-ended question tests your ability to analyze and make critical judgments about what you read. It asks you to make connections between the text and what you already know. It also gives you a chance to express your own ideas. To develop your response, you may go back to the article you have read.

HOW OPEN-ENDED QUESTIONS ARE SCORED

Your response to the performance task will receive a score of level 0, 1, 2 or 3. Level 3 is the highest score, and level 0 is the score for a nonsense answer or no response at all. Your score will be determined based on a **rubric,** an outline that lists the characteristics of a typical response at each level of scoring. Each question will have its own individual rubric. To earn a high score on open-ended questions, use the following tips.

- **Read the question carefully.** Make sure you understand what is being asked.
- **Reply to each part of the question.** Many questions have more than one part. For instance, some questions might ask you to compare **and** contrast. Make sure you have completed each task included in the question.
- **Be specific.** Always give specific examples from the text to support your answer. Check the text again to make sure your examples are correct.
- **Stick to the subject.** Include only information that directly answers the question. Do not include personal experiences or opinions **unless the question asks for them.**
- **Be clear.** Express yourself clearly and simply. Do not try to impress the scorer with difficult language; this will just make your answer harder to read. Be careful to follow correct writing conventions.

The following is an open-ended question for "Life in 999: A Grim Struggle" with one writer's response. As you read the response, think about how *you* would score it. An explanation follows the response.

Explain what your life would be like if you were a teenager in 999. Use information from the article and your own ideas to support your answer.
As you write, be sure to:

- **Tell how life in 999 is different from life today.**
- **Use ideas and details from the article.**
- **Include your own ideas.**
- **Write clearly and neatly.**
- **Use only the space provided.**

In 999, I would probably have been a peasant—hungry, scared, and tired all the time. My life would be like this: My family and I never get enough to eat. We eat pork from a pig we fattened on acorns. We gather wild berries and grow wheat for flour. Our feudal lord takes a big share of what we grow. We hope he will give us a little salt. We need it to preserve the meat we keep for winter.

Information from text

Information from text

I am terrified to go into the forest to cut wood for our fire because wolves and bandits are hiding there. At night, my family and our animals all sleep around the hearth in our little hut, trying to keep warm. We suffer from skin diseases and tuberculosis.

Personal insight

I have had to work in the fields from the time I could walk, and I will have to get married soon. There are no schools for peasants, so I can't read and write. We have to work hard every day from dawn to nightfall. The only thing I have to look forward to is a dance sometimes. I am worn out, and the future looks bleak.

Personal connection to text

Even if I have the good fortune to be a teenage emperor instead of a peasant, I have probably lost my parents by now (since they would be in their forties). I am constantly fighting to protect what I have. Because there are so many other feudal lords, I might lose everything or even be killed by someone with a bigger army.

Personal insight

Moving forward to the present, I can say I am glad to be alive today, when there is not such a big gap between the way rich and poor live and when food and medical care are better. I know that if I stay in school and work hard, I can get a good job. Someday I will make something of myself, an opportunity I could never have had if I lived in 999.

Score 3—This writer shows a good understanding of the text by accurately citing specific details of medieval life and connecting them to personal experience.

Taking the Writing Test

The PSSA writing test is given in two sessions. In each session you will be required to respond to a writing **prompt.** The prompt will direct you to write an essay in one of two modes: **informational** (an essay that shares knowledge and conveys information) or **persuasive** (an essay that persuades readers to take an action or agree with an opinion). Each essay must be at least five paragraphs long, and you will have one hour to complete each essay.

You will also be required to answer multiple-choice editing and revising questions. The multiple-choice editing and revising questions will be based on short passages of text. The passages contain errors, and the questions require you to choose the best way to correct them. Look at this sample passage and question.

Read the passage below and then answer question 1.

1 Yoga is an ancient practice, but it's very popular today. **2** Alexia, who is my yoga instructor, told me that each yoga posture is designed to help improve the health of your organs. **3** Good flexibility is required to do the postures correctly.

1. Which revision of sentence 2 *best* restates the sentence without omitting information?

A Alexia, who is my yoga instructor, told me that yoga postures are good for you.

B Alexia told me that the health of your organs is improved by each yoga posture.

C Each yoga posture is designed to improve the health of your organs, says Alexia, who is my yoga instructor.

D My yoga instructor, Alexia, told me that each yoga posture is designed to improve your organs' health.

EXPLANATION: Options A and B omit information (in A, the organs; in B, the fact that Alexia is the writer's yoga instructor); Option C retains all the facts from the original, but it ends awkwardly with a relative clause. Option D is the best answer as it retains all information and presents that information in a more straightforward way.

THE WRITING PROMPT

Your essay will be evaluated according to a scoring guideline specific to the type, or mode, of writing. You will receive a score of 1, 2, 3, or 4 on each of the following attributes: focus, content development, organization, and style. A score of 3 or 4 is acceptable, while a score of 1 or 2 indicates that your writing is unacceptable.

To help you focus your essay-writing practice, first take a look at the characteristics of a paper that would receive the highest score (4) in each of the modes, informational and persuasive.

CHARACTERISTICS OF EXCELLENT INFORMATIONAL WRITING

Focus. Sharp, distinct controlling point made about a single topic with evident awareness of task and audience.

Content development. Substantial, relevant, and illustrative content that demonstrates a clear understanding of the purpose. Thorough elaboration with effectively presented information consistently supported with well-chosen details.

Organization. Effective organizational strategies and structures, such as logical order and transitions, which develop a controlling idea.

Style. Precise control of language, stylistic techniques, and sentence structures that create a consistent and effective tone.

CHARACTERISTICS OF EXCELLENT PERSUASIVE WRITING

Focus. Sharp, distinct point presented as a position and made convincing through a clear, thoughtful, and substantiated argument with evident awareness of task and audience.

Content development. Substantial, relevant, and illustrative content that demonstrates a clear understanding of the purpose. Thoroughly elaborated argument that includes a clear position consistently supported with precise and relevant evidence. Rhetorical (persuasive) strategies are evident.

Organization. Effective organizational strategies and structures, such as logical order and transitions, to develop a position supported with a purposeful presentation of content.

Style. Precise control of language, stylistic techniques, and sentence structures that create a consistent and effective tone.

STEPS FOR TAKING THE PSSA WRITING TEST

Here are some steps and a suggested timetable for writing a PSSA essay. You'll probably find these steps in the writing process comfortable and familiar.

STEP 1 **Read the writing prompt carefully.** Look for key verbs (such as *analyze, summarize, identify, persuade*) that define your writing task. Identify your audience and purpose.

STEP 2 **Plan what you will write.** You have a total of sixty minutes to plan, write, and proofread your paper, so take about ten minutes for prewriting. Make notes on scratch paper. To help you organize your ideas, make a rough outline, map, or chart. Use a cluster diagram or other graphic organizer to gather main ideas and supporting details. Number your major points in the order you think you will use them.

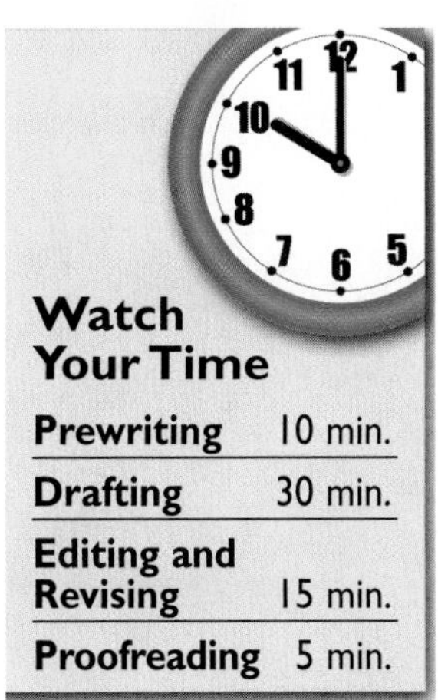

Watch Your Time

Prewriting	10 min.
Drafting	30 min.
Editing and Revising	15 min.
Proofreading	5 min.

STEP 3 **Draft your essay.** Allow about thirty minutes to draft your essay. Try to present your ideas clearly and in an easy-to-follow order. Pay special attention to creating a strong opening paragraph and a definite closing. Make every effort to express your ideas as clearly as you can while making your essay interesting to read. Vary the kinds of sentences (simple, compound, complex, compound-complex) you use. **Remember, you must write at least five paragraphs, including the introduction and conclusion.**

STEP 4 **Edit and revise your draft.** Allow about fifteen minutes to re-read and improve your draft. Make sure your essay is readable! If it isn't, decide whether you have time to copy it over, revising as you go. Look for places where you can add transitions or combine sentences. Be sure to eliminate unnecessary repetition and wordiness. Check your essay by referring to the copy of the *PA Domain Scoring Guide* (provided with the actual test) on the back of the prompt.

STEP 5 **Proofread.** Take at least five minutes to search for and correct errors in grammar, usage, and mechanics. You will not be allowed to use a dictionary, thesaurus, or electronic spellchecker, but don't panic. If you don't know how to spell a word, consider using a different word that has the same meaning.

A SAMPLE WRITING PROMPT

The PSSA's on-demand writing prompts ask you to write informational and persuasive essays in an hour each. Here is a sample prompt for a persuasive essay. A set of five guideline statements follows the prompt.

> Some community leaders have proposed a new youth center for teenagers. The center would provide tutoring, Internet access, job counseling, and sports facilities, but the cost would require cuts in other city services. — **Statement of issue**
>
> Decide whether you support or oppose the proposal, and write an essay to persuade voters in your community to share your point of view. — **Writer's task and audience**

As you write your paper, remember to:

★ Clearly state the issue and your opinion.

★ Use specific reasons, examples, anecdotes, facts, and details to explain your point of view.

★ Present ideas in a logical order, with an introduction, body, and conclusion.

★ Use well-constructed sentences and a variety of words.

★ Correct any errors in grammar, usage, mechanics (capitalization, punctuation, and spelling), and sentence formation.

PREWRITING: ORGANIZING YOUR IDEAS

Form your opinion. The writing prompt presents an issue that you can respond to without doing research or knowing a great deal about the topic.

Gather your ideas. Here's a cluster diagram by a writer who supports the proposal and is coming up with reasons. Before she starts drafting, she'll **evaluate** her support, choosing the **reasons** and **evidence** she thinks will be most likely to convince community members.

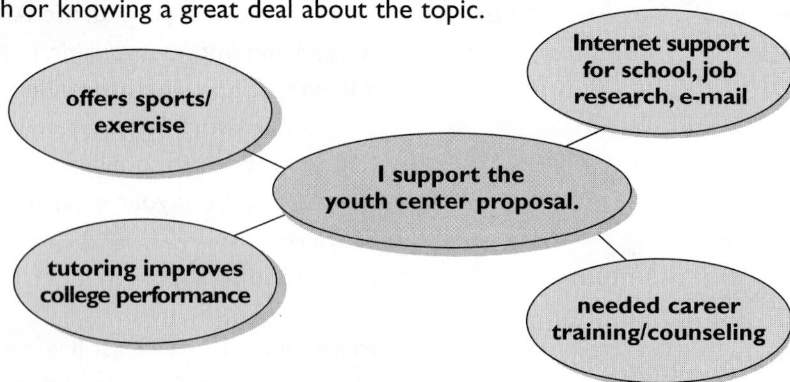

DRAFTING

Time to write. You have a head start because you know what you will say and roughly how you will organize your ideas. Keep in mind your **purpose** and **audience,** and use language appropriate to them.

Keep your focus in mind. Early in your introductory paragraph, include a clear statement of your opinion. Show that you know the type of essay (persuasive) you are writing. This sentence or two is sometimes called your **controlling point, opinion statement,** or **thesis statement.**

Add the details. As you draft, **elaborate** (support) each paragraph's main idea. Support each reason with specific evidence. Try to arrange ideas in an order that your reader will be able to follow easily. Connect ideas and details with transitions.

Find your own voice. Do not use slang, but try to write the way you would sound if you were speaking naturally.

REVISING AND PROOFREADING

Time's almost up. Allow enough time to re-read your paper. Read it once for sense and clarity; and read it a second time for style and sentence variety. Then, proofread it to correct mistakes in grammar, usage, and mechanics.

A SAMPLE ESSAY

Here is one writer's essay in response to the writing prompt on page PA29.

Introduction

When people put money in a savings account, they are saving for the future. The proposed youth center is another way of investing for the future. It's a way that adults in our community can invest in young people—the future of our community.

Controlling point

A youth center would provide recreational, educational, and vocational activities to teenagers. My U.S. history class held a mock vote on the proposal to fund a youth center, and students supported the initiative by passing it unanimously. Unfortunately, we are too young to vote in the city election, so we must convince voting taxpayers that the youth center is a good idea, worth every dollar it will cost. Before the class voted, students identified the following benefits of a youth center.

New sports facilities would give students a safe playing field. A center could also offer exercise classes and a place to hold dances. — **Reason 1**

Some students, including me, cannot afford to buy a computer. Internet access at the youth center would allow us to do homework, research colleges and technical schools, and use e-mail. — **Reason 2**

Students would greatly benefit from tutoring services. A recent report on the evening news indicated that people who were tutored in high school earned better grades in college. — **Reason 3 with fact**

I believe the center's best resource would be career counseling services. According to a recent poll in our local newspaper, half of all seniors are undecided about their careers. Career counseling would help students map out their next steps. — **Reason 4 with statistic**

The youth center would also give students a safe and pleasant place to gather after school and on weekends. We need a place that will be our own, where we won't have to worry about people taking advantage of us or saying, "Move on. There are too many of you teenagers here." — **Reason 5**

To those who fear that a center might eliminate city services, I suggest that the youth center would give teenagers a chance to serve the community. The center could coordinate volunteer work on weekends. We could help clean up the parks, supervise children at playgrounds, and provide company for people in nursing homes. — **Counterargument addressed**

Our willingness to contribute should prove to taxpayers that we teenagers are willing to do our share, accepting the responsibility of citizenship in exchange for a teen center to call our own. — **Conclusion**

HOLT

ELEMENTS OF LITERATURE

Sixth Course

ESSENTIALS OF BRITISH AND WORLD LITERATURE

HOLT

ELEMENTS OF LITERATURE®

Sixth Course

ESSENTIALS OF BRITISH AND WORLD LITERATURE

HOLT, RINEHART AND WINSTON

A Harcourt Education Company

Orlando • **Austin** • New York • San Diego • Toronto • London

Cover
Photo Credits: (Inset) *Houses of Parliament from Westminster Bridge,* 1906 by André Derain (1880–1954). Oil on canvas. 73.6 x 92 cm. © The Cleveland Museum of Art, Leonard C. Hanna, Jr. Fund, 1983.67. © 2005 Artists Rights Society (ARS), New York/ADAGP, Paris. (Background) Big Ben. © Jon Bower/Alamy.

Requests for permission to make copies of any part of the work should be mailed to the following address: Permissions Department, Holt, Rinehart and Winston, 10801 N. MoPac Expressway, Building 3, Austin, Texas 78759-5415.

Acknowledgments appear on pages 1485–1487, which are an extension of the copyright page.

Printed in the United States of America

ISBN 0-03-042419-4 2 3 4 5 048 10 09 08 07 06

Program Authors

Dr. Kylene Beers is the senior program author for *Elements of Literature*. A former middle school teacher who is now a senior reading researcher in the School Development program at Yale University, Dr. Beers has turned her commitment to helping struggling readers into the major focus of her research, writing, speaking, and teaching. She is the author of *When Kids Can't Read: What Teachers Can Do* and *Aliteracy: The Glitch in Becoming a Nation of Readers.* From 1999 to 2006, she was the editor of the National Council of Teachers of English (NCTE) literacy journal *Voices from the Middle.* Additionally, Dr. Beers is the co-editor of *Into Focus: Understanding and Creating Middle School Readers.* Having authored chapters in numerous books and articles in *English Journal, Journal of Adolescent and Adult Literacy, School Library Journal, Middle Matters,* and *Voices from the Middle,* she is a recognized authority on struggling readers, who speaks both nationally and internationally. Dr. Beers has served as the chair of the National Adolescent Literacy Coalition (2005–2007) and has served as a member of the review boards for *English Journal, The ALAN Review,* the Special Interest Group on Adolescent Literature of the International Reading Association, and the Assembly on Literature for Adolescents of the NCTE. She is the 2001 recipient of the Richard W. Halle Award given by NCTE for outstanding contributions to middle school literacy.

Dr. Lee Odell helped establish the pedagogical framework for writing, listening, and speaking for *Elements of Literature*. Dr. Odell is Professor of Composition Theory and Research and, since 1996, Director of the Writing Program at Rensselaer Polytechnic Institute. He began his career teaching English in middle and high schools. More recently he has worked with teachers in grades k–12 to establish a program that involves students from all disciplines in writing across the curriculum and for communities outside their classrooms. Dr. Odell's most recent book (with Charles R. Cooper) is *Evaluating Writing: The Role of Teacher's Knowledge About Text, Learning, and Culture*. He is past chair of the Conference on College Composition and Communication and of NCTE's Assembly for Research.

Writers

John Malcolm Brinnin, author of six volumes of poetry that have received many prizes and awards, was a member of the American Academy and Institute of Arts and Letters. He was a critic of poetry, a biographer of poets, and for a number of years, director of New York's famous Poetry Center. His teaching career included terms at Vassar College, the University of Connecticut, and Boston University, where he succeeded Robert Lowell as Professor of Creative Writing and Contemporary Letters. In addition to other works, Mr. Brinnin wrote *Dylan Thomas in America: An Intimate Journal* and *Sextet: T. S. Eliot & Truman Capote & Others.*

Claire Miller Colombo received a doctorate in English from the University of Texas at Austin and has taught English at both college and secondary levels. She has been a freelance writer of educational materials since 1990.

Robert DeMaria, Jr., is the Henry Noble MacCracken Professor of English Literature at Vassar College, where he has taught since receiving his doctorate from Rutgers University in 1975. He is an expert on eighteenth-century British literature and has edited the college text *British Literature 1640–1789: An Anthology* (Second Edition, 2001). He has also written three books about Samuel Johnson. Most recently Dr. DeMaria has edited an edition of *Gulliver's Travels.*

Donald Gray is Professor Emeritus of English at Indiana University, Bloomington. Dr. Gray has written essays on Victorian poetry and culture and has served as editor of *College English.*

Harley Henry was Professor of English at Macalester College in St. Paul, Minnesota. He has also been a senior Fulbright lecturer in Zimbabwe and a Redfield Visiting Professor at the University of Chicago. In addition to the Romantic period, his teaching specialties include the literature of Zimbabwe, William Faulkner, American fiction from 1945 to 1960, and fiction about baseball.

Rose Sallberg Kam holds a master's in English from California State University, Sacramento, and a master's in biblical studies from the Graduate Theological Union, Berkeley. She taught secondary English for seventeen years, has been a freelance writer of educational materials for nineteen years, and is the author of *Their Stories, Our Stories: Women of the Bible.*

David Adams Leeming was for many years a Professor of English and Comparative Literature at the University of Connecticut. He is the author of several books on mythology, including *Mythology: The Voyage of the Hero; The World of Myth;* and *Encyclopedia of Creation Myths*. For several years, Dr. Leeming taught English at Robert College in Istanbul, Turkey. He also served as secretary and assistant to the writer James Baldwin in New York and Istanbul. He has published the biographies *James Baldwin* and *Amazing Grace: A Life of Beauford Delaney.*

John Leggett is a novelist, biographer, and former teacher. He went to the Writers' Workshop at the University of Iowa in the spring of 1969. In 1970, he assumed temporary charge of the program, and for the next seventeen years he was its director. Mr. Leggett's novels include *Wilder Stone, The Gloucester Branch, Who Took the Gold Away?, Gulliver House*, and *Making Believe*. He is also the author of the highly acclaimed biography *Ross and Tom: Two American Tragedies* and of a biography of William Saroyan, *A Daring Young Man.* Mr. Leggett lives in Napa Valley, California.

C. F. Main was for many years Professor of English at Rutgers University in New Brunswick, New Jersey. He was the editor of *Poems: Wadsworth Handbook and Anthology* and wrote reviews and articles on sixteenth-, seventeenth-, and eighteenth-century literature.

Fannie Safier, a former teacher, has written and edited language arts materials for over thirty-five years.

Mairead Stack has a master's degree in English from New York University. A former teacher, she has edited and written educational materials for literature and language arts for more than twenty years.

Senior Program Consultant

Carol Jago teaches English at Santa Monica High School, in Santa Monica, and directs the California Reading and Literature Project at UCLA. Her classroom experience began with middle school and has included journalism, remedial reading and writing, and honors and advanced placement. She has written a weekly education column for the *Los Angeles Times* and edits the quarterly journal of the California Association of Teachers of English, *California English*. She is the author of several books, including a series on contemporary writers in the classroom: *Alice Walker in the Classroom, Nikki Giovanni in the Classroom,* and *Sandra Cisneros in the Classroom.* She is also the author of *With Rigor for All: Teaching the Classics to Contemporary Students; Beyond Standards: Excellence in the High School English Classroom; Cohesive Writing: Why Concept Is Not Enough; Classics in the Classroom: Designing Accessible Literature Lessons;* and *Papers, Papers, Papers: An English Teacher's Survival Guide.*

ADVISORS

Cynthia A. Arceneaux
Administrative Coordinator
Office of Deputy Superintendent, Instructional Services
Los Angeles Unified School District
Los Angeles, California

Dr. Julie M.T. Chan
Director of Literacy Instruction
Newport-Mesa Unified School District
Costa Mesa, California

Al Desmarais
English Department Chair and Curriculum Specialist in Language Arts
El Toro High School
Saddleback Valley Unified School District
Lake Forest, California

José M. Ibarra-Tiznado
ELL Program Coordinator
Bassett Unified School District
La Puente, California

Dr. Ronald Klemp
Instructor
California State University, Northridge
Northridge, California

Fern M. Sheldon
K–12 Curriculum and Instruction Specialist
Rowland Unified School District
Rowland Heights, California

Jim Shields
Instructor
El Toro High School
Saddleback Valley Unified School District
Lake Forest, California

CRITICAL REVIEWERS

Elmire C. Budak
Lynwood High School
Lynwood, California

Paulette Dewey
Toledo Early College High School
University of Toledo—Scott Park Campus
Toledo, Ohio

Matthew Falk
John A. Rowland High School
Rowland Unified School District
Rowland Heights, California

Terry Filippo
Pendleton High School / Clemson University
Pendleton, South Carolina

R. E. Fisher
Westlake High School
Atlanta, Georgia

Robert V. Gardner
Chaparral High School
Temecula, California

Janice Gauthier
Everett High School
Everett, Massachusetts

Sandra Gilligan
Passaic High School
Passaic, New Jersey

Victor Jaccarino
Herricks High School
New Hyde Park, New York

Diane M. Jackson
Washington Preparatory High School
Los Angeles, California

Barbara Kimbrough
Kane Area High School
Kane, Pennsylvania

Dr. Louisa Kramer-Vida
Oyster Bay-East Norwich SD
Oyster Bay, New York

Martin P. Mushik
Covina High School
Covina, California

Brenda Scheidler
Evansville-Vanderburgh School Corp.
Evansville, Indiana

Mary Ellen Snodgrass
Hickory High School
Hickory, North Carolina

Elaine Sorrell
Marina High School
Huntington Beach, California

David Trimble
Norwin High School
N. Huntingdon, Pennsylvania

Donna Walthour
Greensburg Salem High School
Greensburg, Pennsylvania

John R. Williamson
Highlands High School
Fort Thomas, Kentucky

FIELD-TEST PARTICIPANTS

Barbara A. Briggs
Barberton High School
Barberton, Ohio

Annette Dade
West Orange High School
West Orange, New Jersey

Robert V. Gardner
Chaparral High School
Temecula, California

Bobbye Sykes-Perkins
Luther Burbank High School
Sacramento, California

John R. Williamson
Highlands High School
Fort Thomas, Kentucky

CONTENTS IN BRIEF

COLLECTION 1

The Anglo-Saxons 449–1066

SONGS OF ANCIENT HEROES

COLLECTION 2

The Middle Ages 1066–1485

THE TALES THEY TOLD

COLLECTION 3

The Renaissance 1485–1660

A FLOURISH OF GENIUS

Connecting to World Literature

RENAISSANCE DRAMA

COLLECTION 4

The Restoration and the Eighteenth Century 1660–1800

THE BEST OF ALL POSSIBLE WORLDS

COLLECTION 5

The Romantic Period 1798–1832

THE QUEST FOR TRUTH AND BEAUTY

COLLECTION 6

The Victorian Period 1832–1901

PARADOX AND PROGRESS

COLLECTION 7

The Modern World 1900 to the Present

A REMARKABLE DIVERSITY

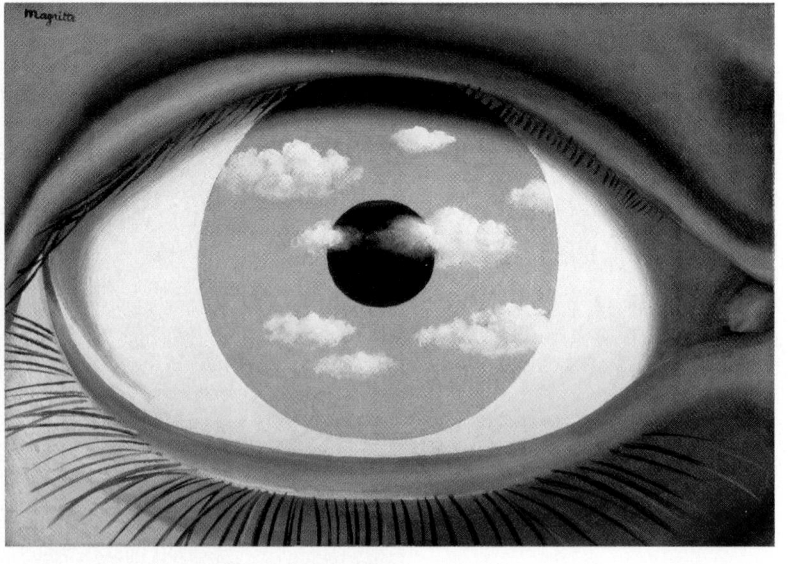
Magritte

CLASHES OF CULTURE

DISCOVERIES AND TRANSFORMATIONS

OURSELVES AMONG OTHERS

Resource Center

SELECTIONS BY ALTERNATIVE THEMES

Selections are listed here in alternative theme groupings.

APPEARANCE VERSUS REALITY

GOOD VERSUS EVIL

HEROES AND ANTIHEROES

HUMOR AND THE STING OF SATIRE

THE INDIVIDUAL AND SOCIETY

INNOCENCE AND EXPERIENCE

LOSS AND DEATH

LOVE'S SORROWS, LOVE'S TRIUMPHS

OPPRESSION AND FREEDOM

PEOPLE AND NATURE

POWER AND AMBITION

THE QUEST AND THE PERILOUS JOURNEY

THE SEARCH FOR WISDOM

THE TRANSFORMING IMAGINATION

THE WAGES OF WAR

SELECTIONS BY GENRE

FICTION

ALLEGORY

ANECDOTES

DEBATE

FABLE

NOVEL EXCERPTS

PARABLES

PARODY

ROMANCE NARRATIVE

TALES / SHORT STORIES

DRAMA

DRAMATIC EXCERPTS

POETRY

BALLADS

DRAMATIC MONOLOGUE

ELEGY

EPICS

HAIKU

LYRICS

SELECTIONS BY GENRE

TANKA

NONFICTION AND INFORMATIONAL TEXT

AXIOMS AND MAXIMS

BIOGRAPHY

CRITICAL COMMENTS

CULTURAL COMMENTARY

DEFINITIONS

DIARY

ESSAYS

HISTORIES

LETTERS

MAGAZINE AND NEWSPAPER ARTICLES

MEDITATION

MEMOIRS

PROVERBS

SACRED TEXTS

TRAVEL BOOK

WEB PAGE

PUBLIC DOCUMENTS

DEBATE

PLATFORM

POLITICAL STATEMENT

SPEECHES

TESTIMONY

SELECTIONS BY REGION

AFRICA

ASIA

EUROPE

GREAT BRITAIN

SELECTIONS BY REGION

NORTH AMERICA

NEW ZEALAND

SOUTH AMERICA

WEST INDIES

SKILLS, WORKSHOPS, AND FEATURES

SKILLS

LITERARY SKILLS

READING SKILLS

READING MATTERS

VOCABULARY SKILLS

WORKSHOPS

WRITING WORKSHOPS

MINI-WORKSHOPS

LISTENING AND SPEAKING WORKSHOPS

MEDIA WORKSHOP

FEATURES

A CLOSER LOOK

COMPARING POINTS OF VIEW

CONNECTING TO WORLD LITERATURE

CRITICAL COMMENTS

PRIMARY SOURCES

REFLECTING ON THE LITERARY PERIOD

GRAMMAR LINK

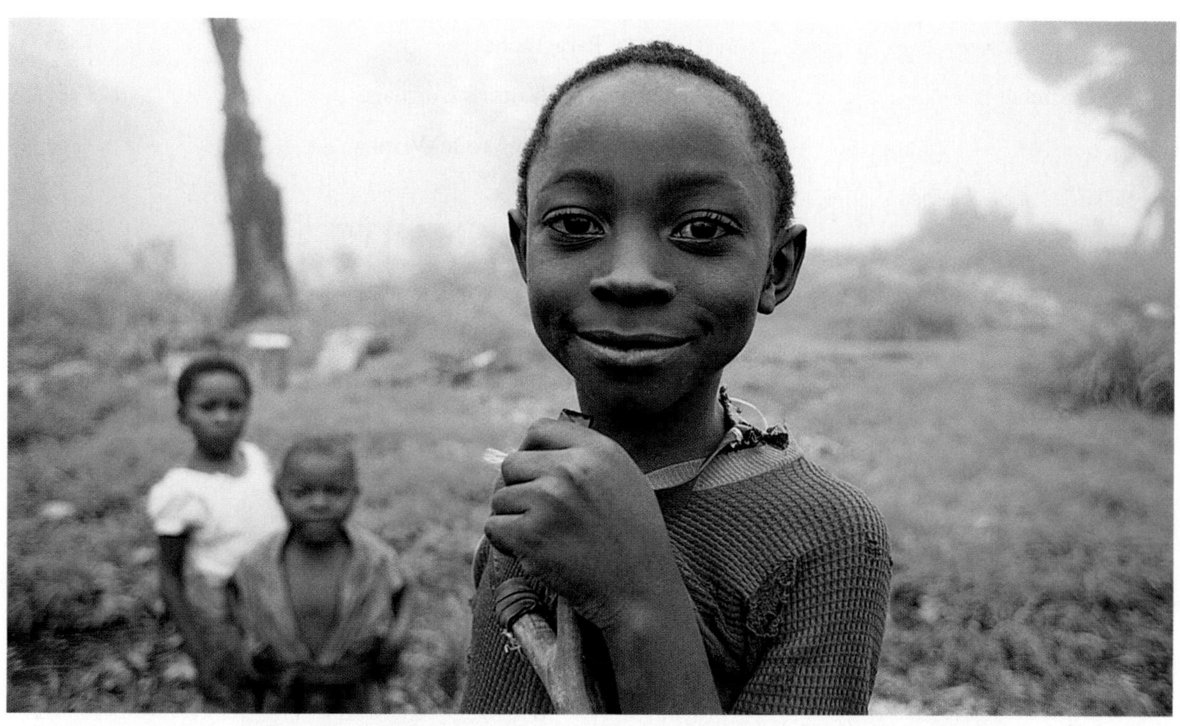

LANGUAGE HANDBOOK

SKILLS REVIEW

THE WORLD OF WORK

WRITER'S HANDBOOK

TEST SMARTS

Elements of Literature on the Internet

TO THE STUDENT

At the *Elements of Literature* Internet site, you can analyze the work of professional writers and learn the inside stories behind your favorite authors. You can also build your word power and analyze messages in the media. As you move through *Elements of Literature*, you will find the best online resources at **go.hrw.com.**

Here's how to log on:

1. Start your Web browser, and enter **go.hrw.com** in the Address or Location field.

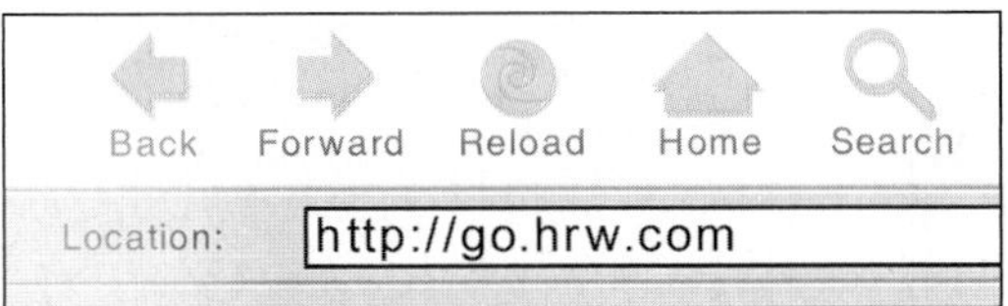

2. Note the keyword in your textbook.

3. Enter the keyword, and click "go."

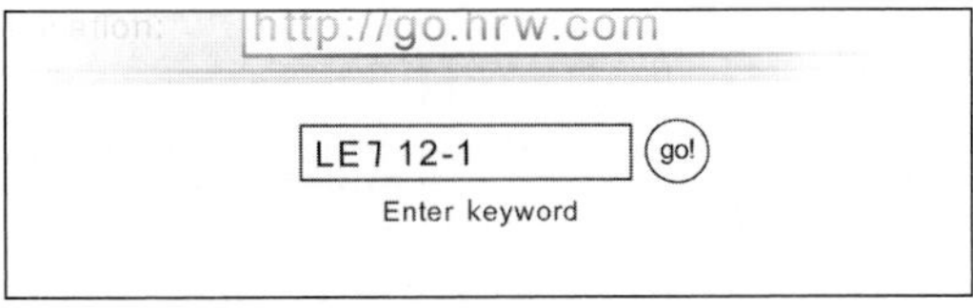

FEATURES OF THE SITE

More About the Writer
Author biographies provide the inside stories behind the lives and works of great writers.

More Writer's Models
Interactive Writer's Models present annotations and reading tips to help you with your own writing. Printable Professional Models and Student Models provide you with quality writing by real writers and students across the country.

Interactive Reading Model
Interactive Reading Workshops guide you through high-interest informational articles and allow you to share your opinions through pop-up questions and polls.

Vocabulary Practice
Interactive vocabulary-building activities help you build your word power.

Projects and Activities
Projects and activities help you extend your study of literature through writing, research, art, and public speaking.

Speeches
Video clips from historical speeches provide you with the tools you need to analyze elements of great speechmaking.

Media Tutorials
Media tutorials help you dissect messages in the media and learn to create your own multimedia presentations.

The British Isles

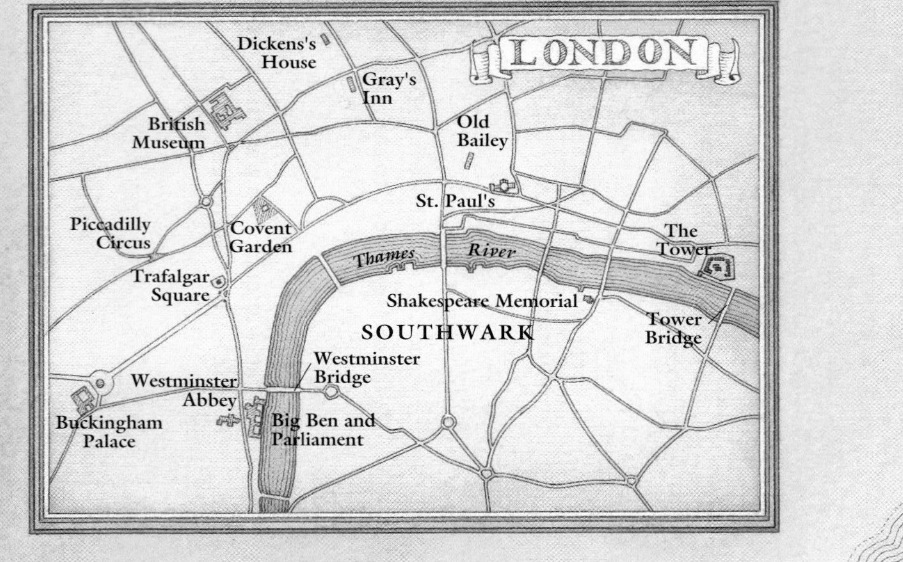
LONDON
Dickens's House
Gray's Inn
British Museum
Old Bailey
St. Paul's
Piccadilly Circus
Covent Garden
The Tower
Thames River
Trafalgar Square
Shakespeare Memorial
SOUTHWARK
Tower Bridge
Westminster Bridge
Westminster Abbey
Buckingham Palace
Big Ben and Parliament

SHETLAND ISLANDS
ORKNEY ISLANDS
HEBRIDES
Inverness
Cawdor
Culloden
Macduff
Loch Ness
Dee R.
Birnam Wood
Glamis
Iona
Dunsinane
Scone
NORTH SEA

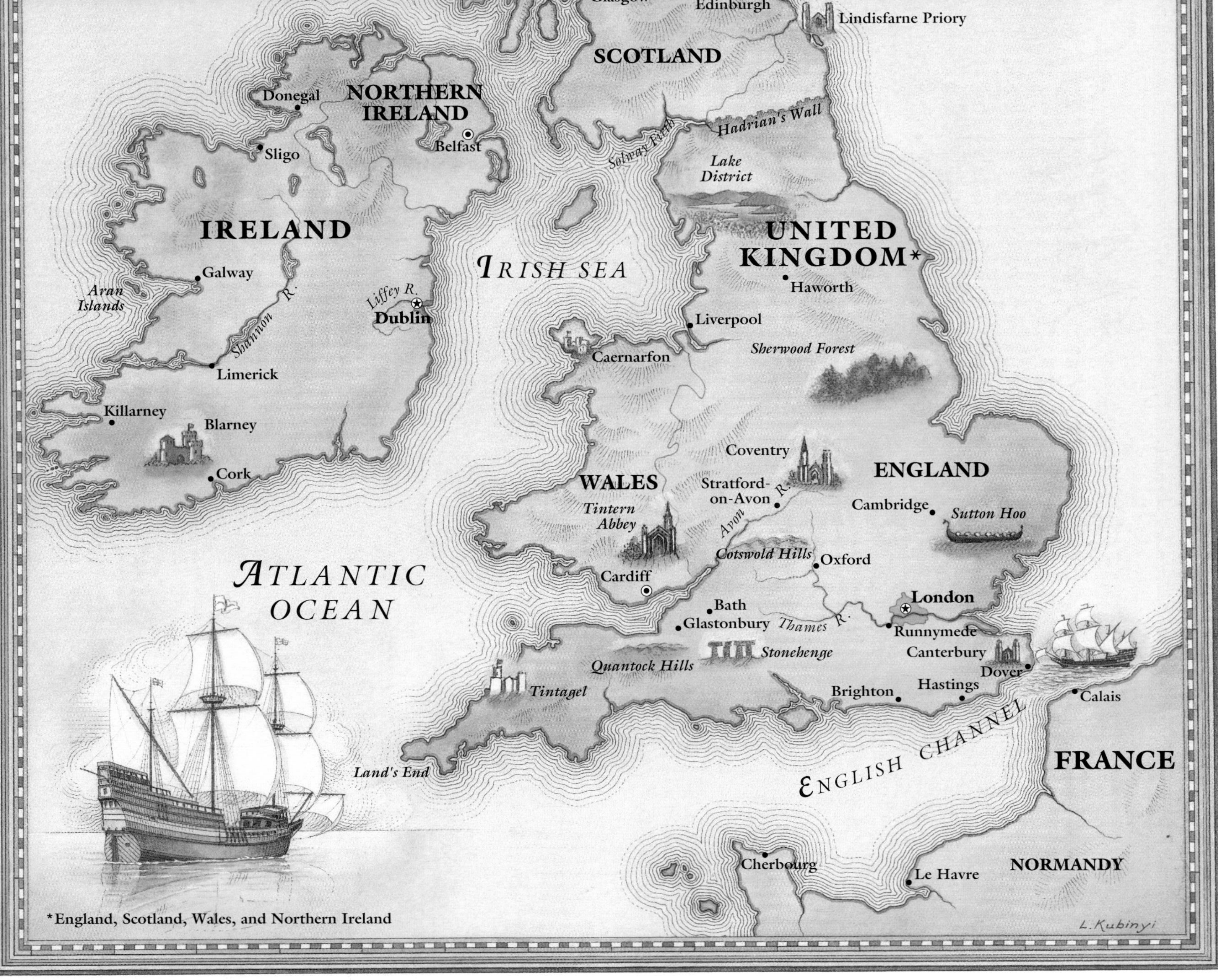
Edinburgh
Lindisfarne Priory
SCOTLAND
Donegal
NORTHERN IRELAND
Belfast
Sligo
Solway Firth
Hadrian's Wall
Lake District
IRELAND
UNITED KINGDOM*
IRISH SEA
Galway
Aran Islands
Shannon R.
Liffey R.
Dublin
Haworth
Liverpool
Caernarfon
Sherwood Forest
Limerick
Killarney
Blarney
Cork
Coventry
ENGLAND
WALES
Stratford-on-Avon
Avon R.
Tintern Abbey
Cambridge
Sutton Hoo
Cotswold Hills
Oxford
ATLANTIC OCEAN
Cardiff
London
Bath
Glastonbury
Thames R.
Runnymede
Canterbury
Stonehenge
Quantock Hills
Dover
Tintagel
Brighton
Hastings
Calais
ENGLISH CHANNEL
Land's End
FRANCE
Cherbourg
Le Havre
NORMANDY
*England, Scotland, Wales, and Northern Ireland
L. Kubinyi

Map of

NORTH AMERICA
Canada
United States
ATLANTIC OCEAN
CARIBBEAN SEA
St. Lucia
Trinidad and Tobago
SOUTH AMERICA
PACIFIC OCEAN
Chile
Argentina

the World

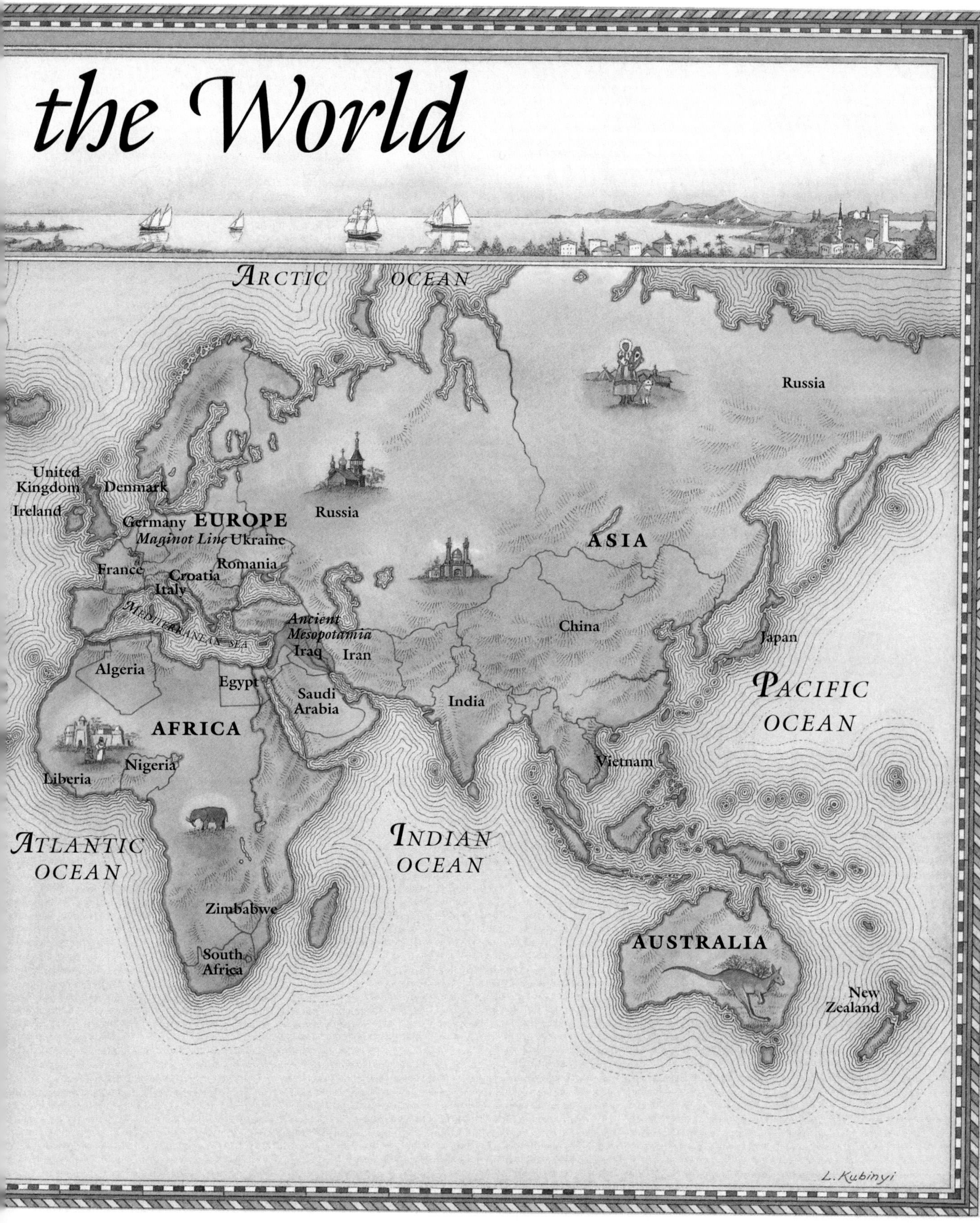

ARCTIC OCEAN

Russia

United Kingdom

Denmark

Ireland

Germany

EUROPE

Russia

Maginot Line

Ukraine

ASIA

France

Romania

Croatia

Italy

MEDITERRANEAN SEA

Ancient Mesopotamia

China

Japan

Iraq

Iran

Algeria

Egypt

Saudi Arabia

India

PACIFIC OCEAN

AFRICA

Nigeria

Liberia

Vietnam

ATLANTIC OCEAN

INDIAN OCEAN

Zimbabwe

AUSTRALIA

South Africa

New Zealand

L. Kubinyi

Invasion of Danes under Hinguar (Ingvar) and Hubba (detail). Page from *Life, Passion, and Miracles of St. Edmund* (c. 1130).

Collection 1

The Anglo-Saxons

449–1066

Songs of Ancient Heroes

And sometimes a proud old soldier
Who had heard songs of the ancient heroes
And could sing them all through, story after story,
Would weave a net of words . . .

—from *Beowulf,* translated by Burton Raffel

go.hrw.com

INTERNET
Collection Resources
Keyword: LE7 12-1

The Anglo-Saxon Period

LITERARY EVENTS

1300 B.C.–A.D. 299

c. 1300 B.C. *Gilgamesh* epic is written down

c. 700 B.C. Homer writes the *Iliad*

307 B.C. Alexandria is center of Greek learning; library under Ptolemy is begun

70 B.C. Roman poet Virgil is born

c. A.D. 5 Roman poet Ovid writes *Metamorphoses*

A.D. 300

late 500s Books are printed in China

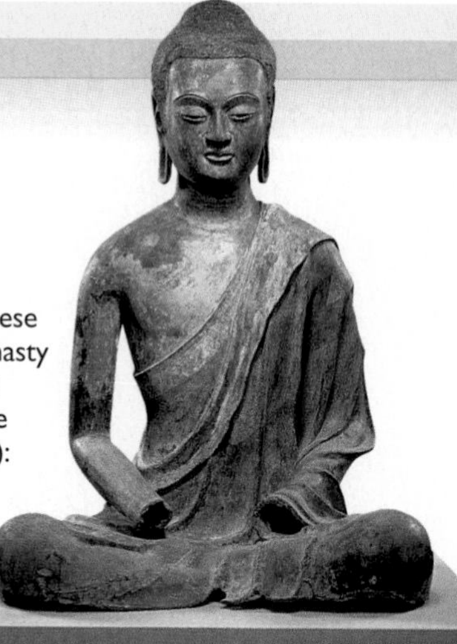

Seated Buddha (c. 650). Chinese sculpture from the Tang Dynasty (618–907). Dry lacquer with traces of gilt and polychrome pigments, H. 38 in. (96.5 cm): W. 27 in. (68.6 cm).

The Metropolitan Museum of Art, Rogers Fund, 1919 (19.186). Photograph by Lynton Gardiner. © 1989 The Metropolitan Museum of Art, New York.

POLITICAL AND SOCIAL EVENTS

1300 B.C.–A.D. 299

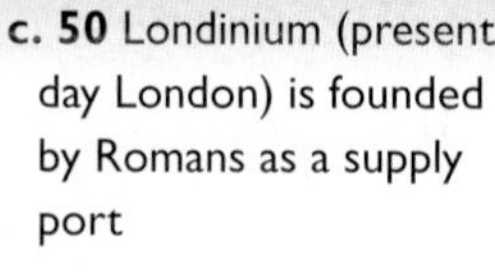

Roman helmet.

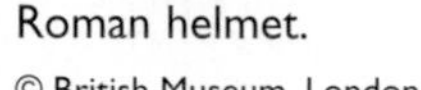

© British Museum, London.

300s B.C. Celts called Brythons live in Britain

55 B.C. Julius Caesar invades Britain

51 B.C. Cleopatra VII becomes last queen of Egypt

c. 50 Londinium (present-day London) is founded by Romans as a supply port

61 Queen Boadicea leads her eastern British tribe in an uprising against the Romans

A.D. 300

c. 313 Christianity is proclaimed lawful religion in the Roman Empire

409 Roman legions withdraw from Britain

c. 449 Angles, Saxons, and Jutes invade Britain

476 Roman Empire falls to Germanic tribes

c. 516 Semilegendary King Arthur rules Celtic tribe

537 King Arthur dies at Battle of Camlann

547 Widespread plague reaches Britain from Europe

552 Buddhism is introduced to Japan

597 Saint Augustine converts Anglo-Saxon King Ethelbert and establishes monastery at Canterbury

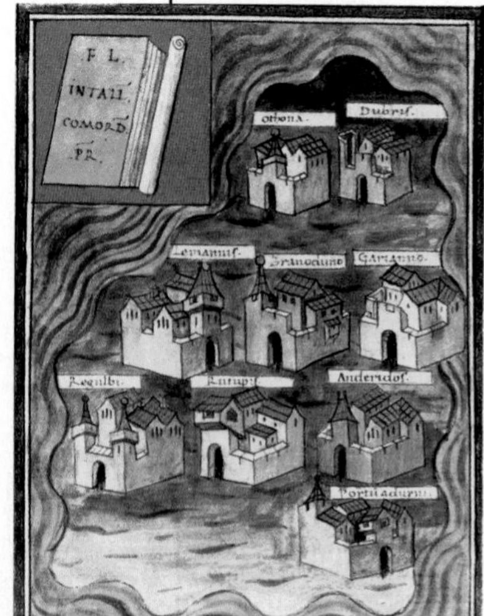

Comes Litoris Saxon per Britaniam (c. 950). Anglo-Saxon map.

Bibliothèque municipale, Rouen, France. The Bridgeman Art Library, New York.

449–1066

Kingston brooch (6th or 7th century).

City of Liverpool Museum, England. The Bridgeman Art Library, New York.

700 | **1066**

600s Lyric poetry of the T'ang period promotes everyday use of Chinese language

640 At Alexandria, Arabs discover the famous library with 300,000 papyrus scrolls

c. 670 Caedmon, the earliest English Christian poet, writes hymns

c. 700 *Beowulf* is first recorded

730 The Venerable Bede, an English cleric, writes the *Ecclesiastical History of the English People*

c. 759 *Manyoshu (Collection of Ten Thousand Leaves),* Japanese anthology of about 4,500 poems, is compiled

760 Monks begin the Book of Kells, an illuminated manuscript of Latin Gospels

c. 850 The *Poetic Edda,* a famous cycle of Norse mythological poems, is composed

900 The Arabian tales *The Thousand and One Nights* are begun

c. 975 *The Exeter Book,* a collection of English poetry, is first copied

c. 1000 In Japan, Lady Murasaki Shikibu writes the world's first novel, *The Tale of Genji*

700 | **1066**

618 Golden age of T'ang dynasty begins in China

c. 625 Mohammed (b. 570), founder of Islam, begins to dictate the Koran

664 Synod of Whitby unites British Christian Church with Roman Church

Coronation of Charlemagne by Pope Leo III. Miniature.

Bibliothèque de l'arsenal, Paris. © Scala/Art Resource, New York.

711 Moors invade Spain

793 Vikings invade Britain, beginning a century of invasions

800 In France, Charlemagne is crowned emperor of the West by Pope Leo III

c. 800 Incas build fortress-city of Machu Picchu in Peru

c. 810 Algebra is devised in Persia

813 School of astronomy is founded at Baghdad

871 Alfred the Great (849–899) becomes king of England

878 Alfred forces the Danes from Wessex

900s Kingdom of Ghana, in Africa, flourishes

1066 Normans defeat Saxons; William the Conqueror becomes English king

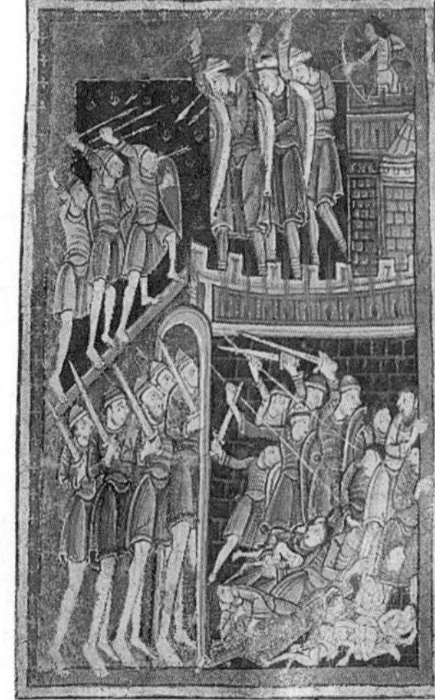

Danes attacking an East Anglian town.

The Pierpont Morgan Library, NY.

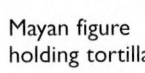

Mayan figure holding tortillas.

Political and Social

Roman Occupation, 55 B.C.–A.D. 409

Roman conquerors arrived with Julius Caesar and remained in Britain for more than four hundred years. They built roads throughout the island and Hadrian's Wall, a seventy-three-mile-long fortification that kept invaders out for several centuries. But when the Romans withdrew completely, in A.D. 409, Britain was left with no government—and again it was vulnerable to invasion.

Hadrian's Wall, a seventy-three-mile defensive barrier (built c. A.D. 122).

Anglo-Saxon Invasion, A.D. 449

In the fifth century the Angles and Saxons, from Germany, and the Jutes, from Denmark, drove the Britons to the perimeter of the country and imposed their

Milestones 449–1066

language and warrior culture on most of Britain. The Anglo-Saxons brought with them a fierce loyalty to their tight-knit communities and to their grim religion. They also greatly esteemed the scops, the storytellers of their society. The scops played the invaluable role of community preservationists, celebrating the heroes of Anglo-Saxon culture through poetic songs.

Divided at first into clans and principalities and later harassed by invading Danes, the Anglo-Saxons were eventually united under King Alfred the Great of Wessex in the ninth century.

(Opposite) Dragon ship. Detail from a manuscript.

By permission of The British Library, London.

The Spread of Christianity, A.D. 400–A.D. 699

Christianity was introduced to Britain during the Roman occupation, but centuries passed before it became the dominant religion of the country. Starting in the early fifth century, Ireland's Christian monks, along with missionaries from Rome and elsewhere on the Continent, began to settle parts of Britain and spread their beliefs. Christian monasteries and Anglo-Saxon culture coexisted for many years. By the late seventh century, however, Christianity had virtually replaced the British pagan religions.

Celtic cross in Cornwall, England.

© Michael Nicholson/CORBIS.

The Norman Invasion, 1066

William the Conqueror crossed the English Channel in 1066 and defeated the Anglo-Saxon armies at the Battle of Hastings. Thus was ended the dominance of Anglo-Saxon culture in the island kingdom.

The battle in which King Harold is killed, from the Bayeux Tapestry (detail) (c. 11th century).

Musée de la tapisserie, Bayeux, France.

The Anglo-Saxons 449–1066

by David Adams Leeming

PREVIEW

Think About . . .

The United States would not be what it is today without its British legacy—in law, literature, and language.

As you read about this period, look for answers to the following questions:

- What specifically did America inherit from Britain in terms of our political system, law, and language?
- What was the influence of Christianity on Britain?
- What was the heroic ideal of Anglo-Saxon Britain?

Collection introduction (pages 4–17) covers **Literary Skills** Evaluate the philosophical, political, religious, ethical, and social influences of a historical period.

Isolated from the European continent, rain-drenched and often fogged in but also green and dotted with thatched cottages, quaint stone churches, and mysterious stone ruins, the island of Great Britain seems made for elves, legends, and poets. If this land of mystery, beauty, and melancholy weather has produced Stonehenge, Robin Hood, and Shakespeare, it has also produced the theory of gravity, the Industrial Revolution, radar, penicillin, and the Beatles.

The British Legacy

We tend to associate the British with their monarchy and their former empire. We should also remember, however, that while most of the world suffered under various forms of tyranny, the British from the time of the Magna Carta (1215) were gradually creating a political system "by and for the people" that remains today a source of envy and inspiration for many nations. Although Americans rebelled against British rule in 1776, the United States would not be what it is today without the legacy of British common law—with its emphasis on personal rights and freedom. Nor would the United States be what it is today without the British parliamentary government, British literature, and the English language.

This relatively small island of Great Britain has been invaded and settled many times: first by ancient people we call the Iberians, then by the Celts (kelts), by the Romans, by the Angles and Saxons, by the Vikings, and by the Normans. Whatever we think of as British today owes something to each of these invaders.

The Spirit of the Celts

When Greek travelers visited what is now Great Britain in the fourth century B.C., they found an island settled by tall blond warriors who called themselves Celts. Among these island Celts was a group called Brythons—Britons—who left their permanent stamp in one of the names eventually adopted for the land they settled (Britain).

The religion of the Celts seems to have been a form of **animism,** from the Latin word for "spirit." The Celts saw spirits everywhere—in rivers, trees, stones, ponds, fire, and thunder. These spirits, or gods, controlled all aspects of existence, and they had to be constantly satisfied. Priests, called Druids, acted as intermediaries between the gods and the people. Sometimes ritual dances were called for, sometimes even human sacrifice. Some think that Stonehenge—that array of huge stones on Salisbury Plain in Wiltshire—was used by the Druids for religious rites having to do with the lunar and solar cycles.

All the Britons dye their bodies with woad, which produces a blue color, and this gives them a more terrifying appearance in battle. They wear their hair long, and shave the whole of their bodies except the head and the upper lip.

—Julius Caesar

Stonehenge, consisting of large sandstone blocks and smaller bluestone pillars.

Boadicea, queen of a Briton tribe, was flogged by the Romans after they had plundered her dead husband's property. She led the Britons in a fierce retaliation.

Boadicea found herself at the head of a numerous army, and nearly all the Britons within reach rallied to her standard. There followed an uprush of hatred from the abyss, which is a measure of the cruelty of the conquest. It was a scream of rage against invincible oppression. . . . Her monument on the Thames Embankment opposite Big Ben reminds us of the harsh cry of liberty or death which has echoed down the ages.

—Winston S. Churchill

The Celtic Heroes and Heroines: A Magical World

The mythology of the Celts has influenced British and Irish writers to this day. Sir Thomas Malory (see page 214), in the fifteenth century, having time on his hands while in jail, gathered together the Celtic legends about a warrior named Arthur. He mixed these stories generously with chivalric legends from the Continent and produced *Le Morte d'Arthur,* about the king who ultimately became the very embodiment of British values.

Early in the twentieth century, William Butler Yeats used the Celtic myths in his poetry and plays in an attempt to make the Irish aware of their lost heroic past.

The Celtic stories are very different from the Anglo-Saxon tales that came later (see page 21), although it is the Anglo-Saxon myths that we tend to study in school. Unlike the male-dominated Anglo-Saxon stories, the Celtic legends are full of strong women, like the tall and fierce and very beautiful Queen Maeve of Connacht (kân′ôt) in Ireland. Maeve once led her troops in an epic battle over the ownership of a fabulous white bull whose back was so broad fifty children could play upon it. Celtic stories, unlike the later, brooding Anglo-Saxon stories, leap into the sunlight (no matter how much blood is spilled). Full of fantastic animals, passionate love affairs, and incredible adventures, the Celtic myths take you to enchanted lands where magic and the imagination rule.

The Romans: The Great Administrators

Beginning with an invasion led by Julius Caesar in 55 B.C. and culminating in one organized by Emperor Claudius about a hundred years later, the Celts were finally conquered by the legions of Rome. Using the administrative genius that enabled them to hold dominion over much of the known world, the Romans provided the armies and organization that prevented further serious invasions of Britain for several hundred years. They built a network of roads (some still used today) and a great defensive wall seventy-three miles long. During Roman rule, Christianity, which would later become a unifying force, gradually took hold under the

A god, perhaps with sacrificial victims, from the Gundestrup caldron (detail) (c. 100 B.C.). Silver.

National Museum, Copenhagen. © Erich Lessing/Art Resource, NY.

King Sweyn and his Danish troops arrive in England, from a manuscript (c. 14th century).

The British Library, London.

leadership of European missionaries. The old Celtic religion began to vanish.

If the Romans had stayed, Londoners today might speak Italian. But the Romans had troubles at home. By A.D. 409, they had evacuated their troops from Britain, leaving roads, walls, villas, and great public baths, but no central government. Without Roman control, Britain was a country of separate clans. The resulting weakness made the island ripe for a series of successful invasions by non-Christian peoples from the Germanic regions of continental Europe.

The Anglo-Saxons Sweep Ashore

This time the attack came from the north. In the middle of the fifth century, the invaders, Angles and Saxons from Germany and Jutes from Denmark, crossed the North Sea. They drove out the old Britons and eventually settled the greater part of Britain. The language of the Anglo-Saxons became the dominant language in the land that was to take a new name—Engla land, or England—from the Angles.

Reconstructed Anglo-Saxon village in West Stow, Suffolk, England. The communal hall is at the right.

The latest newcomers did not have an easy time of it. The Celts put up a strong resistance before they retreated into Wales, in the far west of the country. There traces of their culture, especially their language, can still be found. One of the heroic Celtic leaders was a Welsh chieftain called Arthur, who developed in legend as Britain's "once and future king."

Unifying Forces: Alfred the Great and Christianity

At first, Anglo-Saxon England was no more politically unified than Celtic Britain had been. The country was divided into several independent principalities, each with its own "king." It was not until King Alfred of Wessex (reigned 871–899), also known as Alfred the Great, led the Anglo-Saxons against the invading Danes that England became in any true sense a nation. The Danes were one of the fierce Viking peoples who crossed the cold North

Gold and enamel jewel (9th century) thought to have belonged to King Alfred, possibly the handle to a pointer used for following manuscript text.

Ashmolean Museum, Oxford, England.

Sea in their dragon-prowed boats in the eighth and ninth centuries. Plundering and destroying everything in their path, the Danes eventually took over and settled in parts of northeast and central England.

It is possible that even King Alfred would have failed to unify the Anglo-Saxons had it not been for the gradual reemergence of Christianity in Britain. Irish and Continental missionaries converted the Anglo-Saxon kings, whose subjects converted also. Christianity provided a common faith and common system of morality and right conduct; it also linked England to Europe. Under Christianity and Alfred, Anglo-Saxons fought to protect their people, their culture, and their church from the ravages of the Danes. Alfred's reign began the shaky dominance of Wessex kings in southern England. Alfred's descendants—Ethelfleda, a brilliant military leader and strategist, and her brother Edward—carried on his battle against the Danes.

The battle continued until both the Anglo-Saxons and the Danes were defeated in 1066 by William, duke of Normandy, and his invading force of Normans from northwestern France.

Anglo-Saxon Life: The Warm Hall, the Cold World

In 1939, in Sutton Hoo (in Suffolk, England), archaeologists discovered a treasure that had been under the earth for thirteen hundred years. This enormous ship-grave contained the imprint of a huge wooden ship and a vast treasure trove—all of which had been buried with a great king or noble warrior. There was no trace of the king or warrior himself, but his sword lay there, along with other

What Does "Anglo-Saxon England" Mean?

Here are some key features of this age of warriors:

- Anglo-Saxon society developed from kinship groups led by a strong chief.
- The people farmed, maintained local governments, and created fine crafts, especially metalwork.
- Christianity eventually replaced the old warrior religion, linking England to continental Europe.
- Monasteries served as centers of learning and preserved works from the older oral tradition.
- English—not just the Church's Latin—gained respect as a written language.

The coronation of King Harold, from the Bayeux Tapestry (detail) (11th century).

Musée de la tapisserie, Bayeux, France.

Helmet fragment (7th century) from the Sutton Hoo ship treasure, Suffolk, England.

The Bridgeman Art Library, New York/ British Museum, London.

meticulously decorated treasures of gold, silver, and bronze—his purse, coins, helmet, buckle, serving vessels, and harp. This grave can't help but remind us of the huge burial mound erected in memory of the king Beowulf.

As these Sutton Hoo ship treasures show, the Anglo-Saxons were not barbarians, though they are frequently depicted that way. However, they did not lead luxurious lives either, nor were their lives dominated by learning or the arts. Warfare was the order of the day. As *Beowulf* shows, law and order, at least in the early days, were the responsibility of the leader in any given group, whether family, clan, tribe, or kingdom. Fame and success, even survival, were gained only through loyalty to the leader, especially during war, and success was measured in gifts from the leader. Beowulf, as you will see in the story that follows, makes his name and gains riches by defeating the monsters who try to destroy King Hrothgar.

A CLOSER LOOK: SOCIAL INFLUENCES

Women in Anglo-Saxon Culture

INFORMATIONAL TEXT

Anglo-Saxon culture, with its emphasis on warfare, sounds as if it would be an inhospitable place for women. In fact, women had rights in this society, rights that were sharply curtailed after the Norman Conquest in 1066.

Evidence from wills first used during the later Anglo-Saxon period shows that women inherited and held property. Even when married, women still retained control over their own property. In fact, a prospective husband had to offer a woman a substantial gift (called the *morgengifu,* "morning-gift") of money and land. The woman (not her family or her husband) had personal control over this gift: She could give it away, sell it, or bequeath it as she chose.

Christianity also offered opportunities for women. Women joined religious communities, and some women became powerful abbesses. These abbesses, usually women from noble families, were in charge of large double houses that included both a monastery and a nunnery. Hild (614–680), the abbess of Whitby (in present-day Yorkshire), was one of the most famous of these women. Hild accumulated an immense library and turned Whitby into a center of learning. Vikings sacked Whitby Abbey in the ninth century. The ruins of a monastery later founded at the same site still stand today, high atop cliffs overlooking the wild, gray North Sea.

The ruins of Whitby Abbey, Yorkshire, England.

The Bridgeman Art Library. Private Collection.

This pattern of loyal dependency was basic to Anglo-Saxon life. Such loyalty grew out of a need to protect the group from the terrors of an enemy-infested wilderness—a wilderness that became particularly frightening during the long, bone-chilling nights of winter. In most of England, the Anglo-Saxons tended to live close to their animals in single-family homesteads, wooden buildings that surrounded a communal court or a warm, fire-lit chieftain's hall. This cluster of buildings was protected by a wooden stockade fence. The arrangement contributed to a sense of security and to the close relationship between leader and followers. It also encouraged the Anglo-Saxon tendency to participate in community discussion and rule by consensus.

Three standing figures (Odin, Thor, and Freyr) in tunics, from a Viking tapestry (12th century).

Statens Historiska Museet, Stockholm.

The god Odin being eaten by the wolf Fenrir, from a Viking stone carving.

Manx Museum, Isle of Man, England. © Werner Forman/ Art Resource, New York.

FAST FACTS

Philosophical Views

- The religion of the Celts infuses an imaginative, heroic strain into British culture that surfaces in the medieval legends of King Arthur.
- The brooding fatalism of pagan Anglo-Saxon culture gives the first great British epic, *Beowulf,* its melancholy tone and its emphasis on earthly heroism rather than hope for an afterlife.
- The almost universal adoption of Christianity in the late seventh century unites Britain under a common ethical code.

The Anglo-Saxon Religion: Gods for Warriors

Despite the influence of Christianity, the old Anglo-Saxon religion, with its warrior gods, persisted. A dark, fatalistic religion, it had been brought by the Anglo-Saxons from Germany and had much in common with what we think of as Norse or Scandinavian mythology.

One of the most important Norse gods was Odin, the god of death, poetry, and magic. The Anglo-Saxon name for Odin was Woden (from which we have *Wednesday,* "Woden's day"). Woden could help humans communicate with spirits, and he was associated especially with burial rites and ecstatic trances, important for both poetry and religious mysteries. Not surprisingly, this god of poetry and death played an important role in the lives of people who produced great poetry yet maintained a somber, brooding outlook on life.

The Anglo-Saxon deity named Thunor was essentially the same as Thor, the Norse god of thunder and lightning. His sign was the hammer and possibly also the twisted cross we call the swastika, which is found on so many Anglo-Saxon gravestones. (Thunor's name survives in *Thursday,* "Thor's day.")

Still another significant figure in Anglo-Saxon mythology is the dragon, which seems always, as in *Beowulf,* to be the protector of a treasure. Some scholars suggest that the fiery dragon should be seen as both a personification of "death the devourer" and the guardian of the grave mound, in which a warrior's ashes and his treasure lay.

On the whole the religion of the Anglo-Saxons seems to have been more concerned with ethics than with mysticism—with the earthly virtues of bravery, loyalty, generosity, and friendship.

The Bards: Singing of Gods and Heroes

The Anglo-Saxon communal hall, besides offering shelter and a place for council meetings, provided space for storytellers and their audiences. As in other parts of the ancient world (notably Homeric Greece more than one thousand years earlier), skilled storytellers, or bards, sang of gods and heroes. The Anglo-Saxons did not regard these bards—whom they called **scops** (skäps)—as inferior to warriors. To the Anglo-Saxons, creating poetry was as important as fighting, hunting, farming, or loving.

The poets sang to the strumming of a harp. As sources for their improvisational poetry, the storytellers had a rich supply of heroic tales that reflected the concerns of a people constantly under threat of war, disease, or old age. We are told of the king in *Beowulf:*

> . . . sometimes Hrothgar himself, with the harp
> In his lap, stroked its silvery strings
> And told wonderful stories, a brave king
> Reciting unhappy truths about good

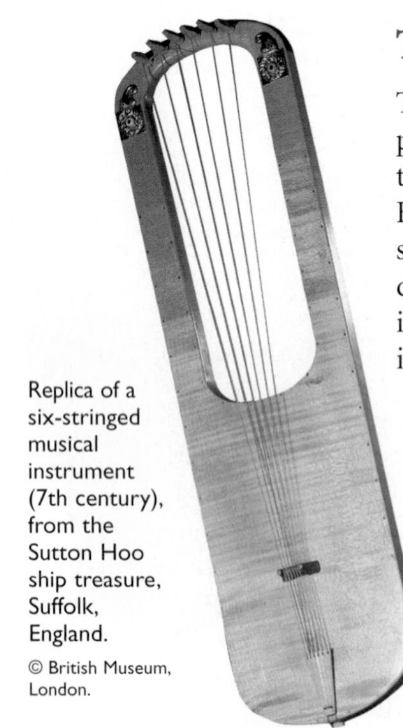

Replica of a six-stringed musical instrument (7th century), from the Sutton Hoo ship treasure, Suffolk, England.

Saint John dictating to the Venerable Bede, from a miscellany (c. 1140). Pen with brown and red ink with color washes on vellum.

And evil—and sometimes he wove his stories
On the mournful thread of old age, remembering
Buried strength and the battles it had won.
He would weep, the old king.

—lines 2107–2114

Hope in Immortal Verse

Anglo-Saxon literature contains many works in this same elegiac, or mournful, strain. Poems such as "The Seafarer" (see page 87), for example, stress the fact that life is hard and ends only in death. For the non-Christian Anglo-Saxons, whose religion offered them no hope of an afterlife, only fame and its commemoration in poetry could provide a defense against death. Perhaps this is why the Anglo-Saxon bards, gifted with the skill to preserve fame in the collective memory, were such honored members of their society.

FAST FACTS

Political Highlights

- The Romans invade in 55 B.C. and organize the fragmented early Britons under a single central government, creating a four-hundred-year period of political stability.
- In the middle of the fifth century, the Angles, Saxons, and Jutes replace the Celts as the dominant political and cultural force in Britain.
- King Alfred of Wessex and his descendants unite Anglo-Saxon England in the late ninth century.

Social Influences

- The bards, or scops, give stories an important position in early British culture.
- Christian monks copy ancient manuscripts and thereby help to preserve classical texts as well as popular Anglo-Saxon literature.

A Light from Ireland

Ireland had historical good luck in the fifth century. Unlike England and the rest of Europe, Ireland, isolated and surrounded by wild seas, was not overrun by the Germanic invaders. Then, in 432, the whole of Celtic Ireland was converted to Christianity by a Romanized Briton named Patricius (Patrick). Patrick had been seized by Irish slave traders when he was a teenager and had been held in bondage by a sheepherder in Ireland for six years. He escaped captivity, became a bishop, and returned to convert his former captors. His success was speedy and undying. From 432 to 750, while Europe and England sank into constant warfare, confusion, and ignorance, Ireland experienced a golden age. The Irish monks founded monasteries that became sanctuaries of learning for refugee scholars from Europe and England. Thus it was in Ireland that Christianity, in the words of Winston Churchill, "burned and gleamed through the darkness."

Opening of *St. Matthew's Gospel*, from the Lindisfarne Gospels (7th century). Note the scribe's comments in the margins.

The British Library, London.

The Christian Monasteries: The Ink Froze

In the death-shadowed world of the Anglo-Saxons, the poets or bards provided one element of hope: the possibility that heroic deeds might be enshrined in the society's memory. Another element of hope was supplied by Christianity. The monasteries served as centers of learning in this period, just as they would in the Middle Ages. In England the cultural and spiritual influence of monasteries existed right alongside the older Anglo-Saxon religion. In fact, the monasteries preserved not only the Latin and Greek classics but also some of the great works of popular literature, such as *Beowulf.*

Monks assigned to the monastery's scriptorium, or writing room, probably spent almost all their daylight hours copying manuscripts by hand. (Printing was still eight hundred years away in England.) The scriptorium was in a covered walkway (the cloister) open to a court. Makeshift walls of oiled paper or glass helped somewhat, but the British Isles in winter are cold; the ink could freeze. Picture a shivering scribe, hunched over sheepskin "paper," called vellum, pressing with a quill pen, obeying a rule of silence: That's how seriously the Church took learning.

The Rise of the English Language

Latin alone remained the language of serious study in England until the time of King Alfred. During his reign, Alfred instituted the *Anglo-Saxon Chronicle,* a lengthy running history of England that covered the earliest days and continued until 1154. Partly because of King Alfred's efforts, English began to gain respect as a language of culture. Only then did the Old English stories and poetry preserved by the monks come to be recognized as great works of literature.

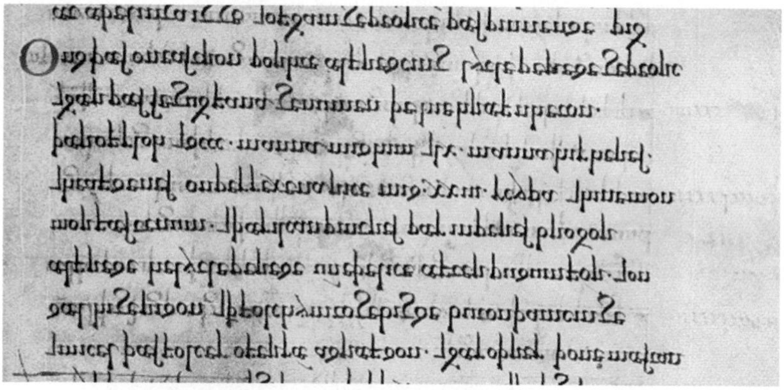

Page from the *Anglo-Saxon Chronicle* (detail).

By permission of The British Library, London.

REVIEW

Talk About . . .

Turn back to the Think About questions at the beginning of this introduction to the Anglo-Saxon period (page 6). Write down your responses, and get together with a classmate to compare and discuss your views.

Write About . . .

Contrasting Literary Periods

Heroism, then and now. The mythology and literature of the early Celts and Anglo-Saxons were filled with larger-than-life heroes. The Anglo-Saxon heroes were exclusively male, but Celtic history and mythology record some powerful female warriors. How do these ancient views of heroism compare with today's notions of personal greatness? In a brief essay, discuss the ways in which individuals gain fame and fortune today. How are their accomplishments celebrated and remembered?

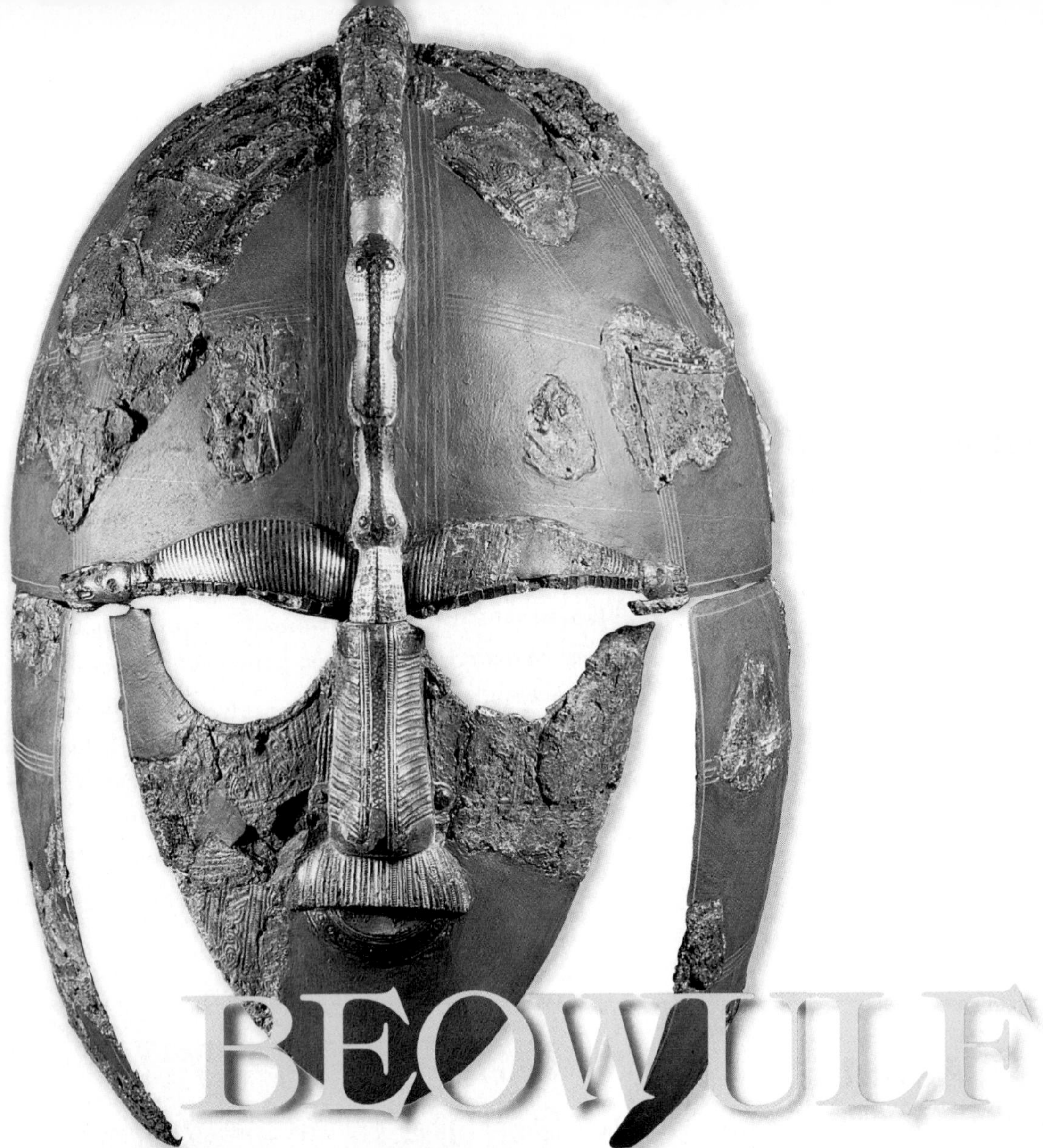

BEOWULF

Sutton Hoo helmet (7th century), from the Sutton Hoo ship treasure, Suffolk, England.
British Museum, London.

Beowulf is to England what Homer's *Iliad* (see page 67) and *Odyssey* are to ancient Greece: It is the first great work of the English national literature—the mythical and literary record of a formative stage of English civilization. It is also an epic of the heroic sources of English culture. As such, *Beowulf* uses a host of traditional **motifs,** or recurring elements, associated with heroic literature all over the world.

The epic tells of Beowulf (his name may mean "bear"), a Geat from Sweden who crosses the sea to Denmark in a quest to rescue King Hrothgar's people from the demonic monster Grendel. Like most early heroic literature, *Beowulf* is an oral epic. It was handed down, with changes and embellishments, from one minstrel to another. The stories of *Beowulf,* like those of all oral epics, are traditional, familiar to the audiences who crowded around the harpist-bards in the communal halls at night. They are the stories of dream and legend, archetypal tales of monsters and god-fashioned weapons, of descents to the underworld and fights with dragons, of the hero's quest and a community threatened by the powers of evil.

The Sources of *Beowulf*

By the standards of Homer, whose epics run to nearly 15,000 lines, *Beowulf* is short—approximately 3,200 lines. It was composed in Old English, probably in Northumbria, in northeastern England, sometime between 700 and 750. The world it depicts, however, is much older, that of the early sixth century. Much of the poem's material is based on early folk legends—some Celtic, some Scandinavian. Since the scenery described is the coast of Northumbria, not Scandinavia, it has been assumed that the poet who wrote the version that has come down to us was Northumbrian. Given the Christian elements in the epic, it is thought that this poet may have been a monk.

The only manuscript of *Beowulf* we have dates from the year 1000 and is now in the British Museum in London. Burned and stained, it was discovered in the eighteenth century: Somehow it had survived Henry VIII's destruction of the monasteries two hundred years earlier.

The Translations of *Beowulf*

Part One of the text you are about to read is from Burton Raffel's popular 1963 translation of the epic. Part Two is from the Irish poet Seamus Heaney's award-winning, bestselling translation of the work, published in 2000.

Prow of the Oseberg ship.

People, Monsters, and Places

Beowulf: a Geat, son of Edgetho (Ecgtheow) and nephew of Higlac (Hygelac), king of the Geats.

Grendel: man-eating monster who lives at the bottom of a foul mere, or mountain lake. His name might be related to the Old Norse *grindill,* meaning "storm," or *grenja,* "bellow."

Herot: golden guest hall built by King Hrothgar, the Danish ruler. It was decorated with the antlers of stags; the name means "hart [stag] hall." Scholars think Herot might have been built near Lejre on the coast of Zealand, in Denmark.

Hrothgar: king of the Danes, builder of Herot. He had once befriended Beowulf's father. His father was called Healfdane (which probably means "half Dane").

Wiglaf: a Geat warrior, one of Beowulf's select band and the only one to help him in his final fight.

Before You Read

from Beowulf

Make the Connection

Quickwrite

This is a story about a hero from the misty reaches of the British past, a hero who faces violence, horror, and even death to save a people in mortal danger. The epic's events took place many centuries ago, but this story still speaks to people today, perhaps because so many of us are in need of a rescuer, a hero.

Take a moment to write about a contemporary hero, real or fictional, and the challenges he or she faces. Describe your hero, and then briefly analyze him or her using these questions:

- What sort of evil or oppression does your hero confront?
- Why does he or she confront evil? What's the motivation?
- For whom does your hero confront evil?
- What virtues does your hero represent?

Literary Focus

The Epic Hero

Beowulf is ancient England's hero, but he is also an **archetype,** or perfect example, of an **epic hero.** In other times, in other cultures, the hero has taken the shape of King Arthur or Gilgamesh (see page 58), or Sundiata or Joan of Arc. In modern America the hero may be a real person, like Martin Luther King, Jr., or a fictional character, like Shane in the western novel of the same name. The hero archetype in *Beowulf* is the dragon slayer, representing a besieged community facing evil forces that lurk in the cold darkness. Grendel, the monster lurking in the depths of the lagoon, may represent all of those threatening forces.

Beowulf, like all epic heroes, possesses superior physical strength and supremely ethical standards. He embodies the highest ideals of Anglo-Saxon culture. In his quest he must defeat monsters that embody dark, destructive powers. At the end of the quest, he is glorified by the people he has saved. If you follow current events, particularly stories concerning people who have gained freedom after years of oppression, you will still see at work this impulse to glorify those people who have set them free. You might also see this impulse in the impressive monuments—and great tourist attractions—in Washington, D.C.

Literary Skills Understand the archetype of the epic hero.

The **epic hero** is the central figure in a long narrative that reflects the values and heroic ideals of a particular society. An **epic** is a quest story on a grand scale.

For more on the Epic, see the Handbook of Literary and Historical Terms.

Vocabulary Development

resolute (rez′ə • lo͞ot′) *adj.:* determined.

vehemently (vē′ə • mənt • lē) *adv.:* violently.

infallible (in • fal′ə • bəl) *adj.:* unable to fail or be wrong.

furled (fûrld) *v.:* rolled up.

lavish (lav′ish) *adj.:* extravagant.

assail (ə • sāl′) *v.:* attack.

extolled (ek • stōld′) *v.:* praised.

INTERNET
Vocabulary Practice
Keyword: LE7 12-1

Viking coin minted in England (10th–11th century). Most such coins consist of precious metals extorted from the British as tribute.
British Museum, London.

Page from the *Beowulf* manuscript (c.1000). Cotton MS Vitellius AXV, f.133.
The Art Archive/British Library, London.

from Beowulf

Part One, translated by Burton Raffel

Viking Warrior Figure, 12th century, Sweden, animal horn.
The Granger Collection, New York.

The Monster Grendel

1

. . . A powerful monster, living down
In the darkness, growled in pain, impatient
As day after day the music rang
Loud in that hall,° the harp's rejoicing
Call and the poet's clear songs, sung
Of the ancient beginnings of us all, recalling
The Almighty making the earth, shaping
These beautiful plains marked off by oceans,
Then proudly setting the sun and moon
To glow across the land and light it;
The corners of the earth were made lovely with trees
And leaves, made quick with life, with each
Of the nations who now move on its face. And then
As now warriors sang of their pleasure:
So Hrothgar's men lived happy in his hall
Till the monster stirred, that demon, that fiend,
Grendel, who haunted the moors, the wild
Marshes, and made his home in a hell
Not hell but earth. He was spawned in that slime,
Conceived by a pair of those monsters born
Of Cain,° murderous creatures banished
By God, punished forever for the crime
Of Abel's death. The Almighty drove
Those demons out, and their exile was bitter,
Shut away from men; they split
Into a thousand forms of evil—spirits
And fiends, goblins, monsters, giants,
A brood forever opposing the Lord's
Will, and again and again defeated.

4. hall: guest-hall or mead-hall. (Mead is a fermented drink made from honey, water, yeast, and malt.) The hall was a central gathering place where Anglo-Saxon warriors could feast, listen to a bard's stories, and sleep in safety.

21. Cain: Grendel is the offspring of one of the descendants of Cain, a son of Adam and Eve. Cain killed his brother, Abel, and became the first murderer. He was eternally cursed by God and, according to legend, fathered all the evil beings that plague humankind: monsters, demons, and evil spirits.

Lines have been renumbered and do not correspond to the New American Library edition or the Farrar, Straus, and Giroux edition.

2

Then, when darkness had dropped, Grendel
Went up to Herot, wondering what the warriors
Would do in that hall when their drinking was done.
He found them sprawled in sleep, suspecting
Nothing, their dreams undisturbed. The monster's
Thoughts were as quick as his greed or his claws:
He slipped through the door and there in the silence
Snatched up thirty men, smashed them
Unknowing in their beds, and ran out with their bodies,
The blood dripping behind him, back
To his lair, delighted with his night's slaughter.
At daybreak, with the sun's first light, they saw
How well he had worked, and in that gray morning
Broke their long feast with tears and laments
For the dead. Hrothgar, their lord, sat joyless
In Herot, a mighty prince mourning
The fate of his lost friends and companions,
Knowing by its tracks that some demon had torn
His followers apart. He wept, fearing
The beginning might not be the end. And that night
Grendel came again, so set
On murder that no crime could ever be enough,
No savage assault quench his lust
For evil. Then each warrior tried
To escape him, searched for rest in different
Beds, as far from Herot as they could find,
Seeing how Grendel hunted when they slept.
Distance was safety; the only survivors
Were those who fled him. Hate had triumphed.
So Grendel ruled, fought with the righteous,
One against many, and won; so Herot
Stood empty, and stayed deserted for years,
Twelve winters of grief for Hrothgar, king
Of the Danes, sorrow heaped at his door
By hell-forged hands. His misery leaped
The seas, was told and sung in all
Men's ears: how Grendel's hatred began,
How the monster relished his savage war
On the Danes, keeping the bloody feud
Alive, seeking no peace, offering
No truce, accepting no settlement, no price
In gold or land, and paying the living
For one crime only with another. No one
Waited for reparation° from his plundering claws:
That shadow of death hunted in the darkness,

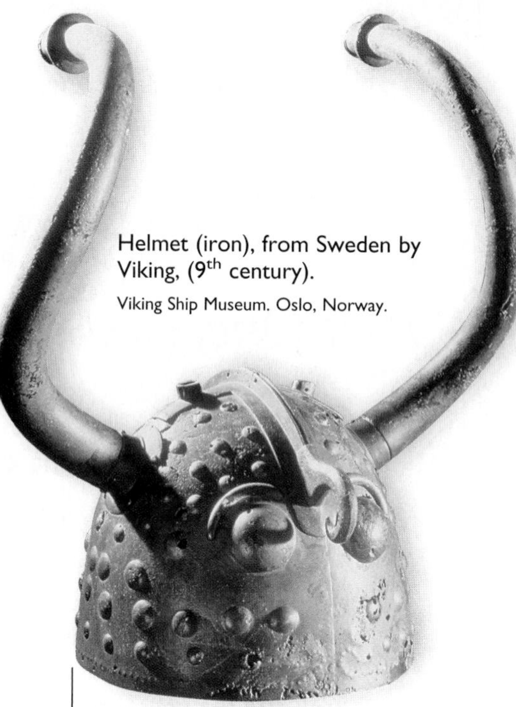

Helmet (iron), from Sweden by Viking, (9th century).
Viking Ship Museum. Oslo, Norway.

53–58. *Why do none of Hrothgar's men challenge Grendel?*

59–64. *How long has Grendel's reign of terror lasted?*

73. **reparation** (rep′ə•rā′shən) *n.:* payment to compensate for wrongdoing.

Stalked Hrothgar's warriors, old
And young, lying in waiting, hidden
In mist, invisibly following them from the edge
Of the marsh, always there, unseen.
So mankind's enemy continued his crimes,
Killing as often as he could, coming
Alone, bloodthirsty and horrible. Though he lived
In Herot, when the night hid him, he never
Dared to touch king Hrothgar's glorious
Throne, protected by God—God,
Whose love Grendel could not know. But Hrothgar's
Heart was bent. The best and most noble
Of his council debated remedies, sat
In secret sessions, talking of terror
And wondering what the bravest of warriors could do.
And sometimes they sacrificed to the old stone gods,
Made heathen vows, hoping for Hell's
Support, the Devil's guidance in driving
Their affliction off. That was their way,
And the heathen's only hope, Hell
Always in their hearts, knowing neither God
Nor His passing as He walks through our world, the Lord
Of Heaven and earth; their ears could not hear
His praise nor know His glory. Let them
Beware, those who are thrust into danger,
Clutched at by trouble, yet can carry no solace°
In their hearts, cannot hope to be better! Hail
To those who will rise to God, drop off
Their dead bodies, and seek our Father's peace!

? **79–89.** *Why is this background information about Grendel and Hrothgar in the poem?*

100. solace (säl′is) *n.:* peace.

3

So the living sorrow of Healfdane's son°
Simmered, bitter and fresh, and no wisdom
Or strength could break it: That agony hung
On king and people alike, harsh
And unending, violent and cruel, and evil.
In his far-off home Beowulf, Higlac's
Follower° and the strongest of the Geats—greater
And stronger than anyone anywhere in this world—
Heard how Grendel filled nights with horror
And quickly commanded a boat fitted out,
Proclaiming that he'd go to that famous king,
Would sail across the sea to Hrothgar,
Now when help was needed. None
Of the wise ones regretted his going, much

104. Healfdane's son: Hrothgar.

110. Higlac's follower: Higlac is Beowulf's uncle and feudal lord.

? **109–116.** *What qualities of the* ***epic hero*** *are conveyed by these lines?*

As he was loved by the Geats: The omens were good,
And they urged the adventure on. So Beowulf
Chose the mightiest men he could find,
The bravest and best of the Geats, fourteen
In all, and led them down to their boat;
He knew the sea, would point the prow°
Straight to that distant Danish shore. . . .

Beowulf arrives in Denmark and is directed to Herot, the mead-hall of King Hrothgar. The king sends Wulfgar, one of his thanes (or feudal lords), to greet the visitors.

The Arrival of the Hero

4

. . . Then Wulfgar went to the door and addressed
The waiting seafarers with soldier's words:
"My lord, the great king of the Danes, commands me
To tell you that he knows of your noble birth
And that having come to him from over the open
Sea you have come bravely and are welcome.
Now go to him as you are, in your armor and helmets,
But leave your battle-shields here, and your spears,
Let them lie waiting for the promises your words
May make."
Beowulf arose, with his men
Around him, ordering a few to remain
With their weapons, leading the others quickly
Along under Herot's steep roof into Hrothgar's
Presence. Standing on that prince's own hearth,
Helmeted, the silvery metal of his mail shirt°
Gleaming with a smith's° high art, he greeted
The Danes' great lord:
"Hail, Hrothgar!
Higlac is my cousin° and my king; the days
Of my youth have been filled with glory. Now Grendel's
Name has echoed in our land: Sailors
Have brought us stories of Herot, the best
Of all mead-halls, deserted and useless when the moon
Hangs in skies the sun had lit,
Light and life fleeing together.
My people have said, the wisest, most knowing
And best of them, that my duty was to go to the Danes'
Great king. They have seen my strength for themselves,
Have watched me rise from the darkness of war,
Dripping with my enemies' blood. I drove

123. prow (prou): front part of a boat.

139. mail shirt: armored garment made of interlocking metal rings.

140. smith's: metalworker's.

142. cousin: any relative.

Five great giants into chains, chased
All of that race from the earth. I swam
In the blackness of night, hunting monsters
Out of the ocean, and killing them one
By one; death was my errand and the fate
They had earned. Now Grendel and I are called
Together, and I've come. Grant me, then,
Lord and protector of this noble place,
A single request! I have come so far,
Oh shelterer of warriors and your people's loved friend,
That this one favor you should not refuse me—
That I, alone and with the help of my men,
May purge all evil from this hall. I have heard,
Too, that the monster's scorn of men
Is so great that he needs no weapons and fears none.
Nor will I. My lord Higlac
Might think less of me if I let my sword
Go where my feet were afraid to, if I hid
Behind some broad linden shield:° My hands
Alone shall fight for me, struggle for life
Against the monster. God must decide
Who will be given to death's cold grip.
Grendel's plan, I think, will be
What it has been before, to invade this hall
And gorge his belly with our bodies. If he can,
If he can. And I think, if my time will have come,
There'll be nothing to mourn over, no corpse to prepare
For its grave: Grendel will carry our bloody
Flesh to the moors, crunch on our bones,
And smear torn scraps of our skin on the walls
Of his den. No, I expect no Danes
Will fret about sewing our shrouds,° if he wins.
And if death does take me, send the hammered
Mail of my armor to Higlac, return
The inheritance I had from Hrethel,° and he
From Wayland.° Fate will unwind as it must!"

5

Hrothgar replied, protector of the Danes:
"Beowulf, you've come to us in friendship, and because
Of the reception your father found at our court.
Edgetho had begun a bitter feud,
Killing Hathlaf, a Wulfing warrior:°
Your father's countrymen were afraid of war,
If he returned to his home, and they turned him away.

? **151–160.** *Beowulf says that he has come to kill Grendel. What proof does he offer that he is up to the task?*

172. linden shield: shield made from wood of the linden tree.

? **180–185.** *Why will Hrothgar not have to hold a funeral if Beowulf dies?*

185. shrouds: cloths used to wrap a body for burial.

188. Hrethel: Beowulf's grandfather, former king of the Geats.
189. Wayland: a smith celebrated for his skill in making swords and mail shirts.

194. Wulfing warrior: The Wulfings were a Germanic tribe. Hrothgar's queen might have been a Wulfing.

Then he traveled across the curving waves
To the land of the Danes. I was new to the throne,
Then, a young man ruling this wide
Kingdom and its golden city: Hergar,
My older brother, a far better man
Than I, had died and dying made me,
Second among Healfdane's sons, first
In this nation. I bought the end of Edgetho's
Quarrel, sent ancient treasures through the ocean's
Furrows to the Wulfings; your father swore
He'd keep that peace. My tongue grows heavy,
And my heart, when I try to tell you what Grendel
Has brought us, the damage he's done, here
In this hall. You see for yourself how much smaller
Our ranks have become, and can guess what we've lost
To his terror. Surely the Lord Almighty
Could stop his madness, smother his lust!
How many times have my men, glowing
With courage drawn from too many cups
Of ale, sworn to stay after dark
And stem that horror with a sweep of their swords.
And then, in the morning, this mead-hall glittering
With new light would be drenched with blood, the benches
Stained red, the floors, all wet from that fiend's
Savage assault—and my soldiers would be fewer
Still, death taking more and more.
But to table, Beowulf, a banquet in your honor:
Let us toast your victories, and talk of the future."
Then Hrothgar's men gave places to the Geats,
Yielded benches to the brave visitors,
And led them to the feast. The keeper of the mead
Came carrying out the carved flasks,
And poured that bright sweetness. A poet
Sang, from time to time, in a clear
Pure voice. Danes and visiting Geats
Celebrated as one, drank and rejoiced.

? 191–207. *What do you think causes Hrothgar to make this speech, reminding Beowulf of the time he helped Beowulf's father? What is the probable effect of these words on Beowulf?*

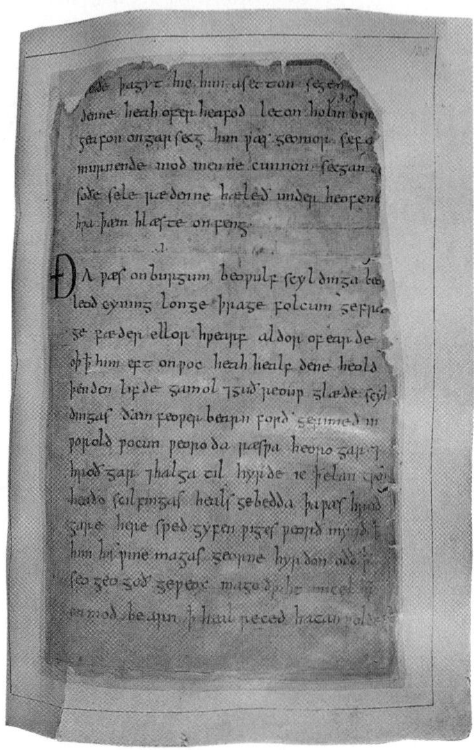

Page from the *Beowulf* manuscript (c.1000). Cotton MS Vitellius AXV, f.133.

The Art Archive/British Library, London.

Unferth's Challenge

6

Unferth spoke, Ecglaf's son,
Who sat at Hrothgar's feet, spoke harshly
And sharp (vexed° by Beowulf's adventure,
By their visitor's courage, and angry that anyone
In Denmark or anywhere on earth had ever

235. vexed (vekst): highly annoyed.

Acquired glory and fame greater
Than his own):
"You're Beowulf, are you—the same
Boastful fool who fought a swimming
Match with Brecca, both of you daring
And young and proud, exploring the deepest
Seas, risking your lives for no reason
But the danger? All older and wiser heads warned you
Not to, but no one could check such pride.
With Brecca at your side you swam along
The sea-paths, your swift-moving hands pulling you
Over the ocean's face. Then winter
Churned through the water, the waves ran you
As they willed, and you struggled seven long nights
To survive. And at the end victory was his,
Not yours. The sea carried him close
To his home, to southern Norway, near
The land of the Brondings, where he ruled and was loved,
Where his treasure was piled and his strength protected
His towns and his people. He'd promised to outswim you:
Bonstan's son° made that boast ring true.
You've been lucky in your battles, Beowulf, but I think
Your luck may change if you challenge Grendel,
Staying a whole night through in this hall,
Waiting where that fiercest of demons can find you."
Beowulf answered, Edgetho's great son:
"Ah! Unferth, my friend, your face
Is hot with ale, and your tongue has tried
To tell us about Brecca's doings. But the truth
Is simple: No man swims in the sea
As I can, no strength is a match for mine.
As boys, Brecca and I had boasted—
We were both too young to know better—that we'd risk
Our lives far out at sea, and so
We did. Each of us carried a naked
Sword, prepared for whales or the swift
Sharp teeth and beaks of needlefish.
He could never leave me behind, swim faster
Across the waves than I could, and I
Had chosen to remain close to his side.
I remained near him for five long nights,
Until a flood swept us apart;
The frozen sea surged around me,
It grew dark, the wind turned bitter, blowing
From the north, and the waves were savage. Creatures
Who sleep deep in the sea were stirred
Into life—and the iron hammered links

? **239–252.** *Why might Unferth think that Beowulf is ashamed of having taken part in the swimming race?*

257. Bonstan's son: Brecca.

? **274–276.** *What is Beowulf's explanation for not leaving Brecca far behind?*

Sutton Hoo Bowl (7th century).
Sutton Hoo ship burial.
Byzantine silver bowl.

The Granger Collection, New York.

Of my mail shirt, these shining bits of metal
Woven across my breast, saved me
From death. A monster seized me, drew me
Swiftly toward the bottom, swimming with its claws
Tight in my flesh. But fate let me
Find its heart with my sword, hack myself
Free; I fought that beast's last battle,
Left it floating lifeless in the sea.

7

"Other monsters crowded around me,
Continually attacking. I treated them politely,
Offering the edge of my razor-sharp sword.
But the feast, I think, did not please them, filled
Their evil bellies with no banquet-rich food,
Thrashing there at the bottom of the sea;
By morning they'd decided to sleep on the shore,
Lying on their backs, their blood spilled out
On the sand. Afterwards, sailors could cross
That sea-road and feel no fear; nothing
Would stop their passing. Then God's bright beacon
Appeared in the east, the water lay still,
And at last I could see the land, wind-swept
Cliff-walls at the edge of the coast. Fate saves
The living when they drive away death by themselves!
Lucky or not, nine was the number
Of sea-huge monsters I killed. What man,
Anywhere under Heaven's high arch, has fought
In such darkness, endured more misery, or been harder
Pressed? Yet I survived the sea, smashed
The monsters' hot jaws, swam home from my journey.
The swift-flowing waters swept me along
And I landed on Finnish soil. I've heard
No tales of you, Unferth, telling
Of such clashing terror, such contests in the night!
Brecca's battles were never so bold;
Neither he nor you can match me—and I mean
No boast, have announced no more than I know
To be true. And there's more: You murdered your brothers,
Your own close kin. Words and bright wit
Won't help your soul; you'll suffer hell's fires,
Unferth, forever tormented. Ecglaf's
Proud son, if your hands were as hard, your heart
As fierce as you think it, no fool would dare
To raid your hall, ruin Herot

? **323–334.** *What is Beowulf's final response to Unferth's challenge?*

And oppress its prince, as Grendel has done.
But he's learned that terror is his alone,
Discovered he can come for your people with no fear
Of reprisal;° he's found no fighting, here,
But only food, only delight.
He murders as he likes, with no mercy, gorges
And feasts on your flesh, and expects no trouble,
No quarrel from the quiet Danes. Now
The Geats will show him courage, soon
He can test his strength in battle. And when the sun
Comes up again, opening another
Bright day from the south, anyone in Denmark
May enter this hall: That evil will be gone!"
Hrothgar, gray-haired and brave, sat happily
Listening, the famous ring-giver sure,
At last, that Grendel could be killed; he believed
In Beowulf's bold strength and the firmness of his spirit.
There was the sound of laughter, and the cheerful clanking
Of cups, and pleasant words. Then Welthow,
Hrothgar's gold-ringed queen, greeted
The warriors; a noble woman who knew
What was right, she raised a flowing cup
To Hrothgar first, holding it high
For the lord of the Danes to drink, wishing him
Joy in that feast. The famous king
Drank with pleasure and blessed their banquet.
Then Welthow went from warrior to warrior,
Pouring a portion from the jeweled cup
For each, till the bracelet-wearing queen
Had carried the mead-cup among them and it was Beowulf's

330. reprisal (ri•prī′zəl) *n.:* punishment in return for an injury.

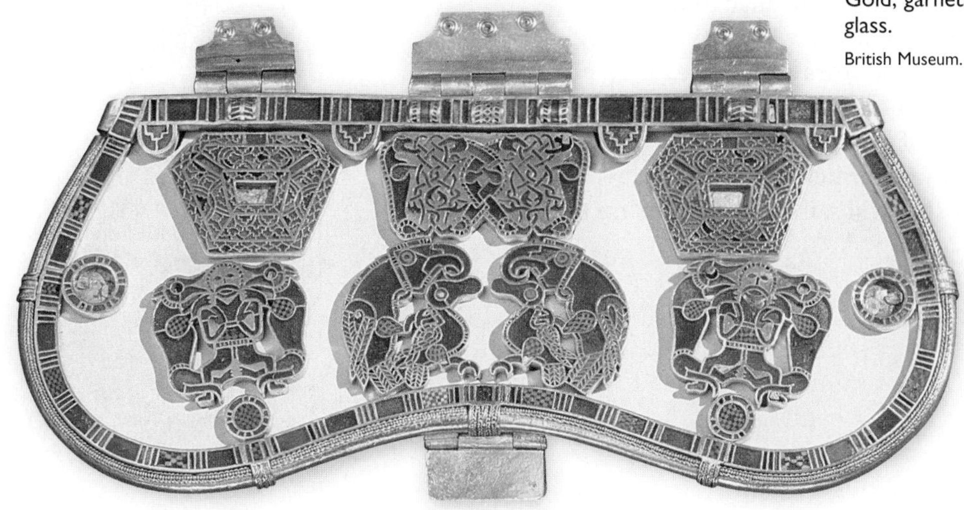

Purse lid, from the Sutton Hoo Ship Burial (c.625–30 A.D.). Gold, garnets and millefiori glass.

British Museum. London, UK.

Turn to be served. She saluted the Geats'
Great prince, thanked God for answering her prayers,
For allowing her hands the happy duty
Of offering mead to a hero who would help
Her afflicted people. He drank what she poured,
Edgetho's brave son, then assured the Danish
Queen that his heart was firm and his hands
Ready:
"When we crossed the sea, my comrades
And I, I already knew that all
My purpose was this: to win the good will
Of your people or die in battle, pressed
In Grendel's fierce grip. Let me live in greatness
And courage, or here in this hall welcome
My death!"
Welthow was pleased with his words,
His bright-tongued boasts; she carried them back
To her lord, walked nobly across to his side.
The feast went on, laughter and music
And the brave words of warriors celebrating
Their delight. Then Hrothgar rose, Healfdane's
Son, heavy with sleep; as soon
As the sun had gone, he knew that Grendel
Would come to Herot, would visit that hall
When night had covered the earth with its net
And the shapes of darkness moved black and silent
Through the world. Hrothgar's warriors rose with him.
He went to Beowulf, embraced the Geats'
Brave prince, wished him well, and hoped
That Herot would be his to command. And then
He declared:
"No one strange to this land
Has ever been granted what I've given you,
No one in all the years of my rule.
Make this best of all mead-halls yours, and then
Keep it free of evil, fight
With glory in your heart! Purge Herot
And your ship will sail home with its treasure-holds full." . . .

364–369. *What does Beowulf's speech here reveal about his* ***character****?*

Saxon brooch discovered at Mitcham, South London (early 6th century). Gold leaf on wood. English School.

The feast ends. Beowulf and his men take the place of Hrothgar's followers and lie down to sleep in Herot. Beowulf, however, is wakeful, eager to meet his enemy.

THE BATTLE WITH GRENDEL

8

Out from the marsh, from the foot of misty
Hills and bogs, bearing God's hatred,
Grendel came, hoping to kill
Anyone he could trap on this trip to high Herot.
He moved quickly through the cloudy night,
Up from his swampland, sliding silently
Toward that gold-shining hall. He had visited Hrothgar's
Home before, knew the way—

Animal head from a Viking ship (c. 800).

Photo: Eirek Irgens Johnsen.

But never, before nor after that night,
Found Herot defended so firmly, his reception
So harsh. He journeyed, forever joyless,
Straight to the door, then snapped it open,
Tore its iron fasteners with a touch,
And rushed angrily over the threshold.
He strode quickly across the inlaid
Floor, snarling and fierce: His eyes
Gleamed in the darkness, burned with a gruesome
Light. Then he stopped, seeing the hall
Crowded with sleeping warriors, stuffed
With rows of young soldiers resting together.
And his heart laughed, he relished the sight,
Intended to tear the life from those bodies
By morning; the monster's mind was hot
With the thought of food and the feasting his belly
Would soon know. But fate, that night, intended
Grendel to gnaw the broken bones
Of his last human supper. Human
Eyes were watching his evil steps,
Waiting to see his swift hard claws.
Grendel snatched at the first Geat
He came to, ripped him apart, cut
His body to bits with powerful jaws,
Drank the blood from his veins, and bolted
Him down, hands and feet; death
And Grendel's great teeth came together,
Snapping life shut. Then he stepped to another
Still body, clutched at Beowulf with his claws,
Grasped at a strong-hearted wakeful sleeper
—And was instantly seized himself, claws
Bent back as Beowulf leaned up on one arm.
That shepherd of evil, guardian of crime,
Knew at once that nowhere on earth
Had he met a man whose hands were harder;
His mind was flooded with fear—but nothing
Could take his talons and himself from that tight
Hard grip. Grendel's one thought was to run
From Beowulf, flee back to his marsh and hide there:
This was a different Herot than the hall he had emptied.
But Higlac's follower remembered his final
Boast and, standing erect, stopped
The monster's flight, fastened those claws
In his fists till they cracked, clutched Grendel
Closer. The infamous killer fought
For his freedom, wanting no flesh but retreat,
Desiring nothing but escape; his claws

Dragonhead from a Viking horse collar (detail) (10th century). Denmark.

National Museum, Copenhagen.

416–418. These lines **foreshadow,** or hint at, the outcome of the battle between Grendel and Beowulf.

? *Grendel has been attacking Herot successfully for years. What will be different about this visit to Herot?*

435–447. "Higlac's follower" is Beowulf. He had earlier sworn to kill Grendel with his bare hands.

? *What details in these lines demonstrate Beowulf's superhuman strength?*

Had been caught, he was trapped. That trip to Herot
Was a miserable journey for the writhing monster!
   The high hall rang, its roof boards swayed,
And Danes shook with terror. Down
The aisles the battle swept, angry
And wild. Herot trembled, wonderfully
Built to withstand the blows, the struggling
Great bodies beating at its beautiful walls;
Shaped and fastened with iron, inside
And out, artfully worked, the building
Stood firm. Its benches rattled, fell
To the floor, gold-covered boards grating
As Grendel and Beowulf battled across them.
Hrothgar's wise men had fashioned Herot
To stand forever; only fire,
They had planned, could shatter what such skill had put
Together, swallow in hot flames such splendor
Of ivory and iron and wood. Suddenly
The sounds changed, the Danes started
In new terror, cowering in their beds as the terrible
Screams of the Almighty's enemy sang
In the darkness, the horrible shrieks of pain
And defeat, the tears torn out of Grendel's
Taut throat, hell's captive caught in the arms
Of him who of all the men on earth
Was the strongest.

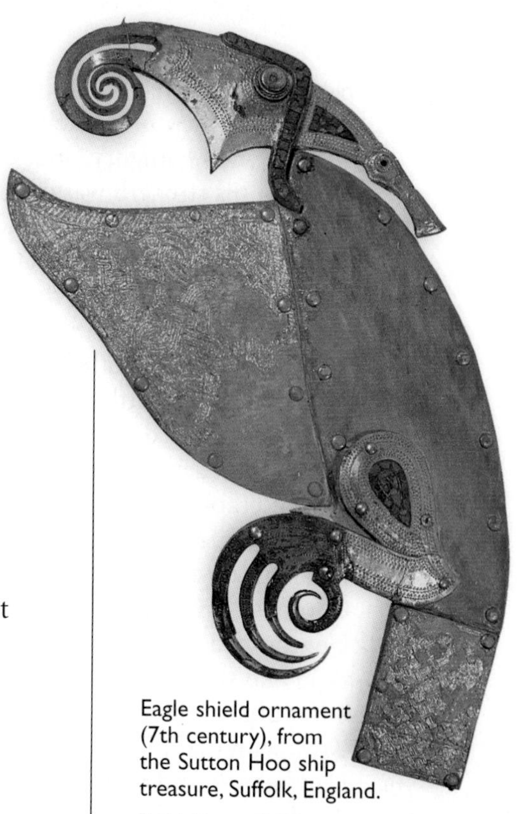

Eagle shield ornament (7th century), from the Sutton Hoo ship treasure, Suffolk, England.
British Museum, London.

? 467–472. *Earlier in the epic it was explained that Grendel is a descendant of Cain, who was cursed by God. In what ways is this battle between Grendel and Beowulf really a battle between good and evil? What details in the description of the battle make this clear?*

? 479–485. *According to these lines, why can't Beowulf's men harm Grendel?*

9

That mighty protector of men
Meant to hold the monster till its life
Leaped out, knowing the fiend was no use
To anyone in Denmark. All of Beowulf's
Band had jumped from their beds, ancestral
Swords raised and ready, determined
To protect their prince if they could. Their courage
Was great but all wasted: They could hack at Grendel
From every side, trying to open
A path for his evil soul, but their points
Could not hurt him, the sharpest and hardest iron
Could not scratch at his skin, for that sin-stained demon
Had bewitched all men's weapons, laid spells
That blunted every mortal man's blade.
And yet his time had come, his days
Were over, his death near; down
To hell he would go, swept groaning and helpless
To the waiting hands of still worse fiends.

Detail of three-ringed gold collar (6th century).

Statens Historiska Museer, Stockholm.

Now he discovered—once the afflictor
Of men, tormentor of their days—what it meant
To feud with Almighty God: Grendel
Saw that his strength was deserting him, his claws
Bound fast, Higlac's brave follower tearing at
His hands. The monster's hatred rose higher,
But his power had gone. He twisted in pain,
And the bleeding sinews deep in his shoulder
Snapped, muscle and bone split
And broke. The battle was over, Beowulf
Had been granted new glory: Grendel escaped,
But wounded as he was could flee to his den,
His miserable hole at the bottom of the marsh,
Only to die, to wait for the end
Of all his days. And after that bloody
Combat the Danes laughed with delight.
He who had come to them from across the sea,
Bold and strong-minded, had driven affliction
Off, purged Herot clean. He was happy,
Now, with that night's fierce work; the Danes
Had been served as he'd boasted he'd serve them; Beowulf,
A prince of the Geats, had killed Grendel,
Ended the grief, the sorrow, the suffering
Forced on Hrothgar's helpless people
By a bloodthirsty fiend. No Dane doubted
The victory, for the proof, hanging high
From the rafters where Beowulf had hung it, was the monster's
Arm, claw and shoulder and all.

490–499. *How does Beowulf defeat Grendel?*

514–517. *How does Beowulf prove his victory over Grendel? Why might he do this?*

10

And then, in the morning, crowds surrounded
Herot, warriors coming to that hall
From faraway lands, princes and leaders
Of men hurrying to behold the monster's
Great staggering tracks. They gaped with no sense
Of sorrow, felt no regret for his suffering,
Went tracing his bloody footprints, his beaten
And lonely flight, to the edge of the lake
Where he'd dragged his corpselike way, doomed
And already weary of his vanishing life.
The water was bloody, steaming and boiling
In horrible pounding waves, heat
Sucked from his magic veins; but the swirling
Surf had covered his death, hidden
Deep in murky darkness his miserable
End, as hell opened to receive him.

522–533. *What has happened to Grendel?*

Then old and young rejoiced, turned back
From that happy pilgrimage, mounted their hard-hooved
Horses, high-spirited stallions, and rode them
Slowly toward Herot again, retelling
Beowulf's bravery as they jogged along.
And over and over they swore that nowhere
On earth or under the spreading sky
Or between the seas, neither south nor north,
Was there a warrior worthier to rule over men.
(But no one meant Beowulf's praise to belittle
Hrothgar, their kind and gracious king!) . . .

Grendel's monstrous mother, in grief for her son, next attacks Herot, and in her dripping claws she carries off one man—Hrothgar's closest friend. The monster also carries off Grendel's arm, which Beowulf had hung high from the rafters. Beowulf is awakened and called for again. In one of the most famous verses in the epic, the old king describes where Grendel and his mother live.

Anglo-Saxon gold buckle (7th century), from the Sutton Hoo ship treasure, Suffolk, England.
British Museum, London.

11

. . . "They live in secret places, windy
Cliffs, wolf-dens where water pours
From the rocks, then runs underground, where mist
Steams like black clouds, and the groves of trees
Growing out over their lake are all covered
With frozen spray, and wind down snakelike
Roots that reach as far as the water
And help keep it dark. At night that lake
Burns like a torch. No one knows its bottom,
No wisdom reaches such depths. A deer,
Hunted through the woods by packs of hounds,
A stag with great horns, though driven through the forest
From faraway places, prefers to die
On those shores, refuses to save its life
In that water. It isn't far, nor is it
A pleasant spot! When the wind stirs
And storms, waves splash toward the sky,
As dark as the air, as black as the rain
That the heavens weep. Our only help,
Again, lies with you. Grendel's mother
Is hidden in her terrible home, in a place
You've not seen. Seek it, if you dare! Save us,
Once more, and again twisted gold,
Heaped-up ancient treasure, will reward you
For the battle you win!"

? **563–569.** *What is Hrothgar asking Beowulf to do?*

Carrying the sword Hrunting, Beowulf goes to the lake where Grendel's mother has her underwater lair. Then, fully armed, he dives to the depths of this watery hell.

The Monster's Mother

12

. . . He leaped into the lake, would not wait for anyone's
Answer; the heaving water covered him
Over. For hours he sank through the waves;
At last he saw the mud of the bottom.
And all at once the greedy she-wolf
Who'd ruled those waters for half a hundred
Years discovered him, saw that a creature
From above had come to explore the bottom
Of her wet world. She welcomed him in her claws,
Clutched at him savagely but could not harm him,
Tried to work her fingers through the tight
Ring-woven mail on his breast, but tore
And scratched in vain. Then she carried him, armor
And sword and all, to her home; he struggled
To free his weapon, and failed. The fight
Brought other monsters swimming to see
Her catch, a host of sea beasts who beat at
His mail shirt, stabbing with tusks and teeth
As they followed along. Then he realized, suddenly,
That she'd brought him into someone's battle-hall,
And there the water's heat could not hurt him,
Nor anything in the lake attack him through
The building's high-arching roof. A brilliant
Light burned all around him, the lake
Itself like a fiery flame.
Then he saw
The mighty water witch, and swung his sword,
His ring-marked blade, straight at her head;
The iron sang its fierce song,
Sang Beowulf's strength. But her guest
Discovered that no sword could slice her evil
Skin, that Hrunting could not hurt her, was useless
Now when he needed it. They wrestled, she ripped
And tore and clawed at him, bit holes in his helmet,
And that too failed him; for the first time in years
Of being worn to war it would earn no glory;
It was the last time anyone would wear it. But Beowulf
Longed only for fame, leaped back

570–594. *Describe how Beowulf comes to the lair of Grendel's mother. What details remind you that Beowulf is not an ordinary man?*

Silver and gold brooch with amber ornaments (9th century). Roscrea, County Tipperary.
National Museum of Ireland, Dublin.

Into battle. He tossed his sword aside,
Angry; the steel-edged blade lay where
He'd dropped it. If weapons were useless he'd use
His hands, the strength in his fingers. So fame
Comes to the men who mean to win it
And care about nothing else! He raised
His arms and seized her by the shoulder; anger
Doubled his strength, he threw her to the floor.
She fell, Grendel's fierce mother, and the Geats'
Proud prince was ready to leap on her. But she rose
At once and repaid him with her clutching claws,
Wildly tearing at him. He was weary, that best
And strongest of soldiers; his feet stumbled
And in an instant she had him down, held helpless.
Squatting with her weight on his stomach, she drew
A dagger, brown with dried blood and prepared
To avenge her only son. But he was stretched
On his back, and her stabbing blade was blunted
By the woven mail shirt he wore on his chest.
The hammered links held; the point
Could not touch him. He'd have traveled to the bottom of
the earth,
Edgetho's son, and died there, if that shining
Woven metal had not helped—and Holy
God, who sent him victory, gave judgment
For truth and right, Ruler of the Heavens,
Once Beowulf was back on his feet and fighting.

? 607–632. *What details in this description of the battle between Grendel's mother and Beowulf add to your suspense about the outcome? At what point do you think Beowulf may not be successful? What saves him?*

Dragon-shaped brooch (2nd century) from the Romano-British period.

13

Then he saw, hanging on the wall, a heavy
Sword, hammered by giants, strong
And blessed with their magic, the best of all weapons
But so massive that no ordinary man could lift
Its carved and decorated length. He drew it
From its scabbard, broke the chain on its hilt,°
And then, savage, now, angry
And desperate, lifted it high over his head
And struck with all the strength he had left,
Caught her in the neck and cut it through,
Broke bones and all. Her body fell
To the floor, lifeless, the sword was wet
With her blood, and Beowulf rejoiced at the sight.
The brilliant light shone, suddenly,
As though burning in that hall, and as bright as Heaven's

638. scabbard . . . hilt: A scabbard is a case that holds the blade of a sword; a hilt is a sword's handle.

? 633–645. *How does Beowulf kill Grendel's mother?*

Own candle, lit in the sky. He looked
At her home, then following along the wall
Went walking, his hands tight on the sword,
His heart still angry. He was hunting another
Dead monster, and took his weapon with him
For final revenge against Grendel's vicious
Attacks, his nighttime raids, over
And over, coming to Herot when Hrothgar's
Men slept, killing them in their beds,
Eating some on the spot, fifteen
Or more, and running to his loathsome moor
With another such sickening meal waiting
In his pouch. But Beowulf repaid him for those visits,
Found him lying dead in his corner,
Armless, exactly as that fierce fighter
Had sent him out from Herot, then struck off
His head with a single swift blow. The body
Jerked for the last time, then lay still. . . .

? **648–665.** *What is Beowulf's final revenge against Grendel? What action of Beowulf's provides a* ***resolution,*** *or wrapping up, of the episode?*

(Left) the Germanic hero Weland at his forge and (right) the adoration of the Magi (8th century), from the Franks casket. Whalebone.

British Museum. © Michael Holford.

In his novel Grendel *(1971), the American writer John Gardner (1933–1982) retells part of* Beowulf *from the point of view of the monster. In this excerpt, Grendel tells his own version of one of his raids on Hrothgar's hall.*

from Grendel

John Gardner

And so I come through trees and towns to the lights of Hrothgar's meadhall. I am no stranger here. A respected guest. Eleven years now and going on twelve I have come up this clean-mown central hill, dark shadow out of the woods below, and have knocked politely on the high oak door, bursting its hinges and sending the shock of my greeting inward like a cold blast out of a cave. "Grendel!" they squeak, and I smile like exploding spring. The old Shaper, a man I cannot help but admire, goes out the back window with his harp at a single bound, though blind as a bat. The drunkest of Hrothgar's thanes come reeling and clanking down from their wall-hung beds, all shouting their meady, outrageous boasts, their heavy swords aswirl like eagles' wings. "Woe, woe, woe!" cries Hrothgar, hoary with winters, peeking in, wide-eyed, from his bedroom in back. His wife, looking in behind him, makes a scene. The thanes in the meadhall blow out the lights and cover the wide stone fireplace with shields. I laugh, crumple over; I can't help myself. In the darkness, I alone see clear as day. While they squeal and screech and bump into each other, I silently sack up my dead and withdraw to the woods. I eat and laugh and eat until I can barely walk, my chest-hair matted with dribbled blood, and then the roosters on the hill crow, and dawn comes over the roofs of the houses, and all at once I am filled with gloom again.

"This is some punishment sent us," I hear them bawling from the hill.

My head aches. Morning nails my eyes.

"Some god is angry," I hear a woman keen. "The people of Scyld and Herogar and Hrothgar are mired in sin!"

My belly rumbles, sick on their sour meat. I crawl through bloodstained leaves to the eaves of the forest, and there peak out. The dogs fall silent at the edge of my spell, and where the king's hall surmounts the town, the blind old Shaper, harp clutched tight to his fragile chest, stares futilely down, straight at me. Otherwise nothing. Pigs root dully at the posts of a wooden fence. A rumple-horned ox lies chewing in dew and shade. A few men, lean, wearing animal skins, look up at the gables of the king's hall, or at the vultures circling casually beyond. Hrothgar says nothing, hoarfrost-bearded, his features cracked and crazed. Inside, I hear the people praying—whimpering, whining, mumbling, pleading—to their numerous sticks and stones. He doesn't go in. The king has lofty theories of his own.

"Theories," I whisper to the bloodstained ground. So the dragon once spoke. ("They'd map out roads through Hell with their crackpot theories!" I recall his laugh.)

Then the groaning and praying stop, and on the side of the hill the dirge-slow shoveling begins. . . .

CONNECTION / MAGAZINE ARTICLE

Life in 999: A Grim Struggle

INFORMATIONAL TEXT

Howard G. Chua-Eoan

from *Time,* October 15, 1992

Today's world is measured in light-years and Mach speed and sheathed in silicon and alloy. In the world of 999, on the eve of the first millennium, time moved at the speed of an oxcart or, more often, of a sturdy pair of legs, and the West was built largely on wood. Europe was a collection of untamed forests, countless mile upon mile of trees and brush and brier, dark and inhospitable. Medieval chroniclers used the word *desert* to describe their arboreal world, a place on the cusp of civilization where werewolves and bogeymen still lunged out of the shadows and bandits and marauders maintained their lairs.

Yet the forests, deep and dangerous as they were, also defined existence. Wood kindled forges and kept alive the hearths of the mud-and-thatch huts of the serfs. Peasants fattened their hogs on forest acorns (pork was crucial to basic subsistence in the cold of winter), and wild berries helped supplement the meager diet. In a world without sugar, honey from forest swarms provided the only sweetness for food or drink. The pleasures of the serfs were few and simple: earthy lovemaking and occasional dances and fests.

Feudal lords ruled over western Europe, taking their share of the harvests of primitive agriculture and making the forests their private hunting grounds. Poaching was not simply theft (usually punishable by imprisonment) but a sin against the social order. Without the indulgence of the nobility, the peasants could not even acquire salt, the indispensable ingredient for preserving meat and flavoring a culinary culture that possessed few spices. Though a true money economy did not exist, salt could be bought with poorly circulated coin, which the lord hoarded in his castle and dispensed to the poor only as alms.

It was in the lord's castle too that peasants and their flocks sought refuge from wolf packs and barbarian invaders. In 999, however, castles, like most other buildings in Europe, were made of timber, far from the granite bastions that litter today's imagined Middle Ages. The peasants, meanwhile, were relegated to their simple huts, where everyone—including the animals—slept around the hearth. Straw was scattered on the floors to collect scraps as well as human and animal waste. Housecleaning consisted of sweeping out the straw.

Illness and disease remained in constant residence. Tuberculosis was endemic, and so were scabrous skin diseases of every kind: abscesses, cankers, scrofula, tumors, eczema, and erysipelas. In a throwback to biblical times, lepers constituted a class of pariahs living on the outskirts of villages and cities. Constant famine, rotten flour, and vitamin deficiencies afflicted huge segments of society with blindness, goiter, paralysis, and bone malformations that created hunchbacks and cripples. A man was lucky to survive 30, and 50 was a ripe old age. Most women, many of them succumbing to the ravages of childbirth, lived less than 30 years. There was no time for what is now considered childhood; children of every class had to grow up immediately and be useful as soon as possible. Emperors were leading armies in their teens; John XI became Pope at the age of 21.

While the general population was growing faster than it had in the previous five cen-

February, from *The Grimani Breviary* (prayer book) (detail).

turies, there was still a shortage of people to cultivate the fields, clear the woodlands, and work the mills. Local taxes were levied on youths who did not marry upon coming of age. Abortion was considered homicide, and a woman who terminated a pregnancy was expelled from the church.

The nobility spent its waking hours battling foes to preserve its prerogatives, the clergy chanting prayers for the salvation of souls, the serfs laboring to feed and clothe everyone. Night, lit only by burning logs or the rare taper, was always filled with danger and terror. The seasons came and went, punctuated chiefly by the occurrence of plentiful church holidays. The calendar year began at different times for different regions; only later would Europe settle on the Feast of Christ's Circumcision, January 1, as the year's beginning.

Thus there was little panic, not even much interest, as the millennium approached in the final months of 999. For what terrors could the apocalypse hold for a continent that was already shrouded in darkness? Rather Europe—illiterate, diseased, and hungry—seemed grimly resigned to desperation and impoverishment. It was one of the planet's most unpromising corners, the Third World of its age.

Response and Analysis

Reading Check

1. What do Hrothgar and his council do to try to save his guest-hall?
2. What prevents Beowulf's men from helping Beowulf in his battle with Grendel?
3. How do the Danes feel about Beowulf after his battle with Grendel?
4. What obstacle does Beowulf face in his confrontation with Grendel's mother? How does he overcome the obstacle?

Thinking Critically

5. In what specific ways does Herot **contrast** with the place where Grendel lives?
6. **Images** are words that help us *see* something, and often hear it, smell it, taste it, and touch it as well. Identify images describing Grendel that associate him with death or darkness. How are these images supposed to make you feel about Grendel?
7. Why do you think it's important to Beowulf and to his image as an **epic hero** that he face Grendel without a weapon? What **symbolism** do you see in the uselessness of human-made weapons against Grendel?
8. What details describe Grendel's mother and her lair? What might Grendel and his mother represent for the Anglo-Saxons?
9. How does Gardner's depiction of Grendel differ from the epic's depiction of him? (See the ***Connection*** on page 39.) Did Gardner make you sympathize with Grendel? Explain.
10. The ***Connection*** on page 40, "Life in 999: A Grim Struggle," describes daily life in late Anglo-Saxon England. What details in this picture of daily life relate to what you've read so far in *Beowulf*? How does life in 999 compare with life today?

Extending and Evaluating

11. Beowulf is the **archetype** of the dragon slayer, the hero who faces death in order to save a threatened community. Does Beowulf remind you of any heroes in real life, in fiction, or in the movies today? What characteristics do the heroes share?

Literary Skills
Analyze the archetype of the epic hero.

INTERNET
Projects and Activities
Keyword: LE7 12-1

Detail of picture stone from Gotland, Sweden.

from Beowulf

Part Two, *translated by* Seamus Heaney

Beowulf carries Grendel's head to King Hrothgar and then returns gift-laden to the land of the Geats, where he succeeds to the throne. After fifty winters pass, Beowulf, now an old man, faces his final task: He must fight a dragon who, angry because a thief has stolen a jeweled cup from the dragon's hoard of gold, is laying waste to the Geats' land. Beowulf and eleven warriors are guided to the dragon's lair by the thief who stole the cup. For Beowulf the price of this last victory will be great.

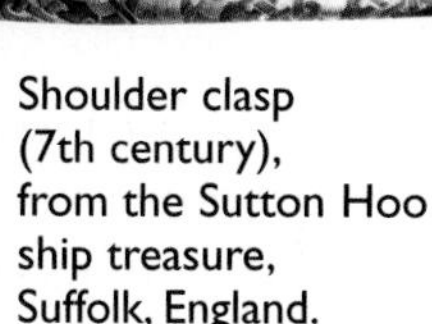

Shoulder clasp (7th century), from the Sutton Hoo ship treasure, Suffolk, England.

British Museum, London/ Photograph © Michael Holford.

The Final Battle

14

Then he addressed each dear companion
one final time, those fighters in their helmets,
resolute and high-born: "I would rather not
use a weapon if I knew another way
to grapple with the dragon and make good my boast
as I did against Grendel in days gone by.
But I shall be meeting molten venom
in the fire he breathes, so I go forth
in mail-shirt and shield. I won't shift a foot
when I meet the cave-guard: what occurs on the wall
between the two of us will turn out as fate,
overseer of men, decides. I am resolved.
I scorn further words against this sky-borne foe.

"Men at arms, remain here on the barrow,°
safe in your armour, to see which one of us
is better in the end at bearing wounds
in a deadly fray. This fight is not yours,
nor is it up to any man except me

666–678. Throughout *Beowulf,* there are many references to the pagan notion of fate (see line 676) as an impersonal force that predetermines the outcome of events in a person's life. This concept, known as *wyrd,* was central to Anglo-Saxon beliefs.

? *How is this older Beowulf different from the Beowulf who slew Grendel and his mother?*

679. **barrow** *n.:* a hill.

Vocabulary

resolute (rez′ə • lo͞ot′) *adj.:* determined.

Viking sword handles, embellished with Viking Age motifs.
Statens Historiska Museer, Stockholm.

to measure his strength against the monster
or to prove his worth. I shall win the gold
by my courage, or else mortal combat,
doom of battle, will bear your lord away."

Then he drew himself up beside his shield.
The fabled warrior in his warshirt and helmet
trusted in his own strength entirely
and went under the crag. No coward path.
Hard by the rock-face that hale° veteran,
a good man who had gone repeatedly
into combat and danger and come through,
saw a stone arch and a gushing stream
that burst from the barrow, blazing and wafting
a deadly heat. It would be hard to survive
unscathed near the hoard, to hold firm
against the dragon in those flaming depths.
Then he gave a shout. The lord of the Geats
unburdened his breast and broke out
in a storm of anger. Under grey stone
his voice challenged and resounded clearly.
Hate was ignited. The hoard-guard recognized
a human voice, the time was over
for peace and parleying.° Pouring forth
in a hot battle-fume, the breath of the monster
burst from the rock. There was a rumble under ground.
Down there in the barrow, Beowulf the warrior
lifted his shield: the outlandish thing
writhed and convulsed and vehemently

679–687. *How does Beowulf's acceptance of fate show his deep sense of responsibility to his people?*

692. hale *adj.:* healthy and energetic.

706. parleying *v.* used as *n.:* discussing.

Vocabulary
vehemently (vē′ə • mənt • lē) *adv.:* violently.

turned on the king, whose keen-edged sword,
an heirloom inherited by ancient right,
was already in his hand. Roused to a fury,
each antagonist struck terror in the other.
Unyielding, the lord of his people loomed
by his tall shield, sure of his ground,
while the serpent looped and unleashed itself.
Swaddled in flames, it came gliding and flexing
and racing towards its fate. Yet his shield defended
the renowned leader's life and limb
for a shorter time than he meant it to:
that final day was the first time
when Beowulf fought and fate denied him
glory in battle. So the king of the Geats
raised his hand and struck hard
at the enamelled scales, but scarcely cut through:
the blade flashed and slashed yet the blow
was far less powerful than the hard-pressed king
had need of at that moment. The mound-keeper
went into a spasm and spouted deadly flames:
when he felt the stroke, battle-fire
billowed and spewed. Beowulf was foiled°
of a glorious victory. The glittering sword,
infallible before that day,
failed when he unsheathed it, as it never should have.
For the son of Ecgtheow, it was no easy thing
to have to give ground like that and go
unwillingly to inhabit another home
in a place beyond; so every man must yield
the leasehold of his days.

It was not long
until the fierce contenders clashed again.
The hoard-guard took heart, inhaled and swelled up
and got a new wind; he who had once ruled
was furled in fire and had to face the worst.
No help or backing was to be had then
from his high-born comrades; that hand-picked troop
broke ranks and ran for their lives
to the safety of the wood. But within one heart
sorrow welled up: in a man of worth
the claims of kinship cannot be denied.

709–720. The image of a lone hero standing up to a fire-breathing dragon or other giant monster is one of the most **archetypal** images in Western heroic literature. **?** *How does the dragon compare with Grendel and Grendel's mother?*

? **720–741.** *In lines 720–736, what goes wrong during Beowulf's battle with the dragon? In lines 737–741, what are you led to believe about Beowulf's ultimate fate?*

733. foiled *v.:* prevented from.

? **746–749.** *How do Beowulf's men react to the sight of the dragon gaining victory over Beowulf?*

Vocabulary

infallible (in•fal′ə•bəl) *adj.:* unable to fail or be wrong.
furled (fʉrld) *v.:* rolled up.

15

His name was Wiglaf, a son of Weohstan's,
a well-regarded Shylfing warrior
related to Aelfhere. When he saw his lord
tormented by the heat of his scalding helmet,
he remembered the bountiful gifts bestowed on him,
how well he lived among the Waegmundings,
the freehold° he inherited from his father before him.
He could not hold back: one hand brandished
the yellow-timbered shield, the other drew his sword— . . .

Sad at heart, addressing his companions,
Wiglaf spoke wise and fluent words:
"I remember that time when mead was flowing,
how we pledged loyalty to our lord in the hall,
promised our ring-giver we would be worth our price,
make good the gift of the war-gear,
those swords and helmets, as and when
his need required it. He picked us out
from the army deliberately, honoured us and judged us
fit for this action, made me these lavish gifts—
and all because he considered us the best
of his arms-bearing thanes.° And now, although
he wanted this challenge to be one he'd face
by himself alone—the shepherd of our land,
a man unequaled in the quest for glory
and a name for daring—now the day has come
when this lord we serve needs sound men
to give him their support. Let us go to him,
help our leader through the hot flame
and dread of the fire. As God is my witness,
I would rather my body were robed in the same
burning blaze as my gold-giver's body
than go back home bearing arms.
That is unthinkable, unless we have first
slain the foe and defended the life
of the prince of the Weather-Geats. I well know
the things he has done for us deserve better.
Should he alone be left exposed
to fall in battle? We must bond together,
shield and helmet, mail-shirt and sword."

758. **freehold** *n.:* estate.

? 761–790. *What arguments does Wiglaf use to convince the men that they must fight with Beowulf?*

772. **thanes** *n. pl.:* in Anglo-Saxon England, group of men who held land of the king in exchange for military service.

Bronze stag atop ceremonial scepter (detail) (7th century), from the Sutton Hoo ship treasure, Suffolk, England.

Vocabulary

lavish (lav′ish) *adj.:* extravagant.

Together Beowulf and the young Wiglaf kill the dragon, but the old king is fatally wounded. Beowulf, thinking of his people, asks to see the monster's treasure. Wiglaf enters the dragon's cave and finds a priceless hoard of jewels and gold.

16

. . . Wiglaf went quickly, keen to get back,
excited by the treasure; anxiety weighed
on his brave heart, he was hoping he would find
the leader of the Geats alive where he had left him
helpless, earlier, on the open ground.
So he came to the place, carrying the treasure,
and found his lord bleeding profusely,
his life at an end; again he began
to swab his body. The beginnings of an utterance
broke out from the king's breast-cage.
The old lord gazed sadly at the gold.

"To the everlasting Lord of All,
to the King of Glory, I give thanks
that I behold this treasure here in front of me,
that I have been thus allowed to leave my people
so well endowed on the day I die.
Now that I have bartered my last breath
to own this fortune, it is up to you
to look after their needs. I can hold out no longer.
Order my troop to construct a barrow
on a headland on the coast, after my pyre has cooled.
It will loom on the horizon at Hronesness
and be a reminder among my people—
so that in coming times crews under sail
will call it Beowulf's Barrow, as they steer
ships across the wide and shrouded waters."

Then the king in his great-heartedness unclasped
the collar of gold from his neck and gave it
to the young thane, telling him to use
it and the warshirt and the gilded helmet well.

"You are the last of us, the only one left
of the Waegmundings. Fate swept us away,

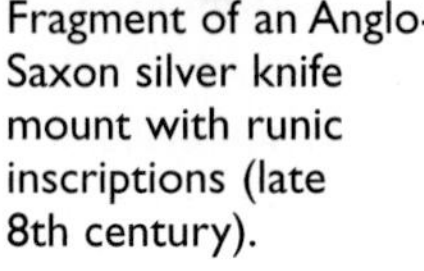

Fragment of an Anglo-Saxon silver knife mount with runic inscriptions (late 8th century).

C. M. Dixon.

802–809. The ultimate purpose of the **epic hero** is to leave something of lasting value to his culture.

? *What has Beowulf left to his people?*

? **810–816.** *What are Beowulf's final wishes?*

The great ax, with depiction of bird-animal (10th century), from Jutland, Denmark.

National Museum of Copenhagen, Denmark. © Werner Forman/Art Resource, New York.

sent my whole brave high-born clan
to their final doom. Now I must follow them."
That was the warrior's last word.
He had no more to confide. The furious heat
of the pyre would assail him. His soul fled from his breast
to its destined place among the steadfast ones.

Wiglaf berates the faithless warriors who did not go to the aid of their king. With sorrow the Geats cremate the corpse of their greatest king. They place his ashes, along with all of the dragon's treasure, in a huge burial tower by the sea, where it can be seen by voyagers.

17

Then twelve warriors rode around the tomb,
chieftains' sons, champions in battle,
all of them distraught, chanting in dirges,
mourning his loss as a man and a king.
They extolled his heroic nature and exploits
and gave thanks for his greatness; which was the proper thing,
for a man should praise a prince whom he holds dear
and cherish his memory when that moment comes
when he has to be convoyed from his bodily home.
So the Geat people, his hearth companions,
sorrowed for the lord who had been laid low.
They said that of all the kings upon the earth
he was the man most gracious and fair-minded,
kindest to his people and keenest to win fame.

829–842. The closing lines of *Beowulf* serve as a kind of **elegy**—a poem that mourns the death of a person or laments something lost.
? *According to these elegiac final lines of the epic, what qualities made Beowulf a great hero?*

Vocabulary
assail (ə • sāl′) *v.:* attack.
extolled (ek • stōld′) *v.:* praised.

A Celtic shield, found in Battersea, near the Thames River, perhaps thrown in the river as an offering to the river god.

Courtesy of the Trustees of the British Museum, London.

INFORMATIONAL TEXT

The Fury of the Northmen

Ellen Ashdown

When the fearsome Vikings began raiding England at the end of the eighth century, the church added a new prayer: "God, deliver us from the fury of the Northmen." Were these Scandinavian warriors—descended from the peoples of *Beowulf*—really such berserk destroyers? The fiercest ones were, indicated by the word *berserk* itself: In Old Norse, a *berserkr* was a "frenzied Norse warrior," so wild and fearless even his comrades kept clear.

Bear or bare?

Berserkr literally means either "bear shirt" or "bare shirt," suggesting that these warriors wore bearskins or perhaps fought "bare"—without armor. Some say the berserkers were religious madmen, followers of Odin, god of death and war. Some say they ate mind-altering plants. Both may be true, because the berserker entered battle in a kind of fit, biting his shield, taunting death, and, like Beowulf, "If weapons were useless he'd use / His hands. . . . So fame / Comes to the men who mean to win it / And care about nothing else!"

Universiteters, Oldsaksamling, Oslo.

Sigurd kills the dragon. Detail of carved portal of Hylestad stave church (12th century).

Dragons from the sea.

The Viking Age spanned the ninth through eleventh centuries, the European continent, and the Atlantic Ocean. Pushed by overpopulation, Vikings from Sweden, Norway, and Denmark struck out for new land. They were farmers at home, but they were a warrior culture too, and they devastated England with nightmarish hit-and-run attacks. Even the name "Viking" comes from a telling phrase: For the Scandinavians, *to go a-viking* meant "to fight as a warrior or pirate."

The Vikings' extraordinary seafaring and shipbuilding skills, honed in their watery land of fiords, or narrow ocean inlets, gave them the advantage of making surprise attacks. The unique Viking warships were long (up to ninety-five feet, manned by thirty rowers), light and swift (to go farther on their provisions), and steady (built with a keel). Shallow-drafted, these dragon-prowed ships could be pulled onto a river shore, swiftly disgorging warriors wielding swords.

Unafraid of the unknown.

But though the Vikings conquered peoples as far away as Spain and Russia (*Rus* was the Slavic word for "Swedes"), their motive was pure wanderlust as much as bloodlust. Expert in navigating by sun, stars, landmarks, and bird flights, the Vikings settled Iceland and Greenland and even explored North America—five hundred years before Columbus. That's why the United States once named a spacecraft *Viking:* to honor the human spirit that dared uncharted seas in the ninth century, and dares uncharted Mars in the twentieth.

Response and Analysis

Pages 50–52 cover
Literary Skills Analyze the universal themes of epic poetry. Understand and analyze alliteration and kennings.
Writing Skills Write a character-analysis essay. Write a descriptive essay.
Listening and Speaking Skills Present a dramatic reading.
Vocabulary Skills Demonstrate word knowledge.

INTERNET
Projects and Activities
Keyword: LE7 12-1

Reading Check

1. Who comes to Beowulf's aid in Beowulf's final battle with the dragon? Why does he help Beowulf?
2. What sad scene concludes the epic?
3. What happens to the dragon's hoard?

Thinking Critically

4. A hoarded treasure in Old English literature is usually a **symbol** of spiritual death or damnation. How does this fact add significance to Beowulf's last fight with the dragon?
5. What details does the poet use to describe the dragon? Keeping those details in mind, explain what the dragon might **symbolize** as Beowulf's final foe.
6. Given what you know about the structure of Anglo-Saxon society, explain what is especially ominous about the behavior of Beowulf's men during the final battle. What does it suggest about the future of the kingdom?
7. The epic closes on a somber, elegiac note—a note of mourning. What words or **images** contribute to this **tone**?
8. Epic poetry usually embodies the attitudes and ideals of an entire culture. What values of Anglo-Saxon society does *Beowulf* reveal? What universal **themes** does it also reveal? Use specific examples from the poem to support your answer.
9. The ***Connection*** on page 49 describes the culture of the Vikings. How does this picture of Viking society relate to what you've read in *Beowulf*?

Literary Criticism

10. **Philosophical approach.** Although the story of Beowulf is set in a pre-Christian era among a people who worshiped stern gods and saw little to hope for beyond the grave, many modern readers see definite strains of a Christian outlook. Review the selections from *Beowulf*. Which passages might reflect a specifically Anglo-Saxon philosophy of life? Which passages might reflect a Christian outlook?

WRITING

Analyzing the Monster

In an **essay,** analyze the monster Grendel, focusing on the character's nature. Begin your **character analysis** of the monster with a sentence stating your general assessment of Grendel as a character. Then, support your assessment with details from the epic. Before you write, organize your details in a chart like the following one:

Character Name	Details from Epic
Actions	
Motives	
Words describing character	
People's responses	
Setting	
Does the character symbolize anything?	

Describe the Mom

In a brief **essay,** describe Grendel's mother. Base your description on the details you find in the text, and add details of your own. Tell what she looked like, how her voice sounded, how she smelled, how she walked. Describe her home. Describe what she ate and how she passed her time. Use as many sensory details as you can: You want your readers to feel they are meeting the monster face to face. How do you want your readers to feel about the monster? Do you want horror, or are you interested in making her somewhat sympathetic? The words you choose will make the difference.

Use "Writing a Descriptive Essay," pages 96–103, for help with this assignment.

LISTENING AND SPEAKING

Being a Bard

Choose any excerpt from the portions of *Beowulf* you have just read, and present a dramatic reading to your classmates as though you were an Anglo-Saxon bard. Choose a section that you feel has particular emotional intensity and suspense, and practice reading it several times before you deliver your reading to the class. Try to find various ways of involving your listeners in the act of storytelling: Vary the rate and pitch of your delivery, make dramatic pauses, and use gestures and even sound effects. For example, a guitar could be used to strike chords at dramatic moments.

Vocabulary Development

Which Word?

resolute	*furled*	*extolled*
vehemently	*lavish*	
infallible	*assail*	

Put your knowledge of the selection Vocabulary to work by answering the following questions with the correct word from the list above:

1. Which word is often used in reference to a flag?
2. Which word describes someone who is stubborn?
3. Which word describes how someone might argue about a subject he or she feels strongly about?
4. Which word is a synonym for *praised*?
5. Which word describes someone who cannot fail?
6. Which word describes someone who gives very generous gifts?
7. Which word is another way of saying *attack*?

Literary Focus

Alliteration and Kennings: Taking the Burden off the Bard

The Anglo-Saxon oral poet was assisted by two poetic devices, alliteration and the kenning.

Alliteration. Alliteration is the repetition of consonant sounds in words close to one another. Anglo-Saxon poetry is often called alliterative poetry. Instead of rhyme unifying the poem, the verse line is divided into two halves separated by a rhythmic pause, or **caesura.** In the first half of the line before the caesura, two words alliterate; in the second half, one word alliterates with the two from the first half. Many lines, however, have only two alliterative words, one in each half. Notice the alliterative *g* and the four primary stresses in this Old English line from *Beowulf*:

Gód mid Géatum Gréndles daéda

Kennings. The kenning, a special metaphor made of compound words, is a staple of Anglo-Saxon literature that also has a place in our language today. *Gas guzzler* and *headhunter* are two modern-day kennings you are likely to have heard.

The earliest and simplest kennings are compound words formed from two common nouns: *sky-candle* for *sun, battle-dew* for *blood,* and *whale-road* for *sea.* Later, kennings grew more elaborate, and compound adjectives joined the compound nouns. A ship became a *foamy-throated ship,* then a *foamy-throated sea-stallion,* and finally a *foamy-throated stallion of the whale-road.* Once a kenning was coined, it was used by the singer-poets over and over again.

In their original languages, kennings are almost always written as simple compounds, with no hyphens or spaces between the words. In translation, however, kennings are often written as hyphenated compounds (*sky-candle, foamy-throated*), as prepositional phrases (*wolf of wounds*), or as possessives (*the sword's tree*).

The work of kennings. Scholars believe that kennings filled three needs: (1) Old Norse and Anglo-Saxon poetry depended heavily on alliteration, but neither language had a large vocabulary. Poets created the alliterative words they needed by combining existing words. (2) Because the poetry was oral and had to be memorized, bards valued ready-made phrases. Such phrases made finished poetry easier to remember, and they gave bards time to think ahead when they were composing new poetry on the spot during a feast or ceremony. (3) The increasingly complex structure of the kennings must have satisfied the early Norse and Anglo-Saxon peoples' taste for elaboration.

Analyzing the text. As you examine these poetic devices, be sure to listen to the way they sound.

1. Read aloud the account of Beowulf's challenge to the dragon (lines 688–734), and listen for the effects of the **alliteration.** What **kennings** can you identify?
2. Look back over lines 392–517. Locate at least two examples of kennings written as **hyphenated compounds,** two written as **prepositional phrases,** and two written as **possessives.** What does each kenning refer to?
3. Compile a list of modern-day kennings, such as *headhunter.*
4. Here is an additional passage from Burton Raffel's translation. How does it compare with the corresponding lines (763–772) in Seamus Heaney's translation (page 46)?

> "I remember how we sat in the
> mead-hall, drinking
> And boasting of how brave we'd be
> when Beowulf
> Needed us, he who gave us these
> swords
> And armor: All of us swore to repay
> him,
> When the time came, kindness for
> kindness
> —With our lives, if he needed
> them. He allowed us to join
> him,
> Chose us from all his great army,
> thinking
> Our boasting words had some
> weight, believing
> Our promises, trusting our swords.
> He took us
> For soldiers, for men."

5. Now that you've read excerpts from two translations of *Beowulf,* think about the similarities and differences you see and hear between them. How does each translator use **figures of speech,** such as **kennings** and **alliteration**?

Vocabulary Development

Anglo-Saxon Legacy: Words and Word Parts

Words from Anglo-Saxon. English has borrowed words from most of the world's languages, but many words in our basic vocabulary come to us from Anglo-Saxon, or Old English. Simple, everyday words, such as the names of numbers (*an* for "one," *twa* for "two," *threo* for "three," *feower* for "four"), words designating family relationships (*fæder* for "father," *modor* for "mother," *sunu* for "son," *dohtor* for "daughter"), names for parts of the body (*heorte* for "heart," *fot* for "foot") and common, everyday things and activities (*æppel* for "apple," *hund* for "hound," *wefan* for "weave") are survivors of Old English words.

Anglo-Saxon affixes. Many English-language conventions can be traced back to Anglo-Saxon times. Both making nouns plural by adding *s* and creating the possessive of a noun by adding *'s* come to us from Old English. Old English has also given us the vowel changes in some irregular verbs like *sing, sang, sung* (*singan, sang, sungen*) and the regular endings for the past tense and past participles of regular verbs (as in *healed, has healed*). The word endings we use to create degrees of comparison with adjectives (as in dark*er*, dark*est*) are also of Anglo-Saxon origin.

Anglo-Saxon has also contributed many important word parts—prefixes and suffixes—to the English language. Some of these affixes just change the tense, person, or number of a word, such as a verb. Others change the entire meaning of a word, and often its part of speech.

Prefixes from Anglo-Saxon	Meanings	Examples
a–	in; on; of; up; to	ashore, aside
be–	around; about; treat as	behind, befriend
for–	away; off; from	forsake, forget
mis–	badly; not; wrongly	misspell, misfire
over–	above; excessive	overtake, oversee
un–	not; reverse of	untrue, unknown

Suffixes from Anglo-Saxon	Meanings	Examples
–en	made of; like	golden, molten
–dom	state; rank; condition	wisdom, kingdom
–ful	full of; marked by	wonderful, useful
–hood	state; condition	brotherhood, neighborhood
–ish	suggesting; like	selfish, childish
–less	lacking; without	hopeless, helpless
–like	like; similar	dreamlike, childlike
–ly	like; characteristic of	friendly, cowardly
–ness	quality; state	kindness, tenderness
–some	apt to; showing	handsome, tiresome
–ward	in the direction of	forward, skyward
–y	showing; suggesting	wavy, hilly, salty

PRACTICE

List examples of modern English words that use each of the Anglo-Saxon prefixes and suffixes shown above.

Vocabulary Skills
Understand and identify Anglo-Saxon words and affixes.

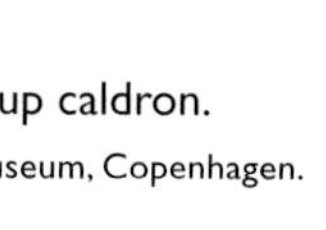

Gundestrup caldron.
National Museum, Copenhagen.

Connecting to World Literature

Epics: Stories on a Grand Scale

by David Adams Leeming

You have just read an excerpt from the Anglo-Saxon epic *Beowulf.* In this Connecting to World Literature feature, you will read excerpts from the following epics from around the world:

A.D. 700
***Beowulf* first recorded**

700 B.C.
Homer writes the *Iliad* and the *Odyssey*

1300 B.C.
The epic of *Gilgamesh* is put into complete form

Pages 54–55 cover **Literary Skills** Understand the epic and the archetype of the epic hero in ancient and modern literature. Compare literary forms of major literary periods.

"I teach kings the history of their ancestors," declares the narrator of the African epic *Sundiata,* "for the world is old, but the future springs from the past." These same words could be applied to epics from all times and places, for an **epic**—a long narrative poem about the exploits of a national hero—is a bridge from the past to the future. Epics carry a culture's history, values, myths, legends, and traditions from one generation to the next.

The Epic Hero: An Eternal Archetype

Whereas the old religious stories, or myths, tended to emphasize the deeds of the gods, epic poems emphasize the deeds of a special kind of human being related to the gods: the **epic hero.** From Gilgamesh to Achilles, epic heroes carry the images and supernatural energies of the gods within themselves. Yet these heroic figures are also, like all of us, subject to the joys and hardships of the human condition.

No matter what the differences may be between epics of different cultures or times, the epic hero remains constant. It is as if each hero wears the particular costume of his or her culture but is really the same figure underneath, facing the same kinds of challenges and ordeals. While the heroes of the Mesopotamian *Gilgamesh* epic, the Greek *Iliad,* and the Anglo-

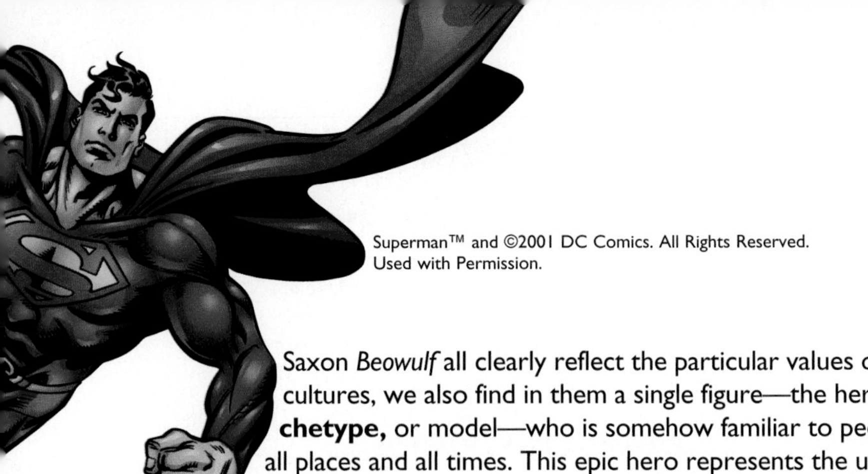

Saxon *Beowulf* all clearly reflect the particular values of their cultures, we also find in them a single figure—the heroic **archetype,** or model—who is somehow familiar to people of all places and all times. This epic hero represents the universal human quest for knowledge and understanding.

An **epic** is a long narrative poem that narrates the great deeds of a larger-than-life hero who embodies the most deeply held values of a particular society.

The Hero's Journey

The epic hero's adventures always involve trials and temptations. As in our own journey through life, there are always obstacles that stand in the way of the hero's goals. Like Gilgamesh, we all have our hopeless desires; like Achilles, we all have our potentially fatal weaknesses; like Beowulf, we must fight our own Grendels and dragons—our inner and outer demons. It is the epic hero's belief in himself (traditionally, epic heroes have always been male) and his own powers that make his success possible in spite of the obstacles.

The Epic Lives On

Today, the epic hero and his quest are alive and well in our own popular culture. In movies, comic books, fantasy novels, television programs, and video games, we meet an endless procession of larger-than-life, sometimes superhuman heroes—both male and female—whom we recognize as descendants of the ancient world's epic heroes. The archetype endures because it is, quite simply, universal and always relevant, a symbol of some of the most deeply held values of humankind. The stories of the epic hero address every aspect of the human experience—its joys, its agonies, its accomplishments, its failures, its sense of its relation to the mysteries of the universe. In Gilgamesh's journey from arrogant kingship to humbled returning pilgrim, in Achilles' passage from pouting adolescent to experienced warrior humbled by the ancient Priam, and in Beowulf's movement from self-seeking adventure to heroic but humble death, we discover a dramatic record of the personal and collective human quest.

Hercules slaying the centaur Eurytion. Detail of a marble sculpture.
Ali Meyer/CORBIS.

The Features of an Epic

- Takes the form of a long narrative poem about a quest, told in formal, elevated language
- Narrates the exploits of a larger-than-life hero who embodies the values of a particular culture
- Begins with a statement of subject and theme and, sometimes, a prayer to a deity
- Deals with events on a large scale
- Uses many of the conventions of oral storytelling, such as repetition, sound effects, figures of speech, and stock epithets
- Often includes gods and goddesses as characters
- Mixes myth, legend, and history

Gilgamesh

A Mesopotamian Epic

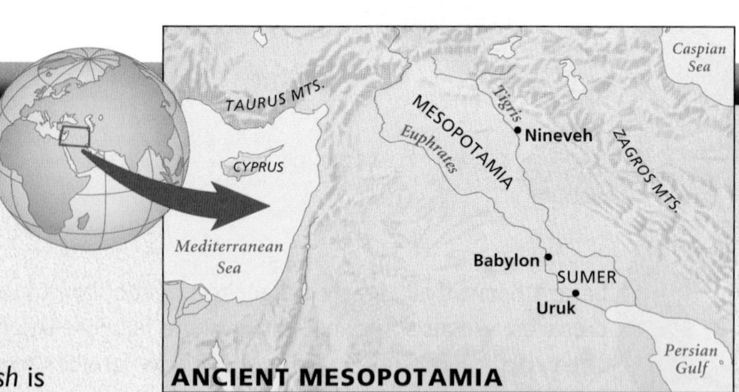

Like most epics, the epic of *Gilgamesh* is based on at least a grain of truth. Many scholars believe that Gilgamesh was an actual king who reigned over the city-state of Uruk, in Sumer, sometime between 2700 and 2500 B.C. Gradually, over the centuries, King Gilgamesh became a legendary figure, rather like King Arthur in the European Middle Ages. Tales of Gilgamesh's exploits grew and were probably recited in verse for centuries before they were recorded in writing. The earliest written fragments date from about 2000 B.C. Later the tale was repeated and reworked by writers from the Sumerian, Babylonian, and Assyrian cultures. Some scholars believe that the epic was finally put into its most complete form by a scribe in 1300 B.C.

The Original Epic Hero?

The Gilgamesh of the epic is a superhuman hero, two parts god and one part human. He thus possesses both supernatural powers and human weaknesses, and in many ways it is his human weaknesses that make him so interesting to us and to the ancient peoples who eagerly listened to and learned from his exploits. He is the leader of his people and the builder of a great city, yet he suffers from excessive pride. In fact, it is because he rejects the love of Ishtar, the goddess of love and war, and insults the gods that he suffers the death of his dear friend, Enkidu. Refusing to accept death—"the common lot of man"—Gilgamesh embarks on a quest for immortality. With superhuman strength, courage, and persistence, he confronts obstacles along the way, but he must ultimately contend with human limitations.

Gilgamesh may, in fact, be the original epic hero. Versions of the epic of *Gilgamesh* have been found at sites almost as far north as the Black Sea and as far south as Jerusalem and from the Mediterranean coast eastward to the Persian Gulf. The epic was so widely known that many scholars believe it served as an **archetype,** or model, for hero myths that would appear later in Greece, India, and Persia.

A New Version of the Epic

The story of Gilgamesh as we know it today is based on eleven clay tablets containing cuneiform (kyo͞o•nē′ə•fôrm′) script—the wedge-shaped characters used as a writing system by ancient Mesopotamians. These tablets were among 25,000 discovered in modern Iraq, at Nineveh, in the buried ruins of the library of King Assurbanipal of Assyria (669–626 B.C.). Nineveh was razed by Persian invaders in 612 B.C., and the original tablets were broken and marred. The recent discovery of older versions of the epic, however, has helped scholars clarify many parts of the story that once were missing or vague.

The epic of *Gilgamesh* reveals a great deal about the ancient Mesopotamians' sometimes pessimistic views of existence, but it also shows us the sensitivity and humanity of these ancient peoples, who are not unlike us in their joys, sorrows, and strivings.

Before You Read

from Gilgamesh: A Verse Narrative

Make the Connection

Quickwrite

Although this story is thousands of years old, its two main characters experience some of the same desires and yearnings for adventure as young people do today. They leave the safety of home together to seek adventure, and they take on challenges that will prove their worth—and, perhaps, help them establish a place in the world. Can you think of a pair of "friends to the end" in a contemporary book or movie who also share important adventures together? How does the bond of their friendship help or hinder them? Describe what happens to each character and to their friendship as a result of the challenges they face together.

Literary Focus

The Foil

Many heroes, such as Beowulf, "go it alone," proudly seeking fame and glory entirely through their own efforts. Sometimes, however, a hero is provided with a companion who serves as his **foil**—a character who sets off the other character through strong contrast. The foil emphasizes the differences between the two characters. A famous example of a foil is Dr. Watson, the practical and down-to-earth companion who accompanies the brilliant, eccentric, and intuitive detective Sherlock Holmes. In *Gilgamesh* the foil is Enkidu, who, in contrast to Gilgamesh, represents the natural man, a pure-hearted and uncomplicated person who is innocent of the ways of civilized society.

A **foil** is a character who helps to define another character by means of contrast.

For more on Foil, see the Handbook of Literary and Historical Terms.

Background

Gilgamesh, who is two-thirds god and one-third human, is handsome, courageous, and strong, but he is also impulsive and willful. His people, upset with his tyrannical treatment of them, pray to the gods for relief. In response the gods send a match for Gilgamesh: the wild man Enkidu, reared by animals and unfamiliar with the ways of civilization. The two become close friends, and Enkidu joins Gilgamesh on a series of adventures. Craving an adventure that will bring them fame, they plan a journey to the cedar forest. There they will confront the monstrous guardian of the forest, the evil giant, Humbaba.

As this part of the story opens, Enkidu is terrified of meeting the monster. Gilgamesh urges him on.

Literary Skills Understand the use of a foil.

Vocabulary Development

austere (ô·stir′) *adj.:* restrained; spare; very plain.

decreed (dē·krēd′) *v.:* ordered; commanded.

contortion (kən·tôr′shən) *n.:* twisted shape or motion.

squall (skwôl) *n.:* violent storm that doesn't last very long.

INTERNET

Vocabulary Practice

Keyword: LE7 12-1

from Gilgamesh
A Verse Narrative

retold by Herbert Mason

Why are you worried about death?
Only the gods are immortal anyway,
Sighed Gilgamesh.
What men do is nothing, so fear is never
Justified. What happened to your power
That once could challenge and equal mine?
I will go ahead of you, and if I die
I will at least have the reward
Of having people say: He died in war
Against Humbaba. You cannot discourage me
With fears and hesitations.
I will fight Humbaba,
I will cut down his cedars.
Tell the armorers to build us two-edged swords
And double shields and tell them
I am impatient and cannot wait long.

Thus Gilgamesh and Enkidu went
Together to the marketplace
To notify the Elders of Uruk
Who were meeting in their senate.
They too were talking of Humbaba,
As they often did,
Edging always in their thoughts
Toward the forbidden.

The one you speak of, Gilgamesh addressed them,
I now must meet. I want to prove
Him not the awesome thing we think he is
And that the boundaries set up by gods
Are not unbreakable. I will defeat him
In his cedar forest. The youth of Uruk
Need this fight. They have grown soft
And restless.

The old men leaned a little forward
Remembering old wars. A flush burned on

Gilgamesh holding a lion. Relief from the palace of Sargon II (8th century B.C.), Khorsabad, Iraq.

Louvre, Paris.

(Top left) detail of mosaic from the Turkish palace of Attalos II (3rd century B.C.).

Pergamon Museum, Berlin. The Bridgeman Art Library.

Their cheeks. It seemed a little dangerous
And yet they saw their king
Was seized with passion for this fight.
Their voices gave the confidence his friend
Had failed to give; some even said
Enkidu's wisdom was a sign of cowardice.
You see, my friend, laughed Gilgamesh,
The wise of Uruk have outnumbered you.

Amidst the speeches in the hall
That called upon the gods for their protection,
Gilgamesh saw in his friend that pain
He had seen before and asked him what it was
That troubled him.

Enkidu could not speak. He held his tears
Back. Barely audibly he said:
It is a road which you have never traveled.

The armorers brought to Gilgamesh his weapons
And put them in his hand. He took his quiver,
Bow and ax, and two-edged sword,
And they began to march.

The Elders gave their austere blessing
And the people shouted: Let Enkidu lead,
Don't trust your strength, he knows the forests,
The one who goes ahead will save his friend.
May Shamash° bring you victory. . . .

After three days they reached the edge
Of the forest where Humbaba's watchman stood.
Suddenly it was Gilgamesh who was afraid,
Enkidu who reminded him to be fearless.
The watchman sounded his warning to Humbaba.
The two friends moved slowly toward the forest gate.

When Enkidu touched the gate his hand felt numb,
He could not move his fingers or his wrist,
His face turned pale like someone's witnessing a death,
He tried to ask his friend for help
Whom he had just encouraged to move on,

Gilgamesh between two demigods supporting the sun. Detail from a stone monument (9th century B.C.), Tell Halaf, Syria.

Archaeological Museum, Aleppo, Syria/Dagli Orti. The Art Archive.

59. Shamash (shä′mäsh): god associated with the sun and human laws.

Vocabulary

austere (ô•stir′) *adj.:* restrained; spare; very plain.

But he could only stutter and hold out
His paralyzed hand.
It will pass, said Gilgamesh.
Would you want to stay behind because of that?
We must go down into the forest together.
Forget your fear of death. I will go before you
And protect you. Enkidu followed close behind
So filled with fear he could not think or speak.
Soon they reached the high cedars.

They stood in awe at the foot
Of the green mountain. Pleasure
Seemed to grow from fear of Gilgamesh.
As when one comes upon a path in woods
Unvisited by men, one is drawn near
The lost and undiscovered in himself;
He was revitalized by danger.
They knew it was the path Humbaba made.
Some called the forest "Hell," and others "Paradise";
What difference does it make? said Gilgamesh.
But night was falling quickly
And they had no time to call it names,
Except perhaps "The Dark,"
Before they found a place at the edge of the forest
To serve as shelter for their sleep.

It was a restless night for both. One snatched
At sleep and sprang awake from dreams. The other
Could not rest because of pain that spread
Throughout his side. Enkidu was alone
With sights he saw brought on by pain
And fear, as one in deep despair
May lie beside his love who sleeps
And seems so unafraid, absorbing in himself the phantoms
That she cannot see—phantoms diminished for one
When two can see and stay awake to talk of them
And search out a solution to despair,
Or lie together in each other's arms,
Or weep and in exhaustion from their tears
Perhaps find laughter for their fears.
But alone and awake the size and nature
Of the creatures in his mind grow monstrous,
Beyond resemblance to the creatures he had known
Before the prostitute had come into his life.

Figure of a man from the Square Temple at Tell Asmar (c. 2750–2600 B.C.), Iraq.

National Museum, Damascus.

Gilgamesh (center) depicted on a Chaldean seal.

Bettmann/CORBIS.

He cried aloud for them to stop appearing over him
Emerging from behind the trees with phosphorescent° eyes
Brought on by rain. He could not hear his voice
But knew he screamed and could not move his arms
But thought they tried to move
As if a heavy weight he could raise
Or wriggle out from underneath
Had settled on his chest,
Like a turtle trapped beneath a fallen branch,
Each effort only added to paralysis.
He could not make his friend, his one companion, hear.

Gilgamesh awoke but could not hear
His friend in agony, he still was captive to his dreams
Which he would tell aloud to exorcise:°
I saw us standing in a mountain gorge,
A rockslide fell on us, we seemed no more
Than insects under it. And then
A solitary graceful man appeared
And pulled me out from under the mountain.
He gave me water and I felt released.

Tomorrow you will be victorious,
Enkidu said, to whom the dream brought chills
(For only one of them, he knew, would be released)
Which Gilgamesh could not perceive in the darkness
For he went back to sleep without responding
To his friend's interpretation of his dream.

114. phosphorescent (fäs′fə·res′ənt) *adj.:* giving off light after being exposed to heat.

126. exorcise *v.:* to drive out.

Did you call me? Gilgamesh sat up again.
Why did I wake again? I thought you touched me.
Why am I afraid? I felt my limbs grow numb
As if some god passed over us drawing out our life.
I had another dream:
This time the heavens were alive with fire, but soon
The clouds began to thicken, death rained down on us,
The lightning flashes stopped, and everything
Which rained down turned to ashes.
What does this mean, Enkidu?

That you will be victorious against Humbaba,
Enkidu said, or someone said through him
Because he could not hear his voice
Or move his limbs although he thought he spoke,
And soon he saw his friend asleep beside him.

At dawn Gilgamesh raised his ax
And struck at the great cedar.
When Humbaba heard the sound of falling trees,
He hurried down the path that they had seen
But only he had traveled. Gilgamesh felt weak
At the sound of Humbaba's footsteps and called to Shamash
Saying, I have followed you in the way decreed;
Why am I abandoned now? Suddenly the winds
Sprang up. They saw the great head of Humbaba
Like a water buffalo's bellowing down the path,
His huge and clumsy legs, his flailing arms
Thrashing at phantoms in his precious trees.
His single stroke could cut a cedar down
And leave no mark on him. His shoulders,
Like a porter's° under building stones,
Were permanently bent by what he bore;
He was the slave who did the work for gods
But whom the gods would never notice.
Monstrous in his contortion, he aroused
The two almost to pity.
But pity was the thing that might have killed.
It made them pause just long enough to show
How pitiless he was to them. Gilgamesh in horror saw
Him strike the back of Enkidu and beat him to the ground
Until he thought his friend was crushed to death.
He stood still watching as the monster leaned to make

Man carrying a goat, from a Sam'al basalt bas-relief (c. 730 B.C.).

Pergamon Museum, Berlin. The Bridgeman Art Library.

168. porter *n.*: person who carries things for other people.

Vocabulary

decreed (dē•krēd′) *v.:* ordered; commanded.
contortion (kən•tôr′shən) *n.:* twisted shape or motion.

His final strike against his friend, unable
To move to help him, and then Enkidu slid
Along the ground like a ram making its final lunge
On wounded knees. Humbaba fell and seemed
To crack the ground itself in two, and Gilgamesh,
As if this fall had snapped him from his daze,
Returned to life
And stood over Humbaba with his ax
Raised high above his head watching the monster plead
In strangled sobs and desperate appeals
The way the sea contorts under a violent squall.
I'll serve you as I served the gods, Humbaba said;
I'll build you houses from their sacred trees.

Enkidu feared his friend was weakening
And called out: Gilgamesh! Don't trust him!
As if there were some hunger in himself
That Gilgamesh was feeling
That turned him momentarily to yearn
For someone who would serve, he paused;
And then he raised his ax up higher
And swung it in a perfect arc
Into Humbaba's neck. He reached out
To touch the wounded shoulder of his friend,

And late that night he reached again
To see if he was yet asleep, but there was only
Quiet breathing. The stars against the midnight sky
Were sparkling like mica° in a riverbed.
In the slight breeze
The head of Humbaba was swinging from a tree.

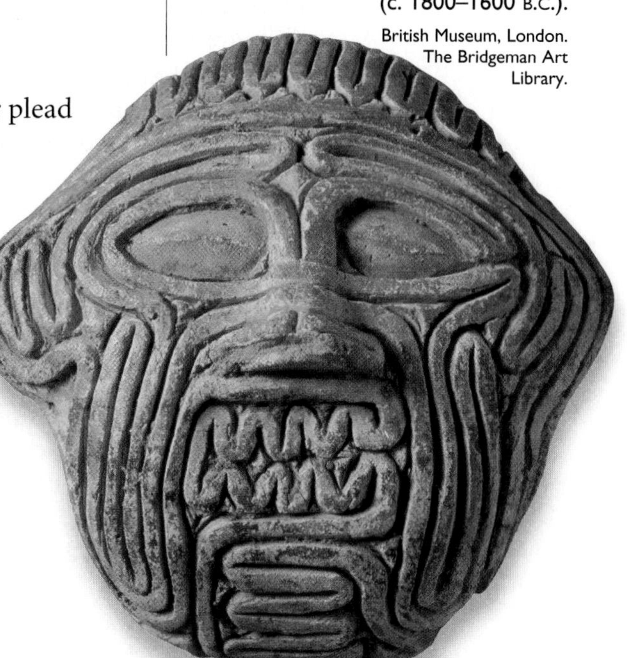

Babylonian sculpture of head of Humbaba carved to resemble intestines (c. 1800–1600 B.C.).

British Museum, London. The Bridgeman Art Library.

206. mica *n.:* kind of thin, crystalline mineral.

Vocabulary

squall (skwôl) *n.:* violent storm that doesn't last very long.

Response and Analysis

Reading Check

1. How do the elders of Uruk respond to Gilgamesh's plan?
2. Summarize what happens in the cedar forest. Do events unfold exactly as Gilgamesh anticipated? Explain.

Thinking Critically

3. Enkidu acts as a **foil** to Gilgamesh. What do you learn about Gilgamesh's strengths and weaknesses by contrasting him with Enkidu?
4. How do Gilgamesh and Enkidu help each other on their adventure? Are there any ways in which they hurt each other? Compare their experiences with those of the friends you wrote about in your Quickwrite notes.
5. Enkidu repeatedly associates Humbaba with death. How does Gilgamesh characterize Humbaba? What are we told about Humbaba's relationship with the gods?
6. Find specific **figures of speech** that describe Humbaba. How do these descriptions make you feel about Humbaba?

Extending and Evaluating

7. After reading this excerpt, do you see Gilgamesh as a hero worthy of unqualified admiration? What lessons, if any, do you think he still needs to learn if he is to be a true **epic hero**?

Comparing Literature

8. How does Humbaba compare with the monster figures in the *Beowulf* epic?
9. How is Gilgamesh like and unlike the epic hero Beowulf? What elements of Gilgamesh's battle with Humbaba are similar to Beowulf's battles with his monsters?

Literary Skills Analyze the use of a foil. Analyze the epic and the archetype of the epic hero in ancient and modern literature. Compare literary forms of major literary periods.

Writing Skills Write an interior monologue.

Vocabulary Skills Demonstrate word knowledge.

WRITING

The Inner Quest

Even though the great early epics are full of action, they also show keen psychological insight. Gilgamesh and Enkidu are guided by internal needs and plagued by inner fears and doubts. These are revealed in the characters' dialogue and in their dreams. Imagine what Gilgamesh or Enkidu is thinking and feeling after the battle with Humbaba. Write an **interior monologue** that expresses what is going through the mind of one of them. Use the first-person pronoun *I*.

Vocabulary Development

Question and Answer

Answer the following questions to test your understanding of the underlined Vocabulary words.

1. What is the opposite of an austere room?
2. What type of person would have decreed something?
3. What could a contortion look like?
4. What is the difference between a light drizzle and a squall?

Sumerian bull's head in bronze, from a musical instrument or piece of furniture (c. 2500 B.C.).

Pergamon Museum, Berlin. The Bridgeman Art Library.

Homer and the *Iliad*

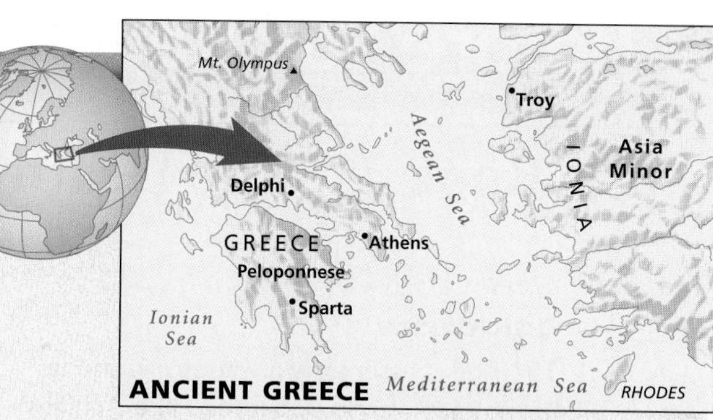

Europe's first and most enduring literary epics, the *Iliad* (il′ē • əd) and the *Odyssey* (äd′i • sē), were composed sometime between 900 and 700 B.C. We know little about Homer, the author of these epics. He was probably a native of the Greek district of Ionia on the western coast of Asia Minor. The name *Homer* may mean "hostage," suggesting that the poet may have been a slave or descended from slaves. Homer belonged to a class of bards who played a vitally important role in Greek society, serving as both oral historians and entertainers. Tradition says Homer was blind, a detail probably based more on convention than on fact: In Greek culture, physical blindness was often a metaphor for profound insight.

The Legend of the Trojan War

Both the *Iliad* and the *Odyssey* tell stories about the heroes and events of the Trojan War. According to oral tradition, the war began not with a battle but with a beauty contest—an unusual beauty contest. Three goddesses—Aphrodite, Athena, and Hera—decided to compete for a golden apple that was inscribed "To the Fairest." The gods, smart enough not to get involved in a potentially hazardous situation, chose a mortal to judge the most beautiful goddess. Paris, a young and handsome but naive prince of Troy, was selected. Each goddess in turn tried to bribe Paris in order to get his vote. The bribe Paris finally accepted was Aphrodite's, for she offered him the most appealing gift of all—marriage to the world's most beautiful woman, Helen, the wife of King Menelaus of Greece. Paris took Helen from Menelaus, and the two sailed for Troy. Outraged by the abduction of Helen, the Greek chieftains, bound by oaths of loyalty, banded together under the leadership of Menelaus's brother, Agamemnon, and attacked Troy. The war party laid siege to Troy, beginning a conflict that would drag on for ten years before the Greeks would finally succeed in sacking Troy and recapturing Helen—thanks to the wiles of the clever hero Odysseus.

Background to the *Iliad*

The *Iliad* opens as the Trojan War enters its tenth year, and it closes several weeks later. The story revolves around two main characters: Achilles, the bravest and handsomest warrior in the Greek army, and his enemy Hector, the honorable warrior-prince of the Trojans. In Book 22 of the epic, the conflict between these two antagonists reaches its tragic climax.

The tragedy that is at the heart of the *Iliad* is set into motion by a human emotion: the anger of Achilles. Human beings are the epic's combatants, but gods and goddesses take sides and profoundly affect the outcome. The Greeks saw their deities as immortal and powerful but in many ways just like humans: interested in human events and actions and capable of the same weaknesses as people—rivalry, jealousy, anger, and pettiness. The Greek gods and goddesses could and did involve themselves in human affairs and could either help or hinder individual people. Ultimately, though, as Homer's epic demonstrates, a person's fate was based as much on his or her own character and actions as on a proper relationship with the gods.

Before You Read

from Book 22: The Death of Hector

Make the Connection

Quickwrite

The *Iliad* is essentially a war story, and its heroes are warriors, but men like Achilles and Hector are not just bloodthirsty killers eager for the next fight. Homer's warriors strive to achieve *arete,* or personal honor and excellence. In their eyes it is honorable to fight bravely for one's king and comrades and dishonorable to seek safety for oneself when one's friends are threatened. To die at the hands of a more powerful enemy is far preferable to them than living with the dishonor of having fled a fight or failed to give one's all in battle. What do the concepts of honor and personal excellence mean to you? How can an ideal of honor make a better society? (Could it also harm a society?) Take some notes on contemporary ideals of honor and how they compare and contrast with the *arete* of Homer's heroes.

Literary Focus

The Epic Simile

Literary Skills Understand the epic simile.

One of the most important features of the *Iliad* is Homer's use of extended comparisons called **epic similes** (also known as **Homeric similes**). Homer's comparisons often extend over many lines and make use of the words *like* and *as.* These complex figures of speech usually compare extraordinary, heroic actions to simple, everyday events that Homer's audience could easily understand. For example, in lines 1–3 of this excerpt from Book 22, Achilles, in hot pursuit of Hector, is compared to a hunting dog: "nonstop / as a hound in the mountains starts a fawn from its lair, / hunting him down the gorges, down the narrow glens." By using the familiar image of a hunt, Homer makes it easy for his listeners to imagine Achilles racing headlong after Hector.

INTERNET

Vocabulary Practice

•

More About Homer

•

Keyword: LE7 12-1

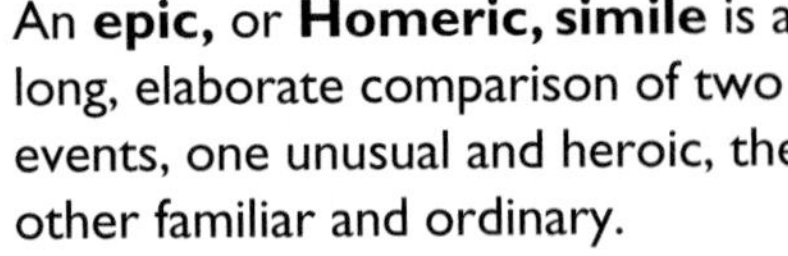

An **epic,** or **Homeric, simile** is a long, elaborate comparison of two events, one unusual and heroic, the other familiar and ordinary.

For more on the Epic, see the Handbook of Literary and Historical Terms.

Background

As the *Iliad* begins, the war between the Greeks and the Trojans has been a stalemate for nearly ten years. Each army has fought bravely, and each has received the help of the gods. Apollo assists Hector and the Trojans, and Athena aids Achilles and the Greeks (who are also referred to as the Achaeans or the Argives). Prior to Book 22, Hector kills Patroclus, Achilles' dearest friend, and strips the corpse of its armor, leaving the body exposed and unburied. Because the Greeks believed that a soul could not find rest until certain burial rites had been performed, Achilles is enraged at Hector and seeks revenge.

Vocabulary Development

groveling (gräv′əl·iŋ) *v.* used as *adj.:* crawling; humiliating oneself in front of authority.

gallant (gal′ənt) *adj.:* noble; brave.

scourge (skʉrj) *n.:* means of inflicting severe punishment. Usually the word refers to a whip.

fawning (fôn′iŋ) *v.* used as *adj.:* cringing and pleading.

the Iliad

from Book 22: The Death of Hector

Homer

translated by **Robert Fagles**

The Characters in the *Iliad*

The Greeks

Achilles (ə•kil′ēz′): son of a mortal king, Peleus, and the sea goddess Thetis; king of the Myrmidons; mightiest of the Greek warriors.

Patroclus (pə•trō′kləs): Greek warrior and dearest friend of Achilles.

The Trojans

Hector (hek′tər): son of King Priam and Queen Hecuba; commander of the Trojan forces.

Paris (par′is): son of King Priam and Queen Hecuba; also known as Alexandros.

Priam (prī′əm): king of Troy; father of Hector and Paris.

Gods and Goddesses

Apollo (ə•päl′ō): god of poetry, music, and prophecy; often referred to only as the son of Zeus and Leto, the daughter of Titans. Apollo sides with the Trojans.

Athena (ə•thē′nə): goddess of wisdom. Athena takes the Greeks' side in the conflict.

Zeus (zo͞os): father-god. Zeus remains more or less neutral throughout the conflict.

The goddess Athena (c. 335 B.C.). Bronze statue.
National Archaeological Museum, Athens. The Bridgeman Art Library.

As Book 22 opens, the exhausted Trojans take refuge behind the walls of their city, but Hector remains outside the gates. As Achilles races toward Troy, Hector's parents urge their son to come back inside the city walls. But Hector resolves to stay exposed outside the gates. After an inner struggle in which he considers simply bargaining with Achilles peacefully, Hector decides to fight to the death. As Achilles bears down on him, though, Hector panics and flees in fear. An epic chase around the walls of Troy begins. Looking down from Mount Olympus, Zeus considers saving Hector from certain death. Athena protests vehemently, however, and Zeus allows her to do as she wishes. Athena races down from Olympus to help Achilles, her favorite. Hector's fate is sealed.

And swift Achilles kept on coursing Hector, nonstop
as a hound in the mountains starts a fawn from its lair,
hunting him down the gorges, down the narrow glens
and the fawn goes to ground, hiding deep in brush
but the hound comes racing fast, nosing him out
until he lands his kill. So Hector could never throw
Achilles off his trail, the swift racer Achilles—
time and again he'd make a dash for the Dardan Gates,°
trying to rush beneath the rock-built ramparts, hoping
men on the heights might save him, somehow, raining spears
but time and again Achilles would intercept him quickly,
heading him off, forcing him out across the plain
and always sprinting along the city side himself—
endless as in a dream . . .
when a man can't catch another fleeing on ahead
and he can never escape nor his rival overtake him—
so the one could never run the other down in his speed

1–18. Achilles repeatedly prevents Hector from nearing the city gates, where his comrades might supply him with extra weapons.
? *What words and comparisons emphasize Achilles' speed?*

8. Dardan Gates: gates of Troy. Dardania, a city built near the foot of Mount Ida, became part of Troy.

Hector and Menelaus fight over the body of Euphorbos (c. 600 B.C.).

The British Museum, London.
The Bridgeman Art Library, New York.

nor the other spring away. And how could Hector have fled
the fates of death so long? How unless one last time,
one final time Apollo had swept in close beside him,
driving strength in his legs and knees to race the wind?
And brilliant Achilles shook his head at the armies,
never letting them hurl their sharp spears at Hector—
someone might snatch the glory, Achilles come in second.
But once they reached the springs for the fourth time,
then Father Zeus held out his sacred golden scales:
in them he placed two fates of death that lays men low—
one for Achilles, one for Hector breaker of horses—
and gripping the beam mid-haft the Father raised it high
and down went Hector's day of doom, dragging him down
to the strong House of Death—and god Apollo left him.
Athena rushed to Achilles, her bright eyes gleaming,
standing shoulder-to-shoulder, winging orders now:
"At last our hopes run high, my brilliant Achilles—
Father Zeus must love you—
we'll sweep great glory back to Achaea's fleet,
we'll kill this Hector, mad as he is for battle!
No way for him to escape us now, no longer—
not even if Phoebus the distant deadly Archer
goes through torments, pleading for Hector's life,
groveling over and over before our storming Father Zeus.
But you, you hold your ground and catch your breath
while I run Hector down and persuade the man
to fight you face-to-face."
So Athena commanded
and he obeyed, rejoicing at heart—Achilles stopped,
leaning against his ashen spearshaft barbed in bronze.
And Athena left him there, caught up with Hector at once,
and taking the build and vibrant voice of Deiphobus°
stood shoulder-to-shoulder with him, winging orders:
"Dear brother, how brutally swift Achilles hunts you—
coursing you round the city of Priam in all his lethal speed!
Come, let us stand our ground together—beat him back."

"Deiphobus!"—Hector, his helmet flashing, called out to her—
"dearest of all my brothers, all these warring years,
of all the sons that Priam and Hecuba produced!
Now I'm determined to praise you all the more,
you who dared—seeing me in these straits—
to venture out from the walls, all for *my* sake,
while the others stay inside and cling to safety."

25–31. *How does Zeus decide the fates of Hector and Achilles? What is the final judgment?*

Athena. Silver coin (c. 324–323 B.C.).

Fitzwilliam Museum, Cambridge, England. The Art Archive/Dagli Orti.

48. Deiphobus (dē·if′ō·bəs): one of Hector's brothers.

34–52. *What does Athena tell Achilles she is going to do? How does Athena trick Hector?*

Vocabulary

groveling (gräv′əl•iŋ) *v.* used as *adj.:* crawling; humiliating oneself in front of authority.

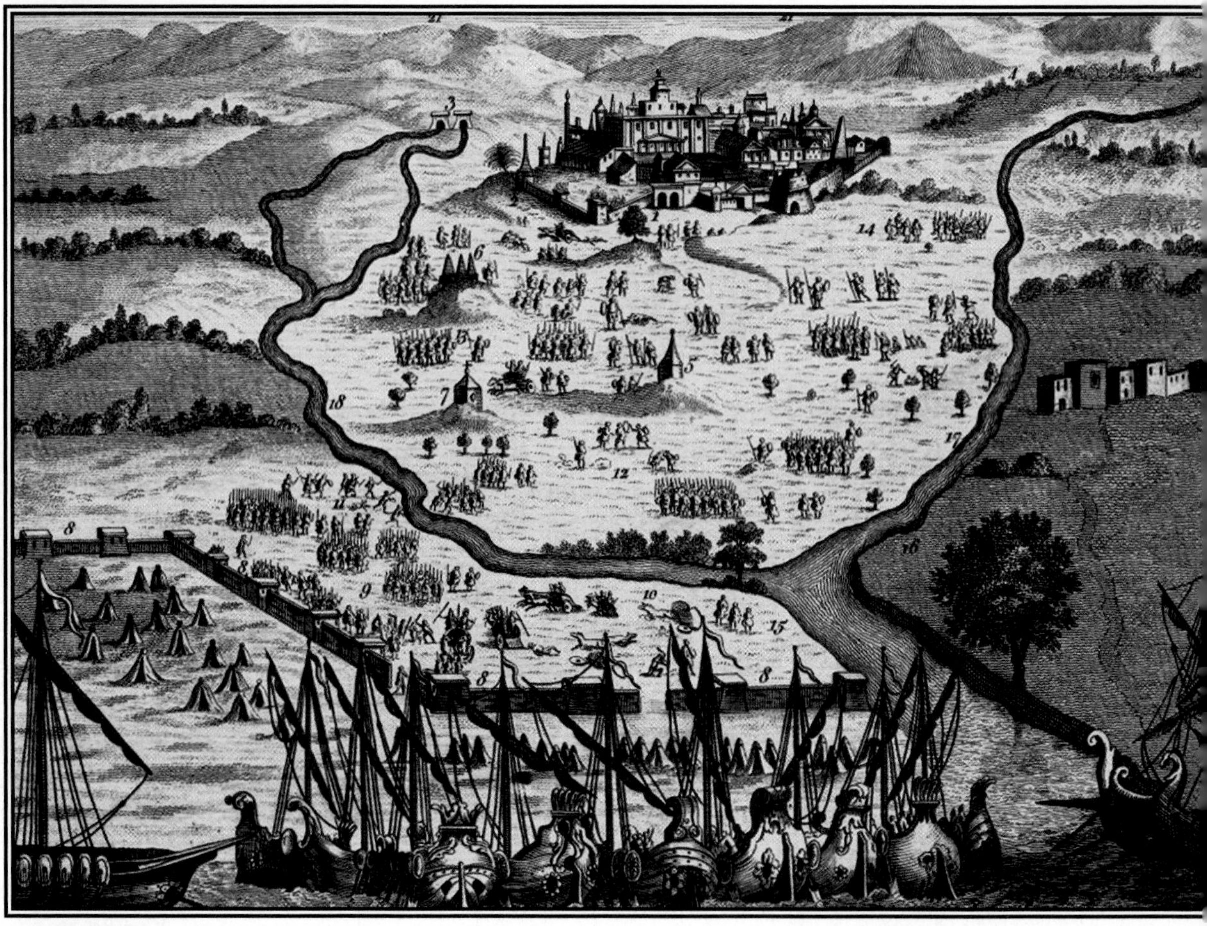

Map of ancient Troy. The Greek ships and encampments are shown outside the walled city.
Bettmann/CORBIS.

The goddess answered quickly, her eyes blazing,
"True, dear brother—how your father and mother both
implored me, time and again, clutching my knees,
and the comrades round me begging me to stay!
Such was the fear that broke them, man for man,
but the heart within me broke with grief for you.
Now headlong on and fight! No letup, no lance spared!
So now, now we'll *see* if Achilles kills us both
and hauls our bloody armor back to the beaked ships
or *he* goes down in pain beneath your spear."

Athena luring him on with all her immortal cunning—
and now, at last, as the two came closing for the kill
it was tall Hector, helmet flashing, who led off:
"No more running from you in fear, Achilles!
Not as before. Three times I fled around
the great city of Priam—I lacked courage then
to stand your onslaught. Now my spirit stirs me
to meet you face-to-face. Now kill or be killed!
Come, we'll swear to the gods, the highest witnesses—
the gods will oversee our binding pacts. I swear

? **73–79.** *What does Hector vow? Why does he now have courage?*

I will never mutilate you—merciless as you are—
if Zeus allows me to last it out and tear your life away.
But once I've stripped your glorious armor, Achilles,
I will give your body back to your loyal comrades.
Swear you'll do the same."
                    A swift dark glance
and the headstrong runner answered, "Hector, stop!
You unforgivable, you . . . don't talk to me of pacts.
There are no binding oaths between men and lions—
wolves and lambs can enjoy no meeting of the minds—
they are all bent on hating each other to the death.
So with you and me. No love between us. No truce
till one or the other falls and gluts with blood
Ares who hacks at men behind his rawhide shield.
Come, call up whatever courage you can muster.
Life or death—now prove yourself a spearman,
a daring man of war! No more escape for you—
Athena will kill you with my spear in just a moment.
Now you'll pay at a stroke for all my comrades' grief,
all you killed in the fury of your spear!"
                    With that,
shaft poised, he hurled and his spear's long shadow flew
but seeing it coming glorious Hector ducked away,
crouching down, watching the bronze tip fly past
and stab the earth—but Athena snatched it up
and passed it back to Achilles
and Hector the gallant captain never saw her.
He sounded out a challenge to Peleus' princely son:
"You missed, look—the great godlike Achilles!
So you knew nothing at all from Zeus about my death—
and yet how sure you were! All bluff, cunning with words,
that's all you are—trying to make me fear you,
lose my nerve, forget my fighting strength.
Well, you'll never plant your lance in my back
as I flee *you* in fear—plunge it through my chest
as I come charging in, if a god gives you the chance!
But now it's for you to dodge *my* brazen spear—
I wish you'd bury it in your body to the hilt.
How much lighter the war would be for Trojans then
if you, their greatest scourge, were dead and gone!"

Shaft poised, he hurled and his spear's long shadow flew
and it struck Achilles' shield—a dead-center hit—

78–98. *What pact has Hector offered Achilles? Why does Achilles refuse the pact?*

106–117. Hector is emboldened by Achilles' unsuccessful attack. *What do Hector's words suggest about the relationship between mortals and gods? What is Hector unaware of?*

Vocabulary

gallant (gal′ənt) *adj.:* noble; brave.

scourge (skurj) *n.:* means of inflicting severe punishment. Usually the word refers to a whip.

but off and away it glanced and Hector seethed,
his hurtling spear, his whole arm's power poured
in a wasted shot. He stood there, cast down . . .
he had no spear in reserve. So Hector shouted out
to Deiphobus bearing his white shield—with a ringing shout
he called for a heavy lance—
but the man was nowhere near
him, vanished—
yes and Hector knew the truth in his heart
and the fighter cried aloud, "My time has come!
At last the gods have called me down to death.
I thought he was at my side, the hero Deiphobus—
he's safe inside the walls, Athena's tricked me blind.
And now death, grim death is looming up beside me,
no longer far away. No way to escape it now. This,
this was their pleasure after all, sealed long ago—
Zeus and the son of Zeus, the distant deadly Archer—
though often before now they rushed to my defense.
So now I meet my doom. Well let me die—
but not without struggle, not without glory, no,
in some great clash of arms that even men to come
will hear of down the years!"
And on that resolve
he drew the whetted sword that hung at his side,
tempered, massive, and gathering all his force
he swooped like a soaring eagle
launching down from the dark clouds to earth
to snatch some helpless lamb or trembling hare.
So Hector swooped now, swinging his whetted sword
and Achilles charged too, bursting with rage, barbaric,
guarding his chest with the well-wrought blazoned shield,
head tossing his gleaming helmet, four horns strong
and the golden plumes shook that the god of fire
drove in bristling thick along its ridge.
Bright as that star amid the stars in the night sky,
star of the evening, brightest star that rides the heavens,
so fire flared from the sharp point of the spear Achilles
brandished high in his right hand, bent on Hector's death,
scanning his splendid body—where to pierce it best?
The rest of his flesh seemed all encased in armor,
burnished, brazen—*Achilles'* armor that Hector stripped
from strong Patroclus when he killed him—true,
but one spot lay exposed,
where collarbones lift the neckbone off the shoulders,
the open throat, where the end of life comes quickest—*there*
as Hector charged in fury brilliant Achilles drove his spear
and the point went stabbing clean through the tender neck

? **123–139.** *What truth does Hector now realize? What does he decide to do?*

? **146–155.** *What descriptive words does Homer use to create a vivid image of Achilles' charge?*

156–165. Here we are reminded that Hector is wearing Achilles' old armor. Achilles had given the armor to his dear friend Patroclus, whom Hector had killed.
? *How does Achilles mortally wound Hector?*

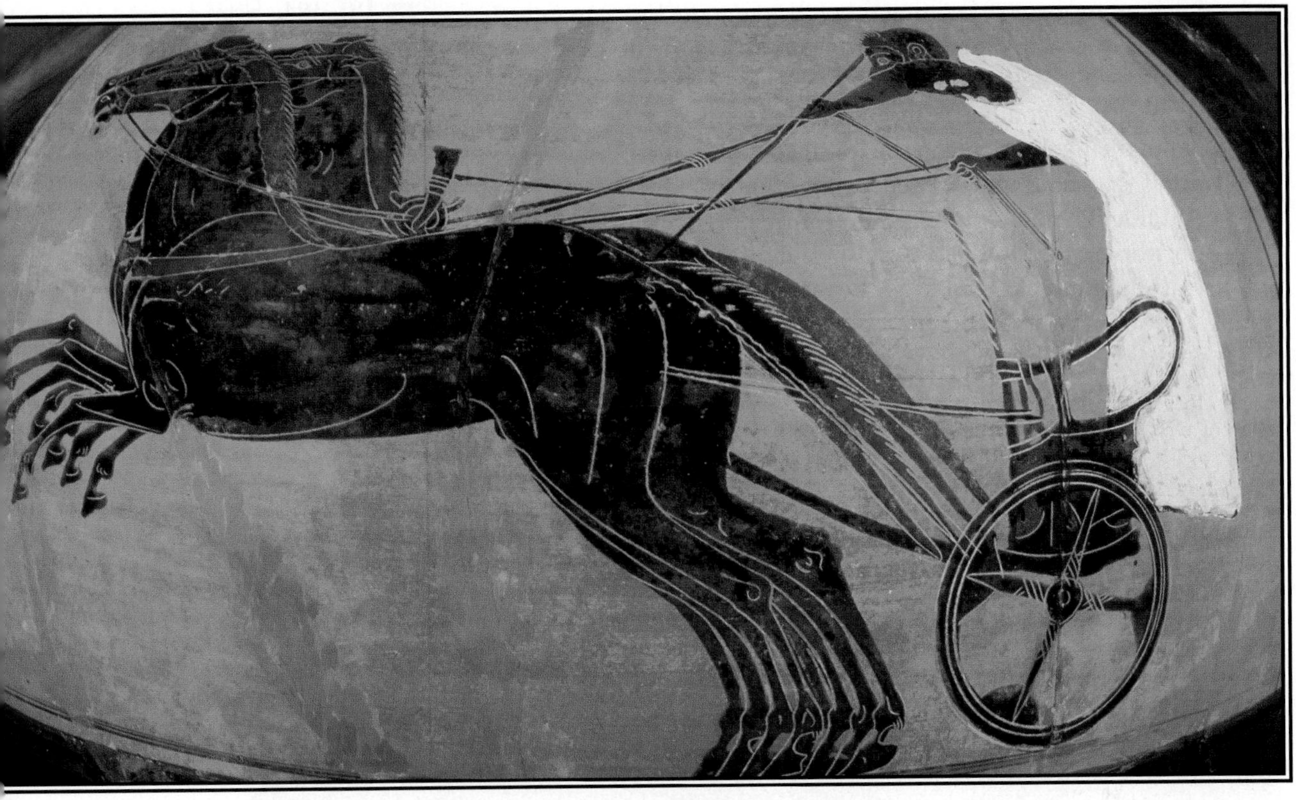

Chariot race depicted on black-figured amphora with white glaze (6th century B.C.).

Louvre, Paris. © Erich Lessing/Art Resource, New York.

but the heavy bronze weapon failed to slash the windpipe—
Hector could still gasp out some words, some last reply . . .
he crashed in the dust—
godlike Achilles gloried over him:
"Hector—surely you thought when you stripped Patroclus' armor
that you, you would be safe! Never a fear of me—
far from fighting as I was—you fool!
Left behind there, down by the beaked ships
his great avenger waited, a greater man by far—
that man was I, and I smashed your strength! And you—
the dogs and birds will maul you, shame your corpse
while Achaeans bury my dear friend in glory!"

Struggling for breath, Hector, his helmet flashing,
said, "I beg you, beg you by your life, your parents—
don't let the dogs devour me by the Argive ships!
Wait, take the princely ransom of bronze and gold,
the gifts my father and noble mother will give you—
but give my body to friends to carry home again,
so Trojan men and Trojan women can do me honor
with fitting rites of fire once I am dead."

175–182. This exchange between Hector and Achilles emphasizes the importance the Greeks and Trojans placed on a proper burial. Without "fitting rites," both men believed, the soul of the departed would never find rest.

? *What does Hector plead?*

Staring grimly, the proud runner Achilles answered,
"Beg no more, you fawning dog—begging me by my parents!
Would to god my rage, my fury would drive me now
to hack your flesh away and eat you raw—
such agonies you have caused me! Ransom?
No man alive could keep the dog-packs off you,
not if they haul in ten, twenty times that ransom
and pile it here before me and promise fortunes more—
no, not even if Dardan Priam should offer to weigh out
your bulk in gold! Not even then will your noble mother
lay you on your deathbed, mourn the son she bore . . .
The dogs and birds will rend you—blood and bone!"

At the point of death, Hector, his helmet flashing,
said, "I know you well—I see my fate before me.
Never a chance that I could win you over . . .
Iron inside your chest, that heart of yours.

? **183–194.** *How does Achilles react to Hector's plea?*

Vocabulary

fawning (fôn′iŋ) *v.* used as *adj.*: cringing and pleading.

Priam begging Achilles to give him the body of Hector (which lies beneath Achilles' couch). Detail from Greek drinking vessel (c. 490 B.C.).

Kunsthistorisches Museum, Vienna. © Erich Lessing/Art Resource, New York.

But now beware, or my curse will draw god's wrath
upon your head, that day when Paris and lord Apollo—
for all your fighting heart—destroy you at the Scaean Gates!"°

Death cut him short. The end closed in around him.
Flying free of his limbs
his soul went winging down to the House of Death,
wailing his fate, leaving his manhood far behind,
his young and supple strength. But brilliant Achilles
taunted Hector's body, dead as he was, "Die, die!
For my own death, I'll meet it freely—whenever Zeus
and the other deathless gods would like to bring it on!"

With that he wrenched his bronze spear from the corpse,
laid it aside and ripped the bloody armor off the back.
And the other sons of Achaea, running up around him,
crowded closer, all of them gazing wonder-struck
at the build and marvelous, lithe beauty of Hector.
And not a man came forward who did not stab his body,
glancing toward a comrade, laughing: "Ah, look here—
how much softer he is to handle now, this Hector,
than when he gutted our ships with roaring fire!"

Standing over him, so they'd gloat and stab his body.
But once he had stripped the corpse the proud runner Achilles
took his stand in the midst of all the Argive troops
and urged them on with a flight of winging orders:
"Friends—lords of the Argives, O my captains!
Now that the gods have let me kill this man
who caused us agonies, loss on crushing loss—
more than the rest of all their men combined—
come, let us ring their walls in armor, test them,
see what recourse the Trojans still may have in mind.
Will they abandon the city heights with this man fallen?
Or brace for a last, dying stand though Hector's gone?
But wait—what am I saying? Why this deep debate?
Down by the ships a body lies unwept, unburied—
Patroclus . . . I will never forget him,
not as long as I'm still among the living
and my springing knees will lift and drive me on.
Though the dead forget their dead in the House of Death,
I will remember, even there, my dear companion.
Now,
come, you sons of Achaea, raise a song of triumph!

200–201. Paris . . . Gates: Hector is foretelling Achilles' ultimate fate. Achilles will later be slain by Paris, who will shoot an arrow into Achilles' heel, the only vulnerable part of his body.

212–218. Achilles' comrades gather around the great warrior and the body of his victim.

? *What do the Greek soldiers do to Hector's body?*

232–237. In the midst of his victory cry, Achilles pauses to remember his dear friend Patroclus, whose death has now been avenged.

Warriors depicted on Mycenaen ceramic vase (detail) (c. 1300–1100 B.C.).

National Archaeological Museum, Athens. © Scala/Art Resource, New York.

Down to the ships we march and bear this corpse on high—
we have won ourselves great glory. We have brought
magnificent Hector down, that man the Trojans
glorified in their city like a god!"
So he triumphed
and now he was bent on outrage, on shaming noble Hector.
Piercing the tendons, ankle to heel behind both feet,
he knotted straps of rawhide through them both,
lashed them to his chariot, left the head to drag
and mounting the car, hoisting the famous arms° aboard,
he whipped his team to a run and breakneck on they flew,
holding nothing back. And a thick cloud of dust rose up
from the man they dragged, his dark hair swirling round
that head so handsome once, all tumbled low in the dust—
since Zeus had given him over to his enemies now
to be defiled in the land of his own fathers.

247. famous arms: Hector's armor.

242–253. Achilles' wrath is so great that he cannot stop at merely killing Hector.
? *How is Hector's body transported from the scene of death? How do you feel as you read this description?*

For centuries people thought that Homer's great stories in the Iliad *were just that—stories, with no basis in historical fact. Then a self-taught German named Heinrich Schliemann (1822–1890) came along. Schliemann had been fascinated with Homer's stories since he was a child. When he was forty-six years old, he abandoned his successful business career and went off to Greece. He wanted to see if he could find evidence that the heroes he loved—Achilles, Patroclus, Hector—had really existed.*

Incredibly, Schliemann was successful. Where Troy had once stood, Schliemann and his workers unearthed seven buried cities. The question was now: Which of these ancient cities was the Troy of the Iliad?

INFORMATIONAL TEXT

Trojan Gold
from Gods, Graves, and Scholars

C. W. Ceram

Schliemann dug and searched. In the second and third levels from the bottom he found traces of fire, the remains of massive walls, and the ruins of a gigantic gate. He was sure that these walls had once enclosed the palace of Priam, and that he had found the famous Scaean Gate.

He unearthed things that were treasures from the scientific point of view. Part of this material he shipped home, part he gave over to experts for examination, material that yielded a detailed picture of the Trojan epoch, the portrait of a people.

It was Heinrich Schliemann's triumph, and the triumph, too, of Homer. He had succeeded, the enthusiastic amateur, in demonstrating the actual existence of what had always counted as mere saga and myth, a figment of the poetic fancy.

A wave of excitement coursed through the intellectual world. Schliemann, whose workers had moved more than 325,000 cubic yards of earth, had earned a breathing spell. Presently, his interests meanwhile having turned to other projects, he set June 15, 1873 as the date for the termination of the diggings. On the day before the last shovelful of earth was to be turned, he found a treasure that crowned his labors with a golden splendor, to the delight of the watching world.

It happened dramatically. Even today, reading about this amazing discovery takes one's breath away. The discovery was made during the early hours of a hot morning. Schliemann, accompanied by his wife, was supervising the excavation. Though no longer seriously expectant of finding anything, nevertheless out of habit he was still keeping close watch on the workmen's every move. They were down twenty-eight feet, at the lower level of the masonry that

Schliemann identified with Priam's palace. Suddenly his gaze was held spellbound. He began to act as if under compulsion. No one can say what the thievish workers would have done if they had seen what met Schliemann's astonished eyes. He seized his wife by the arm. "Gold!" he whispered. She looked at him in amazement. "Quick," he said. "Send the men home at once." The lovely Greek [Schliemann's wife] stammered a protest. "No buts," he told her. "Tell them anything you want. Tell them today is my birthday, that I've just remembered, and that they can all have the rest of the day off. Hurry up, now, hurry!"

The workers left. "Get your red shawl!" Schliemann said to his wife as he jumped down into the hole. He went to work with his knife like a demon. Massive blocks of stone, the debris of millennia, hung perilously over his head, but he paid no attention to the danger. "With all possible speed I cut out the treasure with a large knife," he writes. "I did this by dint of strenuous effort, and in the most frightful danger of losing my life; for the heavy citadel wall, which I had to dig under, might have crashed down on me at any moment. But the sight of so many immeasurably priceless objects made me foolhardy and I did not think of the hazards."

There was the soft sheen of ivory, the jingle of gold. Schliemann's wife held open the shawl to be filled with Priam's treasure. It was the golden treasure of one of the mightiest kings of prehistory, gathered together in blood and tears, the ornaments of a godlike people, buried for three thousand years until dug from under the ruined walls of seven vanished kingdoms. Not for one moment did Schliemann doubt that he had found Priam's treasure-trove. And not until shortly before his death was it proved that Schliemann had been misled in the heat of enthusiasm. Troy lay neither in the second nor in the third layer from the bottom, but in the sixth. The treasure had belonged to a king who had antedated Priam by a thousand years.

Upper part of buildings discovered below a temple of Athena, illustration from Heinrich Schliemann's *Troy and Its Remains* (1875).

The Art Archive.

Response and Analysis

Reading Check

1. How does Athena deceive Hector? Why does Zeus decline to save Hector?
2. What is Hector's dying request, and how does Achilles respond to it?
3. How is Hector's body abused by the Greeks?

Thinking Critically

4. In two extended similes, Hector and Achilles are compared to animals. Find these **epic similes** and others in this part of the story. What comparisons are made in each simile?
5. Achilles and Hector are rival warriors, but are they both heroes? Discuss your opinion of each character in terms of the Greek view of *arete,* or honor, and of your own view of it. You may want to consult the Quickwrite notes you made on contemporary ideals of honor.
6. Homer is concerned with the relationship between *moira,* or fate, and a person's character. Do you feel that Hector was doomed by his noble character, by fate, or by both? Explain.
7. Consider the role of the gods in Book 22. How do they direct or influence events? Do you think their intervention turns the human characters into puppets, or do the humans still make choices that affect their fate? Give reasons for your answer.
8. One of the moving parts of this story is Hector's request that his body be left unmutilated. What episodes in actual wars today, or in movies or stories about war, show that we have this same concern for the bodies of our fallen soldiers?

Extending and Evaluating

9. The *Iliad* is primarily a war epic. In your view, is the *Iliad* a condemnation of the brutality of war, a celebration of the heroism that war can inspire, or an evenly developed examination of both of these aspects? Justify your answer with examples from the epic and from life.
10. The ***Connection*** on page 77 shows that archaeologists have uncovered physical evidence of a walled city where Troy was said to have stood. Do you suppose some of the details in the *Iliad* could be historical? Which events might have happened? Which are definitely fictional?

Literary Criticism

11. **Philosophical approach.** The critic David Denby made the following statement about the *ethos,* or attitudes and ethical beliefs, of the Greek and Trojan warriors of Homer's epic:

> Accepting death in battle as inevitable, the Greek and Trojan aristocrats of the *Iliad* experience the world not as pleasant or unpleasant, nor as good and evil, but as glorious or shameful.

Discuss how the worldview that Denby describes helps to account for, and make sense of, the violent and vengeful elements of Homer's *Iliad* that may seem cruel and immoral to a contemporary reader.

Pages 79–81 cover

Literary Skills
Analyze the epic simile.
Understand conventions of epic poetry.
Compare epics from different literary periods.

Writing Skills
Write an essay comparing and contrasting epic heroes.

Vocabulary Skills
Create semantic maps.

Comparing Literature

12. The theme of friendship is important in both the *Iliad* and the Sumerian epic *Gilgamesh*. Achilles is fiercely loyal to his dead friend Patroclus, and Gilgamesh stands by Enkidu in the gravest danger. Discuss how the specific actions of these epic heroes are influenced by their deeply meaningful friendships.

13. How do the battle scenes in the *Iliad* compare with those in *Beowulf* and *Gilgamesh*? How does each epic hero respond to the sometimes fatal violence that he faces in battle? Are they all equally heroic in their behavior? Explain.

WRITING

Mirror Images?

Consider Achilles and Hector as ideals of the hero in ancient Greece. What special qualities does each hero exhibit? In what ways do they mirror each other? Are their limitations and weaknesses the same, or are they different? Is one hero more "human" than the other? Write a brief essay in which you **compare and contrast** Achilles and Hector as heroes. Cite evidence from the epic to support your findings.

Vocabulary Development

Word Charts

groveling **scourge**
gallant **fawning**

This chart organizes some basic information about the word *gallant*. Using a dictionary, make similar charts for the other Vocabulary words listed above.

gallant
• **Meaning:** noble; brave
• **Origin:** Old English *galaunt*, meaning "merry; brave"
• **Examples:** a very courteous man is gallant; knights are gallant; a person who is sick and does not complain is gallant.

The charioteer of Delphi (detail) (c. 478 B.C.). Bronze statue.

Archaeological Museum, Delphi, Greece.

Literary Focus

Epic Conventions

Certain features of Homer's work were so widely imitated in later written epics, such as Virgil's *Aeneid* and Milton's *Paradise Lost* (see page 403), that they became recognizable characteristics, or **conventions,** of the epic genre. The origins of many of these conventions lie in the oral tradition that gave birth to the *Iliad*. The oral poets used formulas that allowed them to summarize past events rapidly or sketch characters in the epic quickly. Here are some of the epic conventions that occur in the *Iliad:*

1. **Invocation.** The *Iliad* begins with an **invocation,** or formal plea for aid, to the Muse Calliope (kə·lī′ə·pē), one of the nine goddesses who presided over the arts and sciences. The Greeks believed that this "immortal one" spoke through mortal epic poets. The invocation also serves to state the epic's subject and theme. This invocation from the *Iliad* is one of the most famous invocations in all of literature.

> Rage—Goddess, sing the rage of
> Peleus' son Achilles,
> murderous, doomed, that cost the
> Achaeans countless losses,
> hurling down to the House of
> Death so many sturdy souls,
> great fighters' souls, but made
> their bodies carrion,
> feasts for the dogs and birds,
> and the will of Zeus was moving
> toward its end.
> Begin, Muse, when the two first
> broke and clashed,
> Agamemnon lord of men and
> brilliant Achilles.
>
> —*translated by* Robert Fagles

2. ***In medias res.*** The epic plunges us into the middle of the action—that is, *in medias res* (in mā′dē·äs′res′), a Latin term meaning "into the midst of things." **Flashbacks** are then used to inform the audience of events that took place before the narrative's current time.
3. **Epic similes.** One of the most striking features of the language of the *Iliad* is Homer's use of extended, elaborate comparisons, called **epic,** or **Homeric, similes.** Some epic similes are developed over many lines. Such similes compare heroic events to simple, everyday events—events that Homer's audience could easily understand. For example, in another part of Book 22, when Achilles chases Hector, his pursuit is compared to "the wild mountain hawk, the quickest thing on wings, / launching smoothly, swooping down on a cringing dove." Homer's listeners would have been familiar with the image of the birds; this simile would help them understand the epic's action.
4. **Stock epithets.** Another figure of speech that occurs frequently in the *Iliad* is the **stock epithet,** a descriptive adjective or phrase that is repeatedly used with—or in place of—a noun or proper name. Thus, the audience hears of Zeus referred to as "Lord of the lightning" and Athena as "third-born of the gods." The repetition of these kinds of epithets helped the audience follow the narrative; the repetition also helped the rhapsode as he improvised the poem in performance.

Finding epic conventions. Look through the excerpt of the *Iliad* you've just read. Try to find examples of as many of the conventions listed above as possible. How do these conventions add to or detract from the *Iliad*'s appeal?

Grammar Link

Make It Clear: Sentence Fragments and Run-on Sentences

Sentence fragments. What would you think if you came across the following group of words in your reading?

After Agamemnon dishonors Apollo's priest by refusing to surrender Chryseis.

You might be confused by this **sentence fragment** because it does not express a complete thought. Instead, it leaves you wondering: "What happens after Agamemnon dishonors the priest?" A sentence fragment is a group of words that does not express a complete thought but is punctuated as though it were a sentence. Complete sentences, unlike the fragment above, express complete thoughts.

After Agamemnon dishonors Apollo's priest by refusing to surrender Chryseis**,** Apollo punishes the Greeks by sending the plague.

Run-on sentences. In the following sentence it is difficult to tell where one complete thought ends and another begins:

Paris, a prince of Troy, was chosen by the gods to judge the beauty contest, he was offered bribes by each goddess in turn.

A **run-on sentence,** like the example above, contains two or more complete sentences run together as if they were one sentence. You can correct a run-on by separating the two sentences with a period.

Paris, a prince of Troy, was chosen by the gods to judge the beauty contest**.** He was offered bribes by each goddess in turn.

Here is another run-on sentence:

Achilles' mother, Thetis, tried to protect Achilles by dipping him in the River Styx, however, she held him by the heel, making him still vulnerable to attack.

You can correct the run-on by separating the two sentences with a semicolon.

Achilles' mother, Thetis, tried to protect Achilles by dipping him in the River Styx**;** however, she held him by the heel, making him still vulnerable to attack.

Grammar Skills
Identify and correct sentence fragments and run-on sentences.

PRACTICE

Identify each of the following items as a run-on or a fragment. Then, revise each item to make it a complete sentence.

1. Agamemnon wanted Achilles' prize, Achilles refused to give up any part of his spoils.
2. To break up the dispute. Athena grabbed the golden-red hair of Achilles.
3. Because *homer* may mean "hostage" in Greek. Historians have assumed Homer was a slave or descended from slaves.
4. As king of the gods. Zeus remained neutral through much of the battle.
5. Hera was the queen of the gods she was an enemy of the Trojans.

Apply to Your Writing

Review a writing assignment you are working on now or have already completed. Are there any fragments? Are there any run-on sentences? Revise them to make them complete sentences.

For more help, see Sentence Fragments, 9d, and Run-on Sentences, 9e, in the Language Handbook.

PREVIEW

Reflecting on the Literary Period

The Anglo-Saxons: 449–1066

The selections in this feature were written during the same literary period as the other selections in Collection 1, and they share many of the same ideas and concerns. The Focus Question will guide your reading and help you reflect on important aspects of the period.

The Fuller Brooch, Anglo-Saxon, late 9th century.

Think About...

Anglo-Saxon literary works share common themes and ideals of conduct. This literature reflects a society that valued the bond between a lord and his retainers (persons who owed service to the lord); esteemed loyalty, strength, and courage; and considered fame and glory the noblest end of a warrior. Despite the promise of Christian salvation, the Anglo-Saxons maintained a fatalistic, somber attitude toward life, and both Christian and pagan elements coexist in much of their literature.

The three selections included here illustrate traditions that underlie heroic narratives like *Beowulf.* In his *History,* Bede tells the story of an illiterate cowherd, Caedmon, who is inspired to compose religious poetry. Caedmon's Hymn praises God by using some of the same elements used in heroic verse forms. "The Seafarer" and "The Wife's Lament," short reflective poems based on personal experiences, deal with loss and the need for consolation. These **elegies** reflect themes that are prominent in Anglo-Saxon literature—the importance of allegiance to one's leader; the bitterness of exile and isolation; and the belief in the power of fate. Centuries later, these poems still have the power to move us.

Focus Question

As you read each selection, keep in mind this Focus Question and take notes to help you answer it at the end of the feature:

What themes and techniques do poems of the Anglo-Saxon period have in common with heroic narratives like *Beowulf?*

Pages 83–94 cover
Literary Skills
Evaluate the philosophical, political, religious, ethical, and social influences of a historical period.

from A History of the English Church and People

Meet the Writer The Venerable Bede (c. 673–735) was the earliest English historian and the earliest important prose writer. Bede, who was a monk, was known in his own day as a person of great scholarship and learning. His writings include grammatical handbooks, biographies, commentaries on books of the Bible, homilies, and verse. The title "Venerable" was added to his name in recognition of his reputation for wisdom, humility, and scholarship. He seems to have traveled little and spent most of his life, beginning at the age of seven, at the monastery of Jarrow.

Bede's *History of the English Church and People,* originally written in Latin, was translated into Old English during the reign of King Alfred the Great. It became a classic and helped the people of the emerging English nation take pride in their past. The *History* itself is more than a chronicle of events. It also contains legends, lives of saints, local traditions, and stories. From Bede's history one can get a fairly accurate picture of Anglo-Saxon daily life.

Background "Caedmon of Whitby" tells of a miracle in the life of the first known English religious poet. Like the *scops,* or professional poets of the time who celebrated the heroic deeds of their royal patrons, Caedmon celebrates the glorious works of God.

CONNECTING TO THE Focus Question

As you read, consider this question: How does Caedmon's Hymn praise God in terms that would have been admired by Beowulf's society?

from A History of the English Church and People

Bede

translated by **Leo Sherley-Price**

Caedmon of Whitby

In this monastery of [Whitby] lived a brother singularly gifted by God's grace. So skillful was he in composing religious and devotional songs that, when any passage of Scripture was explained to him by interpreters, he could quickly turn it into delightful and moving poetry in his own English tongue. These verses of his have stirred the hearts of many folk to despise the world and aspire to heavenly things. Others after him tried to compose religious poems in English, but none could compare with him; for he did not acquire the art of poetry from men or through any human teacher but received it as a free gift from God. For this reason he could never compose any frivolous or profane[1] verses; but only such as had a religious theme fell fittingly from his devout lips. He had followed a secular[2] occupation

1. **profane:** irreverent; not associated with religious matters.
2. **secular** (sek'yə·lər): worldly, as opposed to religious.

A scribe (probably Bede) writing, by Bede (detail).
British Library, London, UK.

until well advanced in years without ever learning anything about poetry. Indeed it sometimes happened at a feast that all the guests in turn would be invited to sing and entertain the company; then, when he saw the harp coming his way, he would get up from table and go home.

On one such occasion he had left the house in which the entertainment was being held and went out to the stable, where it was his duty that night to look after the beasts. There when the time came he settled down to sleep. Suddenly in a dream he saw a man standing beside him who called him by name. "Caedmon," he said, "sing me a song." "I don't know how to sing," he replied. "It is because I cannot sing that I left the feast and came here." The man who addressed him then said: "But you shall sing to me." "What should I sing about?" he replied. "Sing about the Creation of all things," the other answered. And Caedmon immediately began to sing verses in praise of God the Creator that he had never heard before, and their theme ran thus:

Praise we the Fashioner now of Heaven's fabric,
The majesty of his might and his mind's wisdom,
Work of the world-warden, worker of all wonders,
How he the Lord of Glory everlasting,
Wrought first for the race of men Heaven as a
rooftree,
Then made he Middle Earth to be their mansion.

This is the general sense, but not the actual words that Caedmon sang in his dream; for verses, however masterly, cannot be translated literally from one language into another without losing much of their beauty and dignity. When Caedmon awoke, he remembered everything that he had sung in his dream, and soon added more verses in the same style to a song truly worthy of God.

Early in the morning he went to his superior, the reeve,[3] and told him about this gift that he had received. The reeve took him before the abbess,[4] who ordered him to give an account of his dream and repeat the verses in the presence of many learned men, so that a decision might be reached by common consent as to their quality and origin. All of them agreed that Caedmon's gift had been given him by our Lord. And they explained to him a passage of Scriptural history or doctrine and asked him to render it into verse if he could. He promised to do this, and returned next morning with excellent verses as they had ordered him. The abbess was delighted that God had given such grace to the man, and advised him to abandon secular life and adopt the

3. **reeve:** the manager of an estate; here, the steward in charge of the monastery.
4. **abbess:** the superior of a monastery for nuns and monks.

monastic state.[5] And when she had admitted him into the Community as a brother, she ordered him to be instructed in the events of sacred history. So Caedmon stored up in his memory all that he learned, and like one of the clean animals chewing the cud, turned it into such melodious verse that his delightful renderings turned his instructors into auditors. He sang of the Creation of the world, the origin of the human race, and the whole story of Genesis. He sang of Israel's exodus from Egypt, the entry into the Promised Land, and many other events of Scriptural history. He sang of the Lord's Incarnation,[6] Passion, Resurrection, and Ascension into Heaven, the coming of the Holy Spirit, and the teaching of the Apostles. He also made many poems on the terrors of the Last Judgment, the horrible pains of Hell, and the joys of the Kingdom of Heaven. In addition to these, he composed several others on the blessings and judgments of God, by which he sought to turn his hearers from delight in wickedness and to inspire them to love and do good. For Caedmon was a deeply religious man, who humbly submitted to regular discipline and hotly rebuked all who tried to follow another course. And so he crowned his life with a happy end. ■

5. **monastic state:** Caedmon was originally a lay brother, a non-clergy member, attached to the monastery. Here, the abbess is inviting him to become a full-fledged member of the monastery by taking special vows and participating in the singing of the choir.

6. **Incarnation** (in′kär·nā′shən): appearance in human form.

Response and Analysis

Reading Check

1. What aspects of daily life in Anglo-Saxon England are shown in Bede's *History*?
2. According to Bede, what was Caedmon's gift?

Thinking Critically

3. The story of Caedmon is an account of lowliness exalted. Describe Caedmon's social standing and depth of knowledge before and after he receives his gift from God. Cite passages from the selection to support your response.
4. What religious purpose did Caedmon's poems have? How were they useful for religious instruction?
5. Using details from the selection, respond to **Connecting to the Focus Question** on page 84.

Extending and Evaluating

6. Bede claims that "verses, however masterly, cannot be translated literally from one language into another without losing much of their beauty and dignity." Do you agree? Why or why not?

The Seafarer

Background "The Seafarer," an anonymous poem of uncertain date, was discovered in the Exeter Book, a manuscript of miscellaneous Anglo-Saxon poems dating from around the middle of the tenth century. The Exeter Book is one of the four important collections of Anglo-Saxon poetry that have survived. It contains more than thirty poems and more than ninety riddles. Although the manuscript has been at Exeter (a city in southwest England) since the end of the eleventh century, no one knows where it originated. Some of the manuscript leaves have been damaged by fire, and this has affected the reading of the texts.

"The Seafarer" is a poem of uncommon power and beauty. It is an **elegy**—a poem that mourns the death of a person or laments something lost. The speaker of the poem is an old sailor who has drifted through many winters on ice-cold seas of life. Some interpreters of the poem have suggested that the poem is an **allegory** about the journey of life. Seafaring symbolizes the suffering necessary in the Christian way of life—the seafarer chooses the ascetic life, severe and without worldly pleasures, as a path to salvation.

CONNECTING TO THE
Focus Question

A sense of sadness over the harshness and transience of earthly life is evident in the heroic epic *Beowulf.* As you read this poem, ask yourself: How does "The Seafarer" reflect a similar view of the world?

The Seafarer

translated by **Burton Raffel**

This tale is true, and mine. It tells
How the sea took me, swept me back
And forth in sorrow and fear and pain,
Showed me suffering in a hundred ships,
In a thousand ports, and in me. It tells
Of smashing surf when I sweated in the cold
Of an anxious watch, perched in the bow
As it dashed under cliffs. My feet were cast
In icy bands, bound with frost,
With frozen chains, and hardship groaned
Around my heart. Hunger tore
At my sea-weary soul. No man sheltered
On the quiet fairness of earth can feel
How wretched I was, drifting through winter
On an ice-cold sea, whirled in sorrow,
Alone in a world blown clear of love,
Hung with icicles. The hailstorms flew.

Ship full of Viking warriors. Gotland (10th Century).

The only sound was the roaring sea,
The freezing waves. The song of the swan
Might serve for pleasure, the cry of the sea-fowl,
The death-noise of birds instead of laughter,
The mewing of gulls instead of mead.
Storms beat on the rocky cliffs and were echoed
By icy-feathered terns° and the eagle's screams;
No kinsman could offer comfort there,
To a soul left drowning in desolation.
And who could believe, knowing but
The passion of cities, swelled proud with wine
And no taste of misfortune, how often, how wearily,
I put myself back on the paths of the sea.
Night would blacken; it would snow from the north;
Frost bound the earth and hail would fall,
The coldest seeds. And how my heart
Would begin to beat, knowing once more
The salt waves tossing and the towering sea!
The time for journeys would come and my soul
Called me eagerly out, sent me over
The horizon, seeking foreigners' homes.
But there isn't a man on earth so proud,

24. terns: seabirds related to gulls.

Viking Ship, A.D. 1030

The Granger Collection, New York.

So born to greatness, so bold with his youth,
Grown so brave, or so graced by God,
That he feels no fear as the sails unfurl,
Wondering what Fate has willed and will do.
No harps ring in his heart, no rewards,
No passion for women, no worldly pleasures,
Nothing, only the ocean's heave;
But longing wraps itself around him.
Orchards blossom, the towns bloom,
Fields grow lovely as the world springs fresh,
And all these admonish° that willing mind
Leaping to journeys, always set
In thoughts traveling on a quickening tide.
So summer's sentinel, the cuckoo, sings
In his murmuring voice, and our hearts mourn
As he urges. Who could understand,
In ignorant ease, what we others suffer
As the paths of exile stretch endlessly on?
 And yet my heart wanders away,
My soul roams with the sea, the whales'
Home, wandering to the widest corners
Of the world, returning ravenous° with desire,
Flying solitary, screaming, exciting me
To the open ocean, breaking oaths
On the curve of a wave.
 Thus the joys of God
Are fervent° with life, where life itself
Fades quickly into the earth. The wealth
Of the world neither reaches to Heaven nor remains.
No man has ever faced the dawn
Certain which of Fate's three threats
Would fall: illness, or age, or an enemy's
Sword, snatching the life from his soul.
The praise the living pour on the dead
Flowers from reputation: plant
An earthly life of profit reaped
Even from hatred and rancor,° of bravery
Flung in the devil's face, and death
Can only bring you earthly praise
And a song to celebrate a place
With the angels, life eternally blessed
In the hosts of Heaven.
 The days are gone
When the kingdoms of earth flourished in glory;
Now there are no rulers, no emperors,
No givers of gold, as once there were,

50. admonish: scold mildly.

61. ravenous: very hungry.

65. fervent: passionate.

75. rancor (raŋ′kər): ill will.

When wonderful things were worked among them
And they lived in lordly magnificence.
Those powers have vanished, those pleasures are dead.
The weakest survives and the world continues,
Kept spinning by toil. All glory is tarnished.
The world's honor ages and shrinks.
Bent like the men who mould it. Their faces
Blanch° as time advances, their beards
Wither and they mourn the memory of friends.
The sons of princes, sown in the dust.
The soul stripped of its flesh knows nothing
Of sweetness or sour, feels no pain,
Bends neither its hand nor its brain. A brother
Opens his palms and pours down gold
On his kinsman's grave, strewing his coffin
With treasures intended for Heaven, but nothing
Golden shakes the wrath of God
For a soul overflowing with sin, and nothing
Hidden on earth rises to Heaven.
We all fear God. He turns the earth,
He set it swinging firmly in space,
Gave life to the world and light to the sky.
Death leaps at the fools who forget their God.
He who lives humbly has angels from Heaven
To carry him courage and strength and belief.

91. **blanch:** turn pale.

A man must conquer pride, not kill it,
Be firm with his fellows, chaste for himself,
Treat all the world as the world deserves,
With love or with hate but never with harm,
Though an enemy seek to scorch him in hell,
Or set the flames of a funeral pyre°
Under his lord. Fate is stronger
And God mightier than any man's mind.
Our thoughts should turn to where our home is,
Consider the ways of coming there,
Then strive for sure permission for us
To rise to that eternal joy,
That life born in the love of God
And the hope of Heaven. Praise the Holy
Grace of Him who honored us,
Eternal, unchanging creator of earth. Amen.

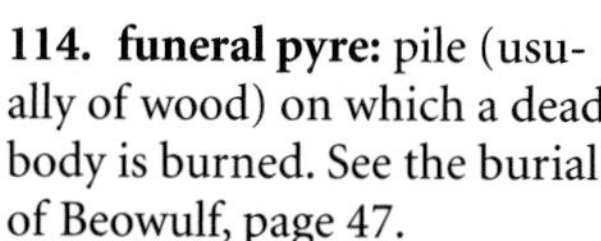

114. funeral pyre: pile (usually of wood) on which a dead body is burned. See the burial of Beowulf, page 47.

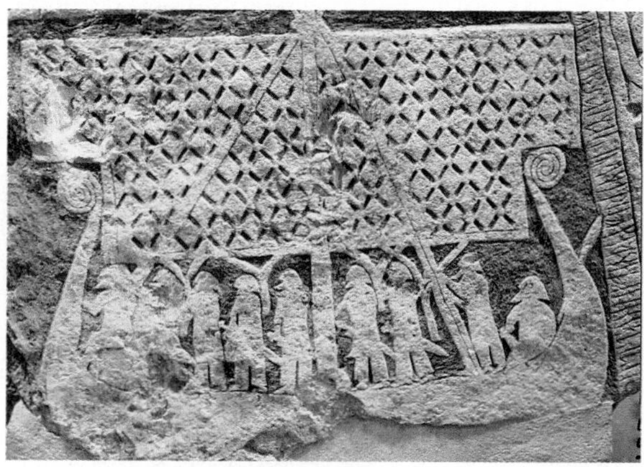

Detail of a picture stone depicting a Viking ship from the Isle of Gotland (stone) by Viking, (9th century).

Historiska Museet, Stockholm, Sweden.

Response and Analysis

Thinking Critically

1. Lines 1–64 express contrasting feelings about seafaring. Describe the feelings and how they change with the seasons.
2. The transitional sentence in lines 64–66 connects seafaring with religion. What is the speaker's attitude toward life on earth?
3. Lines 80–102 contrast the dismal present with the glorious past. How do the speaker's thoughts contribute to the poem's mournful, **elegiac tone**? Cite details from the poem to support your responses.
4. The poem ends with a statement of the speaker's beliefs. What are they?
5. Using details from the selection, respond to **Connecting to the Focus Question** on page 87.

Extending and Evaluating

6. In line 88, the speaker says, "All glory is tarnished." Do you think this idea applies to today's heroes and to present-day life? Explain your response.

The Wife's Lament

Background The female speaker of the anonymous poem "The Wife's Lament" has been separated from her *leodfruma* ("leader of the people"), who is usually assumed to be her husband. It is not clear why she has lost his favor or why she is a "friendless exile."

One interpretation of the poem is that the speaker may have been married to her husband in order to end a dispute between clans. The old feud might have been rekindled and the truce broken. She then would have been separated from her husband and banished.

Another interpretation is that the husband too has turned against her: "I must suffer / The feud of my beloved husband dear" (lines 26–27). Consider your own interpretations as you look for answers to the ambiguities in the poem.

CONNECTING TO THE
Focus Question

"The Wife's Lament" is an elegiac poem that reflects aspects of Anglo-Saxon life and beliefs. As you read, consider this question: How does the poem deal with the experience of loss and the pain of solitude and exile?

The Wife's Lament

translated by **Richard Hamer**

I sing this song about myself, full sad,
My own distress, and tell what hardships I
Have had to suffer since I first grew up,
Present and past, but never more than now;
I ever suffered grief through banishment.
For since my lord departed from this people
Over the sea, each dawn have I had care
Wondering where my lord may be on land.
When I set off to join and serve my lord,
A friendless exile in my sorry plight,
My husband's kinsmen plotted secretly
How they might separate us from each other
That we might live in wretchedness apart
Most widely in the world: and my heart longed.
In the first place my lord had ordered me
To take up my abode here, though I had
Among these people few dear loyal friends;
Therefore my heart is sad. Then had I found
A fitting man, but one ill-starred, distressed,
Whose hiding heart was contemplating crime,
Though cheerful his demeanour. We had vowed
Full many a time that nought should come between us
But death alone, and nothing else at all.

Woman carding wool. Detail of a French tapestry from the series of noblemen in the country.

Louvre, Paris, France.

All that has changed, and it is now as though
Our marriage and our love had never been,
And far or near forever I must suffer
The feud of my beloved husband dear.
So in this forest grove they made me dwell,
Under the oak-tree, in this earthy barrow.
Old is this earth-cave, all I do is yearn.
The dales are dark with high hills up above,
Sharp hedge surrounds it, overgrown with briars,
And joyless is the place. Full often here
The absence of my lord comes sharply to me.
Dear lovers in this world lie in their beds,
While I alone at crack of dawn must walk
Under the oak-tree round this earthy cave,
Where I must stay the length of summer days,
Where I may weep my banishment and all
My many hardships, for I never can
Contrive to set at rest my careworn heart,
Nor all the longing that this life has brought me.
A young man always must be serious,
And tough his character; likewise he should
Seem cheerful, even though his heart is sad
With multitude of cares. All earthly joy
Must come from his own self. Since my dear lord
Is outcast, far off in a distant land,
Frozen by storms beneath a stormy cliff
And dwelling in some desolate abode
Beside the sea, my weary-hearted lord
Must suffer pitiless anxiety.
And all too often he will call to mind
A happier dwelling. Grief must always be
For him who yearning longs for his beloved.

Woman picking flowers. From the sign of Taurus. Fresco. Anonymous. (15th century).
Palazzo della Ragione, Padua, Italy.

Response and Analysis

Thinking Critically

1. Re-read lines 1–29. What events have led to the speaker's banishment to the forest grove?
2. Describe the place where the speaker is forced to live. What words and **images** emphasize its desolation?
3. Beginning at line 43, the speaker makes an attempt to console herself with certain thoughts regarding her husband. What are these thoughts? Is the speaker successful? Explain your responses.
4. What insights does the poem give you into Anglo-Saxon bonds of kinship, the importance of loyalty, and the role of women? Cite details from the poem that support your insights.
5. What questions do you think remain unanswered in "The Wife's Lament"?
6. Using details from the selection, respond to **Connecting to the Focus Question** on page 92.

REVIEW

Reflecting *on the* Literary Period

The Anglo-Saxons: 449–1066

The following questions ask you to compare and analyze the selections in this feature and respond to the Focus Question. Where possible, cite passages from the selections to support your answers.

Bede . . . . *from* **A History of the English Church and People**

Anonymous . . . . **The Seafarer**

Anonymous . . . . **The Wife's Lament**

Comparing Literature

1. Certain **motifs,** or recurring ideas, such as the journey, exile, and fate, appear frequently in many Anglo-Saxon works. What recurrent motifs have you found in the three works presented in this feature? Cite evidence in the text to support your answers.
2. Compare the **elegies** "The Seafarer" and "The Wife's Lament." Discuss the personal experience each poem presents and the speaker's attitude toward the experience. What similarities and differences do you find?
3. The most important bond in Anglo-Saxon society was that between a lord and his retainers. How do "The Seafarer" and "The Wife's Lament" reveal the Anglo-Saxon ideal of loyalty and the tragedy of separation or exile from one's lord?
4. What literary elements do the lines of Caedmon's Hymn have in common with the poetry of *Beowulf?* In your comparison, consider the use of **alliteration**—the repetition of consonant sounds in words that are close to one another—and the words or phrases the poet chooses to praise God. Cite passages from both works to support your response.

RESPONDING TO THE

Focus Question

Review your notes and responses related to the Focus Question for this feature. Using details from the selections, write your answer to the question.

What themes and techniques do poems of the Anglo-Saxon period have in common with heroic narratives like *Beowulf?*

Pages 83–94 cover **Literary Skills** Evaluate the philosophical, political, religious, ethical, and social influences of a historical period.

READ ON: FOR INDEPENDENT READING

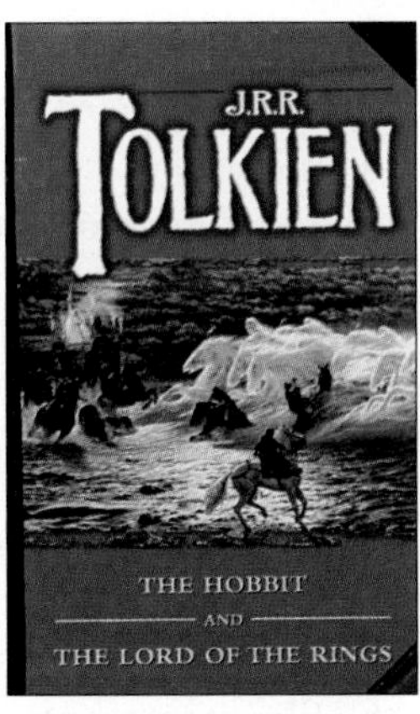

FICTION

"One Ring to Rule Them All . . ."

J.R.R. Tolkien's ***The Lord of the Rings*** is a three-volume fantasy epic that recounts the Great War of the Ring and the ending of the Third Age of Middle-Earth. The hobbit Frodo must embark on a dangerous mission: to destroy the One Ring by casting it into Mount Doom. To do so, Frodo and a brave group of companions must travel across Middle-Earth into the realm of the Dark Lord. ***The Hobbit*** (precursor to ***The Lord of the Rings***) follows Bilbo Baggins, Frodo's uncle, on a hazardous quest to recover stolen treasure from a dragon.

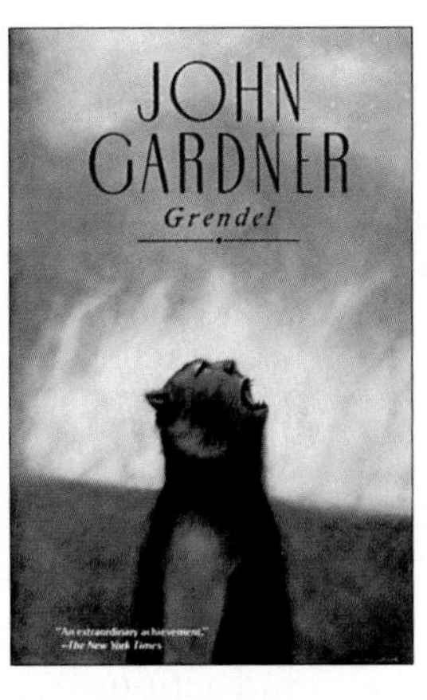

FICTION

Grendel, the Anti-Hero

John Gardner's contemporary novel ***Grendel*** is a retelling of *Beowulf* from the point of view of one of the most frightening monsters in literature. From this viewpoint we come to know Grendel as more than monstrous: He is searching for meaning and questioning the heroic values that depend so heavily on his own death. As in the original Anglo-Saxon epic, Beowulf defeats Grendel in a bloody battle. According to Grendel, however, the defeat is accidental.

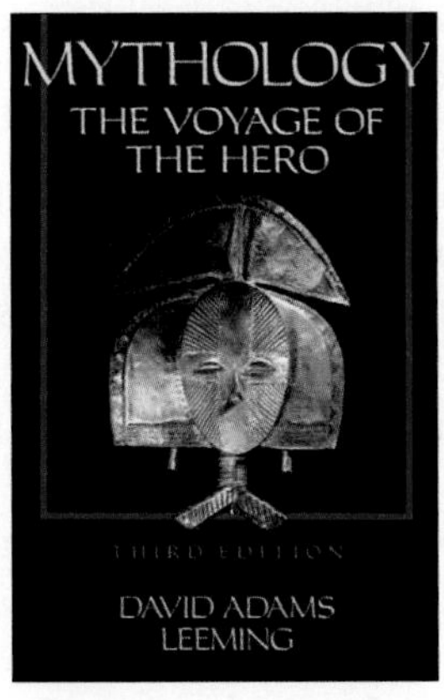

FOLKLORE / MYTHOLOGY

The Universal Hero

David Adams Leeming's ***Mythology: The Voyage of the Hero*** brings together a wide array of narratives that demonstrate the universal themes found in the myths of various cultures. This anthology, which includes English, Navajo, Indonesian, Indian, Chinese, and African tales, shows how myths help societies in their search for meaning. Leeming uses these texts to illustrate the different stages and rites of passage that the mythic hero must go through.

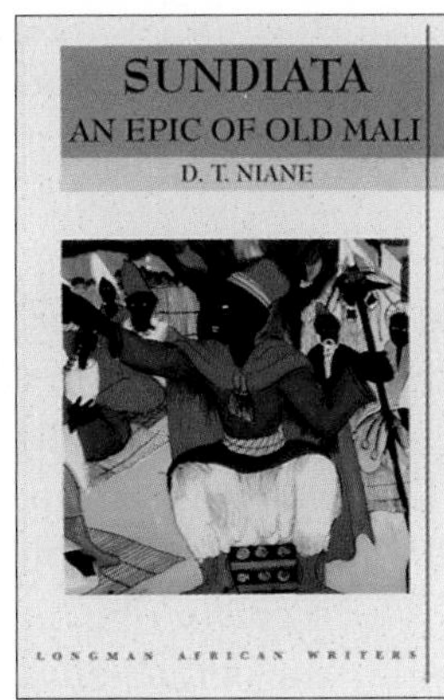

EPIC

Great Deeds of Ages Past

An exciting blend of narrative, poetry, and drama, ***Sundiata: An Epic of Old Mali*** is the best-known African epic. It is the story of the legendary Sundiata, son of the king of Mali some eight hundred years ago. Passed down by griots, Africa's oral historians, the epic reflects the rich complexity of the ancient civilization of Mali.

Writing a Descriptive Essay

Writing Assignment
Write an essay in which you describe a character from a narrative poem.

"Her [Grendel's mother's] body fell / To the floor, lifeless, the sword was wet / With her blood, and Beowulf rejoiced at the sight."
(Beowulf, *lines 643–645*)

In some narrative poetry, such as *Beowulf,* descriptions of the characters are sometimes graphic, but often sparse. Imagine that you are a screenwriter and your job is to describe a character from a narrative poem—such as Hector from the *Iliad,* or Enkidu from *Gilgamesh*—for a scene in a film. You would begin by visualizing your character in context. Then, you would add layers of your own description—for example, the character's speech, thoughts, feelings, and actions—all to help flesh out the scene for the film treatment. For this workshop you will follow a similar procedure in writing a **descriptive essay** of a character from a narrative poem.

Prewriting

Choose a Character

Heroes, Monsters, or None of These As a start for your descriptive essay, find a narrative poem by looking in your textbook for ideas, by consulting with your teacher or school librarian, or by typing in keywords, such as *narrative poem,* on an Internet search. Choose a poem that interests you, and read it. Next, choose a character from the poem that creates a distinctive impression on you. Major characters—like Beowulf or Grendel in *Beowulf,* Hector in the *Iliad,* or Gilgamesh and Enkidu in *Gilgamesh*—may appear throughout the narrative. Minor characters—such as Hector's wife—may appear only briefly at an important point in the narrative.

Whether you choose a major or minor character, focus on just one scene or one bit of action that is important to that character, such as the battle between Beowulf and Grendel in *Beowulf* or the race between Hector and Achilles in the *Iliad.* By adding a variety of details to the information in the poem, you will create a fuller description of the character in that scene.

As you add details, however, remember to keep your description of the character in the context—the literary world of the poem. For example, in *Beowulf,* monsters come up from "secret places" (545) to eat men alive. In the world of ancient Troy in Homer's *Iliad,* Hector is "shackled fast by his deadly fate." A description of Beowulf or Hector should respect the reality of those worlds for the characters, even though they may be worlds very different from yours.

Writing Skills
Write a descriptive essay.

Consider Audience and Purpose

Mass Appeal Your **audience,** or readers, will be your teacher and classmates. Even so, you may need to include background information to show them why the scene you have chosen is important for the character. Your **purpose** is to expand the exact words and phrases from a narrative poem into a descriptive essay. To do so, take phrases that describe the character, such as "noble Hector" (243), and elaborate on them. Notice the way one student brainstormed about audience and purpose for an essay describing the noble Hector at his worst moment.

TIP Document exact words and phrases by including, within parentheses, line numbers from the narrative poem. All citations to the *Iliad* in this Writing Workshop reference line numbers in Robert Fagels's full-length translation of the epic poem.

What do my readers already know about Hector?	They probably know that Hector is one of Homer's great characters—a Trojan hero who has killed many Greeks—and that he is called "noble."
What do I want them to learn about Hector from my description?	Hector has fears that cause him to act like a coward. His actions in a race for his life, however, prove that he is still "noble."

The **form** of your prose description will be different from the poetic narrative. Nonetheless, you should still incorporate natural, fresh, and vivid language; and you should use complete sentences and paragraphs.

Gather, Evaluate, and Organize Support

Hit Your Marks As you plan your descriptive essay, start with what you already know. Re-read the passage you have chosen, and jot down exact words and phrases from the poem that describe how the character looks, speaks, thinks, acts, and feels. Put the words and phrases within quotation marks and write down the line or page numbers for the words and phrases you use. These specific details from the narrative poem will be the basis of your essay—its skeleton.

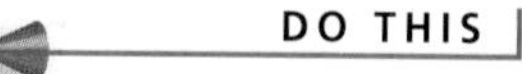
DO THIS

The Full Screen Treatment Add muscle and sinew to your essay by adding to the words and phrases you have taken from the poem. You will use **narrative** and **descriptive details** to expand on

- the character's thoughts, actions, and appearance in the scene
- the sequence of events depicted in the scene—its plot

Narrative details include the character's **actions** and **reactions** (in other words, movements and gestures), **speech,** and **thoughts and feelings**—emotions and responses.

Descriptive details include information about **physical appearance**—a character's facial features, clothing, and so on. Add texture by using **sensory details**—the sights, smells, and sounds of a scene. Shade your writing further with **figurative language**—metaphors, similes—or strong images. Elaborating upon narrative details with descriptive details makes for a rich and full description.

Writing Skills
Determine audience and purpose. Gather and organize supporting details.

Look at the way one student took the exact words of a sentence about Hector from the narrative poem and created a dynamic description. In the scene, Hector doesn't really want to do battle with Achilles, but knows he must. The student added narrative details first, then elaborated with descriptive details to show how and why Hector "wavers" as he waits for Achilles to appear.

Exact words: "So he wavered, waiting there" (lines 156–157).

Narrative details:	**Descriptive details:**
1. Hector waits and dreams about his wife, Andromache. **(feelings)**	1. Hector's craggy face softens, and a dreamy look comes over it. **(physical appearance)** He can almost see Andromache at her loom shuttling the golden threads through the red cloth. **(sensory details)**
2. He thinks about Achilles and becomes angry. **(thoughts, feelings)**	2. Then, he remembers his enemy Achilles, and his eyes harden and his fist curls around his spear. **(figurative language)**
3. Hector adjusts the armor he took from his enemy Patroclus. A dog looks for food around his ankles. **(actions)**	3. As a stray dog snuffs for food around his sandals, Hector pulls at the armor he took from his enemy, Patroclus, loosening it from around his huge neck and biceps. **(physical appearance)**

Director's Cut Think for a moment about how you want to present your prose description to your readers. Choose an order that is logical and makes sense to you. **Chronological order** organizes an essay by time order. **Order of importance** arranges ideas from least important to most important. **Spatial order** presents descriptive information according to directions—left, right, up, down, behind, before, and so on.

Write Your Thesis Statement

In Close Up Before you begin drafting your essay, read back over your notes. What is your distinctive perspective on your subject—your **thesis?** The thesis statement is a summation of what you think about your character and serves to guide the rest of your descriptive essay, as the following example shows.

> As Hector readies himself for the approach of Achilles, his appearance, actions, and thoughts and feelings show how even the most noble of all Trojan warriors fears death.

PRACTICE & APPLY 1 Use the preceding instruction to select a narrative poem and a character to describe, establish your purpose and tone, and gather and organize narrative and descriptive details.

Writing

Writing a Descriptive Essay

A Writer's Framework

Introduction

- Begin with an attention-grabbing opener.
- Give the title of the poem, and include necessary background information.
- Include a clear thesis statement.

Body

- Use narrative details—actions and reactions, speech, and thoughts and feelings.
- Add descriptive details—sensory details, figurative language, and information about physical appearance.

Conclusion

- Review the importance of the chosen scene and character.
- Restate your thesis in an interesting way.
- Close with a dramatic statement.

A Writer's Model

Run, Hector, Run

"Whatever you do," Hector mutters to himself as he spits in the dust, "don't act like a Greek—those cowards." High above him, on the walls of the city, the citizens and soldiers of the city crowd around, talking and calling down to him. His parents—Priam and Hecuba, king and queen of Troy—scream in fear, begging him to come inside the safety of the Trojan gates. Hector, a hero of Homer's the *Iliad,* refuses to obey them, so angry is he over this seemingly endless ten-year-old war between the Trojans and the Greeks.

INTRODUCTION
Attention grabber

Reactions

Background information

"Don't they realize what this moment means?" he asks himself. "What should I do?" he thinks, "Go inside the walls, or offer a treasure to Achilles if he and the Greeks will just go away, or stand and fight?" As Hector readies himself for the approach of Achilles, his appearance, actions, and thoughts and feelings show how even the most noble of all Trojan warriors fears death.

Thoughts

Thesis statement

"Be quiet!" Hector yells up to their pleas. Usually, his resolve is fixed on war. However, something today in the heat and dust has made him nervous. He looks off to his left, over to the tower where inside his beautiful wife is weaving and his young son is sleeping. Hector's craggy face softens, and a dreamy look comes over it. He can almost see Andromache at her loom shuttling the golden threads through the red cloth. Then, he remembers his enemy Achilles, and his eyes harden and his fist curls around his spear. As a stray dog snuffs for food around his sandals, Hector pulls at the armor he took

BODY/Speech
Thoughts and feelings

Sensory details
Figurative language
Physical appearance

(continued)

(continued)

	from his enemy, Patroclus, loosening it from around his huge neck
Actions	and biceps. "That Greek dog," he thinks. He paces up and down, testing his spear, checking his sword, his sandals scuffing in the dust.
Exact words from the poem	He is, after all, Hector, "breaker of horses" (194), "tall Hector" (295), "glorious Hector" (323), "noble Hector" (466), Hector of the "splendid body" (378, 438). He is a Trojan warrior. He is THE Trojan warrior. As he turns to squint into the sun again toward the Greek
Reactions	ships, he sees Achilles, and Hector's mouth goes dry.
Actions	Achilles strides along the sand away from the sea, with the sun reflecting off his brilliant bronze armor breastplate. Hector stands
Figurative language	frozen, staring at Achilles, his memory of earlier battle victories as dull
Physical appearance	as the blue mist rolling in from the sea. Hector stands, all six feet four inches of him, and feels his knees tremble. His eyes widen in terror; he
Sensory details	looks to the right, to the left; the dog near his feet begins to bark. The sounds from the wall—spears clanking, people calling—grow louder
Reactions	and louder. As Achilles seems to glow brighter and more brilliant in the heat, Hector feels his feet, almost in slow motion, begin to churn in the hot, dry dust. He backs up three or four steps toward the city's gate and
Thoughts	hears a voice somewhere within him urging, "Run, you fool, RUN!"
Actions	Hector does run, three times around the city walls, his escape into
Figurative language	the city always blocked by Achilles, who harries him like a hound after a rabbit. Hector hears all the noises swelling in his head until one voice sings out louder than the rest—the voice of his old friend Deiphobus calling encouragement. At that, Hector swings around to face Achilles, the one last soldier in the long line of Greeks that Hector
Speech	has faced and defeated. "No more running from you, Achilles!"
Exact words from the poem	Hector says. "You'll never plant your lance in my back as I flee you in fear!" (334–335)
CONCLUSION	Hector's dramatic turnaround erases any charge of cowardice against him, especially when his actions are compared to those of
Importance of scene for the character	Achilles. Hector—not Achilles—begins the last fight, by swooping down "like a soaring eagle" swinging his whetted, tempered, massive
Reference to thesis	sword. (365, 363, 364). In his last actions and words, Hector's fear and
Final statement	flight of moments before have been cancelled. He is again the awesome, heroic "noble Hector."

INTERNET

More Writer's Models

Keyword: LE7 12-1

PRACTICE & APPLY 2 Using the framework and Writer's Model on these pages as your guide, write the first draft of your descriptive essay.

Evaluate and Revise Your Descriptive Essay

Retakes Sometimes screenwriters must revise their film treatments several times to make sure that they have fully described the character in a scene. You also should look over your descriptive essay and double-check that you have described the character and scene effectively. Use the guidelines below as a think sheet to help you evaluate and revise the content and organization of your descriptive essay. Then, use the guidelines on the next page to revise for style.

PEER REVIEW

Before you revise, exchange your essay with a peer. Have the student read your paper and make suggestions about using sensory details and figurative language.

First Reading: Content and Organization Use the chart below to improve the content and organization of your descriptive essay. As you consider the evaluation questions, take into account your essay's intended audience and your purpose for writing the essay. Use the Tips column to help you mark your essay, and then make the revisions suggested in the Revision Techniques column.

Rubric: Writing a Descriptive Essay

Evaluation Questions	Tips	Revision Techniques
1 Does the introduction name the character, mention the title of the poem, and state the thesis?	**Circle** the character's name and the title of the poem. **Highlight** the thesis statement.	**Add** a sentence that names the character. **Add** the title of the poem. **Add** a sentence that conveys the thesis.
2 Does the essay include exact words and phrases from the poem?	**Bracket** any exact words and phrases from the poem.	**Add** exact words or phrases. Cite line numbers in parentheses.
3 Does the essay include narrative and descriptive details?	**Underline** the narrative details. **Double underline** the descriptive details.	**Elaborate** with the character's actions, speech, and thoughts and feelings. **Add** sensory details and figurative language.
4 Is there an obvious, easy-to-follow organizational pattern?	**Label** important ideas, using numbers for sequence or importance or *top, left,* etc. for location.	**Rearrange** ideas in a consistent pattern. **Add** transitions if necessary.
5 Does the conclusion explain why the chosen scene is important for the character? Does the conclusion restate the thesis and close with a dramatic final statement?	**Put a check** by the sentence that reviews the scene's importance for the character. **Draw a star** by the sentence that restates the thesis. **Draw a box** around the final statement.	**Reword** the conclusion to include a sentence that reviews the importance of the scene for the character. **Add** a sentence that restates the thesis. **Add** a final interesting statement.

Second Reading: Style After reviewing your essay's content and organization, you can focus on your writing style. You may have used some adjectives that are vague or less precise than they could be. For example, describing someone or something as "nice," "bad," or "awesome" doesn't convey as much information as saying, for example, that the "nice" person is "well-mannered and kind." The following chart explains how to replace vague adjectives with more precise words and phrases.

Style Guidelines

Evaluation Question	Tip	Revision Technique
Does the essay include general or vague adjectives, such as "nice," "bad," or "awesome"?	**Draw a line** through adjectives that don't convey much information.	**Replace** vague adjectives with specific adjectives or with words and phrases that convey a more vivid picture.

ANALYZING THE REVISION PROCESS

Study these revisions, and answer the questions that follow.

add — The sounds from the wall [—spears clanking, people calling—] grow louder and louder.

As Achilles seems to glow brighter and more brilliant in the heat, Hector feels his feet, almost in slow motion, begin to

replace — churn in the ~~bad~~ [hot, dry] dust. He backs up three or four steps toward

elaborate — the city's gate and ~~runs~~ [hears a voice somewhere within him urging, "Run, you fool, RUN!"].

Responding to the Revision Process

1. Why do you think the writer expanded the word *sounds* with sensory details in sentence one? What is the effect of such additions?
2. What is the effect of replacing *bad* with *hot, dry* in sentence two?
3. Why do you think the writer added information to sentence three? What is the effect of the addition?

Writing Skills
Revise for content and style.

PRACTICE & APPLY 3 Using the guidelines on these two pages, revise the content, organization, and style of your descriptive essay. Remember to eliminate vague adjectives.

Publishing

Proofread and Publish Your Essay

Last Cut A careful proofreading will ensure that your final paper follows the **conventions** of good writing and is free of errors in grammar, usage, and mechanics. Check through your final paper and correct errors if you find them.

Distribution Rights Now that you have written your descriptive essay, you may want to share it with others. Here are some methods for publishing your essay.

- Adapt your essay into a film or video presentation. Dress your actors to match the descriptions of the characters in your essay, and add a soundtrack that helps bring out the actions and thoughts of your main character.
- Gather several classmates to read and comment on each other's essays.
- E-mail your essay to a Web site for student film productions, or for student screenplays. Ask for your essay to be posted on the Web site, and request feedback from readers.
- Add several illustrations of the narrative poem's scene and character to the text of your descriptive essay. Use illustrations you have drawn, collected from other sources, or generated by computer. Submit your essay to your school's literary magazine.

Reflect on Your Essay

Box Office Receipts Look back over your work on the descriptive essay. To evaluate what you have done, ask yourself the following questions.

- How did your work on this descriptive essay help you understand how screenwriters might create a character for a film based on a narrative poem?
- What was your biggest challenge in adapting the character from the narrative poem to the descriptive essay? Explain why.
- If you were to write a descriptive essay from the perspective of another character in the narrative poem, what changes would you make and why?

PRACTICE & APPLY 4 Use the information on this page to proofread, publish, and reflect on your essay describing a character from a narrative poem.

TIP To make sure that your essay follows the **conventions** of American English, look carefully at the proper names of any characters or places in your description and make sure that you have capitalized them correctly. For more on **capitalization,** see Capitalization, 11a–f, in the Language Handbook.

Writing Skills
Proofread, especially for correct capitalization.

Collection 1: Skills Review

Comparing Literature

Test Practice

The following two poems were written more than nine hundred years apart in two vastly different periods of English history. "The Wanderer," an anonymous Anglo-Saxon poem, was probably written before the tenth century. "Break, Break, Break" is a highly polished poem by the great poet laureate of Victorian England, Alfred, Lord Tennyson (1809–1892) (see page 894). Both poets chose the sea as a central image to express a recurring human yearning that knows no boundaries of time, place, or social circumstance.

DIRECTIONS: Read the following two poems. Then, read each multiple-choice question that follows, and write the letter of the best response.

from The Wanderer

translated by Burton Raffel

This lonely traveller longs for grace,
For the mercy of God; grief hangs on
His heart and follows the frost-cold foam
He cuts in the sea, sailing endlessly,
Aimlessly, in exile. Fate has opened
A single port: memory. He sees
His kinsmen slaughtered again, and cries:
"I've drunk too many lonely dawns,
Grey with mourning. Once there were men
To whom my heart could hurry, hot
With open longing. They're long since dead.
My heart has closed on itself, quietly
Learning that silence is noble and sorrow
Nothing that speech can cure. Sadness
Has never driven sadness off;
Fate blows hardest on a bleeding heart.
So those who thirst for glory smother
Secret weakness and longing, neither
Weep nor sigh nor listen to the sickness
In their souls. So I, lost and homeless,
Forced to flee the darkness that fell
On the earth and my lord.
Leaving everything,
Weary with winter I wandered out
On the frozen waves, hoping to find

Pages 104–107 cover **Literary Skills** Compare and contrast works from different literary periods.

A place, a people, a lord to replace
My lost ones. No one knew me, now,
No one offered comfort, allowed
Me feasting or joy. How cruel a journey
I've travelled, sharing my bread with sorrow
Alone, an exile in every land,
Could only be told by telling° my footsteps.
For who can hear: "friendless and poor,"
And know what I've known since the long cheerful nights
When, young and yearning, with my lord I yet feasted
Most welcome of all. That warmth is dead.
He only knows who needs his lord
As I do, eager for long-missing aid;
He only knows who never sleeps
Without the deepest dreams of longing.
Sometimes it seems I see my lord,
Kiss and embrace him, bend my hands
And head to his knee, kneeling as though
He still sat enthroned, ruling his thanes.°
And I open my eyes, embracing the air,
And see the brown sea-billows heave,
See the sea-birds bathe, spreading
Their white-feathered wings, watch the frost
And the hail and the snow. And heavy in heart
I long for my lord, alone and unloved.
Sometimes it seems I see my kin
And greet them gladly, give them welcome,
The best of friends. They fade away,
Swimming soundlessly out of sight,
Leaving nothing.
How loathsome become
The frozen waves to a weary heart. . . .

31. telling: here, "counting."

43. thanes: people who, in exchange for their military service, held land of a king or lord.

Collection 1: Skills Review

Break, Break, Break

Alfred, Lord Tennyson

Break, break, break,
   On thy cold gray stones, O Sea!
And I would that my tongue could utter
   The thoughts that arise in me.

O, well for the fisherman's boy,
   That he shouts with his sister at play!
O, well for the sailor lad,
   That he sings in his boat on the bay!

And the stately ships go on
   To their haven under the hill;
But O for the touch of a vanished hand,
   And the sound of a voice that is still!

Break, break, break,
   At the foot of thy crags, O Sea!
But the tender grace of a day that is dead
   Will never come back to me.

---

1. In "The Wanderer" the dominant impression of the speaker's life at sea is one of —
   - **A** ceaseless conflict
   - **B** heart-rending loneliness
   - **C** exciting adventure
   - **D** mind-numbing routine

2. In "The Wanderer," the phrase "frost-cold foam" (line 3) is an example of an Anglo-Saxon figure of speech called —
   - **F** pentameter
   - **G** personification
   - **H** kenning
   - **J** elegy

3. Line 23 of "The Wanderer" contains an example of which literary element?
   - **A** alliteration
   - **B** kenning
   - **C** foil
   - **D** allusion

4. In the third stanza of "Break, Break, Break," the speaker grieves over —
   - **F** a sunken ship
   - **G** the loss of a loved one
   - **H** his inability to move on
   - **J** the fisherman's boy

5. What aspect of the sea is emphasized by the repetition of the word *break* in Tennyson's poem?
   - **A** its ability to transform
   - **B** its tender fragility
   - **C** its relentless violence
   - **D** its stark beauty

6. The hardships experienced by the speaker of "Break, Break, Break" differ from those felt by the wanderer in that they —
   - **F** include physical journeys
   - **G** prevent him from sailing again
   - **H** are easily forgotten
   - **J** are emotional rather than physical

7. What attitude toward the sea do the speakers of both poems have in common?
   - **A** Both love the sea and cannot leave it.
   - **B** Both connect the sea with loneliness and loss.
   - **C** Both condemn the sea's destructiveness.
   - **D** Both see the sea as the source of life.

8. How does the Anglo-Saxon speaker of "The Wanderer" differ from the Victorian speaker of "Break, Break, Break"?
   - **F** The Anglo-Saxon speaker refuses to mention his hardships.
   - **G** He is bitter about all that he has suffered.
   - **H** He has never longed for love or companionship.
   - **J** He searches for new companions rather than observing others from afar.

Essay Question

Both "The Wanderer" and "Break, Break, Break" are elegies, or sorrowful poems that lament loss and the inevitable passage of time. In an essay, compare and contrast the source of each speaker's sorrow. Discuss how the language and imagery in each poem convey the sorrowful mood of an elegy. Use details from each poem to support your response.

Collection 1: Skills Review

Vocabulary Skills

Test Practice

Context Clues

DIRECTIONS: Choose the answer that gives the best definition of the underlined word.

1. As Beowulf lifted his shield, the angry beast flailed and thrashed and vehemently attacked the king.
Vehemently means —

A calmly
B timidly
C violently
D feebly

2. After Beowulf's death the Geats extolled the heroic deeds of their fallen king, proclaiming that no other man was so deserving of praise.
Extolled means —

F criticized
G condemned
H exploited
J praised

3. Beowulf never expresses uncertainty about his ability to kill Grendel; he is both proud and resolute.
Resolute means —

A uncertain
B determined
C fearful
D angry

4. Wiglaf encourages his fellow soldiers to join the battle against the dragon by reminding them of the lavish gifts, such as rings and swords and helmets, that Beowulf has given them.
Lavish means —

F extravagant
G useful
H insignificant
J pointless

5. Because Humbaba has huge, flailing limbs and is permanently stooped, he is described as "monstrous in his contortion."
Contortion means —

A monstrosity
B twisted shape
C anger
D beauty

6. King Priam declares that although he is still sane, he is under strain and is harrowed from having suffered so much.
Harrowed means —

F youthful
G mentally distressed
H incapacitated
J helpless

7. Athena tells Achilles that Hector can no longer escape them, not even if the Archer begs for Hector's life, groveling in front of Zeus.
Groveling means —

A humbling oneself in front of authority
B demanding something of an inferior
C escaping for one's life
D refusing to give up

Vocabulary Skills
Use context clues to determine the meanings of words.

Collection 1: Skills Review

Writing Skills

Test Practice

DIRECTIONS: Read the following paragraph from a draft of a student's descriptive essay. Then, answer the questions below it.

(1) In Hrothgar's dark and silent mead hall, Beowulf pulls his cloak around his cold vest of hammered chain mail and looks curiously at his hands, which are growing warmer in the cold, reflecting the heat and fire from the hearth. (2) The mead halls here in Herot are much colder than those in Beowulf's faraway home. (3) He flexes his fingers, then clasps and unclasps his hands on his sword in front of him, remembering that even in battle with sea monsters in the frigid ocean surf, his hands had been warm. (4) Then, in the dark, he hears something. (5) Suddenly, leaning up on one arm, Beowulf stretches out his right hand and seizes Grendel's claws, bending them back in his fierce grip.

1. Which sentence could be added to show thoughts and feelings after sentence 1?

- **A** Beowulf used to feel embarrassed about his hands.
- **B** "Take care of your hands," his mother had always advised him.
- **C** The Geats all thought, "Beowulf is too protective of his hands."
- **D** Nobody in Herot remembered the stories about Beowulf's hands.

2. Which sentence could be deleted to improve the paragraph's organization?

- **F** 2
- **G** 3
- **H** 4
- **J** 5

3. How could sentence 4 be rewritten to include sensory details?

- **A** Because it is quiet in the dark, Beowulf has no trouble hearing something that sounds strange.
- **B** Then, in the very dark hall, he hears something awesome.
- **C** Then, while Beowulf listens in the dark, he hears a sound.
- **D** Then, in the dark, he hears the shadow monster snapping the bones of a fellow Geat.

4. Which reference to the poem could be added after sentence 5 to show a character's feelings?

- **F** Beowulf, "who of all the men on earth/Was the strongest," held the monster fast (lines 471–472).
- **G** Beowulf, the "mighty protector of men," held the monster fast (line 472).
- **H** In fierce pain, Grendel "fought / For his freedom" (lines 444–445).
- **J** In fierce pain, Grendel's "mind was flooded with fear" (line 435).

5. How would you describe the writer's tone in this passage?

- **A** hateful
- **B** apathetic
- **C** suspenseful
- **D** joyous

Writing Skills
Write a descriptive essay.

Scene from *Golf Book of Hours* (detail) (c. 1500).

British Library, London. The Bridgeman Art Library.

Collection 2

THE MIDDLE AGES 1066–1485

The Tales They Told

The medieval world we know was far from perfect. Life expectancy was short, and disease was mostly incontestable. It was a world burdened by royal autocracy and social hierarchy inherited from ancient times. Its piety and devotion were affected by fanaticism and a potential for persecution. Its intellectuals were given to too abstract and not enough practical thinking. But it exhibited as elevated a culture, as peaceful a community, as benign a political system, as high-minded and popular a faith as the world has ever seen.

—Norman F. Cantor

INTERNET

Collection Resources

Keyword: LE7 12-2

The Middle Ages 1066–1485

LITERARY EVENTS

1066 | **1100** | **1150** | **1200**

c. 1100 The French heroic poem *Song of Roland* is written

1131 Omar Khayyám, Persian poet and astronomer, dies

Scene from the *Song of Roland.* Stained-glass window, Chartres Cathedral, France (13th century).

c. 1150 In Spain, paper is first mass-produced

c. 1170s In France, Chrétien de Troyes writes *Lancelot*

1179 Hildegard of Bingen, German abbess, mystic, and poet, dies

c. 1200 The German epic poem the *Nibelungenlied* is begun

1213 Persian poet **Saadi** is born

c. 1216 Marie de France, first known European woman to write narrative poetry, dies

Marie de France.

Bibliothèque Nationale de France.

POLITICAL AND SOCIAL EVENTS

1066 | **1100** | **1150** | **1200**

1066 King Edward the Confessor dies without heir

1066 Duke of Normandy invades England

1086 Domesday Book, a record of all landownership in England, is first compiled

1095 Crusades to free Jerusalem from Turkish control begin

c. 1119 Knights Templar, a religious order whose mission was to protect pilgrims to the Holy Land, is founded

Domesday Book (c. 1085–1086).

1163 Construction of Cathedral of Notre Dame in Paris begins

1170 Thomas à Becket is murdered

1171 Henry II invades Ireland, beginning nearly eight hundred years of British domination

1192 Minamoto Yoritomo becomes first shogun (military ruler) of Japan

1211 Mongol leader Genghis Khan invades China

1215 English barons force King John to sign the Magna Carta

c. 1232 Pope Gregory IX begins the Inquisition

A man and his wife on horseback, from a book of hours (c. 1500).

By permission of the British Library, London.

1250 1300 1350 1400 1485

1266–1273 Thomas Aquinas writes *Summa Theologica*

From *Hours of the Duchess of Burgundy* (c.1450).
Musée Condé, Chantilly, France.

c. 1307 Dante Alighieri begins writing *The Divine Comedy*

1341 Petrarch is crowned poet laureate in Italy

c. 1342 Julian of Norwich, one of the first English women of letters, is born

c. 1343 Geoffrey Chaucer is born

1349–1353 Giovanni Boccaccio writes the *Decameron*

c. 1373 Margery Kempe, author of first autobiography in English, is born

c. 1378 Legendary hero Robin Hood appears in *Piers Plowman*

1380 Entire Bible is translated into English for first time, by followers of John Wycliffe

c. 1387 Chaucer begins *The Canterbury Tales*

1400 Chaucer dies

1455 Gutenberg prints first book with movable type

c. 1475 William Caxton prints first book in English

1485 Thomas Malory's *Le Morte d'Arthur* is first printed by Caxton

1250 1300 1350 1400 1485

c. 1250 First commoners are allowed in British Parliament

1270 Crusades end

Marco Polo in Beijing.
Bibliothèque Nationale de France, Paris.

1275 Venetian traveler Marco Polo visits court of Kublai Khan in China

1296 Edward I invades Scotland and declares himself king

1300s Zimbabwe emerges as major trading empire

1325 Aztecs begin to establish empire in Mexico

1337 Hundred Years' War, between England and France, begins

1348 Black Death strikes England

Jar, China, Ming dynasty, Xuande mark and period (1426–35). Porcelain painted in underglaze blue: H. 19 in. (48.3 cm); Diam. 19 in. (48.3 cm).
The Metropolitan Museum of Art, Gift of Robert E. Tod, 1937. (37.191.1) Photograph by Schecter Lee. Photo © 1986 The Metropolitan Museum of Art.

1368 Ming dynasty begins three-hundred-year rule of China

1381 Peasants' Revolt takes place in England

1399 King Richard II is deposed

1400s Benin Kingdom in West Africa flourishes

1431 In France, Joan of Arc is burned at the stake by the English

c. 1438 Incan Empire is established in Peru

1455–1485 War between the Houses of York and Lancaster (also called the Wars of the Roses) is fought

1473 Nicolaus Copernicus, Polish astronomer, is born

1485 First Tudor king, Henry VII, is crowned

Political and Social

Norman Conquest, 1066

William the Conqueror and his powerful Norman army defeated the English king, Harold, at the Battle of Hastings in 1066. William then installed himself as king of England and divided the land among Norman barons loyal to him alone. This feudal system of landownership that William implemented created a social structure in which every man and woman had a place in a fixed hierarchy, or class system.

William the Conqueror's invasion fleet, from the Bayeux Tapestry (detail) (11th century).

By special permission of the City of Bayeux.

Milestones 1066–1485

A master with his carpenter and stonemason.
British Library, London. The Bridgeman Art Library.

The Age of Feudalism

Feudalism was a system that assigned an economic, political, and social position to every individual at birth. All land was bestowed on lords or barons by the lord over all, the king. Lesser lords, knights, vassals, and serfs served the landowning lords in turn, each with specific obligations to those above them on the feudal ladder. Knights, for instance, were professional warriors who fought their lord's battles, usually against the knights of rival lords. Serfs or peasants, the lowest of the social orders, were bound to the land they tilled and gave most of what they grew to their lord in return for his protection from war and starvation.

The Decline of Feudalism

The tight feudal order gradually broke down as the English people were exposed to other influences and as opportunities arose for them to make money outside the web of feudal obligations. Increased trade with the East created a merchant class. The growth of cities provided people with alternative means of supporting themselves: The growing cities needed carpenters, stonemasons, and other skilled workers. This new, urban middle class was emerging at the same time that the old feudal warriors—the knights—were being replaced by an army made up of yeomen (the class of small landowners). These yeomen used longbows that could even pierce the knights' iron armor.

Two men observe the construction of a house, with formal gardens in the background (15th century).
British Library, London. The Bridgeman Art Library.

The Middle Ages 1066–1485

by David Adams Leeming

PREVIEW

Think About . . .

Anglo-Saxon England was permanently changed by the invasion of the Norman French, led by William the Conqueror in 1066. Despite his name, however, William wished to govern the Anglo-Saxon English, not to conquer them. The Anglo-Norman England that developed under William and his barons combined the older, more democratic Anglo-Saxon traditions with the new social system of the Norman invaders: feudalism.

As you read about this period, look for answers to these questions:

- What effects did the Norman invasion have on the way the English were governed?
- What were the main features of feudalism? How did feudalism change the social structure of Anglo-Saxon England?
- What developments in the fourteenth and fifteenth centuries began to undermine the feudal system?

In October 1066, a daylong battle near Hastings, England, changed the course of history. There, just ten miles from the channel dividing England from France, Duke William of Normandy, France, defeated and killed King Harold of England, the last of the Anglo-Saxon kings. So began the Norman Conquest, an event that radically affected English history, the English character, and the English language. Unlike the Romans, the Normans never withdrew from England.

Collection introduction (pages 114–129) covers **Literary Skills** Evaluate the philosophical, political, religious, ethical, and social influences of a historical period.

William the Conqueror and the Norman Influence

Who was this William the Conqueror? He was the illegitimate son of the previous duke of Normandy, who was in turn a cousin of the English king called Edward the Confessor. Edward had died childless earlier in 1066, and Harold, the earl of Wessex, had been crowned the following day. William claimed, however, that the old king had promised the throne to him. Determined to seize what he considered rightfully his, William sailed across the English Channel with an enormous army.

Norman horsemen chasing defeated English soldiers after the Battle of Hastings, from the Bayeux Tapestry (detail) (11th century).

Musée de la tapisserie, Bayeux, France/Dagli Orti/The Art Archive.

William was an efficient and ruthless soldier, but he wanted to rule the Anglo-Saxons, not eliminate them. Today, as a result, rather than a Norman, French-speaking England (and United States), we find a culture and a language that combine Norman and Anglo-Saxon elements. To the Anglo-Saxons' more democratic and artistic tendencies, the Normans brought administrative ability, an emphasis on law and order, and cultural unity.

Coin depicting William the Conqueror (11th century).

British Museum, London. The Bridgeman Art Library.

One of William's great administrative feats was an inventory of nearly every piece of property in England—land, cattle, buildings—in the Domesday Book. (The title suggests a comparison between William's judgment of his subjects' financial worth and God's final judgment of their moral worth.) For the first time in European history, taxes were based on what people owned.

The Normans Change England

Although the Normans did not erase Anglo-Saxon culture, they did bring significant changes to England. William and many of his successors remained dukes of Normandy as well as kings of England. The powerful Anglo-Norman entity they molded brought England into mainstream European civilization in a new way. For example, William divided the holdings of the fallen English landowners among his own followers. These men and their families brought to England not only a new language—French—but also a new social system—feudalism—which displaced the old Nordic social structure described in *Beowulf.*

An attack on a fortress, from a French manuscript (detail) (13th–14th century).

MS Fr. 1604, fol. 57v. © cliché Bibliothèque Nationale de France, Paris.

Lovers, Garden Scene. French Illumination, 15th century.
akg-images/British Library.

Feudal Relationships

- **king:** all-powerful overlord and landowner.
- **vassal:** aristocratic dependent tenant who received land (a fief) from a lord in exchange for military service and other expressions of loyalty. Vassals could simultaneously serve higher lords and serve as lords themselves by distributing portions of the land they had been allotted.
- **lord:** noble who had the power to grant land to vassals. Lords could also be vassals to other lords.
- **knight:** armored warrior. Vassals had to provide their lords with military service—in the form of knights—for a certain period of time. The larger the fief, the more knights a vassal had to supply.
- **serfs:** peasants who worked on and were bound to vassals' lands. Serfs were not involved in the complicated oaths of loyalty between vassals and lords.

Feudalism: From the Top Down

More than simply a social system, **feudalism** was also a caste system, a property system, and a military system. Ultimately it was based on a religious concept of rank, with God as the supreme overlord. In this sense even a king held land as a **vassal**—a dependent tenant—by "divine right." A king as powerful as William the Conqueror could stand firmly at the top of the pyramid. He could appoint certain barons as his immediate vassals, allotting them portions of his land in return for their economic or military allegiance—or both. In turn, the barons could appoint vassals of their own. The system operated all the way down to the landless knights and to the **serfs,** who were not free to leave the land they tilled. The historian Morris Bishop describes the relationship between lord and vassal in this way:

Granting of land to two knights, from *Life of the Noble Princes of Hainaut* by Jacques de Guise (15th century).

> "The bond between lord and vassal was affirmed or reaffirmed by the ceremony of homage. The vassal knelt, placed his clasped hands within those of his master, declared, 'Lord, I become your man,' and took an oath of fealty. The lord raised him to his feet and bestowed on him a ceremonial kiss. The vassal was thenceforth bound by his oath 'to love what his lord loved and loathe what he loathed, and never by word or deed do aught that should grieve him.'"

The feudal system did not always work. Secure in a well-fortified castle, a vassal might choose not to honor his obligations to a weak overlord. The ensuing battles between iron-clad knights around moated castles account for one of the enduring images of the Middle Ages.

The feudal system carried with it a sense of form and manners that influenced all aspects of the life, art, and literature of the Middle Ages. This sense of formalism came to life most fully in the

A CLOSER LOOK: SOCIAL INFLUENCES

"A Terrible Worm in an Iron Cocoon"

When we hear the term *medieval period*, we inevitably think of knights and their magnificent suits of armor. During the early Middle Ages, armor consisted of a helmet, a shield, and a relatively flexible mail shirt, or *hauberk*, made of countless riveted or welded iron rings. With the crossbow, however, came the need for more protection, so the knight was forced to compromise flexibility and mobility for the sake of heavier armor.

A burden in battle. Held together by rivets, leather straps, hinges, turning pins, buckles, and pegs, a suit of armor replaced mail as the warrior's chief protection. Knights wore a heavily padded undergarment of leather and a mail shirt under the armor, in addition to plate arm, leg, and foot pieces. Mail covered the neck, elbows, and other joints, and gauntlets constructed of linked plates covered the hands. Some suits of armor weighed 120 pounds and contained 200 custom-fitted iron plates. The knight also carried a variety of weapons: lance, dagger, sword, battle-ax, and club-headed mace.

The threat of death in battle was bad enough, but the armor itself could also be fatal—causing death from suffocation, heart failure, even drowning. Battle during hot weather was particularly difficult. Since small slits in the helmet allowed only a limited line of vision and little ventilation, heatstroke—often deadly for the knight—was common. One anonymous poem describes the armored knight as "a terrible worm in an iron cocoon."

Protection at a price. Only aristocratic knights could afford the huge cost of armor, a war horse, packhorses, a mount to ride when not in battle, and servants. The armor's weight and the complex fittings required to piece it together meant that a knight couldn't dress himself for battle. In fact, institution of knighthood and in the related practice, or code, of chivalry.

Knights in Shining Armor

We cannot think of the medieval period without thinking of knights. Since the primary duty of males above the serf class was military service to their lords, boys were trained from an early age to become warriors. Often their training took place in houses other than their own, to be sure that the training was strict. When a boy's training was

A medieval knight in armor.

MS 42130, fol. 202v. By permission of the British Library, London.

INFORMATIONAL TEXT

battles were usually scheduled to allow the warring knights time to be dressed. Servants stood by during battle in case the knight was unhorsed. An armored knight on his back was like an upside-down turtle trying to get on its feet. In this position the knight was vulnerable to his adversary. If he fell into a body of water, he could drown.

From combatant to courtier. During the fifteenth century the knight and his horse were considered invulnerable. This role changed dramatically when the longbow and, later, the musket ball came into warfare. When his armor could no longer protect him in battle, the knight in shining armor became more of a courtier than a combatant. In the last years of their existence, knights participated solely in exhibitions.

Arming a man for fighting on foot. Detail from a manuscript page from *Ordinances of Armory* (15th century). England.

M.775, F.122v. © The Pierpont Morgan Library, New York.

completed, he was dubbed, or ceremonially tapped on his shoulder (originally a hard blow to test the boy's courage). Once knighted, the youth became a man with the title "Sir" and the full rights of the warrior caste.

A woman is a worthy wight:
She serveth a man both daye and nyght;
Thereto she putteth all her might,
And yet she hathe but care and woe.
—Anonymous (fifteenth century)

Knighthood was grounded in the feudal ideal of loyalty, and it was based on a complex system of social codes. Breaking any one of those codes would undermine not only the knight's position but also the very institution of knighthood.

Women in Medieval Society: No Voice, No Choice

Since they were not soldiers, women had no political rights in a system that was primarily military. A woman was always subservient to a man, whether husband, father, or brother. Her husband's or father's social standing determined the degree of respect she commanded. For peasant women, life was a ceaseless round of childbearing, housework, and hard fieldwork. Women of higher stations were occupied with childbearing and household supervision. Such women might even manage entire estates while their men were away on business or at war, but the moment the men returned, the women had to give up their temporary powers.

Off for a day of haying, a peasant pushes his wife to work in a wheelbarrow.

Chivalry and Courtly Love: Ideal but Unreal

Chivalry was a system of ideals and social codes governing the behavior of knights and gentlewomen. The rules of chivalry included taking an oath of loyalty to the overlord and observing certain rules of warfare, such as never attacking an unarmed opponent. In addition, adoring a particular lady (not necessarily one's wife) was seen as a means of self-improvement.

The idea that adoring a lady would make a knight braver and nobler was central to one aspect of chivalry, courtly love. **Courtly love** was, in its ideal form, nonsexual. A knight might wear his lady's colors in battle, he might glorify her in words and be inspired by her, but the lady always remained pure and out of reach. She was set above her admirer, just as the feudal lord was set above his vassal. The fact that such a concept flew in the face of human nature provided a perfect dramatic vehicle for poets and storytellers, as the King Arthur sagas illustrate. When Sir Lancelot and Queen Guinevere, for example, cross the line between courtly and physical love, the whole social system represented by Arthur's Round Table collapses. Camelot crumbles because the sexual code was broken.

Noblewomen watching a tournament, from a German manuscript (c. 14th century).

Cod. Pal. Germ. 848, Codex Manesse, fol. 52v. Universitätsbibliothek, Heidelberg, Germany.

The Rise of the Romance

Chivalry brought about an idealized attitude toward women, but it did little to improve their actual position. A woman's perceived value remained tied to the value of the lands she brought to a marriage. Chivalry did give rise to a new form of literature, the **romance** (see page 215). The greatest English example of the romance is *Sir Gawain and the Green Knight.* The romance hero—who often has the help of magic—undertakes a quest to conquer an evil enemy. J. R. R. Tolkien's *The Lord of the Rings* trilogy shows that the romance is still alive and well today.

The New City Classes: Out from Under the Overlords

For the most part, medieval society centered on the feudal castle, but as the population grew, an increasing number of people lived in towns and cities. Eventually, those population centers would make the feudal system obsolete.

The development of the city classes—lower, middle, and upper middle—is evident in the works of Geoffrey Chaucer (see page 135). Many of his characters make their livings outside the feudal system. Their horizons are defined not by any lord's manor but by such cities as London and Canterbury.

More important, the emerging merchant class had its own tastes in the arts and the ability to pay for what it wanted. As a result, much medieval art is not aristocratic; it is middle class, even "people's art." The people of the cities were free, tied neither to the land nor to knighthood and chivalry. Their point of view was expressed in the **ballads** sung in alehouses and at firesides (see page 130), in the mystery and miracle plays performed outdoors by the new guilds, or craft unions, and even in the great cathedrals and municipal buildings that are synonymous with England to so many people today.

February: Man warming himself, from Ermangol de Beziers, *Breviaire d'amour* (13th century) France.

Provencal codex, fol. 58v. © Giraudon/Art Resource, New York.

The Great Happenings

Against the backdrop of the feudal system imported from the Continent, several events radically influenced the course of English history, as well as English literature.

■ The Crusades: Bloodbath over the Holy Land

In Chaucer's *The Canterbury Tales* we meet a knight who has fought in "heathen" places—along the Mediterranean Sea and in North Africa. The knight's adventures in the fourteenth century were really an extension of the **Crusades** (1095–1270), a series of holy wars waged by European Christians against Muslims. In 1095, the head of the Catholic Church in Rome, Pope Urban II, sent out a plea to Christians of Europe. He upheld that it was their duty to wage war against Muslims occupying Jerusalem and other places in the Middle East that were considered holy to Christians. The pope's call for help set off a

The Crusaders' 1153 attack on Ascalon, a Muslim-held city on the coast of the Holy Land. Scene from *Passages d'Outremer* (detail) (15th century).

MS Fr. 5594, fol. 157v. © cliché Bibliothèque Nationale de France, Paris.

series of disastrous military expeditions that came to be known as the Crusades. For two hundred years, Crusaders set out from Europe to conquer Jerusalem. In their so-called holy wars they slaughtered thousands of Jews and Muslims. Even children were swept up in the cause, when the Children's Crusade was organized in 1212. The Europeans failed to hold Jerusalem, and the carnage they caused was enormous, but Europe benefited greatly from its contact with the sophisticated Middle Eastern civilization. Exposure to Eastern mathematics, astronomy, architecture, and crafts made possible the rich, varied life we find in Chaucer.

■ The Martyrdom of Thomas à Becket: Murder in the Cathedral

When Chaucer's pilgrims set out for Canterbury, their goal was the shrine of Saint Thomas à Becket (c. 1118–1170). Thomas, a Norman, had risen to great power as chancellor (prime minister) under his friend King Henry II (reigned 1154–1189). At that time all Christians belonged to the Catholic Church. Even King Henry was a vassal—of the pope, the head of the Church and God's representative. The pope in those days was enormously powerful and controlled most of the crowned heads of Europe. By appointing his trusted friend Thomas archbishop of Canterbury (head of the Catholic Church in England), Henry hoped to gain the upper hand in disputes with the Church. But the independent Thomas took the pope's side more than once, infuriating the king. In December 1170, Henry raged, "Will no one rid me of this turbulent priest?" Taking his words literally, four of Henry's knights murdered Becket—in his own cathedral. Thomas Grim, an eyewitness, described the gory scene:

Murder of Becket, (detail) from an English psalter (c. 1250).

MS W34, fol. 15v. The Walters Art Museum, Baltimore.

> "Then the third knight inflicted a terrible wound as he lay, by which the sword was broken against the pavement, and the crown which was large was separated from the head; so that the blood white with the brain and the brain red with blood, dyed the surface of the virgin mother Church with the life and death of the confessor and martyr in the colors of the lily and the rose."

Public outrage at Becket's murder led to devotion to Saint Thomas the Martyr and created a backlash against Henry, a significant setback for the monarchy in its power struggles with Rome.

At its worst this setback led to the kinds of liberties taken by several of the clergymen in *The Canterbury Tales*—corruption that the state was in no position to correct. Thus, Chaucer's Monk lives a life of luxury without regard to the poor, his Friar chases women and money, and his Summoner and his Pardoner blackmail people with threats of eternal damnation.

Yet the medieval Church did have one positive effect: It fostered cultural unity—a system of beliefs and symbols that transcended the national cultures of Europe. The Church continued to be the center of learning. Its monasteries were the libraries and publishers of the time, and its language, Latin, remained the international language of educated Europeans. Its leader, the pope, was king of all kings—and his kingdom had no boundaries.

The Magna Carta.

■ The Magna Carta: Power to (Some of) the People

The event that most clearly heralded a return to older, democratic tendencies in England was the signing of the **Magna Carta** ("Great Charter") by King John in 1215, at Runnymede. The vicious but

A CLOSER LOOK: SOCIAL INFLUENCES

Money, Gunpowder, and the Middle Class: The End of an Era

INFORMATIONAL TEXT

The legendary pageantry, the codes of chivalry, the heroic quests undertaken by valiant knights in honor of fair ladies—these images come to mind at the mention of the Middle Ages. But what happened? Why did this period come to an end? In addition to the Black Death's devastating effects, the development of a monetary system and the introduction of gunpowder contributed to changes in medieval England.

Coin of the realm. Before the eleventh century few coins existed in England and western Europe. The English upper classes used gold and silver valued by weight, and foreign coins were usually melted down and formed into ingots. Feudal lords made their own coins for use only on their property, and serfs used a barter system for purchases within the community. The Crusades brought about an economic change, for Crusaders needed money that would be accepted in other lands. Silver was heavy, but gold coins were light and already in use throughout the trade routes. The widespread use of gold coins improved the peasants' buying and selling power; instead of bartering, they were now able to earn gold in exchange for their labor or goods. The new currency also enabled peasants to save money, which hadn't been possible in the barter economy. The minting of coins was essential in the revival of England's economy.

An explosive invention. Chivalric codes governed hand-to-hand combat during much of the Middle Ages. The emergence of guns and gunpowder (and strategic military planning) changed all that. Discovered by the Chinese, gunpowder was introduced into pragmatic John was strongly backed by the pope, but the English barons forced him to sign the document. The signing was a defeat for central papal power. As aristocrats writing for aristocrats, the barons had no interest in the rights of the common people. Still, the Magna Carta later became the basis of English constitutional law, in which such rights as trial by jury and legislative taxation were established.

No freeman shall be taken, or imprisoned, or outlawed, or exiled, or in any way harmed, nor will we go upon him nor will we send upon him, except by the legal judgment of his peers or by the law of the land.

To none will we sell, to none deny or delay, right or justice.

—Magna Carta, clauses 39 and 40

■ The Hundred Years' War (1337–1453): The Arrow Is Mightier Than the Armor

What might be called the first national war was waged by England against France. Fought on the Continent, the **Hundred Years' War** was based on weak claims to the throne of France by two English kings: Edward III (reigned 1327–1377) and Henry V (reigned 1413–1422).

This long war was militarily unsuccessful for the English, but it was an important factor in the gradual development of a British national consciousness. After the war the English were no longer best represented by the knight in shining armor, an import from English warfare around 1325. By 1346, warfare in the Western world had changed forever. In the landmark battle of Crécy, the French outnumbered the English. Yet the English, aided by the longbow and explosives, massacred their opponents. Over the next two hundred years the cannon made even the castle open to attack.

The rules of war and class had changed. Chivalry was at an end, and feudal obligation became a thing of the past. As a result, a free and prosperous middle class developed, revolutionizing the country's social and economic systems.

Mounted knight arrayed in helmet and shirt of mail and carrying a shield. Sculpture-Reliefs (13th century) Spanish. $20\frac{1}{4} \times 10\frac{1}{2} \times 9\frac{3}{8}$ in. ($51.4 \times 26.7 \times 23.8$ cm).

The Metropolitan Museum of Art, New York. Dodge Fund, 1913 (13.21).

Daily Life in London During the Great Plague (1665). Woodcut.

The Art Archive.

the Continent anyway. Instead, they were more accurately represented by the green-clad **yeoman** (small landowner) with his longbow. These English yeomen had formed the nucleus of the English armies in France. Their yard-long arrows could fly over castle walls and pierce the armor of knights. These small landowners now became a dominant force in the new society that grew up from the ruins of feudalism. The old ideals of chivalry lived on only in stories, such as the King Arthur legends retold by Sir Thomas Malory (see page 216).

■ The Black Death

The **Black Death,** or bubonic plague, which struck England in 1348–1349, delivered another blow to feudalism. Highly contagious and spread by fleas from infected rats, the disease was horrifying. The twentieth-century English statesman and historian Sir Winston Churchill described its ravages:

> "The character of the pestilence was appalling. The disease itself, with its frightful symptoms, the swift onset, the blotches, the hardening of the glands under the armpit or in

FAST FACTS

Philosophical Views

- William introduces European feudalism, a system of landownership, which replaces the less centralized, more democratic traditions of Anglo-Saxon England.
- Knights live their lives according to the ideals and social codes associated with chivalry. This code includes remaining loyal to one's lord, adhering to certain rules of warfare, and adoring an admirable, virtuous lady from afar.

Social and Economic Influences

- As Church and papal influence grow stronger in Norman England, the country increasingly becomes a part of the mainstream culture of Catholic Europe.
- Exposure to Eastern civilization as a result of the Crusades broadened Europeans' intellectual horizons.
- The Black Death, or bubonic plague, of 1348–1349 causes a labor shortage that ultimately leads to the serfs' freedom and to the end of feudalism.

the groin, these swellings which no poultice could resolve, these tumors which, when lanced, gave no relief, the horde of virulent carbuncles which followed the dread harbingers of death, the delirium, the insanity which attended its triumph, the blank spaces which opened on all sides in human society, stunned and for a time destroyed the life and faith of the world.”

The plague reduced the nation's population by a third—causing a labor shortage and giving the lower classes more bargaining power against their overlords. One long-term result was the serfs' freedom, which knocked out feudalism's last support. By the time King Henry VII's 1486 marriage reconciled the warring Houses of York and Lancaster, the Middle Ages were ending in England. Henry, a strong king, began the Tudor line that would lead to Elizabeth I. England's Renaissance was about to begin.

FAST FACTS

Political Highlights

- In 1066, the Norman army, led by William the Conqueror, defeats the Anglo-Saxons in the Battle of Hastings.
- In 1215, English barons force King John to sign the Magna Carta in an effort to curb the king's power.
- The English lose the Hundred Years' War with France (1337–1453). With the emergence of the yeomen class (small landowners), modern, democratic England is born.

REVIEW

Talk About . . .

Turn to the Think About questions posed at the start of this introduction to the Middle Ages (page 116). Get together with a group of classmates to discuss your answers.

Write About . . .

Contrasting Literary Periods

Loyalty and honor, then and now. The values of loyalty and honor lay at the heart of the feudal system. The king demanded loyalty from his barons, and these lords expected loyalty from their vassals, knights, and serfs. In turn, those who honorably met their obligations expected certain rewards and protections. Have loyalty and honor remained as important in today's society? To what and whom are people loyal today? What codes of honor do we live by today? Write a brief response to these questions about loyalty and honor then and now.

Before You Read

Ballads

Make the Connection

THREE DEAD SONS VISIT MOTHER FOR DINNER...SLIGHTED WOMAN SPURNS LOVER'S DEATHBED REQUEST...MAIDEN HEADED FOR GALLOWS; FAMILY REFUSES HELP.

These aren't the latest tabloid headlines or current soap-opera summaries; they're the plots of medieval ballads. In the Middle Ages, just as today, certain forms of popular entertainment tended toward the sensational.

Ballads were the poetry of the people, just as popular songs are today, and their subjects were predictably popular—domestic tragedy, false love, true love, the absurdity of husband-wife relationships, and the supernatural. Unlike today's music, ballads were not copyrighted by a composer but were passed down orally from singer to singer. Using a strong beat and repetition, ballads were a gift of story passed from performer to performer, from generation to generation.

Young musician, from *De Musica* (On Music) (14th century) by Anicius Boetius (c. 450–524).

Folio 47R. Biblioteca Nazionale, Naples. The Art Archive/Dagli Orti.

SKILLS FOCUS

Literary Skills Understand the characteristics of ballads.

Literary Focus

Ballad

Ballads are songs or songlike poems that tell stories in simple, rhythmic language. Virtually every ballad includes certain predictable features, or conventions, including sensational or tragic subject matter, omitted details, supernatural events, and a **refrain**—a repeated word, line, or group of lines. (For more on ballads, see pages 133–134.)

A **ballad** is a song or songlike poem that tells a story in a regular pattern of rhythm and rhyme and uses simple, direct language.

For more on Ballads, see the Handbook of Literary and Historical Terms.

Background

The word *ballad* is derived from an Old French word meaning "dancing song." Although the English ballads' connection with dance has been lost, it is clear from their meter and their structure that the original ballads were composed to be sung to music.

The ballads as we know them today probably took their form in the fifteenth century, but they were not printed until Sir Thomas Percy published a number of them in 1765. Inspired by Percy, Sir Walter Scott and others traveled around the British Isles and collected the songs from the people who still sang them.

This ballad is sung in different versions in several countries. The basic story of the song varies little, but Randall is variously known as Donald, Randolph, Ramsay, Ransome, and Durango. Sometimes his last meal consists of fish, sometimes snakes. The dialect of this version is Scottish. This ballad, like many others, is sung entirely as a conversation in a question-and-answer format that builds suspense.

A knight and his lady feeding a falcon, detail from a German manuscript (c. 14th century).

Cod. Pal. Germ. 848, Codex Manesse, fol. 249v. Universitätsbibliothek, Heidelberg, Germany.

Lord Randall

"O where hae ye been, Lord Randall, my son?
O where hae ye been, my handsome young man?"
"I hae been to the wild wood; mother, make my bed soon,
For I'm weary wi' hunting, and fain° wald lie down."

"Where gat ye your dinner, Lord Randall, my son?
Where gat ye your dinner, my handsome young man?"
"I din'd wi' my true-love; mother, make my bed soon,
For I'm weary wi' hunting, and fain wald lie down."

"What gat ye to your dinner, Lord Randall, my son?
What gat ye to your dinner, my handsome young man?"
"I gat eels boil'd in broo;° mother, make my bed soon,
For I'm weary wi' hunting, and fain wald lie down."

"What became of your bloodhounds, Lord Randall, my son?
What became of your bloodhounds, my handsome young man?"
"O they swell'd and they died; mother, make my bed soon,
For I'm weary wi' hunting, and fain wald lie down."

"O I fear ye are poison'd, Lord Randall, my son!
O I fear ye are poison'd, my handsome young man!"
"O yes! I am poison'd; mother, make my bed soon,
For I'm sick at the heart, and I fain wald lie down."

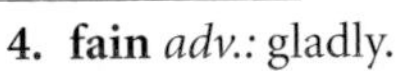

4. **fain** *adv.:* gladly.
11. **broo** *n.:* archaic form of "broth."

The story in this ballad exists in many versions in Europe, Asia, and the Middle East—perhaps illustrating the universal theme called the battle of the sexes. Goodman *and* goodwife *are terms once applied to married men and women, something like* Mr. *and* Mrs. *today.*

The story takes place around November 11—Martinmas, or the feast of Saint Martin of Tours, which was usually celebrated with a big meal.

Get Up and Bar the Door

It fell about the Martinmas time,
And a gay time it was then,
When our goodwife got puddings° to make,
And she's boild them in the pan.

The wind sae cauld blew south and north,
And blew into the floor;
Quoth our goodman to our goodwife,
"Gae out and bar the door."

"My hand is in my hussyfskap,°
Goodman, as ye may see;
An° it should nae be barrd this hundred year,
It's no be barrd for me."

They made a paction tween them twa,
They made it firm and sure,
That the first word whaeer should speak,
Should rise and bar the door.

Then by there came two gentlemen,
At twelve o clock at night,
And they could neither see house nor hall,
Nor coal nor candle-light.

"Now whether is this a rich man's house,
Or whether it is a poor?"
But neer a word ane° o them speak,
For barring of the door.

The Chef (15th century). Woodcut.

And first they ate the white puddings,
And then they ate the black;
Tho muckle° thought the goodwife to hersel,
Yet neer a word she spake.

Then said the one unto the other,
"Here, man, tak ye my knife;
Do ye tak aff the auld man's beard,
And I'll kiss the goodwife."

"But there's nae water in the house,°
And what shall we do than?"
"What ails ye at the pudding-broo,°
That boils into the pan?"

O up then started our goodman,
An angry man was he:
"Will ye kiss my wife before my een,
And scad° me wi pudding-bree?"°

Then up and started our goodwife,
Gied three skips on the floor:
"Goodman, you've spoken the foremost word,
Get up and bar the door."

3. **puddings** *n. pl.:* sausages made with blood.
9. **hussyfskap** (hu'zif·skep) *n.:* archaic word meaning "household chores."
11. **an** *conj.:* archaic word for "if."
23. **ane** *adj.:* archaic word for "one."
27. **muckle** *adj.:* archaic word meaning "much."
33. **but . . . house:** He probably wants water to soften the husband's beard.
35. **what . . . pudding-broo:** What's wrong with using the pudding broth?
40. **scad** *v.:* archaic word meaning "scald." **bree** *n.:* archaic word meaning "broth."

Response and Analysis

Reading Check

1. What has happened to Lord Randall?
2. In "Get Up and Bar the Door," what do the husband and wife argue about? What pact do they make?

Thinking Critically

3. What is the emotional effect of the **refrain's** variation in the fifth stanza of "Lord Randall"?
4. "Lord Randall" provides a good example of **incremental repetition**—the repetition of lines with a new element introduced each time to advance the story until the climax is reached. At what point in this ballad did you discover what is wrong with Lord Randall? How does the incremental repetition increase your suspense?
5. Typical of ballads, "Lord Randall" omits details and ends with only half the story told. Do you think the young man's lover has poisoned him? Explain why or why not. What other questions regarding the **plot** are left unanswered?
6. What prominent parts do puddings or sausages play in the **plot** of "Get Up and Bar the Door"?
7. How is the possibility of violence combined with **ironic** humor in "Get Up and Bar the Door"?
8. As you read "Get Up and Bar the Door," did you find yourself siding with the husband, the wife, or neither? Explain your views.

Extending and Evaluating

9. People often criticize today's media for glorifying violence. Do you think these ballads also glorify violence? Is the issue the same? Explain your responses.

WRITING

Late-Breaking News!

Take one of the basic situations in these ballads, and retell it as a contemporary **news story.** Like a reporter, be sure to tell *what* happened, *where* and *when* it happened, to *whom* it happened, *why* it happened, and *how* it happened. Present your news story in print form, complete with headlines.

LISTENING AND SPEAKING

Bring a Ballad to Life

With a small group, select a traditional or contemporary ballad (or write your own), and prepare to perform it. Have an audience evaluate your first performance according to criteria you all agree on (such as clarity of story, use of ballad conventions, aesthetic effect, and so on). Make sure your performance demonstrates an understanding of the meaning of the ballad you choose. Use your audience's evaluations to perfect your final performance.

SKILLS FOCUS

Pages 133–134 cover
Literary Skills Analyze the characteristics of ballads.
Writing Skills Retell a ballad as a news story.
Listening and Speaking Skills Give an oral performance of a ballad.

Literary Focus

Ballads: Popular Poetry

Ballads come from an oral tradition, so there are no strict rules dictating their form. However, a number of characteristics have come to be associated with ballads, and every ballad reflects at least some of them: **supernatural events; sensational, sordid, or tragic subject matter;** a **refrain;** and the **omission of details.** The ballad singers also used some of the following conventions:

- **incremental repetition** to build up suspense. A phrase or sentence is repeated with a new element added each time until the climax is reached.
- **a question-and-answer format** in which the facts of a story are gleaned little

INTERNET
Projects and Activities
Keyword: LE7 12-2

by little from the answers. Again, this device builds suspense.

- **conventional phrases** understood by listeners to have meaning beyond their literal ones. "Make my bed soon" in "Lord Randall" is an example. Whenever a character in a ballad asks someone to make his bed or to make her bed narrow, it means that the speaker is preparing for death.
- **a strong, simple beat** with verse forms that are relatively uncomplicated. Ballads were sung for a general audience, not an elitist one. Only later, in the era of so-called literary ballads (more sophisticated poems that artfully evoked the atmosphere of the originals), did the rhyme scheme (*abcb*) and meter (a quatrain in which lines of four stresses alternate with lines of three stresses) of the ballad stanza become standard.

Collect a book of ballads. Collect at least three traditional ballads from any culture (including American), or find three variations of the same ballad ("Lord Randall" is supposed to have 103 known variations), and present them in a printed form that can be kept in the classroom for future reference. Write a brief introduction to each ballad, telling what you have learned about its origins and pointing out the conventions it shares with other ballads. If your ballads are not from the English tradition, explain how they are like and unlike traditional British ballads.

The Nine Muses (15th century) by Martin Le Franc.
Bibliothèque de Grenoble, France. The Bridgeman Art Library.

Geoffrey Chaucer

(c. 1343–1400)

By Courtesy of the National Portrait Gallery, London.

Geoffrey Chaucer (1400).

Geoffrey Chaucer, often called the father of English poetry, made the English language respectable.

Ordinary people in Chaucer's England spoke the Anglo-Norman composite now called Middle English, a language that became the ancestor of Modern English. But in Chaucer's time the languages of literature, science, diplomacy, and religion were still Latin and French. Before Chaucer it was not fashionable for serious poets to write in English. People felt that English couldn't possibly convey all the nuances and complexities of serious literature.

By composing in the **vernacular**—the everyday language spoken in London and the East Midlands—Chaucer lent respectability to a language that would develop into the medium for one of the world's greatest bodies of literature. In this sense he is indeed the father of English poetry.

Friends in High Places

Not a great deal is known of Chaucer's life. He was born into a middle-class family in London in the early 1340s, not long after the beginning of the Hundred Years' War. We are told that his father was a wine merchant who had enough money to provide his son with some education. The young Chaucer read a great deal and had some legal training. He became a page to an eminent family from whom he received the finest training in good manners. As he advanced in his government career, he became attached to several noble patrons.

We know, too, that Chaucer was captured in France while serving as a soldier during the Hundred Years' War and that he was important enough to have the king contribute to his ransom. We also know that he married Philippa and had at least two children and that he was on several occasions sent to Europe as the king's ambassador. In 1367, he was awarded the first of several pensions for his services to the Crown. (On April 23, 1374, he was granted the promise of a daily pitcher of wine.) In 1385, he was appointed justice of the peace in the county of Kent, later becoming a member of Parliament. He continued to serve and to enjoy the king's protection.

Writing and Holding a Job

It seems clear that Chaucer was a relatively important government servant and that his work took precedence over his writing. (It would be as if a prominent adviser to the U.S. president were also a highly acclaimed poet.) Yet Chaucer wrote a great deal and sometimes for personal advancement. In about 1369, for example, he composed his first important poem, *The Book of the Duchess,* in memory of his patron's wife, who had just died of the plague.

Despite his government responsibilities, between 1374 and 1386, Chaucer managed to create several great allegorical poems, including *House of Fame* and *Parliament of Fowls,* and his love story *Troilus and Criseyde.*

The Italian Connection

In 1372 and 1378, Chaucer traveled in Italy, where he was very likely influenced by the poems of Dante and Petrarch and by the stories of Giovanni Boccaccio (see page 207). The connection between Boccaccio's collection of tales called the *Decameron* (c. 1348–1353) and Chaucer's *The Canterbury Tales* (c. 1387–1400) is evident. Both use a framing device within which the characters tell their tales, and both include tales based on similar old plots.

Chaucer began writing *The Canterbury Tales* in 1387, during a few years of unemployment when his patron was out of the country. Perhaps because he felt that he had lost his ability to find rhymes, he never completed all the stories. In spite of this, the collection must be considered one of the greatest works in the English language. *The Canterbury Tales* alone—even the Prologue alone, in which each traveler is described—would have been sufficient to place Chaucer in the company of Shakespeare and Milton.

The Force of Personality

What is so great about *The Canterbury Tales?* In part, its greatness lies in Chaucer's language. It also comes from the sheer strength of Chaucer's spirit and personality. John Gardner, one of Chaucer's many biographers, offers a tribute to Chaucer's lasting power:

> "In a dark, troubled age, as it seems to us, he was a comfortable optimist, serene, full of faith. For all his delight in irony—and all his poetry has a touch of that—he affirmed this life, to say nothing of the next, from the bottom of his capacious heart. Joy—satisfaction without a trace of sentimental simple-mindedness—is still the effect of Chaucer's poetry and of Chaucer's personality as it emerges from the poems. It is not the simple faith of a credulous man in a credulous age: No poet has ever written better on the baffling complexity of things. But for all the foggy shiftings of the heart and mind, for all the obscurity of God's huge plan, to Chaucer life was a magnificent affair, though sadly transient; and when we read him now, six centuries later, we are instantly persuaded."

The End of the Old Alliterative Anglo-Saxon World

Chaucer used several metrical forms and some prose in *The Canterbury Tales,* but the dominant meter is based on ten syllables, with an unstressed syllable followed by a stressed syllable. We call this meter **iambic pentameter.** It is a rhythm that most closely matches the way English is spoken. You might hear this rhythm if you read aloud this line in Middle English. (*Bathed* is pronounced with two syllables, bäth′ed; *swich* means "sweet"):

˘ ´ ˘ ´ ˘ ´ ˘ ´ ˘ ´
And bathed every veyne in swich licour

When we read a line such as this, we experience a version of the meter that was to become the most popular metrical line in English. At a stroke we have abandoned the old, alliterative world of the Anglo-Saxons and entered the modern world of Shakespeare, Wordsworth, and even Robert Frost.

The Father in the Family Vault

Chaucer died on October 25, 1400, if we are to believe the date on his tombstone (which an admirer erected in Westminster Abbey in 1556). Chaucer was the very first of those many famous English writers who would be gathered into what we know as the Poets' Corner in Westminster Abbey—one of the great tourist sights in London today. "The Father of English poetry," notes Nevill Coghill, "lies in his family vault."

THE CANTERBURY TALES: SNAPSHOT OF AN AGE

The Canterbury Tales gives us a collection of good stories and a snapshot, a picture of life in the Middle Ages frozen in time. To include the complete range of medieval society in the same picture, Chaucer places his characters on a pilgrimage, a religious journey made to a shrine or holy place. These pilgrims, like a group of people on tour today, are from many stations and stages of life. Together they travel on horseback from London to the shrine of the martyr Saint Thomas à Becket at Canterbury Cathedral, about fifty-five miles to the southeast.

Setting up the frame. The *Tales* begin with a general Prologue, the first lines of which establish that this pilgrimage takes place in the spring, the time of new life and awakening. Fifty-five miles is a long journey by horseback, especially along muddy tracks that would hardly pass as roads today. An inn was always a welcome oasis, even if it provided few luxuries. The poet-pilgrim narrator, whom many consider to be Chaucer himself, starts out at the Tabard Inn in Southwark, a borough in the south of London. There he meets twenty-nine other pilgrims also bound for Canterbury. It is the host of the Tabard who suggests to the pilgrims, as they sit around the fire after dinner, that they exchange tales to pass the time along the way to Canterbury and back to London. The host's suggestion sets up Chaucer's **frame story**—the main story of the pilgrimage that includes each pilgrim's story.

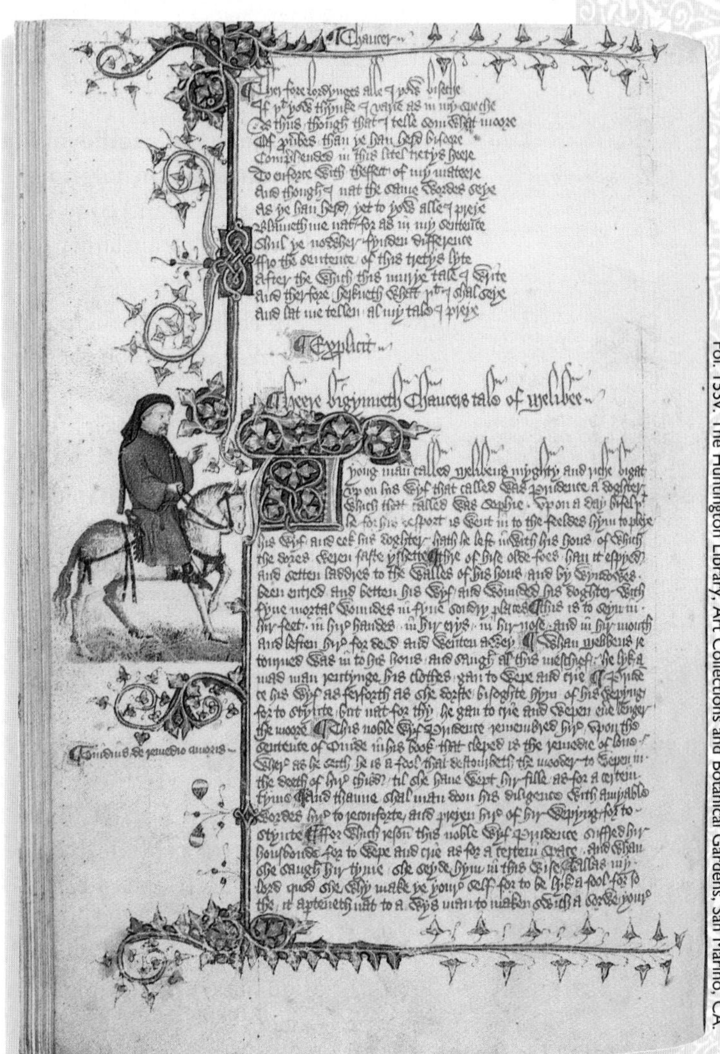

Page from *The Canterbury Tales,* from the Ellesmere manuscript (15th century). The man on the horse is thought to be Chaucer.

A pageant of medieval life. As the Prologue progresses and we are introduced to the pilgrims, Chaucer's brilliant picture of life in late medieval England comes into focus. Here is what Nevill Coghill, one of Chaucer's translators, says about the Prologue:

> "In all literature there is nothing that touches or resembles the *Prologue.* It is the concise portrait of an entire nation, high and low, old and young, male and female, lay and clerical, learned and ignorant, rogue and righteous, land and sea, town and country, but without extremes. Apart from the stunning clarity, touched with nuance, of the characters presented, the most noticeable thing about them is their normality. They are the perennial progeny of men and women. Sharply individual, together they make a party."

Figure thought to be Chaucer, from the Ellesmere manuscript.

Fol. 153v. By permission of The Huntington Library, San Marino, California.

At its most basic level, Chaucer's great work operates on several levels. As a pilgrimage story, it is one of the world's many quest narratives, and it moves from images of spring and awakening at the beginning of the Prologue to images of penance, death, and eternal life in the Parson's tale at the end of the work. The storytellers themselves are pilgrims in search of renewal at the shrine of Thomas à Becket. Coming as they do from all walks of life and all social classes, they cannot help but represent "everyman," or all of us, on our universal pilgrimage through life.

Chaucer's Middle English is here translated into Modern English by Nevill Coghill. While Coghill's version is true to the spirit of Chaucer's original poem, you might attempt to read at least bits of the *Tales* in the wonderfully musical original. (See the beginning of the Prologue in its original Middle English on page 141.)

Chaucer's Canterbury Pilgrims (1810) by William Blake. Engraving.

Private Collection/The Bridgeman Art Library.

Brief Pronunciation Guide to Middle English

Vowels

a: *ah,* as in *father.*
ai, ay, ei, ey: a long *a*, as in *pay.*
au, aw: *ow*, as in *house.*
oo: *oh*, as in *oat.*
e: at times, like a long *a*, as in *mate*. When a double e is used, it is always long. *Eek* is pronounced āk.
e: at times, like a short e, as in *men.*
The final e in Middle English is a separate syllable sounded like a final *ah: soote* rhymes with *soda*. But when the final e precedes a word that starts with a vowel or an *h*, it is not sounded. In "droghte of March," the final e in *droghte* is silent.

Consonants

g: hard *g*, as in *go*, except before e or *i* (in words borrowed from French) where it is sounded like *zh*, as in *garage. Pilgrimage* rhymes with *garage.*
gh, ch: like the German *ch*, as in *nicht.* (These sounds are usually silent in Modern English.) *Knight* is pronounced k•nicht′.
–tion, –cial: The *t* and *c* in such words are not blended with the *i* as they are in Modern English (as in the words *condition* and *special*). The *i* is sounded as a separate syllable. *Special* would have three syllables and *condition* four: kon•di•sē•ôn′. (*C* has the sound of s when it comes before *i.*)

Before You Read

The Prologue to *The Canterbury Tales*

Make the Connection

If you went on a tour today, what types of people would you expect to meet? Most of Chaucer's pilgrims are the kinds of people he would have known and perhaps even observed many times riding toward Canterbury on the old pilgrimage road.

Literary Focus

Characterization

To create the portraits of his pilgrims, Chaucer uses the same methods of **characterization** that writers still use today. He reveals his characters by telling us

- how the character looks and dresses
- how the character speaks and acts
- what the character thinks and feels
- how others respond to the character

He also may tell us directly what the character's nature is—virtuous, vain, clever, and so on.

Frame Story

When Chaucer chooses to have each of his pilgrims tell a story on the way to Canterbury, he is using a popular literary device called the frame story. A **frame story** is a story within a story. Chaucer uses the outer story of the pilgrimage to unite his travelers' individual tales, but the tales themselves also have thematic unity.

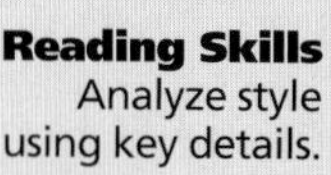

Literary Skills Understand characterization. Understand the characteristics of a frame story.

Reading Skills Analyze style using key details.

INTERNET

Vocabulary Practice

•

More About Geoffrey Chaucer

•

Keyword: LE7 12-2

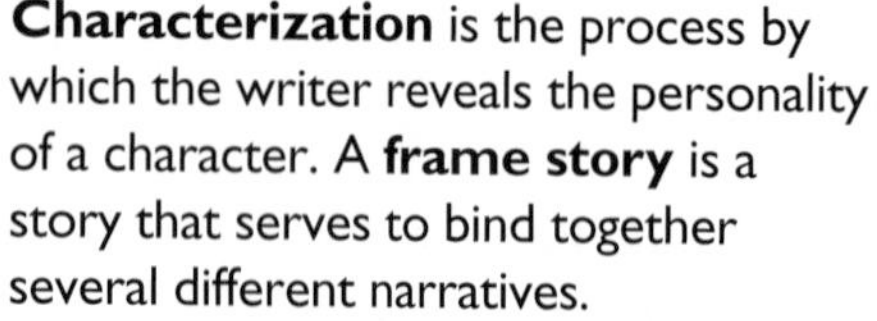

Characterization is the process by which the writer reveals the personality of a character. A **frame story** is a story that serves to bind together several different narratives.

For more on Character and the Frame Story, see the Handbook of Literary and Historical Terms.

Reading Skills

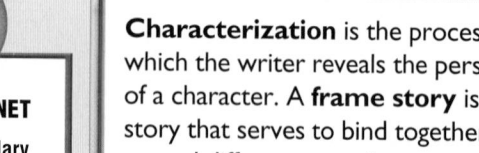

Analyzing Style: Key Details

With twenty-nine pilgrims to introduce in the Prologue, Chaucer could not develop any one character at great length. Instead, he had to provide a few well-chosen details that would make each character stand out vividly.

As you read the descriptions of each pilgrim in the Prologue, jot down striking details of dress, appearance, and behavior that give you an immediate impression of what the character is really like. Note that these telling details often undermine what the characters think of themselves or would like others to think about them.

Vocabulary Development

agility (ə•jil′ə•tē) *n.:* ability to move quickly and easily.

eminent (em′ə•nənt) *adj.:* high-standing; great.

accrue (ə•kro͞o′) *v.:* increase over time.

arbitrate (är′bə•trāt′) *v.:* settle or decide by listening to both sides of an argument.

benign (bi•nīn′) *adj.:* kind; gracious.

guile (gīl) *n.:* sly dealings; skill in deceiving.

obstinate (äb′stə•nət) *adj.:* unreasonably stubborn.

frugal (fro͞o′gəl) *adj.:* thrifty; careful with money.

duress (do͝o•res′) *n.:* pressure.

(Opposite) The opening lines of the Prologue to *The Canterbury Tales,* in the original Middle English.

Here bygynneth the Book of the Tales of Caunterbury.

Whan that Aprill with his shoures soote
The droghte of March hath perced to the roote
And bathed every veyne in swich licour
Of which vertu engendred is the flour,
Whan Zephirus eek with his sweete breeth
Inspired hath in every holt and heeth
The tendre croppes, and the yonge sonne
Hath in the Ram his half cours y-ronne,
And smale foweles maken melodye
That slepen al the nyght with open eye,
So priketh hem Nature in hir corages,
Than longen folk to goon on pilgrymages,
And palmeres for to seken straunge strondes,
To ferne halwes kouthe in sondry londes.
And specially, from every shires ende
Of Engelond, to Caunterbury they wende,
The holy, blisful martir for to seke
That hem hath holpen whan that they were seeke
Bifel that in that sesoun on a day
In Southwerk at the Tabard, as I lay
Redy to wenden on my pilgrymage
To Caunterbury with ful devout corage,
At nyght was come into that hostelrye
Wel nyne-and-twenty in a compaignye
Of sondry folk by aventure y-falle
In felaweshipe, and pilgrymes were they alle
That toward Caunterbury wolden ryde.
The chambres and the stables weren wyde,
And wel we weren esed atte beste;
And shortly, whan the sonne was to reste,
So hadde I spoken with hem everichon
That I was of hir felaweshipe anon;
And made forward erly for to ryse
To take oure wey ther as I yow devyse.
But, nathelees, whil I have tyme and space,
Er that I ferther in this tale pace,
Me thynketh it acordant to resoun
To telle yow al the condicioun
Of ech of hem so as it semed me,
And whiche they weren, and of what degree,
And eek in what array that they were inne;
And at a knyght than wol I first bigynne.

Decorative border from *The Canterbury Tales,* from the Ellesmere manuscript (detail) (15th century).

from The Canterbury Tales

Geoffrey Chaucer
translated by **Nevill Coghill**

The Prologue

When in April the sweet showers fall
And pierce the drought of March to the root, and all
The veins are bathed in liquor of such power
As brings about the engendering of the flower,
When also Zephyrus° with his sweet breath
Exhales an air in every grove and heath
Upon the tender shoots, and the young sun
His half-course in the sign of the *Ram*° has run,
And the small fowl are making melody
That sleep away the night with open eye
(So nature pricks them and their heart engages)
Then people long to go on pilgrimages
And palmers° long to seek the stranger strands
Of far-off saints, hallowed in sundry lands,
And specially, from every shire's end
Of England, down to Canterbury they wend°
To seek the holy blissful martyr, quick
To give his help to them when they were sick.
   It happened in that season that one day
In Southwark, at *The Tabard,* as I lay
Ready to go on pilgrimage and start
For Canterbury, most devout at heart,
At night there came into that hostelry°
Some nine and twenty in a company
Of sundry folk happening then to fall
In fellowship, and they were pilgrims all
That towards Canterbury meant to ride.
The rooms and stables of the inn were wide:
They made us easy, all was of the best.

5. **Zephyrus** (zef′ə·rəs): in Greek mythology, god of the west wind.

8. **Ram:** Aries, first sign of the zodiac. The time is mid-April.

13. **palmers** *n. pl.:* people who had visited the Holy Land and wore palm fronds to show it.

16. **wend** *v.:* go; travel.

23. **hostelry** *n.:* inn. *The Tabard* is a lodging place.

1–18. These lines consist of a single, long sentence that is built on this structure: "When *x* occurs, then *y* happens."
? *When spring brings new life, then—according to the narrator—what do people long to do?*

John Lydgate and the Canterbury pilgrims leaving Canterbury, from a volume of Lydgate's poems (early 16th century).

MS Royal 18 D II, fol. 148. British Library, London.

And, briefly, when the sun had gone to rest,
I'd spoken to them all upon the trip
And was soon one with them in fellowship,
Pledged to rise early and to take the way
To Canterbury, as you heard me say.
But none the less, while I have time and space,
Before my story takes a further pace,
It seems a reasonable thing to say
What their condition was, the full array
Of each of them, as it appeared to me,
According to profession and degree,
And what apparel they were riding in;
And at a Knight I therefore will begin.

The Knight

There was a *Knight,* a most distinguished man,
Who from the day on which he first began
To ride abroad had followed chivalry,
Truth, honor, generousness, and courtesy.
He had done nobly in his sovereign's war
And ridden into battle, no man more,
As well in Christian as in heathen° places,
And ever honored for his noble graces.
When we took Alexandria,° he was there.
He often sat at table in the chair
Of honor, above all nations, when in Prussia.
In Lithuania he had ridden, and Russia,
No Christian man so often, of his rank.
When, in Granada, Algeciras sank
Under assault, he had been there, and in
North Africa, raiding Benamarin;
In Anatolia he had been as well
And fought when Ayas and Attalia fell,
For all along the Mediterranean coast
He had embarked with many a noble host.
In fifteen mortal battles he had been
And jousted for our faith at Tramissene
Thrice in the lists, and always killed his man.
This same distinguished knight had led the van
Once with the Bey of Balat, doing work
For him against another heathen Turk;
He was of sovereign value in all eyes.
And though so much distinguished, he was wise
And in his bearing modest as a maid.
He never yet a boorish thing had said
In all his life to any, come what might;
He was a true, a perfect gentle-knight.
Speaking of his equipment, he possessed
Fine horses, but he was not gaily dressed.
He wore a fustian° tunic stained and dark
With smudges where his armor had left mark;
Just home from service, he had joined our ranks
To do his pilgrimage and render thanks.

The Squire

He had his son with him, a fine young *Squire,*
A lover and cadet, a lad of fire
With locks as curly as if they had been pressed.
He was some twenty years of age, I guessed.

43. Notice that *Knight* appears in italics; so will each new character's designation as the character is introduced.

? *As you read, you might wish to create a list of all the characters introduced in the Prologue.*

49. heathen *adj.:* pagan. Chaucer uses the term to mean non-Christian.

51. Alexandria: city in Egypt captured by the Crusaders in 1365. In the next few lines, Chaucer is indicating the knight's distinguished and extensive career.

The Knight, from the Ellesmere manuscript.

Fol. 10r. By permission of The Huntington Library, San Marino, California.

77. fustian (fus′chən) *adj.:* made of coarse cloth woven from linen and cotton.

The Squire, from the Ellesmere manuscript.

Fol. 115v. By permission of The Huntington Library, San Marino, California.

In stature he was of a moderate length,
With wonderful agility and strength.
He'd seen some service with the cavalry
In Flanders and Artois and Picardy
And had done valiantly in little space
Of time, in hope to win his lady's grace.
He was embroidered like a meadow bright
And full of freshest flowers, red and white.
Singing he was, or fluting° all the day;
He was as fresh as is the month of May.
Short was his gown, the sleeves were long and wide;
He knew the way to sit a horse and ride.
He could make songs and poems and recite,
Knew how to joust and dance, to draw and write.
He loved so hotly that till dawn grew pale
He slept as little as a nightingale.
Courteous he was, lowly and serviceable,
And carved to serve his father at the table.

The Yeoman

There was a *Yeoman* with him at his side,
No other servant; so he chose to ride.
This Yeoman wore a coat and hood of green,
And peacock-feathered arrows, bright and keen
And neatly sheathed, hung at his belt the while
—For he could dress his gear in yeoman style,
His arrows never drooped their feathers low—
And in his hand he bore a mighty bow.
His head was like a nut, his face was brown.
He knew the whole of woodcraft up and down.
A saucy brace was on his arm to ward
It from the bow-string, and a shield and sword
Hung at one side, and at the other slipped
A jaunty dirk,° spear-sharp and well-equipped.
A medal of St. Christopher° he wore
Of shining silver on his breast, and bore
A hunting-horn, well slung and burnished clean,
That dangled from a baldrick° of bright green.
He was a proper forester, I guess.

Vocabulary

agility (ə • jil′ə • tē) *n.:* ability to move quickly and easily.

93. fluting *v.:* whistling.

? **87–102.** *Summarize the narrator's description of the Squire. In what ways does the Squire appear to embody the code of chivalry? (See page 122 for a review of chivalry.)*

The Canon Yeoman, from the Ellesmere manuscript.

Fol. 194r. By permission of The Huntington Library, San Marino, California.

116. dirk *n.:* long dagger.

117. St. Christopher: patron saint of travelers.

120. baldrick (bôl′drik′) *n.:* belt slung over the shoulder and chest to hold a sword.

The Nun

There also was a *Nun,* a Prioress,°
Her way of smiling very simple and coy.
Her greatest oath was only "By St. Loy!"°
And she was known as Madam Eglantyne.
And well she sang a service, with a fine
Intoning through her nose, as was most seemly,
And she spoke daintily in French, extremely,
After the school of Stratford-atte-Bowe;°
French in the Paris style she did not know.
At meat her manners were well taught withal;
No morsel from her lips did she let fall,
Nor dipped her fingers in the sauce too deep;
But she could carry a morsel up and keep
The smallest drop from falling on her breast.
For courtliness she had a special zest,
And she would wipe her upper lip so clean
That not a trace of grease was to be seen
Upon the cup when she had drunk; to eat,
She reached a hand sedately for the meat.
She certainly was very entertaining,
Pleasant and friendly in her ways, and straining
To counterfeit a courtly kind of grace,
A stately bearing fitting to her place,
And to seem dignified in all her dealings.
As for her sympathies and tender feelings,
She was so charitably solicitous
She used to weep if she but saw a mouse
Caught in a trap, if it were dead or bleeding.
And she had little dogs she would be feeding

122. Prioress: head of a convent of nuns.

124. St. Loy: Saint Eligius, known for his perfect manners.

129. Stratford-atte-Bowe: Benedictine convent near London where inferior French was spoken.

? **122–145.** *What details in the description of the Prioress thus far suggest that the narrator thinks she is putting on airs—that is, trying to appear more refined and "high class" than she really is?*

The Prioress, from the Ellesmere manuscript.

Fol. 148v. By permission of The Huntington Library, San Marino, California.

The Nun's Priest, from the Ellesmere manuscript.

Fol. 179r. By permission of The Huntington Library, San Marino, California.

With roasted flesh, or milk, or fine white bread.
And bitterly she wept if one were dead
Or someone took a stick and made it smart;
She was all sentiment and tender heart.
Her veil was gathered in a seemly way,
Her nose was elegant, her eyes glass-gray;
Her mouth was very small, but soft and red,
Her forehead, certainly, was fair of spread,
Almost a span° across the brows, I own;
She was indeed by no means undergrown.
Her cloak, I noticed, had a graceful charm.
She wore a coral° trinket on her arm,
A set of beads, the gaudies tricked in green,°
Whence hung a golden brooch of brightest sheen
On which there first was graven a crowned A,
And lower, *Amor vincit omnia.*°
  Another *Nun,* the secretary at her cell,°
Was riding with her, and *three Priests* as well.

The Monk

  A *Monk* there was, one of the finest sort
Who rode the country; hunting was his sport.
A manly man, to be an Abbott able;
Many a dainty horse he had in stable.
His bridle, when he rode, a man might hear
Jingling in a whistling wind as clear,
Aye, and as loud as does the chapel bell
Where my lord Monk was Prior of the cell.
The Rule of good St. Benet or St. Maur°
As old and strict he tended to ignore;
He let go by the things of yesterday
And took the modern world's more spacious way.
He did not rate that text at a plucked hen
Which says that hunters are not holy men
And that a monk uncloistered is a mere
Fish out of water, flapping on the pier,
That is to say a monk out of his cloister.
That was a text he held not worth an oyster;
And I agreed and said his views were sound;
Was he to study till his head went round
Poring over books in cloisters? Must he toil
As Austin° bade and till the very soil?
Was he to leave the world upon the shelf?
Let Austin have his labor to himself.
  This Monk was therefore a good man to horse;
Greyhounds he had, as swift as birds, to course.°
Hunting a hare or riding at a fence

159. span *n.:* nine inches. A span was supposed to be the distance between the extended thumb and little finger.

162. coral *adj.:* In the Middle Ages, coral was a defense against worldly temptations—but it was also a love charm.

163. a set of beads . . . green: Beads are a rosary, or a set of prayer beads and a crucifix on a string or chain. Every eleventh bead is a gaud, a large bead indicating when the Lord's Prayer is to be said.

166. *Amor vincit omnia* (ä′môr′ vin′chit ôm′nē·ä′): Latin for "Love conquers all."

167. cell *n.:* small convent connected to a larger one.

177. St. Benet or St. Maur: Saint Benet is Benedict (c. 480–c. 547), who founded numerous monasteries and wrote a famous code of regulations for monastic life. Saint Maur is Maurice, a follower of Benedict.

190. Austin: Saint Augustine (354–430), bishop of Hippo in North Africa. He criticized lazy monks and suggested they do hard manual labor.

194. course *v.:* cause to chase game.

The Friar, from the Ellesmere manuscript.
Fol. 76v. By permission of The Huntington Library, San Marino, California.

Was all his fun, he spared for no expense.
I saw his sleeves were garnished at the hand
With fine gray fur, the finest in the land,
And on his hood, to fasten it at his chin
He had a wrought-gold, cunningly fashioned pin;
Into a lover's knot it seemed to pass.
His head was bald and shone like looking-glass;
So did his face, as if it had been greased.
He was a fat and personable priest;
His prominent eyeballs never seemed to settle.
They glittered like the flames beneath a kettle;
Supple his boots, his horse in fine condition.
He was a prelate fit for exhibition,
He was not pale like a tormented soul.
He liked a fat swan best, and roasted whole.
His palfrey° was as brown as is a berry.

193–211. *In what ways does the description of the Monk remind you of the Prioress?*

211. palfrey (pôl′frē) *n.:* horse.

The Friar

There was a *Friar*, a wanton one and merry,
A Limiter,° a very festive fellow.
In all Four Orders° there was none so mellow,
So glib with gallant phrase and well-turned speech.
He'd fixed up many a marriage, giving each
Of his young women what he could afford her.
He was a noble pillar to his Order.
Highly beloved and intimate was he
With County folk within his boundary,
And city dames of honor and possessions;
For he was qualified to hear confessions,
Or so he said, with more than priestly scope;
He had a special license from the Pope.
Sweetly he heard his penitents° at shrift°
With pleasant absolution,° for a gift.
He was an easy man in penance-giving
Where he could hope to make a decent living;
It's a sure sign whenever gifts are given
To a poor Order that a man's well shriven,°
And should he give enough he knew in verity
The penitent repented in sincerity.
For many a fellow is so hard of heart
He cannot weep, for all his inward smart.
Therefore instead of weeping and of prayer
One should give silver for a poor Friar's care.
He kept his tippet° stuffed with pins for curls,
And pocket-knives, to give to pretty girls.
And certainly his voice was gay and sturdy,

213. Limiter: friar having the exclusive right to beg and preach in an assigned (limited) district.
214. Four Orders: The four orders of mendicant (beggar) friars are the Franciscans, the Dominicans, the Carmelites, and the Augustinians.

225. penitents *n. pl.:* people seeking the sacrament of confession so that their sins can be forgiven. **shrift** *n.:* confession.
226. absolution *n.:* formal forgiveness of sins, given by a priest.
230. well shriven: well confessed and absolved (or forgiven) of sins.

237. tippet *n.:* hood or long sleeve (of a robe).

For he sang well and played the hurdy-gurdy.°
At sing-songs he was champion of the hour.
His neck was whiter than a lily-flower
But strong enough to butt a bruiser down.
He knew the taverns well in every town
And every innkeeper and barmaid too
Better than lepers, beggars and that crew,
For in so eminent a man as he
It was not fitting with the dignity
Of his position, dealing with a scum
Of wretched lepers; nothing good can come
Of commerce with such slum-and-gutter dwellers,
But only with the rich and victual-sellers.°
But anywhere a profit might accrue
Courteous he was and lowly of service too.
Natural gifts like his were hard to match.
He was the finest beggar of his batch,
And, for his begging-district, paid a rent;
His brethren did no poaching where he went.
For though a widow mightn't have a shoe,
So pleasant was his holy how-d'ye-do
He got his farthing° from her just the same
Before he left, and so his income came
To more than he laid out. And how he romped,
Just like a puppy! He was ever prompt
To arbitrate disputes on settling days°
(For a small fee) in many helpful ways,
Not then appearing as your cloistered scholar
With threadbare habit hardly worth a dollar,
But much more like a Doctor or a Pope.
Of double-worsted° was the semi-cope°
Upon his shoulders, and the swelling fold
About him, like a bell about its mould
When it is casting, rounded out his dress.
He lisped a little out of wantonness°
To make his English sweet upon his tongue.
When he had played his harp, or having sung,
His eyes would twinkle in his head as bright
As any star upon a frosty night.
This worthy's name was Hubert, it appeared.

Vocabulary

eminent (em′ə•nənt) *adj.:* high-standing; great.
accrue (ə•kroo͞′) *v.:* increase over time.
arbitrate (är′bə•trāt′) *v.:* settle or decide by listening to both sides of an argument.

240. hurdy-gurdy *n.:* lutelike instrument played by turning a crank.

252. victual-sellers: merchants, especially of food.

256–279. *What details in these lines show the Friar's love of luxury? How does this Friar compare with your expectations of a religious figure?*

261. farthing (fär′*th*iŋ) *n.:* former British coin worth one fourth of a penny.

265. settling days: days on which disputes could be settled out of court by independent negotiators. Though friars often acted as negotiators (for a fee), they were officially forbidden to do so.
270. double-worsted: a high-quality woven wool. **semi-cope** *n.:* capelike garment.

274. wantonness *n.:* here, pretense.

The Merchant

There was a *Merchant* with a forking beard
And motley° dress; high on his horse he sat,
Upon his head a Flemish beaver hat
And on his feet daintily buckled boots.
He told of his opinions and pursuits
In solemn tones, he harped on his increase
Of capital; there should be sea-police
(He thought) upon the Harwich-Holland ranges;°
He was expert at dabbling in exchanges.
This estimable Merchant so had set
His wits to work, none knew he was in debt,
He was so stately in administration,
In loans and bargains and negotiation.
He was an excellent fellow all the same;
To tell the truth I do not know his name.

281. motley (mät'lē) *adj.:* multi-colored.

287. Harwich-Holland ranges: sea route between Harwich (a port city on the southeastern coast of England) and Holland.

A CLOSER LOOK: RELIGIOUS INFLUENCES

INFORMATIONAL TEXT

PLACES OF PILGRIMAGE

Chaucer's pilgrims are hardly alone in their faith that visiting a holy site will have spiritual benefits. Besides Canterbury, many Christians of Chaucer's time made pilgrimages to Rome and Jerusalem, both sites that the Wife of Bath, something of a professional pilgrim, had visited. Today Christian pilgrims still travel to Jerusalem and Rome.

In ancient times Jews also made pilgrimages to Jerusalem, during three major festivals: Pesach (Passover), Shavuot (Pentecost), and Sukkot (Tabernacles). These pilgrimages, associated with festivals that mark the Jews' escape from Egypt and journey to Israel, were expected of Jewish men.

For a follower of Islam, no place is more sacred than Mecca, located near the Red Sea in western Saudi Arabia. Mecca is the site of the Kaaba, a sacred, cube-shaped stone building around which Muslim pilgrims must walk. Mohammed, the founder of Islam, decreed that all Muslims who are physically and financially able to make the trip must journey to Mecca at least once in their lifetime.

Varanasi, a city on the Ganges River in India and the site of fifteen hundred temples, is visited by more than one million Hindu pilgrims each year. The Golden Temple, the main Hindu shrine there, is dedicated to the god Shiva. Pilgrims who worship at the Ganges at Varanasi believe they gain special merit in this life, and Hindus who die in Varanasi believe they are guaranteed release from endless rebirths.

The Grand Shrine of Ise, the most sacred site of Japanese Shinto pilgrimages, is located at Ise in Mie Prefecture, Japan. The shrines there are viewed as the dwelling place of two deities, the sun goddess Amaterasu and the agricultural god Toyuke. The history of Ise shrine dates back some two thousand years, but the actual buildings are always fairly new. By tradition the shrines must be rebuilt in the same style every twenty-one years.

The Clerk of Oxford, from the Ellesmere manuscript.

Fol. 88r. By permission of The Huntington Library, San Marino, California.

The Oxford Cleric

An *Oxford Cleric*, still a student though,
One who had taken logic long ago,
Was there; his horse was thinner than a rake,
And he was not too fat, I undertake,
But had a hollow look, a sober stare;
The thread upon his overcoat was bare.
He had found no preferment in the church
And he was too unworldly to make search
For secular employment. By his bed
He preferred having twenty books in red
And black, of Aristotle's° philosophy,
Than costly clothes, fiddle, or psaltery.°
Though a philosopher, as I have told,
He had not found the stone for making gold.°
Whatever money from his friends he took
He spent on learning or another book
And prayed for them most earnestly, returning
Thanks to them thus for paying for his learning.
His only care was study, and indeed
He never spoke a word more than was need,
Formal at that, respectful in the extreme,
Short, to the point, and lofty in his theme.
A tone of moral virtue filled his speech
And gladly would he learn, and gladly teach.

305. Aristotle's (ar′is·tät′′lz): reference to the Greek philosopher (384–322 B.C.).

306. psaltery (sôl′tər·ē) *n.:* stringed instrument that is plucked.

308. stone . . . gold: Alchemists at the time were searching for a stone that was supposed to turn ordinary metals into gold.

? **295–318.** *Which details in the sketch of the Oxford Cleric match the stereotype of the starving student? In what significant ways is the Oxford Cleric different from the Prioress, the Monk, and the Friar?*

The Lawyer

A *Sergeant at the Law* who paid his calls,
Wary and wise, for clients at St. Paul's°
There also was, of noted excellence.
Discreet he was, a man to reverence,
Or so he seemed, his sayings were so wise.
He often had been Justice of Assize
By letters patent,° and in full commission.
His fame and learning and his high position
Had won him many a robe and many a fee.
There was no such conveyancer° as he;
All was fee-simple° to his strong digestion,
Not one conveyance could be called in question.
Though there was nowhere one so busy as he,
He was less busy than he seemed to be.
He knew of every judgment, case, and crime

320. St. Paul's: London cathedral. Lawyers often met outside it to discuss their cases when courts were closed.

325. letters patent: letters from the king permitting people to act as judges at the Assizes, court sessions held periodically.

328. conveyancer *n.:* person who draws up documents transferring ownership of land. The Lawyer is transferring the ownership to himself.

329. fee-simple *n.* used as *adj.:* absolute ownership of real property; in other words, he took absolute possession of everything.

Ever recorded since King William's time.
He could dictate defenses or draft deeds;
No one could pinch a comma from his screeds°
And he knew every statute off by rote.
He wore a homely parti-colored° coat,
Girt with a silken belt of pin-stripe stuff;
Of his appearance I have said enough.

336. **screeds** *n. pl.:* tiresome, lengthy writings.

338. **parti-colored** *adj.:* multicolored.

The Franklin

There was a *Franklin*° with him, it appeared;
White as a daisy-petal was his beard.
A sanguine° man, high-colored and benign,
He loved a morning sop of cake in wine.
He lived for pleasure and had always done,
For he was Epicurus'° very son,
In whose opinion sensual delight
Was the one true felicity in sight.
As noted as St. Julian° was for bounty
He made his household free to all the County.
His bread, his ale were finest of the fine
And no one had a better stock of wine.
His house was never short of bake-meat pies,
Of fish and flesh, and these in such supplies
It positively snowed with meat and drink
And all the dainties that a man could think.
According to the seasons of the year
Changes of dish were ordered to appear.
He kept fat partridges in coops, beyond,
Many a bream and pike were in his pond.
Woe to the cook unless the sauce was hot
And sharp, or if he wasn't on the spot!
And in his hall a table stood arrayed
And ready all day long, with places laid.
As Justice at the Sessions° none stood higher;
He often had been Member for the Shire.°
A dagger and a little purse of silk
Hung at his girdle, white as morning milk.
As Sheriff he checked audit, every entry.
He was a model among landed gentry.

341. **Franklin:** well-to-do landowner who is not of the nobility.

343. **sanguine** (saŋ′gwin) *adj.:* ruddy-complexioned. In Chaucer's day this was considered a sign of a cheerful temperament; today the word signifies optimism.

346. **Epicurus':** Epicurus (341–270 B.C.), an ancient Greek philosopher, taught that the goal of life is pleasure, which is achieved through virtue and moderation. Most people came to think of Epicureans as pleasure seekers.

349. **St. Julian:** patron saint of hospitality.

365. **Justice at the Sessions:** judge at a court meeting.

366. **Member for the Shire:** county representative in Parliament.

Vocabulary

benign (bi•nīn′) *adj.:* kind; gracious.

The Franklin, from the Ellesmere manuscript.

Fol. 123v. By permission of The Huntington Library, San Marino, California.

The Cook, from the Ellesmere manuscript.

Fol. 47r. By permission of The Huntington Library, San Marino, California.

The Guildsmen

A *Haberdasher,*° a *Dyer,* a *Carpenter,*
A *Weaver,* and a *Carpet-maker* were
Among our ranks, all in the livery°
Of one impressive guild-fraternity.
They were so trim and fresh their gear would pass
For new. Their knives were not tricked out with brass
But wrought with purest silver, which avouches°
A like display on girdles and on pouches.
Each seemed a worthy burgess,° fit to grace
A guild-hall with a seat upon the dais.
Their wisdom would have justified a plan
To make each one of them an alderman;°
They had the capital and revenue,
Besides their wives declared it was their due.
And if they did not think so, then they ought;
To be called *"Madam"* is a glorious thought,
And so is going to church and being seen
Having your mantle carried, like a queen.

371. Haberdasher (hab′ər·dash′ər): seller of men's clothing and accessories.

373. livery *n.:* traditional uniform associated with a particular trade.

377. avouches (ə·vouch′iz) *v.:* guarantees.

379. burgess *n.:* citizen.

382. alderman *n.:* head of a guild and therefore a town-council member.

371–388. *Whose characters do you learn more about in these lines: the characters of the guildsmen or the characters of their wives? Explain.*

The Cook

They had a *Cook* with them who stood alone
For boiling chicken with a marrow-bone,
Sharp flavoring-powder and a spice for savor.
He could distinguish London ale by flavor,
And he could roast and seethe and broil and fry,
Make good thick soup, and bake a tasty pie.
But what a pity—so it seemed to me,
That he should have an ulcer on his knee.
As for blancmange,° he made it with the best.

397. blancmange (blə·mônzh′) *n.:* French for "white food." In Chaucer's day this was a sweet dish containing diced chicken, milk, sugar, and almonds.

The Skipper

There was a *Skipper* hailing from far west;
He came from Dartmouth, so I understood.
He rode a farmer's horse as best he could,
In a woollen gown that reached his knee.
A dagger on a lanyard° falling free

402. lanyard (lan′yərd) *n.:* cord.

Hung from his neck under his arm and down.
The summer heat had tanned his color brown,
And certainly he was an excellent fellow.
Many a draught of vintage, red and yellow,
He'd drawn at Bordeaux, while the trader snored.
The nicer rules of conscience he ignored.
If, when he fought, the enemy vessel sank,
He sent his prisoners home; they walked the plank.
As for his skill in reckoning his tides,
Currents, and many another risk besides,
Moons, harbors, pilots, he had such dispatch
That none from Hull to Carthage was his match.
Hardy he was, prudent in undertaking;
His beard in many a tempest had its shaking,
And he knew all the havens as they were
From Gottland to the Cape of Finisterre,
And every creek in Brittany and Spain;
The barge he owned was called *The Maudelayne.*

The Doctor

A *Doctor* too emerged as we proceeded;
No one alive could talk as well as he did
On points of medicine and of surgery,
For, being grounded in astronomy,
He watched his patient closely for the hours
When, by his horoscope, he knew the powers
Of favorable planets, then ascendent,
Worked on the images for his dependent.
The cause of every malady you'd got
He knew, and whether dry, cold, moist, or hot;°
He knew their seat, their humor and condition.
He was a perfect practicing physician.
These causes being known for what they were,
He gave the man his medicine then and there.
All his apothecaries° in a tribe
Were ready with the drugs he would prescribe
And each made money from the other's guile;
They had been friendly for a goodish while.
He was well-versed in Aesculapius° too
And what Hippocrates and Rufus knew
And Dioscorides, now dead and gone,
Galen and Rhazes, Hali, Serapion,

Vocabulary
guile (gīl) *n.:* sly dealings; skill in deceiving.

? 408–410. *Read these lines carefully. What does "sent his prisoners home" actually mean? How does this fit in with the narrator's observation about the Skipper: "The nicer rules of conscience he ignored"?*

The Physician, from the Ellesmere manuscript.

Fol. 133r. By permission of The Huntington Library, San Marino, California.

430. dry . . . hot: People of the time believed that one's physical and mental conditions were influenced by the balance of four major humors, or fluids, in the body—blood (hot and wet), yellow bile (hot and dry), phlegm (cold and wet), and black bile (cold and dry).
435. apothecaries: (ə·päth′ə·ker′ēz) *n. pl.:* pharmacists.
439. Aesculapius: in Greek and Roman mythology, the god of medicine. The names that follow were early Greek, Roman, Middle Eastern, and medieval medical authorities.

Averroes, Avicenna, Constantine,
Scotch Bernard, John of Gaddesden, Gilbertine.
In his own diet he observed some measure;
There were no superfluities° for pleasure,
Only digestives, nutritives and such.
He did not read the Bible very much.
In blood-red garments, slashed with bluish gray
And lined with taffeta, he rode his way;
Yet he was rather close as to expenses
And kept the gold he won in pestilences.
Gold stimulates the heart, or so we're told.
He therefore had a special love of gold.

The Wife of Bath

A worthy *woman* from beside *Bath* city
Was with us, somewhat deaf, which was a pity.
In making cloth she showed so great a bent
She bettered those of Ypres and of Ghent.°
In all the parish not a dame dared stir
Towards the altar steps in front of her,
And if indeed they did, so wrath was she
As to be quite put out of charity.
Her kerchiefs were of finely woven ground;°
I dared have sworn they weighed a good ten pound,
The ones she wore on Sunday, on her head.
Her hose were of the finest scarlet red
And gartered tight; her shoes were soft and new.
Bold was her face, handsome, and red in hue.
A worthy woman all her life, what's more
She'd had five husbands, all at the church door,
Apart from other company in youth;
No need just now to speak of that, forsooth.
And she had thrice been to Jerusalem,
Seen many strange rivers and passed over them;
She'd been to Rome and also to Boulogne,
St. James of Compostella and Cologne,
And she was skilled in wandering by the way.
She had gap-teeth,° set widely, truth to say.
Easily on an ambling horse she sat
Well wimpled° up, and on her head a hat
As broad as is a buckler or a shield;
She had a flowing mantle that concealed
Large hips, her heels spurred sharply under that.
In company she liked to laugh and chat
And knew the remedies for love's mischances,
An art in which she knew the oldest dances.

446. superfluities: (so͞o′pər·flo͞o′ə·tēz) *n. pl.:* excesses.

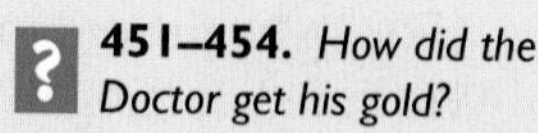
451–454. *How did the Doctor get his gold?*

458. Ypres (ē′pr′) **and of Ghent:** Flemish centers of the wool trade.

463. ground *n.:* type of cloth.

455–486. *Does the Wife of Bath remind you of any comic female stereotypes? Explain.*

478. gap-teeth: In Chaucer's time, gap-teeth on a woman were considered a sign of boldness and were said to indicate an aptitude for love and travel.
480. wimpled *adj.:* A wimple is a linen covering for the head and neck.

The Parson

A holy-minded man of good renown
There was, and poor, the *Parson* to a town,
Yet he was rich in holy thought and work.
He also was a learned man, a clerk,
Who truly knew Christ's gospel and would preach it
Devoutly to parishioners, and teach it.
Benign and wonderfully diligent,
And patient when adversity was sent
(For so he proved in much adversity)
He hated cursing to extort a fee,
Nay rather he preferred beyond a doubt
Giving to poor parishioners round about
Both from church offerings and his property;
He could in little find sufficiency.
Wide was his parish, with houses far asunder,
Yet he neglected not in rain or thunder,
In sickness or in grief, to pay a call
On the remotest, whether great or small,
Upon his feet, and in his hand a stave.°
This noble example to his sheep° he gave
That first he wrought, and afterward he taught;
And it was from the Gospel he had caught
Those words, and he would add this figure too,
That if gold rust, what then will iron do?
For if a priest be foul in whom we trust
No wonder that a common man should rust;
And shame it is to see—let priests take stock—
A shitten shepherd and a snowy flock.
The true example that a priest should give
Is one of cleanness, how the sheep should live.
He did not set his benefice to hire°
And leave his sheep encumbered in the mire
Or run to London to earn easy bread
By singing masses for the wealthy dead,
Or find some Brotherhood and get enrolled.°
He stayed at home and watched over his fold
So that no wolf should make the sheep miscarry.
He was a shepherd and no mercenary.°
Holy and virtuous he was, but then
Never contemptuous of sinful men,
Never disdainful, never too proud or fine,
But was discreet in teaching and benign.
His business was to show a fair behavior
And draw men thus to Heaven and their Savior,

The Parson, from the Ellesmere manuscript.

Fol. 206v. By permission of The Huntington Library, San Marino, California.

505. stave *n.:* staff.

506. sheep *n. pl.:* his parishioners.

487–538. *Contrast the Parson with the Monk and Friar described earlier. Which of the three characters does the narrator present as a true man of God?*

517. He . . . benefice to hire: He did not hire someone else to perform his duties.

521. find . . . enrolled: He did not take a job as a paid chaplain to a guild.

524. mercenary *n.:* someone who will agree to do anything for money.

Unless indeed a man were obstinate;
And such, whether of high or low estate,°
He put to sharp rebuke, to say the least.
I think there never was a better priest.
He sought no pomp or glory in his dealings,
No scrupulosity had spiced his feelings.
Christ and His Twelve Apostles and their lore
He taught, but followed it himself before.

The Plowman

There was a *Plowman* with him there, his brother;
Many a load of dung one time or other
He must have carted through the morning dew.
He was an honest worker, good and true,
Living in peace and perfect charity,
And, as the gospel bade him, so did he,
Loving God best with all his heart and mind
And then his neighbor as himself, repined
At no misfortune, slacked for no content,
For steadily about his work he went
To thrash his corn, to dig or to manure
Or make a ditch; and he would help the poor
For love of Christ and never take a penny
If he could help it, and, as prompt as any,
He paid his tithes in full when they were due
On what he owned, and on his earnings too.
He wore a tabard smock° and rode a mare.
There was a *Reeve,*° also a *Miller*, there,
A College *Manciple*° from the Inns of Court,
A papal *Pardoner*° and, in close consort,
A Church-Court *Summoner,*° riding at a trot,
And finally myself—that was the lot.

The Miller

The *Miller* was a chap of sixteen stone,°
A great stout fellow big in brawn and bone.
He did well out of them, for he could go
And win the ram at any wrestling show.
Broad, knotty, and short-shouldered, he would boast
He could heave any door off hinge and post,
Or take a run and break it with his head.
His beard, like any sow or fox, was red
And broad as well, as though it were a spade;

Vocabulary

obstinate (äbʹstə • nət) *adj.:* unreasonably stubborn.

532. estate *n.:* rank; social standing.

The Miller, from the Ellesmere manuscript.

Fol. 34v. By permission of The Huntington Library, San Marino, California.

539–555. *How is the Plowman like his brother, the Parson? How can you tell that the narrator approves of him?*

555. tabard (tabʹərd) **smock:** short jacket.
556. Reeve: serf who was the steward of a manor. A reeve saw that the estate's work was done and that everything was accounted for.
557. Manciple (manʹsə • pəl): minor employee whose principal duty was to purchase provisions for a college or law firm.
558. Pardoner: minor member of the Church who bought and sold pardons for sinners.
559. Summoner: low-ranking officer who summoned people to appear in church court.
561. sixteen stone: 224 pounds.

The Manciple, from the Ellesmere manuscript.

Fol. 203r. By permission of The Huntington Library, San Marino, California.

The Reeve, from the Ellesmere manuscript.

Fol. 42r. By permission of The Huntington Library, San Marino, California.

And, at its very tip, his nose displayed
A wart on which there stood a tuft of hair
Red as the bristles in an old sow's ear.
His nostrils were as black as they were wide.
He had a sword and buckler at his side,
His mighty mouth was like a furnace door.
A wrangler and buffoon, he had a store
Of tavern stories, filthy in the main.
His was a master-hand at stealing grain.
He felt it with his thumb and thus he knew
Its quality and took three times his due—
A thumb of gold, by God, to gauge an oat!°
He wore a hood of blue and a white coat.
He liked to play his bagpipes up and down
And that was how he brought us out of town.

? **568–575.** *Are any of the comparisons that the narrator makes flattering to the character of the Miller? Explain.*

581. thumb . . . oat: In other words, he pressed on the scale with his thumb to increase the weight of the grain.

The Manciple

The *Manciple* came from the Inner Temple;°
All caterers might follow his example
In buying victuals; he was never rash
Whether he bought on credit or paid cash.
He used to watch the market most precisely
And got in first, and so he did quite nicely.
Now isn't it a marvel of God's grace
That an illiterate fellow can outpace
The wisdom of a heap of learned men?
His masters—he had more than thirty then—
All versed in the abstrusest° legal knowledge,
Could have produced a dozen from their College
Fit to be stewards in land and rents and game
To any Peer in England you could name,
And show him how to live on what he had

585. Inner Temple: one of the four legal societies in London comprising the Inns of Court. Only the Inns were permitted to license lawyers.

595. abstrusest (ab · stro͞os′est) *adj.:* most complex; hardest to understand.

Debt-free (unless of course the Peer were mad)
Or be as frugal as he might desire,
And make them fit to help about the Shire
In any legal case there was to try;
And yet this Manciple could wipe their eye.°

The Reeve

The *Reeve* was old and choleric° and thin;
His beard was shaven closely to the skin,
His shorn hair came abruptly to a stop
Above his ears, and he was docked° on top
Just like a priest in front; his legs were lean,
Like sticks they were, no calf was to be seen.
He kept his bins and garners° very trim;
No auditor could gain a point on him.
And he could judge by watching drought and rain
The yield he might expect from seed and grain.
His master's sheep, his animals and hens,
Pigs, horses, dairies, stores, and cattle-pens
Were wholly trusted to his government.
He had been under contract to present
The accounts, right from his master's earliest years.
No one had ever caught him in arrears.°
No bailiff,° serf, or herdsman dared to kick,
He knew their dodges, knew their every trick;
Feared like the plague he was, by those beneath.
He had a lovely dwelling on a heath,
Shadowed in green by trees above the sward.°
A better hand at bargains than his lord,
He had grown rich and had a store of treasure
Well tucked away, yet out it came to pleasure
His lord with subtle loans or gifts of goods,
To earn his thanks and even coats and hoods.
When young he'd learnt a useful trade and still
He was a carpenter of first-rate skill.
The stallion-cob° he rode at a slow trot
Was dapple-gray and bore the name of Scot.
He wore an overcoat of bluish shade
And rather long; he had a rusty blade
Slung at his side. He came, as I heard tell,
From Norfolk, near a place called Baldeswell.
His coat was tucked under his belt and splayed.
He rode the hindmost of our cavalcade.

Vocabulary
frugal (fro͞o′gəl) *adj.:* thrifty; careful with money.

604. wipe their eye: outdo them. This medieval idiom means something like "steal their thunder" or "show them up."

605. choleric (käl′ər·ik) *adj.:* having too much choler, or yellow bile, and thus (supposedly) bad-tempered.

608. docked *adj.:* clipped short.

611. garners *n. pl.:* granaries.

620. in arrears: behind schedule in paying back debts.

621. bailiff *n.:* here, farm manager.

625. sward (swôrd) *n.:* lawn.

633. stallion-cob: stocky male riding horse.

The Summoner

There was a *Summoner*° with us at that Inn,
His face on fire, like a cherubim,°
For he had carbuncles.° His eyes were narrow,
He was as hot and lecherous as a sparrow.
Black scabby brows he had, and a thin beard.
Children were afraid when he appeared.
No quicksilver, lead ointment, tartar creams,
No brimstone, no boracic, so it seems,
Could make a salve that had the power to bite,
Clean up, or cure his whelks° of knobby white
Or purge the pimples sitting on his cheeks.
Garlic he loved, and onions too, and leeks,
And drinking strong red wine till all was hazy.
Then he would shout and jabber as if crazy,
And wouldn't speak a word except in Latin
When he was drunk, such tags as he was pat in;
He only had a few, say two or three,
That he had mugged up out of some decree;
No wonder, for he heard them every day.
And, as you know, a man can teach a jay°
To call out "Walter" better than the Pope.
But had you tried to test his wits and grope
For more, you'd have found nothing in the bag.
Then *"Questio quid juris"*° was his tag.
He was a noble varlet° and a kind one,
You'd meet none better if you went to find one.
Why, he'd allow—just for a quart of wine—
Any good lad to keep a concubine
A twelvemonth and dispense him altogether!
And he had finches of his own to feather:°
And if he found some rascal with a maid
He would instruct him not to be afraid
In such a case of the Archdeacon's curse
(Unless the rascal's soul were in his purse)
For in his purse the punishment should be.
"Purse is the good Archdeacon's Hell," said he.
But well I know he lied in what he said;
A curse should put a guilty man in dread,
For curses kill, as shriving brings, salvation.
We should beware of excommunication.
Thus, as he pleased, the man could bring duress
On any young fellow in the diocese.

Vocabulary

duress (do͞o•res′) *n.:* pressure.

641. Summoner: A summoner delivers summonses that call people to appear in church courts.
642. cherubim *n.:* in medieval art, a little angel with a rosy face.
643. carbuncles (kär′bun′kəlz) *n. pl.:* pus-filled skin inflammations, something like boils.

650. whelks *n. pl.:* pus-filled sores.

? **641–666.** *How does the Summoner's physical appearance (lines 642–651) match his inner character? How do you know that Chaucer is being ironic in lines 665–666?*

660. jay *n.:* type of bird.

664. *Questio quid juris* (kwest′ē • ō kwid yo͞o′ris): Latin for "I ask what point of the law [applies]." The Summoner uses this phrase to stall and dodge the issue.
665. varlet (vär′lit) *n.:* scoundrel.

670. finches . . . feather: a maxim that means roughly the same as "feathering one's nest"—taking care of one's own interests.

The Summoner, from the Ellesmere manuscript.

Fol. 81r. The Huntington Library, San Marino, CA.

The Pardoner, from the Ellesmere manuscript.

Fol. 138r. By permission of The Huntington Library, San Marino, California.

He knew their secrets, they did what he said.
He wore a garland set upon his head
Large as the holly-bush upon a stake
Outside an ale-house, and he had a cake,
A round one, which it was his joke to wield
As if it were intended for a shield.

The Pardoner

He and a gentle *Pardoner* rode together,
A bird from Charing Cross of the same feather,
Just back from visiting the Court of Rome.
He loudly sang *"Come hither, love, come home!"*
The Summoner sang deep seconds° to this song,
No trumpet ever sounded half so strong.
This Pardoner had hair as yellow as wax,
Hanging down smoothly like a hank of flax.
In driblets fell his locks behind his head
Down to his shoulders which they overspread;
Thinly they fell, like rat-tails, one by one.
He wore no hood upon his head, for fun;
The hood inside his wallet had been stowed,
He aimed at riding in the latest mode;
But for a little cap his head was bare
And he had bulging eye-balls, like a hare.
He'd sewed a holy relic° on his cap;
His wallet lay before him on his lap,
Brimful of pardons° come from Rome, all hot.
He had the same small voice a goat has got.
His chin no beard had harbored, nor would harbor,
Smoother than ever chin was left by barber.
I judge he was a gelding, or a mare.
As to his trade, from Berwick down to Ware
There was no pardoner of equal grace,
For in his trunk he had a pillow-case
Which he asserted was Our Lady's veil.
He said he had a gobbet° of the sail
Saint Peter had the time when he made bold
To walk the waves, till Jesu Christ took hold.
He had a cross of metal set with stones
And, in a glass, a rubble of pigs' bones.
And with these relics, any time he found
Some poor up-country parson to astound,
In one short day, in money down, he drew

693. deep seconds: harmonies.

A Pardoner dispensed pardons granted by the pope.

? **689–704.** *How do such details as "driblets," "like rat-tails," "yellow as wax," and "bulging eye-balls, like a hare" affect the way you feel about this man?*

705. relic *n.:* remains of a saint.

707. pardons *n. pl.:* small strips of parchment with papal seals attached. They were sold as indulgences (pardons for sins), with the proceeds supposedly going to a religious house.

716. gobbet *n.:* fragment.

? **714–734.** *These lines depict the Pardoner as a scam artist. Why do people fall for his tricks?*

More than the parson in a month or two,
And by his flatteries and prevarication°
Made monkeys of the priest and congregation.
But still to do him justice first and last
In church he was a noble ecclesiast.°
How well he read a lesson or told a story!
But best of all he sang an Offertory,°
For well he knew that when that song was sung
He'd have to preach and tune his honey-tongue
And (well he could) win silver from the crowd.
That's why he sang so merrily and loud.
  Now I have told you shortly, in a clause,
The rank, the array, the number, and the cause
Of our assembly in this company
In Southwark, at that high-class hostelry
Known as *The Tabard,* close beside *The Bell.*
And now the time has come for me to tell
How we behaved that evening; I'll begin
After we had alighted at the Inn,
Then I'll report our journey, stage by stage,
All the remainder of our pilgrimage.
But first I beg of you, in courtesy,
Not to condemn me as unmannerly
If I speak plainly and with no concealings
And give account of all their words and dealings,
Using their very phrases as they fell.
For certainly, as you all know so well,
He who repeats a tale after a man
Is bound to say, as nearly as he can,
Each single word, if he remembers it,
However rudely spoken or unfit,
Or else the tale he tells will be untrue,
The things pretended and the phrases new.
He may not flinch although it were his brother,
He may as well say one word as another.
And Christ Himself spoke broad in Holy Writ,
Yet there is no scurrility° in it,
And Plato says, for those with power to read,
"The word should be as cousin to the deed."
Further I beg you to forgive it me
If I neglect the order and degree
And what is due to rank in what I've planned.
I'm short of wit as you will understand.

725. prevarication (pri•var′i•kā′shən) *n.:* telling lies.

728. ecclesiast (e•klē′zē•ast) *n.:* practitioner of church ritual.

730. Offertory *n.:* hymn sung while offerings are collected in church.

? **740–744.** *How will the narrator organize the rest of his narrative?*

? **745–766.** *What is the narrator apologizing for in advance?*

760. scurrility (skə•ril′ə•tē) *n.:* indecency.

The Host

Our *Host* gave us great welcome; everyone
Was given a place and supper was begun.
He served the finest victuals you could think,
The wine was strong and we were glad to drink.
A very striking man our Host withal,
And fit to be a marshal in a hall.
His eyes were bright, his girth a little wide;
There is no finer burgess in Cheapside.°
Bold in his speech, yet wise and full of tact,
There was no manly attribute he lacked,
What's more he was a merry-hearted man.
After our meal he jokingly began
To talk of sport, and, among other things
After we'd settled up our reckonings,
He said as follows: "Truly, gentlemen,
You're very welcome and I can't think when
—Upon my word I'm telling you no lie—
I've seen a gathering here that looked so spry,
No, not this year, as in this tavern now.
I'd think you up some fun if I knew how.
And, as it happens, a thought has just occurred
To please you, costing nothing, on my word.
You're off to Canterbury—well, God speed!
Blessed St. Thomas answer to your need!
And I don't doubt, before the journey's done
You mean to while the time in tales and fun.
Indeed, there's little pleasure for your bones
Riding along and all as dumb as stones.
So let me then propose for your enjoyment,
Just as I said, a suitable employment.
And if my notion suits and you agree
And promise to submit yourselves to me
Playing your parts exactly as I say
Tomorrow as you ride along the way,
Then by my father's soul (and he is dead)
If you don't like it you can have my head!
Hold up your hands, and not another word."
Well, our opinion was not long deferred,
It seemed not worth a serious debate;
We all agreed to it at any rate
And bade him issue what commands he would.
"My lords," he said, "now listen for your good,
And please don't treat my notion with disdain.
This is the point. I'll make it short and plain.
Each one of you shall help to make things slip
By telling two stories on the outward trip

774. Cheapside: district of medieval London.

771–779. *What do you learn about the Host in these lines? How do you think the narrator feels about the Host?*

781–803. *What do words like* fun *(line 786),* pleasure *(line 793), and* enjoyment *(line 795) suggest about the Host's character?*

To Canterbury, that's what I intend,
And, on the homeward way to journey's end
Another two, tales from the days of old;
And then the man whose story is best told,
That is to say who gives the fullest measure
Of good morality and general pleasure,
He shall be given a supper, paid by all,
Here in this tavern, in this very hall,
When we come back again from Canterbury.
And in the hope to keep you bright and merry
I'll go along with you myself and ride
All at my own expense and serve as guide.
I'll be the judge, and those who won't obey
Shall pay for what we spend upon the way.
Now if you all agree to what you've heard
Tell me at once without another word,
And I will make arrangements early for it."
Of course we all agreed, in fact we swore it
Delightedly, and made entreaty° too
That he should act as he proposed to do,
Become our Governor in short, and be
Judge of our tales and general referee,
And set the supper at a certain price.
We promised to be ruled by his advice
Come high, come low; unanimously thus
We set him up in judgment over us.
More wine was fetched, the business being done;
We drank it off and up went everyone
To bed without a moment of delay.
Early next morning at the spring of day
Up rose our Host and roused us like a cock,
Gathering us together in a flock,
And off we rode at slightly faster pace
Than walking to St. Thomas' watering-place;
And there our Host drew up, began to ease
His horse, and said, "Now, listen if you please,
My lords! Remember what you promised me.
If evensong and matins will agree°
Let's see who shall be first to tell a tale.
And as I hope to drink good wine and ale
I'll be your judge. The rebel who disobeys,
However much the journey costs, he pays.
Now draw for cut° and then we can depart;
The man who draws the shortest cut shall start."

? ***811–829.*** *Summarize the rules the Host proposes for the storytelling competition. What's the prize? Who will be the judge?*

825. By "those who won't obey," the Host means those who won't play the game of telling a story when it's their turn. Lines 853–854 further clarify their penalty: Those who won't obey must pay the cost of the entire journey.

831. entreaty *n.:* urgent request.

850. If . . . agree: in other words, if you feel the same way in the evening (at evensong, or evening prayers) as you do in the morning (at matins, or morning prayers).

855. draw for cut: in other words, draw straws.

Response and Analysis

Reading Check

1. When do people "long to go on pilgrimages"?
2. Where is the narrator at the very beginning of the Prologue? Who joins him, and for what purpose?
3. Place each pilgrim within one of these three groups that comprised medieval society: the feudal system (related to the land), the Church, and the city (merchants and professionals).
4. What plan (which becomes the basis of the **frame story**) does the Host propose to the pilgrims? How do the pilgrims respond to his proposal?

Thinking Critically

5. Chaucer is a master at using physical details—eyes, hair, complexion, body type, clothing—to reveal **character.** Describe at least three pilgrims whose inner natures are revealed by their appearance. Refer to your reading notes for help.

Figure thought to be Chaucer; from the Ellesmere manuscript.

Fol. 153v. By permission of The Huntington Library, San Marino, California.

6. Clearly Chaucer **satirizes** the Church of his time. Show how this is true by analyzing two characters connected with the Church. What "good," or honorable, Church people does Chaucer include to balance his satire?
7. What aspects of medieval society does Chaucer **satirize** in his portrayals of the Merchant? of the Franklin? of the Doctor? of the Miller?
8. Which pilgrims do you think Chaucer idealizes?
9. In describing the pilgrims, what has Chaucer as the pilgrim-narrator revealed about his own personality, biases, and values?
10. Which of the pilgrims' professions or trades have survived and exist in society today? Which of Chaucer's character types can be seen today in airports, on pulpits, on farms, in classrooms, on city streets, or in small towns?

WRITING

A Frame Story

Write your own prologue to a modern frame story. Set your frame story in an airport or a bus station where people are waiting or on a tour or a pilgrimage like the ones described in the Closer Look on page 150. Or you might choose to establish your frame by using people stranded by a storm or waiting for rescue from an accident. You will have to decide who your narrator will be and who the travelers will be and what their professions are. Model your prologue on Chaucer's, and describe your travelers in such a way that their inner natures are revealed.

Pages 165–166 cover

Literary Skills Analyze characterization. Analyze characteristics of a frame story. Analyze imagery in characterization.

Reading Skills Analyze style using key details.

Writing Skills Write a prologue to a modern frame story.

Vocabulary Skills Create semantic maps with antonyms.

INTERNET

Projects and Activities

Keyword: LE7 12-2

Vocabulary Development

Antonym Map

agility	guile
eminent	obstinate
accrue	frugal
arbitrate	duress
benign	

Create an antonym map like the one below for each Vocabulary word. First, choose an appropriate antonym for each word in the list. Then, write two sentences based on the Prologue or your responses to it. In the first sentence, use the Vocabulary word. In the second sentence, use the antonym you chose.

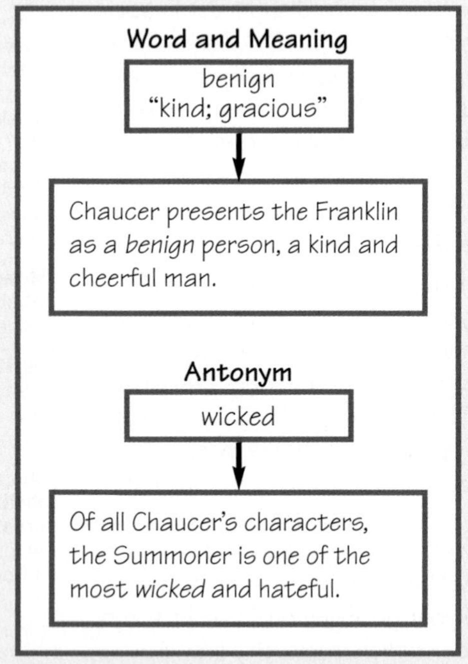

Word and Meaning
benign
"kind; gracious"
Chaucer presents the Franklin as a benign person, a kind and cheerful man.
Antonym
wicked
Of all Chaucer's characters, the Summoner is one of the most wicked and hateful.

Literary Focus

Imagery and Character

Chaucer is a master of **imagery,** language that appeals to the senses. Most images are visual, but imagery can also appeal to our sense of hearing, smell, taste, or touch. In a few vivid words, sometimes using figures of speech, Chaucer creates a cast of characters as real to us as the characters in the latest novel—more real, perhaps, because Chaucer's pilgrims exhibit all the essentials of human nature.

Chaucer relies on his readers' knowledge of physiognomy. Based on some of Aristotle's treatises, physiognomy compares varieties of people with animals and asserts that certain physical characteristics reveal one's true character. Thus, when Chaucer's contemporaries read that the Wife of Bath had "gap-teeth, set widely, truth to say," they knew that the physiognomists believed that a gap between a woman's two front teeth indicated not only that she would travel far but also that she was bold and amorous.

Analyzing Chaucer's imagery. Below is a list of a few physical characteristics and their corresponding physiognomic interpretations. Choose a pilgrim who exhibits each characteristic. How does the physiognomic interpretation reinforce what you already know about the character's nature?

- ramlike appearance = strength
- flaring nostrils = anger
- foxlike appearance = slyness
- high forehead = intelligence
- infected sores = lechery

How do writers reveal character types today? In stories or movies, do any physical features automatically suggest something about character?

Before You Read

from The Pardoner's Tale

Make the Connection

The story in "The Pardoner's Tale" has roots that are old and widespread. Greed as the root of evil is a theme that appears in stories the world over. Starting from the Latin saying *"Radix malorum est cupiditas"*—translated loosely as "The love of money is the root of all evil"—the Pardoner presents us with an **exemplum,** an anecdote that teaches a moral lesson. As in all the tales, Chaucer fits the story to the character of the storyteller. (You may wish to review the description of the Pardoner in lines 689–734 of the general Prologue.)

Literary Focus

Irony

Chaucer is a master of both verbal and situational irony. You use both types of irony yourself all the time. You use **verbal irony** when you say one thing but mean something else. When a friend asks how you liked spending three hours cleaning your room, you might answer, "It was just great." You both know that was not the case, of course. In **situational irony,** what actually happens is different from what you expect. Situational irony occurs when it rains on the weather forecasters' picnic or when the police officer's son robs the bank.

Irony is a contrast or a discrepancy between expectations and reality—between what is said and what is meant, between what is expected and what happens, or between what appears to be true and what actually is true.

For more on Irony, see the Handbook of Literary and Historical Terms.

Background

In the medieval Church, a pardoner was a member of the clergy who had been given power by the pope to forgive sins and grant indulgences. Even when their sins were forgiven in this earthly life, however, many believed that punishment for their sinful deeds awaited them in the next life. Indulgences could help alleviate this problem: They were promises made by the Church to reduce the length and severity of punishments due after death. Forgiving sins and granting indulgences were powers the Church gave the clergy for the spiritual benefit of believers. Such benefits were not supposed to be bought and sold, but greedy clergy sometimes took advantage of people's fear of punishment to demand money. Some, like Chaucer's Pardoner, went so far as to keep the money for themselves instead of turning it over to the Church.

Vocabulary Development

avarice (av′ə • ris) *n.:* too great a desire for wealth.

abominable (ə • bäm′ə • nə • bəl) *adj.:* disgusting; hateful.

superfluity (so͞o′pər • flo͞o′ə • tē) *n.:* excess.

grisly (griz′lē) *adj.:* terrifying.

adversary (ad′vər • ser′ē) *n.:* enemy.

pallor (pal′ər) *n.:* paleness.

prudent (pro͞o′dənt) *adj.:* careful; cautious.

transcend (tran • send′) *v.:* exceed; surpass.

credentials (kri • den′shəlz) *n.:* evidence of a person's position.

absolve (ab • zälv′) *v.:* forgive; make free from blame.

Literary Skills
Understand irony, including verbal and situational irony.

INTERNET

Vocabulary Practice

•

More About Geoffrey Chaucer

•

Keyword: LE7 12-2

The Pardoner, from the Ellesmere manuscript.

Fol. 138r. By permission of The Huntington Library, San Marino, California.

from The Pardoner's Tale

Geoffrey Chaucer

translated by **Nevill Coghill**

from The Pardoner's Prologue

"But let me briefly make my purpose plain;
I preach for nothing but for greed of gain
And use the same old text, as bold as brass,
Radix malorum est cupiditas.°
And thus I preach against the very vice
I make my living out of—avarice.
And yet however guilty of that sin
Myself, with others I have power to win
Them from it, I can bring them to repent;
But that is not my principal intent.
Covetousness° is both the root and stuff
Of all I preach. That ought to be enough.
"Well, then I give examples thick and fast
From bygone times, old stories from the past.
A yokel° mind loves stories from of old,
Being the kind it can repeat and hold.
What! Do you think, as long as I can preach
And get their silver for the things I teach,
That I will live in poverty, from choice?
That's not the counsel of my inner voice!
No! Let me preach and beg from kirk° to kirk
And never do an honest job of work,
No, nor make baskets, like St. Paul, to gain
A livelihood. I do not preach in vain.
There's no apostle I would counterfeit;
I mean to have money, wool and cheese and wheat
Though it were given me by the poorest lad

4. *Radix malorum est cupiditas* (rā′diks ma•lō′rum est ko͞o•pi′di•tas): literally, "The root of evil is desire" (1 Timothy 6:10). The Pardoner has been telling the pilgrims about his preaching methods.

11. Covetousness (kuv′ət•əs•nis) *n.:* quality of craving wealth or possessions; greed.

15. yokel *n.* used as *adj.:* rustic; of the country.

21. kirk *n.:* Scottish for "church."

Vocabulary

avarice (av′ə•ris) *n.:* too great a desire for wealth.

Or poorest village widow, though she had
A string of starving children, all agape.°
No, let me drink the liquor of the grape
And keep a jolly wench in every town!
"But listen, gentlemen; to bring things down
To a conclusion, would you like a tale?
Now as I've drunk a draft of corn-ripe ale,
By God it stands to reason I can strike
On some good story that you all will like.
For though I am a wholly vicious° man
Don't think I can't tell moral tales. I can!
Here's one I often preach when out for winning;
Now please be quiet. Here is the beginning."

29. **agape** *adj.:* open-mouthed.

37. **vicious** *adj.:* here, possessing many faults.

The Pardoner's Tale

In Flanders once there was a company
Of youngsters haunting vice and ribaldry,°
Riot and gambling, stews and public-houses
Where each with harp, guitar, or lute carouses,°
Dancing and dicing° day and night, and bold
To eat and drink far more than they can hold,
Doing thereby the devil sacrifice
Within that devil's temple of cursed vice,
Abominable in superfluity,
With oaths so damnable in blasphemy°
That it's a grisly thing to hear them swear.
Our dear Lord's body they will rend and tear.°. . .
It's of three rioters° I have to tell
Who, long before the morning service bell,
Were sitting in a tavern for a drink.
And as they sat, they heard the hand-bell clink
Before a coffin going to the grave;
One of them called the little tavern-knave°
And said "Go and find out at once—look spry!—
Whose corpse is in that coffin passing by;
And see you get the name correctly too."
"Sir," said the boy, "no need, I promise you;
Two hours before you came here I was told.
He was a friend of yours in days of old,
And suddenly, last night, the man was slain,
Upon his bench, face up, dead drunk again.
There came a privy° thief, they call him Death,

42. **ribaldry** (rib′əl•drē) *n.:* vulgar language or humor.

44. **carouses** (kə•rouz′ez) *v.:* drinks and celebrates noisily.

45. **dicing** *v.:* gambling (throwing dice).

50. **blasphemy** (blas′fə•mē) *n.:* mockery of God.

52. **Our . . . tear:** Their oaths refer to "God's arms" and "God's blessed bones."

53. **rioters** *n. pl.:* people living a wild, unrestrained lifestyle.

58. **tavern-knave:** serving boy.

67. **privy** (priv′ē) *adj.:* archaic usage meaning "secretive; furtive."

Vocabulary

abominable (ə•bäm′ə•nə•bəl) *adj.:* disgusting; hateful.
superfluity (so͞o′pər•flo͞o′ə•tē) *n.:* excess.
grisly (griz′lē) *adj.:* terrifying.

Who kills us all round here, and in a breath
He speared him through the heart, he never stirred.
And then Death went his way without a word.
He's killed a thousand in the present plague,°
And, sir, it doesn't do to be too vague
If you should meet him; you had best be wary.
Be on your guard with such an adversary,
Be primed to meet him everywhere you go,
That's what my mother said. It's all I know."
The publican° joined in with, "By St. Mary,
What the child says is right; you'd best be wary,
This very year he killed, in a large village
A mile away, man, woman, serf at tillage,°
Page in the household, children—all there were.
Yes, I imagine that he lives round there.
It's well to be prepared in these alarms,°
He might do you dishonor." "Huh, God's arms!"
The rioter said, "Is he so fierce to meet?
I'll search for him, by Jesus, street by street.
God's blessed bones! I'll register a vow!
Here, chaps! The three of us together now,
Hold up your hands, like me, and we'll be brothers
In this affair, and each defend the others,
And we will kill this traitor Death, I say!
Away with him as he has made away
With all our friends. God's dignity! Tonight!"
They made their bargain, swore with appetite,
These three, to live and die for one another
As brother-born might swear to his born brother.
And up they started in their drunken rage
And made towards this village which the page
And publican had spoken of before.
Many and grisly were the oaths they swore,
Tearing Christ's blessed body to a shred;
"If we can only catch him, Death is dead!"
When they had gone not fully half a mile,
Just as they were about to cross a stile,°
They came upon a very poor old man
Who humbly greeted them and thus began,
"God look to you, my lords, and give you quiet!"
To which the proudest of these men of riot
Gave back the answer, "What, old fool? Give place!
Why are you all wrapped up except your face?
Why live so long? Isn't it time to die?"

Vocabulary

adversary (ad′vər• ser′ē) *n.:* enemy.

71. present plague: the Black Death, which killed nearly one third of the population of England during the mid–fourteenth century.

77. publican *n.:* tavern keeper; from *public house,* an inn or tavern.

80. tillage *n.:* working the land.

83. alarms *n. pl.:* here, anxious times.

104. stile *n.:* steps used for climbing over a wall.

The old, old fellow looked him in the eye
And said, "Because I never yet have found,
Though I have walked to India, searching round
Village and city on my pilgrimage,
One who would change his youth to have my age.
And so my age is mine and must be still
Upon me, for such time as God may will.
"Not even Death, alas, will take my life;
So, like a wretched prisoner at strife
Within himself, I walk alone and wait
About the earth, which is my mother's gate,°
Knock-knocking with my staff from night to noon
And crying, 'Mother, open to me soon!
Look at me, mother, won't you let me in?
See how I wither, flesh and blood and skin!
Alas! When will these bones be laid to rest?
Mother, I would exchange—for that were best—
The wardrobe in my chamber, standing there
So long, for yours! Aye, for a shirt of hair°
To wrap me in!' She has refused her grace,
Whence comes the pallor of my withered face.
"But it dishonored you when you began
To speak so roughly, sir, to an old man,
Unless he had injured you in word or deed.
It says in holy writ,° as you may read,
'Thou shalt rise up before the hoary° head
And honor it.' And therefore be it said,
'Do no more harm to an old man than you,
Being now young, would have another do
When you are old'—if you should live till then.
And so may God be with you, gentlemen,
For I must go whither I have to go."
"By God," the gambler said, "you shan't do so,
You don't get off so easy, by St. John!
I heard you mention, just a moment gone,
A certain traitor Death who singles out
And kills the fine young fellows hereabout.
And you're his spy, by God! You wait a bit.
Say where he is or you shall pay for it,
By God and by the Holy Sacrament!
I say you've joined together by consent
To kill us younger folk, you thieving swine!"
"Well, sirs," he said, "if it be your design
To find out Death, turn up this crooked way

Vocabulary

pallor (pal′ər) *n.:* paleness.

122. mother's gate: The old man is personifying Death as a mother, her house surrounded by a gate (the earth). Thus, "mother's gate" is the entrance to the grave.

130. shirt of hair: Coarse shirts of woven horsehair were worn as penance. Here, the old man refers to such a shirt used to wrap his body for burial.

136. holy writ: the Bible.

137. hoary *adj.:* white.

The Three Living, the Three Dead, from the *Psalter and Prayer Book of Bonne of Luxembourg, Duchess of Normandy* (before 1349). Fol. 321v.–322r. Tempera, grisaille, ink, and gold leaf on vellum. (4 5/16 × 3 9/16 in. (12.5 × 9.1 cm).

Towards that grove, I left him there today
Under a tree, and there you'll find him waiting.
He isn't one to hide for all your prating.°
You see that oak? He won't be far to find.
And God protect you that redeemed mankind,
Aye, and amend° you!" Thus that ancient man.
At once the three young rioters began
To run, and reached the tree, and there they found
A pile of golden florins° on the ground,
New-coined, eight bushels of them as they thought.
No longer was it Death those fellows sought,
For they were all so thrilled to see the sight,
The florins were so beautiful and bright,
That down they sat beside the precious pile.
The wickedest spoke first after a while.
"Brothers," he said, "you listen to what I say.
I'm pretty sharp although I joke away.
It's clear that Fortune has bestowed this treasure
To let us live in jollity and pleasure.
Light come, light go! We'll spend it as we ought.
God's precious dignity! Who would have thought
This morning was to be our lucky day?
"If one could only get the gold away,
Back to my house, or else to yours, perhaps—
For as you know, the gold is ours, chaps—
We'd all be at the top of fortune, hey?
But certainly it can't be done by day.
People would call us robbers—a strong gang,
So our own property would make us hang.
No, we must bring this treasure back by night
Some prudent way, and keep it out of sight.
And so as a solution I propose
We draw for lots and see the way it goes;
The one who draws the longest, lucky man,
Shall run to town as quickly as he can
To fetch us bread and wine—but keep things dark°—
While two remain in hiding here to mark
Our heap of treasure. If there's no delay,
When night comes down we'll carry it away,
All three of us, wherever we have planned."
He gathered lots and hid them in his hand
Bidding them draw for where the luck should fall.
It fell upon the youngest of them all,
And off he ran at once towards the town.

158. prating *n.:* chattering.

161. amend *v.:* improve.

164. florins *n. pl.:* coins worth twenty-four pence. *Pence* is the British plural of *penny.*

191. keep things dark: do it in secret.

Vocabulary

prudent (pro͞o′dənt) *adj.:* careful; cautious.

As soon as he had gone the first sat down
And thus began a parley° with the other:
"You know that you can trust me as a brother;
Now let me tell you where your profit lies;
You know our friend has gone to get supplies
And here's a lot of gold that is to be
Divided equally among us three.
Nevertheless, if I could shape things thus
So that we shared it out—the two of us—
Wouldn't you take it as a friendly act?"
"But how?" the other said. "He knows the fact
That all the gold was left with me and you;
What can we tell him? What are we to do?"
"Is it a bargain," said the first, "or no?
For I can tell you in a word or so
What's to be done to bring the thing about."
"Trust me," the other said, "you needn't doubt
My word. I won't betray you, I'll be true."
"Well," said his friend, "you see that we are two,
And two are twice as powerful as one.
Now look; when he comes back, get up in fun
To have a wrestle; then, as you attack,
I'll up and put my dagger through his back
While you and he are struggling, as in game;
Then draw your dagger too and do the same.
Then all this money will be ours to spend,
Divided equally of course, dear friend.
Then we can gratify our lusts and fill
The day with dicing at our own sweet will."
Thus these two miscreants° agreed to slay
The third and youngest, as you heard me say.
The youngest, as he ran towards the town,
Kept turning over, rolling up and down
Within his heart the beauty of those bright
New florins, saying, "Lord, to think I might
Have all that treasure to myself alone!
Could there be anyone beneath the throne
Of God so happy as I then should be?"
And so the Fiend,° our common enemy,
Was given power to put it in his thought
That there was always poison to be bought,
And that with poison he could kill his friends.
To men in such a state the Devil sends
Thoughts of this kind, and has a full permission
To lure them on to sorrow and perdition;°
For this young man was utterly content
To kill them both and never to repent.

201. parley *n.:* discussion.

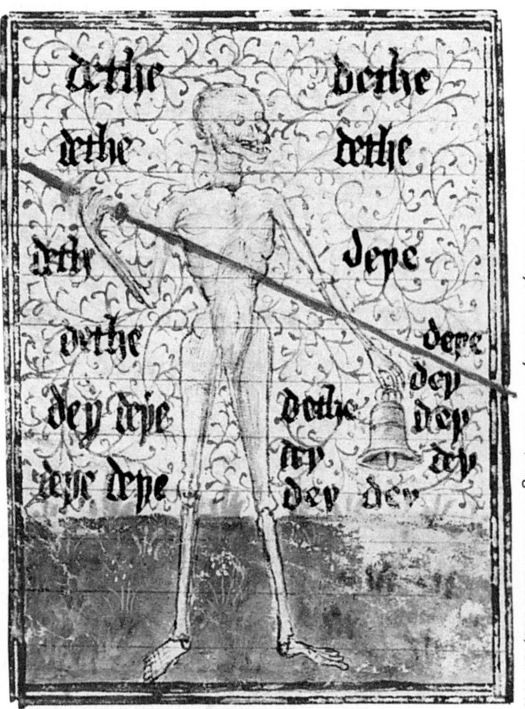

The Bodleian Library, University of Oxford, England. MS Douce 322, fol. 19v.

Death with his spear, from "The Pardoner's Tale."

229. miscreants (mis′krē·ənts) *n. pl.:* criminals; literally, "unbelievers."

238. Fiend: the devil.

244. perdition (pər·dish′ən) *n.:* damnation.

And on he ran, he had no thought to tarry,
Came to the town, found an apothecary°
And said, "Sell me some poison if you will,
I have a lot of rats I want to kill
And there's a polecat too about my yard
That takes my chickens and it hits me hard;
But I'll get even, as is only right,
With vermin that destroy a man by night."
The chemist answered, "I've a preparation
Which you shall have, and by my soul's salvation
If any living creature eat or drink
A mouthful, ere° he has the time to think,
Though he took less than makes a grain of wheat,
You'll see him fall down dying at your feet;
Yes, die he must, and in so short a while
You'd hardly have the time to walk a mile,
The poison is so strong, you understand."
This cursed fellow grabbed into his hand
The box of poison and away he ran
Into a neighboring street, and found a man
Who lent him three large bottles. He withdrew
And deftly poured the poison into two.
He kept the third one clean, as well he might,
For his own drink, meaning to work all night
Stacking the gold and carrying it away.
And when this rioter, this devil's clay,
Had filled his bottles up with wine, all three,
Back to rejoin his comrades sauntered° he.
Why make a sermon of it? Why waste breath?
Exactly in the way they'd planned his death
They fell on him and slew him, two to one.
Then said the first of them when this was done,
"Now for a drink. Sit down and let's be merry,
For later on there'll be the corpse to bury."
And, as it happened, reaching for a sup,
He took a bottle full of poison up
And drank; and his companion, nothing loth,°
Drank from it also, and they perished both.
There is, in Avicenna's° long relation
Concerning poison and its operation,
Trust me, no ghastlier section to transcend
What these two wretches suffered at their end.
Thus these two murderers received their due,
So did the treacherous young poisoner too. . . .

Vocabulary

transcend (tran•send′) *v.:* exceed; surpass.

248. apothecary (ə•päth′ə•ker′ē) *n.:* druggist. Formerly apothecaries prescribed drugs.

258. ere *prep.:* before.

274. sauntered (sôn′tərd) *v.:* strolled.

283. loth (lōth) *adj.:* reluctant; unwilling; alternative spelling of *loath.*

285. Avicenna's (av′i•sen′əz): Avicenna (A.D. 980–1037), a famous Islamic philosopher and doctor, wrote several medical books.

"One thing I should have mentioned in my tale,
Dear people. I've some relics in my bale°
And pardons too, as full and fine, I hope,
As any in England, given me by the Pope.
If there be one among you that is willing
To have my absolution° for a shilling°
Devoutly given, come! and do not harden
Your hearts but kneel in humbleness for pardon;
Or else, receive my pardon as we go.
You can renew it every town or so
Always provided that you still renew
Each time, and in good money, what is due.
It is an honor to you to have found
A pardoner with his credentials sound
Who can absolve you as you ply the spur°
In any accident that may occur.
For instance—we are all at Fortune's beck°—
Your horse may throw you down and break your neck.
What a security it is to all
To have me here among you and at call
With pardon for the lowly and the great
When soul leaves body for the future state!
And I advise our Host here to begin,
The most enveloped of you all in sin.
Come forward, Host, you shall be the first to pay,
And kiss my holy relics right away.
Only a groat.° Come on, unbuckle your purse!"
"No, no," said he,° "not I, and may the curse
Of Christ descend upon me if I do! . . ."

The Pardoner said nothing, not a word;
He was so angry that he couldn't speak.
"Well," said our Host, "if you're for showing pique,°
I'll joke no more, not with an angry man."
The worthy Knight immediately began,
Seeing the fun was getting rather rough,
And said, "No more, we've all had quite enough.
Now, Master Pardoner, perk up, look cheerly!
And you, Sir Host, whom I esteem so dearly,
I beg of you to kiss the Pardoner.
"Come, Pardoner, draw nearer, my dear sir.
Let's laugh again and keep the ball in play."°
They kissed, and we continued on our way.

Vocabulary

credentials (kri•den′shəlz) *n.:* evidence of a person's position.
absolve (ab•zälv′) *v.:* forgive; make free from blame.

292. relics in my bale: Relics are the supposedly holy remains of a saint—bones, teeth, hair, or clothing. A bale is a bundle of goods. In the Middle Ages, many relics were faked.
296. absolution (ab·sə·lo͞o′shən) *n.:* forgiveness. **shilling** *n.:* coin worth twelve pence.

305. ply the spur: In today's terms, this idiom means something like "rev it up" or "put on speed." It refers to the action of a rider digging his spurs into a horse to make it go faster.
307. beck *n.:* summons; in other words, subject to Fortune's will.

317. groat *n.:* silver coin worth four pence.
318. he: the Host.

322. pique (pēk) *n.:* resentment and ill humor.

331. keep the ball in play: continue.

Response and Analysis

Reading Check

1. How does the Pardoner describe his own character and morals in the Prologue to his tale?
2. According to "The Pardoner's Tale," why are the three young rioters looking for Death?
3. Where does the old man tell the rioters to look for Death? How do they treat him?
4. Describe the rioters' plan for the gold and how it proves fatal to all three of them.

Thinking Critically

5. How do the descriptions given by the tavern-knave and the publican **personify** Death? What does the rioters' response to the description of Death tell you about their characters?
6. What do you think the poor old man **symbolizes**?
7. **Irony** is a discrepancy between expectations and reality. What is the central irony in "The Pardoner's Tale"? (What do the rioters expect to find under the tree? What do they *actually* find?)
8. Explain the **irony** in the fact that the Pardoner preaches a story with this particular moral. How do you account for the psychology of the Pardoner? Is he truly evil, simply drunk, or so used to cheating that he does it automatically?
9. What aspects of medieval society (and human nature in general) do you think Chaucer is **satirizing** in "The Pardoner's Tale"?
10. What **moral** does the Pardoner want us to draw from his tale? How is it different from the moral you think Chaucer wants you to draw from "The Pardoner's Tale"?
11. Do people with the Pardoner's ethics exist today—in all sorts of professions? Explain your response.
12. *Is* greed or desire the root of all evil? Discuss the Pardoner's moral.

SKILLS FOCUS

Literary Skills
Analyze irony, including verbal and situational irony.

Writing Skills
Write a character analysis.

Vocabulary Skills
Demonstrate word knowledge.

INTERNET

Projects and Activities

Keyword: LE7 12-2

WRITING

What Makes the Pardoner Tick?

Write a **character analysis** of the Pardoner. Consider in your analysis the Pardoner's Prologue, his tale, and the description of the Pardoner in the general Prologue (see pages 161–162). Before you write, gather details for your analysis in a cluster diagram like the following one:

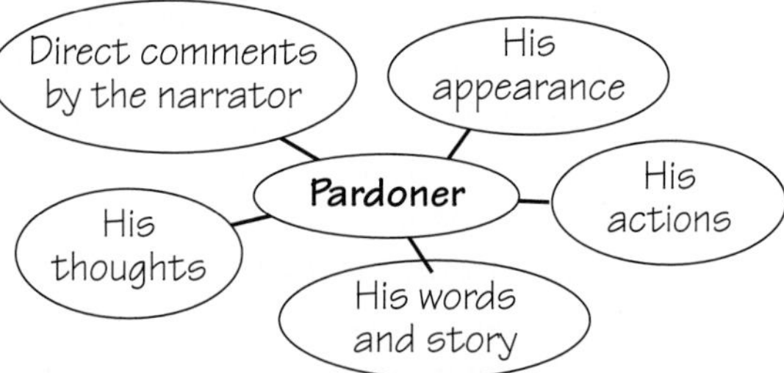

Be sure to quote directly from the text to support your character analysis. If you are so inspired, supply your own illustration (or a cartoon) of the Pardoner.

Vocabulary Development

Question and Answer

Demonstrate your understanding of the underlined Vocabulary words by answering the following questions.

1. Might a person guilty of avarice have a superfluity of possessions?
2. Why might running into an adversary bring a pallor to someone's complexion?
3. Who could absolve a person of an abominable crime?
4. What could you do to transcend your fears if you were faced with a grisly sight?
5. When would it be prudent to check someone's credentials?

The Wife of Bath's Tale

When good King Arthur ruled in ancient days
(A king that every Briton loves to praise)
This was a land brim-full of fairy folk.
The Elf-Queen and her courtiers° joined and broke
Their elfin dance on many a green mead,°
Or so was the opinion once, I read,
Hundreds of years ago, in days of yore.
But no one now sees fairies any more.
For now the saintly charity and prayer
Of holy friars seem to have purged the air;
They search the countryside through field and stream
As thick as motes° that speckle a sun-beam,
Blessing the halls, the chambers, kitchens, bowers,
Cities and boroughs, castles, courts and towers,
Thorpes,° barns and stables, outhouses and dairies,
And that's the reason why there are no fairies.
Wherever there was wont° to walk an elf
To-day there walks the holy friar himself
As evening falls or when the daylight springs,
Saying his matins° and his holy things,
Walking his limit round from town to town.
Women can now go safely up and down
By every bush or under every tree;
There is no other incubus° but he,
So there is really no one else to hurt you
And he will do no more than take your virtue.
   Now it so happened, I began to say,
Long, long ago in good King Arthur's day,
There was a knight who was a lusty liver.°
One day as he came riding from the river
He saw a maiden walking all forlorn
Ahead of him, alone as she was born.
And of that maiden, spite of all she said,
By very force he took her maidenhead.°
   This act of violence made such a stir,
So much petitioning to the king for her,
That he condemned the knight to lose his head
By course of law. He was as good as dead
(It seems that then the statutes° took that view)
But that the queen, and other ladies too,
Implored the king to exercise his grace
So ceaselessly, he gave the queen the case
And granted her his life, and she could choose
Whether to show him mercy or refuse.
   The queen returned him thanks with all her might,
And then she sent a summons to the knight

34. courtiers (kôrt′ē·ərz) *n. pl.:* attendants.

35. mead *n.:* meadow.

42. motes *n. pl.:* dust particles.

45. thorpes *n. pl.:* villages.

47. wont (wänt) *adj.:* accustomed.

50. matins (mat″nz) *n. pl.:* morning prayers.

54. incubus (in′kyə·bəs) *n.:* evil spirit believed to descend on a sleeping woman and make her pregnant.

59. liver *n.:* In medieval times, the liver—not the heart—was believed to be the source of all desires and emotions.

64. maidenhead *n.:* virginity.

69. statutes *n. pl.:* laws.

At her convenience, and expressed her will:
"You stand, for such is the position still,
In no way certain of your life," said she,
"Yet you shall live if you can answer me:
What is the thing that women most desire?
Beware the axe and say as I require.
"If you can't answer on the moment, though,
I will concede you this: You are to go
A twelvemonth and a day to seek and learn
Sufficient answer, then you shall return.
I shall take gages° from you to extort
Surrender of your body to the court."
Sad was the knight and sorrowfully sighed,
But there! All other choices were denied,
And in the end he chose to go away
And to return after a year and day
Armed with such answer as there might be sent
To him by God. He took his leave and went.
He knocked at every house, searched every place,
Yes, anywhere that offered hope of grace.
What could it be that women wanted most?
But all the same he never touched a coast,
Country, or town in which there seemed to be
Any two people willing to agree.
Some said that women wanted wealth and treasure,
"Honor," said some, some "Jollity and pleasure,"
Some "Gorgeous clothes" and others "Fun in bed,"
"To be oft widowed and remarried," said
Others again, and some that what most mattered
Was that we should be cossetted° and flattered.
That's very near the truth, it seems to me;
A man can win us best with flattery.
To dance attendance on us, make a fuss,
Ensnares us all, the best and worst of us.
Some say the things we most desire are these:
Freedom to do exactly as we please,
With no one to reprove our faults and lies,
Rather to have one call us good and wise.
Truly there's not a woman in ten score°
Who has a fault, and someone rubs the sore,
But she will kick if what he says is true;
You try it out and you will find so too.
However vicious we may be within

Vocabulary

concede (kən • sēd′) *v.:* grant.

extort (eks • tôrt′) *v.:* get by threats or violence.

87. gages *n. pl.:* pledges.

MS 493, fol. 74v. Dijon Library, Dijon, France.

Man and woman, from a fifteenth-century manuscript of Virgil's *Aeneid.*

106. cossetted (käs′it·id) *v.:* pampered.

115. ten score: two hundred. A score is twenty.

We like to be thought wise and void of sin.
Others assert we women find it sweet
When we are thought dependable, discreet
And secret, firm of purpose and controlled,
Never betraying things that we are told.
But that's not worth the handle of a rake;
Women conceal a thing? For Heaven's sake!
Remember Midas?° Will you hear the tale?
   Among some other little things, now stale,
Ovid° relates that under his long hair
The unhappy Midas grew a splendid pair
Of ass's ears; as subtly as he might,
He kept his foul deformity from sight;
Save for his wife, there was not one that knew.
He loved her best, and trusted in her too.
He begged her not to tell a living creature
That he possessed so horrible a feature.
And she—she swore, were all the world to win,
She would not do such villainy and sin
As saddle her husband with so foul a name;
Besides to speak would be to share the shame.
Nevertheless she thought she would have died
Keeping this secret bottled up inside;
It seemed to swell her heart and she, no doubt,
Thought it was on the point of bursting out.
   Fearing to speak of it to woman or man,
Down to a reedy marsh she quickly ran
And reached the sedge.° Her heart was all on fire
And, as a bittern° bumbles in the mire,
She whispered to the water, near the ground,
"Betray me not, O water, with thy sound!
To thee alone I tell it: It appears
My husband has a pair of ass's ears!
Ah! My heart's well again, the secret's out!
I could no longer keep it, not a doubt."
And so you see, although we may hold fast
A little while, it must come out at last,
We can't keep secrets; as for Midas, well,
Read Ovid for his story;° he will tell.
   This knight that I am telling you about
Perceived at last he never would find out
What it could be that women loved the best.
Faint was the soul within his sorrowful breast,
As home he went, he dared no longer stay;
His year was up and now it was the day.
   As he rode home in a dejected mood
Suddenly, at the margin° of a wood,

127. Midas: mythical king. Everything he touched turned to gold.

129. Ovid (43 B.C.–c. A.D. 17): Roman poet. Ovid's *Metamorphoses,* a collection of tales, includes one version of the Midas story.

147. sedge *n.:* grasslike plant.

148. bittern *n.:* type of wading bird.

158. Read . . . story: In Ovid's version, it is Midas's barber, not his wife, who tells the secret to a hole in the ground. Reeds grow up from the spot and whisper the secret whenever the wind rustles them.

166. margin *n.:* edge.

He saw a dance upon the leafy floor
Of four and twenty ladies, nay, and more.
Eagerly he approached, in hope to learn
Some words of wisdom ere he should return;
But lo! Before he came to where they were,
Dancers and dance all vanished into air!
There wasn't a living creature to be seen
Save one old woman crouched upon the green.
A fouler-looking creature I suppose
Could scarcely be imagined. She arose
And said, "Sir knight, there's no way on from here.
Tell me what you are looking for, my dear,
For peradventure° that were best for you;
We old, old women know a thing or two."
"Dear Mother," said the knight, "alack the day!
I am as good as dead if I can't say
What thing it is that women most desire;
If you could tell me I would pay your hire."
"Give me your hand," she said, "and swear to do
Whatever I shall next require of you
—If so to do should lie within your might—
And you shall know the answer before night."
"Upon my honor," he answered, "I agree."
"Then," said the crone, "I dare to guarantee
Your life is safe; I shall make good my claim.
Upon my life the queen will say the same.
Show me the very proudest of them all
In costly coverchief or jeweled caul°
That dare say no to what I have to teach.
Let us go forward without further speech."
And then she crooned her gospel in his ear
And told him to be glad and not to fear.
They came to court. This knight, in full array,
Stood forth and said, "O Queen, I've kept my day
And kept my word and have my answer ready."
There sat the noble matrons and the heady
Young girls, and widows too, that have the grace
Of wisdom, all assembled in that place,
And there the queen herself was throned to hear
And judge his answer. Then the knight drew near
And silence was commanded through the hall.
The queen gave order he should tell them all
What thing it was that women wanted most.
He stood not silent like a beast or post,
But gave his answer with the ringing word
Of a man's voice and the assembly heard:

179. peradventure *adv.:* perhaps.

194. coverchief . . . caul (kôl): women's headgear. The coverchief covered the entire head; the caul, a small, netted cap, was sometimes ornamented.

The Knight and the Old Lady.

"My liege° and lady, in general," said he,
"A woman wants the self-same sovereignty°
Over her husband as over her lover,
And master him; he must not be above her.
That is your greatest wish, whether you kill
Or spare me; please yourself. I wait your will."
In all the court not one that shook her head
Or contradicted what the knight had said;
Maid, wife, and widow cried, "He's saved his life!"
And on the word up started the old wife,
The one the knight saw sitting on the green,
And cried, "Your mercy, sovereign lady queen!
Before the court disperses, do me right!
'Twas I who taught this answer to the knight,
For which he swore, and pledged his honor to it,
That the first thing I asked of him he'd do it,
So far as it should lie within his might.
Before this court I ask you then, sir knight,
To keep your word and take me for your wife;
For well you know that I have saved your life.
If this be false, deny it on your sword!"
"Alas!" he said, "Old lady, by the Lord
I know indeed that such was my behest,°
But for God's love think of a new request,
Take all my goods, but leave my body free."
"A curse on us," she said, "if I agree!
I may be foul, I may be poor and old,
Yet will not choose to be, for all the gold
That's bedded in the earth or lies above,
Less than your wife, nay, than your very love!"
"My love?" said he. "By heaven, my damnation!
Alas that any of my race and station
Should ever make so foul a misalliance!"°
Yet in the end his pleading and defiance
All went for nothing, he was forced to wed.
He takes his ancient wife and goes to bed.
Now peradventure some may well suspect
A lack of care in me since I neglect
To tell of the rejoicings and display
Made at the feast upon their wedding-day.
I have but a short answer to let fall;
I say there was no joy or feast at all,
Nothing but heaviness of heart and sorrow.
He married her in private on the morrow

213. liege (lēj) *n.:* lord.

214. sovereignty (säv′rən·tē) *n.:* power.

Medieval knight on horseback.

235. behest *n.:* command; order.

245. misalliance (mis·ə·lī′əns) *n.:* here, a marriage that is unsuitable or inappropriate.

Vocabulary

disperses (di·spurs′iz) *v.:* breaks up.

And all day long stayed hidden like an owl,
It was such torture that his wife looked foul.
Great was the anguish churning in his head
When he and she were piloted to bed;
He wallowed° back and forth in desperate style.
His ancient wife lay smiling all the while;
At last she said "Bless us! Is this, my dear,
How knights and wives get on together here?
Are these the laws of good King Arthur's house?
Are knights of his all so contemptuous?
I am your own beloved and your wife,
And I am she, indeed, that saved your life;
And certainly I never did you wrong.
Then why, this first of nights, so sad a song?
You're carrying on as if you were half-witted
Say, for God's love, what sin have I committed?
I'll put things right if you will tell me how."
"Put right?" he cried. "That never can be now!
Nothing can ever be put right again!
You're old, and so abominably plain,
So poor to start with, so low-bred to follow;
It's little wonder if I twist and wallow!
God, that my heart would burst within my breast!"
"Is that," said she, "the cause of your unrest?"
"Yes, certainly," he said, "and can you wonder?"
"I could set right what you suppose a blunder,
That's if I cared to, in a day or two,
If I were shown more courtesy by you.
Just now," she said, "you spoke of gentle birth,
Such as descends from ancient wealth and worth.
If that's the claim you make for gentlemen
Such arrogance is hardly worth a hen.
Whoever loves to work for virtuous ends,
Public and private, and who most intends
To do what deeds of gentleness he can,
Take him to be the greatest gentleman.
Christ wills we take our gentleness from Him,
Not from a wealth of ancestry long dim,
Though they bequeath their whole establishment
By which we claim to be of high descent.
Our fathers cannot make us a bequest
Of all those virtues that became them best

261. wallowed *v.:* tossed and turned.

HERE BIGYNNETH THE TALE OF THE WIFE OF BATH.

IN THOLDE dayes of the Kyng Arthour,
Of which that Britons speken greet honour,
Al was this land fulfild of faierye.
The elf queene with hir joly compaignye
Daunced ful ofte in manye a grene mede;
This was the olde opinion, as I rede.
I speke of manye hundred yeres ago;
But now kan no man se none elves mo.
For now the grete charitee and prayeres
Of lymytours, and othere hooly freres,
That serchen every lond and every streem,
As thikke as motes in the sonne-beem,
Blessynge halles, chambres, kichenes, boures,
Citees, burghes, castels, hye toures,
Thropes, bernes, shipnes, dayeryes,
This maketh that ther been no faieryes;
For ther as wont to walken was an elf,
Ther walketh now the lymytour hymself,
In undermeles and in morwenynges,
And seyth his matyns and his hooly thynges
As he gooth in his lymytacioun.
Wommen may go saufly up and doun;
In every bussh, or under every tree,
Ther is noon oother incubus but he,
And he ne wol doon hem but dishonour.
AND so bifel it, that this kynge Arthour,
Hadde in his hous a lusty bacheler,
That on a day cam ridynge fro ryver;
And happed that, allone as she was born,
He saugh a mayde walkynge hym biforn,
Of whiche mayde, anon, maugree hir heed,
By verray force he rafte hire maydenhed;
For which oppressioun was swich clamour,
And swich pursute unto the kyng Arthour,
That dampned was this knyght for to be deed

Opening page of the "Tale of the Wife of Bath" (c. 1898) from the Kelmscott *Chaucer*.

Spencer Collection. New York Public Library. Astor, Lenox, and Tilden Foundations.

Vocabulary

contemptuous (kən•temp′cho͞o•əs) *adj.:* scornful.
bequest (bē•kwest′) *n.:* gift left by means of a will.

And earned for them the name of gentlemen,
But bade us follow them as best we can.
"Thus the wise poet of the Florentines,
Dante° by name, has written in these lines,
For such is the opinion Dante launches:
'Seldom arises by these slender branches
Prowess of men, for it is God, no less,
Wills us to claim of Him our gentleness.'
For of our parents nothing can we claim
Save temporal things, and these may hurt and maim.
"But everyone knows this as well as I;
For if gentility were implanted by
The natural course of lineage° down the line,
Public or private, could it cease to shine
In doing the fair work of gentle deed?
No vice or villainy could then bear seed.
"Take fire and carry it to the darkest house
Between this kingdom and the Caucasus,°
And shut the doors on it and leave it there,
It will burn on, and it will burn as fair
As if ten thousand men were there to see,
For fire will keep its nature and degree,
I can assure you, sir, until it dies.
"But gentleness, as you will recognize,
Is not annexed in nature to possessions.
Men fail in living up to their professions;°
But fire never ceases to be fire.
God knows you'll often find, if you inquire,
Some lording° full of villainy and shame.
If you would be esteemed for the mere name
Of having been by birth a gentleman
And stemming from some virtuous, noble clan,
And do not live yourself by gentle deed
Or take your father's noble code and creed,
You are no gentleman, though duke or earl.
Vice and bad manners are what make a churl.°
"Gentility is only the renown
For bounty that your fathers handed down,
Quite foreign to your person, not your own;
Gentility must come from God alone.
That we are gentle comes to us by grace
And by no means is it bequeathed with place.

302. Dante: Dante Alighieri (dän'tā a'lə·gyer'ē) (1265–1321), Italian poet who wrote *The Divine Comedy.*

311. lineage (lin'ē·ij) *n.:* ancestry.

316. Caucasus (kô'kə·səs): mountain range in southeastern Europe, between the Black Sea and the Caspian Sea; in other words, far away.

324. professions *n. pl.:* promises.

327. lording *n.:* alternate form of *lord.*

334. churl *n.:* ill-mannered person.

Vocabulary

prowess (prou'is) *n.:* outstanding ability.
temporal (tem'pə·rəl) *adj.:* limited to this world; not spiritual.

"Reflect how noble (says Valerius)°
Was Tullius surnamed Hostilius,°
Who rose from poverty to nobleness.
And read Boethius,° Seneca° no less,
Thus they express themselves and are agreed:
'Gentle is he that does a gentle deed.'
And therefore, my dear husband, I conclude
That even if my ancestors were rude,
Yet God on high—and so I hope He will—
Can grant me grace to live in virtue still,
A gentlewoman only when beginning
To live in virtue and to shrink from sinning.
"As for my poverty which you reprove,
Almighty God Himself in whom we move,
Believe, and have our being, chose a life
Of poverty, and every man or wife
Nay, every child can see our Heavenly King
Would never stoop to choose a shameful thing.
No shame in poverty if the heart is gay,
As Seneca and all the learned say.
He who accepts his poverty unhurt
I'd say is rich although he lacked a shirt.
But truly poor are they who whine and fret
And covet what they cannot hope to get.
And he that, having nothing, covets not,
Is rich, though you may think he is a sot.°
"True poverty can find a song to sing.
Juvenal° says a pleasant little thing:
'The poor can dance and sing in the relief
Of having nothing that will tempt a thief.'
Though it be hateful, poverty is good,
A great incentive to a livelihood,
And a great help to our capacity
For wisdom, if accepted patiently.
Poverty is, though wanting in estate,
A kind of wealth that none calumniate.°
Poverty often, when the heart is lowly,
Brings one to God and teaches what is holy,
Gives knowledge of oneself and even lends
A glass by which to see one's truest friends.
And since it's no offense, let me be plain;
Do not rebuke my poverty again.
"Lastly you taxed me, sir, with being old.
Yet even if you never had been told

Vocabulary

capacity (kə•pas′i•tē) *n.:* ability to absorb.

341. Valerius (və•lir′ē•əs): first-century A.D. Roman writer who collected historical anecdotes that public speakers could use.

342. Tullius (tul′ē•əs) **surnamed Hostilius** (hos•til′ē•əs): Tullius Hostilius, legendary king of Rome who rose from humble origins.

344. Boethius (bō•ē′thē•əs) (c. A.D. 480–c. 524): Roman philosopher. In his *Consolation of Philosophy*, he argues that rank is no guarantee of honorable conduct. **Seneca** (sen′i•kə) (c. 4 B.C.–A.D. 65): Roman philosopher whose works were popular in the Middle Ages.

366. sot *n.:* fool.

368. Juvenal (jo͞o′və•n′l) (c. A.D. 60–c. 140): Roman satirist.

376. calumniate (kə•lum′nē•āt′) *v.:* slander.

By ancient books, you gentlemen engage
Yourselves in honor to respect old age.
To call an old man 'father' shows good breeding,
And this could be supported from my reading.
"You say I'm old and fouler than a fen.°
You need not fear to be a cuckold,° then.
Filth and old age, I'm sure you will agree,
Are powerful wardens over chastity.
Nevertheless, well knowing your delights,
I shall fulfill your worldly appetites.
"You have two choices; which one will you try?
To have me old and ugly till I die,
But still a loyal, true, and humble wife
That never will displease you all her life,
Or would you rather I were young and pretty
And chance your arm what happens in a city
Where friends will visit you because of me,
Yes, and in other places too, maybe.
Which would you have? The choice is all your own."
The knight thought long, and with a piteous groan
At last he said, with all the care in life,
"My lady and my love, my dearest wife,
I leave the matter to your wise decision.
You make the choice yourself, for the provision
Of what may be agreeable and rich
In honor to us both, I don't care which;
Whatever pleases you suffices° me."
"And have I won the mastery?" said she,
"Since I'm to choose and rule as I think fit?"
"Certainly, wife," he answered her, "that's it."
"Kiss me," she cried. "No quarrels! On my oath
And word of honor, you shall find me both,
That is, both fair and faithful as a wife;
May I go howling mad and take my life
Unless I prove to be as good and true
As ever wife was since the world was new!
And if to-morrow when the sun's above
I seem less fair than any lady-love,
Than any queen or empress east or west,
Do with my life and death as you think best.
Cast up the curtain, husband. Look at me!"
And when indeed the knight had looked to see,
Lo, she was young and lovely, rich in charms.
In ecstasy he caught her in his arms,
His heart went bathing in a bath of blisses
And melted in a hundred thousand kisses,
And she responded in the fullest measure
With all that could delight or give him pleasure.

389. fen *n.:* swamp.

390. cuckold (kuk′əld) *n.:* man whose wife has been unfaithful to him.

411. suffices (sə·fīs′ez) *v.:* satisfies.

Arras 1425–50. Victoria and Albert Museum, London.

A man and woman on horseback, from *The Devonshire Hunting Tapestries* (detail).

So they lived ever after to the end
In perfect bliss; and may Christ Jesus send
Us husbands meek and young and fresh in bed,
And grace to overbid them when we wed.
And—Jesu hear my prayer!—cut short the lives
Of those who won't be governed by their wives;
And all old, angry niggards of their pence,°
God send them soon a very pestilence!

439. niggards (nig′ərdz) **of their pence:** stingy with their money.

Vocabulary

pestilence (pes′tə • ləns) *n.:* plague.

Response and Analysis

Literary Skills Analyze the characteristics of a narrator. Analyze couplets and the use of rhymes.

Reading Skills Interpret character.

Writing Skills Write a historical research report.

Vocabulary Skills Demonstrate word knowledge.

Reading Check

1. Identify (a) the knight's crime; (b) his original punishment; and (c) his second punishment.
2. What bargain do the knight and the old woman strike?
3. What payment for her help does the old woman demand? What is the knight's response?
4. What final choice does the old woman offer the knight at the end of the tale? What is his response?

Thinking Critically

5. **Irony** is a contrast between what seems appropriate or expected and what actually happens. The knight's quest—forced upon him by the queen—is to find out what women want. What **irony** do you see in this punishment?
6. In lines 276–278 the knight moans about having the old woman for his wife. How does she respond to each objection he raises?
7. How does the knight's response to the choice given him by the old woman show that he's learned his lesson about what women want?
8. What opinions does the Wife of Bath express in the tale? What do all her opinions—and her tale itself—tell you about her **character**? Refer to your reading notes for help.
9. Consider the various things the Wife of Bath, as the **narrator** of her tale, says people think women want. What do you think of these proposals? Refer to you Quickwrite notes.
10. Do you think Chaucer's rich portrayal of the Wife of Bath is an indication that he had progressive views about women for his time? Why or why not?
11. What do men and women today think the other wants most out of life or out of a relationship? (Have attitudes changed since Chaucer's time?)

Extending and Evaluating

12. Consider how the knight gets into trouble in the first place, and how things turn out for him. Does the story satisfy you or trouble you in some way? Explain your responses.
13. Examine the old woman's thoughts on poverty (lines 353–382). How do you feel about her opinions?

WRITING

A Historical Report

Both the Middle Ages and Chaucer's tales present many possible topics for historical investigation. Review the introduction to the medieval period (see pages 114–129) and Chaucer's tales to find a topic you are interested in researching. Here are some suggestions:

- the causes and results of the Crusades
- how the Black Death changed history
- the life of a knight
- the lives of women in the Middle Ages

Write a research report of 500 to 750 words on the topic you have chosen.

Use "Reporting Literary Research," pages 240–259, for help with this assignment.

Vocabulary Development

What Would the Wife of Bath Say?

reprove	bequest
concede	prowess
extort	temporal
disperses	capacity
contemptuous	pestilence

Demonstrate your understanding of the Vocabulary words—and of the philosophical views of the Wife of Bath—by using each word listed above in a sentence that expresses an opinion that you think the Wife of Bath would hold. One has already been done for you:

> In marriage, a husband must concede full equality to his wife.

Literary Focus

Couplets: Sound and Sense

Chaucer's favorite rhyme scheme in *The Canterbury Tales* is the **couplet,** two consecutive lines of poetry that rhyme: "When good King Arthur ruled in ancient *days* / (A king that every Briton loves to *praise*)." (When he was growing old, Chaucer complained that his faculty of rhyming was leaving him, which may be the reason he never finished *The Canterbury Tales.*) Nevill Coghill, whose translation of the *Tales* is used here, followed Chaucer's rhyme scheme, though he did not always use Chaucer's own rhyming words.

Analyzing Chaucer's rhymes. Look closely at Chaucer's rhymes.

1. Read aloud parts of the general Prologue (see pages 142–143) to see how the couplets animate the story of the pilgrims. Find some humorous rhymes.
2. Find what you think are the equivalents of these words in the Middle English version of the general Prologue (see page 141): *flower, breath, eye, courage,* and *condition.* The pronunciation of these words has changed since the Middle Ages. According to the words they're rhymed with in the Prologue, how would each of these words have been pronounced in Chaucer's day?
3. Identify at least two couplets in "The Wife of Bath's Tale" that use **half rhymes** (also called **approximate rhymes**), words that share similar but not identical sounds, such as *done/dine.*

Translating Chaucer. Compare the couplets Coghill uses in his translation of the first forty-two lines of the Prologue with the couplets Chaucer uses in his original. Then, try to translate these original lines of the Prologue yourself, perhaps using more of Chaucer's original couplets than Coghill did.

Vocabulary Development

Distinguishing Multiple Meanings of Words

Many words have, over time, accumulated more than one meaning. Consider Chaucer's usage of the word *humor* in the general Prologue:

> The cause of every malady you'd got
> He knew, and whether dry, cold, moist,
> or hot;
> He knew their seat, their humor and
> condition.

Chaucer uses the word *humor* in a sense that was common during the Middle Ages: to refer to the four kinds of bodily fluids (blood, yellow bile, phlegm, and black bile) that were believed to influence a person's well-being. Today, when we refer to someone's general disposition by saying that he is in a bad humor or a good humor, we are invoking this historical meaning of the word. But if we say "My sister has a great sense of humor," we are using the word in a very different sense—the ability to appreciate what is funny or amusing. All of these definitions of *humor* are related, however, in that they share the same origin.

Distinguishing word origins. One of the important pieces of information a dictionary can tell you is the **etymology** of a word—its origin and development over time. Some words that are spelled the same not only have different meanings—they also have different origins. Take the word *host,* for example:

> Our Host gave us great welcome;
> everyone
> Was given a place and supper was begun.

SKILLS FOCUS

Vocabulary Skills
Understand etymologies and multiple-meaning words.

Chaucer uses the word *host* to mean innkeeper: someone who runs an inn or hotel. The following chart shows the different meanings and etymologies, or origins, of *host.*

Word	Origin	Meanings
1. host	Latin *hospes:* "host or guest"	innkeeper; one who entertains guests; an organism in which a parasite lives; radio or television personality who conducts a program on which various guests speak
2. host	Latin *hostis:* "enemy force; stranger; army"	an army; a multitude or great number
3. host	Latin *hostire:* "recompense; repay"	[in Christianity] the eucharistic wafer that represents the body of Christ

PRACTICE

Using a dictionary, look up the **etymology** and different **meanings** of each word listed below. Then, use the word in two different sentences to illustrate two of the word's different meanings.

1. ground
2. shade
3. account
4. draw
5. vain

Connecting to **World Literature**

The Frame Story: A Tale Linking Tales

by David Adams Leeming

You have just read excerpts from Chaucer's *The Canterbury Tales*, an example of a frame story. In this Connecting to World Literature feature you will read excerpts from these other frame stories:

1387
Chaucer begins to write *The Canterbury Tales*

1348–1353
Boccaccio writes the *Decameron*

c. 850
The stories of *The Thousand and One Nights* begin to be collected

100 B.C.–A.D. 500
Stories of the *Panchatantra* are collected

Many—perhaps most—of the tales told by Chaucer's pilgrims in *The Canterbury Tales* did not originate with Chaucer. Instead, they were based on older stories that Chaucer was familiar with—some from the ancient folklore of other cultures. For example, the tale the Pardoner tells (see page 168) is a variation of a story that appears in cultures as diverse as Persia and Tibet.

The Collecting Bug

In the Middle Ages, there was a deliberate effort to collect beloved stories from the oral tradition. These were stories that had formerly been flying about the world by word-of-mouth—from one village and town to the other and even from one country and one continent to the other. These popular tales—fairy tales, legends, moral tales—were the direct ancestors of what we know today as the short story.

The Unifying Frame

How could a grouping of well-told but completely unrelated stories best be collected into one book? The answer came in the form of the **frame story.** We can trace the frame story back at least to the Indian collection of tales called the *Panchatantra* (*pancha* means "five" and *tantra* means "books"), which probably dates from around A.D. 300. A frame story was a means by which a collection of tales could be held together by a common element. Instead of just moving from one unrelated story to another, an outer story (the frame) provided a rationale for the collection.

A Frame to Set Them In

Writers found a variety of ways to frame their collections. The *Panchatantra* is unified by a frame story in which a Hindu wise man, Vishnusharman (vish'nōō • shär'mən), uses a series of fables—stories with a moral—to teach proper behavior to three ignorant and unruly sons of a king. In *The Canterbury Tales*, the frame is the story of pilgrims agreeing to tell tales to kill time on their way to and from Canterbury.

Pages 191–192 cover
Literary Skills
Understand the characteristics of frame stories. Compare frame stories from different cultures and literary periods.

Sindbad the Sailor entertains a group with stories of his seven fantastic voyages, from *The Thousand and One Nights.*

Just before Chaucer's time, in Italy, the writer Giovanni Boccaccio created a frame story in which ten young people flee to a hill town to avoid the Great Plague of 1348 (the Black Death). To while away the ten days of their isolation, they agree to tell ten stories each—hence the title of the collection, the *Decameron* (from the Greek *deca* meaning "ten" and *hemera* meaning "day"). *The Thousand and One Nights* (also known as *The Arabian Nights*), is a famous ninth-century Arabic collection of Indian, Persian, and Arabian tales (finally collected in their present form in about 1450). The frame for this collection is provided by the storytelling of Scheherazade, a wife of the evil sultan, Shahriyar. The sultan is so disgusted by the unfaithfulness of one of his wives that he takes a new bride every day and has her killed at dawn. However, the latest bride, Scheherazade, is such a gifted storyteller that she is able to postpone her death each day by withholding the end of her story until the next night. The sultan doesn't kill her because he can't bear to miss the endings of her stories. What better testament to the power of storytelling?

Panchatantra

(c. 300)

Delhi
HIMALAYAS
Indus
Ganges
Calcutta
INDIA
Bombay
Arabian Sea
Bay of Bengal

The *Panchatantra* (pun′chə • tun′trə) began in ancient India as a tool for teaching statecraft to young princes. The anonymous work consists of a series of **fables,** or brief stories that teach practical lessons about life. The stories are contained within a larger outer story, a narrative framework that gives the tales a thematic unity.

In the outer story, the **frame,** a Brahman priest named Vishnusharman (vish′nōō • shär′mən) tries to teach the art of rulership to three rather dimwitted young princes. The lessons take the form of a series of fables, presented in five sections: how one loses friends, how one wins friends, how one should handle international relations, how one may lose profits and possessions, and how hasty actions can have harmful consequences.

The central theme that runs through the *Panchatantra* is the idea of *niti* (ni′tē), which means "worldly wisdom." A person needs five things in order to achieve *niti:* physical security, freedom from want, resolute action, good friends, and intelligence. A person with *niti* is the sort of person who can triumph over evil or dishonest people by turning the tables on them.

The *Panchatantra* is among the most well-known collections of fables in the world. It was translated into Persian as early as the sixth century. During the Middle Ages it was translated into Arabic, Greek, Hebrew, Latin, German, and Italian. The classic Indian fables have influenced works as diverse as *The Thousand and One Nights* (see page 202), Geoffrey Chaucer's *The Canterbury Tales* (see page 137), and Giovanni Boccaccio's *Decameron* (see page 209). All three of those works, like the *Panchatantra,* rely on a frame story to establish overall unity.

Elephant painting.

City Palace Museum, Udaipur Rajasthan, India. Earl & Nazima Kowall/ CORBIS.

Before You Read

Right-Mind and Wrong-Mind

Make the Connection

Today, if we want to teach someone a moral or practical lesson about life, how do we go about it? Do some people take a direct approach and ask the person to listen to a lecture or to read a self-help manual? Do others try to get the point across in a less direct way—by telling a story, for instance? In your opinion, which way of delivering a lesson is more effective?

Literary Focus

Fable

A **fable** is a brief story in prose or verse that teaches a moral or offers a practical lesson about life. The characters in most fables are animals that speak or act like human beings; this kind of fable is often called a "beast fable." Occasionally, however, the characters in fables are human beings. Whether humans or animals, though, characters in fables often represent abstract qualities—stupidity, trickery, honesty, innocence.

Literary Skills
Understand the characteristics of fables.

A **fable** is a brief story in prose or verse that teaches a moral or gives a practical lesson about life.

For more on Fable, see the Handbook of Literary and Historical Terms.

INTERNET

Vocabulary Practice

Keyword: LE7 12-2

Background

The fable "Right-Mind and Wrong-Mind" is taken from "The Loss of Friends," the first section of the *Panchatantra,* and it illustrates two important literary elements of that ancient Indian collection of fables. The first is the use of the **frame story,** or story-within-a-story device. In this case, the inner story "A Remedy Worse Than the Disease" is used to emphasize the lesson being taught in the main fable, "Right-Mind and Wrong-Mind."

The second literary element is the use of epigrams, which are interspersed throughout the prose narrative. **Epigrams** are brief, clever verses that contain moral or practical advice. In addition to summarizing the lessons of the fables, epigrams add color and flavor to the narratives.

Vocabulary Development

duplicity (do͞o·plis′ə·tē) *n.:* cunning; treachery.

residue (rez′ə·do͞o′) *n.:* leftover portion; remainder.

preliminary (prē·lim′ə·ner′ē) *adj.:* preparing for the main event; introductory.

initiative (i·nish′ə·tiv) *n.:* action of making the first move.

discern (di·sʉrn′) *v.:* recognize (the difference); make out clearly.

Right-Mind and Wrong-Mind

from the Panchatantra

translated by Arthur William Ryder

In a certain city lived two friends, sons of merchants, and their names were Right-Mind and Wrong-Mind. These two traveled to another country far away in order to earn money. There the one named Right-Mind, as a consequence of favoring fortune, found a pot containing a thousand dinars,[1] which had been hidden long before by a holy man. He debated the matter with Wrong-Mind, and they decided to go home, since their object was attained. So they returned together.

When they drew near their native city, Right-Mind said: "My good friend, a half of this falls to your share. Pray take it, so that, now that we are at home, we may cut a brilliant figure before our friends and those less friendly."

But Wrong-Mind, with a sneaking thought of his own advantage, said to the other: "My good friend, so long as we two hold this treasure in common, so long will our virtuous friendship suffer no interruption. Let us each take a hundred dinars, and go to our homes after burying the remainder. The decrease or increase of this treasure will serve as a test of our virtue."

Now Right-Mind, in the nobility of his nature, did not comprehend the hidden duplicity of his friend, and agreed to the proposal. Each then took a certain sum of money. They carefully hid the residue in the ground, and made their entrance into the city.

1. **dinars** (di·närz′) *n.:* A dinar was originally a Roman coin (*denarius*). This currency of varying values was used in many parts of the Mediterranean and the Middle East.

Vocabulary

duplicity (do͞o·plis′ə·tē) *n.:* cunning; treachery.
residue (rez′ə·do͞o′) *n.:* leftover portion; remainder.

Shah Jahan, who ruled India during the Mughal dynasty, from 1628 to 1658. Jahan designed the Taj Mahal to immortalize his favorite wife.

Victoria and Albert Museum, London. The Bridgeman Art Library.

Before long, Wrong-Mind exhausted his preliminary portion because he practiced the vice of unwise expenditure and because his predetermined fate offered vulnerable points. He therefore made a second division with Right-Mind, each taking a second hundred. Within a year this, too, had slipped in the same way through Wrong-Mind's fingers. As a result, his thoughts took this form: "Suppose I divide another two hundred with him, then what is the good of the remainder, a paltry four hundred, even if I steal it? I think I prefer to steal a round six hundred." After this meditation, he went alone, removed the treasure, and leveled the ground.

A mere month later, he took the initiative, going to Right-Mind and saying: "My good friend, let us divide the rest of the money equally." So he and Right-Mind visited the spot and began to dig. When the excavation failed to reveal any treasure, that impudent Wrong-Mind first of all smote his own head with the empty pot, then shouted: "What became of that good lucre?[2] Surely, Right-Mind, you must have stolen it. Give me my half. If you don't, I will bring you into court."

"Be silent, villain!" said the other. "My name is Right-Mind. Such thefts are not in my line. You know the verse:

A man right-minded sees but trash,
Mere clods of earth, in others' cash;
A mother in his neighbor's wife;
In all that lives, his own dear life."

So together they carried their dispute to court and related the theft of the money. And when the magistrates[3] learned the facts, they decreed an ordeal[4] for each. But Wrong-Mind said: "Come! This judgment is not proper. For the legal dictum[5] runs:

Best evidence is written word;
Next, witnesses who saw and heard;
Then only let ordeals prevail
When witnesses completely fail.

In the present case, I have a witness, the goddess of the wood. She will reveal to you which one of us is guilty, which not guilty." And they replied: "You are quite right, sir. For there is a further saying:

To meanest witnesses, ordeals
    Should never be preferred;
Of course much less, if you possess
    A forest goddess's word.

Now we also feel a great interest in the case. You two must accompany us tomorrow morning to that part of the forest." With this they accepted bail from each and sent them home.

Then Wrong-Mind went home and asked his father's help. "Father dear," said he, "the dinars are in my hand. They only require one little word from you. This very night I am going to hide you out of sight in a hole in the mimosa[6] tree that grows near the spot where I dug out the treasure before. In the morning you must be my witness in the presence of the magistrates."

"Oh, my son," said the father, "we are both lost. This is no kind of scheme. There is wisdom in the old story:

The good and bad of given schemes
    Wise thought must first reveal:
The stupid heron saw his chicks
    Provide a mongoose meal."

"How was that?" asked Wrong-Mind. And his father told the story of

2. **lucre** (lo͞o′kər) *n.:* riches; money.
3. **magistrates** *n. pl.:* officials with judicial powers.
4. **ordeal** *n.:* here, a form of trial in which guilt or innocence is determined by subjecting the accused to painful or dangerous tests.
5. **dictum** *n.:* formal pronouncement.

6. **mimosa** *n.:* flowering tree.

Vocabulary

preliminary (prē•lim′ə•ner′ē) *adj.:* introductory.
initiative (i•nish′ə•tiv) *n.:* action of making the first move.

Peacocks and cranes beside a river. Illustration from the *Baburnama* (*The Memoirs of Babur*) (1589–1590). Mughal School.

National Museum of India, New Delhi. The Bridgeman Art Library.

A Remedy Worse Than the Disease

A flock of herons once had their nests on a fig tree in a part of a forest. In a hole in the tree lived a black snake who made a practice of eating the heron chicks before their wings sprouted.

At last one heron, in utter woe at seeing the young ones eaten by a snake, went to the shore of the pond, shed a flood of tears, and stood with downcast face. And a crab who noticed him in this attitude, said: "Uncle, why are you so tearful today?" "My good friend," said the heron, "what am I to do? Fate is against me. My babies and the youngsters belonging to my relatives have been eaten by a snake that lives in a hole in the fig tree. Grieved at their grief, I weep. Tell me, is there any possible device for killing him?"

On hearing this, the crab reflected: "After all, he is a natural-born enemy of my race. I will give him such advice—a kind of true lie—that other herons may also perish. For the proverb says:

Let your speech like butter be;
Steel your heart remorselessly:
Stir an enemy to action
That destroys him with his faction."

And he said aloud: "Uncle, conditions being as they are, scatter bits of fish all the way from the mongoose burrow to the snake's hole. The mongoose will follow that trail and will destroy the villainous snake."

When this had been done, the mongoose followed the bits of fish, killed the villainous snake, and also ate at his leisure all the herons who made their home in the tree.

"And that is why I say:

The good and bad of given schemes, . . .
and the rest of it."

But Wrong-Mind disdained the paternal warning, and during the night he hid his father out of sight in the hole in the tree. When morning came, the scamp took a bath, put on clean garments, and followed Right-Mind and the magistrates to the mimosa tree, where he cried in piercing tones:

"Earth, heaven, and death, the feeling mind,
Sun, moon, and water, fire and wind,
Both twilights, justice, day and night
Discern man's conduct, wrong or right.

O blessed goddess of the wood, which of us two is the thief? Speak."

Then Wrong-Mind's father spoke from his hole in the mimosa: "Gentlemen, Right-Mind took that money." And when all the king's men heard this statement, their eyes blossomed with astonishment, and they searched their minds to discover the appropriate legal penalty for stealing money, in order to visit it on Right-Mind.

Meanwhile, Right-Mind heaped inflammable matter about the hole in the mimosa and set fire to it. As the mimosa burned, Wrong-Mind's father issued from the hole with a pitiful wail, his body scorched and his eyes popping out. And they all asked: "Why, sir! What does this mean?"

"It is all Wrong-Mind's doing," he replied. Whereupon the king's men hanged Wrong-Mind to a branch of the mimosa, while they commended Right-Mind and caused him satisfaction by conferring upon him the king's favor and other things. ■

Vocabulary

discern (di • surn′) *v.:* recognize (the difference); make out clearly.

Tamarind tree (detail) (1590) by Mirza Abd al-Rahim. Mughal school.

The Art Archive/British Library, London.

Response and Analysis

Reading Check

1. What do Right-Mind and Wrong-Mind agree to do with their treasure?
2. How does Wrong-Mind break their agreement?
3. Why does Wrong-Mind hide his father in the mimosa tree?
4. How does Right-Mind expose Wrong-Mind's scheme?

Thinking Critically

5. What **moral lessons** about rulership can be learned from the **fable** "Right-Mind and Wrong-Mind"?
6. What kind of person does the character Wrong-Mind seem to stand for in the fable?
7. How does the story-within-a-story, "A Remedy Worse Than the Disease," connect to the **moral** of "Right-Mind and Wrong-Mind"?
8. An **epigram** is a brief, clever, and often memorable statement. Which of the four-line epigrammatic verses best sums up the overall moral of the fable?
9. Do the lessons taught in "Right-Mind and Wrong-Mind" relate at all to people and their problems today? Think especially in terms of arguments over money and the use of courts to settle disputes. Use examples from the fable to support your opinions.
10. In what other situations could the "remedy" be "worse than the disease"?

Comparing Literature

11. How do these stories from India compare with the stories you've read from *The Canterbury Tales*? Consider these three story elements:
    - characterization
    - use of a frame story
    - use of moral lessons

LISTENING AND SPEAKING

Performing the Fable

Prepare "Right-Mind and Wrong-Mind" for an oral presentation to an audience. You will have to decide how many readers you will need and which parts of the fable you will assign to which reader. Before you present your fable to an audience, try it out before a group of classmates. Have your critics evaluate your performance in terms of clarity, dramatic interest, and originality. Use their evaluation as you make final adjustments in your presentation for the real performance.

Vocabulary Development

Analogies

duplicity preliminary discern
residue initiative

In an **analogy** two pairs of words have the same relationship. They may be antonyms or synonyms, or they may share some other relationship. Work with a partner to complete each analogy below with a Vocabulary word from above.

1. SUM : TOTAL :: residue : remainder
2. SWEET : SOUR :: _______ : final
3. NOISE : SILENCE :: _______ : laziness
4. WISDOM : KNOWLEDGE :: _______ : dishonesty
5. WALK : AMBLE :: _______ : figure out

Literary Skills
Analyze the characteristics of fables. Compare frame stories.

Listening and Speaking Skills
Give an oral performance of a fable.

Vocabulary Skills
Complete word analogies.

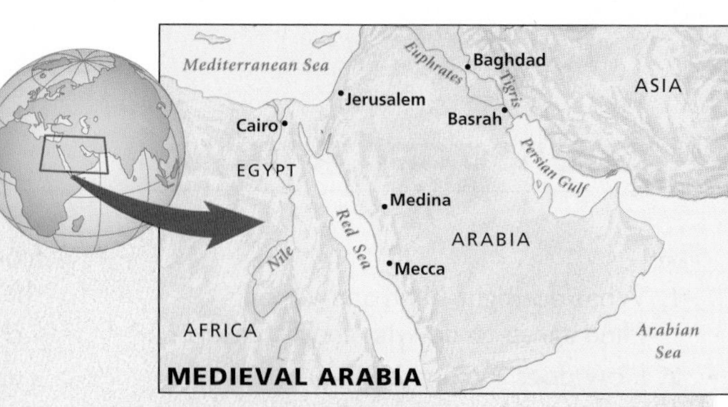

The Thousand and One Nights

(c. 850–c. 1500)

Ever since the writer Antoine Galland translated *The Thousand and One Nights*—or *The Arabian Nights' Entertainments*—into French in the early eighteenth century, this collection of tales has been the best-known and most widely read work of Arabic literature in the West. The often fantastic adventures of the characters Ali Baba, Aladdin, and Sindbad are known throughout the world today.

The original stories in *The Thousand and One Nights* came from many oral and written sources, including such collections as the Indian *Panchatantra* (see page 193) and tales brought by travelers from China, India, and every part of the Middle East. Scholars have identified sources for many of the stories, but the true origins of many others remain unknown because they exist in more than one version and in more than one language.

The earliest references to *The Thousand and One Nights* appear in manuscripts from as early as the ninth century. Kept alive by Arab storytellers throughout the Middle Ages, the collection grew and changed. By the mid–sixteenth century, an unknown Egyptian had put the stories into the form we know today. The tales were first published in Arabic in 1548.

The tales in the collection are loosely held together by a **frame story.** In the frame story a sultan, Shahriyar, is enraged at his wife's unfaithfulness and orders her executed. He then takes a new wife each day but has her killed at dawn the next day because he believes that no woman can ever be faithful. The supply of potential wives is running low when the sultan takes Scheherazade (shə•her'ə•zäd') as his wife.

Scheherazade is a spellbinding storyteller and a clever woman besides. Each night she entertains the sultan with a new tale, but she delays revealing the ending until the following night. The captivated sultan keeps postponing her execution in order to hear the end of each story. After one thousand and one nights of tales, he abandons his plans to kill Scheherazade, and the couple remains happily married.

The Princess in the Kitchens by Edmund Dulac. Illustration for a 1911 edition of *The Arabian Nights.* Lithograph.

Before You Read

from The Third Voyage of Sindbad the Sailor

Make the Connection

Think of monsters you might find in popular stories and movies today. What qualities do these monsters usually have? What does a typical monster or villain look like? What are his or her habits? How does he or she feel about other people? Where do these monsters live—that is, what settings are associated with them?

Literary Focus

Archetypes

An **archetype** is a very old pattern used in storytelling. An archetype can be a plot, a character, a setting, or even just an object. One of the most universal archetypes is the "monster-slaying story." If you have read Homer's *Odyssey,* you might even recognize the monster in this Middle Eastern story. This is a characteristic of archetypes: They cross borders and cultures. In storytelling, archetypes seem to satisfy or excite the most basic human needs and longings.

An **archetype** is the basic pattern or model of a character, a plot, a setting, or an object that recurs in storytelling.

For more on Archetype, see the Handbook of Literary and Historical Terms.

Background

Sindbad is a rich young man from Baghdad (now the capital of Iraq) who goes to sea to regain his fortune after recklessly spending all his wealth. His marvelous adventures at sea are the subjects of the three Sindbad stories that form a story cycle in *The Thousand and One Nights*. Some scholars believe the tales originated in Baghdad, but others argue persuasively that they came from Oman (a country on the southeast coast of the Arabian Peninsula) and only later became associated with Baghdad.

Vocabulary Development

disconsolately (dis•kän′sə•lit•lē) *adv.:* dejectedly; unhappily.

corpulent (kôr′pyo͞o•lənt) *adj.:* fat.

approbation (ap′rə•bā′shən) *n.:* approval.

nimbly (nim′blē) *adv.:* in a quick, light way.

contrived (kən•trīvd′) *v.:* managed.

Sindbad the Sailor being carried by a sea monster, from *One Thousand and One Nights* (18th century).

Archivo Iconografico, S.A./CORBIS.

Literary Skills Understand the characteristics of an archetype.

from The Third Voyage of Sindbad the Sailor

from The Thousand and One Nights

translated by **N. J. Dawood**

Know, my friends, that for some time after my return I continued to lead a happy and tranquil life, but I soon grew weary of my idle existence in Baghdad and once again longed to roam the world in quest of profit and adventure. Unmindful of the dangers of ambition and worldly greed, I resolved to set out on another voyage. I provided myself with a great store of goods and, after taking them down the Tigris,[1] set sail from Basrah,[2] together with a band of honest merchants.

The voyage began prosperously. We called at many foreign ports, trading profitably with our merchandise. One day, however, whilst we were sailing in midocean, we heard the captain of our ship, who was on deck scanning the horizon, suddenly burst out in a loud lament. He beat himself about the face, tore his beard, and rent his clothes.

"We are lost!" he cried, as we crowded round him. "The treacherous wind has driven us off our course toward that island which you see before you. It is the isle of the Zughb, where dwell a race of dwarfs more akin to apes than men, from whom no voyager has ever escaped alive!"

Scarcely had he uttered these words when a multitude of apelike savages appeared on the beach and began to swim out toward the ship. In a few moments they were upon us, thick as a swarm of locusts. Barely four spans[3] in height, they were the ugliest of living creatures, with little gleaming yellow eyes and bodies thickly covered with black fur. And so numerous were they that we did not dare to provoke them or attempt to drive them away, lest they should set upon us and kill us to a man by force of numbers.

They scrambled up the masts, gnawing the cables with their teeth and biting them to shreds. Then they seized the helm and steered the vessel to their island. When the ship had run ashore, the dwarfs carried us one by one to the beach, and, promptly pushing off again, climbed on board and sailed away.

Disconsolately we set out to search for food and water, and by good fortune came upon some fruit trees and a running stream. Here we refreshed ourselves, and then wandered about the island until at length we saw far off among the trees a massive building, where we hoped to pass the night in safety. Drawing nearer, we found that it was a towering palace surrounded by a lofty wall, with a great ebony door which stood wide open. We entered the spacious courtyard, and to our surprise found it deserted. In one corner lay a great heap of bones, and on the far side we saw a broad bench, an open oven, pots and pans of enormous size, and many iron spits for roasting.

1. **Tigris** (tī′gris): river in southwest Asia, flowing from Turkey through Iraq.
2. **Basrah** (bus′rə): port at the head of the Shatt-al-Arab Channel, where the Tigris and Euphrates rivers join.
3. **spans** *n. pl.:* A span was a measurement equal to nine inches, based on the distance between the extended thumb and little finger.

Vocabulary

disconsolately (dis • kän′sə • lit • lē) *adv.:* dejectedly; unhappily.

Colossus by Francisco de Goya y Lucientes.

Exhausted and sick at heart, we lay down in the courtyard and were soon overcome by sleep. At sunset we were awakened by a noise like thunder. The earth shook beneath our feet and we saw a colossal black giant approaching from the doorway. He was a fearsome sight—tall as a palm tree, with red eyes burning in his head like coals of fire; his mouth was a dark well, with lips that drooped like a camel's loosely over his chest, whilst his ears, like a pair of large round discs, hung back over his shoulders: his fangs were as long as the tusks of a boar and his nails were like the claws of a lion.

The sight of this monster struck terror to our hearts. We cowered motionless on the ground as we watched him stride across the yard and sit down on the bench. For a few moments he eyed us one by one in silence; then he rose and, reaching out toward me, lifted me up by the neck and began feeling my body as a butcher would a lamb. Finding me little more than skin and bone, however, he flung me to the ground and, picking up each of my companions in turn, pinched and prodded them and set them down until at last he came to the captain.

Now the captain was a corpulent fellow, tall and broad-shouldered. The giant seemed to like him well. He gripped him as a butcher grips a fatted ram and broke his neck under his foot. Then he thrust an iron spit through his body from mouth to backside and, lighting a great fire in the oven, carefully turned his victim round and round before it. When the flesh was finely roasted, the ogre tore the body to pieces with his fingernails as though it were a pullet,[4] and devoured it limb by limb, gnawing the bones and flinging them against the wall. The monster then stretched himself out on the bench and soon fell fast asleep. His snores were as loud as the grunts and gurgles that issue from the throat of a slaughtered beast.

Thus he slept all night, and when morning came he rose and went out of the palace, leaving us half-crazed with terror.

As soon as we were certain that the monster had gone, we began lamenting our evil fortune. "Would that we had been drowned in the sea or killed by the apes!" we cried. "That would surely have been better than the foul death which now awaits us! But that which Allah has ordained must surely come to pass."

We left the palace to search for some hiding place, but could find no shelter in any part of the island, and had no choice but to return to the palace in the evening. Night came, and with it the black giant, announcing his approach by a noise like thunder. No sooner had he entered than he snatched up one of the merchants and prepared his supper in the same way as the night before. Then, stretching himself out to sleep, he snored the night away.

Next morning, when the giant had gone, we discussed our desperate plight.

"By Allah," cried one of the merchants, "let us rather throw ourselves into the sea than remain alive to be roasted and eaten!"

"Listen, my friends," said another. "We must kill this monster. For only by destroying him can we end his wickedness and save good Muslims from his barbarous cruelty."

This proposal was received with general approbation; so I rose in my turn and addressed the company. "If we are all agreed to kill this monster," I said, "let us first build a raft on which we can escape from this island as soon as we have sent his soul to damnation. Perchance our raft will take us to some other island, where we can board a ship bound for our country. If we are drowned, we shall at least escape roasting and die a martyr's death."

"By Allah," cried the others, "that is a wise plan."

Setting to work at once, we hauled several logs from the great pile of wood stacked beside the oven and carried them out of the palace. Then we fastened them together into a raft, which we left ready on the seashore.

In the evening the earth shook beneath our feet as the black giant burst in upon us, barking and snarling like a mad dog. Once more he seized upon the stoutest of my companions and prepared his meal. When he had eaten his fill, he stretched himself upon the bench as was his custom and soon fell fast asleep.

Noiselessly we now rose, took two of the great iron spits from the oven, and thrust them into the fire. As soon as they were red-hot we carried them over to the snoring monster and plunged their sharpened ends deep into his eyes, exerting our united weight from above to push them home. The giant gave a deafening shriek which filled our hearts with terror and cast us back on the ground many yards away. Totally blinded, he leapt up from the bench groping for us with outstretched hands, while we nimbly dodged his frantic clutches. In despair he felt his way to the ebony door and

4. **pullet** *n.:* chicken.

Vocabulary

corpulent (kôr′pyo͞o•lənt) *adj.:* fat.
approbation (ap′rə•bā′shən) *n.:* approval.
nimbly (nim′blē) *adv.:* in a quick, light way.

Illustration by Edmund Dulac from *Sindbad the Sailor and Other Stories.*

staggered out of the yard, groaning in agonies of pain.

Without losing a moment we made off toward the beach. As soon as we reached the water we launched our raft and jumped aboard; but scarcely had we rowed a few yards when we saw the blind savage running toward us, guided by a foul hag of his own kind. On reaching the shore they stood howling threats and curses at us for a while, and then caught up massive boulders and hurled them at our raft with stupendous force. Missile followed missile until all my companions, save two, were drowned; but we three who escaped soon contrived to paddle beyond the range of their fury. ■

Vocabulary

contrived (kən • trīvd′) *v.:* managed.

Response and Analysis

Reading Check

1. Like all folk tales, this one is built on a simple **plot** structure. Show the story's structure by filling out a chart like the following. (The number of main events may vary.)

Basic situation and conflict	
Main events	
Climax	
Resolution	

Thinking Critically

2. **Archetypes** are very old patterns found in stories across the ages, from many diverse cultures. Archetypes can be characters (the superhuman hero), plots (monster-slaying stories), or places (paradises and hells). How is the giant in this story an example of the archetypal monster who threatens a hero and his people?
3. Storytellers often make the hero's enemy only partly human. How does the storyteller in Sindbad's story make the giant particularly disgusting? Why do you think cannibalism makes an enemy seem especially evil?
4. How do storytellers today (including moviemakers) use the old monster **archetype** found in Sindbad's story?

Literary Skills Analyze the characteristics of an archetype.

Writing Skills Write a story that contains an archetypal hero.

Vocabulary Skills Create semantic maps.

Literary Criticism

5. Some Arab scholars have dismissed *The Thousand and One Nights* as mere popular entertainment that is far from being great literature. These scholars have argued that the stories have crude and simplistic plots and no depth of characterization or theme. If this is true, why do you think *The Thousand and One Nights* has remained popular for hundreds of years?

Comparing Literature

6. How does this monster compare with the monsters that challenge Beowulf (see page 21) and Gilgamesh (see page 58)?

WRITING

Fantastic Foe

Write your own episode about an adventure-seeking hero and his encounter with a monster. You may wish to follow the pattern of the Sindbad story you have just read, but change the details enough so that your story is unique. Before you begin, try mapping out the story details you will include. If you wish, illustrate your story.

Vocabulary Development

Semantic Mapping

disconsolately   *nimbly*
corpulent   *contrived*
approbation

Make a **semantic map** like the following for the Vocabulary words listed above. Be sure to locate the word in the story to determine its meaning in context.

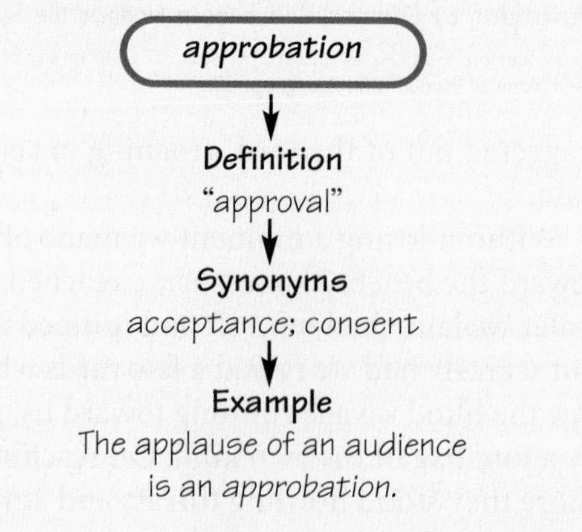

approbation
Definition
"approval"
Synonyms
acceptance; consent
Example
The applause of an audience
is an approbation.

Giovanni Boccaccio

(1313–1375)

Giovanni Boccaccio (bō•käch′ē•ō′) was born in the summer of 1313, perhaps in Florence or possibly in Certaldo, a small Tuscan town twenty miles outside the city. The illegitimate son of an unknown Frenchwoman and a Florentine merchant banker, Boccaccio spent his boyhood with his father. At the age of fourteen, however, he was sent to Naples, where his father had arranged for him to be a clerk in one of his banks.

After finishing his apprenticeship at the bank, Boccaccio entered the University of Naples and earned a degree in law. In 1340, when Boccaccio's father suffered a financial setback, he asked his son to return to Florence. There Boccaccio met Francesco Petrarch, the great Italian poet, who became a lifelong friend and literary advisor. In Florence, too, Boccaccio experienced the most catastrophic event of his lifetime when the Black Death struck the city in 1348. During this plague three out of four Florentines died a gruesome death. The streets of the city were piled high with swollen, reeking corpses covered with black splotches.

Boccaccio used the plague as the backdrop for his masterpiece, the *Decameron*. Written in vernacular Italian—the Italian of everyday speech—instead of Latin, the *Decameron*'s one hundred tales deal with two great subjects: love and the corruption of the clergy. Many of the *Decameron*'s stories are adaptations of popular folk tales, fables, anecdotes, and even jokes that Boccaccio might have overheard on the bustling streets of medieval Florence.

Completed about 1353, the *Decameron* established Boccaccio's literary reputation. Boccaccio, however, did not consider the *Decameron* to be his best work. In fact, he considered it trifling and unimportant. Nevertheless, the *Decameron* has survived the test of time. Geoffrey Chaucer, William Shakespeare, John Milton, and many other writers have used Boccaccio's work as both a model and a source.

Boccaccio (15th century) by Andrea del Castagno.

Uffizi, Florence, Italy.

Before You Read

Federigo's Falcon

Make the Connection

Few experiences are more painful than falling in love with someone who doesn't care about you. We get over it—most of us—and it never (well, almost never) does us serious damage. At the most painful moments, when you think that things can't possibly get worse, they very well might. Or they might, surprisingly, turn around. . . .

Literary Focus

Situational Irony

Situational irony occurs when what actually happens in a story is the opposite of what is expected or appropriate. For example, in Greek mythology, the story of King Midas is loaded with situational irony. Midas, who values wealth above all else, is granted the power to turn anything he touches into gold, but he soon discovers that his touch also turns food, drink, and even his beloved daughter to gold. Thus, far from making him happy, as he expected, Midas's golden touch makes him miserable. Situational irony always produces an unexpected turn of events.

SKILLS FOCUS

Literary Skills Understand situational irony.

Reading Skills Evaluate historical context.

Situational irony occurs when what actually happens is the opposite of what is expected or appropriate.

For more on Irony, see the Handbook of Literary and Historical Terms.

INTERNET

Vocabulary Practice

•

More About Giovanni Boccaccio

•

Keyword: LE7 12-2

Reading Skills

Evaluating Historical Context

Relations between men and women in the Middle Ages were shaped by the social, economic, and ethical realities of the era. Medieval women could not marry without the permission of their male relatives, and family money was usually passed down from male to male. The values of the courtly love tradition required women to be virtuous and withholding, yet capable of inspiring devoted service in a noble man.

Boccaccio may have experienced courtly love firsthand. In his first prose romance, he describes meeting—and immediately falling in love with—a woman named Fiammetta. Fiammetta reappears in many of Boccaccio's works, and it is she who tells the story of Federigo's falcon in the *Decameron*.

As you read Boccaccio's love story, jot down notes on how the historical context affects the plot of the story.

Background

In the **frame story** of the *Decameron,* ten wealthy young Florentines flee to a villa outside the city to escape the ravages of the plague. To pass the time, the young people decide that for each of ten days they will name a king or queen, who, in turn, will choose a theme upon which the others must tell a story. "Federigo's Falcon" is the ninth story told on the fifth day, a day devoted to telling stories with happy endings.

Vocabulary Development

dire (dīr) *adj.:* extreme; desperate.

compensate (käm′pən•sāt′) *v.:* repay; make up (for or to).

presumption (prē•zump′shən) *n.:* act of taking too much for granted.

console (kən•sōl′) *v.:* comfort.

reproached (ri•prōcht′) *v.:* expressed disapproval.

Federigo's Falcon

from the Decameron

Giovanni Boccaccio

translated by **Mark Musa** *and* **Peter Bondanella**

There was once in Florence a young man named Federigo, the son of Messer[1] Filippo Alberighi, renowned above all other men in Tuscany for his prowess in arms and for his courtliness. As often happens to most gentlemen, he fell in love with a lady named Monna[2] Giovanna, in her day considered to be one of the most beautiful and one of the most charming women that ever there was in Florence; and in order to win her love, he participated in jousts and tournaments, organized and gave feasts, and spent his money without restraint; but she, no less virtuous than beautiful, cared little for these things done on her behalf, nor did she care for him who did them. Now, as Federigo was spending far beyond his means and was taking nothing in, as easily happens he lost his wealth and became poor, with nothing but his little farm to his name (from whose revenues he lived very meagerly) and one falcon which was among the best in the world.

More in love than ever, but knowing that he would never be able to live the way he wished to in the city, he went to live at Campi,[3] where his farm was. There he passed his time hawking whenever he could, asked nothing of anyone, and endured his poverty patiently. Now, during the time that Federigo was reduced to dire need, it happened that the husband of Monna Giovanna fell ill, and realizing death was near, he made his last will. He was very rich, and he made his son, who was growing up, his heir, and, since he had loved Monna Giovanna very much, he made her his heir should his son die without a legitimate heir; and then he died.

1. **Messer** (mes'ər): title of address similar to *sir.*
2. **Monna** (mō'nə): In Italian, *Monna* is an abbreviation for *Madonna* (mə·dän'ə), a formal title for a woman, similar to *madam.*
3. **Campi** (käm'pē): small town set in the mountains northwest of Florence. *Campi* literally means "fields."

Detail from Frederick II's *Treatise on Falconry.*

Vocabulary

dire (dīr) *adj.:* extreme; desperate.

Monna Giovanna was now a widow, and as is the custom among our women, she went to the country with her son to spend a year on one of her possessions very close by to Federigo's farm, and it happened that this young boy became friends with Federigo and began to enjoy birds and hunting dogs; and after he had seen Federigo's falcon fly many times, it pleased him so much that he very much wished it were his own, but he did not dare to ask for it, for he could see how dear it was to Federigo. And during this time, it happened that the young boy took ill, and his mother was much grieved, for he was her only child and she loved him enormously. She would spend the entire day by his side, never ceasing to comfort him, and often asking him if there was anything he desired, begging him to tell her what it might be, for if it were possible to obtain it, she would certainly do everything possible to get it. After the young boy had heard her make this offer many times, he said:

"Mother, if you can arrange for me to have Federigo's falcon, I think I would be well very soon."

When the lady heard this, she was taken aback for a moment, and she began to think what she should do. She knew that Federigo had loved her for a long while, in spite of the fact that he never received a single glance from her, and so, she said to herself:

"How can I send or go and ask for this falcon of his which is, as I have heard tell, the best that ever flew, and besides this, his only means of support? And how can I be so insensitive as to wish to take away from this gentleman the only pleasure which is left to him?"

And involved in these thoughts, knowing that she was certain to have the bird if she asked for it, but not knowing what to say to her son, she stood there without answering him. Finally the love she bore her son persuaded her that she should make him happy, and no matter what the consequences might be, she would not send for the bird, but rather go herself for it and bring it back to him; so she answered her son:

"My son, take comfort and think only of getting well, for I promise you that the first thing I shall do tomorrow morning is to go for it and bring it back to you."

The child was so happy that he showed some improvement that very day. The following morning, the lady, accompanied by another woman, as if going for a stroll, went to Federigo's modest house and asked for him. Since it was not the season for it, Federigo had not been hawking for some days and was in his orchard, attending to certain tasks. When he heard that Monna Giovanna was asking for him at the door, he was very surprised and happy to run there. As she saw him coming, she greeted him with feminine charm, and once Federigo had welcomed her courteously, she said:

"Greetings, Federigo!" Then she continued: "I have come to compensate you for the harm you have suffered on my account by loving me more than you needed to; and the compensation is this: I, along with this companion of mine, intend to dine with you—a simple meal—this very day."

To this Federigo humbly replied: "Madonna, I never remember having suffered any harm because of you. On the contrary, so much good have I received from you that if ever I have been worth anything, it has been because of your merit and the love I bore for you; and your generous visit is certainly so dear to me that I would spend all over again that which I spent in the past; but you have come to a poor host."

And having said this, he received her into his home humbly, and from there he led her into his garden, and since he had no one there to keep her company, he said:

"My lady, since there is no one else, this good woman here, the wife of this workman, will keep you company while I go to set the table."

Though he was very poor, Federigo, until now, had never before realized to what extent he had wasted his wealth; but this morning, the fact that he found nothing with which he could honor the lady for the love of whom he had once entertained countless men in the past gave him cause

Vocabulary

compensate (käm′pən • sāt′) *v.:* repay; make up (for or to).

to reflect. In great anguish, he cursed himself and his fortune and, like a man beside himself, he started running here and there, but could find neither money nor a pawnable[4] object. The hour was late and his desire to honor the gracious lady was great, but not wishing to turn for help to others (not even to his own workman), he set his eyes upon his good falcon, perched in a small room; and since he had nowhere else to turn, he took the bird, and finding it plump, he decided that it would be a worthy food for such a lady. So, without further thought, he wrung its neck and quickly gave it to his servant girl to pluck, prepare, and place on a spit to be roasted with care; and when he had set the table with the whitest of tablecloths (a few of which he still had left), he returned, with a cheerful face, to the lady in his garden, saying that the meal he was able to prepare for her was ready.

The lady and her companion rose, went to the table together with Federigo, who waited upon them with the greatest devotion, and they ate the good falcon without knowing what it was they were eating. And having left the table and spent some time in pleasant conversation, the lady thought it time now to say what she had come to say, and so she spoke these kind words to Federigo:

"Federigo, if you recall your past life and my virtue, which you perhaps mistook for harshness and cruelty, I do not doubt at all that you will be amazed by my presumption when you hear what my main reason for coming here is; but if you had children, through whom you might have experienced the power of parental love, it seems certain to me that you would, at least in part, forgive me. But, just as you have no child, I do have one, and I cannot escape the common laws of other mothers; the force of such laws compels me to follow them, against my own will and against good manners and duty, and to ask of you a gift which I know is most precious to you; and it is naturally so, since your extreme condition has left you no other delight, no other pleasure, no other consolation; and this gift is your falcon, which my son is so taken by that if I do not bring it to him, I fear his sickness will grow so much worse that I may lose him. And therefore I beg you, not because of the love that you bear for me, which does not oblige you in the least, but because of your own nobility, which you have shown to be greater

August: Departure for the Hunt with Falcons, from the calendar for the *Très riches heures du duc de Berry* by the Limbourg brothers.

Ms. 65/1284, fol. 8v. Musée Condé, Chantilly, France.

4. **pawnable** *adj.:* able to be given as security in return for a loan of money or goods.

Vocabulary

presumption (prē•zump′shən) *n.:* act of taking too much for granted.

than that of all others in practicing courtliness, that you be pleased to give it to me, so that I may say that I have saved the life of my son by means of this gift, and because of it I have placed him in your debt forever."

When he heard what the lady requested and knew that he could not oblige her since he had given her the falcon to eat, Federigo began to weep in her presence, for he could not utter a word in reply. The lady, at first, thought his tears were caused more by the sorrow of having to part with the good falcon than by anything else, and she was on the verge of telling him she no longer wished it, but she held back and waited for Federigo's reply after he stopped weeping. And he said:

"My lady, ever since it pleased God for me to place my love in you, I have felt that Fortune has been hostile to me in many things, and I have complained of her, but all this is nothing compared to what she has just done to me, and I must never be at peace with her again, thinking about how you have come here to my poor home where, while it was rich, you never deigned to come, and you requested a small gift, and Fortune worked to make it impossible for me to give it to you; and why this is so I shall tell you briefly. When I heard that you, out of your kindness, wished to dine with me, I considered it fitting and right, taking into account your excellence and your worthiness, that I should honor you, according to my possibilities, with a more precious food than that which I usually serve to other people; therefore, remembering the falcon that you requested and its value, I judged it a food worthy of you, and this very day I had it roasted and served to you as best I could; but seeing now that you desired it in another way, my sorrow in not being able to serve you is so great that I shall never be able to console myself again."

And after he had said this, he laid the feathers, the feet, and the beak of the bird before her as proof. When the lady heard and saw this, she first reproached him for having killed such a falcon to serve as a meal to a woman; but then to herself she commended the greatness of his spirit, which no poverty was able or would be able to diminish; then, having lost all hope of getting the falcon and, perhaps because of this, of improving the health of her son as well, she thanked Federigo both for the honor paid to her and for his good will, and she left in grief, and returned to her son. To his mother's extreme sorrow, either because of his disappointment that he could not have the falcon, or because his illness must have necessarily led to it, the boy passed from this life only a few days later.

After the period of her mourning and bitterness had passed, the lady was repeatedly urged by her brothers to remarry, since she was very rich and was still young; and although she did not wish to do so, they became so insistent that she remembered the merits of Federigo and his last act of generosity—that is, to have killed such a falcon to do her honor—and she said to her brothers:

"I would prefer to remain a widow, if that would please you; but if you wish me to take a husband, you may rest assured that I shall take no man but Federigo degli Alberighi."

In answer to this, making fun of her, her brothers replied:

"You foolish woman, what are you saying? How can you want him; he hasn't a penny to his name?"

To this she replied: "My brothers, I am well aware of what you say, but I would rather have a man who needs money than money that needs a man."

Her brothers, seeing that she was determined and knowing Federigo to be of noble birth, no matter how poor he was, accepted her wishes and gave her in marriage to him with all her riches. When he found himself the husband of such a great lady, whom he had loved so much and who was so wealthy besides, he managed his financial affairs with more prudence than in the past and lived with her happily the rest of his days. ■

Vocabulary

console (kən•sōl′) *v.:* comfort.

reproached (ri•prōcht′) *v.:* expressed disapproval.

Response and Analysis

Reading Check

1. How does the young Federigo try to win Monna Giovanna's love? What are the results of his efforts?
2. What does Monna Giovanna do when she learns what Federigo has made for supper?
3. When her brothers urge her to remarry, what does Monna Giovanna remember?

Thinking Critically

4. Why do you think Monna Giovanna does not return Federigo's love at the beginning of the story?
5. How does Federigo's sacrifice change Monna Giovanna's opinion of him? Why will she "take no man but Federigo"?
6. Explain how Monna Giovanna fits the image of the virtuous woman in the medieval courtly love tradition. How does Federigo fit the image of the chivalrous lover? Are there any ways in which these characters depart from the conventional images?
7. The unexpected visit of Monna Giovanna to Federigo after he has lost all his money is an example of **situational irony.** What did you expect would happen? What actually happens?
8. Cite two other examples of situational irony in the story. How is the falcon central to these ironic events?

Comparing Literature

9. What influences of the medieval period help to shape the plots, characters, and themes of the selections you have read from *The Canterbury Tales* and the *Decameron*? How might these stories change if they were set in the twenty-first century? Consult your reading notes.

WRITING

Two Medieval Women

How does Monna Giovanna compare with Chaucer's famous character the Wife of Bath (see page 178)? In an essay, **compare** these medieval female characters. Consider the following:

- their social classes
- their attitudes toward men
- their attitudes toward love and marriage

Vocabulary Development

Etymologies

dire
compensate
presumption
console
reproached

Use a good dictionary to research the origin, or **etymology,** of each Vocabulary word listed above. Use a chart like the one below, which shows the etymology of *dire,* to organize your findings.

Word	Language of Origin	Original Word
dire	Latin (L)	*dirus,* meaning "fearful"

Literary Skills
Analyze situational irony.

Reading Skills
Evaluate historical context. Compare influences of different historical periods.

Writing Skills
Write an essay comparing and contrasting two literary characters.

Vocabulary Skills
Understand etymologies.

Sir Thomas Malory

(c. 1405–1471)

The historical identity of Sir Thomas Malory, the author of Britain's most famous work on King Arthur, is almost as uncertain as the identity of the hero of his *Le Morte d'Arthur (The Death of Arthur)*. All we know for sure about Malory is that he was a knight familiar with chivalric romances who was writing in the years 1469–1470. We know this from a sort of postscript that appears in the manuscript of Malory's work that William Caxton printed in 1485. In this postscript, Malory asks his readers to pray for his deliverance, suggesting that he was in prison during some of the time he was writing his stories about Arthur.

Since the fifteenth century, scholars have been trying to find out more about the actual person who wrote the work Caxton entitled *Le Morte d'Arthur*. At one time as many as five different "historical" Malorys were proposed. However, most scholars have come to accept the Thomas Malory born in Warwickshire as the most likely author of *Le Morte d'Arthur*.

This Warwickshire Malory served in France during the Hundred Years' War and apparently fought at the siege of Calais in 1436. A few years later he married a woman named Elizabeth, who bore him a son. Sir Thomas was elected to Parliament at least once and died in 1471, perhaps from the plague.

The record of this aristocratic war hero, however, also contains a series of arrests for theft, burglary, and assault, including the robbing of an abbey in which he supposedly broke eighteen doors and roughed up the monks.

But the charges against Malory were merely accusations, and there is no record of any trials or convictions. The late fifteenth century was a time of great political partisanship and civil disorder, so it is very possible that Malory's imprisonment was politically motivated. He might simply have backed the wrong side in a political conflict.

The Arthur in Malory's work is not the historical sixth-century general who helped his fellow Britons defend themselves against the invading Saxons. No, Malory's Arthur is a consolidation of later legends that developed in England and on the Continent. Using Celtic and Continental sources, Malory created a mythic Arthur who later became the very embodiment of British values.

Le Morte d'Arthur, coming as it does at the end of the fifteenth century, serves as a kind of literary swan song to the feudal order of the Middle Ages, with its castles, knights, and chivalric codes. Malory's readers lived in a different world. Cities were growing, and money and competition were replacing the old feudal ways of barter and mutual obligation. Something in the chivalric order that Malory portrayed, however, seems to have answered a longing in his audience for a more orderly world.

Detail from fifteenth-century French manuscript of *Le roman du roi Arthur et les compagnons de la Table Ronde* by Chrétien de Troyes.

The Art Archive/Biblioteca Nazionale Turin/Dagli Orti.

Before You Read

from The Day of Destiny

Make the Connection

People hate to let go of their heroes. In fact, many cultures tell stories in which the hero promises to return in an hour of need to help the people once again. How do we try to keep our heroes alive? We build statues to them and record their portraits on canvas, coins, and film. Most of all, though, we tell their stories—stories that we hope will keep our heroes and the values they respect alive in the memories of future generations.

Literary Focus

The Romance Hero

From the thirteenth century onward ***romance*** was a term applied to a verse narrative that traces the adventures of a brave knight or other hero who has to overcome danger for the love of a noble lady or some other high ideal. The typical medieval romance is a narrative set in a world in which the ordinary laws of nature are suspended and idealized heroes fight, and almost always conquer, the forces of evil.

Malory's Arthur is in many ways the archetypal, or typical, romance hero—the medieval descendent of the epic hero. The **romance hero** is usually born under mysterious circumstances, grows up in obscurity, and undergoes a childhood initiation involving a magic weapon. In his maturity he fights to defeat evil and promote peace. Throughout his life he is aided by magic weapons and wise mentors. Mysterious events surround his departure from this world, suggesting that he may return when his people need him the most.

A **romance hero** is a larger-than-life figure, usually of mysterious origins, who performs extraordinary deeds with the aid of magic.

For more on the Romance, see the Handbook of Literary and Historical Terms.

Background

Malory's *Le Morte d'Arthur* contains a series of tales about the birth, education, adventures, and death (or disappearance) of King Arthur. In the early tales, Arthur persuades his knights to unite in the fellowship of the Round Table and to dedicate themselves to the chivalric code of honor. For a while, Arthur's vision is realized, and justice prevails in the kingdom. But human frailties, including Arthur's own, gradually corrupt the fellowship of the Round Table. Arthur becomes vulnerable to evil forces, personified by Sir Modred, who is Arthur's own illegitimate son.

In this last episode, Arthur is about to meet his wicked son in battle.

Vocabulary Development

righteous (rī′chəs) *adj.:* morally right.

prevailed (prē·vāld′) *v.:* gained the desired effect.

dissuade (di·swād′) *v.:* advise against.

brandishing (bran′dish·iŋ) *v.* used as *adj.:* shaking in a threatening way.

piteous (pit′ē·əs) *adj.:* deserving of pity.

Literary Skills
Understand the archetype of the romance hero.

INTERNET

Vocabulary Practice

Keyword: LE7 12-2

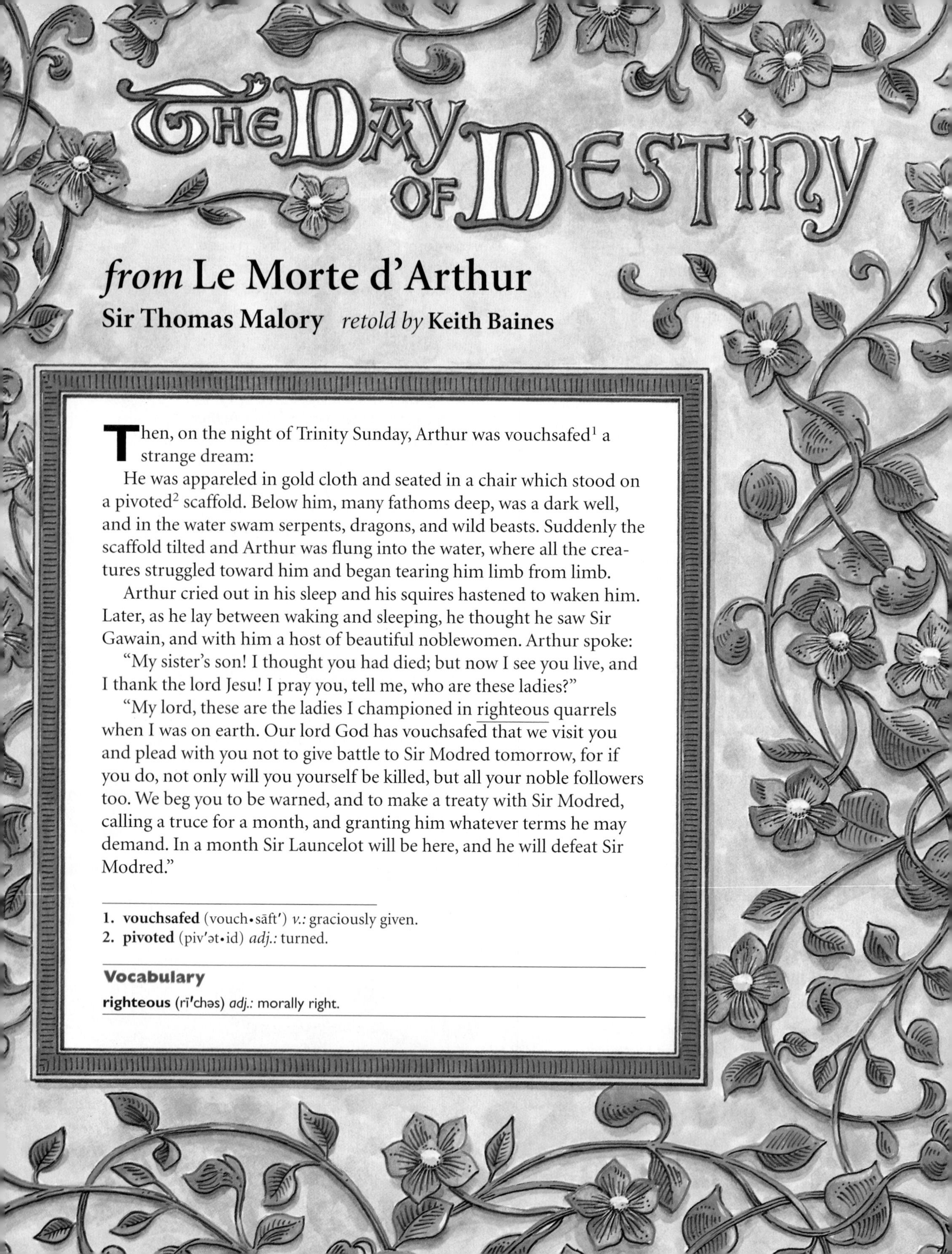

The Day of Destiny

from Le Morte d'Arthur

Sir Thomas Malory *retold by* **Keith Baines**

Then, on the night of Trinity Sunday, Arthur was vouchsafed[1] a strange dream:

He was appareled in gold cloth and seated in a chair which stood on a pivoted[2] scaffold. Below him, many fathoms deep, was a dark well, and in the water swam serpents, dragons, and wild beasts. Suddenly the scaffold tilted and Arthur was flung into the water, where all the creatures struggled toward him and began tearing him limb from limb.

Arthur cried out in his sleep and his squires hastened to waken him. Later, as he lay between waking and sleeping, he thought he saw Sir Gawain, and with him a host of beautiful noblewomen. Arthur spoke:

"My sister's son! I thought you had died; but now I see you live, and I thank the lord Jesu! I pray you, tell me, who are these ladies?"

"My lord, these are the ladies I championed in righteous quarrels when I was on earth. Our lord God has vouchsafed that we visit you and plead with you not to give battle to Sir Modred tomorrow, for if you do, not only will you yourself be killed, but all your noble followers too. We beg you to be warned, and to make a treaty with Sir Modred, calling a truce for a month, and granting him whatever terms he may demand. In a month Sir Launcelot will be here, and he will defeat Sir Modred."

1. **vouchsafed** (vouch•sāft′) *v.:* graciously given.
2. **pivoted** (piv′ət•id) *adj.:* turned.

Vocabulary

righteous (rī′chəs) *adj.:* morally right.

Battle between King Arthur and Modred, from *St. Alban's Chronicle* (late 15th century).
Ms. 6, fol. 66v. Lambeth Palace Library, London/The Bridgeman Art Library.

Thereupon Sir Gawain and the ladies vanished, and King Arthur once more summoned his squires and his counselors and told them his vision. Sir Lucas and Sir Bedivere were commissioned to make a treaty with Sir Modred. They were to be accompanied by two bishops and to grant, within reason, whatever terms he demanded.

The ambassadors found Sir Modred in command of an army of a hundred thousand and unwilling to listen to overtures of peace. However, the ambassadors eventually prevailed on him, and

Vocabulary

prevailed (prē•vāld′) *v.:* gained the desired effect.

in return for the truce granted him suzerainty[3] of Cornwall and Kent, and succession to the British throne when King Arthur died. The treaty was to be signed by King Arthur and Sir Modred the next day. They were to meet between the two armies, and each was to be accompanied by no more than fourteen knights.

Both King Arthur and Sir Modred suspected the other of treachery, and gave orders for their armies to attack at the sight of a naked sword. When they met at the appointed place, the treaty was signed and both drank a glass of wine.

Then, by chance, one of the soldiers was bitten in the foot by an adder which had lain concealed in the brush. The soldier unthinkingly drew his sword to kill it, and at once, as the sword flashed in the light, the alarums were given, trumpets sounded, and both armies galloped into the attack.

"Alas for this fateful day!" exclaimed King Arthur, as both he and Sir Modred hastily mounted and galloped back to their armies. There followed one of those rare and heartless battles in which both armies fought until they were destroyed. King Arthur, with his customary valor, led squadron after squadron of cavalry into the attack, and Sir Modred encountered him unflinchingly. As the number of dead and wounded mounted on both sides, the active combatants continued dauntless until nightfall, when four men alone survived.

King Arthur wept with dismay to see his beloved followers fallen; then, struggling toward him, unhorsed and badly wounded, he saw Sir Lucas the Butler and his brother, Sir Bedivere.

"Alas!" said the king, "that the day should come when I see all my noble knights destroyed! I would prefer that I myself had fallen. But what has become of the traitor Sir Modred, whose evil ambition was responsible for this carnage?"

Looking about him King Arthur then noticed Sir Modred leaning with his sword on a heap of the dead.

"Sir Lucas, I pray you give me my spear, for I have seen Sir Modred."

"Sire, I entreat you, remember your vision—how Sir Gawain appeared with a heaven-sent message to dissuade you from fighting Sir Modred. Allow this fateful day to pass; it is ours, for we three hold the field, while the enemy is broken."

"My lords, I care nothing for my life now! And while Sir Modred is at large I must kill him: there may not be another chance."

"God speed you, then!" said Sir Bedivere.

3. **suzerainty** (so͞o′zə•rin′tē) *n.:* position of feudal lord.

Vocabulary

dissuade (di•swād′) *v.:* advise against.

Arthur is mortally wounded, from *Roman du Saint Graal* (detail) (early 14th century).
The British Library, London.

When Sir Modred saw King Arthur advance with his spear, he rushed to meet him with drawn sword. Arthur caught Sir Modred below the shield and drove his spear through his body; Sir Modred, knowing that the wound was mortal, thrust himself up to the handle of the spear, and then, brandishing his sword in both hands, struck Arthur on the side of the helmet, cutting through it and into the skull beneath; then he crashed to the ground, gruesome and dead.

King Arthur fainted many times as Sir Lucas and Sir Bedivere struggled with him to a small chapel nearby, where they managed to ease his wounds a little. When Arthur came to, he thought he heard cries coming from the battlefield.

"Sir Lucas, I pray you, find out who cries on the battlefield," he said.

Wounded as he was, Sir Lucas hobbled painfully to the field, and there in the moonlight saw the camp followers stealing gold and jewels from the dead, and murdering the wounded. He returned to the king and reported to him what he had seen, and then added:

"My lord, it surely would be better to move you to the nearest town?"

Vocabulary

brandishing (bran′dish•iŋ) *v.* used as *adj.:* shaking in a threatening way.

"My wounds forbid it. But alas for the good Sir Launcelot! How sadly I have missed him today! And now I must die—as Sir Gawain warned me I would—repenting our quarrel with my last breath."

Sir Lucas and Sir Bedivere made one further attempt to lift the king. He fainted as they did so. Then Sir Lucas fainted as part of his intestines broke through a wound in the stomach. When the king came to, he saw Sir Lucas lying dead with foam at his mouth.

"Sweet Jesu, give him succor!"[4] he said. "This noble knight has died trying to save my life—alas that this was so!"

Sir Bedivere wept for his brother.

"Sir Bedivere, weep no more," said King

4. **succor** (suk′ər) *n.:* help.

A CLOSER LOOK: SOCIAL INFLUENCES

The Archetype of Arthur

INFORMATIONAL TEXT

If you remember your old myths and fairy tales, you'll recognize many of the same elements in Arthur's story. Even movies and cartoons today use these **archetypes** of the romance hero. (For more about the heroic archetype, see pages 54–55.)

In Malory's mythic form, Arthur has the mysterious birth typical of the romance hero. His childhood points to his kinship with such mythic and romance heroes as the Greek Theseus and the German Siegfried. His strange death, departure, and promised return also place him among other "once and future kings"—heroes whose return is always hoped for.

The Arthurian tales were carried into the Elizabethan age. They were resurrected in the nineteenth century by Alfred, Lord Tennyson (see page 894), in his group of poems called *Idylls of the King*. Tennyson brought Arthur and his knights back at a time when the English nation, embarked upon building an empire, needed a reminder of its heroic past and special destiny.

The Arthurian legend was revived yet again in the twentieth century by T. H. White in his bestselling book *The Once and Future King* (1958). Though White's treatment of the Arthurian material is ironic (in keeping with an ironic age), it still inspired the 1960s musical play and movie *Camelot,* which capture the romantic imagination of another generation struggling with disillusion and social disorder.

The Lady of the Lake, from *Morte d'Arthur,* illustrated by Aubrey Beardsley (1872–1898).

The Art Archive.

Arthur, "for you can save neither your brother nor me; and I would ask you to take my sword Excalibur[5] to the shore of the lake and throw it in the water. Then return to me and tell me what you have seen."

"My lord, as you command, it shall be done."

Sir Bedivere took the sword, but when he came to the water's edge, it appeared so beautiful that he could not bring himself to throw it in, so instead he hid it by a tree, and then returned to the king.

"Sir Bedivere, what did you see?"

"My lord, I saw nothing but the wind upon the waves."

"Then you did not obey me; I pray you, go swiftly again, and this time fulfill my command."

Sir Bedivere went and returned again, but this time too he had failed to fulfill the king's command.

"Sir Bedivere, what did you see?"

"My lord, nothing but the lapping of the waves."

"Sir Bedivere, twice you have betrayed me! And for the sake only of my sword: it is unworthy of you! Now I pray you, do as I command, for I have not long to live."

This time Sir Bedivere wrapped the girdle around the sheath and hurled it as far as he could into the water. A hand appeared from below the surface, took the sword, waved it thrice, and disappeared again. Sir Bedivere returned to the king and told him what he had seen.

"Sir Bedivere, I pray you now help me hence, or I fear it will be too late."

Sir Bedivere carried the king to the water's edge, and there found a barge in which sat many beautiful ladies with their queen. All were wearing black hoods, and when they saw the king, they raised their voices in a piteous lament.

"I pray you, set me in the barge," said the king.

Sir Bedivere did so, and one of the ladies laid the king's head in her lap; then the queen spoke to him:

5. **Excalibur:** Arthur's sword, given to him by the mysterious Lady of the Lake.

"My dear brother, you have stayed too long: I fear that the wound on your head is already cold."

Thereupon they rowed away from the land and Sir Bedivere wept to see them go.

"My lord King Arthur, you have deserted me! I am alone now, and among enemies."

"Sir Bedivere, take what comfort you may, for my time is passed, and now I must be taken to Avalon[6] for my wound to be healed. If you hear of me no more, I beg you pray for my soul."

The barge slowly crossed the water and out of sight while the ladies wept. Sir Bedivere walked alone into the forest and there remained for the night.

In the morning he saw beyond the trees of a copse a small hermitage.[7] He entered and found a hermit kneeling down by a fresh tomb. The hermit was weeping as he prayed, and then Sir Bedivere recognized him as the Archbishop of Canterbury, who had been banished by Sir Modred.

"Father, I pray you, tell me, whose tomb is this?"

"My son, I do not know. At midnight the body was brought here by a company of ladies. We buried it, they lit a hundred candles for the service, and rewarded me with a thousand bezants."[8]

"Father, King Arthur lies buried in this tomb."

Sir Bedivere fainted when he had spoken, and when he came to he begged the Archbishop to allow him to remain at the hermitage and end his days in fasting and prayer.

"Father, I wish only to be near to my true liege."[9]

"My son, you are welcome; and do I not recognize you as Sir Bedivere the Bold, brother to Sir Lucas the Butler?"

6. **Avalon:** legendary island, sometimes identified with the earthly Paradise.
7. **hermitage** (hur′mə•tij) *n.:* secluded home.
8. **bezants** (bez′ənts) *n. pl.:* gold coins of Byzantium.
9. **liege** (lēj) *n.:* lord or sovereign.

Vocabulary

piteous (pit′ē•əs) *adj.:* deserving of pity.

Bedivere returning Excalibur to the lake upon the death of Arthur, from *Roman du Saint Graal* (early 14th century).
The British Library, London.

Thus the Archbishop and Sir Bedivere remained at the hermitage, wearing the habits of hermits and devoting themselves to the tomb with fasting and prayers of contrition.[10]

Such was the death of King Arthur as written down by Sir Bedivere. By some it is told that there were three queens on the barge: Queen Morgan le Fay, the Queen of North Galys, and the Queen of the Waste Lands; and others include the name of Nyneve, the Lady of the Lake who had served King Arthur well in the past, and had married the good knight Sir Pelleas.

10. **contrition** (kən·trish′ən) *n.:* here, remorse for having offended God.

In many parts of Britain it is believed that King Arthur did not die and that he will return to us and win fresh glory and the Holy Cross[11] of our Lord Jesu Christ; but for myself I do not believe this, and would leave him buried peacefully in his tomb at Glastonbury, where the Archbishop of Canterbury and Sir Bedivere humbled themselves, and with prayers and fasting honored his memory. And inscribed on his tomb, men say, is this legend:

HIC IACET ARTHURUS, REX QUONDAM REXQUE FUTURUS.[12] ■

11. **Holy Cross:** cross on which Jesus was crucified.
12. Latin for "Here lies Arthur, the once and future King."

Response and Analysis

Reading Check

1. What does King Arthur dream of on Trinity Sunday?
2. What is Sir Lucas's advice to Arthur? What does Arthur do?
3. What happens when Arthur and Sir Modred meet?
4. Where does Sir Bedivere take the wounded king? What happens to Bedivere?

Thinking Critically

5. "The Day of Destiny" includes many romance motifs, or **archetypes,** that often occur in epics, legends, myths, and folk tales. Fill in this graphic organizer to show how each of the archetypes listed appears in the story of Arthur.

Romance Motif	Arthur Story
Faithful follower	
Wise old man	
Dreams	
Number 3	
Magic	
Testing of follower	
Betrayal	

6. Over the centuries many people have searched for Arthur's grave. According to this old story, what should archaeologists look for in their search for the tomb?
7. What mysterious details surround Arthur's last hours? How could these details—combined with the inscription on Arthur's tomb—suggest that Arthur did not die?

WRITING

Comparing Heroes

In a brief essay, discuss the ways in which King Arthur is like the ancient epic heroes who preceded him—heroes like Gilgamesh (see page 58), Achilles (see page 67), and, especially, the first archetypal British hero, Beowulf (see page 21). How is Arthur *unlike* such heroes? Use specific examples from the texts to back up your ideas. Before you write, gather information from the texts about these details that pertain to heroes:

- is a leader of the people
- has devoted followers
- has superhuman strength
- is courageous
- fights evil
- has magic weapons
- encounters supernatural elements

Literary Skills Analyze the archetype of the romance hero.

Writing Skills Write an essay comparing and contrasting archetypal heroes.

Vocabulary Skills Understand etymologies.

Vocabulary Development

Etymologies

righteous **dissuade** **piteous** **prevailed** **brandishing**

For each Vocabulary word listed above, look up its **etymology** in a dictionary. If a word has a prefix or suffix, look up its meaning as well. Make a chart like the one below for each word. Remember that prefixes and suffixes are defined separately in the dictionary.

Word	Prefix or suffix	Origin
righteous	*–ous*, "full of; characterized by"	(OE) *rihtwis*, meaning "right"

INTERNET

Projects and Activities

Keyword: LE7 12-2

Grammar Link

Linking It Up: Combining Sentences with Coordinating and Subordinating Conjunctions

Read these sentences aloud. How could they be improved?

> Then King Arthur summoned his knights. King Arthur told them to assemble his noble lords and bishops. He was ready to meet with Modred.

When two or more sentences express related ideas that are equally important, you may be able to combine them with a kind of connective word called a **coordinating conjunction.** Coordinating conjunctions—*and, but, for, nor, or, so,* and *yet*—enable you to combine subjects, verbs, objects, or even entire sentences.

> Then King Arthur summoned his knights and told them to assemble his noble lords and bishops**,** for he was ready to meet with Modred.

How could you improve these sentences?

> All the black-hooded women in the barge saw Arthur. They wailed piteously.

When two or more sentences express related ideas that are of unequal importance, you can combine the sentences by making the more important sentence a main, or independent, clause and the less important idea a subordinate, or dependent, clause. To show the relationship between the clauses, you must use a connective word called a **subordinating conjunction,** which begins a subordinate clause and connects it to a main clause. Among the most commonly used subordinating conjunctions are *after, although, as, because, before, how, if, since, then, that, though, unless, until, when, where,* and *while.* A subordinating conjunction may appear between the clauses it connects, or it can come at the beginning of a sentence to add emphasis or sentence variety.

> All the black-hooded women in the barge wailed piteously when they saw King Arthur.

> When they saw King Arthur**,** all the black-hooded women in the barge wailed piteously.

Grammar Skills
Combine sentences using coordinating and subordinating conjunctions.

PRACTICE

Combine each of the following sentences into one sentence by using coordinating or subordinating conjunctions or a combination of the two, as appropriate. You can combine subjects, verbs, objects, or entire sentences. You may have to add, change, or delete words and punctuation to make the resulting combined sentence read smoothly and make sense. Bear in mind that the sentences can be combined in a number of ways.

1. Sir Gawain appeared to King Arthur in a dream. He warned of Arthur's impending death.
2. King Arthur told his men to consider the treaty broken if they saw any sword drawn. Sir Modred told his men to do the same.
3. Sir Bedivere threw Excalibur into the lake. A hand appeared out of the lake. The hand caught the sword.

Apply to Your Writing

Read over a writing assignment you are working on now or have already completed. Are there any short, choppy sentences that have a clear relationship to one another? (It is often easier to determine this if you read your work aloud.) Where appropriate, use coordinating and subordinating conjunctions to combine any such sentences.

For more help, see Coordinating Ideas and Subordinating Ideas, 9a and 9b, in the Language Handbook.

PREVIEW

Reflecting *on the* Literary Period

The Middle Ages: 1066–1485

The selections in this feature were written during the same literary period as the other selections in Collection 2, and they share many of the same ideas and concerns. The Focus Question will guide your reading and help you reflect on important aspects of the period.

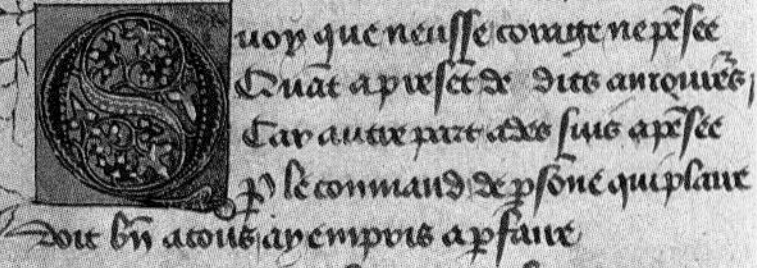

Lover telling of love to lady (Christine de Pisan), mid 15th century.

The Art Archive/British Library.

Think About...

Great storytellers flourished during the Middle Ages. Two types of medieval narratives that continue to resonate with contemporary readers are the **ballad** and the **romance.**

The **popular ballad** or **folk ballad** is a form of folk poetry that reflects the everyday life of common people. The most popular themes, often tragic, were disappointed love, jealousy, revenge, sudden disaster, and deeds of adventure and daring. Sometimes the ballad deals with only a single incident, which may be the climax of the action. Often, the plot has to be inferred from dialogue and from whatever action is revealed in the ballad. The ballad doesn't provide comment or interpretation, and there is little characterization or description. Yet, the ballad is extremely dramatic and suspenseful. It is effective precisely because of what is not told but what is hinted at.

Medieval romances, which were composed for an aristocratic audience, were markedly different from ballads. *Sir Gawain and the Green Knight,* one of the most well-known English romances, reflects the system of ideals and social codes known as chivalry—the standard for behavior among knights and their gentlewomen. The style of a romance, with its vivid description of settings and characters and with its detailed plot, is strikingly different from the simple style of the ballad.

Pages 225–238 cover **Literary Skills** Evaluate the philosophical, political, religious, ethical, and social influences of a historical period.

Focus Question

As you read each selection, keep in mind this Focus Question and take notes to help you answer it at the end of the feature:

How do the ballads and romances of the Middle Ages reflect medieval views of love and honor?

Edward, Edward

Background "Edward, Edward" is an international ballad, one found across northern Europe and brought to England and Scotland by travelers and sailors. Sir Thomas Percy, who in the 1760s compiled many popular ballads, found the same characters in a Swedish ballad and also noted that another version of the ballad appeared with the title "Son Davie, Son Davie." Another collection changed the hero's name to Edward.

(For more information about the characteristics of ballads, see page 133.)

CONNECTING TO THE Focus Question

As you read, consider these questions: Why would ballads like "Edward, Edward" have been recited or sung in alehouses and at firesides? What does the ballad reveal about popular attitudes?

Edward, Edward

"Why does your brand sae drop wi' blude,°
Edward, Edward?
Why does your brand sae drop wi' blude,
And why sae sad gang ye,° O?"—
"O I hae kill'd my hawk sae gude,°
Mither, mither;
O I hae kill'd my hawk sae gude,
And I had nae mair° but he, O."

"Your hawk's blude was never sae red,
Edward, Edward;
Your hawk's blude was never sae red,
My dear son, I tell thee, O."—
"O I hae kill'd my red-roan steed,
Mither, mither;
O I hae kill'd my red-roan steed,
That erst° was sae fair and free, O."

"Your steed was auld,° and ye hae got mair,
Edward, Edward;
Your steed was auld, and ye hae got mair;
Some other dule ye dree,° O."—
"O I hae kill'd my father dear,
Mither, mither;
O I hae kill'd my father dear,
Alas, and wae is me, O!"

1. **brand . . . blude:** sword so drip with blood.
4. **gang ye:** go you.
5. **gude:** good.
8. **nae mair:** no more.
16. **erst:** before.
17. **auld:** old.
20. **dule ye dree:** grief you suffer.

"And whatten penance will ye dree° for that,
Edward, Edward?
Whatten penance will ye dree for that?
My dear son, now tell me, O."—
"I'll set my feet in yonder boat,
Mither, mither;
I'll set my feet in yonder boat,
And I'll fare over the sea, O."

"And what will ye do wi' your tow'rs and your ha',°
Edward, Edward?
And what will ye do wi' your tow'rs and your ha',
That were sae fair to see, O?"—
"I'll let them stand till they doun fa',
Mither, mither;
I'll let them stand till they doun fa',
For here never mair maun° I be, O."

25. whatten . . . dree: what punishment for sin will you suffer.

33. ha': hall; that is, ancestral home.

40. maun: must.

Lovers, Garden Scene (detail). French Illumination, 15th century.

akg-images/British Library.

"And what will ye leave to your bairns° and your wife,
Edward, Edward?
And what will ye leave to your bairns and your wife,
When ye gang owre the sea, O?"—
"The warld's room: let them beg through life,
Mither, mither;
The warld's room: let them beg through life;
For them never mair will I see, O."

"And what will ye leave to your ain° mither dear,
Edward, Edward?
And what will ye leave to your ain mither dear,
My dear son, now tell me, O?"—
"The curse of hell frae me sall ye bear,
Mither, mither;
The curse of hell frae me sall ye bear:
Sic° counsels ye gave to me, O!"

41. **bairns:** children.

49. **ain:** own.

56. **sic:** such.

Response and Analysis

Thinking Critically

1. What questions are unanswered in "Edward, Edward"? Cite details from the ballad to support your answer.
2. Like many ballads, "Edward, Edward" builds up suspense with **incremental repetition**—the repetition of lines with a new element introduced each time to advance the story until the **climax** is reached. At what point does the ballad reach a climax?
3. What could be the implications of Edward's last response to his mother in the final stanza of the ballad?
4. Using details from the selection, respond to **Connecting to the Focus Question** on page 226.

Extending and Evaluating

5. Imagine a modern version of the events recounted in this ballad. How might they become a subject for today's tabloids? Explain.

from Sir Gawain and the Green Knight

Background The **romance** *Sir Gawain and the Green Knight* was probably written around 1375, at a time when the old ideals of knightly conduct—courage, loyalty, and courtesy—were beginning to erode.

Sir Gawain and the Green Knight is about one of the knights at the court of King Arthur. As the poem opens, King Arthur and his knights are at a Christmas-season party. Suddenly, an enormous green stranger armed with a huge ax rides into the hall and challenges any knight to "exchange one blow for another." Gawain, the best of knights, accepts and beheads the challenger. The Green Knight coolly picks up his own head, mounts his horse, repeats his challenge, and gallops off with the head in his arms. Gawain must submit to the same treatment in a year and a day.

Gawain sets off on a long journey before Christmas of the next year to honor his pledge. In the wilds of north Wales he comes upon a splendid castle, where the lord invites him to stay and suggests an odd "game." The lord says he will go hunting each day and will give Gawain whatever he wins in the hunt. In return, Gawain must give the lord anything he has won that day.

Gawain is tempted on three successive days by his host's wife. He accepts only kisses the first two days, and true to his bargain, gives his host the kisses when he returns from hunting. On the morning of the third day, the lady gives Gawain not only kisses but also a magical green girdle, or sash, that she claims will protect him from any harm. When the lord returns, Gawain again gives him the kisses but keeps the sash a secret.

In the excerpt included here, Gawain sets off on New Year's Day to find the Green Chapel and the dreaded Green Knight. Gawain leaves the castle with the green sash wrapped around his armor. He is certain he is headed for his death.

CONNECTING TO THE Focus Question

As you read, consider these questions: How does the author of this poem reveal a familiarity with aristocratic life? What attitude does the poem take toward the code of chivalric honor and heroism?

from Sir Gawain and the Green Knight

translated by **John Gardner**

He put his spurs to Gringolet,° plunged down the path,
Shoved through the heavy thicket grown up by the woods
And rode down the steep slope to the floor of the valley;
He looked around him then—a strange, wild place,
And not a sign of a chapel on any side
But only steep, high banks surrounding him,
And great, rough knots of rock and rugged crags

1. **Gringolet:** Gawain's horse.

That scraped the passing clouds, as it seemed to him.
He heaved at the heavy reins to hold back his horse
And squinted in every direction in search of the Chapel,
And still he saw nothing except—and this was strange—
A small green hill all alone, a sort of barrow,°
A low, smooth bulge on the bank of the brimming creek
That flowed from the foot of a waterfall,
And the water in the pool was bubbling as if it were boiling.
Sir Gawain urged Gringolet on till he came to the mound
And lightly dismounted and made the reins secure
On the great, thick limb of a gnarled and ancient tree;
Then he went up to the barrow and walked all around it,
Wondering in his wits what on earth it might be.
It had at each end and on either side an entrance,
And patches of grass were growing all over the thing,
And all the inside was hollow—an old, old cave
Or the cleft of some ancient crag, he couldn't tell which
it was.
"Whoo, Lord!" thought the knight,
"Is *this* the fellow's place?
Here the Devil might
Recite his midnight mass.

"Dear God," thought Gawain, "the place is deserted enough!
And it's ugly enough, all overgrown with weeds!
Well might it amuse that marvel of green
To do his devotions here, in his devilish way!
In my five senses I fear it's the Fiend himself
Who's brought me to meet him here to murder me.
May fire and fury befall this fiendish Chapel,
As cursed a kirk° as I ever yet came across!"
With his helmet on his head and his lance in hand
He leaped up onto the roof of the rock-walled room
And, high on that hill, he heard, from an echoing rock
Beyond the pool, on the hillside, a horrible noise.
Brrrack! It clattered in the cliffs as if to cleave them,
A sound like a grindstone grinding on a scythe!°
Brrrack! It whirred and rattled like water on a mill wheel!
Brrrrrack! It rushed and rang till your blood ran cold.
And then: "Oh God," thought Gawain, "it grinds, I think,
For me—a blade prepared for the blow I must take
as my right!
God's will be done! But here!
He may well get his knight,
But still, no use in fear;
I won't fall dead of fright!"

12. barrow: grave mound.

The Headless Green Knight in Arthur's Hall, an alliterative poem in 1212 lines, English, by the Pearl Poet.

British Library, London, UK.

37. kirk: Scottish for "church."

43. scythe (sī*th*): long-handled cutting tool.

And then Sir Gawain roared in a ringing voice,
"Where is the hero who swore he'd be here to meet me?
Sir Gawain the Good is come to the Green Chapel!
If any man would meet me, make it now,
For it's now or never, I've no wish to dawdle here long."
"Stay there!" called someone high above his head,
"I'll pay you promptly all that I promised before."
But still he went on with that whetting noise a while,
Turning again to his grinding before he'd come down.
At last, from a hole by a rock he came out into sight,
Came plunging out of his den with a terrible weapon,
A huge new Danish ax to deliver his blow with,
With a vicious swine of a bit bent back to the handle,
Filed to a razor's edge and four foot long,
Not one inch less by the length of that gleaming lace.
The great Green Knight was garbed as before,
Face, legs, hair, beard, all as before but for this:
That now he walked the world on his own two legs,
The ax handle striking the stone like a walking-stave.°
When the knight came down to the water he would not wade
But vaulted across on his ax, then with awful strides
Came fiercely over the field filled all around
with snow.
Sir Gawain met him there
And bowed—but none too low!
Said the other, "I see, sweet sir,
You go where you say you'll go!

"Gawain," the Green Knight said, "may God be your guard!
You're very welcome indeed, sir, here at my place;
You've timed your travel, my friend, as a true man should.
You recall the terms of the contract drawn up between us:
At this time a year ago you took your chances,
And I'm pledged now, this New Year, to make you my payment.
And here we are in this valley, all alone,
And no man here to part us, proceed as we may;
Heave off your helmet then, and have here your pay;
And debate no more with me than I did then
When you severed my head from my neck with a single swipe."
"Never fear," said Gawain, "by God who gave
Me life, I'll raise no complaint at the grimness of it;
But take your single stroke, and I'll stand still
And allow you to work as you like and not oppose
you here."

71. walking-stave (stāv): staff.

He bowed toward the ground
And let his skin show clear;
However his heart might pound,
He would not show his fear.

Quickly then the man in the green made ready,
Grabbed up his keen-ground ax to strike Sir Gawain;
With all the might in his body he bore it aloft
And sharply brought it down as if to slay him;
Had he made it fall with the force he first intended
He would have stretched out the strongest man on earth.
But Sir Gawain cast a side glance at the ax
As it glided down to give him his Kingdom Come,°
And his shoulders jerked away from the iron a little,
And the Green Knight caught the handle, holding it back,
And mocked the prince with many a proud reproof:°
"*You* can't be Gawain," he said, "who's thought so good,
A man who's never been daunted on hill or dale!
For look how you flinch for fear before anything's felt!
I never heard tell that Sir Gawain was ever a coward!
I never moved a muscle when *you* came down;
In Arthur's hall I never so much as winced.
My head fell off at my feet, yet I never flickered;
But you! You tremble at heart before you're touched!
I'm bound to be called a better man than you, then,
my lord."
Said Gawain, "I shied once:
No more. You have my word.
But if my head falls to the stones
It cannot be restored.

"But be brisk, man, by your faith, and come to the point!
Deal out my doom if you can, and do it at once,
For I'll stand for one good stroke, and I'll start no more
Until your ax has hit—and that I swear."
"Here goes, then," said the other, and heaves it aloft
And stands there waiting, scowling like a madman;
He swings down sharp, then suddenly stops again,
Holds back the ax with his hand before it can hurt,
And Gawain stands there stirring not even a nerve;
He stood there still as a stone or the stock of a tree
That's wedged in rocky ground by a hundred roots.
O, merrily then he spoke, the man in green:
"Good! You've got your heart back! Now I can hit you.
May all that glory the good King Arthur gave you

107. his Kingdom Come: life after death.

110. reproof: rebuke; scolding.

Sir Gawain in bed is visited by Guinevere, the wife of the castle's lord. Illustration to the metric romance: Sir Gawain and the Green Knight (1360). Ms Cotton Nero A.X., fol. 129.

akg-images/British Library.

Prove efficacious now—if it ever can—
And save your neck." In rage Sir Gawain shouted,
"*Hit* me, hero! I'm right up to here with your threats!
Is it *you* that's the cringing coward after all?"
"Whoo!" said the man in green, "he's wrathful, too!
No pauses, then; I'll pay up my pledge at once,

I vow!"
He takes his stride to strike
And lifts his lip and brow;
It's not a thing Gawain can like,
For nothing can save him now!

He raises that ax up lightly and flashes it down,
And that blinding bit bites in at the knight's bare neck—
But hard as he hammered it down, it hurt him no more
Than to nick the nape of his neck, so it split the skin;
The sharp blade slit to the flesh through the shiny hide,
And red blood shot to his shoulders and spattered the ground.
And when Gawain saw his blood where it blinked in the snow
He sprang from the man with a leap to the length of a spear;
He snatched up his helmet swiftly and slapped it on,
Shifted his shield into place with a jerk of his shoulders,
And snapped his sword out faster than sight; said boldly—
And, mortal born of his mother that he was,
There was never on earth a man so happy by half—
"No more strokes, my friend; you've had your swing!
I've stood one swipe of your ax without resistance;

If you offer me any more, I'll repay you at once
With all the force and fire I've got—as you
will see.
I take one stroke, that's all,
For that was the compact we
Arranged in Arthur's hall;
But now, no more for me!"

The Green Knight remained where he stood, relaxing on his ax—
Settled the shaft on the rocks and leaned on the sharp end—
And studied the young man standing there, shoulders hunched,
And considered that staunch° and doughty° stance he took,
Undaunted yet, and in his heart he liked it;
And then he said merrily, with a mighty voice—
With a roar like rushing wind he reproved the knight—
"Here, don't be such an ogre on your ground!
Nobody here has behaved with bad manners toward you
Or done a thing except as the contract said.
I owed you a stroke, and I've struck; consider yourself
Well paid. And now I release you from all further duties.
If I'd cared to hustle, it may be, perchance, that I might

Uprising of 9000 inhabitants of Meaux (Beauvais) (detail) (1358). Chronicles illustrated by Loyset Liedet.

Bibliotheque Nationale, Paris, France.

175. staunch (stônch): steadfast. **doughty** (dout'ē): courageous.

Have hit somewhat harder, and then you might well be cross!
The first time I lifted my ax it was lighthearted sport,
I merely feinted and made no mark, as was right,
For you kept our pact of the first night with honor
And abided by your word and held yourself true to me,
Giving me all you owed as a good man should.
I feinted a second time, friend, for the morning
You kissed my pretty wife twice and returned me the kisses;
And so for the first two days, mere feints, nothing more
severe.
A man who's true to his word,
There's nothing he needs to fear;
You failed me, though, on the third
Exchange, so I've tapped you here.

"That sash you wear by your scabbard° belongs to me;
My own wife gave it to you, as I ought to know.
I know, too, of your kisses and all your words
And my wife's advances, for I myself arranged them.
It was I who sent her to test you. I'm convinced
You're the finest man that ever walked this earth.
As a pearl is of greater price than dry white peas,
So Gawain indeed stands out above all other knights.
But you lacked a little, sir; you were less than loyal;
But since it was not for the sash itself or for lust
But because you loved your life, I blame you less."
Sir Gawain stood in a study° a long, long while,
So miserable with disgrace that he wept within,
And all the blood of his chest went up to his face
And he shrank away in shame from the man's gentle words.
The first words Gawain could find to say were these:
"Cursed be cowardice and covetousness both,
Villainy and vice that destroy all virtue!"
He caught at the knots of the girdle° and loosened them
And fiercely flung the sash at the Green Knight.
"There, there's my fault! The foul fiend vex it!
Foolish cowardice taught me, from fear of your stroke,
To bargain, covetous, and abandon my kind,
The selflessness and loyalty suitable in knights;
Here I stand, faulty and false, much as I've feared them,
Both of them, untruth and treachery; may they see sorrow
and care!
I can't deny my guilt;
My works shine none too fair!
Give me your good will
And henceforth I'll beware."

199. scabbard (skab′ərd): case that holds the blade of a sword.

210. stood in a study: stood thinking deeply.

217. girdle: sash.

At that, the Green Knight laughed, saying graciously,
"Whatever harm I've had, I hold it amended
Since now you're confessed so clean, acknowledging sins
And bearing the plain penance of my point;
I consider you polished as white and as perfectly clean
As if you had never fallen since first you were born.
And I give you, sir, this gold-embroidered girdle,
For the cloth is as green as my gown. Sir Gawain, think
On this when you go forth among great princes;
Remember our struggle here; recall to your mind
This rich token. Remember the Green Chapel.
And now, come on, let's both go back to my castle
And finish the New Year's revels with feasting and joy,
not strife,
I beg you," said the lord,
And said, "As for my wife,
She'll be your friend, no more
A threat against your life."

Sir Gawain and the Green Knight (1952) by Dorothea Braby.

Rare Books and Manuscripts Division, The New York Public Library.

Response and Analysis

Reading Check

1. Where does Gawain find the Green Knight, and what is the Green Knight doing?
2. Who does the Green Knight turn out to be?

Thinking Critically

3. In what ways is Gawain a superhuman **romance hero**? In what ways is he weak or flawed, just as an ordinary person might be? Cite details from the poem to support your response.
4. What **images** make the setting of the confrontation seem demonic? Do you think there is any **symbolism** in the setting? Explain.
5. How would you describe the writer's **tone**—or attitude—in this tale? Is he entirely serious, or do you find moments of humor? Find passages in the text to support your answer.
6. Using details from the selection, respond to **Connecting to the Focus Question** on page 229.

Extending and Evaluating

7. Do you think people today long to find heroes like Gawain? What might be a modern hero's quest, and what form would tests of the hero's honor or courage take?

REVIEW

Reflecting on the Literary Period

The Middle Ages: 1066–1485

The following questions ask you to compare and analyze the selections in this feature and respond to the Focus Question. Where possible, cite passages from the selections to support your answers.

Comparing Literature

1. **Tone**—the attitude taken toward a subject or a character—is created through the writer's choice of words and details. Compare the tone of "Edward, Edward" and of "Lord Randall" (see page 131). What similarities or differences do you find?
2. **Dialogue** is an important narrative element in both "Edward, Edward" and in *Sir Gawain and the Green Knight.* How is dialogue used to advance the action in each selection? What kind of effects does the dialogue create?
3. Compare the attitudes toward knighthood and chivalry in the **romances** *Sir Gawain and the Green Knight* and Malory's *Le Morte d'Arthur* (see "The Day of Destiny," page 216). How does each romance address the knightly values of courage, loyalty, and courtesy?
4. The legends of King Arthur and his knights remain enduringly popular in English literature. What aspects of the legends continue to resonate with contemporary readers? How do Arthur and his knights embody the ideals of character and leadership?

RESPONDING TO THE

Focus Question

Review your notes and responses related to the Focus Question for this feature. Using details from the selections, write your answer to the question.

How do the ballads and romances of the Middle Ages reflect medieval views of love and honor?

Pages 225–238 cover **Literary Skills** Evaluate the philosophical, political, religious, ethical, and social influences of a historical period.

READ ON: FOR INDEPENDENT READING

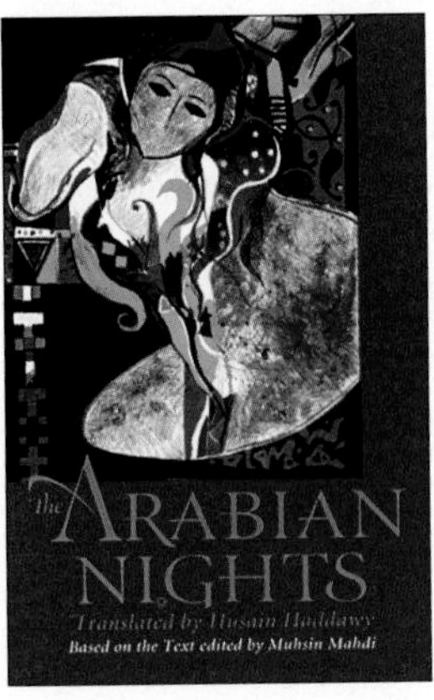

FICTION

Stories That Save a Life

Perhaps you have been entranced by the story of Sindbad's fantastic voyages—just one of the many tales in ***The Arabian Nights*** (translated by Husain Haddawy), a framework of stories that date back to the ninth century. Princess Scheherazade, whose husband intends to murder her, saves her own life by telling a dazzling variety of tales but stopping each night at the most suspenseful moment, thereby postponing her death.

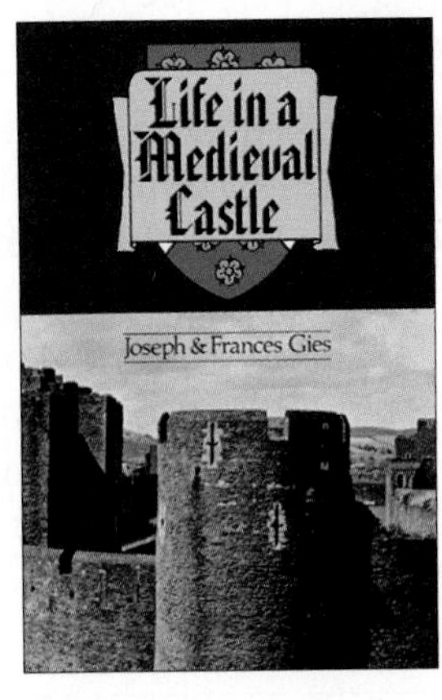

NONFICTION

Within Castle Walls

The romance of the medieval castle lives on in literature, in film, and in our collective impression of what life in a castle entails. We think of creaking drawbridges, dungeons, sword fights, and grand dinners for ravenous knights. In Joseph and Frances Gies's ***Life in a Medieval Castle,*** the romance is tempered with a truth more interesting than fiction.

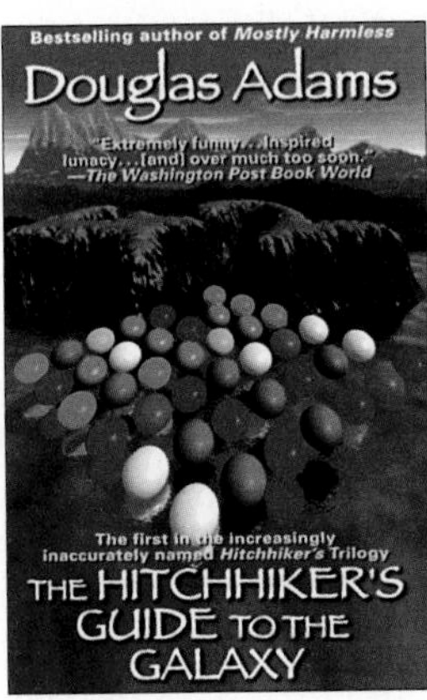

FICTION

Pilgrims in Outer Space

Join Earthling Arthur Dent and his trusty sidekick from Betelgeuse, Ford Prefect, on a cosmic (and comic) quest through the galaxy. In ***The Hitchhiker's Guide to the Galaxy,*** by Douglas Adams, you may "finally learn once and for all the plain and simple answer to all those nagging little problems of Life, the Universe, and Everything!"

FICTION

A Lasting Hero

The English writer T. H. White wrote his version of the Arthurian legend, ***The Sword in the Stone,*** before World War II, when England was in need of a hero to bolster its national pride. He later expanded this story into a four-part novel, ***The Once and Future King,*** that explores the problems of war, justice, and national identity. Though White views Arthur's quest as a tragedy, he balances this somber theme with humorous characters and comic fun.

Reporting Literary Research

Writing Assignment
Write a formal research paper of at least 1,500 words on a topic that links literature and historical investigation.

To what extent did the clergy of Chaucer's *The Canterbury Tales* represent the clergy of the fourteenth century? Was Malory's King Arthur based, at least in part, on an actual historical figure? **Literary research** arises from questions such as these and involves a study not only of works of literature but also of sources that illuminate the literature, such as scholarly writings on history. By researching such sources, you can expand your understanding of the literary work, its author, and the culture that produced it.

Prewriting

Choose and Narrow a Research Topic

My Kingdom for a Topic Literary research is a labor-intensive process that can be intensely rewarding for what it tells you about a literary subject. If a research topic that fascinates you doesn't immediately come to mind, scan your textbook, searching for authors and works that look intriguing. Jot down a list of several possibilities, and do a little preliminary research in your textbook, in general reference works like encyclopedias, and on the Internet to gather some information on the works and authors on your list. Then, from your list choose a general literary topic, such as Chaucer's *The Canterbury Tales,* for your research. You'll have the opportunity to narrow your topic later.

Once you've chosen a general topic, decide on an appropriate historical approach you'd like to take in your research. You might need to do some more preliminary research to get an idea of the historical significance of the topic you've chosen. Here are some examples of topics appropriate for literary and historical investigation.

- Investigate how Geoffrey Chaucer's life as a civil servant in fourteenth-century England influenced his writing.
- Investigate how accurately *Beowulf* reflects the history and culture of the ancient Germanic tribes who populate its pages.
- Investigate how Christianity spread among the Angles, Saxons, and Jutes of England and influenced their literature.
- Investigate how the writing of John Stuart Mill or Charles Dickens influenced social and economic reforms of the Victorian period.

Writing Skills
Write a literary research paper.

Tailor to Fit Narrow your subject so that you can cover it adequately. For example, the cultural history of England as reflected in Geoffrey Chaucer's *The Canterbury Tales* is much too broad for a research paper of 1,500 words. To narrow a topic, keep challenging yourself to be more specific by asking yourself a series of increasingly specific questions, as one student did in the following example.

Subject: *Geoffrey Chaucer*

What interests me about Chaucer?	—how Chaucer's *The Canterbury Tales* reflects the culture of medieval (fourteenth-century) England
What interests me about Chaucer's portrayal of medieval English culture?	—how Chaucer portrays women of medieval English culture in *The Canterbury Tales*
What interests me about the women in *The Canterbury Tales*?	—how the women in *The Canterbury Tales* reflect women in medieval English society

Limited topic: the complex female characters in Chaucer's *The Canterbury Tales* reflect medieval society at that time and the conflicting ideas about women's roles

Consider Purpose, Audience, and Tone

Why? Who? and What? Your **purpose** for writing this paper is to inform your **audience**—usually your teacher and your classmates—about the topic you've chosen. Your research paper will be an original **synthesis,** or combination, of information you gather from research, the conclusions you draw from that research information, and your insights into the topic. You will use a combination of rhetorical strategies—**exposition, narration,** and **description**—to communicate your synthesis and to support your main idea or proposition. The **tone** of your paper should be objective and formal without being stuffy. Avoid first- and second-person pronouns, slang, exclamation marks, and flowery language.

Make a Research Plan

Look Before You Leap Know what questions you want your research to answer by directing your research. Develop a list of **research questions,** like one writer researching Chaucer's depiction of women devised when she used the *5W-How?* method. (The *5W-How?* method answers the questions *Who? What? When? Where? Why?* and *How?*)

- Who are some of the female characters in *The Canterbury Tales*?
- What personalities do these female characters possess?
- When did medieval women become involved in business?
- Where did medieval women work or spend their leisure time?
- Why were women restricted in their activities?
- How did men treat women during Chaucer's time?

Writing Skills
Determine audience and purpose. Develop research questions.

Now, jot down a list of research questions of your own. If you come across a source of information not relevant to these questions, do not use that source.

Get an Overview and Find Sources

The Big Picture Start the search for answers to your research questions by consulting a general reference work, such as a print or CD-ROM encyclopedia or an Internet site or page containing related key words. Such general works will give you an overview of your topic, as well as valuable background information and knowledge of other sources you can use in your research. Once you have an adequate overview of your topic, you're ready to look for specific sources of information. Of course, in your search for information, you'll want to explore both print and nonprint sources. Here is a general source guide.

INFORMATION RESOURCES

Library Resources	
Source	**What to Look For**
Card catalog or online catalog	Books, records, audiotapes, and videotapes (Print and audiovisual listings are in separate catalogs in some libraries.)
***Readers' Guide to Periodical Literature* or online periodical indexes**	Magazines and some journal articles indexed by subject and author
Indexes to newspapers, essays, and articles	Articles from major newspapers, such as *The New York Times;* possibly local newspapers (Newspapers are frequently on microfilm.)
Specialized reference books and CD-ROMs	Encyclopedias of special subjects, such as *Contemporary Authors, Twentieth Century Authors;* almanacs; biographical references like *Current Biography*
Microfilm or microfiche and online databases	Indexes to major newspapers, back issues of some newspapers and magazines
Community Resources	
Source	**What to Look For**
World Wide Web and online services	Articles, interviews, bibliographies, pictures, videos, and sound recordings
Museums, historical societies, and government offices	Exhibits, records, and experts
Schools and colleges	Libraries, experts, exhibits, special collections, and records
Television and radio, video stores	Documentary and instructional programs and videos

Getting Specific If your topic involves a classic author like Chaucer, your search for information may leave you drowning in sources. If so, toss yourself a life jacket with these guidelines.

- **Balance primary and secondary sources. Primary sources** consist of firsthand, original information, such as letters, autobiographies, works of literature and art, and historical documents. **Secondary sources** consist of information derived from, or about, primary sources or other secondary sources. Examples include encyclopedias, documentary films, biographies, history books, and interviews with historians. For one student, Chaucer's *The Canterbury Tales* is a major primary source. A journal article written by a Chaucer scholar is a secondary source.
- **Check the reliability and validity of sources.** A source is reliable and valid when its facts are accurate and when its ideas are presented objectively. Unfortunately, however, both primary and secondary sources can be biased, or slanted, and inaccurate. Seek information published by major universities or established, credible publishing companies. These sources can serve as a kind of benchmark by which you can judge other sources.
- **Cover all relevant perspectives.** Develop **research strategies** to find information from **relevant** perspectives, or points of view, on your topic. Look for sources that reveal the perspectives of a variety of literary and historical scholars who have written about matters related to your topic. For example, the student writing about women in *The Canterbury Tales* uses the perspectives of both men and women and of scholars in history and English literature.

TIP Evaluate the reliability and validity of sources on the World Wide Web more than in print materials because information from Web sites is not held to the same standards as most books and journal articles.

Note Sources

Keep an Address Book Readers of your research paper may want to consult *your* sources for additional information on your topic. In a *Works Cited* list or a *Bibliography* at the end of your report, you'll provide precise details about every source you used. Use the following suggestions to help you record your sources.

- **Make a *source card,* or *bibliography card,* for every source you use.** You may keep your list on 3- × 5-inch index cards, in a computer file, or simply on several pages of a notebook.
- **Number your sources.** Assign each source a number. Use the number, rather than the author and title, when you are taking notes from a given source.
- **Record all publishing information.** Record everything you might need for your list of *Works Cited,* such as author and title, city, publisher, and date. This collection uses the Modern Language Association of America (MLA) format. Different formats include those of *The Chicago Manual of Style* or the American Psychological Association (APA).

Writing Skills
Consult a variety of research sources. Evaluate the reliability of sources. Record sources for a *Works Cited* list.

- **Annotate your source card.** Turn your source cards into an annotated bibliography by writing a short note about the contents of the source and your evaluation of the source.
- **Note the call number or location of the source.** This information will save you time if you must go back to a source later.

source number	(1)
publishing information	Hallissy, Margaret. A Companion to Chaucer's Canterbury Tales. Westport: Greenwood Publishing Group, 1995.
annotation	An introduction to the tales and characters. Has a guide to the language and a bibliography.
call number	821.C393h

Research and Take Notes

A Great Leap Forward Now you are ready to leap into the major phase of your research project—the search for specific information to answer your research questions. Here are some guidelines for creating **note cards** to record information.

GUIDELINES FOR NOTE CARDS

1. **Use a separate note card, sheet of paper, or computer file for each source and for each main idea.** Separate records for each source and main idea make sorting and grouping your notes easier.
2. **Write the source number in the upper right-hand corner and the page number(s) at the bottom of the note card.** Both numbers are essential for correct documentation. The source number gives you access to the publication data on your corresponding source card. The page number(s) must be supplied if you use the information in your paper.
3. **Write a heading at the top of the card showing the main idea.** The headings will let you see content at a glance and will be useful later as you prepare your outline.
4. **Re-read the note to make sure you understand it.** Decipher any abbreviations or note-taking shortcuts that might be unclear when you are writing your paper.

Writing Skills
Take notes on note cards.

Now, as you take notes, use the guidelines below and on the next page to decide how to record each piece of information—direct quotation, paraphrase, or summary.

- **Direct quotation** Quote an author directly and exactly, including his or her punctuation, capitalization, and spelling, when a passage is phrased in a memorable way or if you want to capture the technical accuracy of a passage. Enclose the passage in quotation marks. Since your paper should be a synthesis of information you derive from outside sources and your own analysis and conclusions, avoid using too many direct quotations and long quotations.

When you do use direct quotations in your paper, smoothly integrate them into your sentences and paragraphs. If you need only part of a quotation, you might need to use ellipsis points to show omissions from quoted text. If you need to insert your words into a quotation to clarify or explain it, put brackets around those insertions. (For more on the use of **ellipsis points** and **brackets** with quotations, see 13e and 13o in the Language Handbook.)

- **Paraphrase** When you want to use material from a source without directly quoting the source, paraphrase the information. Paraphrasing means that you completely rewrite a passage in your own words and style. A paraphrase is usually about the same length as the original.
- **Summary** When you want to use the general idea presented in a source, summarize the information. A typical summary is highly condensed—one fourth to one third the length of the original passage.

TIP Avoid **plagiarizing,** or failing to give credit to an author whose words or ideas you have used, by completely rewriting the passages. Simply substituting synonyms for some of the words from your source is not enough.

(3) — source card number

Structure of The Canterbury Tales — heading

"Structurally regarded, The Canterbury Tales is a kind of Human Comedy. From this point of view, the Pilgrims are the Dramatis personae, and their stories are only speeches that are somewhat longer than common." — note (quotation)

page 130 — page number

The structure of The Canterbury Tales is much like the structure of a drama. The characters in this drama are the Pilgrims, who present their stories as long speeches. — note (paraphrase)

page 130 — page number

The Pilgrims are like characters in a drama. They tell their stories in long speeches. — note (summary)

page 130 — page number

Analyze Research Information

The Good, the Bad, and the Useless Analyze the information you uncovered to see if it is relevant and useful for your topic and to account for any differences in scholarly records. Start by dividing your notes into categories based on their headings. The student writing about Chaucer's female characters, for example, first divided her cards into two stacks, one each for the Prioress and the Wife of Bath. Then she subdivided each set on the basis of what aspect of each character the note dealt with, discarding notes that turned out to be irrelevant to her topic as she did so. Her notes became the source of the specific examples and supporting details she used to develop the main ideas in her paper. Her method of organizing became the basis of her formal outline.

TIP Your teacher may require that you develop two or more main ideas from your information. Keep in mind that if you use only two main ideas, each one must be fully elaborated in your research paper.

Next, analyze the notes, both for consistency of factual information and for interpretation of factual information. If two sources are inconsistent in their presentation of facts, check each source for reliability and validity by using the suggestions on page 243. Use the information from the most reliable and valid source or the information that is verified in other reputable sources.

If two reliable sources disagree on an interpretation of facts, subject both interpretations to logical analysis and common sense. Attempt to **explain** the difference using information from the primary or secondary source to support your point. A difference in interpretation might be a simple matter of differing perspectives. For example, scholars' differing perspectives on the attitudes of men toward women during the Middle Ages might well lead to different interpretations of the female characters in *The Canterbury Tales* or of customs regarding the role of women in the Middle Ages. Explaining such differences will enhance your paper.

Write a Thesis Statement

Assert Yourself Your **thesis statement** is a sentence or two identifying the main idea that you intend to set forth in your paper. Writing a thesis statement is an act of *synthesis.* You draw a conclusion about the information you have analyzed, thus synthesizing your topic and your conclusion about it. In effect, your thesis statement reflects the answers to your original research questions. Here is the thesis statement of the student writing about Chaucer's depiction of women. At this point, any thesis statement is preliminary. You might change it later for reasons of content or style.

Writing Skills
Analyze information. Write a thesis statement.

> Chaucer reflects the social changes taking place for women by creating complex, often inconsistent female characters who echo the contradictions of the times.

Make an Outline

Mapping the Territory Create an outline by taking your note cards and arranging them according to the main-idea headings you put on them. Keep rearranging them until you find an order that makes sense. You will probably end up using a combination of organizational patterns—chronological order, order of importance, and logical order—for both your main ideas and your specific examples and supporting details.

- **Chronological order** can be used to discuss events in an author's or character's life in the order in which they occurred.
- **Order of importance** can be used to discuss main ideas about an author's work. The most important idea is often discussed last.
- **Logical order** groups ideas by the relationships among them—for example, cause-and-effect or comparison-contrast.

Organizing your notes paves the way for a **formal outline,** which, in its final form, can also serve as a table of contents for the finished paper. Follow standard outline format, as shown below in the partial outline of the Writer's Model on page 252.

II. The Prioress: Spiritual Concerns and Worldly Concerns
  A. Appearance
    1. Fine forehead
      a. Takes pride in forehead
      b. Shows forehead despite conventions of the time
    2. Jewelry
      a. Wears green-beaded rosary
      b. Has gold brooch with motto
  B. Interests/pleasures
    1. French language
    2. Aristocratic manners
    3. Animal lover
      a. Keeps dogs
      b. Feeds dogs from the table

TIP You can also use the major divisions of your outline as **headings** within the paper to make it easier to follow, as the writer of the model on page 252 did.

Document Sources

Reveal Your Sources To document a paper means to identify the sources from which the information in your paper came. Although the rules for *how* to document sources are clearly set forth in whichever style guide you follow, the rules about *what* to document are not so distinct. In general, document all but the most widely known quotations; all theories, ideas, and opinions other than your own; all data from surveys, research studies, and interviews conducted by

Writing Skills
Make an outline.

TIP Your teacher may prefer a style of documentation different from parenthetical citations, such as footnotes or endnotes. **Footnotes** are placed at the bottom of the same page where you used the source information. **Endnotes** are identical to footnotes but are compiled in a list at the end of the paper.

someone other than you; and all obscure information represented as factual. You don't need to document common knowledge—information that can be found in several sources or standard reference works.

Point the Way Place **parenthetical citations** (sources enclosed in parentheses) within the body of your paper as close as possible to the information they document. They direct readers to the *Works Cited* list at the end of your paper for more complete information on each source.

Parenthetical citations should be as brief as possible. For most citations, use the last name of the author and the page number. If you name the author in the sentence, give only the page number in parentheses. The chart below gives guidelines for citing sources.

GUIDELINES FOR GIVING CREDIT WITHIN A PAPER

Types of Sources	Content of Citation/Example
Sources with one author	**Author's last name and a page reference, if any** (Chaucer 25)
Separate passages in a single source	**Author's last name and page references, if any** (Bishop 37, 39)
Sources with more than one author	**All authors' last names; if over three, use first author's last name and *et al.* ("and others")** (Thompson and Johnson 322) (Anderson, et al. 313)
Multivolume sources	**Author's last name, plus volume and page reference** (Prucha 2: 214–15)
Sources with a title only	**Full title (if short) or shortened version and page** (World Almanac 38)
Literary sources published in many editions	**Author's last name, title, and division references (act, scene, canto, book, chapter, part, and line numbers) in place of page numbers** (Shakespeare, The Tempest 3.2.51–52)
Indirect sources	**Abbreviation *qtd. in* (quoted in) before the source** (qtd. in Blamires 29)
More than one source in the same citation	**Citations separated with semicolons** (Chute 30; Sheehan 64)

Parenthetical citations are usually inserted near the end of the information they are documenting. The following sample passage contains information from three sources.

> Although their status was changing dramatically (Bishop 37), women were paid less for doing the same work as their husbands (Gies and Gies, Women 181), and within marriages husbands still expected the same compliance that seemed "natural" to the medieval male (Kittredge 143).

Writing Skills
Include a *Works Cited* list.

Follow the Forms The ***Works Cited*** list is a list of the sources, print and nonprint, that you use in your paper. If you don't cite a source in your paper, don't put it in your *Works Cited* list. Here are guidelines for preparing your *Works Cited* list.

- **Center the words *Works Cited.***
- **Begin each entry on a separate line.** Position the first line of the entry even with the left margin, and indent all other lines five spaces, or one-half inch if you are using a word processor. Double-space all entries.
- **Alphabetize the sources by the authors' last names.** If there is no author, alphabetize by title, ignoring *A, An,* and *The* and using the first letter of the next word.
- **If you use two or more sources by the same author, include the author's name only in the first entry.** For all other entries, put three hyphens in place of the author's name, followed by a period (---.).

TIP Your teacher may prefer that you call the list of works in your paper a *bibliography* if you cite only print publications. *Bibliography* refers to printed materials exclusively.

The following sample entries are a reference for preparing your *Works Cited* list. Notice that you include page numbers only for sources that are one part of a whole work, such as one essay in a book of essays.

SAMPLE ENTRIES FOR *WORKS CITED* LIST

Standard Reference Works

NOTE: When an author or editor is credited in a standard reference work, the source is listed under that person's name. Otherwise, the source is listed by the title of the book or article. Page and volume numbers are not needed if the work alphabetizes entries. For common reference works, the edition year is sufficient publication information.

Print Encyclopedia Article

Lumiansky, R. M. "Chaucer, Geoffrey." The New Encyclopaedia Britannica: Macropaedia. 15th ed. 1987.

"Canterbury Cathedral." Academic American Encyclopedia. 1996 ed.

Article in a Biographical Reference Book

"Geoffrey Chaucer (c.1343–1400)." The Cambridge Biographical Encyclopedia. 2nd edition. Ed. David Crystal. Cambridge: Cambridge UP, 1998.

Books

NOTE: Use shortened forms of publishers' names. For the words *University* and *Press,* use *U* and *P.*

One Author

Knapp, Peggy. Chaucer and the Social Contest. New York: Routledge, 1990.

Two Authors

Allen, Judson Boyce, and Theresa Anne Moritz. A Distinction of Stories: The Medieval Unity of Chaucer's Fair Chain of Narratives for Canterbury. Columbus: Ohio State UP, 1981.

Three Authors

Klibansky, Raymond, Erwin Panofsky, and Fritz Saxl. Saturn and Melancholy: Studies in the History of Natural Philosophy, Religion, and Art. London: Nelson, 1964.

(continued)

(continued)

Four or More Authors

Davis, Norman, et al. A Chaucer Glossary. Oxford: Oxford UP, 1979.

No Author Shown

An Exhibition of Fifteenth-Century Manuscripts and Books in Honor of the Six Hundredth Anniversary of the Birth of Geoffrey Chaucer (1340–1400). Chicago: U of Chicago P, 1941.

Editor of a Collection of Writings

Miller, Robert P., ed. Chaucer: Sources and Backgrounds. New York: Oxford UP, 1977.

Two or Three Editors

Evans, Rudy, and Lesley Johnson, eds. Feminist Readings in Middle English Poetry: The Wife of Bath and All Her Sect. London: Routledge, 1995.

Translation

Chaucer, Geoffrey. The Canterbury Tales. Trans. Nevill Coghill. New York: Penguin Classics, 1977.

Bibliography Published as a Book

Lagorio, Valerie Marie, and Ritamary Bradley. The 14th-Century English Mystics: A Comprehensive Annotated Bibliography. New York: Garland, 1981.

Unpublished Thesis or Dissertation

Lee, Chong-kyung. "To Pursue a Life of Perfection: Distinctive Forms of Female Monastic Life in the Early Middle Ages." Diss. U of Texas, 1997.

Selections Within Books

From a Book of Works by One Author

Chaucer, Geoffrey. The Canterbury Tales: Nine Tales and the General Prologue. Ed. Glending Olson and V. A. Kolve. New York: W. W. Norton and Company, 1989.

From a Book of Works by Several Authors

Donaldson, E. Talbot. "Chaucer the Pilgrim." Chaucer Criticism: The Canterbury Tales. Ed. Richard J. Schoeck and Jerome Taylor. Vol. 1. Notre Dame: U of Notre Dame P, 1960. 1–13.

Introduction, Preface, Foreword, or Afterword

Hieatt, A. Kent, and Constance Hieatt. Introduction. The Canterbury Tales. By Geoffrey Chaucer. Ed. A. Kent Hieatt and Constance Hieatt. New York: Bantam, 1981. ix–xxiv.

Articles from Magazines, Newspapers, and Journals

From a Weekly Magazine

Hughes, Robert. "Blazing Exceptions to Nature." Time 30 Nov. 1987: 94–96.

From a Monthly or Quarterly Magazine

Huneycutt, Lois. "Medieval Queenship." History Today June 1989: 16–23.

No Author Shown

"History in the Media." History Today. 01 Mar 01: 7.

From a Scholarly Journal

Green, Richard Firth. "Women in Chaucer's Audience." The Chaucer Review 18.2 (1983): 146–54.

From a Daily Newspaper, Without a Byline

"20th-Century Tools Analyzing Chaucer's 14th-Century Tome." Fort Worth Star-Telegram 27 Aug. 1998, final morning ed.

Unsigned Editorial from a Daily Newspaper, No City in Paper's Title

"Woman's Hour." Editorial. Christian Science Monitor 16 July 1998: 16.

(continued)

Other Sources

Personal Interview

Landow, Charles. Personal interview. 20 Oct. 2002.

Telephone Interview

Barnes, Elaine. Telephone interview. 17 Aug. 2002.

Published Interview with Title

Midgeley, Abigail. "Men Always Made the Big Decisions." Generations: A Century of Women Speak About Their Lives. By Myriam Miedzian and Alisa Malinovich. New York: Atlantic Monthly P, 1997. 241–45.

Broadcast or Recorded Interview with Title

Campbell, Joseph. "Love and the Goddess." The Power of Myth. Prod. Joan Konner and Alvin H. Perlmutter. Videocassette. Mystic Fire, 1988.

Published Letter

Paston, Margaret. "To Her Husband, John Paston." 14 Dec. 1441. Letter in Women's Lives in Medieval Europe: A Sourcebook. Ed. Emilie Amt. New York: Routledge, 1993. 170–71.

Personal Letter or E-Mail Message

Grau, Katherine. Letter to the author. 22 Jan 2002.

Rodholm, Kai. E-mail to the author. 9 July 2001.

Sound Recording

Dyson, George. The Canterbury Pilgrims. Perf. Yvonne Kenny, Robert Tear, and Stephen Roberts. London Symphony Chorus. Cond. Malcolm Hicks. London Symphony Orch. Cond. Richard Hickox. Chandos, 1997.

Film or Video Recording

NOTE: Always include the title, director (if known) distributor, and year. You may include the producer. For video recordings, add a description of the medium (*Videotape* or *Videocassette*) before the distributor's name.

"The Wife of Bath" by Geoffrey Chaucer. Videocassette. Films for the Humanities and Sciences, 1996.

Material Accessed Through the Internet

"Courtly Love." Geoffrey Chaucer Page. Harvard U. 31 Jan. 2002. <http://icg.fas.harvard.edu/~chaucer/special/lifemann/love>.

Article from a CD-ROM Reference Work

Miller, Robert P. "Chaucer, Geoffrey." The 1998 Grolier's Multimedia Encyclopedia. CD-ROM. Danbury: Grolier Interactive Inc., 1998.

Full-Text Magazine, Newspaper, or Journal Article from a CD-ROM Database

"Middle Ages." History Today Apr. 1998: 51. MAS FullTEXT Select Version 5.0. CD-ROM. EBSCO Publishing, 1996.

PRACTICE & APPLY 1 Using the preceding instructions, select a topic for your literary research paper. Then, locate and record information from primary and secondary sources. Write a thesis statement and plan your paper's documentation. Be sure to follow the guidelines for making source cards (page 243) and taking notes (page 244).

Writing

Literary Research Paper

A Writer's Framework

Introduction

- Hook your readers with an intriguing opening.
- Provide background information about the author, his or her work(s), and the period in which he or she wrote.
- Include a clear thesis statement.

Body

- Choose one or a combination of organizational patterns.
- Develop each main idea that supports your thesis.
- Add facts, details, and examples from your research.
- Use sources offering different perspectives.

Conclusion

- Restate your thesis.
- Bring your paper to a close by providing a final insight into your research.

A Writer's Model

Chaucer's Female Characters: A Reflection of Change

INTRODUCTION
Intriguing opening
Primary source

In the Prologue to Geoffrey Chaucer's *The Canterbury Tales,* the Prioress wears a gold brooch inscribed with the motto *"Amor Vincit Omnia"* (Chaucer 25)—"Love Conquers All"—a motto that could mean spiritual love or romantic love. If the Prioress represents nuns in general in the late fourteenth century, then the motto is ironic. Later in the Prologue, Chaucer introduces the independent and gregarious Wife of Bath, proud widow of five husbands. She, too, seems to represent an ironic version of fourteenth-century wives in general.

Direct quotation
Secondary source
Background information
Source by two authors
Thesis statement

Chaucer, "one of the most wonderful observers in the whole of English literature" (Power 94), reports everything he observes about people with accuracy—even if he sees contradictions. His ability to "tell a good story" with "vivid and familiar" character types and a "wickedly modern sense of irony" is well known to contemporary readers ("Remembering Geoffrey Chaucer"). The last half of the fourteenth century was a time of contradictions (Thompson and Johnson 863). Most of the traditional relationships of society were changing, and "the times were filled with war, plague, suffering, and anger" (Bishop 334). Amid all this upheaval, the relation of women to society was also changing. By creating complex, often inconsistent female characters who echo the contradictions of the times, Chaucer reflects the social changes taking place for women.

The Prioress: Spiritual Concerns and Worldly Concerns

Heading

BODY

First main idea

The Prioress (Madame Eglantine) appears in the General Prologue as both a woman of the Church and a vain woman with worldly interests. Her simple but coy smile seems an affectation, and her graceful manner calls attention to herself. She takes pride in her "well-shaped head, / Almost a span across the brows" (Chaucer 25). Madame Eglantine does not hesitate to show off one of her finest features, even though, as Eileen Power points out, "The nuns were supposed to wear their veils pinned tightly down to their eyebrows, so that their foreheads were completely hidden" (89). The Prioress also has "a set of beads, the gaudies tricked in green," from which hangs the gold brooch that proclaims her faith in the power of love (Chaucer 25); yet she coyly refrains from specifying whether that love is spiritual or romantic.

Author of quotation named in text

Her interests range further than devotion to God and singing "the service" (Chaucer 24) or the medieval hymn "Angelus ad Virginem" (Wood). She speaks good French and has the perfect manners of an aristocratic lady. She goes to great lengths to make sure that no crumb falls from her lips and that no trace of grease appears on her drinking cup. In addition, she has a tender sympathy for animals, weeping for a mouse caught in a trap. She feeds several dogs "roasted flesh, or milk and fine white bread" from the table (Chaucer 25). In all these ways, she indulges her taste in the pleasures of the world and gives more than a usual sympathy for animals, rather than in the practices of self-denial and attention to human need, as might be expected of a nun.

Specific examples

Writer's conclusion

Chaucer's picture of the Prioress seemingly matches the lives of nuns at this time. Morris Bishop comments that in the late Middle Ages nuns often entered convents not because they have a spiritual calling but because they were "surplus or unmarriageable daughters of the noble and bourgeois classes." He calls the convents "aristocratic spinsters' clubs" (174). They were aristocratic because, although not formally required, a payment to the convent was necessary before a girl would be accepted as a novitiate (Gies and Gies, <u>Women</u> 64). Under these conditions of admission, many of the nuns were not devoted to a spiritual life and were openly rebellious toward the restrictions that the Church tried to impose on them.

Connection of literature and history

Writer's conclusion

Among the Church's prohibitions were pets, which the bishops believed interfered with discipline. Such a ruling, however, did not rid the convent of animals (Power 90). Like Chaucer's Prioress, the nuns enjoyed having pets and kept them as companions. Life in the convent was limited even further because nuns were not supposed to travel.

Specific examples

(continued)

(continued)

In 1300, a Papal Bull, a special decree or edict from the Pope, ordered that nuns be confined in the convents except under the most exceptional of circumstances. In response, the nuns of one convent chased the bishop who brought the order to the gate of the nunnery and "when he was riding away . . . threw the Bull at his head, screaming that they would never obey it" (Power 93). The model for Chaucer's Prioress, then, is rooted in history: Nuns may be devoted to the Church but also strongly interested in worldly affairs.

Ellipsis within quotation

Writer's conclusion

The Wife of Bath: Dominance and Dependence

Heading

Second main idea

For the Wife of Bath, the conflict is between a desire for dominance and a desire for a strong husband; she wants power, but she also wants a conventional marriage relationship (Patterson 142). Chaucer describes her in the Prologue as an independent woman, yet always refers to her, as she always refers to herself, as a "Wife" (Patterson 136). She has had five husbands, and she says, in introducing her tale, "Welcome the sixth, whenever he appears" (Chaucer 218). From her friendly manner and engaging conversation she appears to have joined the other pilgrims to Canterbury to look for another husband.

Writer's conclusion

The Wife of Bath, a weaver by trade, is a woman with money and the respect of society. She has wealth enough to travel three times to Jerusalem and through Italy and France. She makes her social position obvious by her clothing, especially the kerchiefs she wears as a headdress, which "weighed a good ten pound, / The ones she wore on Sunday" (Chaucer 34). Such clothing denoted status (Carroll). Although she wants to be admired and respected for her money and position, ironically she does not want to "change the system" completely (Patterson 142). She wants to be a special kind of wife—an understandable desire when considered within her historical context.

Summary of primary source

Online source

Writer's conclusion

In the two centuries before Chaucer, conditions for women had been oppressive and unchangeable (Thompson and Johnson 322). Women were expected both by custom and by law to be subservient to their husbands and were valued in some cases for little else than their ability to bear children (Thompson and Johnson 322) and do menial work (Bishop 37). One commentary of the Middle Ages proposed that if God had intended women to be equal to men, Eve would have been derived from Adam's head instead of his rib (Coulton 190). The men of the time agreed that "women were inferior beings" (Rowling 72). However, comparing the Wife of Bath to the accepted social conventions of marriage produces surprising results. Because the Wife of Bath has outlived five husbands, she is not

Information from secondary sources

Writer's conclusion

physically inferior. Because she has independent wealth, she is not financially inferior. She is an ironic representation of the traditional woman of the times.

In fact, Chaucer's Wife of Bath argues to readjust the system. She wants to be married, but she wants power over men within the home and an end to men's control, particularly economic control, of women. She does not advocate independence from men. She understands that in marriage "sovereignty is synonymous with economic control" and that by achieving economic independence, she gains "independence of spirit, the freedom to give freely" (Carruthers). Once she feels she has "sovereignty in wedlock," she is "as kind to him / As any wife from Denmark to the rim / Of India, and as true" (Chaucer 237).

Historically, women during Chaucer's time, like the Wife of Bath, could be in "business for themselves and were considered legally capable of controlling funds for their business and of answering for that business in borough court" (Sheehan 32). Moreover, a woman could work with her husband, and "when a man die[d] his widow carrie[d] on the trade" (Gies and Gies, Life 53). However, women were paid less for doing the same work as their husbands (Gies and Gies, Women 181), and within marriages husbands still expected the same compliance that seemed "natural" to the medieval male (Kittredge 143). Georges Duby says that women were almost nonexistent in a social sense unless they had husbands (98). The irony about the Wife of Bath is her *managing* so many husbands.

In the prologue to Chaucer's dream-vision poem, *The Legend of Good Women,* the god of love punishes Chaucer by having him write only about stereotypically good women instead of stereotypically bad (Lumiansky). A decade later, in *The Canterbury Tales,* using his keen powers of observation, Chaucer creates women who escape both stereotypical molds, women who are real people, mirroring the contradictory times in which they lived. In the Prioress and the Wife of Bath, Chaucer focuses our attention on women whose complexity parallels the complexity of the times. Since these characters are not at all simple, they remain still fresh and alive after six hundred years.

Analysis of primary source

Online source

Connection of history and literature

Brackets within quotations

Paraphrase

Writer's conclusion

CONCLUSION

Primary source

Restatement of thesis

Final insight

Works Cited

Bishop, Morris. The Middle Ages. New York: American Heritage P, 1970.

Carroll, Sharon. "Women's Clothing in the Middle Ages." Millersville U. 10 May 2001 <http://www.millersv.edu/~english/homepage/duncan/medfem/cloth.html>.

(continued)

TIP Research reports and *Works Cited* lists are normally double-spaced. See a double-spaced Writer's Model at go.hrw.com.

(continued)

Carruthers, Mary. “The Wife of Bath and the Painting of Lions.” Geoffrey Chaucer Page. Harvard U. 10 May 2001 <http://icg.fas.harvard.edu/~chaucer/canttales/wbpro/carruth.htm>.

Chaucer, Geoffrey. The Canterbury Tales. Trans. Nevill Coghill. New York: Penguin Classics, 1977.

Coulton, G. G. Chaucer and His England. London: Methuen, 1963.

Duby, Georges. Love and Marriage in the Middle Ages. Trans. Jane Dunnett. Chicago: U of Chicago P, 1994.

Gies, Joseph, and Frances Gies. Life in a Medieval City. New York: Harper, 1969.

---. Women in the Middle Ages. New York: Harper, 1978.

Kittredge, George Lyman. “Chaucer’s Discussion of Marriage.” Chaucer Criticism: The Canterbury Tales. Ed. Richard J. Schoeck and Jerome Taylor. Vol. 1. Notre Dame: U of Notre Dame P, 1960. 130–59.

Lumiansky, R. M. “Chaucer, Geoffrey.” Encyclopaedia Britannica Online. 10 May 2001. <http://www.eb.com:180>.

Patterson, Lee. “‘Experience woot well it is nought so’: Marriage and the Pursuit of Happiness in the Wife of Bath’s Prologue and Tale.” Geoffrey Chaucer: The Wife of Bath. Ed. Peter G. Beidler. Case Studies in Contemporary Criticism. Boston: Bedford Books of St. Martin’s, 1996. 133–54.

Power, Eileen. Medieval People. New York: Barnes, 1968.

“Remembering Geoffrey Chaucer.” All Things Considered. Host. Linda Wertheimer. Nat’l. Public Radio. KUT, Austin. 27 October 2000.

Rowling, Marjorie. Life in Medieval Times. New York: Capricorn, 1973.

Sheehan, Michael M. “The Wife of Bath and Her Four Sisters: Reflections on a Woman’s Life in the Age of Chaucer.” Medievalia et Humanistica. Ed. Paul M. Clogan. New Ser. 13. Totowa, NJ: Rowman & Allanheld, 1985. 23–42.

Thompson, James Westfall, and Edgar Nathaniel Johnson. An Introduction to Medieval Europe 300–1500. New York: Norton, 1937.

Wood, Carol. “Angelus ad Virginem.” The Chaucer Songbook. Audio CD. Mel Bay Publications, Inc., 2000.

PRACTICE & APPLY 2 Use the framework and the Writer's Model to draft and document your literary research paper and to create a *Works Cited* list for it.

Revising

Evaluate and Revise Your Literary Research Paper

The Best It Can Be Because doing all that a research paper entails is difficult and time-consuming, you want your paper to be as good as you can make it. Therefore, take the time to revise it. Careful revisions can turn a run-of-the-mill research paper into a superior paper. Read your paper at least twice. First, evaluate and revise the content and organization of your paper. Second, evaluate and revise its style.

PEER REVIEW

Before you revise, trade papers with a peer. He or she may be able to point out ideas in your paper that need more or better supporting details.

First Reading: Content and Organization Use the guidelines in the following chart to evaluate and revise the content and organization of your research paper. To answer the evaluation questions in the first column, use the tips in the second column. Then, if necessary, use the revision techniques suggested in the third column.

editor in charge

Rubric: Reporting Literary Research

Evaluation Questions	Tips	Revision Techniques
1 Does the introduction hook the reader's attention, give background information, and clearly state the thesis?	**Circle** the hook, **underline** background information, and **bracket** the thesis statement.	**Add** a quotation or interesting detail to hook readers. **Add** necessary background. **Add** a thesis statement.
2 Does the body include only main ideas and supporting details that are relevant to the thesis?	With a colored marker, **highlight** the main ideas. **Number** supporting details for each.	**Delete** irrelevant ideas and details. **Add** details to support ideas with fewer than three supporting details.
3 Are facts and ideas stated mainly in the writer's own words?	**Star** sentences containing direct quotations. If more than one third of the sentences are starred, revise.	**Replace** unnecessary direct quotations with paraphrases and summaries.
4 Are sources credited when necessary? Are citations correctly placed and punctuated?	**Place check marks** by material from outside sources that requires documentation.	**Add** parenthetical citations. **Correct** placement and punctuation of citations.
5 Does the conclusion restate the thesis? Is the *Works Cited* list complete and correctly formatted?	**Bracket** the restatement of the thesis. **Place an X** beside *Works Cited* entries of each source cited in the body of the paper.	**Add** a sentence or two restating the thesis. **Add** and **correct** *Works Cited* entries.

Second Reading: Style To keep your readers' attention fixed firmly on the ideas in your paper, avoid long series of sentences that follow the same pattern. For example, avoid beginning every sentence with the same subject-verb pattern. Instead, use a variety of sentence patterns to keep your style fresh and lively. The guidelines below will help you improve **sentence variety** in your paper.

Style Guidelines

Evaluation Question	Tip	Revision Technique
Do many of the sentences begin in the same familiar subject-verb pattern?	**Underline** the first five words of each sentence. If three sentences in a row begin with the subject-verb pattern, revise.	**Rearrange** or **combine** sentences to place dependent clauses at the beginning. Rephrase when necessary.

ANALYZING THE REVISION PROCESS

Study these revisions, and answer the questions that follow.

Most of the traditional relationships of society, ~~such as the relationship between knight and lord,~~ were changing, and "the times were filled with war, plague, suffering and anger" (Bishop 334). Amid all this upheaval, the relation of women to society was also changing. By creating complex, often inconsistent female characters who echo the contradictions of the times, Chaucer reflects the social changes taking place for women.

delete

add

rearrange

Responding to the Revision Process

1. Why did the writer delete information from the first sentence and add information to the second sentence?
2. Why did the writer rearrange the last sentence?

Writing Skills
Revise for content and style.

PRACTICE & APPLY 3 Using the guidelines in this section, first evaluate and revise the content and organization of your research paper. Then, evaluate and revise the style of your paper, particularly the way you begin your sentences.

Proofread and Publish Your Paper

Polish the Prose When you went to all the trouble to research and write a literary research paper, you became an authority on your topic. Don't allow careless errors in grammar, usage, and mechanics to destroy your credibility as an authority. Instead, finish the job by proofreading your paper very carefully. Meticulously correct every error you find. While good content, organization, and style are the most impressive aspects of a paper, an error-free paper is also impressive.

TIP As you proofread, be sure to see that you have followed the **conventions** of standard American English. Look in particular for dangling modifiers, modifiers that do not clearly and sensibly modify a word or group of words in a sentence. It is easy to write a dangling modifier when you explain complex ideas, as you often do in research papers. For more on **dangling modifiers,** see Placement of Modifiers, 5h, in the Language Handbook.

Publish Your Essay

Share the Wealth (of Knowledge) Your research paper is a synthesis of a great deal of information, the conclusions you have drawn about that research, and your interpretations and insights. Don't let it go to waste after sharing it with your teacher and classmates. Make it available to others. Consider these publishing ideas.

- Save your literary research project as a writing sample to submit for a college or job application.
- If the topic is one that would be of interest to students in another class, offer to present the report to the class, complete with appropriate **visuals** and **graphics.**
- If your school has a Web site, or you know of a Web site on a topic related to your paper, submit the paper to the creators of the site for possible inclusion.

COMPUTER TIP

If you have access to a computer and advanced publishing software, consider using those tools to design and format graphics and visuals to enhance the content of your research paper. For more on **graphics** and **visuals,** see *Designing Your Writing* in the Writer's Handbook.

Reflect on Your Essay

Consider the Road You've Traveled Responding to the following questions will help you think about what this research project has meant to you and what you've learned about yourself as a writer. Keep your answers along with a copy of your paper, and refer to both the next time you write a research paper.

- What was the most intriguing discovery your research produced? Why?
- What questions did your research answer that you had not asked or anticipated? Describe them.
- What passage in your paper was the most effective combination of research and conclusions drawn from that research? Why?

PRACTICE & APPLY 4 Following the guidelines in this section, first proofread your research paper to correct any errors. Then, publish your essay in an appropriate source and reflect on your literary research paper.

Writing Skills
Proofread, especially for correct use of modifiers. Design and format a research paper, including visuals and graphics.

Presenting Literary Research

Speaking Assignment
Adapt your literary research paper for an oral presentation to an audience.

Scholars in various fields—science, history, literature, anthropology—put the results of their research into the forms of books and articles, which are published in scholarly or professional journals. No doubt you ran across many such writings in your research. These same scholars also make oral presentations of the results of their research before their peers at various meetings and conferences. In this workshop you will do the same—adapt your written report for an oral presentation to your peers.

Adapt Your Literary Research Paper

Adapt to Your Environment The **purpose** of your oral report will be to share the results of your literary research with an **audience**—in this case, your classmates. Because your listeners will not be able to stop and think about or re-read information, you may need to simplify and clarify the material from your paper. Try the following suggestions for adapting your literary research paper.

- Liven up your **introduction.** Look for an interesting fact or an intriguing quotation to seize the immediate attention of your audience.
- State your **thesis** clearly in the introduction, perhaps even repeating important parts for emphasis, to focus the attention of your audience.
- Make the most of your **conclusion** by hammering home your thesis. Communicate a final insight into your topic with a relevant anecdote or a compelling quotation.
- Simplify your vocabulary, and break up long sentences into shorter ones. Doing both these things will make your oral presentation easier to understand. Also, maintain a combination of **exposition, narration,** and **description** from your written report to support your thesis and to make your report both informative and entertaining.
- Include information from as many of the **primary** and **secondary sources** you used in your written report as your time allows. Be sure to include information from all **relevant perspectives** on the topic. Explain the differences in information from your sources.
- Do not cite sources except to identify the author of important quotations or striking facts or conclusions. To integrate an important quotation into your oral presentation, you might say, "According to Eileen Power, Chaucer was 'one of the most wonderful observers in the whole of English literature.'" At the beginning of your presentation, tell your audience that you will be using information from a variety of sources.

Listening and Speaking Skills
Present a literary research paper.

Rehearse Your Presentation

Formally Speaking Since you will be speaking as an authority on the subject of your presentation, deliver your presentation **extemporaneously.** This means that you'll rehearse your presentation until you are thoroughly familiar and comfortable with your material, but you will not memorize it. Maintain a formal, objective tone suitable for a research presentation. Create note cards with reminders of important points and the full text of important quotations. Be sure to arrange your note cards in the order of your presentation.

Perfect Practice Once you are comfortable with the content of your presentation, start rehearsals to perfect it. Try one or more of these rehearsal strategies: videotape your presentation, practice in front of a mirror, or present your report to your family or friends. As you rehearse, pay attention not only to the content of your presentation but also to performance details such as those presented in the chart below.

Quick guide!

PERFORMANCE TECHNIQUES

Technique	Tips
Diction	• Use standard American English, and speak clearly. • Define any technical terms for your audience. • Avoid the use of informal expressions.
Emphasis	Emphasize important points by changing the volume or tone of your voice.
Pauses	• Pause to give your audience time to think about what you have just said. • Pause to emphasize the point you are about to make.
Facial Expressions	Make your facial expressions complement the content of your presentation—serious expressions for serious content and lively ones for light content.
Gestures	Use natural, relaxed gestures, and don't be afraid to move around as you speak.
Eye Contact	Engage your audience by making eye contact with as many people as possible.

The Eyes Have It Perhaps your presentation is one that could be enhanced through the use of **visuals**—charts, graphs, photographs, or exhibits. If so, think carefully about how you want to present your visuals and include them in your rehearsals. Visuals should be large enough for the audience to see clearly and obviously relevant to the part of the oral presentation you're making at the time you use them. Direct your audience's attention to your visuals, if necessary.

Listening and Speaking Skills
Rehearse effective performance techniques.

Follow the instructions in this workshop to adapt your literary research paper for an oral presentation. Rehearse your presentation thoroughly before presenting it to your class.

Collection 2: Skills Review

Comparing Literature

Test Practice

The two poems that follow tell essentially the same story. The first, "The Twa Corbies," is an anonymous medieval Scottish folk ballad passed down orally. The second poem is a literary ballad, carefully constructed in 1828 by the great Russian poet Alexander Pushkin. Like many Romantic poets of his day, Pushkin admired the songs and stories of the common people, both inside and outside of Russia. He freely borrowed from such popular sources as ballads and folk tales when composing his own poetry.

DIRECTIONS: Read the following poems. Then, read each multiple-choice question that follows, and write the letter of the best response.

The Twa Corbies

Anonymous

As I was walking all alane
I heard twa corbies making a mane;°
The tane unto the t'other say,
'Where sall we gang and dine today?'

'—In behint yon auld fail dyke,°
I wot° there lies a new-slain Knight;
And naebody kens° that he lies there,
But his hawk, his hound, and lady fair.

'His hound is to the hunting gane,
His hawk to fetch the wild-fowl hame,
His lady's ta'en another mate,
So we may mak our dinner sweet.

'Ye'll sit on his white hause-bane,°
And I'll pick out his bonny blue een:°
Wi' ae lock o' his gowden hair
We'll theek° our nest when it grows bare.

'Mony a one for him makes mane,
But nane sall ken where he is gane;
O'er his white banes, when they are bare,
The wind sall blaw for evermair.'

2. **mane** *n.:* moan.
5. **fail dyke:** earth bank.
6. **wot** *v.:* know.
7. **kens** *v.:* knows.
13. **hause-bane:** neck-bone.
14. **een** *n. pl.:* eyes.
16. **theek** *v.:* thatch.

Pages 262–265 cover **Literary Skills** Compare and contrast works of major literary periods.

Raven doth to raven fly

Alexander Pushkin

translated by Walter Arndt

Raven doth to raven fly,
Raven doth to raven cry:
Raven, where is fallen meat?
What shall be the morning's treat?

Raven answers raven thus:
Well I know of meat for us;
On the fallow, by the willow
Lies a knight, a clod his pillow.

Why he died, who dealt the blow,
That his hawk alone can know,
And the sable mare that bore him,
And his bride who rode before him.

But the hawk now sails the air,
And the foe bestrode the mare,
And the bride a wreath is wreathing
For a new love, warm and breathing.

Collection 2: Skills Review

1. In "The Twa Corbies," which of the following phrases *most* helps you realize that the *corbies* are birds?
   - **A** "I heard the twa corbies making a mane"
   - **B** "Ye'll sit on his white hause-bane"
   - **C** "We'll theek our nest when it grows bare"
   - **D** "So we may mak our dinner sweet"

2. In "The Twa Corbies," what question does one corbie ask the other in the first stanza?
   - **F** Where is the rest of our gang?
   - **G** Where will I find a faithful mate?
   - **H** Where is the slain Knight?
   - **J** Where shall we go and dine today?

3. In "The Twa Corbies," the lady reacts to the Knight's death by —
   - **A** taking another mate
   - **B** killing his hawk and hound
   - **C** becoming grief-stricken
   - **D** searching for him forever

4. In "The Twa Corbies," what is the attitude of the corbies toward the dead Knight?
   - **F** They regret that he died so young.
   - **G** They believe he will be remembered forever.
   - **H** They are pleased to make a meal of him.
   - **J** They pity those who are left behind to grieve.

5. Which of the following is a supernatural element found in "The Twa Corbies"?
   - **A** birds feasting on a dead Knight
   - **B** the lady taking another mate
   - **C** talking birds
   - **D** a hound hunting fowl

6. What is similar about the first two stanzas of both ballads?
   - **F** The first stanza poses a question, and the second one answers it.
   - **G** Both stanzas are written in dialect.
   - **H** Each stanza has an *abcb* rhyme scheme.
   - **J** The speaker of each stanza is a knight.

7. What does the third stanza of "Raven doth to raven fly" imply about how the knight died?
   - A He fell off his horse.
   - B He was slain by an enemy.
   - C His bride poisoned him.
   - D He died in a hunting accident.

8. Unlike "The Twa Corbies," the last stanza of "Raven doth to raven fly" emphasizes —
   - F the knight's decay
   - G the lady's lack of grief
   - H the corbies' meal
   - J the hound's hunting activities

9. A theme common to both ballads is —
   - A the beauty of nature
   - B the peacefulness of death
   - C the importance of friendship
   - D the failure of love

10. What word *best* describes the tone of both ballads?
    - F warmhearted
    - G unsentimental
    - H humorous
    - J romantic

Essay Question

These two ballads tell similar stories about the death of a knight. Both are told from the point of view of the birds that are about to devour the dead man. Yet for all their similarities, there are differences in details that subtly distinguish each ballad. Write an essay in which you point out the differences between the ballads. Be sure to describe the emotional effect of each ballad.

Collection 2: Skills Review

Vocabulary Skills

Test Practice

Words with Multiple Meanings

DIRECTIONS: Choose the answer in which the underlined word is used in the same way as it is used in the lines from *The Canterbury Tales*.

1. "He stood not silent like a beast or post,
   But gave his answer with the ringing word . . ."
   - A The student planned to post an ad.
   - B The soldier would not leave her post.
   - C All that's left of that old barn is a rotted post.
   - D She gladly accepted the post when her boss offered it to her.

2. "But let me briefly make my purpose plain . . ."
   - F The wind-swept plain stretched far and wide.
   - G I prefer plain yogurt.
   - H He's not handsome; his face is very plain.
   - J I thought she had made it plain that she would be leaving tomorrow.

3. "I preach for nothing but for greed of gain . . ."
   - A The doctor will gain nothing but respect for all her charity work.
   - B Too many crimes have been committed for petty gain.
   - C If I could just gain their interest, I know they'd hire me.
   - D We could probably gain more speed if we shift gears.

4. "Become our Governor in short, and be
   Judge of our tales and general referee . . ."
   - F In the armed forces, a general ranks higher than a colonel.
   - G There's a general feeling that we're being too strict.
   - H He buys his supplies at the general store.
   - J In general, the salesperson preferred to work weekends.

5. "And set the supper at a certain price."
   - A Once Mira has set her mind on a goal, there's no way to stop her.
   - B The fine was set at five hundred dollars.
   - C Is there a set number of players needed for this game?
   - D We need help getting this set ready for the play.

Vocabulary Skills
Understand multiple-meaning words.

Collection 2: Skills Review

Writing Skills

Test Practice

DIRECTIONS: Read the following paragraph from a draft of a student's historical research paper. Then, answer the questions below it.

(1) Anglo-Saxon literature has similarities with the literature of the Middle Ages. (2) Because the English epic *Beowulf* tells a story that predates the arrival of Christianity in England, it is saturated with pagan ideas and symbolism. (3) However, it also contains Christian themes and references to Christian symbols. (4) In fact, some scholars believe that monks may have added Christian elements to the original *Beowulf* story. (5) By the Middle Ages, Christian themes in literature had largely replaced pagan themes. (6) *Beowulf* is also effective as an exciting adventure story.

1. Which sentence states the main idea of the passage better than sentence 1?

A *Beowulf* is an example of Anglo-Saxon literature that combines pagan and Christian elements.

B Christian themes are dominant in the most enduring literature of the Middle Ages.

C *Beowulf* and *The Canterbury Tales* are the literary high points of their respective ages.

D Anglo-Saxon literature reflects paganism, but medieval literature reflects Christianity.

2. To strengthen support for the main idea, the writer could

F discuss the history of the medieval Christian church

G mention a differing opinion from a secondary source

H include an analysis of *Beowulf's* pagan and Christian themes

J contrast the religious beliefs of various medieval writers

3. Which sentence, if added, would support the idea in sentence 5?

A Grendel, the monster in *Beowulf*, is a pagan symbol.

B *The Canterbury Tales* depicts the perfect Christian knight.

C During the Middle Ages, feudal themes dominated literature.

D The Church's influence on medieval literature was extensive.

4. Which sentence should be deleted to improve the passage's organization?

F 2 **H** 5

G 3 **J** 6

5. While presenting this passage in an oral presentation, the speaker could

A pause to emphasize important ideas

B avoid making eye contact in order to focus on the message

C stand perfectly still while speaking

D speak softly so others may practice their presentations

Writing Skills
Write a historical research paper.

The Ambassadors (1533) by Hans Holbein the Younger. Oil on canvas. The ambassadors are Jean de Dintville and Georges de Selve, from the court of King Henri II of France. The objects on the table represent the arts and sciences.

Collection 3

The Renaissance 1485-1660

A Flourish of Genius

O England! model to thy inward greatness,
Like little body with a mighty heart . . .

—William Shakespeare

Grammar students with their teacher (c. 1330–1338) by Andrea Pisano. Bas relief.

The Art Archive/Duomo Florence/ Dagli Orti (A).

INTERNET

Collection Resources

Keyword: LE7 12-3

The Renaissance 1485–1660

LITERARY EVENTS

1485

1513 Niccolò Machiavelli writes *The Prince*

Martin Luther's sermon (detail) (16th century), from a triptych by Lucas Cranach the Elder.
Church of St. Marien, Wittenberg.

1515

1516 Thomas More's *Utopia* is published

1538 Book-licensing laws are introduced in England

1540

1557 *Tottel's Miscellany* (including poems of Wyatt and Surrey) is published

1564 William Shakespeare, the Bard of Avon, is born

1566

1572 In France, Montaigne begins his *Essais*

c. 1586 Okuni, a former priestess, forms first kabuki theater company in Japan

1590 Edmund Spenser publishes first three books of *The Faerie Queene*

Portrait of Queen Elizabeth I within the Armada jewel (16th century) by Nicholas Hilliard.
The Victoria and Albert Museum, London.

POLITICAL AND SOCIAL EVENTS

1485

1485 Richard III is killed in battle

1492 Christopher Columbus reaches the Americas

1498 Vasco da Gama reaches India via Cape of Good Hope

c. 1503 Leonardo da Vinci paints *Mona Lisa*

1509 Henry VIII is crowned king of England

1513 Balboa crosses Isthmus of Panama and sights Pacific Ocean

1515

1517 Martin Luther posts his ninety-five theses on a church door in Wittenberg, Germany, beginning the Protestant Reformation

1517 First Africans are taken to Americas as slaves

1519–1521 Magellan leads first expedition to circumnavigate the globe

1521 Hernando Cortés conquers Mexico, destroying Aztec Empire

c. 1534 With the Supremacy Act, Henry VIII proclaims himself head of Church of England

1540

1543 Polish astronomer Nicolaus Copernicus publishes theory that planets orbit the sun

1553–1558 Mary Tudor—"Bloody Mary"—reigns, restoring papal authority in England

1558 Elizabeth I becomes queen of England

1566

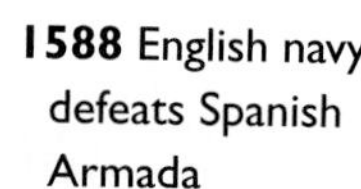

1588 English navy defeats Spanish Armada

English astrolabe (1559), a navigational instrument, made for Queen Elizabeth I by Thomas Gemini.
Museum of the History of Science, University of Oxford.

1590 | 1610 | 1640 | 1660

1593–1594 In London, outbreak of plague forces theaters to close

1599 Globe Theatre is built in London

1605 Cervantes publishes Part I of *Don Quixote* (Part II is published in 1615)

1605–1606 Shakespeare writes *King Lear* and *Macbeth*

1609 Shakespeare's sonnets (written c. mid-1590s) are published

1610–1611 John Donne writes *Holy Sonnets*

1611 King James Bible is published

1621 Newspapers are first published in London

1642–1660 Puritans close all theaters in England

1650 American poet Anne Bradstreet's *The Tenth Muse Lately Sprung Up in America* is published in London

c. 1658 John Milton begins *Paradise Lost*

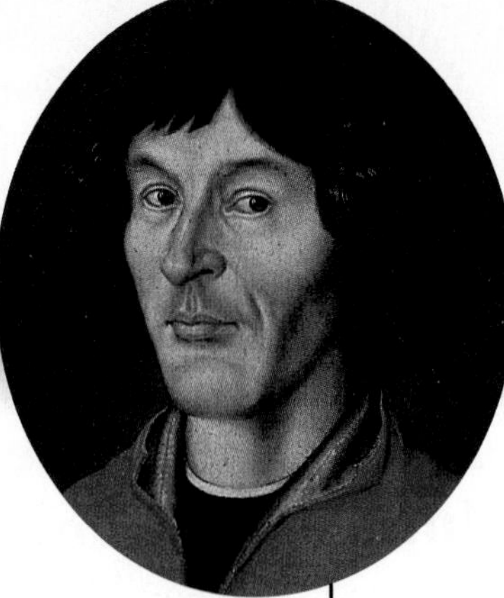

Nicolaus Copernicus (detail) (1575). German School.

Museum of Torun, Poland.

1610 | 1640 | 1660

1600 British East India Company founded for trade with Asia

1605 Gunpowder Plot, an attempt by Guy Fawkes and others to blow up Parliament and assassinate James I, is averted

1607 First permanent English settlement in North America is established at Jamestown, Virginia

1609 In Italy, Galileo is first to study sky with telescope

1620 The *Mayflower* lands at Plymouth Rock, Massachusetts

1628 English physician William Harvey explains the circulation of blood

c. 1632–1649 Taj Mahal is built near Agra, India

1639 Japan expels all Europeans except the Dutch

1642–1651 English Civil Wars are fought

1649 Charles I is beheaded

1652 Dutch establish settlement in South Africa

1653–1658 Oliver Cromwell rules England as lord protector

1655 Jews are legally readmitted to England (after being expelled in 1290)

1660 Puritan Commonwealth ends; monarchy is restored with Charles II

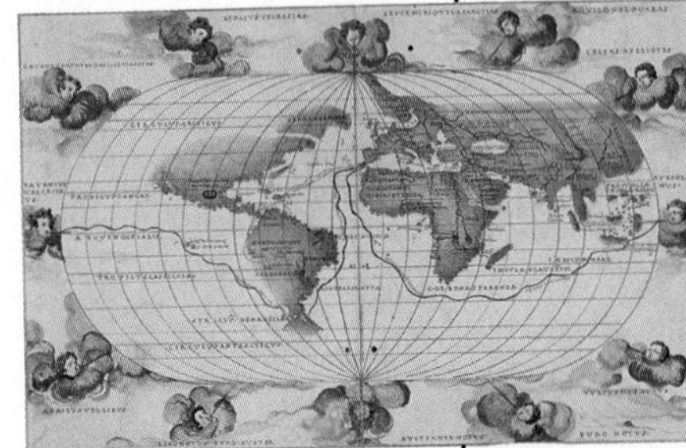

The world map (c. 1540), from the *Portolan Atlas of the World* by Battista Agnese of Venice.

Royal Geographic Society, London.

Hernando Cortés (1485–1547), Spanish explorer, meeting Montezuma II (c. 1480–1520), Aztec emperor.

Political and Social

Humanism: A New Intellectual Movement

During the Renaissance educated people began to embrace an intellectual movement known as humanism. The movement took its name from the *studia humanitatis* (humane studies)—the fields of study we today call the humanities, such as philosophy, history, languages, and the arts. Humanists looked not only to the Bible but also to the Latin and Greek classics for wisdom and knowledge. They combined classical ideals with traditional Christian thought in order to teach people how to live and rule. The invention of the printing press helped spread this new emphasis on the humanities, as more books became available to more people than ever before.

St. Jerome in His Study (detail) (1480) by Domenico Ghirlandaio.

Chiesadi Ognissanti, Florence, Italy.

Milestones 1485–1660

Henry VIII Breaks with the Roman Catholic Church, 1534

The pope refused to grant Henry VIII an annulment of his marriage to his first wife, Catherine of Aragon. In response, Henry denied the authority of the pope and declared himself head of the Church in England. This marked the beginning of the Protestant Reformation in England. Many of Henry's subjects viewed his bold move as an opportunity to achieve much-needed reform of the Church. They wished to put an end to the widespread corruption among the clergy and to the political power that Rome and its ally Spain wielded over English affairs. Some of Henry's subjects remained loyal to the Roman Catholic Church, however, and many of them lost their lives or their property by refusing to recognize Henry as head of the new Church of England.

(Opposite) *King Henry VIII* (1542) by Hans Holbein the Younger. Oil and tempura on oak. This portrait was painted after Catherine Howard's execution.

From the Castle Howard Collection, York, England.

The English Navy Defeats the Spanish Armada, 1588

The most decisive event in England's emergence as a naval power and independent political force in northern Europe was the defeat of the great armada of Spanish ships by the Royal Navy in 1588. (An *armada* is a fleet of warships.) Never again would the Spanish Empire be the undisputed ruler of the oceans of the known world.

Launch of Fireships Against the Armada (16th century). Netherlands School.

The Renaissance 1485–1660

by C. F. Main

PREVIEW

Think About . . .

The Renaissance era in Europe and in England was marked by a change in the way people thought about themselves and the world. No longer content with the fixed religious beliefs of the Middle Ages, people became more interested in expanding their knowledge of history, art, science, and especially the classic texts of ancient Greece and Rome. The Roman Catholic Church was challenged on a number of fronts. By the end of the sixteenth century, the Church had lost its position as the supreme moral and political power in Europe.

As you read about this period, look for answers to these questions:

- What questions interested the humanist thinkers?
- What social and economic developments during the Renaissance fostered a growing interest in reading and learning?
- What forces led people to challenge the power of the Roman Catholic Church in England and on the Continent?

SKILLS FOCUS

Collection introduction (pages 272–292) covers **Literary Skills** Evaluate the philosophical, political, religious, ethical, and social influences of a historical period.

What do you think people living a hundred years from now will call the age we live in today? Will they say we lived in the space age, the age of computers, the age of anxiety, the age of violence? We might be given a label we can't even imagine.

Just as we don't know what people of the future will think of us, the people of Europe living in the 1400s, 1500s, and 1600s didn't know that they were living in the Renaissance. Historical periods—the Middle Ages, the Renaissance, the Romantic period—are historians' inventions, useful labels for complex phenomena. The Middle Ages in England did not end on a certain night in 1485, when King Richard III's naked body, trussed up like a turkey, was thrown into an unmarked grave. The English Renaissance did not begin the moment a Tudor nobleman was crowned King Henry VII. The changes in people's values, beliefs, and behavior that marked the emerging Renaissance occurred gradually. Much that could be called medieval lingered on long after the period known as the

(Opposite) *A Marriage Fête at Bermondsey* (c. 1570) by J. Hoefnagel. Oil on panel. Hatfield House, Hertfordshire, England. © Marquess of Salisbury Collection.

Sir Francis Bacon.

Some books are to be tasted, others to be swallowed, and some few to be chewed and digested.
—Francis Bacon (1625)

Middle Ages was past. Historical periods cannot be rigidly separated from one another, but they can be distinguished.

Rediscovering Ancient Greece and Rome

The term ***renaissance*** is a French word meaning "rebirth." It refers particularly to renewed interest in classical learning—the writings of ancient Greece and Rome. During the long period of the Middle Ages, most European scholars had forgotten the Greek language, and they used a form of Latin that was very different from the Latin of ancient Rome. Few ordinary people could read. Those who could read were encouraged to study texts explaining Church doctrine. In the Renaissance, however, people discovered the marvels of old Greek and Latin classics—books that had been tucked away on the cobweb-covered shelves of monasteries for hundreds of years. Now people learned to read Greek once more and reformed the Latin that they read, wrote, and spoke.

The Spirit of Rebirth

Some people became more curious about themselves and their world than people generally had been in the Middle Ages, so that gradually there was a renewal of the human spirit—a renewal of curiosity and creativity. New energy seemed to be available for creating beautiful things and thinking new, even daring thoughts.

Ladies and Gentlemen Dancing in a Sumptuous Interior by Paulus Vredeman de Vries (1567–c. 1630).
Christie's, London.

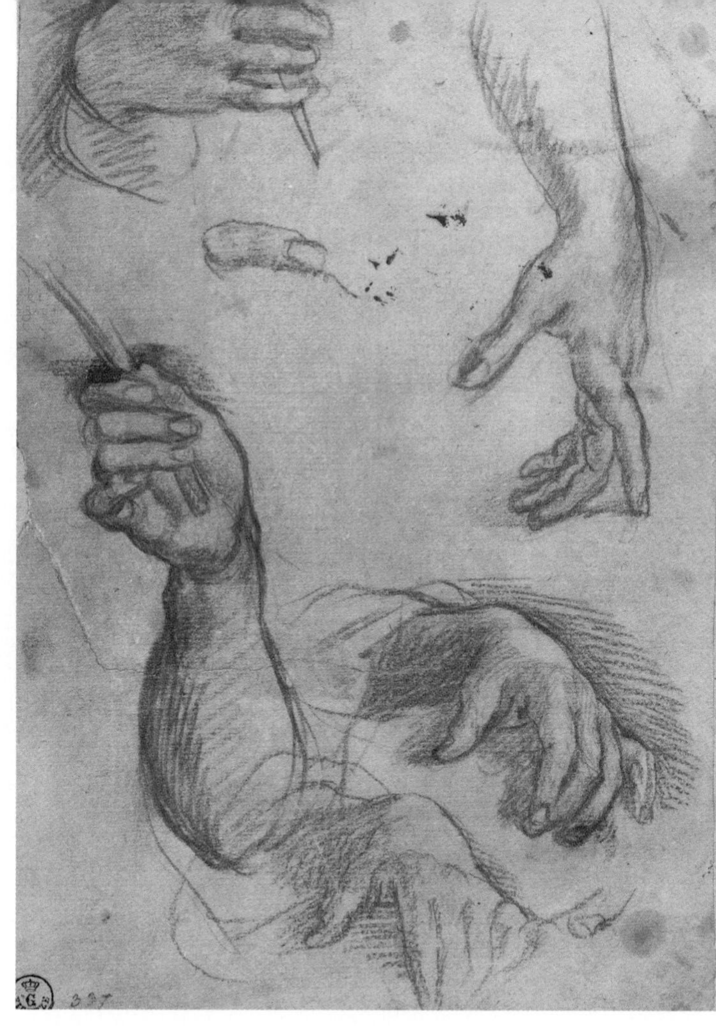

Study of Hands (16th century) by Andrea del Sarto.

Today we still use the term *Renaissance person* for an energetic and productive human being who is interested in science, literature, history, art, and other subjects. (In America, Virginia's Thomas Jefferson, author of the Declaration of Independence, is referred to as a Renaissance man.)

Telescopes owned by Galileo.

It All Began in Italy: A Flourish of Genius

The new energy and creativity started in Italy, where considerable wealth had been generated from banking and trade with the East. The Renaissance began in Italy in the fourteenth century and lasted into the sixteenth. Thinking about just a few of the extraordinary people who flourished in this period—artists such as Leonardo da Vinci and Michelangelo, explorers such as Christopher Columbus, or scientists such as Galileo—reminds us how remarkably rich this period was and how much we owe to it.

Almost everyone in Europe and Britain at this time was Roman Catholic, in name anyway, so the Church was very rich and powerful, even in political affairs, in ways we would probably object to today. Many of the popes were lavish patrons of artists, architects, and scholars. Pope Julius II, for example, commissioned the artist

The creation of Adam (detail), from the Sistine Chapel ceiling (16th century) by Michelangelo.

Michelangelo to paint gigantic scenes from the Bible on the ceiling of the Sistine Chapel, a small church in the pope's "city" that was called, as it is today, the Vatican. Lying on his back on a scaffold, Michelangelo painted the Creation, the Fall of Man and Woman, the Flood, and other biblical subjects. His bright, heroic figures, which are still admired by thousands of visitors to Rome each year, show individual human beings who are noble and capable of perfection. This optimistic view of humanity was expressed by many other Renaissance painters and writers as well.

Knowledge is power.
—Francis Bacon (1597)

Humanism: Questions About the Good Life

Refreshed by the classics, the new writers and artists were part of an intellectual movement known as **humanism.** The humanists went to the old Latin and Greek classics to discover new answers to such questions as "What is a human being?" "What is a good life?" and "How do I lead a good life?" Of course, Christianity provided complete answers to these questions, answers that the Renaissance humanists accepted as true. Renaissance humanists found no essential conflicts between the teachings of the Church and those of an ancient Roman moralist like Cicero. They sought instead to harmonize these two great sources of wisdom: the Bible and the classics. Their aim was to use the classics to strengthen, not discredit, Christianity.

The humanists' first task was to recover accurate copies of these ancient writings. Their searches through Italian monasteries turned up writers and works whose very existence had been forgotten. Their next task was to share their findings. So they became teachers, especially of the young men who would become the next generation's rulers—wise and virtuous rulers, they hoped. From the Greek writer Plutarch, for instance, these humanist teachers would learn that the aim of life is to attain virtue, not success or money or fame, because virtue is the best possible human possession and the only source of true happiness.

The New Technology: A Flood of Print

The computer has radically transformed how we get information today. Similarly, the printing press transformed the way information was exchanged during the Renaissance. Before this all books were laboriously written out by hand—you can imagine how difficult and expensive this was and how few books were available.

The inventor of printing with movable type was a German named Johannes Gutenberg (1400?–1468). He printed the first complete

Printing Shop (1580s) by Jan van der Straet. Engraving.

book, an immense Latin Bible, at Mainz, Germany, around 1455. From there the art and craft of printing spread to other cities in Germany, the Low Countries (the Netherlands, Belgium, and Luxembourg), and northern Italy. By 1500, relatively inexpensive books were available throughout western Europe. In 1476, printing reached England, then regarded as an island remote from the centers of civilization. In that year, William Caxton (1422?–1491), a merchant, diplomat, and writer who had been living in the Low Countries, set up a printing press in Westminster (now part of London). In all, Caxton's press issued about one hundred different titles, initiating a flood of print in English that is still increasing.

Two Friends—Two Humanists

When you hear people speak of humanism, you may hear the name Erasmus. Desiderius Erasmus (1466?–1536) is today perhaps the best known of all the Renaissance humanists. Erasmus was a Dutch monk, but he lived outside the monastery and loved to travel, visit-

Sir Thomas More (detail) (16th century) by Hans Holbein the Younger.

© The Frick Collection, New York.

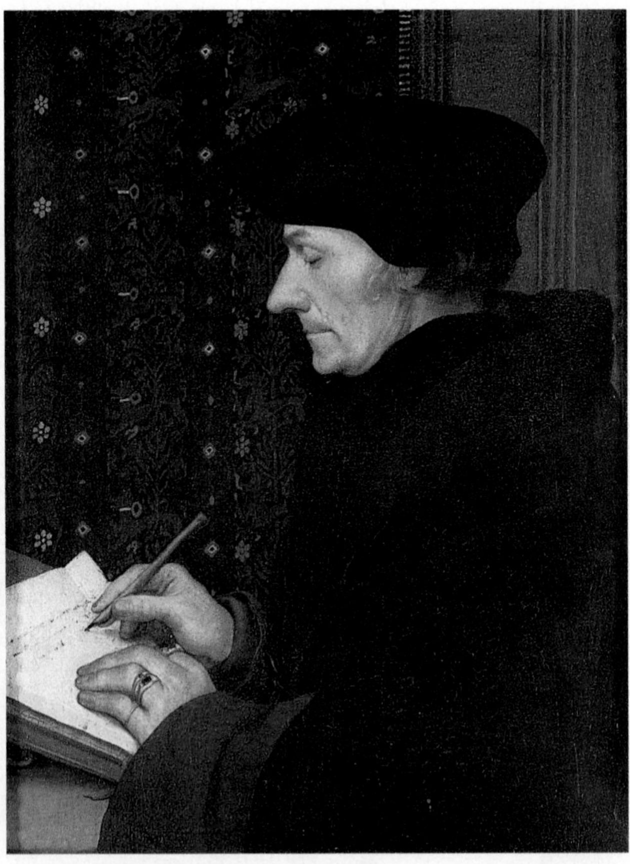

Erasmus of Rotterdam (detail) (c. 1523) by Hans Holbein the Younger. Oil on wood (42 cm × 32 cm).

Louvre, Paris.

Bird's-eye view of London, from *Atlas Civitatis Orbis Terrarum* (c. 1574) by Georg Braun.
Map L85c 27. By permission of The Folger Shakespeare Library, Washington, D.C.

ing many of the countries in Europe, including Italy, France, Germany, and England. He belonged, then, to all Europe. Because he wrote in Latin, he could address his many writings to all the educated people of western Europe.

On his visits to England, Erasmus taught Greek at Cambridge University and became friendly with a number of important people, among them a young lawyer named Thomas More (1477?–1535). More and Erasmus had much in common: They both loved life, laughter, and classical learning, and they both were dedicated to the Church, though they were impatient with some of the Church's corrupt practices at that time.

Like Erasmus, More wrote in Latin—poems, pamphlets, biographies, and his famous treatise on human society, *Utopia* (yo͞o · tō′ pē · ə) (1516). *Utopia* became immediately popular, and it has been repeatedly translated into English and many other languages. Hundreds of writers have imitated or parodied it, and it has given us a useful adjective for describing impractical social schemes: *utopian.* More himself was far from impractical; he held a number of important offices, rose to the very top of his profession, was knighted, and as lord chancellor became one of the king's chief ministers. More continues to fascinate people today. The play and film *A Man for All Seasons,* by Robert Bolt, is about More and his tragic standoff with King Henry VIII over a matter of law (see page 283).

The Reformation: Breaking with the Church

Martin Luther (1529) by Lucas Cranach the Elder.

Galleria degli Uffizi, Florence, Italy/The Bridgeman Art Library.

Superstition, idolatry, and hypocrisy have ample wages, but truth goes a-begging.

—Martin Luther
from *Table Talk* (1569)

While the Renaissance was going on throughout Europe, there occurred in some countries another important series of events, called the **Reformation.** In England these two vast movements were closely related, and their forces were felt by all English writers. Although the exact nature of the Reformation varied from country to country, one feature was common to all Reformers: They rejected the authority of the pope and the Italian churchmen. In England, conflicts with the papacy had occurred off and on over the centuries, but adjustments had always been made on both sides. By the 1530s, an open break with the Roman Catholic Church could no longer be avoided.

By then a number of circumstances made such a break possible. Strong feelings of patriotism and national identity made the English people resent the financial burdens imposed on them by the Vatican—the pope, after all, was a foreign power in far-off Italy. Moreover, new religious ideas were coming into England from the Continent, especially from Germany. There, a monk named Martin Luther (1483–1546) had founded a new kind of Christianity, based not on what the pope said but on a personal understanding of the Bible. Like any institution that has been around for a long time and has ignored corruption within its ranks, the Church needed reform. Right at home in England, humanists like More and Erasmus were ridiculing old superstitions, as well as the ignorance and idleness of monks and the loose living and personal wealth of priests and bishops.

King Versus Pope: All for an Heir

The generations-old conflict between the pope and the king of England came to a climax when Henry VIII wanted to get rid of his wife of twenty-four years. Divorce was not allowed, especially for kings (until recently that was still true in Britain), so Henry needed a loophole. He asked Pope Clement VII to declare that he, Henry, was not properly married to his Spanish wife, Catherine of Aragon, because she had previously been wedded—for all of five months—to his older brother Arthur, now dead. (It was against Church law to marry a dead sibling's spouse; the biblical basis for the law is in Leviticus.)

Henry had two motives for wanting to get rid of Catherine. First, although she had borne him a princess, she was too old to give him

An Allegory of the Tudor Succession: The Family of Henry VIII (c. 1589–1595). British School, possibly after Lucas de Heere. Oil on panel (45″ × 71¾″).

Yale Center for British Art, Paul Mellon Collection, New Haven, Connecticut.

the male heir that he thought he must have. (Catherine had lost five babies.) What is more, another, younger woman had won Henry's dangerous affections: The king now wished to marry Anne Boleyn, who had been his "favorite" for several years. (Henry had earlier seduced Anne's sister.) The pope was not able to grant Henry the annulment of his marriage, even if he had wanted to, because the pope was controlled by Queen Catherine's nephew, the emperor of Spain. So, upon receiving the pope's refusal in 1533, Henry appointed a new archbishop of Canterbury, who obligingly declared Henry's marriage to Catherine invalid. In 1534, Henry concluded the break with Rome by declaring himself head of the English Church.

The Protestant Reformation

With Catherine packed away under house arrest—since she refused to accept the annulment of her marriage—Henry closed all of England's monasteries and sold the rich buildings and lands to his subjects. While the vast majority of his subjects agreed with Henry's changes in the Church, some of them did not. The best known of those who remained loyal to the pope was Sir Thomas More, now the lord chancellor of England. More felt he could not legally recognize his friend Henry as head of the Church. For More's stubbornness, Henry ordered that his lord chancellor be beheaded.

Anne Boleyn (detail), from *Memoirs of the Court of Queen Elizabeth* by Sarah, countess of Essex.

Reminding us of a point in astronomy, which is that the longer the days are the farther off is the sun and yet the hotter; so is it with our love, for although by absence we are parted it nevertheless keeps its fervency, at least in my case and hoping the like of yours . . .

—King Henry VIII, from a letter to Anne Boleyn (1528)

It wasn't the first—or the last—time that Henry would execute a friend.

This was the very beginning of Protestantism in England. Many people were dissatisfied with the new church for reasons just the opposite of More's. They felt that it was not reformed enough, that it was merely a copy of Catholicism, as in some respects it was. These people later became known as Puritans, Baptists, Presbyterians, Dissenters, and Nonconformists. All of them wanted to get rid of many things they called "popish," such as the bishops, the prayer book, the priest's vestments, and even the church bells and the stained-glass windows. Some of them said that religion was solely a matter between the individual and God. This idea, which is still the foundation of most Protestant churches, is directly traceable to the teachings of those Renaissance humanists who emphasized the freedom of all human beings.

Henry VIII: Renaissance Man and Executioner

The five Tudor rulers of England are easy to remember: They consist of a grandfather, a father, and three children. The grandfather was Henry VII (1457–1509), a Welsh nobleman who seized the throne after England was exhausted by the long struggle called the Wars of the Roses. (Both factions involved used a rose as their emblem, one red, one white.) Henry VII was a shrewd, patient, and stingy man who restored peace and order to the kingdom; without these there could never have been a cultural Renaissance.

The Great Harry (detail) (1546) from the Anthony Roll manuscript.

The Pepys Library, Magdalene College, Cambridge, England.

His son Henry VIII (reigned 1509–1547) had six wives: After Catherine of Aragon and Anne Boleyn, there were Jane Seymour, Anne of Cleves, Catherine Howard, and Catherine Parr. The fates of these unfortunate women are summarized in a jingle:

> Divorced, beheaded, died,
> Divorced, beheaded, survived.

The sexual intrigues of the court trapped two of Henry's wives: The king could play around, but he couldn't tolerate any suspicion of his wives' fidelity. The price paid by two young wives was heavy: Like Thomas More, Anne Boleyn and Catherine Howard lost their heads on the chopping block.

Despite his messy home life, Henry VIII was an important figure. He created the Royal Navy, which put a stop to foreign invasions of England and provided the means for this island kingdom to spread its political power, language, and literature all over the globe. If we overlook his use of the sword against his enemies (and friends), Henry VIII himself deserves the title Renaissance man. He wrote poetry and played many musical instruments well; he was a champion athlete and a hunter; and he supported the new humanistic learning. In his old age, however, Henry was also coarse, dissolute, arrogant, and a womanizer. He died without knowing that the child he ignored because she was female would become the greatest ruler England ever had.

Catherine of Aragon (16th century) by M. Sittou.
Kunsthistorisches Museum, Vienna.

The Boy King and Bloody Mary

Henry VIII was survived by three children: Mary, daughter of the Spanish princess Catherine of Aragon; Elizabeth, daughter of Anne Boleyn, a lady-in-waiting at the court; and Edward, son of the noblewoman Jane Seymour, who died twelve days after her son's birth. According to the laws of succession, a son had to be crowned first, and so at age nine the son of Henry and Jane Seymour became Edward VI (reigned 1547–1553). An intelligent but sickly boy, he ruled in name only while his relatives wielded the actual power.

When Edward died (of tuberculosis) he was followed by his half-Spanish half-sister Mary (reigned 1553–1558). Mary was a devout, strong-willed Catholic determined to avenge the wrongs done to her mother. She restored the pope's power in England and ruthlessly hunted down Protestants.

Had she lived longer and had she exercised better judgment, Mary might have undone all her father's accomplishments.

Mary Tudor (16th century).
Musée Condé, Chantilly, France.

The Armada portrait of Elizabeth I (c. 1588) attributed to George Gower.

> *Fain would I climb, yet fear I to fall.*
> —Sir Walter Raleigh to Elizabeth I, scratched on a windowpane
>
> *If thy heart fails thee, climb not at all.*
> —Elizabeth's reply, scratched underneath

She made a strategic error, however, when she burned about three hundred of her subjects at the stake. She further lost the support of her people when she married Philip II, king of Spain, a country England was beginning to fear and hate. (Mary was thirty-seven and Philip only twenty-six.) Mary's executions earned her the name Bloody Mary. The queen died of a fever. Because she was childless, she was succeeded by her sister Elizabeth.

Elizabeth: The Virgin Queen

Elizabeth I (reigned 1558–1603) was one of the most brilliant and successful monarchs in history. Since she inherited a kingdom torn by fierce religious feuds, her first task was to restore law and order. She reestablished the Church of

England and again rejected the pope's authority. The pope excommunicated her. To keep Spain happy, she pretended that she just might marry her widowed brother-in-law, King Philip.

Philip was the first of a long procession of noblemen, both foreign and English, who wanted to wed her. However, Elizabeth resisted marriage all her life and officially remained "the Virgin Queen" (thereby giving the American colony Virginia its name). She knew that her strength lay in her independence and in her ability to play one suitor off against another. "I am your anointed Queen," she told a group from Parliament who urged her to marry. "I will never be by violence constrained to do anything. I thank God I am endued with such qualities that if I were turned out of the realm in my petticoat, I were able to live in any place in Christendom."

A True Daughter

A truly heroic person, Elizabeth survived many plots against her life. Several of these plots were initiated by her cousin, another Mary—Mary Stuart, Queen of Scots. As Elizabeth

> *Then she, lying very still upon the block, one of the executioners holding her slightly with one of his hands, she endured two strokes of the other executioner with an axe, she making very small noise or none at all, and not stirring any part of her from the place where she lay: and so the executioner cut off her head, saving one little gristle, which being cut asunder, he lift up her head to the view of all the assembly and bade God save the Queen. Then, her dress of lawn falling from off her head, it appeared as gray as one of threescore and ten years old, polled very short, her face in a moment being so much altered from the form she had when she was alive, as few could remember her by her dead face. Her lips stirred up and down a quarter of an hour after her head was cut off.*
>
> —Robert Wynkfielde, eyewitness to the execution of Mary, Queen of Scots (1587)

Execution of Mary, Queen of Scots (detail) (16th century) by a Dutch artist.
Scottish National Portrait Gallery, Edinburgh.

English Ships and the Spanish Armada, August 1588 (detail). English School. Oil. National Maritime Museum, London.

> *As for her face, it is and appears to be very aged. It is long and thin and her teeth are very yellow and unequal, compared with what they were formerly, so they say, and on the left side less than on the right. Many of them are missing so that one cannot understand her easily when she speaks quickly. Her figure is fair and tall and graceful in whatever she does; so far as may be she keeps her dignity . . .*
>
> —André Hurault, French ambassador, writing about Elizabeth I (1597)

had no children, Mary was heir to England's throne because she too was a direct descendant of Henry VII. A Catholic, Mary was eventually deposed from her throne in Protestant Scotland. Put under house arrest, she lived as a royal exile in England, carefully watched by her cousin Elizabeth. Elizabeth endured Mary and her plots for twenty years and then, a true daughter of her father, sent her Scottish cousin to the chopping block.

The Spanish Armada Sinks: A Turning Point in History

King Philip of Spain, ever watchful for an opportunity to hammer at England, used Mary's execution as an excuse to invade England. He assembled a vast fleet of warships for that purpose: the famous Spanish Armada. In 1588, England's Royal Navy, assisted greatly by nasty weather in the Irish Sea, destroyed the Armada. This victory assured England's and all of northern Europe's independence from the powerful Catholic countries of the Mediterranean. It was a great turning point in history and Elizabeth's finest moment. If Spain had prevailed, history would have been quite different: All of North America, like most of South America, might be speaking Spanish instead of English.

All my possessions for a moment of time.

—Elizabeth I's last words (1603)

A Flood of Literature

What is the connection between these political events and English literature? With their own religious and national identity firmly established, the English started writing as never before. After the defeat of the Armada, Elizabeth became a beloved symbol of peace, security, and prosperity to her subjects, and she provided inspiration to scores of English authors. They represented her mythologically in poetry, drama, and fiction—as Gloriana, Diana, the Faerie Queene, and Cynthia. Literary works that did not directly represent her were dedicated to her because authors knew she was a connoisseur of literature, a person of remarkably wide learning, and something of a writer herself.

A Dull Man Succeeds a Witty Woman

Elizabeth died childless. She was succeeded by her second cousin, James VI of Scotland. James was the son of Elizabeth's cousin Mary, whom Elizabeth had beheaded years before. As James I of England (reigned 1603–1625), he lacked Elizabeth's ability to resolve (or postpone) critical issues, especially religious and economic ones. James was a spendthrift where Elizabeth had been thrifty; he was thick tongued and goggle-eyed where she had been glamorous and witty; he was essentially a foreigner where she had been a complete Englishwoman.

James I tried hard. He wrote learned books in favor of the divine right of kings and against tobacco; he patronized Shakespeare; he sponsored a new translation of the Bible; and he was in many respects an admirable man and a benevolent, peaceful ruler. Yet his relationship with many of his subjects, especially with pious, puritanically minded merchants, went from bad to worse.

The Decline of the Renaissance

The difficulties of James's reign became the impossibilities of his son's. Charles I (reigned 1625–1649) turned out to be remote, autocratic, and self-destructive. Some of his most powerful subjects had him beheaded in 1649. For the next eleven years, England was ruled by Parliament and the Puritan dictator Oliver Cromwell, not by an anointed king. When Charles's self-indulgent son came to power eleven years later, in 1660, England had changed in many important ways.

FAST FACTS

Philosophical Views

- Intellectuals who are part of the humanist movement use Latin and Greek classics along with the Bible to teach people a better way to live and rule.
- Strong feelings of patriotism and new ideas coming from the Continent encourage people to question the authority of the Catholic Church and to object to the financial burdens imposed on them by the pope in Rome.

Political Highlights

- The Protestant Reformation begins in 1534, when King Henry VIII rejects the authority of the pope and declares himself head of the English Church.
- Henry's daughter Elizabeth I succeeds to her father's throne in 1558 and reestablishes the Church of England.
- In 1588, the Royal Navy defeats the Spanish Armada.

Of course the Renaissance did not end in 1660 when Charles II returned from exile in France, just as it had not begun on a specific date. Renaissance values, which were primarily moral and religious, gradually eroded, and Renaissance energies gradually gave out. The last great writer of the English Renaissance was John Milton, who lived on into an age in which educated people were becoming more worldly in their outlook. Scientific truths were soon to challenge long-accepted religious beliefs.

The English Renaissance was over.

FAST FACTS

Social and Economic Influences

- The invention of the printing press in Germany in the mid-1400s makes books more widely available than ever and fosters an explosion of learning.
- The rise of a rich merchant and banking class provides the wealth that makes possible the growth in art, literature, and learning.

REVIEW

Talk About . . .

Turn back to the Think About questions posed at the start of this introduction to the Renaissance (see page 274). Discuss these questions with a group of classmates.

Write About . . .

Contrasting Literary Periods

Revolutions in reading, then and now. Gutenberg's invention of the printing press in Germany in the mid-1400s made it possible for people in Europe to obtain and read a greater variety of books and printed materials than ever before. In time this invention revolutionized people's view of the world and created a desire for even more books on a wider range of subjects. In the contemporary world the inventions of the computer and the Internet have also created an explosion of access to information and a demand for even greater access. At the same time there are predictions that the printed book as we know it will soon disappear and that literacy itself may suffer. Compare and contrast these two great technological revolutions—printing and the computer. Discuss the impact of each technology on literature and the pursuit of knowledge.

The Glass of Fashion

INFORMATIONAL TEXT

They displayed their new costumes from ten o'clock in the morning till noon, strolling up and down the center aisle of St. Paul's Church. They insisted on rich fabrics: velvet, taffeta, gold brocade, and fur. They wore the finest silk stockings and cork platform shoes. They curled their hair, perfumed their gloves, and (if daring) wore makeup. They showed off favorite jewels—pearls, perhaps—in earrings, bracelets, and designs sewn all over their clothes. The men in the Renaissance were peacocks indeed!

Exquisite excess. Women also dressed flamboyantly in the Renaissance. Elizabeth I herself owned eighty wigs and three thousand gowns at her death.

In the 1580s and 1590s, the Renaissance silhouette was ridiculously exaggerated. Starched linen neck ruffs stretched from shoulder to shoulder. Shoulders themselves were extended with "wings" that make even the most exaggerated of today's shoulder pads look like cotton balls. Hoop skirts (called farthingales) could be four feet wide at the hips, and men's full, thigh-length pants were padded to what critics called "monstrous and outrageous greatness."

Women corseted their waists to produce a

Portrait of a lady said to be Lady Style (detail) (16th century) by the circle of William Larkin.

Christie's, London.

Portrait of Elizabeth Vernon, countess of Southampton (c. 1610).

By permission of the duke of Buccleuch, Kettering, England.

Portrait of a nobleman in garter robes, said to be the seventh earl of Shrewsbury (detail) (16th century) by Paul van Somer.

Christie's, London.

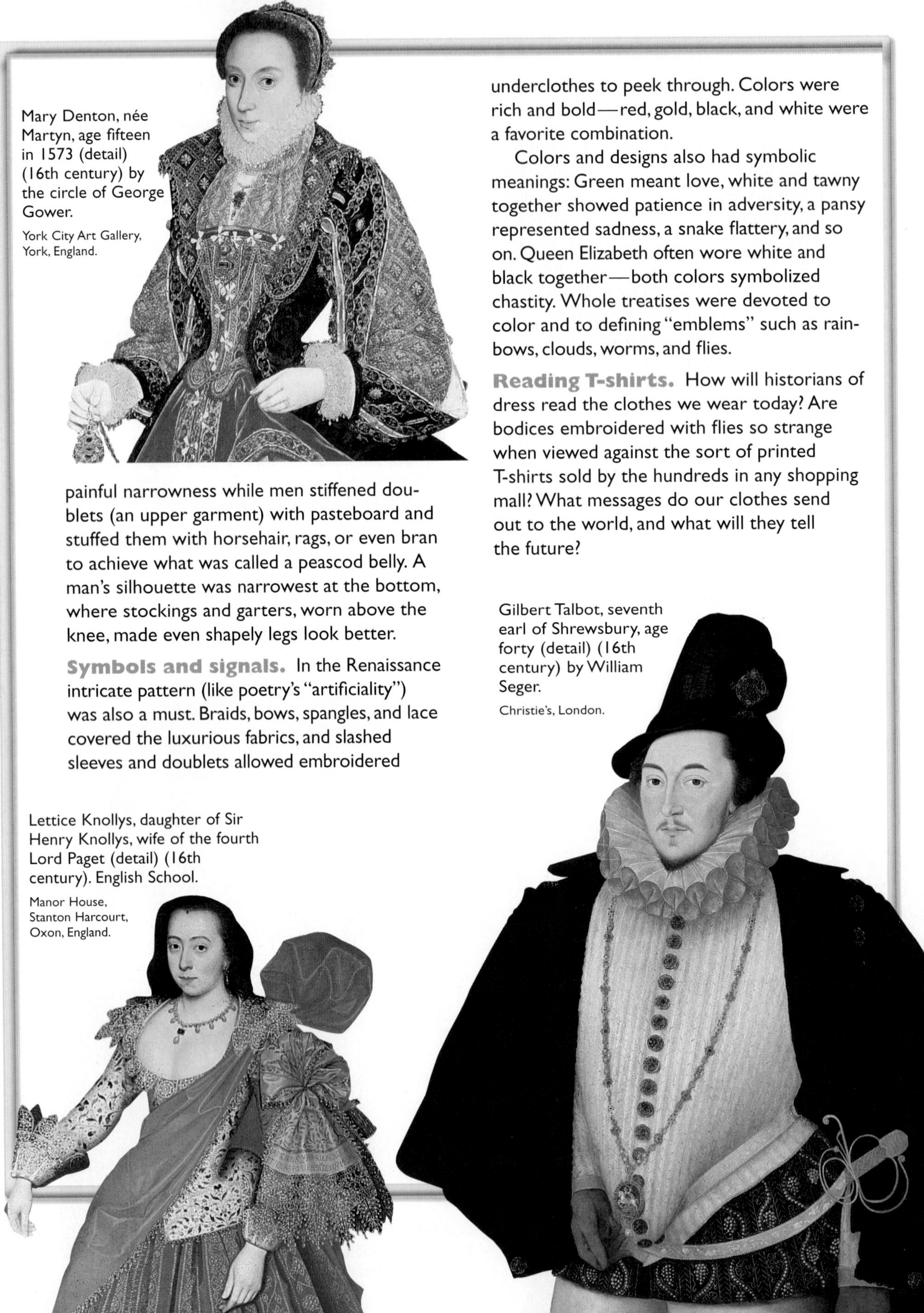

Mary Denton, née Martyn, age fifteen in 1573 (detail) (16th century) by the circle of George Gower.

York City Art Gallery, York, England.

painful narrowness while men stiffened doublets (an upper garment) with pasteboard and stuffed them with horsehair, rags, or even bran to achieve what was called a peascod belly. A man's silhouette was narrowest at the bottom, where stockings and garters, worn above the knee, made even shapely legs look better.

Symbols and signals. In the Renaissance intricate pattern (like poetry's "artificiality") was also a must. Braids, bows, spangles, and lace covered the luxurious fabrics, and slashed sleeves and doublets allowed embroidered underclothes to peek through. Colors were rich and bold—red, gold, black, and white were a favorite combination.

Colors and designs also had symbolic meanings: Green meant love, white and tawny together showed patience in adversity, a pansy represented sadness, a snake flattery, and so on. Queen Elizabeth often wore white and black together—both colors symbolized chastity. Whole treatises were devoted to color and to defining "emblems" such as rainbows, clouds, worms, and flies.

Reading T-shirts. How will historians of dress read the clothes we wear today? Are bodices embroidered with flies so strange when viewed against the sort of printed T-shirts sold by the hundreds in any shopping mall? What messages do our clothes send out to the world, and what will they tell the future?

Gilbert Talbot, seventh earl of Shrewsbury, age forty (detail) (16th century) by William Seger.

Christie's, London.

Lettice Knollys, daughter of Sir Henry Knollys, wife of the fourth Lord Paget (detail) (16th century). English School.

Manor House, Stanton Harcourt, Oxon, England.

Before You Read

The Passionate Shepherd to His Love
The Nymph's Reply to the Shepherd

Make the Connection

You've heard it before. On the radio or in a music video, a singer passionately appeals to a woman to be his love. Although the specific lyrics may vary, the message is always the same. What you may not know is that people have heard this message for centuries. The "invitation to love" is an old poetic tradition. It was especially common in Renaissance England, and it lives on today—not only in the lyrics of popular music but also in the letters, poems, and e-mails that people write to those whose love they seek.

Literary Focus

The Pastoral

Marlowe's poem is a **pastoral,** from the Latin word *pastor,* meaning "shepherd." Pastoral poems are set in an idealized countryside inhabited by handsome shepherds and beautiful nymphs (young women) all living in harmony with nature. Although the characters in the Elizabethan pastorals are presented as simple country people, the diction, imagery, and arguments of these rustic speakers are highly sophisticated. This gives pastoral poems an elegance and an artificiality that do not really correspond to their naive, uncomplicated characters and settings. Many pastorals express a longing or nostalgia for simpler, more innocent times.

Pastoral poems depict country life in idyllic, idealized terms. The characters in pastoral poems are naive and innocent yet express themselves with poetic sophistication.

For more on the Pastoral, see the Handbook of Literary and Historical Terms.

A woman, possibly personifying Summer (detail) (late 17th century). Satin embroidered with silk, metal thread, and beads.

Literary Skills
Understand the characteristics of pastoral poems.

Christopher Marlowe

(1564–1593)

Marlowe belonged to the first generation of Elizabethan dramatists. His career ended about the time Shakespeare's began, although he was only two months older than Shakespeare. The son of a Canterbury shoemaker, Marlowe won scholarships to the King's School in Canterbury and then to Cambridge University. While still a student, he translated some love poems by Ovid, the Roman poet. The poems were declared too erotic by the bishop of London, who had the books burned.

In 1587, before completing his studies, Marlowe apparently became a spy. Elizabeth's government maintained an elaborate espionage system to keep track of Roman Catholics, but just what spying Marlowe did for the government remains uncertain. It *is* certain that Marlowe had only six more years to live when, at twenty-three, he came down to London from Cambridge. He associated with a number of other recent university graduates living near the London theaters and supporting themselves by writing plays and pamphlets. Excitement and danger were part of their lives. Marlowe himself was jailed for his involvement in a street fight that ended with one man murdered.

Another brush with the law came when Marlowe's roommate, a fellow dramatist named Thomas Kyd, accused him of making scandalous, seditious, and atheistic speeches. Marlowe was arrested. A few days before the case was to be heard, he went with some rather shady characters down the Thames, to a tavern in Deptford. After supper the men got into a violent fight over the bill; Marlowe was stabbed above the eye and died instantly. The court acquitted his assailant on the grounds of self-defense, though it is very possible that all the testimony in this case was fabricated and that Marlowe was assassinated for reasons not yet discovered. Theories about Marlowe's life and death are abundant; there are even a few people today who believe, without any evidence, that Marlowe wasn't murdered but lived on to write all of Shakespeare's plays for him.

Today Marlowe's most famous play is probably *The Tragicall History of Dr. Faustus,* about the man who makes a bargain with Satan. Faustus and all of Marlowe's other tragic heroes have been called overreachers: self-driven, power-hungry men who refuse to recognize either their limitations as human beings or their responsibilities to God and their fellow creatures. Marlowe's heroes all want to be more than mere men, and only death can put an end to their monstrous ambitions. To express these grandiose themes, Marlowe created wild and soaring poetry, like nothing ever heard before on the stage. Although Marlowe did not write Shakespeare's plays, he showed Shakespeare what was possible in dramatic poetry.

Reputed portrait of Christopher Marlowe (1585). French School. Oil.

The Master and Fellows of Corpus Christi College, Cambridge, England.

This poem is part of two literary traditions. It is an example of a **pastoral** *poem (it is, in fact, probably the most famous of the English pastorals), and it is part of the* carpe diem *tradition. The* **carpe diem** *poem (see page 299) is a call to "seize the day"—live life to the fullest in the here and now. Marlowe's poem has often been set to music, and several poets have written answers or sequels to it. (The most famous reply to this poem, by Sir Walter Raleigh, follows on page 297.)*

Young man leaning against a tree among roses, by Nicholas Hilliard. Miniature.

©Victoria and Albert Museum, London/Art Resource, New York.

The Passionate Shepherd to His Love

Christopher Marlowe

Come live with me, and be my love,
And we will all the pleasures prove°
That valleys, groves, hills, and fields,
Woods, or steepy mountain yields.

And we will sit upon the rocks,
Seeing the shepherds feed their flocks
By shallow rivers, to whose falls
Melodious birds sing madrigals.°

And I will make thee beds of roses,
And a thousand fragrant posies,
A cap of flowers, and a kirtle,°
Embroidered all with leaves of myrtle.

A gown made of the finest wool
Which from our pretty lambs we pull,
Fair linèd slippers for the cold,
With buckles of the purest gold.

A belt of straw and ivy buds,
With coral clasps and amber studs,
And if these pleasures may thee move,
Come live with me, and be my love.

The shepherd swains° shall dance and sing
For thy delight each May morning.
If these delights thy mind may move,
Then live with me, and be my love.

2. **prove** *v.:* experience.

8. **madrigals**(ma′dri·gəlz) *n. pl.:* complicated songs for several voices.

11. **kirtle** (kʉrt′'l) *n.:* archaic word for "dress," "gown," or "skirt."

21. **swains** *n. pl.:* young boys.

Sir Walter Raleigh

(c. 1552–1618)

Sir Walter Raleigh (16th century) by Nicholas Hilliard.
By Courtesy of the National Portrait Gallery, London.

Raleigh (also spelled Ralegh) is one of the most colorful figures of a very colorful age. A handsome, expensively dressed, and probably arrogant man, at the peak of his success he was Queen Elizabeth's confidential secretary and captain of her guard. He fought brilliantly for England in France, Spain, Ireland, and America. He was passionately devoted to the cause of colonizing the Americas, and to advertise its products, he became one of the first bold Englishmen to smoke tobacco and grow potatoes.

In his rise to power, Raleigh made many enemies, some of whom saw their chance to destroy him when the queen died. They poisoned King James's mind against him, and—on trumped-up evidence—he was convicted of treason. Raleigh was sentenced to death in 1603, though his execution was not carried out until 1618.

Imprisoned in the Tower of London during this long interval, he conducted chemical experiments and wrote a *History of the World* that runs from Adam and Eve to the establishment of the Roman Empire. He also dreamed of another expedition to Guiana, a region on the northern coast of South America; he had explored Guiana earlier in his life and believed it contained vast hoards of gold and jewels. In 1617, still under a death sentence, he was allowed to undertake his last voyage to Guiana. It was a disaster. The English obtained no treasure, and the Spanish killed many of Raleigh's men, including his beloved son. Very ill with fever, Raleigh sailed home to face a certain and shameful death. According to the verdict of history, however, the shame is King James's, not Raleigh's. Raleigh was sacrificed to satisfy the Spanish, who were clamoring for his death as a condition for maintaining peaceful relations with England.

In his speech on the scaffold, Raleigh described himself as "a seafaring man, a soldier, and a courtier." He did not think of himself as a writer. He was carefree with his poems; only about thirty-five of them have survived, and they have been slowly assembled by literary researchers over the past four centuries. His most ambitious poem is the *Ocean to Cynthia,* one of the hundreds of literary works that Queen Elizabeth's subjects wrote to express their love and devotion. It survives only in fragments. This is unfortunate, because Raleigh's poems have considerable merit. They are powerful, outspoken, even blunt, and suffused with the courage of a man who was always ready to accept without self-pity whatever life might bring him. He could have been thinking of himself when he wrote in his *History,* "There is no man so assured of his honor, of his riches, health, or life, but that he may be deprived of either or all, the very next hour or day to come."

Here is Raleigh's reply to Marlowe's "Passionate Shepherd." Elizabethan London was a small place, and Raleigh's and Marlowe's paths must have crossed more than once. Other poets, including John Donne and Robert Herrick, replied to Marlowe, but Raleigh wrote the best answer. His speaker is identified as a nymph, which means a young woman. Like her creator, she has a strong character.

Embroidered wall hanging (detail) (1601).

Schweizerisches Landesmuseum, Zurich, Switzerland.

The Nymph's Reply to the Shepherd

Sir Walter Raleigh

If all the world and love were young,
And truth in every shepherd's tongue,
These pretty pleasures might me move
To live with thee and be thy love.

But Time drives flocks from field to fold,°
When rivers rage and rocks grow cold,
And Philomel° becometh dumb;
The rest complains of cares to come.

The flowers do fade, and wanton° fields
To wayward winter reckoning yields;
A honey tongue, a heart of gall°
Is fancy's spring, but sorrow's fall.

Thy gowns, thy shoes, thy beds of roses,
Thy cap, thy kirtle, and thy posies.
Soon break, soon wither, soon forgotten,
In folly ripe, in reason rotten.

Thy belt of straw and ivy buds,
Thy coral clasps and amber studs,
All these in me no means can move
To come to thee and be thy love.

But could youth last and love still breed,
Had joys no date, nor age no need,
Then these delights my mind might move
To live with thee and be thy love.

5. **fold** *n.:* pen where sheep are kept in winter.

7. **Philomel:** the nightingale.

9. **wanton** *adj.:* luxuriant.

11. **gall** *n.:* bitter substance.

Response and Analysis

The Passionate Shepherd to His Love
The Nymph's Reply to the Shepherd

Thinking Critically

1. Describe the life that the shepherd invites his love to share with him in "The Passionate Shepherd to His Love." How will they be dressed? How will they spend their time?
2. In **pastoral** writing the harsh realities of country life do not exist. Which details of the shepherd's description in "The Passionate Shepherd to His Love" seem distinctly idealistic? What realistic, gritty details of a shepherd's life can you imagine?
3. In "The Nymph's Reply to the Shepherd," what flaws does the nymph find in the shepherd's idyllic vision? On what conditions would she agree to live with him?
4. What is the **tone** of the nymph's response in "The Nymph's Reply to the Shepherd"?

Extending and Evaluating

5. Idyllic escape with a loved one still has a strong appeal, whether the retreat is a remote island or a mountaintop hideaway. How is this romantic escape motif used today in literature, television, movies, and advertising?

WRITING

Donne Replies

The poet John Donne (see page 336) wrote "The Bait," a poem that was clearly inspired by Marlowe's "Passionate Shepherd." Read Donne's poem here. Then, in a brief **essay,** explain whether this poem is an answer to Marlowe's poem, an imitation of it, or neither. Remember to provide specific references to both poems.

Literary Skills Analyze the characteristics of pastoral poems.

Writing Skills Write an essay comparing and analyzing two poems.

The Bait

John Donne

Come live with me, and be my love,
And we will some new pleasures prove,
Of golden sands, and crystal brooks,
With silken lines, and silver hooks.

There will the river whispering run,
Warmed by thy eyes more than the sun,
And there the enamored fish will stay,
Begging themselves they may betray.

When thou wilt swim in that live bath,
Each fish, which every channel hath,
Will amorously to thee swim,
Gladder to catch thee, than thou him.

If thou, to be so seen, beest loth,
By sun or moon, thou darkenest both;
And if myself have leave to see,
I need not their light, having thee.

Let others freeze with angling reeds,
And cut their legs with shells and weeds,
Or treacherously poor fish beset
With strangling snare, or windowy net.

Let coarse bold hands from slimy nest
The bedded fish in banks out-wrest,
Or curious traitors, sleave-silk flies,
Bewitch poor fishes' wand'ring eyes.

For thee, thou need'st no such deceit,
For thou thyself art thine own bait;
The fish that is not catched thereby,
Alas, is wiser far than I.

Before You Read

To the Virgins, to Make Much of Time
To His Coy Mistress

Make the Connection

Today we frequently and openly talk about a person's willingness or unwillingness to commit himself or herself to a relationship. It seems that people have been struggling with such indecision for centuries. The Elizabethans Robert Herrick and Andrew Marvell wrote poems in which a speaker urges a woman—or women in general—to, in effect, hurry up and love. In the poems that follow, both speakers pressure women with what may really be the oldest line in the world: "We are all going to die one day, so take your pleasures now, while you still can."

Literary Focus

Carpe Diem

Herrick's and Marvell's poems reflect an ancient theme the Romans called ***carpe diem*** (kär′pe dē′em), meaning "seize the day." *Carpe diem* is a call to live life to the fullest right now: "Let us eat and drink, for tomorrow we die," as the Roman poet Horace said. *Carpe diem* poems are the literary counterpart of the human skull that was sometimes part of the decor at wild Roman parties—a grisly reminder of the fate none of us can escape.

Carpe diem—literally, "seize the day"—is a literary theme that urges living and loving in the present moment, since life and earthly pleasure cannot last.

For more on Carpe Diem, *see the Handbook of Literary and Historical Terms.*

The Outdoor Concert (detail) (16th century). Italian School.
Hotel Lallemand, Bourges, France.

SKILLS FOCUS

Literary Skills
Understand *carpe diem* poetry.

Robert Herrick
(1591–1674)

Robert Herrick (18th century) by Schiavonetti.

By Courtesy of the National Portrait Gallery, London.

We first hear of Herrick as an apprentice to his uncle, a London goldsmith and jeweler; it is pleasant to think that the future poet may have acquired his taste for small, beautiful things in his uncle's workshop. Herrick apparently lacked ambition and drive, since he did not enter a university until he was twenty-two, a very late age in those days, and he did not leave it until he was twenty-nine. For the next few years he had no regular occupation but enjoyed himself in London as a member of the playwright Ben Jonson's circle of young friends (see page 353). At some point he was ordained a priest, but the serious part of Herrick's life did not begin until he was thirty-nine.

Herrick was then called to a parish in Dean Prior, in Devonshire, far from London, in the West Country, which Londoners habitually regarded as wretched and barbaric. According to some of Herrick's poems, this was an intolerable exile; according to others, it was heaven on earth. At any rate, Herrick's stay in Dean Prior came abruptly to an end in 1647 with the arrival of Cromwell's army, which deprived him of his parish and substituted in his place a clergyman of a more puritanical stripe. (It would not be easy to find a less puritanical priest than Herrick.) When the king was restored some thirteen years later, so was Herrick, and he lived on at Dean Prior until he died, at the age of eighty-three.

While deprived of his parish and living in London, Herrick published a fat little volume containing about fourteen hundred poems. The book was called *Hesperides, or the Works Both Human and Divine of Robert Herrick, Esq.* (1648). Less than a fourth of the poems fit into the "divine" category, and these are mainly witty verses on biblical characters and events. All the rest of the poems are definitely "human," though the book's last line—"Jocund his Muse was; but his Life was chaste"—suggests that Herrick's life was a bit less lively than his poetry. The word *Hesperides* in the title is borrowed from classical mythology; it is the collective name for the nymphs who live in a garden where they watch over a tree that bears golden apples. The title implies that Herrick's book is a garden full of precious things.

Herrick borrowed more than his title from classical antiquity. He was so steeped in Latin poetry that he frequently wrote his poems as if he were an ancient Roman, imposing pagan customs, creeds, and rituals on the English countryfolk and his own household. He imitated the Latin love poets, especially Catullus, when he addressed poems to beautiful women with such classical names as Julia, Corinna, Perilla, Anthea, and Electra.

Herrick also wrote about his small house, his spaniel named Tracy, the royal family in far-off London—whatever came into his mind. Altogether his poems give us a picture of "Merrie England," which is not so much the England of any particular time or place but an ideal, pastoral state where sadness is momentary and pleasure innocent. It is only recently that scholars have started to see, behind the seeming innocence of Herrick's joyful poems, that the "jocund" poet often hid his political views behind the harmless guise of pastoral poetry.

The first line of this little lyric, Herrick's most popular poem, has been a metaphorical part of our language ever since the nineteenth century, when Herrick was "discovered" by people interested in Renaissance literature. Instead of courting one woman, as in most **carpe diem** *poems, Herrick addresses all "virgins," or young women. As you read, remember that Herrick was a priest.*

To the Virgins, to Make Much of Time

Robert Herrick

Gather ye rosebuds while ye may,
 Old Time is still a-flying;
And this same flower that smiles today,
 Tomorrow will be dying.

The glorious lamp of heaven, the sun,
 The higher he's a-getting,
The sooner will his race be run,
 And nearer he's to setting.

That age is best which is the first,
 When youth and blood are warmer;
But being spent, the worse, and worst
 Times still° succeed the former.

Then be not coy,° but use your time;
 And while ye may, go marry:
For having lost but once your prime,
 You may forever tarry.°

12. still *adv.:* always.

13. coy *adj.:* cold; inaccessible; aloof.

16. tarry *v.:* delay; linger.

Spring (detail) (1595) by Lucas van Valkenborch.

Victoria and Albert Museum, London.

Andrew Marvell

(1621–1678)

Andrew Marvell (c. 1655–1660).
Oil on canvas (23½″ × 18½″).
By Courtesy of the National Portrait Gallery, London.

Marvell, whose very English name should be accented on its first syllable, like *marvelous,* was the son of a clergyman, who sent him to Cambridge University. There he must have received an excellent education, because the poet John Milton (see page 397), who was not easily impressed by other men's learning, said that Marvell was "well read in the Greek and Latin classics." After receiving his bachelor's degree, Marvell traveled for several years in Holland, France, Italy, and Spain. There is, surprisingly, no record of Marvell's having been involved in the great upheaval of the 1640s. He seems to have survived the Civil Wars without allying himself with either the Royalists or the Parliamentarians. About 1650, he became a tutor to Mary Fairfax, an heiress and a daughter of Sir Thomas Fairfax, who had served as lord general of the Parliamentary armies. The Fairfaxes had several large estates, one of them at a place called Nun Appleton, and there Marvell wrote a remarkable long poem, "Upon Appleton House." However, he did not publish this or any of the other poems that are so highly regarded today. In the best Renaissance fashion, he wrote only for his friends' and his own entertainment.

After leaving the Fairfax household, where presumably he wrote his best poems, Marvell became tutor to a ward of Oliver Cromwell, the lord protector and virtual dictator of England in the 1650s. Then, in 1657, he became assistant to Cromwell's secretary of state, having been strongly recommended for the post by his friend and fellow poet John Milton. Marvell became active in politics, serving as a member of Parliament for his native city, Hull, from 1659 until his death. When King Charles II was restored and the Commonwealth government dissolved in 1660, Marvell somehow had enough influence with the Royalists to save Milton's life. At this point in his career, Marvell began to publish verse satires of his political opponents and prose pamphlets on issues of the day. Still, his lyric poems remained in manuscript until after his death, when his housekeeper, calling herself Mary Marvell and claiming to be his wife, sold them to a publisher, who brought them out.

Marvell's posthumous volume, called *Miscellaneous Poems,* made little impression when it appeared in 1681. Styles in poetry had changed after 1660, so that Marvell's witty, ingenious metaphors must have seemed old-fashioned to readers who admired the lucid, rational poems of the Restoration writers. Today we are in a better position to appreciate Marvell. To many judicious critics his poems sum up much that is admirable in Renaissance lyric poetry. He is a master craftsman, always in control of his materials. His poems have precision, urbanity, and lightness of touch. Many of Marvell's poems are also, under their graceful surfaces, deep and thoughtful, like those of John Donne (see page 336). No wonder Marvell is sometimes called the "most major" of the minor poets in English.

This poem is the most famous invitation to love in English. Nobody has ever assumed that Marvell, a bachelor, was writing to a particular woman, yet the poem is much deeper than others of its kind. Its speaker dwells on the details of human mortality with morbid precision, to make his beloved feel that even immoral behavior while alive is preferable to being good but dead. The title could be rephrased as "To his cold, standoffish girlfriend"; at the time, mistress *did not mean a sexual partner.*

To His Coy Mistress

Andrew Marvell

Had we but world° enough, and time,
This coyness,° Lady, were no crime.
We would sit down, and think which way
To walk, and pass our long love's day.
Thou by the Indian Ganges' side
Shouldst rubies find; I by the tide
Of Humber° would complain.° I would
Love you ten years before the Flood,°
And you should, if you please, refuse
Till the conversion of the Jews.°
My vegetable° love should grow
Vaster than empires and more slow;
An hundred years should go to praise
Thine eyes, and on thy forehead gaze;
Two hundred to adore each breast,
But thirty thousand to the rest;
An age at least to every part,
And the last age should show your heart.
For, Lady, you deserve this state,°
Nor would I love at lower rate.
But at my back I always hear
Time's wingèd chariot hurrying near;
And yonder all before us lie
Deserts of vast eternity.
Thy beauty shall no more be found,
Nor, in thy marble vault, shall sound
My echoing song; then worms shall try
That long-preserved virginity,
And your quaint honor turn to dust,

1. world *n.:* geographical space.
2. coyness *n.:* reluctance to make a commitment.

7. Humber: muddy river in Marvell's hometown of Hull; here, ironically compared to the grand Ganges in India.
complain *v.:* utter complaints about not being loved.
8. Flood: biblical flood, described in Genesis.
10. conversion of the Jews: Christians once believed that all Jews would be converted to Christianity immediately before the Last Judgment.
11. vegetable *adj.:* plantlike; having the power to grow very large, like oak trees.
19. state *n.:* ceremony.

Two lovers (detail) (15th century), from an Italian plate.

And into ashes all my lust:
The grave's a fine and private place,
But none, I think, do there embrace.
    Now therefore, while the youthful hue
Sits on thy skin like morning dew,
And while thy willing soul transpires°
At every pore with instant fires,
Now let us sport us while we may,
And now, like amorous birds of prey,
Rather at once our time devour
Than languish in his slow-chapped° power.
Let us roll all our strength and all
Our sweetness up into one ball,
And tear our pleasures with rough strife
Through the iron gates of life;
Thus, though we cannot make our sun
Stand still, yet we will make him run.

35. transpires *v.:* breathes out.

40. slow-chapped: slow-jawed. Time is seen as consuming life.

INFORMATIONAL TEXT

Most young people of Marlowe's and Marvell's time—those who didn't come from wealthy families or didn't acquire generous patrons—had difficult, exhausting lives. For them witty conceits praising adored ladies were as foreign as the moon—and life was consumed with making ends meet.

Give Us This Day Our Daily Bread

from Shakespeare Alive!

Joseph Papp *and* Elizabeth Kirkland

You are living in England in the late years of the sixteenth century. Like most people, you live with your family in the countryside, eking out a meager existence as best you can. If you're lucky, your father is a yeoman farmer who owns enough land to support his family, or a "husbandman" who has less property but supplements his income by wage earning.

The land you live in is full of contradictions. A woman, Queen Elizabeth, rules the nation, while within the family, men still rule women. A highly educated elite enjoys the fruits of literature, while many people can't even read. The government invests huge sums of money in voyages of exploration and wars with other nations, while science and medicine remain in an appallingly primitive state. In London, the royal court glitters with jewels and finery, while misery reigns in rural hovels. Rich young men wander around Europe for fun, while in England, thousands of homeless people wander from parish to parish, begging and stealing to survive.

The gap between the rich and the poor seems to have widened in the 1570s and 1580s; wealth and power are concentrated in the hands of the few, and many people can't even find a job.

You come from a family of laborers. You don't have much land at all, hardly even a vegetable garden you can call your own, and you are completely dependent on whatever wages you can get by harvesting other people's crops and doing odd jobs around the village. There is no money for such "extras" as education or nice clothes or red meat. In fact, your father's daily income, even when combined with yours, barely covers the cost of feeding you and your brothers and sisters; thank goodness your mother is able to bring in a few extra pennies from her spinning.

Your dependent status as a tenant makes your perch in life still more precarious. To an unjust and unscrupulous landlord, profit is more important than principles, and yours feels no obligation to look out for your best interests. If he decides to "enclose" the land—to stop using it for farming and turn it into grazing pastures for sheep—he has endless means of forcing you out: He might make you give up your lease, or renew it only at great expense, or, most commonly, charge you exorbitant rent.

Three Peasants (detail) (16th or 17th century) by Albrecht Dürer. Oil on panel.

Kunsthistorisches Museum, Vienna.

While your family has been struggling against these odds and worrying about how to make ends meet from day to day, larger forces have been at work that are going to affect you drastically. First, England has been undergoing a huge increase in population. The two-and-a-half million English people who were alive when your grandparents were born will practically have doubled by the time your grandchildren die. This unprecedented population growth is already being translated into inflated prices, as too many people chase after scarce resources. It also means that wages stay unacceptably low; with so many laborers on the job market, farmers and other employers can easily find people willing to work for the pathetically low wages they offer if you're not interested.

Getting and spending have been a constant battle, and staying on the winning side has depended on plentiful harvests, which bring the twofold benefit of jobs and low grain prices. But in recent years the battle has become a losing one: The heavy rains of the last two summers have ruined the harvests, the population has been growing faster than the crops, and famine has begun to cast its long, thin shadow across your life.

Grain—whether you eat the oatmeal cakes of northern England or the coarse wheat bread of the southerners—is a staple of your diet and, if you have no land and have to buy all your grain on the market, your single biggest expense. When prices shoot up, as they do in bad harvest years, it spells disaster for many a citizen; the Carriers in Shakespeare's *Henry IV Part 1* remember a comrade who "never joyed since the price of oats rose. It was the death of him." You try to find cheaper kinds of grain than your usual wheat, supplementing your diet with stomach-filling peas and beans—but even the prices of these are rising now, and you begin to realize, horrifying though it is, that there aren't many alternatives. Starvation seems inevitable.

You wonder how you and your family are going to cope with the steady advance of such hunger, the hair falling out and the skin turning gray and the bleak prospect of watching your fellow villagers "starving and dying in our streets and in the fields [because] of lack of bread," as a contemporary in the northern town of Newcastle writes.

To make matters worse, there has been an economic recession too, mainly because of a slump in the cloth trade that your mother had been depending on for her livelihood. Many people rely on the cloth and wool trades for their living, and now, "the deadness of that trade and want of money is such that they are for the most part without work, and know not how to live," as an official of one parish reports.

Summer (detail) (16th century) by Jorg Breu the Elder.

Response and Analysis

To the Virgins, to Make Much of Time
To His Coy Mistress

Thinking Critically

1. In "To the Virgins, to Make Much of Time" and "To His Coy Mistress," what do Herrick and Marvell say about time and its effects on youth and beauty?
2. A famous **image** of time appears in couplet form in Marvell's "To His Coy Mistress," in lines 21–22. To what does he compare time? What does this image make you see?
3. What does the **speaker** in Herrick's "To the Virgins" say about marriage? How do you think the speaker in Marvell's "To His Coy Mistress" feels about marriage?
4. Marvell's "To His Coy Mistress" contains both **hyperbole,** or exaggeration, and **understatement.** Find examples of each rhetorical device.
5. The image of the sun appears in both "To the Virgins" (line 5) and "To His Coy Mistress" (line 45). How does each poet use the reference to the sun? How would you **paraphrase** the last two lines of Marvell's "To His Coy Mistress"?

Extending and Evaluating

6. In two or three sentences, explain how the difficult existence described in "Give Us This Day Our Daily Bread" (see the ***Connection*** on page 305) corresponds to your previous notion of life in the late 1500s. In light of this information, what is surprising—or, perhaps, *not* surprising—about the visions of life presented in the pastoral poems you have just read?
7. Herrick, in "To the Virgins," and Marvell, in "To His Coy Mistress," have similar objectives but different approaches. Is one poet more persuasive than the other? How are their arguments both similar and different?

WRITING

Carpe Diem Song

Write **lyrics** for your own *carpe diem* song in any style. You might try to imitate the melancholic, romantic tone of the poems you've read, or you might adopt the more modern style of today's songs, which are sometimes romantic, sometimes plaintive, sometimes humorous.

Carpe Diem Comparison

In a short essay, **compare and contrast** any two of the four ***carpe diem*** poems you have read by Marlowe, Raleigh, Herrick, and Marvell. Include in your essay your own response to the poems. Use a chart like the following to gather details for your essay.

	Poem 1	Poem 2
Tone		
Images		
Figures of speech		
Theme		
Setting		
My response:		

Literary Skills Analyze *carpe diem* poetry.

Writing Skills Write lyrics for a *carpe diem* song. Write an essay comparing and contrasting two poems.

INTERNET

Projects and Activities

Keyword: LE7 12-3

William Shakespeare

(1564–1616)

William Shakespeare, attributed to John Taylor (d. 1651).
By courtesy of the National Portrait Gallery, London.

Every literate person has heard of Shakespeare, the author of more than thirty-six remarkable plays and more than 150 poems. Over the centuries these literary works have made such a deep impression on the human race that all sorts of fancies, legends, and theories have been invented about their author. Some critics claim that somebody other than Shakespeare wrote the works that bear his name, although they cannot agree on who, among a dozen candidates, this other author actually was. Controversy about the authorship of Shakespeare's plays rests on two assumptions. First, some people assume that someone with Shakespeare's modest education (he was not a university graduate) could not possibly have written plays that show such a wide range of knowledge. Second, some people assume that we do not know much about Shakespeare. They say that a great number of contemporary references would have been made about a man who wrote such successful plays.

In fact, Shakespeare's life is better documented than the life of any other dramatist of the time, except perhaps Ben Jonson (see page 353), a writer who seems almost modern in the way he publicized himself. Jonson was an honest, blunt, and outspoken man who knew Shakespeare well; for a time the two dramatists wrote for the same theater company, and Shakespeare even acted in Jonson's plays. Often severe in his judgments of other writers, Jonson published a poem praising Shakespeare, asserting that he was superior to all Greek, Roman, and English dramatists, predicting that he would be "not of an age, but for all time." Jonson's judgment is now commonly accepted, and his prophecy has come true.

The Years in Stratford-on-Avon

Shakespeare was born in Stratford-on-Avon, a historic and prosperous market town in Warwickshire, and was christened in the parish church there on April 26, 1564. His father was John Shakespeare, a glovemaker who was active in the town government; his mother—born Mary Arden—came from a prominent family in the county. Presumably, for seven years or so, Shakespeare attended the King's New School, where he obtained an excellent education in Latin and the Bible. (Little English was taught except when students had to translate Latin works into English and then back into Latin.) After leaving school, Shakespeare may have become a teacher himself, but because he shows in his plays very detailed knowledge of many different crafts and trades, speculators have proposed a number of different occupations that he could have had.

At eighteen, Shakespeare married Anne Hathaway, the twenty-six-year-old daughter of a farmer living near Stratford. They had three children, a daughter named Susanna and twins named Hamnet and Judith. We don't know how the young Shakespeare supported his family, but his needs and ambitions soon drew him to London. The two daughters grew up and eventually married; the son died when he was eleven.

The "Upstart Crow"

How did Shakespeare first become interested in the theater? Presumably by seeing plays. We know that traveling acting companies frequently visited Stratford, and we assume that he attended their performances and that he also went to the nearby city of Coventry, where a famous cycle of religious plays was put on every year. To be a dramatist, however, one had to be in London, where theater was flourishing in the 1580s. Exactly when Shakespeare left his family and moved to London (there is no evidence that his wife was ever in the city) is uncertain; scholars say that he probably arrived there in 1587. It is certain that he was busy and successful in the London theater by 1592, when a fellow dramatist named Robert Greene attacked him in print and ridiculed a passage in his early play *Henry VI.* Greene, a down-and-out Cambridge graduate, warned other university men then writing plays to beware of this mere actor who was writing plays—an "upstart crow beautified with our feathers." Greene died of dissipation just as his ill-natured attack was being published, but a friend of his named Henry Chettle immediately apologized in print to Shakespeare and commended Shakespeare's acting and writing abilities and his personal honesty.

Actor and Author

From 1592 on, there is ample documentation of Shakespeare's life and works. We know where he lived in London, at least approximately when his plays were produced and printed, and even how he spent his money. From 1594 until his retirement in about 1613, he was a member of one company, which also included the great tragic actor Richard Burbage and the popular clown Will Kemp. Although actors and others connected with the theater had a very low status legally, in practice they enjoyed the patronage of noblemen and even royalty. It is a mistake to think of Shakespeare as an obscure actor who somehow wrote great plays; he was well-known even as a young man.

Rubbing Shoulders with the Aristocracy

By 1596, Shakespeare was beginning to prosper. He had his father apply to the Heralds' College for a coat of arms that the family could display, signifying that they were "gentlefolk," or people of high social standing. On Shakespeare's family crest is a falcon shaking a spear. To support this claim to gentility, Shakespeare bought New Place, a handsome house and grounds in Stratford, a place so spacious and elegant that the queen of England once stayed there after Shakespeare's daughter Susanna inherited it. Shakespeare also, in 1599, joined with a few other members of his company, called the Lord Chamberlain's Men, to finance a new theater—the famous Globe—on the south side of the Thames. The "honey-tongued Shakespeare," as he was called in a book about English literature published in 1598, was now earning money as a playwright, an actor, and a shareholder in a theater. By 1600, Shakespeare was regularly associating with members of the aristocracy, and six of his plays had been given command performances at the court of Queen Elizabeth.

The King's Men

Shakespeare prospered even more under Elizabeth's successor, King James of Scotland. Fortunately for Shakespeare's company, as it turned out, James's royal entry into London in 1603 had to be postponed for several months because the plague was raging in the city. While waiting for the epidemic to subside, the royal court stayed in various palaces outside

London. Shakespeare's company took advantage of this situation and, since the city theaters were closed, performed several plays for the court and the new king. Shakespeare's plays delighted James, for he loved literature and was starved for pleasure after the grim experience of ruling Scotland for many years. He immediately took the company under his patronage, renamed it the King's Men, gave it patents to perform anywhere in the realm, provided the men with special clothing for state occasions, increased their salaries, and appointed their chief members, including Shakespeare, to serve as grooms of the royal chamber. All this patronage brought such prosperity to Shakespeare that he was able to make some very profitable real estate investments in Stratford and London.

An Active Retirement

In about 1610, Shakespeare decided that, having made a considerable sum from his plays and theatrical enterprises, he would retire to his handsome house in Stratford, a place he had never forgotten, though he seems to have kept his life there rather separate from his life in London. His retirement was not complete, for the records show that after he returned to Stratford, he still took part in the management of the King's Men and their two theaters: the Globe, an octagonal building opened in 1599 and used for performances in good weather, and the Blackfriars, acquired in 1608 and used for indoor performances. Shakespeare's works in this period show no signs of diminished creativity, except that in some years he wrote one play instead of the customary two, and they continue to illustrate the great diversity of his genius.

The Last Years

Shakespeare's last recorded visit to London was made with his son-in-law Dr. John Hall in November 1614, though he may have gone down to the city afterward because he continued to own property there, including a building very near the Blackfriars theater. Probably, though, he spent most of the last two years of his life at New Place, with his daughter Susanna Hall (and his granddaughter Elizabeth) living nearby. He died on April 23, 1616, and was buried under the floor of Stratford Church, with this epitaph warning posterity not to dig up his remains and transfer them to the graveyard outside the church—a common practice in those days to make room for newer corpses:

Good friend, for Jesus' sake forbear
To dig the dust enclosèd here!
Blest be the man that spares these stones,
And curst be he that moves my bones.

For Independent Reading

These plays by Shakespeare are recommended:

- *A Midsummer Night's Dream* (comedy)
- *Hamlet* (tragedy)
- *Othello* (tragedy)
- *The Tempest* (comedy)

Christopher Walken (top) and Raul Julia in *Othello*, performed for the New York Shakespeare Festival (1991).

Shakespeare's Sonnets: The Mysteries of Love

Shakespeare. The name calls to mind the great plays whose characters have come to life on stages around the world: *Hamlet, Macbeth, Romeo and Juliet, Othello.* Yet had Shakespeare written no plays at all, his reputation as a poet, as the author of the *Sonnets* (1609), would still have been immense. There are 154 sonnets altogether; their speaker is male, and their chief subject is love. Beyond those three points, however, there is little agreement, only questions:

- Is the sonnets' speaker a dramatic character invented by Shakespeare, like Romeo, Macbeth, or Hamlet, or is he the poet himself?
- If the sonnets are about the real man Shakespeare, then who are the real people behind the characters the sonnets mention?
- Is the order in which the sonnets were originally published (probably without Shakespeare's consent) the correct or the intended sequence? Could they be arranged to tell a more coherent story? *Should* they be so arranged?
- In the 1609 publication, who is the "Mr. W. H." mentioned as the "only begetter" of the sonnets: the young man? someone else?

These and dozens of other questions about the sonnets have been asked and answered over and over again—but never to everybody's satisfaction. We have hundreds of conflicting theories but no absolutely convincing answers.

About the individual sonnets, though, if not the whole sequence, agreement is perfect: They are among the supreme utterances in English. They say profound things about important human experiences, and they say them with great art.

Emblems and Devices of Love (detail) (early 16th century), a French text by Pierre Sala.

Stowe 955 fol. 12b–13. British Library, London.

The Sonnet in the Renaissance

The word *sonnet* is derived from the Italian word *sonetto,* meaning "little sound; song." A **sonnet** is a fourteen-line lyric poem that conforms to strict patterns of rhythm and rhyme.

In Italy the sonnet form was perfected by Francesco Petrarca, known in English as Petrarch. The form he popularized is called the **Italian,** or **Petrarchan, sonnet.** The Petrarchan sonnet has two parts: an eight-line section, called the **octave,** followed by a six-line section, called the **sestet.** This form makes the Italian sonnet perfectly suited for a two-part statement: question-answer, problem-solution, or theme-comment. The transition between the two parts, called the **volta,** or turn, is usually found in the ninth line—the beginning of the sestet—as in Petrarch's Sonnet 42, below.

SONNET 42
PETRARCH

The spring returns, the spring wind softly blowing *a*
Sprinkles the grass with gleam and glitter of showers, *b*
Powdering pearl and diamond, dripping with flowers, *b*
Dropping wet flowers, dancing the winters going; *a*
The swallow twitters, the groves of midnight are glowing *a*
With nightingale music and madness; the sweet fierce powers *b*
Of love flame up through the earth; the seed-soul towers *b*
And trembles; nature is filled to overflowing . . . *a*
The spring returns, but there is no returning *c*
Of spring for me. O heart with anguish burning! *c*
She that unlocked all April in a breath *d*
Returns not . . . And these meadows, blossoms, birds *e*
These lovely gentle girls—words, empty words *e*
As bitter as the black estates of death! *d*

Octave (lines 1–8)
Volta (line 9)
Sestet (lines 9–14)

Translated by Joseph Auslander

The Shakespearean Sonnet Form

Each of Shakespeare's sonnets has its formal organization, established by the rules of the sonnet form. Each sonnet also has a logical organization of ideas, also established by the sonnet form.

In the English sonnet form known as the **Shakespearean sonnet,** the fixed requirements are fourteen iambic pentameter lines divided into three quatrains and a couplet, with the rhyme scheme *abab cdcd efef gg.* Here is how Shakespeare structured Sonnet 18 to make these two organizations cooperate in a way that seems natural, not forced.

Logical Organization	Sonnet 18 William Shakespeare		Formal Organization
A question and tentative answers	Shall I compare thee to a summer's day?	*a*	First quatrain
	Thou art more lovely and more temperate.	*b*	
	Rough winds do shake the darling buds of May,	*a*	
	And summer's lease hath all too short a date.	*b*	
	Sometime too hot the eye of heaven shines,	*c*	Second quatrain
	And often is his gold complexion dimmed;	*d*	
	And every fair from fair sometime declines,	*c*	
	By chance, or nature's changing course untrimmed.	*d*	
The turn	But thy eternal summer shall not fade,	*e*	Third quatrain
	Nor lose possession of that fair thou owest,	*f*	
	Nor shall Death brag thou wander'st in his shade	*e*	
	When in eternal lines to time thou grow'st.	*f*	
A final answer	So long as men can breathe, or eyes can see,	*g*	Couplet
	So long lives this, and this gives life to thee.	*g*	

The logical organization of ideas, of course, varies from sonnet to sonnet. In Sonnet 18, the first line's question is followed by negative answers: The speaker's beloved does bear some resemblances to a summer's day, but only superficial ones. The first two quatrains concentrate on the summer day's imperfections rather than on the loved one.

Then in line 9 comes the **turn**—a shift in focus or thought. The speaker turns from the faulty summer's day to the beloved, and by the end of the third quatrain, the speaker has entirely abandoned the opening comparison. Like most literary terms, the word *turn* is a metaphor; the speaker, figuratively speaking, is turning from one thing to another.

Sonnet 18, with its turn after line 8, follows the pattern of the Petrarchan sonnet; in an English sonnet the final couplet is often a second turn of great impact: a final summary or explanation of all that came before. In this sonnet the couplet says, perhaps with some exaggeration, that by being addressed in this poem, the beloved person has become immortal.

Before You Read

Sonnets 29, 30, 71, 73, 116, 130

Make the Connection

What is it that makes us happy, that lets us look back over years receding into the past, and ahead to the inevitable conclusion, without sorrow or despair? Wealth hasn't answered the question satisfactorily for many people. Power always seems to dwindle or be wrenched out of our hands in an instant. Fame evaporates faster than the early-morning dew. If there is any answer to this question, for many people it is love. Time passes and death is inescapable, but love, if we are fortunate enough to find it or create it, sustains us through it all.

In these six sonnets, Shakespeare speculates on what love is and what it does to us and for us.

Literary Focus

Shakespearean Sonnet

English poets, limited by their "rhyme-poor" language, created the **English,** or **Shakespearean, sonnet,** which allows more rhymes than the Petrarchan sonnet. The Shakespearean sonnet is fourteen lines long and uses three four-line units, called **quatrains,** followed by a final two-line **couplet.** The organization of thought in the sonnet usually corresponds to this structure: The three quatrains often express related ideas, and the couplet sums up the poet's message. The Shakespearean sonnet is written in a particular **meter,** or rhythmic pattern, called **iambic pentameter,** with each line consisting of five unstressed syllables alternating with five stressed syllables. The typical rhyme scheme of the Shakespearean sonnet is *abab cdcd efef gg.*

Literary Skills
Understand the characteristics of Shakespearean sonnets.

INTERNET

More About William Shakespeare

Keyword: LE7 12-3

The **Shakespearean sonnet** is written in iambic pentameter and has three four-line units, or **quatrains,** followed by a concluding two-line unit, or **couplet.**

For more on the Shakespearean Sonnet, see Sonnet in the Handbook of Literary and Historical Terms.

Background

Shakespeare's greatest nondramatic poetry is in a group of 154 sonnets. In addition to their richness of language and imagery, Shakespeare's sonnets have an unusual depth of perception and feeling, extending beyond the conventional subject of love to a contemplation of the beauty of life and the mortality of man. In his first 126 sonnets, Shakespeare celebrates his devoted friendship with a young man, which he presents as a higher, less selfish relationship than his passionate love for a particular woman (the "dark lady"), who is the subject of the remaining twenty-eight sonnets. The identities of the young man and the dark lady to whom the sonnets are addressed have never been determined with certainty.

Portrait by Nicholas Hilliard. Miniature on vellum.

In this sonnet the speaker describes how he rids himself of such ugly emotions as envy, self-pity, self-hatred, and the dismal belief that everybody else is luckier than he is.

Sonnet 29

William Shakespeare

When, in disgrace° with Fortune and men's eyes,
I all alone beweep my outcast state,
And trouble deaf heaven with my bootless° cries,
And look upon myself and curse my fate,
Wishing me like to one more rich in hope,
Featured like him, like him° with friends possessed,
Desiring this man's art,° and that man's scope,°
With what I most enjoy contented least;
Yet in these thoughts myself almost despising,
Haply° I think on thee, and then my state,
Like to the lark° at break of day arising
From sullen° earth, sings hymns at heaven's gate;
For thy sweet love remembered such wealth brings
That then I scorn to change my state with kings.

1. **disgrace** *n.:* loss of favor.

3. **bootless** *adj.:* useless; futile.

5–6. **one . . . him . . . him:** three men whom the speaker envies.

7. **art** *n.:* literary ability. **scope** *n.:* power.

10. **haply** *adv.:* by chance.

11. **lark** *n.:* English skylark, a bird whose song seems to pour down from the sky.

12. **sullen** *adj.:* gloomy.

Response and Analysis

Thinking Critically

1. Like many of Shakespeare's sonnets, Sonnet 29 is actually a single sentence. In the long introductory clause, what does the speaker say he envies?
2. The main clause begins the **turn.** In what line does the turn occur? What remembrance changes the speaker's state of mind?
3. How does the speaker's **tone,** or attitude, change after the turn?
4. What **simile** does the speaker use in lines 11–12 to describe his new state of mind? Does this simile strike you as a good description of joy?
5. Do you think that love has this power to transform our feelings? Discuss your responses to the poem.

WRITING

Solace from a Sonnet

In Sonnet 29, Shakespeare describes how he overcomes feelings of despair and failure by remembering his love. People today also experience temporary periods of depression when they feel their looks, possessions, friends, or accomplishments don't measure up. Write a modern version of Shakespeare's Sonnet 29, either following the sonnet form or writing the poem entirely in couplets. To get ideas for your **poem,** consider these questions: What might people today envy in their neighbors? What might help a modern person feel more satisfied?

Literary Skills
Analyze the characteristics of Shakespearean sonnets.

Writing Skills
Write a sonnet.

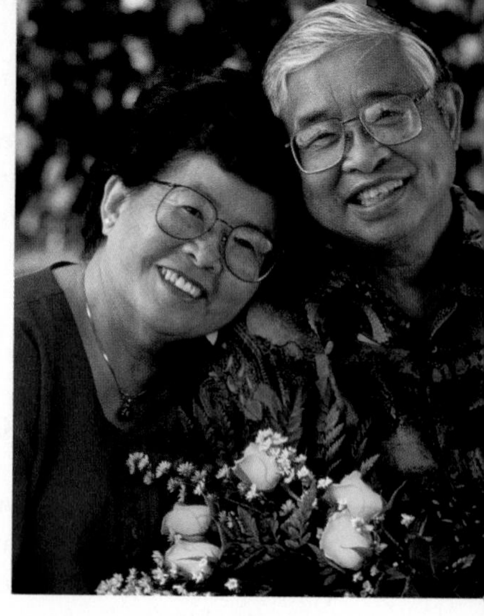

Shakespeare's best sonnets are remarkable for their original, imaginative **metaphors**—*their comparisons of two unlike things. Sonnet 30 begins with such a metaphor: Periods of quiet meditation are called* sessions, *as though they were court trials in which one's thoughts come to the bar of justice to hear their cases tried. Notice how line 2 continues the legal metaphor.*

Sonnet 30

William Shakespeare

When to the sessions of sweet silent thought
I summon up remembrance of things past,
I sigh the lack of many a thing I sought,
And with old woes new wail° my dear time's waste.°
Then can I drown an eye (unused to flow)
For precious friends hid in death's dateless° night,
And weep afresh love's long since canceled woe,
And moan th' expense° of many a vanished sight.°
Then can I grieve at grievances foregone,
And heavily from woe to woe tell° o'er
The sad account of fore° bemoanèd moan,
Which I new pay as if not paid before.
　But if the while I think on thee, dear friend,
　All losses are restored and sorrows end.

4. new wail: again lament. **my . . . waste:** the damage that time has done to things dear to me.
6. dateless *adj.:* endless.
8. expense *n.:* loss. **vanished sight:** things gone, such as dead friends.
10. tell *v.:* count.
11. fore *adv.:* already.

Response and Analysis

Literary Skills
Analyze the characteristics of Shakespearean sonnets.

Thinking Critically

1. What are the various grievances the speaker remembers?
2. What thoughts cheer him up?
3. Where does the **turn** take place in this sonnet?
4. What **metaphors** in this sonnet compare the speaker's sadness to things having to do with law? (Look for legal terms like *summon, canceled, expense, grievances, account, pay.*)
5. Point out where in this sonnet Shakespeare uses **alliteration**—the repetition of consonant sounds. Read the sonnet aloud to hear the effect of these repeated sounds.
6. What similarities can you find in the main ideas expressed in Sonnet 30 and Sonnet 29?

In several of Shakespeare's sonnets, the speaker emphasizes the difference between his age and his beloved's: He is much older, and so presumably he will die first. This sonnet says, surprisingly, that he does not want his loved one to remember him at all. "Forget me," he says, "as soon as you hear my funeral bell."

Sonnet 71

William Shakespeare

No longer mourn for me when I am dead
Than you shall hear the surly sullen bell
Give warning to the world that I am fled
From this vile world, with vilest worms to dwell.
Nay, if you read this line, remember not
The hand that writ it; for I love you so
That I in your sweet thoughts would be forgot
If thinking on me then should make you woe.
O, if, I say, you look upon this verse
When I, perhaps, compounded am with clay,
Do not so much as my poor name rehearse,
But let your love even with my life decay,
    Lest the wise world should look into your moan
    And mock you with me after I am gone.

A man aged twenty-four, by Nicholas Hilliard.

Response and Analysis

Thinking Critically

1. What does the speaker tell his loved one to do after he has died?
2. What two reasons does the speaker give for wanting his beloved to forget about him?
3. The shift in **mood** in Sonnet 71 is more subtle than that in the preceding sonnets. Where does the **turn** occur? What mood does the speaker shift into?
4. Where in this sonnet do you hear **alliteration**—the repetition of consonant sounds?
5. How does the speaker use **irony** in line 13 when he calls the world "wise"?
6. Think about the **tone** of this sonnet—the speaker's attitude toward his subject, which is his own death. How would you describe his tone?
7. What does this speaker imply about the way in which the world views him?

Literary Skills
Analyze the characteristics of Shakespearean sonnets.

As in Sonnet 71, the speaker of Sonnet 73 dwells on his advanced years. This sonnet is rich in striking metaphors, with each quatrain developing a single metaphor.

Sonnet 73

William Shakespeare

That time of year thou mayst in me behold
When yellow leaves, or none, or few, do hang
Upon those boughs which shake against the cold,
Bare ruined choirs° where late the sweet birds sang.
In me thou see'st the twilight of such day
As after sunset fadeth in the west,
Which by and by black night doth take away,
Death's second self, that seals up all in rest.
In me thou see'st the glowing of such fire,
That on the ashes of his youth doth lie
As the deathbed whereon it must expire,
Consumed with that which it was nourished by.°
    This thou perceivest, which makes thy love more strong,
    To love that well which thou must leave ere long.

4. **choirs** *n. pl.:* parts of a church or cathedral in which services are held. The landscape of Shakespeare's England was dotted with church ruins, a result of Henry VIII's destruction of monasteries.

12. **consumed . . . nourished by:** choked by the ashes of the wood that once fed its flame.

Response and Analysis

Thinking Critically

1. What three **metaphors** does this speaker use to describe himself? What contrast between the speaker and his beloved is implied?
2. What seasonal **images** do you see in this poem? How do these images contribute to the poem's **tone** of loss and sadness?
3. Find the **turn** in this sonnet. What does the speaker tell his beloved in the final couplet?
4. The idea in line 12 is somewhat compressed. **Paraphrase** it in your own words, after you have thought about what originally fed ("nourished") the speaker's fires—fires that are now choked ("consumed").
5. How do you feel about the main idea of this sonnet, expressed in the last couplet?

Literary Skills Analyze the characteristics of Shakespearean sonnets.

Writing Skills Write an essay comparing and contrasting two sonnets.

WRITING

Tone Poems

Both Sonnet 71 and Sonnet 73 have particular tones and moods. In a brief **essay, compare and contrast** the sonnets by focusing on each speaker's **tone.** Discuss how word choice, figurative language, imagery, and sound effects work together to create a very specific tone in each poem.

Perhaps the most famous of Shakespeare's sonnets, Sonnet 116 defines true love metaphorically as "the marriage of true minds." Such love is completely firm against all "impediments," a word taken from the priest's remarks to those attending a Church of England wedding service: "If any of you know cause or just impediment why these persons should not be joined together . . ."

Sonnet 116

William Shakespeare

Let me not to the marriage of true minds
Admit impediments. Love is not love
Which alters when it alteration finds,
Or bends with the remover to remove.
Oh no! It is an ever-fixèd mark°
That looks on tempests and is never shaken.
It is the star to every wandering bark,°
Whose worth's unknown, although his height be taken.°
Love's not Time's fool, though rosy lips and cheeks
Within his bending sickle's compass° come.
Love alters not with his brief hours and weeks,
But bears it out° even to the edge of doom.
    If this be error and upon me proved,
    I never writ, nor no man ever loved.

5. **mark** *n.:* seamark; a prominent object on shore that serves as a guide to sailors.
7. **bark** *n.:* boat.
8. **height be taken:** altitude measured to determine a ship's position.
10. **compass** *n.:* range; reach.
12. **bears it out:** survives.

Response and Analysis

Thinking Critically

1. What **metaphors** in this sonnet describe the steadiness of love?
2. Where does the speaker define love by what it is *not* and by what it does *not* do?
3. How is time **personified** in this poem?
4. Where does the **turn** in this sonnet take place? How do you think the speaker's voice might change as he speaks this line?
5. What single quality of true love does this sonnet emphasize?
6. How could this sonnet be used to justify a difference in the lovers' ages?
7. This poem is read at both weddings and funerals. Do you think the poem is equally appropriate for either occasion? Explain why or why not.

Literary Skills
Analyze the characteristics of Shakespearean sonnets.

The Lady with the Ermine (15th century) by Leonardo da Vinci.

Czartoryski Museum, Krakow, Poland/The Bridgeman Art Library.

This sonnet ridicules the fashionable, exaggerated metaphors some of Shakespeare's fellow poets were using to describe the women they loved: Your eyes are suns that set me on fire, your cheeks are roses, your breasts are white as snow. Such metaphors, known as ***conceits,*** *are traceable to Petrarch, but by 1600 they had become, through overuse, tiresome or laughable. (Note that the word* mistress *in this poem simply meant "girlfriend" in the Renaissance.)*

Sonnet 130

William Shakespeare

My mistress' eyes are nothing like the sun,
Coral is far more red than her lips' red.
If snow be white, why then her breasts are dun,°
If hairs be wires, black wires grow on her head.
I have seen roses damasked,° red and white,
But no such roses see I in her cheeks.
And in some perfumes is there more delight
Than in the breath that from my mistress reeks,
I love to hear her speak, yet well I know
That music hath a far more pleasing sound.
I grant I never saw a goddess go,
My mistress, when she walks, treads on the ground.
And yet, by Heaven, I think my love as rare
As any she belied° with false compare.

3. dun *adj.:* dull, grayish brown.

5. damasked *v.:* variegated in two colors.

14. belied *v.:* misrepresented.

Response and Analysis

Literary Skills Analyze the characteristics of Shakespearean sonnets.

Writing Skills Write a response to a sonnet. Write an essay comparing and contrasting two sonnets.

Thinking Critically

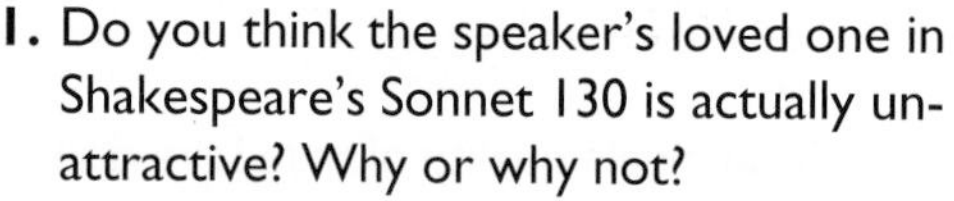

1. Do you think the speaker's loved one in Shakespeare's Sonnet 130 is actually unattractive? Why or why not?
2. Sonnet 130 could have been written by someone who had read too many **Petrarchan sonnets.** What details in the sonnet poke fun at sonnet conventions?
3. Why is the **couplet** absolutely necessary to keep Shakespeare's Sonnet 130 from being misunderstood?
4. Which remarks in Shakespeare's sonnet did you find humorous?

WRITING

A Reply

Suppose you are the beloved of the speaker of Shakespeare's Sonnet 130. Write a **response** to his description of you, or write a comic **description** of another beloved who falls short of perfection.

Louise Labé's Sonnet 23 is written in the style of Petrarch and responds to the conceits that Shakespeare mocks in Sonnet 130. Labé (1524?–1566), a wealthy and well-educated Frenchwoman, was married to an elderly manufacturer. Two unhappy love affairs might explain the tone of her sonnet.

Sonnet 23

Louise Labé

translated by **Willis Barnstone**

What good is it to me if long ago
you eloquently praised my golden hair,
compared my eyes and beauty to the flare
of two suns where, you say, love bent the bow,
sending the darts that needled you with grief?
Where are your tears that faded in the ground?
Your death? by which your constant love is bound
in oaths and honor now beyond belief?
Your brutal goal was to make *me* a slave
beneath the ruse° of being served by you.
Pardon me, friend, and for once hear me through:
I am outraged with anger and I rave.
Yet I am sure, wherever you have gone,
your martyrdom is hard as my black dawn.

10. ruse *n.:* trick.

Portrait of a Young Woman (1569) (detail).
Tate Gallery, London/Art Resource, New York.

WRITING

Sonnets Side by Side

How does Louise Labé's sonnet compare with Shakespeare's Sonnet 130? To gather details for your **comparison,** fill out a chart like the following one. Use the block method to write your comparison: First, tell how Shakespeare uses the following elements of poetry; then, tell how Labé uses them.

	Shakespeare	Labé
Speaker		
Person addressed		
Images		
Tone		
Message		
Sonnet form		

Use "Comparing and Contrasting Literature," pages 1002–1009, for help with this assignment.

INTERNET

Projects and Activities

Keyword: LE7 12-3

Before You Read

Songs from Shakespeare

Make the Connection

In Shakespeare's time, when people went to the Globe, the Swan, or any other London theater, they expected not only to see a tragedy or comedy performed but also to hear music, both vocal and instrumental. Shakespeare included a great variety of songs in his plays: some melancholy, some comic, some thoughtful. Each song is particularly adapted to the play and scene in which it appears and to the character who performs it.

Think of the ways songs and instrumental music are used in films, television programs, and plays today. What various purposes—dramatic and otherwise—do such songs serve in the context of the larger work?

Literary Focus

Dramatic Song

The **songs** in Shakespeare's plays are the best of this kind that have come down to us, for Shakespeare excelled in lyric and dramatic poetry. Shakespeare's songs serve a variety of dramatic purposes: Some advance the play's action; some help establish the mood of a scene; some reveal character. The songs, which use a variety of poetic techniques, rely heavily on **onomatopoeia,** language that sounds like what it means.

SKILLS FOCUS

Literary Skills Understand the characteristics of dramatic songs.

A **dramatic song** is a type of poem found in many of Shakespeare's plays. The songs serve to advance the action, create a mood, or reveal character. Like most songs, the dramatic songs rely on a variety of poetic techniques.

For more on Dramatic Song, see the Handbook of Literary and Historical Terms.

INTERNET

More About William Shakespeare

Keyword: LE7 12-3

Background

Although many of Shakespeare's songs are written for female characters, all the women's roles in the plays were filled by boys. These were boys who had been trained to sing as well as act and who probably sang in high, pure voices that sounded very feminine. Unfortunately, most of the original music for the songs has been lost, but just as the plays themselves have inspired many composers of music for opera, orchestra, and ballet, so have the songs from the plays been set to music by many composers, right up to the present time.

Couple courting, from a Bible manuscript said to have been owned by Pope John XXII (15th century).

The Art Archive/Musée Atger Montpellier/Dagli Orti.

A character named Amiens sings this song in As You Like It *(Act II, Scene 7), a comedy about a group of sophisticated courtiers exiled from their palaces and living in a very comfortable wilderness, the Forest of Arden. This song makes a playful comment on a common human failing: ingratitude. In comparison with people's ungrateful behavior, the cruel winter weather seems kind.*

Blow, Blow, Thou Winter Wind

William Shakespeare

Blow, blow, thou winter wind,°
Thou art not so unkind
As man's ingratitude;
Thy tooth is not so keen,
Because thou art not seen,
Although thy breath be rude.
Heigh-ho! Sing, heigh-ho! Unto the green holly:
Most friendship is feigning, most loving mere folly:
Then, heigh-ho, the holly!
This life is most jolly.

Freeze, freeze, thou bitter sky,
That dost not bite so nigh
As benefits forgot:
Though thou the waters warp°
Thy sting is not so sharp
As friend remembered not.
Heigh-ho! Sing, heigh-ho! Unto the green holly:
Most friendship is feigning, most loving mere folly:
Then, heigh-ho, the holly!
This life is most jolly.

1. wind *n.:* pronounced to rhyme with *find.*
14. warp *v.:* make rough by freezing.

Winter by William Blake.

This song in Shakespeare's late play Cymbeline *(Act IV, Scene 2) is recited, not sung, by two young princes, Guiderius and Arviragus. They claim they cannot sing because their voices have suddenly "got the mannish crack" or, as we would say, have started to change. So they take turns reciting the lines, as indicated, over the body of their sister Imogen, who looks very dead but as it turns out later has only drunk a sleeping potion.*

The song is an ***elegy****—a kind of poem lamenting the dead and consoling the living. When such a poem is designed to be sung or performed at a funeral, it is usually called a* ***dirge.*** *Some of the content of this particular dirge is traditional. One of its themes, that of "death the leveler," makes the point that we all—high and low, rich and poor—die. Its other theme is called the consolation theme. It recounts unpleasant experiences in life from which the dead person is free.*

Fear No More the Heat o' the Sun

William Shakespeare

Guiderius Fear no more the heat o' the sun
Nor the furious winter's rages;
Thou thy worldly task hast done,
Home art gone, and ta'en thy wages.
Golden lads and girls all must,
As° chimney sweepers, come to dust.

Arviragus Fear no more the frown o' the great;
Thou art past the tyrant's stroke.
Care no more to clothe and eat;
To thee the reed° is as the oak.
The scepter, learning, physic, must
All follow this and come to dust.

Guiderius Fear no more the lightning flash—
Arviragus Nor th' all-dreaded thunderstone;°
Guiderius Fear not slander, censure rash;

6. as *prep.:* like.

10. reed *n.:* proverbially frail plant.

14. thunderstone *n.:* type of stone, formerly associated with the noise of thunder.

Arviragus Thou hast finished joy and moan.
Both All lovers young, all lovers must
Consign to° thee and come to dust.

Guiderius No exorciser° harm thee!
Arviragus Nor no witchcraft charm thee!
Guiderius Ghost unlaid° forbear thee!
Arviragus Nothing ill come near thee!
Both Quiet consummation° have,
And renowned be thy grave!

18. consign to: agree with.

19. exorciser *n.:* conjurer; magician.

21. unlaid *v.:* not properly laid to rest in the grave, condemned to walk the earth forever.

23. consummation *n.:* finality.

Chateau de Chaumont Tapestry Set: Time, French (c. 1500–1510) (338.9 × 439.10 cm). Tapestry weave: silk and wool. The inscription, translated from the French, reads, "Sometimes we see Time adorned with green foliage, as pleasant as an angel; and then suddenly he changes and becomes very strange. Never does Time persist in one state."

Ariel, the "airy spirit" of The Tempest, *sings this brief song in Act I, Scene 2, to Prince Ferdinand, who has lost his father at sea in the dreadful storm that opens the play. But the father is not really dead. Unknown to Ferdinand, he has been washed up onto the island on which the play takes place.*

Full Fathom Five

William Shakespeare

Full fathom five thy father lies;
  Of his bones are coral made:
Those are pearls that were his eyes:
  Nothing of him that doth fade,
But doth suffer a sea change
Into something rich and strange.
Sea nymphs hourly ring his knell:°
  Ding-dong.
Hark! I hear them—Ding-dong, bell.

7. **knell** (nel) *n.:* tolling of bells at a funeral.

Response and Analysis

Songs from Shakespeare

Thinking Critically

1. What aspects of human nature does the singer of "Blow, Blow" criticize?
2. How does man's bite compare with winter's in "Blow, Blow"?
3. The song "Blow, Blow" is sung by a character named Amiens. What would you say this song reveals about Amiens's **character**?
4. **Personification** is when a nonhuman thing or quality is talked about as if it were human. What details personify the wind and the sky in "Blow, Blow"?
5. How does the merry-sounding chorus of "Blow, Blow" affect the impression created by the preceding verses?
6. According to the dirge "Fear No More," what are the advantages of being dead? What are the dangers?
7. Identify the lines in "Fear No More" that convey the **theme** of death as a leveler—a force that makes all people equal in the end.
8. Re-read the famous **simile** in lines 5–6 of "Fear No More." How are the "golden lads and girls" different from "chimney sweepers"? How are these two types of people also the same?
9. When the singer of "Fear No More" refers to *scepter, learning,* and *physic* in line 11, he is using a figure of speech called **metonymy** (mə•tän′ə•mē)—something closely related to a person or thing is substituted for the person or thing itself. When we say, "The White House vetoed the bill," we are using metonymy. We are substituting something closely associated with the president (the White House) for the president himself. What professions do the words in line 11 refer to?
10. "Thy father"—the subject of "Full Fathom Five"—is King Alonso, a thoroughly bad man who, in the course of the play, becomes a good man. What other "sea changes" are identified in this dirge?
11. Which lines of "Full Fathom Five" suggest that Ariel has a playful and cheerful character?
12. Identify the **alliteration** in the first line of "Full Fathom Five." What other **sound effects** do you hear in this song?
13. Think about the subjects of these three songs. Do songs today deal with these same subjects? Could these songs be put in modern musical settings? Discuss your responses.

WRITING

Song Sense

"Blow, Blow" is probably one of the first dramatic songs to characterize the singer. Since Shakespeare's day this practice has been commonplace in musicals and operas—even rock operas. Find the lyrics of a song from a musical that is sung by a particular character and reveals something about that character's personality or nature. Write a brief **interpretation** of the character based on the song's lyrics. If you can find a recording of the song, play it for the class, and then share your interpretation.

LISTENING AND SPEAKING

Sounds Like Shakespeare

Select one of these songs and one of the sonnets, and prepare them for a performance before a group of classmates. You will have to decide if you want to do a solo reading, a group reading, or a choral reading. The refrains, for example, could be read by a chorus. Be sure to think carefully about how you will use your voice, where you will speak loudly or softly, and where you will pause or come to a full stop. What words or lines in the poems do you think should receive emphasis?

Literary Skills
Analyze the characteristics of dramatic songs.

Writing Skills
Write a character interpretation.

Listening and Speaking Skills
Present an oral interpretation of a sonnet and a dramatic song.

Before You Read

Famous Shakespearean Speeches

Make the Connection

What do you do when you want to think through a personal problem or experience or analyze your feelings? Do you talk to a friend or relative, write an e-mail, or sit down with your journal? In drama, characters often express their thoughts and conflicts in long speeches, called soliloquies and monologues.

Literary Focus

Monologue and Soliloquy

Most of the words spoken in a play occur in conversation, or verbal exchange between characters—that is, in dialogue. Renaissance playwrights frequently used two other devices for revealing to an audience a dramatic character's thoughts and feelings: monologues and soliloquies. A **monologue** is a long, usually formal speech spoken by one character to another character or the audience. A **soliloquy** (sə•lil′ə•kwē) is a meditative kind of monologue in which the speaker, usually alone onstage, shares his or her true inner thoughts and feelings directly with the audience.

Literary Skills Understand the uses of monologue and soliloquy in drama.

A **monologue** is a long speech made by one character in a play to another character or the audience.

In the type of monologue known as a **soliloquy,** a single character, usually alone onstage, speaks directly to the audience about his or her private thoughts and feelings.

For more on Monologue and Soliloquy, see the Handbook of Literary and Historical Terms.

INTERNET

More About William Shakespeare

Keyword: LE7 12-3

Background

The Elizabethan soliloquy, or solo speech, derives from classical sources, particularly the Latin orations that Shakespeare and his contemporaries studied as schoolboys and later imitated when writing their plays. It was Shakespeare, however, who developed the art of the soliloquy far beyond anything his predecessors or contemporaries accomplished. Particularly in his great tragedies, he overcame the natural artificiality of the soliloquy (people do not usually speak their thoughts out loud in poetic, formal language). He did this by making the words and rhythms fit his characters and their situations, so that the speeches sound completely natural.

An actor stepping to the front of the stage to deliver a soliloquy, at the new Globe Theatre on London's South Bank.

Hamlet, the young prince of Denmark, has been told by the ghost of his father (the elder Hamlet) that his uncle, Claudius, now married to Hamlet's mother, murdered the elder Hamlet. The prince is plagued by doubts, conflicting impulses, and confusing emotions. He both desires and fears to take revenge on his uncle. In this most famous of Shakespearean soliloquies, Hamlet weighs the case for action against inaction. The soliloquy is from Hamlet, *Act III, Scene 1.*

To be, or not to be

William Shakespeare

Hamlet.

To be, or not to be—that is the question.
Whether 'tis nobler in the mind to suffer
The slings and arrows of outrageous° fortune,
Or to take arms against a sea of troubles,
And by opposing end them. To die, to sleep—
No more, and by a sleep to say we end
The heartache and the thousand natural shocks
That flesh is heir to. 'Tis a consummation°
Devoutly to be wished. To die, to sleep,
To sleep—perchance to dream. Aye, there's the rub,°
For in that sleep of death what dreams may come
When we have shuffled off this mortal coil°
Must give us pause. There's the respect
That makes calamity of so long life.°
For who would bear the whips and scorns of time,
The oppressor's wrong, the proud man's contumely,°
The pangs of despised love, the law's delay,
The insolence of office, and the spurns
That patient merit of the unworthy takes,°
When he himself might his quietus° make
With a bare bodkin?° Who would fardels° bear,
To grunt and sweat under a weary life,
But that the dread of something after death,
The undiscovered country from whose bourn
No traveler returns, puzzles the will,
And makes us rather bear those ills we have
Than fly to others that we know not of?

3. outrageous *adj.:* cruel.

8. consummation *n.:* ending.

10. rub *n.:* obstacle.

12. coil *n.:* turmoil (but also life's entanglements).

13–14. the respect . . . life: the reason that makes living so long a calamity; also, the reason that makes calamity so long-lived.

16. contumely *n.:* insult.

18–19. the spurns . . . takes: the insults from the unworthy that people of merit must endure patiently.

20. quietus (kwī·ēt'əs) *n.:* release.

21. bare bodkin: mere dagger (less likely meaning is "unsheathed dagger"). **fardels** *n. pl.:* burdens.

Thus conscience does make cowards of us all,
And thus the native hue° of resolution
Is sicklied o'er with the pale cast° of thought,
And enterprises of great pitch and moment
With this regard their currents turn awry
And lose the name of action. . . .°

29. native hue: reddish complexion.

30. cast *n.:* color.

32–33. with . . . action: Brooding on this thought causes great enterprises to be diverted from their course and left undone.

Kevin Kline as Hamlet, performed for the New York Shakespeare Festival.
Martha Swope/Timepix.

This scene, from Act V, Scene 5, of Macbeth, *occurs after a long series of betrayals and murders, set in motion by Macbeth and his wife. Now, having gained the throne of Scotland through violence and treachery, the two are racked with guilt and fear of their enemies. Lady Macbeth, sleepless and haunted, takes her own life. Preoccupied with the approach of the rightful heirs to the throne and their armed allies, Macbeth, alone in his castle, reacts to the news of his wife's death with this soliloquy.*

Tomorrow, and tomorrow, and tomorrow

William Shakespeare

Macbeth.

Tomorrow, and tomorrow, and tomorrow
Creeps in this petty pace from day to day,
To the last syllable of recorded time;
And all our yesterdays have lighted fools
The way to dusty death. Out, out, brief candle!
Life's but a walking shadow, a poor player
That struts and frets his hour upon the stage
And then is heard no more. It is a tale
Told by an idiot, full of sound and fury,
Signifying nothing.

Raul Julia as Macbeth, performed for the New York Shakespeare Festival.

Martha Swope/Timepix.

Young Prince Hal assumes the throne of England at the death of his father and becomes King Henry V. To consolidate his power at home, the new king decides to cross the English Channel and seize the French crown, which he believes rightfully belongs to England. Under Henry's able leadership the small but brave English army defeats the French forces at Harfleur. Now sick, tired, and underfed, Henry's troops face a much larger French force at Agincourt.

A noble has just wished aloud that the English had more fighting men. This is the king's answer, from Henry V, *Act IV, Scene 3.*

Saint Crispin's Day Speech

William Shakespeare

King.

What's° he that wishes so?
My cousin Westmorland? No, my fair cousin.
If we are marked to die, we are enough
To do our country loss; and if to live,
The fewer men, the greater share of honor.
God's will, I pray thee, wish not one man more.
By Jove, I am not covetous for gold,
Nor care I who doth feed upon my cost;
It yearns° me not if men my garments wear;
Such outward things dwell not in my desires.
But if it be a sin to covet honor
I am the most offending soul alive.
No, faith, my coz, wish not a man from England.
God's peace, I would not lose so great an honor
As one man more, methinks, would share from me
For the best hope I have. O, do not wish one more!
Rather proclaim it, Westmorland, through my host°
That he which hath no stomach to this fight,
Let him depart; his passport shall be made
And crowns for convoy put into his purse.
We would not die in that man's company
That fears his fellowship to die with us.

1. **what's:** who's.

9. **yearns** *v.:* saddens.

17. **host** *n.:* army.

This day is called the Feast of Crispian.°
He that outlives this day and comes safe home
Will stand a-tiptoe when this day is named
And rouse him at the name of Crispian.
He that shall see this day and live old age
Will yearly on the vigil feast his neighbors
And say, "Tomorrow is Saint Crispian."
Then will he strip his sleeve and show his scars,
And say, "These wounds I had on Crispin's Day."
Old men forget; yet all shall be forgot,
But he'll remember with advantages°
What feats he did that day. Then shall our names,
Familiar in his mouth as household words—
Harry the King, Bedford and Exeter,
Warwick and Talbot, Salisbury and Gloucester—
Be in their flowing cups freshly remembered.
This story shall the good man teach his son;
And Crispin Crispian shall ne'er go by,
From this day to the ending of the world,
But we in it shall be rememberèd—
We few, we happy few, we band of brothers.
For he today that sheds his blood with me
Shall be my brother; be he ne'er so vile,
This day shall gentle his condition.°
And gentlemen in England now abed
Shall think themselves accursed they were not here,
And hold their manhoods cheap whiles any speaks
That fought with us upon Saint Crispin's Day.

23. Feast of Crispian: Saint Crispin's Day, October 25. Crispinus and Crispianus were martyrs who fled Rome in the third century. Because they worked as shoemakers, they became that craft's patron saints after they were martyred.

33. advantages *n. pl.:* additions of his own.

46. gentle his condition: bring him up to the position of gentleman.

Andre Braugher as Henry V, performed for the New York Shakespeare Festival (1996).

In The Tempest, *Prospero, the rightful duke of Milan, is forced out of office by his villainous brother, Antonio. Prospero has lived for twelve years on a remote island with his daughter, Miranda. On the island, Prospero, who has magic powers, rules over all. He commands a company of helpful spirits as well as a hideous creature named Caliban, whom Prospero keeps as a kind of prisoner. The island's peace is disturbed when a shipwrecked party from Milan comes ashore. Miranda falls in love with one of the survivors, the handsome young Ferdinand. Meanwhile, Caliban sees his opportunity for freedom and plots to overthrow Prospero.*

In Act IV, Scene 1, Prospero orders his spirits to celebrate the future marriage of Miranda and Ferdinand. But the old magician abruptly breaks off the revels, or celebration, when he remembers that Caliban intends to kill him.

Patrick Stewart as Prospero in *The Tempest,* performed for the New York Shakespeare Festival.

Our revels now are ended

William Shakespeare

Prospero.

Our revels now are ended. These our actors,
As I foretold you, were all spirits and
Are melted into air, into thin air;
And, like the baseless fabric of this vision,
The cloud-capped towers, the gorgeous palaces,
The solemn temples, the great globe itself,
Yea, all which it inherit, shall dissolve,
And, like this insubstantial pageant faded,
Leave not a rack° behind. We are such stuff
As dreams are made on, and our little life
Is rounded with a sleep. Sir, I am vexed.
Bear with my weakness. My old brain is troubled.
Be not disturbed with my infirmity.
If you be pleased, retire into my cell
And there repose. A turn or two I'll walk
To still my beating mind.

9. rack *n.:* cloud.

Response and Analysis

Famous Shakespearean Speeches

Thinking Critically

1. What action is Hamlet considering at the opening of his speech?
2. What is Hamlet afraid will happen in "that sleep of death"?
3. According to lines 15–20 of "To be, or not to be," what trials in life do we put up with?
4. According to lines 21–27 of "To be, or not to be," why do we bear all those burdens in life?
5. What do you think Hamlet means when he says, "Conscience does make cowards of us all" (line 28)? Do you agree?
6. With what emotions does Macbeth receive the news of his wife's death?
7. What **metaphors** does Macbeth use to characterize life?
8. How would you describe Macbeth's view of life? Given Macbeth's crimes, are you surprised at the tone of his speech?
9. What are your reactions to the idea expressed by Macbeth that life "is a tale / Told by an idiot, full of sound and fury, / Signifying nothing"? Explain.
10. In his Saint Crispin's Day speech, how does Henry V use **persuasive language** to make a small army seem like an advantage? Use examples from the monologue.
11. What can you infer about Henry V as a man and a military leader from his speech? What effect do you think his words had on his soldiers?
12. Could portions of the Saint Crispin's Day Speech be used in situations today? Explain your response.
13. What **metaphors** does Prospero use to describe us and our lives?
14. Some critics have read Prospero's speech as Shakespeare's farewell to the stage. (*The Tempest* is a late play.) Which words and phrases in the speech support this interpretation?

WRITING

In Your Own Words

Take one of these soliloquies or monologues, and **paraphrase** it—that is, restate the speech using your own words. When you paraphrase, you must rephrase figures of speech to demonstrate that you understand them; you must supply missing words; and you should rephrase sentences that are not in subject-verb-complement order.

The purpose of a paraphrase is to show that you understand a text. If you were to paraphrase Hamlet's opening question, you might write: "To live or not to live—that's what I have to decide." A paraphrase is different from a summary. A **summary** cites the main points or main events in a text; a paraphrase must rephrase every detail. A summary is shorter than the original text. A paraphrase is usually longer than the original text, and it is never as interesting.

LISTENING AND SPEAKING

Performing a Speech

Imagine that you are an actor preparing to perform one of these monologues or soliloquies in a new performance of a play. To bring the speech alive, you will have to do more than just memorize the lines. You will have to decide how to use your voice and your body. When should you speak quickly? slowly? loudly? softly? What words and lines should you emphasize? What gestures and facial expressions should you use? The best way to make these decisions is to work with a partner—the way an actor works with a director—and together study the words, images, rhythms, and clues to character in Shakespeare's text. When you are ready, perform your speech for an audience.

Literary Skills
Analyze the uses of monologue and soliloquy in drama.

Writing Skills
Write a paraphrase of a monologue or soliloquy.

Listening and Speaking Skills
Give an oral performance of a monologue or soliloquy.

John Donne
(1572–1631)

Donne (a Welsh name pronounced "dun") wrote learned, passionate, argumentative poetry, most of which he never published, since he never wished to be known publicly as a poet. His first aim in life was to be a "courtier"—that is, a member of the queen's government. He had a serious disadvantage, however: He was born into a prominent Roman Catholic family, being descended from no less a person than Sir Thomas More, the lord chancellor whom Henry VIII had beheaded in 1535.

When Donne was only twelve years old, he was already studying at Oxford. Barred from taking a degree because of his religion, Donne returned to his native city of London and in his late teens became a law student at Lincoln's Inn, one of the Inns of Court where lawyers were trained. He had no financial worries since his father, a prosperous iron merchant, had died when Donne was four and left him some money. He now became "Jack" Donne, a handsome, well-dressed youth who devoted his mornings to heavy reading in philosophy and foreign literature and his afternoons to circulating in society. A friend described him as "a great visitor of ladies, a great frequenter of plays, a great writer of conceited [metaphorical] verses."

After various adventures, including joining two naval expeditions against Spain, Donne became private secretary to Sir Thomas Egerton, lord keeper of the great seal. This was an important post for Donne—the start of a brilliant career in government—for by now he had abandoned his Catholicism and spent his inheritance. Then, in 1601, he blasted all his hopes and ambitions by secretly marrying a seventeen-year-old, Anne More (no relation).

John Donne (c. 1595)
Private Collection.

Marriage with a minor, without her father's consent, was then a serious crime against both Church and state. As soon as Anne's father heard about it, he had Donne arrested, jailed, and dismissed from his position. In jail, Donne wrote his shortest poem:

John Donne,
Anne Donne,
Undone.

Though he was not kept in prison long, Donne never did recover his position, and for years he and Anne had to live off the bounty of friends and relatives. They certainly needed help, since they eventually had twelve children, though five died in infancy.

In the early 1600s, Donne continued to read voraciously and to write poetry for private circulation and prose for public consumption. He wrote against the Church of Rome so effectively that he became known as an important defender of the Church of England. The new king, James I, persuaded Donne to become a clergyman in 1615. His brilliant, theatrical sermons immediately won him advancement in the Church, and he rose to be dean of St. Paul's, the principal cathedral of England, in London.

Donne died full of years and honors, and a portrait showing how he looked in his death shroud can still be seen in St. Paul's.

Before You Read

Song

Make the Connection

Unlike the multitude of Renaissance songs idealizing women, the following song by Donne satirizes women, using **hyperbole** (hī·pur′bə·lē), or extreme exaggeration. Imagine a lover who has fallen hard for the "perfect woman" once too often—and now has a cynical view of all women.

Literary Focus

Metaphysical Poetry

The term **metaphysical poetry** has been applied to the work of John Donne, Andrew Marvell, and other seventeenth-century poets whose detached, intellectual style stands in sharp contrast to the emotional extravagance of most of the Elizabethan love poets who preceded them. Metaphysical poetry is known for its startling and unexpected imagery, its intricate figures of speech, its philosophical musings and references to esoteric fields of knowledge, its irregular meter, and its sheer verbal wit.

Metaphysical poetry is a seventeenth-century poetic style that is intellectual and abstract. It is distinguished by its ingenious and obscure imagery, philosophical and religious speculations, rough-sounding meter, and witty word play.

For more on Metaphysical Poetry, see the Handbook of Literary and Historical Terms.

Background

Donne's love poems are collectively known as his songs and sonnets, but that label is misleading, since most of the poems are too intellectually demanding to be called songs, and none is a sonnet by strict, modern definition. We know, however, that the following poem is indeed a song—music for accompaniment was included in one manuscript version.

Bond of Union (1956) by Maurits Cornelius Escher.

Literary Skills
Understand the characteristics of metaphysical poetry.

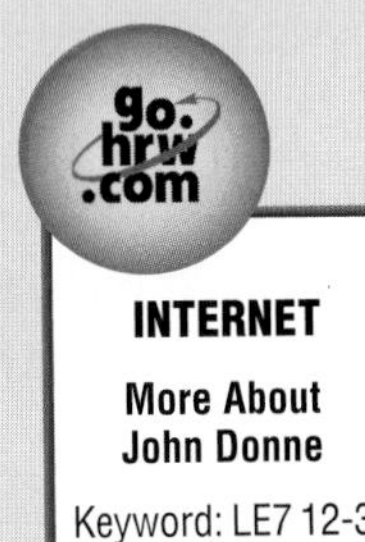

INTERNET

More About John Donne

Keyword: LE7 12-3

Portrait of a lady with a large ruff. The armillary sphere in the background was used to teach the concepts of astronomy (16th century). English School.

Johnny van Haeften Gallery, London.

Song

John Donne

Go, and catch a falling star,
Get with child a mandrake° root,
Tell me, where all past years are,
Or who cleft° the devil's foot,
Teach me to hear mermaids° singing,
Or to keep off envy's stinging,
And find
What wind
Serves to advance an honest mind.

If thou be'st born to strange sights,
Things invisible to see,
Ride ten thousand days and nights,
Till age snow white hairs on thee,
Thou, when thou return'st, wilt tell me
All strange wonders that befell thee,
And swear
Nowhere
Lives a woman true, and fair.

If thou find'st one, let me know,
Such a pilgrimage were sweet;
Yet do not, I would not go,
Though at next door we might meet,
Though she were true, when you met her,
And last, till you write your letter,
Yet she
Will be
False, ere I come, to two, or three.

2. mandrake *n.:* plant whose forked root is said to resemble a human being's torso and legs.
4. cleft *v.:* split.
5. mermaids *n. pl.:* sirens of Greek mythology. The song of these sea nymphs lured sailors and led them to crash their ships on rocky shores.

Response and Analysis

Thinking Critically

1. To whom is this **speaker** talking? What do you think might have occasioned the writing of the poem?
2. In the second stanza, what does the speaker say his listener will discover about a woman both "true, and fair"?
3. In the last stanza, what does the speaker say he will not do? Why?
4. What **hyperbole,** or exaggeration, does the speaker use to make his points?
5. How would you describe the speaker's **tone**? List at least three words that reveal his attitude. Do you think he is being serious?

WRITING

Coining Commands

Imitate the first stanza of "Song" by constructing some **exaggerated** commands of your own to show the impossibility of something. You might want to respond to the points Donne raises in "Song."

Literary Focus

Metaphysical Poetry

In the nineteenth century, Samuel Coleridge (see page 757) described Donne's inventiveness as a "forge and fire-blast" that could twist "iron pokers into true-love knots." In the 1590s, when Donne started writing, this blazing poetic style was truly revolutionary. Most poets then aimed for sweet, smooth, musical-sounding verse. Donne would have none of that. "I sing not siren-like, to tempt, for I am harsh," he says in one poem. The new style he forged came to be called, by later critics, **metaphysical poetry**—a term that reflected its intensity of intellect, its self-conscious invention, and its bold emotion.

For the most part, Donne based the rhythm and sounds of his poems on colloquial—that is, spoken—English. "For God's sake hold your tongue and let me love," he begins one poem. The speaker in his poems frequently sounds blunt and angry, or he broods to himself, or he seems to be thinking out loud. At times the speaker almost seems to be lecturing the woman he is addressing.

Whatever his tone, Donne's speaker is always using his brains and bringing into the poems ideas from scholarly disciplines, especially philosophy and theology. He also brings in images from everyday activities and trades and from learned disciplines like law, medicine, and science. Reading a metaphysical poem is frequently like figuring out the solution to a riddle—or trying to untangle a complicated knot.

To their critics, metaphysical poets were showoffs. They were accused of writing poems just to display their learning and wit.

Responding to the metaphysical poets. The seventeenth-century poet and critic John Dryden, who disliked it, said metaphysical poetry "perplexed the minds of the fair sex with nice [here meaning 'paltry' or 'foolish'] speculations of philosophy." How do you feel about this kind of intellectual poetry? Can you see a connection between the metaphysical poets' imagery and the art by Escher on page 337? Explain.

Literary Skills
Analyze the characteristics of metaphysical poetry.

Writing Skills
Write an imitation of a metaphysical poem.

Before You Read

A Valediction: Forbidding Mourning

Make the Connection

Quickwrite

Leaving someone you love for a long time is never easy. If this poem is autobiographical—as Izaak Walton, Donne's friend and biographer, claimed—Donne was trying to ease a parting of great pain. The poem is typical of Donne's work in that it is set on a particular dramatic occasion. The speaker, a man about to take a long journey, says goodbye ("valediction") to the woman he loves, telling her not to cry or feel sad ("forbidding mourning").

If you were leaving for a long time, what would you say to someone you love whom you were leaving behind? If you were the one left behind, what would you want to hear? Take notes on your thoughts.

Literary Focus

Metaphysical Conceits

This poem contains the most famous of all **metaphysical conceits.** These are odd and surprising figures of speech in which one thing is compared to another thing that is very much unlike it. The metaphysical poets—as their name suggests—used such conceits for an analytic and psychological investigation of love and life. Here are some examples of these unusual conceits: A lover's tears are newly minted coins; the king's court is a bowling alley; a man is a world; lovers are holy saints. In this poem, the lovers are compared to the two prongs of a compass (the kind used to draw circles in geometry).

Metaphysical conceits are especially complex and clever figures of speech that make surprising connections between two seemingly dissimilar things.

For more on Conceits, see the Handbook of Literary and Historical Terms.

Background

Walton said Donne wrote this poem for his wife when he left for a diplomatic mission to France. She urged him not to go because she was pregnant and unwell, but he felt obligated to the mission's leader, Sir Robert Drury. Two days after arriving in Paris, Donne had a vision which he described to Sir Robert: "I have seen my dear wife pass twice by me through this room, with her hair hanging about her shoulders, and a dead child in her arms." A messenger sent back to England returned with the news that "Mrs. Donne . . . after a long and dangerous labor . . . had been delivered of a dead child" on the very day Donne had the vision.

SKILLS FOCUS

Literary Skills Understand metaphysical conceits.

INTERNET

More About John Donne

Keyword: LE7 12-3

Mrs. Pemberton (16th century) by Hans Holbein the Younger.
The Victoria and Albert Museum, London.

A Valediction: Forbidding Mourning

John Donne

As virtuous men pass mildly away,
And whisper to their souls, to go,
Whilst some of their sad friends do say,
The breath goes now, and some say, no:

So let us melt, and make no noise,
No tear-floods, nor sigh-tempests move,
'Twere profanation° of our joys
To tell the laity° our love.

Moving of th' earth° brings harms and fears,
Men reckon what it did and meant,°
But trepidation of the spheres,°
Though greater far, is innocent.°

Dull sublunary° lovers' love
(Whose soul° is sense°) cannot admit
Absence, because it doth remove
Those things which elemented° it.

But we by a love, so much refined,
That ourselves know not what it is,
Interassurèd of the mind,
Care less eyes, lips, and hands to miss.

Our two souls therefore, which are one,
Though I must go, endure not yet
A breach,° but an expansion,
Like gold to airy thinness beat.

If they be two, they are two so
As stiff twin compasses are two,
Thy soul the fixed foot, makes no show
To move, but doth, if th' other do.

And though it in the center sit,
Yet when the other far doth roam,
It leans, and hearkens after it,
And grows erect, as that comes home.

Such wilt thou be to me, who must
Like th' other foot, obliquely° run;
Thy firmness° makes my circle just,°
And makes me end, where I begun.

7. profanation *n.:* lack of reverence.
8. laity *n.:* laypersons; here, those unable to understand the "religion" of true love.
9. moving of th' earth: earthquake.
10. meant: "What does it mean?" was a question ordinarily asked of any unusual phenomenon.
11. trepidation of the spheres: irregularities in the movements of remote heavenly bodies.
12. innocent *adj.:* unobserved and harmless compared with earthquakes.
13. sublunary *adj.:* under the moon, therefore subject to change.
14. soul *n.:* essence. **sense** *n.:* the body with its five senses; that is, purely physical rather than spiritual.
16. elemented *v.:* comprised; composed.

23. breach *n.:* break; split.

34. obliquely *adv.:* off course.
35. firmness *n.:* fidelity. **just** *adj.:* perfect. A circle symbolizes perfection, hence wedding rings.

Response and Analysis

Thinking Critically

1. How would you paraphrase the **simile** in lines 1–8? What emotions does this figure of speech evoke?
2. The **speaker** tells his wife that their love is different from that of other couples. What difference does he see, and how does he express it?
3. Why do you think Donne refers to irregular events on earth and in the heavens in lines 9–12? What kind of event is like the separation of lovers?
4. How would you explain the **conceit** Donne uses in lines 25–36? What does it suggest about the nature of love?
5. Why does the speaker insist that the lovers—obviously two people—are actually one?
6. What unusual **images** and references to specialized fields of knowledge mark this as a metaphysical poem? What emotions do these images evoke?
7. What impression of the speaker did you form as you read and discussed this poem? What sort of man does he seem to be?

Literary Criticism

8. The eighteenth-century writer Samuel Johnson disapproved of metaphysical conceits. He described them as "the discovery of occult [hidden] resemblances in things apparently unlike. . . . The most heterogeneous [dissimilar] ideas are yoked by violence together." Do you think Donne's conceits are forced (or violent)? Do you think they work—that is, can you draw meaning from the connections they make between such dissimilar things? Explain your own responses to Donne's poetry.

WRITING

Your Own Valediction

Suppose that you, like Donne, are leaving a loved one behind for a long, possibly dangerous journey. Write your own "valediction" in a brief **letter.** Be sure to refer to the thoughts you wrote down for the Quickwrite on page 340.

A Wooded Landscape at Evening (detail) (19th century) by Carl Bondel.
Bonhams, London.

Literary Skills Analyze metaphysical conceits.

Writing Skills Write a letter.

Before You Read

Meditation 17

Make the Connection

There is one farewell that everyone must make, one parting and passage that time holds in store for all of us, whether we prepare ourselves for the journey or not. In 1624, prompted by a serious illness, Donne wrote a series of meditations—thoughtful reflections on a topic or theme. The opening of Meditation 17 refers to the practice, in Donne's time, of ringing church bells to announce the death of a church member.

Literary Focus

Tone

Writers deliberately express certain attitudes toward or feelings about a subject. For instance, one writer may express an idealistic attitude on the subject of love and another a bitter and disillusioned view. The writer's attitude toward or feelings about the subject, the reader, or a character constitute the **tone** of a work. Writers convey their tone by the words, images, and details they choose. In Meditation 17, Donne's tone reinforces his solemn and sad message.

Tone is the attitude a writer takes toward the reader, the subject, or a character in a work.

For more on Tone, see the Handbook of Literary and Historical Terms.

(Opposite and right) Marble effigy of John Donne in his shroud, from St. Paul's Cathedral, London.

Literary Skills
Understand the use of tone.

INTERNET

More About John Donne

Keyword: LE7 12-3

Meditation 17

John Donne

Nunc lento sonitu dicunt, Morieris.	Now, this bell tolling softly for another, says to me, Thou must die.

Perchance he for whom this bell tolls, may be so ill, as that he knows not it tolls for him; and perchance I may think myself so much better than I am, as that they who are about me, and see my state, may have caused it to toll for me, and I know not that. The Church is catholic, universal, so are all her actions; all that she does belongs to all. When she baptizes a child, that action concerns me; for that child is thereby connected to that Head[1] which is my Head too, and engrafted into that body, whereof I am a member. And when she buries a man, that action concerns me: All mankind is of one Author, and is one volume; when one man dies, one chapter is not torn out of the book, but translated[2] into a better language; and every chapter must be so translated; God employs several translators; some pieces are translated by age, some by sickness, some by war, some by justice; but God's hand is in every translation; and his hand shall bind up all our scattered leaves[3] again, for that Library where every book shall lie open to one another: ❶ As therefore the bell that rings to a sermon, calls not upon the preacher only, but upon the congregation to come; so this bell calls us all: but how much more me, who am brought so near the door by this sickness. There was a contention as far as a suit[4] (in which both piety and dignity, religion and estimation,[5] were mingled), which of the religious orders should ring to prayers first in the morning; and it was determined, that they should ring first that rose earli-

❶

Donne says that humanity is a book and God its author.

? *How does Donne extend, or develop, this metaphor? How does this metaphor help to organize or clarify the idea Donne is trying to get across?*

1. **Head:** Christ.
2. **translated** *v.:* spiritually carried across from one realm to another.
3. **leaves** *n. pl.:* pages.
4. **contention . . . suit:** argument that went as far as a lawsuit.
5. **estimation** *n.:* self-esteem.

est. If we understand aright the dignity of this bell that tolls for our evening prayer, we would be glad to make it ours, by rising early, in that application, that it might be ours, as well as his, whose indeed it is. The bell doth toll for him that thinks it doth; and though it intermit[6] again, yet from that minute, that that occasion wrought upon him, he is united to God. Who casts not up his eye to the sun when it rises? but who takes off his eye from a comet when that breaks out?[7] Who bends not his ear to any bell, which upon any occasion rings? but who can remove it from that bell, which is passing a piece of himself out of this world? No man is an island, entire of itself; every man is a piece of the continent, a part of the main;[8] if a clod be washed away by the sea, Europe is the less, as well as if a promontory were, as well as if a manor of thy friends or of thine own were; any man's death diminishes me, because I am involved in mankind; and therefore never send to know for whom the bell tolls; it tolls for thee. ❷ Neither can we call this a begging of misery or a borrowing of misery, as though we were not miserable enough of ourselves, but must fetch in more from the next house, in taking upon us the misery of our neighbors. Truly it were an excusable covetousness if we did; for affliction[9] is a treasure, and scarce any man hath enough of it. No man hath affliction enough that is not matured, and ripened by it, and made fit for God by that affliction. If a man carry treasure in bullion, or in a wedge of gold, and have none coined into current monies, his treasure will not defray[10] him as he travels. Tribulation is treasure in the nature of it, but it is not current money in the use of it, except we get nearer and nearer our home, Heaven, by it. Another man may be sick too, and sick to death, and this affliction may lie in his bowels, as gold in a mine, and be of no use to him; but this bell, that tells me of his affliction, digs out, and applies that gold to me; if by this consideration of another's danger I take mine own into contemplation, and so secure myself by making my recourse[11] to my God, who is our only security. ❸ ■

❷

In this mystical passage, Donne suggests that all human souls are connected and that when one soul passes from this world to the next, all souls lose a measure of life.

? *In your opinion, what phrase from this passage best captures its main idea?*

Donne's logic here is this: We must take upon ourselves the pain of our dying neighbor, because this pain, while no longer of use to the neighbor, might motivate us to improve our lives by strengthening our relationship with God.

? *What effect does Donne achieve with the repetition of the word* affliction *in this passage? Do you agree or disagree that suffering can, in one sense, be thought of as "gold"?*

6. **intermit** *v.:* cease.
7. **comet . . . out:** Comets were regarded as signs of disaster to come.
8. **main** *n.:* mainland.
9. **affliction** *n.:* suffering.
10. **defray** *v.:* pay for.
11. **making my recourse:** turning for aid.

Response and Analysis

Thinking Critically

1. What sound prompts the speaker to begin his meditation?
2. Several of Donne's **metaphors** suggest something about the relationship of people to one another. Identify two of those metaphors. What do they imply about society?
3. Why does the speaker feel that affliction is a treasure? In what ways is tribulation like money?
4. How would you explain what Donne means by saying, "The bell . . . tolls for thee"?
5. What do you think Donne's **main ideas** are in this meditation? Do you agree with them all? Explain why or why not.
6. How would you describe the speaker's **tone:** solemn, sad, depressed, angry, resigned, or something else? Which words in the meditation reinforce this tone?
7. **Rhetoric** refers to the art of using words effectively to communicate. How does Donne's **tone** in this meditation support the point he is trying to make?
8. Do any lines from this meditation have particular relevance to our lives today? Explain your response.

WRITING

Meditation on Metaphors

In a brief **essay,** take two of the **metaphors** from Meditation 17, and show how Donne uses them to make his points. Explain the comparisons the metaphors are based on. Show how Donne extends the metaphors. Describe the emotions that each metaphor evokes.

Literary Skills Analyze the use of tone.

Writing Skills Write an essay explaining the author's use of metaphors.

Grammar Link

Appropriate Additions: Adjective Clauses and Adverb Clauses

How can you combine short, choppy sentences to form sentences that flow smoothly? Try using adjective and adverb clauses. An **adjective clause** modifies a noun or a pronoun and usually begins with *who, whom, whose, which, that,* or *where.* Here are two choppy sentences:

John Donne became the dean of St. Paul's Cathedral. St. Paul's Cathedral is in London.

By turning one of these sentences into an adjective clause, we can combine the two choppy sentences.

John Donne became the dean of St. Paul's Cathedral**,** which is in London.

If an adjective clause is not essential to the meaning of a sentence, it is a **nonrestrictive clause** (as in the sentence above) and must be set off from the rest of the sentence with a comma or commas.

If an adjective clause is essential to the meaning of a sentence, it is a **restrictive clause** (*The poem **that I like the best** is "Song."*), and no commas are necessary.

An **adverb clause** modifies a verb, an adjective, or an adverb. An adverb clause begins with a subordinating conjunction, such as *after, although, because, before, if, since, until, when,* or *while.* Here are two more choppy sentences:

John Donne studied at Oxford. He was only twelve years old.

By turning one of these sentences into an adverb clause, you can combine the choppy sentences.

When John Donne was only twelve years old, he studied at Oxford.

When you place an adverb clause at the beginning of a sentence, separate it from the independent clause with a comma.

PRACTICE

Combine each pair of sentences that follows by using either an adjective clause or an adverb clause. Identify the kind of clause that you use for each item.

1. John Donne was related to Sir Thomas More. Sir Thomas More was beheaded by Henry VIII in 1535.
2. John Donne was jailed for marrying Anne More. He had not asked her father's permission.
3. In Meditation 17, Donne compares humanity to chapters in a book. The chapters have been authored by God.
4. John Donne became private secretary to Sir Thomas Egerton. He had had many adventures.

Apply to Your Writing

Take out a writing assignment you are working on now or have already completed. Are there any short, choppy sentences? Add variety to your writing by combining those sentences using adjective or adverb clauses.

For more help, see The Adjective Clause, 7d, and The Adverb Clause, 7f, in the Language Handbook.

Grammar Skills
Understand and use adjective clauses and adverb clauses.

Before You Read

Death be not proud

Make the Connection

Quickwrite

Although death is inescapable, it is not, for everyone, unconquerable. For those who believe in the immortality of the soul—as Donne firmly did—death is merely a station on the soul's journey, the moment of its delivery from the confines of the body to the bliss of eternal life.

Write the labels "Defeat" and "Triumph" at the top of two columns. Under each label, list ways in which you think death can be seen as either a triumph or a defeat. For example, dying to save someone's life may be triumph and dying in a needless accident may be defeat.

Literary Focus

Paradox

A **paradox** is a statement that at first glance seems impossible or illogical ("The child is the father of the man") but, when looked at more closely, expresses a deeper truth than was immediately apparent ("What we are as adults is very much influenced by our childhood experiences"). Paradoxes are useful because they capture our attention and force us to think more deeply about issues we might otherwise take for granted.

Literary Skills
Understand the use of paradox.

> A **paradox** is a seeming contradiction that is actually true.
>
> *For more on Paradox, see the Handbook of Literary and Historical Terms.*

INTERNET

More About John Donne

Keyword: LE7 12-3

Background

In Donne's collected poems, which are grouped by type, "Death be not proud" is one of nineteen Holy Sonnets included in the category of "Divine Poems." Because Donne never published the Holy Sonnets and because they are arranged in different ways in contemporary manuscripts and in books printed after his death, we do not know the order in which he wanted us to read them.

Italian Landscape (18th century) by Hubert Robert.

Musée Calvet, Avignon, France/Peter Willi/The Bridgeman Art Library.

The Ruins of Holyrood Chapel (c. 1824) by Louis Jacques Mandé Daguerre.
Board of Trustees of the National Museums and Galleries on Merseyside (Walker Art Gallery), Liverpool, England.

Death be not proud

John Donne

Death be not proud, though some have callèd thee
Mighty and dreadful, for thou art not so,
For those whom thou think'st thou dost overthrow,
Die not, poor Death, nor yet canst thou kill me.
From rest and sleep, which but thy pictures° be,
Much pleasure,° then from thee, much more must flow,
And soonest our best men with thee do go,
Rest of their bones, and soul's delivery.°
Thou art slave to fate, chance, kings, and desperate men,
And dost with poison, war, and sickness dwell,
And poppy,° or charms° can make us sleep as well,
And better than thy stroke; why swell'st° thou then?
One short sleep past, we wake eternally,
And death shall be no more; Death, thou shalt die.

5. pictures *n. pl.:* images. A sleeping person can resemble a dead person.
6. much pleasure: That is, rest and sleep give much pleasure.
8. rest . . . delivery: Death gives the body rest and delivers the soul from the bondage of the body.
11. poppy *n.:* opium. **charms** *n. pl.:* magic; hypnotism.
12. swell'st *v.:* swell with pride.

Margaret Edson's Pulitzer Prize–winning play, W;t, *tells the story of Vivian Bearing, an English professor who has devoted her career to studying the Holy Sonnets of John Donne. At the beginning of the play, Bearing has been diagnosed with terminal cancer. Rather than succumbing to despair, however, she views her illness and her life with logic and humor.*

In this scene, Bearing recalls a confrontational meeting with one of her college English literature professors (E. M. Ashford) about Donne's Holy Sonnet Six, or "Death be not proud."

The scene is a flashback to Bearing's days in college, twenty-eight years earlier. At that time, Bearing was twenty-two years old.

from W;t

Margaret Edson

E.M. Please sit down. Your essay on Holy Sonnet Six, Miss Bearing, is a melodrama, with a veneer of scholarship unworthy of you—to say nothing of Donne. Do it again.

Vivian. I, ah . . .

E.M. You must begin with a text, Miss Bearing, not with a feeling.

Death be not proud, though some have
called thee
Mighty and dreadfull, for, thou art not soe.

You have entirely missed the point of the poem, because, I must tell you, you have used an edition of the text that is inauthentically punctuated. In the Gardner edition—

Vivian. That edition was checked out of the library—

E.M. Miss Bearing!

Vivian. Sorry.

E.M. You take this too lightly, Miss Bearing. This is Metaphysical Poetry, not The Modern Novel. The standards of scholarship and critical reading which one would apply to any other text are simply insufficient. The effort must be total for the results to be meaningful. Do you think the punctuation of the last line of this sonnet is merely an insignificant detail?

The sonnet begins with a valiant struggle with death, calling on all the forces of intellect and drama to vanquish the enemy. But it is ultimately about overcoming the seemingly insuperable barriers separating life, death, and eternal life.

In the edition you chose, this profoundly simple meaning is sacrificed to hysterical punctuation:

And Death—*capital D*—shall be no
more—*semicolon!*

Death—*capital D—comma*—thou shalt
die—*exclamation point!*

If you go in for this sort of thing, I suggest you take up Shakespeare.

Gardner's edition of the Holy Sonnets returns to the Westmoreland manuscript source of 1610—not for sentimental reasons, I assure you, but because Helen Gardner is a *scholar.* It reads:

And death shall be no more, *comma,* Death
thou shalt die.

[*As she recites this line, she makes a little gesture at the comma.*]

Nothing but a breath—a comma—separates life from life everlasting. It is very simple really. With the original punctuation restored, death is no longer something to act out on a stage, with exclamation points. It's a comma, a pause.

This way, the *uncompromising* way, one learns something from this poem, wouldn't you say? Life, death. Soul, God. Past, present. Not insuperable barriers, not semicolons, just a comma.

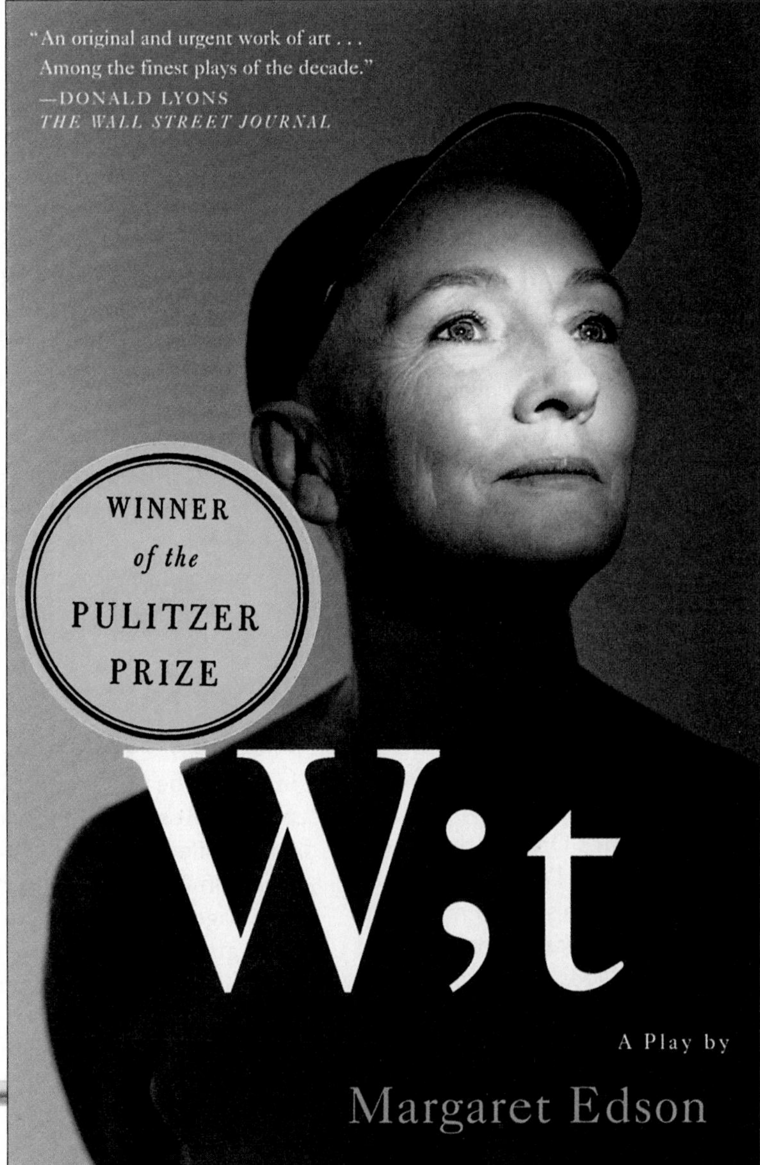

"An original and urgent work of art . . .
Among the finest plays of the decade."
—DONALD LYONS
THE WALL STREET JOURNAL
WINNER of the PULITZER PRIZE
W;t
A Play by
Margaret Edson

Response and Analysis

Still Life with a Skull and a Writing Quill, (1628) by Pieter Claesz. Oil on wood. 9½ x 14⅛ in. (24.1 × 35.9 cm).

The Metropolitan Museum of Art, Rogers Fund, 1949 (49.107).
Photograph ©2004, The Metropolitan Museum of Art.

Thinking Critically

1. According to the poem, why shouldn't Death be proud? Whom must Death serve as a slave?
2. Explain how rest and sleep are the "pictures" of Death (line 5).
3. Show how, as the sonnet develops, the speaker shifts the grounds of his attack on Death.
4. How does the sonnet resolve its **paradoxes:** that those who die do not die and that Death itself will die?
5. What is the speaker's **tone** in this poem—how does he feel toward Death? What words reveal his attitude?
6. Did you find any of your Quickwrite ideas in Donne's poem? Did any of his taunts of Death seem especially original to you? Explain.
7. Donne **personifies** Death—that is, he speaks of Death as if Death were a person. How does this poem make you feel about Death? (Does it make Death less frightening? Does it give you a new way of looking at Death?)
8. Is this a **Shakespearean** or a **Petrarchan sonnet** (see pages 311–313)? Demonstrate how you arrived at your answer.

SKILLS FOCUS

Literary Skills
Analyze the use of paradox.

Writing Skills
Write an essay comparing and contrasting personification in two poems.

Extending and Evaluating

9. The last line of this version of "Death be not proud" is punctuated differently from the version that the professor in the ***Connection*** on page 350 prefers. Is there any important difference between the use of a comma and the use of a semicolon in the last line? What feeling might the semicolon subtly evoke?

WRITING

Death Personified

In "Death be not proud," Donne forcefully **personifies** Death. How does Donne's image differ from that of the personified Death in Chaucer's "The Pardoner's Tale" (see page 168)?

In an **essay, compare and contrast** the two portrayals of Death. Consider these points:

- Death's characteristics and power
- how people respond to Death

Ben Jonson

(1572?–1637)

Benjamin Jonson (early 17th century) after Abraham van Blyenberch. Oil on canvas (18½″ × 16½″).

By Courtesy of the National Portrait Gallery, London.

Although Jonson was christened Benjamin, he was, and is, always known as Ben. He was probably born in the same year as his friend John Donne, and if his friend William Shakespeare had never existed, Jonson would probably be regarded as the chief dramatist of the age.

Ben's father died before he was born. His stepfather, a bricklayer, intended to make him a bricklayer too, but while still a boy, Jonson became acquainted with William Camden, a scholar and headmaster of the superb Westminster School. Camden enrolled young Ben in his school and educated him at his own expense.

Jonson never attended a university, but he had an immense knowledge of Latin literature and a small acquaintance with Greek. He was no mere pedant or bookish recluse. After leaving Westminster, Ben joined the English army and fought against the Spanish in Flanders. There, while the two massed armies watched, he engaged in single combat with the Spanish champion and killed him. Back in England he became a playwright and an actor, specializing in loud and roaring parts. He had two brushes with the law: once when he killed a fellow actor in a duel and escaped hanging by demonstrating that he could read; once when he went to prison for making derogatory remarks about Scotland in a play. In short, Jonson was very much a part of the tough, violent life of the time—a complete Londoner, holding forth at the Mermaid Tavern, where his witty combats with Shakespeare and others are mentioned in contemporary writings.

Gradually Jonson became known as a dramatist. He was particularly good at devising masques (elaborate, expensively mounted productions) for the court of King James. Jonson also wrote tragedies and comedies for the public theaters.

Jonson's attitude toward his writing was different from Donne's and Shakespeare's; Jonson was more like today's writers, who are, for the most part, eager for public notice. In 1616, Jonson astonished the reading public by publishing a number of his plays and poems under the title *Works,* a label traditionally reserved for more intellectual subjects, such as theology and history. Jonson believed that poems and plays are serious works of art, as serious in their own way as history and theology and as worthy of high regard.

At the height of his career, Jonson was a sort of literary dictator in London—opinionated and crusty but admired by a number of younger writers, who became known as the tribe of Ben or the sons of Ben. They stood by Jonson in his old age, when he was sick and poor and neglected because his blunt and forthright manner had made him many enemies. Jonson was buried near Chaucer in Westminster Abbey, in what later became known as the Poets' Corner. His inscription required only four words: "O rare Ben Jonson."

For Independent Reading

You may want to read these poems by Jonson:

- "Song: Still to Be Neat"
- "On My First Daughter"

Before You Read

On My First Son
Song: To Celia

Make the Connection

When you hear the word *love,* do you first think of romantic love? If you do, this is a natural response. However, the ties of love bind us powerfully to family, friends, mentors, even pets—not just to the objects of our romantic affection. One of love's ironies is that a strong bond of love, so strengthening and fulfilling—even inspiring—also opens us to crushing heartache when the bond is cut. The two poems by Ben Jonson that follow explore two very different kinds of love—and two very different outcomes for love.

Literary Focus

The Epigram

Both of the following Ben Jonson poems were published in his collection *Epigrams* (1616). The **epigram**—a brief, cleverly worded, memorable statement, usually in rhymed verse—was a classical form Jonson favored in contrast to both Elizabethan romanticism and the metaphysical complexity of a John Donne poem (see page 337). For the ancients an epigram was written to give permanence to an event or observation; it was pointed, polished, and striking—like an engraved motto on a monument. Jonson's epigrams take the form of short poems, often with a two-part structure: The first part establishes the mood or the event; the second makes a concise point.

An **epigram** is a brief, clever, and usually memorable poem or short verse.

For more on Epigram, see the Handbook of Literary and Historical Terms.

Background

Jonson once said that he always wrote out his poems in prose before turning them into verse, just as his headmaster Camden had taught him to. At times, it must be admitted, the prose that he versified was not his own but someone else's. For example, the poem "Song: To Celia" was crafted out of five different prose passages that Jonson found in the *Epistles* of the Greek philosopher Philostratus (A.D. 170?–245).

Throughout most of his life, Jonson's enemies taunted him for once having been a bricklayer. In a sense he remained a bricklayer all his creative life, a builder whose tiniest literary construction is solid and seamless.

Literary Skills
Understand the characteristics of epigrams.

Details from *The Grimani Breviary.*
Archivo Iconografico, S.A./CORBIS.

This poem is about Ben Jonson's son, Benjamin, who died of the plague on his seventh birthday. (Jonson and his wife also lost a daughter, Mary, in infancy.) The name Benjamin *in Hebrew means "child of the right hand" and, ironically, connotes a "lucky, clever child." Pay special attention to the famous* **epitaph,** *or inscription on a grave, that appears in quotation marks at the end of the poem.*

On My First Son

Ben Jonson

Farewell, thou child of my right hand, and joy;
  My sin was too much hope of thee, loved boy:
Seven years thou wert lent to me, and I thee pay,°
  Exacted° by thy fate, on the just° day.
Oh, could I lose all father° now! for why
  Will man lament the state he should envy—
To have so soon 'scaped world's and flesh's rage,
  And if no other misery, yet age?
Rest in soft peace, and asked, say, "Here doth lie
  Ben Jonson his best piece of poetry;
For whose sake henceforth all his vows be such
  As what he loves may never like too much."

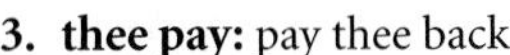

3. thee pay: pay thee back.

4. exacted *v.:* forced. **just** *adj.:* exact. Loans were often made for exactly seven years.

5. father *n.:* sense of fatherhood; the need to mourn like a father.

Portrait of a boy (16th century) by Robert Peake the Elder.

Christie's, London.

This poem has a very famous tune that many people still know. Thomas Arne (1710–1778), who also composed the British national anthem, "Rule, Britannia," created music for Ben Jonson's poem and called it "Drink to Me Only with Thine Eyes." The song can still be found in many old songbooks.

Song: To Celia

Ben Jonson

Drink to me only with thine eyes,
And I will pledge with mine;
Or leave a kiss but in the cup,
And I'll not look for wine.
The thirst that from the soul doth rise
Doth ask a drink divine;
But might I of Jove's nectar° sup,
I would not change° for thine.
I sent thee late a rosy wreath,
Not so much honoring thee
As giving it a hope, that there
It could not withered be.
But thou thereon didst only breathe,
And sent'st it back to me;
Since when it grows, and smells, I swear,
Not of itself but thee.

7. Jove's nectar: Jove, more commonly called Jupiter, is the supreme god in Roman mythology. Nectar was the drink that kept the gods immortal.
8. change *v.:* exchange.

Response and Analysis

On My First Son
Song: To Celia

Thinking Critically

1. According to line 2 of "On My First Son," what was the speaker's (Jonson's) "sin"? What do you think he means by this declaration?
2. Explain the **metaphor** Jonson uses in lines 3–4 of "On My First Son." What does this comparison tell you about how Jonson views life?
3. In lines 7–8 of "On My First Son," what comfort does Jonson suggest is possible? Do you feel that he, the speaker, is comforted by this idea? Explain, using evidence from the text.
4. What does Jonson vow at the end of "On My First Son"?
5. Jonson borrowed some of the features of "On My First Son" from Latin works: The direct address to the dead boy in line 9 and the first three words of the **epitaph,** or inscription, "Here doth lie . . ." are straight out of Latin classics. However, the ideas contained in the epitaph are original to Jonson, especially the central **metaphor** in line 10. To what does Jonson compare his son? What do you think of this comparison?
6. In "Song: To Celia," what do you think it means to "drink" and "pledge" with the eyes?
7. What does "thine" refer to in line 8 of "Song: To Celia"?
8. How would you **paraphrase** lines 9–16 of "Song: To Celia"?

WRITING

On Love and Loss

In "On My First Son," Jonson resolves never again to love so strongly, because his loss is so unbearable. What do you think of Jonson's resolution? What effect could a vow like this have on someone? In a **letter** to the writer, explain what you think of his vow to never again love too much.

LISTENING AND SPEAKING

Reciting a Poem

Choose either of the Jonson poems you have just read, and prepare an oral reading. Before you begin, be sure to mark copies of the poems with appropriate pauses and stopping points so that you can read the poem in a natural, convincing way. Be sure that the **tone** of your reading—whether it is exuberant or restrained, grave or lively—matches the tone of the poem you have chosen. Recite your poem for the class, and ask for critiques of your delivery.

Motets (16th century) by Richard Sampson. Canon, with circular staves and rose at center.
Roy 11 E XI fol. 2v. British Library, London.

Literary Skills
Analyze the characteristics of epigrams.

Writing Skills
Write a letter to the poet.

Listening and Speaking Skills
Give an oral presentation of a poem.

Introduction Comparing Points of View

Education and Equality

Main Reading

Connected Readings

You will be reading the three selections listed above in this Comparing Points of View feature on education and equality. In the top corner of the pages in this feature, you'll find three stars. Smaller versions of these stars appear next to the questions on page 364 that focus on education and equality. On page 371, you'll compare the points of view expressed in the selections.

Examining the Issue: Education and Equality

With the advent of humanism, education was no longer restricted to the clergy. In fact, men of the privileged classes were now expected to study a wide array of subjects, from philosophy and economics to music and science. Education for Renaissance women, however, was a different story. Only women of noble birth had access to education, and the goal of education was to produce better wives and mothers, since education was linked to growth in moral virtue and since women directed the early education of their children.

Although education was held up as a primary good during the Renaissance, it was certainly not available to all—and its goal was not to create equality, either between classes or between men and women.

Make the Connection

Quickwrite

Jot down your ideas about the role of education in bringing women closer to equality with men. Does the struggle for equality between the sexes continue today? What other kinds of equality can education help to create?

Pages 358–371 cover
Literary Skills Analyze points of view on a topic.
Reading Skills Draw inferences.

Reading Skills

Drawing Inferences

When you read thoughtfully, you make **inferences**—you draw certain conclusions from a text based on the evidence. The selections that follow differ greatly in purpose and subject matter, but they are all firmly rooted in their authors' times. From what these writers say—and how they say it—you can draw inferences about the social and political realities of their time. Take careful notes as you read.

Francis Bacon
(1561–1626)

From his earliest days, Francis Bacon knew that he was an important person. When he was about nine, Queen Elizabeth asked him how old he was, and he is said to have replied, "Two years younger than your Majesty's happy reign." A boy who speaks like this will go far, and Bacon went far. He rose in his chosen profession, the law, until he reached the very top and became lord chancellor and keeper of the great seal, an office that his father, Sir Nicholas Bacon, had also held. He was elevated to the peerage, the British nobles who could govern as members of the House of Lords, and he amassed a large fortune, though he was often in debt because of his extravagant lifestyle. At the height of his political career, he was found guilty of taking bribes and was removed from office. Bacon retired to his country estate, where he devoted himself full time to thinking and writing about new ways to discover knowledge.

In a now famous letter to his uncle, Lord Burghley, Elizabeth's secretary of state, Bacon wrote, "I have taken all knowledge to be my province." Of course, he did not master all knowledge, but he did make important contributions to many different branches of knowledge: political science, economics, biology, physics, music, architecture, botany, constitutional law, industrial development, philosophy, theology, mythology, astronomy, chemistry, landscape gardening, and literature. He is most famous, however, for his vision of humanity's future, when knowledge would be based on verifiable experimentation and science would be separate from theology.

Bacon's best-known literary works, the *Essays*, are intended to help people get ahead in life. Bacon was the first Englishman to use the word *essay* to designate a brief discourse in prose. He took the word from the French writer Montaigne (män·tān′), whose delightful *essais* are mainly about a fascinating person, Montaigne himself. Bacon writes instead about humanity in general.

Bacon had embarked on a new career as a practicing scientist when death overtook him. One wintry day he descended from his carriage carrying a dead chicken, intending to freeze it in the snow and thereby test the preservative powers of cold. Today this seems like a painfully obvious thing to do, but nobody had tried it in a systematic way before 1626. Suddenly, in the midst of the experiment, Bacon took a chill. His servants carried him into nearby Highgate, the house of the earl of Arundel. In poor health most of his life, Bacon died there of complications resulting from exposure.

In all his works, Bacon's aim was to make the world better. As the destroyer of old Aristotelian ways of thinking and as the stimulator of "modern" ones, Bacon has no equal.

Sir Francis Bacon, Viscount of St. Albans (detail) (late 16th–early 17th century) by Paul van Somer. Oil.

Private Collection.

Before You Read

Of Studies

Points *of* View

Quickwrite

Two well-known sayings express contrasting views on the relationship of books and learning to success in life. According to one axiom, "Knowledge is power." According to the other, more cynical saying, "It's not what you know but who you know." Bacon himself coined the first saying, but he probably would have agreed with both views, since he was both extremely learned and very well connected to powerful people. What is your view of the value of reading and learning? Write down your views and the reasons you feel as you do.

Literary Focus

Parallelism

Bacon's sentences have been studied for centuries as models of **parallelism,** or **parallel structure**—the repetition of words, phrases, or sentences that have a similar grammatical structure. Parallelism is a powerful rhetorical device that enhances a passage's clarity and makes it rhythmic and memorable. Bacon also uses parallel structure to present contrasting ideas. Reading aloud and paying attention to punctuation and parallel structure will help you make sense of Bacon's long, complex sentences.

Parallelism is the repetition of words, phrases, or sentences that have a similar grammatical structure.

For more on Parallelism, see the Handbook of Literary and Historical Terms.

Reading Skills

Analyzing Arguments

In this persuasive essay, Bacon is expressing his point of view on the value of study and arguing to convince his readers that his viewpoint is correct. Bacon's essay is only one paragraph in length, but it is packed with ideas. In your first reading, look for any explicit, or direct, statements that express Bacon's overall point of view on the topic—his **main idea.** Such statements often occur at the beginning or end of persuasive essays. Then, in a second or third reading, take note of the reasons, examples, and details that Bacon uses to support his arguments and persuade his readers. Finally, consider whether Bacon has convinced you of his arguments, and explain why or why not.

Vocabulary Development

discourse (dis′kôrs′) *n.:* speech.

sloth (slôth) *n.:* laziness.

affectation (af′ek•tā′shən) *n.:* artificial behavior designed to impress others.

diligence (dil′ə•jəns) *n.:* care; carefulness.

impediment (im•ped′ə•mənt) *n.:* obstacle; stumbling block.

Literary Skills Analyze points of view on a topic. Understand the use of parallelism.

Reading Skills Analyze arguments.

INTERNET

Vocabulary Practice

Keyword: LE7 12-3

Of Studies

Francis Bacon

Studies serve for delight, for ornament, and for ability. Their chief use for delight is in privateness and retiring;[1] for ornament, is in discourse; and for ability, is in the judgment and disposition[2] of business. ❶ For expert men can execute, and perhaps judge of particulars, one by one; but the general counsels, and the plots and marshaling of affairs, come best from those that are learned. To spend too much time in studies is sloth; to use them too much for ornament is affectation; to make judgment wholly by their rules is the humor[3] of a scholar. They perfect nature and are perfected by experience; for natural abilities are like natural plants that need pruning by study; and studies themselves do give forth directions too much at large, except they be bounded in by experience. Crafty men contemn[4] studies; simple men admire[5] them; and wise men use them: For they teach not their own use; but that is a wisdom without them[6] and above them, won by observation. Read not to contradict and confute;[7] nor to believe and take for granted; nor to find talk and discourse; but to weigh and consider. ❷ Some books are to be tasted, others to be swallowed, and some few to be chewed and digested: That is, some books are to be read only in parts; others to be read, but not curiously;[8] and some few to be read wholly, and with diligence and attention. ❸ Some books also may be read by deputy, and extracts made of them by others; but that would be only in the less important arguments, and the meaner sort of books; else distilled books are like common distilled waters,[9] flashy[10] things. Reading maketh a full man; conference[11] a ready man; and writing an exact man. And therefore, if a man write little, he had need have a great memory; if he confer little, he had need have a present wit;[12] and if he read little, he had need have much cunning, to seem to know that[13] he doth not.

❶ ? *What three things can studies (reading, writing, and discussion) be helpful for? How can studies be used for each of these things?*

❷ ? *In the sentence that begins "Read not to contradict and confute . . . ," what does Bacon conclude that reading should be used for? What should it not be used for?*

❸ ? *According to Bacon, what is the difference among books that are meant to be "tasted," books that are meant to be "swallowed," and books that are meant to be "chewed and digested"?*

---

1. **privateness and retiring:** privacy and leisure. 2. **disposition** *n.:* thoughtful placement. 3. **humor** *n.:* whim. 4. **contemn** *v.:* despise. 5. **admire** *v.:* archaic for "marvel at." 6. **without them:** separate from them; outside them. 7. **confute** *v.:* dispute. 8. **curiously** *adv.:* carefully. 9. **common distilled waters:** homemade remedies. 10. **flashy** *adj.:* superficial; empty. 11. **conference** *n.:* conversation; discussion. 12. **present wit:** ability to think fast. 13. **that** *pron.:* what.

Vocabulary

discourse (dis′kôrs′) *n.:* speech.
sloth (slôth) *n.:* laziness.
affectation (af′ək • tā′shən) *n.:* artificial behavior designed to impress others.
diligence (dil′ə • jens) *n.:* care; carefulness.

Histories make men wise; poets witty;[14] the mathematics subtle; natural philosophy deep; moral grave; logic and rhetoric able to contend. *Abeunt studia in mores.*[15] Nay, there is no stond[16] or impediment in the wit but may be wrought[17] out by fit studies: like as diseases of the body may have appropriate exercises. Bowling is good for the stone and reins;[18] shooting for the lungs and breast; gentle walking for the stomach; riding for the head; and the like. So if a man's wit be wandering, let him study the mathematics; for in demonstrations, if his wit be called away never so little, he must begin again: If his wit be not apt to distinguish or find differences, let him study the Schoolmen;[19] for they are *cymini sectores:*[20] If he be not apt to beat over[21] matters, and to call one thing to prove and illustrate another, let him study the lawyers' cases; so every defect of the mind may have a special receipt.[22] ❹ ■

❹
Bacon uses an extended analogy to argue the value of "fit studies."
? *Summarize Bacon's analogy: Studies are to the mind as ________ is to ________*

14. **witty** *adj.:* imaginative. 15. ***Abeunt . . . mores:*** Latin for "Studies help form character," from *Heroides* by Ovid (43 B.C.–c. A.D. 17). 16. **stond** *n.:* stoppage. 17. **wrought** *v.:* worked. 18. **stone and reins:** archaic for "kidney stones and the kidneys." 19. **schoolmen** *n. pl.:* medieval philosophers. 20. **cymini sectores:** Latin for "hairsplitters"; literally, dividers of the cumin seed. 21. **beat over:** thoroughly discuss. 22. **receipt:** *n.:* remedy.

Vocabulary

impediment (im • ped′ə • mənt) *n.:* obstacle; stumbling block.

A Still Life with Books (detail) (17th century) by Charles E. Bizet d'Annonay.

Musée de l'Ain, Bourg-en-Bresse, France.

Bacon's essays are written in a terse, compressed style that demands a reader's full attention. For the most part, Bacon does not develop his ideas in paragraphs. Instead, he writes a sentence containing one idea, then follows it with a sentence containing another idea. While the sentences are all related to the topic of the essay, they are related in different ways—and they could be rearranged without much damage to the whole. The effect is like a string of beads all the same size.

Many of the sentences contain nuggets of wisdom known as **axioms** *or adages. Like proverbs, axioms do not argue or explain but merely make positive statements. Here is a sampling of some of Bacon's most memorable axioms.*

Musée de l'Ain, Bourg-en-Bresse, France.

Axioms
from the Essays

Francis Bacon

Men fear death as children fear to go in the dark; and as that natural fear in children is increased with tales, so is the other.

—"Of Death"

Revenge is a kind of wild justice, which the more man's nature runs to, the more ought law to weed it out.

—"Of Revenge"

The virtue of prosperity is temperance; the virtue of adversity is fortitude.

—"Of Adversity"

He that hath wife and children hath given hostages to fortune.

—"Of Marriage and Single Life"

There was never proud man thought so absurdly well of himself as the lover doth of the person loved: And therefore it was well said, *That it is impossible to love and to be wise.*

—"Of Love"

They that deny a God destroy man's nobility, for certainly man is of kin to the beasts by his body, and if he be not of kin to God by his spirit, he is a base and ignoble creature.

—"Of Atheism"

A principal fruit of friendship is the ease and discharge of the fullness and swellings of the heart.

—"Of Friendship"

As the baggage is to an army, so is riches to virtue.

—"Of Riches"

No man prospers so suddenly as by others' errors.

—"Of Fortune"

There is no excellent beauty that hath not some strangeness in the proportion.

—"Of Beauty"

It were better to have no opinion of God at all than such an opinion as is unworthy of him.

—"Of Superstition"

Response and Analysis

Reading Check

1. What are some of the ways in which studies can be misused?
2. What should reading be used for? What should it *not* be used for?
3. What do these kinds of readings do for us: histories, poems, mathematics, natural philosophy, moral philosophy, logical rhetoric?

Thinking Critically

4. In no more than three sentences, state what you think is Bacon's **main idea** in "Of Studies." Then, quote **details** from the essay that support your statement of its main idea.
5. Bacon says that too much studying is "sloth"—laziness. Do you agree? Explain how this **paradox,** or seeming contradiction, can be true.
6. Bacon had the reputation of being a hard, ambitious man, and his essays are frequently said to be cynical and lacking in warmth. Find remarks in "Of Studies" that could support this view.
7. Which sentence from the essay best sums up Bacon's views on the value of study? Cite reasons and examples he offers to support his argument. Has Bacon convinced you of his **point of view**? Explain. You may want to consult your reading notes.

Extending and Evaluating

8. Bacon's fondness for **parallelism** and balanced sentences is apparent in "Of Studies," which uses parallel structures to state, restate, and elaborate his main idea. For example, "Some books are to be tasted, others to be swallowed, and some few to be chewed and digested." Find other examples of parallelism in the essay, and explain how it improves the essay's clarity.
9. "Of Studies" was written almost four hundred years ago. Do you think Bacon's views are still relevant today? Are any of his points dated? Do you disagree with anything Bacon says? Explain. Consult your Quickwrite notes.

WRITING

Talking Back to Bacon

Write an **essay** of your own in response to Bacon's reflections on studies or in response to one of the axioms in the ***Primary Source*** on page 363. Your response to Bacon may range from total disagreement to total approval of all he says. In your opening statement, tell what the topic of your essay will be. Be sure to bring in examples and experiences from real life to support or refute Bacon. Give your essay a title that uses the word *Of.*

Literary Skills Analyze points of view on a topic. Analyze the use of parallelism.

Reading Skills Analyze arguments.

Writing Skills Write a response essay.

Vocabulary Skills Demonstrate word knowledge.

Vocabulary Development

Stating Opinions

discourse, diligence, sloth, impediment, affectation

Use each of the words above to state an opinion or make an assertion that could be argued in a persuasive essay. One has been done for you below.

> Children who show signs of sloth will grow up to be lazy adults.

Connected Readings

Education and Equality

You have just read Sir Francis Bacon's persuasive essay "Of Studies," which praises the virtues of reading and learning and expresses a solidly Renaissance view of the value of knowledge and education. The next two selections you will be reading—a speech by Queen Elizabeth I and a selection of dramatic monologues in the form of a literary debate by Margaret Cavendish—also shed light (in both direct and indirect ways) on Renaissance views of the value of education. Although immense emphasis was placed on education during the Renaissance, formal education of the type extolled by Sir Francis Bacon was not available to the majority of the population, and particularly not to women. It was, however, available to women of the privileged classes—and some of these women took full advantage of the opportunity, becoming as intellectually accomplished as their male peers.

After you have read these selections, answer the questions on page 371, which ask you to compare all three selections—and to consider the relationship between education and equality today.

Points *of* View

Before You Read

King Henry VIII appointed humanist scholars to tutor both his son and his daughters. His younger daughter eventually became Queen Elizabeth I (1533–1603), the most influential of England's educated women. She could translate Greek and Latin classics into polished English, and she spoke and read six languages. She was also proficient in areas common to most gentlewomen—riding, music, astronomy, geography, philosophy, mathematics, and needlepoint. As queen, Elizabeth dazzled poets, dramatists, and court ambassadors with her superb literary training and political and diplomatic skills. One of her tutors, Roger Ascham, went so far as to exclaim, "It is your shame (I speak to you all, you young gentlemen of England) that one maid should go beyond you all in excellency of learning and knowledge of diverse tongues."

Many of Elizabeth's aristocratic countrywomen also gained excellent educations, yet what could they do with their knowledge? No professorships were open to them, nor could they join the ranks of the clergy. Aside from the personal satisfaction available from study, few women found themselves in a position where they could actually make use of their education.

Queen Elizabeth I wrote poems, letters, prayers, sermons, and translations—at the same time that she governed the country, conducted foreign policy, fostered the arts, and dedicated herself fervently to the new religion of her reign. She also wrote masterful speeches and political addresses. One of her best-known orations is the Tilbury Speech, given in 1588 before news of the destruction of the Spanish Armada reached England. Elizabeth's goal was to rouse her land forces to defend England against Spanish invasion.

SPEECH

Tilbury Speech

Queen Elizabeth I

My loving people: We have been persuaded by some that are careful of our safety to take heed how we commit ourself to armed multitudes for fear of treachery, but I assure you I do not desire to live to distrust my faithful and loving people. Let tyrants fear. I have always so behaved myself that, under God, I have placed my chiefest strength and safeguard in the loyal hearts and goodwill of my subjects. And therefore I am come amongst you, as you see, at this time, not for my recreation and disport, but being resolved in the midst and heat of the battle to live or die amongst you all, to lay down for my God, and for my kingdom, and for my people, my honor and my blood, even in the dust. I know I have the body but of a weak and feeble woman, but I have the heart and stomach of a king—and of a king of England too—and think foul scorn that Parma, or Spain, or any prince of Europe should dare to invade the borders of my realm. To which, rather than any dishonor shall grow by me, I myself will take up arms, I myself will be your general, judge, and rewarder of every one of your virtues in the field. I know already for your forwardness you have deserved rewards and crowns, and we do assure you, in the word of a prince, they shall be duly paid you.

—Elizabeth I

The Rainbow Portrait (c. 1600) of Elizabeth I, attributed to Isaac Oliver. The inscription next to the rainbow reads *"Non sine sole iris,"* which means "No rainbow without the sun." Elizabeth would have been the sun. Note the eyes and ears embroidered on her gown.

Points of View

Before You Read

Margaret Cavendish, duchess of Newcastle (1623–1673), was an eccentric gentlewoman who reached adulthood some decades after Elizabeth's death and the troubled times that followed. As a member of the aristocracy, Cavendish had both access to education and the freedom to write what she pleased. Although she was viewed as an oddity, she openly tackled such controversial topics as the situation of women in a male-dominated society. Some called her "the crazy duchess." Despite this kind of criticism, however, Cavendish published many unique works of prose and poetry during her lifetime—a time when women were considered daring if they wrote anything at all.

Female Orations is a fictional debate between women, representing a range of viewpoints on the role of women in society. Cavendish's speculations on the meaning of femininity are unusually sophisticated in their insight into the complexity of women's cultural situation in the mid–seventeenth century.

DEBATE

from Female Orations

Margaret Cavendish, duchess of Newcastle

I

Ladies, gentlewomen, and other inferior women, but not less worthy: I have been industrious to assemble you together, and wish I were so fortunate as to persuade you to make frequent assemblies, associations, and combinations amongst our own sex, that we may unite in prudent counsels, to make ourselves as free, happy, and famous as men; whereas now we live and die as if we were produced from beasts, rather than from men; for men are happy, and we women are miserable; they possess all the ease, rest, pleasure, wealth, power, and fame; whereas women are restless with labor, easeless with pain, melancholy for want of pleasures, helpless for want of power, and die in oblivion, for want of fame. ❶ Nevertheless, men are so unconscionable[1] and cruel against us that they endeavor to bar us of all sorts of liberty, and will not suffer us freely to associate amongst our own sex; but would fain[2] bury us in their houses or beds, as in a grave. The truth is, we live like bats or owls, labor like beasts, and die like worms.

❶ The first speaker in the debate welcomes the participants and expresses her wish that women would assemble for such discussion and debate more frequently.
? *How does this speaker contrast the situation of women with that of men?*

1. **unconscionable** (un • kän′shən • ə • bəl) *adj.:* not fair.
2. **fain** *adv.:* eagerly; gladly.

II

Ladies, gentlewomen, and other inferior women: The lady that spoke to you hath spoken wisely and eloquently, in expressing our unhappiness; but she hath not declared a remedy, or showed us a way to come out of our miseries; but, if she could or would be our guide, to lead us out of the labyrinth[3] men have put us into, we should not only praise and admire her, but adore and worship her as our goddess: but alas! men, that are not only our tyrants but our devils, keep us in the hell of subjection, from whence I cannot perceive any redemption or getting out; we may complain and bewail our condition, yet that will not free us; we may murmur and rail against men, yet they regard not what we say. In short, our words to men are as empty sounds; our sighs, as puffs of winds; and our tears, as fruitless showers; and our power is so inconsiderable, that men laugh at our weakness. ❷

❷ Cavendish structures the fictional debate so that each speaker in turn (there are seven speakers in all) responds to the points made by the speaker or speakers before her. ? *What criticism does the second speaker make of the first speaker? How would you characterize this speaker based on her comments?*

III

Ladies, gentlewomen, and other inferior women: The former orations were exclamations against men, repining[4] at their condition and mourning for our own; but we have no reason to speak against men, who are our admirers and lovers; they are our protectors, defenders, and maintainers; they admire our beauties, and love our persons; they protect us from injuries, defend us from dangers, are industrious for our subsistence, and provide for our children; they swim great voyages by sea, travel long journeys by land, to get us rarities and curiosities; they dig to the center of the earth for gold for us; they dive to the bottom of the sea for jewels for us: they build to the skies houses for us: they hunt, fowl, fish, plant, and reap for food for us. All which, we could not do ourselves; and yet we complain of men, as if they were our enemies, whenas[5] we could not possibly live without them, which shows we are as ungrateful as inconstant. But we have more reason to murmur against Nature, than against men, who hath made men more ingenious, witty, and wise than women; more strong, industrious, and laborious than women; for women are witless and strengthless, and unprofitable creatures, did they not bear children.

Wherefore, let us love men, praise men, and pray for men; for without men, we should be the most miserable creatures that Nature hath made or could make. . . . ❸

Margaret Cavendish, duchess of Newcastle (17th century). English School. Engraving.

Private Collection/The Bridgeman Art Library.

❸ ? *How is the third speaker unlike the two speakers who preceded her? Summarize her views of men. How might a modern feminist react to this speaker's ideas?*

---

3. **labyrinth** *n.:* maze.
4. **repining** *v.* used as *adj.:* complaining.
5. **whenas:** *conj.:* while on the other hand.

Woman reading *Tristan und Isolde* by W. Hauschild.

The Art Archive/Neuschwanstein Castle, Germany/Dagli Orti (A).

Several other viewpoints are expressed as the debate continues in parts IV–VI. Part VII, which follows, is the last section of the debate.

VII

Noble ladies, honorable gentlewomen, and worthy female-commoners: ❹ The former oratoress's speech was to persuade us out of ourselves and to be that which Nature never intended us to be, to wit, masculine. But why should we desire to be masculine, since our own sex and condition is far the better? For if men have more courage, they have more danger; and if men have more strength, they have more labor than women have; if men are more eloquent in speech, women are more harmonious in voice; if men be more active, women are more graceful; if men have more liberty, women have more safety; ❺ for we never fight duels nor battles; nor do we go long travels or dangerous voyages; we labor not in building nor digging in mines, quarries, or pits, for metal, stone, or coals; neither do we waste or shorten our lives with university or scholastical studies, questions, and disputes; we burn not our faces with smiths' forges or chemists' furnaces; and hundreds of other actions which men are employed in; for they would not only fade the fresh beauty, spoil the lovely features, and decay the youth of women, causing them to appear old, when they are young; but would break their small limbs, and destroy their tender lives. Wherefore women have no reason to complain against Nature or the god of Nature, for although the gifts are not the same as they have given to men, yet those gifts they have given to women are much better; for we women are much more favored by Nature than men, in giving us such beauties, features, shapes, graceful demeanor, and such insinuating[6] and enticing attractives, that men are forced to admire us, love us, and be desirous of us; ❻ insomuch that rather than not have and enjoy us, they will deliver to our disposals their power, persons, and lives, enslaving themselves to our will and pleasures; also, we are their saints, whom they adore and worship; and what can we desire more than to be men's tyrants, destinies, and goddesses? ❼

---

6. **insinuating** *v.* used as *adj.:* suggestive.

❹ **?** *What can you infer about the seventh and final speaker from the way she addresses her audience? (Review the way the first three speakers opened their comments.)*

❺ **?** *What is the effect of this speaker's repeated use of an "If . . . then" parallel structure in these sentences?*

❻ **?** *Why, according to this speaker, do women have no reason to complain?*

❼ **?** *How would you summarize this speaker's argument? Do you agree or disagree with her? Explain.*

Analysis *Comparing Points of View*

Education and Equality

The questions on this page ask you to analyze the views on education and equality in the preceding three selections.

Francis Bacon . . . . **Of Studies**
Queen Elizabeth I . . . . **Tilbury Speech**
Margaret Cavendish . . . . *from* **Female Orations**

Thinking Critically

1. In light of the selections you've just read, how do you think Francis Bacon intended to use the word *man* throughout "Of Studies"? Was he using it to mean any human being, male or female, or did he intend to apply his ideas only to males? What evidence from Renaissance history—or simply the essay itself—supports your conclusion?
2. In the Tilbury Speech, Queen Elizabeth says that she has the body of "a weak and feeble woman" but "the heart and stomach of a king." What **inference** can you draw about implicit and explicit ideas and assumptions of her time toward women—and men? (An **implicit** idea is one that is not stated directly and must be inferred from details. An **explicit** idea is stated directly.) Why do you think she finds it necessary to mention her gender? Consult your reading notes from page 358.
3. Review the excerpts from Margaret Cavendish's *Female Orations*. Characterize the speaker of each section. What arguments does each speaker present? What assumptions about women may have been valid in the seventeenth century but are no longer valid today?
4. In the sixteenth and seventeenth centuries, an "inferior" was someone of lower social status than an aristocrat or a noble. Even when you know the meaning of this word, what effect does Cavendish's repeated use of the phrase "Ladies, gentlewomen, and other inferior women" have on you as a modern reader? Why do you think Cavendish has her first three speakers use this opening address?

WRITING

Letter to the Past

Write a letter to Queen Elizabeth I or to Margaret Cavendish, duchess of Newcastle, in which you express your thoughts about their writings and attitudes. Begin by explaining that you have just read something the writer wrote more than three centuries ago. Identify the work, and tell the writer how attitudes or realities have changed since her time. (See your Quickwrite notes from page 358 for ideas.) Explain to her our contemporary views on education and equality. Conclude by telling the writer what you think of her achievements.

Pages 358–371 cover
Literary Skills
Analyze and compare points of view on a topic.

Reading Skills
Draw inferences.

Writing Skills
Write a letter to one of the writers.

The King James Bible (1611): A Masterpiece by a Committee

One of the first acts of James I after he was crowned king of England was to sponsor a new translation of the Bible. There were many translations of the Bible available, but the king, like others, disliked the interpretive comments included in the existing translations. Moreover, Renaissance scholarship had made people more historically minded and sensitive to textual inaccuracies. The new translation would be checked against the most authoritative Hebrew and Greek texts available.

The King's Scholars

To produce the translation, the king appointed a team of fifty-four learned clergymen. They broke up into groups, each with a section of the Scriptures to translate and each with a pair of scholars to check the work. Seven years later, after a committee of bishops gave it a final review, the new translation was published. It has become known variously as the King James Bible, because James sponsored it; as the Authorized Version, because the Anglican Church authorized its use; and simply as the English Bible, because it has been so important to the civilization and literature of all English-speaking countries.

The Influence of the English Bible

If English-speaking people living before our time read anything, they read the English Bible. And if they read nothing themselves, they regularly heard the Bible read in church. For nearly four centuries most writers in English have been influenced, consciously or unconsciously, by the English Bible. They have quoted it, echoed it, paraphrased it, alluded to it, imitated it, and retold its fascinating stories over and over.

Everyday English speech is full of words and phrases from the English Bible: "lovingkindness," "tender mercy," "long-suffering." We "cast pearls before swine" and "wait until the eleventh hour" before acting. We speak of the "wisdom of Solomon" and the "patience of Job." Many biblical words (such as *scapegoat*) are by now so embedded in our language that we use them without knowing we are using biblical language.

Today, the King James Bible stands with Shakespeare as an exemplar of English when the language was, as many people believe, more flexible and eloquent than at any other time, and more capable of stirring people's hearts and minds.

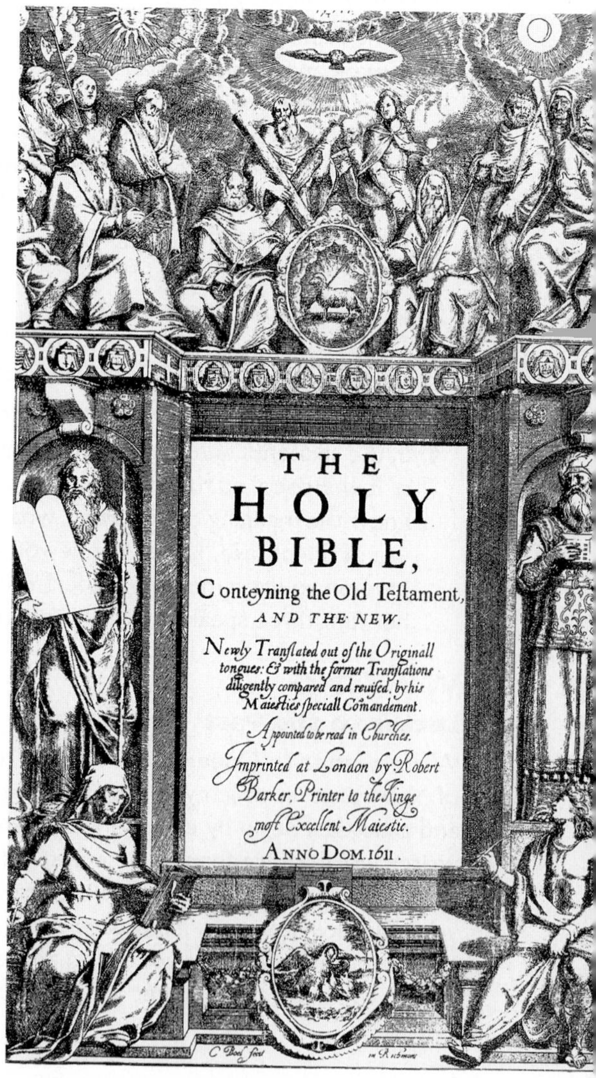

THE
HOLY
BIBLE,
Conteyning the Old Teſtament,
AND THE NEW.
Newly Tranſlated out of the Originall
tongues: & with the former Tranſlations
diligently compared and reuiſed, by his
Maieſties ſpeciall Cōmandement.
Appointed to be read in Churches.
Imprinted at London by Robert
Barker, Printer to the Kings
moſt Excellent Maieſtie.
ANNO DOM. 1611.

Title page from the King James Bible (1611). Printed by Robert Barker, London.

The Pierpont Morgan Library, NY.

Illuminated *P* (detail) (c. 1500) from a Flemish Bible.

Victoria and Albert Museum, London.

salms: Worship Through Poetry

The Bible is full of poetry. Every book of it contains poems or fragments of poems inserted into the prose, and much of the prose itself is highly rhythmical. One book, Psalms, consists entirely of poems, some of which were set to music and sung during worship services in the ancient Temple in Jerusalem. The Book of Psalms preserves 150 of these songs, a fraction of the total number that the ancient Hebrews knew and sang. Psalms were used as hymnals and included songs appropriate for many types of worship: thanksgiving, lament, praise, and devotion. Modern scholars now agree that the psalms were written by many authors over many centuries, but seventy-three of the psalms are said to be "for David" or "concerning David," the heroic Hebrew king.

Faithful to the source. In English a collection of psalms is called a psalter (the *p* is silent in both *psalm* and *psalter*). (In Hebrew the name for the collection is *Tehillim,* or "songs of praise.") There have been dozens of English psalters besides the one in the King James Bible, but none of them has lasted so well and so long. King James's translators did not try to impose rhyme on their versions because there is no rhyme in the originals. Instead, they imitated such Hebrew poetic devices as **repetition** and **parallel structure** (the use of sentences or phrases similar in structure):

> Let the floods clap their hands,
> Let the hills be joyful together.
> —Psalm 98:8

The psalmists were fond of saying essentially the same thing twice, in different words ("thy rod and thy staff" in Psalm 23). The King James Bible uses the numbering of the ancient Hebrew manuscripts; some other Bibles use a different numbering system, derived from a Greek translation of the Hebrew, and these Bibles have an extra psalm, number 151.

Ancient yet modern. Biblical poetry, then, is much like modern free verse in that it does not have rhyme and meter but it does have other patterns of repetition, balance, antithesis, and parallelism. Metaphors and similes abound, and so do images drawn from nature and everyday experience:

> My God, in him will I trust.
> Surely he shall deliver thee from the snare of the fowler,
> And from the noisome pestilence.
> He shall cover thee with his feathers,
> And under his wings shalt thou trust:
> His truth shall be thy shield and buckler.
> Thou shalt not be afraid for the terror by night;
> Nor for the arrow that flieth by day;
> Nor for the pestilence that walketh in darkness;
> Nor for the destruction that wasteth at noonday.
> —Psalm 91:2–6

Before You Read

Psalms 23 *and* 137

Make the Connection

You may be familiar with one or both of the following psalms. Psalm 23 is a song of trust that affirms the speaker's confidence in God. Psalm 137 is a cry from the heart of the speaker, a captive Israelite in Babylon who is experiencing life's perils firsthand.

What troubling events in modern history might inspire people to seek the comforting presence of God?

Literary Focus

Parallelism

Parallelism is the repetition of words, phrases, or sentences that have the same grammatical structure or restate a similar idea. Parallelism is common in literature meant to be sung or recited, such as the poems in the Bible's Book of Psalms. Instead of relying on rhyme, meter, or other modern poetic devices, the psalms use parallel structure to create a sense of rhythm, balance, and order; to show the relationships among ideas; and to heighten emotional impact.

Parallelism is the repetition of words, phrases, or sentences that have the same grammatical structure or restate a similar idea.

For more on Parallelism, see the Handbook of Literary and Historical Terms.

Background

The Book of Psalms is the Bible's songbook. The Greek word *psalmos*, which means "plucking of strings," tells us that the poems were sung to musical accompaniment. The Hebrew title of the book, *Tehillim,* means "songs of praise." The book's 150 lyric poems express not only praise, however, but a wide range of emotions. They evoke everything from the heights of joy and gratitude to the depths of anguish and bitterness.

Some, like Psalm 137, connect directly to the history of the people of Israel. In the sixth century B.C., King Nebuchadnezzar of Babylonia conquered Jerusalem and deported many Israelites to his own capital, Babylon. (Ancient Babylon is now a ruin; it lies on the Euphrates River south of Baghdad, in Iraq.)

Nebuchadnezzar admires the Hanging Gardens of Babylon. Illustration by E. Wallcousins from *Myths of Babylonia and Assyria.*

Mary Evans Picture Library.

Literary Skills
Understand the use of parallelism.

Psalm 23 is probably the best-known religious poem in the Western world. The opening verses, comparing God to a shepherd, use the kind of pastoral imagery found throughout the Bible. (This song was sung by a pastoral people, so the comparison of the Lord to a shepherd is particularly appropriate.) Then the metaphors in the psalm change, and the Lord becomes a host providing a banquet for the speaker, whose enemies watch him enviously as he eats, not daring to harm him. Among the images of the poem, there is also a suggestion of the speaker as a pilgrim traveling through a dangerous world.

Shepherds. Bas-relief on the lintel over the west portal of Chartres Cathedral in France.

Chartres Cathedral, France.

Psalm 23

The Lord is my shepherd; I shall not want.
He maketh me to lie down in green pastures:
He leadeth me beside the still waters.
He restoreth my soul:
He leadeth me in the paths of righteousness for his name's sake.°
Yea, though I walk through the valley of the shadow of death,
I will fear no evil: For thou art with me;
Thy rod and thy staff they comfort me.
Thou preparest a table before me in the presence of mine
    enemies:
Thou anointest my head with oil; my cup runneth over.
Surely goodness and mercy shall follow me all the days of my life:
And I will dwell in the house of the Lord forever.

5. his name's sake: That is, he will live up to his name as shepherd.

Clusters of stone ruins from ancient Babylon, now Iraq.

Nik Wheeler/Black Star Publishing/ Picture Quest.

This is a song of entreaty on the occasion of a national catastrophe: Many Israelites are being held captive in Babylon. This lament over a remembered home has been recited by many captives in the thousands of years since it was first sung in ancient Babylon.

The speaker of Psalm 137 is a captive Israelite, bitterly lamenting his people's exile. The Babylonians have asked their captives to sing to entertain them, but what do the captives have to sing about?

Psalm 137

By the rivers of Babylon, there we sat down, yea, we wept,
When we remembered Zion.°
We hanged our harps
Upon the willows in the midst thereof.
For there they that carried us away captive required of us a song;
And they that wasted us required of us mirth,
Saying, "Sing us one of the songs of Zion."
How shall we sing the Lord's song
In a strange land?
If I forget thee, O Jerusalem,
Let my right hand forget her cunning.
If I do not remember thee,
Let my tongue cleave° to the roof of my mouth;
If I prefer not Jerusalem above my chief joy.
Remember, O Lord, the children of Edom° in the day of
    Jerusalem;
Who said, "Raze it,° raze it, even to the foundation thereof."
O daughter of Babylon,° who art to be destroyed;
Happy shall he be, that rewardeth thee
As thou hast served us.
Happy shall he be, that taketh
And dasheth thy little ones against the stones.

2. Zion: a hill in Jerusalem that is often a symbol for the whole of Israel.

13. cleave *v.:* adhere; stick.

15. children of Edom: The Edomites, neighbors of the Israelites, rejoiced when the Israelites' kingdom was conquered and most of its population was deported.

16. Raze it: Level it to the ground.

17. daughter of Babylon: the Babylonian people.

Response and Analysis

Thinking Critically

1. An **extended metaphor** is a comparison that is developed at length, perhaps over several lines of writing or even an entire work, such as a poem. In Psalm 23, how does the speaker extend the metaphor that compares God to a shepherd? What feeling does this metaphor evoke?
2. The second **metaphor** in Psalm 23 compares God to a generous host. (In the ancient Middle East, it was a sign of hospitality to anoint a guest's head and dusty feet with oil.) How does the speaker extend this metaphor of God as a gracious host, with the speaker as his guest?
3. Which lines of Psalm 23 hint at the idea that life is a perilous journey?
4. Psalm 23 is often read at funerals or memorial services. Why might people find the images in the psalm consoling?
5. The speaker in Psalm 137 is both homesick and vengeful. Which lines convey each of these emotions? How do you react to the final line of the psalm?
6. On what occasion might Psalm 137 be sung? Does the text of the psalm have any relevance for people today?
7. Both psalms contain examples of **parallelism,** or parallel structure—places where the same grammatical structure is repeated or an idea is restated in different words. Read aloud at least one example of parallelism in each psalm.

WRITING

Psalm Similarities

The version of Psalm 23 that follows appeared in a psalter translated by the Massachusetts Puritans and published in the *Bay Psalm Book* (1640). In a brief **essay, compare and contrast** this version with the version in the King James Bible. Tell which version you prefer and why, using examples from each text.

Psalm 23

The Lord to me a shepherd is;
want therefor shall not I.
He in the folds of tender grass
doth cause me down to lie.
To waters calm me gently leads,
restore my soul doth he;
He doth in paths of righteousness for his name's sake lead
me.
Yea, though in valley of death's
shade I walk, none ill I'll fear,
Because thou art with me; thy rod
and staff my comfort are.
For me a table thou hast spread in
presence of my foes;
Thou dost anoint my head with
oil; my cup it overflows.
Goodness and mercy surely shall
all my days follow me.
And in the Lord's house I shall
dwell so long as days shall be.

Before you begin writing, gather your details in a chart like the following one.

	King James	Bay Psalms
Images		
Main idea		
Sound effects		
Syntax (sentence patterns)		

Literary Skills Analyze the use of parallelism.

Writing Skills Write an essay comparing and contrasting two versions of a psalm.

Before You Read

The Parable of the Prodigal Son

Make the Connection

Quickwrite

The Bible contains about forty **parables,** or moral lessons, which occur in all four Gospels. They are attributed to Jesus, who, like other Jewish teachers, used them to make his messages clear. The parables of Jesus tend to be down-to-earth and easy to grasp on a literal level. They involve ordinary events that people of his time could relate to: a shepherd searching for a sheep that has strayed from the flock; sleeping bridesmaids who are unprepared for the arriving bridal party; a poor woman who loses a coin. The underlying messages of these parables concern deep truths about conduct and morality.

Jot down brief notes about a modern situation that would make a good parable—an anecdote that teaches a lesson about life. It may be something you have experienced or something you have heard about.

Literary Focus

Parable

A **parable** is a short, allegorical story that teaches a moral or religious lesson about life. The word *parable* comes from a Greek word meaning "comparison; analogy." Parables convey their lessons about life through the use of **allegory:** The simple characters, places, and events in the story symbolize broader, more complex concepts. Because symbols can be interpreted in multiple ways, even a brief allegory can yield more than one meaning. The biblical parables draw their lessons from characters and situations that would have been familiar to people of Jesus' time: a shepherd and his lost sheep, a problem son, a victim of a highway robbery.

Literary Skills
Understand the characteristics of parables.

A **parable** is a short, allegorical story that teaches a moral lesson about life.

For more on Parable, see the Handbook of Literary and Historical Terms.

Background

In ancient Israel—Jesus' homeland—the oldest son in a family would inherit a double share of his father's wealth and become the head of the family upon his father's death. In this parable we encounter a family situation that would have been common: The elder son is set to receive two thirds of his father's estate, and the younger son, one third. During his lifetime a father was under no obligation to divide up his estate or cash in any part of it for the sake of his sons.

You may notice that the word *prodigal,* used for centuries to identify this parable, never occurs in the story itself. The word usually means "recklessly extravagant; wasteful," but it can also mean "lavish; abundant." As you read "The Parable of the Prodigal Son," keep these different meanings in mind. Determine which characters could be called prodigal and why.

The Prodigal Son (1975–1976) by Marc Chagall.

The Parable of the Prodigal Son

And he[1] said, A certain man had two sons:

And the younger of them said to his father, Father, give me the portion of goods that falleth to me. And he divided unto them his living.

And not many days after the younger son gathered all together, and took his journey into a far country, and there wasted his substance with riotous living.

And when he had spent all, there arose a mighty famine in that land; and he began to be in want.

And he went and joined himself to a citizen of that country; and he sent him into his fields to feed swine.[2]

And he would fain have filled his belly with the husks that the swine did eat: and no man gave unto him.

And when he came to himself, he said, How many hired servants of my father's have bread enough and to spare, and I perish with hunger!

I will arise and go to my father, and will say unto him, Father, I have sinned against heaven, and before thee,

And am no more worthy to be called thy son: make me as one of thy hired servants.

And he arose, and came to his father. But when he was yet a great way off, his father saw him, and had compassion, and ran, and fell on his neck, and kissed him.

And the son said unto him, Father, I have sinned against heaven, and in thy sight, and am no more worthy to be called thy son.

But the father said to his servants, Bring forth the best robe, and put it on him; and put a ring on his hand, and shoes on his feet:

And bring hither the fatted calf, and kill it; and let us eat, and be merry:

For this my son was dead, and is alive again; he was lost, and is found. And they began to be merry.

Now his elder son was in the field: and as he came and drew nigh to the house, he heard musick and dancing.

And he called one of the servants, and asked what these things meant.

And he said unto him, Thy brother is come; and thy father hath killed the fatted calf, because he hath received him safe and sound.

And he was angry, and would not go in: therefore came his father out, and intreated him.

And he answering said to his father, Lo, these many years do I serve thee, neither transgressed I at any time thy commandment: and yet thou never gavest me a kid,[3] that I might make merry with my friends:

But as soon as this thy son was come, which hath devoured thy living with harlots,[4] thou hast killed for him the fatted calf.

And he said unto him, Son, thou art ever with me, and all that I have is thine.

It was meet that we should make merry, and be glad: for this thy brother was dead, and is alive again; and was lost, and is found.

—Luke 15:11–32

1. **he:** Jesus.

2. **swine** *n.:* pigs. The ancient Israelites considered swine ritually taboo, or unclean, and they avoided any contact with them. Tending pigs would thus have been considered degrading work.

The Prodigal Son (detail) (1975–1976) by Marc Chagall.

3. **kid** *n.:* baby goat.

4. **harlots** *n. pl.:* prostitutes.

Response and Analysis

Reading Check

1. How does the younger son acquire his money? How does he then lose it?
2. Why does the younger son decide to return home?
3. What is his father's reaction to the younger son's return? What is his brother's reaction?

Thinking Critically

4. At the end of the **parable,** whose position do you understand better, that of the father or that of the elder son? Why?
5. As an **allegory** this parable can be understood on both a literal and a symbolic level. The literal level concerns two sons, an inheritance, and a loving father. On that level, state in your own words the **theme** of the story—the comment it makes about life.
6. On a **symbolic** level this parable carries religious messages about God, sin, and forgiveness. On that level the father symbolizes God, and his welcoming attitude symbolizes forgiveness. What do the following elements of the allegory most probably symbolize?
   - the younger son
   - working as a swineherd
   - the elder son's resentment
7. What contemporary situations could this parable apply to?

Literary Criticism

8. Some commentators point out that the title "The Parable of the Prodigal Son" is misleading—because the plot hinges on the actions of a prodigal *father* who gives lavishly of his goods and love to *both* of his sons. Consider all of the meanings of the word *prodigal.* How do they apply to the father? Do they apply more to the son than to the father? How might readers' perceptions of the story change if it were called "The Parable of the Prodigal Parent"?

WRITING

Plotting a Parable

Using your Quickwrite notes as a basis, write a modern **parable.** To be sure that the characters and plot of your parable carry both literal and symbolic meanings, make a chart of each element of the story and its symbolic meaning before you write.

You may want to rewrite "The Parable of the Prodigal Son" instead, using language, situations, and references that a modern reader would understand. For example, your setting might be a high school, your characters might be female instead of male, and so on. To plan your update, make a chart like the one below, listing the features of the original parable, their allegorical meanings, and the features of the updated parable. The allegorical meanings should remain the same when you update the various features.

Features of Original Parable	Allegorical Meaning	Features of Updated Parable
Characters:		Characters:
Places:		Places:
Events:		Events:

Literary Skills Analyze the characteristics of parables.

Writing Skills Write a modern parable.

Connecting to World Literature

Worlds of Wisdom: Wisdom Literature

c. 1213–1292
Saadi lives

1191
Zen is introduced to Japan

651–652
The Koran is written

c. 300 B.C.–c. A.D. 300
The *Bhagavad-Gita* is written

c. 400–c. 100 B.C.
Taoist anecdotes are created

479 B.C.
Confucius dies

c. 571 B.C.
Lao Tzu is born

1000–100 B.C.
Hebrew Bible is written and assembled

You have just read two psalms and a parable from the King James Bible. In this Connecting to World Literature feature, you will read excerpts from wisdom literature from around the world:

From age to age and culture to culture, people have wrestled with the same fundamental questions: What is the meaning of life? How can I become my truest self? What is justice? What is my place in the grand scheme of things?

Society after society has distilled its answers to such questions to create "wisdom literature"—poems, stories, and sayings that provide guidance on everything from rearing children to preparing for the afterlife. Wisdom literature thus serves a **didactic,** or instructional, purpose: It teaches people how to live.

Oral Roots, Sacred Roots

The literary forms represented in this feature—fable, parable, scripture, anecdote, and proverb—spring from the **oral tradition.** Just as Jesus wrote no books, neither did the Taoist teachers, Confucius, or the masters of Zen Buddhism. Their disciples wrote down their teachings for later ages and, in doing so, retained many features of their masters' oral styles. Thus you will find wisdom literature rich in rhetorical techniques, such as **parallelism, repetition,** and **figures of speech.**

Like the wisdom literature in the Bible, many of these selections have a **sacred,** or religious, context. For example, the Arabic Koran, the holy book of the Islamic faith, contains didactic writings that teach people how to relate to God and how to live a moral life.

Literary Skills
Compare wisdom literature from different cultures and literary periods.

Scene from the life of Confucius and his disciples (early 18th century). Ink, watercolor, and sepia wash.

Bibliothèque Nationale, Paris, France/Giraudon-Bridgeman Art Library.

Revealed Truths and Hidden Meanings

Both sacred and secular wisdom may be taught indirectly through stories. A **parable**—from a Greek word meaning "comparison; analogy"—is a brief allegorical story that teaches a moral, or lesson, about life. (See page 378.) Jesus and the twelfth-century masters of Zen Buddhism often taught by means of parables.

An **anecdote** is another type of brief story. An anecdote usually focuses on a single interesting incident or event, often one that reveals the character of an important person. Taoist teachers in China and Sufi masters in Persia often taught by means of anecdotes.

Witty Wisdom

Much of the world's wisdom is condensed into witty one-liners. **Proverbs, aphorisms, axioms,** and **maxims** are all brief sayings—sometimes blunt and to the point, sometimes poetic and obscure. These sayings are widely accepted as true—for example, "Don't cry over spilled milk." Similar proverbs pop up the world over. For instance, English speakers say, "A bird in the hand is worth two in the bush," while the Ashanti people of Ghana say, "One bird in your hand is worth ten birds in the sky." Proverbs sometimes contradict one another: "Absence makes the heart grow fonder" and "Out of sight, out of mind" offer totally opposing views, yet taken separately, each proverb expresses a truth about human nature.

Reflecting its roots, wisdom literature—especially the proverb—employs a variety of catchy oral techniques and literary devices, such as **metaphor**

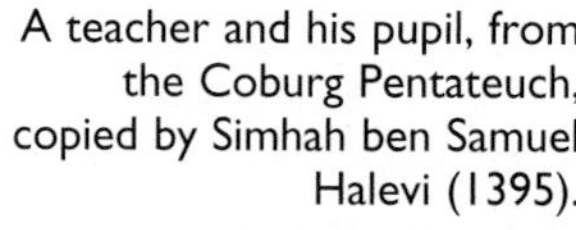

A teacher and his pupil, from the Coburg Pentateuch, copied by Simhah ben Samuel Halevi (1395).

British Library, London, UK/ The Bridgeman Art Library.

("The squeaky wheel gets the grease"), **alliteration** ("It takes two to tango"), **parallelism** ("The bigger they are, the harder they fall"), and **rhyme** ("Birds of a feather flock together").

Lasting Legacy

Many classics of Eastern wisdom, from Islamic Sufi poetry to Zen parables, have gained immense popularity in the West. The Chinese *Tao Te Ching* and the Indian *Bhagavad-Gita,* along with the Bible, have been translated more often than any other books in the world. How do these works manage to transcend barriers of place, time, and culture? A partial answer lies in the beauty of their expression: The sayings, poems, and stories speak timeless truths in timeless voices.

A deeper answer lies in the sheer commonality of human experience. In the sixth century B.C., Confucius taught, "Never do to others what you would not like them to do to you." In the first century B.C., Rabbi Hillel of Israel taught, "What is hateful to you, do not do to your neighbor." Christians attribute another version of the same teaching to Jesus and call it the golden rule: "Do unto others as you would have them do unto you."

Before You Read

Worlds of Wisdom

Make the Connection

Probably every society that has ever existed on earth has developed its own sets of instructions for how to lead a good life: how we should conduct ourselves in everyday life, how we should deal with the difficulties that confront us, how we can find meaning and purpose in our existence. Where do we look today for answers to these and other profound human questions? What is the wisdom literature of contemporary life? How is it different from—or the same as—the wisdom literature that has come down to us from the past?

Literary Focus

Didactic Literature

A literary work that is meant to instruct, give advice, or convey a philosophy or a moral message is known as **didactic literature.** A great deal of the world's wisdom literature—works as diverse as the Taoist anecdotes and the biblical parables—comes in the form of sacred texts. Secular works such as proverbs, fables, anecdotes, folk tales, and maxims can also serve as didactic literature. Most didactic literature ultimately derives from an oral tradition.

> **Didactic literature** is literature that instructs or conveys a philosophy or moral message.
>
> *For more on Didactic Literature, see the Handbook of Literary and Historical Terms.*

The Ascent of the Prophet Mohammed to Heaven, from a sixteenth-century manuscript. Gouache, ink, and gold on paper.

Art Resource, New York.

Literary Skills
Understand the characteristics of didactic literature.

The Koran, the holy book of Islam, is believed to contain God's revelation to Mohammed by the angel Gabriel. The text was first written down in Arabic in the middle of the seventh century. (Koran—qu'ran—is an Arabic word meaning "recitation," showing that the text is believed to be the actual transcript of God's revelations to Mohammed.) The central theme of the Koran is that there is only one all-powerful God—Allah—who created the world. This God is merciful and compassionate, but he is also the God of Judgment Day. The proper response to Allah is to submit to his will (the word Islam *means "submission," and one who accepts Islam is a Muslim, or "one who submits to God"), be generous to the poor, and lead an upright life. Every individual has a choice between following the good, which leads to an afterlife of eternal bliss, or giving in to evil, which leads to eternal damnation.*

The Koran consists of 114 suras, or chapters. Each sura begins with the invocation "In the Name of Allah, the Compassionate, the Merciful." Although the Koran has been translated into various languages, including English, translations are considered paraphrases of the original Arabic and thus cannot be used for religious ceremonies.

Qur'an manuscript, Islamic, Eastern Islamic Lands (11th century). Ht. 12⅞ in. (32.7 cm) W. 9 in. (22.9 cm).

The Metropolitan Museum of Art, Rogers Fund, 1940 (40.164.2a).

Night

from the Koran

translated by N. J. Dawood

In the Name of Allah, the Compassionate, the Merciful

By the night, when she lets fall her darkness, and by the radiant day! By Him that created the male and the female, your endeavors have different ends!

For him that gives in charity and guards himself against evil and believes in goodness, We shall smooth the path of salvation; but for him that neither gives nor takes and disbelieves in goodness, We shall smooth the path of affliction. When he breathes his last, his riches will not avail him.

It is for Us to give guidance. Ours is the life of this world, Ours the life to come. I warn you, then, of the blazing fire, in which none shall burn save the hardened sinner, who denies the truth and gives no heed. But the good man who purifies himself by almsgiving[1] shall keep away from it: and so shall he that does good works for the sake of the Most High only, not in recompense[2] for a favor. Such men shall be content. ■

1. **almsgiving** *n.:* performing deeds of charity.
2. **recompense** *n.:* repayment.

The Bhagavad-Gita, *literally "Song of the Lord," is an episode that interrupts the Indian epic* Mahabharata*—perhaps the longest poem ever composed in any language. The* Gita, *as it is affectionately known, consists of a dialogue between a character from the main epic, Arjuna, and his charioteer, Krishna (who is both Arjuna's human brother-in-law and—unbeknownst to Arjuna—the earthly embodiment of Vishnu, one of the most important of the Hindu gods). Their argument takes place just before a great battle with Arjuna's relatives.*

The Gita *has been called the "bedside book" of every pious Hindu, and the teachings of this ancient poem played a major role in shaping the philosophy of Mahatma Gandhi (1869–1948), the charismatic social reformer who led India to independence from Britain in 1947. The teachings of the* Gita *also have indirectly but critically affected modern American society: Gandhi's philosophy of nonviolent protest profoundly influenced Martin Luther King, Jr., during the civil rights movement of the 1960s.*

The Gita *is divided into eighteen sections, or "teachings," and is a fine example of* ***didactic verse,*** *or poetry meant to convey a philosophy. In this excerpt, Krishna urges Arjuna to fulfill his* dharma, *or sacred duty, by waging battle, but Arjuna hesitates to fight members of his family.*

from Philosophy and Spiritual Discipline

from the Bhagavad-Gita
translated by Barbara Stoler Miller

Lord Krishna

When he gives up desires in his mind,
is content with the self within himself,
then he is said to be a man
whose insight is sure, Arjuna.

When suffering does not disturb his mind,
when his craving for pleasures has
vanished,
when attraction, fear, and anger are gone,
he is called a sage whose thought is sure.

When he shows no preference
in fortune or misfortune
and neither exults nor hates,
his insight is sure.

When, like a tortoise retracting
its limbs, he withdraws his senses
completely from sensuous objects,
his insight is sure.

Arjuna and His Charioteer Lord Krsna Confront Carna (detail) Indian, Darhwal School.
Philadelphia Museum of Art: Purchased with the Edith H. Bell Fund 1975.

Sensuous objects fade
when the embodied self abstains from
food;
the taste lingers, but it too fades
in the vision of higher truth.

Even when a man of wisdom
tries to control them, Arjuna,
the bewildering senses
attack his mind with violence.

Controlling them all,
with discipline he should focus on me;
when his senses are under control,
his insight is sure.

Brooding about sensuous objects
makes attachment to them grow;
from attachment desire arises,
from desire anger is born.

From anger comes confusion;
from confusion memory lapses;
from broken memory understanding is
lost;
from loss of understanding, he is ruined.

But a man of inner strength
whose senses experience objects
without attraction and hatred,
in self-control, finds serenity.

The parables illustrating the insights of Zen Buddhism are drawn from an austere philosophical and religious tradition within Buddhism that originated in China and then flowered in Japan starting in the twelfth century. The object of Zen is to free the mind of everyday, conventional logic through meditation. Instead of imparting facts in a clear and logical way, the Zen master first tries to confuse his students, to force them to abandon all preconceived notions of what knowledge is. He might, for example, ask a nonsensical question that has no answer, such as "What is the sound of one hand clapping?" or "What did your face look like before you were born?" This technique prepares the students to understand the lessons inherent in these deceptively simple ***parables,*** *or brief allegorical stories that teach lessons or morals about life.*

Zen Parables

compiled by **Paul Reps**

The Moon Cannot Be Stolen

Ryokan, a Zen master, lived the simplest kind of life in a little hut at the foot of a mountain. One evening a thief visited the hut only to discover there was nothing in it to steal.

Ryokan returned and caught him. "You may have come a long way to visit me," he told the prowler, "and you should not return empty-handed. Please take my clothes as a gift."

The thief was bewildered. He took the clothes and slunk away.

Ryokan sat naked, watching the moon. "Poor fellow," he mused, "I wish I could give him this beautiful moon."

Temper

A Zen student came to Bankei and complained: "Master, I have an ungovernable temper. How can I cure it?"

"You have something very strange," replied Bankei. "Let me see what you have."

"Just now I cannot show it to you," replied the other.

"When can you show it to me?" asked Bankei.

"It arises unexpectedly," replied the student.

"Then," concluded Bankei, "it must not be your own true nature. If it were, you could show it to me at any time. When you were born, you did not have it, and your parents did not give it to you. Think that over."

The Gates of Paradise

A soldier named Nobushige came to Hakuin, and asked: "Is there really a paradise and a hell?"

"Who are you?" inquired Hakuin.

"I am a samurai," the warrior replied.

"You, a soldier!" exclaimed Hakuin. "What kind of ruler would have you as his guard? Your face looks like that of a beggar."

Nobushige became so angry that he began to draw his sword, but Hakuin continued: "So you have a sword! Your weapon is probably much too dull to cut off my head."

As Nobushige drew his sword, Hakuin remarked: "Here open the gates of hell!"

At these words the samurai, perceiving the master's discipline, sheathed his sword and bowed.

"Here open the gates of paradise," said Hakuin.

The First Principle

When one goes to Obaku temple in Kyoto, he sees carved over the gate the words "The First Principle." The letters are unusually large, and those who appreciate calligraphy° always admire them as being a masterpiece. They were drawn by Kosen two hundred years ago.

When the master drew them he did so on paper, from which workmen made the larger carving in wood. As Kosen sketched the letters, a bold pupil was with him who had made several gallons of ink for the calligraphy and who never failed to criticize his master's work.

° **calligraphy** *n.:* the art of beautiful handwriting.

"That is not good," he told Kosen after the first effort.

"How is that one?"

"Poor. Worse than before," pronounced the pupil.

Kosen patiently wrote one sheet after another until eighty-four First Principles had accumulated, still without the approval of the pupil.

Then, when the young man stepped outside for a few moments, Kosen thought: "Now is my chance to escape his keen eye," and he wrote hurriedly, with a mind free from distraction:

"The First Principle."

"A masterpiece," pronounced the pupil. ■

Confucius, the founder of an important and lasting Chinese philosophical system, left no written works. After his death, in around 479 B.C., his disciples gathered his sayings in a collection known as The Analects*—"selected sayings." The sayings in* The Analects *range from brief statements, or* ***maxims,*** *to more extended dialogues between Confucius and his students. Confucius, who followed the ancient "way of goodness," believed that studying ancient teachings enabled people to join the continuous chain of minds from the past to their own time.*

In The Analects, *Confucius—called "the Master"—speaks about the concept of* chung-yung, *usually translated as "the golden mean," an ideal of universal moral and social harmony.* The Analects *instructs the individual on how to achieve moderation in all things through moral education, the building of a harmonious family life, and the development of virtues such as loyalty, obedience, and integrity. Confucius also emphasizes filial piety—the carrying out of basic obligations to one's living parents or dead ancestors.*

from The Analects of Confucius

translated and annotated by Arthur Waley

The Master said, "Yu, shall I teach you what knowledge is? When you know a thing, to recognize that you know it, and when you do not know a thing, to recognize that you do not know it. That is knowledge."

The Master said, "Even when walking in a party of no more than three I can always be certain of learning from those I am with. There will be good qualities that I can select for imitation and bad ones that will teach me what requires correction in myself."

Tzu-kung asked, saying, "Is there any single saying that one can act upon all day and every day?" The Master said, "Perhaps the saying about consideration: 'Never do to others what you would not like them to do to you.'" ■

A portrait of Confucius carved on a stone stele, from the Tang dynasty (618–906).

The Tao Te Ching *(dou dā jiŋ), or "Classic of the Way of Power," is a brief collection of sayings and poetry that teach the nature of Taoism. It is attributed to the philosopher Lao Tzu (lou'dzu'), who, according to legend, was born as an old, bearded, white-haired man and lived to the ripe old age of 160. The* Tao Te Ching *was intended to provide guidance for rulers who wished to govern according to* Tao, *or "the Way." Passages from the* Tao Te Ching, *like those in the Confucian* Analects, *often teach through* ***maxims,*** *or brief sayings about life, and use parallel language and other repetitive devices. The heart of the* Tao Te Ching *is the presence of "the Master" who has become one with the* Tao.

Broadly defined, Taoism consists of the joyful acceptance of life and a willingness to yield to the natural world, becoming one with it. Confucianism, with which it is often contrasted, emphasizes the individual's obligation to act responsibly and sensibly, carrying out prescribed duties to family and society. Chinese people see the two philosophies as offering complementary, rather than opposing, views.

Mountain landscape (16th century). Silk scroll.

from the Tao Te Ching

Lao Tzu

translated by **Stephen Mitchell**

The supreme good is like water,
which nourishes all things without trying to.
It is content with the low places that people disdain.
Thus it is like the Tao.

In dwelling, live close to the ground.
In thinking, keep to the simple.
In conflict, be fair and generous.
In governing, don't try to control.
In work, do what you enjoy.
In family life, be completely present.

When you are content to be simply yourself
and don't compare or compete,
everybody will respect you.

Followers of Taoism have long used ***anecdotes,*** *or brief stories, to convey indirectly the teachings of their philosophy. The stories are intended to impart the spiritual teachings of Taoism, with its focus on oneness with the world and the unchangeable nature of the Way.*

Taoist Anecdotes

translated and edited by **Moss Roberts**

Gold, Gold

Many, many years ago there was a man of the land of Ch'i who had a great passion for gold. One day at the crack of dawn he went to the market—straight to the gold dealers' stalls, where he snatched some gold and ran. The market guards soon caught him. "With so many people around, how did you expect to get away with it?" a guard asked.

"When I took it," he replied, "I saw only the gold, not the people."

—Lieh Tzu

A Clever Judge

In the days when Ch'en Shu-ku was a magistrate in Chienchou, there was a man who had lost an article of some value. A number of people were arrested, but no one could discover exactly who the thief was. So Shu-ku laid a trap for the suspects. "I know of a temple," he told them, "whose bell can tell a thief from an honest man. It has great spiritual powers."

The magistrate had the bell fetched and reverently enshrined in a rear chamber. Then he had the suspects brought before the bell to stand and testify to their guilt or innocence. He explained to them that if an innocent man touched the bell it would remain silent, but that if the man was guilty it would ring out.

Then the magistrate led his staff in solemn worship to the bell. The sacrifices concluded, he had the bell placed behind a curtain, while one of his assistants secretly smeared it with ink. After a time he took the suspects to the bell and had each one in turn extend his hands through the curtain and touch the bell. As each man withdrew his hands, Shu-ku examined them. Everyone's hands were stained except for those of one man, who confessed to the theft under questioning. He had not dared touch the bell for fear it would ring. ■

—Chang Shih-nan

Homage to the First Principle (detail) (c. 1325).
Royal Ontario Museum/CORBIS.

The poet Saadi, whose real name was Musharrif Od-Din Muslih Od-Din, lived in thirteenth-century Persia (now Iran). As a follower of Sufism (so͞o'fiz'əm), a mystical sect of Islam, he believed in the holiness of all creation. His witty, practical sayings and lush lyrics made him one of Persia's best-loved poets.

For Sufis, Sufism is not only a religion or a philosophy, but also a way of life. Sufi mystics withdrew from the material world and devoted themselves to a stark, homeless existence, begging for their living and wandering from place to place as they meditated on God's love. Even today, Sufis are not attached to belongings and places, and they are not driven by concerns of time, money, or achievement. They concentrate instead on the development of the human mind and on reaching a higher plane of understanding through a gradual process of thought and practice.

Sayings of Saadi

translated by **Idries Shah**

The Unfed Dervish

When I see the poor dervish° unfed
My own food is pain and poison to me.

Information and Knowledge

However much you study, you cannot know
without action.
A donkey laden with books is neither an
intellectual nor a wise man.
Empty of essence, what learning has he—
Whether upon him is firewood or book?

The Elephant Keeper

Make no friendship with an elephant keeper
If you have no room to entertain an elephant.

° **dervish** *n.:* Muslim monk dedicated to a life of poverty.

Safety and Riches

Deep in the sea are riches beyond compare.
But if you seek safety, it is on the shore.

The Fox and the Camels

A fox was seen running away in terror. Someone asked what was troubling it. The fox answered: "They are taking camels for forced labor." "Fool!" he was told, "the fate of camels has nothing to do with you, who do not even look like one." "Silence!" said the fox, "for if an intriguer were to state that I was a camel, *who* would work for my release?" ■

Portrait of a Sufi, Islamic, India, Deccan probably Bijapur, Adil Shahi period (1490–1686) (First quarter of 17th century). Ink, colors and gold on paper: Page: 15⅛ × 9¾ in. (38.4 × 24.8 cm) Painting 8⅞ × 9¾ in. (22.6 × 24.8 cm).

In the oral literatures of Africa, ***proverbs*** *represent a poetic form that achieves great depth of meaning using very few words. In cultures that have no written literature, proverbs function as the distilled essence of a people's values and knowledge. They are used to settle legal disputes, resolve ethical dilemmas, and teach children the philosophy of their people. Because proverbs often contain puns, rhymes, and clever allusions, they also provide entertainment. Like poetry, they compress complicated ideas into a few thoughtfully crafted words. The following proverbs are from several different African cultures.*

An Ashanti head. The Ashanti are famous for their goldwork.

Werner Forman Archive, Wallace Collection, London/Art Resource, New York.

African Proverbs

compiled by **Charlotte** *and* **Wolf Leslau**

Only when you have crossed the river, can you say the crocodile has a lump on his snout.
—*Ashanti*

When a man is wealthy, he may wear an old cloth.
—*Ashanti*

The ruin of a nation begins in the homes of its people.
—*Ashanti*

He who cannot dance will say: "The drum is bad."
—*Ashanti*

It is the fool's sheep that break loose twice.
—*Ashanti*

No one tests the depth of a river with both feet.
—*Ashanti*

Wood may remain ten years in the water, but it will never become a crocodile.
—*Zaire*

Evil enters like a needle and spreads like an oak tree.
—*Ethiopia*

The witness of a rat is another rat.
—*Ethiopia*

The frog wanted to be as big as the elephant, and burst.
—*Ethiopia*

When the heart overflows, it comes out through the mouth.
—*Ethiopia*

When spider webs unite, they can tie up a lion.
—*Ethiopia*

Confiding a secret to an unworthy person is like carrying grain in a bag with a hole.
—*Ethiopia*

I have a cow in the sky, but cannot drink her milk.
—*Ethiopia*

If you offend, ask for pardon; if offended, forgive.
—*Ethiopia*

A fool and water will go the way they are diverted.
—*Ethiopia*

Response and Analysis

Thinking Critically

1. According to "Night," a sura from the Koran, what kind of life should a person live? What will happen to those who live otherwise?
2. **Parallelism,** or **parallel structure,** is the repetition of words or phrases that have the same grammatical structure. For example, lines 5–7 of the excerpt you read from "Philosophy and Spiritual Discipline" illustrate a parallel arrangement of words in each line. How does the poet use parallelism throughout the rest of the excerpt?
3. How would you summarize the lesson taught in the Taoist anecdote "Gold, Gold"?
4. Across cultures we find many similar ideas expressed in religious and philosophical texts. What is the main difference between Confucius's saying and the Bible's golden rule, "Do unto others as you would have them do unto you"?
5. In the passage you read from the *Tao Te Ching,* in what two ways is water described as being like the *Tao*? What must one do to gain people's respect?
6. In Saadi's saying "Information and Knowledge," what does the speaker mean by "you cannot know without action"? How would you sum up the difference between information and knowledge?
7. Name at least three of these pieces of wisdom literature that directly relate to our lives today. Think about family life, love, relationships, wisdom, and responsibility.

Literary Skills Analyze the characteristics of didactic literature. Compare and contrast wisdom literature from different countries.

Writing Skills Write an essay comparing and contrasting different views of life. Write a modern proverb.

Extending and Evaluating

8. Didactic literature often uses **metaphor** and conveys its moral or message indirectly. Do you think using metaphor illuminates the message more clearly or obscures it? Explain.

Comparing Literature

9. As with Jesus' **parables** in the Bible, readers must draw their own lessons or meanings from the Zen parables. While some of the morals are obvious, many of these parables have more than one level of meaning. Compare and contrast the lessons of the Zen parables with "The Parable of the Prodigal Son" (see page 380) or other biblical parables you are familiar with. Which parables do you find easier to understand? Why?

WRITING

Worldly Wisdom

Some of the didactic literature you have just read may express attitudes toward life that you find surprising, baffling, or in conflict with your own views and beliefs. Other pieces may strike you as accurately reflecting your beliefs. Choose one piece of wisdom literature that either expresses a view quite different from your own or reflects your own beliefs. Then, write a brief **essay** explaining the similarities or differences between your view of life and the view you find reflected in the selection.

Proverbial Truths

The most memorable proverbs stand the test of time because they address general truths. Think of a general truth of modern life, and write it in the form of a **proverb.** If you can't think of a fresh topic, try updating a well-known proverb.

John Milton
(1608–1674)

John Milton (1670) by William Faithorne. Colored engraving.

The Granger Collection, New York.

Early in his life, John Milton resolved to be a great poet. His teachers and his parents encouraged him in this ambition because they believed, as Milton said later in his life, that he "might perhaps leave something so written to aftertimes as they should not willingly let it die." Time has confirmed his parents' and his teachers' confidence: Milton's *Paradise Lost,* his major epic, is one of the most brilliant achievements in English poetry and perhaps the richest and most intricately beautiful poem in the world. Posterity has not let *Paradise Lost* die.

Fortunate Beginnings

Milton was fortunate in his parents. His father, a musician and prosperous businessman, had Milton educated at St. Paul's School (which he loved) and Cambridge University (which he hated). Indulged in every way by his parents, Milton spent the next eight years after college (1632–1640) continuing his education by himself, since he firmly believed that a poet must be a person of learning, familiar with ancient and contemporary philosophy, history, languages, and literatures.

Political Activity: Intelligent Devotion

In the 1640s, an ongoing struggle between King Charles and his Parliament came to a head. Milton, believing that a poet must be active in the life of his time, entered the paper warfare that accompanied the conflict and started publishing prose works—some of them very elaborate and a few of them very insulting—in support of the Parliamentary party. For this reason some people have referred to Milton as a Puritan, but this is a label that has only limited application to a person of Milton's stature. If he shared some of the Puritans' ideas and attitudes, such as their extreme dislike of kings and bishops, he also differed greatly from them in other important ways. For instance, he advocated divorce for incompatible married couples, and he argued that the press should be free from government censorship and interference. Although we take these freedoms for granted, most people in the seventeenth century, particularly most Puritans, considered them dangerously radical.

During part of this period, Milton served in the government of England under Oliver Cromwell, who, with the title of lord protector, ruled England after the Parliamentary party had won the Civil Wars and executed King Charles. As Latin secretary to the Council of State, Milton was responsible for translating all correspondence with foreign countries, Latin then being the language of diplomacy.

Milton's eyesight was gradually failing. By 1652, he could only distinguish day from night; otherwise, by the age of forty-four, before he had finished his life's work, Milton was totally blind.

All for Nothing: Milton the Traitor

To Milton the ideal government was a republic in which the most capable, intelligent, and virtuous men would serve as leaders. To establish and maintain such a government in England, he had devoted most of his intelligence and energy for twenty years. Then suddenly, in 1660, the cause for which he had worked so hard became totally discredited; the English recalled their dead king's son from exile and crowned him as King Charles II. Overnight Milton found himself stripped of his possessions and under arrest as a traitor. Fortunately influential friends, including the poet Andrew Marvell (see page 302), intervened, and Milton was allowed to go into retirement rather than to the scaffold. From then on, he lived in seclusion with his three daughters and his third wife, his first two wives and only son having died. By reading aloud to him, his daughters enabled him to carry on the studies he thought necessary for a poet.

A Subject Fit for an Epic

Being a poet, in Milton's view, meant imitating the great writers of antiquity, the epic poets Homer and Virgil and the Greek dramatists Aeschylus, Sophocles, and Euripides. Because those writers chose subjects drawn from their own nations' histories, Milton first pondered various English subjects for his works, especially King Arthur and the knights of the Round Table. After years of thinking and reading, however, Milton decided that King Arthur's exploits were mainly fictitious, and so he settled on subjects drawn from the Bible.

Paradise Lost: The Work of a Lifetime

Milton published *Paradise Lost* twice: first in a ten-book version in 1667 and then in twelve books in 1674, the year of his death. It's no exaggeration to say that Milton in one way or another worked on this epic all his life. He made many different plans and even once thought of it as a tragedy with Satan, the fallen archangel transformed into the chief devil, as its protagonist. In the finished poem, Satan is still very conspicuous. The first two books are devoted mainly to him, he appears frequently in Books III–X, and Milton lavishes on him some of his most glorious writing. It's not surprising, then, that many readers have regarded Satan as the secret hero of the poem, especially since he receives no such grand treatment in the Bible. Milton was "of the Devil's party without knowing it," asserted the poet and artist William Blake (see page 718). Yet this argument is convincing only to those who concentrate on certain parts of the poem and ignore the rest of it. Moreover, in literary works, evil frequently seems more interesting than good, and if any part of *Paradise Lost* fails from a literary point of view, it is Milton's portrayal of God.

A Profound Work of Art

In *Paradise Lost*, Milton took relatively few verses from the Bible, mainly Genesis, and developed them into a 10,565-line poem. He used the conventions and devices of the classical epic to make the poem a work of art; he used his great learning and wide experience of human affairs to make the poem profound. Although the poem ranges back and forth between Hell and Heaven, the most important action takes place on Earth, where the first human beings, Adam and Eve, are given the choice of obeying or disobeying God. They choose to disobey, and having done so, they accept their punishment and make the best of the life that is left to them. They are the heroes of Milton's epic, and they represent us all.

The Fallen Angels Entering Pandemonium, an illustration by John Martin for *Paradise Lost,* Book I, (exhibited 1841).
Tate Gallery, London/Art Resource, New York.

Paradise Lost: Milton's Epic

At the very beginning of *Paradise Lost,* Milton describes the content of his epic as "things unattempted yet in prose or rhyme" (line 16). His allusions to Homer, Virgil, Dante, and a host of lesser epic poets leave no doubt that Milton wanted *Paradise Lost* to sum up and also surpass all previous epics. To write his great literary epic (a **literary epic,** as distinguished from an epic from the oral tradition, is the product of the imagination of an individual writer), Milton followed the examples of the past by using the conventions of the epic. He begins with an invocation to the Muse, he starts the action *in medias res* ("in the middle of things"), and he writes about a grand subject. Above all, Milton follows the epic tradition by casting his poem in an **elevated style** suited to the grand events he is describing, using ornate language, complex syntax, multiple **allusions,** and elaborate comparisons called **epic similes.** (For more about epic conventions, see page 81.) The quality that would set Milton's epic apart, of course, was that it dealt with great deeds on a cosmic scale at the dawn of Creation—rather than with earthly matters.

A Grand Subject

There is a formal, set way to begin an epic. At the outset, an epic poet does two things: The speaker invokes the Muse (one of the nine Greek goddesses who inspire poets and other practitioners of the arts and sciences) to speak or sing through the poet; and the speaker states the subject of the poem. Milton does both these things in the first, complicated sentence (lines 1–16) of *Paradise Lost.* Grammatically, this sentence begins in line 6 with the command, "Sing, Heavenly Muse." "Sing," says Milton, and now we move back to line 1, "Of man's first disobedience," which is Adam and Eve's first act of disobedience against God, who has forbidden them to eat the fruit of a particular tree in Eden. The result, or "fruit," of their disobedience is expulsion from and loss of Paradise, another name for the Garden of Eden. Yet all is not lost, because a "greater Man" (line 4), Jesus Christ, has restored the possibility of Paradise for the human race.

Milton's Great Argument

Milton calls this argument "great" (line 24), for he is attempting to resolve a dilemma that has puzzled many people throughout the ages. On the one hand, we are told that through his Eternal Providence (line 25) God takes loving care of Creation; on the other hand, we know that there are many very bad things in the world, such as war, crime, poverty, disease, oppression, and injustice. In *Paradise Lost,* Milton asserts that God is not responsible for these evils; instead, Adam and Eve's disobedience to God "Brought death into the world, and all our woe" (line 3). God gave Adam and Eve the freedom to choose between good and evil, and the strength to resist evil; yet they chose evil, and their offspring—all of us—have suffered the effects of their choice ever since.

This explanation is not original to Milton; many Christians have accepted it for centuries. Yet a reader need not accept this traditional explanation of the evil in the world in order to enjoy and admire the poem. (Indeed, some readers have found evidence in the poem that Milton himself did not really believe it.) The poem is rich enough to provide support for many different interpretations.

Reading *Paradise Lost*

Milton decided to write his epic in his native language and in Shakespeare's meter, which is **blank verse,** or unrhymed iambic pentameter. Though blank verse was the usual meter in dramatic poetry, it was not used at all for nondramatic poems in Milton's day and for long after. Most of Milton's sentences are long, and many of them are not in normal word order (subject-verb-object). Also, his vocabulary includes words not used in ordinary prose today. (Unfamiliar proper nouns are explained in the notes, but they still have to be understood in their context.)

Paradise Within

In Milton's heroic, optimistic view of life, goodness was not goodness unless it resulted from a struggle to overcome evil. God purposely let Satan escape from Hell and establish himself on Earth, not only so that Satan's deeds would damn him further but also so that human beings would have something to fight against—and with God's help triumph over. In one of his prose tracts, *Areopagitica* (1644), Milton describes life as a race in which good must compete with bad. Virtue, he says, is not virtue unless it is won in the "dust and heat" of the conflict with evil. And so, when Adam and Eve lose Paradise, they also gain something: the opportunity to prove themselves in the real world. The Archangel Michael, who comes to turn them out of their perfect garden, tells them how to live in the new, imperfect world. Practice good deeds, he says, and patience, temperance, faith, and love, and

> then wilt thou be not loath
> To leave this Paradise, but shalt possess
> A Paradise within thee, happier far.
> —Book XII, lines 585–587

Before You Read

The Fall of Satan

Make the Connection

Why does evil exist? What is the source of its power to fascinate? The struggle of good versus evil is central to *Paradise Lost*—in this case, the conflict exists on a truly epic scale, as Satan first rebels against God (in Book I) and then ensnares Adam and Eve to do likewise (in Book IX). In Milton's epic and in the Bible, this original choice of evil over good explains the sufferings and the burdens of humanity and our fateful tendencies to misuse reason and freedom, to let pride override fear of God.

Literary Focus

Style

The unique manner in which writers use language to express their ideas is called **style.** An author's style is closely connected to **diction,** or word choice, and **syntax,** or the way sentences are constructed. A writer's style can be categorized as formal or casual, plain or ornate, abstract or concrete—or by any of a number of other descriptive words.

> **Style** is the unique manner in which writers use language to express their ideas. Two of the main aspects of style are diction and syntax.
>
> *For more on Style, see the Handbook of Literary and Historical Terms.*

Reading Skills

Milton's Style

Milton wrote in the 1600s, and on first reading you may be daunted by his style. As you read Milton, you will find it helpful to identify areas of difficulty and apply strategies to deal with them. If you are stalled by an unfamiliar word, try using **context clues** to figure it out. Make use of the **side glosses** that are provided to help you with unfamiliar names and terms. Read and answer the **reading stop** annotations and questions for help understanding key ideas as you go along.

Milton is challenging—just as many good things are. Once you have solved the puzzles posed by Milton's style, though, you should be hooked by this story of the primal battle between the forces of good and the forces of evil.

Vocabulary Development

transgress (trans•gres′) *v.:* sin against; violate a limit.

infernal (in•fur′nəl) *adj.:* hellish; fiendish.

guile (gīl) *n.:* cunning.

affliction (ə•flik′shən) *n.:* suffering.

contention (kən•ten′shən) *n.:* struggle.

ignominy (ig′nə•min′ē) *n.:* dishonor; disgrace.

impetuous (im•pech′o͞o•əs) *adj.:* forceful; violent.

desolation (des′ə•lā′shən) *n.:* utter misery; extreme loneliness.

reiterated (rē•it′ə•rāt′id) *v.* used as *adj.:* repeated.

malice (mal′is) *n.:* ill will; evil intentions.

Literary Skills Understand the use of style.

Reading Skills Understand Milton's style.

INTERNET

Vocabulary Practice

•

More About John Milton

•

Keyword: LE7 12-3

The Fall of Satan
from Paradise Lost
John Milton

Of man's first disobedience, and the fruit
Of that forbidden tree, whose mortal taste
Brought death into the world, and all our woe,
With loss of Eden, till one greater Man°
Restore us, and regain the blissful seat,
Sing, Heavenly Muse,° that on the secret top
Of Oreb, or of Sinai,° didst inspire
That shepherd,° who first taught the chosen seed°
In the beginning how the Heavens and Earth
Rose out of Chaos; or if Sion hill°
Delight thee more, and Siloa's brook° that flowed
Fast by the oracle of God, I thence
Invoke thy aid to my adventurous song,
That with no middle flight intends to soar
Above the Aonian mount,° while it pursues
Things unattempted yet in prose or rhyme.
And chiefly thou, O Spirit,° that dost prefer
Before all temples the upright heart and pure,
Instruct me, for thou know'st; thou from the first
Wast present, and with mighty wings outspread
Dove-like sat'st brooding on the vast abyss
And mad'st it pregnant: what in me is dark
Illumine, what is low raise and support;
That to the height of this great argument
I may assert Eternal Providence,
And justify the ways of God to men.
Say first, for Heaven hides nothing from thy view,
Nor the deep tract of Hell, say first what cause
Moved our grand parents° in that happy state,
Favored of Heaven so highly, to fall off
From their Creator, and transgress his will
For one restraint,° lords of the world besides?°
Who first seduced them to that foul revolt?
The infernal Serpent;° he it was, whose guile,

Vocabulary

transgress (trans • gres′) *v.:* sin against; violate a limit.
infernal (in • fur′nəl) *adj.:* hellish; fiendish.
guile (gīl) *n.:* cunning.

(Opposite) *The Angel of Divine Presence* (detail) by William Blake. Watercolor.

Fitzwilliam Museum, University of Cambridge, UK/The Bridgeman Art Library.

4. one greater Man: Christ.

6. Heavenly Muse: Urania, muse of astronomy and sacred poetry. Milton hopes to be inspired by Urania, just as Moses was inspired to receive God's word for the Hebrews.
7. Oreb . . . Sinai: names for the mountain where Moses received God's inspiration.
8. shepherd *n.:* Moses. **chosen seed:** the Hebrews.
10. Sion hill: Zion, a hill near Jerusalem.
11. Siloa's brook: stream that flowed past the Temple, "the oracle of God," on Mount Zion.
15. Aonian mount: in Greek mythology, Mount Helicon, the home of the Muses.
17. Spirit: Holy Spirit; divine inspiration.

? **1–16.** *Paraphrase the first sentence of the epic. What will the subject of Milton's story be? (See lines 1–5.)*

29. grand parents: Adam and Eve.

32. one restraint: the command not to eat of the fruit of the tree of knowledge. **besides** *adv.:* in every other way.
34. Serpent: Milton is referring to Satan's final form.

? **26.** *According to line 26, what is Milton's purpose? State this purpose in your own words.*

Stirred up with envy and revenge, deceived
The mother of mankind, what time his pride
Had cast him out from Heaven, with all his host
Of rebel angels, by whose aid aspiring
To set himself in glory above his peers,°
He trusted to have equaled the Most High,
If he opposed; and with ambitious aim
Against the throne and monarchy of God,
Raised impious war in Heaven and battle proud
With vain attempt. Him the Almighty Power
Hurled headlong flaming from the ethereal° sky
With hideous ruin and combustion down
To bottomless perdition,° there to dwell
In adamantine° chains and penal° fire,
Who durst° defy the Omnipotent to arms.
Nine times the space that measures day and night
To mortal men, he with his horrid crew
Lay vanquished, rolling in the fiery gulf,
Confounded though immortal. But his doom
Reserved him to more wrath; for now the thought
Both of lost happiness and lasting pain
Torments him; round he throws his baleful eyes,
That witnessed huge affliction and dismay
Mixed with obdurate° pride and steadfast hate.
At once as far as angels ken° he views
The dismal situation waste and wild:
A dungeon horrible on all sides round
As one great furnace flamed, yet from those flames
No light, but rather darkness visible
Served only to discover sights of woe,
Regions of sorrow, doleful shades, where peace
And rest can never dwell, hope never comes
That comes to all; but torture without end
Still urges,° and a fiery deluge, fed
With ever-burning sulfur unconsumed:
Such place Eternal Justice had prepared
For those rebellious, here their prison ordained
In utter darkness, and their portion set
As far removed from God and light of Heaven
As from the center thrice to the utmost pole.°
O how unlike the place from whence they fell!
There the companions of his fall, o'erwhelmed
With floods and whirlwinds of tempestuous fire,
He soon discerns, and weltering° by his side

Vocabulary

affliction (ə•flik'shən) *n.:* suffering.

39. peers *n. pl.:* equals; the other archangels.

45. ethereal *adj.:* heavenly.

47. perdition *n.:* damnation.
48. adamantine (ad'ə•man'tin) *adj.:* unbreakable. **penal** *adj.:* punishing.
49. durst *v.:* dared.

53–56. Milton explains that the archangel Satan, jealous of God's power, has rebelled against the Almighty and thus been expelled from Heaven. The action of the poem begins at this point, *in medias res* ("in the middle of things")—the customary starting point of classical epics.

? *What most torments Satan in Hell?*

58. obdurate *adj.:* stubborn; unrepentant.
59. ken *n.:* range of view.
68. still urges: always afflicts.

? **61–77.** *What images does Milton use to describe Hell?*

74. center . . . pole: three times the distance from Earth, or "center," to the outermost point in the universe. In Milton's cosmos, Earth is the center of ten concentric spheres.
78. weltering *v.:* used as *adj.:* rolling about.

The Fallen Angels on the Wing by Gustave Doré. Engraving.

Culver Pictures.

One next himself in power, and next in crime,
Long after known in Palestine, and named
Beelzebub.° To whom the Arch-Enemy,
And then in Heaven called Satan,° with bold words
Breaking the horrid silence thus began:
"If thou beest he—but O how fallen! how changed
From him, who in the happy realms of light
Clothed with transcendent brightness didst outshine
Myriads though bright—if he whom mutual league,
United thoughts and counsels, equal hope
And hazard in the glorious enterprise,
Joined with me once, now misery hath joined
In equal ruin: into what pit thou seest
From what height fallen! so much the stronger proved
He with his thunder;° and till then who knew
The force of those dire arms? Yet not for those,
Nor what the potent Victor in his rage
Can else inflict, do I repent or change,
Though changed in outward luster, that fixed mind
And high disdain, from sense of injured merit,
That with the Mightiest raised me to contend,
And to the fierce contention brought along
Innumerable force of spirits armed

81. Beelzebub (bē·el′zə·bub′): next in power to Satan; described as prince of the devils in Matthew 12:24.
82. Satan: Hebrew for "adversary; opposer."

93. He . . . thunder: God.

93–124. In this speech, Satan claims that although he has been defeated by God (the "potent Victor"), he will not surrender.
? *What details in Satan's speech show that he sees himself and God as the generals of two opposing armies? What is Satan's attitude toward his defeat?*

Vocabulary
contention (kən • ten′shən) *n.:* struggle.

The Angel Michael Binding Satan ("He Cast him into the Bottomless Pit, and Shut him up") (c. 1805) by William Blake (1757–1827, London).

Courtesy of the Fogg Art Museum, Harvard University Art Museums, Gift of W. A. White, 1915.8. Photo Credit: Rick Stafford.

That durst dislike his reign, and, me preferring,
His utmost power with adverse power opposed
In dubious battle on the plains of Heaven,
And shook his throne. What though the field be lost?
All is not lost; the unconquerable will,
And study° of revenge, immortal hate,
And courage never to submit or yield:
And what is else not to be overcome?
That glory never shall his wrath or might
Extort from me. To bow and sue for grace
With suppliant° knee, and deify his power
Who from the terror of this arm so late
Doubted° his empire, that were low indeed,
That were an ignominy and shame beneath
This downfall; since by fate the strength of gods

107. study *n.:* pursuit.

112. suppliant *adj.:* humble.

114. doubted *v.:* archaic for "feared for."

Vocabulary

ignominy (ig′nə • min′ē) *n.:* dishonor; disgrace.

And this empyreal substance° cannot fail,
Since through experience of this great event,
In arms not worse, in foresight much advanced,
We may with more successful hope resolve
To wage by force or guile eternal war
Irreconcilable to our grand Foe,
Who now triumphs, and in the excess of joy
Sole reigning holds the tyranny of Heaven."
So spake the apostate° Angel, though in pain,
Vaunting° aloud, but racked with deep despair;
And him thus answered soon his bold compeer:°
"O Prince, O Chief of many thronèd Powers,
That led the embattled Seraphim° to war
Under thy conduct, and in dreadful deeds
Fearless, endangered Heaven's perpetual King,
And put to proof his high supremacy,
Whether upheld by strength, or chance, or fate;
Too well I see and rue the dire event,°
That with sad overthrow and foul defeat
Hath lost us Heaven, and all this mighty host
In horrible destruction laid thus low,
As far as gods and heavenly essences
Can perish: for the mind and spirit remains
Invincible, and vigor soon returns,
Though all our glory extinct, and happy state
Here swallowed up in endless misery.
But what if he our Conqueror (whom I now
Of force° believe almighty, since no less
Than such could have o'erpowered such force as ours)
Have left us this our spirit and strength entire
Strongly to suffer and support our pains,
That we may so suffice° his vengeful ire,
Or do him mightier service as his thralls°
By right of war, whate'er his business be,
Here in the heart of Hell to work in fire,
Or do his errands in the gloomy deep?
What can it then avail,° though yet we feel
Strength undiminished, or eternal being
To undergo eternal punishment?"
Whereto with speedy words the Arch-Fiend replied:
"Fallen Cherub, to be weak is miserable,
Doing or suffering:° But of this be sure,
To do aught° good never will be our task,

117. empyreal (em·pir′ē·əl) **substance:** heavenly—and therefore indestructible—substance of which all angels (including Satan) are made.

125. apostate *adj.:* guilty of abandoning one's beliefs. Satan is apostate.

126. vaunting *v.* used as *adj.:* boasting.

127. compeer *n.:* companion; equal. Now Beelzebub speaks.

129. Seraphim: highest order of angels.

134. event *n.:* archaic for "outcome."

143–145. *What does Beelzebub admit about God? How is his attitude different from Satan's?*

144. of force: of necessity.

148. suffice *v.:* archaic for "satisfy."

149. thralls *n. pl.:* slaves.

153. avail *v.:* be of help or advantage.

158. doing or suffering: whether active or passive.

159. aught *n.* used as *adj.:* anything; whatever.

But ever to do ill our sole delight,
As being the contrary to his high will
Whom we resist. If then his providence
Out of our evil seek to bring forth good,
Our labor must be to pervert that end,
And out of good still° to find means of evil;
Which ofttimes may succeed, so as perhaps
Shall grieve him, if I fail not, and disturb
His inmost counsels from their destined aim.
But see the angry Victor° hath recalled
His ministers of vengeance and pursuit
Back to the gates of Heaven; the sulfurous hail
Shot after us in storm, o'erblown hath laid
The fiery surge, that from the precipice
Of Heaven received us falling, and the thunder,
Winged with red lightning and impetuous rage,
Perhaps hath spent his shafts, and ceases now
To bellow through the vast and boundless deep.
Let us not slip° the occasion, whether scorn
Or satiate° fury yield it from our Foe.
Seest thou yon dreary plain, forlorn and wild,
The seat of desolation, void of light,
Save what the glimmering of these livid flames
Casts pale and dreadful? Thither let us tend
From off the tossing of these fiery waves,
There rest, if any rest can harbor there,
And reassembling our afflicted powers,
Consult how we may henceforth most offend
Our Enemy, our own loss how repair,
How overcome this dire calamity,
What reinforcement we may gain from hope,
If not, what resolution from despair."
Thus Satan talking to his nearest mate
With head uplift above the wave, and eyes
That sparkling blazed; his other parts besides,
Prone on the flood, extended long and large,
Lay floating many a rood,° in bulk as huge
As whom the fables name of monstrous size,
Titanian or Earth-born, that warred on Jove,
Briareos or Typhon,° whom the den
By ancient Tarsus held, or that sea-beast
Leviathan,° which God of all his works
Created hugest that swim the ocean stream:

Vocabulary

impetuous (im • pech′o͞o • əs) *adj.:* forceful; violent.
desolation (des′ə • lā′shən) *n.:* utter misery; extreme loneliness.

156–168. *What does Satan vow? In what ways might this be considered the essence of evil?*

165. still *adv.:* always.

169. angry Victor: God.

178. slip *v.:* lose.
179. satiate *v.* used as *adj.:* satisfied

192–210. Milton uses an epic simile to describe Satan lying in repose on the lake of fire (lines 196–209). *To what is Satan being compared? What does this comparison suggest about Satan?*

196. rood *n.:* old unit of measure varying locally from about six to eight yards.
198–200. Titanian . . . Typhon: In an epic simile, Milton compares Satan to the Titans and giants of Greek mythology. Briareos, a hundred-handed giant, helped Zeus (Jove) battle the Titans. Typhon, a hundred-headed serpent-monster from Cilicia (near Tarsus), attacked heaven and was imprisoned by Zeus.
201. Leviathan: biblical sea monster, either a reptile or a whale.

Satan in His Original Glory by William Blake. Watercolor.
Tate Gallery, London.

Him haply slumbering on the Norway foam,
The pilot of some small night-foundered° skiff,
Deeming some island, oft, as seamen tell,
With fixèd anchor in his scaly rind
Moors by his side under the lee, while night
Invests° the sea, and wishèd morn delays:
So stretched out huge in length the Arch-Fiend lay
Chained on the burning lake; nor ever thence
Had risen or heaved his head, but that the will
And high permission of all-ruling Heaven
Left him at large to his own dark designs,
That with reiterated crimes he might
Heap on himself damnation, while he sought
Evil to others, and enraged might see
How all his malice served but to bring forth
Infinite goodness, grace, and mercy shown
On man by him seduced, but on himself
Treble confusion, wrath, and vengeance poured.
  Forthwith upright he rears from off the pool
His mighty stature; on each hand the flames

204. night-foundered: overtaken by night.

208. invests *v.:* covers.

214–220. Milton reminds his readers that Satan remains at the mercy of God and that God plans to use Satan's evil to bring good into the world.
? *Why has God left Satan "to his own dark designs"? Paraphrase what Milton says in lines 214–220.*

Vocabulary

reiterated (rē • it′ə • rāt′id) *v.* used as *adj.:* repeated.
malice (mal′is) *n.:* ill will; evil intentions.

Driven backward slope their pointing spires, and rolled
In billows, leave in the midst a horrid vale.
Then with expanded wings he steers his flight
Aloft, incumbent° on the dusky air
That felt unusual weight, till on dry land
He lights, if it were land that ever burned
With solid, as the lake with liquid fire;
And such appeared in hue, as when the force
Of subterranean wind transports a hill
Torn from Pelorus,° or the shattered side
Of thundering Etna,° whose combustible
And fueled entrails thence conceiving fire,
Sublimed° with mineral fury, aid the winds,
And leave a singèd bottom all involved°
With stench and smoke: such resting found the sole
Of unblest feet. Him followed his next mate,
Both glorying to have scaped the Stygian° flood
As gods, and by their own recovered strength,
Not by the sufferance° of supernal° power.
"Is this the region, this the soil, the clime,"
Said then the lost Archangel, "this the seat
That we must change for Heaven, this mournful gloom
For that celestial light? Be it so, since he
Who now is sovereign can dispose and bid
What shall be right: farthest from him is best,
Whom reason hath equaled, force hath made supreme
Above his equals. Farewell, happy fields,
Where joy forever dwells! Hail, horrors! hail,
Infernal world! and thou, profoundest° Hell,
Receive thy new possessor; one who brings
A mind not to be changed by place or time.
The mind is its own place, and in itself
Can make a Heaven of Hell, a Hell of Heaven.
What matter where, if I be still the same,
And what I should be, all but less than he
Whom thunder hath made greater? Here at least
We shall be free; the Almighty hath not built
Here for his envy, will not drive us hence:
Here we may reign secure, and in my choice
To reign is worth ambition, though in Hell:
Better to reign in Hell than serve in Heaven.
But wherefore let we then our faithful friends,
The associates and copartners of our loss,
Lie thus astonished° on the oblivious° pool,
And call them not to share with us their part
In this unhappy mansion, or once more
With rallied arms to try what may be yet
Regained in Heaven, or what more lost in Hell?"

226. incumbent *adj.:* lying.

221–238. *To what natural forces is Satan compared? Paraphrase the actions of Satan described in these lines. What impression of Satan does Milton create here?*

232. Pelorus: headland in Sicily, Italy; now called Cape Faro.
233. Etna: volcano in Sicily, Italy.
235. sublimed *v.* used as *adj.:* vaporized.
236. involved *adj.:* enveloped.
239. Stygian (stij′ē·ən): of or like the river Styx; infernal, hellish. In Greek mythology the river Styx encircles the underworld.
241. sufferance *n.:* permission. **supernal** *adj.:* heavenly.

251. profoundest *adj.:* lowest; deepest.

254–255. Satan accepts his fate, bids farewell to Heaven, and declares himself the sovereign ruler of Hell.
How would you paraphrase what Satan says in these lines? In what ways is his declaration true? In what ways is it false?

266. astonished *v.* used as *adj.:* dazed. **oblivious** *adj.:* causing forgetfulness.

Response and Analysis

Reading Check

1. Whom does Milton call upon at the beginning of his epic (lines 6–16)? What question does he ask about Adam and Eve (lines 27–33)?
2. What is Milton's purpose in writing this epic poem (lines 24–26)?
3. Why was Satan cast out of Heaven (lines 41–43)?
4. In his first speech, what does Satan tell Beelzebub that he will never do (line 96)? What course does he favor instead (lines 105–124)?
5. According to lines 210–220, who allows Satan the freedom to pursue his evil intentions?
6. In his last speech (lines 258–263), what does Satan claim are the advantages of life in Hell?

Thinking Critically

7. According to Milton, how is the rebellion of Satan and the angels against God connected to "man's first disobedience" and the origin of evil in the world? How does Milton explain the existence of evil in a world created by a loving God?
8. Re-read Milton's first description of Hell in lines 53–74. How is Hell both a psychological state and a physical place? What do you make of the poet's use of an **oxymoron** in the phrase "darkness visible" (line 63)? (An oxymoron is a figure of speech that relies on a **paradox,** or a self-contradictory idea.)
9. In his opening speech, Satan vows never to "repent or change" (line 96). Nevertheless, where can you catch hints that the angel longs for his former state? How might this yearning relate to Milton's mention of "the thought . . . of lost happiness" in lines 54–55?
10. In lines 210–220, the speaker offers a solemn assurance that despite all Satan's power and grandeur, the devil is still subject to God's purposes. How do these lines contribute a level of **dramatic irony** to Satan's ringing assertion of freedom in lines 242–270?
11. How do people today still use the arguments and rationalizations used by Satan and his old crony Beelzebub in lines 143–168?

Extending and Evaluating

12. Judging by this excerpt from *Paradise Lost,* does Milton succeed in explaining the causes of evil and suffering in this world? Explain your thinking.

Literary Criticism

13. Many critics see Satan as the real hero of *Paradise Lost.* Like many literary villains, Satan is a compelling figure—but can he really be considered a heroic figure from any perspective? Use evidence from the text—including descriptions of Satan's appearance, his words, his actions, and his effect on others—to support your point of view.

WRITING

True Words?

Among the most famous passages in *Paradise Lost* are these words from Satan's last speech (lines 254–255):

> The mind is its own place,
> and in itself
> Can make a Heaven of Hell,
> a Hell of Heaven.

In a brief **essay,** explain what these words mean and whether they address something that is true about the human condition. In your opinion, are Satan's words an accurate description of what the mind can do? Draw from your own knowledge and experience to find examples of ways in which these words are (or are not) true in everyday life.

Pages 411–412 cover

Literary Skills
Analyze the use of style. Analyze epic similes, irregular syntax, and blank verse.

Reading Skills
Understand Milton's style.

Writing Skills
Write an essay analyzing a passage from the selection. Write a paraphrase of a speech from the selection.

Vocabulary Skills
Identify word relationships.

Paraphrase a Speech

Write a **paraphrase** of one of the long speeches in this text. You might try Satan's speech in lines 84–124, Beelzebub's speech in lines 157–191, or Satan's speech in lines 242–270. In your paraphrase, make the text very clear by following these guidelines:

- Put Milton's sentences in subject-verb-complement order.
- Provide words missing in Milton's text.
- Rephrase figures of speech to be sure you understand them.
- Replace archaic, or old-fashioned, words with modern words.

Imagine that you are writing a paraphrase to explain the text to a reader who is having trouble understanding it.

Vocabulary Development

Identifying Word Relationships

1. infernal, impetuous, contention
2. reiterated, guile
3. ignominy, desolation, affliction
4. malice, transgress

On a separate sheet of paper, write down the meanings of the Vocabulary words in each set above. Then, explain what relationship the words in each set share. Sometimes a word may have to be considered as it appears in the context of the poem.

Literary Focus

Milton's Poetic Style 

Analyzing epic similes. The word *as* in Milton's epic tells us that a simile is coming, an elaborate **epic simile** in which something in the poem is compared to something quite outside the poem—often an animal, sometimes a human being or a human action. These epic similes allow Milton to bring to his epic a variety of nonbiblical material. Note the **analogies,** or similarities between two unlike things, that the similes are based on.

1. What epic similes are used to describe Satan's bulk in lines 196–208? What is compared to what? How are these things alike?
2. What epic simile describes Satan's landing on dry land in lines 230–237? What is compared to what? How are these things alike?

Reading irregular syntax. To accommodate the demands of his meter, Milton often **omits words** and **inverts syntax,** wrenching some of his sentences out of the usual subject-verb-complement order. If you are having problems finding the **subject** and **verb** in one of his long or inverted sentences, re-read the sentence until you can locate these core sentence parts.

3. In lines 76–78, what are the **subject,** the **verb,** and the **direct object**? What additional words should be supplied in lines 78–81 to make sense of the rest of this sentence?
4. Using normal English syntax, how would you rephrase lines 157–162?

Reading blank verse. Milton uses **blank verse,** or unrhymed iambic pentameter, to give his epic an exalted tone. In iambic pentameter each line of a poem has ten syllables, with five strong stresses alternating with five weaker stresses (the lines begin with an unstressed syllable and end with a stressed one). An **iamb** is an unstressed syllable followed by a stressed one, as in the word *refér.*

5. Choose a passage to read aloud so that you can hear the beat of the iambs. Where does Milton vary the meter to give his verse variety and to prevent a singsong rhythm?

Vocabulary Development

Scientific and Mathematical Words Derived from Greek and Latin

Many of the scientific and mathematical terms that we use today are derived from ancient Greek and Latin, the classical languages that were rediscovered and embraced by scholars during the Renaissance. Developing a knowledge of Greek and Latin roots and affixes can help you feel more at home in the world of complex scientific and mathematical words. If you become a scientist or a mathematician yourself, you might go to Greek and Latin when you need to make up names for your discoveries.

Words are built on a base, or **root,** which contains the core of the word's meaning. The root *–bio–,* for instance, comes from a Greek word meaning "life." The words *biorhythm, biome,* and *biodegradable* contain this root. These words also contain **affixes**—word parts added to the beginning (prefixes) or end (suffixes) of a root to change its meaning. For instance, by adding the **suffix** *–logy,* meaning "study of," to the root *–bio–*, the word *biology*—"the study of life"—is formed. The **prefix** *micro–* added to *biology* creates the word *microbiology,* "the study of very small [*microscopic*] life-forms."

Some common roots, prefixes, and suffixes from Greek and Latin are listed in the charts below. Knowing these word parts will help you determine the meanings of unfamiliar scientific and mathematical terms when you come across them in various texts.

Greek and Latin Roots	Meaning	Example
–aero–	air; gas	aerobic; aerial
–anthr–, –anthrop–, –andro–	human	anthropology; androgyny
–baro–	weight	barometric
–cal–, –calor–	heat	calorie; calorimeter
–geo–	earth; ground	geography; geology
–gon–	angle	polygon; pentagon; trigonometry
–hydr–, –hydro–	water	hydrogen; hydrate
–iso–	alike; equal	isosceles; isometric
–morph–	shape; form	morphology; polymorphous
–patho–	disease	pathology; pathological
–psych–	mind	psychology; psychoanalysis
–zo–	life; animal	zoology; protozoa

Pages 413–414 cover **Vocabulary Skills** Understand and use words derived from Greek and Latin.

Greek and Latin Affixes	Meaning	Example
ana–	upward; throughout; similar to	analysis; analog
anti–	against	antibiotic; antidote
–gen	something that produces or is produced	oxygen; hydrogen
hemi–	half	hemisphere
hypo–	under; below; too little	hypodermic
meta–	change; over; through	metastasis
–osis	state; condition; formation	meiosis; mitosis; symbiosis
–quadro–, quadr–	four	quadratic; quadruped
sub–	under	subtract; suborbital
–tomy	cutting	anatomy
trans–	across; over; beyond	transversal; transduce
tri–	three	triangle

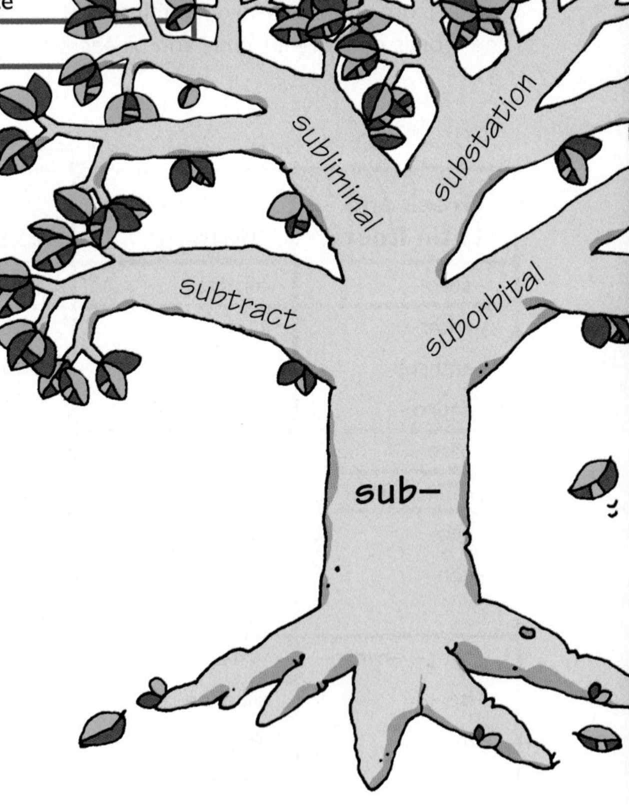

PRACTICE

Each of the following words is used in mathematical or scientific fields of study. Use the charts above and your own knowledge of words to guess as best you can each word's meaning, based on its root or affixes. Then, check your guess by looking up the definition of the word in a dictionary. Write down how the root or affix of each word helped you determine the word's meaning.

1. anthropomorphic
2. aerobiology
3. pathogen
4. psychopathology
5. metamorphosis
6. transcontinental

Before You Read

When I consider how my light is spent

Make the Connection

Quickwrite

Our lives are filled with turning points—successes and failures, tests and triumphs, beginnings and endings. Sometimes we recognize the turning points only in hindsight. In the sonnet that follows, Milton writes about a turning point in his life: the onset of blindness during middle age.

People of every era, at any age, often face questions similar to the ones Milton ponders: "Where do I go from here?" and "Now that tragedy has struck, how can I possibly go on?" Jot down four or five critical turning points that a person might face during his or her life, and list the questions that those events might force a person to consider.

Literary Focus

Allusion

An **allusion** is a reference to a statement, person, place, event, or thing that is known from literature, history, religion, mythology, politics, sports, science, or popular culture.

In ordinary conversation we may allude to a famous figure by calling an intelligent person an Einstein or a good baseball player a Babe Ruth. We might allude to a parable in the Gospel of Luke in the Bible by calling someone who has helped us change a flat tire a good Samaritan. Literary works frequently allude to past literary classics: Ernest Hemingway's novel *For Whom the Bell Tolls* takes its title from John Donne's Meditation 17 (see page 344), and the title of John Steinbeck's novel *The Grapes of Wrath* comes from the "Battle Hymn of the Republic." As you saw in "The Fall of Satan" from *Paradise Lost,* Milton himself took delight in alluding to everything from geographic locations to biblical passages.

An **allusion** is a reference to a statement, a person, a place, an event, or a thing that is known from literature, history, religion, mythology, politics, sports, science, or popular culture.

For more on Allusion, see the Handbook of Literary and Historical Terms.

Background

Altogether Milton wrote eighteen sonnets in English and five in Italian. In both form and subject matter, his sonnets differ from those of his English predecessors, Sidney, Spenser, and Shakespeare. Milton's sonnets closely follow the Italian, or Petrarchan, sonnet form and are about events and persons in his own public and private life. In "When I consider how my light is spent," however, he introduces a variation into the Petrarchan sonnet by making the turn, or change, before line 9. (For more information about the Petrarchan sonnet, see page 312.)

Literary Skills
Understand the use of allusion.

INTERNET

More About John Milton

Keyword: LE7 12-3

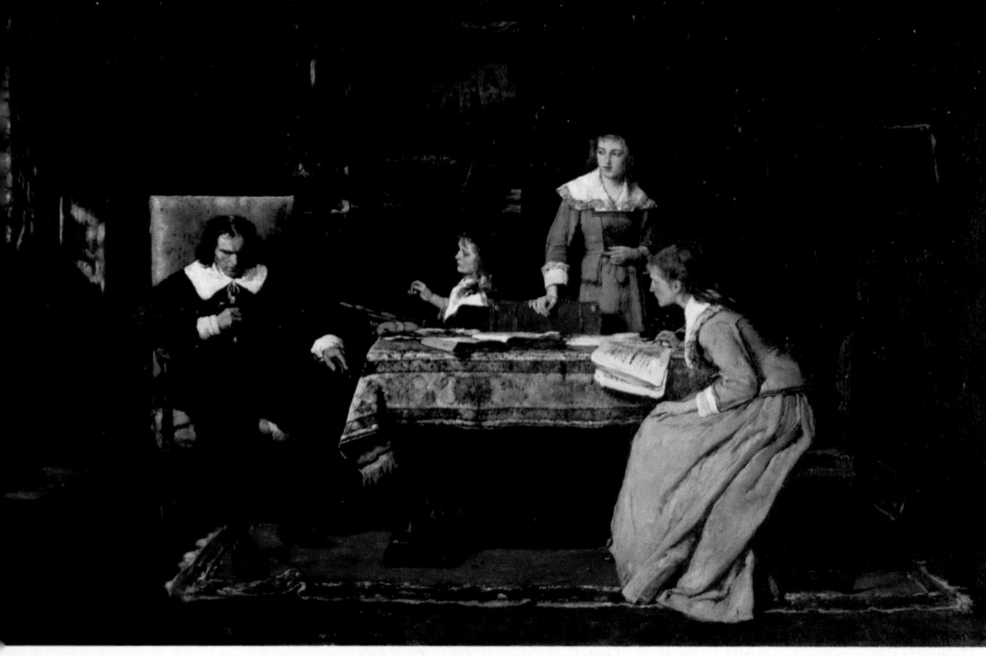

The Blind Milton Dictating Paradise Lost *to His Daughters* (1877) by Mihály Munkácsy.

Collection of the New York Public Library. Astor, Lenox and Tilden Foundations.

In "When I consider how my light is spent," sometimes titled "On His Blindness," Milton dramatizes a calamity that hit him in middle age: blindness. Long before he had accomplished his life's work, he lost his sight. Deeply religious and believing firmly that everyone is accountable to God, Milton asks in the first part of the sonnet, "How can I continue to do the work that God expects of me?" He proposes an answer in the remainder of the sonnet.

When I consider how my light is spent

John Milton

When I consider how my light is spent
　Ere half my days in this dark world and wide,
　And that one talent° which is death to hide
　Lodged with me useless, though my soul more bent
To serve therewith my Maker, and present
　My true account, lest He returning chide,
　"Doth God exact day-labor, light denied?"
　I fondly° ask. But Patience, to prevent
That murmur, soon replies, "God doth not need
　Either man's work or His own gifts. Who best
　Bear His mild yoke, they serve Him best. His state
Is kingly: Thousands° at His bidding speed,
　And post o'er land and ocean without rest;
　They also serve who only stand and wait."

3. talent *n.:* reference to the parable of the talents (Matthew 25:14–30), in which a servant is scolded for burying his one talent, or coin, in the earth instead of putting it to good use.
8. fondly *adv.:* foolishly.

12. thousands: of angels.

Response and Analysis

Thinking Critically

1. What question does the speaker ask of God in the first eight lines? How would you paraphrase this question—that is, how would you restate it in your own words?
2. The answer to the question indicates the turn in this sonnet. What is Patience's reply to the question in the last six lines? How would you paraphrase that answer in your own words?
3. The word *talent* in line 3 is both a pun and an **allusion** to a biblical **parable** that Milton's readers would have recognized instantly. In Matthew 25:14–30, three servants are given coins called talents. The first two servants invest their talents and double their value, while the third is punished for burying the one talent he received, accomplishing nothing at all. What is Milton's "one talent"? How is his situation similar to or different from that of the third servant in the parable?
4. The phrase "mild yoke" in line 11 refers to the words of Jesus in Matthew 11:30: "For my yoke is easy, and my burden is light." What is Milton's "yoke," or burden? By making such an **allusion,** what is Milton saying about his situation?
5. In this sonnet, how well does Milton answer the fundamental questions, "Where do I go from here?" and "How can I go on, now that tragedy has struck?" Would his answers have satisfied people of his own time? How well does the sonnet speak to people of today? Be sure to explain your responses. You may want to consult your Quickwrite notes for help.

WRITING

Those Who Stand and Wait

In a brief **essay,** explore the ways in which the quotation "They also serve who only stand and wait" might apply to your life. Think of some situations in which it would be appropriate to stand and wait. What dangers, or pitfalls, do you also see in the statement? That is, how might people use it to avoid doing something that is demanded by justice or fairness? What do you think Milton meant by the phrase?

LISTENING AND SPEAKING

Two Speakers

Present this sonnet using two speakers, one to present the problem in the octave and the other to present the response in the sestet. Before you present the poem, be sure you understand the structure of Milton's sentences. Then, determine exactly where you must pause and when you must make full stops. It will help to write or print the poem out first. On the copy, write directions for your oral reading.

Literary Skills
Analyze the use of allusion.

Writing Skills
Write an essay analyzing a line of a sonnet.

Listening and Speaking Skills
Recite a sonnet that has two speakers.

John Bunyan
(1628–1688)

John Bunyan (17th century) by Robert White.
British Library, London, UK/The Bridgeman Art Library.

Unlike most of the other writers represented in this anthology, John Bunyan came from England's lowest social class. He worked with his hands, as a brazier, or tinker—a maker and mender of cooking pots and pans. He was not an ordinary tinker, however, but the author of a book that, next to the Bible, has been the most widely read of all English books: *The Pilgrim's Progress from This World to That Which Is to Come* (1678), commonly called *The Pilgrim's Progress.*

What we know about Bunyan comes mainly from his autobiographical work *Grace Abounding to the Chief of Sinners* (1666), the Chief of Sinners being himself. In this book he describes his childhood poverty, his service in the army fighting King Charles I, and his marriage. He and his wife, he tells us, were "as poor as poor might be, with not so much household stuff as a dish or spoon betwixt us both." Aside from a very few details like these, *Grace Abounding* is concerned entirely with the state of Bunyan's soul and his relationship with God. To Bunyan these were the only important matters in life.

Although he had never been formally educated or ordained as a minister, Bunyan felt called upon to preach to his fellow Baptists. He began holding services in private houses and then, as his eloquence and piety attracted many people, in the woods outside his hometown of Elstow. Such Puritan sects as the Baptists flourished during the years when England was without a king (1649–1660), but with the restoration of Charles II, the government soon reestablished the Church of England and outlawed all other forms of religion. Inevitably Bunyan found it impossible to obey the law requiring attendance at the Church of England and forbidding all other religious gatherings. In 1660, he was arrested and jailed for preaching without a license. For twelve years he remained imprisoned, preaching to other inmates and writing religious books. A short period of freedom followed this imprisonment—a time when the authorities were lax in enforcing the laws. Then, in 1675, Bunyan was locked up again.

During his second confinement he wrote *The Pilgrim's Progress,* which was such a great success that, like the producers of popular movie sequels today, he published a second part. When the laws against Dissenters were eventually relaxed, Bunyan also became famous as a preacher—even in London, where an audience of several thousand would go to hear him on a Sunday. When told about Bunyan, King Charles expressed astonishment that a tinker could draw such crowds.

Before You Read

from The Pilgrim's Progress

Make the Connection

How many times have you heard life referred to as a journey? This familiar metaphor has formed the basis for many literary works—from Homer's *Odyssey* to the latest science fiction book or movie. The journey is a fitting metaphor for life, because beyond having a beginning and an end, journeys usually confront the traveler with unexpected challenges and tests. Such challenges can be physical, mental, or moral, but the most compelling combine all three.

Literary Focus

Allegory

In the literary form known as **allegory,** two stories are told at once. The characters, settings, and events stand not only for themselves but also for abstract, or intangible, ideas. An allegorical story operates on two levels of meaning: one literal and one symbolic. Since the purpose of most allegories is to teach, the **literal,** or surface, story is a means of conveying the **symbolic,** or submerged, story, which is concerned with mental, emotional, and moral developments. In *The Pilgrim's Progress,* these dual levels of storytelling are reflected in the names of the people, places, and events in the story.

An **allegory** is a story in which the characters, settings, and events stand for abstract ideas.

For more on Allegory, see the Handbook of Literary and Historical Terms.

Background

The narrator of *The Pilgrim's Progress* is a dreamer. Asleep, he dreams about a man named Christian who lives with his family in a city called Destruction. Besides living in a city with this appalling name, Christian has another problem: On his back he bears a burden that he cannot get rid of. It is like a part of himself. And so he decides to leave home and go on a *progress,* or journey, to a wonderful place he has heard of, called the Celestial City. On this trip (which takes up most of the first part of the book), Christian has a few pleasant experiences, but most of his adventures are unpleasant, even dangerous. He falls into the Slough of Despond (a *slough* is a mudhole; the word rhymes with *cow*), climbs the Hill Difficulty, fights a dragonlike monster called Apollyon, and is arrested and unjustly punished in a worldly town called Vanity, with its outdoor market, Vanity Fair. He also encounters numerous sly characters who try to distract him from his goal: Mr. Worldly Wiseman, Little-Faith, and Ignorance, for example. Finally, after he has overcome all these obstacles, Christian enters the Celestial City.

Vocabulary Development

allure (ə • lo͝or′) *v.:* tempt; attract.

reproachfully (ri • prōch′fəl • ē) *adv.:* accusingly.

confounded (kən • foun′did) *adj.:* confused.

implacable (im • plak′ə • bəl) *adj.:* unchangeable; fixed.

respite (res′pit) *n.:* postponement; reprieve.

transfigured (trans • fig′yərd) *v.:* changed the form of.

Literary Skills
Understand the use of allegory.

INTERNET

Vocabulary Practice

Keyword: LE7 12-3

Plan of the road from the City of Destruction to the Celestial City, from *The Pilgrim's Progress* (19th century). Engraving.

Private Collection/The Bridgeman Art Library.

from The Pilgrim's Progress

John Bunyan

Bunyan tells the story of Christian's journey as if he, the narrator, were recounting his own dream. At this point in the story, Christian and his traveling companion, Faithful, enter a town called Vanity in which the local fair, or outdoor market, is in full swing. In Bunyan's day, merchants from all over Europe would sell their wares at such events, and the buying and selling would be accompanied by eating, drinking, sport, and general merriment.

Then I saw in my dream that when they were got out of the wilderness they presently saw a town before them, and the name of that town is Vanity; and at the town there is a fair kept called Vanity-Fair. It is kept all the year long; it beareth the name of Vanity-Fair, because the town where 'tis kept is lighter than vanity; and also, because all that is there sold, or that cometh thither, is Vanity. As is the saying of the wise, *All that cometh is vanity.*

This Fair is no new erected business, but a thing of ancient standing; I will show you the original of it.

Almost five thousand years agone, there were pilgrims walking to the Celestial City, as these two honest persons are; and Beelzebub, Apollyon, and Legion,[1] with their companions, perceiving by the path that the Pilgrims made that their way to the City lay through this town of Vanity, they contrived here to set up a fair; a fair wherein should be sold of all sorts of vanity, and that it should last all the year long. Therefore at this Fair are all such merchandise sold, as houses, lands, trades, places, honours, preferments,[2] titles, countries, kingdoms, lusts, pleasures, and delights of all sorts, as whores, bawds, wives, husbands, children, masters, servants, lives, blood, bodies, souls, silver, gold, pearls, precious stones, and what not.

And moreover, at this Fair there is at all times to be seen jugglings, cheats, games, plays, fools, apes, knaves, and rogues, and that of all sorts.

Here are to be seen too, and that for nothing, thefts, murders, adulteries, false-swearers, and that of a blood-red colour.

And as in other fairs of less moment there are the several rows and streets under their proper names, where such and such wares are vended: so here likewise, you have the proper places, rows, streets (*viz.*[3] countries and kingdoms), where the wares of this Fair are soonest to be found: here is the Britain Row, the French Row, the Italian Row, the Spanish Row, the German Row, where several sorts of vanities are to be sold. But as in other fairs, some one commodity is as the chief of all the fair, so the ware of Rome and her merchandise is greatly promoted in this Fair: only our English nation, with some others, have taken a dislike thereat.

Now, as I said, the way to the Celestial City lies just through this town, where this lusty Fair is kept; and he that will go to the City, and yet not go through this town, must needs go out of the world. The Prince of Princes himself, when here, went through this Town[4] to his own country, and that upon a fair-day too. Yea, and as I think it was Beelzebub, the chief lord of this Fair, that invited him to buy of his vanities; yea, would have made him lord of the Fair, would he but have done him reverence as he went through the town. Yea, because he was such a person of honour, Beelzebub had him from street to street, and showed him all the kingdoms of the world in a little time, that he might if possible allure that Blessed One, to cheapen[5] and buy some of his vanities. But he had no mind to the merchandise, and therefore left the town without laying out so much as one farthing upon these vanities. This Fair therefore is an ancient thing, of long standing, and a very great Fair.

Now these pilgrims, as I said, must needs go through this Fair: well, so they did; but behold, even as they entered into the Fair, all the people in the Fair were moved, and the town itself as it were in a hubbub about them; and that for several reasons: for,

First, the pilgrims were clothed with such kind of raiment as was diverse from the raiment of any that traded in that Fair. The people therefore of the Fair made a great gazing upon them: Some

1. **Beelzebub** (bē·el'zə·bub'): here, Satan. **Apollyon** (ə·päl'yən): in the book of Revelation, the angel of the bottomless pit. **Legion**: unclean spirits or devils.
2. **preferments** *n. pl.:* appointments to political or religious positions.
3. ***viz.*** *adv.:* namely.
4. **The Prince of Princes . . . Town:** reference to the temptation of Christ (Matthew 4:1–11).
5. **cheapen** *v.:* ask the price of.

Vocabulary

allure (ə • loor') *v.:* tempt; attract.

said they were fools, some they were bedlams,[6] and some 'They are outlandish-men.'[7]

Secondly, and as they wondered at their apparel so they did likewise at their speech; for few could understand what they said; they naturally spoke the language of Canaan;[8] but they that kept the Fair, were the men of this world: so that from one end of the Fair to the other, they seemed barbarians each to the other.

Thirdly, but that which did not a little amuse the merchandisers was that these pilgrims set very light by all their wares, they cared not so much as to look upon them; and if they called upon them to buy, they would put their fingers in their ears, and cry, *Turn away mine eyes from beholding vanity;* and look upwards, signifying that their trade and traffic was in Heaven.

One chanced mockingly, beholding the carriages of the men, to say unto them, 'What will ye buy?' but they, looking gravely upon him, said, 'We buy the truth.' At that there was an occasion taken to despise the men the more; some mocking, some taunting, some speaking reproachfully, and some calling upon others to smite them. At last things came to a hubbub and great stir in the Fair; insomuch that all order was confounded. Now was word presently brought to the great one of the Fair, who quickly came down and deputed some of his most trusty friends to take these men into examination about whom the Fair was almost overturned. . . .

The townspeople at Vanity Fair are immediately suspicious of Christian and Faithful, and they arrest the two pilgrims and bring them to trial. Three witnesses, Envy, Superstition, and Pick-thank, a favor-seeker, testify against Faithful. His fate is turned over to a jury of townspeople.

Then went the jury out, whose names were Mr. Blind-man, Mr. No-good, Mr. Malice, Mr. Love-lust, Mr. Live-loose, Mr. Heady, Mr. High-mind, Mr. Enmity, Mr. Liar, Mr. Cruelty, Mr. Hate-light, and Mr. Implacable, who every one gave in his private verdict against him among themselves, and afterwards unanimously concluded to bring him in guilty before the Judge. And first Mr. Blind-man, the foreman, said, "I see clearly that this man is an heretic." Then said Mr. No-good, "Away with such a fellow from the earth." "Ay," said Mr. Malice, "for I hate the very looks of him." Then said Mr. Love-lust, "I could never endure him."

6. **bedlams** *n. pl.:* mental patients from Bethlehem Hospital, the notorious hospital for the insane in London.
7. **outlandish-men:** foreigners.
8. **Canaan:** Promised Land. The "language of Canaan" is the language of the Bible.

Vocabulary

reproachfully (ri • prōch′fəl • ē) *adv.:* accusingly.
confounded (kən • foun′did) *adj.:* confused.
implacable (im • plak′ə • bəl) *adj.:* unchangeable; fixed.

THE
Pilgrim's Progrefs
FROM
THIS WORLD,
TO
That which is to come
Delivered under the Similitude of a
DREAM
Wherein is Difcovered,
The Manner of his fetting out,
His Dangerous JOURNEY,
AND
fe Arrival at the Defired Countrey.

By JOHN BUNYAN.

he Fourth Edition, with Additions.

ave ufed Similitudes. *Hofea*, 12. 10.

cenfed and Entred according to Order.

DONDON,
inted for *Nath. Ponder*, at the *Peacock*
in the *Poultrey* near the Church, 1680.

Frontispiece of *The Pilgrim's Progress* (1680) by John Bunyan. English School. Engraving.

"Nor I," said Mr. Live-loose, "for he would always be condemning my way." "Hang him, hang him," said Mr. Heady. "A sorry scrub," said Mr. High-mind. "My heart riseth against him," said Mr. Enmity. "He is a rogue," said Mr. Liar. "Hanging is too good for him," said Mr. Cruelty. "Let's dispatch him out of the way," said Mr. Hate-light. Then said Mr. Implacable, "Might I have all the world given me, I could not be reconciled to him, therefore let us forthwith bring him in guilty of death." And so they did, therefore he was presently condemned to be had from the place where he was, to the place from whence he came, and there to be put to the most cruel death that could be invented.

They therefore brought him out to do with him according to their law; and first they scourged him, then they buffeted him, then they lanced his flesh with knives; after that they stoned him with stones, then pricked him with their swords; and last of all they burned him to ashes at the stake. Thus came Faithful to his end. Now, I saw that there stood behind the multitude a chariot and a couple of horses, waiting for Faithful, who (so soon as his adversaries had dispatched him) was taken up into it, and straightway was carried up through the clouds, with sound of trumpet, the nearest way to the Celestial Gate. But as for Christian, he had some respite, and was remanded back to prison; so he there remained for a space: but he that over-rules all things, having the power of their rage in his own hand, so wrought it about that Christian for that time escaped them, and went his way. . . .

Christian continues on his journey and finds another companion, the convert Hopeful. After more trials and tests of faith, the two reach their long-awaited destination: the Gates of the Celestial City.

Now I saw in my dream, that these two men went in at the Gate; and lo, as they entered they were transfigured, and they had raiment put on that shone like gold. There was also that met them with harps and crowns, and gave them to them, the harp to praise withal, and the crowns in token of honour. Then I heard in my dream, that all the bells in the City rang again for joy; and that it was said unto them, "*Enter ye into the joy of your Lord.*" I also heard the men themselves, that they sang with a loud voice, saying, "*Blessing, honour, glory, and power, be to him that sitteth upon the throne, and to the Lamb for ever and ever.*"

Now just as the Gates were opened to let in the men, I looked in after them; and behold, the City shone like the sun, the streets also were paved with gold, and in them walked many men with crowns on their heads, palms in their hands, and golden harps to sing praises withal. ■

Vocabulary

respite (res′pit) *n.:* postponement; reprieve.
transfigured (trans • fig′yərd) *v.:* changed the form of.

Response and Analysis

Reading Check

1. What is offered at Vanity Fair?
2. What characteristics of the two pilgrims disturb the people at Vanity Fair?
3. What happens to Faithful after he is arrested and tried?
4. What becomes of Christian after his imprisonment?

Thinking Critically

5. True to the spirit of **allegory,** Vanity Fair is both a **literal** and a **symbolic** place. What are some of the concrete details that give Bunyan's creation the feel of an actual English marketplace?
6. What is the **allegorical,** or symbolic, significance of the town of Vanity Fair in Christian's spiritual journey?
7. What do you think is the main reason the townspeople arrest Christian and Faithful? What really upsets them?
8. What attitude toward Faithful do all the members of the jury have in common? How do their names and their words reveal their **characters**?
9. Who or what are the modern counterparts to the allegorical characters on Faithful's jury and to the challenges that the two pilgrims face in Vanity Fair?
10. What does Bunyan wish to teach by means of the Vanity Fair episode? Do you think this lesson still has meaning in the modern world? Explain your response.

Literary Skills
Analyze the use of allegory.

Writing Skills
Write an allegory.

Vocabulary Skills
Understand and use synonyms.

Extending and Evaluating

11. Is **allegory** an effective way of getting a moral message across today? Why or why not?

Literary Criticism

12. Biblical characters, cosmology, and quotations abound in *The Pilgrim's Progress,* yet the work has been translated widely and read by people of many cultures and religions. In fact, next to the Bible itself, it has been the most widely read of all English books. Discuss how Bunyan's narrative transcends its Christian framework to achieve universal appeal.

WRITING

The Jury Is In

One of the most enjoyable parts of the Vanity Fair episode is the commentary of the delightfully named jurors. Try writing your own **allegory** by expanding this scene. Invent other allegorical characters that might have appeared in the courtroom that day. Give your characters names, and write dialogue for them that reflects their names. Like Bunyan, you may want to use humor and satire.

Vocabulary Development

Venn Diagrams

allure	implacable
reproachfully	respite
confounded	transfigured

Using a dictionary or the definitions on page 419, find a synonym for each Vocabulary word listed above. Then, explore the similarities among and the differences between the two synonymous words by making a Venn diagram like the one below. In the overlapping area, write the meanings that apply to both words.

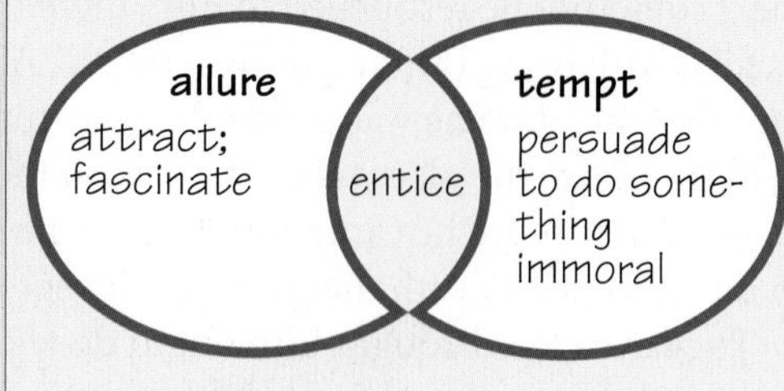

Collection 3:
The Renaissance

Renaissance Drama

Shakespeare

Life's but a walking shadow,
a poor player
That struts and frets his hour
upon the stage
And then is heard no more.
It is a tale
Told by an idiot, full of sound
and fury,
Signifying nothing.

—*The Tragedy of Macbeth*
(Act V, Scene 5)

Macbeth at the Royal Opera House, London

The Renaissance Theater

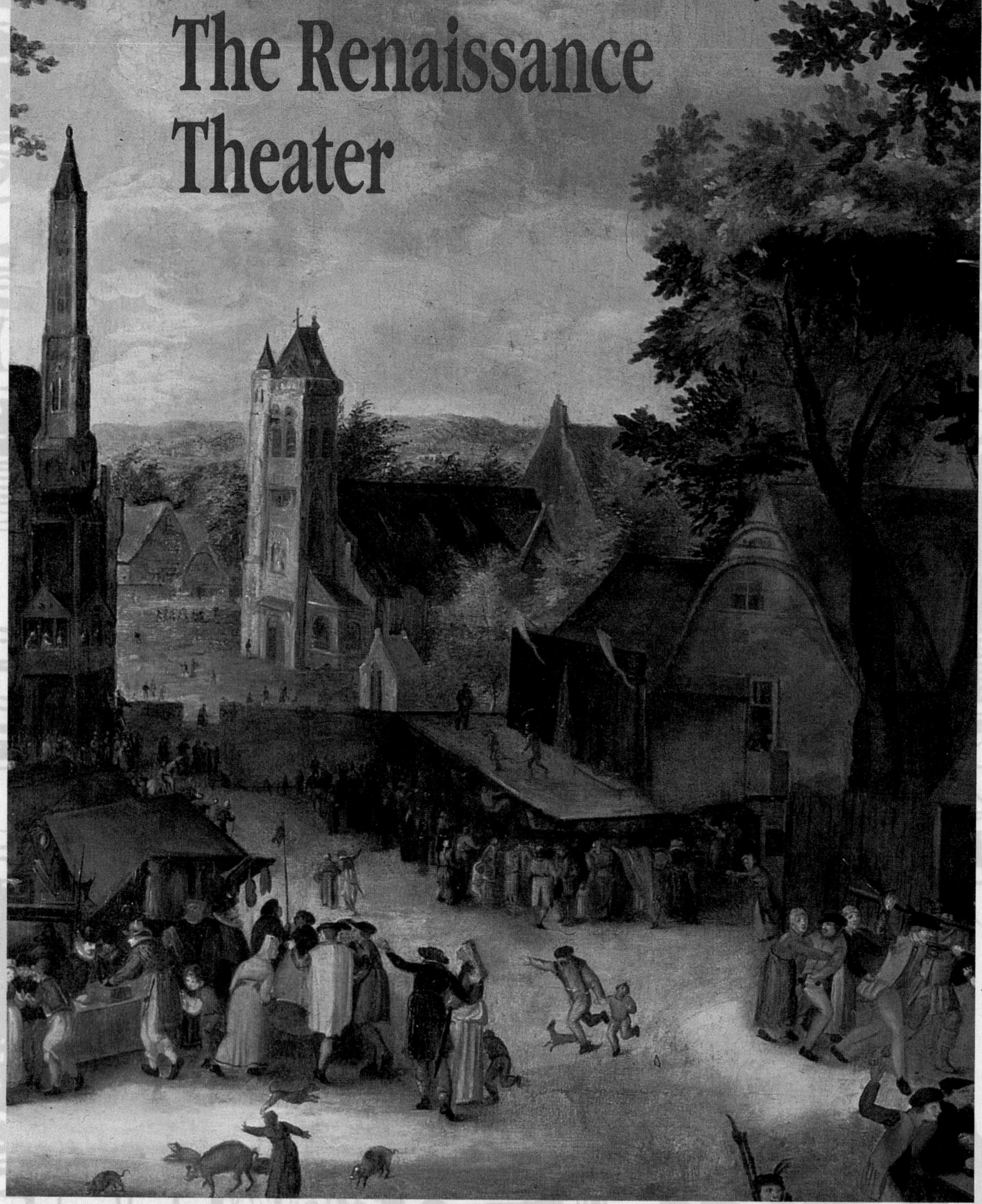

A *Flemish Fair* (detail) (late 16th to early 17th century) by Isaac Claesz Swanenburgh.

Cheltenham Art Gallery & Museums, Gloucestershire, UK.

Drama as Teacher: The Forerunners

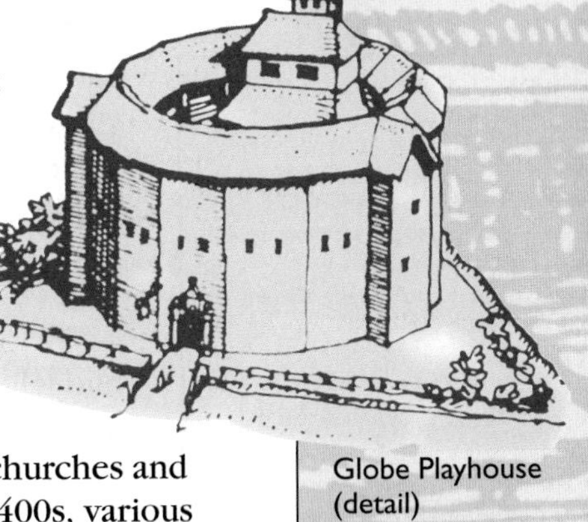
Globe Playhouse (detail) (c. 1599–1613) by C. Walter Hodges.

Even before the Renaissance, the English had been writing and performing plays for several centuries. Some scholars believe that medieval drama evolved from church ceremonies such as the dialogue songs performed at Easter Eve services. In these tiny playlets, three women would appear at a door representing the tomb of Christ and guarded by an angel. The angel would ask in Latin, "Whom do you seek?" and then he would announce the Resurrection.

From this obscure beginning, drama moved out of the churches and into the marketplaces of towns. There, in the 1300s and 1400s, various workers' guilds cooperated in staging cycles of plays that dramatized the whole history of the human race as then understood: its creation by God, its fall through the wiles of Satan, its life in Old Testament times, its redemption by Christ, and its final judgment at the end of the world. Parts of four cycles of these plays have been preserved, and they are named after the towns where they probably originated: York, Chester, Coventry, and Wakefield. Gradually, the plays became less religious, often relying on *deus ex machina* (an artificial device arbitrarily used to resolve a plot), and comedy was incorporated into them. The wife of Noah, for instance, makes a great fuss about entering the ark and is carried kicking and screaming aboard. Comic scenes like this one provide an early example of English skill in mixing the comic with the serious in drama. The most notable play of the period just before the Renaissance is *Everyman,* based on a Dutch original.

Representation of a Mystery Play (detail) (1825) by David Jee.

By permission of the British Library, London.

Several kinds of plays, then, were written and produced before the Renaissance: **miracle** and **mystery plays** that taught people stories from the Bible and saints' legends; **moralities** that taught people how to live and die; and, starting in the early 1500s, a new kind of play called an **interlude.** Interludes were one-act plays, some of them indistinguishable from moralities, others rowdy and farcical. With the interludes the playwrights stopped being anonymous. Even before the new humanist learning came in, there were strong dramatic traditions that the great Renaissance playwrights knew about.

Old Traditions, New Theaters

By the mid–sixteenth century, the art of drama in England was three centuries old, but the idea of housing it in a permanent building was new. Even after theaters had been built, plays were still regularly performed in improvised spaces when acting companies toured the provinces or presented their plays in the large houses of royalty and nobility.

In 1576, James Burbage, the father of Shakespeare's partner and fellow actor Richard Burbage, built the first public theater and called it, appropriately, the Theater. Shortly thereafter, a second playhouse, called the Curtain, was erected. Both of these were in a northern suburb of London, where they would not offend the staid residents of London proper. Then came the Rose, the Swan, the Fortune, the Globe, the Red Bull, and the Hope—far more public theaters than in any other European capital.

The Globe: "This Wooden O"

The Globe is the most famous of the public theaters because the company that Shakespeare belonged to owned it. Many of his plays received their first performances there. It was built out of timbers salvaged from the Theater, which was demolished in 1599. Unfortunately, the plans for the Globe have not survived, though there still exist old, panoramic drawings of London in which its exterior is pictured. But the most important sources of information about the theater's structure are the plays themselves, with their stage directions and other clues.

Most scholars now accept as accurate the reconstruction of the Globe published by C. Walter Hodges, whose drawing appears on this page. Notice that the theater has three main parts: the building proper, the stage, and the tiring house, or backstage area, with the flag flying from its peak to indicate that there will be a performance that day.

KEY

- **a** Main entrance
- **b** The yard
- **c** Entrance to lowest gallery
- **d** Entrance to staircase and upper galleries
- **e** Corridor serving the different sections of the middle gallery
- **f** Middle gallery ("Twopenny Rooms")
- **g** "Gentlemen's Rooms" or "Lords' Rooms"
- **h** The stage
- **j** The hanging being put up round the stage
- **k** The "hell" under the stage
- **l** The stage trap, leading down to the hell
- **m** Stage doors
- **n** Curtained "place behind the stage"
- **o** Gallery above the stage, used as required sometimes by musicians, sometimes by spectators, and often as part of the play
- **p** Backstage area (the tiring house)
- **q** Tiring-house door
- **r** Dressing rooms
- **s** Wardrobe and storage
- **t** The hut housing the machine for lowering enthroned gods, etc., to the stage
- **u** The "heavens"
- **w** Hoisting the playhouse flag

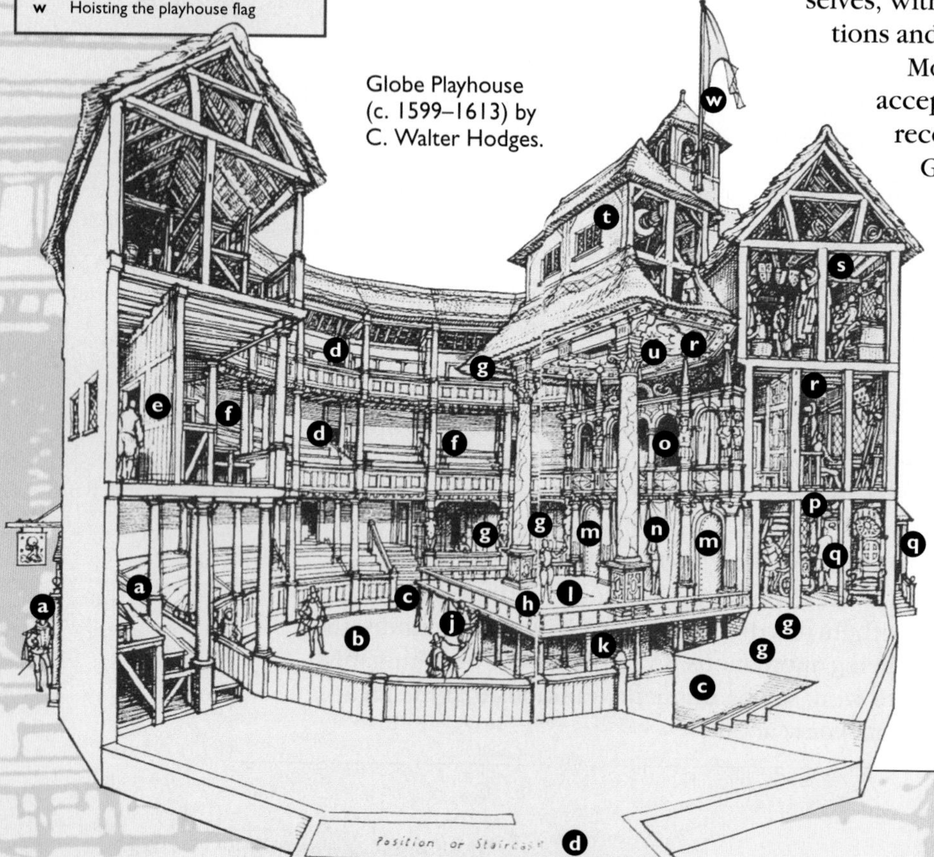

Globe Playhouse (c. 1599–1613) by C. Walter Hodges.

A wooden structure three stories high, the building proper surrounded a spacious inner yard open to the sky. It was probably a sixteen-sided polygon. Any structure with that many sides would appear circular, so it is not surprising that Shakespeare referred to the Globe as "this wooden O" in his play *Henry V.* There were probably only two entrances to the building, one for the public and one for the theater company. But there may have been another public door used as an exit, because when the Globe burned down in 1613, the crowd escaped quickly and safely.

General admission to the theater cost one penny; this entitled a spectator to be a groundling, which meant he or she could stand in the yard. Patrons paid a little more to mount up into the galleries, where there were seats and a better view of the stage. The most expensive seats were chairs set right on the stage along its two sides. People who wanted to be conspicuous rented them, though they must have been a great nuisance to the rest of the audience and the actors. A public theater held a surprisingly large number of spectators—three thousand, according to two contemporary accounts. Since the spectators must have been squeezed together, it is no wonder that the authorities always closed the theaters during plague epidemics.

Up Close and Personal

The stage jutted halfway out into the yard, so that the actors were in much closer contact with the audience than actors are in modern theaters. Thus, every tiny nuance of an actor's performance could affect the audience. The actors were highly trained, and they could sing, dance, declaim, wrestle, fence, clown, roar, weep, and whisper. Large, sensational effects were also plentiful. Spectators loved to see witches or devils emerge through the trapdoor in the stage, which everybody pretended led down to Hell, just as everybody pretended that the ceiling over part of the stage was the Heavens. This ceiling was painted with elaborate suns, moons, and stars, and it contained a trapdoor through which angels, gods, and spirits could be lowered on a wire and even flown over the other actors' heads.

Behind the Scenes

The third part of the theater was the tiring (from *tire,* an archaic form of "attire") house, a tall building that contained machinery and dressing rooms and that provided a two-story back wall for the stage. Hodges's drawing of the Globe shows that this wall contained a gallery above and a curtained space below. The gallery had multiple purposes, depending on what play was being performed: Spectators could sit there, musicians could perform there, or parts of the play could be acted there—as if on balconies, towers, hills, and the like. The curtained area below the gallery was used mainly for "discoveries" of things prepared in advance and hidden from the audience until the proper time. In Shakespeare's *Merchant of Venice,* for example, the curtain is drawn to reveal three small chests, one of which hides the heroine's picture. Apparently, this curtained area was too small, too shallow, and too far out of the sight of some spectators to be used as a performance space. If a performer were "discovered" behind the curtains (as Marlowe's Dr. Faustus is discovered in his study), he would quickly move out onto the stage to be seen and heard better. When large properties such as thrones, beds, desks, and so on were pushed through the curtains onto the stage, the audience would know at once that the action was taking place indoors. When the action shifted to the outdoors, the property could be pulled back behind the curtain.

Globe Theater at Bankside (detail) (17th century). Watercolor.

The Power of Make-Believe

Renaissance audiences took for granted that the theater cannot show "reality": Whatever happens on the stage is make-believe. When the people in the audience saw actors carrying lanterns, they knew it was night, even though the sun was shining brightly overhead. Often, instead of seeing a scene, they heard it described, as when Shakespeare has a character exclaim over a sunrise,

> But look, the morn in russet mantle clad
> Walks o'er the dew of yon high eastward hill.
>
> —*Hamlet,* Act I, Scene I, lines 166–167

When a forest setting was called for, there was no painted scenery imitating real trees, bushes, flowers, and so on. Instead, a few bushes and small trees might be pushed onto the stage, and then the actors spoke lines that evoked images in the spectators' minds. In *As You Like It,* Rosalind simply looks around and announces, "Well, this is the forest of Arden." As the theatrical historian Gerald Bentley put it, Renaissance drama was "a drama of persons, not a drama of places."

Pomp and Pageantry

The scenery may have been kept to a minimum, but the theaters themselves were ornate. The interiors were painted brightly, with many decorations, and the space at the rear of the stage could be covered with colorful tapestries or hangings. Costumes were rich, elaborate, and expensive. The manager-producer Philip Henslowe once paid twenty pounds (then an enormous sum) for a single cloak for one of his actors to wear. Henslowe's lists of theatrical properties mention chariots, fountains, dragons, beds, tents, thrones, booths, and wayside crosses, among other things.

The audience also enjoyed the processions—religious, royal, military—that occurred in many plays. These would enter the stage from one door, cross the stage, and then exit by the other door. A few quick costume changes as the actors passed through the tiring house could double and triple the apparent number of people in a procession.

Music Most Eloquent

When people went to the London theater, they expected not only to see a tragedy or comedy acted but also to hear music, both vocal and instrumental. Trumpets announced the beginning of the play and important arrivals and departures within the play. High up in the gallery, musicians played between acts and at other appropriate times during the performance. And scattered throughout most of the plays, especially the comedies, were songs.

The songs in Shakespeare's plays are the best of this kind that have come down to us, for Shakespeare excelled in lyric and in dramatic poetry. He included a great variety of songs in his plays: sad, happy, comic, thoughtful songs, each one adapted to the play and scene in which it occurs and to the character who performs it. Some of the songs advance the dramatic action, some help establish the mood of a scene, and some reveal character. Like this invitation to love (from the comedy *Twelfth Night*), all of these songs are fresh and spontaneous, not contrived and artificial.

O mistress mine, where are you roaming?
O, stay and hear, your true love's coming,
   That can sing both high and low.
Trip no further, pretty sweeting;
Journeys end in lovers meeting,
   Every wise man's son doth know . . .

What is love? 'tis not hereafter;
Present mirth hath present laughter;
   What's to come is still unsure.
In delay there lies no plenty;
Then come kiss me, sweet and twenty;
Youth's a stuff will not endure.

Lady Masquer (detail) (c. 1610) by Inigo Jones.

Unfortunately, most of the original music for Shakespeare's songs has been lost. But just as the plays themselves have inspired many composers of music for opera, orchestra, and ballet, so have the songs from the plays been set to music right up to the present.

Varying the Venue

The acting companies performed in two other kinds of spaces: in the great halls of castles and manor houses, and in indoor, fully covered theaters in London.

For performances in a great hall, a theater company must have had a portable stage. In these buildings, the usual entertainment was a bear being attacked by dogs. The bear pits were vile places, but their temporary stages could easily accommodate any play except for scenes requiring the use of Heavens overhanging the stage.

Something like this stage may also have been used in private theaters like the Blackfriars, which Shakespeare's company, the King's Men, acquired in 1608. One great advantage of the Blackfriars—a disused monastery that was entirely roofed over—was that the company could perform there in cold weather and, since artificial lighting always had to be used, at night. Thus, the King's Men could put on plays all during the year, increasing profits for the shareholders, among them Shakespeare.

Groundlings Get Close Look

LONDON June 12, 1997—Attending Shakespeare's Globe means pondering seemingly impertinent questions: As you're deciding what seats to buy, box office personnel ask, "Would you like to be a groundling?"

Excuse me? Soon, you learn that the word comes from Elizabethan theater. Groundlings were grimy, snaggle-toothed creatures who stood on the ground without seats, eating, picking pockets.

At the Globe, groundlings still get away with a lot. They prop their elbows on the lip of the stage for the ultimate front-row seat. Moshing is not yet outlawed. Only when you pull out a camera do ushers discreetly intervene.

At last Thursday's *Henry V,* people in the seats seemed so drawn in that they moved down to stand among the groundlings. That's not surprising: The lack of the usual theatrical artifice makes you want to get closer to the play.

—*from USA Today*

(Below) Aerial view of the new Globe Theatre on London's South Bank.

(Below) A 1997 production of Shakespeare's *Henry V* at the new Globe Theatre, London.

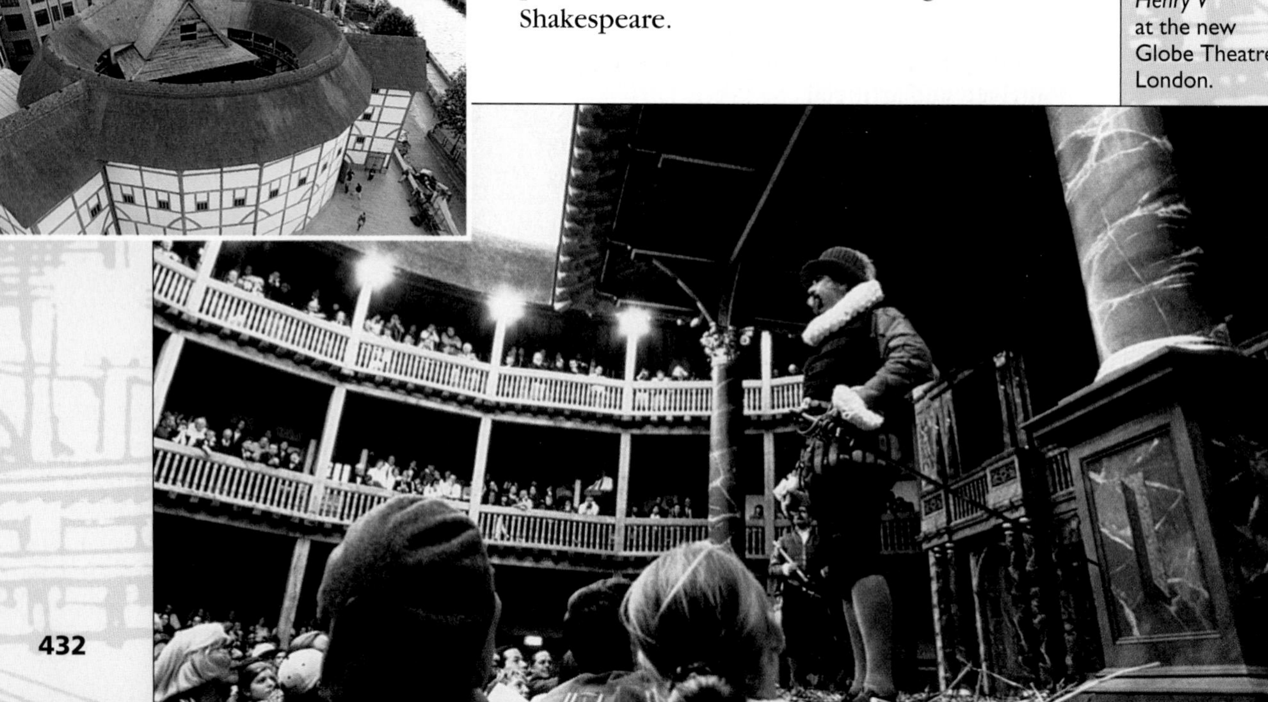

William Shakespeare

(1564–1616)

What sort of man was William Shakespeare? This is a very hard question to answer because he left no letters, diaries, or other private writings containing his personal views. Instead, he left us plays filled with characters representing a vast range of human emotions and attitudes.

William Shakespeare, attributed to John Taylor (d. 1651).
By courtesy of the National Portrait Gallery, London.

The Early Plays

Among Shakespeare's earliest plays, which he wrote in the early 1590s, are *Richard III,* a chronicle or history play about a deformed usurper who became king of England; *The Comedy of Errors,* a rowdy farce about mistaken identity, based on a Latin play; *Titus Andronicus,* a blood-and-thunder tragedy full of rant and atrocities; and *Romeo and Juliet,* a poetic tragedy about ill-fated lovers—the Shakespeare play most frequently taught in schools. The extraordinary thing about these plays is not so much their immense variety—each one is quite different from all the others—but that they are all still regularly revived and performed worldwide.

Years of Prosperity

In the late 1590s, near the end of Elizabeth I's reign, Shakespeare completed his cycle of plays about England during the Wars of the Roses: *Richard II,* both parts of *Henry IV,* and *Henry V.* Also in this period he wrote the tragedy *Julius Caesar* and the comedies that are most frequently performed today, such as *A Midsummer Night's Dream* and *The Merchant of Venice.* Around this time, he also wrote or rewrote *Hamlet* (1600–1601), the tragedy that, of all his tragedies, has provoked the most varied and controversial interpretations from critics, scholars, and actors.

Shakespeare indeed prospered under Queen Elizabeth; according to an old tradition, she asked him to write *The Merry Wives of Windsor* because she wanted to see the merry, fat old knight Sir John Falstaff (of the Henry plays) in love.

The "Tragic Period"

In the early years of the seventeenth century, Shakespeare wrote his greatest tragedies: *Hamlet, Othello, King Lear, Macbeth,* and *Antony and Cleopatra.* Because these famous plays are so preoccupied with evil, violence, and death, some critics feel that Shakespeare must have been unhappy and depressed when he wrote them. And so, these critics invent a "tragic period" in Shakespeare's biography, and they search for personal crises in his private life. To be sure, in 1607, an actor named Edmund Shakespeare, who may well have been William's younger brother, died in London; but by 1607, Shakespeare's alleged "tragic period" was almost over. However, instead of "tragic" we should think of the years 1600–1607 as glorious, because in them Shakespeare's productivity was at its peak.

Retirement

Shakespeare seems to have retired to Stratford around 1610, though he continued to write for the London stage. His last English history play, *Henry VIII,* contained a tribute to Queen Elizabeth—a somewhat tardy tribute, because, unlike most of the other poets of the day, Shakespeare did not praise her in print when she died in 1603. During the first performance of *Henry VIII,* in June of 1613, the firing of the cannon at the end of Act I set the Globe on fire (it had a thatched roof), and it burned to the ground. No injuries were recorded, although a bottle of ale had to be poured on a man whose breeches were burning.

A Complete Man of the Theater

Shakespeare created works specifically for his own acting company and his own stage. He had, for instance, to provide good parts in every play for the principal performers in the company, including the comedians acting in tragedies. Since there were no actresses, he had to limit the number of female parts in his plays and create them in such a way that they could readily be taken over by boys. For instance, although there are many fathers in the plays, there are very few mothers: While boys could be taught to flirt and play shy, acting maternally would be difficult for them. Several of Shakespeare's young women characters disguise themselves as young men early in Act I—an easy solution to the problem of boys playing girls' parts.

Since many of the plays contain many characters, and since there were a limited number of actors in the company, Shakespeare had to arrange for doubling and even tripling of roles: That is, a single actor would have to perform more than one part. Since, of course, an actor could portray only one character at a time, Shakespeare had to plan his scenes carefully, so that nobody would ever have to be on stage in two different roles at the same time. A careful study of the plays shows that Shakespeare handled very masterfully all these technical problems of dramaturgy.

Never Out of Print

From earliest times the public has wanted to read Shakespeare's plays as well as see them staged. In every generation, people have felt that the plays contain so much wisdom, so much knowledge of human nature, and so much remarkable poetry that they need to be pondered in private as well as enjoyed in public. Most readers have agreed with what the poet John Dryden said about Shakespeare's "soul": The man who wrote the plays may be elusive, but he was obviously a great genius whose lofty imagination is matched by his sympathy for all kinds of human behavior.

Shakespeare's contemporaries were so eager to read his plays that enterprising publishers did everything possible, including stealing them, to make them available. Of course, the company generally tried to keep the plays unpublished because they did not want them performed by rival companies. Even so, eighteen plays were published in small books called quartos before Shakespeare's partners collected them together and published them after his death. This collection, known as the "first folio" because of its large size, was published in 1623. Surviving copies of this folio are regarded as valuable treasures today.

Of course, the general reader need not consult any of the original texts of Shakespeare, because his works never go out of print; they are always available in many different languages and formats. The plays that exist in two different versions (one in a quarto and one in a folio) have provided scholars with endless matter for speculation about what Shakespeare actually intended the correct text to be. Indeed, every aspect of Shakespeare has been, and continues to be, thoroughly studied and written about by literary and historical scholars, actors and critics, experts in many fields, and amateurs of every stripe.

(For more information about William Shakespeare, see page 308.)

The Tragedy of Macbeth: The Sources of the Play

Orson Welles in his film production of *Macbeth* (1948).

Poster for *Macbeth,* featuring Raul Julia, at the Public Theater, New York (1990).

Shakespeare's play *Macbeth* conforms to the general rule of Renaissance tragedies, in which the drama had to be about real people whose deeds are recorded in history. (Renaissance comedies, on the other hand, concerned the imaginary doings of fictitious characters.) Shakespeare took the main events of Macbeth's career as king of Scotland (1040–1057) from Raphael Holinshed's *Chronicles of England, Scotland, and Ireland* (1577), the book that provided Shakespeare with historical material for many of his plays. But there are striking differences between his account of Macbeth and Holinshed's. The historical Macbeth had a much more legitimate claim to King Duncan's throne than Shakespeare's Macbeth did. The historical Macbeth gained the throne with the help of other nobles dissatisfied with King Duncan, and he ruled rather successfully. In contrast, Shakespeare's Macbeth has no supporters except his wife, whose strong and ambitious nature Shakespeare develops from a brief statement in the history. And in the play, the reign of Macbeth and his wife brings nothing but violence and disaster to Scotland.

A witch placing a crown on Macbeth's head in the Faux-Real production of *Htebcam* (1994) ("Macbeth" spelled backward).

One explanation for these changes to Holinshed's story is that Shakespeare wanted to explore—from a safe distance—the events and attitudes of his own time. Contemporary audiences have all but lost sight of the scandal that was a backdrop for the play: the Gunpowder Plot of 1605, in which several Catholic zealots plotted to blow up King James I and his Protestant Parliament. Garry Wills, a professor and political columnist, says that for its Elizabethan audience, *Macbeth* was a thriller. (For Wills, the Gunpowder Plot would compare to a plan to bomb the U.S. Capitol building during a presidential address.) The threat to an anointed king, and the perceived evil behind it, was relived in Macbeth's complete threat to the social order in a Scotland of the distant past.

Shakespeare altered his source text, in ways both small and large, in order to pay homage to his own king and country; his changes were

Ellen Terry as Lady Macbeth (detail) (1888–1889) by John Singer Sargent.

Tate Gallery, London.

The three witches in Roman Polanski's film production of *Macbeth* (1971).

intended for an audience of his *particular* moment in history. If he ever saw it, *Macbeth* must have pleased King James, the patron of Shakespeare's company. Since James had recently survived the Gunpowder Plot, he was especially interested in attacks on kings. James always defended the idea that he ruled by divine right. Moreover, he was a Scot and claimed to be a direct descendant of Banquo, to whom the third witch says, "Thou shalt get kings, though thou be none." For these reasons, scholars have for a long time thought of *Macbeth* as a play written for a command performance at court, though there is absolutely no proof that it was. James refused to sit through long plays, and this royal shortcoming has even been used to explain the fact that *Macbeth* is one of Shakespeare's shortest plays.

We can also say that Shakespeare made many changes in Holinshed's story because he was much more interested in psychological truth than in historical fact. And in this sense, *Macbeth* is also about *real* people, men and women tempted by ambition and power, caught up in a web of wants and needs. In playing out these real feelings and desires, Shakespeare's Macbeth transcends the historical Macbeth and gives us a portrait and a play for all times. As the critic Sylvan Barnet notes, "When one reads or sees *Macbeth,* one cannot help feeling that one is experiencing a re-creation or representation of what a man is, in the present, even in the timeless."

The Banquet (detail) by an unknown artist, from Act III, Scene 4, of *Macbeth* at London's Princess Theatre (1853).

Victoria and Albert Museum, London.

Before You Read

The Tragedy of Macbeth

Make the Connection

Quickwrite

Have you ever wondered how just one action—whether tremendous or trivial—might affect the entire course of your life? Could one selfish impulse lead to a chain of decisions you will reflect on with the greatest anguish?

In *Macbeth,* a brave and intelligent man deliberately murders one to whom he owes loyalty—his friend, his kinsman, his guest, his king—and then he must immediately, as a consequence of his murder, kill two other innocent men. After that, he cannot turn away from his evil course: Macbeth's lust for power brings absolute destruction on himself and his family.

Literary Skills Understand the characteristics of tragedy.

Think of people in actual life and in fiction who are obsessed with power and will go to extreme measures to obtain what they want. What are some of the consequences of such shameless ambition? Write down your thoughts.

Literary Focus

Tragedy

Macbeth is a **tragedy:** a kind of play in which human actions have inevitable consequences, in which the characters' bad deeds, errors, and crimes are never forgiven or rectified. By contrast, the characters in a comedy do not live under this iron law of cause and effect; they can do whatever they please as long as they amuse their audience and as long as the funny mess they have made is easily cleaned up at the end of the play. But in a tragedy, an ill-judged action will remorselessly lead to a catastrophe, usually but not necessarily a death or multiple deaths.

A **tragedy** is a literary work depicting serious events in which the main character, who is often high-ranking and dignified, comes to an unhappy end.

For more on Tragedy, see the Handbook of Literary Terms.

INTERNET

More About William Shakespeare

Keyword: LE7 12-3

The Tragedy of Macbeth

William Shakespeare

CHARACTERS

Duncan, king of Scotland
Malcolm, **Donalbain** — his sons
Macbeth, **Banquo**, **Macduff**, **Lennox**, **Ross**, **Menteith**, **Angus**, **Caithness** — noblemen of Scotland
Fleance, son to Banquo
Siward, earl of Northumberland, general of the English forces
Young Siward, his son
Seyton, an officer attending on Macbeth
Son to Macduff
An English Doctor
A Scottish Doctor
A Porter
An Old Man
Three Murderers
Lady Macbeth
Lady Macduff
A Gentlewoman attending on Lady Macbeth
Hecate
Witches
Apparitions
Lords, Officers, Soldiers, Attendants, and Messengers

Setting: Scotland; England

From Roman Polanski's film production of *Macbeth* (1971).

ACT I

Scene 1. *An open place.*

Thunder and lightning. Enter three WITCHES.

First Witch.
When shall we three meet again?
In thunder, lightning, or in rain?
Second Witch.
When the hurlyburly's done,
When the battle's lost and won.
Third Witch.
That will be ere the set of sun.
First Witch.
Where the place?
Second Witch. Upon the heath.
Third Witch.
There to meet with Macbeth.
First Witch.
I come, Graymalkin.°
Second Witch.
Paddock° calls.
Third Witch. Anon!°
All.
Fair is foul, and foul is fair.
Hover through the fog and filthy air. [*Exeunt.*]

? 2. *This scene, played against thunder and lightning, sets the mood of the play. The witches might have made their appearance through the trapdoor on the stage. Thunder would have been produced by rolling cannonballs in the area above the stage. How could these actresses (actors in Shakespeare's day) convey a sense of menace?*

8. **Graymalkin:** the witches' attendant, a gray cat.

9. **Paddock:** toad. **Anon!:** Soon!

Scene 2. *A camp.*

Alarum within.° Enter KING DUNCAN, MALCOLM, DONALBAIN, LENNOX, *with* ATTENDANTS, *meeting a bleeding* CAPTAIN.

King.
What bloody man is that? He can report,
As seemeth by his plight, of the revolt
The newest state.
Malcolm. This is the sergeant
Who like a good and hardy soldier fought
'Gainst my captivity. Hail, brave friend!
Say to the king the knowledge of the broil°
As thou didst leave it.
Captain. Doubtful it stood,
As two spent swimmers, that do cling together
And choke their art.° The merciless Macdonwald—
Worthy to be a rebel for to that
The multiplying villainies of nature
Do swarm upon him—from the Western Isles°
Of kerns and gallowglasses° is supplied;
And Fortune, on his damnèd quarrel smiling,
Showed like a rebel's whore: but all's too weak:
For brave Macbeth—well he deserves that name—
Disdaining Fortune, with his brandished steel,

Alarum within: trumpets offstage.

6. **broil:** quarrel.

? 7. *The captain is bloody and could be carried in or supported by others. How would he speak his lines?*

9. **choke their art:** hinder each other's ability to swim.

12. **Western Isles:** a region of West Scotland comprising the Outer Hebrides.

13. **kerns and gallowglasses:** lightly armed Irish soldiers and heavily armed soldiers.

Photofest

"Fair is foul, and foul is fair. / Hover through the fog and filthy air."

Which smoked with bloody execution,
Like valor's minion° carved out his passage
Till he faced the slave;
Which nev'r shook hands, nor bade farewell to him,
Till he unseamed him from the nave to th' chops,°
And fixed his head upon our battlements.

King.
O valiant cousin! Worthy gentleman!

Captain.
As whence the sun 'gins his reflection°
Shipwracking storms and direful thunders break,
So from that spring whence comfort seemed to come
Discomfort swells. Mark, King of Scotland, mark:
No sooner justice had, with valor armed,
Compelled these skipping kerns to trust their heels
But the Norweyan° lord, surveying vantage,°
With furbished arms and new supplies of men,
Began a fresh assault.

King. Dismayed not this
Our captains, Macbeth and Banquo?

19. minion: favorite.

22. unseamed . . . chops: split him from navel to jaws.

? **23.** *Notice how this horrible action is described by a messenger, not shown on stage. What did Macbeth do to the rebellious Macdonwald?*

25. 'gins his reflection: rises.

31. Norweyan: Norwegian. **surveying vantage:** seeing an opportunity.

Captain. Yes;
As° sparrows eagles, or the hare the lion.
If I say sooth,° I must report they were
As cannons overcharged with double cracks;
So they doubly redoubled strokes upon the foe.
Except° they meant to bathe in reeking wounds,
Or memorize another Golgotha,°
I cannot tell—
But I am faint; my gashes cry for help.

King.
So well thy words become thee as thy wounds;
They smack of honor both. Go get him surgeons.

[*Exit* CAPTAIN *attended.*]

[*Enter* ROSS *and* ANGUS.]

Who comes here?

Malcolm. The worthy Thane° of Ross.

Lennox.
What a haste looks through his eyes! So should he look
That seems to° speak things strange.

Ross. God save the king!

King.
Whence cam'st thou, worthy thane?

Ross. From Fife, great king;
Where the Norweyan banners flout the sky
And fan our people cold.
Norway himself,° with terrible numbers,
Assisted by that most disloyal traitor
The Thane of Cawdor, began a dismal conflict;
Till that Bellona's bridegroom,° lapped in proof,°
Confronted him with self-comparisons,°
Point against point, rebellious arm 'gainst arm,
Curbing his lavish° spirit: and, to conclude,
The victory fell on us.

King. Great happiness!

Ross. That now
Sweno, the Norways' king, craves composition;°
Nor would we deign him burial of his men
Till he disbursèd, at Saint Colme's Inch,°
Ten thousand dollars to our general use.

King.
No more that Thane of Cawdor shall deceive
Our bosom interest:° go pronounce his present° death,
And with his former title greet Macbeth.

Ross.
I'll see it done.

King.
What he hath lost, noble Macbeth hath won. [*Exeunt.*]

35. As: No more than.

? **35.** *This line can be delivered in several ways. How do you imagine the captain speaks it?*

36. sooth: truth.

39. Except: unless.

40. memorize another Golgotha: make the place as memorable as Golgotha, where Christ was crucified.

? **44.** *Duncan can be played in several ways: as a strong but aging king; as a frail old man; as a kind but foolish old man who doesn't understand what's going on. As the play goes on, decide how you interpret Duncan's character.*

45. Thane: Scottish title of nobility.

47. seems to: seems about to.

51. Norway himself: that is, the king of Norway.

54. Bellona's bridegroom: Bellona is the goddess of war. Macbeth, who is a great soldier, is called her mate. **lapped in proof:** clad in armor.

55. self-comparisons: countermovements.

57. lavish: insolent; rude.

59. composition: peace terms.

61. Saint Colme's Inch: island off the coast of Scotland.

64. bosom interest: heart's trust. **present:** immediate.

? **67.** *As you read, notice how later events relate to the king's words. How would you have him say these lines?*

Scene 3. *A heath.*

Thunder. Enter the three WITCHES.

First Witch.
Where hast thou been, sister?
Second Witch.
Killing swine.
Third Witch.
Sister, where thou?
First Witch.
A sailor's wife had chestnuts in her lap,
And mounched, and mounched, and mounched. "Give me,"
quoth I.
"Aroint thee,° witch!" the rump-fed ronyon° cries.
Her husband's to Aleppo gone, master o' th' *Tiger:*
But in a sieve° I'll thither sail,
And, like a rat without a tail,
I'll do, I'll do, and I'll do.
Second Witch.
I'll give thee a wind.
First Witch.
Th' art kind.
Third Witch.
And I another.
First Witch.
I myself have all the other;
And the very ports they blow,°
All the quarters that they know
I' th' shipman's card.°
I'll drain him dry as hay:
Sleep shall neither night nor day
Hang upon his penthouse lid;°
He shall live a man forbid:°
Weary sev'nights nine times nine
Shall he dwindle, peak,° and pine:
Though his bark cannot be lost,
Yet it shall be tempest-tossed.
Look what I have.
Second Witch.
Show me, show me.
First Witch.
Here I have a pilot's thumb,
Wracked as homeward he did come.

[*Drum within.*]

Third Witch.
A drum, a drum!
Macbeth doth come.

6. **Aroint thee:** begone. **rump-fed ronyon:** fat-rumped, scabby creature.

8. **But . . . sieve:** Witches were believed to have the power to sail in sieves.

15. **ports they blow:** harbors they blow into.

17. **card:** compass.

20. **penthouse lid:** eyelid.

21. **forbid:** cursed.

23. **peak:** grow pale.

All.

The weird sisters, hand in hand,
Posters° of the sea and land,
Thus do go about, about:
Thrice to thine, and thrice to mine,
And thrice again, to make up nine.
Peace! The charm's wound up.

[*Enter* MACBETH *and* BANQUO.]

Macbeth.

So foul and fair a day I have not seen.

Banquo.

How far is't called to Forres?° What are these
So withered, and so wild in their attire,
That look not like th' inhabitants o' th' earth,
And yet are on't? Live you, or are you aught
That man may question? You seem to understand me,
By each at once her choppy° finger laying

33. Posters: travelers.

? **38.** *What words is Macbeth echoing here? Why, given the weather, does Macbeth think the day is "fair"?*

39. Forres: a town in northeast Scotland and site of King Duncan's castle.

? **39.** *What should Banquo do as he sees the witches? How should his voice change between the words* Forres *and* What?

44. choppy: chapped; sore.

"All hail, Macbeth! Hail to thee, Thane of Glamis!"

Photofest

Upon her skinny lips. You should° be women,
And yet your beards forbid me to interpret
That you are so.

Macbeth. Speak, if you can: what are you?

First Witch.
All hail, Macbeth! Hail to thee, Thane of Glamis!

Second Witch.
All hail, Macbeth! Hail to thee, Thane of Cawdor!

Third Witch.
All hail, Macbeth, that shalt be king hereafter!

Banquo.
Good sir, why do you start, and seem to fear
Things that do sound so fair? I' th' name of truth,
Are ye fantastical, or that indeed
Which outwardly ye show? My noble partner
You greet with present grace and great prediction
Of noble having and of royal hope,
That he seems rapt withal:° to me you speak not.
If you can look into the seeds of time,
And say which grain will grow and which will not,
Speak then to me, who neither beg nor fear
Your favors nor your hate.

First Witch. Hail!

Second Witch. Hail!

Third Witch. Hail!

First Witch.
Lesser than Macbeth, and greater.

Second Witch.
Not so happy,° yet much happier.

Third Witch.
Thou shalt get° kings, though thou be none.
So all hail, Macbeth and Banquo!

First Witch.
Banquo and Macbeth, all hail!

Macbeth.
Stay, you imperfect° speakers, tell me more:
By Sinel's death I know I am Thane of Glamis;
But how of Cawdor? The Thane of Cawdor lives,
A prosperous gentleman; and to be king
Stands not within the prospect of belief,
No more than to be Cawdor. Say from whence
You owe° this strange intelligence?° Or why
Upon this blasted heath you stop our way
With such prophetic greeting? Speak, I charge you.

[WITCHES *vanish.*]

Banquo.
The earth hath bubbles as the water has,
And these are of them. Whither are they vanished?

45. should: must.

? **51.** *Banquo's words give a clue as to how Macbeth reacts to the witches. What is Macbeth doing? When Banquo asks, "Are ye fantastical," whom is he addressing?*

57. rapt withal: entranced by it.

? **61.** *What does Banquo ask the witches?*

66. happy: lucky.

67. get: beget.

70. imperfect: incomplete.

? **71.** *Sinel is Macbeth's father. What do you think Macbeth's tone is here? Is he overeager? or just casually curious?*

76. owe: own; have. **intelligence:** information.

? **Stage direction.** *The witches on Shakespeare's stage would have vanished through the trapdoor. Is Banquo, in his next speech, intrigued or disturbed? How does Macbeth feel?*

Macbeth.
Into the air, and what seemed corporal° melted
As breath into the wind. Would they had stayed!

Banquo.
Were such things here as we do speak about?
Or have we eaten on the insane root°
That takes the reason prisoner?

Macbeth.
Your children shall be kings.

Banquo. You shall be king.

Macbeth.
And Thane of Cawdor too. Went it not so?

Banquo.
To th' selfsame tune and words. Who's here?

[*Enter* ROSS *and* ANGUS.]

Ross.
The king hath happily received, Macbeth,
The news of thy success; and when he reads°
Thy personal venture in the rebels' fight,
His wonders and his praises do contend
Which should be thine or his. Silenced with that,
In viewing o'er the rest o' th' selfsame day,
He finds thee in the stout Norweyan ranks,
Nothing afeard of what thyself didst make,
Strange images of death.° As thick as tale
Came post with post,° and every one did bear
Thy praises in his kingdom's great defense,
And poured them down before him.

Angus. We are sent
To give thee, from our royal master, thanks;
Only to herald thee into his sight,
Not pay thee.

Ross.
And for an earnest° of a greater honor,
He bade me, from him, call thee Thane of Cawdor;
In which addition,° hail, most worthy thane!
For it is thine.

Banquo. What, can the devil speak true?

Macbeth.
The Thane of Cawdor lives: why do you dress me
In borrowed robes?

Angus. Who was the thane lives yet,
But under heavy judgment bears that life
Which he deserves to lose. Whether he was combined
With those of Norway, or did line° the rebel
With hidden help and vantage, or that with both
He labored in his country's wrack, I know not;
But treasons capital,° confessed and proved,
Have overthrown him.

81. corporal: corporeal (bodily, physical).

84. insane root: henbane, believed to cause insanity.

90. reads: considers.

97. Nothing . . . death: killing, and not being afraid of being killed.

98. post with post: messenger with a message.

104. earnest: pledge.

106. addition: title.

112. line: support.

115. capital: deserving death.

Macbeth (*aside*). Glamis, and Thane of Cawdor:
The greatest is behind. (*To* ROSS *and* ANGUS.) Thanks for your pains.
(*Aside to* BANQUO.) Do you not hope your children shall be kings,
When those that gave the Thane of Cawdor to me
Promised no less to them?

Banquo (*aside to* MACBETH). That, trusted home,°
Might yet enkindle you unto the crown,°
Besides the Thane of Cawdor. But 'tis strange:
And oftentimes, to win us to our harm,
The instruments of darkness tell us truths,
Win us with honest trifles, to betray 's
In deepest consequence.
Cousins,° a word, I pray you.

Macbeth (*aside*). Two truths are told
As happy prologues to the swelling act
Of the imperial theme.—I thank you, gentlemen.—
(*Aside*.) This supernatural soliciting
Cannot be ill, cannot be good. If ill,
Why hath it given me earnest of success,
Commencing in a truth? I am Thane of Cawdor:
If good, why do I yield to that suggestion
Whose horrid image doth unfix my hair
And make my seated heart knock at my ribs,
Against the use of nature? Present fears
Are less than horrible imaginings.
My thought, whose murder yet is but fantastical,
Shakes so my single° state of man that function
Is smothered in surmise, and nothing is
But what is not.°

Banquo. Look, how our partner's rapt.

Macbeth (*aside*).
If chance will have me king, why, chance may crown me,
Without my stir.

Banquo. New honors come upon him,
Like our strange° garments, cleave not to their mold
But with the aid of use.

Macbeth (*aside*). Come what come may,
Time and the hour runs through the roughest day.

Banquo.
Worthy Macbeth, we stay upon your leisure.

Macbeth.
Give me your favor.° My dull brain was wrought
With things forgotten. Kind gentlemen, your pains
Are registered where every day I turn
The leaf to read them. Let us toward the king.
(*Aside to* BANQUO.) Think upon what hath chanced, and at more time,

? **117.** *"Behind" here means "to follow." How should this important aside be spoken? What is Macbeth's mood?*

120. trusted home: trusted all the way.

121. enkindle . . . crown: arouse in you the ambition to become king.

? **126.** *How does this speech show Banquo as part of the conscience of the play?*

127. Cousins: This word is used frequently by Shakespeare to mean "fellows" or "kindred friends" of some sort.

? **Stage direction.** *When a character is delivering an aside, the director or the playwright must arrange for the others on stage to be involved in some way so that it would be natural for them not to notice the character delivering the aside. Where should Macbeth go on stage to deliver this important aside? What do you think he meant by the "swelling act" in line 128? Where are Banquo, Angus, and Ross?*

? **137.** *What do you suppose Macbeth is thinking of that makes his seated (fixed) heart knock at his ribs in an unnatural way?*

140. single: unaided; weak.

142. nothing . . . not: Nothing is real to me except my imaginings.

? **142.** *What might Macbeth do as Banquo notices him brooding?*

145. strange: new.

? **145.** *What does Banquo compare Macbeth and his new honors to? Is Banquo's mood different from Macbeth's?*

149. favor: pardon.

The interim having weighed it, let us speak
Our free hearts each to other.

Banquo. Very gladly.

Macbeth.
Till then, enough. Come, friends. [*Exeunt.*]

Scene 4. *Forres. The palace.*

Flourish.° *Enter* KING DUNCAN, LENNOX, MALCOLM, DONALBAIN, *and* ATTENDANTS.

King.
Is execution done on Cawdor? Are not
Those in commission yet returned?

Malcolm. My liege,
They are not yet come back. But I have spoke
With one that saw him die, who did report
That very frankly he confessed his treasons,
Implored your highness' pardon and set forth
A deep repentance: nothing in his life
Became him like the leaving it. He died
As one that had been studied in his death
To throw away the dearest thing he owed°
As 'twere a careless trifle.

King. There's no art
To find the mind's construction in the face:
He was a gentleman on whom I built
An absolute trust.

[*Enter* MACBETH, BANQUO, ROSS, *and* ANGUS.]

O worthiest cousin!
The sin of my ingratitude even now
Was heavy on me: thou art so far before,
That swiftest wing of recompense is slow
To overtake thee. Would thou hadst less deserved,
That the proportion° both of thanks and payment
Might have been mine! Only I have left to say,
More is thy due than more than all can pay.

Macbeth.
The service and the loyalty I owe,
In doing it, pays itself.° Your highness' part
Is to receive our duties: and our duties
Are to your throne and state children and servants;
Which do but what they should, by doing everything
Safe toward° your love and honor.

King. Welcome hither.
I have begun to plant thee, and will labor
To make thee full of growing. Noble Banquo,
That hast no less deserved, nor must be known
No less to have done so, let me enfold thee
And hold thee to my heart.

Flourish: of trumpets.

? **8.** *What does this famous line mean: "nothing in his life / Became him like the leaving it"?*

10. owed: owned.

? **12.** *What irony would you feel here? What does Duncan fail to realize about another face?*

19. proportion: greater amount.

23. pays itself: is its own reward.

27. safe toward: safeguarding.

? **32.** *You know Macbeth's thoughts. How do you feel about him as the king lavishes praise on him? Is the king's reception of Banquo even warmer? How might Macbeth react here?*

"We will establish our estate upon Our eldest, Malcolm."

From Roman Polanski's film production of *Macbeth* (1971).

Banquo. There if I grow,
The harvest is your own.
King. My plenteous joys,
Wanton in fullness, seek to hide themselves
In drops of sorrow. Sons, kinsmen, thanes,
And you whose places are the nearest, know,
We will establish our estate upon
Our eldest, Malcolm, whom we name hereafter
The Prince of Cumberland: which honor must
Not unaccompanied invest him only,
But signs of nobleness, like stars, shall shine
On all deservers. From hence to Inverness,°
And bind us further to you.
Macbeth.
The rest is labor, which is not used for you.°
I'll be myself the harbinger,° and make joyful
The hearing of my wife with your approach;
So, humbly take my leave.
King. My worthy Cawdor!
Macbeth (*aside*).
The Prince of Cumberland! That is a step
On which I must fall down, or else o'erleap,
For in my way it lies. Stars, hide your fires;
Let not light see my black and deep desires:
The eye wink at the hand;° yet let that be
Which the eye fears, when it is done, to see. [*Exit.*]
King.
True, worthy Banquo; he is full so valiant,
And in his commendations° I am fed;
It is a banquet to me. Let's after him,
Whose care is gone before to bid us welcome.
It is a peerless kinsman. [*Flourish. Exeunt.*]

? **35.** *There's a clue in this line that shows how moved the king is. What is the king doing at the words "drops of sorrow"?*

42. Inverness: Macbeth's castle.

? **43.** *Who is to inherit Duncan's crown?*

44. The rest . . . you: When rest is not used for you, it is labor.

45. harbinger: sign of something to come.

52. wink . . . hand: be blind to the hand's deed.

? **53.** *Where in this speech do we begin to hear Macbeth talk in terms of darkness?*

55. his commendations: praises of him.

Scene 5. *Inverness. Macbeth's castle.*

Enter Macbeth's wife, LADY MACBETH, *alone, with a letter.*

Lady Macbeth (*reads*). "They met me in the day of success; and I have learned by the perfect'st report they have more in them than mortal knowledge. When I burned in desire to question them further, they made themselves air, into which they vanished. Whiles I stood rapt in the wonder of it, came missives° from the King, who all-hailed me 'Thane of Cawdor'; by which title, before, these weird sisters saluted me, and referred me to the coming on of time, with 'Hail, king that shalt be!' This have I thought good to deliver thee, my dearest partner of greatness, that thou mightst not lose the dues of rejoicing, by being ignorant of what greatness is promised thee. Lay it to thy heart, and farewell."

Glamis thou art, and Cawdor, and shalt be
What thou art promised. Yet do I fear thy nature;
It is too full o' th' milk of human kindness
To catch the nearest way. Thou wouldst be great,
Art not without ambition, but without
The illness° should attend it. What thou wouldst highly,
That wouldst thou holily; wouldst not play false,
And yet wouldst wrongly win. Thou'dst have, great Glamis,
That which cries, "Thus thou must do" if thou have it;
And that which rather thou dost fear to do

? **Stage direction.** *As you picture Lady Macbeth reading this letter, try to imagine what she would be doing on stage and what her mood would be, especially at the words "Thane of Cawdor."*

6. missives: messengers.

? **13.** *What does Lady Macbeth do with the letter? Whom is she addressing here with "thou" and "thy"? How would you explain "th' milk of human kindness"?*

18. illness: wickedness; evil nature.

"My dearest love,
Duncan comes here tonight."
Photofest

Than wishest should be undone. Hie thee hither,
That I may pour my spirits in thine ear,
And chastise with the valor of my tongue
All that impedes thee from the golden round
Which fate and metaphysical° aid doth seem
To have thee crowned withal.

[*Enter* MESSENGER.]

What is your tidings?

Messenger.
The king comes here tonight.

Lady Macbeth. Thou'rt mad to say it!
Is not thy master with him, who, were't so,
Would have informed for preparation?

Messenger.
So please you, it is true. Our thane is coming.
One of my fellows had the speed of him,°
Who, almost dead for breath, had scarcely more
Than would make up his message.

Lady Macbeth. Give him tending;
He brings great news. [*Exit* MESSENGER.]
The raven himself is hoarse
That croaks the fatal entrance of Duncan
Under my battlements. Come, you spirits
That tend on mortal° thoughts, unsex me here,
And fill me, from the crown to the toe, top-full
Of direst cruelty! Make thick my blood,
Stop up th' access and passage to remorse,
That no compunctious visitings of nature°
Shake my fell° purpose, nor keep peace between
Th' effect and it! Come to my woman's breasts,
And take my milk for gall,° you murd'ring ministers,°
Wherever in your sightless° substances
You wait on nature's mischief! Come, thick night,
And pall° thee in the dunnest° smoke of hell,
That my keen knife see not the wound it makes,
Nor heaven peep through the blanket of the dark,
To cry "Hold, hold!"

[*Enter* MACBETH.]

Great Glamis! Worthy Cawdor!
Greater than both, by the all-hail hereafter!
Thy letters have transported me beyond
This ignorant present, and I feel now
The future in the instant.

Macbeth. My dearest love,
Duncan comes here tonight.

Lady Macbeth. And when goes hence?

Macbeth.
Tomorrow, as he purposes.

26. *What do you guess the "golden round" is?*

27. metaphysical: supernatural.

33. had . . . him: had more speed than he did.

36. *Who is the raven she refers to as being hoarse? Why does she call him a raven?*

39. mortal: deadly.

43. compunctious . . . nature: natural feelings of compassion.

44. fell: savage.

46. gall: a bitter substance; bile. **murd'ring ministers:** agents of murder.

47. sightless: invisible.

49. pall: cover with a shroud, a burial cloth. **dunnest:** darkest.

52. *How has Lady Macbeth reinforced the witches' statement: "Fair is foul, and foul is fair . . ."?*

57. *Is their passion for each other as great as their passion for power? If you feel it is, how might a director illustrate it here?*

Lady Macbeth. O, never
Shall sun that morrow see!
Your face, my thane, is as a book where men
May read strange matters. To beguile the time,°
Look like the time; bear welcome in your eye,
Your hand, your tongue: look like th' innocent flower,
But be the serpent under't. He that's coming
Must be provided for: and you shall put
This night's great business into my dispatch;°
Which shall to all our nights and days to come
Give solely sovereign sway and masterdom.

Macbeth.
We will speak further.

Lady Macbeth. Only look up clear.°
To alter favor ever is to fear.°
Leave all the rest to me. [*Exeunt.*]

61. beguile the time: deceive people of the day.

66. dispatch: management.

? **69.** *How is Macbeth feeling?*

69. clear: undisturbed.

70. To alter . . . fear: To show an altered face is dangerous.

Scene 6. *Before Macbeth's castle.*

Hautboys° and torches. Enter KING DUNCAN, MALCOLM, DONALBAIN, BANQUO, LENNOX, MACDUFF, ROSS, ANGUS, *and* ATTENDANTS.

Hautboys: oboes.

King.
This castle hath a pleasant seat;° the air
Nimbly and sweetly recommends itself
Unto our gentle senses.

Banquo. This guest of summer,
The temple-haunting martlet,° does approve°
By his loved mansionry° that the heaven's breath
Smells wooingly here. No jutty,° frieze,
Buttress, nor coign of vantage,° but this bird
Hath made his pendent bed and procreant° cradle.
Where they most breed and haunt, I have observed
The air is delicate.

[*Enter* LADY MACBETH.]

King. See, see, our honored hostess!
The love that follows us sometime is our trouble,
Which still we thank as love. Herein I teach you
How you shall bid God 'ield° us for your pains
And thank us for your trouble.

Lady Macbeth. All our service
In every point twice done, and then done double,
Were poor and single business to contend
Against those honors deep and broad wherewith
Your majesty loads our house: for those of old,
And the late dignities heaped up to them,
We rest your hermits.°

King. Where's the Thane of Cawdor?
We coursed° him at the heels, and had a purpose

1. seat: situation; setting.

4. martlet: a bird that builds nests in churches. **approve:** prove.

5. mansionry: nest (dwelling).

6. jutty: projection.

7. coign of vantage: advantageous corner (of the castle).

8. procreant: breeding.

? **9.** *This scene contrasts strongly with the previous one. Again, what irony do you feel as Duncan admires the castle? How do you imagine Lady Macbeth acts as she now enters to greet her guests?*

13. 'ield: reward.

20. We rest your hermits: We'll remain dependents who will pray for you.

21. coursed: chased.

"See, see, our honored hostess!"

From Roman Polanski's film production of *Macbeth* (1971).

To be his purveyor:° but he rides well,
And his great love, sharp as his spur, hath holp° him
To his home before us. Fair and noble hostess,
We are your guest tonight.

Lady Macbeth. Your servants ever
Have theirs, themselves, and what is theirs, in compt,°
To make their audit at your highness' pleasure,
Still° to return your own.

King. Give me your hand.
Conduct me to mine host: we love him highly,
And shall continue our graces toward him.
By your leave, hostess. [*Exeunt.*]

22. purveyor: advance man.

23. holp: helped.

26. in compt: in trust.

28. Still: always.

? **31.** *How do you imagine the scene ends?*

Scene 7. *Macbeth's castle.*

Hautboys. Torches. Enter a SEWER,° *and diverse* SERVANTS *with dishes and service, and pass over the stage. Then enter* MACBETH.

Macbeth.
If it were done when 'tis done, then 'twere well
It were done quickly. If th' assassination
Could trammel up the consequence, and catch,
With his surcease,° success; that but this blow
Might be the be-all and the end-all—here,
But here, upon this bank and shoal of time,

Sewer: butler.

? **1.** *This is one of Shakespeare's great soliloquies, in which Macbeth voices his indecision and possibly his conscience. What are his conflicts?*

4. his surcease: Duncan's death.

We'd jump° the life to come. But in these cases
We still have judgment here; that we but teach
Bloody instructions, which, being taught, return
To plague th' inventor: this even-handed° justice
Commends° th' ingredients of our poisoned chalice
To our own lips. He's here in double trust:
First, as I am his kinsman and his subject,
Strong both against the deed; then, as his host,
Who should against his murderer shut the door,
Not bear the knife myself. Besides, this Duncan
Hath borne his faculties° so meek, hath been
So clear° in his great office, that his virtues
Will plead like angels trumpet-tongued against
The deep damnation of his taking-off;°
And pity, like a naked newborn babe,
Striding the blast, or heaven's cherubin horsed
Upon the sightless couriers° of the air,
Shall blow the horrid deed in every eye,
That° tears shall drown the wind. I have no spur
To prick the sides of my intent, but only
Vaulting ambition, which o'erleaps itself
And falls on th' other——

[*Enter* LADY MACBETH.]

How now! What news?

Lady Macbeth.
He has almost supped. Why have you left the chamber?

Macbeth.
Hath he asked for me?

Lady Macbeth. Know you not he has?

Macbeth.
We will proceed no further in this business:
He hath honored me of late, and I have bought
Golden opinions from all sorts of people,
Which would be worn now in their newest gloss,
Not cast aside so soon.

Lady Macbeth. Was the hope drunk
Wherein you dressed yourself? Hath it slept since?
And wakes it now, to look so green° and pale
At what it did so freely? From this time
Such I account thy love. Art thou afeard
To be the same in thine own act and valor
As thou art in desire? Wouldst thou have that
Which thou esteem'st the ornament of life,°
And live a coward in thine own esteem,
Letting "I dare not" wait upon° "I would,"
Like the poor cat i' th' adage?°

Macbeth. Prithee, peace!
I dare do all that may become a man;
Who dares do more is none.

7. jump: risk. (Macbeth knows he will be condemned to hell for the sin of murder.)

10. even-handed: impartial.

11. Commends: offers.

17. faculties: powers.

18. clear: clean.

20. taking-off: murder.

23. sightless couriers: winds.

25. That: so that.

? **26.** *Macbeth says he has no spur to prick the sides of his intent. Is that true?*

37. green: sickly.

42. ornament of life: crown.

44. wait upon: follow.

45. poor . . . adage: saying about a cat who wants fish but won't wet its paws.

Lady Macbeth. What beast was't then
That made you break° this enterprise to me?
When you durst do it, then you were a man;
And to be more than what you were, you would
Be so much more the man. Nor time nor place
Did then adhere,° and yet you would make both.
They have made themselves, and that their fitness now
Does unmake you. I have given suck, and know
How tender 'tis to love the babe that milks me:
I would, while it was smiling in my face,
Have plucked my nipple from his boneless gums,
And dashed the brains out, had I so sworn as you
Have done to this.

Macbeth. If we should fail?

Lady Macbeth. We fail?
But° screw your courage to the sticking-place,°
And we'll not fail. When Duncan is asleep—
Whereto the rather shall his day's hard journey
Soundly invite him—his two chamberlains
Will I with wine and wassail° so convince,°
That memory, the warder of the brain,
Shall be a fume, and the receipt of reason
A limbeck only:° when in swinish sleep
Their drenchèd natures lie as in a death,
What cannot you and I perform upon
Th' unguarded Duncan, what not put upon
His spongy officers, who shall bear the guilt
Of our great quell?

Macbeth. Bring forth men-children only;
For thy undaunted mettle° should compose
Nothing but males. Will it not be received,
When we have marked with blood those sleepy two
Of his own chamber, and used their very daggers,
That they have done't?

Lady Macbeth. Who dares receive it other,
As we shall make our griefs and clamor roar
Upon his death?

Macbeth. I am settled, and bend up
Each corporal agent to this terrible feat.
Away, and mock the time° with fairest show:
False face must hide what the false heart doth know.

[*Exeunt.*]

48. break: disclose; reveal.

52. adhere: suit.

? **54.** *How does Lady Macbeth try to intimidate her husband in this speech? Watch what she says about herself in the next lines. There has been some question as to whether "We fail?" (line 59) should be a question. How does the meaning change if the line is spoken as a statement?*

60. But: only. **sticking-place:** the notch in a crossbow.

64. wassail: drinking. **convince:** overcome.

67. the receipt . . . only: The reasoning part of the brain would become like a **limbeck** (or still), distilling only confused thoughts.

? **72.** *"Quell" is murder. What are Lady Macbeth's plans?*

73. mettle: spirit.

81. mock the time: deceive the world.

? **81.** *Should Macbeth pause here? How should these key words be spoken?*

? **82.** *How is this yet another echo of the witches' words in Scene 1?*

Response and Analysis

Act I

Reading Check

1. In Scene 1, where do the witches plan to meet again, and why?
2. What does the king determine to do for Macbeth? Why?
3. What do the witches tell Macbeth and Banquo in Scene 3?
4. What are Lady Macbeth's plans for Duncan when he visits the castle?

Thinking Critically

5. How does the weather in the brief opening scene of *Macbeth* reflect the human passions revealed in the rest of the act?
6. Explain the **paradox,** or the apparently contradictory nature, of the witches' greeting to Banquo in Scene 3: "Lesser than Macbeth, and greater." How is this paradox true?
7. How does Banquo's reaction to the witches differ from Macbeth's? What do you think Macbeth's reaction suggests about his **character**?
8. What **conflict** rages in Macbeth after he hears the witches' prophecy? What **resolution** to this conflict does Macbeth express in his aside in Scene 4, lines 48–53?
9. Find details in the play that show the contrasts between Lady Macbeth's **character** and her husband's. Who is more single-minded and logical? Who is more argumentative and sensitive?

Extending and Evaluating

10. One critic has said that the witches are "in some sense representative of potentialities within" Macbeth. How could that statement be explained? Is there any evidence in Act I that Macbeth has wanted to be king before? Explain.

Literary Focus

Blank Verse

Almost all of *Macbeth* is written in **blank verse,** or unrhymed **iambic pentameter,** a form of poetry that comes close to imitating the natural rhythms of English speech. An **iamb** is a metrical foot that has one unstressed syllable followed by one stressed syllable. (Each of the following is an iamb: *Macbeth, success, to win.*) **Pentameter** means that each line of verse has five feet, so one line of iambic pentameter has five iambs. Read this line aloud to hear the meter.

> **Banquo:** Gŏod sír, whȳ dó yŏu stárt,
> ănd seém tŏ feár . . .

Analyzing blank verse. Some lines in *Macbeth* are irregular, with fewer feet or with feet that are not iambs. The play even has a few prose passages, indicated by lines that are set full measure; that is, they extend across the width of the page.

1. Scan one major speech by Macbeth and one by Lady Macbeth anywhere in Act I. What variations in iambic pentameter do you find? Why do you think these variations exist—how do sound and sense relate to each other?
2. Do the witches speak in blank verse? Why do you suppose Shakespeare wrote their speeches in this way?
3. Find a prose passage in Act I. Why do you think Shakespeare chose to use prose in this passage?

Literary Skills Analyze the characteristics of tragedy, including character, conflict, and resolution. Analyze the characteristics of blank verse.

ACT II Scene 1. *Inverness. Court of Macbeth's castle.*

Enter BANQUO, *and* FLEANCE, *with a torch before him (on the way to bed).*

Banquo.
How goes the night, boy?

Fleance.
The moon is down; I have not heard the clock.

Banquo.
And she goes down at twelve.

Fleance. I take't, 'tis later, sir.

Banquo.
Hold, take my sword. There's husbandry° in heaven.
Their candles are all out. Take thee that too.
A heavy summons° lies like lead upon me,
And yet I would not sleep. Merciful powers,
Restrain in me the cursèd thoughts that nature
Gives way to in repose!

[*Enter* MACBETH, *and a* SERVANT *with a torch.*]

Give me my sword!
Who's there?

Macbeth.
A friend.

Banquo.
What, sir, not yet at rest? The king's a-bed:
He hath been in unusual pleasure, and
Sent forth great largess to your offices:°
This diamond he greets your wife withal,
By the name of most kind hostess; and shut up°
In measureless content.

Macbeth. Being unprepared,
Our will became the servant to defect,°
Which else should free have wrought.

Banquo. All's well.
I dreamt last night of the three weird sisters:
To you they have showed some truth.

Macbeth. I think not of them.
Yet, when we can entreat an hour to serve,
We would spend it in some words upon that business,
If you would grant the time.

Banquo. At your kind'st leisure.

Macbeth.
If you shall cleave to my consent, when 'tis,°
It shall make honor for you.

Banquo. So° I lose none
In seeking to augment it, but still keep
My bosom franchised° and allegiance clear,°
I shall be counseled.

? **Stage direction.** *Who is Fleance? What would you remember of the witches' prophecy when you see him here? Do we know if Macbeth and his wife have any children?*

4. **husbandry:** economizing.

6. **summons:** call to sleep.

14. **largess to your offices:** gifts to your servants' quarters.

16. **shut up:** concluded.

18. **to defect:** to insufficient preparations.

? 24. *This is the second time Macbeth has suggested he and Banquo talk. Do you think he might want to confide in Banquo? Does he want to get Banquo on his side? How would you characterize his motives?*

25. **cleave . . . 'tis:** join my cause, when the time comes.

26. **So:** provided that.

28. **franchised:** free (from guilt). **clear:** clean.

Macbeth. Good repose the while!

Banquo.
Thanks, sir. The like to you!

[*Exit* BANQUO, *with* FLEANCE.]

Macbeth.
Go bid thy mistress, when my drink is ready,
She strike upon the bell. Get thee to bed.

[*Exit* SERVANT.]

Is this a dagger which I see before me,
The handle toward my hand? Come, let me clutch thee.
I have thee not, and yet I see thee still.
Art thou not, fatal vision, sensible°
To feeling as to sight, or art thou but
A dagger of the mind, a false creation,
Proceeding from the heat-oppressèd brain?
I see thee yet, in form as palpable°
As this which now I draw.
Thou marshal'st me the way that I was going;
And such an instrument I was to use.
Mine eyes are made the fools o' th' other senses,
Or else worth all the rest. I see thee still;
And on thy blade and dudgeon° gouts° of blood,
Which was not so before. There's no such thing.
It is the bloody business which informs°
Thus to mine eyes. Now o'er the one half-world
Nature seems dead, and wicked dreams abuse°
The curtained sleep; witchcraft celebrates

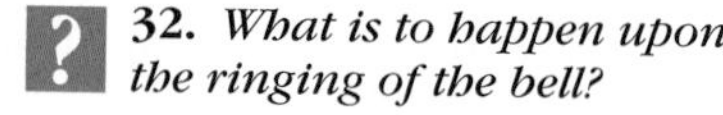

32. *What is to happen upon the ringing of the bell?*

36. **sensible:** perceptible to the senses.

40. **palpable:** obvious.

? 41. *What does Macbeth do at this moment? If you were directing the play, would you suspend a dagger in front of Macbeth during this speech? Why or why not?*

46. **dudgeon:** hilt. **gouts:** large drops.

48. **informs:** gives shape.

50. **abuse:** deceive.

"I have done the deed."

Photofest

Pale Hecate's° offerings; and withered murder,
Alarumed° by his sentinel, the wolf,
Whose howl's his watch, thus with his stealthy pace,
With Tarquin's° ravishing strides, towards his design
Moves like a ghost. Thou sure and firm-set earth,
Hear not my steps, which way they walk, for fear
Thy very stones prate of my whereabout,
And take the present horror from the time,
Which now suits with it.° Whiles I threat, he lives:
Words to the heat of deeds too cold breath gives.

[*A bell rings.*]

I go, and it is done: the bell invites me.
Hear it not, Duncan, for it is a knell
That summons thee to heaven, or to hell. [*Exit.*]

52. Hecate's: Hecate (hek′it), goddess of sorcery.

53. Alarumed: called to action.

55. Tarquin's: Tarquin was a Roman tyrant who raped a woman named Lucrece.

60. now suits with it: now seems suitable to it.

? **64.** *Trace in this soliloquy a vision, a call to action, and a leave-taking. What should you be feeling as an audience as Macbeth exits?*

Scene 2. *Macbeth's castle.*

Enter LADY MACBETH.

Lady Macbeth.
That which hath made them drunk hath made me bold;
What hath quenched them hath given me fire. Hark! Peace!
It was the owl that shrieked, the fatal bellman,
Which gives the stern'st good-night.° He is about it.
The doors are open, and the surfeited grooms
Do mock their charge with snores. I have drugged their possets,°
That death and nature do contend about them,
Whether they live or die.

Macbeth (*within*). Who's there? What, ho?

Lady Macbeth.
Alack, I am afraid they have awaked.
And 'tis not done! Th' attempt and not the deed
Confounds° us. Hark! I laid their daggers ready;
He could not miss 'em. Had he not resembled
My father as he slept, I had done't.

[*Enter* MACBETH.]

My husband!

Macbeth.
I have done the deed. Didst thou not hear a noise?

Lady Macbeth.
I heard the owl scream and the crickets cry.
Did not you speak?

Macbeth. When?

Lady Macbeth. Now.

Macbeth. As I descended?

Lady Macbeth. Ay.

? **3.** *What sound would you hear here? In this soliloquy, who are the "them" and who is "He"?*

4. stern'st good-night: The owl's call is supposed to portend death. The bellman was a person who rang a bell outside a condemned person's cell the night before his execution, to warn him to confess his sins.

6. possets: bedtime drinks.

11. Confounds: ruins.

? **13.** *How should Lady Macbeth say this last line, which reveals why the plans have changed? Do you think she is beginning to show remorse?*

"My hands are of your color, but I shame
To wear a heart so white."
Photofest

Macbeth. Hark!
Who lies i' th' second chamber?
Lady Macbeth. Donalbain.
Macbeth. This is a sorry sight.
Lady Macbeth.
A foolish thought, to say a sorry sight.
Macbeth.
There's one did laugh in 's sleep, and one cried "Murder!"
That they did wake each other. I stood and heard them.
But they did say their prayers, and addressed them
Again to sleep.
Lady Macbeth. There are two lodged together.
Macbeth.
One cried "God bless us!" and "Amen" the other,
As they had seen me with these hangman's hands:
List'ning their fear, I could not say "Amen,"
When they did say "God bless us!"
Lady Macbeth. Consider it not so deeply.
Macbeth.
But wherefore could not I pronounce "Amen"?
I had most need of blessing, and "Amen"
Stuck in my throat.
Lady Macbeth. These deeds must not be thought
After these ways; so, it will make us mad.

? **33.** *Is Lady Macbeth fighting for control here?*

Macbeth.
Methought I heard a voice cry "Sleep no more!
Macbeth does murder sleep"—the innocent sleep,
Sleep that knits up the raveled sleave° of care,
The death of each day's life, sore labor's bath,
Balm of hurt minds, great nature's second course,°
Chief nourisher in life's feast——

Lady Macbeth. What do you mean?

Macbeth.
Still it cried "Sleep no more!" to all the house:
"Glamis hath murdered sleep, and therefore Cawdor
Shall sleep no more: Macbeth shall sleep no more."

Lady Macbeth
Who was it that thus cried? Why, worthy thane,
You do unbend your noble strength, to think
So brainsickly of things. Go get some water,
And wash this filthy witness from your hand.
Why did you bring these daggers from the place?
They must lie there: go carry them, and smear
The sleepy grooms with blood.

Macbeth. I'll go no more.
I am afraid to think what I have done;
Look on 't again I dare not.

Lady Macbeth. Infirm of purpose!
Give me the daggers. The sleeping and the dead
Are but as pictures. 'Tis the eye of childhood
That fears a painted devil. If he do bleed,
I'll gild the faces of the grooms withal,
For it must seem their guilt. [*Exit. Knock within.*]

Macbeth. Whence is that knocking?
How is't with me, when every noise appalls me?
What hands are here? Ha! They pluck out mine eyes!
Will all great Neptune's ocean wash this blood
Clean from my hand? No; this my hand will rather
The multitudinous seas incarnadine,°
Making the green one red.

[*Enter* LADY MACBETH.]

Lady Macbeth.
My hands are of your color, but I shame
To wear a heart so white. (*Knock.*) I hear a knocking
At the south entry. Retire we to our chamber.
A little water clears us of this deed:
How easy is it then! Your constancy
Hath left you unattended.° (*Knock.*) Hark! more knocking.
Get on your nightgown, lest occasion call us
And show us to be watchers.° Be not lost
So poorly in your thoughts.

36. raveled sleave: tangled thread.

38. second course: sleep (the less substantial first course is food).

? **41.** *Who else complained about sleep? In what way has Glamis "murdered sleep"?*

? **46.** *What is the "filthy witness"? What actions are the couple engaged in here? In the next line, Lady Macbeth discovers the daggers. Why is she so alarmed at seeing them in her husband's hands? How could Macbeth have been carrying them so they weren't visible before?*

? **55.** *What will Lady Macbeth do to the grooms if Duncan bleeds enough?*

61. incarnadine: make red.

? **63.** *Based on this speech, what does Lady Macbeth look like?*

68. Your . . . unattended: Your firmness has deserted you.

70. watchers: that is, up late.

? **71.** *What is Macbeth acting like?*

Photofest

"...drink, sir, is a great provoker of three things."

Macbeth.
To know my deed, 'twere best not know myself.

[*Knock.*]

Wake Duncan with thy knocking! I would thou couldst!
[*Exeunt.*]

Scene 3. *Macbeth's castle.*

Enter a PORTER. *Knocking within.*

Porter. Here's a knocking indeed! If a man were porter of hell gate, he should have old° turning the key. (*Knock.*) Knock, knock, knock! Who's there, i' th' name of Beelzebub?° Here's a farmer, that hanged himself on th' expectation of plenty. Come in time! Have napkins enow° about you; here you'll sweat for 't. (*Knock.*) Knock, knock! Who's there, in th' other devil's name? Faith, here's an equivocator,° that could swear in both the scales against either scale; who committed treason enough for God's sake, yet could not equivocate to heaven. O, come in, equivocator. (*Knock.*) Knock, knock, knock! Who's there? Faith, here's an English tailor come hither for stealing out of a French hose:° come in, tailor. Here you may roast your goose.° (*Knock.*) Knock,

? **Stage direction.** *In the theater, this sharp, loud knocking is frightening. In the next line, what might Macbeth wish the knocking could awake in himself?*

? **Stage direction.** *Note that the porter is drunk. What would he be doing during this long speech while the knocking persists?*

2. have old: grow old.

3. Beelzebub: the Devil.

5. enow: enough.

7. equivocator: The porter means a Jesuit (who allegedly used false arguments in his zeal for souls).

12. French hose: tightfitting stocking.

13. goose: iron used by a tailor for pressing.

knock; never at quiet! What are you? But this place is too cold for hell. I'll devil-porter it no further. I had thought to have let in some of all professions that go the primrose way to th' everlasting bonfire. (*Knock.*) Anon, anon! (*Opens an entrance.*) I pray you, remember the porter.

[*Enter* MACDUFF *and* LENNOX.]

Macduff.
Was it so late, friend, ere you went to bed,
That you do lie so late?

Porter. Faith, sir, we were carousing till the second cock:° and drink, sir, is a great provoker of three things.

Macduff. What three things does drink especially provoke?

Porter. Marry, sir, nose-painting, sleep, and urine. Lechery, sir, it provokes and unprovokes; it provokes the desire, but it takes away the performance: therefore much drink may be said to be an equivocator with lechery: it makes him and it mars him; it sets him on and it takes him off; it persuades him and disheartens him; makes him stand to and not stand to; in conclusion, equivocates him in a sleep, and giving him the lie, leaves him.

Macduff. I believe drink gave thee the lie° last night.

Porter. That it did, sir, i' the very throat on me: but I requited him for his lie, and, I think, being too strong for him, though he took up my legs sometime, yet I make a shift to cast° him.

Macduff. Is thy master stirring?

[*Enter* MACBETH.]

Our knocking has awaked him; here he comes.

Lennox.
Good morrow, noble sir.

Macbeth. Good morrow, both.

Macduff.
Is the king stirring, worthy thane?

Macbeth. Not yet.

Macduff.
He did command me to call timely° on him:
I have almost slipped the hour.

Macbeth. I'll bring you to him.

Macduff.
I know this is a joyful trouble to you;
But yet 'tis one.

Macbeth.
The labor we delight in physics° pain.
This is the door.

Macduff. I'll make so bold to call,
For 'tis my limited service.° [*Exit* MACDUFF.]

Lennox.
Goes the king hence today?

21. second cock: about 3 A.M.

32. gave thee the lie: pun meaning "called you a liar" and "stretched you out, lying in bed."

35. cast: here, a pun meaning "to cast in plaster" and "to vomit" (cast out).

? **36.** *All the time this humorous bantering is going on, what do we know these king's men are about to discover?*

40. timely: early.

44. physics: cures.

46. limited service: appointed duty.

Macbeth. He does: he did appoint so.

Lennox.
The night has been unruly. Where we lay,
Our chimneys were blown down, and, as they say,
Lamentings heard i' th' air, strange screams of death,
And prophesying with accents terrible
Of dire combustion° and confused events
New hatched to th' woeful time: the obscure bird
Clamored the livelong night. Some say, the earth
Was feverous and did shake.

Macbeth. 'Twas a rough night.

Lennox.
My young remembrance cannot parallel
A fellow to it.

[*Enter* MACDUFF.]

Macduff.
O horror, horror, horror! Tongue nor heart
Cannot conceive nor name thee.

Macbeth and Lennox. What's the matter?

Macduff.
Confusion now hath made his masterpiece.
Most sacrilegious murder hath broke ope
The Lord's anointed temple,° and stole thence
The life o' th' building.

Macbeth. What is't you say? The life?

Lennox.
Mean you his majesty?

Macduff.
Approach the chamber, and destroy your sight
With a new Gorgon:° do not bid me speak;
See, and then speak yourselves. Awake, awake!

[*Exeunt* MACBETH *and* LENNOX.]

Ring the alarum bell. Murder and treason!
Banquo and Donalbain! Malcolm! Awake!
Shake off this downy sleep, death's counterfeit,
And look on death itself! Up, up, and see
The great doom's image! Malcolm! Banquo!
As from your graves rise up, and walk like sprites,
To countenance° this horror. Ring the bell.

[*Bell rings. Enter* LADY MACBETH.]

Lady Macbeth.
What's the business,
That such a hideous trumpet calls to parley°
The sleepers of the house? Speak, speak!

Macduff. O gentle lady,
'Tis not for you to hear what I can speak:

? **47.** *How must Macbeth be feeling?*

52. combustion: tumult; uproar.

? **54.** *In Elizabethan times, people often believed that nature mirrored terrible things happening to human beings, especially to kings. How did this weather mirror what was happening to the king in Macbeth's castle?*

? **55.** *A single line, but full of irony. How would Macbeth say it?*

62. Lord's anointed temple: body of the king.

? **63.** *How would you explain Macduff's metaphors?*

66. Gorgon: creature from Greek mythology whose face could turn an onlooker to stone.

74. countenance: be in keeping with.

76. parley: conference of war.

The repetition, in a woman's ear,
Would murder as it fell.

[*Enter* BANQUO.]

O Banquo, Banquo!
Our royal master's murdered.

Lady Macbeth. Woe, alas!
What, in our house?

Banquo. Too cruel anywhere.
Dear Duff, I prithee, contradict thyself,
And say it is not so.

[*Enter* MACBETH, LENNOX, *and* ROSS.]

Macbeth.
Had I but died an hour before this chance,
I had lived a blessèd time; for from this instant
There's nothing serious in mortality:°
All is but toys. Renown and grace is dead,
The wine of life is drawn, and the mere lees°
Is left this vault° to brag of.

[*Enter* MALCOLM *and* DONALBAIN.]

Donalbain.
What is amiss?

Macbeth. You are, and do not know't.
The spring, the head, the fountain of your blood
Is stopped; the very source of it is stopped.

Macduff.
Your royal father's murdered.

Malcolm. O, by whom?

Lennox.
Those of his chamber, as it seemed, had done't:
Their hands and faces were all badged° with blood;
So were their daggers, which unwiped we found
Upon their pillows. They stared, and were distracted.
No man's life was to be trusted with them.

Macbeth.
O, yet I do repent me of my fury,
That I did kill them.

Macduff. Wherefore did you so?

Macbeth.
Who can be wise, amazed, temp'rate and furious,
Loyal and neutral, in a moment? No man.
The expedition° of my violent love
Outrun the pauser, reason. Here lay Duncan,
His silver skin laced with his golden blood,
And his gashed stabs looked like a breach in nature
For ruin's wasteful entrance: there, the murderers,
Steeped in the colors of their trade, their daggers

? **82.** *The emphasis on Lady Macbeth's gentleness and fairness when we know the foulness underneath might well merit a snicker from the audience. The snicker might be expected to grow into a laugh when she says, "What, in our house?" These are difficult moments to act. How do you think Lady Macbeth should be behaving?*

87. mortality: life.

89. lees: dregs.

90. vault: pun on "wine vault" and the "vault of heaven."

? **94.** *Macbeth and Lady Macbeth might well look at each other at this moment. Does Lennox draw the conclusion they wanted him to draw: that the servants killed Duncan?*

96. badged: marked.

104. expedition: haste.

Unmannerly breeched with gore.° Who could refrain,°
That had a heart to love, and in that heart
Courage to make 's love known?

Lady Macbeth. Help me hence, ho!

Macduff.
Look to the lady.

Malcolm (*aside to* DONALBAIN). Why do we hold our tongues,
That most may claim this argument for ours?°

Donalbain (*aside to* MALCOLM).
What should be spoken here,
Where our fate, hid in an auger-hole,°
May rush, and seize us? Let's away:
Our tears are not yet brewed.

Malcolm (*aside to* DONALBAIN). Nor our strong sorrow
Upon the foot of motion.°

Banquo. Look to the lady.

[LADY MACBETH *is carried out.*]

And when we have our naked frailties hid,°
That suffer in exposure, let us meet
And question° this most bloody piece of work,
To know it further. Fears and scruples° shake us.
In the great hand of God I stand, and thence
Against the undivulged pretense° I fight
Of treasonous malice.

Macduff. And so do I.

All. So all.

Macbeth.
Let's briefly° put on manly readiness,
And meet i' th' hall together.

All. Well contented.

[*Exeunt all but* MALCOLM *and* DONALBAIN.]

Malcolm.
What will you do? Let's not consort with them.
To show an unfelt sorrow is an office°
Which the false man does easy. I'll to England.

Donalbain.
To Ireland, I; our separated fortune
Shall keep us both the safer. Where we are
There's daggers in men's smiles; the near in blood,
The nearer bloody.

Malcolm. This murderous shaft that's shot
Hath not yet lighted, and our safest way
Is to avoid the aim. Therefore to horse;
And let us not be dainty of° leave-taking,
But shift away. There's warrant° in that theft
Which steals itself° when there's no mercy left.

[*Exeunt.*]

110. unmannerly breeched with gore: unbecomingly covered with blood, as if wearing red trousers. **refrain:** check oneself.

114. That . . . ours: who are the most concerned with this topic.

116. auger-hole: unsuspected place.

119. Our tears . . . motion: We have not yet had time for tears, nor to express our sorrows in action.

120. naked frailties hid: poor bodies clothed.

122. question: discuss.

123. scruples: suspicions.

125. undivulged pretense: hidden purpose.

127. briefly: quickly.

130. office: function.

138. dainty of: fussy about.

139. warrant: justification.

140. steals itself: steals oneself away.

Scene 4. *Outside Macbeth's castle.*

Enter ROSS *with an* OLD MAN.

Old Man.
Threescore and ten I can remember well:
Within the volume of which time I have seen
Hours dreadful and things strange, but this sore° night
Hath trifled former knowings.°

Ross. Ha, good father,
Thou seest the heavens, as troubled with man's act,
Threatens his bloody stage. By th' clock 'tis day,
And yet dark night strangles the traveling lamp:°
Is't night's predominance,° or the day's shame,
That darkness does the face of earth entomb,
When living light should kiss it?

Old Man. 'Tis unnatural,
Even like the deed that's done. On Tuesday last
A falcon, tow'ring in her pride of place,°
Was by a mousing° owl hawked at and killed.

Ross.
And Duncan's horses—a thing most strange and certain—
Beauteous and swift, the minions° of their race,
Turned wild in nature, broke their stalls, flung out,°
Contending 'gainst obedience, as they would make
War with mankind.

Old Man. 'Tis said they eat° each other.

Ross.
They did so, to th' amazement of mine eyes,
That looked upon't.

[*Enter* MACDUFF.]

Here comes the good Macduff.
How goes the world, sir, now?

Macduff. Why, see you not?

Ross.
Is't known who did this more than bloody deed?

Macduff.
Those that Macbeth hath slain.

Ross. Alas, the day!
What good could they pretend?°

Macduff. They were suborned:°
Malcolm and Donalbain, the king's two sons,
Are stol'n away and fled, which puts upon them
Suspicion of the deed.

Ross. 'Gainst nature still.
Thriftless° ambition, that will ravin up°
Thine own life's means!° Then 'tis most like
The sovereignty will fall upon Macbeth.

3. sore: grievous.

4. trifled former knowings: made trifles of former experiences.

7. traveling lamp: sun.

8. predominance: astrological supremacy.

12. tow'ring . . . place: soaring at her summit.

13. mousing: normally mouse-eating.

15. minions: darlings.

16. flung out: lunged wildly.

18. eat: ate.

24. pretend: hope for. **suborned:** bribed.

28. Thriftless: wasteful. **ravin up:** greedily devour.

29. own life's means: parent.

CONNECTION / ESSAY

from On the Knocking at the Gate in *Macbeth*

INFORMATIONAL TEXT

Thomas De Quincey

From my boyish days I had always felt a great perplexity on one point in *Macbeth.* It was this: The knocking at the gate which succeeds to the murder of Duncan produced to my feelings an effect for which I never could account. The effect was that it reflected back upon the murderer a peculiar awfulness and a depth of solemnity; yet, however obstinately I endeavored with my understanding to comprehend this, for many years I never could see *why* it should produce such an effect.

. . . At length I solved it to my own satisfaction; and my solution is this: —Murder, in ordinary cases, where the sympathy is wholly directed to the case of the murdered person, is an incident of coarse and vulgar horror; and for this reason—that it flings the interest exclusively upon the natural but ignoble instinct by which we cleave to life: an instinct which, as being indispensable to the primal law of self-preservation, is the same in kind (though different in degree) amongst all living creatures. This instinct, therefore, because it annihilates all distinctions, and degrades the greatest of men to the level of "the poor beetle that we tread on," exhibits human nature in its most abject and humiliating attitude. Such an attitude would little suit the purposes of the poet. What then must he do? He must throw the interest on the murderer. Our sympathy must be with *him* (of course I mean a sympathy of comprehension, a sympathy by which we enter into his feelings, and are made to understand them—not a sympathy of pity or approbation). In the murdered person, all strife of thought, all flux and reflux of passion and of purpose, are crushed by one overwhelming panic; the fear of instant death smites him "with its petrific mace."[1] But in the murderer, such a murderer as a poet will condescend to, there must be raging some great storm of passion—jealousy, ambition, vengeance, hatred—which will create a hell within him; and into this hell we are to look.

In *Macbeth,* for the sake of gratifying his own enormous and teeming faculty of creation, Shakespeare has introduced two murderers: and, as usual in his hands, they are remarkably discriminated: but—though in Macbeth the strife of mind is greater than in his wife, the tiger spirit not so awake, and his feelings caught chiefly by contagion from her—yet, as

1. **petrific mace:** stone club. This is an allusion to Milton's *Paradise Lost* (Book X, line 294), in which Death wields a "mace petrific."

Macduff.
He is already named,° and gone to Scone°
To be invested.°

Ross. Where is Duncan's body?

Macduff.
Carried to Colmekill,°
The sacred storehouse of his predecessors
And guardian of their bones.

Ross. Will you to Scone?

Macduff.
No, cousin, I'll to Fife.

31. **named:** elected. **Scone** (sko͞on).

32. **invested:** installed as king.

33. **Colmekill:** Iona Island, the ancient burying place of Scottish kings. (It was founded by St. Colm.)

both were finally involved in the guilt of murder, the murderous mind of necessity is finally to be presumed in both. This was to be expressed; and, on its own account, as well as to make it a more proportionable antagonist to the unoffending nature of their victim, "the gracious Duncan," and adequately to expound "the deep damnation of his taking off," this was to be expressed with peculiar energy. We were to be made to feel that the human nature—i.e., the divine nature of love and mercy, spread through the hearts of all creatures, and seldom utterly withdrawn from man—was gone, vanished, extinct, and that the fiendish nature had taken its place. And, as this effect is marvellously accomplished in the *dialogues* and *soliloquies* themselves, so it is finally consummated by the expedient under consideration; and it is to this that I now solicit the reader's attention. If the reader has ever witnessed a wife, daughter, or sister in a fainting fit, he may chance to have observed that the most affecting moment in such a spectacle is *that* in which a sigh and a stirring announce the recommencement of suspended life.

. . . All action in any direction is best expounded, measured, and made apprehensible, by reaction. Now, applying this to the case in *Macbeth:* Here, as I have said, the retiring of the human heart and the entrance of the fiendish heart was to be expressed and made sensible. Another world has stepped in; and the murderers are taken out of the region of human things, human purposes, human desires. They are transfigured: Lady Macbeth is "unsexed"; Macbeth has forgot that he was born of woman; both are conformed to the image of devils; and the world of devils is suddenly revealed. But how shall this be conveyed and made palpable? In order that a new world may step in, this world must for a time disappear. The murderers and the murder must be insulated—cut off by an immeasurable gulf from the ordinary tide and succession of human affairs—locked up and sequestered in some deep recess; we must be made sensible that the world of ordinary life is suddenly arrested, laid asleep, tranced, racked into a dread armistice; time must be annihilated, relation to things without abolished; and all must pass self-withdrawn into a deep syncope[2] and suspension of earthly passion. Hence it is that, when the deed is done, when the work of darkness is perfect, then the world of darkness passes away like a pageantry in the clouds: The knocking at the gate is heard, and it makes known audibly that the reaction has commenced; the human has made its reflux upon the fiendish; the pulses of life are beginning to beat again; and the reestablishment of the goings-on of the world in which we live first makes us profoundly sensible of the awful parenthesis that had suspended them.

2. **syncope** (siŋ′kə·pē): unconsciousness.

Ross. Well, I will thither.

Macduff.
Well, may you see things well done there. Adieu,
Lest our old robes sit easier than our new!

Ross.
Farewell, father.

Old Man.
God's benison° go with you, and with those
That would make good of bad, and friends of foes!
[*Exeunt omnes.*]

40. **benison:** blessing.

INFORMATIONAL TEXT

Macbeth's Porter

Why does Macbeth's comic porter—speaking a gross, drunken rigmarole—appear in Scene 3, right after the murder of Duncan? Is this not a monstrous interruption?

One way to account for the scene is to remind ourselves that Shakespeare was writer-in-residence to a company of actors and therefore bound to provide parts for every member in every play—even a part for the chief comedian in a tragedy. But this is not a satisfactory explanation because it was not characteristic of Shakespeare merely to do what was expected of him as a professional writer; he always did something more, almost making a virtue out of theatrical necessity. And so, as a second explanation of the porter's scene, some critics have argued that it is designed to provide **comic relief** from the tense aftermath of Duncan's murder. But this also is not a convincing reason, because the scene actually increases tension rather than relieves it. As Macbeth and his wife stand whispering about the evil thing they have done, they—and the audience—are startled to hear a loud and totally unexpected knocking on the main gate of the castle. Even a hardened criminal would be startled by the coincidence of these events, and Macbeth and his wife are mere beginners in crime. While they hastily retreat into their bedroom, the porter (a word meaning "door tender") shuffles on stage to answer the knocking at his leisure, thus prolonging the interval between the murder and its discovery and greatly increasing suspense. And, after all, suspense is what makes drama interesting.

Theatergoers in Shakespeare's day were accustomed to comic porters; they were familiar figures in miracle plays, in which they kept the gates of hell. They were expected to be droll and at the same time sinister. "Who's there, i' th' name of Beelzebub?" asks Macbeth's porter, referring to one of the chief devils and implying that the castle is a place the Devil occupies. And indeed it already has become hell, which is as much a state of mind as a particular place. Lady Macbeth has called for the "smoke of hell" in Act I, and Macbeth has been unable to say "Amen" when Duncan's men cried "God bless us!" in Act II. To cut out the porter's scene, as many directors have done (and also many editors of school texts), is to weaken the fabric of the play.

Richard Wordsworth as the porter from a production of *Macbeth* by the Old Vic Company.

Response and Analysis

Act II

Reading Check

1. Describe the vision that Macbeth has at the end of Scene 1. What details **foreshadow** the action to come?
2. In Scene 2, as Macbeth kills Duncan, what does Lady Macbeth hear? What does Macbeth hear?
3. In Scene 2, how does Macbeth respond to Lady Macbeth's suggestion that he go wash the "filthy witness" from his hands?
4. Why has Macduff come?
5. What reason does Macbeth give for killing Duncan's two guards?
6. In Scene 4, whom does Macduff suspect of Duncan's murder?

Thinking Critically

7. Though Macbeth encounters no actual opposition until long after Duncan is murdered, Shakespeare must **foreshadow** some trouble for him. To build up **suspense,** Shakespeare edges one character toward suspicion of Macbeth. Who is this character, and what inkling does he give of his dissatisfaction with Macbeth?
8. In Act I, Lady Macbeth seemed to be planning to murder Duncan herself. But at the last moment, in Act II, she is unable to wield her dagger. What reason does she give? What do her actions and explanation reveal about her **character**?
9. Lady Macbeth's fainting spell, like everything else she has done so far, has a purpose. What message do you think Lady Macbeth wants her fainting spell to convey?
10. Macduff becomes an important character in the three remaining acts. Describe how Shakespeare **characterizes** him in Act II.
11. What would you say is the **mood** of Act II? What **images** and actions help to create this mood? Why might images of blood and water appear in Scene 2, and what do they **symbolize**?
12. Review De Quincey's interpretation of the porter's scene in the ***Connection*** on page 468, and review also the Critical Comment on page 470. What **purpose** do you see for this scene? Is it just for **comic relief,** or does it have other dramatic functions? Give reasons for your interpretation.

Extending and Evaluating

13. A terrible murder is committed in this act. How do various characters respond to the violence? How would people today react to the news that a ruler has been assassinated in cold blood and that a nation is in political chaos?
14. In some productions of *Macbeth,* Scene 4 is cut. Why would this be done? Is there any dramatic purpose for keeping it? Why do you think the Old Man is included in this scene?

WRITING

Truth or Lies?

In Scene 3, when Duncan's corpse is discovered, Macbeth utters what sounds like a hypocritical lament beginning, "Had I but died . . ." (line 85). But is it really hypocritical? The critic A. C. Bradley argues that, although the speech is meant to be a lie, it actually contains "Macbeth's profoundest feelings." Write a **brief** essay analyzing Macbeth's **internal conflict.** How does Macbeth feel about having murdered Duncan? What clues tell you how he feels? Cite evidence from the play to support your response.

Literary Skills
Analyze the characteristics of tragedy, including suspense, character, and comic relief.

Writing Skills
Write an essay analyzing a character's internal conflict.

ACT III Scene 1. *Forres. The palace.*

Enter BANQUO.

Banquo.
Thou hast it now: king, Cawdor, Glamis, all,
As the weird women promised, and I fear
Thou play'dst most foully for't. Yet it was said
It should not stand° in thy posterity,
But that myself should be the root and father
Of many kings. If there come truth from them—
As upon thee, Macbeth, their speeches shine—
Why, by the verities on thee made good,
May they not be my oracles as well
And set me up in hope? But hush, no more!

[*Sennet° sounded. Enter* MACBETH *as king,* LADY MACBETH, LENNOX, ROSS, LORDS, *and* ATTENDANTS.]

Macbeth.
Here's our chief guest.

Lady Macbeth. If he had been forgotten,
It had been as a gap in our great feast,
And all-thing° unbecoming.

Macbeth.
Tonight we hold a solemn supper, sir,
And I'll request your presence.

Banquo. Let your highness
Command upon me, to the which my duties
Are with a most indissoluble tie
For ever knit.

Macbeth.
Ride you this afternoon?

Banquo. Ay, my good lord.

Macbeth.
We should have else desired your good advice
(Which still° hath been both grave and prosperous°)
In this day's council; but we'll take tomorrow.
Is't far you ride?

Banquo.
As far, my lord, as will fill up the time
'Twixt this and supper. Go not my horse the better,°
I must become a borrower of the night
For a dark hour or twain.

Macbeth. Fail not our feast.

Banquo.
My lord, I will not.

Macbeth.
We hear our bloody cousins are bestowed°
In England and in Ireland, not confessing

4. **stand:** continue.

? 10. *What would you say Banquo's mood is? Is he envious or thoughtful and troubled?*

Sennet: trumpet.

13. **all-thing:** altogether.

21. **still:** always. **grave and prosperous:** weighty and profitable.

25. **Go not my horse the better:** unless my horse goes faster than I expect.

29. **are bestowed:** have taken refuge.

Their cruel parricide, filling their hearers
With strange invention.° But of that tomorrow,
When therewithal we shall have cause of state
Craving us jointly.° Hie you to horse. Adieu,
Till you return at night. Goes Fleance with you?

Banquo.
Ay, my good lord: our time does call upon 's.

Macbeth.
I wish your horses swift and sure of foot,
And so I do commend you to their backs.
Farewell. [*Exit* BANQUO.]
Let every man be master of his time
Till seven at night. To make society
The sweeter welcome, we will keep ourself
Till supper-time alone. While° then, God be with you!

[*Exeunt* LORDS *and all but* MACBETH *and a* SERVANT.]

Sirrah, a word with you: attend° those men
Our pleasure?

Attendant.
They are, my lord, without the palace gate.

Macbeth.
Bring them before us. [*Exit* SERVANT.]
To be thus° is nothing, but° to be safely thus—
Our fears in Banquo stick deep,
And in his royalty of nature reigns that
Which would be feared. 'Tis much he dares;
And, to° that dauntless temper° of his mind,
He hath a wisdom that doth guide his valor
To act in safety. There is none but he
Whose being I do fear: and under him
My genius is rebuked,° as it is said
Mark Antony's was by Caesar. He chid the sisters,
When first they put the name of king upon me,
And bade them speak to him; then prophetlike
They hailed him father to a line of kings.
Upon my head they placed a fruitless crown
And put a barren scepter in my gripe,
Thence to be wrenched with an unlineal hand,
No son of mine succeeding. If't be so,
For Banquo's issue have I filed° my mind;
For them the gracious Duncan have I murdered;
Put rancors° in the vessel of my peace
Only for them, and mine eternal jewel°
Given to the common enemy of man,°
To make them kings, the seeds of Banquo kings!
Rather than so, come, fate, into the list,°
And champion me to th' utterance!° Who's there?

32. invention: lies.

34. us jointly: our joint attention.

? **35.** *Macbeth has asked three important questions in this scene. What are they? How do you think he would ask them?*

? **42.** *Notice that Macbeth uses the "royal we"; that is, he speaks of himself as "we," as a representative of all the people. Why do you think he wants to be alone?*

43. While: until.

44. attend: await.

48. thus: king. **but:** unless.

52. to: added to. **temper:** quality.

56. genius is rebuked: guardian spirit is cowed.

? **63.** *What is an "unlineal hand"? What is a "barren scepter"? What is eating at Macbeth now?*

65. filed: defiled; dirtied.

67. rancors: bitter enmity.

68. eternal jewel: immortal soul.

69. common enemy of man: Satan.

71. list: battle.

72. champion me to th' utterance: fight against me till I give up.

? **72.** *Why exactly is Macbeth so angry? What has he given up in order to make Banquo's sons kings?*

[*Enter* SERVANT *and two* MURDERERS.]

Now go to the door, and stay there till we call.

[*Exit* SERVANT.]

Was it not yesterday we spoke together?

Murderers.
It was, so please your highness.

Macbeth. Well then, now
Have you considered of my speeches? Know
That it was he in the times past, which held you
So under fortune,° which you thought had been
Our innocent self: this I made good to you
In our last conference; passed in probation° with you,
How you were borne in hand,° how crossed; the instruments,°
Who wrought with them, and all things else that might
To half a soul° and to a notion° crazed
Say "Thus did Banquo."

First Murderer. You made it known to us.

Macbeth.
I did so; and went further, which is now
Our point of second meeting. Do you find
Your patience so predominant in your nature,
That you can let this go? Are you so gospeled,°
To pray for this good man and for his issue,
Whose heavy hand hath bowed you to the grave
And beggared yours forever?

First Murderer. We are men, my liege.

Macbeth.
Ay, in the catalogue ye go for° men;
As hounds and greyhounds, mongrels, spaniels, curs,
Shoughs, water-rugs° and demi-wolves, are clept°
All by the name of dogs: the valued file°
Distinguishes the swift, the slow, the subtle,
The housekeeper, the hunter, every one
According to the gift which bounteous nature
Hath in him closed,° whereby he does receive
Particular addition, from the bill°
That writes them all alike: and so of men.
Now if you have a station in the file,
Not i' th' worst rank of manhood, say't,
And I will put that business in your bosoms
Whose execution takes your enemy off,
Grapples you to the heart and love of us,
Who wear our health but sickly in his life,°
Which in his death were perfect.

Second Murderer. I am one, my liege,
Whom the vile blows and buffets of the world
Hath so incensed that I am reckless what
I do to spite the world.

? **74.** *What do you imagine the murderers would be like: the all-too-common "hit men" of contemporary movies? Or could they simply be officers who have a grudge against Banquo? (They have been portrayed in many ways.)*

78. held you / So under fortune: kept you from good fortune.

80. probation: review.

81. borne in hand: deceived. **instruments:** tools.

83. soul: brain. **notion:** mind.

88. gospeled: so meek from reading the Gospel (of Jesus).

? **91.** *What techniques is Macbeth using on the murderers? Does it remind you of the way Lady Macbeth goaded him into killing Duncan?*

92. go for: pass as.

94. Shoughs, water-rugs: shaggy dogs and long-haired water dogs. **clept:** called.

95. valued file: classification by valuable traits.

99. closed: enclosed.

100. bill: list.

107. who wear . . . life: who are "sick" while he (Banquo) still lives.

From Roman Polanski's film production of *Macbeth* (1971).

"It is concluded: Banquo, thy soul's flight,
If it find heaven, must find it out tonight."

First Murderer. And I another
So weary with disasters, tugged with fortune,
That I would set° my life on any chance,
To mend it or be rid on't.

Macbeth. Both of you
Know Banquo was your enemy.

Both Murderers. True, my lord.

Macbeth.
So is he mine, and in such bloody distance°
That every minute of his being thrusts
Against my near'st of life:° and though I could
With barefaced power sweep him from my sight
And bid my will avouch° it, yet I must not,
For° certain friends that are both his and mine,
Whose loves I may not drop, but wail his fall
Who I myself struck down: and thence it is
That I to your assistance do make love,
Masking the business from the common eye
For sundry weighty reasons.

113. set: risk.

116. distance: quarrel.

118. near'st of life: vital spot.

120. avouch: justify.

121. For: because of.

126. *How is Macbeth justifying to the murderers the fact that he has to ask them to do the job of killing Banquo?*

Second Murderer. We shall, my lord,
Perform what you command us.

First Murderer. Though our lives——

Macbeth.
Your spirits shine through you. Within this hour at most
I will advise you where to plant yourselves,
Acquaint you with the perfect spy° o' th' time,
The moment on't; for't must be done tonight,
And something° from the palace; always thought°
That I require a clearness:° and with him—
To leave no rubs° nor botches in the work—
Fleance his son, that keeps him company,
Whose absence is no less material to me
Than is his father's, must embrace the fate
Of that dark hour. Resolve yourselves apart:°
I'll come to you anon.

Murderers. We are resolved, my lord.

Macbeth.
I'll call upon you straight. Abide within.

130. perfect spy: exact information.

132. something: some distance. **thought:** remembered.

133. clearness: freedom from suspicion.

134. rubs: flaws.

138. apart: alone (make up your minds by yourselves).

? **140.** *What has Macbeth arranged with the murderers? What is his mood here? Does Lady Macbeth have any part in arranging these next murders?*

From Roman Polanski's film production of *Macbeth* (1971).

"Gentle my lord, sleek o'er your rugged looks."

It is concluded: Banquo, thy soul's flight,
If it find heaven, must find it out tonight. *[Exeunt.]*

Scene 2. *The palace.*

Enter LADY MACBETH *and a* SERVANT.

Lady Macbeth.
Is Banquo gone from court?

Servant.
Ay, madam, but returns again tonight.

Lady Macbeth.
Say to the king, I would attend his leisure
For a few words.

Servant. Madam, I will. *[Exit.]*

Lady Macbeth. Nought's had, all's spent,
Where our desire is got without content:
'Tis safer to be that which we destroy
Than by destruction dwell in doubtful joy.

[Enter MACBETH.*]*

How now, my lord! Why do you keep alone,
Of sorriest fancies your companions making,
Using those thoughts which should indeed have died
With them they think on? Things without° all remedy
Should be without regard: what's done is done.

Macbeth.
We have scorched° the snake, not killed it:
She'll close° and be herself, whilst our poor malice°
Remains in danger of her former tooth.
But let the frame of things disjoint,° both the worlds° suffer,
Ere we will eat our meal in fear, and sleep
In the affliction of these terrible dreams
That shake us nightly: better be with the dead,
Whom we, to gain our peace, have sent to peace,
Than on the torture of the mind to lie
In restless ecstasy.° Duncan is in his grave;
After life's fitful fever he sleeps well.
Treason has done his worst: nor steel, nor poison,
Malice domestic,° foreign levy,° nothing,
Can touch him further.

Lady Macbeth. Come on.
Gentle my lord, sleek° o'er your rugged° looks;
Be bright and jovial among your guests tonight.

Macbeth.
So shall I, love; and so, I pray, be you:
Let your remembrance apply to Banquo;°
Present him eminence,° both with eye and tongue:
Unsafe the while, that we must lave°
Our honors in these flattering streams

? 7. *What reversal of attitudes is taking place here?*

11. **without:** beyond.

? 12. *This scene can be played in several ways. Is Lady Macbeth hostile to her husband and angry with him? Or can she be shown to have some tenderness in this scene?*

13. **scorched:** slashed.

14. **close:** heal. **malice:** enmity; hatred.

16. **frame of things disjoint:** universe collapse. **worlds:** heaven and earth.

22. **ecstasy:** frenzy.

25. **Malice domestic:** domestic war (civil war). **foreign levy:** exaction of tribute by a foreign country.

? 26. *What do you picture the couple doing in this scene? Are they sitting together? Are they close, or is there a distance between them?*

27. **sleek:** smooth. **rugged:** furrowed.

30. **Let . . . Banquo:** That is, focus your thoughts on Banquo.

31. **eminence:** honors.

32. **lave:** wash.

INFORMATIONAL TEXT

The Bard and the Database

In literary circles it's known as the "Authorship Question": Did William Shakespeare, the actor from Stratford-on-Avon, really write the greatest poetry the world has ever known?

This question has been around since the 1700s, and over the years people have proposed as many as fifty-eight various writers as possible authors of Shakespeare's plays and poems, ranging from Sir Francis Bacon to Sir Walter Raleigh to Queen Elizabeth I herself.

Matching Shakespeare. Hoping to apply computer technology to this centuries-old problem, Professor Ward Elliott of Claremont McKenna College near Los Angeles created a database of Renaissance literature, including the King James Bible, all of Shakespeare's poetry, and material from twenty-seven of the most promising candidates, and embarked upon his "Matching Shakespeare" study. Elliott's plan was first to identify Shakespeare's unique style through computer analysis and then to compare this to the styles of various writers to see if any matched up.

Elliott's "Matching Shakespeare" study applied dozens of different linguistic tests, but five conventional tests and a powerful new one proved most accurate. The conventional tests measured features like the number of relative clauses and hyphenated compound words and length of words and sentences, and the new test used a pattern recognition technique.

And the real Shakespeare is. What have the tests shown? Did Shakespeare write Shakespeare? Based on his studies, Elliott believes that he has been able to eliminate all the principal

And make our faces vizards° to our hearts,
Disguising what they are.

Lady Macbeth. You must leave this.

Macbeth.
O, full of scorpions is my mind, dear wife!
Thou know'st that Banquo, and his Fleance, lives.

Lady Macbeth.
But in them nature's copy's not eterne.°

Macbeth.
There's comfort yet; they are assailable.
Then be thou jocund. Ere the bat hath flown
His cloistered flight, ere to black Hecate's summons
The shard-borne° beetle with his drowsy hums
Hath rung night's yawning peal, there shall be done
A deed of dreadful note.

Lady Macbeth. What's to be done?

Macbeth.
Be innocent of the knowledge, dearest chuck,°
Till thou applaud the deed. Come, seeling° night,
Scarf up° the tender eye of pitiful day,
And with thy bloody and invisible hand
Cancel and tear to pieces that great bond

34. vizards: masks.

? **35.** *With what degree of urgency must Lady Macbeth say this line?*

38. nature's copy's not eterne: That is, they won't live forever.

42. shard-borne: carried on scaly wings.

45. chuck: chick (a term of endearment).

46. seeling: eye-closing; blinding.

47. Scarf up: blindfold.

candidates. Every writer failed at least one of the conventional tests, with some failing four or five.

On the other hand, Shakespeare's writings all fell within a consistent profile. Although the study does not definitively prove that it was Shakespeare himself who wrote the works attributed to him, Elliott (along with most reputable scholars) feels that it does demonstrate that one individual *did* write them all.

Why has such a fuss been made about the authorship of Shakespeare's works? In part, it's because people cannot believe that someone who led such a seemingly ordinary life could have been such a genius. Shakespeare still confounds all the scholarly detectives who continue to debate the "Authorship Question."

Which keeps me pale! Light thickens, and the crow
Makes wing to th' rooky° wood.
Good things of day begin to droop and drowse,
Whiles night's black agents to their preys do rouse.
Thou marvel'st at my words: but hold thee still;
Things bad begun make strong themselves by ill:
So, prithee, go with me. [*Exeunt.*]

51. rooky: full of rooks, or crows.

Scene 3. *Near the palace.*

Enter three MURDERERS.

First Murderer.
But who did bid thee join with us?
Third Murderer. Macbeth.
Second Murderer.
He needs not our mistrust; since he delivers
Our offices and what we have to do
To the direction just.°
First Murderer. Then stand with us.
The west yet glimmers with some streaks of day.
Now spurs the lated° traveler apace

? **1.** *The identity of the Third Murderer is not made clear. Whom would you name as possible suspects?*

4. He needs . . . just: We need not mistrust him (the Third Murderer) since he describes our duties according to our exact directions.

6. lated: belated.

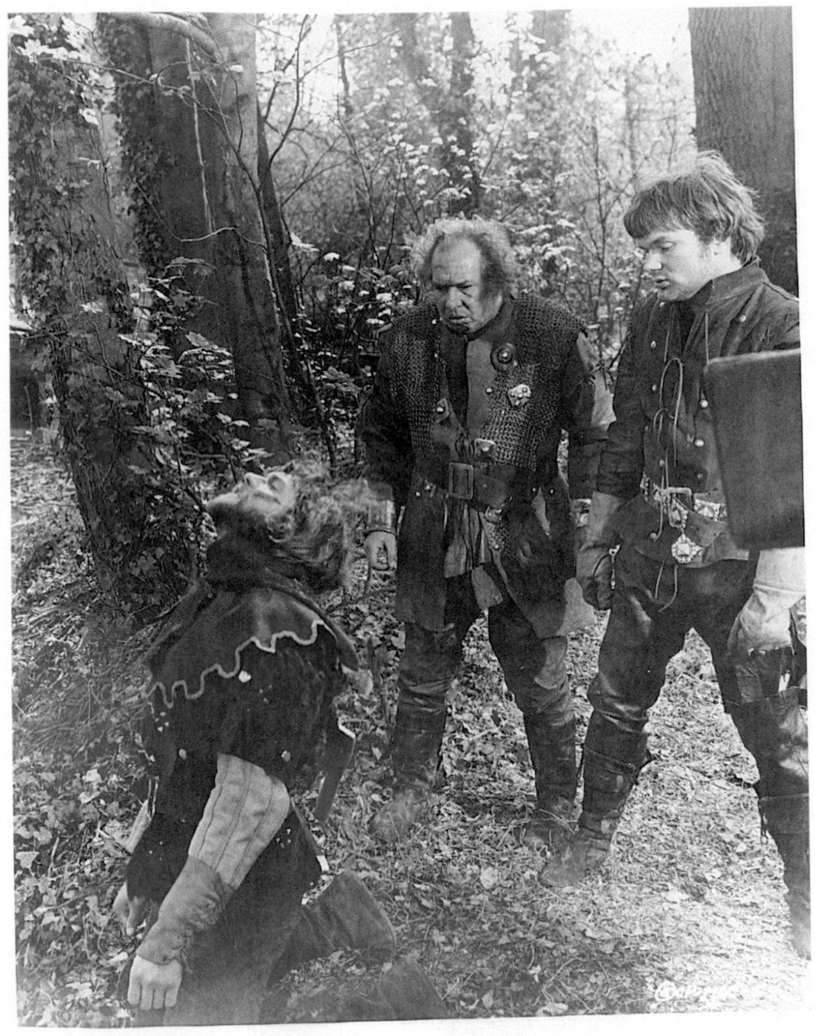

"O, treachery! Fly, good Fleance, fly, fly, fly!"

From Roman Polanski's film production of *Macbeth* (1971).

To gain the timely inn, and near approaches
The subject of our watch.

Third Murderer. Hark! I hear horses.

Banquo (*within*). Give us a light there, ho!

Second Murderer. Then 'tis he. The rest
That are within the note of expectation°
Already are i' th' court.

First Murderer. His horses go about.

Third Murderer.
Almost a mile: but he does usually—
So all men do—from hence to th' palace gate
Make it their walk.

[*Enter* BANQUO *and* FLEANCE, *with a torch.*]

Second Murderer.
A light, a light!

Third Murderer. 'Tis he.

First Murderer. Stand to't.

10. within . . . expectation: on the list of expected guests.

Banquo.
It will be rain tonight.

First Murderer. Let it come down.

[*They set upon* BANQUO.]

Banquo.
O, treachery! Fly, good Fleance, fly, fly, fly!

[*Exit* FLEANCE.]

Thou mayst revenge. O slave! [*Dies.*]

Third Murderer.
Who did strike out the light?

First Murderer. Was't not the way?°

> ? **19.** *What would the murderers be doing as the light goes out?*
>
> **19. way:** thing to do.

Third Murderer.
There's but one down; the son is fled.

Second Murderer.
We have lost best half of our affair.

First Murderer.
Well, let's away and say how much is done. [*Exeunt.*]

> ? **21.** *Disposal of bodies is always a problem for directors of Shakespeare's plays. How would you have Banquo's body carried off? By whom?*
>
> ? **22.** *This scene, so necessary to the play, is often called the play's turning point or technical climax. What have been Macbeth's good fortunes so far?*

Scene 4. *The palace.*
Banquet prepared. Enter MACBETH, LADY MACBETH, ROSS, LENNOX, LORDS, *and* ATTENDANTS.

Macbeth.
You know your own degrees;° sit down:
At first and last, the hearty welcome.

> **1. degrees:** ranks.
>
> ? **2.** *This crucial scene is often called the dramatic climax of the play; it is tremendously exciting when staged well. Notice where Macbeth's subjects become aware of his capacity for irrational behavior.*

Lords.
Thanks to your majesty.

Macbeth.
Oneself will mingle with society°
And play the humble host.
Our hostess keeps her state,° but in best time
We will require° her welcome.

> **4. society:** the company.
>
> **6. keeps her state:** remains seated in her chair of state.
>
> **7. require:** request.

Lady Macbeth.
Pronounce it for me, sir, to all our friends,
For my heart speaks they are welcome.

[*Enter* FIRST MURDERER.]

Macbeth.
See, they encounter° thee with their hearts' thanks.
Both sides are even: here I'll sit i' th' midst:
Be large in mirth; anon we'll drink a measure°
The table round. (*Goes to* FIRST MURDERER.) There's blood upon thy face.

> **10. encounter:** meet.
>
> **12. measure:** goblet.

Murderer.
'Tis Banquo's then.

Macbeth.
'Tis better thee without than he within.°
Is he dispatched?

> **15. thee . . . within:** outside you than inside him.

"The fit is momentary; upon a thought / He will again be well."
Photofest

Murderer. My lord, his throat is cut;
That I did for him.
Macbeth. Thou are the best o' th' cutthroats.
Yet he's good that did the like for Fleance;
If thou didst it, thou art the nonpareil.
Murderer.
Most royal sir, Fleance is 'scaped.
Macbeth (*aside*).
Then comes my fit again: I had else been perfect,
Whole as the marble, founded° as the rock,
As broad and general as the casing air:°
But now I am cabined, cribbed,° confined, bound in
To saucy° doubts and fears.—But Banquo's safe?
Murderer.
Ay, my good lord: safe in a ditch he bides,
With twenty trenchèd° gashes on his head,
The least a death to nature.
Macbeth. Thanks for that.
(*Aside.*) There the grown serpent lies; the worm° that's fled
Hath nature that in time will venom breed,
No teeth for th' present. Get thee gone. Tomorrow
We'll hear ourselves° again. [*Exit* FIRST MURDERER.]

? **20.** *How would Macbeth react to this line?*

22. founded: firmly based.

23. broad . . . casing air: unconfined as the surrounding air.

24. cribbed: penned up.

25. saucy: insolent.

27. trenchèd: trenchlike.

29. worm: serpent.

32. hear ourselves: talk it over.

Lady Macbeth. My royal lord,
You do not give the cheer.° The feast is sold
That is not often vouched, while 'tis a-making,
'Tis given with welcome. To feed were best at home;°
From thence, the sauce to meat° is ceremony;
Meeting were bare without it.

[*Enter the* GHOST OF BANQUO, *and sits in Macbeth's place.*]

Macbeth. Sweet remembrancer!°
Now good digestion wait on appetite,
And health on both!

Lennox. May't please your highness sit.

Macbeth.
Here had we now our country's honor roofed,°
Were the graced person of our Banquo present—
Who may I rather challenge for unkindness
Than pity for mischance!°

Ross. His absence, sir,
Lays blame upon his promise. Please't your highness
To grace us with your royal company?

Macbeth.
The table's full.

Lennox. Here is a place reserved, sir.

Macbeth.
Where?

Lennox.
Here, my good lord. What is't that moves your highness?

Macbeth.
Which of you have done this?

Lords. What, my good lord?

Macbeth.
Thou canst not say I did it. Never shake
Thy gory locks at me.

Ross.
Gentlemen, rise, his highness is not well.

Lady Macbeth.
Sit, worthy friends. My Lord is often thus,
And hath been from his youth. Pray you, keep seat.
The fit is momentary; upon a thought°
He will again be well. If much you note him,
You shall offend him and extend his passion.°
Feed, and regard him not.—Are you a man?

Macbeth.
Ay, and a bold one, that dare look on that
Which might appall the devil.

Lady Macbeth. O proper stuff!
This is the very painting of your fear.
This is the air-drawn dagger which, you said,
Led you to Duncan. O, these flaws° and starts,
Imposters to° true fear, would well become

33. cheer: sense of cordiality.

35. The feast . . . home: The feast seems sold (not given) when the host fails to welcome the guests. Mere eating is best done at home.

36. meat: food.

? **37.** *Lady Macbeth has summoned her husband to her area of the stage. What mood is she in?*

? **Stage direction.** *The ghost is crucial to this scene. From what you read here, should the ghost be imagined? Or should it actually appear on stage? How should it look, if so?*

37. remembrancer: reminder.

40. our . . . roofed: our nobility under one roof.

43. Who . . . mischance: whom I hope I may reprove because he is unkind rather than pity because he has encountered an accident.

? **46.** *When Macbeth says this line, what does he see?*

? **49.** *How should Macbeth ask this question? Whom should he be talking to?*

? **51.** *According to Macbeth's speech here, what is the ghost doing? Does anyone else see the ghost? How should the others be acting?*

? **53.** *Do you think this is true? Or is Lady Macbeth desperately trying to cover for her husband?*

55. upon a thought: as quick as a thought.

57. extend his passion: lengthen his fit.

? **58.** *Where do you think Lady Macbeth has taken her husband so that she can whisper this intimidating line?*

63. flaws: gusts; outbursts.

64. to: compared with.

A woman's story at a winter's fire,
Authorized° by her grandam. Shame itself!
Why do you make such faces? When all's done,
You look but on a stool.

Macbeth. Prithee, see there!
Behold! Look! Lo! How say you?
Why, what care I? If thou canst nod, speak too.
If charnel houses° and our graves must send
Those that we bury back, our monuments
Shall be the maws of kites.° [*Exit* GHOST.]

Lady Macbeth. What, quite unmanned in folly?

Macbeth.
If I stand here, I saw him.

Lady Macbeth. Fie, for shame!

Macbeth.
Blood hath been shed ere now, i' th' olden time,
Ere humane statute purged the gentle weal;°
Ay, and since too, murders have been performed
Too terrible for the ear. The time has been
That, when the brains were out, the man would die,
And there an end; but now they rise again,
With twenty mortal murders on their crowns,°
And push us from our stools. This is more strange
Than such a murder is.

Lady Macbeth. My worthy lord,
Your noble friends do lack you.

Macbeth. I do forget.
Do not muse at me, my most worthy friends;
I have a strange infirmity, which is nothing
To those that know me. Come, love and health to all!
Then I'll sit down. Give me some wine, fill full.

[*Enter* GHOST.]

I drink to th' general joy o' th' whole table,
And to our dear friend Banquo, whom we miss;
Would he were here! To all and him we thirst,°
And all to all.°

Lords. Our duties, and the pledge.

Macbeth.
Avaunt! and quit my sight! Let the earth hide thee!
Thy bones are marrowless, thy blood is cold;
Thou hast no speculation° in those eyes
Which thou dost glare with.

Lady Macbeth. Think of this, good peers,
But as a thing of custom; 'tis no other.
Only it spoils the pleasure of the time.

Macbeth.
What man dare, I dare.
Approach thou like the rugged Russian bear,
The armed rhinoceros, or th' Hyrcan° tiger;

66. Authorized: vouched for.

? **68.** *What could the actor playing Banquo do here in mockery of Macbeth?*

? **70.** *What action is Macbeth engaged in here? What is his tone?*

71. charnel houses: vaults containing bones.

73. our . . . kites: Our tombs shall be the bellies of rapacious birds.

? **75.** *Whom is Macbeth talking to?*

76. purged . . . weal: cleansed the state and made it gentle.

81. mortal . . . crowns: deadly wounds on their heads.

? **85.** *What impression is Macbeth trying to create?*

91. thirst: desire to drink.

92. all to all: Let everybody drink to everybody.

? **93.** *Whom is Macbeth talking to now? According to this speech, what might the ghost be doing?*

95. speculation: sight.

101. Hyrcan: of Hyrcania (near the Caspian Sea).

Take any shape but that, and my firm nerves°
Shall never tremble. Or be alive again,
And dare me to the desert° with thy sword.
If trembling I inhabit then, protest me
The baby of a girl.° Hence, horrible shadow!
Unreal mock'ry, hence! [*Exit* GHOST.]
Why, so: being gone,
I am a man again. Pray you, sit still.

Lady Macbeth.
You have displaced the mirth, broke the good meeting,
With most admired° disorder.

Macbeth. Can such things be,
And overcome us° like a summer's cloud,
Without our special wonder? You make me strange
Even to the disposition that I owe,°
When now I think you can behold such sights,
And keep the natural ruby of your cheeks,
When mine is blanched with fear.

Ross. What sights, my lord?

Lady Macbeth.
I pray you, speak not: he grows worse and worse;
Question enrages him: at once, good night.
Stand not upon the order of your going,°
But go at once.

Lennox. Good night; and better health
Attend his majesty!

Lady Macbeth. A kind good night to all!

[*Exeunt* LORDS.]

Macbeth.
It will have blood, they say: blood will have blood.
Stones have been known to move and trees to speak;
Augurs and understood relations° have
By maggot-pies and choughs and rooks brought forth°
The secret'st man of blood. What is the night?°

Lady Macbeth.
Almost at odds with morning, which is which.

Macbeth.
How say'st thou, that Macduff denies his person
At our great bidding?

Lady Macbeth. Did you send to him, sir?

Macbeth.
I hear it by the way,° but I will send:
There's not a one of them but in his house
I keep a servant fee'd.° I will tomorrow,
And betimes° I will, to the weird sisters:
More shall they speak, for now I am bent° to know
By the worst means the worst. For mine own good
All causes° shall give way. I am in blood
Stepped in so far that, should I wade no more,

102. nerves: sinews.

104. desert: lonely place.

106. If . . . girl: If then I tremble, proclaim me a baby girl.

? **108.** *How "brave" should Macbeth appear to be with all the "brave" talk in these lines? What is his mood when he says "I am a man again"?*

110. admired: amazing.

? **110.** *Lady Macbeth and her husband converse in private again. What would the other guests be doing?*

111. overcome us: come over us.

113. You . . . owe: You make me wonder what my nature is.

? **117.** *What clue here would tell the actor playing Macbeth how he is to be behaving?*

119. Stand . . . going: Do not insist on departing in your order of rank.

? **122.** *Read this speech carefully, and decide how Macbeth would deliver it: Slow? Fast? What is his mood?*

124. Augurs . . . relations: auguries (omens) and comprehended reports.

125. By . . . forth: by magpies, crows, and rooks (telltale birds) revealed.

126. What . . . night: What time of night is it?

? **127.** *Is the old fire still present in Lady Macbeth? Or is she suddenly tired and broken?*

130. by the way: incidentally.

132. fee'd: that is, paid to spy.

133. betimes: quickly.

134. bent: determined.

136. causes: considerations.

Photofest

"Come, let's make haste; she'll soon be back again."

Returning were as tedious as go o'er.
Strange things I have in head that will to hand,
Which must be acted ere they may be scanned.°

Lady Macbeth.
You lack the season of all natures,° sleep.

Macbeth.
Come, we'll to sleep. My strange and self-abuse°
Is the initiate fear that wants hard use.°
We are yet but young in deed. [*Exeunt.*]

Scene 5. *A witches' haunt.*

Thunder. Enter the three WITCHES, *meeting* HECATE.

First Witch.
Why, how now, Hecate! you look angerly.

Hecate.
Have I not reason, beldams° as you are,
Saucy and overbold? How did you dare
To trade and traffic with Macbeth
In riddles and affairs of death;

? **140.** *Does the prospect of a new adventure animate Macbeth? Or is he spent and exhausted?*

140. may be scanned: can be examined.

141. season . . . natures: seasoning (preservative) of all living creatures.

142. self-abuse: delusion.

143. initiate . . . use: beginner's fear that lacks hardening practice.

? **144.** *How might Lady Macbeth react to this last line?*

? **Scene 5.** Macbeth *was published in the first folio in 1623, seven years after Shakespeare had died. Some people think that this scene was written by someone else because the play was short and needed fleshing out. After you read the scene, decide if you think it "sounds" like the rest of the play.*

2. beldams: hags.

And I, the mistress of your charms,
The close contriver° of all harms,
Was never called to bear my part,
Or show the glory of our art?
And, which is worse, all you have done
Hath been but for a wayward son,
Spiteful and wrathful; who, as others do,
Loves for his own ends, not for you.
But make amends now: get you gone,
And at the pit of Acheron°
Meet me i' th' morning: thither he
Will come to know his destiny.
Your vessels and your spells provide,
Your charms and everything beside.
I am for th' air; this night I'll spend
Unto a dismal and a fatal end:
Great business must be wrought ere noon.
Upon the corner of the moon
There hangs a vap'rous drop profound;°
I'll catch it ere it come to ground:
And that distilled by magic sleights°
Shall raise such artificial sprites°
As by the strength of their illusion
Shall draw him on to his confusion.°
He shall spurn fate, scorn death, and bear
His hopes 'bove wisdom, grace, and fear:
And you all know security°
Is mortal's chiefest enemy. [*Music and a song.*]
Hark! I am called; my little spirit, see,
Sits in a foggy cloud and stays for me. [*Exit.*]

[*Sing within,* "Come away, come away," *etc.*]

First Witch.
Come, let's make haste; she'll soon be back again.
[*Exeunt.*]

7. close contriver: secret inventor.

15. Acheron: river of Hades.

24. profound: heavy.

26. sleights: arts.

27. artificial sprites: spirits created by magic arts.

29. confusion: ruin.

32. security: overconfidence.

Scene 6. *The palace.*

Enter LENNOX *and another* LORD.

Lennox.
My former speeches have but hit your thoughts,°
Which can interpret farther. Only I say
Things have been strangely borne.° The gracious Duncan
Was pitied of Macbeth: marry, he was dead.
And the right-valiant Banquo walked too late;
Whom, you may say, if't please you, Fleance killed,
For Fleance fled. Men must not walk too late.
Who cannot want the thought,° how monstrous
It was for Malcolm and for Donalbain
To kill their gracious father? Damnèd fact!°

1. My . . . thoughts: My recent words have only coincided with what you have in your mind.

3. borne: managed.

8. cannot . . . thought: cannot help but think.

10. fact: evil deed.

How it did grieve Macbeth! Did he not straight,
In pious rage, the two delinquents tear,
That were the slaves of drink and thralls° of sleep?
Was not that nobly done? Ay, and wisely too;
For 'twould have angered any heart alive
To hear the men deny't. So that I say
He has borne all things well: and I do think
That, had he Duncan's sons under his key—
As, an 't° please heaven, he shall not—they should find
What 'twere to kill a father. So should Fleance.
But, peace! for from broad words,° and 'cause he failed
His presence at the tyrant's feast, I hear,
Macduff lives in disgrace. Sir, can you tell
Where he bestows himself?

Lord. The son of Duncan,
From whom this tyrant holds the due of birth,°
Lives in the English court, and is received
Of the most pious Edward° with such grace
That the malevolence of fortune nothing
Takes from his high respect.° Thither Macduff
Is gone to pray the holy king, upon his aid°
To wake Northumberland° and warlike Siward;°
That by the help of these, with Him above
To ratify the work, we may again
Give to our tables meat, sleep to our nights,
Free from our feasts and banquets bloody knives,
Do faithful homage and receive free° honors:
All which we pine for now. And this report
Hath so exasperate the king that he
Prepares for some attempt of war.

Lennox. Sent he to Macduff?

Lord.
He did: and with an absolute "Sir, not I,"
The cloudy° messenger turns me his back,
And hums, as who should say "You'll rue the time
That clogs° me with this answer."

Lennox. And that well might
Advise him to a caution, t' hold what distance
His wisdom can provide. Some holy angel
Fly to the court of England and unfold
His message ere he come, that a swift blessing
May soon return to this our suffering country
Under a hand accursed!

Lord. I'll send my prayers with him.
[*Exeunt.*]

13. thralls: slaves.

19. an 't: if it.

21. for . . . words: because of frank talk.

? **24.** *Lennox is sometimes called the "ironic" character of the play. Do you agree? What tone would he use in this speech?*

25. due of birth: birthright.

27. Edward: Edward the Confessor (reigned 1042–1066).

29. nothing . . . respect: does not diminish the high respect in which he is held.

30. upon his aid: to aid him (Malcolm).

31. To wake Northumberland: that is, to arouse the people in an English county near Scotland. **Siward:** earl of Northumberland.

36. free: freely granted.

41. cloudy: disturbed.

43. clogs: burdens.

? **49.** *This is basically an "information" scene. Can you summarize what it tells you about the plot?*

Response and Analysis

Act III

Reading Check

1. In the **soliloquy** that opens Scene 1, what does Banquo reveal that he knows about Macbeth? What does Banquo decide to do?
2. How and why does Macbeth arrange Banquo's murder? Is Lady Macbeth involved in the murder?
3. In Scene 3, who escapes the murderers?
4. What happens in Scene 4 when Ross, Lennox, and the other lords invite Macbeth to share their table? What does Macbeth do? What does Lady Macbeth do?
5. Macduff does not appear at all in Act III. Where is he, and why?
6. By Scene 6, what opinion do Lennox and the other lord hold of Macbeth?

Thinking Critically

7. Macbeth does not kill Banquo with his own hands, as he killed Duncan and his two guards. What can you infer about Macbeth's changing **character** after seeing how he engages in this complex plan involving professional murderers?
8. The relationship between Macbeth and Lady Macbeth has changed in several ways since they became rulers of Scotland. Find details in this act that reveal some of these changes. What reasons can you suggest for these changes?
9. In Shakespeare's tragedies, a **turning point**—an event that moves the action ever downward to its tragic conclusion—usually occurs in the third act. How is Fleance's escape a turning point in this play?
10. How does the banquet scene blur the clear-cut and common-sense distinction that most of us make between the real and the imaginary? In what other scenes has this distinction also been blurred?
11. Nobody except Macbeth sees Banquo's ghost. In some productions of the play, the ghost does not appear onstage; in others, it does. If you were the director, which would you choose? What effect is created by having Banquo appear at the banquet, made up as a ghost? What is gained by having it appear as though no real person is the **motivation** for Macbeth's terrifying behavior?

Extending and Evaluating

12. After his vision of Banquo's ghost in Scene 4, Macbeth finally accepts that "blood will have blood" (line 122). What does this phrase mean? Is it relevant to today's world? How?
13. Shakespeare never reveals the identity of the Third Murderer, introduced in Scene 3. Who do you think the murderer is? Do you think the introduction of this Third Murderer is a flaw in the play? Explain.

WRITING

A Modern Macbeth

Write a contemporary version of the banquet scene (Scene 4), in which Macbeth reacts to the sight of Banquo's ghost. Change the setting to a modern time and place, and allow the characters to speak in today's language. For example, after Macbeth's bizarre behavior at the banquet, Lady Macbeth might explain to her guests that her husband is suffering from overwork and stress.

Literary Skills
Analyze the characteristics of tragedy, including soliloquy, character, and turning point.

Writing Skills
Write a modern version of a scene.

ACT IV Scene 1. *A witches' haunt.*

Thunder. Enter the three WITCHES.

First Witch.
Thrice the brinded° cat hath mewed.
Second Witch.
Thrice and once the hedge-pig° whined.
Third Witch.
Harpier° cries, 'Tis time, 'tis time.
First Witch.
Round about the caldron go:
In the poisoned entrails throw.
Toad, that under cold stone
Days and nights has thirty-one
Swelt'red venom sleeping got,°
Boil thou first i' th' charmèd pot.
All.
Double, double, toil and trouble;
Fire burn and caldron bubble.
Second Witch.
Fillet° of a fenny° snake,
In the caldron boil and bake;
Eye of newt and toe of frog,
Wool of bat and tongue of dog,
Adder's fork° and blindworm's° sting,
Lizard's leg and howlet's° wing,
For a charm of pow'rful trouble,
Like a hell-broth boil and bubble.
All.
Double, double, toil and trouble;
Fire burn and caldron bubble.

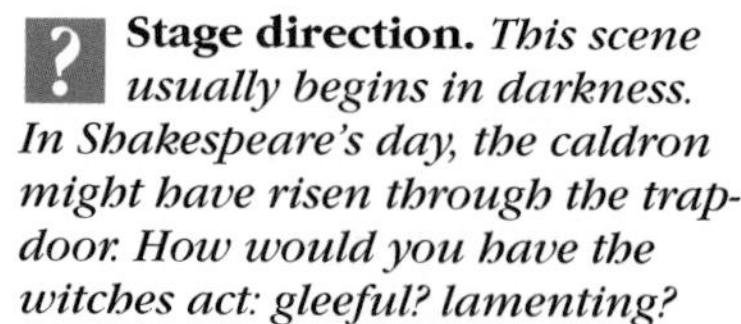

Stage direction. *This scene usually begins in darkness. In Shakespeare's day, the caldron might have risen through the trapdoor. How would you have the witches act: gleeful? lamenting?*

1. brinded: brindled.

2. hedge-pig: hedgehog.

3. Harpier: an attendant spirit like Graymalkin and Paddock in Act I, Scene 1.

8. Swelt'red . . . got: venom sweated out while sleeping.

12. Fillet: slice. **fenny:** from a swamp.

16. fork: forked tongue. **blindworm's:** legless lizard's.

17. howlet's: owl's.

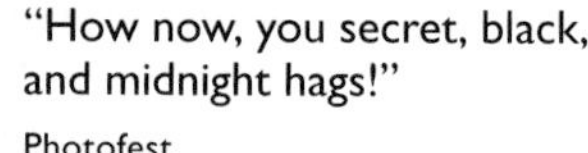

"How now, you secret, black, and midnight hags!"
Photofest

Third Witch.
Scale of dragon, tooth of wolf,
Witch's mummy,° maw and gulf°
Of the ravined° salt-sea shark,
Root of hemlock digged i' th' dark,
Liver of blaspheming Jew,
Gall of goat, and slips of yew
Slivered in the moon's eclipse,
Nose of Turk and Tartar's lips,
Finger of birth-strangled babe
Ditch-delivered by a drab,°
Make the gruel thick and slab:°
Add thereto a tiger's chaudron,°
For th' ingredients of our caldron.

All.
Double, double, toil and trouble;
Fire burn and caldron bubble.

Second Witch.
Cool it with a baboon's blood,
Then the charm is firm and good.

[*Enter* HECATE *and the other three* WITCHES.]

Hecate.
O, well done! I commend your pains;
And every one shall share i' th' gains:
And now about the caldron sing,
Like elves and fairies in a ring,
Enchanting all that you put in.

[*Music and a song:* "Black Spirits," *etc.*]

[*Exeunt* HECATE *and the other three* WITCHES.]

Second Witch.
By the pricking of my thumbs,
Something wicked this way comes:
Open, locks,
Whoever knocks!

[*Enter* MACBETH.]

Macbeth.
How now, you secret, black, and midnight hags!
What is't you do?

All. A deed without a name.

Macbeth.
I conjure you, by that which you profess,
Howe'er you come to know it, answer me:
Though you untie the winds and let them fight
Against the churches; though the yesty° waves
Confound° and swallow navigation up;

23. Witch's mummy: mummified flesh of a witch. **maw and gulf:** stomach and gullet.

24. ravined: ravenous.

31. drab: harlot.

32. slab: slimy.

33. chaudron: entrails.

? *This exciting scene has five major sections, each with its own intensity. See if you can identify them when you're finished.*

? **48.** *How has Macbeth's attitude toward the witches changed since his earlier encounters with them?*

53. yesty: foamy.

54. Confound: destroy.

Though bladed corn be lodged° and trees blown down;
Though castles topple on their warders' heads;
Though palaces and pyramids do slope°
Their heads to their foundations; though the treasure
Of nature's germens° tumble all together,
Even till destruction sicken,° answer me
To what I ask you.

First Witch. Speak.

Second Witch. Demand.

Third Witch. We'll answer.

First Witch.
Say, if th' hadst rather hear it from our mouths,
Or from our masters?

Macbeth. Call 'em, let me see 'em.

First Witch.
Pour in sow's blood, that hath eaten
Her nine farrow;° grease that's sweaten°
From the murderer's gibbet° throw
Into the flame.

All. Come, high or low,
Thyself and office° deftly show!

[*Thunder.* FIRST APPARITION: *an Armed Head.*°]

Macbeth.
Tell me, thou unknown power——

First Witch. He knows thy thought:
Hear his speech, but say thou nought.

First Apparition.
Macbeth! Macbeth! Macbeth! Beware Macduff!
Beware the Thane of Fife. Dismiss me: enough.

[*He descends.*]

Macbeth.
Whate'er thou art, for thy good caution thanks:
Thou hast harped° my fear aright. But one word more——

First Witch.
He will not be commanded. Here's another,
More potent than the first.

[*Thunder.* SECOND APPARITION: *a Bloody Child.*]

Second Apparition.
Macbeth! Macbeth! Macbeth!

Macbeth.
Had I three ears, I'd hear thee.

Second Apparition.
Be bloody, bold, and resolute! Laugh to scorn
The pow'r of man, for none of woman born
Shall harm Macbeth. [*Descends.*]

55. bladed . . . lodged: grain in the ear be beaten down.

57. slope: bend.

59. nature's germens: seeds of all life.

60. sicken: sicken at its own work.

? **61.** *These exchanges are spoken rapidly. Do the witches now see Macbeth as a participant in evil?*

65. farrow: young pigs. **sweaten:** sweated.

66. gibbet: gallows.

? **67.** *What are the witches doing all during this scene?*

68. office: function.

Armed Head: helmeted head.

? **71.** *Why does the helmeted head deliver this message? How does the form of the apparition support the warning the apparition gives?*

74. harped: hit upon; struck the note of.

Macbeth.
Then live, Macduff: what need I fear of thee?
But yet I'll make assurance double sure,
And take a bond of fate.° Thou shalt not live;
That I may tell pale-hearted fear it lies,
And sleep in spite of thunder.

[*Thunder.* THIRD APPARITION: *a Child Crowned, with a tree in his hand.*]

What is this,
That rises like the issue° of a king,
And wears upon his baby-brow the round
And top of sovereignty?°

All. Listen, but speak not to't.

Third Apparition.
Be lion-mettled, proud, and take no care
Who chafes, who frets, or where conspirers are:
Macbeth shall never vanquished be until
Great Birnam Wood to high Dunsinane Hill
Shall come against him. [*Descends.*]

Macbeth. That will never be.
Who can impress° the forest, bid the tree
Unfix his earth-bound root? Sweet bodements,° good!
Rebellious dead, rise never, till the Wood
Of Birnam rise, and our high-placed Macbeth
Shall live the lease of nature,° pay his breath
To time and mortal custom.° Yet my heart
Throbs to know one thing. Tell me, if your art
Can tell so much: shall Banquo's issue ever
Reign in this kingdom?

All. Seek to know no more.

Macbeth.
I will be satisfied.° Deny me this,
And an eternal curse fall on you! Let me know.
Why sinks that caldron? And what noise° is this?

[*Hautboys.*]

First Witch. Show!
Second Witch. Show!
Third Witch. Show!

All.
Show his eyes, and grieve his heart;
Come like shadows, so depart!

[*A show of eight* KINGS *and* BANQUO, *last* KING *with a glass° in his hand.*]

Macbeth.
Thou art too like the spirit of Banquo. Down!
Thy crown does sear mine eyelids. And thy hair,

? **82.** *Macbeth takes the child's message to mean he need not fear Macduff. Nonetheless, why should the second apparition's message be approached with caution?*

84. take . . . fate: get a guarantee from fate (that is, he will kill Macduff and thus will compel fate to keep its word).

87. issue: offspring.

89. round . . . sovereignty: that is, crown.

? **93.** *What does the third apparition prophesy? What must be Macbeth's mental state at this point?*

95. impress: conscript; draft.

96. bodements: prophecies.

99. lease of nature: natural life span.

100. mortal custom: natural death.

? **102.** *What is Macbeth's mood? How might his tone change when he asks about Banquo's issue, or children?*

104. satisfied: that is, fully informed.

106. noise: music.

? **Stage direction.** *A parade of eight Stuart kings passes before Macbeth. These are the kings of Banquo's line. The last king holds up a mirror* (**glass**) *to suggest an infinite number of descendants. Banquo appears last. According to the next speech, how does Banquo act toward Macbeth?*

Thou other gold-bound brow, is like the first.
A third is like the former. Filthy hags!
Why do you show me this? A fourth! Start,° eyes!
What, will the line stretch out to th' crack of doom?°
Another yet! A seventh! I'll see no more.
And yet the eighth° appears, who bears a glass
Which shows me many more; and some I see
That twofold balls and treble scepters° carry:
Horrible sight! Now I see 'tis true;
For the blood-boltered° Banquo smiles upon me,
And points at them for his.° What, is this so?

First Witch.
Ay, sir, all this is so. But why
Stands Macbeth thus amazedly?
Come, sisters, cheer we up his sprites,°
And show the best of our delights:
I'll charm the air to give a sound,
While you perform your antic round,°
That this great king may kindly say
Our duties did his welcome pay.

[*Music. The* WITCHES *dance, and vanish.*]

Macbeth.
Where are they? Gone? Let this pernicious hour
Stand aye accursèd in the calendar!
Come in, without there!

[*Enter* LENNOX.]

Lennox. What's your grace's will?

Macbeth.
Saw you the weird sisters?

Lennox. No, my lord.

Macbeth.
Came they not by you?

Lennox. No indeed, my lord.

Macbeth.
Infected by the air whereon they ride,
And damned all those that trust them! I did hear
The galloping of horse.° Who was't came by?

Lennox.
'Tis two or three, my lord, that bring you word
Macduff is fled to England.

Macbeth. Fled to England?

Lennox.
Ay, my good lord.

Macbeth (*aside*).
Time, thou anticipat'st° my dread exploits.
The flighty purpose never is o'ertook
Unless the deed go with it.° From this moment

116. Start: that is, from the sockets.

117. crack of doom: blast (of a trumpet) at Doomsday.

119. eighth: King James I of England (the present king).

121. twofold . . . scepters: coronation emblems.

123. blood-boltered: matted with blood.

124. his: his descendants.

? **124.** *What does Banquo look like? What must be Macbeth's mental state now?*

127. sprites: spirits.

130. antic round: grotesque, circular dance.

? **136.** *How would the mood on stage change as Lennox appears? What crucial information does he give Macbeth?*

140. horse: horses (or horsemen).

144. anticipat'st: foretold.

146. The flighty . . . it: The fleeting plan is never accomplished unless an action accompanies it.

The very firstlings of my heart° shall be
The firstlings of my hand. And even now,
To crown my thoughts with acts, be it thought and done:
The castle of Macduff I will surprise;°
Seize upon Fife; give to th' edge o' th' sword
His wife, his babes, and all unfortunate souls
That trace him in his line.° No boasting like a fool;
This deed I'll do before this purpose cool:
But no more sights!—Where are these gentlemen?
Come, bring me where they are. [*Exeunt.*]

147. firstlings . . . heart: that is, first thoughts, impulses.

150. surprise: attack suddenly.

153. trace . . . line: are of his lineage.

156. *By this speech, how does Macbeth show he has fallen ever deeper into evil? How different is Macbeth now from the reluctant murderer of the first part of the play? Why does Macbeth want to murder Macduff's children?*

Stage direction. *In many productions, the mood of this scene contrasts dramatically with the previous scenes of horror. How would you stage this domestic scene to suggest the vulnerability of Lady Macduff and her children?*

Scene 2. *Macduff's castle.*

Enter Macduff's wife LADY MACDUFF, *her* SON, *and* ROSS.

Lady Macduff.
What had he done, to make him fly the land?

Ross.
You must have patience, madam.

Lady Macduff. He had none:
His flight was madness. When our actions do not,
Our fears do make us traitors.

Ross. You know not
Whether it was his wisdom or his fear.

Lady Macduff.
Wisdom! To leave his wife, to leave his babes,
His mansion and his titles,° in a place
From whence himself does fly? He loves us not;
He wants the natural touch:° for the poor wren,
The most diminutive of birds, will fight,
Her young ones in her nest, against the owl.
All is the fear and nothing is the love;
As little is the wisdom, where the flight
So runs against all reason.

Ross. My dearest coz,°
I pray you, school° yourself. But, for your husband,
He is noble, wise, judicious, and best knows
The fits o' th' season.° I dare not speak much further:
But cruel are the times, when we are traitors
And do not know ourselves; when we hold rumor
From what we fear,° yet know not what we fear,
But float upon a wild and violent sea
Each way and move. I take my leave of you.
Shall not be long but I'll be here again.
Things at the worst will cease,° or else climb upward
To what they were before. My pretty cousin,
Blessing upon you!

Lady Macduff.
Fathered he is, and yet he's fatherless.

7. titles: possessions.

9. wants . . . touch: that is, lacks natural affection for his wife and children.

14. coz: cousin.

15. school: control.

17. fits . . . season: disorders of the time.

17. *How could Ross show his fear in line 17?*

20. hold . . . fear: believe rumors because we fear.

24. cease: cease worsening.

Ross.
I am so much a fool, should I stay longer,
It would be my disgrace° and your discomfort.
I take my leave at once. [*Exit* ROSS.]
Lady Macduff. Sirrah,° your father's dead:
And what will you do now? How will you live?
Son.
As birds do, mother.
Lady Macduff. What, with worms and flies?
Son.
With what I get, I mean; and so do they.
Lady Macduff.
Poor bird! thou'dst never fear the net nor lime,°
The pitfall nor the gin.°
Son.
Why should I, mother? Poor birds they are not set for.
My father is not dead, for all your saying.
Lady Macduff.
Yes, he is dead: how wilt thou do for a father?
Son. Nay, how will you do for a husband?
Lady Macduff. Why, I can buy me twenty at any market.
Son. Then you'll buy 'em to sell° again.
Lady Macduff.
Thou speak'st with all thy wit, and yet, i' faith,
With wit enough for thee.°
Son.
Was my father a traitor, mother?
Lady Macduff. Ay, that he was.
Son. What is a traitor?
Lady Macduff. Why, one that swears and lies.°
Son. And be all traitors that do so?
Lady Macduff. Every one that does so is a traitor, and must be hanged.
Son. And must they all be hanged that swear and lie?
Lady Macduff. Every one.
Son. Who must hang them?
Lady Macduff. Why, the honest men.
Son. Then the liars and swearers are fools; for there are liars and swearers enow° to beat the honest men and hang up them.
Lady Macduff. Now, God help thee, poor monkey! But how wilt thou do for a father?
Son. If he were dead, you'd weep for him. If you would not, it were a good sign that I should quickly have a new father.
Lady Macduff. Poor prattler, how thou talk'st!

[*Enter a* MESSENGER.]

Messenger.
Bless you, fair dame! I am not to you known,
Though in your state of honor I am perfect.°

29. It . . . disgrace: That is, I would weep.

? **30.** *In taking his leave, how would Ross show affection for Lady Macduff and her young son? Would you have Ross be younger or older than Lady Macduff?*

30. Sirrah: here, an affectionate address to a child.

? **31.** *How would you have Lady Macduff act in this scene? Frightened? Bitter? Loving? Resigned?*

34. lime: birdlime (smeared on branches to catch birds).

35. gin: trap.

41. sell: betray.

43. for thee: for a child.

47. swears and lies: takes an oath and breaks it.

55. enow: enough.

62. in . . . perfect: That is, I am fully informed of your honorable rank.

I doubt° some danger does approach you nearly:
If you will take a homely° man's advice,
Be not found here; hence, with your little ones.
To fright you thus, methinks I am too savage;
To do worse to you were fell° cruelty,
Which is too nigh your person. Heaven preserve you!
I dare abide no longer. [*Exit* MESSENGER.]

Lady Macduff. Whither should I fly?
I have done no harm. But I remember now
I am in this earthly world, where to do harm
Is often laudable, to do good sometime
Accounted dangerous folly. Why then, alas,
Do I put up that womanly defense,
To say I have done no harm?—What are these faces?

[*Enter* MURDERERS.]

Murderer.
Where is your husband?

Lady Macduff.
I hope, in no place so unsanctified
Where such as thou mayst find him.

Murderer. He's a traitor.

Son.
Thou li'st, thou shag-eared° villain!

Murderer. What, you egg!

[*Stabbing him.*]

Young fry° of treachery!

Son. He has killed me, mother:
Run away, I pray you! [*Dies.*]

[*Exit* LADY MACDUFF, *crying* "Murder!" *followed by* MURDERERS.]

63. doubt: fear.

64. homely: plain.

67. fell: fierce.

? **69.** *Some readers think that this messenger has been sent by Lady Macbeth. Is there any support for this theory? Would it be within her character? What must Lady Macduff do when she hears this terrible message?*

? **75.** *What would Lady Macduff and her son do as they see the murderers enter the room?*

79. shag-eared: hairy-eared.

80. fry: spawn.

Scene 3. *England. Before the king's palace.*

Enter MALCOLM *and* MACDUFF.

Malcolm.
Let us seek out some desolate shade, and there
Weep our sad bosoms empty.

Macduff. Let us rather
Hold fast the mortal° sword, and like good men
Bestride our down-fall'n birthdom.° Each new morn
New widows howl, new orphans cry, new sorrows
Strike heaven on the face, that° it resounds
As if it felt with Scotland and yelled out
Like syllable of dolor.°

Malcolm. What I believe, I'll wail;
What know, believe; and what I can redress,

3. mortal: deadly.

4. Bestride . . . birthdom: protectively stand over our native land.

6. that: so that.

8. Like . . . dolor: similar sound of grief.

As I shall find the time to friend,° I will.
What you have spoke, it may be so perchance.
This tyrant, whose sole° name blisters our tongues,
Was once thought honest:° you have loved him well;
He hath not touched you yet. I am young; but something
You may deserve of him through me;° and wisdom°
To offer up a weak, poor, innocent lamb
T' appease an angry god.

Macduff.
I am not treacherous.

Malcolm. But Macbeth is.
A good and virtuous nature may recoil
In° an imperial charge. But I shall crave your pardon;
That which you are, my thoughts cannot transpose:°

10. to friend: to be friendly, favorable.

12. sole: very.

13. honest: good.

? **14.** *What great irony would the audience feel upon hearing this line, given what has just taken place in the previous scene?*

15. deserve . . . me: that is, earn by betraying me to Macbeth. **wisdom:** it may be wise.

20. recoil / In: give way under.

21. transpose: transform.

"Now, God help thee, poor monkey! But how wilt thou do for a father?"

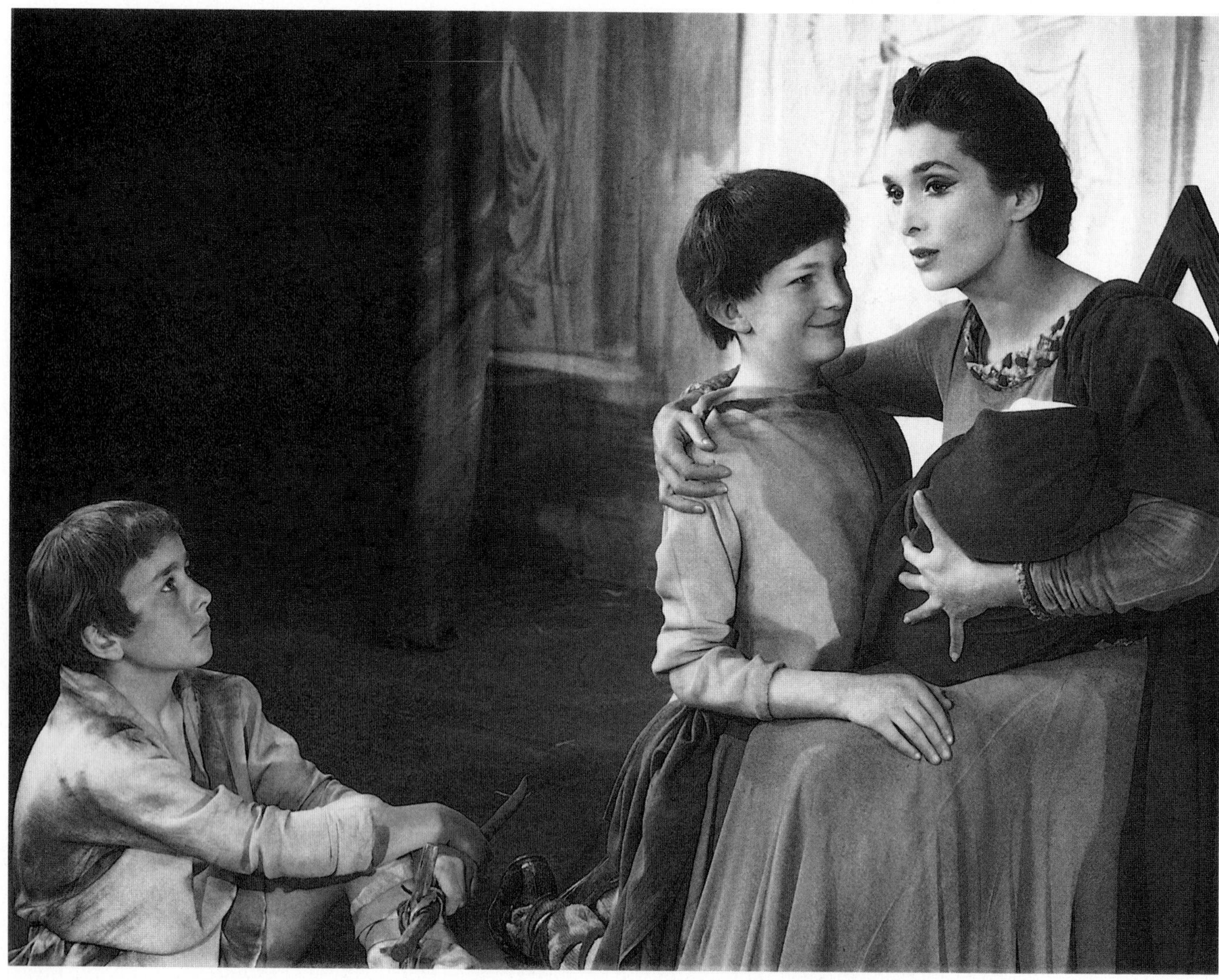

Angels are bright still, though the brightest° fell:
Though all things foul would wear° the brows of grace,
Yet grace must still look so.°

Macduff. I have lost my hopes.

Malcolm.
Perchance even there where I did find my doubts.
Why in that rawness° left you wife and child,
Those precious motives, those strong knots of love,
Without leave-taking? I pray you,
Let not my jealousies° be your dishonors,
But mine own safeties. You may be rightly just°
Whatever I shall think.

Macduff. Bleed, bleed, poor country:
Great tyranny, lay thou thy basis° sure,
For goodness dare not check° thee: wear thou thy wrongs;
The title is affeered.° Fare thee well, lord:
I would not be the villain that thou think'st
For the whole space that's in the tyrant's grasp
And the rich East to boot.

Malcolm. Be not offended:
I speak not as in absolute fear of you.
I think our country sinks beneath the yoke;
It weeps, it bleeds, and each new day a gash
Is added to her wounds. I think withal°
There would be hands uplifted in my right;°
And here from gracious England° have I offer
Of goodly thousands: but, for° all this,
When I shall tread upon the tyrant's head,
Or wear it on my sword, yet my poor country
Shall have more vices than it had before,
More suffer, and more sundry ways than ever,
By him that shall succeed.

Macduff. What should he be?

Malcolm.
It is myself I mean, in whom I know
All the particulars° of vice so grafted°
That, when they shall be opened,° black Macbeth
Will seem as pure as snow, and the poor state
Esteem him as a lamb, being compared
With my confineless harms.°

Macduff. Not in the legions
Of horrid hell can come a devil more damned
In evils to top Macbeth.

Malcolm. I grant him bloody,
Luxurious,° avaricious, false, deceitful,
Sudden,° malicious, smacking of every sin
That has a name: but there's no bottom, none,
In my voluptuousness:° your wives, your daughters,
Your matrons and your maids, could not fill up

22. the brightest: Lucifer, the angel who led the revolt of the angels and was thrown out of heaven; Satan.

23. would wear: desire to wear.

24. so: like itself.

26. rawness: unprotected condition.

29. jealousies: suspicions.

30. rightly just: perfectly honorable.

32. basis: foundation.

33. check: restrain.

34. affeered: legally confirmed.

? 37. *This speech might present a problem for the actor playing Macduff because it does not clearly relate to what has gone before it. It seems too grand and philosophical at this point in the play. How would you have the actor deliver this speech?*

41. withal: moreover.

42. in my right: on behalf of my claim.

43. England: the king of England.

44. for: despite.

51. particulars: special kinds. **grafted:** engrafted.

52. opened: in bloom (that is, revealed).

55. confineless harms: unbounded evils.

? 57. *How has Macduff responded to this speech?*

58. Luxurious: lecherous.

59. Sudden: violent.

61. voluptuousness: lust.

The cistern of my lust, and my desire
All continent° impediments would o'erbear,
That did oppose my will. Better Macbeth
Than such an one to reign.

Macduff. Boundless intemperance
In nature° is a tyranny; it hath been
Th' untimely emptying of the happy throne,
And fall of many kings. But fear not yet
To take upon you what is yours: you may
Convey° your pleasures in a spacious plenty,
And yet seem cold, the time° you may so hoodwink.
We have willing dames enough. There cannot be
That vulture in you, to devour so many
As will to greatness dedicate themselves,
Finding it so inclined.

Malcolm. With this there grows
In my most ill-composed affection° such
A stanchless° avarice that, were I king,
I should cut off the nobles for their lands,
Desire his jewels and this other's house:
And my more-having would be as a sauce
To make me hunger more, that I should forge
Quarrels unjust against the good and loyal,
Destroying them for wealth.

Macduff. This avarice
Sticks deeper, grows with more pernicious root
Than summer-seeming° lust, and it hath been
The sword of our slain kings.° Yet do not fear.
Scotland hath foisons to fill up your will
Of your mere own.° All these are portable,°
With other graces weighed.

Malcolm.
But I have none: the king-becoming graces,
As justice, verity, temp'rance, stableness,
Bounty, perseverance, mercy, lowliness,
Devotion, patience, courage, fortitude,
I have no relish of° them, but abound
In the division of each several crime,°
Acting it many ways. Nay, had I pow'r, I should
Pour the sweet milk of concord into hell,
Uproar° the universal peace, confound
All unity on earth.

Macduff. O Scotland, Scotland!

Malcolm.
If such a one be fit to govern, speak:
I am as I have spoken.

Macduff. Fit to govern!
No, not to live. O nation miserable!
With an untitled° tyrant bloody-sceptered,

64. continent: restraining.

? **66.** *Why do you think Malcolm is drawing attention to his vices? What could he hope to accomplish?*

67. nature: man's nature.

71. Convey: secretly manage.

72. time: here, people.

77. ill-composed affection: evilly compounded character.

78. stanchless: never-ending.

? **84.** *How do you imagine Malcolm delivering this speech? How could his delivery affect Macduff's response?*

86. summer-seeming: youthful, or transitory.

87. sword . . . kings: the cause of death to our kings.

89. foisons . . . own: enough abundance of your own to satisfy your covetousness. **portable:** bearable.

95. relish of: taste for.

96. division . . . crime: variations of each kind of crime.

99. Uproar: put into a tumult.

104. untitled: having no right to the throne.

When shalt thou see thy wholesome days again,
Since that the truest issue of thy throne
By his own interdiction° stands accursed,
And does blaspheme his breed?° Thy royal father
Was a most sainted king: the queen that bore thee,
Oft'ner upon her knees than on her feet,
Died° every day she lived. Fare thee well!
These evils thou repeat'st upon thyself
Hath banished me from Scotland. O my breast,
Thy hope ends here!

Malcolm. Macduff, this noble passion,
Child of integrity, hath from my soul
Wiped the black scruples,° reconciled my thoughts
To thy good truth and honor. Devilish Macbeth
By many of these trains° hath sought to win me
Into his power; and modest wisdom° plucks me
From over-credulous haste: but God above
Deal between thee and me! For even now
I put myself to° thy direction, and
Unspeak mine own detraction;° here abjure
The taints and blames I laid upon myself,
For° strangers to my nature. I am yet
Unknown to woman, never was forsworn,
Scarcely have coveted what was mine own,
At no time broke my faith, would not betray
The devil to his fellow, and delight
No less in truth than life. My first false speaking
Was this upon myself. What I am truly,
Is thine and my poor country's to command:
Whither indeed, before thy here-approach,
Old Siward, with ten thousand warlike men,
Already at a point,° was setting forth.
Now we'll together, and the chance of goodness
Be like our warranted quarrel!° Why are you silent?

Macduff.
Such welcome and unwelcome things at once
'Tis hard to reconcile.

[*Enter a* DOCTOR.]

Malcolm.
Well, more anon. Comes the king forth, I pray you?

Doctor.
Ay, sir. There are a crew of wretched souls
That stay° his cure: their malady convinces
The great assay of art;° but at his touch,
Such sanctity hath heaven given his hand,
They presently amend.°

Malcolm. I thank you, doctor.

[*Exit* DOCTOR.]

107. interdiction: curse; exclusion.

108. breed: ancestry.

111. Died: that is, prepared for heaven.

? **114.** *How might the tone change here? How has Macduff proved himself?*

116. scruples: suspicions.

118. trains: plots.

119. modest wisdom: prudence.

122. to: under.

123. detraction: slander.

125. For: as.

135. at a point: prepared.

137. the chance . . . quarrel: May our chance of success equal the justice of our cause.

? **137.** *Where should Malcolm pause in this line? Should he act puzzled, or matter-of-fact?*

142. stay: await.

143. convinces . . . art: defies the efforts of medical science.

145. presently amend: immediately recover.

Macduff.
What's the disease he means?
Malcolm. 'Tis called the evil:°
A most miraculous work in this good king,
Which often since my here-remain in England
I have seen him do. How he solicits heaven,
Himself best knows: but strangely visited° people,
All swoll'n and ulcerous, pitiful to the eye,
The mere° despair of surgery, he cures,
Hanging a golden stamp° about their necks,
Put on with holy prayers: and 'tis spoken,
To the succeeding royalty he leaves
The healing benediction. With this strange virtue°
He hath a heavenly gift of prophecy,
And sundry blessings hang about his throne
That speak° him full of grace.

[*Enter* ROSS.]

Macduff. See, who comes here?
Malcolm.
My countryman; but yet I know him not.
Macduff.
My ever gentle° cousin, welcome hither.
Malcolm.
I know him now: good God, betimes° remove
The means that makes us strangers!
Ross. Sir, amen.
Macduff.
Stands Scotland where it did?
Ross. Alas, poor country!
Almost afraid to know itself! It cannot
Be called our mother but our grave, where nothing°
But who knows nothing is once seen to smile;
Where sighs and groans, and shrieks that rent the air,
Are made, not marked;° where violent sorrow seems
A modern ecstasy.° The dead man's knell
Is there scarce asked for who, and good men's lives
Expire before the flowers in their caps,
Dying or ere they sicken.
Macduff. O, relation
Too nice,° and yet too true!
Malcolm. What's the newest grief?
Ross.
That of an hour's age doth hiss the speaker;°
Each minute teems° a new one.
Macduff. How does my wife?
Ross.
Why, well.
Macduff. And all my children?

146. evil: scrofula, called "the king's evil" because it allegedly could be cured by the king's touch.

150. strangely visited: oddly afflicted.

152. mere: utter.

153. stamp: coin.

156. virtue: power.

159. speak: proclaim.

? **Stage direction.** *Ross is Macduff's countryman. What news do you anticipate he brings with him?*

161. gentle: noble.

162. betimes: quickly.

166. nothing: no one.

169. marked: noticed.

170. modern ecstasy: ordinary emotion.

174. relation / Too nice: tale too accurate.

175. That . . . speaker: The report of the grief of an hour ago is hissed as stale news.

176. teems: gives birth to.

? **176.** *Does Ross look at Macduff on this line, or does he turn away?*

Ross. Well too.
Macduff.
The tyrant has not battered at their peace?
Ross.
No; they were well at peace when I did leave 'em.
Macduff.
Be not a niggard of your speech: how goes't?
Ross.
When I came hither to transport the tidings,
Which I have heavily° borne, there ran a rumor
Of many worthy fellows that were out;°
Which was to my belief witnessed° the rather,
For that I saw the tyrant's power° afoot.
Now is the time of help. Your eye in Scotland
Would create soldiers, make our women fight,
To doff their dire distresses.
Malcolm. Be't their comfort
We are coming thither. Gracious England hath
Lent us good Siward and ten thousand men;
An older and a better soldier none
That Christendom gives out.°
Ross. Would I could answer
This comfort with the like! But I have words
That would° be howled out in the desert air,
Where hearing should not latch° them.
Macduff. What concern they?
The general cause or is it a fee-grief
Due to some single breast?°
Ross. No mind that's honest
But in it shares some woe, though the main part
Pertains to you alone.
Macduff. If it be mine,
Keep it not from me, quickly let me have it.
Ross.
Let not your ears despise my tongue forever,
Which shall possess them with the heaviest sound
That ever yet they heard.
Macduff. Humh! I guess at it.
Ross.
Your castle is surprised;° your wife and babes
Savagely slaughtered. To relate the manner,
Were, on the quarry° of these murdered deer,
To add the death of you.
Malcolm. Merciful heaven!
What, man! Ne'er pull your hat upon your brows;
Give sorrow words. The grief that does not speak
Whispers the o'er-fraught heart,° and bids it break.
Macduff.
My children too?

? 179. *What is the double meaning of this line?*

182. **heavily:** sadly.

183. **out:** up in arms.

184. **witnessed:** attested.

185. **power:** army.

192. **gives out:** reports.

194. **would:** should.

195. **latch:** catch.

197. **fee-grief . . . breast:** that is, personal grief belonging to an individual.

? 203. *Macduff's pain becomes visible. How should we see it?*

204. **surprised:** suddenly attacked.

206. **quarry:** heap of slaughtered game.

210. **Whispers . . . heart:** whispers to the overburdened heart.

? 211. *How full, or soft, a voice would you have Macduff use in this line?*

Ross. Wife, children, servants, all
That could be found.
Macduff. And I must be from thence!
My wife killed too?
Ross. I have said.
Malcolm. Be comforted.
Let's make us med'cines of our great revenge,
To cure this deadly grief.
Macduff.
He has no children. All my pretty ones?
Did you say all? O hell-kite!° All?
What, all my pretty chickens and their dam°
At one fell swoop?
Malcolm.
Dispute° it like a man.
Macduff. I shall do so;
But I must also feel it as a man.
I cannot but remember such things were,
That were most precious to me. Did heaven look on,
And would not take their part? Sinful Macduff,

216. *How would Macduff say this line: "He has no children"?*

217. hell-kite: hellish bird of prey.

218. dam: mother.

220. Dispute: counter.

220. *Is Malcolm being critical or encouraging here?*

"Bring thou this fiend of Scotland and myself;
Within my sword's length set him."

Photofest

They were all struck for thee! Naught° that I am,
Not for their own demerits but for mine
Fell slaughter on their souls. Heaven rest them now!

Malcolm.
Be this the whetstone of your sword. Let grief
Convert to anger; blunt not the heart, enrage it.

Macduff.
O, I could play the woman with mine eyes,
And braggart with my tongue! But, gentle heavens,
Cut short all intermission;° front to front°
Bring thou this fiend of Scotland and myself;
Within my sword's length set him. If he 'scape,
Heaven forgive him too!

Malcolm. This time goes manly.
Come, go we to the king. Our power is ready;
Our lack is nothing but our leave.° Macbeth
Is ripe for shaking, and the pow'rs above
Put on their instruments.° Receive what cheer you may.
The night is long that never finds the day. [*Exeunt.*]

225. Naught: wicked.

232. intermission: interval. **front to front:** forehead to forehead (that is, face to face).

237. Our lack . . . leave: We need only to take our leave.

239. Put . . . instruments: arm themselves.

CRITICAL COMMENT

The King's Evil

INFORMATIONAL TEXT

In Act IV, Scene 3, Malcolm and Macduff, exiled from Scotland, discuss the characteristics of a good king and praise King Edward, who has given them political asylum in England. Edward, a saintly monarch known to history as "the Confessor," was believed to have the gift of healing any of his subjects who suffered from an ailment known as the king's evil, a kind of scrofula or tuberculosis of the lymphatic glands and primarily a disease of children. Long before Shakespeare's time, the custom of being touched by the king was abandoned, but King James revived the practice and his successors continued it for a century or so. The eighteenth-century writer Samuel Johnson, scrofulous as a child, was one of the last English people to receive the royal touch.

The National Gallery, London.

Edward the Confessor (detail of the Wilton Diptych).

The conversation between Malcolm and Macduff not only compliments King James indirectly, but also implicitly condemns Macbeth, a kingly killer rather than a healer of children. Edward cures evil; Macbeth *is* evil.

INFORMATIONAL TEXT

Hecate: Queen of the Night

Hecate (here pronounced in two syllables, with the accent on the first: hek´it) is a figure from Greek mythology, a queen of the night and protector of witches and enchanters. This character comes from books, unlike the witches, who were based on older, usually widowed women, whose solitary lives placed them at the margins of Scottish society. Every theatergoer would find the witches believable, and every educated person would know that King James had written an important treatise called *Daemonologie,* asserting that witches "are channels through which the malignity of evil spirits might be visited upon human beings."

Most Shakespearean scholars believe that the scenes involving Hecate (Act III, Scene 5; Act IV, Scene 1) were written by somebody other than Shakespeare and introduced into *Macbeth* at some time before 1623, when the play was first printed. This other writer has never been positively identified, although some people think he was Thomas Middleton (d. 1627), a contemporary of Shakespeare and a fellow writer for the King's Men. Two songs, the first beginning with the words "Come away" (Act III, Scene 5) and the second with "Black Spirits" (Act IV, Scene 1), were also added to the Hecate scenes, and these songs are indeed by Middleton, the complete texts of them occurring in his thriller *The Witch.*

And so the practice of adding things to *Macbeth* began very early, and it has continued throughout most of the play's long stage history. The supernatural elements seem to invite directors to devise spectacles and take liberties, especially with the witches, who have been flown on wires in some productions and whose parts have been played by ballet dancers in others.

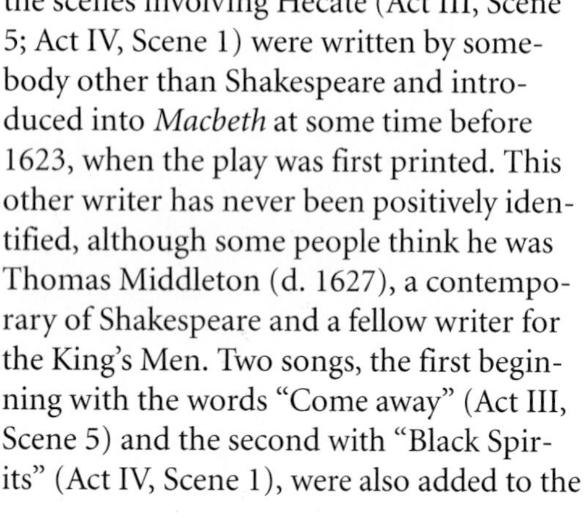

Macbeth and the Witches by Henry Fuseli.

Response and Analysis

Act IV

Reading Check

1. What ingredients go into the witches' stew? What **symbolic** purpose does this vile concoction have?
2. What has Macbeth come to ask the witches, and how do they answer?
3. Briefly describe the three apparitions. What does each apparition tell Macbeth?
4. Which nobleman does Macbeth plan to murder after talking with the witches? How is his plan foiled?
5. At the end of Scene 1, what does Macbeth vow? How is his vow carried out in Scene 2?
6. According to the conversation between Malcolm and Macduff in Scene 3, what has happened to Scotland during Macbeth's reign?

Thinking Critically

7. In this act, Macbeth seeks out the witches, just as they initiated the encounter in Act I. How has Macbeth's situation changed since he last talked with the witches? How has his moral **character** deteriorated? Find lines and actions that support your interpretation.
8. Do you think the witches have caused any of the changes in Macbeth's **character,** either directly or indirectly? Explain your reasons.
9. In Scene 1, the eight kings appear in what was called in Shakespeare's time a **dumb show**—an interpolated brief scene in which nothing is said. What is the point of this particular dumb show?
10. In Scene 2, the lines spoken by Macduff's wife and son illustrate Shakespeare's great skill at **characterization.** Using only a few words, he brings the woman and the child to life. How would you describe Lady Macduff? How would you describe the boy?
11. Both the murderer and Lady Macduff herself call Macduff a traitor. In what sense does each mean it? Do you think Macduff is a traitor, in either sense?
12. In Scene 3, Malcolm deliberately lies to Macduff. What does this behavior, and the reason for it, reveal about Malcolm?

Extending and Evaluating

13. The murder of Macduff's small son is one of the most pitiful and shocking scenes in Shakespeare. Do you think reporting the murder after the fact might have been better than showing the carnage onstage? What would be lost and what would be gained by this change?
14. In Scene 3, Malcolm and Macduff decry the chaos that Macbeth's rule has brought to Scotland, as if Macbeth's disorder has become Scotland's. Does that happen today—does the weakness or the evil of a nation's leader become that of a nation itself? Explain your response.

WRITING

Things to Come

The final outcome of a **tragedy** is never in doubt. However, the matter of when, where, or how the main character will meet his or her fate is usually not foretold, although in Act IV careful readers can see hints of Macbeth's end. In a brief **essay,** discuss what you think will be Macbeth's final undoing. How does Shakespeare use the apparitions and the witches to indicate the consequences of evil deeds and to **foreshadow** Macbeth's fate?

Literary Skills Analyze the characteristics of tragedy, including character and dumb show.

Writing Skills Write an essay exploring a writer's use of foreshadowing.

ACT V Scene 1. *Dunsinane. In the castle.*

Enter a DOCTOR *of physic and a waiting* GENTLEWOMAN.

Doctor. I have two nights watched with you, but can perceive no truth in your report. When was it she last walked?

Gentlewoman. Since his majesty went into the field, I have seen her rise from her bed, throw her nightgown upon her, unlock her closet,° take forth paper, fold it, write upon't, read it, afterwards seal it, and again return to bed; yet all this while in a most fast sleep.

Doctor. A great perturbation in nature, to receive at once the benefit of sleep and do the effects of watching!° In this slumb'ry agitation, besides her walking and other actual performances,° what, at any time, have you heard her say?

5. closet: chest.

9. effects of watching: deeds of one awake.

11. actual performances: deeds.

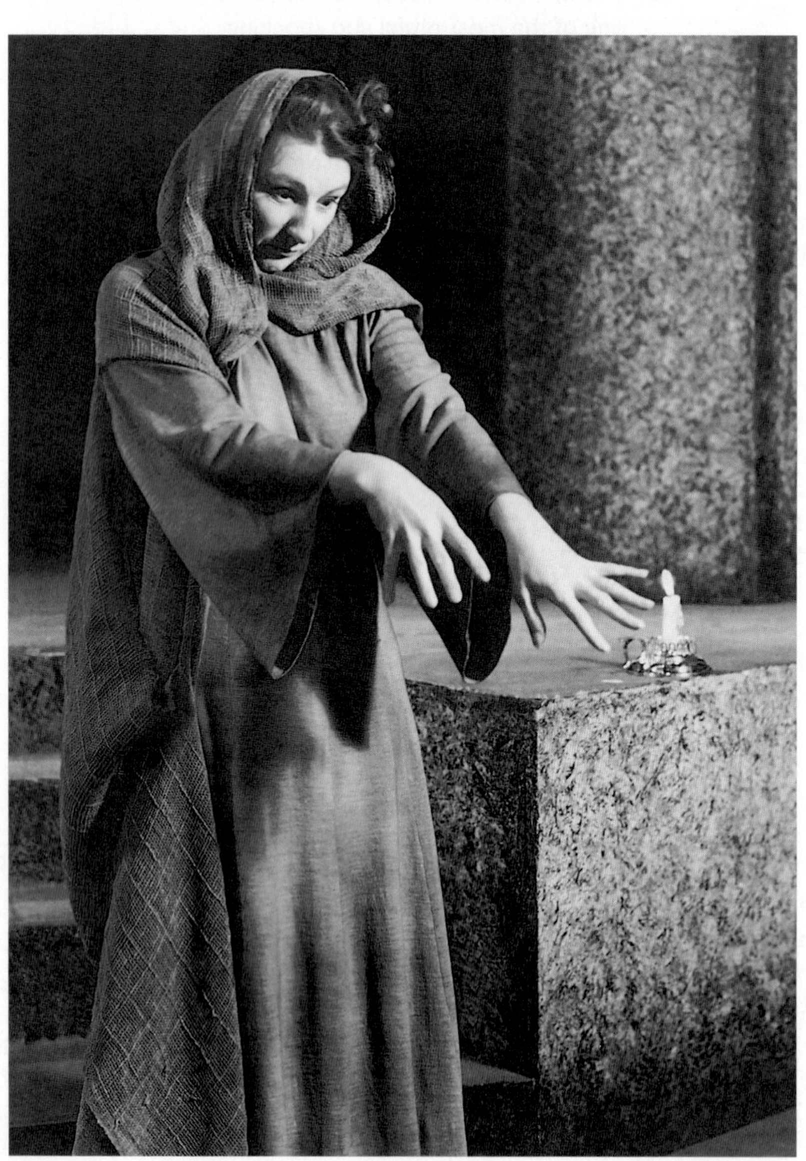

"What, will these hands ne'er be clean?"

Photofest

Gentlewoman. That, sir, which I will not report after her.

Doctor. You may to me, and 'tis most meet° you should.

Gentlewoman. Neither to you nor anyone, having no witness to confirm my speech.

[*Enter* LADY MACBETH, *with a taper.*]

Lo you, here she comes! This is her very guise,° and, upon my life, fast asleep! Observe her; stand close.°

Doctor. How came she by that light?

Gentlewoman. Why, it stood by her. She has light by her continually. 'Tis her command.

Doctor. You see, her eyes are open.

Gentlewoman. Ay, but their sense° are shut.

Doctor. What is it she does now? Look, how she rubs her hands.

Gentlewoman. It is an accustomed action with her, to seem thus washing her hands: I have known her continue in this a quarter of an hour.

Lady Macbeth. Yet here's a spot.

Doctor. Hark! she speaks. I will set down what comes from her, to satisfy° my remembrance the more strongly.

Lady Macbeth. Out, damned spot! Out, I say! One: two: why, then 'tis time to do't. Hell is murky. Fie, my lord, fie! A soldier, and afeard? What need we fear who knows it, when none can call our pow'r to accompt?° Yet who would have thought the old man to have had so much blood in him?

Doctor. Do you mark that?

Lady Macbeth. The Thane of Fife had a wife. Where is she now? What, will these hands ne'er be clean? No more o' that, my lord, no more o' that! You mar all with this starting.

Doctor. Go to,° go to! You have known what you should not.

Gentlewoman. She has spoke what she should not, I am sure of that. Heaven knows what she has known.

Lady Macbeth. Here's the smell of the blood still. All the perfumes of Arabia will not sweeten this little hand. Oh, oh, oh!

Doctor. What a sigh is there! The heart is sorely charged.°

Gentlewoman. I would not have such a heart in my bosom for the dignity° of the whole body.

Doctor. Well, well, well——

Gentlewoman. Pray God it be, sir.

Doctor. This disease is beyond my practice.° Yet I have known those which have walked in their sleep who have died holily in their beds.

Lady Macbeth. Wash your hands; put on your nightgown; look not so pale! I tell you yet again, Banquo's buried. He cannot come out on 's° grave.

Doctor. Even so?

Lady Macbeth. To bed, to bed! There's knocking at the gate.

13. meet: suitable.

16. guise: custom.

17. close: hidden.

? **20.** *Why must Lady Macbeth have light by her continually?*

22. sense: powers of sight.

? **28.** *After setting down the taper on a table, what does Lady Macbeth do with her hands?*

30. satisfy: confirm.

34. to accompt: into account.

? **35.** *What does she think is still on her hands?*

? **37.** *Who is the Thane of Fife?*

40. Go to: an exclamation.

? **43.** *What action is suggested by this line?*

45. charged: burdened.

47. dignity: worth; rank.

50. practice: professional skill.

55. on 's: of his.

? **55.** *Whom does she think she is speaking to here?*

Come, come, come, come, give me your hand! What's done cannot be undone. To bed, to bed, to bed!
[*Exit* LADY MACBETH.]

Doctor. Will she go now to bed?
Gentlewoman. Directly.
Doctor.
Foul whisp'rings are abroad. Unnatural deeds
Do breed unnatural troubles. Infected minds
To their deaf pillows will discharge their secrets.
More needs she the divine° than the physician.
God, God forgive us all! Look after her;
Remove from her the means of all annoyance,°
And still° keep eyes upon her. So good night.
My mind she has mated° and amazed my sight:
I think, but dare not speak.
Gentlewoman. Good night, good doctor.
[*Exeunt.*]

59. *Once again there is a sudden dramatic change. What echo from the past brings it about? How do you think Lady Macbeth leaves the stage?*

65. divine: priest.

67. annoyance: injury.

68. still: continuously.

69. mated: baffled.

70. *What do the doctor and gentlewoman know? Why won't they speak out?*

Scene 2. *The country near Dunsinane.*

Drum and colors. Enter MENTEITH, CAITHNESS, ANGUS, LENNOX, SOLDIERS.

Menteith.
The English pow'r° is near, led on by Malcolm,
His uncle Siward and the good Macduff.
Revenges burn in them; for their dear° causes
Would to the bleeding and the grim alarm°
Excite the mortified° man.
Angus. Near Birnam Wood
Shall we well meet them; that way are they coming.
Caithness.
Who knows if Donalbain be with his brother?
Lennox.
For certain, sir, he is not. I have a file°
Of all the gentry: there is Siward's son,
And many unrough° youths that even now
Protest° their first of manhood.
Menteith. What does the tyrant?
Caithness.
Great Dunsinane he strongly fortifies.
Some say he's mad; others, that lesser hate him,
Do call it valiant fury: but, for certain,
He cannot buckle his distempered° cause
Within the belt of rule.°
Angus. Now does he feel
His secret murders sticking on his hands;
Now minutely revolts upbraid° his faith-breach.
Those he commands move only in command,
Nothing in love. Now does he feel his title

1. pow'r: army.

3. dear: heartfelt.

4. alarm: call to arms.

5. mortified: half dead.

5. *Where have you heard about Birnam Wood before?*

8. file: list.

10. unrough: beardless.

11. Protest: assert.

15. distempered: swollen with disease.

16. rule: self-control.

18. minutely revolts upbraid: rebellions every minute rebuke.

Hang loose about him, like a giant's robe
Upon a dwarfish thief.

Mentieth. Who then shall blame
His pestered° senses to recoil and start,
When all that is within him does condemn
Itself for being there?

Caithness. Well, march we on,
To give obedience where 'tis truly owed.
Meet we the med'cine° of the sickly weal,°
And with him pour we, in our country's purge,
Each drop of us.°

Lennox. Or so much as it needs
To dew° the sovereign° flower and drown the weeds.
Make we our march towards Birnam.

[*Exeunt, marching.*]

23. pestered: tormented.

27. med'cine: that is, Malcolm. **weal:** commonwealth.

29. Each . . . us: that is, every last drop of our blood.

30. dew: bedew; water (and thus make grow). **sovereign:** royal; also, remedial.

? **31.** *The "falling action" of a Shakespearean play is usually swift. How does this scene show that the hero's enemies are now rallying to crush him? What group is shown in this scene?*

Scene 3. *Dunsinane. In the castle.*

Enter MACBETH, DOCTOR, *and* ATTENDANTS.

Macbeth.
Bring me no more reports; let them fly all!
Till Birnam Wood remove to Dunsinane
I cannot taint° with fear. What's the boy Malcolm?
Was he not born of woman? The spirits that know
All mortal consequences° have pronounced me thus:
"Fear not, Macbeth; no man that's born of woman
Shall e'er have power upon thee." Then fly, false thanes,
And mingle with the English epicures.
The mind I sway° by and the heart I bear
Shall never sag with doubt nor shake with fear.

[*Enter* SERVANT.]

The devil damn thee black, thou cream-faced loon!°
Where got'st thou that goose look?

Servant.
There is ten thousand——

Macbeth. Geese, villain?

Servant. Soldiers, sir.

Macbeth.
Go prick thy face and over-red° thy fear,
Thou lily-livered boy. What soldiers, patch?°
Death of° thy soul! Those linen° cheeks of thine
Are counselors to fear. What soldiers, whey-face?

Servant.
The English force, so please you.

Macbeth.
Take thy face hence. [*Exit* SERVANT.]
Seyton!—I am sick at heart,
When I behold—Seyton, I say!—This push°

3. taint: become infected.

5. mortal consequences: future human events.

9. sway: move.

11. loon: fool.

? **12.** *Macbeth is in an extreme state of agitation. Which of the apparitions' prophecies is he relying on? How would you stage his treatment of the servant, which follows?*

14. over-red: cover with red.

15. patch: fool.

16. of: upon. **linen:** pale.

20. push: effort.

Will cheer me ever, or disseat° me now.
I have lived long enough. My way of life
Is fall'n into the sear,° the yellow leaf,
And that which should accompany old age,
As honor, love, obedience, troops of friends,
I must not look to have; but, in their stead,
Curses not loud but deep, mouth-honor, breath,
Which the poor heart would fain deny, and dare not.
Seyton!

[*Enter* SEYTON.]

Seyton.
What's your gracious pleasure?

Macbeth. What news more?

Seyton.
All is confirmed, my lord, which was reported.

Macbeth.
I'll fight, till from my bones my flesh be hacked.
Give me my armor.

Seyton. 'Tis not needed yet.

Macbeth.
I'll put it on.
Send out moe° horses, skirr° the country round.
Hang those that talk of fear. Give me mine armor.
How does your patient, doctor?

Doctor. Not so sick, my lord,
As she is troubled with thick-coming fancies
That keep her from her rest.

Macbeth. Cure her of that.
Canst thou not minister to a mind diseased,
Pluck from the memory a rooted sorrow,
Raze out° the written troubles of the brain,
And with some sweet oblivious° antidote
Cleanse the stuffed bosom of that perilous stuff
Which weighs upon the heart?

Doctor. Therein the patient
Must minister to himself.

Macbeth.
Throw physic° to the dogs, I'll none of it.
Come, put mine armor on. Give me my staff.
Seyton, send out.—Doctor, the thanes fly from me.—
Come, sir, dispatch.° If thou couldst, doctor, cast
The water° of my land, find her disease
And purge it to a sound and pristine health,
I would applaud thee to the very echo,
That should applaud again.—Pull't off, I say.—
What rhubarb, senna, or what purgative drug,
Would scour these English hence? Hear'st thou of them?

21. disseat: unthrone (with wordplay on *cheer;* pronounced *chair*).

? **22.** *What mood is Macbeth in now?*

23. sear: withered.

35. moe: more. **skirr:** scour.

? **37.** *Who is the doctor's patient?*

42. Raze out: erase.

43. oblivious: causing forgetfulness.

47. physic: medical science.

50. dispatch: hurry.

51. cast/The water: literally, analyze the urine.

? **56.** *Lines 47–56 contain almost a roller coaster of emotions. Can you cite some?*

Doctor.
Ay, my good lord; your royal preparation
Makes us hear something.

Macbeth. Bring it° after me.
I will not be afraid of death and bane°
Till Birnam Forest come to Dunsinane.

Doctor (*aside*).
Were I from Dunsinane away and clear,
Profit again should hardly draw me here. [*Exeunt.*]

58. it: the armor.

59. bane: destruction.

? **60.** *Is Macbeth truly courageous here? Or would you suggest that he is merely coasting on a kind of false bravery lent to him by the witches' prophecies?*

Scene 4. *Country near Birnam Wood.*

Drum and colors. Enter MALCOLM, SIWARD, MACDUFF, *Siward's son* YOUNG SIWARD, MENTEITH, CAITHNESS, ANGUS, *and* SOLDIERS, *marching.*

Malcolm.
Cousins, I hope the days are near at hand
That chambers will be safe.°

Menteith. We doubt it nothing.°

Siward.
What wood is this before us?

Menteith. The Wood of Birnam.

Malcolm.
Let every soldier hew him down a bough
And bear't before him. Thereby shall we shadow
The numbers of our host, and make discovery°
Err in report of us.

Soldiers. It shall be done.

Siward.
We learn no other but° the confident tyrant
Keeps still in Dunsinane, and will endure°
Our setting down before't.

Malcolm. 'Tis his main hope,
For where there is advantage to be given°
Both more and less° have given him the revolt,
And none serve with him but constrainèd things
Whose hearts are absent too.

Macduff. Let our just censures
Attend the true event,° and put we on
Industrious soldiership.

Siward. The time approaches,
That will with due decision make us know
What we shall say we have and what we owe.°
Thoughts speculative their unsure hopes relate,
But certain issue strokes must arbitrate:°
Towards which advance the war.° [*Exeunt, marching.*]

2. That . . . safe: that a man will be safe in his bedroom. **nothing:** not at all.

? **5.** *Stop and describe what the soldiers are to do here and why.*

6. discovery: Macbeth's scouts.

? **7.** *Malcolm seems to have more authority at this point in the play. Can you find specific instances where his new authority could be dramatized?*

8. no other but: nothing but that.

9. endure: allow.

11. advantage . . . given: afforded an opportunity.

12. more and less: high and low.

15. just . . . event: true judgments await the actual outcome.

18. owe: own. The contrast is between "what we shall say we have" and "what we shall really have."

20. certain . . . arbitrate: The definite outcome must be decided by battle.

21. war: army.

"Tomorrow, and tomorrow, and tomorrow
Creeps in this petty pace from day to day,
To the last syllable of recorded time."

From Orson Welles's film production of *Macbeth* (1948).

Scene 5. *Dunsinane. Within the castle.*

Enter MACBETH, SEYTON, *and* SOLDIERS, *with drum and colors.*

Macbeth.
Hang out our banners on the outward walls.
The cry is still "They come!" Our castle's strength
Will laugh a siege to scorn. Here let them lie
Till famine and the ague° eat them up.
Were they not forced° with those that should be ours,
We might have met them dareful,° beard to beard,
And beat them backward home.

[*A cry within of women.*]

What is that noise?

Seyton.
It is the cry of women, my good lord. [*Exit.*]

Macbeth.
I have almost forgot the taste of fears:
The time has been, my senses would have cooled
To hear a night-shriek, and my fell° of hair
Would at a dismal treatise° rouse and stir
As life were in't. I have supped full with horrors.
Direness, familiar to my slaughterous thoughts,
Cannot once start° me.

4. **ague:** fever.

5. **forced:** reinforced.

6. **met them dareful:** that is, met them on the battlefield boldly.

? 7. *Macbeth should contrast with Malcolm now. How should he be acting?*

11. **fell:** pelt.

12. **treatise:** story.

15. **start:** startle.

[*Enter* SEYTON.]

Wherefore was that cry?

Seyton.
The queen, my lord, is dead.

Macbeth.
She should° have died hereafter;
There would have been a time for such a word.°
Tomorrow, and tomorrow, and tomorrow
Creeps in this petty pace from day to day,
To the last syllable of recorded time;
And all our yesterdays have lighted fools
The way to dusty death. Out, out, brief candle!
Life's but a walking shadow, a poor player
That struts and frets his hour upon the stage
And then is heard no more. It is a tale
Told by an idiot, full of sound and fury,
Signifying nothing.

[*Enter a* MESSENGER.]

Thou com'st to use thy tongue; thy story quickly!

Messenger.
Gracious my lord,
I should report that which I say I saw,
But know not how to do't.

Macbeth. Well, say, sir.

Messenger.
As I did stand my watch upon the hill,
I looked toward Birnam, and anon, methought,
The wood began to move.

Macbeth. Liar and slave!

Messenger.
Let me endure your wrath, if't be not so.
Within this three mile may you see it coming;
I say a moving grove.

Macbeth. If thou speak'st false,
Upon the next tree shalt thou hang alive,
Till famine cling° thee. If thy speech be sooth,°
I care not if thou dost for me as much.
I pull in resolution,° and begin
To doubt° th' equivocation of the fiend
That lies like truth: "Fear not, till Birnam Wood
Do come to Dunsinane!" And now a wood
Comes toward Dunsinane. Arm, arm, and out!
If this which he avouches° does appear,
There is nor flying hence nor tarrying here.
I 'gin to be aweary of the sun,
And wish th' estate° o' th' world were now undone.
Ring the alarum bell! Blow wind, come wrack!
At least we'll die with harness° on our back. [*Exeunt.*]

17. should: inevitably would.

18. word: message.

28. *A scene that began in defiance changes with the great speech beginning "She should have died hereafter." What is Macbeth's new mood? Does Macbeth speak only for himself here, or for the general human condition?*

35. *What is Macbeth thinking of now?*

40. cling: wither. **sooth:** truth.

42. pull in resolution: restrain confidence.

43. doubt: suspect.

47. avouches: asserts.

50. th' estate: the orderly condition.

52. harness: armor.

52. *Macbeth ends the scene in a state of great emotion. How would you characterize his mental state?*

Scene 6. *Dunsinane. Before the castle.*

Drum and colors. Enter MALCOLM, SIWARD, MACDUFF, *and their* ARMY, *with boughs.*

Malcolm.
Now near enough. Your leavy° screens throw down,
And show like those you are. You, worthy uncle,
Shall, with my cousin, your right noble son,
Lead our first battle.° Worthy Macduff and we°
Shall take upon 's what else remains to do,
According to our order.°

Siward. Fare you well.
Do we° but find the tyrant's power° tonight,
Let us be beaten, if we cannot fight.

Macduff.
Make all our trumpets speak; give them all breath,
Those clamorous harbingers of blood and death.
[*Exeunt. Alarums continued.*]

1. **leavy:** leafy.

4. **battle:** battalion. **we:** Malcolm uses the royal "we."

6. **order:** plan.

7. **Do we:** if we do. **power:** forces.

"Make all our trumpets speak; give them all breath,
Those clamorous harbingers of blood and death."
Photofest

Scene 7. *Another part of the field.*

Enter MACBETH.

Macbeth.
They have tied me to a stake; I cannot fly,
But bearlike I must fight the course.° What's he
That was not born of woman? Such a one
Am I to fear, or none.

[*Enter* YOUNG SIWARD.]

Young Siward.
What is thy name?

Macbeth. Thou'lt be afraid to hear it.

Young Siward.
No; though thou call'st thyself a hotter name
Than any is in hell.

Macbeth. My name's Macbeth.

Young Siward.
The devil himself could not pronounce a title
More hateful to mine ear.

Macbeth. No, nor more fearful.

Young Siward.
Thou liest, abhorrèd tyrant; with my sword
I'll prove the lie thou speak'st.

[*Fight, and* YOUNG SIWARD *slain.*]

Macbeth. Thou wast born of woman.
But swords I smile at, weapons laugh to scorn,
Brandished by man that's of a woman born. [*Exit.*]

[*Alarums. Enter* MACDUFF.]

Macduff.
That way the noise is. Tyrant, show thy face!
If thou be'st slain and with no stroke of mine,
My wife and children's ghosts will haunt me still.
I cannot strike at wretched kerns,° whose arms
Are hired to bear their staves.° Either thou, Macbeth,
Or else my sword, with an unbattered edge,
I sheathe again undeeded.° There thou shouldst be;
By this great clatter, one of greatest note
Seems bruited.° Let me find him, Fortune!
And more I beg not. [*Exit. Alarums.*]

[*Enter* MALCOLM *and* SIWARD.]

Siward.
This way, my lord. The castle's gently rend'red:°
The tyrant's people on both sides do fight;
The noble thanes do bravely in the war;
The day almost itself professes° yours,

2. course: bout; round. (He has in mind an attack of dogs or men upon a bear chained to a stake.)

? **4.** *What is Macbeth desperately clinging to now?*

17. kerns: foot soldiers (contemptuous).

18. staves: spears.

20. undeeded: that is, having done nothing.

22. bruited: reported.

24. gently rend'red: surrendered without a struggle.

27. itself professes: declares itself.

And little is to do.
Malcolm. We have met with foes
That strike beside us.°
Siward. Enter, sir, the castle.
[*Exeunt. Alarum.*]

Scene 8. *Another part of the field.*

Enter MACBETH.

Macbeth.
Why should I play the Roman fool, and die
On mine own sword? Whiles I see lives,° the gashes
Do better upon them.

[*Enter* MACDUFF.]

Macduff. Turn, hell-hound, turn!
Macbeth.
Of all men else I have avoided thee.
But get thee back! My soul is too much charged°
With blood of thine already.

29. **That . . . us:** that is, who deliberately miss us.

2. **Whiles . . . lives:** so long as I see living men.

5. **charged:** burdened.

"I have no words: / My voice is in my sword, thou bloodier villain / Than terms can give thee out!"
From Roman Polanski's film production of *Macbeth* (1971).

Macduff. I have no words:
My voice is in my sword, thou bloodier villain
Than terms can give thee out!° [*Fight. Alarum.*]

Macbeth. Thou losest labor:
As easy mayst thou the intrenchant° air
With thy keen sword impress° as make me bleed:
Let fall thy blade on vulnerable crests;°
I bear a charmèd life, which must not yield
To one of woman born.

Macduff. Despair° thy charm,
And let the angel° whom thou still hast served
Tell thee, Macduff was from his mother's womb
Untimely ripped.

Macbeth.
Accursèd be that tongue that tells me so,
For it hath cowed my better part of man!°
And be these juggling fiends no more believed,
That palter° with us in a double sense;
That keep the word of promise to our ear,
And break it to our hope. I'll not fight with thee.

Macduff.
Then yield thee, coward,
And live to be the show and gaze o' th' time:°
We'll have thee, as our rarer monsters° are,
Painted upon a pole,° and underwrit,
"Here may you see the tyrant."

Macbeth. I will not yield,
To kiss the ground before young Malcolm's feet,
And to be baited° with the rabble's curse.
Though Birnam Wood be come to Dunsinane,
And thou opposed, being of no woman born,
Yet I will try the last. Before my body
I throw my warlike shield. Lay on, Macduff;
And damned be him that first cries "Hold, enough!"

[*Exeunt, fighting. Alarums.*]

[*Reenter fighting, and* MACBETH *slain. Exit* MACDUFF, *with* MACBETH. *Retreat and flourish.*° *Enter, with drum and colors,* MALCOLM, SIWARD, ROSS, THANES, *and* SOLDIERS.]

Malcolm.
I would the friends we miss were safe arrived.

Siward.
Some must go off;° and yet, by these I see,
So great a day as this is cheaply bought.

Malcolm.
Macduff is missing, and your noble son.

Ross.
Your son, my lord, has paid a soldier's debt:
He only lived but till he was a man;
The which no sooner had his prowess confirmed

8. terms . . . out: words can describe you.

9. intrenchant: incapable of being cut.

10. impress: make an impression on.

11. vulnerable crests: heads that can be wounded.

13. Despair: despair of.

14. angel: that is, fallen angel; fiend.

? **16.** *What is the meaning of lines 15–16? How do they relate to the prophecy?*

18. better . . . man: manly spirit.

20. palter: equivocate.

24. gaze . . . time: spectacle of the age.

25. monsters: freaks.

26. Painted . . . pole: pictured on a banner set by a showman's booth.

29. baited: assailed (like a bear by dogs).

Retreat and flourish: trumpet call to withdraw, and fanfare.

36. go off: die (theatrical metaphor).

In the unshrinking station° where he fought,
But like a man he died.

Siward. Then he is dead?

Ross.
Ay, and brought off the field. Your cause of sorrow
Must not be measured by his worth, for then
It hath no end.

Siward. Had he his hurts before?

Ross.
Ay, on the front.

Siward. Why then, God's soldier be he!
Had I as many sons as I have hairs,
I would not wish them to a fairer death:
And so his knell is knolled.

Malcolm. He's worth more sorrow,
And that I'll spend for him.

Siward. He's worth no more:
They say he parted well and paid his score:°
And so God be with him! Here comes newer comfort.

[*Enter* MACDUFF, *with Macbeth's head.*]

Macduff.
Hail, king! for so thou art: behold, where stands
Th' usurper's cursèd head. The time is free.°
I see thee compassed° with thy kingdom's pearl,
That speak my salutation in their minds,
Whose voices I desire aloud with mine:
Hail, King of Scotland!

All. Hail, King of Scotland!

[*Flourish.*]

Malcolm.
We shall not spend a large expense of time
Before we reckon with your several loves,°
And make us even with you. My thanes and kinsmen,
Henceforth be earls, the first that ever Scotland
In such an honor named. What's more to do,
Which would be planted newly with the time°—
As calling home our exiled friends abroad
That fled the snares of watchful tyranny,
Producing forth the cruel ministers°
Of this dead butcher and his fiendlike queen,
Who, as 'tis thought, by self and violent hands°
Took off her life—this, and what needful else
That calls upon us,° by the grace of Grace
We will perform in measure, time, and place:°
So thanks to all at once and to each one,
Whom we invite to see us crowned at Scone.

[*Flourish. Exeunt omnes.*]

42. unshrinking station: that is, place at which he stood firmly.

52. parted . . . score: departed well and settled his account.

? **53.** *What character traits does Malcolm show in this scene? How is old Siward like a military man to the end?*

? **Stage direction.** *Macduff enters with Macbeth's head on a pole. A great shout goes up. What is Macduff's tone in the next speech?*

55. The time is free: The world is liberated.

56. compassed: surrounded.

61. reckon . . . loves: reward the devotion of each of you.

65. What's . . . time: What else must be done that should be newly established in this age.

68. ministers: agents.

70. self . . . hands: her own violent hands.

72. calls upon us: demands my attention.

73. in . . . place: fittingly, at the appropriate time and place.

? **75.** *Scone (skōōn) is a village in Scotland. For centuries, all Scottish kings were crowned in Scone on the Stone of Destiny. The stone was taken to England in 1296 and was returned to Scotland, to Edinburgh Castle, in 1996. How would you have the characters exit? Who would exit last?*

Soliloquies and Asides

INFORMATIONAL TEXT

Renaissance playwrights had two useful devices for revealing to an audience or reader a dramatic character's inmost thoughts and feelings: soliloquies and asides.

A **soliloquy** is a meditative kind of speech in which a character, usually alone on stage and pretending that the audience is not present, thinks out loud. Everybody understands that the speaker of a soliloquy tells the truth freely and openly, however discreditable that truth may be. For instance, in his famous soliloquy beginning "To be or not to be," Shakespeare's Hamlet admits to the audience that he is thinking of committing suicide.

Asides are much shorter than soliloquies, but just as truthful. **Asides** are a character's private comments on what is happening at a given moment in a play. They are spoken out of the side of the mouth, so to speak, for the benefit of the audience; the other characters on stage pretend that they do not hear them. For example, Macbeth's asides in Act I, Scene 3, tell us that he cannot put the witches' prophecies out of his mind.

Macbeth's tragic decline can be best traced in his solo speeches—his asides and soliloquies. The most important of these, which are what make the play so interesting psychologically, occur as follows:

Act I, Scene 3, lines 130–142
Act I, Scene 4, lines 48–53
Act I, Scene 7, lines 1–28
Act II, Scene 1, lines 33–64
Act III, Scene 1, lines 48–72
Act IV, Scene 1, lines 144–156
Act V, Scene 3, lines 19–29
Act V, Scene 5, lines 9–15

The early soliloquies show Macbeth's indecision and his fierce inner conflict; then, after he succumbs to evil, they show the terror in his soul and his inability to recover his lost innocence. At times they even show that he is reconciled to his murderous career, especially after the second set of prophecies gives him a false sense of security. But finally the soliloquies show his despair and loss of feeling about, and interest in, life itself. All these changing states of mind are expressed in powerful images that help the audience share Macbeth's suffering. In contrast, we see Lady Macbeth mainly from the outside, though an attentive reader can find speeches in which she also reveals feelings. In *Macbeth,* the inner spiritual catastrophe parallels the outer physical catastrophe.

Peter O'Toole as Macbeth in a 1980 performance.

The Mystery of Evil

INFORMATIONAL TEXT

Macbeth fascinates us because it shows, perhaps more clearly than any of Shakespeare's other tragedies, how a character can change as a result of what he does. *Macbeth* also shows that crime does not pay, but that smug cliché is not very relevant to the play: Macbeth is "caught" as soon as he understands the witches' prophecy, and his mental anguish begins before he commits any crimes.

At the start of the play, the mere thought of committing a murder terrifies Macbeth, although he is no novice at carving up men in battle. But it is one thing to fight openly, quite another to kill stealthily. His wife says her great warrior-husband Macbeth is "too full o' th' milk of human kindness." Shakespeare apparently wants us to think of Macbeth as a good man and to feel sympathetic toward him even after he becomes a murderer. When Duncan's body is found, Macbeth does not feel excited about becoming king; instead, he mutters to himself, "The wine of life is drawn." He can't enjoy his kingly state; he is too terrified by what he is doing. "Full of scorpions is my mind," he says to his wife. He lives in such constant terror that by the end of the play he is numb to all feeling—even to the death of his beloved wife. A "dead butcher," Malcolm calls him: an automatic killer.

Lady Macbeth's deterioration is different from her husband's but just as dramatic. Legally, she is only an accomplice, never an actual murderer. But she is the first to decide that Duncan must die; Macbeth wavers right up to the last moment. After the first murders, she exerts immense self-control over herself while he surrenders to his nerves. But she does eventually crack under the strain. Malcolm might not have called her a "fiendlike queen" after her death had he known how much she suffered from pangs of conscience. Both Macbeth and his wife are moral beings who excite our pity rather than our contempt or disgust.

But why do they commit their crimes? The customary answer to this question—that they are ambitious—leads only to another question: Why are they so ambitious that they are willing to commit such crimes? Ultimately, these questions are unanswerable, because evil is as mysterious as it is real. Shakespeare makes no attempt to solve the mystery; instead, in *Macbeth*, he uses language to make it even more mysterious. The world of *Macbeth* is filled, from beginning to end, with mysterious and repulsive images of evil.

The Imagery: Darkness, Night, Blood

First of all, there are the witches. The play opens with the three witches performing their sinister rites and chanting, "Fair is foul, and foul is fair," blurring the differences between these opposites. Macbeth's first speech joins the same opposites, as though they were synonyms: "So foul and fair a day I have not seen." Macbeth's speech thus establishes a connection between himself and the witches even before he meets them.

Shakespeare's audience would have immediately recognized the witches as embodiments of evil in league with Satan himself. Several times they refer to themselves as the "weird sisters"—*weird* here meaning maliciously and perversely supernatural, possessing harmful powers given them by evil spirits in the form of nasty pet animals such as old gray tomcats and toads. English and Scottish witches are not to be regarded as the Fates of Greek mythology whose baleful influence could not be resisted. Rather, they are tempters of a kind that Shakespeare's contemporaries believed they should always avoid. One of the witches seems to foretell Macbeth's future by saying, "All hail, Macbeth, that shalt be king hereafter!" After an inner struggle, and under the influence of his wife's goading, Macbeth chooses to make "hereafter" happen immediately. Nowhere in the play do the witches *cause* Macbeth to make this wicked decision. Rather, he voluntarily surrenders himself, following a visionary dagger—a manifestation of his decision—that leads him into Duncan's bedroom. Having once given in to evil, Macbeth is thereafter under the control of evil forces stronger than his own moral sense.

Shakespeare expresses these evil forces in images of darkness, night, and blood. He has Banquo call the weird sisters "instruments of darkness," linking them to the thick gloom that pervades the whole play and provides a cover under which evil can do its work. Even in daylight Macbeth and his wife invoke the night: "Come, thick night," Lady Macbeth cries as part of her prayer asking evil spirits to "unsex" her. Macbeth also calls for night to come, to blindfold "the tender eye of pitiful day" so that the killers he has hired can safely murder innocent Banquo and his son.

By setting many of the violent scenes at night and by making the scenes in *Macbeth* "murky," full of "fog and filthy air," and pierced by the cries of owls, Shakespeare suppresses all the pleasant associations night might have, especially as the time for refreshing sleep. Just as he commits his first murder, Macbeth thinks he hears a horrible voice crying, "Macbeth does murder sleep"; thereafter, he becomes an insomniac and his wife a sleepwalker. Darkness, voices, ghosts, hallucinations—these are used to express Macbeth's and his wife's surrender to evil and their subsequent despair.

Evil in *Macbeth* takes the form of violence and bloodshed. Right after the opening scene with the witches, a man covered with gashes appears before King Duncan, who asks, "What bloody man is that?" Between this scene and the final one, in which Macbeth's bleeding and "cursèd" head is displayed on a pike, human blood hardly stops running. Images of blood appeal not only to our sense of sight but also to our sense of touch (Macbeth's bloody and secret murders are "sticking on his hands" in the last act), and even to our sense of smell ("Here's the smell of the blood still," Lady Macbeth moans in Act V as she holds out her "little hand"). Such imagery is designed to make us feel moral revulsion, not just physical disgust: Bloodshed leads only to more bloodshed.

The Poetry: Expressing the Dark Night

All this imagery reminds us that *Macbeth* is a poem as well as a play—a dramatic poem sharing many of the characteristics of lyric poetry. The most obvious of these is **meter,** here the unrhymed iambic pentameter or **blank verse** that Shakespeare's predecessor Christopher Marlowe established as the appropriate medium for tragedy. Poetry is to tragedy as singing is to opera: It elevates and enhances the emotional impact of the experience being communicated. Indeed, without the poetry there could be no tragedy, because without it Shakespeare could not have expressed the dark night into which Macbeth's soul sinks. And a tragic poet is much more concerned with states of mind and feeling than with physical action. Macbeth shares with Shakespeare's other great tragic heroes—Hamlet, Lear, Othello—the ability to express in eloquent, moving language whatever he is feeling. One of the most famous speeches of this kind occurs when, near the end of his bloody career, Macbeth sums up what life means to him:

> Out, out, brief candle!
> Life's but a walking shadow, a poor player
> That struts and frets his hour upon the stage
> And then is heard no more. It is a tale
> Told by an idiot, full of sound and fury,
> Signifying nothing.
>
> —Act V, Scene 5, lines 23–28

The bitter nihilism of these metaphors suggests that Macbeth is already dead in spirit, although his body must undergo a last battle. By murdering Duncan, he has murdered more than sleep: He has destroyed himself.

INFORMATIONAL TEXT

Nothing is impervious to ***parody,*** *not even the high seriousness of a play like Shakespeare's Macbeth. In the following piece from* Twisted Tales from Shakespeare, *Richard Armour presents another view of the three weird sisters. You and your classmates might want to write a parody of your own.*

Macbeth and the Witches

Richard Armour

Three witches, extremely weird sisters, are having a picnic amidst thunder and lightning somewhere in Scotland. Judging from their appearance, they were placed one-two-three in the Edinburgh Ugly Contest.

"When shall we three meet again in thunder, lightning, or in rain?" asks one of them. They hate nice weather and are happiest when they are soaking wet and their hair is all stringy.

"When the hurly-burly's[1] done, when the battle's lost and won," another replies. A battle is going on between the forces of Duncan, the King of Scotland, and some Norwegians, assisted by the rebel Thane of Cawdor. At the moment it's looking good for Duncan, because two of his generals, Macbeth and Banquo, have cunningly put bagpipes into the hands of the enemy, who are blowing their brains out.

The witches hear some dear friend[2] calling and depart. "Fair is foul, and foul is fair," they comment philosophically as they leave. This must have been pretty upsetting to any moralists, semanticists, or baseball umpires who chanced to overhear them.

Shortly afterward, the battle having been won by Macbeth and the weather having turned bad enough to be pleasant, the witches meet again.

"Where hast thou been, Sister?" asks one.

"Killing swine," the second replies. All three of them have been busy doing similar diverting things, and one of them happily shows the others the thumb of a drowned sailor which she is adding to her thumb collection.[3]

Macbeth and Banquo come by at this point, on their way to inform the King that they have defeated the rebels. They would rather tell him in person than render a report in triplicate.

"Speak, if you can," says Macbeth boldly to the hags. "What are you?" He rather thinks they are witches but would like to hear it from their own skinny lips.

The witches start hailing.[4] They hail Macbeth as Thane of Glamis and Thane of Cawdor and say he will be King Hereafter. Not to leave Banquo out, they hail him as "lesser than Macbeth, and greater." (The witches are masters of gobbledyspook.) He won't be a king, they say, but he'll beget kings, and now they have to begetting along.

Macbeth knows he is Thane of Glamis, but has no idea (or didn't have until now) of becoming Thane of Cawdor or King Hereafter.

1. See also hurdy-gurdy, hunky-dory, and okey-dokey.
2. A cat and a toad. Witches have to make friendships where they can.
3. In a comedy, this would be considered tragic relief.
4. Until now it has been raining.

The three witches and Lady Macbeth (in front) from the Faux-Real production of *Htebcam* (1994).

"Stay, you imperfect speakers, tell me more," he commands. But the witches, perhaps not liking the way he refers to their elocution, vanish into thin air, making it slightly thicker.

While Macbeth is meditating about what the witches have forecast for him, a couple of the King's henchmen, straight from a busy day of henching, ride up. They bring word that Duncan is liquidating the Thane of Cawdor and giving his title to Macbeth, it being an inexpensive gift. (Duncan, as King of Scotland, was Scotcher than anybody.)

"Look how our partner's rapt," remarks Banquo, noticing that Macbeth, stunned with all the good news, acts as if he has been struck on the noggin. But Macbeth is only lost in thought and will find his way out presently. Thus far the witches have been batting 1,000, and Macbeth is beginning to take more than a casual interest in Duncan's health.[5]

5. Henceforth, when he says "How are you?" to the King, it will be a bona fide question.

[These are Richard Armour's footnotes.]

Response and Analysis

Act V

Reading Check

1. Why, according to the doctor, is Lady Macbeth walking in her sleep?
2. In Scene 2, what opinion of Macbeth do the Scottish lords now hold?
3. When does Lady Macbeth die?
4. What is Macbeth's plan for dealing with the attacking troops? Why has he been forced to choose this plan?
5. What changes in personality does Macbeth describe in Scene 5, lines 9–15?
6. In the speech in Scene 5 that begins "Tomorrow, and tomorrow, and tomorrow . . ." (lines 19–28), how does Macbeth describe life? What **metaphors** does he use?
7. How are the prophecies proclaimed by the three apparitions in Act IV, Scene 1, fulfilled in Act V?
8. At the end of the play, what has become of Macbeth? Who becomes King?

Thinking Critically

9. Theatrically, the spectacle of Lady Macbeth walking in her sleep is one of the most striking scenes in the play. It is entirely Shakespeare's invention, not found or suggested in his source. Why do you suppose Shakespeare has her walk in her sleep? How is this scene related to the remarks that Macbeth makes about sleep in Act II, Scene 2, just after he kills Duncan?
10. In the sleepwalking scene, Lady Macbeth refers to many of her waking experiences. For example, the words "One: two" may refer to the moment in Act II, Scene 1, when she struck the bell signaling Macbeth to go kill Duncan. Find traces of other experiences in what she says while sleepwalking.
11. At the end of Act IV, Malcolm says, "The night is long that never finds the day" (line 240). In what metaphorical sense does he use the terms *night* and *day*? How does his remark **foreshadow** the outcome of the play?
12. The last act of *Macbeth* contains the play's **climax**—the most emotional and suspenseful part of the action—the moment when the characters' **conflict** is finally resolved. Which part of Act V do you consider the climax? Explain.
13. Shakespeare gave most of his **tragic heroes** an impressive dying speech in which they say something significant about their own life and death. Although he did not write such a speech for Macbeth, which speech of Macbeth's do you think serves in the play as his dying speech? Explain why you select this speech rather than some other one.
14. In his closing speech at the end of the play, Malcolm refers to Macbeth and Lady Macbeth as "this dead butcher and his fiendlike queen" (line 69). Do you think these are accurate descriptions of Macbeth and his wife? Explain your answer, citing evidence from the play.

Extending and Evaluating

15. In Act V, Scene 5, Macbeth expresses the idea that life "is a tale / Told by an idiot, full of sound and fury, / Signifying nothing." What are your reactions to this idea? Do you agree or disagree? Explain your response.

Literary Skills
Analyze the characteristics of tragedy, including tragic hero, climax, and resolution. Analyze imagery and figurative language.

The Play as a Whole

Thinking Critically

16. "Nothing in his life / Became him like the leaving it," says Malcolm in Act I, referring to the traitorous Thane of Cawdor. Malcolm also says that the Thane of Cawdor threw away the dearest thing he owned. How might these two statements

also apply to Macbeth? Could these lines apply to any people in actual life?

17. One of the **themes** of *Macbeth* centers on evil, which Shakespeare saw as a force beyond human understanding. Do you think Shakespeare also saw evil as stronger than the forces of good? Support your answer with events from the play.
18. The philosopher Aristotle argued that a bad man cannot be the principal character of a **tragedy.** Does Shakespeare keep you from losing all sympathy for Macbeth in spite of Macbeth's increasing viciousness? Was there a point at which you lost sympathy for Macbeth? If so, where?
19. One critic has observed that a part of Macbeth's tragedy is the fact that many of his strengths are also his weaknesses. Explain this apparent contradiction. What are Macbeth's strengths? Which ones also work against him?
20. **Internal conflicts** rage within Macbeth, as well as **external conflicts** with other characters. Explain some of the play's main conflicts, and trace their **resolution.**

Extending and Evaluating

21. Do you think people should **parody** a great tragic play like *Macbeth,* the way Richard Armour does in "Macbeth and the Witches" (see the ***Connection*** on page 524)? Why or why not?
22. What modern figure, real or fictional, had a downfall, like Macbeth's, that came after an attempt to gain great power? How is this modern figure like Macbeth, and how different? Would this modern figure make a good **tragic hero**? Refer to your Quickwrite notes (see page 438) as you answer this question.

Literary Focus

Imagery and Figurative Language

Macbeth's poetry is rich in **imagery** and **figurative language** that help to create atmosphere and reveal character and theme.

1. Powerful **images** in the play contrast the natural and the unnatural, as in Lady Macbeth's speech in Act I, Scene 7, lines 54–59:

   . . . I have given suck, and know
   How tender 'tis to love the babe that
   milks me:
   I would, while it was smiling in my face,
   Have plucked my nipple from his bone-
   less gums,
   And dashed the brains out, had I so
   sworn as you
   Have done to this.

   a. What unnatural sounds and events are reported in Act II, Scenes 2–4? Look at the **context** of these images. What **mood** do they create?

   b. Look at the witches' scenes. What would you say is the emotional effect of each scene? Besides the witches themselves, what unnatural images occur in these scenes?

2. We hear about sleep and sleeplessness throughout the play. How is sleep described in these **figures of speech**?

   a. **First Witch.** . . . I'll drain him dry
   as hay:
   Sleep shall neither night nor day
   Hang upon his penthouse lid; . . .
   —Act I, Scene 3, lines 18–20

   b. **Macbeth.** Methought I heard a
   voice cry "Sleep no more!
   Macbeth does murder sleep"—the
   innocent sleep,
   Sleep that knits up the raveled
   sleave of care,
   The death of each day's life, sore
   labor's bath,
   Balm of hurt minds, great nature's
   second course,
   Chief nourisher in life's feast—
   —Act II, Scene 2, lines 34–39

WRITING

Choose from among the following assignments to respond to the play.

1. **Is She a Monster?**

   Lady Macbeth is sometimes regarded as a monster, ruthlessly ambitious and fiendishly cruel. What clues can you find in the play suggesting that Shakespeare did not want us to judge her so severely? In a brief essay, write a **character analysis** of Lady Macbeth. Study her character as it is revealed through her words and actions and her relationship with Macbeth. Then, form a **thesis statement,** a clear statement of your main idea or argument. In your essay, be sure to include details from the play to elaborate on and support your points.

2. **Critiquing a Tragedy**

   Traditionally, critics have thought of the following as the classic elements of a Shakespearean tragedy: (a) a **protagonist,** the **tragic hero,** a man of high estate whose desires or conflicts set the action in motion; (b) an **antagonist** who blocks this protagonist; (c) a **rising action** in which **complications** develop, leading in the third act to a **turning point;** (d) a **falling action** that inexorably leads to a tragic climax; (e) a **resolution,** in which the social order that had been torn asunder by the action is restored. Write a **critical review** of *Macbeth* in which you discuss ways in which the play does or does not follow this traditional tragic pattern.

3. **The Playwright's Purpose**

   When Macbeth discovers how Macduff entered the world (Act V, Scene 8), he also discovers that the witches are "juggling fiends" who have given him a false sense of security. Why do you think Shakespeare shows Macbeth taken in by their prophecies? What might Shakespeare be implying about Macbeth's **character**? about the witches' powers? Is he suggesting that Macbeth might be a victim of mysterious evil forces? Write a brief **essay** in which you explore Shakespeare's purpose in "conjuring up" the witches in the play to influence Macbeth's actions with their prophecies.

4. **Rethinking the Final Act**

   Imagine a single event or series of events that could have taken place at any point in the play and averted Macbeth's or Lady Macbeth's tragic end in the last act. Write a narrative description of your proposed plot changes and alternative ending to *Macbeth.* Be sure to describe how your new twists to the plot affect the outcome of the play.

5. **Taking on a Critic**

   In his introduction to the play, critic Harold Bloom writes of Macbeth, "His imagination is so strong . . . that we can see that it *is* imagination, rather than ambition or the witches, that victimizes and destroys Macbeth." Could the apparitions that haunt Macbeth throughout the play be figments of his own imagination? Do you find Bloom's point of view convincing, or would you argue that a combination of factors brings about Macbeth's downfall? Write a **persuasive essay** in which you respond to Bloom's assertion. Defend your point of view using evidence from the play.

LISTENING AND SPEAKING

6. **Performing a Soliloquy**

   With a small group, select one of Macbeth's soliloquies and "perform" it in the way a choir interprets a song: Vary voice pitches, volume, tempo, rhythm, meter, and tone. Repeat key lines as a refrain, and use echoing words, vocal sound effects, harmony, and chanting to accentuate and enhance the words. (For an explanation of soliloquies and a list of examples in *Macbeth,* see the Critical Comment on page 521.)

Writing Skills
Write a character analysis. Write a critical review analyzing the tragic pattern of a play. Write an essay analyzing the writer's purpose. Write a new outcome for a play. Write a persuasive essay.

Listening and Speaking Skills
Give an oral performance of a soliloquy.

Reflecting *on the* Literary Period

The Renaissance: 1485–1660

The selections in this feature were written during the same literary period as the other selections in Collection 3, and they share many of the same ideas and concerns. The Focus Question will guide your reading and help you reflect on important aspects of the period.

The Four Sons of Aymond (detail) (1472) by David Aubert. Bibliotheque Nationale.

akg-images/Visioars.

Think About . . .

A century or more separates the sonnets of Sir Thomas Wyatt from the lyric poetry of Sir John Suckling and Richard Lovelace. During this period, English poetry evolved in several directions, and lyric poems underwent dramatic changes in tone and style.

Renaissance poets were expected to adhere to formal patterns and specific subjects. The challenge during this time was to create something fresh and original within these strict conventions, or guidelines. The conventions of the English sonnet, which were based on the sonnets of the Italian poet Petrarch (page 312), were introduced into English literature by Sir Thomas Wyatt. Wyatt's sonnets ushered in a style that inspired a number of great sonnets by such writers as Edmund Spenser and William Shakespeare (page 308). These lyrics are notable for the expression of the speaker's personal feelings; their central theme was the speaker's love for a beautiful but unattainable woman.

Toward the end of the Renaissance in England, another kind of love poetry emerged. Cavalier poets Sir John Suckling and Richard Lovelace wrote light, witty poems that emphasize clarity and precision of form.

Pages 529–540 cover **Literary Skills** Evaluate the philosophical, political, religious, ethical, and social influences of a historical period.

Focus Question

As you read each selection, keep in mind this Focus Question and take notes to help you answer it at the end of the feature:

What themes and characteristics of Renaissance love poems give them a timeless quality and universal appeal?

Whoso List to Hunt

Meet the Writer **Sir Thomas Wyatt** (1503–1542) was a courtier and diplomat who served Henry VIII and spent much of his life traveling abroad as an ambassador for the king.

Wyatt is remembered today as a literary innovator who helped change the nature of English poetry. Up to Wyatt's time, poetry was still essentially medieval in subject matter, style, and form. Wyatt greatly admired Italian poetry, and he frequently translated and adapted the sonnets of Petrarch, the great fourteenth-century Italian poet. Because he brought this new kind of poem, the love sonnet, to England from Italy, Wyatt is credited with introducing the fourteen-line sonnet into English poetry.

As a courtier, Wyatt had no ambition to have his work published and publicly distributed. He was expected to compose songs and verses, just as he was expected to do battle for his king, joust in tournaments, dance, and carry on intrigues with the ladies. Wyatt circulated his poems privately among his friends, in handwritten copies. After his death, many of his poems appeared in an anthology now known as *Tottel's Miscellany,* published by an enterprising printer named Richard Tottel. Because Wyatt's meter was considered to be rough, Tottel "improved" the poems by changing many words so that the poems sounded smoother to his ears. Modern editors have restored the original texts, using manuscript copies of the poems and Wyatt's own corrections.

Background According to traditional gossip, this poem is about Wyatt's longing for Anne Boleyn, a beautiful young woman at court. When he realized that King Henry also fancied Anne, Wyatt gave up the pursuit to whoever else wanted to "hunt" her. Regardless of the story's truth, Anne did become the second of Henry's six wives.

The sonnet "Whoso List to Hunt" is an adaptation of one of Petrarch's poems. Wyatt also took from Petrarch's commentators the story about Julius Caesar's tame deer (line 13), whose collars were inscribed *Noli me tangere* (Latin for "touch me not"), warning hunters not to molest Caesar's property.

CONNECTING TO THE
Focus Question

A common metaphor for love is a contest between hunter and prey: *the thrill of the chase; a good catch; Cupid's arrow.* As you read, consider the idea of love as a hunt. Why do you think so many metaphors for love suggest pursuit, wounds, and conquests?

Anne Boleyn (late 16th century) by an unknown artist. Oil on panel (21 3/8″ x 16 3/8″).

By Courtesy of the National Portrait Gallery, London.

Whoso List to Hunt

Sir Thomas Wyatt

Whoso list° to hunt, I know where is an hind,°
But as for me, alas, I may no more.
The vain travail° hath wearied me so sore
I am of them that farthest cometh behind.
Yet may I, by no means, my wearied mind
Draw from the deer, but as she fleeth afore,
Fainting I follow. I leave off therefore,
Since in a net I seek to hold the wind.

Who list her hunt, I put him out of doubt,°
As well as I, may spend his time in vain.
And graven with diamonds in letters plain
There is written, her fair neck round about,
"*Noli me tangere,* for Caesar's I am,
And wild for to hold, though I seem tame."

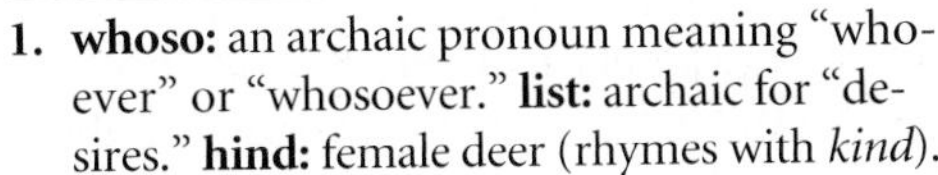

1. **whoso:** an archaic pronoun meaning "who-ever" or "whosoever." **list:** archaic for "de-sires." **hind:** female deer (rhymes with *kind*).
3. **travail:** hard work.
9. **put him out of doubt:** assure him (that he).

Ms 18 fol. 84v Charles the Bold, Duke of Burgundy receiving the envoys from France and Guyenne (16th century) (vellum).

Musee Dobree, Nantes, France.

Response and Analysis

Thinking Critically

1. How does this poem describe a love triangle? Using the Background note on page 530, identify the **speaker,** the hind, and Caesar.
2. What warning does the speaker give to those who desire to hunt the hind? What **image** shows that the speaker has given up the chase as hopeless?
3. The last line of the sonnet refers to the hind as "wild for to hold." Do you think the speaker is referring to the woman or to Caesar's claim on her? Explain.
4. Using details from the selection, respond to **Connecting to the Focus Question** on page 530.

Extending and Evaluating

5. What do you think about Wyatt's description of love as a hunt or a conquest? Do you agree or disagree with this idea? Is it still common today? Explain your answer.

Sonnets 30 and 75

Meet the Writer Because his influence on later poets was considerable, **Edmund Spenser** (1552–1599) is often referred to as "the poet's poet." He attended Cambridge University as a "sizar," or poor scholar. After graduating from the university, he served as personal secretary to the queen's favorite, the earl of Leicester. In Leicester's household he came to know Sir Philip Sidney, and during the later 1570s they often met to discuss literature and to read each other's poetry.

In 1579, Spenser published a series of pastoral poems, *The Shepheardes Calender,* which he dedicated to Sidney. This work was a major literary event. Although Spenser used deliberately archaic language, his skillful musical effects and metrical inventions marked a turning point for Elizabethan poetry.

In 1580, Spenser went to Ireland as secretary to the lord deputy of Ireland. Except for two or three visits to England, he was to spend the rest of his life in that war-torn country. English troops had invaded and conquered Ireland, but the Irish resisted. They particularly resented people like Spenser, who was given an Irish castle and a vast estate in County Cork.

Spenser was working on an ambitious epic called *The Faerie Queene* when Sir Walter Raleigh encouraged him to go to London and publish the completed portions of the poem. After the first three books were published in 1590, Spenser was recognized as a major English poet.

In 1591, Spenser returned to Ireland, where conditions remained unsettled and dangerous. He managed to continue work on *The Faerie Queene* and other poems. In 1596, three additional books of *The Faerie Queene* appeared. Spenser had dedicated the poem to the queen, but he never received the secure position that he longed for at Elizabeth's court.

As the century drew to a close, the Irish intensified their efforts to expel the English from their land. During one of these raids, Spenser's castle was burned and his infant son killed. Spenser escaped to London, where he died suddenly in 1599. He was buried near Chaucer in the part of Westminster Abbey that has become known as the Poets' Corner. Today, Spenser is generally acknowledged to be one of England's greatest nondramatic poets.

Background *Amoretti* ("little Cupids" or "little love poems") is a sequence of eighty-nine sonnets recording a man's two-year courtship of a woman named Elizabeth (Spenser's second wife). In Sonnet 30, Spenser uses, in an original way, the convention of the burning man and the icy lady. Sonnet 75 uses another convention, the writer's "eternizing conceit": Submit to my love, and I'll immortalize you through my writing. Again, Spenser gives this long-established notion a new twist. For his sonnet sequence, Spenser invented a form known as the **Spenserian sonnet,** which is based on an intricate pattern of interlocking rhymes.

CONNECTING TO THE
Focus Question

As you read, consider this question: How do the speakers in Spenser's sonnets use the resources of language to convey their experiences?

from Amoretti

Sonnet 30

Edmund Spenser

My love is like to ice, and I to fire;
How comes it then that this her cold so great
Is not dissolved through my so hot desire,
But harder grows the more I her entreat?
Or how comes it that my exceeding heat
Is not delayed° by her heart frozen cold,
But that I burn much more in boiling sweat,
And feel my flames augmented manifold?°
What more miraculous thing may be told
That fire which all thing melts, should harden ice,
And ice which is congealed° with senseless cold,
Should kindle fire by wonderful device?°
Such is the power of love in gentle mind,
That it can alter all the course of kind.°

6. delayed: tempered.

8. augmented manifold: increased in many ways.

11. congealed: thickened.

12. device: trick.

14. kind: nature.

Unknown Man with Flame Background (16th century) by Nicholas Hilliard.
Ham House, Surrey, England.

Sonnet 75

Edmund Spenser

One day I wrote her name upon the strand,°
But came the waves and washèd it away;
Again I wrote it with a second hand,
But came the tide, and made my pains his prey.
"Vain man," said she, "that doest in vain assay,°
A mortal thing so to immortalize,
For I myself shall like to this decay,
And eke° my name be wipèd out likewise."
"Not so," quod° I, "let baser things devise°
To die in dust, but you shall live by fame:
My verse your virtues rare shall eternize,
And in the heavens write your glorious name.
Where whenas death shall all the world subdue,
Our love shall live, and later life renew."

---

1. **strand:** beach.
5. **assay:** try.
8. **eke:** archaic for "also."
9. **quod:** quoth; said. **devise:** plan.

Portrait of an Unknown Lady (16th century) by Nicholas Hilliard.
Victoria and Albert Museum, London.

Response and Analysis

Sonnets 30 and 75

Thinking Critically

1. A **paradox** is an apparent contradiction that is somehow true. What paradoxes can you find in Sonnet 30? Explain them.
2. In Sonnet 30, the **speaker** says something serious about love. What is it?
3. In what sense has the love of the two people in Sonnet 75 survived today?
4. In Sonnet 75, what **image** does Spenser use to represent love's impermanence?
5. Using details from the selections, respond to **Connecting to the Focus Question** on page 532.

Extending and Evaluating

6. Some attitudes toward love and toward men and women have changed since these sonnets were written. Do you find the speaker's feelings dated or still relevant? Cite details from the poems to explain your response.

Why So Pale and Wan, Fond Lover?

To Lucasta, on Going to the Wars

To Althea, from Prison

Meet the Writers **Sir John Suckling** (1609–1642) and **Richard Lovelace** (1618–1657) were Royalists; that is, they supported King Charles in the English Civil Wars of the 1640s. Because of their politics, they are known as Cavalier poets. *Cavalier* was the name for a supporter of the king, and Roundheads were supporters of the Parliamentary forces.

Suckling and Lovelace had more than politics in common, however; they also shared a mutual literary goal—to write poems that sound like elegant conversation.

Sir John Suckling was born rich, but he lost his fortune through gambling and extravagant living. When war broke out, he raised a company of one hundred men, outfitted in scarlet coats and white doublets, to fight for the king. He plotted to deliver one of the king's chief advisors from imprisonment in the Tower of London. However, the plot was discovered, and Suckling was forced to flee to France. There, at the age of thirty-three, he died. Historians are not sure whether he took his own life or was murdered.

Like his fellow Cavalier poets, **Richard Lovelace** (pronounced "love-less") came from a wealthy family. His good looks and elegant manners created a stir when he was at Oxford University. After Oxford, Lovelace became a favorite courtier to King Charles and Queen Henrietta Maria. Lovelace became an ardent Royalist and, when the Civil Wars broke out, he fought bravely for King Charles but was imprisoned twice by the opposing Parliamentary forces. Like Suckling, he lost all his wealth and land, and he died in poverty at age thirty-nine.

Background The poems of Suckling and Lovelace epitomize what we think of as the Cavalier manner: witty, charming, and graceful. Lovelace is on the whole more serious than "natural, easy Suckling."

At its best, the poetry of both Suckling and Lovelace is tinged with a slight element of desperation or melancholy, which suggests that behind a facade of gallantry and elegance, their careless, aristocratic lives were crumbling away.

CONNECTING TO THE Focus Question

Like their Elizabethan counterparts, the lyrics of the seventeenth century are rich in love poetry that introduces new modes of expression and a new tone. As you read these poems, consider this question: What attitudes do the speakers of these poems have toward women, love, and honor?

In Renaissance literature, young men suffer horribly from unrequited love. Part of this literary convention is that the women whom the men admire show no pity. In fact, they ignore pleas for attention so firmly that the men become "pale and wan"—that is, sickly looking—like the young fellow whom the speaker of this poem is so irritated with.

Why So Pale and Wan, Fond Lover?

Sir John Suckling

Why so pale and wan, fond lover?
   Prithee, why so pale?
Will, when looking well can't move her,
   Looking ill prevail?
   Prithee, why so pale?

Why so dull and mute, young sinner?
   Prithee, why so mute?
Will, when speaking well can't win her,
   Saying nothing do't?
   Prithee, why so mute?

Quit, quit, for shame; this will not move,
   This cannot take her.
If of herself she will not love,
   Nothing can make her:
   The devil take her!

Henry Percy, 9th Earl of Northumberland (1595) by Nicholas Hilliard.

The English Civil Wars are the backdrop for this poem. The poem takes the form of a lover's farewell to his beloved. It is tempting to identify Lovelace himself with the speaker, for the poet was an idealist about king and country, ready to sacrifice his happiness, fortune, and life in their service.

To Lucasta, on Going to the Wars

Richard Lovelace

Tell me not, sweet, I am unkind,
   That from the nunnery°
Of thy chaste breast and quiet mind
   To war and arms I fly.

True, a new mistress now I chase,
   The first foe in the field;
And with a stronger faith embrace
   A sword, a horse, a shield.

Yet this inconstancy is such
   As you too shall adore;
I could not love thee, dear, so much,
   Loved I not honor more.

2. **nunnery:** literally, a convent for nuns; here, a metaphor for a pure, safe place.

George Clifford, 3rd Earl of Cumberland (16th century) by Nicholas Hilliard.

National Maritime Museum, London.

Like "To Lucasta, on Going to the Wars," this poem follows the fashion of giving women in poems classical names. We do not know whether real women are behind the names Lucasta *and* Althea. *Lovelace was imprisoned during the Civil Wars, and it seems likely that he would have been visited by a female admirer.*

To Althea, from Prison

Richard Lovelace

When Love with unconfinèd wings
   Hovers within my gates,
And my divine Althea brings
   To whisper at the grates;
When I lie tangled in her hair
   And fettered to her eye,
The gods° that wanton° in the air
   Know no such liberty.

When flowing cups run swiftly round,
   With no allaying Thames,°
Our careless heads with roses bound,
   Our hearts with loyal flames;
When thirsty grief in wine we steep,
   When healths and drafts go free,
Fishes that tipple in the deep
   Know no such liberty.

---

7. **gods:** In many seventeenth-century versions of this poem, "gods" is replaced by "birds." **wanton:** frolic.
10. **allaying Thames** (temz): That is, the wine is not diluted with water from the Thames River.

A Man Holding a Hand from a Cloud (miniature) (16th century) by Nicholas Hilliard.
Victoria and Albert Museum, London

When, like committed linnets,° I
With shriller throat shall sing
The sweetness, mercy, majesty,
And glories of my King;°
When I shall voice aloud how good
He is, how great should be,
Enlargèd° winds that curl the flood°
Know no such liberty.

Stone walls do not a prison make,
Nor iron bars a cage:
Minds innocent and quiet take
That for an hermitage.°
If I have freedom in my love,
And in my soul am free,
Angels alone, that soar above,
Enjoy such liberty.

17. committed linnets: caged birds.

20. my King: Charles I, king of England from 1625 to 1649.

23. enlargèd: released. **flood:** sea.

28. hermitage: holy refuge.

Response and Analysis

Why So Pale and Wan, Fond Lover? To Lucasta, on Going to the Wars To Althea, from Prison

Thinking Critically

1. In "Why So Pale and Wan, Fond Lover?" what advice does the speaker give the pale lover? What is his **tone,** and how does it differ from Lovelace's tone in "To Lucasta" and "To Althea"?
2. In "To Lucasta," what **metaphors** of love are used to describe war? What do you think of these romantic ways of talking about war?
3. The speaker in "To Lucasta" implies two **paradoxes:** that his inconstancy (line 9) is really constancy; and that to be loyal, he must be disloyal. According to the speaker, how can these seemingly contradictory statements be true?
4. In "To Althea," what comparison is made in each stanza's final two-line **refrain**? What is different about the last comparison?
5. Lines 25–26 in "To Althea" are famous. What **paradox** is contained in these lines? What makes the jailed speaker free?
6. Imagine Suckling and Lovelace discussing their conceptions of love. On what would they agree and disagree? Cite details from the poems to support your response.
7. What does "To Althea" imply about the meaning of the word *prison*? Do you agree or disagree?
8. Using details from the selections, respond to **Connecting to the Focus Question** on page 535.

Extending and Evaluating

9. Here we have three poems that are either addressed to women or about a woman's treatment of a man—but the women's feelings remain unknown. What do you imagine a modern woman's response would be to each speaker?

REVIEW

Reflecting on the Literary Period

The Renaissance: 1485–1660

The following questions ask you to compare and analyze the selections in this feature and respond to the Focus Question. Where possible, cite passages from the selections to support your answers.

Sir Thomas Wyatt .... **Whoso List to Hunt**

Edmund Spenser .... *from* **Amoretti**
Sonnet 30
Sonnet 75

Sir John Suckling .... **Why So Pale and Wan, Fond Lover?**

Richard Lovelace .... **To Lucasta, on Going to the Wars**

.... **To Althea, from Prison**

Comparing Literature

1. The fourteen-line sonnet has a strict pattern of **rhythm** and **rhyme.** The main idea or argument is developed logically through the poem's structure. Often there is a **turn,** where a shift in focus or thought occurs. (See "The Sonnet in the Renaissance" on page 312.) Examine the structure of the sonnets by Wyatt and Spenser. How does Wyatt use the **octave** and the **sestet** to present his theme and comment? How does Spenser use the final **couplet** in his sonnets?
2. Compare Shakespeare's Sonnet 18 (page 313) with Spenser's Sonnet 75. How do the poets treat the theme of love's immortality?
3. Re-read the last stanza of "Why So Pale and Wan, Fond Lover?" and the final two lines of "To Lucasta." Contrast the philosophies of the two poems as expressed in these lines. How do they differ?
4. What **images,** ideas, and attitudes expressed by these Renaissance poems are still used in contemporary poems about love?

Pages 529–540 cover **Literary Skills** Evaluate the philosophical, political, religious, ethical, and social influences of a historical period.

RESPONDING TO THE
Focus Question

Review your notes and responses related to the Focus Question for this feature. Using details from the selections, write your answer to the question.

What themes and characteristics of Renaissance love poems give them a timeless quality and universal appeal?

READ ON: FOR INDEPENDENT READING

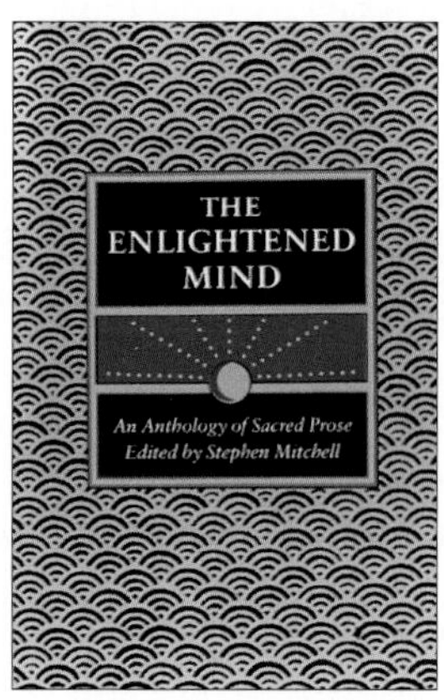

NONFICTION

Wisdom Through the Ages

If you're looking for an eye-opener, ***The Enlightened Mind: An Anthology of Sacred Prose***, edited by Stephen Mitchell, might be just the book for you. This inspiring compilation highlights sacred writings from many cultures and traditions. It includes essays, sermons, and aphorisms from such diverse writers and thinkers as Plato, the Zen masters, and the Renaissance poet George Herbert.

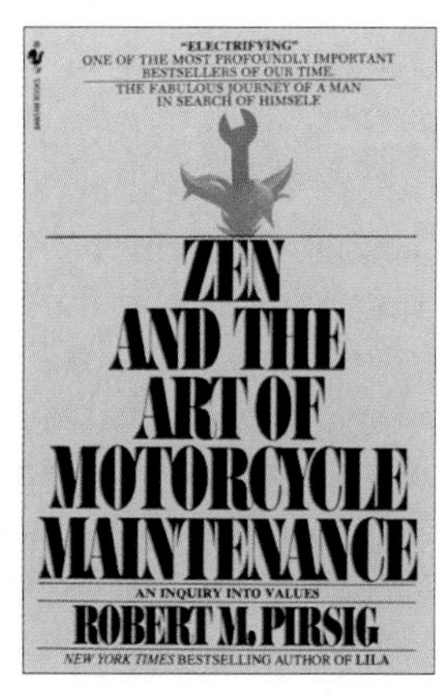

NONFICTION

Motorcycle Meditations

Part travelogue, part meditation, part rambling discourse, Robert Pirsig's ***Zen and the Art of Motorcycle Maintenance*** is above all an inquiry into human values. While taking an extended motorcycle trip, Pirsig pursues the same questions that intrigued Francis Bacon and John Milton: What is the nature of the universe, and what is our place in it? How should we conduct our lives?

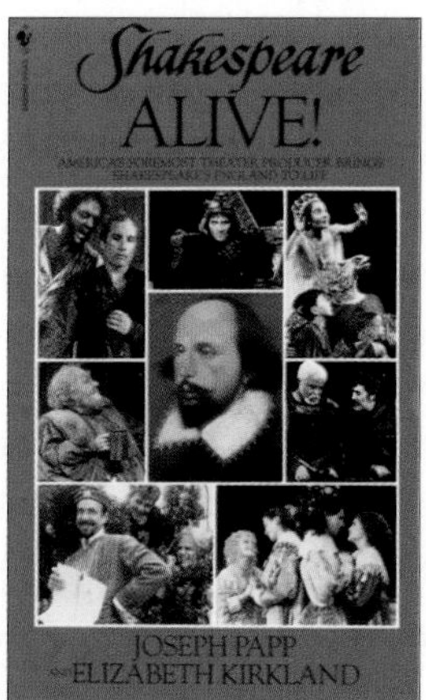

NONFICTION

The Bard's Background and Playground

People flocked in droves to Renaissance London, where the theater was a major attraction. Shakespeare was an integral part of this world, but there's been a tendency to divorce the man from his background. ***Shakespeare Alive!*** by Joseph Papp and Elizabeth Kirkland helps bring the legend back to life, placing Shakespeare in the theatrical and social context where he thrived.

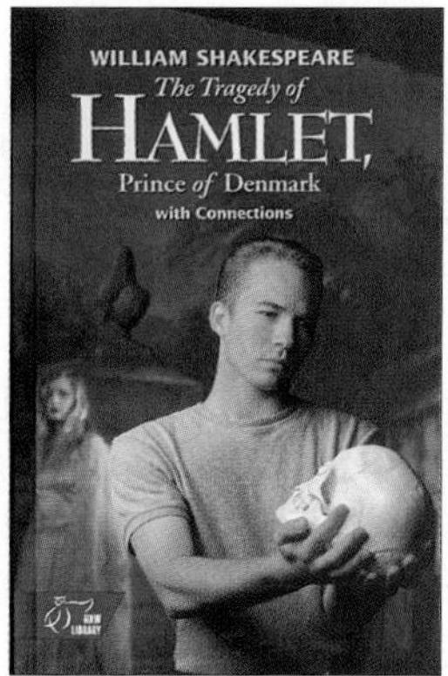

PLAY

Justice Gone Awry

What are the consequences of seeking justice at any cost? In William Shakespeare's play ***Hamlet,*** the young, brooding prince of Denmark is tormented by the need to avenge his father's death. Hamlet's decision to seek justice sets in motion a catastrophic chain of events that shatters the royal court. *Hamlet* is often considered Shakespeare's greatest tragedy, acclaimed for its intense psychological depth, riveting action, and wonderful poetry.

This title is available in the HRW Library.

Analyzing Literature

Writing Assignment
Write an essay in which you analyze the literary elements of a poem.

When you read the literary selections in this collection, your initial responses, whether positive or negative, enthusiastic or indifferent, were personal and subjective. You're not required to defend your first thoughts and feelings about a work. However, when you dig deeper and begin to analyze a work of literature, you must become more critical and objective because you must be able to support your conclusions. When you write a **literary analysis,** you examine a selection's parts, or literary elements, and how they work together to produce an overall effect. In this workshop you will focus your critical attention on the elements of a poem.

Prewriting

Choose and Analyze a Poem

A Work of Substance To begin your analysis, choose a poem of moderate length, approximately ten to twenty lines. Because your literary analysis should be at least 1,500 words long, the poem should be rich in meaning and complex enough to require careful analysis. To find a suitable poem, re-read poems you have enjoyed in the past. Also, page through this book, or ask your teacher, a librarian, family members, or friends to recommend poems that they've found especially memorable or moving.

I Spy with a Critical Eye . . . After you've chosen a poem, read it carefully, examining the poem critically to discover its unique aspects—what distinguishes it from other poems. Read it as many times as it takes to feel comfortable in your understanding of the ideas it expresses. The following chart explains the basic **literary elements** you'll find in poetry and provides analysis questions for each.

LITERARY ELEMENTS

Element	Analysis Questions
Speaker is the imaginary voice, or persona, assumed by a writer.	Who is the speaker? Is his or her voice immediately identifiable? Is the speaker speaking about himself or herself or about others? Is the speaker speaking to someone? Is the speaker describing a scene or emotion or is the speaker narrating a story?

(continued)

(continued)

Stylistic devices are the techniques a writer uses to control **language** to create effects.	How does **diction** (word choice) affect the poem's tone? What effects does the poet create through **rhythm, rhyme, alliteration,** and **onomatopoeia?** Does the poet use **figurative language,** such as similes or metaphors, to suggest feelings or ideas? Does the poet use **imagery** that appeals to readers' senses? How do these images affect the mood of the poem?
Theme is the central idea or insight of a work of literature.	What main idea does the poem express about its subject? Does the poem examine a universal theme, common problem, or life experience? Does it reveal any insight into the human condition?
Tone is the attitude a poet takes toward the reader or subject of the poem.	What's the poet's attitude toward the subject? sarcastic? reverent? What's the speaker's attitude toward the audience? intimate? condescending? What words and details convey the tone? How does the tone affect your response to the poem?

Repeat the process of critical reading until you have a comprehensive understanding of the **significant ideas** in the poem and a firm grip on the elements that help communicate those ideas. Because there are often many elements working at once to create a poem's overall effect, plan to focus your essay on just one or two elements. In poems of ten to twenty lines, one or two elements usually dominate.

Digging Deeper A deep, thoughtful literary analysis identifies the **ambiguities, nuances,** and **complexities** of a work and elaborates on their impact on the poem. The chart below provides definitions of these characteristics as well as student examples based on Shakespeare's "Sonnet 73" (page 318).

Quick guide!

AMBIGUITIES, NUANCES, AND COMPLEXITIES

Definitions	Examples
Ambiguities are lines or words that lend themselves to more than one interpretation.	The word "consumed" in the third quatrain is ambiguous. It can mean that the speaker's youth has been destroyed by a metaphorical fire. It could also mean that he has wastefully spent his youth or that he's engrossed or obsessed with thinking about his youth.
Nuances are changes in the tone or meaning of the poem.	"Sonnet 73" begins with a somber tone in the first three quatrains and ends with a happier, hopeful tone in the final couplet.
Complexities result when a poem is rich in meaning but difficult to interpret.	The first quatrain of "Sonnet 73" uses a complex metaphor, going beyond the traditional association between winter and old age to create the image of an elderly person whose thin arms and legs (boughs, or limbs) shake in the cold.

TIP Use the **literary present** tense whenever you summarize the plot or subject matter of a literary work or refer to an author's relationship to his or her work; for example, " 'Sonnet 73' **begins** with a somber tone" and "Shakespeare **writes** about the universal theme of love and loss."

State Your Thesis and Gather Support

A Statement of Intent Review your notes, and pull together all your information to determine what your essay will say about the poem. To do this, ask yourself the following questions.

- Do one or two literary elements stand out as more interesting or significant than others?
- What overall effect do the elements create?

DO THIS

Using your answers to these questions, draft a **thesis statement,** like the student example below, that identifies the one or two elements you have chosen to analyze and states your main idea about their effects.

> In "Sonnet 73" Shakespeare develops a solemn metaphor for old age, leading up to a final statement of the poem's hope-filled theme: Love grows strong in the face of approaching death.

TIP You may also wish to consult professional or academic analyses of the poem for evidence others have gathered. If you quote or paraphrase any of these analyses in your essay, be sure to document them appropriately. For more on **documenting sources,** see page 247.

The Evidence Will Show Your literary analysis is an interpretation, your unique viewpoint, that you must support through evidence and elaboration. Select three to five **key points**—the ideas about the literary elements you are discussing that are most important to proving your thesis. Support your key points by gathering **literary evidence**—direct quotations and paraphrases of lines or passages. You may need to review the poem repeatedly to find accurate and detailed **references** from the text of the poem that support your key points and thesis. **Elaborate** on the evidence you find by explaining its meaning and tying it to your thesis statement.

The Importance of Being Orderly A strong thesis and compelling evidence won't convince readers that your interpretation is valid if your essay's organization is hard to follow. Your essay's focus will help you determine how you organize your ideas. If your essay focuses on a single literary element, you may want to use **chronological order,** tracing the development of the element from its first appearance in the poem to its last. If it focuses upon two literary elements, you may want to organize them by **order of importance,** from most important to least, or vice versa.

Writing Skills
Write a literary analysis of a poem. Assess, organize, and analyze information. Draft a thesis statement.

PRACTICE & APPLY 1 Analyze a poem by critically examining the poet's use of literary elements. Develop a thesis, gather your support, and organize your analysis.

Writing

Analyzing Literature

A Writer's Framework

Introduction

- Create an engaging opening with an interesting quotation or a bold statement.
- Introduce the poem you're analyzing by title and author.
- State a clear thesis that identifies the literary elements and your main idea about their effects.

Body

- Discuss the key points of your analysis.
- Provide literary evidence from the text of the poem.
- Elaborate on your evidence.
- Organize your essay by order of importance or by chronological order.

Conclusion

- Restate your thesis in a memorable way.
- Leave readers with a closing thought to consider.

A Writer's Model

Metaphor and Theme in Shakespeare's "Sonnet 73"

There's an old saying: "You don't miss the water, 'til the well runs dry." We often do not appreciate what we have until it is gone. However, what happens when we foresee an approaching loss? In "Sonnet 73" Shakespeare considers this question by discussing aging and dying. He develops a solemn metaphor for old age, leading up to a final statement of the poem's hope-filled theme: Love grows strong in the face of approaching death.

INTRODUCTION
Engaging opener
Title and author
Thesis statement

First, in the opening quatrain, the speaker compares himself to a tree in winter, a tree whose "yellow leaves, or none, or few, do hang / Upon those boughs which shake against the cold" (lines 2–3). Beginning this poem on a somber note, this complex metaphor goes beyond the traditional association between winter and old age to create the image of an elderly person whose thin arms and legs (boughs, or limbs) shake in the cold. The metaphor suggests that death is natural.

BODY
First key point
Evidence: quotation
Complexity
Elaboration

Next, in the second quatrain, the speaker compares himself to the twilight of the day, that time of day just before dark, "after sunset fadeth in the west" (6). This metaphor suggests that the speaker is very near the end of his life because "by and by black night" (7) will take away all remaining light. Shakespeare enriches the metaphor by

Second key point
Chronological order
Evidence: quotations

(continued)

(continued)

Elaboration

personifying death and night, "Death's second self" (8). Again, Shakespeare takes advantage of traditional associations between the cycle of the day and the cycle of life to emphasize that death is an inevitable and natural part of life.

Third key point

Evidence: quotation

Elaboration

Evidence: paraphrase

Elaboration

Ambiguity

Elaboration

Then, in the third quatrain, Shakespeare develops a complex metaphor of fire to suggest the progression through life to death. The speaker compares himself to the ember stage of a fire. The fire, the "deathbed whereon [the speaker] must expire" (11), is now a bed of ashes. The ashes represent all the years the speaker has lived up to this point. Ultimately, then, the speaker will be consumed by what once nourished him, the wood—now ash—that will finally suffocate the last glowing embers of life. The association of the life cycle with the natural phenomenon of fire paints death as merely the last step in a natural process. This metaphor has a degree of ambiguity, as well. Shakespeare uses the word *consumed* (12), which has many meanings. Readers should assume the primary definition, which is that the speaker's youth has been destroyed by fire. However, to appreciate the richness of the metaphor, readers should also consider the other definitions: Perhaps the speaker's youth has been spent wastefully or the speaker is engrossed or obsessed with thoughts of his youth. With any of these definitions, the image and tone remain somber.

Fourth key point

Evidence: paraphrase

Evidence: quotation

Elaboration

Nuance

Finally, in the concluding couplet, the speaker shifts from metaphors about aging to his theme. The speaker addresses his friend, saying that the friend clearly sees that the speaker's death is fast approaching, but that the effect of this knowledge is to make "thy love more strong, / To love that well which thou must leave ere long" (13–14). The speaker seems to say that his friend's love grows stronger as he or she realizes that death will soon separate them. His tone, then, shifts from the somber tone of the first three quatrains to a happier, more hopeful tone in the closing couplet.

CONCLUSION

Thesis restated

Closing thought

Shakespeare's metaphors lead the reader to a universal truth of human existence: As death nears, the bonds of friendship are strengthened and intensified. Perhaps the intensity of emotion we feel for someone we love at the approach of the inevitable and natural end of life is nature's way of telling us to cherish the people we love while we can.

INTERNET

More Writer's Models

Keyword: LE7 12-3

PRACTICE & APPLY 2 Refer to the framework on page 545 and the Writer's Model that begins on the same page as you write the first draft of your literary analysis of a poem.

Revising

Evaluate and Revise Your Analysis

In Pursuit of Perfection Like artists who paint multiple versions of their subjects, good writers know that their work can always be improved upon. A word, sentence, paragraph, or even the whole organizational structure may need adjusting. When you begin the revision process, start by evaluating and revising the content and organization of your analysis, using the guidelines below. Then, evaluate and revise the sentence style of your analysis using the guidelines on the next page.

PEER REVIEW

Before you begin revising, ask a peer to read your paper and offer constructive criticism. He or she may be able to point out places where you need more evidence from the poem's text to support your ideas.

First Reading: Content and Organization Use the chart below to look for ways to improve the content and organization of your literary analysis.

editor in charge

Rubric: Analyzing Literature

Evaluation Questions	Tips	Revision Techniques
1 Does the introduction engage the reader's interest and introduce the subject of the analysis?	**Put parentheses** around the engaging opening. **Circle** the title of the poem and the name of the author.	If necessary, **add** a quotation or a bold statement. **Add** the name of the poem and author.
2 Does the introduction include a thesis statement that clearly identifies the literary elements and states a main idea about their effects?	**Highlight** the thesis statement. **Bracket** the literary elements and the main idea about their effects.	If needed, **add** a thesis statement that identifies the poem's literary elements and states your main idea about their effects.
3 Are the key points clear? Do they support the thesis?	**Underline** the key points. **Draw an arrow** from the key points to the thesis.	**Rewrite** key points that are not clearly expressed. **Replace** key points that don't support the thesis with ones that do.
4 Does literary evidence support all key points about the thesis? Does the essay elaborate upon all evidence?	**Put a check mark** by each direct quotation or paraphrase from the poem. **Put an X** by elaboration of literary evidence.	If necessary, **add** literary evidence for key points, or **add** elaboration to all evidence.
5 Are the key points arranged logically so that they are easy to follow?	**Review** the underlined key points to see if their arrangement is logical.	**Rearrange** key points by order of importance or by chronological order.
6 Does the conclusion restate the thesis? Does it include a thought-provoking closing thought?	**Highlight** the sentence restating the thesis. **Underline** the sentence or sentences containing the closing thought.	**Add** a sentence restating the thesis or a closing thought, if either is needed.

Second Reading: Style Once you've revised *what* you say in your analysis, you can concentrate on *how* you say it—your writing style. Since a literary analysis can often be complex and difficult to follow, you can improve the sentence style of your essay by using **transitional words and phrases** to connect your ideas and to guide readers through your analysis.

To show chronology in your analysis, use transitions such as *first, next, then,* and *finally.* To show order of importance, use such transitions as *most important, last,* and *mainly.* To help you add transitional words and phrases to your analysis, use the guidelines in the chart below.

Style Guidelines

Evaluation Question	Tip	Revision Technique
Does the essay include transitional words and phrases that guide the reader?	**Draw a box** around transitional words and phrases. If there are none, revise.	**Add** transitional words and phrases to make the connection of ideas in the analysis clear.

ANALYZING THE REVISION PROCESS

Study these revisions, and answer the questions that follow.

add — *Then, in the third quatrain,* ^ Shakespeare develops a complex metaphor of fire to suggest the progression through life to death. The speaker compares

add — himself to the ember stage of a fire. The fire ^ *, the "deathbed whereon [the speaker] must expire" (11),* is now a bed of

add — ashes. ^ *The ashes represent all the years the speaker has lived up to this point.*

Responding to the Revision Process

1. How does adding the transition to the first sentence help the reader understand the flow of the ideas?
2. How does the added quotation improve the passage?
3. Why do you think the writer added the sentence at the end of this passage?

PRACTICE & APPLY 3 Following the guidelines on this page and the previous one, evaluate and revise the content, organization, and style of your analysis. If possible, collaborate with a classmate throughout the revision process.

Writing Skills
Revise for content and style.

Publishing

Proofread and Publish Your Analysis

Bottom of the Ninth Before you publish your analysis, proofread it and make any last-minute changes. Search for and eliminate errors in grammar, usage, and mechanics. Such errors can distract your readers from your message, lessening the impact of your analysis and making all your hard work less meaningful.

Share Your Expertise Analyzing the poem you chose has made you something of an authority on that particular poem. Now you can share with others the knowledge and insight you have gained from writing your analysis. Here are some ideas for publishing your work.

- If the poem you analyzed is by a living poet, send a copy of your analysis to him or her and ask for feedback.
- Around the world, people celebrate the birthdays of noteworthy poets. Create a pamphlet about the poet whose work you've studied. Include graphics (such as a drawing or photo of the poet), some background information about him or her, plus the poem you analyzed and your analysis. Distribute the pamphlet to friends, family, and classmates on the poet's birthday.
- Search the Internet for Web sites devoted to the poet whose work you have analyzed. If the site or sites you find accept submissions, send them your analysis for possible posting.
- Present a memorized recitation of the poem you have analyzed. After the recitation, share with your audience the insights about the poem that you've gained through analyzing it. For more on **reciting literature,** see page 550.

Reflect on Your Analysis

Look Back for the Future Use the following questions to determine what lessons you've learned from writing a literary analysis and how those lessons might benefit your future writing efforts.

- How did writing a literary analysis help you to better understand the poem? How will this new understanding help you approach reading other poems?
- Do you think the skills you used in writing a literary analysis will carry over to other types of writing? Why or why not?

PRACTICE & APPLY 4 Following the guidelines on this page, first proofread your analysis for errors in grammar, usage, and mechanics. Then, publish your analysis for a wider audience and reflect on the writing experience.

TIP Proofreading will help ensure that your literary analysis follows the **conventions** of standard American English. For example, identify and correct punctuation errors you've made in incorporating direct quotations from the poem. For more on **quotation marks,** see Quotation Marks, 13c–d, in the Language Handbook.

COMPUTER TIP

If you have access to publishing software and design programs, you can use them to make a more professional-looking pamphlet. For more on **page design, type,** and **visuals,** see *Designing Your Writing* in the Writer's Handbook.

Writing Skills
Proofread, especially for correct use of quotation marks.

Reciting Literature

Speaking Assignment
Prepare and present a recitation of a poem, a speech, or a dramatic soliloquy.

Reading and analyzing poetry on paper is certainly a rewarding challenge. Yet some people believe that poetry is not fully experienced unless it is read or listened to aloud. Through the ages, people have gathered to hear Shakespeare's plays and poetry brought to life through performance and recitations. Literary readings still attract attentive audiences today. When you present a memorized **recitation** of a literary work, you can enrich your understanding of the work and make it live and breathe for your listeners.

Prepare Your Recitation

Choose a Text Start by finding an appropriate poem, speech, or dramatic soliloquy—one that you find meaningful or moving, that will appeal to your audience, and that you can recite in the amount of time your teacher allows. Browse through this book, literary magazines, and anthologies of collected works for possible selections. Select the literary work that best fits the following criteria.

SELECTION CRITERIA FOR A RECITATION

Criteria	Questions
Aptness	Are the content and tone appropriate for your audience and the occasion?
Artistic merit	Does the selection use precise, vivid language? Are ideas clearly expressed? Will the selection appeal to the listeners' emotions as well as their intellects?
Originality	Does the selection present a unique perspective on life or human nature?
Relevance	Does the selection deal with universal themes such as life and death, love, justice, or personal identity?

Analyze the Text A good recitation is more than just a display of your memorization skills: It's an **interpretation**—an expression of your personal understanding of the selection's meaning. The following tips will help you analyze the text in order to create your interpretation.

- **Identify** the selection's speaker, including his or her motivations.
- **Look up** the definitions and pronunciations of any unfamiliar words.
- **Paraphrase** to check your understanding of the text by restating the ideas in your own words.
- **Research** to clarify material that you don't understand. Check for historical allusions in an encyclopedia. Look up classical or literary allusions in an unabridged or specialized dictionary.

Listening and Speaking Skills
Present a recitation of a poem, speech, or dramatic soliloquy.

Deliver Your Recitation

Rehearse Your Material A recitation should deliver your interpretation clearly and forcefully while creating an aesthetic effect through skillful **artistic staging**. Practice your presentation until you achieve a comfortable command of the text. Experiment with various ways of expressing the selection's meaning with your voice and body. If possible, research and analyze professional recitations for models of how you can effectively vocalize and use body language yourself. The following strategies will help you polish your delivery.

- **Stress** or **pause** to emphasize certain words or phrases.
- Vary the **pitch** and **tone** of your voice to reveal the speaker's feelings. A rising tone often suggests uncertainty, while a falling tone expresses conviction.
- Vary your **rate of speaking** to convey the mood of the passage. A slower rate can suggest contemplation or hesitation; a quicker pace may signal excitement, nervousness, anger, or joy.
- Use **facial expressions** and natural **gestures** and **movements** to convey the meaning and mood of the material. A smile and a flourish with the hand may suggest a lighter mood, while a snarl and a raised fist may hint at anger in the speaker.

Mark up a double-spaced copy of the text with notes on the decisions you make during rehearsals. This marked copy can help you commit your delivery strategies to memory. Here are markings you can use to translate textual cues into a meaningful interpretation.

TIP Give your listeners a brief introduction to your selection. Along with the title and the author's name, include background information and reasons why you chose the selection.

MARKING TEXT FOR DELIVERY Quick guide

Markings	Interpretive Technique
Draw a single slash (/) after each comma or semicolon. **Draw a double slash (//)** after each colon, dash, and period.	Pause for each single slash; pause longer for each double slash.
Underline italicized words.	Stress or speak these words more loudly.
Draw an arrow with a rising curve over each question mark.	Speak with a rising tone.
Highlight significant words, phrases, or lines.	Adjust pitch, volume, or rate for emphasis.

PRACTICE & APPLY 5 Using the directions in this workshop, prepare a recitation of a poem, speech, or dramatic soliloquy. Pay close attention to performance details. Present your final recitation to an audience, such as your classmates or family.

Listening and Speaking Skills
Rehearse and deliver your presentation.

Collection 3: Skills Review

Comparing Literature

The subject of love, with its great joys and deep sorrows, has engaged lyric poets of every age. Renaissance poets, so keenly aware of the individual in the here and now, were particularly fascinated by the tension between the urgency of love and the shortness of time. The French poet Pierre de Ronsard (1524–1585) explored this theme in his sonnet "When You Are Old," one of a collection of poems addressed to a lady, Helene, who apparently rejected the aging poet. Three centuries later the young Irish poet William Butler Yeats (1865–1939) found in Ronsard's poignant clause a suitable beginning for his own address to another reluctant woman.

DIRECTIONS: Read the poems that follow. Then, read each multiple-choice question that follows, and write the letter of the best response.

When You Are Old

Pierre de Ronsard

translated by Humbert Wolfe

When you are old, at evening candle-lit
  beside the fire bending to your wool,
read out my verse and murmur, "Ronsard writ
  this praise for me when I was beautiful."
And not a maid but, at the sound of it,
  though nodding at the stitch on broidered stool,
will start awake, and bless love's benefit
  whose long fidelities bring Time to school.
I shall be thin and ghost beneath the earth
  by myrtle shade in quiet after pain,
but you, a crone,° will crouch beside the hearth
  mourning my love and all your proud disdain.
And since what comes tomorrow who can say?
Live, pluck the roses of the world today.

---

11. crone *n.:* old woman.

Pages 552–555 cover **Literary Skills** Compare and contrast works from different literary periods.

When You Are Old

William Butler Yeats

When you are old and grey and full of sleep,
And nodding by the fire, take down this book,
And slowly read, and dream of the soft look
Your eyes had once, and of their shadows deep;

How many loved your moments of glad grace,
And loved your beauty with love false or true,
But one man loved the pilgrim soul in you,
And loved the sorrows of your changing face;

And bending down beside the glowing bars,
Murmur, a little sadly, how Love fled
And paced upon the mountains overhead
And hid his face amid a crowd of stars.

Collection 3: Skills Review

1. The speaker in both poems is asking the woman he is addressing to imagine that she —
   - **A** is happy in her solitude
   - **B** is still beautiful in old age
   - **C** has not been forgotten
   - **D** is old and reading his poetry

2. The last two lines of Ronsard's poem are an example of the literary theme known as —
   - **F** *carpe diem*
   - **G** caesura
   - **H** metaphysical conceit
   - **J** kenning

3. What do the last two lines of Ronsard's poem reveal about the speaker's purpose in addressing the woman?
   - **A** He wishes to get even with her for rejecting him.
   - **B** He is trying to persuade her to marry him now.
   - **C** He wishes to immortalize her in a love poem.
   - **D** He is trying to stop her from pursuing him.

4. The roses in the last line of Ronsard's poem symbolize —
   - **F** broken promises
   - **G** flowers
   - **H** opportunities
   - **J** compliments

5. Ronsard's poem is an example of which poetic form?
   - **A** Shakespearean sonnet
   - **B** literary epic
   - **C** Petrarchan sonnet
   - **D** ballad

6. In Yeats's poem the image "pilgrim soul" in line 7 suggests that the woman the speaker loves is —
   - **F** homeless
   - **G** a restless seeker after truth
   - **H** a religious dissenter
   - **J** logical and sure of herself

7. What emotion do both poets hope to evoke in the women they are addressing?
   - **A** pity
   - **B** revenge
   - **C** regret
   - **D** joy

8. The attitude of Yeats's speaker toward the woman differs from that of Ronsard's speaker in that Yeats's speaker —
   - **F** desires revenge
   - **G** has not given up on the possibility of winning her
   - **H** is more sad than angry
   - **J** is more offended by her rejection

9. How does the attitude toward time expressed in Ronsard's poem reflect Renaissance attitudes on that subject?
   - **A** Ronsard's speaker is acutely aware of the brevity of youth, beauty, and earthly life.
   - **B** Ronsard's speaker is focused on the afterlife rather than earthly life.
   - **C** Ronsard's speaker feels he has more than enough time to accomplish what he wants in life.
   - **D** Ronsard's speaker expects that time inevitably will bring greater happiness.

10. Which statement about these poems is *not* true?
    - **F** Both poems use rhyme.
    - **G** Both poems follow a regular meter.
    - **H** Each speaker asks a woman to read his verses.
    - **J** Both poems are bitter in tone.

Essay Question

In a brief essay, compare and contrast these two poems. Focus on how each poet uses each of these elements: speaker, person addressed, message, tone, key word or phrase, and form and structure (use of sound effects, meter, figurative language). Arrange your essay in the block style: First, tell how Ronsard uses these elements; then, tell how Yeats uses them.

Collection 3: Skills Review

Vocabulary Skills

Test Practice

Synonyms

DIRECTIONS: Words that have similar meanings are called **synonyms.** For example, *benign* and *kind* are synonyms. In the sentences below, choose the word or group of words whose meaning is most similar to the meaning of the underlined word.

1. To transgress a law is to —
- **A** question it
- **B** break it
- **C** explain it
- **D** apply it

2. An impetuous person is —
- **F** overly helpful
- **G** dangerously manipulative
- **H** extremely impulsive
- **J** unreasonably stubborn

3. An impediment is —
- **A** an obstacle
- **B** an architectural feature
- **C** a commandment
- **D** a plea

4. Guile is the same as —
- **F** innocence
- **G** bitterness
- **H** awe
- **J** deceit

5. Someone who is implacable is —
- **A** fearful
- **B** relentless
- **C** vigilant
- **D** confused

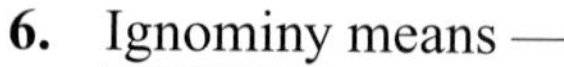

6. Ignominy means —
- **F** ignorance
- **G** disgrace
- **H** aggression
- **J** retaliation

7. A person who studies with diligence is —
- **A** inconsistent
- **B** careless
- **C** unfocused
- **D** persevering

8. Someone who looks at you reproachfully is —
- **F** studying you
- **G** admiring you
- **H** blaming you
- **J** afraid of you

9. Something with allure is —
- **A** fascinating
- **B** flattering
- **C** repulsive
- **D** threatening

10. If you have reiterated a statement, you have —
- **F** denied it
- **G** explained it
- **H** repeated it
- **J** contradicted it

Vocabulary Skills
Use synonyms.

Collection 3: Skills Review

Writing Skills

Test Practice

DIRECTIONS: Read the following paragraph from a draft of a student's analysis of a poem. Then, answer the questions below it.

(1) The speaker in Andrew Marvell's poem "To His Coy Mistress" urges his lady to accept his love by gradually changing the tone of his requests. (2) He begins with an idealistic tone, describing how extravagant his love would be if time were not an issue. (3) Soon his tone admonishes her, trying to frighten her into accepting his advances before it is too late. (4) He describes "Time's wingèd chariot hurrying near" (line 22) to show that there is little time left for them to act. (5) The winged chariot is an allusion to Greek mythology. (6) The tone becomes urgent by the poem's end as the speaker persuades his lady to "tear our pleasures with rough strife / Through the iron gates of life" (lines 43–44).

1. Which of these transitions could be added to the beginning of sentence 2?
   - **A** However,
   - **B** As a result,
   - **C** For example,
   - **D** Additionally,

2. Which reference could the student add to support the ideas in sentence 2?
   - **F** He predicts "The grave's a fine and private place, / But none, I think, do there embrace" (lines 31–32).
   - **G** He offers to spend a hundred years "to praise / Thine eyes, and on thy forehead gaze" (lines 13–14).
   - **H** The speaker tries to persuade her by saying, "Now let us sport us while we may" (line 37).
   - **J** He insists that she act "while the youthful hue / Sits on thy skin like morning dew" (lines 33–34).

3. The best way to add depth to the passage would be to
   - **A** compare courtship practices of Marvell's time to those of today
   - **B** relate other stylistic devices to the nuances in tone
   - **C** add an overview of the interesting facts of Andrew Marvell's life
   - **D** elaborate on the allusions to the Ganges and Humber rivers

4. Which sentence should be deleted to improve the passage's organization?
   - **F** 2
   - **G** 3
   - **H** 4
   - **J** 5

5. To recite Marvell's poem orally, the student should
   - **A** elaborate on any metaphors the listeners might not understand
   - **B** read directly from a marked-up copy of the poem
   - **C** briefly introduce the poem to explain its context
   - **D** deliver each line with the same pitch and tone

Writing Skills
Write a literary analysis of a poem.

Coronation Procession of Charles II to Westminster from the Tower of London (detail) (1661) by Dirck Stoop.
Museum of London.

Collection 4

The Restoration and the EIGHTEENTH CENTURY 1660–1800

The Best of All Possible Worlds

There are seven groups in English society

1. The Great, who live profusely.
2. The Rich, who live very plentifully.
3. The Middle Sort, who live well.
4. The Working Trades, who labor hard, but feel no want.
5. The Country People, Farmers, etc., who fare indifferently.
6. The Poor, that fare hard.
7. The Miserable, that really pinch and suffer want.

—Daniel Defoe

Detail from *The Old Fleet Prison*. Culver Pictures.

INTERNET

Collection Resources

Keyword: LE7 12-4

The Restoration and the

LITERARY EVENTS

1660

1660 Samuel Pepys begins his diary

1660s London theaters reopen; actresses appear onstage for the first time

1666 In France, Jean Baptiste Molière's *The Misanthrope* is first performed

Opening page of Samuel Pepys's *Diary* (1659–1660).

The Pepys Library, Magdalene College, Cambridge, England.

1670

1678 John Bunyan publishes *The Pilgrim's Progress,* Part 1 (Part 2 appears in 1684)

1680s Poems of **Bashō** help popularize haiku poetry in Japan

1688 Aphra Behn publishes *Oroonoko,* an early antislavery novel

1690

1691 In Mexico, Sor Juana Inés de la Cruz publishes *Respuesta a Sor Filotea* (*Reply to Sister Philotea*), a defense of women's intellectual rights

1709 First issue of Addison and Steele's *The Tatler* is printed (*The Spectator* is begun in 1711)

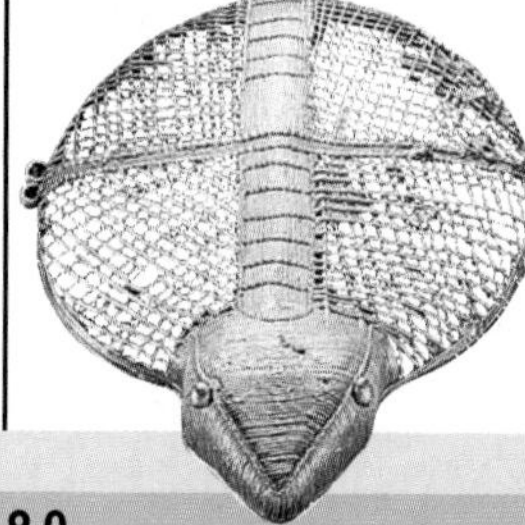

Gold turtle-shaped Ashanti emblem (17th or 18th century) from Ghana.

1710

1712 Alexander Pope publishes part of *The Rape of the Lock*

1719 Daniel Defoe publishes *Robinson Crusoe*

1726 Jonathan Swift publishes *Gulliver's Travels*

1729 Swift publishes *A Modest Proposal,* protesting English treatment of Irish poor

POLITICAL AND SOCIAL EVENTS

1660

1660 Charles II is proclaimed king of England (crowned in 1661)

1665 Plague claims more than 68,000 people in London

1666 Great Fire destroys much of London

The Great Fire of London (17th century).

1670

c. 1670s Ashanti Empire is formed in Africa

1673 English Test Act bans Roman Catholics from public office

1685–1688 James II, king of England, tries to reestablish Catholic Church

1687 Newton publishes *Mathematical Principles of Natural Philosophy*

1688–1689 Glorious (Bloodless) Revolution: James II is succeeded by Protestant rulers William and Mary

1690

1690 John Locke publishes *An Essay Concerning Human Understanding*

1695 English Parliament enacts Penal Laws, depriving Irish Catholics of civil rights

1707 England, Wales, and Scotland are politically unified as Great Britain

1710

1714 George I, a German who could not speak English, becomes king of England

1718 In England, Lady Mary Wortley Montagu introduces Turkish practice of inoculation against smallpox

Signature of Charles II. The *R* stands for *Rex,* Latin for "king."

The Bridgeman Art Library.

Eighteenth Century 1660–1800

1740 | 1765 | 1780 | 1800

1740 Samuel Richardson publishes *Pamela, or Virtue Rewarded*

1755 Samuel Johnson publishes his *Dictionary of the English Language*

1759 In France, **Voltaire** publishes *Candide*

1773 African American poet Phillis Wheatley's *Poems on Various Subjects, Religious and Moral* is published in London

Frontispiece of Phillis Wheatley's *Poems on Various Subjects, Religious and Moral* (1773).

1789 Olaudah Equiano, once held in slavery in Colonial America, publishes his autobiography in Britain

1791 James Boswell's *The Life of Samuel Johnson* is published

1792 Mary Wollstonecraft publishes *A Vindication of the Rights of Woman*

1798 Wordsworth and **Coleridge** publish *Lyrical Ballads*

1740 | 1765 | 1780 | 1800

An Early London Coffeehouse (detail) (c. 1705) signed A. S.

British Museum, London.

1752 Benjamin Franklin invents the lightning rod

1760 George III is crowned king of England; becomes known as the king who lost the American Colonies

1762 Catherine II (Catherine the Great) becomes czarina of Russia

1765 British Parliament passes Stamp Act for taxing American Colonies

1765 Mozart writes *Symphony No. 1* at age nine

1773 Boston Tea Party occurs

1775 American Revolution begins

French Revolution button (c. 1789–1793). The motto may be translated as "Liberty or Death." Brass with miniatures painted on ivory.

1789 French Revolution begins with storming of the Bastille

1798 British crush Irish nationalist rebellion led by Theobald Wolfe Tone

1799 Rosetta stone (key to deciphering Egyptian hieroglyphics) is found in Egypt

1799 Napoleon heads revolutionary government in France

Political and Social

The Restoration of Charles II, 1660

When the Stuart King Charles II was returned to the throne in 1660, the Church of England regained its power. The life of the aristocratic courtier became the model for a sophisticated age of taste, refinement, and luxury. London theaters reopened, and censorship of the arts declined. However, religious persecution became increasingly widespread, causing many dissenters to immigrate to other countries in search of religious freedom.

The Return of Charles II to Whitehall in 1660 (1867) by Alfred Barron Clay. Oil on canvas.

The Bridgeman Art Library.

An Early London Coffeehouse (detail) (c. 1705) signed A. S.

British Museum, London.

The Bloodless Revolution, 1688

When Charles II died, in 1685, without a legitimate heir, his brother James II, a Roman Catholic, became king. Protestant English political leaders, fearing domination by Rome, acted quickly to transfer power to James's Protestant daughter Mary. Mary's Dutch husband, William of Orange, then attacked England and

Milestones 1660–1800

forced King James to flee. Parliament invited William and Mary to assume the English throne. They accepted and were installed in 1689 without a drop of blood having been shed. Thus, the Protestant succession to the throne of England was secured in what has come to be called the Glorious (Bloodless) Revolution.

OATS. *n. ſ.* [aten, Saxon.] A grain, which in England is generally given to horſes, but in Scotland ſupports the people.

Definition from Samuel Johnson's *A Dictionary of the English Language.*

The Growth of a New Reading Public

As the eighteenth century progressed, more and more writers were focusing on values and concerns associated with middle-class rather than upper-class life. These concerns included thrift, work, domestic relations, and social respectability. Writers like Daniel Defoe, Richard Steele, and Joseph Addison began practicing a new profession, journalism, in which they not only reported on contemporary social and political events but also urged improvement in public manners and morals. Other new literary forms, such as the novel, also found an eager audience in the middle classes, especially among women.

Gulliver awakens in Lilliput, where everyone is about the size of a finger. Illustration.

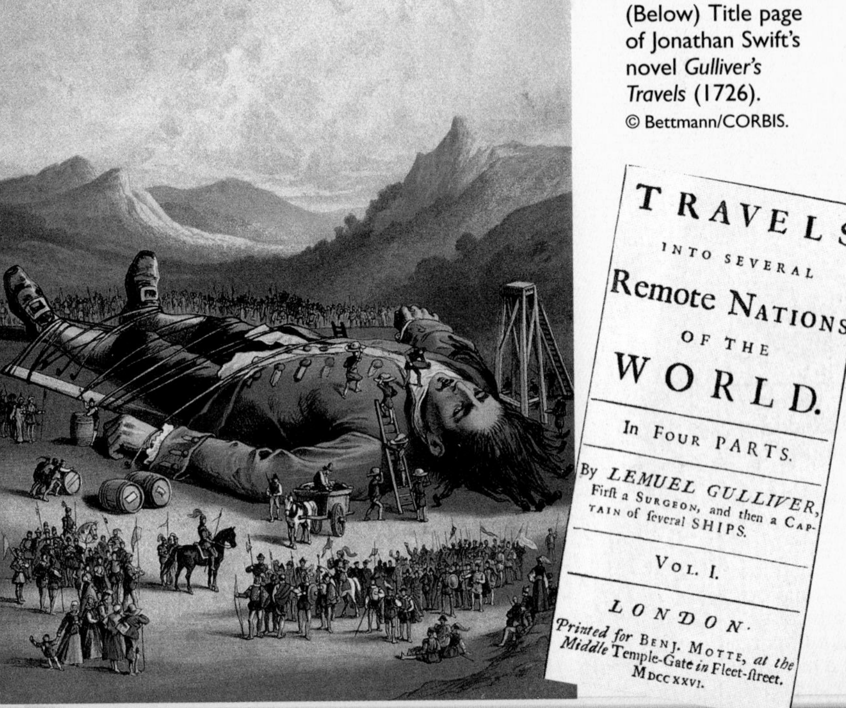

TRAVELS
INTO SEVERAL
Remote NATIONS
OF THE
WORLD.
In FOUR PARTS.
By LEMUEL GULLIVER,
Firſt a SURGEON, and then a CAPTAIN of ſeveral SHIPS.
VOL. I.
LONDON:
Printed for BENJ. MOTTE, at the Middle Temple-Gate in Fleet-ſtreet.
MDCCXXVI.

(Below) Title page of Jonathan Swift's novel *Gulliver's Travels* (1726).

The Restoration and the Eighteenth Century 1660–1800

by C. F. Main

PREVIEW

Think About . . .

In 1660, the English monarchy was restored after nearly twenty years of civil war and repressive Puritan rule. Then plague descended, followed by a devastating fire in London. No wonder, then, that the English were ready for a period of stability in which the conservative values of order, decorum, and clarity were of the utmost importance.

As you read about this period, look for answers to these questions:

- What was new about the way in which nature was regarded and analyzed in the eighteenth century?
- How did Enlightenment values affect religious beliefs?
- What new forms of popular literature developed in the eighteenth century?

From 1660 to 1800, people from England and Europe were pouring into North America. These eager voyagers not only sought freedom from religious and political persecution; they also saw money to be made in the American continent's rich lands and forests—in furs, tobacco, and timber for British sailing ships. They transported Africans for use as slave labor in the Americas. In 1775, these Colonies rebelled against British rule and eventually won their freedom. The United States was a raw, vigorous, brand-new nation. Across the Atlantic, things were very different.

Collection introduction (pages 562–578) covers **Literary Skills** Evaluate the philosophical, political, religious, ethical, and social influences of a historical period.

From Tumult to Calm

In 1660, England was utterly exhausted from nearly twenty years of civil war. By 1700, it had lived through a devastating plague and a fire that left more than two thirds of Londoners homeless. By the middle of the eighteenth century, however, England had settled into a period of calm and order, at least among the upper classes. Despite the loss of the American Colonies, the reinvigorated British military forces established new settlements around the globe. And though life for many was wretched, the middle class grew. Throughout this period in a very old nation with tastes much more

The Orrery (1766) by Joseph Wright of Derby. Oil on canvas.
An orrery is a mechanical device that shows the positions of the earth, sun, and moon.
The Bridgeman Art Library.

refined than raw, British men and women also produced many brilliant works of philosophy, art, and literature.

This long period of time in England—from 1660 to 1800—has been given several labels: the Augustan Age, the neoclassical period, the Enlightenment, and the Age of Reason. Each of these labels applies to some characteristics of these 140 years, but none applies to all.

Augustan and Neoclassical: Comparisons with Rome

Many people liked to find similarities between England in this period and ancient Rome, especially during the reign of the

The Execution of King Charles I at Whitehall, London, January 30, 1649. Woodcut.

The Granger Collection, New York.

emperor Octavian (63 B.C.–A.D. 14). When he became emperor, Octavian was given the high-sounding name *Augustus,* meaning "the exalted one." Augustus restored peace and order to Rome after Julius Caesar's assassination. Similarly, the Stuart monarchs of England restored peace and order to England after the civil wars that led to the execution of King Charles I in 1649—wars that continued even after the king was dead.

The people of both Rome and England were weary of war, suspicious of revolutionaries and radicals, and ready to settle down, make money, and enjoy life. The Roman Senate had hailed Augustus as the second founder of Rome; in 1660, the English people brought back the son of Charles I from his exile in France, crowned him King Charles II, and hailed him as their savior. As a warning to revolutionaries, they dug up the corpse of Oliver Cromwell, who had ruled England between Charles I and Charles II, and cut off its head. The monarchy was restored without shedding a drop of blood in warfare.

In this age, many English writers consciously modeled their works on the old Latin classics, which they had studied in school and university. These writings that imitate Latin works were called **neoclassical**—"new classical." The classics, it was generally agreed, were valuable because they represented what was permanent and universal in human experience. All educated people knew the Latin classics better than they knew their own English literature.

We, therefore, the Representatives of the United States of America, in General Congress, Assembled, . . . do, in the Name, and by Authority of the good People of these Colonies, solemnly Publish and Declare, . . . that all political Connection between them and the State of Great Britain, is and ought to be totally dissolved. . . .

— Declaration of Independence, Philadelphia (July 4, 1776)

Nothing of importance happened today.

— Diary entry reportedly made by King George III (July 4, 1776)

Reason and Enlightenment: From Why? to How?

Labels like the "Age of Reason" and the "Enlightenment" reveal how people were gradually changing their view of themselves and the world. For instance, Shakespeare, the greatest writer of the Renaissance, expressed a commonly held view when he described the unusual events that preceded the assassination of Julius Caesar—"a tempest dropping fire" and "blue lightning." These unnatural events, says a character in the play *Julius Caesar,* are "instruments of fear and warning." For centuries, people had believed that before a great public disaster like the assassination of a ruler, the earth and sky gave warnings. People believed that unusual events such as earthquakes, comets, and even babies born with malformations had some kind of meaning, and that they were sent as punishments for past misdoings or as warnings of future troubles. People did not ask, "*How* did this unusual event take place?" but "*Why* did this unusual event take place, and what does it *mean*?"

Throughout the Enlightenment, people gradually stopped asking *why?* questions and started asking *how?* questions, and the answers to those questions—about everything from the workings of the human body to the laws of the universe—became much less frightening and superstitious. For instance, the astronomer Edmond Halley (1656–1742) took the terror out of celestial phenomena by calculating when they were going to occur. He computed, with "immense labor," he said, the orbit of the comet that still bears his name. He predicted it would appear in 1758, 1834, 1910, and 1986—and it did. And how did he know it would reappear at seventy-six-year intervals? Because that was the time it took to complete its orbit. This reasonable explanation made no connection between the comet and human affairs.

The truth is, the science of Nature has been already too long made only a work of the brain and the fancy: It is now high time that it should return to the plainness and soundness of observations on material and obvious things.

—Robert Hooke

Interior of Henry VII's Chapel, Westminster Abbey (c. 1750) by Canaletto.

Museum of London.

Newton's reflecting telescope (1688).

Royal Society, London.

Changes in Religion: More Questions

The new scientific and rational explanations of phenomena gradually began to affect some people's religious views. If comets were not sent by God to warn people, perhaps God didn't interfere at all in human affairs. Perhaps the universe was like an immense piece of clockwork, set in motion by a Creator who more or less withdrew from this perfect mechanism and let it run by itself. Such a view, part of an ideology known as deism, could make people feel self-satisfied and complacent, especially if they believed, as Alexander Pope (see page 597) noted, that "Whatever is, is right." Some philosophers even argued that "in this best of all possible worlds, . . . all is for the best"—a view that the French writer Voltaire ridiculed in his novel *Candide* (1759). (See page 619.) But other than a tiny minority of "enlightened" rationalists and materialists,

A CLOSER LOOK: SOCIAL INFLUENCES

Life Among the Haves . . .

INFORMATIONAL TEXT

According to the law, all men were equal, but some were more equal than others—especially England's wealthy, during the Restoration and the eighteenth century. Famous for its excesses, this artificial age offered extreme luxuries to those known as "quality" or "polite" society—the rich.

Gossip and gambling. Greatly influenced by the French in manners, dress, furniture, gardens, and recreation, the elite gathered regularly at London's fashionable coffeehouses—numbering three thousand by the early eighteenth century. These centers of news, gossip, and gambling were places to see and to be seen in. Another meeting place, the city's formal gardens, offered illuminated groves, dining, and fireworks.

Powder and plumage. Whatever their haunt, both men and women devoted themselves to colorful and extravagant fashion. Men carried snuffboxes and wore velvet or satin coats, lace ruffles, silk knee breeches, high-heeled shoes with gold or silver buckles, and broad-brimmed hats decorated with feathers. Women wore low-cut silk dresses with hoops made from whalebones. Their elaborate petticoats were fashioned from colorful silk, velvet, or chintz, often quilted or trimmed with silver.

By 1664, wigs and makeup were the rage for men and women. Powdered and stuffed with horsehair, women's headdresses grew to enormous proportions. Jewels, flowers, ribbons, plumage, and even fruit decorated these monstrous structures—reaching two to three feet in height. Men also wore their hair in pigtails—tied with a bow and powdered. In 1795, a tax was created to generate income from the rich—a guinea on every powdered head. Cosmetics were made from ingredients such as borax, vinegar, bread, eggs, and pigeon wings. Black patches, or fake beauty marks, were an important fashion accessory.

most people, including great philosophers and scientists like Sir Isaac Newton (1642–1727) and John Locke (1632–1704), remained religious. Christianity in its various forms continued to exercise an undiminished power over almost all Europeans in this period, just as it had in the Middle Ages and the Renaissance.

Alexander Pope.

Nature and Nature's
laws lay hid in night:
God said, Let Newton
be! and all was light.

—Alexander Pope,
epitaph intended
for Sir Isaac Newton

Religion and Politics: Repression of Minority Sects

Religion determined people's politics in this period. Charles II reestablished the Anglican Church as the official church of the country, which it continues to be in England to this day. (In the United States it is called the Episcopal Church.) With the approval of Parliament, the king attempted to outlaw all the various Puritan and Independent sects—dozens of them, all happily disagreeing

The pursuit of pleasure. The wealthy divided the year between London residences, country estates, and fashionable spas. A whirlwind of masked balls, dances, and formal dinner parties, known as the London season, ended by the first week in June. Summers were often spent in seaside towns and at freshwater springs. Daniel Defoe described one trendy spa: "[The attendants] present you with a little floating dish like a basin, in which the lady puts her handkerchief and a nosegay, of late the snuffbox is added, and some patches; through the bath occasioning a little perspiration, the patches do not stick as kindly as they should."

It was a careless, pleasure-seeking time centered on dancing, dining, drinking, theatergoing, card playing, and gambling. As is always the case with fashion, change was inevitable. By the end of the eighteenth century, the lifestyle of the wealthy leaned toward simplicity and sobriety.

Cartoon mocking the huge wigs worn by rich women (1771). Lithograph.

William of Orange receiving his crown from the lords in the Houses of Parliament, while his wife, Mary II, looks on.

among themselves—that had caused so much uproar during the preceding thirty years. Persecution of these various sects continued throughout the eighteenth century.

The Bloodless Revolution

Charles II had a number of illegitimate children, but no legal heir. When he died in 1685, he was succeeded by his brother James II, a practicing Roman Catholic. Most English people were utterly opposed to James. After all, it was widely believed that Roman

A CLOSER LOOK: SOCIAL INFLUENCES

. . . and Life Among the Have-Nots

INFORMATIONAL TEXT

For the poor, life is always hard, but during the Restoration and the eighteenth century, the poor lived in deplorable conditions, without the aid of doctors or police, and beyond the reach of education, religion, and charity. As if that were not enough, the poor also lived under the threat of debtors' prisons, where torture was common.

Neither space nor air. Overcrowding in London's tenements and workhouses reached an all-time high during the period. Entire families lived together in one-room garrets or cellars infested with rats, lice, snails, and bedbugs. Unhealthy conditions worsened with the institution of a window tax in 1696. In order to avoid the tax, many blocked up their windows, creating stagnant air and cutting off light. Space and air seemed luxuries that only the rich could afford. Adding to the filth and discomfort, household garbage and human waste were thrown out into the streets. Butcher shops and slaughterhouses matter-of-factly tossed bloody remnants into open drains that intersected with streets and walkways.

Superstition, not science. Although medical science had begun to develop, superstition still marked the treatment of the sick in the early part of the eighteenth century. For example, smallpox was commonly treated with a black powder made by burning thirty to forty live toads. Bleeding served as a remedy for most ailments. As odd as it might seem today, the connection between dirt and disease hadn't been made by the medical profession. And since physicians practiced medicine almost exclusively with the upper classes, they knew little of the ailments of the poor. Personal hygiene, or the lack of it, certainly contributed to the general state of health. One observer described a pauper woman's petticoats as "standing alone with dirt."

Brief unhappy lives. During the first part of the eighteenth century, the overall death rate surpassed the birthrate. In the worst years, more than 74 percent of London's children died before the age of five. Many of those children who did survive

Catholics had not only set fire to London and caused other disasters but also were actively plotting to hand the country over to the pope. When James's queen produced a little boy—a Catholic heir—English political leaders transferred power to James's daughter Mary, who was married to the Dutch William of Orange, a Protestant prince. Late in 1688, William attacked England. King James fled the country, and early in 1689 Parliament declared William and Mary king and queen, thus restoring Protestant rule. These events are known as the Glorious (bloodless) Revolution. Ever since, the rulers of England have been, at least in name, Anglicans.

The hatred between the supporters of William of Orange (King Billy) and those of King James festered for more than three hundred years—and still explodes in violence in the streets of Northern Ireland.

were forced to work for a living as soon as physically able, and sometimes sooner. Often they suffered abuse by their guardians or employers.

A deadly escape. It's no wonder that many sought comfort and warmth in inexpensive alcohol. Starting in 1720 and for the next thirty years, cheap gin was readily available in the capital. The poor were especially susceptible to the disastrous effects of gin—high crime and death rates throughout most of the century. In fact, during a two-year period, 12,000 people out of London's population of 800,000 were convicted of illegally selling gin.

Hope returns. Eventually, improvements in agriculture created a demand for manure, and a use for street filth was found. That, coupled with the Paving Acts of 1762, did much to clean up London's streets. In 1769, a dispensary movement provided free advice and medicine for the underprivileged. Only then was the belief dispelled that the London poor were sick because they were immoral.

Night (18th century) by William Hogarth.

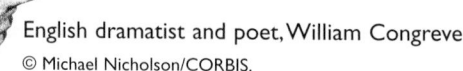

Covent Garden with St. Paul's Church (c. 1737) by Balthasar Nebot.
Guildhall Art Gallery, London.

Addicted to the Theater

For eighteen years, while the Puritans held power, the theaters in England were closed. During the exile of the royal court in France, Charles had become addicted to theatergoing, so one of the first things he did after regaining his throne was to repeal the ban on play performances, imposed in 1642. Charles and his brother James patronized companies of actors. Boys and men no longer acted the female roles. The new theater had real actresses, like the famous Nell Gwyn, and the new plays emphasized the sexual relations of men and women in very unsentimental and unromantic ways. The great, witty comedies produced during this period (such as William Wycherley's *The Country Wife* and William Congreve's *The Way of the World*) reflected the life of the rich and leisured people of that time—the Frenchified, pleasure-loving upper classes—and their servants and hangers-on. In addition to dramatists, a large number of prose and verse writers, many of them Dissenters (people who did not belong to the Anglican Church), did not cater to the tastes of sophisticated people but wrote solely for ordinary readers.

English dramatist and poet, William Congreve.

The Age of Satire: Attacks on Immorality and Bad Taste

Today, Alexander Pope and Jonathan Swift are regarded as the most accomplished literary artists of the early eighteenth century. Though their era became known as the Age of Pope, both men had a profound influence on succeeding writers. During their own lifetimes, however, Pope and Swift were frequently out of harmony with the values of the age, and both often criticized it severely.

Although Pope addressed his works exclusively to the educated and leisured classes, he also attacked the members of these classes for their immorality and their bad taste, two failings that were usually associated in Pope's mind. Pope loved order, discipline, and craftsmanship; both he and Swift were appalled by the squalor and shoddiness—in art, manners, and morals—that underlay the polished surfaces of Augustan life. This violent, filthy underside of

> *It is an age, indeed, which is only fit for satire, and the sharpest I have shall never be wanting to lance its villainies. . . .*
>
> —John Dryden, from dedication to his *Life of Plutarch* (1683)

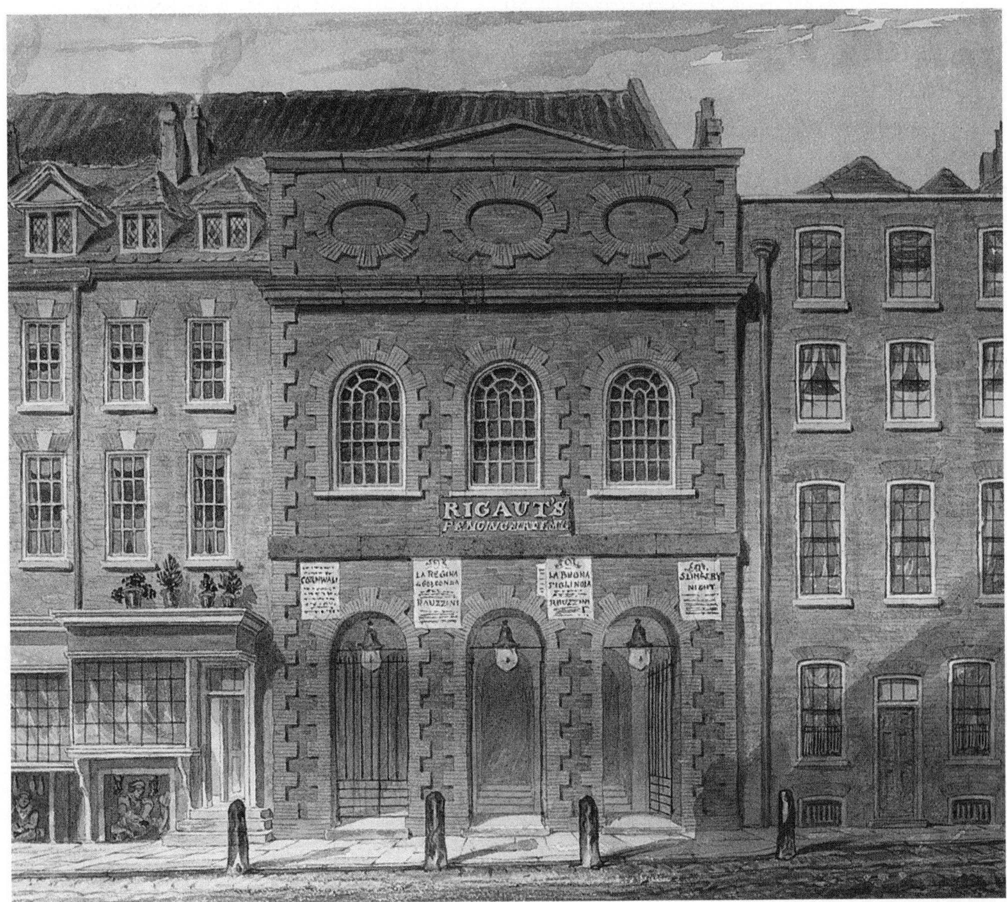

The First Opera House in the Haymarket (18th century) by William Capon.

Guildhall Library. Corporation of London.

The newspapers! Sir, they are the most villainous—licentious—abominable—infernal—Not that I ever read them—no—I make it a rule never to look into a newspaper.

—Richard Sheridan
from *The Critic*

eighteenth-century life is illustrated in the paintings and engravings of William Hogarth (1697–1764). Swift shared many of Pope's attitudes and ideals, and in his exposure of the mean and sordid in human behavior, Swift's works resemble Hogarth's art. Neither Swift nor Pope felt smug or satisfied with the world, as many English people did. Both writers hated the corrupt politics of the time and the growing commercialism and materialism of the English people.

Journalism: A New Profession

In contrast with Swift and Pope and their aristocratic values, a writer named Daniel Defoe (1660–1731) stood for values that we think of as being middle class: thrift, prudence, industry, and respectability. Defoe (see page 647) had no interest in polished manners and social poise. Swift and Pope looked down their noses at him. "Defoe has written a vast many things," Pope once said, "and none bad, though none excellent."

The Laughing Audience (1733) by William Hogarth.

Defoe, like the essayists Joseph Addison and Sir Richard Steele, followed a new profession: journalism. Eighteenth-century journalists did not merely describe contemporary political and social matters; they also saw themselves as reformers of public manners and morals. Journalists today—using both print and video—still see themselves in reformer roles.

A Poetry of Mind, Not of Soul

Today when we think of great poetry, we think of great lyrics: the sonnets of Shakespeare, Keats, and Wordsworth; the religious poems of Donne and Eliot; the private poems of Emily Dickinson; and the lyrics of such twentieth-century poets as William Butler Yeats, Robert Frost, and Elizabeth Bishop. These poets reveal in their poems their innermost thoughts and feelings, their honest and original responses to life. "Genuine poetry," said Matthew Arnold, a nineteenth-century poet and critic, "is conceived and composed in the soul."

Later critics like Matthew Arnold criticized the poetry of people such as Alexander Pope because, Arnold said, it was conceived and

Mr. and Mrs. William Chase (18th century) by Joseph Wright of Derby.
Agnew and Sons, London.

composed in their "wits"—that is, in their minds, not their souls. But these so-called Augustan poets did not define poetry in Arnold's way and so should not be judged by his standards. They had no desire to expose their souls; they thought of poetry as having a public rather than a private function.

A Public Poetry Conceived in Wit

Augustan poets would write not merely a poem but a particular kind of poem. They would decide in advance the kind of poem, much as a carpenter decides on the kind of chair to make. The best Augustan poems are like things artfully made for a particular purpose, usually a public purpose. Many of the popular kinds of poetry were inherited from classical antiquity.

If, for instance, a grand person such as a general or a titled lady died, a poet would celebrate that dead person in an **elegy,** the appropriate kind of poem for the occasion. Augustan elegies did

FAST FACTS

Political Highlights

- In 1660, civil war in England comes to an end, and an era of peace begins with the restoration of Charles II to the throne.
- Charles II reestablishes the Anglican Church as the official church of England. Other sects are outlawed and persecuted.
- William and Mary assume the English throne in 1689 after the forced exile of the Catholic king James II; Protestant rule is continued without violence.

Social Influences

- Upon his return from France, Charles II reopens the London theaters. For the first time, women are allowed to act in plays.
- A growing middle class provides an audience for new literary forms, such as journalism, essays, and novels.

not tell the truth about a dead person, even if the truth could be determined; rather, they said the very best things that the poet could think of saying.

At the opposite extreme, a poet might decide that a certain type of behavior, or even a certain conspicuous person, should be exposed to public ridicule. The poet would then write a **satire,** a kind of writing that does not make a fair and balanced judgment of people and their behavior but rather says the worst things about them that the poet can think of saying.

Another important kind of poem was the **ode**—an ambitious, often pompous poetic utterance expressing a public emotion, like the jubilation felt after a great naval victory.

Regardless of its kind, every poem had to be carefully and artificially constructed; every poem had to be dressed in exact meter and rhyme. Poems were not to sound like spontaneous and impromptu utterances, just as people were not to appear in public except in fancy dress. Those who could afford it adorned themselves with vast wigs, ribboned and jeweled clothing, and red shoes with high heels. People's movements were dignified and stately in public. Nothing was what we would today call natural—neither dress nor manners nor poetry.

The First English Novels

By the mid–eighteenth century, people were writing—and others, including women, were eagerly buying (or borrowing)—long fictional narratives called novels ("something new"). These novels, which were a development of the middle class, were often broad and comical—the adventures, for example, of a handsome ne'er-do-well or lower-class beauty, frequently recounted in

Front cover of Daniel Defoe's novel *Robinson Crusoe* (1881).

The Bridgeman Art Library.

Tom Jones Refused Admittance by the Nobleman's Porter (18th century) by Thomas Rowlandson. Illustration for Henry Fielding's *Tom Jones.*

endless episodes or through a series of letters. Authorities disagree as to whether *Robinson Crusoe* and Defoe's other fictional narratives are true novels, but many agree that the novel began either with Defoe or with the writers of the next generation.

The novels of one of the most prominent eighteenth-century novelists, Henry Fielding (1707–1754), are literally crammed with rough and rowdy incidents, and though Fielding does manage to make his characters seem good, they are never soft or sentimental. Fielding's rollicking novel *Tom Jones* has even been made into an Oscar-winning movie, proof that his high-spirited characters are still fresh and funny today. Samuel Richardson (1689–1761) was perhaps the first novelist to explore in great detail the emotional life of his characters, especially his heroines (in *Pamela* and *Clarissa*). The novels of Laurence Sterne (1713–1768) are experimental and whimsical—and still unique despite the efforts of many imitators to copy them. All these novels tell us something of what life at this time was like. They also help us understand the joys and disappointments of human experience in all ages.

FAST FACTS

Philosophical Views

- Natural phenomena are increasingly explained by scientific observation.
- Deism, a complex set of ideas with an emphasis on the cosmos as a perfect mechanism set in motion by God, influences the religious beliefs of some.
- Writers like Pope and Swift use satire to expose the moral corruption and crass commercialism of the day. Journalists—and the reforms they advocate—also become increasingly important.

Searching for a Simpler Life

By the last decade of the century, the world was changing in disturbing ways. The Industrial Revolution was turning English cities and towns into filthy, smoky slums. Across the English Channel, the French were about to murder a king and set their whole society on a different political course. The eighteenth century was closing, and—just as at the end of the twentieth century, when people sensed that a new era was about to begin—people in England knew that the age of elegance, taste, and reason was over.

As a reflection of all this change, writers were developing new interests. Appalled at the industrial blight, they were turning to external nature and writing about the effect of the natural landscape on the human soul. Disgusted with the excessive focus on the upper classes and "good taste," they were looking back at the past and searching out the simple poems and songs composed by nameless, uneducated folk poets. They were even becoming interested in the literary possibilities of the humble life and were trying to enter into the consciousness of the poor and simple. Nothing could be less Augustan than these tendencies. In short, a new literary age was beginning.

REVIEW

Talk About . . .

Turn back to the Think About questions posed at the start of this introduction to the Restoration and the eighteenth century (page 564). Discuss your responses with a group of classmates.

Write About . . .

Contrasting Literary Periods

Fashion, art, and literature, then and now. Eighteenth-century tastes in fashion and art tended toward the formal and the artificial. Even a brief look at the favored attire of the aristocratic classes of Restoration England, with their powdered wigs, satin breeches, and high-heeled shoes, will reveal their taste for artful elaboration. In literature too, eighteenth-century tastemakers encouraged the use of strict forms and classical unities rather than spontaneity or naturalness. How do these eighteenth-century tastes compare with today's trends in fashion, art, and literature? Find examples (of paintings, prints, costumes, poetry) from both eras, and discuss how standards of taste have changed or remained the same.

Jonathan Swift

(1667–1745)

Jonathan Swift (c. 1718) by Charles Jervas.
Oil on canvas ($48\frac{1}{2}'' \times 38\frac{1}{4}''$).

By Courtesy of the National Portrait Gallery, London.

Jonathan Swift is the principal prose writer of the early eighteenth century and England's greatest satirist. He was an Anglo-Irishman, a label applied to people who live in Ireland but who regard themselves as more English than Irish. Swift was born in Dublin of English parents, seven months after the death of his father. Abducted by his nurse, he spent three years in England before being returned to Ireland, where he was cared for by his uncle.

Although Swift was poor, his prosperous uncle paid for his education. Hoping to advance himself, Swift went to England and became secretary to Sir William Temple, a distant relative—a writer, a wealthy country gentleman, and a statesman. The job gave Swift the opportunity to mingle with public figures, read, and look about for a more important and permanent position. Unfortunately, nothing came of Temple's patronage. After several years of disappointment, Swift took his life into his own hands, obtained a master's degree from Oxford University, and was ordained a priest in the Church of Ireland, a counterpart to the Church of England.

Swift seemed fated to live in Ireland, although he desperately wanted a career in England. Now, as a priest, he was assigned to remote parishes in the Irish countryside. To Swift, Ireland seemed a cultural desert, inhabited mainly by Roman Catholic natives and Scottish Presbyterian immigrants—people whom Swift neither admired nor respected. He escaped to England whenever possible. Swift hoped to be made an English bishop, but his political friends fell from power, and the only appointment he could obtain was back in Ireland, as the dean of St. Patrick's Cathedral in Dublin. Swift returned to his native city, was installed as dean, and held that office for the remaining thirty years of his life.

Swift did not write for fame or money; most of his books and pamphlets were published anonymously. Nor did he write simply to divert or entertain. Swift's aim in writing was to improve human conduct, to make people more decent and humane. *Gulliver's Travels* (1726) attacks many different varieties of human misbehavior, vice, and folly. Swift even became an Irish patriot in his pamphlets, defending the Irish against the oppressive policies of their English rulers. The most famous of his pamphlets is *A Modest Proposal* (1729). In a letter to Pope, Swift justified these pro-Irish writings: "What I do is owing to perfect rage and resentment, and the mortifying sight of slavery, folly, and baseness about me, among which I am forced to live."

Swift's last days were sad: He suffered from a disease of the inner ear which made him dizzy, deaf, and disoriented. He was buried in his cathedral in Dublin, where groups of tourists now pause every day of the year to read his epitaph, which ends: "Go, traveler, and imitate, if you can, one who strove with all his strength to champion liberty."

Before You Read

A Modest Proposal

Make the Connection

What if nobody listened to the good ideas you proposed for solving one of society's most pressing problems? How could you get people's attention? Jonathan Swift found himself in this predicament. In the late 1720s, Irish harvests had been so poor for several years that farmers couldn't afford to pay the rents demanded by their English landlords. Beggars and starving children appeared everywhere. Money was in short supply, and most of it was shipped off to England. England's policies kept the Irish poor.

In response to this problem, Swift wrote a pamphlet that offered an outrageous solution to these problems of famine and human misery—perhaps the most outrageous solution ever offered. His purpose was to use shocking satire to make English society conscious of an unspeakable wrong—and, hopefully, to correct it.

Literary Skills Understand verbal irony.

Reading Skills Understand persuasive techniques (logical, emotional, and ethical appeals).

Literary Focus

Verbal Irony

Verbal irony occurs when a writer or speaker says one thing but really means something quite different—usually the direct opposite. In speech, tone of voice alerts listeners to irony. Let's say you have a bad case of the flu, for instance, and someone asks, "How are you?" Your response—"Marvelous!"—spoken in an unmistakably sarcastic tone, makes your irony clear. Since writers cannot depend on tone of voice to convey sarcasm, they often pile irony upon irony until no attentive reader could possibly miss the point. Swift's essay is a classic example of verbal irony extended to its limit.

Verbal irony is a contrast between what is said and what is really meant.

For more on Irony, see the Handbook of Literary and Historical Terms.

INTERNET

Vocabulary Practice

•

More About Jonathan Swift

•

Keyword: LE7 12-4

Reading Skills

Recognizing Persuasive Techniques

Swift's essay is perhaps the most famous and most skilled example of persuasive writing used for the purpose of satire. As you read, watch for examples of these persuasive techniques: **logical appeals** (using evidence such as facts or statistics to support a position), **emotional appeals** (passages that use words that arouse strong feelings), and **ethical appeals** (passages that establish the writer's qualifications and sincerity). Use the questions and comments alongside key passages as a guide to your reading.

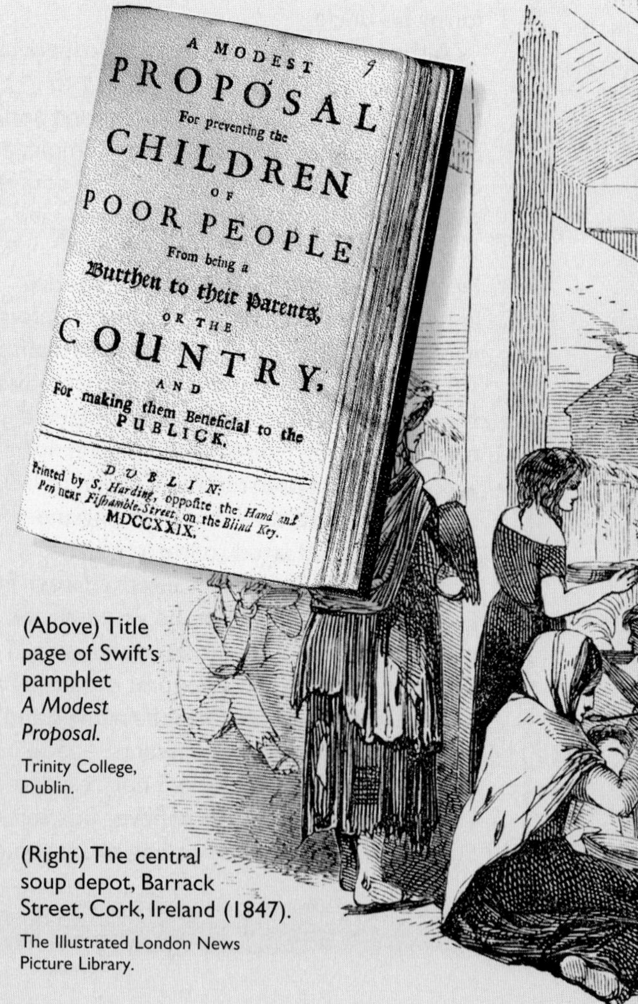

A MODEST PROPOSAL For preventing the CHILDREN OF POOR PEOPLE From being a Burthen to their Parents, OR THE COUNTRY, AND For making them Beneficial to the PUBLICK.

DUBLIN: Printed by S. Harding, opposite the Hand and Pen near Fishamble-Street, on the Blind Key. MDCCXXIX.

(Above) Title page of Swift's pamphlet *A Modest Proposal.*

Trinity College, Dublin.

(Right) The central soup depot, Barrack Street, Cork, Ireland (1847).

The Illustrated London News Picture Library.

Vocabulary Development

sustenance (sus′tə • nəns) *n.:* food or money to support life.

glutted (glut′id) *v.* used as *adj.:* overfilled.

deference (def′ər • əns) *n.:* respect.

scrupulous (skro͞op′yə • ləs) *adj.:* extremely careful and precise in deciding what is right or wrong.

censure (sen′shər) *v.:* condemn.

expedient (ek • spē′dē • ənt) *n.:* convenient means to an end.

digressed (di • grest′) *v.:* wandered off the subject.

procure (prō • kyoor′) *v.:* obtain; get.

brevity (brev′ə • tē) *n.:* being brief; shortness.

animosities (an′ə • mäs′ə • tēz) *n. pl.:* hostilities; violent hatreds or resentments.

Background

Swift makes his modest proposal all the more outrageous by assuming the voice of a practical economic planner. He pretends to be objective, full of common sense, even sensitive and kind. It is this difference between sober, straightforward style and appalling content that gives Swift's pamphlet its force. Ultimately, Swift is protesting against a purely statistical view of humanity—a view that would reduce people to breeders and babies to meat. Swift risks appearing as a monster himself in order to expose the monstrous behavior of others.

A Modest Proposal

Jonathan Swift

FOR PREVENTING THE CHILDREN OF POOR PEOPLE IN IRELAND FROM BEING A BURDEN TO THEIR PARENTS OR COUNTRY, AND FOR MAKING THEM BENEFICIAL TO THE PUBLIC

It is a melancholy object to those, who walk through this great town,[1] or travel in the country, when they see the streets, the roads, and cabin doors, crowded with beggars of the female sex, followed by three, four, or six children, all in rags, and importuning every passenger for an alms.[2] These mothers instead of being able to work for their honest livelihood, are forced to employ all their time in strolling, to beg sustenance for their helpless infants, who, as they grow up either turn thieves for want[3] of work, or leave their dear native country to fight for the Pretender[4] in Spain, or sell themselves to the Barbadoes.[5]

I think it is agreed by all parties, that this prodigious number of children, in the arms, or on the backs, or at the heels of their mothers, and frequently of their fathers, is in the present deplorable state of the kingdom, a very great additional grievance; and therefore whoever could find out a fair, cheap, and easy method of making these children sound and useful members of the commonwealth would deserve so well of the public, as to have his statue set up for a preserver of the nation. ❶

But my intention is very far from being confined to provide only for the children of professed beggars; it is of a much greater extent, and shall take in the whole number of infants at a certain age, who are born of parents in effect as little able to support them, as those who demand our charity in the streets.

As to my own part, having turned my thoughts, for many years, upon this important subject, and maturely weighed the several schemes of other projectors,[6] I have always found them grossly mistaken in their computation. It is true a child, just dropped from its dam,[7] may be supported by her milk, for a solar year[8] with little other nourishment, at most not above the value of two shillings, which the mother may certainly get, or the value in scraps, by her lawful occupation of begging, and it is exactly at one year old that I propose to provide for them, in such a manner, as, instead of being a charge upon their parents, or the parish, or wanting food and raiment[9] for the rest of their lives, they shall, on the contrary, contribute to the feeding and partly to the clothing of many thousands. ❷

❶ ? *What problem does the speaker describe in the first two paragraphs?*

❷ ? *At what age does the speaker suggest that children are ready to be made useful to society through his plan?*

1. **town** *n.:* Dublin.
2. **importuning . . . alms:** asking passersby for a handout.
3. **want** *n.:* lack; need.
4. **the Pretender:** James Edward (1688–1766), son of England's last Catholic king, the deposed James II (1633–1701). James Edward kept trying to gain the throne.
5. **sell . . . Barbadoes:** go to the West Indies and work as indentured servants.
6. **projectors** *n. pl.:* speculators; schemers.
7. **dam** *n.:* mother (ordinarily used only of animals).
8. **solar year:** from the first day of spring in one year to the last day of winter in the next.
9. **raiment** (rā'mənt) *n.:* clothing.

Vocabulary

sustenance (sus'tə·nəns) *n.:* food or money to support life.

(Opposite) Bridget O'Donnel of West Cork and her children.

The Illustrated London News Picture Library.

There is likewise another great advantage in my scheme, that it will prevent those voluntary abortions, and that horrid practice of women murdering their bastard children, alas! too frequent among us, sacrificing the poor innocent babes, I doubt,[10] more to avoid the expense, than the shame, which would move tears and pity in the most savage and inhuman breast.

The number of souls[11] in Ireland being usually reckoned one million and a half, of these I calculate there may be about two hundred thousand couples whose wives are breeders, from which number I subtract thirty thousand couples, who are able to maintain their own children, although I apprehend there cannot be so many under the present distresses of the kingdom, but this being granted, there will remain an hundred and seventy thousand breeders. I again subtract fifty thousand for those women who miscarry, or whose children die by accident, or disease within the year. There only remain an hundred and twenty thousand children of poor parents annually born: The question therefore is, how this number shall be reared, and provided for, which, as I have already said, under the present situation of affairs, is utterly impossible by all the methods hitherto proposed, for we can neither employ them in handicraft,[12] or agriculture; we neither build houses (I mean in the country) nor cultivate land: They can very seldom pick up a livelihood by stealing until they arrive at six years old, except where they are of towardly parts,[13] although, I confess they learn the rudiments much earlier, during which time, they can however be properly looked upon only as probationers,[14] as I have been informed by a principal gentleman in the county of Cavan,[15] who protested to me, that he never knew above one or two instances under the age of six, even in a part of the kingdom so renowned for the quickest proficiency in that art.[16] ❸

> ❸
> In this essay, Swift uses a series of small ironies to construct his larger satire.
> ? *What is ironic about the speaker's comments on stealing?*

I am assured by our merchants, that a boy or girl, before twelve years old, is no saleable commodity, and even when they come to this age, they will not yield above three pounds, or three pounds and half a crown at most on the exchange, which cannot turn to account[17] either to the parents or the kingdom, the charge of nutriment and rags having been at least four times that value.

I shall now therefore humbly propose my own thoughts, which I hope will not be liable to the least objection.

I have been assured by a very knowing American[18] of my acquaintance in London, that a young healthy child well nursed is at a year old a most delicious, nourishing, and wholesome food, whether stewed, roasted, baked, or boiled, and I make no doubt that it will equally serve in a fricassee,[19] or ragout.[20]

I do therefore humbly offer it to public consideration, that of the hundred and twenty thousand children, already computed, twenty thousand may be reserved for breed, whereof only one-fourth part to be males, which is more than we allow to sheep, black cattle, or swine, and my reason is that these children are seldom the fruits of marriage, a circumstance not much regarded by our savages; therefore one male will be sufficient to serve four females. That the remaining hundred thousand may at a year old be offered in sale to the persons of quality, and fortune, through the kingdom, always advising the mother to let them suck plentifully in the last month, so as to render them plump, and fat for a

---

10. **doubt** *v.:* suspect.
11. **souls** *n. pl.:* people.
12. **handicraft** *n.:* manufacturing.
13. **of towardly parts:** exceptionally advanced or mature for their age.
14. **probationers** *n pl.:* apprentices.
15. **Cavan:** inland county in Ireland that is remote from Dublin.
16. **that art:** stealing.
17. **turn to account:** be profitable.
18. **American:** To Swift's readers this label would suggest a barbaric person.
19. **fricassee** (frik′ə·sē′) *n.:* stew with a light gravy.
20. **ragout** (ra·go͞o′) *n.:* highly flavored stew.

An Irish cabin.
National Library of Ireland, Dublin.

good table. A child will make two dishes at an entertainment for friends, and when the family dines alone, the fore or hind quarter will make a reasonable dish, and seasoned with a little pepper or salt will be very good boiled on the fourth day, especially in winter. ❹

> ❹
> The speaker "humbly" offers his proposal.
> ? *What horrible plan is he actually proposing?*

I have reckoned upon a medium, that a child just born will weigh twelve pounds, and in a solar year if tolerably nursed increaseth to twenty-eight pounds.

I grant this food will be somewhat dear,[21] and therefore very proper for landlords, who, as they have already devoured[22] most of the parents, seem to have the best title to the children.

Infant's flesh will be in season throughout the year, but more plentiful in March, and a little before and after, for we are told by a grave author,[23] an eminent French physician, that fish being a prolific diet, there are more children born in Roman Catholic countries about nine months after Lent, than at any other season, therefore reckoning a year after Lent, the markets will be more glutted than usual, because the number of popish[24] infants, is at least three to one in this kingdom, and therefore it will have one other collateral advantage by lessening the number of papists among us. ❺

> ❺
> Re-read this paragraph carefully.
> ? *What bias does the speaker of this essay reveal?*

I have already computed the charge of nursing a beggar's child (in which list I reckon all cottagers,[25] laborers, and four-fifths of the farmers) to be about two shillings per annum,[26] rags included, and I believe no gentleman would repine to give ten shillings for the carcass of a good fat child, which, as I have said will make four dishes of excellent nutritive meat, when he hath only some particular friend, or his own family to dine with him. Thus the squire will learn to be a good landlord, and grow popular among his tenants, the mother will have eight shillings net profit, and be fit for work until she produceth another child. ❻

> ❻
> ? *In discussing the economics of his proposal, what kind of appeal is the speaker making?*

Those who are more thrifty (as I must confess the times require) may flay[27] the carcass; the skin of which, artificially[28] dressed, will make admirable gloves for ladies, and summer boots for fine gentlemen.

As to our city of Dublin, shambles[29] may be appointed for this purpose, in the most convenient parts of it, and butchers we may be assured will not be wanting, although I rather recommend buying the children alive, and dressing them hot from the knife, as we do roasting pigs. ❼

> ❼
> ? *When the speaker suggests "dressing" children "hot from the knife," what effect does he expect his word choice to create?*

21. **dear** *adj.:* expensive.
22. **devoured** *v.:* made poor by charging high rents.
23. **grave author:** The French satirist François Rabelais. His work is comic, not "grave."
24. **popish** *adj.:* derogatory term meaning "Roman Catholic."
25. **cottagers** *n. pl.:* tenant farmers.
26. **per annum:** Latin for "by the year"; annually.
27. **flay** *v.:* remove the skin of.
28. **artificially** *adv.:* with great artifice; skillfully.
29. **shambles** *n.:* slaughterhouse.

Vocabulary

glutted (glut′id) *v.* used as *adj.:* overfilled.

A very worthy person, a true lover of his country, and whose virtues I highly esteem, was lately pleased, in discoursing on this matter, to offer a refinement upon my scheme. He said, that many gentlemen of this kingdom, having of late destroyed their deer, he conceived that the want of venison might be well supplied by the bodies of young lads and maidens, not exceeding fourteen years of age, nor under twelve, so great a number of both sexes in every country being now ready to starve, for want of work and service:[30] and these to be disposed of by their parents if alive, or otherwise by their nearest relations. But with due deference to so excellent a friend, and so deserving a patriot, I cannot be altogether in his sentiments, for as to the males, my American acquaintance assured me from frequent experience, that their flesh was generally tough and lean, like that of our schoolboys, by continual exercise, and their taste disagreeable, and to fatten them would not answer the charge. Then as to the females, it would, I think with humble submission,[31] be a loss to the public, because they soon would become breeders themselves: And besides it is not improbable that some scrupulous people might be apt to censure such a practice (although indeed very unjustly) as a little bordering upon cruelty, which, I confess, hath always been with me the strongest objection against any project, how well soever intended.

An Irish peasant.
National Library of Ireland, Dublin.

But in order to justify my friend, he confessed that this expedient was put into his head by the famous Sallmanaazor,[32] a native of the island Formosa, who came from thence to London, above twenty years ago, and in conversation told my friend, that in his country when any young person happened to be put to death, the executioner sold the carcass to persons of quality, as a prime dainty, and that, in his time, the body of a plump girl of fifteen, who was crucified for an attempt to poison the emperor, was sold to his imperial majesty's prime minister of state, and other great mandarins[33] of the court, in joints[34] from the gibbet,[35] at four hundred crowns. Neither indeed can I deny, that if the same use were made of several plump young girls in this town, who, without one single groat to their fortunes, cannot stir abroad without a chair,[36] and appear at the playhouse, and assemblies in foreign fineries, which they never will pay for; the kingdom would not be the worse.

Some persons of a desponding spirit are in great concern about that vast number of poor people, who are aged, diseased, or maimed, and I have been desired to employ my thoughts what course may be taken, to ease the nation of so grievous an encumbrance. But I am not in the least pain upon that matter, because it is very well known, that they are every day dying, and rotting, by cold, and famine, and filth, and vermin,[37] as fast as can be reasonably expected. And as to the younger laborers they are now in almost as

30. **service** *n.:* employment as servants.
31. **with humble submission:** with all due respect to those who hold such opinions.
32. **Sallmanaazor:** George Psalmanazar (c. 1679–1763), a Frenchman who pretended to be from Formosa, an old Portuguese name for Taiwan. His writings were fraudulent.

33. **mandarins** (man′də·rinz) *n. pl.:* officials. The term comes from *mandarim,* the Portuguese word describing high-ranking officials in the Chinese Empire, with which the Portuguese traded.
34. **joints** *n. pl.:* large cuts of meat, including the bone.
35. **gibbet** (jib′it) *n.:* gallows.
36. **chair** *n.:* sedan chair; a covered seat carried by servants.
37. **vermin** *n. pl.:* pests such as lice, fleas, and bedbugs.

Vocabulary

deference (def′ər·əns) *n.:* respect.
scrupulous (skro͞op′yə·ləs) *adj.:* extremely careful in deciding what is right or wrong.
censure (sen′shər) *v.:* condemn.
expedient (ek·spē′dē·ənt) *n.:* convenient means to an end.

hopeful[38] a condition. They cannot get work, and consequently pine away for want of nourishment, to a degree, that if at any time they are accidentally hired to common labor, they have not strength to perform it, and thus the country and themselves are in a fair way[39] of being soon delivered from the evils to come. 8

> 8
> **?** *What other problem does the speaker take up? What is his solution, and how is it similar to his main proposal?*

I have too long digressed, and therefore shall return to my subject. I think the advantages by the proposal which I have made are obvious and many as well as of the highest importance.

For first, as I have already observed, it would greatly lessen the number of papists, with whom we are yearly overrun, being the principal breeders of the nation, as well as our most dangerous enemies, and who stay at home on purpose with a design to deliver the kingdom to the Pretender, hoping to take their advantage by the absence of so many good Protestants,[40] who have chosen rather to leave their country, than stay at home, and pay tithes[41] against their conscience, to an idolatrous Episcopal curate.

Secondly, the poorer tenants will have something valuable of their own, which by law may be made liable to distress,[42] and help to pay their landlord's rent, their corn and cattle being already seized, and money a thing unknown.

Thirdly, whereas the maintenance of an hundred thousand children, from two years old, and upwards, cannot be computed at less than ten shillings apiece per annum, the nation's stock will be thereby increased fifty thousand pounds per annum, besides the profit of a new dish, introduced to the tables of all gentlemen of fortune in the kingdom, who have any refinement in taste, and the money will circulate among ourselves, the goods being entirely of our own growth and manufacture.[43]

Fourthly, the constant breeders, besides the gain of eight shillings sterling per annum, by the sale of their children, will be rid of the charge of maintaining them after the first year.

Fifthly, this food would likewise bring great custom to taverns, where the vintners[44] will certainly be so prudent as to procure the best receipts[45] for dressing it to perfection, and consequently have their houses frequented by all the fine gentlemen, who justly value themselves upon their knowledge in good eating, and a skillful cook, who understands how to oblige his guests will contrive to make it as expensive as they please.

Sixthly, this would be a great inducement to marriage, which all wise nations have either encouraged by rewards, or enforced by laws and penalties. It would increase the care and tenderness of mothers toward their children, when they were sure of a settlement for life to the poor babes, provided in some sort by the public to their annual profit instead of expense, we should soon see an honest emulation[46] among the married women, which of them could bring the fattest child to the market, men would become as fond of their wives, during the time of their pregnancy, as they are now of their mares in foal, their cows in calf, or sows when they are ready to farrow,[47] nor offer to beat or kick them (as is too frequent a practice) for fear of a miscarriage. 9

> 9
> **?** *List the six advantages of the speaker's proposal. Who profits from these "advantages"? Who suffers?*

38. **hopeful** *adj.:* actually, hopeless. Swift is using the word with intentional irony.
39. **are in a fair way:** have a good chance.
40. **good Protestants:** that is, in Swift's view, bad Protestants, because they object to the Church of Ireland's bishops and regard them as "idolatrous."
41. **tithes** (tīthz) n. pl.: monetary gifts to the church equivalent to one tenth of each donor's income.
42. **liable to distress:** that is, the money from the sale of their children may be seized by their landlords.
43. **own growth and manufacture:** homegrown, edible children, not imported ones.
44. **vintners** (vint′nərz) *n. pl.:* wine merchants.
45. **receipts** *n. pl.:* archaic for "recipes."
46. **emulation** (em′yo͞o·lā′shən) *n.:* competition.
47. **farrow** (far′ō) *v.:* produce piglets.

Vocabulary

digressed (di·grest′) *v.:* wandered off the subject.
procure (prō·kyoor′) *v.:* obtain; get.

Many other advantages might be enumerated. For instance, the addition of some thousand carcasses in our exportation of barreled beef. The propagation of swine's flesh, and improvement in the art of making good bacon, so much wanted among us by the great destruction of pigs, too frequent at our tables, which are no way comparable in taste, or magnificence to a well-grown, fat yearling child, which roasted whole will make a considerable figure at a Lord Mayor's feast, or any other public entertainment. But this, and many others I omit being studious of brevity.

Supposing that one thousand families in this city, would be constant customers for infants' flesh, besides others who might have it at merry meetings, particularly weddings and christenings, I compute that Dublin would take off annually about twenty thousand carcasses, and the rest of the kingdom (where probably they will be sold somewhat cheaper) the remaining eighty thousand.

I can think of no one objection, that will possibly be raised against this proposal, unless it should be urged that the number of people will be thereby much lessened in the kingdom. This I freely own, and it was indeed one principal design in offering it to the world. I desire the reader will observe, that I calculate my remedy for this one individual kingdom of Ireland, and for no other that ever was, is, or, I think, ever can be upon earth. ⑩

> ⑩
> ? *What objection does the speaker anticipate? How does he answer this objection?*

Therefore let no man talk to me of other expedients:[48] *Of taxing our absentees[49] at five shillings a pound; of using neither clothes, nor household furniture, except what is of our own growth and manufacture; of utterly rejecting the materials and instruments that promote foreign luxury; of curing the expensiveness of pride, vanity, idleness, and gaming[50] in our women; of introducing a vein of parsimony,[51] prudence, and temperance; of learning to love our country, wherein we differ even from Laplanders, and the inhabitants of Topinamboo;[52] of quitting our animosities, and factions,[53] nor act any longer like the Jews, who were murdering one another at the very moment their city[54] was taken; of being a little cautious not to sell our country and consciences for nothing; of teaching landlords to have at least one degree of mercy toward their tenants. Lastly of putting a spirit of honesty, industry, and skill into our shopkeepers, who, if a resolution could now be taken to buy only our native goods, would immediately unite to cheat and exact[55] upon us in the price, the measure, and the goodness, nor could ever yet be brought to make one fair proposal of just dealing, though often and earnestly invited to it.* ⑪

> ⑪
> This italicized section is a list of ideas that Swift sees as reasonable and actually proposed for Ireland.
> ? *Determine where each separate idea begins, and then paraphrase each idea.*

Therefore I repeat, let no man talk to me of these and the like expedients, till he hath at least a glimpse of hope, that there will ever be some hearty and sincere attempt to put them in practice.

---

48. **other expedients:** At one time or another, Swift had advocated all these measures for the relief of Ireland, but they were all ignored by the government. This section was italicized in all editions printed during Swift's lifetime to indicate that Swift made these proposals sincerely rather than ironically.
49. **absentees** *n. pl.:* English landowners who refused to live on their Irish property.
50. **gaming** *v.* used as *n.:* gambling.
51. **parsimony** (pär′sə·mō′nē) *n.:* thriftiness; economy.
52. **Topinamboo:** Swift is referring to a region of Brazil populated by native peoples collectively called the Tupinambá. Here Swift suggests that if Brazilian peoples and Laplanders can love their seemingly inhospitable lands, the Irish should love Ireland.
53. **factions** *n. pl.:* political groups that work against the interests of other such groups or against the main body of government.
54. **their city:** Jerusalem, which the Roman emperor Titus destroyed in A.D. 70 while Jewish factions fought one another.
55. **exact** *v.:* force payment.

Vocabulary

brevity (brev′ə·tē) *n.:* briefness; shortness.

animosities (an′ə·mäs′ə·tēz) *n. pl.:* hostilities; violent hatreds or resentments.

Judy O'Donnel's "home" under the bridge at Donnbeg, Clare, Ireland (1849).

The Illustrated London News Picture Library.

But as to myself, having been wearied out for many years with offering vain, idle, visionary thoughts, and at length utterly despairing of success, I fortunately fell upon this proposal, which as it is wholly new, so it hath something solid and real, of no expense and little trouble, full in our own power, and whereby we can incur no danger in disobliging[56] England. For this kind of commodity will not bear exportation, the flesh being of too tender a consistence, to admit a long continuance in salt, although perhaps I could name a country,[57] which would be glad to eat up our whole nation without it.

After all I am not so violently bent upon my own opinion, as to reject any offer, proposed by wise men, which shall be found equally innocent, cheap, easy, and effectual. But before something of that kind shall be advanced in contradiction to my scheme, and offering a better, I desire the author, or authors will be pleased maturely to consider two points. First, as things now stand, how they will be able to find food and raiment for a hundred thousand useless mouths and backs. And secondly, there being a round million of creatures in human figure, throughout this kingdom, whose whole subsistence[58] put into a common stock would leave them in debt two millions of pounds sterling, adding those who are beggars by profession to the bulk of farmers, cottagers, and laborers, with their wives and children, who are beggars in effect; I desire those politicians, who dislike my overture, and may perhaps be so bold to attempt an answer, that they will first ask the parents of these mortals, whether they would not at this day think it a great happiness to have been sold for food at a year old, in the manner I prescribe, and thereby have avoided such a perpetual scene of misfortunes, as they have since gone through, by the oppression of landlords, the impossibility of paying rent without money or trade, the want of common sustenance, with neither house nor clothes to cover them from inclemencies of weather, and the most inevitable prospect of entailing[59] the like, or great miseries, upon their breed forever.

I profess in the sincerity of my heart that I have not the least personal interest in endeavoring to promote this necessary work, having no other motive than the public good of my country, by advancing our trade, providing for infants, relieving the poor, and giving some pleasure to the rich. I have no children, by which I can propose to get a single penny; the youngest being nine years old, and my wife past childbearing. ⓬ ■

⓬ The speaker concludes with an ethical appeal to show that he is fair and trustworthy and has no ulterior motive.

? *Identify the ironies in this concluding paragraph.*

56. **disobliging** *v.* used as *n.:* offending.

57. **a country:** England.

58. **whole subsistence:** all their possessions.

59. **entailing** *v.* used as *n.:* passing on to the next generation.

Top of the Food Chain

T. Coraghessan Boyle

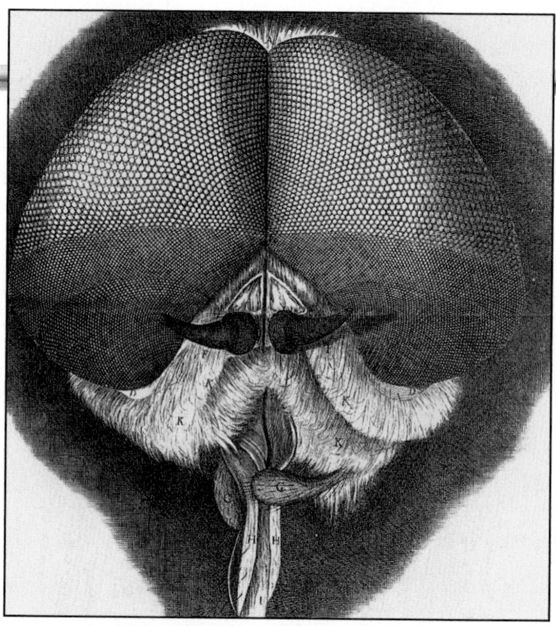

Eye of a Fly by Robert Hooke, from *Micrographia* (1665).

Rare Books and Manuscripts Division. The New York Public Library. Astor, Lenox and Tilden Foundations.

The thing was, we had a little problem with the insect vector[1] there, and believe me, your tamer stuff, your Malathion and pyrethrum and the rest of the so-called environmentally safe products,[2] didn't begin to make a dent in it, not a dent, I mean it was utterly useless—we might as well have been spraying Chanel No. 5 for all the good it did. And you've got to realize these people were literally covered with insects day and night—and the fact that they hardly wore any clothes just compounded the problem. Picture if you can, gentlemen, a naked little two-year-old boy so black with flies and mosquitoes it looks like he's wearing long johns, or the young mother so racked with the malarial shakes she can't even lift a Diet Coke to her lips—it was pathetic, just pathetic, like something out of the Dark Ages. . . . Well, anyway, the decision was made to go with DDT.[3] In the short term. Just to get the situation under control, you understand.

Yes, that's right, Senator, *DDT:* Dichlorodiphenyltrichloroethane.

Yes, I'm well aware of that fact, sir. But just because *we* banned it domestically, under pressure from the bird-watching contingent and the hopheads down at the EPA, it doesn't necessarily follow that the rest of the world—especially the developing world—was about to jump on the bandwagon. And that's the key word here, Senator: developing. You've got to realize this is Borneo we're talking about here, not Port Townsend or Enumclaw. These people don't know from square one about sanitation, disease control, pest eradication. It rains a hundred and twenty inches a year, minimum.[4] They dig up roots in the jungle. They've still got headhunters along the Rajang River, for god's sake.

And please don't forget they *asked* us to come in there, practically begged us—and not only the World Health Organization but the Sultan of Brunei and the government in Sarawak too. We did what we could to accommodate them and reach our objective in the shortest period of time and by the most direct and effective means.

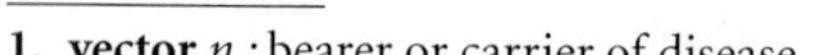

1. **vector** *n.:* bearer or carrier of disease.
2. **Malathion** (mal′ə•thī′än′) **and pyrethrum** (pī•reth′rəm): insecticides made from organic substances. Though they are less toxic than synthetic insecticides, their safety is still debated.
3. **DDT:** synthetic compound first discovered to be an insecticide in 1939. Widely used during World War II, DDT was later found to cause such toxic effects in other animal populations that its use was severely restricted in the United States in 1972.
4. **hundred and twenty inches . . . minimum:** In comparison, the average yearly rainfall in most of the United States is less than half this figure.

We went to the air. Obviously. And no one could have foreseen the consequences, no one, not even if we'd gone out and generated a hundred environmental impact statements—it was just one of those things, a freak occurrence, and there's no defense against that. Not that I know of, anyway. . . .

Caterpillars? Yes, Senator, that's correct. That was the first sign: caterpillars.

But let me backtrack a minute here. You see, out in the bush they have these roofs made of thatched palm leaves—you'll see them in the towns too, even in Bintulu or Brunei—and they're really pretty effective, you'd be surprised. A hundred and twenty inches of rain, they've got to figure a way to keep it out of the hut, and for centuries, this was it. Palm leaves. Well, it was about a month after we sprayed for the final time and I'm sitting at my desk in the trailer thinking about the drainage project at Kuching, enjoying the fact that for the first time in maybe a year I'm not smearing mosquitoes all over the back of my neck, when there's a knock at the door. It's this elderly gentleman, tattooed from head to toe, dressed only in a pair of running shorts—they love those shorts, by the way, the shiny material and the tight machine stitching, the whole country, men and women both, they can't get enough of them. . . . Anyway, he's the headman of the local village and he's very excited, something about the roofs—*atap,* they call them. That's all he can say, *atap, atap,* over and over again.

It's raining, of course. It's always raining. So I shrug into my rain slicker, start up the 4 × 4, and go have a look. Sure enough, all the *atap* roofs are collapsing, not only in his village but throughout the target area. The people are all huddled there in their running shorts, looking pretty miserable, and one after another the roofs keep falling in, it's bewildering, and gradually I realize the headman's diatribe has

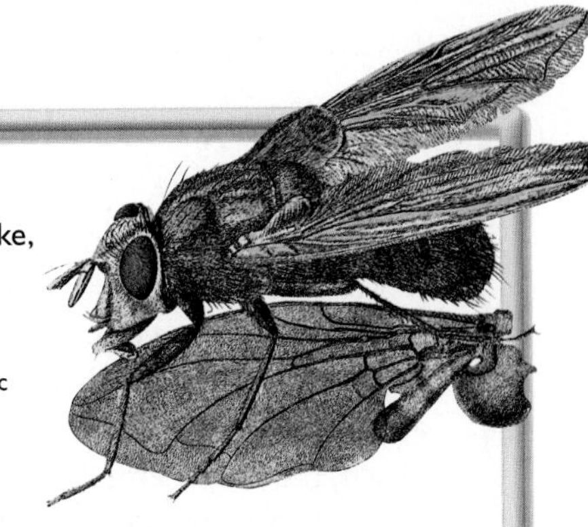

Blue Fly by Robert Hooke, from *Micrographia* (1665).

Rare Books and Manuscripts Division. The New York Public Library. Astor, Lenox and Tilden Foundations.

begun to feature a new term I was unfamiliar with at the time—the word for caterpillar, as it turns out, in the Iban dialect. But who was to make the connection between three passes with the crop duster and all these staved-in roofs?

Our people finally sorted it out a couple weeks later. The chemical, which, by the way, cut down the number of mosquitoes exponentially, had the unfortunate side effect of killing off this little wasp—I've got the scientific name for it somewhere in my report here, if you're interested—that preyed on a type of caterpillar that in turn ate palm leaves. Well, with the wasps gone, the caterpillars hatched out with nothing to keep them in check and chewed the roofs to pieces, which was unfortunate, we admit it, and we had a real cost overrun on replacing those roofs with tin . . . but the people were happier, I think, in the long run, because, let's face it, no matter how tightly you weave those palm leaves, they're just not going to keep the water out like tin. Of course, nothing's perfect, and we had a lot of complaints about the rain drumming on the panels, people unable to sleep, and what-have-you. . . .

Yes, sir, that's correct—the flies were next.

Well, you've got to understand the magnitude of the fly problem in Borneo, there's nothing like it here to compare it with, except maybe a garbage strike in New York. Every minute of every day you've got flies everywhere, up your nose, in your mouth, your ears, your eyes, flies in your rice, your Coke, your Singapore sling, and your gin rickey. It's enough to drive you to distraction, not to mention the diseases these things carry, from dysentery to typhoid to cholera and back round the loop again. And once the mosquito population was down, the flies seemed to breed up to fill in the gap—Borneo wouldn't be Borneo without some damned insect blackening the air.

Of course, this was before our people had tracked down the problem with the caterpillars and the wasps and all of that, and so we figured we'd had a big success with the mosquitoes, why not a series of ground sweeps, mount a fogger in the back of a Suzuki Brat, and sanitize the huts, not to mention the open sewers, which as you know are nothing but a breeding ground for flies, chiggers, and biting insects of every sort. At least it was an error of commission rather than omission. At least we were trying.

I watched the flies go down myself. One day they were so thick in the trailer I couldn't even *find* my paperwork, let alone attempt to get through it, and the next they were collecting on the windows, bumbling around like they were drunk. A day later they were gone. Just like that. From a million flies in the trailer to none. . . .

Well, no one could have foreseen that, Senator.

The geckos ate the flies, yes. You're all familiar with geckos, I assume, gentlemen? These are the lizards you've seen during your trips to Hawaii, very colorful, patrolling the houses for roaches and flies, almost like pets, but of course they're wild animals, never lose sight of that, and just about as unsanitary as anything I can think of, except maybe flies.

Yes, well don't forget, sir, we're viewing this with twenty-twenty hindsight, but at the time no one gave a thought to geckos or what they ate—they were just another fact of life in the tropics. Mosquitoes, lizards, scorpions, leeches—you name it, they've got it. When the flies began piling up on the windowsills like drift, naturally the geckos feasted on them, stuffing themselves till they looked like sausages crawling up the walls. Where before they moved so fast you could never be sure you'd seen them, now they waddled across the floor, laid around in the corners, clung to the air vents like magnets—and even then no one paid much attention to them till they started turning belly-up in the streets. Believe me, we confirmed a lot of things there about the buildup of these products[5] as you move up the food chain and the efficacy—or lack thereof—of certain methods, no doubt about that. . . .

The cats? That's where it got sticky, really sticky. You see, nobody really lost any sleep over a pile of dead lizards—though we did tests routinely and the tests confirmed what we'd expected, that is, the product had been concentrated in the geckos because of the number of contaminated flies they consumed. But lizards are one thing and cats are another. These people really have an affection for their cats—no house, no hut, no matter how primitive, is without at least a couple of them. Mangy-looking things, long-legged and scrawny, maybe, not at all the sort of animal you'd see here, but there it was: They loved their cats. Because the cats were functional, you understand—without them, the place would have been swimming in rodents inside of a week.

You're right there, Senator, yes—that's exactly what happened.

You see, the cats had a field day with these feeble geckos—you can imagine, if any of you have ever owned a cat, the kind of joy these

5. **these products:** insecticides.

animals must have experienced to see their nemesis, this ultra-quick lizard, and it's just barely creeping across the floor like a bug. Well, to make a long story short, the cats ate up every dead and dying gecko in the country, from snout to tail, and then the cats began to die . . . which to my mind would have been no great loss if it wasn't for the rats. Suddenly there were rats everywhere—you couldn't drive down the street without running over half-a-dozen of them at a time. They fouled the grain supplies, fell in the wells and died, bit infants as they slept in their cradles. But that wasn't the worst, not by a long shot. No, things really went down the tube after that. Within the month we were getting scattered reports of bubonic plague, and of course we tracked them all down and made sure the people got a round of treatment with antibiotics, but still we lost a few and the rats kept coming. . . .

It was my plan, yes. I was brainstorming one night, rats scuttling all over the trailer like something out of a cheap horror film, the villagers in a panic over the threat of the plague and the stream of nonstop hysterical reports from the interior—people were turning black, swelling up and bursting, that sort of thing—well, as I say, I came up with a plan, a stopgap, not perfect, not cheap, but at this juncture, I'm sure you'll agree, something had to be implemented.

We wound up going as far as Australia for some of the cats, cleaning out the SPCA facilities and what-have-you, though we rounded most of them up in Indonesia and Singapore—approximately fourteen thousand in all. And yes, it cost us—cost us upfront purchase money and aircraft fuel and pilots' overtime and all the rest of it—but we really felt there was no alternative. It was like all nature had turned against us.

And yet still, all things considered, we made a lot of friends for the U.S.A. the day we dropped those cats, and you should have seen them, gentlemen, the little parachutes and harnesses we'd tricked up, fourteen thousand of them, cats in every color of the rainbow, cats with one ear, no ears, half a tail, three-legged cats, cats that could have taken pride of show in Springfield, Massachusetts, and all of them twirling down out of the sky like great big oversized snowflakes. . . .

It was something. It was really something.

Of course, you've all seen the reports. There were other factors we hadn't counted on, adverse conditions in the paddies and manioc fields[6]—we don't to this day know what predatory species were inadvertently killed off by the initial sprayings, it's just a mystery—but the weevils[7] and whatnot took a pretty heavy toll on the crops that year, and by the time we dropped the cats, well—the people were pretty hungry, and I suppose it was inevitable that we lost a good proportion of them right then and there. But we've got a CARE program going there now and something hit the rat population—we still don't know what, a virus, we think—and the geckos, they tell me, are making a comeback.

So what I'm saying is it could be worse, and to every cloud a silver lining, wouldn't you agree, gentlemen?

---

6. **paddies and manioc fields:** Paddies, or rice paddies, are small, flooded fields used to grow rice in eastern and southern Asia. Manioc, also called cassava, is a kind of tuber cultivated in tropical areas.
7. **weevils** *n. pl:* snouted beetles extremely destructive to rice and grain crops.

Response and Analysis

Reading Check

1. Why does the speaker of *A Modest Proposal* think the food he proposes is "very proper for landlords"?
2. Why does the speaker reject the idea of selling and eating twelve- to fourteen-year-olds?
3. About midway in the pamphlet, the speaker lists the advantages of his proposal. What are the six principal advantages?
4. Describe the one objection that the speaker anticipates to his proposal.

Thinking Critically

5. What is **ironic** in Swift's use of the word *modest* to describe his proposal? (In what sense is he using the word *modest*?) Why does the speaker express the hope that his plan "will not be liable to the least objection" just before he introduces it?
6. How would you state the **purpose** of this essay? Whom or what is Swift trying to reform?
7. How would you describe the **tone** of this essay? What evidence supports your interpretation?
8. Describe the speaker's real meaning when he asserts that England will not mind if Ireland kills and eats its babies. What element of **satire** is evident here?
9. Near the end of the pamphlet, the speaker lists "other expedients" that might help lessen the present distress in Ireland. Some of these options are very constructive. Why, then, does the speaker brush aside these ideas for reform in favor of this horrible proposal?
10. Find places in the proposal where the speaker uses **logical appeals** to support his suggestions. You may want to consult your reading notes.
11. Find sentences in which the speaker uses **ethical appeals** by describing himself favorably and claiming to possess virtues that—considering the nature of his proposal—he could not possibly have. (Check your reading notes.)
12. The speaker also uses **emotional appeals** to support his suggestions—in particular, ironic word choices that arouse strong feelings by equating human beings with animals. For example, early in the essay he speaks of a child as "dropped from its dam," language usually used only when speaking of animals. Where else does the speaker use emotionally loaded words that equate babies or their parents with animals? (Check your reading notes.)
13. How is Boyle's satire in "Top of the Food Chain" (see the ***Connection*** on page 590) similar to and different from Swift's proposal? In your response, consider the content, purpose, and language techniques used in each text.
14. What other human disasters resulting from bureaucratic incompetence around the world could be targets for another "modest proposal"?

Extending and Evaluating

15. Is Swift's **irony** effective in *A Modest Proposal,* or does it risk being taken seriously by readers and arousing nothing more than disgust or outrage at the author? Explain your thinking.

Literary Skills Analyze verbal irony, diction, and connotations.

Reading Skills Analyze persuasive techniques.

Writing Skills Write an ironic proposal. Generate research topics.

Vocabulary Skills Compare word meanings.

INTERNET

Projects and Activities

Keyword: LE7 12-4

WRITING

A New Modest Proposal

Swift approached the subjects of corruption in England and poverty in Ireland from the point of view of a benevolent humanitarian. Pretend you are a modern social worker, educator, environmentalist, or military advisor to the president. Attack an evil you see in the world by writing an ironic **proposal** for its solution—a proposal so outrageous that readers will see at once the severity of the problem. Remember that some readers may miss your irony and attack you for insensitivity, just as some people attacked Swift. To lessen this possibility, make your moral outrage clear by the sheer outrageousness of your exaggerations.

Swift Investigation

This essay is rich in possibilities for research. Review the essay and the footnotes that accompany it. Review Swift's biography. Then, make a list of topics that you might investigate for a **research paper.** Remember that when you find a research topic that interests you, you must make sure your topic is narrow enough to be handled in a paper of about seven to ten pages. For example, suppose you want to investigate Irish history. You might start with the topic "Britain and the Irish problem." You might then narrow that broad topic to these more manageable topics:

- how Britain came to colonize Ireland
- absent landlords in Irish history
- British and Irish relations today

Vocabulary Development

Intensity Scale

sustenance, expedient, glutted, digressed, deference, procure, scrupulous, brevity, censure, animosities

You can reinforce your understanding of a word by comparing it to other words with similar meanings. One way to compare words is to arrange them on a scale that shows high and low intensities. Make an intensity scale like the one below for each remaining Vocabulary word listed above. Note that the Vocabulary words needn't necessarily go in the "High Intensity" column.

High Intensity	Low Intensity
scrupulous	careful

Literary Focus

Connotations

Diction, or word choice, is especially important in **persuasive writing.** Swift is particularly skillful in choosing words with strong **connotations**—that is, words loaded with strong feelings, associations, or even judgments. Some of Swift's loaded words follow.

savages	beggars	filth
male and female	rags	idolatrous
popish infants	breeders	carcasses

In each instance, another word or term could have been chosen to create a different, less harsh effect. For example, *male* and *female*—as opposed to *man* and *woman*—make us think of animals, not human beings, which is Swift's intention.

1. Find the places in the text where the words listed above are used. What is the emotional effect of each word choice?
2. What tamer or more positive words could have been used to create different emotional effects?

Vocabulary Development

Analyzing Word Analogies

An **analogy** is a similarity or likeness between two things that are unlike in other ways. When you state an analogy, you compare two things to show how they are alike. A **word analogy** is a formally written statement that compares two pairs of words.

Reading word analogies. A word analogy depends upon the relationship between the first pair of words being the same as the relationship between the second pair of words. For example, *cool* and *chilly* have a synonymous relationship to each other, just as *mad* and *angry* have. Here's how a word analogy using these words is written:

COOL : CHILLY :: mad : angry

The colon (:) stands for the phrase "is related to." The double colon (::) between the two pairs of words stands for the phrase "in the same way that." Here are two ways to read the analogy:

COOL [is related to] CHILLY [in the same way that] *mad* [is related to] *angry*.

COOL is to CHILLY as *mad* is to *angry*.

Identifying relationships. Two types of relationships frequently expressed in word analogies are **synonyms** and **antonyms.** The example used above (COOL : CHILLY :: mad : angry) expresses a synonymous relationship. The following word analogy expresses an antonymous, or opposite, relationship.

SOILED : CLEAN :: careless : careful

Soiled is the opposite of *clean,* just as *careless* is the opposite of *careful.*

Vocabulary Skills
Analyze word analogies.

Solving word analogies. Use the following steps to solve an analogy question:

1. Identify the relationship between the capitalized pair of words. (Note also the part of speech of each word.)
2. Look for the same relationship and the same parts of speech in the pairs of words in the answer choices. Eliminate those that do not have that relationship.
3. Choose the pair of words whose relationship and word order match those of the capitalized pair.

PRACTICE

For each of the following items, choose the pair of words that expresses a relationship that is most similar to the relationship between the pair of capitalized words. Write the letter of your answer, and identify the type of relationship expressed in each analogy.

1. MELANCHOLY : SAD ::
   - **a.** dismayed : happy
   - **b.** awkward : silly
   - **c.** cluttered : tidy
   - **d.** jubilant : cheerful
2. PROLIFIC : FERTILE ::
   - **a.** foolish : intense
   - **b.** courageous : brave
   - **c.** agitated : calm
   - **d.** sensible : sensitive
3. CENSURE : PRAISE ::
   - **a.** change : alter
   - **b.** cautious : careless
   - **c.** wealthy : prosperous
   - **d.** deny : admit
4. CHARITY : PITILESSNESS ::
   - **a.** order : chaos
   - **b.** emotion : happiness
   - **c.** select : choose
   - **d.** acceptable : forbidden

Alexander Pope

(1688–1744)

Alexander Pope, the most important poet of the early eighteenth century, was a child prodigy. As a very little boy, he later admitted, he "lisped in numbers." That is, he could speak in meter even before he could pronounce English properly. Such a talented youth would ordinarily be educated at Cambridge or Oxford. Pope's family was Roman Catholic, however, and therefore prohibited from attending these universities, as well as from voting, from holding public office, and even from practicing their religion.

Pope's father, a retired linen merchant, could afford to educate his son at home, which was perhaps the best place for Pope since his health was very delicate. Early in life he contracted a kind of tuberculosis that stunted his growth and disfigured his body, so that eventually his servants had to lace him into a canvas brace before he could sit upright. Since he continually suffered pains in his head, bones, and joints, it is no wonder he spoke of his life as "this long disease."

In spite of all of this, Pope led a remarkably busy and productive life. When he was twenty-three, he published *An Essay on Criticism,* a poem inspired in part by the Latin poet Horace's *Art of Poetry.* At twenty-four, he published a miniature classical epic, *The Rape of the Lock.* During his thirties he translated into English two enormous Greek epics, Homer's *Iliad* and, with the help of two assistants, Homer's *Odyssey.* In these works, Pope was not at all limited by his classical models, but used them to make works that were fresh and original. For this reason, he is sometimes referred to as a neoclassical (that is, new classical) poet.

Pope's early, brilliant successes inspired envy in lesser writers, who ridiculed him. To defend himself he turned to satire, a kind of writing highly suited to his temperament. The great satires of Pope's maturity include *The Dunciad* (1728, enlarged and revised in 1743), which attacks dull, uninteresting writers of all kinds and shows the forces of stupidity, ignorance, and folly taking over the world; and the *Moral Essays* (1731–1735), which pass judgment on certain immoral men and women as well as on very rich people who lack common sense and good taste.

As a man Pope was, and still is, both loved and hated. In his lifetime and long after, he had a reputation for cruelty, malice, and ill nature. But Pope had a large circle of friends, men and women, including some of the best writers of the day, who found him good-natured, generous, and brilliant in conversation. His agreeable manners, his large expressive eyes, and his way of dressing elegantly in bright colors charmed his friends. Pope became rich and famous; as for the people who raged against him, most of them are remembered today only because they disliked Alexander Pope.

Alexander Pope and Dog Bounce (detail) (c. 1718) attributed to Jonathan Richardson.
Hagley Hall, Worcestershire, England.

Before You Read

Heroic Couplets ♦ *from* An Essay on Man

Make the Connection

For the writers of Pope's time, the purpose of poetry was both to please and to instruct. The clarity, elegance, and compression of Pope's style ensured that his works would more than fulfill this ideal. With the exception of Shakespeare, Pope is probably the most widely quoted writer in English literature, in part because his rhyming couplets are so pleasing and easy to remember.

Literary Focus

Antithesis

Pope habitually expresses himself in antitheses. An **antithesis** (an•tith'ə•sis) uses parallel structure to present a balanced contrast: "Give me liberty, or give me death." ("Give me liberty, or kill me" fails as an antithesis because it isn't parallel or balanced.) By compressing elements of similarity and difference, antithesis helps make a statement more forceful and (often) more memorable.

> **Antithesis** is a contrast of ideas expressed in a grammatically balanced statement.
>
> *For more on Antithesis, see the Handbook of Literary and Historical Terms.*

Reading Skills

Identifying the Writer's Stance

Pope's purpose was to uplift his audience as well as delight them, and his poetry reflects his moral and social values as well as his literary brilliance. He uses the **heroic couplet** structure (two rhyming lines of iambic pentameter) to concisely and explicitly express his views on subjects such as human nature, proper education, and good writing. As you read Pope's couplets, try to rephrase his views in your own words, and then think about what his beliefs and values reveal about him as an individual and as a representative of the age in which he lived.

The Author and His Publisher (1784) by Thomas Rowlandson. Gray wash and watercolor over pencil on laid paper.

Yale Center for British Art, Paul Mellon Collection, USA. The Bridgeman Art Library.

Literary Skills Understand antithesis.

Reading Skills Identify the writer's stance.

Pope is the greatest master of the ***heroic couplet,*** *so-called because both he and his predecessor John Dryden used this form in their translations of the epic poems of antiquity. Each heroic couplet consists of two rhymed lines of* ***iambic pentameter.*** *(For variety, Pope occasionally introduces a* ***triplet.****) Many couplets express a thought in a complete sentence—such a couplet is called* ***closed:***

> *Trust not yourself; but your defects to know,*
> *Make use of every friend—and every foe.*

Although this couplet from An Essay on Criticism *is part of a long and carefully organized explanation, it still makes good sense when it is plucked out of its context and allowed to stand by itself. Yet removing couplets from the poems in which they are embedded is dangerous, because it may lead us to think of the poems as strings of beads that can be easily broken apart. In reality, Pope's couplets are so carefully arranged into verse paragraphs that they are more like the forged links of an iron chain than separable units.*

Heroic Couplets

Alexander Pope

1 Music resembles poetry: in each
Are nameless graces[1] which no methods[2] teach,
And which a master hand alone can reach.
—*An Essay on Criticism,* lines 143–145

2 A little learning is a dangerous thing;
Drink deep, or taste not the Pierian[3] spring.
—*An Essay on Criticism,* lines 215–216

3 Be not the first by whom the new are tried,
Nor yet the last to lay the old aside.
—*An Essay on Criticism,* lines 335–336

4 True ease in writing comes from art, not chance,
As those move easiest who have learned to dance.
—*An Essay on Criticism,* lines 362–363

5 Be thou the first true merit to befriend;
His praise is lost, who stays till all commend.
—*An Essay on Criticism,* lines 474–475

6 Good nature and good sense must ever join;
To err is human, to forgive, divine.
—*An Essay on Criticism,* lines 524–525

1. **nameless graces:** pleasing passages that cannot be explained.
2. **methods** *n. pl.:* instruction books showing how to write poems.
3. **Pierian** (pī·ir′ē·ən): an allusion to the Muses, Greek goddesses of the arts and literature. The Muses were said to live in a district of Greece called Pieria.

7 Hope springs eternal in the human breast:
Man never is, but always to be blest.
—*An Essay on Man,* Epistle I, lines 95–96

8 'Tis education forms the common mind,
Just as the twig is bent, the tree's inclined.
—*Moral Essays,* Epistle I, lines 149–150

9 But when to mischief mortals bend their will,
How soon they find fit instruments of ill!
—*The Rape of the Lock,* Canto III, lines 125–126

10 Satire's my weapon, but I'm too discreet
To run amuck, and tilt[4] at all I meet.
—*Imitations of Horace, Satire I,* Book II, lines 69–70

4. **tilt** *v.:* charge at or thrust a weapon toward an opponent.

View Across Greenwich Park Toward London (detail) (18th century) by Jean Rigaud.
Roy Miles Gallery, London.

An Essay on Man is Pope's long (1,304 lines) philosophical poem, published when he was forty-five. A lifetime of reading, in both English and foreign languages, contributed to its composition. The poem is concerned not only with "man," by which Pope means the whole human race, but with the entire universe as well. It's important to know that the ideas in the poem are not merely the private notions of Pope and his friends, but that they come from many authors, including Plato, Aristotle, St. Thomas Aquinas, Dante, Erasmus, Shakespeare, Bacon, and Milton.

from An Essay on Man

Alexander Pope

Know then thyself,° presume not God to scan;°
The proper study of mankind is man.
Placed on this isthmus of a middle state,°
A being darkly wise, and rudely great:
With too much knowledge for the skeptic° side,
With too much weakness for the Stoic's pride,°
He hangs between; in doubt to act, or rest;
In doubt to deem himself a god, or beast;
In doubt his mind or body to prefer;
Born but to die, and reasoning but to err;
Alike in ignorance, his reason such,
Whether he thinks too little, or too much:
Chaos of thought and passion, all confused;
Still° by himself abused, or disabused;°
Created half to rise, and half to fall;
Great lord of all things, yet a prey to all;
Sole judge of truth, in endless error hurled:
The glory, jest, and riddle of the world!

1. Know . . . thyself: moral precept of Socrates and other ethical philosophers. **scan** *v.:* pry into; speculate about.

3. middle state: that is, having the rational intellect of angels and the physical body of beasts.

5. skeptic *n.* used as *adj.:* The ancient Skeptics doubted that humans can gain accurate knowledge of anything. They emphasized the limitations of human knowledge.

6. Stoic's pride: The ancient Stoics' ideal was a calm acceptance of life and an indifference to both pain and pleasure. Stoics are called proud because they refused to recognize human limitations.

14. still *adv.:* always; continually. **disabused** *v.:* undeceived.

Alexander Pope. Portrait in oil.

Bryn Mawr College, Bryn Mawr, Pennsylvania.

Response and Analysis

Heroic Couplets
from An Essay on Man

Thinking Critically

1. What explicit value or point of view does Pope directly express in each of the heroic couplets? **Paraphrase** or express each couplet in your own words. You may want to refer to your reading notes.
2. Think of some examples of how a little learning could be a dangerous thing (couplet 2).
3. Pope habitually uses **antithesis** to focus and clarify his meaning. List all the antitheses you can find in the heroic couplets. What parallel elements can you find?
4. In almost every sentence in this excerpt from *An Essay on Man,* Pope says something flattering about the human race, only to follow it with something critical. What characteristics does he think we should be proud of? ashamed of?
5. In what ways do you think human beings could be seen as the "glory" of this world? as its "jest"? as its "riddle" (line 18 of the *Essay*)?

Literary Skills Analyze antithesis and epigrams.

Reading Skills Analyze the writer's stance.

Writing Skills Write an essay comparing literary works.

Listening and Speaking Skills Present an oral interpretation of a poem.

Extending and Evaluating

6. Do you disagree with any of Pope's opinions and pronouncements—in the couplets or in the *Essay*? Explain.
7. Which opinions of Pope's do you think are most true or most valuable—even in the world today?

WRITING

Pope Versus Shakespeare

In an **essay,** compare Pope's view of humanity with the view expressed by William Shakespeare's Hamlet in the following lines:

> What a piece of work is a man! how noble in reason! how infinite in faculties! in form and moving how express and admirable! in action how like an angel! in apprehension how like a god! the beauty of the world, the paragon of animals!
>
> —*Hamlet,* Act II, Scene 2

Conclude your analysis by stating which point of view is closer to your own. Cite a few reasons to support your response.

LISTENING AND SPEAKING

Read Aloud: A Pope Performance

Present "Two Minutes of Pope" to the class. Read a selection of couplets aloud to feel the effect of **antitheses, rhymes,** and **alliteration.** Be sure to practice alternative readings before you make your presentation.

Literary Focus

Epigrams

Pope had a dog named Bounce, one of whose puppies he gave to his friend Frederick, Prince of Wales, who lived in Kew. Pope had an epigram engraved on the puppy's collar. An **epigram** is a short poem, often satirical, that ends in a witticism or clever turn of thought. To whom do you think the epigram is addressed? (Don't say "the prince," because surely the prince knows his own dog.)

Epigram Engraved on the Collar of a Dog

I am his Highness's dog at Kew;
Pray tell me sir, whose dog are you?

Before You Read

from The Rape of the Lock

Make the Connection

Quickwrite

If you look at the newspapers and magazines displayed at a supermarket checkout, you'll probably agree that many Americans like to read about rich and famous people—those who have made it big in politics, sports, business, and entertainment. Many readers find it especially interesting to read about the trivial problems and petty quarrels of these well-known people. *The Rape of the Lock* tells the story of a petty quarrel among members of the eighteenth-century nobility. Take a few minutes to think about why people today (and people in the eighteenth century) are fascinated by the lives of the rich and famous. Has the appeal of "celebrity gossip" changed very much since Pope's day? Why or why not? Write down your thoughts.

Literary Focus

Mock Epic

The Rape of the Lock is a **mock epic.** Its comedy arises from the discrepancy between its trivial subject matter (the snipping of a curl) and its grandiose treatment. (In mock epics, cracked teacups become major catastrophes.) Pope achieves this comic discrepancy by putting all the traditional devices found in serious epics (like Homer's *Iliad,* Virgil's *Aeneid,* and Milton's *Paradise Lost*) into a tame, domestic context where little is at risk. For instance, the classical epics all have gods and goddesses who intervene in human affairs. Following these models, Pope creates tiny, airy spirits (called "sylphs") who try, in vain, to prevent the "rape" of Belinda's curl. Similarly, Pope includes a hotly contested game of cards and an outburst of temper to satisfy the requirement that every epic contain battles.

A **mock epic** is a comic narrative poem, written in dignified language, that parodies the serious epic genre by treating a trivial subject in a lofty, grand manner.

For more on Mock Epic, see the Handbook of Literary and Historical Terms.

Background

The title of Pope's comic masterpiece means "the violent theft of a lock of hair." The poem is based on a real incident. The lock in question belonged to a certain rich and fashionable young lady named Arabella Fermor. The theft in question was committed by a certain rich and fashionable young man named Robert, Lord Petre. When Robert snipped a curl from Arabella's hairdo, he set off a quarrel between the Fermor and the Petre families. Had the two families been less sensible, their row might have escalated into bitter hatred. As it turned out, the feud subsided into laughter—thanks to Alexander Pope.

Literary Skills Understand the characteristics of a mock epic.

Vocabulary Development

exulting (eg•zult'iŋ) *v.* used as *adj.:* rejoicing.

repast (ri•past') *n.:* meal.

desist (di•zist') *v.:* stop.

recesses (rē'ses•iz) *n. pl.:* secluded or hidden places.

titillating (tit''l•āt'iŋ) *v.* used as *adj.:* exciting; stimulating.

dejects (dē•jekts') *v.:* casts down; dispirits.

INTERNET

Vocabulary Practice

Keyword: LE7 12-4

A Woman in Blue (Portrait of the Duchess of Beaufort) (late 1770s) by Thomas Gainsborough.
Hermitage, St. Petersburg. The Bridgeman Art Library.

Pope's poem is divided into five sections called **cantos.** *Canto I begins like a proper epic, with a statement of the subject and an invocation to the Muse—a female deity who was supposed to inspire poets and other artists. Pope, however, clearly signals his comic intentions in the very first couplet:*

What dire offense from amorous causes springs,
What mighty contests rise from trivial things,
I sing—

In Canto II, Belinda and her friends take a boat up the river Thames to a party. All who see her admire the two beautiful curled locks that hang down her back. And despite the small army of sprites (spirits) assigned to protect Belinda's beautiful hair, the Baron resolves to possess these locks.

from The Rape of the Lock

Alexander Pope

from Canto III

Close by those meads, forever crowned with flowers,
Where Thames with pride surveys his rising towers,
There stands a structure° of majestic frame,
Which from the neighboring Hampton takes its name.
Here Britain's statesmen oft the fall foredoom
Of foreign tyrants, and of nymphs° at home;
Here thou, great Anna!° whom three realms obey,
Dost sometimes counsel take—and sometimes tea.
Hither the heroes and the nymphs resort,
To taste awhile the pleasures of a court;
In various talk th' instructive hours they passed,
Who gave the ball, or paid the visit last;
One speaks the glory of the British queen,
And one describes a charming Indian screen;
A third interprets motions, looks, and eyes;
At every word a reputation dies.

1–16. In lines 1–8, notice how Pope juxtaposes, or places side by side, the grandiose and the trivial: At Hampton Court, statesmen discuss the fall of tyrants—and also of young ladies. Meanwhile, Queen Anne is sometimes served political counsel—and at other times, tea.

? *What does line 16 tell you about life at Hampton Court?*

3. **structure** *n.:* Hampton Court, a royal residence on the river Thames, upstream from London.
6. **nymphs** *n. pl.:* young ladies.
7. **Anna:** Queen Anne (1665–1714), who ruled England, Ireland, and Scotland.

Snuff,° or the fan,° supply each pause of chat,
With singing, laughing, ogling, and all that.
   Meanwhile, declining from the noon of day,
The sun obliquely shoots his burning ray;
The hungry judges soon the sentence sign,
And wretches hang that jurymen may dine. . . .
Belinda now, whom thirst of fame invites,
Burns to encounter two adventurous knights,
At omber° singly to decide their doom;
And swells her breast with conquests yet to come. . . .
The nymph exulting fills with shouts the sky;
The walls, the woods, and long canals reply.
   Oh thoughtless mortals! ever blind to fate,
Too soon dejected and too soon elate.
Sudden, these honors shall be snatched away,

21–22. These clever lines have been quoted for centuries.

? *What do these two lines mean?*

? **23–28.** *What is Belinda's ambition? How does Pope describe Belinda?*

---

17. snuff *n.:* powdered tobacco product sniffed or rubbed on the teeth and gums. **fan** *n.:* standard equipment for a lady.
25. omber *n.:* card game for three players, popular in the eighteenth century.

Vocabulary

exulting (eg·zult'iŋ) *v.* used as *adj.:* rejoicing.

View of Hampton Court, Herefordshire (c. 1806) by J.M.W. Turner.

The Bridgeman Art Library. Yale Center for British Art, Paul Mellon Collection, New Haven, Connecticut.

And cursed forever this victorious day.
For lo! the board with cups and spoons is crowned,
The berries° crackle, and the mill° turns round;
On shining altars of Japan° they raise
The silver lamp; the fiery spirits blaze:
From silver spouts the grateful liquors glide,
While China's earth° receives the smoking tide.°
At once they gratify their scent and taste,
And frequent cups prolong the rich repast.
Straight hover round the fair her airy band;
Some, as she sipped, the fuming liquor fanned,
Some o'er her lap their careful plumes displayed,
Trembling, and conscious of the rich brocade.
Coffee (which makes the politician wise,
And see through all things with his half-shut eyes)
Sent up in vapors to the Baron's brain
New stratagems, the radiant lock to gain.
Ah, cease, rash youth! desist ere 'tis too late,
Fear the just gods, and think of Scylla's fate!°
Changed to a bird, and sent to flit in air,
She dearly pays for Nisus' injured hair!
But when to mischief mortals bend their will,
How soon they find fit instruments of ill!
Just then, Clarissa drew with tempting grace
A two-edged weapon from her shining case:
So ladies in romance assist their knight,
Present the spear, and arm him for the fight.
He takes the gift with reverence, and extends
The little engine° on his fingers' ends;
This just behind Belinda's neck he spread,
As o'er the fragrant steams she bends her head.
Swift to the lock a thousand sprites repair,
A thousand wings, by turns, blow back the hair;

33–52. In this verse paragraph, Pope sets the scene for the grand offense. The rich are gathered in a sitting room at Hampton Court, drinking endless cups of coffee.

? *What are Belinda's companions doing? What is the Baron doing?*

? **55–62.** *What action is described in these lines?*

---

34. berries *n. pl.:* coffee beans. **mill** *n.:* coffee grinder.

35. altars of Japan: small lacquered tables.

38. China's earth: cups made of earthenware. **smoking tide:** coffee.

50. Scylla's fate: In Greek mythology, Scylla (sil'ə) is turned into a seabird by the gods after she betrays her father Nisus by cutting off his purple lock of hair, on which his life and kingdom depend.

60. engine *n.:* instrument.

Vocabulary

repast (ri·past') *n.:* meal.
desist (di·zist') *v.:* stop.

And thrice they twitched the diamond in her ear;
Thrice she looked back, and thrice the foe drew near.
Just in that instant, anxious Ariel° sought
The close recesses of the virgin's thought;
As on the nosegay in her breast reclined,
He watched th' ideas rising in her mind,
Sudden he viewed, in spite of all her art,
An earthly lover lurking at her heart.°
Amazed, confused, he found his power expired,
Resigned to fate, and with a sigh retired.
   The peer now spreads the glittering *forfex*° wide,
T' enclose the lock; now joins it, to divide.
Even then, before the fatal engine closed,
A wretched sylph too fondly interposed;
Fate urged the shears, and cut the sylph in twain,
(But airy substance soon unites again).
The meeting points the sacred hair dissever
From the fair head, forever, and forever!
   Then flashed the living lightning from her eyes,
And screams of horror rend th' affrighted skies.
Not louder shrieks to pitying Heaven are cast,
When husbands, or when lapdogs breathe their last;
Or when rich china vessels fallen from high,
In glittering dust, and painted fragments lie!
   "Let wreaths of triumph° now my temples twine,"
The victor cried, "the glorious prize is mine!
While fish in streams, or birds delight in air,
Or in a coach and six° the British fair,
As long as *Atalantis*° shall be read,
Or the small pillow grace a lady's bed,
While visits shall be paid on solemn days,
When numerous wax lights in bright order blaze,
While nymphs take treats, or assignations give,

63–74. Having been armed by an accomplice, the Baron advances toward Belinda's back and then retreats three times in rapid sequence. This comical image mimics the rhythms of fencing.

? **75–82.** *How is the theft of the lock accomplished?*

83–88. Belinda screams in horror at the abduction of her lock.
? *What three kinds of shrieks is Belinda's shriek compared to?*

---

67. **Ariel:** chief of the heavenly sprites sent to protect Belinda.
72. **earthly lover . . . heart:** If in her heart Belinda wants the Baron to succeed, the sprites cannot protect her.
75. ***forfex:*** Latin for "scissors."
89. **wreaths of triumph:** like the ones worn by athletic and military heroes in ancient times.
92. **coach and six:** coach with six horses.
93. ***Atalantis:*** *The New Atalantis* (1709), a fashionable novel by Mrs. Delarivière Manley that thinly disguises some contemporary scandals.

Vocabulary

recesses (rē′ses · iz) *n. pl.:* secluded or hidden places.

So long my honor, name, and praise shall live!
What time would spare, from steel receives its date,°
And monuments, like men, submit to fate!"...

*In Canto IV, Pope describes an incident that occurs in all proper epics: a descent into the underworld. Just as Virgil had Aeneas travel down to Hades, Pope has Umbriel, a "melancholy sprite," fly down to a dismal, imaginary place called the Cave of Spleen. (*Spleen *was the eighteenth century's name for what we call depression; rich, idle people were particularly subject to spleen in Pope's day.) In the cave, Umbriel obtains a vial of "soft sobs, melting griefs, and flowing tears," as well as an immense bag full of "sighs, sobs, and passions," which somewhat resembles the bag of unfavorable winds in Homer's* Odyssey, *given to Odysseus to keep tightly closed so his ship won't be blown off course. Umbriel then returns to the earth's surface and empties the contents of the bag and vial over Belinda and her girlfriend, who is even angrier than Belinda. The canto ends with Belinda lamenting to the Baron:*

"O, hadst thou, cruel! been content to seize
Hairs less in sight, or any hairs but these!"

The others in Belinda's tea-party audience shed tears of pity, but the Baron ignores her pleas: "Fate and Jove had stopped the Baron's ears."

89–100. Like a victorious epic hero, the Baron sings of his mighty conquest, observing that while men and monuments shall pass away, his name shall live forever.

? *Why is the Baron's attitude amusing? How long will the Baron's reputation really last—and how can you tell?*

from Canto V

..."To arms, to arms!" the fierce virago° cries,
And swift as lightning to the combat flies.
All side in parties, and begin th' attack;
Fans clap, silks rustle, and tough whalebones° crack;
Heroes' and heroines' shouts confus'dly rise,
And bass and treble voices strike the skies.
No common weapons in their hands are found,
Like gods they fight, nor dread a mortal wound.°...
See, fierce Belinda on the Baron flies,
With more than usual lightning in her eyes:
Nor feared the chief th' unequal fight to try,

? **1–8.** *What is being described in these lines?*

---

99. date *n.:* destruction.

1. virago *n.:* ferocious woman; here, Belinda's girlfriend, who leads the attack on the Baron and his friends.

4. whalebones *n. pl.:* Whalebones were used to shape and stiffen women's clothing.

8. like gods . . . mortal wound: Like gods, who are immortal and have no fear of physical wounds, these fighters do not fear the wounds inflicted by words.

Who sought no more than on his foe to die.
But this bold lord with manly strength endued,
She with one finger and a thumb subdued:
Just where the breath of life his nostrils drew,
A charge of snuff the wily virgin threw;
The gnomes direct, to every atom just,
The pungent grains of titillating dust.
Sudden with starting tears each eye o'erflows,
And the high dome re-echoes to his nose.
"Now meet thy fate," incensed Belinda cried,
And drew a deadly bodkin° from her side. . . .
"Boast not my fall," he cried, "insulting foe!
Thou by some other shalt be laid as low.
Nor think, to die dejects my lofty mind:
All that I dread is leaving you behind!
Rather than so, ah, let me still survive,
And burn in Cupid's flames—but burn alive."
"Restore the lock!" she cries; and all around
"Restore the lock!" the vaulted roofs rebound.
Not fierce Othello° in so loud a strain
Roared for the handkerchief that caused his pain.
But see how oft ambitious aims are crossed,
And chiefs contend till all the prize is lost!
The lock, obtained with guilt, and kept with pain,
In every place is sought, but sought in vain:
With such a prize no mortal must be blessed,
So Heaven decrees! with Heaven who can contest?
Some thought it mounted to the lunar sphere,
Since all things lost on earth are treasured there.
There heroes' wits are kept in ponderous vases,
And beaux'° in snuffboxes and tweezer cases.
There broken vows and deathbed alms are found,
And lovers' hearts with ends of riband bound. . . .
But trust the Muse—she saw it upward rise,
Though marked by none but quick, poetic eyes: . . .

9–20. Belinda revenges herself on the Baron by throwing snuff in his face to make him sneeze.

? *How is this silly action in keeping with the* ***mock-epic*** *genre?*

? **29–38.** *Paraphrase this verse paragraph. Why, according to the speaker, is the lock unable to be found?*

22. **bodkin** *n.:* long, ornamental hairpin shaped like a dagger.
31. **Othello:** Shakespeare's tragic hero Othello gave his wife a handkerchief, which his enemy stole and then used as false evidence of the wife's unfaithfulness.
42. **beaux':** fashionable gentlemen's.

Vocabulary

titillating (tit′'l·āt′iŋ) *v.* used as *adj.:* exciting; stimulating.
dejects (dē·jekts′) *v.:* casts down; dispirits.

Sir Plume Demands the Restoration of the Lock (1854) by C. R. Leslie. Oil.
Private Collection.

A sudden star, it shot through liquid air,
And drew behind a radiant trail of hair.°. . .
    Then cease, bright nymph! to mourn thy ravished hair,
Which adds new glory to the shining sphere!
Not all the tresses that fair head can boast,
Shall draw such envy as the lock you lost.
For, after all the murders° of your eye,
When, after millions slain, yourself shall die;
When those fair suns shall set, as set they must,
And all those tresses shall be laid in dust,
This lock, the Muse shall consecrate to fame,
And midst the stars inscribe Belinda's name.

? **45–48.** *What has become of the lock?*

49–58. Even though the lock is gone forever, its very loss will ensure Belinda's lasting fame. ? *Who, according to the poet, is the true (though comic) hero?*

48. trail of hair: The word *comet* derives from a Greek word for "long-haired."

53. murders *n. pl.:* Just as Belinda's eyes are said to "eclipse the day" (Canto I, line 14), here they are said to murder the young men who admire her. Both compliments are ancient and overused in love poetry.

Response and Analysis

Reading Check

1. Summarize the main events of Pope's poem in **chronological** order. Be sure to include all the main events that lead up to and follow the theft of the lock of hair.

Thinking Critically

2. Who, if anyone, do you think is victorious at the end of the poem? Cite lines from the poem to support your opinion.
3. In the satirical passage that opens Canto III (lines 1–18), what seems to be Pope's **tone**—his attitude toward the queen and her courtiers? Is he scornful or amused? How can you tell?
4. The world outside the poem and the world inside it come together in Canto III (lines 7–8). What is the effect of the three words after the dash?
5. In Canto III (line 86), Pope juxtaposes—that is, places side by side—dying husbands and dying lapdogs. What is the effect of this juxtaposition? Find other surprising juxtapositions in the poem, and describe their effects.
6. A **mock epic** amusingly parodies the style and conventions of the serious epic. Ever since Homer, a hallmark of the epic has been the elaborate **epic simile,** or extended comparison between two unlike things. What things are being compared in Canto III (lines 57–58 and 85–88) and Canto V (lines 31–32)?
7. In the complete poem, Pope frequently makes **satirical** remarks about the world outside the privileged ranks to which Belinda and her friends belong. Examples of such remarks occur in Canto III (lines 21–22 and 45–46). Who or what are Pope's targets in these **couplets**?
8. Belinda's victory at cards in Canto III (lines 23–28) and her cries of triumph are ironic because her happiness is so momentary; it's about to be shattered by the theft of her lock. Since **irony** always involves a discrepancy of some kind, explain how Belinda's victory over the Baron in Canto V (lines 13–22) also might be considered ironic.
9. Based on the extracts you have read, how would you state Pope's **theme**—his central message—in this mock epic? Who or what are the objects of his satire?
10. Does the epic apply in any way to any aspects of contemporary life? Can you find passages that could serve as satiric commentaries on people's behavior today? Be sure to review your Quickwrite notes before you answer.

Literary Skills Analyze the characteristics of a mock epic.

Writing Skills Write an essay comparing and contrasting epics. Write a description in mock-heroic style.

Vocabulary Skills Create etymology maps.

INTERNET

Projects and Activities

Keyword: LE7 12-4

King Charles Spaniels (1845) (detail) by Sir Edwin Henry Landseer.

WRITING

Mocking Epics

In a brief **essay, compare and contrast** Pope's **mock epic** with a serious epic: *Beowulf* (see page 21), Homer's *Iliad* (see page 67), Milton's *Paradise Lost* (see page 403), or if you know it well, Homer's *Odyssey.* Consider these elements of the epic: invocations to the Muse, statement of subject, intervention of gods and goddesses, epic battles, a hero or heroine who reflects the values of a particular society, and use of elevated language. What aspects of Pope's mock epic most successfully parody the great epics of the past?

Your Mock-Heroic Style

In Canto III, Pope describes making and drinking coffee in rich, elevated, and roundabout language (lines 33–40). This mock-heroic writing style breaks the elementary rule that says writers must try to use simple, direct language when describing simple activities. As an exercise in mock-heroic writing, write a prose **description** of a common activity (such as riding a bicycle or cooking and eating a hamburger), using inflated language and rich images.

Worcester teapot.
The Bridgeman Art Library.

Vocabulary Development

Etymology Maps

exulting **desist** **titillating**
repast **recesses** **dejects**

In keeping with his mock-heroic style, Alexander Pope used a great deal of vocabulary based on Latin words in *The Rape of the Lock.* Use a dictionary to find out the origin, or **etymology,** of the Vocabulary words above. Then, fill out an etymology map for each word. The first word has been done for you.

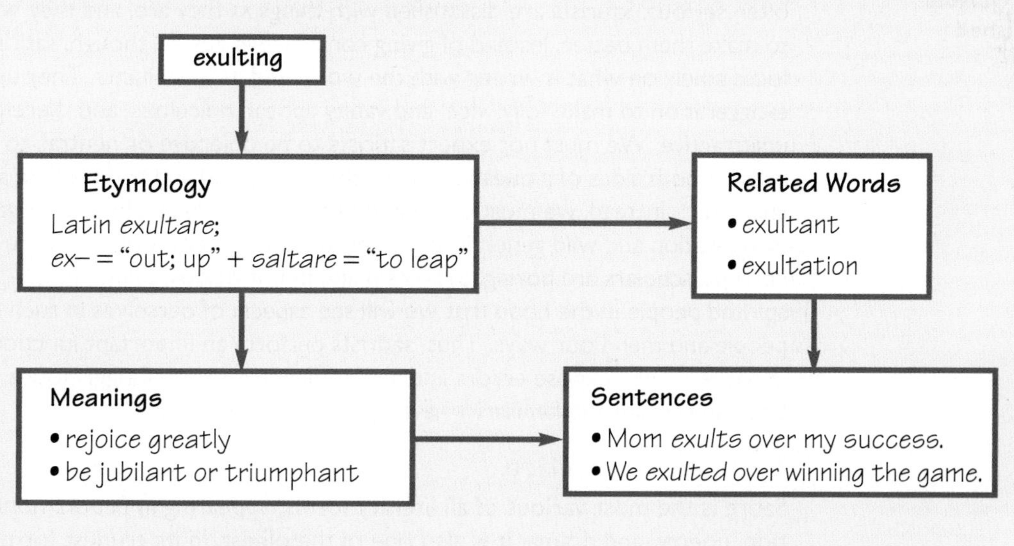
exulting
Etymology
Latin exultare;
ex– = "out; up" + saltare = "to leap"
Related Words
• exultant
• exultation
Meanings
• rejoice greatly
• be jubilant or triumphant
Sentences
• Mom exults over my success.
• We exulted over winning the game.

Connecting to **World Literature**

The Sting of Satire

by Robert DeMaria, Jr.

1759
Candide published

1729
A Modest Proposal published

1605
Don Quixote published

You have just read the famous English satire *A Modest Proposal* by Jonathan Swift and an excerpt from Alexander Pope's mock-epic poem *The Rape of the Lock*. In this Connecting to World Literature feature, you will read excerpts from two famous satirical novels from other parts of the world:

A **satire** is any piece of writing designed to make its readers feel critical—of themselves, of their fellow human beings, of their society. Some satires, like Alexander Pope's *The Rape of the Lock* (see page 605), are intended to make us laugh at human foolishness and weakness; these satires are good-natured and laugh-provoking. Other satires, like Swift's *A Modest Proposal* (see page 582), may make us laugh, but it is often laughter of a bitter kind, arising from anger and indignation at human vices and crimes.

Neither Nice Nor Neutral: The Purposes of Satire

No matter how humorous a satire may be, its ultimate purpose is most often serious: Satirists are dissatisfied with things as they are, and they want to make them better. Instead of giving constructive advice, though, satirists focus solely on what is wrong with the world and its inhabitants. They use exaggeration to make folly, vice, and vanity appear ridiculous, and therefore unattractive. We must not expect satirists to be objective or neutral, to present both sides of a question, or to show the good and bad traits of a character. Instead, we must understand that satire is fueled by extravagant exaggeration and wild generalization: Lawyers are greedy, politicians are corrupt, scholars are boring. Satirists make fun of vicious, selfish, mean-spirited people in the hope that we will see aspects of ourselves in such people and mend our ways. Thus, satirists perform an important function in society: They expose errors and absurdities that we no longer notice because custom and familiarity have blinded us to them.

Pages 614–616 cover **Literary Skills** Understand the characteristics of satire. Compare satires from different cultures and literary periods.

The Uses of Satire

Satire is the most various of all literary forms, appearing in fiction, nonfiction, poetry, and drama. It is also one of the oldest. In its crudest form, invective (another word for "name-calling") satire is probably as old as civilization. The more formal satire found in the literature of the West was mostly influenced by ancient Greek and Roman writers.

The Royal Academy Exhibition by Thomas Rowlandson.

Throughout history, satire has traditionally thrived whenever repressive governments are in power and their obvious corruptions can be ridiculed. Times of prosperity and indulgence, when reckless spending and greed prevail—when upper classes "sup" while the lower classes starve—are likewise eras when satirists flourish.

Scathing Humor: The Weapon of the Satirist

One of the most useful techniques available to the satirist is **parody,** a mocking imitation of a writer's style or of a particular genre. Often, the style being parodied is applied to a trivial subject. Pope's *The Rape of the Lock,* for example, parodies the epic style to describe the theft of a lock of hair. Miguel de Cervantes's *Don Quixote* (see page 627) parodies the chivalric romance, finding its satire in the incongruity that arises from the clash between the romantic and the real. Parody can only be used successfully by writers who are familiar with many works of literature and who understand and appreciate style.

The Great Age of Satire

Satire thrived across western Europe, beginning early in Italy and cropping up later in Spain, most famously in Cervantes's parody of medieval romances, *Don Quixote* (1605). Throughout his comic novel, Cervantes ridicules the often tangled and confusing passages that are hallmarks of chivalric romances. The narrator tells us that Don Quixote read so many romances that "his brain dried up." Many passages from such tales are so convoluted that "Aristotle himself would not have been able to understand them, even if he had been resurrected for that sole purpose." Wickedly, Cervantes quotes literally from a tale by a sixteenth-century writer whose language is so exaggerated that Cervantes does not need to embellish it further: "The reason of the unreason that afflicts my reason, in such a manner weakens my reason that I with reason lament me of your comeliness."

The great age of Western satire began in the latter half of the seventeenth century and lasted until the middle of the eighteenth century—a time of great social stability, especially in England and France.

The Fate of Satire: Make Way for Romanticism

At the end of the eighteenth century, the American Revolution, the French Revolution, and several other events shattered the peaceful climate that had prevailed until then. Most European governments became less restrictive, and the kind of oppositional temper that marks satire and parody became harder for writers to call forth. Amid the efforts to build new nations, satire and parody gave way to attempts to recapture the grandeur of the old epics and romances. Human nature was celebrated as naturally good and noble rather than criticized as corrupt and mean.

While some later writers, such as Lord Byron and Charles Dickens, did write masterful satirical works, people, for the most part, sought to glory in the achievements of their cultures. The Romantic lyric, the extended elegy, and the epic narrative became the most popular literary forms in the West in the early part of the nineteenth century. Too much critical honesty finally seemed to be more than society could bear. As one character in Molière's play *The Misanthrope* says:

> “In certain cases it would be uncouth
> And most absurd to speak the naked truth;
> With all respect for your exalted notions,
> It's often best to veil one's true emotions.
> Wouldn't the social fabric come undone
> If we were wholly frank with everyone?”

Jonathan Swift.

Voltaire

(1694–1778)

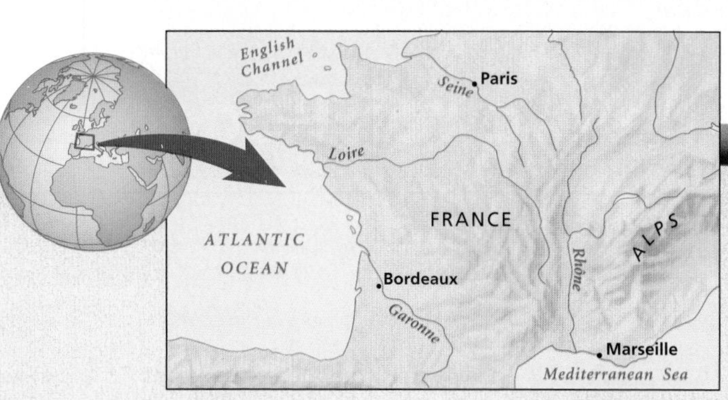

François-Marie Arouet (àr • we), better known by his pen name, Voltaire, is remembered chiefly for his lifelong fight against injustice. Throughout his life, he implored his fellow philosophers to "crush the infamous," by which he meant all things inhumane and oppressive. As a satirist, philosopher, historian, dramatist, and poet, Voltaire continually criticized the wastefulness of war, the intolerance of organized religion, and indifference to the plight of the poor.

Born in Paris to middle-class parents, Voltaire studied law for a time but soon gave it up to become a writer. His reputation was established early, based on his classical tragedies and his lampoons of the government. Still, even his celebrity did not prevent Voltaire from being brutally beaten at the hands of an offended nobleman, imprisoned in the Bastille, and exiled to England in 1726.

In London, Voltaire met Jonathan Swift and Alexander Pope and was deeply influenced by the works of Bacon, Newton, and Locke, which emphasize the experimental method in science. When he returned to Paris, Voltaire wrote philosophical essays and historical studies that reflect this influence. Voltaire debunked traditional approaches to writing history, preferring to write philosophical treatises on morals. These essays were not abstract, but focused on how people actually lived and worked according to their moral principles. His efforts were not well-received, however, by the people in power. The publication of his most formidable work, *Essay on the Morals and the Spirit of the Nations from Charlemagne to Louis XIII,* caused the book to be banned and Voltaire to be exiled.

Aside from his voluminous correspondence and hundreds of pamphlets on every issue of his time, Voltaire wrote in every literary genre. Of his numerous romances and tales, *Candide* has proved to be the most enduring. Voltaire had little patience for purely metaphysical speculation. This emphasis on modest but practical achievement is reflected in the last page of *Candide:* "Let us work without arguing . . . it's the only way to make life endurable."

Voltaire lived much of his later life near the Swiss border with France. He died during a rare visit to Paris, taken at age eighty-three to see his last play produced. Initially refused a Christian burial, Voltaire's remains were interred in Paris with great ceremony thirteen years later, following the revolution so greatly influenced by his ideas for reform.

Voltaire (1833), engraved by James Mollison from an original by Nicolas de Largillière.

Before You Read

from Candide

Make the Connection

Voltaire's *Candide* tells the tale of the woes that befall a naive young man named Candide. The novel's subtitle, "Optimism," reflects the fact that Candide is brought up to believe that his world is the best of all possible worlds. (Many people liked to believe this during the Enlightenment.) Candide and his beloved, Cunegonde, suffer a series of disasters, which Voltaire narrates with verve and wit. Yet the humor never obscures Voltaire's deeper messages: Optimism is foolish in a world where people's lives are all too often shaped by cruel social forces, and humankind and its social institutions stand in need of reform.

Literary Focus

Satire

Satire is a kind of writing that ridicules human weakness, vice, or folly in order to bring about social reform. Satires often try to persuade the reader to do or believe something by showing the opposing view as absurd, vicious, or inhumane. Expert satirists use a variety of tools to undermine their opponents' beliefs. As you read the excerpts from *Candide*, look for five techniques in particular: outrageous exaggerations, deadpan understatements, warped logic (absurdities dressed up as common sense), improbable situations, and ridiculous names.

Literary Skills
Understand the characteristics of satire.

INTERNET

Vocabulary Practice

•

More About Voltaire

•

Keyword: LE7 12-4

> **Satire** is a kind of writing that ridicules human weakness, vice, or folly in order to bring about social reform.
>
> *For more on Satire, see the Handbook of Literary and Historical Terms.*

Background

In the tumultuous social climate of eighteenth-century Europe, writers, scientists, and philosophers questioned accepted truths in ways they never had before. Yet direct challenges to authority can be dangerous. Thus satire, with its indirect criticism and deflating humor, became for many the weapon of choice. In *Candide,* Voltaire satirizes the calamities that befall Candide, an innocent who has been schooled by the repellent Doctor Pangloss to believe that everything happens for the best. In the first two chapters, Voltaire holds up for ridicule the castle and the army—two of the most important social institutions of eighteenth-century Europe. He also targets the theories of the German philosopher Gottfried Leibniz, who believed that a rational God made a rational world in which everything, including evil, has a place and a purpose. Voltaire's Doctor Pangloss directly echoes Leibniz every time he proclaims, "In this best of all possible worlds, . . . all is for the best."

Vocabulary Development

endowed (en•doud′) *v.* used as *adj.:* provided with.

candor (kan′dər) *n.:* honesty; directness.

pensive (pen′siv) *adj.:* reflective; thoughtful.

vivacity (vī•vas′ə•tē) *n.:* liveliness; high-spiritedness.

consternation (kän′stər•nā′shən) *n.:* bewilderment; dismay.

prodigy (präd′ə•jē) *n.:* someone gifted from childhood with an exceptional quality or talent.

clemency (klem′ən•sē) *n.:* mercy; leniency.

from Candide

Voltaire

translated by
Richard Aldington

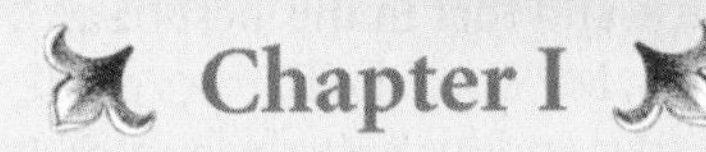

Chapter I

How Candide was brought up in a noble castle and how he was expelled from the same

In the castle of Baron Thunder-ten-tronckh in Westphalia[1] there lived a youth, endowed by Nature with the most gentle character. His face was the expression of his soul. His judgment was quite honest and he was extremely simple-minded; and this was the reason, I think, that he was named Candide. Old servants in the house suspected that he was the son of the Baron's sister and a decent honest gentleman of the neighborhood, whom this young lady would never marry

1. **Westphalia** (west·fā'lē·ə): region in western Germany noted for its excellent ham. In a letter to his niece, Voltaire described Westphalia as "vast, sad, sterile, detestable."

Vocabulary

endowed (en·doud') *v.* used as *adj.*: provided with.

Candide (played by Mark Baker) and his beloved Cunegonde (played by Maureen Brennan) in the 1974 Broadway revival of the musical *Candide*. © Martha Swope/TimePix.

because he could only prove seventy-one quarterings,[2] and the rest of his genealogical tree was lost, owing to the injuries of time. The Baron was one of the most powerful lords in Westphalia, for his castle possessed a door and windows. His Great Hall was even decorated with a piece of tapestry. The dogs in his stableyards formed a pack of hounds when necessary; his grooms were his huntsmen; the village curate was his Grand Almoner.[3] They all called him "My Lord," and laughed heartily at his stories. The Baroness weighed about three hundred and fifty pounds, was therefore greatly respected, and did the honors of the house with a dignity which rendered her still more respectable. Her daughter Cunegonde,[4] aged seventeen, was rosy-cheeked, fresh, plump, and tempting. The Baron's son appeared in every respect worthy of his father. The tutor Pangloss[5] was the oracle of the house, and little Candide followed his lessons with all the candor of his age and character. Pangloss taught metaphysico-theologo-cosmolonigology.[6] He proved admirably that there is no effect without a cause and that in this best of all possible worlds, My Lord the Baron's castle was the best of castles and his wife the best of all possible Baronesses. "'Tis demonstrated," said he, "that things cannot be otherwise; for, since everything is made for an end, everything is necessarily for the best end. Observe that noses were made to wear spectacles; and so we have spectacles. Legs were visibly instituted to be breeched, and we have breeches. Stones were formed to be quarried and to build castles; and My Lord has a very noble castle; the greatest Baron in the province should have the best house; and as pigs were made to be eaten, we eat pork all the year round; consequently, those who have asserted that all is well talk nonsense; they ought to have said that all is for the best." Candide listened attentively and believed innocently; for he thought Mademoiselle Cunegonde extremely beautiful, although he was never bold enough to tell her so. He decided that after the happiness of being born Baron of Thunder-ten-tronckh, the second degree of happiness was to be Mademoiselle Cunegonde; the third, to see her every day; and the fourth to listen to Doctor Pangloss, the greatest philosopher of the province and therefore of the whole world. One day when Cunegonde was walking near the castle, in a little wood which was called The Park, she observed Doctor Pangloss in the bushes, giving a lesson in experimental physics to her mother's waiting-maid, a very pretty and docile brunette. Mademoiselle Cunegonde had a great inclination for science and watched breathlessly the reiterated experiments she witnessed; she observed clearly the Doctor's sufficient reason, the effects and the causes, and returned home very much excited, pensive, filled with the desire of learning, reflecting that she might be the sufficient reason of young Candide and that he might be hers. On her way back to the castle she met Candide and blushed; Candide also blushed. She bade him good morning in a hesitating voice; Candide replied without knowing what he was saying. Next day, when they left the table after dinner, Cunegonde and Candide found themselves behind a screen; Cunegonde dropped her handkerchief, Candide picked it up; she innocently held his hand; the young man innocently kissed the young lady's hand with remarkable vivacity, tenderness, and grace; their lips met, their eyes sparkled, their knees

2. **quarterings** *n. pl.:* divisions on a coat of arms or family tree. Seventy-one is an absurdly high number, tracing a person's genealogy over two thousand years.
3. **Grand Almoner:** member of a noble household responsible for allotting charity to the poor.
4. **Cunegonde** (kyo͞o'nā·gônd').
5. **Pangloss:** Greek for "all tongue."
6. **metaphysico-theologo-cosmolonigology:** This nonsense term is a satirical poke at the philosopher Leibniz and his followers, especially the embedded syllable *–nig–*, a shortened form of *nigaud*, which is French for "simpleton."

Vocabulary

candor (kan'dər) *n.:* honesty; directness.
pensive (pen'siv) *adj.:* reflective; thoughtful.
vivacity (vī·vas'ə·tē) *n.:* liveliness; high-spiritedness.

trembled, their hands wandered. Baron Thunder-ten-tronckh passed near the screen, and, observing this cause and effect, expelled Candide from the castle by kicking him in the backside frequently and hard. Cunegonde swooned; when she recovered her senses, the Baroness slapped her in the face; and all was in consternation in the noblest and most agreeable of all possible castles.

Chapter II

What happened to Candide among the Bulgarians

Candide, expelled from the earthly paradise, wandered for a long time without knowing where he was going, turning up his eyes to Heaven, gazing back frequently at the noblest of castles which held the most beautiful of young Baronesses; he lay down to sleep supperless between two furrows in the open fields: It snowed heavily in large flakes. The next morning the shivering Candide, penniless, dying of cold and exhaustion, dragged himself toward the neighboring town, which was called Wald-berghoff-trarbk-dikdorff. He halted sadly at the door of an inn. Two men dressed in blue noticed him. "Comrade," said one, "there's a well-built young man of the right height."[7] They went up to Candide and very civilly invited him to dinner. "Gentlemen," said Candide with charming modesty, "you do me a great honor, but I have no money to pay my share." "Ah, sir," said one of the men in blue, "persons of your figure and merit never pay anything; are you not five feet five tall?" "Yes, gentlemen," said he, bowing, "that is my height." "Ah, sir, come to table; we will not only pay your expenses, we will never allow a man like you to be short of money; men were only made to help each other." "You are in the right," said Candide, "that is what Doctor Pangloss was always telling me, and I see that everything is for the best." They begged him to accept a few crowns,[8] he took them and wished to give them an IOU, they refused to take it, and all sat down to table. "Do you not love tenderly . . ." "Oh, yes," said he. "I love Mademoiselle Cunegonde tenderly." "No," said one of the gentlemen. "We were asking if you do not tenderly love the King of the Bulgarians." "Not a bit," said he, "for I have never seen him." "What! He is the most charming of kings, and you must drink his health." "Oh, gladly, gentlemen." And he drank. "That is sufficient," he was told. "You are now the support, the aid, the defender, the hero of the Bulgarians, your fortune is made, and your glory assured." They immediately put irons on his legs and took him to a regiment. He was made to turn to the right and left, to raise the ramrod and return the ramrod, to take aim, to fire, to march double time, and he was given thirty strokes with a stick; the next day he drilled not quite so badly, and received only twenty strokes; the day after, he only had ten and was looked on as a prodigy by his comrades. Candide was completely mystified and could not make out how he was a hero. One fine spring day he thought he would take a walk, going straight ahead, in the belief that to use his legs as he pleased was a privilege of the human species as well as of animals. He had not gone two leagues[9] when four other heroes, each six feet tall, fell upon him, bound him, and dragged him back to a cell. He was asked by his judges whether he would rather be thrashed thirty-six times by the whole regiment or receive a dozen lead bullets at once in his brain. Although he protested that men's wills are free and that he wanted neither one nor the other, he had to make

7. **height** *n.:* Voltaire is making fun of the recruiting practices of the "King of the Bulgarians"—Voltaire's satiric name for King Frederick the Great of Prussia—who chose and organized soldiers according to their height.

8. **crowns** *n. pl.:* units of money.
9. **leagues** *n. pl.:* unit of distance equal to about three miles.

Vocabulary

consternation (kän′stər·nā′shən) *n.:* bewilderment; dismay.

prodigy (präd′ə·jē) *n.:* someone gifted from childhood with an exceptional quality or talent.

© Martha Swope/TimePix.

Dr. Pangloss (played by Lewis J. Stadlen), the greatest philosopher in the universe, in the 1974 Broadway revival of the musical *Candide*.

a choice; by virtue of that gift of God which is called liberty, he determined to run the gauntlet[10] thirty-six times and actually did so twice. There were two thousand men in the regiment. That made four thousand strokes which laid bare the muscles and nerves from his neck to his backside. As they were about to proceed to a third turn, Candide, utterly exhausted, begged as a favor that they would be so kind as to smash his head; he obtained this favor; they bound his eyes and he was made to kneel down. At that moment the King of the Bulgarians came by and inquired the victim's crime, and as this King was possessed of a vast genius, he perceived from what he learned about Candide that he was a young metaphysician[11] very ignorant in worldly matters, and therefore pardoned him with a clemency which will be praised in all newspapers and all ages. An honest surgeon healed Candide in three weeks with the ointments recommended by Dioscorides.[12] He had already regained a little skin and could walk when the King of the Bulgarians went to war with the King of the Abares.[13] ■

10. **run the gauntlet:** run between two rows of soldiers who strike the victim with clubs or other weapons.
11. **metaphysician** (met′ə·fə·zish′ən) *n.:* philosopher who studies the nature of reality and the origin and structure of the universe.

12. **Dioscorides** (dī′əs·kôr·ə·dēz′): Greek army physician who wrote a treatise on medicine in the first century A.D. Even in Voltaire's day, Dioscorides' work was out-of-date.
13. **Abares** (a·bär′): that is, the French, who fought against the "Bulgarians," or Prussians, in the Seven Years' War (1756–1763).

Vocabulary

clemency (klem′ən·sē) *n.:* mercy; leniency.

Response and Analysis

Reading Check

1. Who is Candide and what do we know of his background and character? (Where did his name come from?)
2. What is Doctor Pangloss's philosophy?
3. Why is Candide expelled from the Baron's castle?
4. How does Candide become a soldier in the Bulgarian army?
5. Why is Candide sentenced to run the gauntlet?

Thinking Critically

6. **Satire** relies on many techniques usually associated with comedy. Five such techniques are exaggeration, understatement, warped logic, improbable situations, and ridiculous names. On a sheet of paper, draw a chart like the one below and list as many examples of each technique as you can find in this excerpt from *Candide*. Your list will be very long!

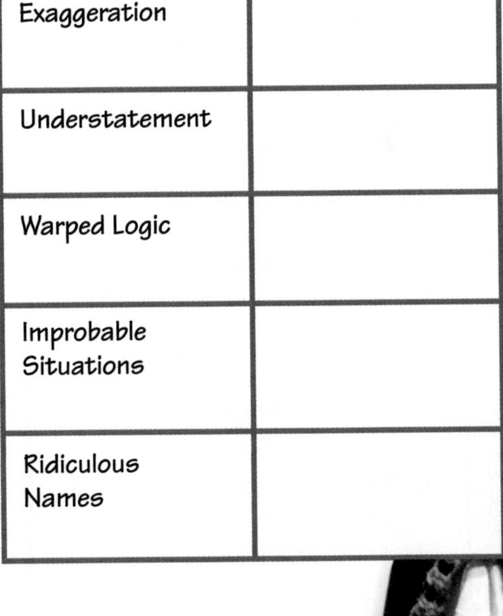

Exaggeration	
Understatement	
Warped Logic	
Improbable Situations	
Ridiculous Names	

7. Do people like Doctor Pangloss still exist in today's worlds of education, politics, or religion? Where and why do you still hear people saying things like "It's all for the best"?
8. How does Voltaire use **exaggeration** in Chapter II to satirize disciplinary practices in the Prussian Army? What point do you think he is trying to make?
9. As Chapter II illustrates, Candide suffers every time he exercises what he believes to be his free will. According to Voltaire, what forces get in the way of a person's exercise of free will?
10. What details of character and plot in *Candide* **parody,** or mock, the popular romances that still appear on today's bestseller lists or in the movies or on TV soap operas? Why do you think such romances continue to appeal to many people?

Extending and Evaluating

11. Voltaire wrote *Candide* more than 230 years ago. In your opinion, how well has his satire held up? What value, if any, does *Candide* hold for someone growing up in today's world? Does Voltaire's underlying message against intolerance, cruelty, and smugness still apply? Explain your response.

Literary Skills
Analyze the characteristics of satire. Compare satires from different cultures and literary periods.

Writing Skills
Write an essay analyzing a literary work. Write a brief play.

Vocabulary Skills
Understand the meanings and origins of words.

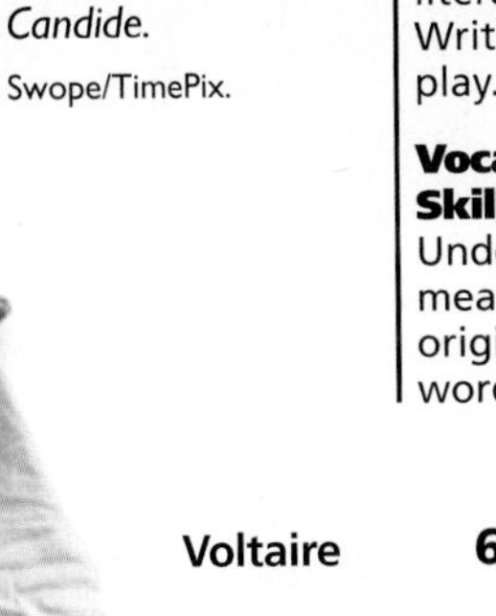

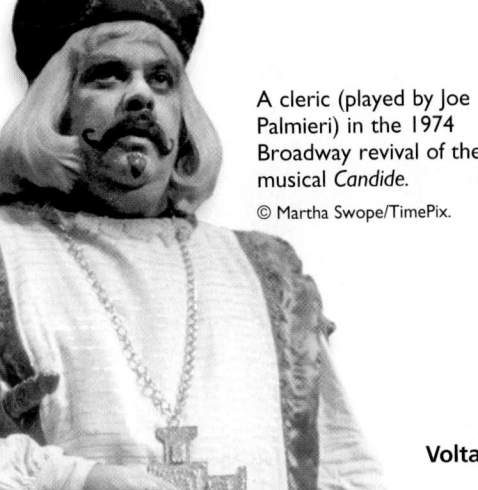

A cleric (played by Joe Palmieri) in the 1974 Broadway revival of the musical *Candide*.

Comparing Literature

12. In what ways is Voltaire's satire like Alexander Pope's in *The Rape of the Lock* (see page 605)? Consider these techniques of satire as you compare the two texts:

- target of the satire
- use of humor
- use of exaggeration
- use of improbable situations
- use of ridiculous names
- expression of tone (lighthearted or bitter?)

WRITING

Analyzing Humor

Refer to the chart you filled out for question number 6 on page 623. Use the details you gathered on that chart to write a brief **analysis** of Voltaire's humor. When you analyze something, you take it apart and examine its elements to see how it works. The chart will show you many techniques used by Voltaire to ridicule his characters and to make us laugh. At the end of your essay, describe the targets of Voltaire's satire.

Use "Writing a Literary Essay," pages 684–691, for help with this assignment.

Candide Onstage

In 1956, Leonard Bernstein and Richard Wilbur brought their musical comedy based on *Candide* to the Broadway stage. (The photographs in the text are from a later production of that musical.) Try your hand at adapting these two chapters of *Candide* as a **play** for the stage. You will have to identify your main characters and the sets. You can pick up a great deal of your dialogue from the text itself.

Program from a 1996 production of *Candide* at Arena Stage, Washington, D.C.

Illustration by Scott McKowen.

Vocabulary Development

Word Information Charts

endowed
consternation
candor
prodigy
pensive
clemency
vivacity

Using a dictionary, make a chart of basic information about each Vocabulary word listed above. The first one has been done for you.

endowed
• **Meaning:** "provided with" • **Origin:** Old French *en–*, "in," and *dotare*, "to endow" • **Related Words:** *endow* (v.); *endowment* (n.) • **Examples** (things that can be endowed): money, talent, scholarships

Miguel de Cervantes

(1547–1616)

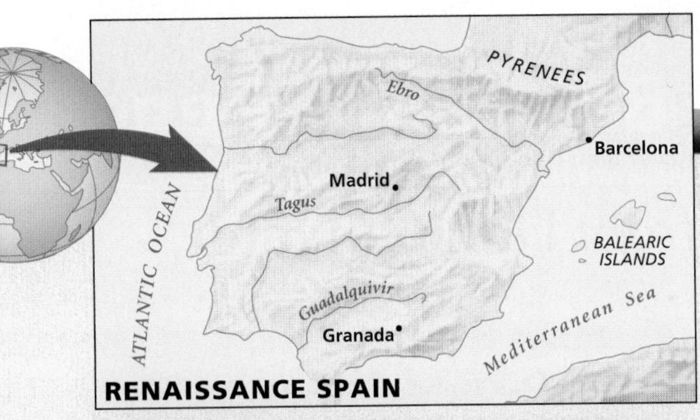

Miguel de Cervantes (sər•vän′tēz′), son of a wandering apothecary, or druggist, was born near Madrid, Spain, in 1547. In 1569, Cervantes, seeing no prospects at home, enlisted in the army, fought valiantly, and was wounded at the Battle of Lepanto in 1571. His left hand was crippled, earning him the nickname *el manco de Lepanto*—"the one-handed man of Lepanto."

Cervantes hoped to be promoted to an army captain after the war, but his plans were ruined when he was captured by Barbary pirates and held as a slave for five years in Algeria. He returned to Spain in 1580, jobless, in debt, and without any hope of regaining his army career. Over the years he worked as a playwright, bureaucrat, and tax collector before finally landing in jail for failure to pay his debts. Many of those debts had accrued as a result of his family's scraping together the ransom money to buy his freedom from the pirates.

According to legend, it was while he was in jail that the idea for *Don Quixote* came to Cervantes. His hero, Don Quixote, is a poor, aging landowner who reads nothing but romantic tales of chivalry. As he teeters on the edge of insanity, the old man becomes convinced that he is a knight-errant, even though the age of knights is long past.

The Ingenious Gentleman Don Quixote of La Mancha was published in January of 1605 and immediately caused a sensation. Once the first edition sold out, pirated (illegally printed) copies began to appear. Six editions were issued in the first year, and translations into French and English appeared within ten years.

Miguel de Cervantes.

It seemed that everyone in Spain, and soon everyone in Europe, was laughing at the adventures of the ridiculous knight Don Quixote.

Cervantes, at the age of fifty-eight, was now a famous author, but he was still poor. As was common until the nineteenth century, authors were at the mercy of publishers and were seldom able to retain the copyrights on their books. Thus, *Don Quixote's* publisher, not Cervantes, reaped the lion's share of the book's profits. Spain's greatest writer died in poverty on April 22, 1616—one day before Shakespeare. To his family, Cervantes left many debts. To the world he left a comic masterpiece that earned him the title of father of the modern novel.

Before You Read

from Don Quixote

Make the Connection

Don Quixote is a comic lampoon of the medieval romances that audiences of Cervantes's era continued to devour. But beneath the parody, *Don Quixote* makes a poignant comment on universal human qualities. Even as we laugh at Don Quixote, we realize that there is something of him in all of us. Like Don Quixote, who wished he had lived in an earlier age, and like Cervantes himself, who wished he were a military hero, most of us cherish unlikely dreams. In *Man of La Mancha*, Dale Wasserman's musical adaptation of *Don Quixote* for the stage, Quixote sings of his need "to dream the impossible dream." We can no more relinquish our dreams than he could, without giving up an important part of our inner selves.

The "impossible dream" aspect of Cervantes's novel led to a new adjective in English: *quixotic* (kwik·sät′ik). The word describes a dreamer who is well-intentioned but impractical. What quixotic heroes can you think of—from movies, comic strips, television shows, or books? What traits do they share? What keeps them going, no matter what happens?

Literary Skills
Understand the characteristics of parody.

Literary Focus

Parody

A literary **parody** is an imitation of a work of literature for amusement or instruction. Parodies often make the characteristics of someone or something seem ridiculous by transferring them to a ridiculous subject. To achieve this, parodies use exaggeration, verbal irony (saying one thing and meaning another), incongruity (deliberately pairing things that don't belong together), and humorously twisted imitation. Cervantes pokes fun at every aspect of the medieval romance and its heroic knights. Quixote sees himself as a knight of old, but his armor is rusty, his horse is a nag, and the giants he battles turn out to be windmills.

INTERNET

Vocabulary Practice

•

More About Miguel de Cervantes

•

Keyword: LE7 12-4

Parody is the imitation of a work of literature for amusement or instruction.

For more on Parody, see the Handbook of Literary and Historical Terms.

Background

Initially, Cervantes intended *Don Quixote* to lampoon tales of chivalry and courtly romances, stories from the medieval period about romantic love and knightly adventure, which were still eagerly read by the audience of Cervantes's time. In these stories, idealized knights fought villains, dragons, and monsters, and embarked on quests in honor of ladies to whom they had sworn their love. Such heroes stood for military values such as honor, courage, and loyalty, combined with Christian values such as piety, courtesy, and chastity.

Vocabulary Development

succor (suk′ər) *v.:* help in time of distress.

enmity (en′mə·tē) *n.:* hostility.

victuals (vit′′lz) *n. pl.:* provisions; pieces of food.

vigil (vij′əl) *n.:* staying watchfully awake.

flaccid (flas′id) *adj.:* limp; flabby.

disposition (dis′pə·zish′ən) *n.:* natural qualities of personality.

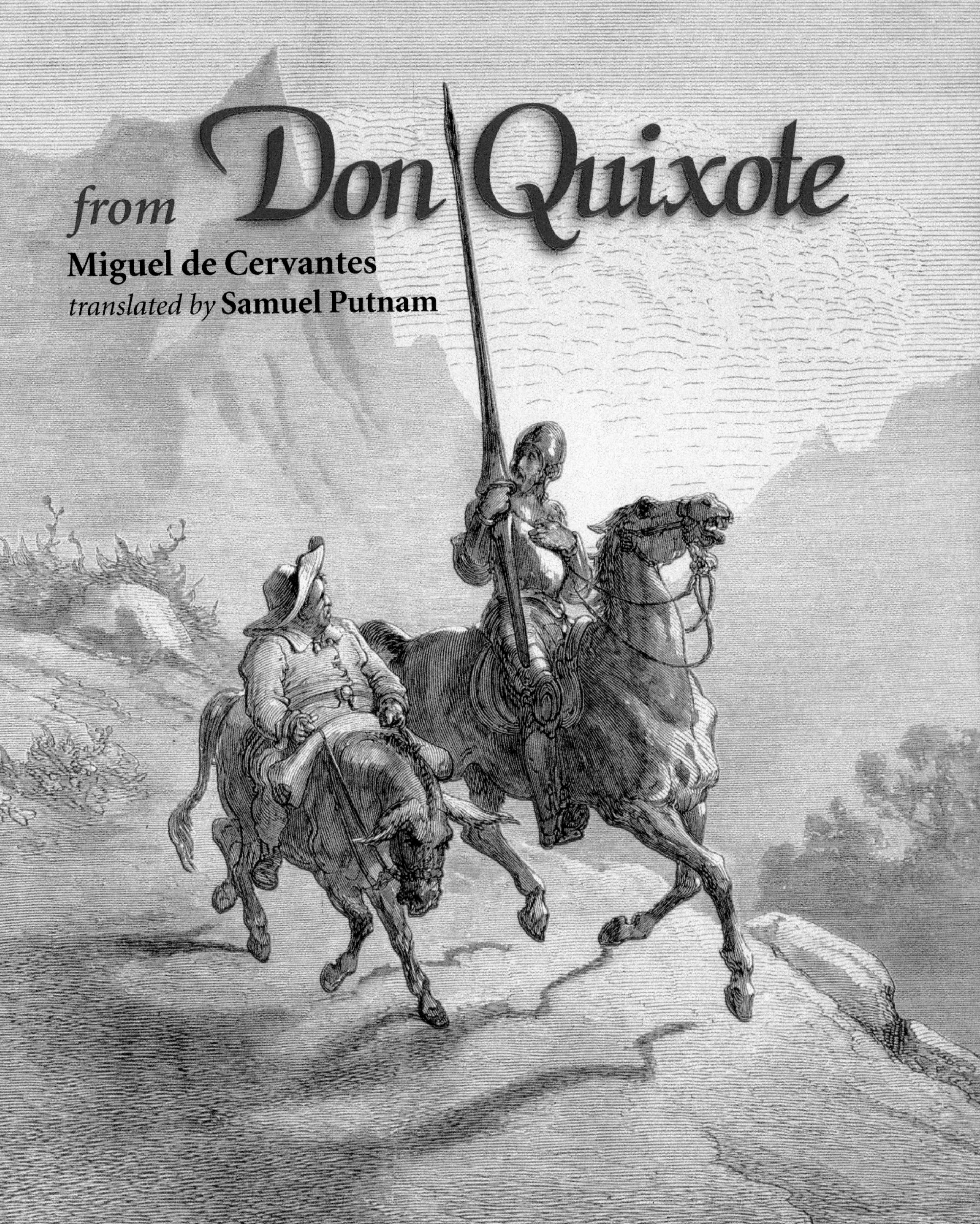

from Don Quixote

Miguel de Cervantes

translated by **Samuel Putnam**

Don Quixote is a middle-aged gentleman of La Mancha. Unlike most gentlemen, he no longer hunts or attends to his property but spends all of his time reading books about chivalry. As a result of his constant preoccupation with these fanciful tales, he goes mad.

With his mind full of images of adventure and enchantment from his books, Don Quixote decides to become a knight-errant and go forth in search of adventure. He takes down the family's rusty armor and names his bony old nag Rocinante. He knows that as a knight-errant, he must also have a fair lady to whom he may dedicate his dangerous battles and noble deeds. He chooses a country girl whom he hardly knows, Aldonza Lorenzo, and renames her Dulcinea del Toboso.

Don Quixote sets out to right all the injustices in the world, but before his adventures can really begin, his friends and family trick him into returning home. They treat him as a lunatic and refuse to let him read the books that led him into his madness.

Back in his home village, Don Quixote meets a poor farmer named Sancho Panza whom he persuades to serve as his squire. One night, Don Quixote and Sancho secretly ride out and begin their adventures.

The excerpt you are about to read from Chapter 8 relates what happens when Don Quixote and Sancho catch sight of thirty or forty windmills.

from Chapter 8

Of the good fortune which the valorous Don Quixote had in the terrifying and never-before-imagined adventure of the windmills, along with other events that deserve to be suitably recorded.

At this point they caught sight of thirty or forty windmills which were standing on the plain there, and no sooner had Don Quixote laid eyes upon them than he turned to his squire and said, "Fortune is guiding our affairs better than we could have wished; for you see there before you, friend Sancho Panza, some thirty or more lawless giants with whom I mean to do battle. I shall deprive them of their lives, and with the spoils from this encounter we shall begin to enrich ourselves; for this is righteous warfare, and it is a great service to God to remove so accursed a breed from the face of the earth."

"What giants?" said Sancho Panza.

"Those that you see there," replied his master, "those with the long arms, some of which are as much as two leagues in length."

"But look, your Grace, those are not giants but windmills, and what appear to be arms are their wings which, when whirled in the breeze, cause the millstone to go."

"It is plain to be seen," said Don Quixote, "that you have had little experience in this matter of adventures. If you are afraid, go off to one side and say your prayers while I am engaging them in fierce, unequal combat."

Saying this, he gave spurs to his steed Rocinante, without paying any heed to Sancho's warning that these were truly windmills and not giants that he was riding forth to attack. Nor even when he was close upon them did he perceive what they really were, but shouted at the top of his lungs, "Do not seek to flee, cowards and vile creatures that you are, for it is but a single knight with whom you have to deal!"

At that moment a little wind came up and the big wings began turning.

"Though you flourish as many arms as did the giant Briareus,"[1] said Don Quixote when

(Page 627) Don Quixote and Sancho setting out (detail) (1863) by Gustave Doré. Engraving.

The Bridgeman Art Library.

1. **Briareus** (brī·är′ē·əs): in Greek mythology, a giant with a hundred arms who helped Zeus overthrow the Titans.

he perceived this, "you still shall have to answer to me."

He thereupon commended himself with all his heart to his lady Dulcinea, beseeching her to succor him in this peril; and, being well covered with his shield and with his lance at rest, he bore down upon them at a full gallop and fell upon the first mill that stood in his way, giving a thrust at the wing, which was whirling at such a speed that his lance was broken into bits and both horse and horseman went rolling over the plain, very much battered indeed. Sancho upon his donkey came hurrying to his master's assistance as fast as he could, but when he reached the spot, the knight was unable to move, so great was the shock with which he and Rocinante had hit the ground.

"God help us!" exclaimed Sancho, "did I not tell your Grace to look well, that those were nothing but windmills, a fact which no one could fail to see unless he had other mills of the same sort in his head?"

"Be quiet, friend Sancho," said Don Quixote. "Such are the fortunes of war, which more than any other are subject to constant change. What is more, when I come to think of it, I am sure that this must be the work of that magician Frestón, the one who robbed me of my study and my books, and who has thus changed the giants into windmills in order to deprive me of the glory of overcoming them, so great is the enmity that he bears me; but in the end his evil arts shall not prevail against this trusty sword of mine."

"May God's will be done," was Sancho Panza's response. And with the aid of his squire the knight was once more mounted on Rocinante, who stood there with one shoulder half out of joint. And so, speaking of the adventure that had just befallen them, they continued along the Puerto Lápice highway; for there, Don Quixote said, they could not fail to find many and varied adventures, this being a much-traveled thoroughfare. The only thing was, the knight was exceedingly downcast over the loss of his lance.

"I remember," he said to his squire, "having read of a Spanish knight by the name of Diego Pérez de Vargas, who, having broken his sword in battle, tore from an oak a heavy bough or branch and with it did such feats of valor that day, and pounded so many Moors, that he came to be known as Machuca,[2] and he and his descendants from that day forth have been called Vargas y Machuca. I tell you this because I too, intend to provide myself with just such a bough as the one he wielded, and with it I propose to do such exploits that you shall deem yourself fortunate to have been found worthy to come with me and behold and witness things that are almost beyond belief."

"God's will be done," said Sancho. "I believe everything that your Grace says; but straighten yourself up in the saddle a little, for you seem to be slipping down on one side, owing, no doubt, to the shaking up that you received in your fall."

"Ah, that is the truth," replied Don Quixote, "and if I do not speak of my sufferings, it is for the reason that it is not permitted knights-errant to complain of any wound whatsoever, even though their bowels may be dropping out."

"If that is the way it is," said Sancho, "I have nothing more to say; but, God knows, it would suit me better if your Grace did complain when something hurts him. I can assure you that I mean to do so, over the least little thing that ails me—that is, unless the same rule applies to squires as well."

Don Quixote laughed long and heartily over Sancho's simplicity, telling him that he might complain as much as he liked and where and when he liked, whether he had good cause or not; for he had read nothing to the contrary in the ordinances[3] of chivalry. Sancho then called his master's attention to the fact that it was time

2. **Machuca** (mä·chōō′kä): literally, "the pounder," the hero of an old ballad.
3. **ordinances** (ôrd′'n·əns·əz) *n. pl.:* authoritative commands.

Vocabulary

succor (suk′ər) *v.:* help in time of distress.
enmity (en′mə·tē) *n.:* hostility.

The adventure with the windmills (c. 1868) by Gustave Doré. Engraving.

The Bridgeman Art Library.

to eat. The knight replied that he himself had no need of food at the moment, but his squire might eat whenever he chose. Having been granted this permission, Sancho seated himself as best he could upon his beast, and, taking out from his saddlebags the provisions that he had stored there, he rode along leisurely behind his master, munching his victuals and taking a good, hearty swig now and then at the leather flask in a manner that might well have caused the biggest-bellied tavern-keeper of Málaga to envy him. Between drafts he gave not so much as a thought to any promise that his master might have made him, nor did he look upon it as any hardship, but rather as good sport, to go in quest of adventures however hazardous they might be.

The short of the matter is, they spent the night under some trees, from one of which Don Quixote tore off a withered bough to serve him as a lance, placing it in the lance head from which he had removed the broken one. He did not sleep all night long for thinking of his lady Dulcinea; for this was in accordance with what he had read in his books, of men of arms in the forest or desert places who kept a wakeful vigil, sustained by the memory of their ladies fair. Not so with Sancho, whose stomach was full, and not with chicory water.[4] He fell into a dreamless slumber, and had not his master called him, he would not have been awakened either by the rays of the sun in his face or by the many birds who greeted the coming of the new day with their merry song.

Upon arising, he had another go at the flask, finding it somewhat more flaccid than it had been the night before, a circumstance which grieved his heart, for he could not see that they were on the way to remedying the deficiency within any very short space of time. Don Quixote did not wish any breakfast; for, as has been said, he was in the habit of nourishing himself on savorous memories. They then set out once more along the road to Puerto Lápice, and around three in the afternoon they came in sight of the pass that bears that name.

"There," said Don Quixote as his eyes fell upon it, "we may plunge our arms up to the elbow in what are known as adventures. But I must warn you that even though you see me in the greatest peril in the world, you are not to lay hand upon your sword to defend me, unless it be that those who attack me are rabble and men of low degree, in which case you may very well come to my aid; but if they be gentlemen, it is in no wise permitted by the laws of chivalry that you should assist me until you yourself shall have been dubbed a knight."

"Most certainly, sir," replied Sancho, "your Grace shall be very well obeyed in this; all the more so for the reason that I myself am of a peaceful disposition and not fond of meddling in the quarrels and feuds of others. However, when it comes to protecting my own person, I shall not take account of those laws of which you speak, seeing that all laws, human and divine, permit each one to defend himself whenever he is attacked."

"I am willing to grant you that," assented Don Quixote, "but in this matter of defending me against gentlemen you must restrain your natural impulses."

"I promise you I shall do so," said Sancho. "I will observe this precept as I would the Sabbath day. . . ." ■

4. **chicory water:** inexpensive coffee substitute.

Vocabulary

victuals (vit′'lz) *n. pl.:* provisions; food.
vigil (vij′əl) *n.:* staying watchfully awake.
flaccid (flas′id) *adj.:* limp; flabby.
disposition (dis′pə·zish′ən) *n.:* natural qualities of personality.

Response and Analysis

Reading Check

1. After being knocked down by the windmill, how does Don Quixote explain the fact that he has not killed a giant?
2. What natural human needs does Don Quixote ignore? How does Sancho Panza, in contrast, satisfy those same needs?

Thinking Critically

3. In his **parody,** Cervantes uses the techniques of **exaggeration, verbal irony, incongruity,** and **humorous imitation.** List one example of each technique used in this selection.
4. Cervantes directly pokes fun at the medieval romance every time Don Quixote obeys one of the rules of knighthood, or "ordinances of chivalry," as he understands them. List three such "rules" that Don Quixote cites.
5. Put simply, an idealist, or romantic, views the world as he or she thinks it ought to be; a realist views the world as it is. Is Don Quixote an idealist or a realist? Which role does Sancho Panza fit? Cite evidence from the text to support your conclusions.
6. A **foil** is a character who is used as a contrast to another character. In what ways is Sancho Panza a foil to Don Quixote? Identify the behaviors of the two men that suggest they are opposites.

Comparing Literature

7. How do Don Quixote's optimism and idealism compare with Candide's (see page 619)? Do both of these characters "tilt at windmills," or do they manifest their philosophies in profoundly different ways? Explain your responses.
8. Cervantes parodies the medieval romance in *Don Quixote*, and Alexander Pope mocks the literary epic in *The Rape of the Lock* (see page 605). What satiric techniques do these two lampoons share?

Literary Skills Analyze the characteristics of parody. Compare works from different cultures and literary periods.

Writing Skills Write a parody.

Vocabulary Skills Demonstrate word knowledge.

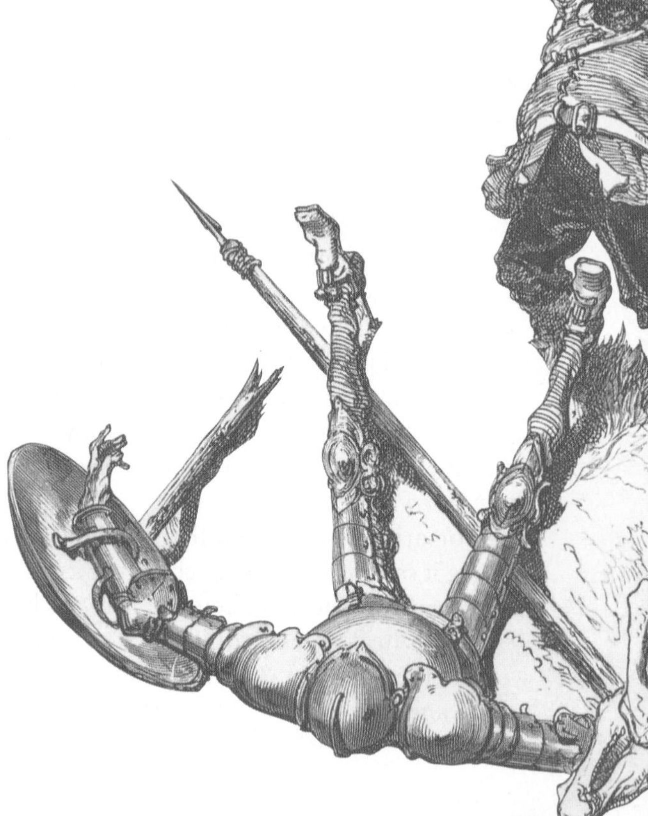

Don Quixote and the windmill (detail) by Gustave Doré.

Giraudon/Art Resource, New York. Bibliothèque Nationale, Paris, France.

WRITING

A Modern-Day Parody

Imagine Cervantes writing a parody today. Select some form of written communication that you imagine he would relish lampooning, and then write a **parody** of your own. You may choose from such forms of writing as the multiple-choice test, the memoir, the business memo, the advice-column letter, or the political-campaign speech. Before you begin writing your parody, decide what the target of your satire will be. Then, use one or more of Cervantes's tools—exaggeration, verbal irony, incongruity, humorous imitation—to write a parody of your own.

Vocabulary Development

Question and Answer Charts

succor	victuals	flaccid
enmity	vigil	disposition

Work with a group or alone to find out what you know about the meanings of the Vocabulary words listed above. Make up two questions about each word, and organize your answers in a chart. After you've completed charts for all the words, invite someone else to answer your questions. The first word has been done for you.

succor	
Questions	**Answers**
How would you succor someone who has been injured?	• get medical help • try to make him or her comfortable
In what situations might you be required to succor someone?	• when someone falls off a horse • when someone faints

Introduction Comparing Points of View

Women's Rights

You will be reading the three selections listed above in this Comparing Points of View feature on women's rights. In the top corner of the pages in this feature, you'll find three stars. Smaller versions of the stars appear next to the questions on page 644 that focus on women's rights. At the end of the feature (page 650), you'll compare the various points of view expressed in the selections.

Examining the Issue: Women's Rights

The women's rights movement, an ongoing series of political movements aimed at attaining educational, social, and political equality for women, arose primarily in England and the United States. Its roots lay both in humanistic thought (see page 278) and in the Industrial Revolution of the eighteenth and nineteenth centuries—two important influences that, in very different ways, contributed to the creation of a more democratic society.

According to the dictates of both theology and law, married women of the eighteenth century still could not own property, run a business, or control their own lives or those of their children. Social critics (both male and female) began to contrast this state of affairs with the ideal of freedom that inspired the American and French Revolutions of the late eighteenth century. Since then, there have been countless advances and setbacks in campaigns for the rights of women to study, to own property, to vote, to pursue a career, and, in general, to control their own lives. The readings in this Comparing Points of View feature present some of the earliest shots fired in the battle for women's rights.

Pages 634–650 cover **Literary Skills** Analyze points of view on a topic.

Reading Skills Understand and analyze rhetorical devices.

Make the Connection

Quickwrite

The basic concept behind the issue of women's rights is that women and men are equally human and should have equal stature in society. Few westerners now challenge that concept, yet many dislike or reject such labels as "feminism," preferring instead to speak of "human rights" or "women's rights." What do these three labels mean to you? Write a brief explanation of which term you find most meaningful and why you prefer it over the other two terms.

Reading Skills

Analyzing Rhetorical Devices

Rhetorical devices are methods writers or speakers use to make their language more effective or to reinforce a particular point. Rhetorical devices are particularly important in any kind of communication that seeks to win the reader over to a writer's point of view. Speeches, policy statements, debates, political and religious tracts, arguments, persuasive essays, and many other kinds of public documents freely employ a variety of rhetorical devices, such as the following:

- **rhetorical question:** The writer, for effect, asks a question for which an answer is not expected—usually because the writer expects that the audience will agree with the opinion being expressed.
- **argument by analogy:** The writer points out a parallel between two subjects or situations in order to make a point.
- **historical allusion:** The writer cites a person, a place, or an event from history that relates to the topic at hand.
- **repetition** or **restatement:** The writer repeats the main idea in different ways.
- **counterargument:** The writer anticipates the audience's objections or concerns and openly addresses them.
- **appeal to authority:** The writer cites the opinions of experts on the subject.
- **illustrative anecdote or example:** The writer uses a brief story or cites a particular case in order to support his or her point.

In the following selections on the topic of women's rights, be alert for various rhetorical devices. How does each writer use them to reinforce his or her main points?

The Art Class (late 19th century) by Arturo Ricci.

Mary Wollstonecraft
(1759–1797)

Mary Wollstonecraft Godwin (c. 1797) by John Opie. Engraving after painting.

The Granger Collection, New York.

English feminism begins with Mary Wollstonecraft, who demanded "JUSTICE for one half of the human race"—that is, women. The last place Wollstonecraft felt she would ever find justice in eighteenth-century England was in the institution of marriage. "I will not marry," she announced, a decision born from years of emotionally and physically protecting her mother from the abuse and anger of a husband and father who had squandered his fortune in futile attempts to become a successful gentleman farmer. Wollstonecraft's upbringing had left her with good reason to distrust the bond of marriage.

Nineteen and self-educated, Wollstonecraft left home to work in some of the few occupations legally available to single women. Eventually, she became a governess for a wealthy Irish family and witnessed the "dissipated lives the women of quality lead," with their single-minded obsession with "matrimony and dress."

Wollstonecraft left Ireland and moved to London to work as an editorial assistant. There she met some of the radical political thinkers of the day, including Thomas Paine, an American agitator and patriot, and William Godwin, a political philosopher. (At a dinner party, Wollstonecraft and Godwin disagreed with each other on every topic discussed.)

In 1789, the French Revolution erupted, an upheaval that terrified monarchs in Europe and thrilled radicals with its slogan "liberty, equality, fraternity." Wollstonecraft published *A Vindication of the Rights of Men* (1790), which vigorously defended the principles of human equality underlying the French Revolution. She then topped that with her masterpiece, *A Vindication of the Rights of Woman* (1792), an impassioned criticism of social and economic institutions that sanctioned women's inequality. Critics—especially those who refused to read her book or answer her arguments—attacked her swiftly; one critic called her "a hyena in petticoats."

Eventually—and ironically—Wollstonecraft became romantically involved with William Godwin, the dinner companion with whom she had argued vehemently years before. Godwin had spent years arguing for the abolition of all institutions, especially government, organized religion, and marriage. The two put aside their objections, however, and married, discovering to their delight that they were very happy with each other.

Such domestic joy, however, was short-lived; eleven days after giving birth to their daughter, Mary Wollstonecraft died from septicemia, the result of a botched operation to correct a complication from her pregnancy. Daughter Mary survived, grew up to marry the poet Percy Bysshe Shelley, and wrote the famous novel *Frankenstein* (1818). William Godwin erected a stone at Wollstonecraft's grave with the inscription: "Mary Wollstonecraft Godwin, Author of *A Vindication of the Rights of Woman.*" No other words were necessary.

Before You Read

from A Vindication of the Rights of Woman

Points *of* View

In much of today's world, the same educational opportunities are available to both genders. Women share the vote with men, and women may study for and pursue virtually any career they wish. These opportunities, often taken for granted, were not always available to women. In England, during the Restoration, the educated woman was the exception to the rule, and women were not allowed to vote. Keep these facts in mind as you read this excerpt from a famous feminist's essay. How much of what she says still rings true today? How far have we—or haven't we—come since the late 1700s?

Literary Focus

Tone

Tone is the attitude a writer takes toward the reader or toward his or her topic. Writers establish tone through the careful choice of details and words. One way that writers control tone is through the use of words with specific **connotations**—those associations and emotions that have come to be attached to a word through usage. For example, the words *economical* and *frugal* are both synonyms for *thrifty,* but *economical* connotes that a person is simply managing expenditures so as to avoid wasting money, while *frugal* connotes that a person has cut down on all but necessary expenses and is counting every penny. Be alert to Wollstonecraft's choice of "loaded" words—words with strong connotations.

> **Tone** is the attitude a writer takes toward the reader, the subject, or a character.
>
> *For more on Tone, see the Handbook of Literary and Historical Terms.*

Reading Skills

Noting Patterns of Organization

Persuasive arguments, like the ones in this famous essay, usually state a position, clarify that position, offer supporting arguments for it, and conclude by restating the position or making recommendations or judgments based upon it. The excerpt that follows is the introduction to Wollstonecraft's essay. Introductions typically prepare the reader for the text that follows, by explaining why the text is called for and presenting its arguments in brief form. As you read the introduction, take note of sections that explain why the essay as a whole is necessary and sections that present an overview of the arguments the essay will propose.

The word *vindication* is used here to mean "justification."

Literary Skills Analyze points of view on a topic. Understand tone and connotations.

Reading Skills Understand patterns of organization.

Vocabulary Development

solicitude (sə•lis′ə•to͞od′) *n.:* care; concern.

partial (pär′shəl) *adj.:* biased.

deplore (dē•plôr′) *v.:* regret; strongly disapprove of.

fastidious (fa•stid′ē•əs) *adj.:* picky; overly fussy.

specious (spē′shəs) *adj.:* showy but false; lacking genuineness.

abrogated (ab′rə•gāt′id) *v.* used as *adj.:* abolished; repealed.

cursory (kʉr′sə•rē) *adj.:* hasty; superficial.

vitiate (vish′ē•āt) *v.:* impair; weaken; spoil.

insipid (in•sip′id) *adj.:* dull; flat.

propensity (prə•pen′sə•tē) *n.:* natural inclination or tendency.

INTERNET

Vocabulary Practice

•

More About Mary Wollstonecraft

•

Keyword: LE7 12-4

Mr. B. Finds Pamela Writing (18th century) by Joseph Highmore. Illustration for *Pamela, or Virtue Rewarded* (1740) by Samuel Richardson. Oil on canvas.
Pamela is the servant of Mr. B's mother. The novel involves Mr. B's dishonorable pursuit of Pamela.
The Bridgeman Art Library.

from A Vindication of the Rights of Woman

Mary Wollstonecraft

Introduction

After considering the historic page, and viewing the living world with anxious solicitude, the most melancholy emotions of sorrowful indignation have depressed my spirits, and I have sighed when obliged to confess, that either nature has made a great difference between man and man, or that the civilization which has hitherto taken place in the world has been very partial. I have turned over various books written on the subject of education, and patiently observed the conduct of parents and the management of schools; but what has been the result?—a profound conviction that the neglected education of my fellow-creatures is the grand source of the misery I deplore; and that women, in particular, are rendered weak and wretched by a variety of concurring causes, originating from one hasty conclusion. The conduct and manners of women, in fact, evidently prove that their minds are not in a healthy state; for, like the flowers which are planted in too rich a soil, strength and usefulness are sacrificed to beauty; and the flaunting leaves, after having pleased a fastidious eye, fade, disregarded on the stalk, long before the season when they ought to have arrived at maturity. —One cause of this barren blooming I attribute to a false system of education, gathered from the books written on this subject by men who, considering females rather as women than human creatures, have been more anxious to make them alluring mistresses than affectionate wives and rational mothers; ❶

❶ In the first paragraph, Wollstonecraft sets up her argument by asserting that women are denied proper educations.

? *What loaded words does she use in this opening paragraph?*

Vocabulary

solicitude (sə·lis′ə·to͞od′) *n.:* care; concern.

partial (pär′shəl) *adj.:* biased.

deplore (dē·plôr′) *v.:* regret; strongly disapprove of.

fastidious (fa·stid′ē·əs) *adj.:* picky; overly fussy.

and the understanding of the sex has been so bubbled[1] by this specious homage, that the civilized women of the present century, with a few exceptions, are only anxious to inspire love, when they ought to cherish a nobler ambition, and by their abilities and virtues exact[2] respect.

In a treatise, therefore, on female rights and manners, the works which have been particularly written for their improvement must not be overlooked; especially when it is asserted, in direct terms, that the minds of women are enfeebled by false refinement; that the books of instruction, written by men of genius, have had the same tendency as more frivolous productions; and that, in the true style of Mahometanism,[3] they are treated as a kind of subordinate beings, and not as a part of the human species, when improvable[4] reason is allowed to be the dignified distinction which raises men above the brute creation, and puts a natural scepter[5] in a feeble hand.

Yet, because I am a woman, I would not lead my readers to suppose that I mean violently to agitate the contested question respecting the equality or inferiority of the sex; but as the subject lies in my way, and I cannot pass it over without subjecting the main tendency of my reasoning to misconstruction,[6] I shall stop a moment to deliver, in a few words, my opinion. ❷—

❷
In this paragraph and the next, Wollstonecraft asserts that she will acknowledge and draw upon the work of other people who share her view, but that it is her primary intention to express her own opinions.

? *What two opinions does Wollstonecraft then express?*

1. **bubbled** *v.:* be deluded with "bubbles," that is, flimsy evidence.
2. **exact** *v.:* demand; require.
3. **Mahometanism:** Islam, the religion of Muslims. Europeans mistakenly thought that the Koran teaches that women have no souls. On the contrary, the Koran teaches that women are to be treated as equals to men.
4. **improveable** *adj.:* capable of being improved.
5. **scepter** (sep′tər) *n.:* ornamental staff symbolizing a monarch's authority.
6. **misconstruction** *n.:* misunderstanding.

In the government of the physical world it is observable that the female in point of strength is, in general, inferior to the male. This is the law of nature; and it does not appear to be suspended or abrogated in favor of woman. A degree of physical superiority cannot, therefore, be denied—and it is a noble prerogative![7] But not content with this natural pre-eminence, men endeavor to sink us still lower, merely to render us alluring objects for a moment; and women, intoxicated by the adoration which men, under the influence of their senses, pay them, do not seek to obtain a durable interest in their hearts, or to become the friends of the fellow creatures who find amusement in their society.

I am aware of an obvious inference:—from every quarter have I heard exclamations against masculine women; but where are they to be found? If by this appellation[8] men mean to inveigh[9] against their ardour in hunting, shooting, and gaming, I shall most cordially join in the cry; but if it be against the imitation of manly virtues, or, more properly speaking, the attainment of those talents and virtues, the exercise of which ennobles the human character, and which raise females in the scale of animal being, when they are comprehensively termed mankind;—all those who view them with a philosophic eye must, I should think, wish with me, that they may every day grow more and more masculine. ❸

❸
In this paragraph Wollstonecraft anticipates her readers' concerns and presents a counterargument explaining why women should aspire to be "masculine."

? *What does Wollstonecraft understand the word* masculine *to mean? What implicit assumptions underlie her use of the word?*

7. **prerogative** *n.:* privilege.
8. **appellation** *n.:* name.
9. **inveigh** *v.:* complain loudly.

Vocabulary

specious (spē′shəs) *adj.:* showy but false; lacking genuineness.

abrogated (ab′rə·gāt′id) *v.* used as *adj.:* abolished; repealed.

This discussion naturally divides the subject. I shall first consider women in the grand light of human creatures, who, in common with men, are placed on this earth to unfold their faculties; and afterwards I shall more particularly point out their peculiar designation. ❹

> ❹
> **?** *How will the writer divide her subject?*

I wish also to steer clear of an error which many respectable writers have fallen into; for the instruction which has hitherto been addressed to women, has rather been applicable to *ladies,* if the little indirect advice, that is scattered through Sandford and Merton,[10] be excepted; but, addressing my sex in a firmer tone, I pay particular attention to those in the middle class, because they appear to be in the most natural state. Perhaps the seeds of false refinement, immorality, and vanity, have ever been shed by the great. Weak, artificial beings, raised above the common wants and affections of their race, in a premature unnatural manner, undermine the very foundation of virtue, and spread corruption through the whole mass of society! As a class of mankind they have the strongest claim to pity; the education of the rich tends to render them vain and helpless, and the unfolding mind is not strengthened by the practice of those duties which dignify the human character.—They only live to amuse themselves, and by the same law which in nature invariably produces certain effects, they soon only afford barren amusement. ❺

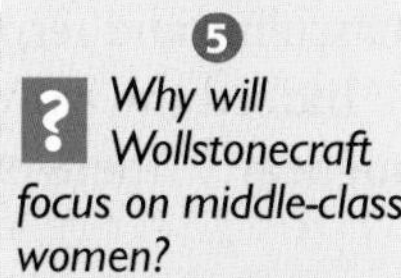

> ❺
> **?** *Why will Wollstonecraft focus on middle-class women?*

But as I purpose[11] taking a separate view of the different ranks of society, and of the moral character of women in each, this hint is, for the present, sufficient; and I have only alluded to the subject, because it appears to me to be the very essence of an introduction to give a cursory account of the contents of the work it introduces.

My own sex, I hope, will excuse me, if I treat them like rational creatures, instead of flattering their *fascinating* graces, and viewing them as if they were in a state of perpetual childhood, unable to stand alone. I earnestly wish to point out in what true dignity and human happiness consists—I wish to persuade women to endeavor to acquire strength, both of mind and body, and to convince them that the soft phrases, susceptibility of heart, delicacy of sentiment, and refinement of taste, are almost synonymous with epithets[12] of weakness, and that those beings who are only the objects of pity and that kind of love, which has been termed its sister, will soon become objects of contempt. ❻

> ❻
> This and the next paragraph contain a rough sketch of Wollstonecraft's essay.
>
> **?** *What is Wollstonecraft trying to persuade her readers of?*

Dismissing then those pretty feminine phrases, which the men condescendingly use to soften our slavish dependence, and despising that weak elegancy of mind, exquisite sensibility, and sweet docility of manners, supposed to be the sexual characteristics of the weaker vessel, I wish to shew[13] that elegance is inferior to virtue, that the first object of laudable[14] ambition is to obtain a character as a human being, regardless of the distinction of sex; and that secondary views should be brought to this simple touchstone.[15]

This is a rough sketch of my plan; and should I express my conviction with the energetic emotions that I feel whenever I think of the subject,

---

10. **Sandford and Merton:** reference to *The History of Sandford and Merton,* a children's book. A character in the book often cites the moral superiority of a poor boy over a rich one.
11. **purpose** *v.:* intend.
12. **epithets** (ep′ə·thets′) *n. pl.:* names.
13. **shew** *v.:* archaic spelling of *show.*
14. **laudable** *adj.:* praiseworthy.
15. **touchstone** *n.:* criterion; originally a stone used for testing the quality of gold and silver alloys by the color of the streak produced by rubbing them upon it.

Vocabulary

cursory (kur′sə·rē) *adj.:* hasty; superficial.

the dictates of experience and reflection will be felt by some of my readers. Animated by this important object, I shall disdain to cull[16] my phrases or polish my style;—I aim at being useful, and sincerity will render me unaffected; for, wishing rather to persuade by the force of my arguments, than dazzle by the elegance of my language, I shall not waste my time in rounding periods, or in fabricating the turgid bombast[17] of artificial feelings, which, coming from the head, never reach the heart.—I shall be employed about things, not words!—and, anxious to render my sex more respectable members of society, I shall try to avoid that flowery diction which has slided from essays into novels, and from novels into familiar letters and conversation. ❼

> ❼
> ? *What kind of language will Wollstonecraft use, and why?*

These pretty superlatives,[18] dropping glibly from the tongue, vitiate the taste, and create a kind of sickly delicacy that turns away from simple unadorned truth; and a deluge of false sentiments and overstretched feelings, stifling the natural emotions of the heart, render the domestic pleasures insipid, that ought to sweeten the exercise of those severe duties, which educate a rational and immortal being for a nobler field of action.

The education of women has, of late, been more attended to than formerly; yet they are still reckoned a frivolous sex, and ridiculed or pitied by the writers who endeavor by satire or instruction to improve them. It is acknowledged that they spend many of the first years of their lives in acquiring a smattering of accomplishments; meanwhile strength of body and mind are sacrificed to libertine[19] notions of beauty, to the desire of establishing themselves,—the only way women can rise in the world,—by marriage. And this desire making mere animals of them, when they marry they act as such children may be expected to act:—they dress; they paint, and nickname God's creatures. —Surely these weak beings are only fit for a seraglio![20] —Can they be expected to govern a family with judgment, or take care of the poor babes whom they bring into the world? ❽

> ❽
> ? *What, according to Wollstonecraft, is women's main ambition in life?*

If then it can be fairly deduced from the present conduct of the sex, from the prevalent fondness for pleasure which takes place of ambition and those nobler passions that open and enlarge the soul; that the instruction which women have hitherto received has only tended, with the constitution[21] of civil society, to render them insignificant objects of desire—mere propagators[22] of fools!—if it can be proved that in aiming to accomplish them, without cultivating their understandings, they are taken out of their sphere of duties, and made ridiculous and useless when the short-lived bloom of beauty is over,* I presume that *rational* men will excuse me for endeavoring to persuade them to become more masculine and respectable. ❾

> ❾
> This paragraph consists of a single sentence.
>
> ? *Break it down by locating the two if statements in the sentence. Then, paraphrase both of them, as well as the implied then statement in the final clause.*

Indeed the word masculine is only a bugbear:[23] there is little reason to fear that

---

*A lively writer, I cannot recollect his name, asks what business women turned of forty have to do in the world?

---

16. **cull** *v.:* sort out.
17. **turgid bombast:** pompous rant or utterance.
18. **superlatives** *n.:* exaggerations.
19. **libertine** *adj.:* sensual.
20. **seraglio** (si·ral'yō) *n.:* place in a Muslim house where wives live; a harem.
21. **constitution** *n.:* composition.
22. **propagators** *n. pl.:* spreaders.
23. **bugbear** *n.:* anything causing needless fear.

Vocabulary

vitiate (vish'ē·āt) *v.:* impair; weaken; spoil.
insipid (in·sip'id) *adj.:* dull; flat.

The Bridgeman Art Library.

Marriage à la Mode: The Marriage Contract (c. 1743) by William Hogarth. Oil on canvas.

women will acquire too much courage or fortitude; for their apparent inferiority with respect to bodily strength, must render them, in some degree, dependent on men in the various relations of life; but why should it be increased by prejudices that give a sex to virtue, and confound simple truths with sensual reveries? [24]

Women are, in fact, so much degraded by mistaken notions of female excellence, that I do not mean to add a paradox when I assert, that this artificial weakness produces a propensity to tyrannize, and gives birth to cunning, the natural opponent of strength, which leads them to play off those contemptible infantine airs that undermine esteem even whilst they excite desire. Let men become more chaste and modest, and if women do not grow wiser in the same ratio, it will be clear that they have weaker understandings. It seems scarcely necessary to say, that I now speak of the sex in general. Many individuals have more sense than their male relatives; and, as nothing preponderates[25] where there is a constant struggle for equilibrium, without it has naturally more gravity, some women govern their husbands without degrading themselves, because intellect will always govern. ⑩ ■

24. **reveries** *n. pl.:* musings.

25. **preponderates** *v.:* predominates.

⑩ Wollstonecraft points out a curious **paradox,** or seeming contradiction, that has occurred as a result of women's oppression.

? *What is this paradox?*

Vocabulary

propensity (prə·pen′sə·tē) *n.:* natural inclination or tendency.

Response and Analysis

Reading Check

1. Outline the main points of this essay, and show the details the writer uses to support them. Your answers to the questions posed in the text will guide you in making your outline.
2. In the final four paragraphs (beginning "The education of women . . ."), what test does the author propose for judging the value of educating women?

Thinking Critically

3. Overall, what basic roles for women does the author continue to accept? In her view, how would better education help women fulfill these roles?
4. The author uses wit and **satire** throughout the essay whenever she discusses the qualities conventionally assigned to men and to women. List some of those qualities. How does the writer satirize the belief that educating women will make them masculine?
5. In paragraphs five through nine, how does the author outline her topic? You might want to refer to your reading notes for help.
6. In her concluding paragraph, how does Wollstonecraft explain women's use of cunning to get their way? What solution does she propose?
7. How would you describe the **tone** of Wollstonecraft's text? What particular words, phrases, or longer passages contribute to this tone?

Literary Criticism

8. **Political approach.** Explain the basic political viewpoint that Wollstonecraft advances regarding the education of middle-class women. In what way is her view a radical one for the time in which she lived? Are there any ways in which her argument is limited by the political realities of her time?

Literary Skills
Analyze points of view on a topic. Analyze tone.

Reading Skills
Analyze patterns of organization.

Writing Skills
Write an essay.

Vocabulary Skills
Demonstrate word knowledge.

Grammar Skills
Use correct subject-verb agreement.

WRITING

Then and Now

In a brief **essay,** evaluate the relevance of Wollstonecraft's essay to our time. Do her observations about the role of women hold true today, or are her arguments limited to the social realities of the eighteenth century? Which, if any, of her observations about men and women remain valid in the twenty-first century? Use details from the text and examples from real life to support your response.

Vocabulary Development

Question and Answer

Be prepared to justify your answer to each question.

1. Name something that a parent would feel solicitude for.
2. What is the opposite of a partial juror?
3. What word is the opposite of *deplore*?
4. What is the opposite of a fastidious person?
5. Why would you reject a specious argument?
6. If you have abrogated your responsibilities, have you abandoned them or embraced them?
7. What is the opposite of a cursory investigation?
8. If you vitiate an argument, do you strengthen it or weaken it?
9. What is the opposite of an insipid argument?
10. If you have a propensity for lying, how would people react to you?

Grammar Link

Make Sure It Agrees: Subject-Verb Agreement

Read the following paragraph about Mary Wollstonecraft.

> Doubts about the institution of marriage was always uppermost in Mary Wollstonecraft's mind. Marriage, along with domestic life, were a kind of slavery to her. To her great surprise, however, she found a true soul mate in William Godwin. Wollstonecraft and Godwin was in some ways an unlikely couple. Neither Wollstonecraft nor Godwin were "the marrying kind." Yet they found solace and support in each other. One of their favorite pastimes were exchanging witty notes.

The writer has trouble with some tricky subject-verb combinations. In many English sentences and clauses the subject comes right before the verb. When you vary this standard sentence pattern, however, agreement problems can occur. These problems can be solved and mastered.

1. Subject-verb agreement means that a singular verb takes a singular subject and plural subjects take plural verbs. A subject's number is not changed by a following phrase or clause.

   Doubts about the institution of marriage were always uppermost in Mary Wollstonecraft's mind.

2. In formal usage, a singular subject followed by a parenthetical phrase such as *along with* . . . , *as well as* . . . , or *in addition to* . . . remains singular.

   Marriage, along with domestic life, was a kind of slavery to her.

3. A compound subject is two or more subjects having the same verb. A compound subject joined by *and* usually takes a plural verb, even if one subject is singular.

   Wollstonecraft and Godwin were in some ways an unlikely couple.

4. When a compound subject is joined by *or* or *nor*, the verb agrees with the subject closer to the verb.

   Neither Wollstonecraft nor Godwin was "the marrying kind."

5. When a singular indefinite pronoun is the subject, it takes a singular verb.

   One of their favorite pastimes was exchanging witty notes.

PRACTICE

On a separate sheet of paper, correct any problems with subject-verb agreement in the following sentences. If the subject and verb agree, write *correct*.

1. Women who rise to the upper class lives only to amuse themselves, according to Wollstonecraft.
2. Marriage to wealthy men were the only way women could improve their status.
3. One of Wollstonecraft's early novels were partly autobiographical.
4. Wollstonecraft thought that neither beauty nor weakness make women attractive.
5. The goal of Wollstonecraft's writings is to educate and bring about social reform.

Apply to Your Writing

Review a writing assignment you are working on now or have already completed. Are there any sentences in which the subjects and verbs do not agree? Revise to correct the subject-verb agreement.

For more help, see Agreement of Subject and Verb, 2a–i, in the Language Handbook.

Connected Readings

Mary, Lady Chudleigh ...... **To the Ladies**
Daniel Defoe .... *from* **The Education of Women**

You have just read an excerpt from Mary Wollstonecraft's persuasive essay *A Vindication of the Rights of Woman* and considered the views it expresses about women's rights. Each of the next two selections you will be reading presents another point of view on women's rights. As you read, ask yourself how these views are alike and how they are different. After you have read these selections, answer the questions on page 650, which ask you to compare all three selections.

Points *of* View

Before You Read

The poems and essays of Mary, Lady Chudleigh (1656–1710), addressed the concerns of women of her time and explored a philosophy of how to live a peaceful life. She adamantly opposed the idea that wives should submit to the will of their husbands, and she expressed this view in many of her works. While none of her writings were published until 1701, Chudleigh wrote for members of her London literary circle for years. Even though four of her children died at a very young age and she herself suffered years of excruciating rheumatism that ultimately caused her death, her poems and essays demonstrate that she had the time and freedom to acquire an impressive knowledge of philosophy, science, and history.

"To the Ladies" is Chudleigh's most anthologized poem; it appeared in print in 1703 and was so popular that it has been found copied onto the flyleaves of other books. Chudleigh's marriage may have been somewhat unrewarding and may have contributed to the bitter tone in this poem.

POEM

To the Ladies

Mary, Lady Chudleigh

Wife and Servant are the same,
But only differ in the Name:
For when that fatal Knot is ty'd,
Which nothing, nothing can divide:
When she the word *obey* has said,
And Man by Law supreme has made,
Then all that's kind is laid aside,
And nothing left but State° and Pride:
Fierce as an Eastern Prince he grows,
And all his innate Rigor shows:
Then but to look, to laugh, or speak,
Will the Nuptial Contract break.
Like Mutes she Signs alone must make,
And never any Freedom take:
But still be govern'd by a Nod,
And fear her Husband as her God:
Him still must serve, him still obey,
And nothing act, and nothing say,
But what her haughty Lord thinks fit,
Who with the Pow'r, has all the Wit.
Then shun, oh! shun that wretched State,
And all the fawning Flatt'rers hate:
Value your selves, and Men despise,
You must be proud, if you'll be wise.

8. **State** *n.:* ostentation; pretentiousness.

Points *of* View

Before You Read

Daniel Defoe (1660–1731) was at various times a businessman and a spy, but he was always a man who wrote and wrote and wrote—more than five hundred works in all, on every conceivable subject, from the choice of a wife to the history of the devil to the manufacture of glass. He wrote in every literary form: political pamphlets, treatises on economic theory, satiric verse, popular novels, and journalistic accounts of sensational events. During Defoe's lifetime, his political writings led to notoriety, arrests, public punishment, and even jail time. It is a great irony of literary history that the prolific Defoe is now primarily remembered as the author of only one book, a novel about a survivor—a shipwrecked sailor named *Robinson Crusoe* (1719).

Daniel Defoe (1706).
The Granger Collection, New York.

Reading informational materials: analyzing an argument. In order to convince audiences to think or act in a certain way, writers use **argument,** a form of persuasion that appeals to reason, rather than to emotion. Underlying any argument is the writer's **point of view,** an attitude shaped by the writer's background and values. No matter how logical and well-reasoned an argument is, the careful reader can often discern a particular leaning, or **bias,** on the part of a writer—a value judgment or preference that prevents the author from being completely impartial.

ESSAY

from The Education of Women

Daniel Defoe

I have often thought of it as one of the most barbarous customs in the world, considering us as a civilized and a Christian country, that we deny the advantages of learning to women. ❶ We reproach the sex every day with folly and impertinence; while I am confident, had they the advantages of education equal to us, they would be guilty of less than ourselves.

> ❶ What is Defoe's central claim?

One would wonder, indeed, how it should happen that women are conversible at all; since they are only beholden to natural parts, for all their knowledge. Their youth is spent to teach them to stitch and sew or make baubles. They are taught to read, indeed, and perhaps to write their names, or so; and that is the height of a woman's education. And I would but ask

Reading Skills
Analyze a writer's argument.

The Young Schoolmistress (1740) by Jean-Baptiste Chardin. Oil on canvas.
The Bridgeman Art Library.

any who slight the sex for their understanding, what is a man (a gentleman, I mean) good for, that is taught no more? I need not give instances, or examine the character of a gentleman, with a good estate, or a good family, and with tolerable parts; and examine what figure he makes for want of education.

The soul is placed in the body like a rough diamond; and must be polished, or the luster of it will never appear. And 'tis manifest, that as the rational soul distinguishes us from brutes; so education carries on the distinction, and makes some less brutish than others. ❷ This is too evident to need any demonstration. But why then should women be denied the benefit of instruction? If knowledge and understanding had been useless additions to the sex, GOD Almighty would never have given them capacities; for he made nothing needless. Besides, I would ask such, What they can see in ignorance, that they should think it a necessary ornament to a woman? or how much worse is a wise woman than a fool? or what has the woman done to forfeit the privilege of being taught? Does she plague us with her pride and impertinence? Why did we not let her learn, that she might have had more wit? Shall we upbraid women with folly, when 'tis only the error of this inhuman custom, that hindered them from being made wiser? ❸

❷
Defoe uses an analogy to advance his argument.

? *In the analogy,* polish *is to* diamond *as* educate *is to* ______.

❸
In a series of rhetorical questions, Defoe explores (and implicitly dismisses) several reasons why women are kept in ignorance.

? *Paraphrase two of these reasons.*

The capacities of women are supposed to be greater, and their senses quicker than those of the men; and what they might be capable of being bred to, is plain from some instances of female wit, which this age is not without. Which upbraids us with Injustice, and looks as if we denied women the advantages of education, for fear they should *vie* with the men in their improvements. . . . ❹

> ❹ ? *What conclusion does Defoe draw about the true reason for the neglect of women's education?*

[They] should be taught all sorts of breeding suitable both to their genius and quality. And in particular, Music and Dancing; which it would be cruelty to bar the sex of, because they are their darlings. But besides this, they should be taught languages, as particularly French and Italian: and I would venture the injury of giving a woman more tongues than one. They should, as a particular study, be taught all the graces of speech, and all the necessary air of conversation; which our common education is so defective in, that I need not expose it. They should be brought to read books, and especially history; and so to read as to make them understand the world, and be able to know and judge of things when they hear of them.

To such whose genius would lead them to it, I would deny no sort of learning; but the chief thing, in general, is to cultivate the understandings of the sex, that they may be capable of all sorts of conversation; that their parts and judgments being improved, they may be as profitable in their conversation as they are pleasant. ❺

> ❺ ? *What does Defoe believe women should be taught, and for what purpose?*

Women, in my observation, have little or no difference in them, but as they are or are not distinguished by education. Tempers, indeed, may in some degree influence them, but the main distinguishing part is their Breeding. . . .

The great distinguishing difference, which is seen in the world between men and women, is in their education; and this is manifested by comparing it with the difference between one man or woman, and another.

And herein it is that I take upon me to make such a bold assertion, That all the world are mistaken in their practice about women. For I cannot think that GOD Almighty ever made them so delicate, so glorious creatures; and furnished them with such charms, so agreeable and so delightful to mankind; with souls capable of the same accomplishments with men: and all, to be only Stewards of our Houses, Cooks, and Slaves. ❻

> ❻ ? *Do you detect any subtle biases against women in Defoe's argument?*

Not that I am for exalting the female government in the least: but, in short, *I would have men take women for companions, and educate them to be fit for it.* A woman of sense and breeding will scorn as much to encroach upon the prerogative of man, as a man of sense will scorn to oppress the weakness of the woman. But if the women's souls were refined and improved by teaching, that word would be lost. To say, the *weakness* of the sex, as to judgment, would be nonsense; for ignorance and folly would be no more to be found among women than men.

I remember a passage, which I heard from a very fine woman. She had wit and capacity enough, an extraordinary shape and face, and a great fortune: but had been cloistered up all her time; and for fear of being stolen, had not had the liberty of being taught the common necessary knowledge of women's affairs. And when she came to converse in the world, her natural wit made her so sensible of the want of education, that she gave this short reflection on herself: "I am ashamed to talk with my very maids," says she, "for I don't know when they do right or wrong. I had more need go to school, than be married.". . . ❼

> ❼ ? *How does Defoe use this anecdote to reinforce his main idea?*

'Tis a thing will be more easily granted than remedied. . . . ■

Analysis Comparing Points *of* View

Women's Rights

The questions on this page ask you to analyze the views on women's rights in the preceding three selections.

Mary Wollstonecraft . . . *from* **A Vindication of the Rights of Woman**

Mary, Lady Chudleigh . . **To the Ladies**

Daniel Defoe . . . . *from* **The Education of Women**

Thinking Critically

1. Why would readers of the eighteenth century have found the opening line of Lady Chudleigh's poem somewhat shocking? What details of the poem support the meaning of this line?
2. In his essay "The Education of Women," what types of learning does Defoe particularly recommend for women? Why?
3. Which of Defoe's arguments sound outdated today? Why?
4. Compare Defoe's essay with Wollstonecraft's. What arguments are advanced by both writers for granting women "the advantages of learning"? What arguments are advanced only by one writer or the other?
5. Compare the second to last sentence of Defoe's essay—"'I had more need go to school, than be married'"—with the last two lines of Chudleigh's poem. How are the ideas related?
6. Each of these writings makes strong claims about the rights of women. Discuss the effectiveness of each text, not only for *what* it says, but for *how* it gets its message across. What **rhetorical devices** do these writers use? Which writer, in your opinion, creates the most powerful and memorable argument? You may want to refer to your reading notes from page 635.

Pages 634–650 cover
Literary Skills Analyze and compare points of view on a topic.
Reading Skills Analyze rhetorical devices.
Writing Skills Write an essay explaining a political philosophy.

WRITING

Defining a Philosophy

In a short paper, summarize your understanding of the philosophical stance that underlies women's rights movements. Then, discuss appropriate names for that philosophy. Was *feminism* originally a good name for it? Is it still a suitable name, or would some other phrase or title speak more clearly to people of the twenty-first century? See your Quickwrite notes for ideas.

PREVIEW

Reflecting *on the* Literary Period

The Restoration and the Eighteenth Century: 1660–1800

The selections in this feature were written during the same literary period as the other selections in Collection 4, and they share many of the same ideas and concerns. The Focus Question will guide your reading and help you reflect on important aspects of the period.

The Connoisseurs (1783) by David Allan.

Think About...

The span of time between the Renaissance and the Romantic period is often called the Age of Reason or the Enlightenment. In an era that prided itself on its belief in human reason and common sense, writers tended to focus on the problems of society and the universal truths of human experience.

In *Gulliver's Travels,* Jonathan Swift uses satire to expose social ills and question the idea of humans as rational animals. Daniel Defoe, in *A Journal of the Plague Year,* strives for a plain style to communicate how a society reacted during a time of unimaginable horror.

Applying reason to human experience, Samuel Johnson emphasizes his belief in traditional virtues, social order, and the role of common sense. Thomas Gray, in his famous elegy, expresses his views on mortality and humility, while creating a mood that foreshadows the writings of the Romantic poets.

Pages 651–682 cover
Literary Skills
Evaluate the philosophical, political, religious, ethical, and social influences of a historical period.

Focus Question

As you read each selection, keep in mind this Focus Question and take notes to help you answer it at the end of the feature:

How does eighteenth-century literature demonstrate the significant role played by reason and common sense in dealing with society's problems and the universal truths of human experience?

from Gulliver's Travels

Meet the Writer **Jonathan Swift** (1667–1745) is one of the greatest masters of clear and simple writing. He once said that the secret of good prose is "proper words in proper places," and nothing is more difficult than that.

(For more information about Jonathan Swift, see page 579.)

Background In 1726, Swift's masterpiece, *Gulliver's Travels,* was published anonymously and became a sensational success. It can be read on two levels: As an entertaining and inventive fantasy, *Gulliver's Travels* has always been loved by young readers; as a satire, it rises to deep moral indignation against what Swift elsewhere referred to as "that animal called man."

The narrator of *Gulliver's Travels* is Lemuel Gulliver, a well-meaning but not very bright Englishman who describes whatever he sees with simple innocence. A *gull* was a term for someone easily duped, or gullible; therefore, it is up to the reader to see the truths that Gulliver misses.

Through Gulliver, Swift exposes the corruption in English institutions. In "A Voyage to Lilliput," the pretentious English politicians and court are made ridiculous by being reduced in scale. In "A Voyage to Brobdingnag," Swift mocks the immorality and cruelty of English society. The third voyage to Laputa is a satire on showy displays of learning. Swift's most biting satire occurs in the land of the Houyhnhnms, where intelligent and noble horses govern the Yahoos, a breed of filthy, brutish humans.

As a result of his travels, Gulliver realizes that people are not always what they seem to be and that evil is present wherever people exist.

CONNECTING TO THE
Focus Question

As you read, ask yourself: What follies and vices are the targets of Swift's satire in *Gulliver's Travels?*

Gulliver's Travels in Lilliput illustrated by Gennady Spirin.

The first voyage, describing the visit to Lilliput, opens with an account of Gulliver's early life: his birth, parentage, and scholarship. After studying medicine, Gulliver becomes a ship's doctor and embarks on a long voyage; when the ship breaks up in a storm somewhere in the South Pacific, he manages to swim ashore and, exhausted, falls into a deep sleep.

from Gulliver's Travels

from Part 1: A Voyage to Lilliput

Jonathan Swift

I lay down on the grass, which was very short and soft, where I slept sounder than ever I remember to have done in my life, and, as I reckoned, above nine hours; for when I awaked, it was just daylight. I attempted to rise, but was not able to stir: For as I happened to lie on my back, I found my arms and legs were strongly fastened on each side to the ground; and my hair, which was long and thick, tied down in the same manner. I likewise felt several slender ligatures[1] across my body, from my armpits to my thighs. I could only look upward; the sun began to grow hot, and the light offended my eyes. I heard a confused noise about me, but in the posture I lay, could see nothing except the sky.

In a little time I felt something alive moving on my left leg, which advancing gently forward over my breast, came almost up to my chin; when bending my eyes downward as much as I could, I perceived it to be a human creature not six inches high, with a bow and arrow in his hands, and a quiver at his back. In the meantime, I felt at least forty more of the same kind (as I conjectured[2]) following the first. I was in the utmost astonishment, and roared so loud, that they all ran back in a fright; and some of them, as I was afterward told, were hurt with the falls they got by leaping from my sides upon the ground. However, they soon returned, and one of them, who ventured so far as to get a full sight of my face, lifting up his hands and eyes by way of admiration, cried out in a shrill, but distinct voice, *Hekinah degul:*[3] The others repeated the same words several times, but then I knew not what they meant. I lay all this while, as the reader may believe, in great uneasiness: At length, struggling to get loose, I had the fortune to break the strings, and wrench out the pegs that fastened my left arm to the ground; for, by lifting it up to my face, I discovered the methods they had taken to bind me, and at the same time with a violent pull, which gave me excessive pain, I a little loosened the strings that tied down my hair on the left side, so that I was just able to turn my head about two inches. But the creatures ran off a second time, before I could seize them; whereupon there was a great shout in a very shrill accent, and after it ceased, I heard one of them cry aloud, *Tolgo phonac;* when in an instant I felt above an hundred arrows discharged on my left hand, which pricked me like so many needles; and besides, they shot another flight into the air, as we do bombs in Europe, whereof many, I suppose, fell on my body (though I felt them not), and some on my face, which I immediately covered with my left

1. **ligatures** (lig′ ə•chərz): ties or bonds.
2. **conjectured** (kən•jek′ chərd): reasoned; guessed.

3. ***Hekinah degul:*** This and other examples of the Lilliputian (lil′ə•pyo͞o′ shən) tongue are mainly nonsense words. Swift was fond of puns, pig Latin, and other kinds of word games.

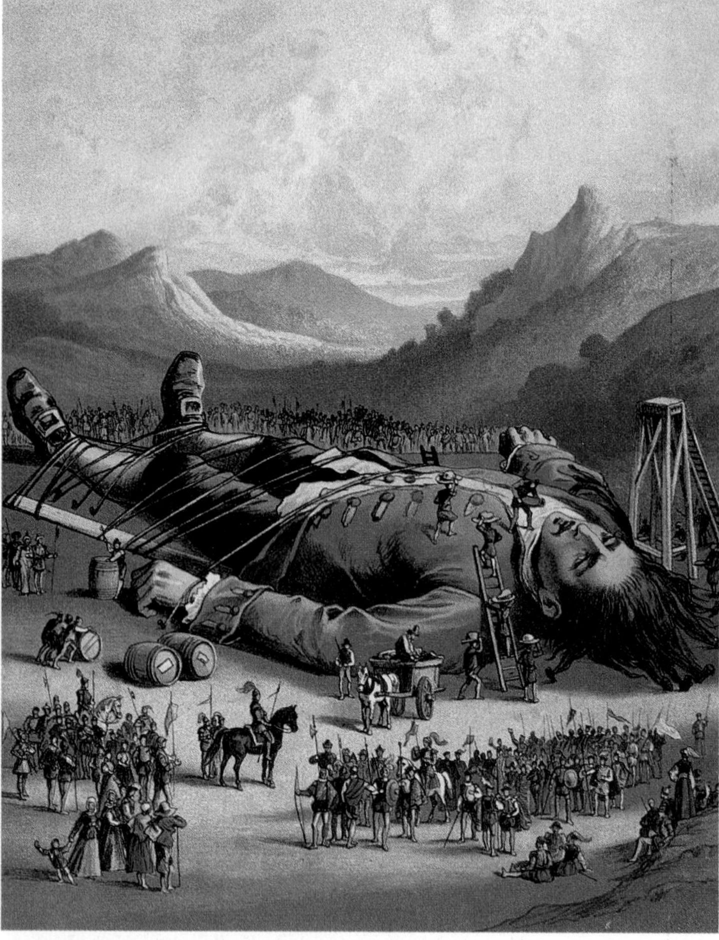

Gulliver is tied down by the people of Lilliput. First published: 1726.

hand. When this shower of arrows was over, I fell a-groaning with grief and pain, and then striving again to get loose, they discharged another volley larger than the first, and some of them attempted with spears to stick me in the sides; but, by good luck, I had on me a buff jerkin,[4] which they could not pierce. I thought it the most prudent method to lie still, and my design was to continue so till night, when, my left hand being already loose, I could easily free myself: And as for the inhabitants, I had reason to believe I might be a match for the greatest armies they could bring against me, if they were all of the same size with him that I saw. But fortune disposed otherwise of me.

When the people observed I was quiet, they discharged no more arrows; but, by the noise increasing, I knew their numbers were greater; and about four yards from me, over against my right ear, I heard a knocking for above an hour, like that of people at work; when turning my head that way, as well as the pegs and strings would permit me, I saw a stage erected, about a foot and a half from the ground, capable of holding four of the inhabitants, with two or three ladders to mount it: From whence one of them, who seemed to be a person of quality, made me a long speech, whereof I understood not one syllable. But I should have mentioned, that before the principal person began his oration, he cried out three times, *Langro dehul san* (these words and the former were afterward repeated and explained to me). Whereupon immediately about fifty of the inhabitants came and cut the strings that fastened the left side of my head, which gave me the liberty of turning it to the right, and of observing the person and gesture of him who was to speak. He appeared to be of a middle age, and taller than any of the other three who attended him, whereof one was a page who held up his train, and seemed to be somewhat longer than my middle finger; the other two stood one on each side to support him. He acted every part of an orator, and I could observe many periods of threatenings, and others of promises, pity, and kindness.

I answered in a few words, but in the most submissive manner, lifting up my left hand, and both my eyes to the sun, as calling him for a witness; and being almost famished with

4. **buff jerkin:** short, closefitting leather jacket, often without sleeves.

hunger, having not eaten a morsel for some hours before I left the ship. I found the demands of nature so strong upon me, that I could not forbear showing my impatience (perhaps against the strict rules of decency) by putting my finger frequently on my mouth, to signify that I wanted food. The *Hurgo*[5] (for so they call a great lord, as I afterward learnt) understood me very well. He descended from the stage, and commanded that several ladders should be applied to my sides, on which above an hundred of the inhabitants mounted and walked toward my mouth, laden with baskets full of meat,[6] which had been provided and sent thither by the King's orders, upon the first intelligence[7] he received of me. I observed there was the flesh[8] of several animals, but could not distinguish them by the taste. There were shoulders, legs, and loins, shaped like those of mutton, and very well dressed, but smaller than the wings of a lark. I ate them by two or three at a mouthful, and took three loaves at a time, about the bigness of musket bullets. They supplied me as fast as they could, showing a thousand marks of wonder and astonishment at my bulk and appetite.

I then made another sign that I wanted drink. They found by my eating, that a small quantity would not suffice me; and being a most ingenious people, they slung up with great dexterity one of their largest hogsheads,[9] then rolled it toward my hand, and beat out the top; I drank it off at a draft, which I might well do, for it hardly held half a pint, and tasted like a small wine of Burgundy, but much more delicious. They brought me a second hogshead, which I drank in the same manner, and made signs for more, but they had none to give me. When I had performed these wonders, they shouted for joy, and danced upon my breast, repeating several times as they did at first, *Hekinah degul.* They made me a sign that I should throw down the two hogsheads, but first warned the people below to stand out of the way, crying aloud, *Borach mivola,* and when they saw the vessels in the air, there was an universal shout of *Hekinah degul.* I confess I was often tempted, while they were passing backward and forward on my body, to seize forty or fifty of the first that came in my reach, and dash them against the ground. But the remembrance of what I had felt, which probably might not be the worst they could do, and the promise of honor I made them, for so I interpreted my submissive behavior, soon drove out those imaginations. Besides, I now considered myself as bound by the laws of hospitality to a people who had treated me with so much expense and magnificence. However, in my thoughts, I could not sufficiently wonder at the intrepidity of these diminutive mortals, who durst venture to mount and walk on my body, while one of my hands was at liberty, without trembling at the very sight of so prodigious a creature as I must appear to them.

After some time, when they observed that I made no more demands for meat, there appeared before me a person of high rank from his Imperial Majesty. His Excellency, having mounted on the small of my right leg, advanced forward up to my face, with about a dozen of his retinue. And producing his credentials under the Signet Royal,[10] which he applied close to my eyes, spoke about ten minutes, without any signs of anger, but with a kind of determinate resolution; often pointing forward, which, as I afterward found, was toward the capital city, about half a mile distant, whither it was agreed by his Majesty in council that I must be conveyed. I answered in few words, but to no purpose, and made a sign with my hand that was loose, putting it to the other (but over his Excellency's

5. ***Hurgo:*** This Lilliputian word is perhaps a partial anagram (a word formed by rearranging the letters of another word) of the English word *rogue.* It would be characteristic of Swift to call a "great lord" a rogue.
6. **meat:** archaic word for "food."
7. **intelligence:** news.
8. **flesh:** meat.
9. **hogsheads** (hôgz′ hedz′): barrels.
10. **Signet Royal:** royal seal; the seal used as a signature to mark documents as official.

head for fear of hurting him or his train) and then to my own head and body, to signify that I desired my liberty. It appeared that he understood me well enough, for he shook his head by way of disapprobation, and held his hand in a posture to show that I must be carried as a prisoner. However, he made other signs to let me understand that I should have meat and drink enough, and very good treatment. Whereupon I once more thought of attempting to break my bonds; but again, when I felt the smart of their arrows, upon my face and hands, which were all in blisters, and many of the darts still sticking in them, and observing likewise that the number of my enemies increased, I gave tokens[11] to let them know that they might do with me what they pleased. Upon this, the *Hurgo* and his train withdrew, with much civility and cheerful countenances.

Soon after I heard a general shout, with frequent repetitions of the words, *Peplom selan,* and I felt great numbers of people on my left side relaxing the cords to such a degree, that I was able to turn upon my right, and to ease myself with making water; which I very plentifully did, to the great astonishment of the people, who conjecturing by my motions what I was going to do, immediately opened to the right and left on that side, to avoid the torrent which fell with such noise and violence from me. But before this, they had daubed my face and both my hands with a sort of ointment very pleasant to the smell, which in a few minutes removed all the smart of their arrows. These circumstances, added to the refreshment I had received by their victuals and drink, which were very nourishing, disposed me to sleep. I slept about eight hours, as I was afterward assured; and it was no wonder, for the physicians, by the Emperor's order, had mingled a sleeping potion in the hogshead of wine. . . .

My gentleness and good behavior had gained so far on the Emperor and his court, and indeed upon the army and people in general, that I began to conceive hopes of getting my liberty in a short time. I took all possible methods to cultivate this favorable disposition. The natives came by degrees to be less apprehensive of any danger from me. I would sometimes lie down, and let five or six of them dance on my hand. And at last the boys and girls would venture to come and play at hide-and-seek in my hair. I had now made a good progress in understanding and speaking their language. The Emperor had a mind one day to entertain me with several of the country shows, wherein they exceed all nations I have known, both for dexterity and

Gulliver is measured by the tailors (c. late 19th to early 20th century); illustration by Arthur Rackham.

11. **gave tokens:** here used to mean "signaled."

magnificence. I was diverted with none so much as that of the rope dancers,[12] performed upon a slender white thread, extended about two foot, and twelve inches from the ground. Upon which I shall desire liberty, with the reader's patience, to enlarge a little.

This diversion is only practiced by those persons who are candidates for great employments, and high favor, at court. They are trained in this art from their youth, and are not always of noble birth, or liberal education. When a great office is vacant, either by death or disgrace (which often happens), five or six of those candidates petition the Emperor to entertain his Majesty and the court with a dance on the rope, and whoever jumps the highest without falling, succeeds in the office. Very often the chief ministers themselves are commanded to show their skill, and to convince the Emperor that they have not lost their faculty. Flimnap, the Treasurer, is allowed to cut a caper on the straight rope, at least an inch higher than any other lord in the whole empire. I have seen him do the summerset[13] several times together upon a trencher[14] fixed on the rope, which is no thicker than a common packthread[15] in England. My friend Reldresal, principal Secretary for Private Affairs, is, in my opinion, if I am not partial, the second after the Treasurer; the rest of the great officers are much upon a par.

These diversions are often attended with fatal accidents, whereof great numbers are on record. I myself have seen two or three candidates break a limb. But the danger is much greater when the ministers themselves are commanded to show their dexterity; for, by contending to excel themselves and their fellows, they strain so far, that there is hardly one of them who hath not received a fall, and some of them two or three. I was assured that a year or two before my arrival, Flimnap would have infallibly broke his neck, if one of the King's cushions, that accidentally lay on the ground, had not weakened the force of his fall.

There is likewise another diversion, which is only shown before the Emperor and Empress, and first minister, upon particular occasions. The Emperor lays on the table three fine silken threads of six inches long. One is blue, the other red, and the third green. These threads are proposed as prizes for those persons whom the Emperor hath a mind to distinguish by a peculiar mark of his favor. The ceremony is performed in his Majesty's great chamber of state, where the candidates are to undergo a trial of dexterity very different from the former, and such as I have not observed the least resemblance of in any other country of the Old or the New World. The Emperor holds a stick in his hands, both ends parallel to the horizon, while the candidates advancing one by one, sometimes leap over the stick, sometimes creep under it backward and forward several times, according as the stick is advanced or depressed. Sometimes the Emperor holds one end of the stick, and his first minister the other; sometimes the minister has it entirely to himself. Whoever performs his part with most agility, and holds out the longest in leaping and creeping, is rewarded with the blue-colored silk; the red is given to the next, and the green to the third, which they all wear girt[16] twice round about the middle; and you see few great persons about this court, who are not adorned with one of these girdles. . . .

One morning, about a fortnight after I had obtained my liberty, Reldresal, principal Secretary (as they style him) of Private Affairs, came to my house attended only by one servant. He ordered his coach to wait at a distance, and

12. **rope dancers:** tightrope dancers.
13. **summerset:** archaic word for "somersault."
14. **trencher:** wooden platter usually used for serving food.
15. **packthread:** twine.
16. **girt:** encircled.

desired I would give him an hour's audience; which I readily consented to, on account of his quality and personal merits, as well as of the many good offices he had done me during my solicitations at court. I offered to lie down, that he might the more conveniently reach my ear; but he chose rather to let me hold him in my hand during our conversation. He began with compliments on my liberty, said he might pretend to some merit in it; but, however, added, that if it had not been for the present situation of things at court, perhaps I might not have obtained it so soon. "For," said he, "as flourishing a condition as we appear to be in to foreigners, we labor under two mighty evils: a violent faction at home, and the danger of an invasion by a most potent enemy from abroad. As to the first, you are to understand, that for about seventy moons past there have been two struggling parties in this empire, under the names of *Tramecksan* and *Slamecksan,* from the high and low heels on their shoes, by which they distinguish themselves. It is alleged indeed, that the high heels are most agreeable to our ancient constitution: But however this be, his Majesty hath determined to make use of only low heels in the administration of the government, and all offices in the gift of the Crown, as you cannot but observe; and particularly, that his Majesty's Imperial heels are lower at least by a *drurr* than any of his court; (*drurr* is a measure about the fourteenth part of an inch). The animosities between these two parties run so high, that they will neither eat nor drink, nor talk with each other. We compute the *Tramecksan,* or High-Heels, to exceed us in number; but the power is wholly on our side. We apprehend his Imperial Highness, the Heir to the Crown, to have some tendency toward the High-Heels; at least we can plainly discover one of his heels higher than the other, which gives him a hobble in his gait. Now, in the midst of these intestine[17] disquiets, we are threatened with an invasion from the island of Blefuscu, which is the other great empire of the universe, almost as large and powerful as this of his Majesty. For as to what we have heard you affirm, that there are other kingdoms and states in the world inhabited by human creatures as large as yourself, our philosophers are in much doubt, and would rather conjecture that you dropped from the moon, or one of the stars; because it is certain, that an hundred mortals of your bulk would, in a short time, destroy all the fruits and cattle of his Majesty's dominions. Besides, our histories of six thousand moons make no mention of any other regions, than the two great empires of Lilliput and Blefuscu. Which two mighty powers have, as I was going to tell you, been engaged in a most obstinate war for six and thirty moons past. It began upon the following occasion. It is allowed on all hands, that the primitive way of breaking eggs[18] before we eat them, was upon the larger end: But his present Majesty's grandfather, while he was a boy, going to eat an egg, and breaking it according to the ancient practice, happened to cut one of his fingers. Whereupon the Emperor his father published an edict, commanding all his subjects, upon great penalties, to break the smaller end of their eggs. The people so highly resented this law, that our histories tell us there have been six rebellions raised on that account; wherein one Emperor lost his life, and another his crown. These civil commotions were constantly fomented by the monarchs of Blefuscu; and when they were quelled[19], the exiles always fled for refuge to that empire. It is computed, that eleven thousand persons have, at several times, suffered death, rather than submit to break their eggs at the smaller end. Many hundred large volumes have been published upon this controversy: But the books of the Big-Endians have been long forbidden, and the whole party rendered incapable by law of holding employments. During the course of

17. **intestine:** internal.

18. **primitive way of breaking eggs:** The English eat a boiled egg by standing it up in an egg cup, cutting off one end with a knife, and scooping out the contents with a spoon.

19. **quelled** (kweld): subdued.

these troubles, the emperors of Blefuscu did frequently expostulate by their ambassadors, accusing us of making a schism[20] in religion, by offending against a fundamental doctrine of our great prophet Lustrog, in the fifty-fourth chapter of the Brundrecal (which is their Alcoran).[21] This, however, is thought to be a mere strain upon the text, for the words are these: *That all true believers shall break their eggs at the convenient end;* and which is the convenient end, seems, in my humble opinion, to be left to every man's conscience, or at least in the power of the chief magistrate to determine. Now the Big-Endian exiles have found so much credit in the Emperor of Blefuscu's court, and so much private assistance and encouragement from their party here at home, that a bloody war has been carried on between the two empires for six and thirty moons with various success; during which time we have lost forty capital ships, and a much greater number of smaller vessels, together with thirty thousand of our best seamen and soldiers; and the damage received by the enemy is reckoned to be somewhat greater than ours. However, they have now equipped a numerous fleet, and are just preparing to make a descent upon us; and his Imperial Majesty, placing great confidence in your valor and strength, has commanded me to lay this account of his affairs before you."

I desired the Secretary to present my humble duty to the Emperor, and to let him know, that I thought it would not become me, who was a foreigner, to interfere with parties; but I was ready, with the hazard of my life, to defend his person and state against all invaders.

---

20. **schism** (siz′ əm): division.
21. **Alcoran:** archaic English name for the Koran, Islam's sacred book.

Lilliput (19th century); illustration by Grandville.

Response and Analysis

Reading Check

1. What test do the candidates for high office in Lilliput have to undergo? What disaster almost happens to Flimnap?
2. Explain how the war between Lilliput and Blefuscu began.

Thinking Critically

3. Is there any relationship between the physical size of the Lilliputians and the way Swift wants us to evaluate their behavior? Does their size **symbolize** some other kind of "smallness"? Explain.
4. How are the qualifications of officeholders in Lilliput **satirized**? How does Swift use **irony** in his description of the Lilliputian officials?
5. How would you describe Swift's **tone**—his attitude toward the Lilliputians? What words or passages support your answer?
6. The institutions for which Swift urges reform here include politics and religion. What does he think of the differences that divide people into factions and sects? What other aspects of Lilliputian (and by implication English) life does Swift suggest are ripe for reform?

Extending and Evaluating

7. Swift draws parallels between Lilliputian politics and the British politics of his time. What parallels can you detect between Lilliput and what you know of modern politics, in either this country or some other one?

On his second voyage, Gulliver finds himself in Brobdingnag (bräb′ diŋ•nag′), *a country Swift locates in Alaska. Here everything is twelve times larger than in England. The situation in Part 1 is now reversed, and Gulliver discovers what it is like to be an insignificant, timid creature among giants. At court he tries to impress the king and queen with his importance and the importance of England and its civilization. Although its inhabitants look like large and ugly brutes, Brobdingnag is a kind of utopia, a model society with an enlightened and benevolent king. Note how the king treats Gulliver despite his opinion of Gulliver's size and civilization.*

from Part 2: A Voyage to Brobdingnag

Jonathan Swift

It is the custom that every Wednesday (which, as I have before observed, was their Sabbath) the King and Queen, with the royal issue of both sexes, dine together in the apartment of his Majesty, to whom I was now become a favorite; and at these times my little chair and table were placed at his left hand, before one of the saltcellars.[1] This prince took a pleasure in conversing with me, inquiring into the manners, religion, laws, government, and learning of Europe; wherein I gave him the best account I was able. His apprehension was so clear, and his judgment so exact, that he made very wise reflections and observations upon all I said. But, I confess, that after I had been a little too copious[2] in talking of my own beloved country, of our trade, and wars by sea and land, of our schisms in religion, and parties in the state; the prejudices of his education prevailed[3] so far, that he could not forbear taking me up in his right hand, and stroking me gently with the other, after an hearty fit of laughing, asked me, whether I were a Whig or a Tory.[4] Then turning to his first minister, who waited behind him with a white staff, near as tall as the mainmast of the *Royal Sovereign*,[5] he observed how contemptible a thing was human grandeur, which could be mimicked by such diminutive insects as I. "And yet," said he, "I dare engage, those creatures have their titles and distinctions of honor, they contrive little nests and burrows, that they call houses and cities; they make a figure in dress and equipage;[6] they love, they fight, they dispute, they cheat, they betray." And thus he continued on, while my color came and went several times, with indignation to hear our noble country, the mistress of arts and arms, the scourge of France, the arbitress of Europe, the seat of virtue, piety, honor, and truth, the pride and envy of the world, so contemptuously treated.

But as I was not in a condition to resent injuries, so, upon mature thoughts, I began to doubt whether I were injured or no. For, after having been accustomed several months to the sight and converse of this people, and observed every object upon which I cast my eyes, to be of proportionable magnitude, the horror I had first conceived from their bulk and aspect was so far worn off, that if I had then beheld a company of English lords and ladies in their finery and

1. **saltcellars:** dishes of salt.
2. **copious** (kō′ pē•əs): wordy; profuse.
3. **prevailed:** predominated; held sway.
4. **Whig . . . Tory:** the two chief political parties of eighteenth-century Great Britain.
5. ***Royal Sovereign:*** one of the largest British warships of Swift's age. A white staff is the symbol of the office of the British treasurer.
6. **equipage** (ek′ wi•pij′): carriage and horses with attendant servants.

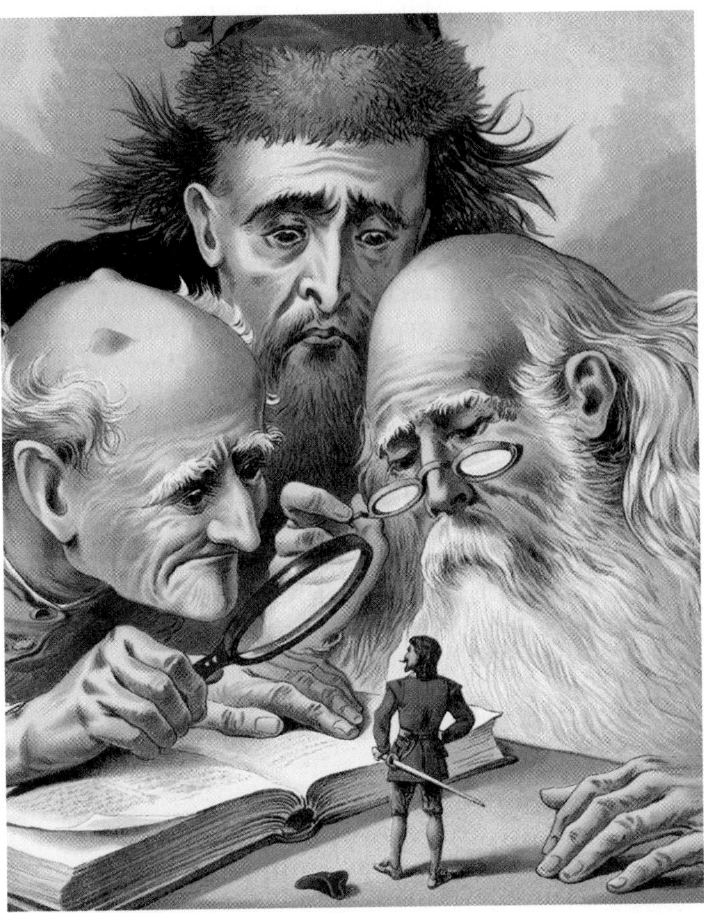

Gulliver is questioned by the scholars of Lorbruldrud. First published: 1726.

birthday clothes,[7] acting their several parts in the most courtly manner, of strutting, and bowing, and prating;[8] to say the truth, I should have been strongly tempted to laugh as much at them as this King and his grandees[9] did at me. Neither indeed could I forbear smiling at myself, when the Queen used to place me upon her hand toward a looking glass, by which both our persons appeared before me in full view together; and there could be nothing more ridiculous than the comparison; so that I really began to imagine myself dwindled many degrees below my usual size. . . .

I was frequently rallied[10] by the Queen upon account of my fearfulness, and she used to ask me whether the people of my country were as great cowards as myself. The occasion was this: The kingdom is much pestered with flies in summer; and these odious[11] insects, each of them as big as a Dunstable lark, hardly gave me any rest while I sat at dinner, with their continual humming and buzzing about my ears. They would sometimes alight upon my victuals, and leave their loathsome excrement or spawn behind, which to me was very visible, though not to the natives of that country, whose large optics were not so acute as mine in viewing smaller objects. Sometimes they would fix upon my nose or forehead, where they stung me to the quick, smelling very offensively, and I could easily trace that viscous[12] matter, which our naturalists tell us enables those creatures to walk with their feet upward upon a ceiling. I had much ado to defend myself against these detestable animals, and could not forbear starting when they came on my face. It was the common practice of the dwarf to catch a number of these insects in his hand, as schoolboys do among us, and let them out suddenly under my nose, on purpose to frighten me, and divert the Queen. My remedy was to cut them in pieces with my knife as they flew in the air, wherein my dexterity was much admired. . . .

He [the King] was perfectly astonished with the historical account I gave him of our affairs during the last century, protesting it was only an

7. **birthday clothes:** new outfits worn on a royal's birthday.
8. **prating:** talking pompously.
9. **grandees** (gran•dēz′): important persons; from *grande,* Spanish and Portuguese for "a nobleman of the highest rank."
10. **rallied:** teased.
11. **odious** (ō′ dē•əs): hateful; offensive.
12. **viscous** (vis′ kəs): having the form of a sticky fluid.

heap of conspiracies, rebellions, murders, massacres, revolutions, banishments; the very worst effects that avarice, faction, hypocrisy, perfidiousness, cruelty, rage, madness, hatred, envy, lust, malice, and ambition, could produce.

His Majesty, in another audience, was at the pains to recapitulate the sum of all I had spoken; compared the questions he made with the answers I had given; then taking me into his hands, and stroking me gently, delivered himself in these words, which I shall never forget, nor the manner he spoke them in. "My little friend Grildrig,[13] you have made a most admirable panegyric[14] upon your country. You have clearly proved that ignorance, idleness, and vice, are the proper ingredients for qualifying a legislator: that laws are best explained, interpreted, and applied by those whose interest and abilities lie in perverting, confounding, and eluding them. I observe among you some lines of an institution, which in its original might have been tolerable, but these half erased, and the rest wholly blurred and blotted by corruptions. It doth not appear from all you have said, how any one perfection[15] is required toward the procurement of any one station among you; much less that men are ennobled on account of their virtue, that priests are advanced for their piety or learning, soldiers for their conduct or valor, judges for their integrity, senators for the love of their country, or counselors for their wisdom. As for yourself (continued the King), who have spent the greatest part of your life in traveling, I am well disposed to hope you may hitherto have escaped many vices of your country. But by what I have gathered from your own relation, and the answers I have with much pains wringed and extorted from you, I cannot but conclude the bulk of your natives to be the most pernicious[16] race of little odious vermin that nature ever suffered to crawl upon the surface of the earth." ■

13. **Grildrig:** the Brobdingnagians' name for Gulliver.
14. **panegyric** (pan′ə • jir′ik): a speech full of praise.
15. **perfection:** here used to mean virtue.
16. **pernicious** (pər•nish′əs): wicked; extremely harmful.

Response and Analysis

Reading Check

1. What do English people think of themselves, according to Gulliver?
2. According to the king, what are the qualifications for being an English legislator?

Thinking Critically

3. How does Swift **characterize** the king of Brobdingnag? What actions show the king's personality traits?
4. Where does Swift use **verbal irony** to make his points?
5. What evidence suggests that Gulliver is learning little from his experiences in Brobdingnag?
6. What are the main targets of Swift's **satire** in this episode? Cite evidence in the text to support your response.

Extending and Evaluating

7. Choose at least one passage in the Brobdingnag episode that could apply to politics in the U.S. today, and explain how it relates.

. . .

Using details from Parts 1 and 2 of this excerpt from *Gulliver's Travels,* respond to **Connecting to the Focus Question** on page 652.

from A Journal of the Plague Year

Meet the Writer Daniel Defoe (1660–1731), a merchant's son, was born Daniel Foe. He added the aristocratic prefix *De* to his name when he was about thirty-five.

Defoe led a long and busy life and was an extremely prolific writer. His plain and vigorous style was filled with detailed practical knowledge appropriate to his characters and subject matter. Among several types of works, he wrote journalistic accounts of sensational events, such as *A Journal of the Plague Year* (1722). He is best remembered by far for his novel *The Life and Strange Surprising Adventures of Robinson Crusoe* (1719), an adventure tale many consider the first realistic novel.

(For more information about Daniel Defoe, see page 647.)

Background In 1721, there was much worry in England about a new outbreak of bubonic plague in mainland Europe. *A Journal of the Plague Year,* which Defoe published in 1722, pretends to be a firsthand account of an epidemic of bubonic plague that had ravaged London fifty-seven years before, in 1665. To tell the story, Defoe invented a narrator called H. F., who may be modeled on Defoe's real-life uncle, Henry Foe. Defoe's sources for this grim narrative are his own childhood memories; the reminiscences of his uncle and other eyewitnesses; city records; and pamphlets, books, and sermons about the plague.

CONNECTING TO THE
Focus Question

As you read, consider how Defoe attempts to use reason to alert his readers to the dangers of plague and possible means of controlling it. How does he create a convincing picture of human behavior in a time of great stress?

from A Journal of the Plague Year

Daniel Defoe

1. The Infection Spreads

Here the opinion of the physicians agreed with my observation afterward, namely, that the danger was spreading insensibly, for the sick could infect none but those that came within reach of the sick person; but that one man who may have really received the infection and knows it not, but goes abroad and about as a sound person, may give the plague to a thousand people, and they to greater numbers in proportion, and neither the person giving the infection or the persons receiving it know anything of it, and perhaps not feel the effects of it for several days after.

For example, many persons in the time of this visitation never perceived that they were infected till they found to their unspeakable surprise, the tokens come out upon them; after which they seldom lived six hours; for those spots they called the tokens were really gangrene spots, or mortified flesh[1] in small knobs as broad as a little silver penny, and hard as a piece of callus or horn; so that, when the disease was come up to that length, there was nothing could follow but certain death; and yet, as I said, they knew nothing of their being infected, nor found themselves so much as

1. **gangrene . . . flesh:** decay of soft tissues from a blockage of blood flow.

Londoners fleeing into the countryside to escape the plague. Woodcut.
The Granger Collection, New York.

out of order, till those mortal[2] marks were upon them. But everybody must allow that they were infected in a high degree before, and must have been so some time, and consequently their breath, their sweat, their very clothes, were contagious for many days before. . . .

2. Dismal Scenes

I had some little obligations, indeed, upon me to go to my brother's house, which was in Coleman Street[3] parish and which he had left to my care, and I went at first every day, but afterward only once or twice a week.

In these walks I had many dismal scenes before my eyes, as particularly of persons falling dead in the streets, terrible shrieks and screechings of women, who, in their agonies, would throw open their chamber windows and cry out in a dismal, surprising manner. It is impossible to describe the variety of postures in which the passions of the poor people would express themselves.

Passing through Tokenhouse Yard, in Lothbury, of a sudden a casement[4] violently opened just over my head, and a woman gave three frightful screeches, and then cried, "Oh! death, death, death!" in a most inimitable[5] tone, and which struck me with horror and a chillness in my very blood. There was nobody to be seen in the whole street, neither did any other window open, for people had no curiosity now in any case, nor could anybody help one another, so I went on to pass into Bell Alley.

Just in Bell Alley, on the right hand of the passage, there was a more terrible cry than that, though it was not so directed out at the window; but the whole family was in a terrible fright, and I could hear women and children run screaming about the rooms like distracted, when a garret[6] window opened and somebody from a window on the other side the alley called and asked, "What is the matter?" upon which, from the first window, it was answered, "Oh Lord, my old master has hanged himself!" The other asked again, "Is he quite dead?" and the first answered, "Ay, ay, quite dead; quite dead and cold!" This person was a merchant and a deputy alderman, and very rich. I care not to mention the name, though I knew his name too, but that would be an hardship to the family, which is now flourishing again.

But this is but one; it is scarce credible what dreadful cases happened in particular families every day. People in the rage of the distemper, or

2. **mortal:** fatal.
3. **Coleman Street:** This place and other places Defoe names are all within the old City of London, unless otherwise noted.
4. **casement:** hinged window.
5. **inimitable** (i•nim′i•tə•bəl): difficult or impossible to imitate.
6. **garret:** attic.

in the torment of their swellings, which was indeed intolerable, running out of their own government,[7] raving and distracted, and oftentimes laying violent hands upon themselves, throwing themselves out at their windows, shooting themselves, etc.; mothers murdering their own children in their lunacy,[8] some dying of mere grief as a passion, some of mere fright and surprise without any infection at all, others frighted into idiotism and foolish distractions, some into despair and lunacy, others into melancholy madness.

The pain of the swelling was in particular very violent, and to some intolerable; the physicians and surgeons may be said to have tortured many poor creatures even to death. The swellings in some grew hard, and they applied violent drawing plasters or poultices[9] to break them, and if these did not do they cut and scarified[10] them in a terrible manner. In some those swellings were made hard partly by the force of the distemper and partly by their being too violently drawn, and were so hard that no instrument could cut them, and then they burnt them with caustics,[11] so that many died raving mad with the torment, and some in the very operation. In these distresses, some, for want of help to hold them down in their beds, or to look to them, laid hands upon themselves as above. Some broke out into the streets, perhaps naked, and would run directly down to the river if they were not stopped by the watchman or other officers, and plunge themselves into the water wherever they found it.

It often pierced my very soul to hear the groans and cries of those who were thus tormented, but of the two this was counted the most promising particular in the whole infection, for if these swellings could be brought to a head, and to break and run, or, as the surgeons call it, to digest, the patient generally recovered; whereas those who, like the gentlewoman's daughter, were struck with death at the beginning, and had the tokens come out upon them, often went about indifferent easy till a little before they died, and some till the moment they dropped down, as in apoplexies[12] and epilepsies is often the case. Such would be taken suddenly very sick, and would run to a bench or bulk,[13] or any convenient place that offered itself, or to their own houses if possible, as I mentioned before, and there sit down, grow faint, and die. This kind of dying was much the same as it was with those who die of common mortifications,[14] who die swooning, and, as it were, go away in a dream. Such as died thus had very little notice of their being infected at all till the gangrene was spread through their whole body; nor could physicians themselves know certainly how it was with them till they opened their breasts or other parts of their body and saw the tokens.

3. Escape from Quarantine

I remember one citizen who, having thus broken out of his house in Aldersgate Street or thereabout, went along the road to Islington;[15] he attempted to have gone in at the Angel Inn, and after that the White Horse, two inns known still by the same signs, but was refused; after which he came to the Pied Bull, an inn also still continuing the same sign. He asked them for lodging for one night only, pretending to be going into Lincolnshire,[16] and assuring them of his being very sound and free from the infection, which also at that time had not reached much that way.

---

7. **out of their own government:** unable to control themselves.
8. **lunacy:** madness.
9. **drawing plasters or poultices** (pōl′tis•iz): hot packs used to soften sores and draw infection to the skin's surface.
10. **scarified** (skar′ə•fīd′): punctured.
11. **caustics:** chemicals that can burn or eat away flesh.
12. **apoplexies** (ap′ə•plek′sēz): strokes.
13. **bulk:** archaic word for a low stall projecting from a wall or storefront.
14. **mortifications** (môrt′ə•fi•kā′shənz): archaic word for gangrene.
15. **Islington:** suburb north of London.
16. **Lincolnshire:** county on the east coast of England.

They told him they had no lodging that they could spare but one bed up in the garret, and that they could spare that bed for one night, some drovers being expected the next day with cattle; so, if he would accept of that lodging, he might have it, which he did. So a servant was sent up with a candle with him to show him the room. He was very well dressed, and looked like a person not used to lie in a garret; and when he came to the room he fetched a deep sigh, and said to the servant, "I have seldom lain in such a lodging as this." However, the servant assuring him again that they had no better, "Well," says he, "I must make shift; this is a dreadful time; but it is but for one night." So he sat down upon the bedside, and bade the maid, I think it was, fetch him up a pint of warm ale. Accordingly the servant went for the ale, but some hurry in the house, which perhaps employed her other ways, put it out of her head, and she went up no more to him.

The next morning, seeing no appearance of the gentleman, somebody in the house asked the servant that had showed him upstairs what was become of him. She started. "Alas!" says she, "I never thought more of him. He bade me carry him some warm ale, but I forgot." Upon which, not the maid, but some other person was sent up to see after him, who, coming into the room, found him stark dead and almost cold, stretched out across the bed. His clothes were pulled off, his jaw fallen, his eyes open in a most frightful posture, the rug of the bed being grasped hard in one of his hands, so that it was plain he died soon after the maid left him; and 'tis probable, had she gone up with the ale, she had found him dead in a few minutes after he sat down upon the bed. The alarm was great in the house, as anyone may suppose, they having been free from the distemper till that disaster, which, bringing the infection to the house, spread it immediately to other houses round about it. . . . ■

Lord, have mercy on London. Woodcut.
The Granger Collection, New York.

Response and Analysis

Reading Check

1. What were the symptoms of the plague?
2. What attempts were made to cure people?

Thinking Critically

3. How might the **tone** of the journal—the attitude of the writer toward the events he is recounting—have been different if the work had actually been written during the London plague?
4. What effect does Defoe create by using **first-person point of view** in his account? Cite examples from the text to support your response.
5. Using details from the selection, respond to **Connecting to the Focus Question** on page 663.

Extending and Evaluating

6. What is meant by the expression "morbid curiosity"? Where does this kind of curiosity appear in contemporary life, and how do you account for it?
7. How might experiencing a plague change a person's views of life and death?

from A Dictionary of the English Language

Meet the Writer **Samuel Johnson** (1709–1784) was the dominant literary figure in England during the latter part of the eighteenth century. In fact, the period between Pope and Wordsworth is often referred to as the Age of Johnson. A wise man, a moralist, a talker, an eminent writer and critic, a beloved friend of people rich, poor, young and old, Johnson became in his own day an English institution. He remains a vivid figure because so many of his contemporaries recorded their impressions of him.

Johnson is famous for a great variety of works and for three large projects: *A Dictionary of the English Language* (1755); an edition of Shakespeare with an important critical preface and useful notes (1765); and *The Lives of the English Poets* in ten volumes (1779–1781), a series of biographical-critical prefaces.

In 1763, Johnson met James Boswell, who would soon begin recording Johnson's conversations for posterity. Johnson loved argument, but his temper was not malicious. As his friend Hester Thrale remarked, "No man loved laughing better."

Johnson was deeply conservative in his values and committed to the established church and political order. He was the most learned man of his day, but he always insisted that knowledge was useless unless it helped people live in the real world.

Background Johnson's *Dictionary*, published in 1755, was the first comprehensive and authoritative dictionary in English. It contains about 40,000 words and 114,000 illustrative passages. To compile his dictionary, Johnson gathered information from many literary, religious, philosophical, scientific, and technical books, marking passages and underlining key words. Then, he had six copyists write out the marked passages on slips of paper, which were later pasted into eighty notebooks. Finally, using the passages, Johnson wrote definitions of the key words.

Johnson's *Dictionary* was the basis of all subsequent English dictionaries. It lives on today because it reflects its author's interesting character and sense of humor.

CONNECTING TO THE Focus Question

Johnson never hesitated to question authorities or beliefs that he thought were mistaken. As you read, consider this question: How is Johnson's insistence on thinking for himself reflected in the dictionary entries?

from A Dictionary of the English Language

Samuel Johnson

alligator. The crocodile. This name is chiefly used for the crocodile of America, between which, and that of Africa, naturalists have laid down this difference, that one moves the upper, and the other the lower jaw; but this is now known to be chimerical,[1] the lower jaw being equally moved by both.

1. **chimerical** (kī•mer′i•kəl): fanciful.

athletick. Strong of body; vigorous; lusty; robust.

> Science distinguishes a man of honor from one of those *athletick* brutes, whom undeservedly we call heroes.
>
> —Dryden.

autopsy. Ocular demonstration; seeing a thing oneself.

balderdash. Anything jumbled together without judgment; rude mixture; a confused discourse.

bedpresser. A heavy lazy fellow.

> This sanguine coward, this *bedpresser*, this horseback-breaker, this huge hill of flesh.
>
> —Shakespeare, *Henry IV,* Part 1.

catsup. A kind of pickle, made from mushrooms.

companion. A familiar term of contempt; a fellow.

> I scorn you, scurvy *companion*! What? you poor, base, rascally, cheating, lack-linen mate: Away, you moldy rogue, away.
>
> —Shakespeare, *Henry IV,* Part 2.

cough. A convulsion of the lungs, vellicated by some sharp serosity. It is pronounced *coff.*

dedication. A servile address to a patron.

dull. Not exhilarating; not delightful; as, *to make dictionaries is* dull *work.*

essay. A loose sally of the mind; an irregular indigested piece; not a regular and orderly composition.

excise. A hateful tax levied upon commodities, and adjudged not by the common judges of property, but wretches hired by those to whom excise is paid.

favorite. One chosen as a companion by his superior; a mean wretch whose whole business is by any means to please.

fillip. A jerk of the finger let go from the thumb.

frightfully. Disagreeably; not beautifully. A woman's word.

fun. (A low cant[2] word.) Sport; high merriment; frolicsome delight.

goose. A large waterfowl proverbially noted, I know not why, for foolishness.

gravy. The serous juice that runs from flesh not much dried by the fire.

> They usually boil and roast their meat until it falls almost off from the bones; but we love it half raw, with the blood trickling down from it, delicately terming it the *gravy,* which in truth looks more like an ichorous or raw bloody matter.
>
> —Harvey, *On Consumptions.*

to hiss. To utter a noise like that of a serpent and some other animals. It is remarkable, that this word cannot be pronounced without making the noise which it signifies.

immaterial. (1) Incorporeal; void of matter. (2) Unimportant; without weight; impertinent; without relation. This sense has crept into the conversation and writings of barbarians; but ought to be utterly rejected.

jogger. One who moves heavily and dully.

lexicographer. A writer of dictionaries; a harmless drudge, that busies himself in tracing the original, and detailing the signification of words.

lingo. Language; tongue; speech. A low cant word.

lunch, luncheon. As much food as one's hand can hold.

merrythought. A forked bone on the body of fowls; so called because boys and girls pull in play at the two sides, the longest part broken off betokening priority of marriage.

mushroom. An upstart; a wretch risen from the dunghill; a director of a company.

network. Anything reticulated or decussated, at equal distances, with interstices between the intersections.

osprey. The sea-eagle, of which it is reported, that when he hovers in the air, all the fish in the water turn up their bellies, and lie still for him to seize which he pleases.

parody. A kind of writing, in which the words of an author or his thoughts are taken, and by a slight change adapted to some new purpose.

---

2. **cant:** a word Johnson uses to describe language he disapproves of because he perceives it to be of base origins.

patron. One who countenances, supports, or protects. Commonly a wretch who supports with insolence, and is paid with flattery.

pension. An allowance made to anyone without an equivalent. In England it is generally understood to mean pay given to a state hireling for treason to his country.

to period. To put an end to. A bad[3] word.

rhinoceros. A vast beast in the East Indies armed with a horn in his front.

romance. A tale of wild adventures in war and love.

to romp. To play rudely, noisily, and boisterously.

> A stool is the first weapon taken up in a general *romping* or skirmish.
>
> —Swift, *Rules to Servants.*

to sneeze. To emit wind audibly by the nose.

sonnet. A short poem consisting of fourteen lines, of which the rhymes are adjusted by a particular rule. It is not very suitable to the English language, and has not been used by any man of eminence since Milton.

3. **bad:** here used to mean "low" or "vulgar."

stammel. Of this word I know not the meaning.

tittletattle. Idle talk; prattle; empty gabble.

torpedo. A fish which while alive, if touched even with a long stick, benumbs the hand that so touches it, but when dead is eaten safely.

tory. (A cant term, derived, I suppose, from an Irish word signifying a savage.) One who adheres to the ancient constitution of the state, and the apostolical hierarchy of the Church of England, opposed to a whig.

unkindly. Unnatural; contrary to nature.

vivacious. Long-lived.

whale. The largest of fish.

whig. The name of a faction.

to worm. To deprive a dog of something, nobody knows what, under his tongue, which is said to prevent him, nobody knows why, from running mad.

zed. The name of the letter *z.*

Response and Analysis

Thinking Critically

1. Which definitions contain what we would regard as errors of fact?
2. What is Johnson's attitude toward slang, which he calls "low" or "cant" words?
3. How does Johnson's personality come through in the voice of the *Dictionary*? Which definitions show the writer's sense of humor? Which show his political bias, religious preferences, and independence of mind?
4. Based on your own experiences and the answers to the preceding questions, what inferences can you make about the English language, especially about the way it changes? Cite examples from the *Dictionary.*
5. Using details from the selection, respond to **Connecting to the Focus Question** on page 667.

Extending and Evaluating

6. Explain who, in your opinion, should decide a word's meaning and pronunciation.

from The Life of Samuel Johnson

Meet the Writer James Boswell (1740–1795) is the author of what many people consider the world's greatest biography—*The Life of Samuel Johnson*, published in 1791.

In 1763, Boswell met Johnson, who was then fifty-three and famous for his *Dictionary*. Under Johnson's sponsorship, Boswell was admitted to the select Literary Club, where he discovered a purpose for his life: to become Johnson's biographer—a job that took nearly thirty years. Boswell explained his purpose in the opening pages of *Life:* "I will venture to say that he [Johnson] will be seen in this work more completely than any man who has ever yet lived."

Wherever he went, Boswell kept a written record of his own and other people's behavior and conversation by training his memory to recall exact details of an event and later writing these down in private. To create his biography, begun four years after Johnson's death, Boswell used as sources his journals, Johnson's writings and letters, and information collected from Johnson's friends. Boswell's *Life* reveals more than the character of Johnson; it also offers us a window into the literary world of London during the second half of the eighteenth century.

Background Throughout the biography we often see Boswell provoking Johnson to speak out on a topic or manipulating the conversation for dramatic effect, in much the same way a playwright manages the dialogue of his or her characters. It is precisely this detail—the large number of conversations he reports—that sets Boswell's *Life* apart from other early biographies.

CONNECTING TO THE Focus Question

Although Johnson's views were conservative and traditional, he prided himself on his independence of mind. As you read these excerpts from Boswell's biography, ask yourself: What impression do you get of Johnson's intellect and capacity for reason?

from The Life of Samuel Johnson

James Boswell

Boswell's First Meeting with Johnson, 1763

This is to me a memorable year; for in it I had the happiness to obtain the acquaintance of that extraordinary man whose memoirs I am now writing; an acquaintance which I shall ever esteem as one of the most fortunate circumstances in my life. Though then but two-and-twenty, I had for several years read his works with delight and instruction, and had the highest reverence for their author, which had grown up in my fancy into a kind of mysterious veneration, by figuring to myself a state of solemn elevated abstraction, in which I supposed him to live in the immense metropolis of London. . . .

Mr. Thomas Davies the actor, who then kept a bookseller's shop in Russel Street, Covent Garden, told me that Johnson was very much his friend, and came frequently to his house, where he more than once invited me to meet him; but by some unlucky accident or other he was prevented from coming to us. . . .

At last, on Monday the 16th of May, when I was sitting in Mr. Davies's back parlor, after having drunk tea with him and Mrs. Davies, Johnson unexpectedly came into the shop; and Mr. Davies having perceived him through the glass door in the room in which we were sitting, advancing toward us—he announced his awful[1] approach to me, somewhat in the manner of an actor in the part of Horatio, when he addresses Hamlet on the appearance of his father's ghost, "Look, my Lord, it comes." I found that I had a very perfect idea of Johnson's figure, from the portrait of him painted by Sir Joshua Reynolds soon after he had published his *Dictionary,* in the attitude of sitting in his easy chair in deep meditation, which was the first picture his friend did for him, which Sir Joshua very kindly presented to me, and from which an engraving has been made for this work. Mr. Davies mentioned my name, and respectfully introduced me to him. I was much agitated; and recollecting his prejudice against the Scotch, of which I had heard much, I said to Davies, "Don't tell where I come from."—"From Scotland," cried Davies roguishly. "Mr. Johnson (said I), I do indeed come from Scotland, but I cannot help it." I am willing to flatter myself that I meant this as light pleasantry to soothe and conciliate him, and not as an humiliating abasement at the expense of my country. But however that might be, this speech was somewhat unlucky; for with that quickness of wit for which he was so remarkable, he seized the expression "come from Scotland," which I used in the sense of being of that country, and, as if I had said that I had come away from it, or left it, retorted, "That, Sir, I find, is what a very great many of your countrymen cannot help." This stroke stunned me a good deal; and when we had sat down, I felt myself not a little embarrassed, and apprehensive of what might come next. He then addressed himself to Davies. "What do you think of Garrick?[2] He has refused me an order for the play for Miss Williams, because he knows the house will be full, and that an order would be worth three shillings." Eager to take any opening to get into conversation with him, I ventured to say, "O, Sir, I cannot think Mr. Garrick would grudge such a trifle to you." "Sir (said he, with a stern look), I have known David Garrick longer than you have done: and I know no right you have to talk to me on the subject." Perhaps I deserved this check; for it was rather presumptuous in me, an entire stranger, to express any doubt of the justice of his animadversion[3] upon his old acquaintance and pupil. I now felt myself much mortified, and began to think that the hope which I had long indulged of obtaining his acquaintance was blasted. And, in truth, had not my ardor been uncommonly strong, and my resolution uncommonly per-

1. **awful:** here, used to mean producing awe; now, more commonly, "awesome."

2. **Garrick:** the English actor David Garrick (1717–1779), a former pupil of Johnson's.
3. **animadversion** (an′i•məd•vʉr′zhən): critical comment.

An Early London Coffeehouse (detail) (c. 1705) signed A. S.
British Museum, London.

severing, so rough a reception might have deterred[4] me forever from making any further attempts. Fortunately, however, I remained upon the field not wholly discomfited. . . .

I was highly pleased with the extraordinary vigor of his conversation, and regretted that I was drawn away from it by an engagement at another place. I had, for a part of the evening, been left alone with him, and had ventured to make an observation now and then, which he received very civilly; so that I was satisfied that though there was a roughness in his manner, there was no ill nature in his disposition. Davies followed me to the door, and when I complained to him a little of the hard blows which the great man had given me, he kindly took upon him to console me by saying, "Don't be uneasy. I can see he likes you very well."

4. **deterred:** prevented.

Boswell's First Visit to Johnson

A few days afterward I called on Davies, and asked him if he thought I might take the liberty of waiting on Mr. Johnson at his Chambers in the Temple.[5] He said I certainly might, and that Mr. Johnson would take it as a compliment. So upon Tuesday the 24th of May, . . . I boldly repaired to Johnson. His Chambers were on the first floor of No. 1, Inner-Temple-lane, and I entered them with an impression given me by the Reverend Dr. Blair,[6] of Edinburgh, who had been introduced to him not long before, and described his having "found the Giant in his den," an expression, which, when I came to be pretty well acquainted with Johnson, I repeated to him, and he was diverted at this picturesque account of himself. . . .

5. **Temple:** area in London where lawyers and other professional people lived and worked.
6. **Blair:** Hugh Blair (1718–1800), a Presbyterian clergyman and writer.

He received me very courteously; but, it must be confessed, that his apartment, and furniture, and morning dress, were sufficiently uncouth. His brown suit of clothes looked very rusty; he had on a little old shriveled unpowdered wig, which was too small for his head; his shirtneck and knees of his breeches were loose; his black worsted stockings ill drawn up; and he had a pair of unbuckled shoes by way of slippers. But all these slovenly[7] particularities were forgotten the moment that he began to talk. Some gentlemen, whom I do not recollect, were sitting with him; and when they went away, I also rose; but he said to me, "Nay, don't go." "Sir (said I), I am afraid that I intrude upon you. It is benevolent to allow me to sit and hear you." He seemed pleased with this compliment, which I sincerely paid him, and answered, "Sir, I am obliged to any man who visits me."...

Boswell Quizzes Johnson

I know not how so whimsical a thought came into my mind, but I asked, "If, Sir, you were shut up in a castle, and a newborn child with you, what would you do?" JOHNSON. "Why, Sir, I should not much like my company." BOSWELL. "But would you take the trouble of rearing it?" He seemed, as may well be supposed, unwilling to pursue the subject: but upon my persevering in my question, replied, "Why yes, Sir, I would; but I must have all conveniences. If I had no garden, I would make a shed on the roof, and take it there for fresh air. I should feed it, and wash it much, and with warm water to please it, not with cold water to give it pain." BOSWELL. "But, Sir, does not heat relax?" JOHNSON. "Sir, you are not to imagine the water is to be very hot. I would not *coddle*[8] the child. No, Sir, the hardy method of treating children does no good. I'll take you five children from London, who shall cuff[9] five Highland children. Sir, a man bred in London will carry a burden, or run, or wrestle, as well as a man brought up in the hardiest manner in the country." BOSWELL. "Good living, I suppose, makes the Londoners strong." JOHNSON. "Why, Sir, I don't know that it does. Our chairmen[10] from Ireland, who are as strong men as any, have been brought up upon potatoes. Quantity makes up for quality." BOSWELL. "Would you teach this child that I have furnished you with, anything?" JOHNSON. "No, I should not be apt to teach it." BOSWELL. "Would not you have a pleasure in teaching it?" JOHNSON. "No, Sir, I should *not* have a pleasure in teaching it." BOSWELL. "Have you not a pleasure in teaching men? *There* I have you. You have the same pleasure in teaching men, that I should have in teaching children." JOHNSON. "Why, something about that."...

Johnson's Eccentricities

... Talking to himself was, indeed, one of his singularities ever since I knew him. I was certain that he was frequently uttering pious ejaculations; for fragments of the Lord's Prayer have been distinctly overheard. His friend Mr. Thomas Davies, of whom Churchill[11] says, "That Davies hath a very pretty wife," when Dr. Johnson muttered "lead us not into temptation," used with waggish and gallant humor to whisper [to] Mrs. Davies, "You, my dear, are the cause of this."

He had another particularity, of which none of his friends ever ventured to ask an explanation. It appeared to me some superstitious habit, which he had contracted early, and from which he had never called upon his reason to disentangle him. This was his anxious care to go out or in at a door

7. **slovenly:** untidy.
8. ***coddle:*** cook in hot water. Johnson is having fun with the two distinct meanings of the word, the other being "treat tenderly."
9. **cuff:** win a fight or scuffle with.
10. **chairmen:** here, used to mean porters who transported people through the London streets in sedan chairs (covered seats).
11. **Churchill:** Charles Churchill (1731–1764), author of satirical and comic poems.

Oliver Goldsmith, James Boswell, and Samuel Johnson (left to right).

or passage by a certain number of steps from a certain point, or at least so as that either his right or his left foot (I am not certain which) should constantly make the first actual movement when he came close to the door or passage. Thus I conjecture: For I have, upon innumerable occasions, observed him suddenly stop, and then seem to count his steps with a deep earnestness; and when he had neglected or gone wrong in this sort of magical movement, I have seen him go back again, put himself in a proper posture to begin the ceremony, and, having gone through it, break from his abstraction, walk briskly on, and join his companion. A strange instance of something of this nature, even when on horseback, happened when he was in the Isle of Skye.[12] Sir Joshua Reynolds has observed him to go a good way about rather than cross a particular alley in Leicesterfields;[13] but this Sir Joshua imputed to his having had some disagreeable recollection associated with it.

That the most minute singularities which belonged to him, and made very observable parts of his appearance and manner, may not be omitted, it is requisite to mention, that while talking or even musing as he sat in his chair, he commonly held his head to one side toward his right shoulder, and shook it in a tremulous manner, moving his body backward and forward, and rubbing his left knee in the same direction, with the palm of his hand. In the intervals of articulating he made various sounds with his mouth, sometimes as if ruminating, or what is called chewing the cud, sometimes giving a half whistle, sometimes making his tongue play backward from the roof of his mouth, as if clucking like a hen, and sometimes protruding it against his upper gums in front, as if pronouncing quickly under his breath, *too, too, too:* all this accompanied sometimes with a thoughtful look, but more frequently with a smile. Generally when he had concluded a period, in the course of a dispute, by which time he was a good deal exhausted by violence and vociferation, he used to blow out his breath like a whale. This I supposed was a relief to his lungs; and seemed in him to be a contemptuous mode of expression, as if he had made the arguments of his opponent fly like chaff before the wind.

I am fully aware how very obvious an occasion I here give for the sneering jocularity of such as have no relish of an exact likeness; which to render complete, he who draws it must not disdain the slightest strokes. But if witlings[14] should be inclined to attack this

12. **Isle of Skye:** largest of the Inner Hebrides, a group of islands off the west coast of Scotland.

13. **Leicesterfields** (les′tər•fēldz): square in London.

14. **witlings:** people who think they are witty.

account, let them have the candor[15] to quote what I have offered in my defense. . . .

Johnson's Love of Argument

. . . I mentioned a new gaming club,[16] of which Mr. Beauclerk[17] had given me an account, where the members played to a desperate extent. JOHNSON. "Depend upon it, Sir, this is mere talk. *Who* is ruined by gaming? You will not find six instances in an age. There is a strange rout made about deep play: Whereas you have many more people ruined by adventurous trade,[18] and yet we do not hear such an outcry against it."

15. **candor:** honesty.
16. **gaming clubs:** gambling club.
17. **Beauclerk:** Topham Beauclerk (1739–1780), a fashionable gentleman descended from King Charles II.
18. **trade:** business.

THRALE. "There may be few people absolutely ruined by deep play; but very many are much hurt in their circumstances by it." JOHNSON. "Yes, Sir, and so are very many by other kinds of expense." I had heard him talk once before in the same manner; and at Oxford he said, "he wished he had learnt to play at cards." The truth, however, is, that he loved to display his ingenuity in argument; and therefore would sometimes in conversation maintain opinions which he was sensible were wrong, but in supporting which, his reasoning and wit would be most conspicuous. He would begin thus: "Why, Sir, as to the good or evil of card playing—" "Now (said Garrick), he is thinking which side he shall take." He appeared to have a pleasure in contradiction, especially when any opinion whatever was delivered with an air of confidence; so that there was hardly any topic, if not one of the great truths of religion and morality, that he might not have been incited to argue, either for or against. . . . ■

Response and Analysis

Reading Check

1. How was Johnson dressed when Boswell first visited him in his study?
2. Describe the mannerisms Johnson exhibited while he was talking.
3. Why, according to Boswell, did Johnson sometimes express opinions that he did not really believe?

Thinking Critically

4. Judging from these accounts, what do you think was Johnson's greatest strength as a person? What was his greatest fault?
5. Cite specific details from the biography that reflect Johnson's independent attitudes.
6. Using details from the selection, respond to **Connecting to the Focus Question** on page 670.

Extending and Evaluating

7. In this **biography,** Boswell often mentions himself—his own feelings, impressions, and conclusions about Johnson. Do you think these references contribute significantly to Boswell's work, or should he have been more detached and objective? Explain your answer.
8. Do you think Johnson would have been more or less interesting had his behavior been more conventional? Why is eccentricity of behavior important to society? How is eccentricity regarded in our society today?

Elegy Written in a Country Churchyard

Meet the Writer Thomas Gray (1716–1771), writer of the widely admired "Elegy Written in a Country Churchyard," was considered England's foremost lyric poet by his contemporaries. Even Johnson, who found most of Gray's poetry dull, recognized the universal appeal of "Elegy" when he wrote, "The Churchyard abounds with images which find a mirror in every mind, and with sentiments to which every bosom returns an echo."

Painfully shy, Gray led a quiet life as a scholar at Cambridge University—reading literature in a variety of languages, studying an assortment of subjects, painting landscapes, and playing the harpsichord.

The great crisis of Gray's life came when Richard West, a close friend, died of tuberculosis. Gray sought consolation in writing poetry. Reluctant to publish, he carefully and fastidiously revised and rewrote his verses. It took him nine years to complete "Elegy," which was published in 1751.

Although his verse has ties to the neoclassical tradition, Gray is sometimes designated as a forerunner of Romantic poetry. Like the Romantic poets, he turns to country life and nature, he expresses sympathy with common humanity, and he uses the first-person point of view.

Background An **elegy** is a poem that mourns the death of a person or laments something lost. Gray's "Elegy" combines elements from several literary traditions. First, it is a **pastoral** elegy, that is, it is set outdoors in a beautiful landscape, with rural people who are idealized types. A second element is the **Gothic**—the "moping owl," the graveyard, the general gloominess—which helps create atmosphere. Gray follows other writers of the time by also including another element—polished **generalizations** about life and death.

CONNECTING TO THE
Focus Question

Gray's "Elegy" has been called a classic because it expresses well-known truths in a memorable way. As you read, ask yourself how the poem illustrates Alexander Pope's definition of true wit: "What oft was thought but ne'er so well expressed."

Ode to a Country Churchyard (*Gray's Elegy*) (detail) (1883) by Jasper F. Cropsey. Oil on canvas (13½" x 25⅕").

The Newington-Cropsey Foundation, Hasting-on-Hudson, New York.

Elegy Written in a Country Churchyard

Thomas Gray

The curfew tolls the knell of parting day,
The lowing herd wind slowly o'er the lea,°
The plowman homeward plods his weary way,
And leaves the world to darkness, and to me.

Now fades the glimmering landscape on the sight,
And all the air a solemn stillness holds;
Save where the beetle wheels his droning flight,
And drowsy tinklings lull the distant folds.

Save that from yonder ivy-mantled tower
The moping owl does to the moon complain
Of such, as wand'ring near her secret bower,
Molest her ancient solitary reign.

Beneath those rugged elms, that yew tree's shade,
Where heaves the turf in many a mold'ring heap,
Each in his narrow cell forever laid,
The rude° forefathers of the hamlet sleep.

The breezy call of incense-breathing morn,
The swallow twitt'ring from the straw-built shed,°
The cock's shrill clarion, or the echoing horn,°
No more shall rouse them from their lowly bed.

For them no more the blazing hearth shall burn,
Or busy housewife ply her evening care:
No children run to lisp their sire's return,
Or climb his knees the envied kiss to share.

Oft did the harvest to their sickle yield,
Their furrow oft the stubborn glebe° has broke;
How jocund did they drive their team afield!
How bowed the woods beneath their sturdy stroke!

Let not Ambition mock their useful toil,
Their homely joys and destiny obscure;
Nor Grandeur hear with a disdainful smile,
The short and simple annals of the poor.

2. lea: meadow.

16. rude: uneducated; unpolished.

18. shed: nest.

19. horn: hunting horn.

26. glebe: soil.

Ode to a Country Churchyard (Gray's Elegy) (1883) by Jasper F. Cropsey. Oil on canvas (13½″ x 25⅕″).

The Newington-Cropsey Foundation, Hasting-on-Hudson, New York.

The boast of heraldry,° the pomp of power,
And all that beauty, all that wealth e'er gave,
Awaits alike th' inevitable hour.
The paths of glory lead but to the grave.

Nor you, ye proud, impute to these the fault,
If Mem'ry o'er their tomb no trophies° raise,
Where through the long-drawn aisle and fretted vault°
The pealing anthem swells the note of praise.

Can storied urn° or animated° bust
Back to its mansion call the fleeting breath?
Can Honor's voice provoke° the silent dust,
Or Flatt'ry soothe the dull cold ear of Death?

Perhaps in this neglected spot is laid
Some heart once pregnant with celestial fire,
Hands that the rod of empire might have swayed,
Or waked to ecstasy the living lyre.

33. boast of heraldry: pride in one's ancestry. Heraldry is the study of family coats of arms.
38. trophies: monuments.
39. fretted vault: elaborately ornamented church ceiling.

41. storied urn: an urn with an inscription on it. **animated:** lifelike.
43. provoke: evoke; call forth.

But Knowledge to their eyes her ample page
Rich with the spoils of time did ne'er unroll;
Chill Penury° repressed their noble rage,°
And froze the genial current° of the soul.

Full many a gem of purest ray serene,
The dark unfathomed caves of ocean bear:
Full many a flower is born to blush unseen,
And waste its sweetness on the desert air.

Some village Hampden° that with dauntless breast
The little tyrant of his fields withstood;
Some mute inglorious Milton here may rest,
Some Cromwell° guiltless of his country's blood.

Th' applause of list'ning senates to command,
The threats of pain and ruin to despise,
To scatter plenty o'er a smiling land,
And read their hist'ry in a nation's eyes

Their lot forbade: nor circumscribed alone
Their growing virtues, but their crimes confined;
Forbade to wade through slaughter to a throne,
And shut the gates of mercy on mankind,

The struggling pangs of conscious° truth to hide,
To quench the blushes of ingenuous° shame,
Or heap the shrine of Luxury and Pride
With incense, kindled at the Muse's flame.°

Far from the madding° crowd's ignoble strife,
Their sober wishes never learned to stray;
Along the cool sequestered vale of life
They kept the noiseless tenor° of their way.

Yet ev'n these bones from insult to protect
Some frail memorial° still erected nigh,
With uncouth° rhymes and shapeless sculpture decked,
Implores the passing tribute of a sigh.

Their name, their years, spelt by th' unlettered muse,°
The place of fame and elegy supply:
And many a holy text around she strews,
That teach the rustic moralist to die.

51. penury: poverty.
rage: emotion; feeling.
52. genial current: warm impulses.

57. village Hampden: an obscure person who, with opportunity, might have been famous like John Hampden (1594–1643), an English statesman who defied the king over unjust taxation shortly before the English Civil Wars.
60. Cromwell: Lord Protector Oliver Cromwell, who ruled England from 1653 to 1658.

69. conscious: guiltily aware; conscientious.
70. ingenuous: naively innocent.
72. incense . . . flame: tributes paid to them by poets.
73. madding: frenzied.

76. tenor: course.

78. frail memorial: modest tombstone, in contrast to the elaborate tombs inside the church.
79. uncouth: unsophisticated; artless.
81. unlettered muse: humble engraver of the tombstone.

For who to dumb Forgetfulness a prey,
This pleasing anxious being e'er resigned,
Left the warm precincts of the cheerful day,
Nor cast one longing ling'ring look behind?

On some fond breast the parting soul relies,
Some pious drops° the closing eye requires;
Ev'n from the tomb the voice of Nature cries,
Ev'n in our ashes live their wonted fires.

For thee,° who mindful of th' unhonored dead
Dost in these lines their artless tale relate;
If chance, by lonely Contemplation led,
Some kindred spirit shall inquire thy fate,

Haply° some hoary-headed swain° may say,
"Oft have we seen him at the peep of dawn
Brushing with hasty steps the dews away
To meet the sun upon the upland lawn.

"There at the foot of yonder nodding beech
That wreathes its old fantastic roots so high,
His listless length at noontide would he stretch,
And pore upon the brook that babbles by.

"Hard° by yon wood, now smiling as in scorn,
Mutt'ring his wayward fancies he would rove,
Now drooping, woeful wan, like one forlorn,
Or crazed with care, or crossed in hopeless love.

"One morn I missed him on the customed hill,
Along the heath, and near his fav'rite tree;
Another came; nor yet beside the rill,°
Nor up the lawn, nor at the wood was he.

"The next with dirges due in sad array
Slow through the churchway path we saw him borne.
Approach and read (for thou canst read)° the lay,
Graved on the stone beneath yon aged thorn."°

90. drops: mourners' tears.

93. thee: Gray himself.

97. haply: perhaps. **hoary-headed swain:** white-haired countryman.

105. hard: close.

111. rill: brook.

115. thou canst read: The "swain" who is speaking is apparently illiterate.

116. thorn: hawthorn bush.

The Epitaph

Here rests his head upon the lap of Earth
A youth to Fortune and to Fame unknown:
Fair Science frowned not on his humble birth,°
And Melancholy marked him for her own.

Large was his bounty, and his soul sincere,
Heaven did a recompense as largely send:
He gave to Mis'ry all he had, a tear:
He gained from Heaven ('twas all he wished) a friend.

No farther seek his merits to disclose,
Or draw his frailties from their dread abode,
(There they alike in trembling Hope repose)
The bosom of his Father and his God.

119. fair . . . birth: He was educated—*science* meant learning in general—despite his modest beginnings.

Response and Analysis

Reading Check

1. Where is the speaker, and what time of day is it? What, according to the **images** in stanzas 2 and 3, does he hear?
2. What does the speaker imagine these humble people might have become if they had had the chance (lines 45–60)?

Thinking Critically

3. The poet **personifies** ambition and grandeur in lines 29 and 31. What does he warn them not to do? What other examples of personification can you find in the poem?
4. The poem contains two statements that are still frequently quoted because of the truths they express so memorably: "The paths of glory lead but to the grave" (line 36) and "Full many a flower is born to blush unseen, / And waste its sweetness on the desert air" (lines 55–56). How do you interpret these lines, and how do they relate to the poem's **theme**?
5. According to lines 77–92, what evidence in their gravestones shows that humble, ordinary people also wish to be remembered?
6. Using details from the poem, respond to **Connecting to the Focus Question** on page 676.

Extending and Evaluating

7. In one sense, most Enlightenment writers thought the purpose of literature was to convey ideas. Most Romantic writers, by contrast, wanted to convey emotions. Judging by his **elegy,** in which group do you think Gray seems to fit? Cite evidence in the text to support your answer.
8. What ideas in the poem relate to ideas and feelings people have today?

REVIEW

Reflecting on the Literary Period

The Restoration and the Eighteenth Century: 1660–1800

The following questions ask you to compare and analyze the selections in this feature and respond to the Focus Question. Where possible, cite passages from the selections to support your answers.

Jonathan Swift .... *from* **Gulliver's Travels**
.... *from* **Part 1: A Voyage to Lilliput**
.... *from* **Part 2: A Voyage to Brobdingnag**

Daniel Defoe .... *from* **A Journal of the Plague Year**

Samuel Johnson .... *from* **A Dictionary of the English Language**

James Boswell .... *from* **The Life of Samuel Johnson**

Thomas Gray .... **Elegy Written in a Country Churchyard**

Comparing Literature

1. In *Gulliver's Travels,* which device do you think creates a more effective **satire:** a hero who is a giant among Lilliputians or one who is tiny among Brobdingnagians? Or do you find them equally effective? Explain.
2. Contrast the satiric **tone** of Swift's *Gulliver's Travels* with the realism of Defoe's *Journal of the Plague Year.* Cite details that contribute to each.
3. What characteristics of Johnson's personality as seen in Boswell's *Life of Samuel Johnson* can also be seen in Johnson's *Dictionary* entries?
4. Defoe's *Journal of the Plague Year* and Gray's "Elegy Written in a Country Churchyard" both deal with death but in very different ways. How does each reflect eighteenth-century concerns and sensibilities?
5. Swift, Defoe, and Gray all deal in their separate ways with problems of society and universal human truths. Compare and contrast the selections in terms of author's purpose, subjects addressed, **tone,** and **theme.**

Pages 651–682 cover **Literary Skills** Evaluate the philosophical, political, religious, ethical, and social influences of a historical period.

RESPONDING TO THE

Focus Question

Review your notes and responses related to the Focus Question for this feature. Using details from the selections, write your answer to the question.

How does eighteenth-century literature demonstrate the significant role played by reason and common sense in dealing with society's problems and the universal truths of human experience?

READ ON: FOR INDEPENDENT READING

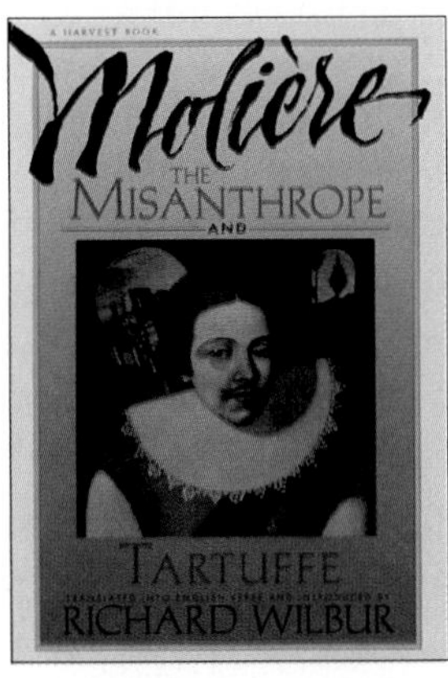

DRAMA

The Rogue and the Recluse

The French playwright Molière had a remarkable genius for exposing and satirizing the ills of society. In Richard Wilbur's translations of ***Tartuffe*** and ***The Misanthrope,*** you'll meet two men whom Molière considered representative of his age: one a roguish hypocrite who charms everyone he meets and the other an eccentric recluse who shuns hypocrisy at a great cost to himself. Molière's comedies of manners, so relevant when they were first written, have lost none of their potency and humor today.

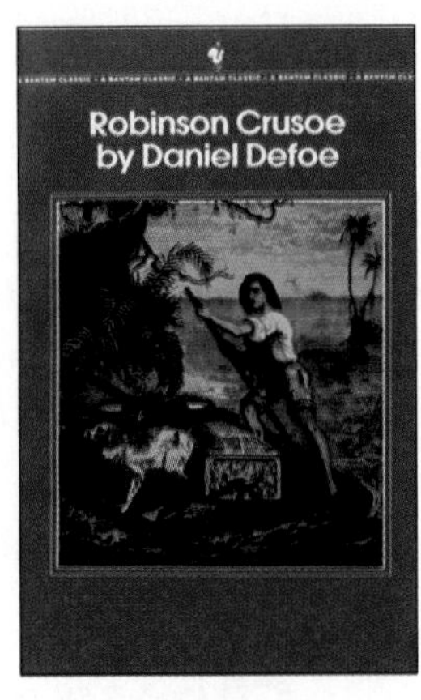

FICTION

Diary of a Castaway

Since its publication in 1719, Daniel Defoe's ***Robinson Crusoe*** has spawned countless imitations and adaptations. Perhaps the story contained in Crusoe's fictional autobiography has endured because it poses age-old questions. How might we react if we were plucked from our ordinary lives and set on a barren island? Could we face the physical hardships and mental isolation of such an extraordinary new life?

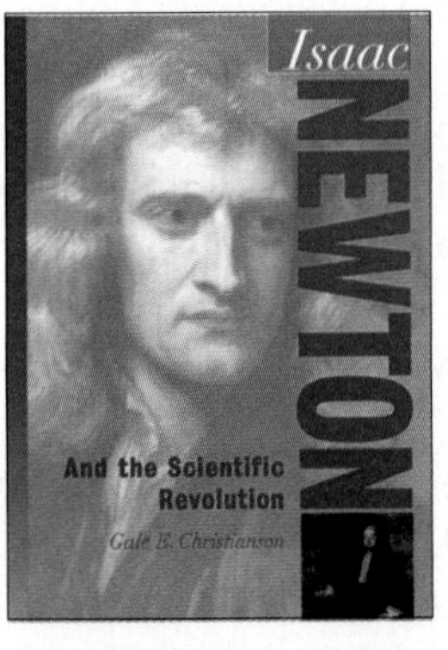

NONFICTION

Pioneer of Science

Restoration England was an age marked by avid amateur experimentation and heated public debates about the mysteries of science. Sir Isaac Newton single-handedly unraveled many of the world's great puzzles: He invented calculus, formulated the three laws of motion, and realized, as no one else had, that gravity accounts for both orbiting planets and falling apples. You can read about the man and his works in ***Isaac Newton and the Scientific Revolution*** by Gale E. Christianson.

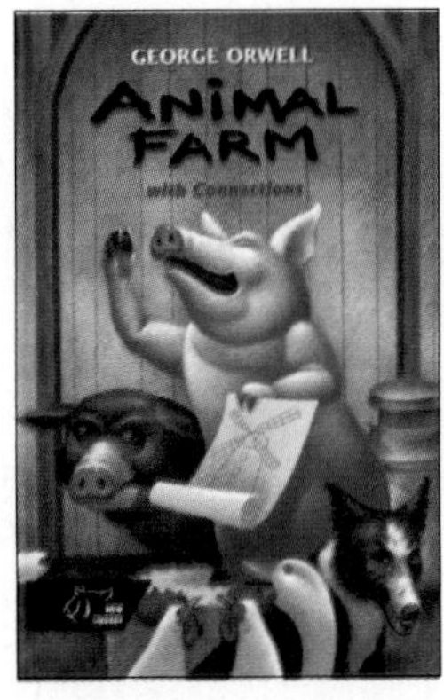

FICTION

Down on the Farm

Like Pope and Swift, George Orwell uses satire to reveal the absurdities of human nature. In his famous novel ***Animal Farm*** (1945), Orwell satirizes the problems of a supposedly equal society. The animals of Manor Farm revolt against their incompetent owner and install the "Seven Commandments of Animalism," which the sheep simply remember as "four legs good, two legs bad." The pigs Napoleon and Snowball eventually disagree about the future of the farm, and a rivalry for power ensues.

This title is available in the HRW Library.

Writing Workshop

Writing a Literary Essay

Writing Assignment
Write a literary essay that shows how multiple works reflect the same literary trend.

Because they reflect universal human feelings and experiences, great works of literature such as Miguel de Cervantes' *Don Quixote* transcend time. Yet every work of literature is shaped by the era in which it is produced. In this workshop you'll write a **literary essay** that analyzes three works from the same literary period to discover how they reflect the literary trends of the time in which they were written.

Prewriting

Choose a Topic

A Trendy Topic Start by choosing a literary period on which to focus. You may want to investigate the literary period of one of your favorite authors or works, or you might get ideas about important literary periods by talking to your teacher or school librarian. Below is a list of literary periods you might consider.

- Renaissance (1485–1660)
- Victorian Period (1832–1901)
- Romantic Period (1798–1832)
- Twentieth Century (1901–2000)

Once you've chosen a literary period, do research to identify the **literary trends,** such as changes in style or the development of new literary genres, of that period and the works that reflect those trends. Find information about literary trends and works by looking through this textbook—particularly at the introduction to the literary period you've chosen—or by checking out library books that discuss the literary period.

Select one literary trend and three works by three different writers that reflect that trend. If the works you choose are long works, such as novels or epic poems, you will probably need to deal with a single section of each work to provide a thorough analysis in a 1,500-word essay. For example, one student who selected the eighteenth century as the focus of his literary essay chose to write about "A Voyage to Laputa" from Jonathan Swift's *Gulliver's Travels,* Book I of Alexander Pope's *The Dunciad,* and all of Voltaire's short novel *Candide* to show how they reflect a dominant trend in eighteenth-century literature—satire.

Writing Skills
Write an essay analyzing works of literature.

Analyze Literary Works

The Evidence Will Show . . . Through your research, you already know that your three works reflect a literary trend. Now you'll demonstrate *how* each work reflects that trend. To do that, read each work critically, following the guidelines on the next page.

- First, as you read each work, ask yourself, "What **evidence** shows that this work illustrates the literary trend I've chosen?" Jot down your responses to this question.
- Next, once you've read and responded to one work, analyze your responses to see what **major point** most of the evidence supports.

DO THIS

When you've gone through this process for each work, you should have the major points you'll discuss in your essay and the evidence supporting them. The partial chart below shows one student's major point about Swift's work and the literary evidence that led him to it.

Evidence	Major Point
Members of the Laputian nobility regard themselves as scientists; their heads are tilted and their eyes are strangely arranged; tailors take measurements with scientific instruments, but the clothes they make don't fit.	Swift uses satire to ridicule the impractical ideas and practices of some of the scientists of his time.

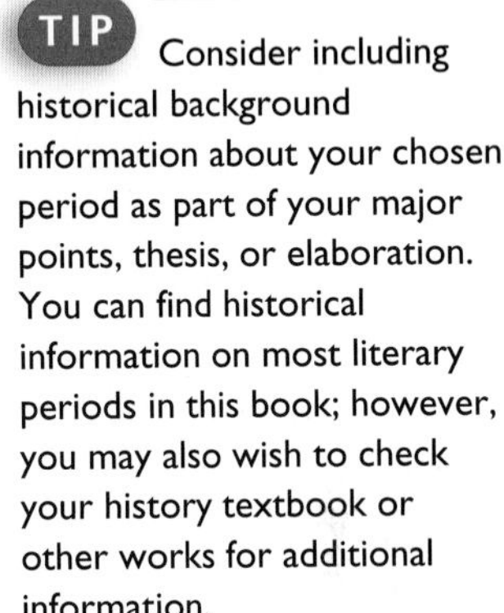

TIP Consider including historical background information about your chosen period as part of your major points, thesis, or elaboration. You can find historical information on most literary periods in this book; however, you may also wish to check your history textbook or other works for additional information.

Write a Thesis Statement

Tying the Knot Now that you've analyzed each work and identified the major points you will discuss in your essay, you can tie those points together in a **thesis statement**—a sentence or two that expresses the main idea of your essay. Your thesis statement should also identify the literary period, the literary trend, and the authors whose works you'll discuss. Remember, it's likely that you'll revise your thesis statement—for reasons of content or style—by the time you write your final draft. Here is one student's working thesis statement.

> Jonathan Swift, Alexander Pope, and Voltaire used satire to ridicule the intellectual folly of the eighteenth century.

Elaborate on the Evidence

Building Your Case A compelling case in a literary essay consists of the major points that support your thesis, plus at least two pieces of **literary evidence** that support each major point. Use **precise and relevant examples** as support; however, don't merely state a major point and then follow it with only literary evidence from the work in question. Instead, **elaborate** upon the evidence by interpreting it for your readers. In other words, explain precisely how the evidence supports the major point. Look at how one student structured part of his argument about Pope in the notes on the next page. Notice how he wrote down a **parenthetical citation,** showing where in the work he found the quote; then, he elaborated on this literary evidence.

Writing Skills
Analyze works of literature.
Write a thesis statement.
Support ideas with references to the text.

Major Point: Pope uses satire to chastise writers who create dull, nonsensical works.

Literary Evidence: In a prayer to the goddess Dulness, the poet Bays asks her to "spread a healing mist before the mind" and to replace reason with cobwebs (l, 174).

Elaboration: Bays wants a mist, or fog, to obscure his vision. He wants cobwebs instead of reason in his mind. This is an ironic contrast to what we expect writers to want—clear vision and clear reason. Pope uses irony—the contrast between expectation and reality—to satirize writers who create illogical works.

Reference Note

For more on **parenthetical citations,** see page 248.

TIP Writers from every period use **stylistic devices**—figurative language, irony, imagery, diction—that suit their purposes. Some styles of literature require certain stylistic devices—so much so that the literary style and the device can hardly be separated. Such is the case with irony and satire, the literary style that holds human vice and folly up to ridicule. If part of your literary evidence involves a writer's use of a stylistic device, be sure to explain the relationship between the stylistic device and the trend. For more on **stylistic devices,** see page 543.

Organize Your Essay

TIP When writing about literature, use the **literary present tense.** The characters and actions depicted in literature are forever unfolding for new readers. For example, instead of writing "In *Gulliver's Travels,* Swift **used** satire . . . ," you would write "In *Gulliver's Travels,* Swift **uses** satire. . . ."

Setting Forth Plan to **structure** your arguments and ideas in a sustained way. Since this essay deals with three works by different writers, plan to discuss one work at a time, starting with the one published first and ending with the one published last. By organizing the works chronologically, you can show how each not only reflects the literary trend you're discussing, but also contributes to establishing that trend. Here is part of a student's working outline for an essay on satire in the works of Swift, Pope, and Voltaire.

—Introduction
—Background information
—Thesis statement
—Swift on scientists
—Major point
—First example of literary evidence
—Elaboration
—Second example of literary evidence
—Elaboration

Writing Skills
Use a clear structure and system of organization.

PRACTICE & APPLY 1 Follow the guidelines in this section to analyze three works from one literary period. Find literary evidence to support your major points, elaborate on your evidence, and organize your essay chronologically.

Writing

Writing a Literary Essay

A Writer's Framework

Introduction

- Introduce the literary period and provide background information about that period.
- In a thesis statement, identify the literary period, the literary trend, and the authors discussed in the essay.

Body

- Develop the major points that support the thesis.
- Use at least two pieces of fully elaborated literary evidence to support each point.
- Organize the essay in chronological order.

Conclusion

- Restate, but don't repeat, your thesis.
- Close with a final observation on the literary works or on the literary period.

A Writer's Model

Satire in the Eighteenth Century

The eighteenth century was known as the Enlightenment and the Age of Reason for its emphasis on reason and common sense. Some scientists, writers, and philosophers, however, divorced reason from common sense. The result was reason carried to ludicrous extremes. Jonathan Swift, Alexander Pope, and Voltaire—three of the most important writers of the eighteenth century—used satire to ridicule the intellectual folly of the day.

INTRODUCTION
Literary period and background information
Thesis statement

In *Gulliver's Travels,* Swift uses satire to present a humorous characterization of scientists and to expose some of their impractical ideas. Swift creates a fictional island, Laputa, where members of the nobility regard themselves as scientists. These Laputians' heads are always tilted to one side as if they are in deep thought. In addition, their eyes are strangely arranged—one of them turns inward, and the other turns straight up to show that their thoughts are fixed on themselves and on higher ideas. Swift turns the mental characteristics of the Laputians into humorous physical characteristics. The position of their heads suggests that they are lost in thought and cannot look at anything straight on. In addition, due to the position of their eyes, they cannot see the ground and so they are not down to earth. As evidence of the Laputians' impracticality, the tailor sent to make clothes for Gulliver takes measurements with scientific instruments made for other tasks. Ironically, the result is that Gulliver's new clothes don't fit.

BODY
Major point
Evidence: summary
Elaboration
Evidence: summary

(continued)

(continued)

Elaboration

Like the scientists of the eighteenth century, the Laputians have become so carried away with knowledge for its own sake that they have lost sight of common sense.

Major point
Evidence: summary
Elaboration

Alexander Pope satirizes the literature of the time in his long poem *The Dunciad*, which praises a goddess named Dulness. The title *The Dunciad* makes fun of poems written by stupid people—dunces. The goddess named Dulness implies that these poets are inspired by dullness. In other words, Pope is saying that the poets of his day value dullness and write boring poems. His character, a poet named Bays, prays to Dulness, asking her to "spread a healing mist before the mind" and to replace reason with cobwebs (I, 174). Instead of asking for his mind to be sharp and clear, as one would expect, Bays wants the opposite. Pope uses the stylistic device of irony to ridicule the dull and dimwitted writers of his day.

Evidence: quotation
Elaboration

Major point
Evidence: summary

In *Candide,* Voltaire makes fun of eighteenth-century philosophers who teach that the world is a rational, perfect place. To ridicule this kind of thinking, Voltaire creates a character named Pangloss, who is a philosopher. Pangloss teaches the young Candide a popular philosophy of the day: In this "best of all possible worlds," everything happens for the best (20). However, when Candide goes out to experience this "best of all possible worlds," he encounters one misfortune after another—he is kicked out of his home, separated from the woman he loves, kidnapped, forced to take part in a brutal war, beaten, nearly killed and eaten, cheated, robbed, shipwrecked, and caught in an earthquake. As Candide suffers, he echoes Pangloss's ridiculous teachings to others who suffer terrible misfortunes, making this philosophy seem more and more ridiculous. The novel's irony is the contrast between the optimistic philosophy of some eighteenth-century thinkers and Candide's actual experience.

Evidence: quotation/summary

Elaboration

CONCLUSION
Restatement of thesis
Final observation

Just as the best scientists, writers, and philosophers of the eighteenth century exposed superstitions to the light of reason, Swift, Pope, and Voltaire exposed the misguided reasoning of lesser scientists, writers, and philosophers. In doing so, they established the trend of using satire to fight folly.

INTERNET
More Writer's Models
Keyword: LE7 12–4

PRACTICE & APPLY 2 Using the framework on page 687 and the Writer's Model above as guides, write the first draft of your literary essay. Be sure to cite all literary evidence used in your essay.

Revising

Evaluate and Revise Your Draft

Polish Your Prose A literary essay is a sophisticated piece of writing that requires much effort. To be sure that your essay is as clearly developed and organized as you want it to be, read through your draft at least twice. On your first reading, consider the content and organization of your essay. On your second, consider the style.

PEER REVIEW

Before you revise, trade papers with a peer. He or she may be able to offer advice on how to improve your elaboration of literary evidence.

First Reading: Content and Organization Use the following chart to help you evaluate and revise the content and organization of your literary essay. Answer the questions in the left-hand column by using the tips in the middle column. If revisions are necessary, use the revision techniques in the right-hand column.

Rubric: Writing a Literary Essay

Evaluation Questions	Tips	Revision Techniques
1 Does the introduction introduce the literary period and give necessary background information?	**Box** the literary period. **Bracket** background information about the literary period.	**Add** sentences that introduce the literary period and give necessary background information.
2 Does the introduction contain a thesis statement that identifies the literary period, the literary trend, and the authors being discussed?	**Underline** the thesis statement. **Double underline** the mention of the literary period, the literary trend, and the authors.	**Add** information to identify the literary period, the literary trend, and the authors whose works the essay discusses.
3 Are the major points that support the thesis clear? Are the works organized chronologically?	**Star** the major points that support the thesis statement. **List** each work's publication date in the margin.	**Add** major points, or **rewrite** them so they clearly support the thesis statement. **Rearrange** major points to put works in chronological order.
4 Is each major point supported by at least two pieces of literary evidence? Is the evidence fully elaborated through explanations and interpretation?	**Circle** each piece of literary evidence. **Highlight** sentences or parts of sentences that elaborate upon the literary evidence.	**Add** literary evidence, if necessary. **Elaborate** upon literary evidence by explaining how it supports a significant idea and by interpreting the evidence.
5 Does the conclusion restate the thesis and make a final observation about the literary works or period?	**Draw a squiggly line** under the restatement of the thesis. **Double underline** the final observation.	**Add** a sentence that restates the thesis. **Add** a final observation about the literary works or period.

Second Reading: Style The second time you read your draft, focus on evaluating and revising your style—the way you express yourself. One way to improve your style is to **introduce quotations** gracefully so that a reader doesn't hesitate or stumble. Look at the examples below, and then use the style guidelines in the chart to improve the style of your essay.

Awkward Pangloss stands by his philosophy even when faced with his own misfortune. He says that "it would be unbecoming for me to recant" (136).

Smooth Even when faced with his own misfortune, Pangloss clings to his optimistic philosophy, saying "it would be unbecoming for me to recant" (136).

Style Guidelines

Evaluation Question	Tip	Revision Technique
Are quotations introduced smoothly so that they don't interrupt the flow of thought?	**Highlight** the introductions to all quotations.	**Add** introductory phrases to quotations or **combine** quotations with other sentences.

ANALYZING THE REVISION PROCESS

Study these revisions, and answer the questions that follow.

combine

His character, a poet named Bays, prays to Dulness~~, Bays says,~~ *, asking her to* "~~S~~pread a healing mist before the mind" *and* to replace reason with cobwebs (I, 174). *Instead of asking for his mind to be sharp and clear, as one would expect, Bays wants the opposite.* Pope uses the stylistic device of irony to ridicule the dull and dimwitted writers of his day.

elaborate

Responding to the Revision Process

1. Why did the writer combine the first two sentences?
2. How does the writer's elaboration of the literary evidence contained in this passage improve the draft?

PRACTICE & APPLY 3 Using the guidelines on pages 689 and 690, first evaluate and revise the content and organization of your literary essay. Then, evaluate and revise its style, introducing quotations gracefully.

Writing Skills
Revise for content and style.

Publishing

Proofread and Publish Your Essay

Say What You Mean Errors in basic grammar, usage, and mechanics can ruin the value of an otherwise excellent literary essay. To ensure that your audience will focus on your ideas and not on your mistakes, proofread your essay with care before you submit your final draft.

Far and Wide In your literary essay, you collected and interpreted information that might be of interest to other readers. With a classmate, brainstorm imaginative publishing ideas, or try one of these suggestions to share your essay with a wider audience.

- With classmates, create a Web site that contains your essays along with links that lead to a variety of sites related to the literary works and periods you discussed.
- Submit your essay to one of the many online literary magazines published by high school students.
- Ask a history teacher who teaches the period that your essay examines to make your essay available to his or her classes.
- Adapt your essay into an oral response to literature, and present it to an audience of your classmates. For more on **presenting a literary response,** see page 692.

TIP As you proofread, make sure your essay follows the **conventions** of standard American English. Look in particular to see that you use quotation marks and italics correctly in punctuating the titles of the literary works you discuss. For more on **punctuating titles,** see Italics, 13b, and Quotation Marks, 13d, in the Language Handbook.

Reflect on Your Literary Essay

Know Yourself You've created a complex analysis. Take a few minutes now to reflect on your essay in order to grasp how much you've accomplished—how much you learned about your topic and about your writing process. Write responses to the following questions, and include them with a final copy of your essay.

- Did your thesis change by the time you wrote your final draft? If so, explain how and why.
- What major revisions did you make to your draft? How did they improve the essay?
- Did writing the essay deepen your understanding of the works and the literary period you chose? Why or why not?
- What kinds of resources were helpful to you in developing your topic? For what other types of assignments, for this class and others, might resources such as these also be useful? Explain your response.

PRACTICE & APPLY 4 Proofread the final draft of your essay for errors in the conventions of grammar, usage, and mechanics. Then, publish and reflect on your literary essay using the suggestions and questions above.

Writing Skills
Proofread, especially for correct punctuation of titles.

Presenting a Literary Response

Speaking Assignment
Adapt your literary essay for an oral response to literature, and present it to your class.

Writing a literary essay about a specific literary period probably helped you understand that period better. You can share that understanding with your classmates by adapting your literary essay for an **oral response to literature** and delivering it to your class.

Adapt Your Written Essay

Go with the Flow You can follow the same basic organization of your written essay, but you might need to adjust the introduction, body, and conclusion to make your oral presentation effective.

- The **introduction** to an oral presentation needs to be more dramatic than a written introduction so your listeners won't tune you out before you get started. Consider beginning with one of the **unique aspects** of the works you'll discuss. For example, a unique aspect of *The Dunciad* is Alexander Pope's use of the mock-epic genre to ridicule some poets of his day. End your introduction with a strong but simple **thesis statement** that leaves listeners with no misconceptions about the literary period, literary trend, or authors whose works you plan to discuss.
- The **body** of your oral presentation should cover the main points of your essay as well as the **literary evidence**—quotations and detailed references to the works—and elaboration that interprets or explains the evidence. Make clear the significant ideas in the works. Explain for listeners the effects of any **stylistic devices,** such as imagery or language, that the authors use. Be especially thorough in your explanation of the **ambiguities** (events or passages subject to more than one interpretation), **nuances** (subtle shades of meaning), and **complexities** (passages rich in meaning, but difficult to understand). Remember, listeners must immediately understand the ideas you present, so explain these challenging elements simply and clearly.
- The **conclusion** for your oral response serves the same purpose as your written conclusion: It wraps up your ideas. To impress listeners, it should also be memorable. Consider using a **rhetorical device** such as a rhetorical question, repetition, or parallelism when restating your thesis. When you make a final observation about your topic, consider framing it in terms of the **universal themes** shared by the works you are discussing. For example, a universal theme in the works of Swift, Pope, and Voltaire is that human beings are capable of reform, despite their foolishness.

Listening and Speaking Skills
Deliver an oral response to literature.

Rehearse and Deliver Your Oral Response

Naturally Speaking Because you want your presentation to sound natural and relaxed, don't memorize it. Instead, speak **extemporaneously.** Make **concise notes** to use now as you rehearse and later when you deliver your presentation. On note cards, write key words or phrases about main points and brief reminders of evidence you'll use in your presentation. Write quotations out word for word so you can present them accurately. Arrange the note cards in the order in which you want to present the information on them.

A Polished Performance Merely standing up, staring straight ahead, and delivering the content of your presentation in a natural sounding voice will not make your presentation effective. You must use certain delivery techniques, too, including those in the chart below.

Quick guide

DELIVERY TECHNIQUES

Technique	Tips
Pronunciation and enunciation	Pronounce the words you are using correctly, clearly, and distinctly. Don't slur words.
Emphasis	Emphasize important points by changing the volume or tone of your voice.
Pauses	Pause to give your audience time to think about what you have just said and to emphasize the point you are about to make.
Facial expressions	Make your facial expressions complement the content of your presentation—serious expressions for serious content and light expressions for light content.
Gestures	Use natural, relaxed gestures, and don't be afraid to move around as you speak.
Eye contact	Engage your audience by making eye contact with as many people as possible.

TIP Be sure to use **standard American English** when you deliver your presentation. Avoid using slang and colloquialisms in an oral response to literature. Your listeners could misunderstand nonstandard language.

Stand and Deliver Rehearse your presentation until you are thoroughly familiar and comfortable with the content and the delivery techniques you intend to use when you actually present your response. If possible, rehearse in front of an audience of friends or family, and ask for feedback on how you might improve your presentation.

PRACTICE & APPLY 5 Use the instructions in this workshop to adapt your written literary essay for an oral presentation. Speak extemporaneously, and use delivery techniques effectively as you present your oral response to literature.

Listening and Speaking Skills
Use effective verbal and nonverbal techniques.

Collection 4: Skills Review

Comparing Literature

Test Practice

The following excerpts provide two accounts of disastrous fires that occurred over sixteen hundred years apart. The fire described by the Roman historian Tacitus (c. A.D. 56–c. 117) in "The Burning of Rome" occurred in A.D. 64. It is perhaps best remembered as the occasion when Emperor Nero, a particularly heartless, despotic ruler, "fiddled while Rome burned." Samuel Pepys (1633–1703; pronounced "peeps"), the most famous diarist of the English Restoration, kept a secret, multivolume diary from 1660 to 1669. He recorded "The First Day of the Great Fire of London" alongside entries describing his public and private experiences in daily life. The Great Fire, which occurred in 1666, was a horrible national disaster for England.

DIRECTIONS: Read the following excerpts. Then, read each multiple-choice question that follows, and write the letter of the best response.

from The Burning of Rome

from The Annals

Tacitus

translated by **George Gilbert Ramsay**

And now came a calamitous fire—whether it was accidental or purposely contrived by the Emperor remains uncertain for on this point authorities are divided—more violent and destructive than any that ever befell our city. It began in that part of the Circus[1] which adjoins the Palatine and Caelian hills.[2] Breaking out in shops full of inflammable merchandise, it took hold and gathered strength at once; and being fanned by the wind soon embraced the entire length of the Circus, where there were no mansions with protective walls, no temple-enclosures, nor anything else to arrest its course. Furiously the destroying flames swept on, first over the level ground, then up the heights, then again plunging into the hollows, with a rapidity which outstripped all efforts to cope with them, the ancient city lending itself to their progress by its narrow tortuous streets and its misshapen blocks of buildings. The shrieks of panic-stricken women; the weakness of the aged, and the helplessness of the young; the efforts of some to save themselves, of others to help their neighbors; the hurrying of those who dragged their sick along, the lingering of those who waited for them—all made up a scene of inextricable confusion.

Many persons, while looking behind them, were enveloped from the front or from the side; or having escaped to the nearest place of safety, found this, too, in posses-

1. **Circus:** Circus Maximus, a great arena used for chariot races.
2. **Palatine** (paˈlə·tīnˈ) **and Caelian** (sēˈlē·ən) **hills:** two of seven hills of ancient Rome.

Pages 694–697 cover **Literary Skills** Compare and contrast works from different literary periods.

sion of the flames, and even places which they had thought beyond their reach in the same plight with the rest. At last, not knowing where to turn, or what to avoid, they poured into the roads or threw themselves down in the fields: some having lost their all, not having even food for the day; others, though with means of escape open to them, preferred to perish for love of the dear ones whom they could not save. And none dared to check the flames; for there were many who threatened and forced back those who would extinguish them, while others openly flung in torches, saying that *they had their orders;*—whether it really was so, or only that they wanted to plunder undisturbed.

from The Diary of Samuel Pepys

Samuel Pepys

September 2, 1666
The First Day of the Great Fire of London

Lord's Day. Some of our maids sitting up late last night to get things ready against our feast today, Jane called us up, about three in the morning, to tell us of a great fire they saw in the City.[1] So I rose, and slipped on my nightgown and went to her window, and thought it to be on the backside of Mark Lane at the furthest; but being unused to such fires as followed, I thought it far enough off, and so went to bed again and to sleep. About seven rose again to dress myself, and there looked out at the window and saw the fire not so much as it was, and further off. So to my closet[2] to set things to rights after yesterday's cleaning. By and by Jane comes and tells me that she hears that above three hundred houses have been burned down tonight by the fire we saw, and that it was now burning down all Fish Street by London Bridge. So I made myself ready presently, and walked to the Tower[3] and there got up upon one of the high places, Sir. J. Robinson's little son going up with me; and there I did see the houses[4] at that end of the bridge all on fire, and an infinite great fire on this and the other side of the end of the bridge—which, among other people, did trouble me for poor little Michell and our Sarah[5] on the bridge. So down, with my heart full of trouble, to the Lieutenant of the Tower, who tells me that it begun this morning in the King's baker's house in Pudding Lane, and that it hath burned down St. Magnes Church and most part of Fish Street

1. **City:** London. The Great Fire started in a bakery, raged for four days and four nights, and destroyed some 13,000 residences. It leveled four fifths of the city and left about 100,000 people homeless.
2. **closet** *n.:* private room.
3. **Tower:** Tower of London, a short walk from Pepys's house.
4. **houses** *n. pl.:* Shops and dwellings were built on London Bridge.
5. **Sarah:** maid whom Mrs. Pepys discharged on December 5, 1662. Pepys wrote: "The wench cried, and I was ready to cry too."

Collection 4: Skills Review

already. So I down to the waterside and there got a boat and through bridge, and there saw a lamentable fire. Poor Michell's house, as far as the Old Swan,[6] already burned that way and the fire running further, that in a very little time it got as far as the Steelyard while I was there. Everybody endeavoring to remove their goods, and flinging into the river or bringing them into lighters[7] that lay off. Poor people staying in their houses as long as till the very fire touched them, and then running into boats or clambering from one pair of stair by the waterside to another. And among other things, the poor pigeons I perceive were loath to leave their houses, but hovered about the windows and balconies till they were some of them burned, their wings, and fell down.

6. **Michell's house . . . Old Swan:** Betty Michell, a former sweetheart of Pepys, lost her house in the fire. The Old Swan was a tavern on Thames Street, near London Bridge.
7. **lighters** *n. pl.:* large, open barges.

Having stayed, and in an hour's time seen the fire rage every way, and nobody to my sight endeavoring to quench it, but to remove their goods and leave all to the fire; and having seen it get as far as the Steelyard, and the wind mighty high and driving it into the City, and everything, after so long a drought, proving combustible, even the very stones of churches, and among other things, the poor steeple by which pretty Mrs. —— lives, and whereof my old schoolfellow Elborough is parson, taken fire in the very top and there burned till it fall down—I to Whitehall with a gentleman with me who desired to go off from the Tower to see the fire in my boat—to Whitehall, and there up to the King's closet in the chapel, where people came about me and I did give them an account dismayed them all; and word was carried in to the King, so I was called for and did tell the King and Duke of York what I saw, and that unless his Majesty did command houses to be pulled down, nothing could stop the fire. . . .

---

1. Tacitus describes the scene of the fire as being one of —

A confusion

B heroism

C orderliness

D anticipation

2. A distinctive feature of Tacitus's style is his —

F use of parallel structure

G use of words with strong connotations

H offering of two different causes or explanations for an event

J all of the above

Collection 4: Skills Review

3. Which of the following is true of both "The Burning of Rome" and "The First Day of the Great Fire of London"?
   - **A** Both express contempt for the victims.
   - **B** Both describe scenes of beauty.
   - **C** Both describe people making the fire worse on purpose.
   - **D** Both describe the power of the fire.

4. What word best describes Tacitus's tone?
   - **F** enthusiastic
   - **G** critical
   - **H** sentimental
   - **J** neutral

5. In which of the following ways does Pepys's literary technique differ from Tacitus's?
   - **A** Pepys describes the fire scene.
   - **B** Pepys writes in the third person.
   - **C** Pepys romanticizes the beauty of the fire.
   - **D** Pepys describes his personal feelings.

6. According to Pepys's diary entry, after he first sees the fire from a window, he goes back to sleep because —
   - **F** he is too terrified to go outdoors
   - **G** the fire seems far away
   - **H** he thinks it is a dream
   - **J** he is ill

7. Pepys's descriptions of the "lamentable fire" and the "poor pigeons" typify his tone of —
   - **A** cynicism
   - **B** superiority
   - **C** disgust
   - **D** compassion

8. What is Pepys's reaction to the fire?
   - **F** He finds the sight worrisome.
   - **G** He wishes the flames were bigger.
   - **H** He becomes enraged.
   - **J** He has no reaction at all.

9. One aspect of Restoration life depicted in Pepys's account is —
   - **A** commercialism
   - **B** a clear-cut class system
   - **C** the popularity of satire
   - **D** vast scientific progress

Essay Question

The excerpts you have read are accounts of great tragedies recounted by two very different writers from very different time periods—a historian from ancient Rome and a diarist from Restoration England. In a short essay, compare and contrast the texts. In your essay consider these elements of each text:

- audience
- purpose
- writer's perspective
- use of personal details
- tone

Collection 4: Skills Review

Vocabulary Skills

Test Practice

Analogies: Synonyms and Antonyms

DIRECTIONS: For each item, choose the lettered pair of words that expresses a relationship that is most similar to the relationship between the pair of capitalized words.

1. GLUTTED : EMPTIED ::
- **A** hurried : tarried
- **B** ran : jumped
- **C** shut : closed
- **D** freed : liberated

2. SCRUPULOUS : CARELESS ::
- **F** eager : indifferent
- **G** miserly : stingy
- **H** thin : slender
- **J** annoyed : angry

3. BREVITY : SHORTNESS ::
- **A** restlessness : turmoil
- **B** calmness : distress
- **C** gratitude : thankfulness
- **D** honor : disgrace

4. ANIMOSITIES : HOSTILITIES ::
- **F** exercises : athletes
- **G** truths : deceits
- **H** crimes : punishments
- **J** blunders : errors

5. SOLICITUDE : ANTAGONISM ::
- **A** fidelity : disloyalty
- **B** transitory : permanent
- **C** serious : solemn
- **D** hopeless : unfortunate

6. DESIST : CEASE ::
- **F** congratulate : ridicule
- **G** release : snare
- **H** modify : alter
- **J** avoid : invite

7. FLACCID : FLABBY ::
- **A** timid : outspoken
- **B** restful : restless
- **C** tardy : punctual
- **D** empty : vacant

8. SPECIOUS : GENUINE ::
- **F** interested : bored
- **G** limber : flexible
- **H** aggressive : hostile
- **J** flavorful : healthful

Vocabulary Skills
Analyze word analogies.

Collection 4: Skills Review

Writing Skills

Test Practice

DIRECTIONS: Read the following paragraph from a draft of a student's literary essay. Then, answer the questions below it.

(1) The first English novels, developed during the eighteenth century, examined middle-class life and values. (2) Daniel Defoe's *Robinson Crusoe* was published during this time. (3) Robinson Crusoe, the first-person narrator, describes himself as being from a middle-class family, "the third son of the family, and not bred to any trade" (1). (4) Throughout his adventures, Crusoe challenges the belief systems of the time about work, trade, class systems, and human dignity. (5) Defoe published the novel when he was nearly sixty.

1. Which sentence would best replace sentence 2 to sustain the paragraph's overall idea?

- **A** The exciting characters in Defoe's *Robinson Crusoe* reflect the growing Protestant movement of the time.
- **B** Defoe's *Robinson Crusoe* exemplifies the literary trend of basing novels on the middle class.
- **C** Defoe's *Robinson Crusoe* shows how the Age of Reason brought about new criticisms of Christianity.
- **D** Defoe's *Robinson Crusoe* is a classic tale involving shipwrecks, cannibalism, and life on a deserted island.

2. To elaborate the idea in sentence 3, the student could

- **F** recount the entire plot of the novel
- **G** describe the character of the cannibal, whom Crusoe named Friday
- **H** explain the meaning of the quotation as it relates to the novel
- **J** present the biography of Defoe's life

3. To relate Defoe's work to the overall trends in eighteenth-century literature, the student could

- **A** compare Crusoe to heroes in other eighteenth-century novels
- **B** explain how Defoe's novel comments on Protestantism
- **C** contrast eighteenth-century novels with Romantic poetry
- **D** contrast Defoe's writing style with the scientific writing of the time

4. Which sentence should be deleted or moved to another paragraph in order to improve the organization of the passage?

- **F** 1
- **G** 3
- **H** 4
- **J** 5

5. To present the paragraph as part of an oral response, the student could

- **A** avoid referring to the novel in order to save time
- **B** recite a summary of the entire novel to increase the audience's interest
- **C** change the tone of her voice to emphasize important points
- **D** read her response word for word from note cards

Writing Skills
Write an essay analyzing works of literature.

Worcester (detail) (19th century) by Sir John Gilbert.

Guildhall Art Gallery, Corporation of London. The Bridgeman Art Library.

Collection 5

The Romantic Period 1798–1832

The Quest for Truth and Beauty

The divine arts of imagination: imagination, the real & eternal world of which this vegetable universe is but a faint shadow.

—William Blake

Brickmakers (1821) by Sir John Gilbert.

INTERNET

Collection Resources

Keyword: LE7 12-5

The Romantic Period 1798–1832

LITERARY EVENTS

1786 1794 1802 1809

1786 Robert Burns publishes *Poems, Chiefly in the Scottish Dialect*

1789 William Blake publishes *Songs of Innocence*

1792 Mary Wollstonecraft critiques female educational restrictions in *A Vindication of the Rights of Woman*

1794 Ann Radcliffe's *The Mysteries of Udolpho* popularizes the Gothic novel

1798 William Wordsworth and **Samuel Taylor Coleridge** publish *Lyrical Ballads*

1800 Maria Edgeworth's *Castle Rackrent,* the first historical novel in English, satirizes absentee landowners in Ireland

1807 Charles and Mary Lamb publish *Tales from Shakespeare*

1808 Johann Wolfgang von Goethe publishes Part I of *Faust*

Jane Austen (c. 1790).
The Granger Collection, New York.

1812 Charles Dickens is born

1812 Lord Byron publishes first two cantos of *Childe Harold's Pilgrimage*

1812 Brothers Grimm begin to publish *Grimm's Fairy Tales*

1813 Jane Austen publishes *Pride and Prejudice*

POLITICAL AND SOCIAL EVENTS

1786 1794 1802 1809

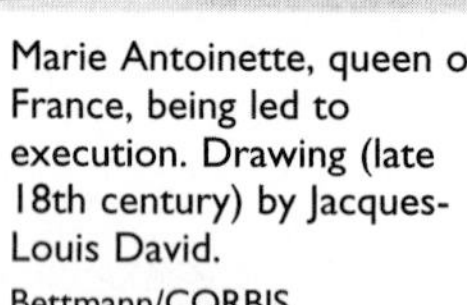

Marie Antoinette, queen of France, being led to execution. Drawing (late 18th century) by Jacques-Louis David.
Bettmann/CORBIS.

1789 French Revolution begins with storming of Bastille

1793 King Louis XVI of France is beheaded

1793 France declares war on England

1800 Thomas Jefferson is elected U.S. president

1800 Napoleon conquers parts of Italy

1801 Act of Union creates United Kingdom of Great Britain and Ireland

Napoleon in his study (19th century) by Hippolyte (Paul) Delaroche.
Agnew & Sons, London. The Bridgeman Art Library.

1802 Workday of pauper children is limited to twelve hours in England

1803 United States purchases Louisiana Territory from France

1804 Napoleon crowns himself emperor in France

1805 Egypt gains independence from Ottoman Turks

1805 Lord Nelson defeats Napoleon's navy at Battle of Trafalgar

1806 Construction begins on Arc de Triomphe

1808 United States bans importation of slaves from Africa

1810 Simón Bolívar begins series of South American rebellions against Spain

1811 Venezuela declares independence from Spain

1811 English artisans called Luddites riot and destroy textile machines, fearing that industrialism threatens their livelihoods

1812 Napoleon invades Russia

1812 United States declares war on Great Britain

Scarlet Ibis (1837) by John James Audubon.
Collection of New-York Historical Society (Acc. No. 1863.17.397).

1814 **1819** **1822** **1829**

1814 Noted actor Edmund Kean debuts as Shylock in Shakespeare's *The Merchant of Venice*

1818 Mary Shelley, daughter of **Mary Wollstonecraft,** publishes *Frankenstein*

1819 Sir Walter Scott publishes *Ivanhoe*

1819 John Keats writes his greatest poems between January and September

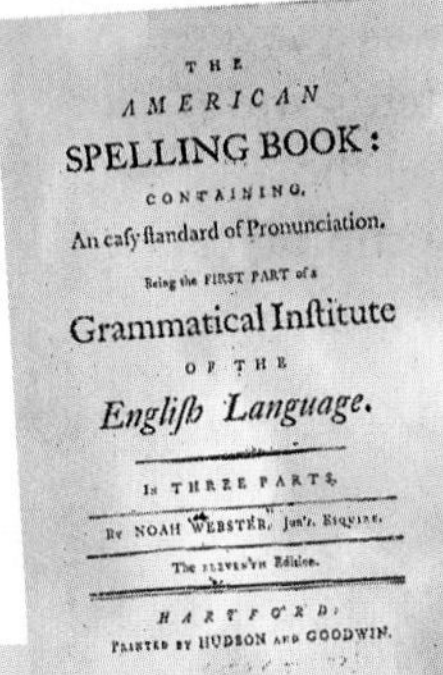

THE
AMERICAN
SPELLING BOOK:
CONTAINING,
An easy standard of Pronunciation.
Being the FIRST PART of a
Grammatical Institute
OF THE
English Language.
In THREE PARTS.
By NOAH WEBSTER, Jun'r. Esquire.
The ELEVENTH Edition.
HARTFORD:
PRINTED BY HUDSON AND GOODWIN.

Title page of the first known edition of Noah Webster's *The American Spelling Book* (1788).
The Granger Collection, New York.

1823 Alexander Pushkin begins his novel in verse, *Eugene Onegin*

1826 James Fenimore Cooper publishes *The Last of the Mohicans*

1827 John James Audubon begins publishing *The Birds of America*

1828 Noah Webster publishes *An American Dictionary of the English Language*

1830 Emily Dickinson is born in Amherst, Massachusetts

1831 Victor Hugo publishes *The Hunchback of Notre Dame*

1814 **1819** **1822** **1829**

1814 British forces burn Washington, D.C.

1815 Allied British, Dutch, and German forces defeat Napoleon at Waterloo

1815 German confederation is created to replace Holy Roman Empire

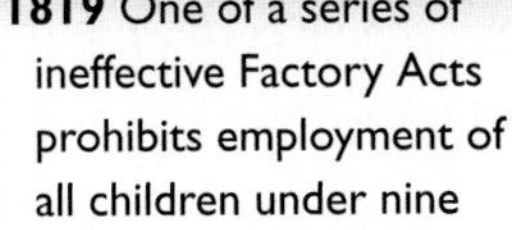

1819 One of a series of ineffective Factory Acts prohibits employment of all children under nine

1819 First steamship, the *Savannah,* crosses the Atlantic in twenty-nine days

1820 Antarctica is sighted by Russian, British, and American ships

1820 George III, mentally unstable since 1810, dies

1821 Cherokee system of writing is created by Sequoyah

1821 Mexico declares its independence from Spain

1822 Liberia is founded as home for former U.S. slaves

1822 Rosetta stone is deciphered, allowing Egyptian hieroglyphics to be read

1823 In the United States, Monroe Doctrine closes the Americas to further European colonization

1824 First labor unions are permitted in Great Britain

1829 Catholic Emancipation Act allows British Roman Catholics to hold public office

1831 Charles Darwin serves as naturalist on HMS *Beagle* during expedition along the coast of South America

HMS *Beagle*.
The Granger Collection, New York.

1831 Nat Turner leads slave rebellion in Virginia

1832 Reform Act extends voting rights in Britain to upper-middle-class men

1833 Slavery is abolished in British Empire

Se-Quo-Yah (Inventor of Cherokee Alphabet). Lithograph printed by Lehman and Duval after a painting by Charles Bird King.
Philadelphia Museum of Art: Gift of Miss William Adger, 1937.

Political and Social

The American Revolution, 1776–1783

The beginning of the end of the worldwide British Empire began with the revolt of the thirteen American Colonies. Britain's defeat in the American War of Independence was a severe economic blow, leaving the country with massive war debts and without the American revenue which had been enriching the British economy. The loss of the Colonies was also a psychological blow to England.

The Death of General Mercer at the Battle of Princeton, January 3, 1777 (detail) (c. 1789–1831) by John Trumbull.

The French Revolution and the Era of Napoleon, 1789–1815

In July of 1789, an angry crowd of Frenchmen stormed the Bastille, a prison in Paris, to protest the oppressive policies of the French monarchy. This event marked the first step in a long series of violent political upheavals and radical changes in the French national government. These revolutionary experiments, which were intended to introduce "liberty, fraternity, and equality" into French society, instead often resulted in a loss of freedom, civility, and safety. Events

Milestones 1798–1832

The guillotine.
Musée de la Ville de Paris, Musée Carnavalet, Paris. © Giraudon/Art Resource, New York.

such as the massacre of clergy and nobility in September of 1792, the execution of King Louis XVI in 1793, and finally the rise to power of Napoleon (a military dictator with world-conquering ambitions) dashed the hopes of British liberals and strengthened the conservative side. The British liberals had initially looked to revolutionary France for new models of political freedom, but now rich and powerful British conservatives could point a finger at French excesses to justify their repressive policies.

The Motto of the Republic of France (18th century).
Musée de la Revolution Française, Vizille, France. The Bridgeman Art Library.

Interior of a coal mine in South Staffordshire, England.
Ironbridge Gorge Museum, Telford, Shropshire, England. The Bridgeman Art Library.

The Industrial Revolution in England

With the invention of efficient machines to do work formerly done at home by hand, nineteenth-century England began moving from a traditional rural, agricultural society to a more modern, urban, and industrialized state. Masses of landless people now had no choice but to move to crowded cities and work in squalid, dangerous factories for low wages. The wealthy owners of these new factories and mills embraced the hands-off economic theory of *laissez faire* (les′ā fer′)—"let people do as they please"—to justify doing nothing to improve the appalling conditions in which their labor force lived and worked. This laissez-faire approach was even applied to rationalize the use of young children of the poor for back-breaking labor.

Child working in a brick factory.
Bettmann/CORBIS.

The Romantic Period 1798–1832

by Harley Henry

PREVIEW

Think About . . .

Beginning in the late eighteenth century, English society was being rocked by great political, economic, and social changes. The neoclassical faith in reason and its reverence for order and tradition, which had dominated English thought and literature for more than a century, seemed inadequate in the face of these profound upheavals. New ways of thinking, feeling, and responding to change seemed needed.

As you read about this period, look for answers to these questions:

- How did political events in America and France in the late eighteenth and early nineteenth centuries affect English society?
- How did the industrialization of England revolutionize the ways in which people lived and worked?
- What political and economic theories developed in response to the changes brought about by England's rapid industrialization?
- What new values and responses to change did the Romantic poets offer?

Collection introduction (pages 704–717) covers **Literary Skills** Evaluate the philosophical, political, religious, ethical, and social influences of a historical period.

During the spring of 1798, two young English poets sold some of their poems to raise money for a trip to Germany. Each had published books of poetry, but their new joint work was to be anonymous. As Samuel Taylor Coleridge, the younger of the pair, told the printer: "Wordsworth's name is nothing . . . mine *stinks.*"

Soon after they left England, their book, *Lyrical Ballads, with a Few Other Poems,* appeared. Among the "few other poems" was Coleridge's long narrative *The Rime of the Ancient Mariner* (see page 765) and a last-minute addition, Wordsworth's "Lines Composed a Few Miles Above Tintern Abbey" (see page 736). Both of these works are now among the most important poems in English literature.

So began what is now called the "Romantic period" in England. Literary historians have found other momentous events to mark its beginning and end, but we should remember the casual, modest appearance of *Lyrical Ballads* as we consider the Romantic period and the writers associated with it.

The Wanderer Above the Sea of Clouds (1818) by Caspar David Friedrich. Oil on canvas.
Hamburg Kunsthalle, Germany. The Bridgeman Art Library.

> *It was the best of times, it was the worst of times, it was the age of wisdom, it was the age of foolishness, it was the epoch of belief, it was the epoch of incredulity, it was the season of Light, it was the season of Darkness, it was the spring of hope, it was the winter of despair, we had everything before us, we had nothing before us, we were all going direct to Heaven, we were all going direct the other way. . . .*
>
> —Charles Dickens
> from *A Tale of Two Cities*

Turbulent Times, Bitter Realities

Another way to date the Romantic period is to say that it started with the French Revolution in 1789 and ended with the Parliamentary reforms of 1832 that laid the political foundations for modern Britain. The era has been most often identified with six poets: Three (William Blake, William Wordsworth, and Samuel Taylor Coleridge) were born before the period began and lived through most or all of it, while three others (the "second generation" of Percy Bysshe Shelley, John Keats, and George Gordon, Lord Byron) began their short careers in the second decade of the new century but died before 1825. It was a turbulent, revolutionary age, one in which England changed from an agricultural society to an industrial nation with a large and restless working class concentrated in the teeming mill towns.

We think about this era in terms of some important historic developments. Beginning in America in 1776, an age of revolution swept across western Europe, releasing political, economic, and social forces that produced, during the next century, some of the most radical changes ever experienced in human life.

The French Revolution

The American Revolution had lost for England its thirteen Colonies. This was a great economic loss, but it was also a loss of prestige and of confidence. The more radical revolution in France, which started with the storming of the prison called the Bastille on July 14, 1789, had far more ominous repercussions. For the ruling classes in England, the French Revolution came to represent their worst fears: the overthrow of an anointed king by a democratic mob. To English conservatives, the French Revolution meant the triumph of radical principles, and they feared that the revolutionary fever would spread across the Channel.

Tragic End of Louis XVI (18th century).
Musée Carnavelet, Paris. Photo Bulloz.

Storming of the Bastille (18th century).
Chateaux de Versailles, et de Trianon, France.

The "New Regime"

But democratic idealists and liberals like Wordsworth felt exhilarated by the events in France. During the revolution's early years, they even made trips to France to view the new regime firsthand, as if it were a tourist attraction like the Acropolis in Greece. Wordsworth later wrote, "Bliss was it in that dawn to be alive, / But to be young was very heaven!"

Even Wordsworth became disillusioned, however, when in 1792 the "September massacre" took place in France. Hundreds of French aristocrats and some members of the clergy—some with only the slightest ties to the regime of King Louis XVI—had their heads severed from their bodies by a grisly new invention, the guillotine.

In 1793, France and England declared war on each other. Many English liberals, including Wordsworth and Coleridge, turned against France. In the midst of the blood and turmoil and calls from France for worldwide revolution, control of the French government changed hands again. Napoleon Bonaparte, an officer in the French army, emerged first as dictator and then, in 1804, as emperor of France. In the end, Napoleon—whose very name today suggests a tyrant—became as ruthless as the executed king himself had been.

The Executioners, desperate lest themselves be murdered . . . seize the hapless Louis: six of them desperate, him singly desperate, struggling there; and bind him to their plank. Abbé Edgeworth, stooping, bespeaks him: "Son of Saint Louis, ascend to Heaven." The Axe clanks down; a King's Life is shorn away.

—Thomas Carlyle, describing the execution of Louis XVI on January 21, 1793

Bedlam Furnace, Madeley Dale, Shropshire (1803) by Paul Sandby Munn.
Private Collection.

London, 1802

Milton! thou shouldst be living at this hour;
England hath need of thee; she is a fen
Of stagnant waters: altar, sword, and pen,
Fireside, the heroic wealth of hall and bower,
Have forfeited their ancient English dower
Of inward happiness. We are selfish men;
Oh! raise us up, return to us again;
And give us manners, virtue, freedom, power.
Thy soul was like a star, and dwelt apart;
Thou hadst a voice whose sound was like the sea;
Pure as the naked heavens, majestic, free,
So didst thou travel on life's common way,
In cheerful godliness; and yet thy heart
The lowliest duties on herself did lay.

—William Wordsworth

The Conservatives Clamp Down

The bewildering changes in western Europe made conservatives in England more rigid than ever. England instituted severe repressive measures: It outlawed collective bargaining and kept suspected spies or agitators in prison without a trial. After a brief peace in 1802–1803, England began a long war against Napoleon. English guns first defeated Napoleon's navy at the Battle of Trafalgar and finally—in 1815 with the help of allies—sent Napoleon's army packing at Waterloo, Belgium.

The conservatives in England felt they had saved their country from a tyrant and from chaos; the early supporters of the revolution felt betrayed. For them, Waterloo was simply the defeat of one tyrant by another. Still, the Romantics clung to their hopes for the "dawn of a new era" through peaceful change—hopes provoked and shaped by upheavals in English life brought about by the Industrial Revolution.

Card makers (c. 1800).

The Industrial Revolution Finds a Foothold

England was the first nation in the world to experience the effects of the Industrial Revolution. Previously, goods had been made by hand, at home. Now, production switched to factories, where machines worked many times faster than human beings could work by hand. Since factories were in cities, the city populations increased, resulting in desperate living conditions that would appall even the most hardened social worker today.

In addition, the communal land once shared by small farmers was taken over by individual owners. Some of these rich owners transformed the fields into vast private parks, generously stocked with deer for their own Christmas hunts. Others divided the land neatly into privately held fields. Whatever happened to the land, it was no longer communally owned. This resulted in large numbers of landless people. Just as some unemployed and homeless people do today, these landless people migrated to cities in search of work, or relied on the forms of charity of the time, the poorhouse and begging.

A Surrey Cornfield (19th century) by George Vicat Cole.

Children pushing a coal cart through a mine shaft (1842).

The Tyranny of Laissez Faire

The economic philosophy that kept all this misery going was a policy called **laissez faire** (les′ā fer′), "let (people) do (as they please)." According to this policy, the new economic forces should be allowed to operate freely without government interference. The result of laissez faire was that the rich grew richer, and the poor suffered even more. The system, of course, had its most tragic effects on the helpless, especially children. Small children of the poor were often used as beasts of burden. In the coal pits, for example, very small children were even harnessed to carts for dragging coal, just as if they had been small donkeys.

The Rebellion of the Romantic Poets

The six Romantic poets in this collection were all, in their own ways, deeply aware of their revolutionary times and dedicated to bringing about change. They had no illusions about their very limited political power, but they believed in the force of literature. Frustrated by England's resistance to political and social change that would improve conditions, the Romantic poets turned from the formal, public verse

The Sleeping Princess (19th century) by Sir Edward Burne-Jones.

of the eighteenth-century Augustans to a more private, spontaneous, lyric poetry. These lyrics expressed the Romantics' belief that imagination, rather than mere reason, was the best response to the forces of change. Wordsworth spoke of imagination this way:

> "... spiritual love acts not nor can exist
> Without imagination, which, in truth,
> Is but another name for absolute power
> And clearest insight, amplitude of mind,
> And Reason in her most exalted mood."
>
> —from *The Prelude*

What Does "Romantic" Mean?

The word *romantic* comes from the term *romance,* one of the most popular genres of medieval literature (see page 215). Later, Romantic writers self-consciously used the elements of romance in an attempt to go back beyond the refinements of neoclassical literature to older types of writing that they saw as more "genuine." The romance genre also allowed writers to explore new, more psychological and mysterious aspects of human experience.

Today, the word *romantic* is often a negative label used to describe sentimental writing. The word is particularly applied to bestselling paperback "romances" about love—a subject that many people mistakenly think the Romantic poets popularized. As a historical term, however, *romantic* has at least three useful meanings, all of them relevant to the Romantic poets.

■ A Child's Sense of Wonder

First, the term *romantic* signifies a fascination with youth and innocence, particularly the freshness and wonder of a child's perception of the world. This perception seemed to resemble the age's sense of a "new dawn" and what Wordsworth saw in his first experience in France as "human nature being born again."

■ Social Idealism

Second, the term *romantic* refers to a view of the cyclical development of human societies. This is the stage when people need to question tradition and authority in order to imagine better—that is, happier, fairer, and healthier—ways to live. *Romantic* in this sense is associated with idealism. (The 1966–1975 period in the United States might be called a romantic era.)

■ Adaptation to Change

Finally, the term *romantic* suggests an ability to adapt to change—an acceptance of change rather than a rigid rejection of it. In the so-called Romantic period of the first half of the nineteenth century (up to the Civil War in America), Western societies met the

What Was Romanticism?

Romanticism is characterized by these general features:

- Romanticism turned away from the eighteenth-century emphasis on reason and artifice. Instead, the Romantics embraced imagination and naturalness.
- Romantic-era poets rejected the public, formal, and witty works of the previous century. They preferred poetry that spoke of personal experiences and emotions, often in simple, unadorned language.
- Many Romantics turned to a past or an inner dream world that they felt was more picturesque and magical than the ugly industrial age they lived in.
- Most Romantics believed in individual liberty and sympathized with those who rebelled against tyranny.
- The Romantics thought of nature as transformative; they were fascinated by the ways nature and the human mind "mirrored" each other's creative properties.

conditions necessary for industrialization. This demanded that people acquire a stronger and stronger awareness of change, and that they try to find ways to adapt to it. In this sense, we still live with the legacy of the Romantic period.

A New Kind of Poetry

Lyrical Ballads did not remain unnoticed or anonymous for long. In 1800, with Coleridge looking over his shoulder, Wordsworth

A CLOSER LOOK: SOCIAL INFLUENCES

INFORMATIONAL TEXT

View of Strawberry Hill, Middlesex from the gardens (19th century) by Gustave Ellinthorpe Sintzenich. Watercolor, pencil, and body color.

Mallett & Sons Antiques Ltd., London. The Bridgeman Art Library.

The Lure of the Gothic

Literature of the Romantic period is filled with examples of the eerie and supernatural: Samuel Coleridge's haunting *The Rime of the Ancient Mariner* and Mary Shelley's famously horrible *Frankenstein*. The Romantics' taste for terror grew from a sensibility called "Gothic" that set stories in gloomy medieval castles. The intention of the Gothic? To make readers' blood run cold.

A "little gothick Castel." Much credit for the popularity of the Gothic style must go to a dramatically unorthodox construction project. In 1747, Horace Walpole (1717–1797) began building what he called a "little gothick Castel." A more conventional choice by the son of wealthy, powerful Prime Minister Robert Walpole (1676–1745) would have been a mansion in the popular neoclassical style. Neoclassical architecture—like the White House in the United States—is inspired by ancient Roman and Greek models and emphasizes balance and symmetry. In stark contrast, the Gothic revels in rustic irregularity: quirky battlements (medieval-style fortifications with openings for defenders) or overgrown landscaping. Walpole's home, named Strawberry Hill, was designed to be gloriously imperfect. When its odd medieval battlements collapsed, the ruin only enhanced its charm and intensified its melancholy atmosphere.

Making monsters. Walpole had constructed a Gothic ruin; in 1764, he filled it with monsters. His novel *The Castle of Otranto* uses composed the Preface for the expanded collection. In it he declared that he was writing a new kind of poetry that he hoped would be "well adapted to interest mankind permanently. . . ." The subject matter would be different from that of earlier giants of poetry—like Alexander Pope—who used poetry to satirize, or to persuade the reader with argumentative techniques. For Wordsworth, good poetry was "the spontaneous overflow of powerful feelings." Such poetry should use simple, unadorned language to deal with

> *I will not Reason & Compare: my business is to Create.*
> —William Blake

ghosts, living statues, and an eerie forest cave to illustrate a royal family's collapse. With this terrifying, imaginative story, Walpole created the first Gothic novel, a genre of horror tales that we recognize today.

The effects of Walpole's creations were far-reaching. The model of his crumbling house and of stories that provoked violent emotions helped begin the Romantic period's love affair with all things Gothic. Contemporary tastes thought that Gothic architecture reflected the wild, unpredictable aspects of nature; its ruins reflected human aspirations and failures. A melancholy painting or a desolate landscape could enhance spiritual awareness. Ann Radcliffe (1764–1823), one of the best-known Gothic novelists, describes this ideal awareness in *The Mysteries of Udolpho* (1794). In twilight gloom, a character finds "that delicious melancholy which no person, who had felt it once, would resign for the gayest pleasures. They awaken our best and purest feelings; disposing us to benevolence, pity, and friendship."

Exploring unseen evils. The turn from rational enlightenment to Gothic sensationalism indicated more than just a fad for terrifying tales and quirky architecture. The Gothic was one way in which people of the age expressed a sense of helplessness about forces beyond their control: frightening revolutions in Europe and industrialization's unsettling economic changes. The familiar, sensational trappings of the Gothic novel that we know today were less important than its ability to let readers, if only for a moment, share their fears about the age's suffering, injustice, and other unseen evils.

Two Men Contemplating the Moon (1819) by Caspar David Friedrich.

Staatliche Kunstsammlungen Dresden, Gemäldegalerie Neue Meister.

> *"I see everything I paint in this world, but everybody does not see alike. To the eyes of a miser, a guinea [a coin] is more beautiful than the sun, & a bag worn with the use of money has more beautiful proportions than a vine filled with grapes. . . . But to the eyes of the man of imagination nature is imagination itself. As a man is, so he sees. . . . To me this world is all one continued vision of fancy or imagination."*
>
> —William Blake

commonplace subjects. Its form is often a lyric that lends itself to spontaneity, immediacy, a quick burst of emotion, and self-revelation. Furthermore, Wordsworth focused on rural life instead of city life, because in the country "the passions of men are incorporated with the beautiful and permanent forms of Nature." Wordsworth found hope in "certain inherent and indestructible qualities of the human mind, and likewise . . . certain powers in the great and permanent objects that act upon it, which are equally inherent and indestructible." In other words, there is a permanent and interactive bond between the human mind and nature. Wordsworth reveals and celebrates this bond in "Tintern Abbey" (see page 736).

The Mystery of Imagination

It is a mistake to think of the Romantics as "nature poets." They were "mind poets" who sought a deeper understanding of the bond between human beings and the world of the senses. Their search led them to a third, more mysterious element present in both the mind and nature. In "Tintern Abbey" Wordsworth describes this link as "something far more deeply interfused." This "something" is a creative power that makes things happen. The Romantics identified this power as the imagination, a faculty superior to human reasoning.

Each of the Romantics had his or her own special view of the imagination. But all of them seem to have believed that the imagination could be stimulated by both nature and the mind itself. They had a strong sense of nature's mysterious forces, which both inspire the poet—as they do in Shelley's "Ode to the West Wind" (see page 806)—and hint at the causes of the great changes taking place in the world. Romantic poems usually present imaginative experiences as very powerful or moving. This suggests that the human imagination is also a kind of desire—a motive that drives the mind to discover things that it cannot learn by rational or logical thinking.

In the Preface, Wordsworth says that the poet considers "the mind of man as naturally a mirror of the fairest and most interesting properties of nature." Yet his long autobiographical poem, *The Prelude,* ends by pledging that poets will reveal "how the mind of Man becomes / A thousand times more beautiful than the earth / On which he dwells." Whatever we may call the creative power interfused in nature, the human imagination also moves the mind in mysterious ways to imitate (without being sacrilegious) the powers of its Maker. The purpose of this imitation is to create new realities in the mind and (as a result) in poetry.

FAST FACTS

Social and Economic Influences

- A laissez-faire economic philosophy is embraced by English capitalists to block reform in the early days of the Industrial Revolution.
- The growing industrialization of Britain leads to the growth of urban populations and a rise in the numbers of poor workers.

The Romantic Poet

In the Preface, Wordsworth makes it clear that the poet is special, "endowed with more lively sensibility, more enthusiasm and tenderness . . . a greater knowledge of human nature, and a more comprehensive soul, than are supposed to be common among mankind." Though the word *supposed* (meaning "thought") may suggest that Wordsworth thought his fellow citizens had too low an estimate of much of humankind, all of the Romantic poets described the poet in such lofty terms.

For William Blake, for example, the poet was the bard, an inspired revealer and teacher. The poet, wrote Coleridge, "brings the whole soul of man into activity" by employing "that synthetic and magical power . . . the imagination." Shelley called poets "the unacknowledged legislators of the world." Keats wrote that a poet is a "physician" to all humanity and "pours out a balm upon the world." Wordsworth wrote in *The Prelude,*

. . . what we have loved,
Others will love, and we will teach them how;
Instruct them how the mind of man becomes
A thousand times more beautiful than the earth
On which he dwells, above this frame of things
(Which, 'mid all revolution in the hopes
And fears of men, doth still remain unchanged)
In beauty exalted, as it is itself
Of quality and fabric more divine.

The poet, in sum, is someone human beings and society cannot do without.

FAST FACTS

Political Highlights

- The French and American Revolutions in the late 1700s deeply affect England. Conservative economic and political measures and a lengthy war against Napoleon strengthen the power of the rich.

Philosophical Views

- Romanticism arises as a response to social and economic changes caused by the Industrial Revolution.

REVIEW

Talk About . . .

Turn back to the Think About questions posed at the start of this introduction to the Romantic period (see page 706), and discuss your responses with a group of classmates.

Write About . . .

Contrasting Literary Periods

The role of the poet, then and now. Wordsworth and the Romantics saw a very special place for the poet or the artist in society. In fact, the Romantics saw the poet in a role similar to that of a priest, teacher, or master. In the Romantic view, the poet functions as a sort of spiritual guide to the inner realms of intuition, feeling, and imagination. Do people see poets and artists in this light today, or are they viewed and valued differently? Write your opinions on the role of artists in today's society.

William Blake
(1757–1827)

William Blake (detail) (1807) by Thomas Phillips. Oil on canvas (35¼" × 17¼").

The Granger Collection, New York.

William Blake's life is not as "romantic" or "poetic" as the lives of Coleridge, Shelley, and Keats were. By all accounts, he was somewhat happily married to the same woman for much of his life. He never traveled, and he lived outside London for only three years (1800–1803). He began his artistic training at ten, when his father, a London shopkeeper, sent him to one of the best drawing schools. Apprenticed to an engraver at fourteen, Blake worked steadily at his craft as an engraver and as a professional artist throughout a long life.

During his lifetime, Blake's work received very little attention, and a great deal of his poetry was never published in the sense of being public. When his work was noticed, readers and viewers too often decided that it, and therefore Blake himself, was weird, confused, or mad. What we really know of Blake—from the enormous energy and variety of his poetry, paintings, drawings, and engravings—is that he was quite simply a great artist in the fullest sense.

A woman at a gathering is said to have asked Blake *where* he had come upon the scene he had just vividly described to her. "*Here*, madam," he said, pointing his finger at his forehead. To paraphrase Blake, if we see with imagination, we see all things in the infinite. But if we see only with reason, we see only ourselves. "I know that this world is a world of imagination & vision," he wrote.

The history of Blake the poet cannot really be separated from that of Blake the visual artist. Not only did he provide illustrations for most of his poems, but he also printed much of his poetry himself (and sometimes only for himself), using engraving methods he himself had created. According to Blake's nineteenth-century biographer Alexander Gilchrist, "the poet and his wife did everything in making the book [*Songs of Innocence* (1789)]—writing, designing, printing, engraving—everything except manufacturing the paper; the very ink, or color rather, they did make. Never before surely was a man so literally the author of his own book."

A good deal of what Blake wrote other than his poems is cryptic and needs illumination from his art. But one characteristic of the man himself shines through clearly—the optimism sustained by his continuous joy in the "one continued vision" of his art. As one acquaintance described Blake, "He was a man without a mask; his aim single, his path straightforward, and his wants few; so he was free, noble, and happy."

Blake's Poems: Innocence to Experience

William Blake first published *Songs of Innocence* in 1789. In 1794, this collection and *Songs of Experience* were issued together in one volume, the title page promising a demonstration of "the two Contrary States of the Human Soul."

Innocence and experience. Blake conceived the first of these states, "Innocence," as a state of genuine love and naive trust toward all humankind, accompanied by unquestioned belief in Christian doctrine. Though a firm believer in Christianity, Blake thought that its doctrines were being used by the English Church and other institutions as a form of social control: to encourage among the people passive obedience and acceptance of oppression, poverty, and inequality. Recognition of this marks what Blake called the state of "Experience," a profound disillusionment with human nature and society. One entering the state of "Experience" sees cruelty and hypocrisy only too clearly but is unable to imagine a way out. Blake also conceived of a third, higher state of consciousness that he called "Organized Innocence," which is expressed in his later works. In this state, one's sense of the divinity of humanity coexists with oppression and injustice, though involving continued recognition of and active opposition to them.

Reading Blake. When reading *Songs of Innocence* and, to a lesser extent, *Songs of Experience,* it is important to remember that Blake intended them not as simple expressions of religious faith. The poems are demonstrations of viewpoints that are necessarily limited or distorted by each narrator's or speaker's state of consciousness.

The Ghost of Samuel Appearing to Saul (1800) by William Blake. Pen and ink with watercolor over graphite (12 9/16" × 13 1/2").

Before You Read

The Tyger
The Lamb

Make the Connection

William Blake's poetry and art reflect his fascination with the Bible and his struggle to find answers to questions that profoundly disturbed him: What is the source of evil in the world? Why does God allow the innocent to suffer? Can evil be transformed or transcended?

One of Blake's early conclusions about the problem of good and evil was that "without contraries is no progression." To Blake, "The Tyger" and "The Lamb" reflect "two contrary states of the human soul," both of which are as essential to humanity as joy and sadness, innocence and experience.

Literary Focus

Symbol

A **symbol** is a person, place, animal, thing, or event that stands for both itself and something more than itself. In literature, symbols function on two levels: They have a literal, or exact, meaning and a figurative, or metaphorical, one. The metaphorical meaning involves states, feelings, and experiences that are hard to articulate yet are of great importance to people, such as love, death, danger, or hope.

The meanings of some symbols are widely recognized, such as the dove as a sign of peace, but poets and writers often create new symbols whose meaning can only be discovered by exploring the structure, language, and imagery of the works in which they appear.

A **symbol** is a person, place, animal, thing, or event that stands for itself and for something beyond itself.

For more on Symbol, see the Handbook of Literary and Historical Terms.

Background

Blake's poems have a surface simplicity that masks a very complex view of human life and of Christianity. As a religious visionary, Blake saw the entire material world as a set of signs or symbols representing religious or mystical realities. In addition, any one of Blake's symbols—the "tyger," for instance—has such a rich array of meanings that we cannot expect ever to understand fully what such a symbol meant to him.

Elohim Creating Adam (1795–1805) by William Blake.
Tate Gallery, London.

Literary Skills
Understand symbols.

While almost everyone agrees that "The Tyger" is one of the most powerful of Blake's Songs of Experience, *there has been much disagreement about the meaning of the poem's central* **symbol,** *the tiger itself. One possibility is that the tiger represents a strong revolutionary energy that can enlighten and transform society—a positive but volatile force Blake believed was operating in the French Revolution. The poem's speaker, at any rate, cannot comprehend such a startling energy, and can only wonder whether it is demonic or godlike.*

The Tyger (1793) by William Blake, from his book *Songs of Experience*. Hand-colored etching.

Library of Congress, Washington, D.C.

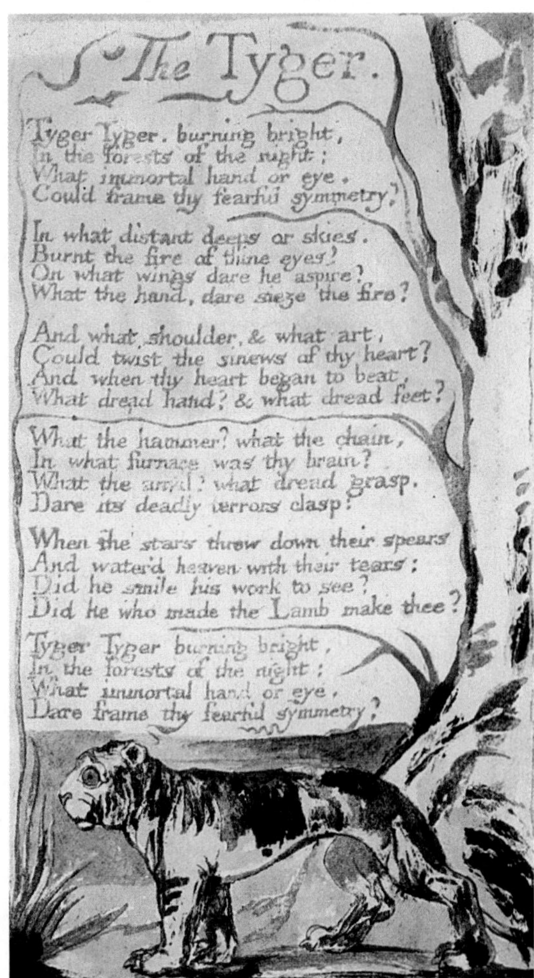
The Tyger.

Tyger Tyger. burning bright,
In the forests of the night;
What immortal hand or eye.
Could frame thy fearful symmetry?

In what distant deeps or skies.
Burnt the fire of thine eyes?
On what wings dare he aspire?
What the hand, dare sieze the fire?

And what shoulder, & what art,
Could twist the sinews of thy heart?
And when thy heart began to beat,
What dread hand? & what dread feet?

What the hammer? what the chain,
In what furnace was thy brain?
What the anvil? what dread grasp,
Dare its deadly terrors clasp!

When the stars threw down their spears
And waterd heaven with their tears:
Did he smile his work to see?
Did he who made the Lamb make thee?

Tyger Tyger burning bright,
In the forests of the night:
What immortal hand or eye,
Dare frame thy fearful symmetry?

The Tyger

from Songs of Experience

William Blake

Tyger! Tyger! burning bright
In the forests of the night,
What immortal hand or eye
Could frame thy fearful symmetry?

In what distant deeps or skies
Burnt the fire of thine eyes?
On what wings dare he aspire?
What the hand dare seize the fire?

And what shoulder, and what art,
Could twist the sinews of thy heart?
And when thy heart began to beat,
What dread hand? and what dread feet?

What the hammer? what the chain?
In what furnace was thy brain?
What the anvil? what dread grasp
Dare its deadly terrors clasp?

When the stars threw down their spears,°
And watered heaven with their tears,
Did he smile his work to see?
Did he who made the Lamb make thee?

Tyger! Tyger! burning bright
In the forests of the night,
What immortal hand or eye,
Dare frame thy fearful symmetry?

17. stars . . . spears: reference to the angels who fell with Satan and threw down their spears after losing the war in heaven.

PRIMARY SOURCE / LETTER

Charles Lamb (1775–1834), perhaps the most accomplished Romantic essayist, sings the praises of William Blake in a letter to Bernard Barton.

"Blake Is a Real Name . . ."

Blake is a real name, I assure you, and a most extraordinary man, if he be still living. He is the Robert [William] Blake, whose wild designs accompany a splendid folio edition of the *Night Thoughts,* which you may have seen, in one of which he pictures the parting of soul and body by a solid mass of human form floating off, God knows how, from a lumpish mass (facsimile to itself) left behind on the dying bed. He paints in water-colors marvelous strange pictures, visions of his brain, which he asserts that he has seen. They have great merit. He has *seen* the old Welsh bards on Snowden—he has seen the beautifulest, the strongest, and the ugliest man, left alone from the massacre of the Britons by the Romans, and has painted them from memory (I have seen his paintings), and asserts them to be as good as the figures of Raphael and Angelo, but not better, as they had precisely the same retrovisions and prophetic visions with himself. The painters in oil (which he will have it that neither of them practiced) he affirms to have been the ruin of art, and affirms that all the while he was engaged in his water paintings, Titian was disturbing him, Titian the III Genius of Oil Painting. His pictures—one in particular, the *Canterbury Pilgrims* (far above Stothard's)—have great merit, but hard, dry, yet with grace. He has written a catalogue of them with a most spirited criticism on Chaucer, but mystical and full of vision. His poems have been sold hitherto only in manuscript. I never read them; but a friend at my desire procured the Sweep Song. There is one to a tiger, which I have heard recited, beginning:

> Tiger, Tiger, burning bright,
> Thro' the desarts of the night,

which is glorious. But, alas! I have not the book; for the man is flown, whither I know not, to Hades or a madhouse—But I must look on him as one of the most extraordinary persons of the age.

—Charles Lamb

The Agony in the Garden (c. 1799–1800) (detail) by William Blake.
Tate Gallery, London.

The Lamb (c. 1789–1794) by William Blake, from his book *Songs of Innocence and of Experience*. Relief etching finished in pen and watercolor.

Fitzwilliam Museum, University of Cambridge, England.

One of the Songs of Innocence, *this poem has often been read as a statement of Christian faith. However, we know that Blake's other writings show Christ as an active fighter against injustice, not the "meek" and "mild" lamb—a common symbol for Christ—with which this innocent speaker identifies. The speaker's viewpoint is thus an incomplete representation of Blake's beliefs—just one aspect of Blake's worldview.*

The Lamb

from Songs of Innocence

William Blake

Little Lamb, who made thee?
Dost thou know who made thee?
Gave thee life, and bid thee feed
By the stream and o'er the mead,°
Gave thee clothing of delight,
Softest clothing, wooly, bright;
Gave thee such a tender voice,
Making all the vales° rejoice?
Little Lamb, who made thee?
Dost thou know who made thee?

Little Lamb, I'll tell thee,
Little Lamb, I'll tell thee:
He° is called by thy name,
For He calls himself a Lamb.
He is meek, and he is mild;
He became a little child.
I a child, and thou a lamb,
We are called by his name.
Little Lamb, God bless thee!
Little Lamb, God bless thee!

4. mead *n.:* meadow.

8. vales *n. pl.:* valleys.

13. He: Christ.

Response and Analysis

The Tyger
The Lamb

Thinking Critically

1. What question does the speaker of "The Tyger" ask over and over? What answer is implied?
2. Where in the poem does the speaker wonder if the tiger may have been created by God? What **imagery** tells us that the speaker also suspects that the tiger could be a demonic creation? List the images that suggest a human creator—like a blacksmith or a goldsmith.
3. What **imagery** suggests that the tiger could be a force of enlightenment? of revolutionary violence?
4. What do you think Blake means by the tiger's "fearful symmetry"? (Picture a tiger's stripes.)
5. The last stanza of "The Tyger" virtually repeats the first. What is the significance of the one word changed in the last stanza?
6. How does "The Tyger" represent people's simultaneous attraction toward and repulsion from evil?
7. What does the creator do for his creation in the first stanza of "The Lamb"?
8. How does the second stanza of "The Lamb" respond to the questions asked in the first stanza?
9. What are you told directly about the **speaker** of "The Lamb"? What inferences can you draw from this information?
10. Christ called himself a lamb because, like the Passover lamb slain to save the people of Israel, he sacrificed himself for the people. What might this imply about the fate of the young **speaker** in this poem?
11. How do you think the voice of the speaker in "The Lamb" is different from the voice of the speaker in "The Tyger"? Why do you think the questions in "The Lamb" get answers?
12. If you had to choose your own symbols for the qualities represented by Blake's tiger and lamb, what would they be? Explain.

Extending and Evaluating

13. Why do human beings commit evil? Why does God allow innocent children to suffer? Such questions profoundly disturbed Blake. One of his early conclusions about the problem of good and evil is his idea that "Without contraries [opposites] there is no progression [growth]." How do "The Tyger" and "The Lamb" reflect what Blake termed "two contrary states of the human soul"? In what sense are these contrasting states essential to human beings?

Literary Skills Analyze symbols.

Writing Skills Compare and contrast the early draft with the final version of a poem.

WRITING

Second-Guessing Blake

In an early draft of "The Tyger," Blake inserted the following lines after the third stanza:

Could fetch it from the furnace deep
And in thy horrid ribs dare steep
In the well of sanguine wee
In what clay and in what mold
Were thy eyes of fury rolled

This early version also lacked the fifth stanza of the final version. In a brief **essay, compare and contrast** the early draft with the final version of "The Tyger," commenting on why you think Blake made the changes he made.

Before You Read

The Chimney Sweeper *from* Songs of Innocence
The Chimney Sweeper *from* Songs of Experience

Make the Connection

Quickwrite

In these two poems, the first from *Songs of Innocence* and the second from *Songs of Experience,* Blake speaks for the poor children of his day who were forced to do backbreaking labor. In Blake's London, buildings were heated by coal- or wood-burning fireplaces, so every house had at least one chimney that had to be cleaned regularly. Poor children were often used to do this dirty and hazardous work because they could fit into the narrow chimney passages. In fact, some parents were so poverty stricken that they sold their children to "masters" who managed crews of young sweepers. The work was dangerous, and the children were badly treated by masters concerned only with profits.

If you could cry out against an evil of our day—and get people to listen—which social injustice would you protest? Take a few minutes to jot down your thoughts.

A row of rooftops above a street of terraced houses in Britain.

Literary Focus

Parallelism

When words, phrases, or sentences are arranged in balanced grammatical structures, they are said to be **parallel.** Poets, dramatists, preachers, and speechwriters (whose work is meant to be spoken aloud) are particularly likely to employ parallelism because the repetition it introduces enhances the rhythmic and emotional effect of their lines and makes them easier to understand and remember. Blake's use of parallelism contributes to the childlike simplicity of the surface of his poems.

Parallelism is the repetition of words, phrases, or sentences that have the same grammatical structure or that restate a similar idea.

For more on Parallelism, see the Handbook of Literary and Historical Terms.

Background

In the late 1700s, prices increased sharply and work became scarce. Blake saw starving people rooting through garbage, homeless families sleeping in doorways, and children begging on the streets or working at horrible jobs. Most members of the upper class believed that they deserved their comfortable stations in life, and that the poor must be innately evil, deserving the hunger and appalling conditions that they endured.

Blake was said to be mad, not only because he saw visions, but also because his poems cry out against the social problems he saw all around him: the growing division between classes, the wretched working conditions, and child labor. No one should go hungry, he said, in a land as green and wealthy as England.

Literary Skills Understand parallelism.

Drawing depicting a young English chimney sweep covered with soot (1850).
MANSELL/TimePix.

This poem from Songs of Innocence *features a child speaker who tries to cheer himself and his fellow chimney sweep, Tom Dacre, with the thought that the oppression and poverty they endure will be compensated for by endless joy in heaven.*

The Chimney Sweeper
from Songs of Innocence

William Blake

When my mother died I was very young,
And my father sold me while yet my tongue
Could scarcely cry "'weep! 'weep! 'weep! 'weep!"°
So your chimneys I sweep, and in soot I sleep.

There's little Tom Dacre, who cried when his head,
That curled like a lamb's back, was shaved: so I said
"Hush, Tom! never mind it, for when your head's bare
You know that the soot cannot spoil your white hair."

And so he was quiet, and that very night,
As Tom was a-sleeping, he had such a sight!—
That thousands of sweepers, Dick, Joe, Ned, and Jack,
Were all of them locked up in coffins of black.

And by came an Angel who had a bright key,
And he opened the coffins and set them all free;
Then down a green plain leaping, laughing, they run,
And wash in a river, and shine in the Sun.

Then naked and white, all their bags left behind,
They rise upon clouds and sport in the wind;
And the Angel told Tom, if he'd be a good boy,
He'd have God for his father, and never want° joy.

And so Tom awoke; and we rose in the dark,
And got with our bags and our brushes to work.
Though the morning was cold, Tom was happy and warm;
So if all do their duty they need not fear harm.

3. **"'weep . . . 'weep":** the child's attempt at the chimney sweepers' cry of "Sweep! Sweep!"

20. **want** *v.:* lack.

Unlike the sweeper in Songs of Innocence, *this sweeper does not accept oppression and poverty believing he will be rewarded in heaven. This little speaker recognizes that the people who pray for him (his parents) are the same ones who sold him into a life of hard labor.*

The first three lines are spoken by an adult who comes upon the pitiful child and asks him where his parents are. The rest of the poem is the child's bitter answer to that sad question.

The Chimney Sweeper

from Songs of Experience

William Blake

A little black thing among the snow
Crying "'weep, 'weep," in notes of woe!
"Where are thy father and mother? say?"
"They are both gone up to the church to pray.

"Because I was happy upon the heath,
And smil'd among the winter's snow;
They clothed me in the clothes of death,
And taught me to sing the notes of woe.

"And because I am happy, and dance and sing,
They think they have done me no injury,
And are gone to praise God and his Priest and King,
Who make up a heaven of our misery."

"The Chimney Sweeper," plate 37 from *Songs of Innocence and of Experience,* copy AA (c. 1815–26), by William Blake. Etching, ink, and watercolor.

Fitzwilliam Museum, University of Cambridge, England. The Bridgeman Art Library.

In 1831, Michael Sadler (1780–1835) introduced a bill in Parliament that proposed limiting the hours of workers under eighteen years of age to ten hours a day. Parliament did not pass this bill, but in April of 1832, it established a committee to investigate the conditions of children working in textile factories. With Sadler as chairman, this committee interviewed factory owners, workers, and doctors who treated people who worked in the factories. After the Sadler Committee's report was published, Parliament passed the Factory Act of 1833. This act limited working hours to twelve hours a day for textile workers aged thirteen to seventeen, and eight hours a day for those aged nine to twelve. The interview printed here is representative of the kinds of testimony heard by the Sadler Committee. The examiner's questions are followed by Peter Smart's answers, which are indicated by dashes.

from Evidence Given Before the Sadler Committee

Peter Smart, called in; and Examined.
You say you were locked up night and day?
—Yes.

Do the children ever attempt to run away?
—Very often.

Were they pursued and brought back again?
—Yes, the overseer pursued them, and brought them back.

Did you ever attempt to run away?
—Yes, I ran away twice.

And you were brought back?
—Yes; and I was sent up to the master's loft, and thrashed with a whip for running away.

Were you bound[1] to this man?
—Yes, for six years.

By whom were you bound?
—My mother got 15s.[2] for the six years.

1. **bound** *v.:* legally obliged to work for.
2. **s.:** one shilling was equal to one twentieth of a pound.

Do you know whether the children were, in point of fact, compelled to stop during the whole time for which they were engaged?
—Yes, they were.

By law?
—I cannot say by law; but they were compelled by the master; I never saw any law used there but the law of their own hands.

To what mill did you next go?
—To Mr. Webster's, at Battus Den, within eleven miles of Dundee.

In what situation did you act there?
—I acted as overseer.

At 17 years of age?
—Yes.

Did you inflict the same punishment that you yourself had experienced?
—I went as overseer; not as a slave, but as a slave-driver.

What were the hours of labor in that mill?
—My master told me that I had to produce a certain quantity of yarn; the hours were at that time fourteen; I said that I was not able to produce the quantity of yarn that was required; I told him if he took the timepiece out of the mill I would produce that quantity, and after that time I found no difficulty in producing the quantity.

How long have you worked per day in order to produce the quantity your master required?
—I have wrought nineteen hours.

Was this a water-mill?
—Yes, water and steam both.

To what time have you worked?
—I have seen the mill going till it was past 12 o'clock on the Saturday night.

So that the mill was still working on the Sabbath morning?
—Yes.

Were the workmen paid by the piece, or by the day?
—No, all had stated wages.

Did not that almost compel you to use great severity to the hands then under you?
—Yes; I was compelled often to beat them, in order to get them to attend to their work, from their being over-wrought.

Were not the children exceedingly fatigued at that time?
—Yes, exceedingly fatigued.

Were the children bound in the same way in that mill?
—No; they were bound from one year's end to another, for twelve months.

Did you keep the hands locked up in the same way in that mill?
—Yes, we locked up the mill; but we did not lock the bothy.[3]

Did you find that the children were unable to pursue their labor properly to that extent?
—Yes; they have been brought to that condition, that I have gone and fetched up the doctor to them, to see what was the matter with them, and to know whether they were able to rise or not able to rise; they were not at all able to rise; we have had great difficulty in getting them up.

When that was the case, how long have they been in bed, generally speaking?
—Perhaps not above four or five hours in their beds.

Children at work in a cotton factory (1839). Engraving.
MANSELL/TimePix.

3. **bothy** *n.:* hut.

Response and Analysis

The Chimney Sweeper *from* Songs of Innocence
The Chimney Sweeper *from* Songs of Experience

Thinking Critically

1. What details of the speaker's history do you learn in the first poem? What is his present life like?
2. In the first poem, how does the angel reassure Tom Dacre in his dream? What **moral lesson** does the speaker in the first poem draw from Tom's dream?
3. How does Tom Dacre's dream contrast with the actual conditions of his daily life?
4. In the second poem, how does the young chimney sweeper answer the adult's question? What do you think are his "clothes of death"?
5. How would you **paraphrase** the last two lines of the second poem?
6. How would you describe the **tone** of the second poem? How does this sweeper's attitude toward his life and his parents contrast with the attitude of the sweeper in the first poem?
7. How does Blake's use of **parallelism** in both poems add to their emotional effect? Discuss specific examples of parallelism in the poems.
8. In each poem, what is the emotional effect of the child's mispronunciation of the chimney sweeper's cry?
9. Do people today sometimes take the attitude expressed by the speaker of the first poem: If you are good, if you do your duty, you need not fear harm? Expand on your response.
10. Do these poems remind you of any cases of exploitation or injustice in modern life? Consult your Quickwrite notes.

Literary Skills Analyze parallelism.

Writing Skills Write part of a prose narrative.

WRITING

Down the Chimney

Based on details from both "The Chimney Sweeper" poems, the information in the ***Primary Source*** on page 728, and any other research materials you want to use, write the opening or closing paragraphs of a prose narrative that tells about the daily life of a child laborer in Blake's London. You may want to write in the first person, as if for an autobiography.

Engraving depicting a young English chimney sweep sitting on top of a chimney, reading (1800).

MANSELL/TimePix.

Before You Read

A Poison Tree

Make the Connection

Quickwrite

What happens to anger that is allowed to grow and fester; anger that is nurtured and held dear? In this poem, one of Blake's *Songs of Experience,* the speaker describes what happens when anger is left unresolved. As you read, notice the images Blake uses to describe anger and how it works on the individual psychologically. Before you begin, jot down some notes describing the ways anger can be destructive, not only to the object of the anger, but also to the person feeling it.

Literary Focus

Theme

The **theme** of a work of literature is its central idea or main insight about human nature or human life. The theme of a work is not the same as its subject; rather, the theme is the writer's point of view on the subject. In the case of "A Poison Tree," Blake's subject is anger, and his theme is his insight into what anger is and does. In poetry the theme is rarely stated directly. More often, it is implied by all the details, images, and symbols of the poem and must be deciphered by the reader.

The **theme** of a work of literature is the main idea or central insight into human nature or human life that the writer conveys either directly or indirectly.

For more on Theme, see the Handbook of Literary and Historical Terms.

A Poison Tree
from Songs of Experience

William Blake

I was angry with my friend:
I told my wrath, my wrath did end.
I was angry with my foe:
I told it not, my wrath did grow.

And I watered it in fears,
Night and morning with my tears;
And I sunned it with smiles,
And with soft deceitful wiles.°

And it grew both day and night,
Till it bore an apple bright;
And my foe beheld it shine,
And he knew that it was mine,

And into my garden stole
When the night had veiled the pole:
In the morning glad I see
My foe outstretched beneath the tree.

8. **wiles** *n. pl.:* cunning tricks.

Literary Skills Understand theme.

Response and Analysis

Thinking Critically

1. What two ways of handling anger are mentioned in the poem? What is different about the two situations?
2. What **imagery** is used to describe the second way in which the speaker handles anger?
3. What happens to the speaker's foe in the last stanza? Of whom or what is he a victim?
4. What do you think the "apple bright" (line 10) **symbolizes**? What is the "poison tree"?
5. How is the speaker of the poem a victim? Do you see the speaker as good or evil or both? Give examples from the poem.
6. What do you see as the **theme** of the poem? How does this theme comment on human nature? Give specific details from the poem to support your interpretation.
7. What is Blake alluding to in his reference to forbidden fruit in the third stanza?
8. Does the poem describe ways in which anger can be destructive that are similar to the ways you wrote about in your Quickwrite notes? Does it offer any insights on anger that you did not consider?

Extending and Evaluating

9. Blake's use of **parallel structure** and simple diction gives "A Poison Tree" an air of straightforward, even childlike, simplicity. Do you think this tone supports or undercuts the points being made about anger and its consequences? Explain.

Literary Skills Analyze theme.

Writing Skills Write an essay analyzing a poem.

Grammar Skills Use verb tenses consistently.

INTERNET

Projects and Activities

Keyword: LE7 12-5

WRITING

Contrary States

Blake's two groups of poems, *Songs of Innocence* and *Songs of Experience,* depict two contrary states of the human soul. The speakers in *Songs of Innocence* are usually children or childlike. The speakers in *Songs of Experience* are usually adults. In an **essay,** analyze "A Poison Tree." Tell what you believe its theme is and explain why the poem is an appropriate *Song of Experience* and not a *Song of Innocence.* What comment does the poem make on the cosmos of "Mercy, Pity, Peace, and Love," which Blake describes for *Songs of Innocence?*

A Poison Tree (1794) by William Blake, from his book *Songs of Experience.* Relief etching with watercolor and pen additions.

Private Collection.

Grammar Link

The Right Tense for Sense: Verb Tense Consistency

You use tenses to show when something happened. Unnecessarily changing verb tense in midsentence can create awkwardness and confusion. When you write about events occurring at the same time, use verbs that are in the same tense. Use different tenses only to indicate that events occur at different times.

Two events occurring at the same time:

INCORRECT Blake began writing poetry at the age of twelve, but he intends to become a painter.

CORRECT Blake began writing poetry at the age of twelve, but he intended to become a painter.

Two events occurring at different times:

UNCLEAR By the time Blake was twenty-seven, he published his first work of poetry.

CLEAR By the time Blake was twenty-seven, he had published his first work of poetry. [This sentence makes it clear that Blake published his work before he turned twenty-seven.]

"Auguries of Innocence" by William Blake (transcribed c. 1807) from the Pickering, or Ballads, manuscript.

The Pierpont Morgan Library, NY.

PRACTICE

Check for consistency of verb tenses in the following sentences. If the tenses are consistent, write *correct.* If the tenses are not consistent, rewrite the sentence with the correct verb tense.

1. Blake not only wrote his poetry, but he illustrates it as well.
2. Blake was an innovative artist; he invented many of his own printing techniques.
3. In his own time, Blake's art fails to attract attention, but now, his art is appreciated by many people worldwide.
4. By the time Blake died in 1827, he illustrated the works of many famous authors, including John Milton, Thomas Gray, and Edward Young.

Apply to Your Writing

Review a writing assignment you are working on now or have already completed. Are there any sentences with unnecessary shifts in verb tense? Correct these shifts to avoid awkwardness and confusion.

For more help, see Tenses and Their Uses, 3b–c, in the Language Handbook.

William Wordsworth

(1770–1850)

William Wordsworth (1842) by Benjamin Robert Haydon. Oil on canvas (49″ × 39″).

By Courtesy of the National Portrait Gallery, London.

Surveying Wordsworth's life can be like walking around a large statue, awed by its presence and puzzled by its apparent importance. Sometimes Wordsworth must have felt the same way. As he thought about his early life and re-created it in his autobiographical poem *The Prelude,* Wordsworth said he felt as if he were "two consciousnesses"—one remembering, the other one remembered.

When Wordsworth's mother died in 1778, he and his three brothers were sent to school at Hawkshead in the Lake District. His sister, Dorothy, aged seven, had to live with relatives. When their father died in 1783, the children were placed under the guardianship of two uncles. William managed to get a degree from Cambridge in 1791. As an educated man with no title, wealth, or head for business, he had little interest in the few careers open to him—the main one being the Church. In late 1791, Wordsworth went to France to learn the language and, as it turned out, discovered the bliss of being young in that time of birth and rebirth known as the French Revolution. Thus began a decade of painful growth, as he searched for and eventually found his vocation as a poet.

After he returned from France in 1792, war broke out between France and England. Wordsworth was sickened by the war, and he gradually became deeply disillusioned about his hopes for change. Late in 1793, he went on a long walking tour. This experience—and the collapse of his radical hope of perfecting society—drove him to poetry.

In 1795, his fortunes began to change. He was reunited with his sister, Dorothy, who became a constant companion and inspiration. When he inherited some money from a friend, he and Dorothy took up residence in a rent-free cottage, and the poet Samuel Taylor Coleridge suddenly burst upon their lives. By June 1797, when he and Dorothy moved to a country house four miles from the village where Coleridge lived, Wordsworth had produced a good deal of new poetry, none yet published, including a play and some stark narratives. Coleridge and Wordsworth quickly became powerful influences on each other's work. *Lyrical Ballads* (1798) was the fruit of their friendship and mutual influence. During the following decade, Wordsworth wrote many of his most widely read works.

The distinguishing quality of Wordsworth's best lyric poetry comes from his simple delight in the nature of experience itself and in the mind's capacity to shape everyday experience into something lasting and poetic. Poetry, he wrote in the Preface to *Lyrical Ballads,* is the "spontaneous overflow of powerful feelings"; but, he added, poems of lasting value are produced only by someone who has "thought long and deeply." The marriage of feeling and thought, as Coleridge recognized, made Wordsworth "the best poet of the age."

Before You Read

Lines Composed a Few Miles Above Tintern Abbey

Make the Connection

William Wordsworth loved nature in all of its forms, and he believed that nature helped him to "see into the life of things." Loving nature, he writes in this poem, quiets his mind, lightens his mood, guides him to kind acts, and brings him closer to God.

Literary Focus

Blank Verse

Wordsworth composed poetry in his head while he walked—"his jaws working the whoal time," recalled a person in the country who observed him. He spoke the words aloud to memorize them and to get the rhythm right. When Wordsworth was a child, under the direction of his father, he memorized and recited long passages in **blank verse** (unrhymed iambic pentameter) from the works of Shakespeare and Milton. In "Tintern Abbey," Wordsworth uses for the first time a less formal, "conversational" blank verse that gives his poem the flowing rhythm of natural speech.

Blank verse is poetry written in unrhymed **iambic pentameter.** Each line contains five iambs; each iamb, or metrical foot, is an unstressed syllable followed by a stressed syllable.

For more on Blank Verse, see the Handbook of Literary and Historical Terms.

Reading Skills

Recognizing Patterns of Organization

Before you read this poem aloud, look for the end punctuation and the indents that signal the end of one stanza and the beginning of another. (How many stanzas are in the poem?) Then, as you read, make notes on how Wordsworth uses these stanzas to organize his ideas.

Background

"Tintern Abbey" (which refers to the ruined abbey mentioned only in the title) is one of the most important short lyric works in English literature. A major step forward in Wordsworth's writing and a definitive statement of some of the Romantics' ideas, it has inspired and guided many poets since. The ease with which Wordsworth wrote it is therefore even more astonishing. In July 1798, Wordsworth and his sister, Dorothy, went on a vigorous walking tour in southern Wales. Shortly after leaving the Wye River Valley, Wordsworth, by his own account, began to compose this poem about revisiting the valley, finishing it "just as I was entering Bristol in the evening after a ramble of four or five days. . . . Not a line of it was altered, and not any part of it written down till I reached Bristol. It was published almost immediately after."

Wordsworth had learned something important from Coleridge: the use of a flowing blank verse and the easy maneuvering of the meditative poem.

Literary Skills Understand blank verse.

Reading Skills Recognize patterns of organization.

INTERNET

More About William Wordsworth

Keyword: LE7 12-5

Lines Composed a Few Miles Above Tintern Abbey

On Revisiting the Banks of the Wye During a Tour. July 13, 1798

William Wordsworth

Five years have past; five summers, with the length
Of five long winters! and again I hear
These waters, rolling from their mountain springs
With a soft inland murmur.—Once again
Do I behold these steep and lofty cliffs,
That on a wild secluded scene impress
Thoughts of more deep seclusion; and connect
The landscape with the quiet of the sky.
The day is come when I again repose
Here, under this dark sycamore, and view
These plots of cottage ground, these orchard tufts,
Which at this season, with their unripe fruits,
Are clad in one green hue, and lose themselves
'Mid groves and copses.° Once again I see
These hedgerows,° hardly hedgerows, little lines
Of sportive wood run wild: these pastoral° farms,
Green to the very door; and wreaths of smoke
Sent up, in silence, from among the trees!
With some uncertain notice, as might seem
Of vagrant dwellers in the houseless woods,
Or of some Hermit's cave, where by his fire
The Hermit sits alone.
These beauteous forms,
Through a long absence, have not been to me
As is a landscape to a blind man's eye:
But oft, in lonely rooms, and 'mid the din
Of towns and cities, I have owed to them
In hours of weariness, sensations sweet,
Felt in the blood, and felt along the heart;
And passing even into my purer mind,
With tranquil restoration:—feelings too
Of unremembered pleasure: such, perhaps,

1–22. The speaker describes a beloved place in nature to which he has returned after five years.
? *Look for the verbs* hear, behold, view, *and* see. *What does the speaker hear? What does he see?*

14. copses *n. pl.:* areas densely covered with shrubs and small trees.
15. hedgerows *n. pl.:* rows of bushes, shrubs, and small trees that serve as fences.
16. pastoral *adj.:* relating to herds or flocks, pasture land, and country life.

Tintern Abbey (1834) by J.M.W. Turner.
British Museum, London.

As have no slight or trivial influence
On that best portion of a good man's life,
His little, nameless, unremembered acts
Of kindness and of love. Nor less, I trust,
To them I may have owed another gift,
Of aspect more sublime; that blessed mood,
In which the burden of the mystery,
In which the heavy and the weary weight
Of all this unintelligible world,
Is lightened:—that serene and blessed mood,
In which the affections° gently lead us on,—
Until, the breath of this corporeal° frame
And even the motion of our human blood
Almost suspended, we are laid asleep
In body, and become a living soul:
While with an eye made quiet by the power

? **23–41.** *According to the speaker, how have memories of this beloved landscape affected him?*

42. affections *n. pl.:* feelings.
43. corporeal *adj.:* bodily.

Landscape (detail) (19th century) by Patrick Nasmyth.
Roy Miles Fine Painting, London, UK.

Of harmony, and the deep power of joy,
We see into the life of things.
                    If this
Be but a vain belief, yet, oh! how oft—
In darkness and amid the many shapes
Of joyless daylight; when the fretful stir
Unprofitable, and the fever of the world,
Have hung upon the beatings of my heart—
How oft, in spirit, have I turned to thee,
O sylvan° Wye! thou wanderer through the woods,
How often has my spirit turned to thee!

? **49.** *What visual clue signals that a new stanza is beginning here? How does the speaker's focus or emphasis change in the new stanza?*

56. sylvan *adj.:* associated with the forest or woodlands.

And now, with gleams of half-extinguished thought,
With many recognitions dim and faint,
And somewhat of a sad perplexity,
The picture of the mind° revives again:
While here I stand, not only with the sense
Of present pleasure, but with pleasing thoughts
That in this moment there is life and food
For future years. And so I dare to hope,
Though changed, no doubt, from what I was when first
I came among these hills; when like a roe°
I bounded o'er the mountains, by the sides

61. picture of the mind: primarily the picture in the mind, but also the picture the individual mind has of itself.

67. roe *n.:* deer.

Of the deep rivers, and the lonely streams,
Wherever nature led: more like a man
Flying from something that he dreads, than one
Who sought the thing he loved. For nature then
(The coarser pleasures of my boyish days,
And their glad animal movements all gone by)
To me was all in all.—I cannot paint
What then I was. The sounding cataract°
Haunted me like a passion: the tall rock,
The mountain, and the deep and gloomy wood,
Their colors and their forms, were then to me
An appetite; a feeling and a love,
That had no need of a remoter charm,°
By thought supplied, nor any interest
Unborrowed from the eye.—That time is past,
And all its aching joys are now no more,
And all its dizzy raptures. Not for this
Faint° I, nor mourn nor murmur; other gifts
Have followed; for such loss, I would believe,
Abundant recompense.° For I have learned
To look on nature, not as in the hour
Of thoughtless youth; but hearing oftentimes
The still, sad music of humanity,
Nor harsh nor grating, though of ample power
To chasten and subdue. And I have felt
A presence that disturbs me with the joy
Of elevated thoughts; a sense sublime
Of something far more deeply interfused,
Whose dwelling is the light of setting suns,
And the round ocean and the living air,
And the blue sky, and in the mind of man:
A motion and a spirit, that impels
All thinking things, all objects of all thought,
And rolls through all things. Therefore am I still
A lover of the meadows and the woods,
And mountains; and of all that we behold
From this green earth; of all the mighty world
Of eye, and ear,—both what they half create,
And what perceive; well pleased to recognize
In nature and the language of the sense
The anchor of my purest thoughts, the nurse,
The guide, the guardian of my heart, and soul
Of all my moral being.
Nor perchance,
If I were not thus taught, should I the more
Suffer° my genial° spirits to decay:
For thou art with me here upon the banks

65–85. With a hint of nostalgia, the speaker remembers the exhilarating times he spent in nature as a youth.
? *How would you describe the speaker's relationship to nature when he was a boy?*

76. cataract *n.:* waterfall.

81. remoter charm: appeal other than the scene itself.

86. faint *v.:* become weak; lose heart.

88. recompense *n.:* repayment.

? **93–102.** *Re-read these lines. In your own words, what is the "presence" (line 94) that the speaker describes?*

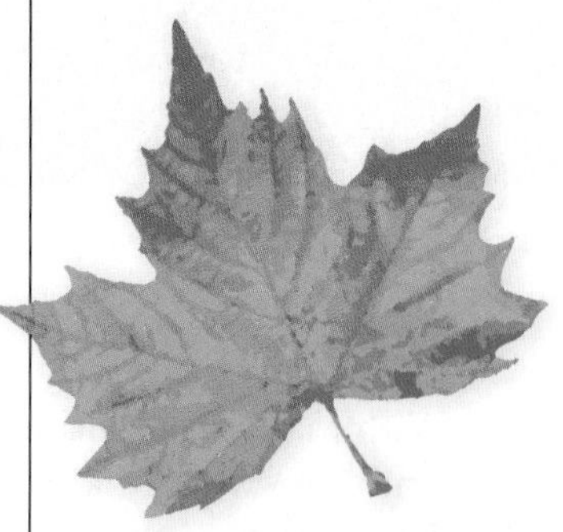

? **111–115.** *What shift takes place in this final stanza?*

113. suffer *v.:* allow. **genial** *adj.:* creative.

Of this fair river; thou my dearest Friend,°
My dear, dear Friend; and in thy voice I catch
The language of my former heart, and read
My former pleasures in the shooting lights
Of thy wild eyes. Oh! yet a little while
May I behold in thee what I was once,
My dear, dear Sister! and this prayer I make,
Knowing that Nature never did betray
The heart that loved her; 'tis her privilege,
Through all the years of this our life, to lead
From joy to joy: for she can so inform
The mind that is within us, so impress
With quietness and beauty, and so feed
With lofty thoughts, that neither evil tongues,
Rash judgments, nor the sneers of selfish men,
Nor greetings where no kindness is, nor all
The dreary intercourse° of daily life,
Shall e'er prevail against us, or disturb
Our cheerful faith, that all which we behold
Is full of blessings. Therefore let the moon
Shine on thee in thy solitary walk;
And let the misty mountain winds be free
To blow against thee: and, in after years,
When these wild ecstasies shall be matured
Into a sober pleasure; when thy mind
Shall be a mansion for all lovely forms,
Thy memory be as a dwelling place
For all sweet sounds and harmonies; oh! then,
If solitude, or fear, or pain, or grief,
Should be thy portion, with what healing thoughts
Of tender joy wilt thou remember me,
And these my exhortations!° Nor, perchance—
If I should be where I no more can hear
Thy voice, nor catch from thy wild eyes these gleams
Of past existence—wilt thou then forget
That on the banks of this delightful stream
We stood together; and that I, so long
A worshipper of Nature, hither came
Unwearied in that service: rather say
With warmer love—oh! with far deeper zeal
Of holier love. Nor wilt thou then forget,
That after many wanderings, many years
Of absence, these steep woods and lofty cliffs,
And this green pastoral landscape, were to me
More dear, both for themselves and for thy sake!

115. my dearest Friend: Wordsworth's sister, Dorothy.

? 121–159. *What prayer does the speaker make in these concluding lines? Whom is the prayer for? Paraphrase the speaker's thoughts.*

? 116–134. *What makes these lines conversational?*

131. intercourse *n.:* dealings; social contacts.

146. exhortations *n. pl.:* strong advice.

Response and Analysis

Reading Check

1. What is the speaker experiencing at the beginning of the poem (lines 1–22)?
2. What has the speaker lost since he first "came among these hills" (line 67)?
3. What does the speaker see in his "dear Sister" that makes him more aware of what he "was once" (lines 120–121)?

Thinking Critically

4. What do you think is meant by "the burden of the mystery" (line 38)?
5. What "gifts" (line 86) and "abundant recompense" (line 88) does the speaker believe he has received for his "loss" (line 87)?
6. What do you think the speaker means when he says, in lines 90–91, that he has heard "the still, sad music of humanity"?
7. What role does the speaker's sister play in this poem?
8. What would you say is Wordsworth's attitude toward his past, his present, and his future?
9. Wordsworth's **blank verse** is best read aloud in the long, rolling movements of his stanzas, or verse paragraphs. Slowly and carefully read aloud a stanza of the poem, observing the punctuation and **run-on lines.** Then, state whether you think the stanza you have chosen is unified by one **main idea.** If so, what is that main idea? You may want to consult your reading notes.
10. Summarize and comment on the significance of the speaker's conclusion, beginning at line 102. Have you ever had to come to terms with losing part of your past? How did you resign yourself to the loss?

Literary Skills Analyze blank verse.

Reading Skills Analyze patterns of organization.

Writing Skills Write a conversation poem in blank verse.

Extending and Evaluating

11. How is this poem an example of the idea that poetry "takes its origin from emotion recollected in tranquillity"?

WRITING

Poetic Conversation

In "Tintern Abbey," Wordsworth explores a form he and Coleridge termed the "conversation poem." The conversation poem is usually a deeply personal meditation, seemingly spoken to a silent listener or to a loved one who is absent or asleep. Imagine that you have been away from a special place that holds many memories for you. Write a brief **conversation poem** in blank verse in which you tell someone else how you feel as you return to this place for the first time in five years. Use a conversational tone.

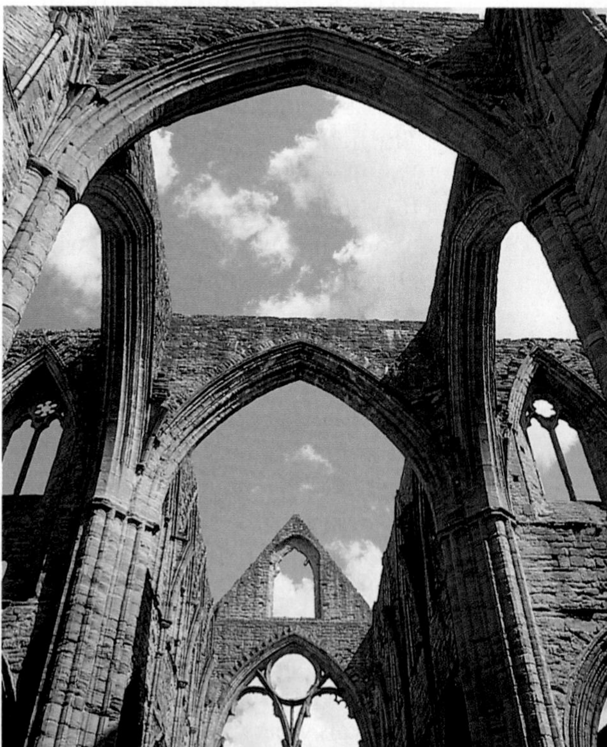

The ruins of Tintern Abbey today.

Before You Read

Composed upon Westminster Bridge

Make the Connection

Wordsworth chose to spend most of his time in the English countryside, especially in the beautiful Lake District where, he believed, nature had made him a poet. First published in 1807, this sonnet shows that Wordsworth the nature lover could be moved not only by mountains and waterfalls, but also by the majesty of a sleeping city—in this case, London. But this is clearly a different London from the one of Blake's chimney sweepers (see pages 726–727) and from the one known as the "great wen [boil]" that shocked many of Wordsworth's contemporaries with its filth and poverty. It is London seen from a distance, and by a man happily journeying to France. Here, London's filth and poverty are disguised and transfigured by the poet's imagination.

Literary Focus

Personification

Wordsworth breathes life into his sonnet by using **personification,** a kind of metaphor in which a nonhuman thing is talked about as if it were human. Look for details that personify the city, the sun, the river, even the houses of London.

Personification is a kind of metaphor in which a nonhuman thing or quality is talked about as if it were human.

For more on Personification, see the Handbook of Literary and Historical Terms.

Westminster Bridge (1855). Wood engraving.

Literary Skills Understand personification.

INTERNET

More About William Wordsworth

Keyword: LE7 12-5

Composed upon Westminster Bridge
September 3, 1802

William Wordsworth

Earth has not anything to show more fair:
Dull would he be of soul who could pass by
A sight so touching in its majesty:
This City now doth, like a garment, wear
The beauty of the morning; silent, bare,
Ships, towers, domes, theaters, and temples lie
Open unto the fields, and to the sky;
All bright and glittering in the smokeless air.
Never did sun more beautifully steep
In his first splendor, valley, rock, or hill;
Ne'er saw I, never felt, a calm so deep!
The river glideth at his own sweet will:
Dear God! the very houses seem asleep;
And all that mighty heart is lying still!

Westminster Bridge, London (detail) (late 19th or early 20th century) by Louis H. Grimshaw.

Response and Analysis

Literary Skills Analyze personification.

Writing Skills Write a description using personification.

Thinking Critically

1. What details and features of the city are mentioned by the speaker?
2. What details **personify** the city? How does this personification make you feel?
3. What **paradox,** or seeming contradiction, do you find in the poem's last line?
4. What quality, or characteristic, of the scene seems to move the speaker most deeply?
5. What seems to be the **mood** of the speaker in this poem?

Extending and Evaluating

6. How do the **themes** and **images** of this poem classify Wordsworth as a typical Romantic poet?

WRITING

A City as a Person

Write a **description,** in prose or verse, of a city or town that you know well. Use **personification** to characterize your city or town. You might open with Wordsworth's first line: "Earth has not anything to show more fair."

Before You Read

The World Is Too Much with Us

Make the Connection

Quickwrite

The "world" is sometimes thought of as the world of material objects—the world of money and status symbols, the world of power, competition, and ambition. In seeking out the pleasures of this material world, what could a person lose? Jot down some answers to this question.

Literary Focus

Allusion

An **allusion** is a reference to a person, place, thing, or event that is recognizable from literature, history, religion, mythology, politics, sports, science, or popular culture. Allusions are often used to lend deeper meaning to a literary passage or work. In Wordsworth's poem "The World Is Too Much with Us," the poet alludes to two sea gods from Greek mythology—Proteus and Triton. By making reference to these gods, Wordsworth underscores an earlier sentiment in the poem. Look for this connection as you read.

An **allusion** is a reference to something from literature, history, religion, mythology, politics, sports, science, or popular culture.

For more on Allusion, see the Handbook of Literary and Historical Terms.

Background

Wordsworth wrote his final draft of this sonnet in 1804, at a time when he realized that his imaginative powers were beginning to fail. Although he continued to compose new works and to edit *The Prelude,* a long poem published after his death, he knew he was no longer responding to nature with the youthful passion that had inspired his earlier poems.

This sonnet counterattacks the ferocious criticism that Wordsworth was receiving from conservative reviewers, especially Francis Jeffrey in the *Edinburgh Review.* Jeffrey accused Wordsworth of using unpoetic language, but, even more, of conspiring against society, brooding needlessly over problems "instead of contemplating the wonders and pleasures which civilization has created for mankind." Jeffrey considered Wordsworth an enemy of progress because of his "idle discontent with the existing institutions of society" and his yearning for an earlier, less civilized time when people lived in harmony with nature.

Mosaic of Tritons, Nereids, and a sea antelope (1st century) from Ostia, Italy.

Museo Ostiense, Ostia, Italy.

Literary Skills Understand allusion.

INTERNET

More About William Wordsworth

Keyword: LE7 12-5

A Country Road with Trees and Figures by John Constable.
Victoria and Albert Museum, London. The Bridgeman Art Library.

The World Is Too Much with Us

William Wordsworth

The world is too much with us; late and soon,
Getting and spending, we lay waste our powers:
Little we see in Nature that is ours;
We have given our hearts away, a sordid boon!°
This Sea that bares her bosom to the moon;
The winds that will be howling at all hours,
And are up-gathered now like sleeping flowers;
For this, for everything, we are out of tune;
It moves us not.—Great God! I'd rather be
A Pagan suckled in a creed outworn;
So might I, standing on this pleasant lea,°
Have glimpses that would make me less forlorn;
Have sight of Proteus° rising from the sea;
Or hear old Triton° blow his wreathèd horn.

4. sordid boon: foul gift. That is, the act of giving our hearts away is shameful.

11. lea *n.:* meadow.

13. Proteus (prō′tē·əs): in Greek mythology, a sea god who can change shape at will.

14. Triton (trī′tən): in Greek mythology, a sea god who controls the waves by blowing a conch shell. (See the mosaic on page 745.)

Response and Analysis

Thinking Critically

1. What does the speaker mean by the "world"? What do you think the speaker means when he says, "We have given our hearts away" (line 4)? Explain why you agree or disagree with the speaker.
2. Why do you think the speaker would "rather be / A Pagan" (lines 9–10)?
3. What is Wordsworth's purpose in alluding to mythology in the last lines of the poem? What emotions do these **allusions** evoke?
4. Identify the two parts of this sonnet. How is the **tone** of the second part different from the tone of the first part? How does this difference affect the meaning of the poem?
5. Identify the central **theme** of the poem. Does Wordsworth state this theme directly, or is it implied? How does the **personification** of the sea and the wind contribute to the theme?
6. How are the ideas about materialism and progress in this poem relevant to today's world? You may want to refer to your Quickwrite notes.

Extending and Evaluating

7. What is your reaction to the speaker's attack on modern life? Do you agree with Wordsworth that if people were in tune with nature they would be happier and less materialistic? Explain why or why not.

WRITING

Typically Romantic

In a brief **essay,** identify the elements in "The World Is Too Much with Us" that make the poem "typically Romantic"—that is, representative of Romantic lyric poetry. Consider the **allusions** and **images** Wordsworth uses, as well as the **theme** of the poem. Be sure to quote specific lines from the poem to support your points.

Literary Focus

Romantic Lyric Forms

The poems in this section represent a number of lyric forms—from variations on traditional sonnet schemes and experiments with the ode to the distinctive Romantic lyric form, the "meditative poem."

Sonnet. The sonnet was popular in Romantic poetry as a traditional type of occasional poem written on an important subject, public or private. Milton, for example, had used the sonnet in this way. But for the Romantics the sonnet was also used for experimentation. Coleridge's early sonnets, called "effusions" to excuse their looseness, helped him create the meditative poem. Keats's sonnets shaped the stanza forms for his odes. The main sonnet form was the **Italian,** or **Petrarchan,** composed of an octave (eight lines) and a sestet (six lines). But the Romantics also used the **Shakespearean sonnet** of three quatrains (four lines) and a couplet (two lines) form.

Ode. The Romantic ode was a self-conscious use of a classical form that had been brought into English literature in the seventeenth and eighteenth centuries. The structure of the Romantic ode was certainly influenced by the Romantic meditative poem. Sometimes a poem in the manner of an ode was called a "hymn." A traditional ode has two distinctive features: (1) It uses heightened, impassioned language, and (2) it addresses some object. The ode may speak to, or **apostrophize,** objects (an urn), creatures (a nightingale), and presences or powers (the west wind). The speaker invokes the object and then creates a relationship with it, through praise or prayer.

Meditative poem. The Romantics developed the meditative poem and passed it on to later generations of poets. It is the best

Literary Skills
Analyze allusion. Analyze Romantic lyric forms (sonnet, ode, meditative poem).

Writing Skills
Write an essay identifying the Romantic elements in a poem.

example of the artful illusion of the lyric in which we are to imagine a person speaking. The perfect example of the form—Wordsworth's "Tintern Abbey"—is in a flowing **blank verse** in which the stanzas are the equivalent of paragraphs, beginning and ending where sense, rather than strict form, dictates. The tone of these lyrics is much easier and more colloquial than the tone of the odes. Coleridge called one of his meditative lyrics a "conversation poem."

Recognizing speakers and tone. Re-read Wordsworth's lyrics aloud, paying attention to the voices you hear. As you read, think about the speakers: the bard or prophet who speaks about matters of great concern; the wanderer who happens upon something that turns out to be revealing; and the lover of poetic experiences who finds beauty in all the details of life. Which of these **speakers** do you see in each of Wordsworth's poems?

Study of Sky and Trees by John Constable.
Victoria and Albert Museum. © Scala/Art Resource, New York.

Connecting to **World Literature**

Tanka and Haiku

You have just read Romantic poems by William Blake and William Wordsworth. In this Connecting to World Literature feature, you will read two very different forms of poetry—Japanese tanka and haiku—that, like Romantic poetry, use images of nature. Unlike Romantic poetry, however, these Japanese forms are concise and rigidly structured.

1715–1826
Taniguchi Buson and Kobayashi Issa live

1644–1738
Matsuo Bashō and Uejima Onitsura live

A.D. 794–1185
Tanka thrives during Heian period

The **tanka** (täŋ′kə) and the **haiku** (hī′ko͞o′) are two of the most beloved forms of Japanese poetry. Both are very old, tanka dating from the eighth century A.D. and haiku from the thirteenth and fourteenth centuries. Both forms of poetry demand the compression of ideas and images into the space of a few words.

Borrowed Words, New Beginnings

In early times, Japanese was exclusively a spoken language; there was no system for writing it down. The earliest Japanese poets wrote in Chinese. Between the fifth and eighth centuries, a system for writing Japanese was developed: Chinese letters, or characters, were adapted to represent Japanese sounds. These phonetic characters came to be known as kana (kä′nə), meaning "borrowed names."

Toward the end of this period—during the eighth century—a collection of poems called the *Manyoshu* (man′yō·shū), or *Collection of Ten Thousand Leaves,* appeared. By this time, Japanese poets had begun to appreciate the lyrical power of their own language. Indeed, the Japanese view the *Manyoshu* as the beginning of a written literature that they could call entirely their own.

The Origin of Tanka

It is in the *Manyoshu* that the earliest-known tanka appear. **Tanka,** meaning "short songs," are brief and lyrical. Like other lyric poems, each tanka expresses a private emotion or thought, often on the theme of change, solitude, or love. The traditional tanka consists of exactly thirty-one syllables divided among five lines. Three of the poem's lines have seven syllables, and the other two have five.

Lovers composed and exchanged tanka as expressions of affection. Aristocrats amused themselves by playing a game in which one person would invent the first three lines of a tanka and another would finish it.

Literary Skills
Understand tanka and haiku. Compare and contrast Japanese poetry with Romantic poetry.

Haiku Happenings

Eventually, tanka inspired an even more condensed poetic form—the haiku. A **haiku** is a brief, unrhymed, three line poem. In Japanese, the first and last lines have five syllables each and the middle line has seven.

Examples of short verses similar to haiku have been found in thirteenth- and fourteenth-century Japanese literature. However, the art of haiku was not perfected until later in the seventeenth century, when the greatest of the classical haiku poets, Matsuo Bashō (ba'shō), lived. When English authors such as John Milton were composing epic, intricate poems, Bashō and his pupils were writing strikingly pure, compressed verses only a few words long. In the centuries since Bashō, the haiku form has been adopted by poets all over the world.

Unlike many Western poets, the classical haiku masters do not present similes, metaphors, or other figures of speech. Rather, haiku poets present simple, unadorned images, and the reader must make an imaginative leap to understand the connection between them.

Birds on a Snowy Plum Bough by Muryu.

British Library, London, UK/ The Bridgeman Art Library.

To Say or Not to Say?

By their precision, their simple beauty, and their economy of words, tanka and haiku embody an important principle of Japanese art and culture: What is *not* said is often as important as what *is* said. Understandably, this principle creates certain challenges for translators of both haiku and tanka.

One difficulty faced by translators is that the Japanese language differs greatly from English. For example, it has no articles and rarely uses pronouns. To accommodate these differences, the English translators of tanka and haiku sometimes choose to make their English versions rhyme, though this is not in keeping with Japanese tradition. In other cases, the English translations do not have the exact number of syllables per line as prescribed by the Japanese form.

Although form must sometimes be sacrificed, the main work of translating any poem is to preserve its essence—the transcendent quality that stretches across the miles and the years to connect a single author and a single reader at any given moment. This essence of Japanese poetry is summarized by Ki Tsurayuki (kē tso͞o·rä·yo͞o'kē), one of the editors of the great tenth-century tanka anthology, *Kokinshu,* in his preface to the collection:

> “When we hear the notes of the nightingale among the blossoms, when we hear the frog in the water, we know that every living being is capable of song. Poetry, without effort, can move heaven and earth, can touch the gods and spirits . . . it turns the hearts of man and woman to each other and it soothes the soul of the fierce warrior.”

Though his comments were written over a thousand years ago, they still hold true for much of Japanese verse.

Before You Read

Tanka and Haiku

Make the Connection

Quickwrite

Tanka and haiku are highly visual poetic forms, presenting subtle images of nature and the changing seasons to suggest a variety of moods and emotions, from quiet joy to bittersweet reflection. The best tanka and haiku use simple sensory images—tree branches, streams, the stirrings of an autumn breeze—to imply far more than they state directly. How would you suggest a mood through a single image? If you were a photographer, what scenes or objects would you photograph to convey the following moods: loneliness, nostalgia, contentment? Freewrite for a few minutes, describing in detail the images you would photograph, and explaining your reasons for choosing these images.

Literary Focus

Imagery

Imagery is language that appeals to the senses—to sight, hearing, smell, touch, and taste. The Japanese tanka and haiku writers relied on imagery—often from nature—to subtly and indirectly suggest moods and themes. What is left out is as important as what is included, and it is up to the reader to make the connection between the images and the emotions they imply. Thus, the image of a fallen cherry blossom may suggest the brevity of love or even of life itself, and the image of the full moon may prompt philosophical musings about change and eternity. The reader must ponder the images in order to grasp the meaning of the poem.

Imagery is language that appeals to the senses of sight, hearing, smell, touch, and taste.

For more on Imagery, see the Handbook of Literary and Historical Terms.

Background

The five tanka you will read (see page 753) were composed by five different Japanese poets over a period of five centuries, yet they share a similar form and similar themes. Although each poem reflects its author's individual age, social position, and philosophy of life, all evoke equally strong images and emotions.

Because all the tanka presented here are translations from the Japanese, they necessarily differ from the originals. For example, only one of the five translated poems actually follows the traditional tanka formula of thirty-one syllables. The translated poems also do not have the same rhythm or cadence as the Japanese originals. Yet in other respects the translated poems are faithful to the traditions of Japanese tanka. They are unrhymed, for instance, which is in keeping with classical tanka style, and they make use of **assonance,** the repetition of similar vowel sounds in nearby words.

The first three haiku you will read are by the greatest seventeenth-century haiku master, Bashō. In all three poems, Bashō finds beauty in seemingly insignificant or ordinary objects or events. This practice is inspired by the Buddhist belief that, through contemplation, anyone can find great significance in even the humblest of things.

Literary Skills Understand imagery.

Tanka Poets

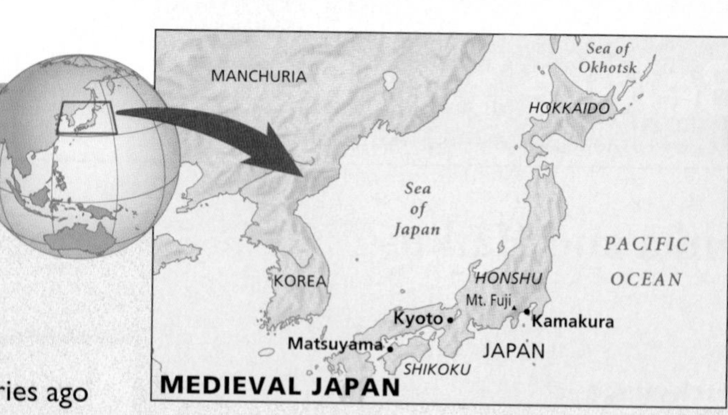

The poets who wrote tanka centuries ago are still widely read in Japan. In fact, their poems are so familiar that they are the basis of a popular "poem-card" game traditionally played in Japan at the New Year. In this game one player reads the first half of a poem from the thirteenth-century anthology *The Verses of a Hundred Poets*. The other players must then choose the correct ending to the poem from among the hundred cards spread on the floor. Ironically, very few facts are known about these early masters whose words have become so deeply ingrained in Japanese culture.

Princess Nukada

(seventh century)

Princess Nukada (n o͞o • kä′dä) was a favorite at the court of two emperors and was the most accomplished female poet of her time. We know little else about her, however. The only clues we have to her character are her poems, which are delicate and passionate. Some of them, including the one reproduced here, were written for her elder sister, Princess Kagami (kä • gä′mē).

Oshikochi Mitsune

(late ninth century)

Oshikochi Mitsune (ō′shē • kō′chē mē • tso͞o′nā) was among the greatest poets of the early Heian era. He was one of the editors of the *Kokinshu,* and some of his verses appear in that anthology. Many of his poems are melancholy, but they are never sentimental.

Ki Tsurayuki

(884–946)

Another editor of the *Kokinshu,* Ki Tsurayuki (kē′ tso͞o • rä • yo͞o′kē) was a high court official as well as an accomplished writer and calligrapher. In addition to his fine tanka poems, he wrote a travel diary that interwove poetry with prose. At the time most cultured Japanese men chose to write prose in Chinese. Generally only women and those men who could not afford a classical education wrote in Japanese. Because Ki Tsurayuki preferred to write in Japanese, and did not want to invite ridicule, he published his diary under a woman's name.

Ono Komachi

(mid–tenth century)

Of all the poets whose tanka appeared in the *Kokinshu,* Ono Komachi (ō′nō kō·mä′chē) is perhaps the most revered. Her great physical beauty and the emotional power of her verse made her a celebrated figure in her time. More than three centuries after her death, Kan'ami Kiyotsugu, a Noh dramatist, wrote a play about Ono Komachi, whom he described as

The brightest flower long ago
Her dark brows arched
Her face bright-powdered always
When cedar-scented halls could scarce
contain
Her damask robes.

Saigyo

(1118–1190)

Among the most accomplished twelfth-century tanka poets was Saigyo (sä′ē·gyō), who abandoned his position as a royal bodyguard at the age of twenty-three to become a priest. His tanka were written during his years of wandering through the Japanese countryside.

Tanka

I waited and I
Yearned for you.
My blind
Stirred at the touch
Of the autumn breeze.
—Princess Nukada

The end of my journey
Was still far off,
But in the tree-shade
Of the summer mountain
I stood, my mind floating.
—Oshikochi Mitsune

Now, I cannot tell
What my old friend is thinking:
But the petals of the plum
In this place I used to know
Keep their old fragrance.
—Ki Tsurayuki

How helpless my heart!
Were the stream to tempt,
My body, like a reed
Severed at the roots,
Would drift along, I think.
—Ono Komachi

Every single thing
Changes and is changing
Always in this world.
Yet with the same light
The moon goes on shining.
—Priest Saigyo

These tanka are translated by Geoffrey Bownas and Anthony Thwaite.

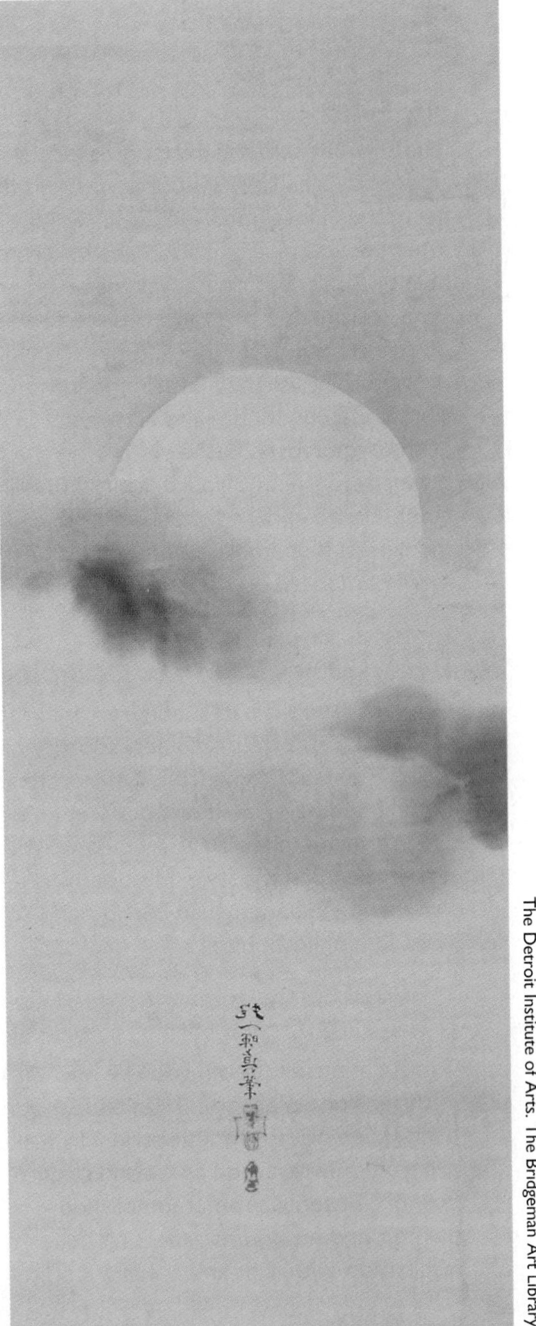

Hanging Scroll Depicting the Autumnal Moon (detail), from a triptych of three seasons (early 19th century) by Sakai Hoitsu. Ink on silk.

Haiku Poets

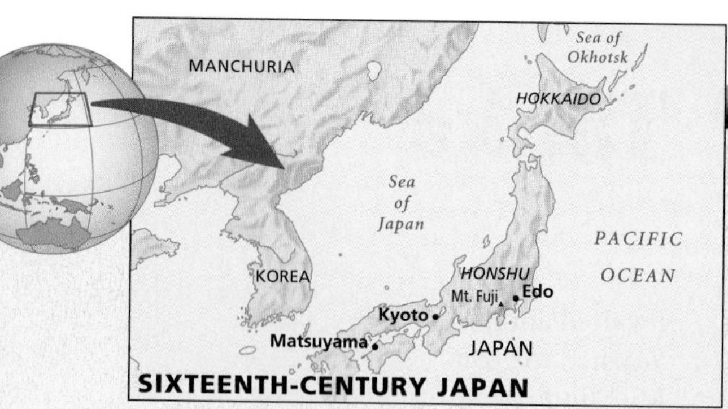

Matsuo Bashō

(1644–1694)

The son of a samurai, Matsuo Bashō (mät′so͞o • ō ba′shō) spent his youth in the service of a local lord. He began writing verses when he was nine and soon showed remarkable promise. Before he was thirty, he had won acclaim as a poet and had started his own poetry school.

Two things shaped Bashō's poetry: his devotion to Zen Buddhism and his travels. In 1684, at the age of forty, Bashō set out on the first of his many journeys through Japan. Traveling alone, Bashō endured great discomforts and loneliness. Nonetheless, some of his best haiku were composed on these lonely journeys.

Uejima Onitsura

(1660–1738)

One of Bashō's greatest admirers was Uejima Onitsura (o͞o • ā • jē′mä ō • nēt • so͞o′ra). Like Bashō, Onitsura came from a samurai background and began writing poetry at an early age. Though Onitsura admired Bashō, he did not imitate Bashō's style. His poems are more joyful and exuberant than Bashō's and somewhat less philosophical.

Taniguchi Buson

(1715–1783)

Taniguchi Buson (ta • ni • go͞o′chē bo͞o′sän), a younger contemporary of Onitsura, soon established his own poetic style. His haiku are generally regarded as second only to Bashō's. Buson was an accomplished painter, and his poems reflect his fascination with light and color.

Kobayashi Issa

(1762–1826)

Kobayashi Issa (kō • bə • yä′shē ē′sä) is one of the most beloved of Japan's haiku masters. His life was extraordinarily sad. His mother died when he was an infant, and his relations with his stepmother were so poor that his father sent him away from home to study when he was only fourteen. His first wife bore him five children, but all of them died in infancy. Eventually his wife succumbed to illness. Possibly because of these many sorrows, Issa's verses are taut with emotion, though rarely sentimental.

Bashō (17th century) by Ran-ku.

Haiku

On a withered branch
A crow has settled—
autumn nightfall.
—Matsuo Bashō

A village where they ring
no bells!—Oh, what *do* they do
at dusk in spring?
—Matsuo Bashō

No rice?—In that hour
we put into the gourd
a maiden-flower.
—Matsuo Bashō

Even stones in streams
of mountain water compose
songs to wild cherries.
—Uejima Onitsura

Blossoms on the pear;
and a woman in the moonlight
reads a letter there. . . .
—Taniguchi Buson

A morning-glory vine
all blossoming has thatched
this hut of mine.
—Kobayashi Issa

Lady Chiyo, a famous calligrapher and writer of haiku (18th century) by Tsukioka Yoshitoshi.

Asian Art and Archaeology, Inc./CORBIS.

The haiku by Bashō, Buson, and Issa are translated by Harold G. Henderson. The haiku by Onitsura is translated by Peter Beilenson and Harry Behn.

Response and Analysis

Tanka and Haiku

Thinking Critically

1. List one **image** from nature found in three of the **tanka.** What human thought or feeling does each natural image suggest or imply?
2. Which of the **tanka** do you think most strongly suggests a **mood** of loneliness or quiet reflection? What image or images does the poet use to convey this mood?
3. If you were asked to make a generalization about the **themes** of tanka poetry based on these poems, what would your generalization be?
4. Haiku poets often delight readers by revealing an unexpected relationship between two dissimilar things. Find examples of unexpected relationships in the three haiku by Bashō.
5. What **images** does Buson use in his haiku? What emotions do these images evoke?
6. What two things are contrasted in Issa's poem? What might each of these things **symbolize,** or stand for?
7. The six **haiku** reprinted here are translations from the Japanese, and like all translations, they do not follow the originals exactly. What departures from strict haiku form (unrhymed poems of seventeen syllables) can you see in these translations?
8. Seasonal **images** are common in haiku. What seasonal images do you find in these haiku? What **mood** or emotions do these images convey?

Comparing Literature

9. Based on these tanka and haiku, how would you compare the poets' views on the relationship between human beings and nature with the views of an English Romantic poet like William Wordsworth (see page 734)? Describe the single most important way that tanka and haiku are like Romantic poetry. In what respect are they most different?

Literary Skills
Analyze imagery, tanka, and haiku. Compare and contrast Japanese poetry with Romantic poetry.

Writing Skills
Write a tanka or a haiku.

WRITING

The Power of Suggestion

Try writing your own tanka or haiku, using an original image from nature to make an indirect comment on human life or to express a particular mood or feeling. You may want to go back to your Quickwrite notes to find an image that is meaningful to you. You do not have to keep to the strict syllable counts of tanka or haiku, but your poem should be unrhymed, and it should contain five lines if it is a tanka or three lines if it is a haiku. Read your poem to a few classmates, and ask them to discuss what they think you are suggesting about the human experience through your use of imagery.

From the series *Illustrated Collection of Butterflies* (c. 1804–1818) by Kubo Shunman. Woodblock print.

Fitzwilliam Museum, University of Cambridge, England. The Bridgeman Art Library.

Samuel Taylor Coleridge

(1772–1834)

Samuel Taylor Coleridge (1792) by Peter Vandyke. Oil on canvas (21½″ × 17½″).

By Courtesy of the National Portrait Gallery, London.

He was "the most wonderful man that I have ever known," said Wordsworth. The two poems that follow are only sketches in comparison with the full portrait of Coleridge, a man who was unquestionably a genius.

The youngest child of a village parson, Coleridge began his classical education at home. When he arrived at Cambridge University in 1792, he already had a reputation for insatiable curiosity and wide reading in "out-of-the-way" books.

He left the university in 1794 without a degree but with a commitment to a utopian colony in America. The experiment never materialized, but Coleridge gave radical lectures and married one of the prospective utopians. In 1796, he moved to a village in Somerset, with one book of poetry published but no prospects of a career. The next twenty months, which ended when he and Wordsworth went to Germany to study, were a time of miracles. In 1798, *Lyrical Ballads* was published, and by then English Romanticism had begun.

Wordsworth and Coleridge became catalysts for each other, and the friendship helped Coleridge write most of his best poems. But convinced that Wordsworth was "the best poet of the age," the poet in Coleridge hid in the giant's shadow. After the year in Germany, Wordsworth returned in late 1799 to his native Lake District. Coleridge abandoned his own roots and followed (as he told a friend) "a great, a true poet, I am only a kind of metaphysician."

Despite this characteristic modesty, Coleridge was, if only in brief periods, a "true poet" and, moreover, a profound philosopher. The middle period of his life, from 1800 to 1818, produced great achievements, most notably his lectures on Shakespeare and his work on philosophy and criticism.

But for Coleridge this period was also a time of pain and despair, memorialized in "Dejection: An Ode" (1802) and played out in the collapse of his marriage, his increasing addiction to opium (prescribed for painful attacks of arthritis), and his inability to discipline his wonderful mind.

By 1816, Coleridge had put himself under the care of a kindly physician, Dr. James Gillman. Despite the effect he had on others, Coleridge himself was lonely. His loneliness came from a lifelong need for affection and support—a need that made the isolation of the writer's life often unbearable for him. His addiction to opium, which began before he was thirty, was not controlled until his residence with the Gillmans.

Coleridge's addiction to opium was made worse by the laudanum he took to relieve the discomforts he suffered when he tried to stop using the drug. Laudanum was commonly used in Coleridge's time and was even given to infants. Little was known then about withdrawal symptoms. Although scholars disagree about the destructive effect of opium on his achievements, there is no question that Coleridge was badly addicted.

Coleridge was truly magnanimous, generous of his intellect and spirit, and devoted to the good of his fellow human beings. The full portrait of Coleridge, however, is too great for anyone to master. Anyone, that is, except someone like Coleridge himself.

Before You Read

Kubla Khan

Make the Connection

Quickwrite

The poem you are about to read may challenge the limits of your imagination. Fantastical and strange, it is like a vivid yet incomprehensible dream. Coleridge, in fact, suggested that the poem came to him in a dream. Like a dream, the poem contains allusions to the deepest human desires—for pleasure, order, beauty, even chaos and war. It also holds within it the moment when, upon waking, the vividness and the supposed logic of the dream are suddenly—perhaps forever—lost to the dreamer.

Think about some dreams that you have had. Then, jot down some notes that describe how dreams seem to work. Are they logical or illogical? How do they progress? Do they tell coherent stories or do they consist mostly of images and fragments of stories? As you read, think about how the poem may imitate or reproduce this process.

Literary Focus

Alliteration

Alliteration—the repetition of a consonant sound in words that are close to one another—can have several effects. Coleridge uses alliteration throughout "Kubla Khan" to help create the poem's enchanted mood. Alliteration can impart a musical quality to a poem, emphasize a particular line or idea, or help establish a rhythm. As in lines 25–26 of "Kubla Khan," alliteration can also suggest a certain kind of movement: "Five *m*iles *m*eandering with a *m*azy *m*otion, / Through wood and dale the sacred river ran. . . ." Here the repeated *m* sound evokes and imitates the lazy, serpentine flow of the river. As you read the poem, look for—and listen to—other examples of alliteration.

Literary Skills
Understand alliteration.

INTERNET

More About Samuel Taylor Coleridge

Keyword: LE7 12-5

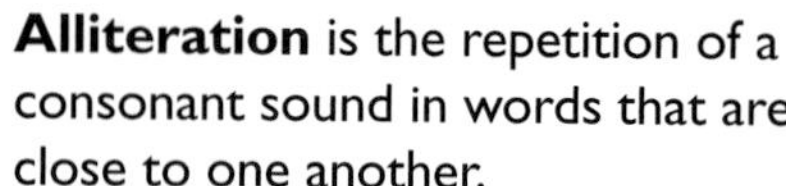

Alliteration is the repetition of a consonant sound in words that are close to one another.

For more on Alliteration, see the Handbook of Literary and Historical Terms.

Background

"Kubla Khan" has a lyrical tone and manner that resemble a meditative ode. Full of mystery and dread, "Kubla Khan" was composed at about the same time (late 1797 or early 1798) as *The Rime of the Ancient Mariner.*

"Kubla Khan" has always intrigued readers, including the poet Byron, who, after reading it in manuscript, apparently persuaded Coleridge to publish it in 1816. At the time, Coleridge added a prose introduction that offered a rational account of the poem's origins. He claimed it was written in a reverie brought on by opium taken after he had read a provocative passage in a seventeenth-century travel book. Coleridge asserted that he woke from his dream and was interrupted by a visitor while composing the poem. After the visitor departed an hour later, a mere fragment of his dream-poem could be reproduced, he claimed.

Kubla Khan (c. 1216–1294), the grandson of Genghis Khan, was the Mongol conqueror of China.

Kublai Khan, from the Yüan dynasty, China.
National Palace Museum, Taipei Taiwan, Republic of China.

Palace of Kublai Khan at Peking (14th century). Miniature from the *Livre des Merveilles*.

(MS Fr. 2810, fol. 37)

Kubla Khan

Samuel Taylor Coleridge

In Xanadu did Kubla Khan
A stately pleasure-dome decree:
Where Alph,° the sacred river, ran
Through caverns measureless to man
   Down to a sunless sea.
So twice five miles of fertile ground
With walls and towers were girdled round:
And there were gardens bright with sinuous rills,°
Where blossomed many an incense-bearing tree;
And here were forests ancient as the hills,
Enfolding sunny spots of greenery.

But oh! that deep romantic chasm which slanted
Down the green hill athwart a cedarn cover!°
A savage place! as holy and enchanted

3. Alph: probably a reference to the Greek river Alpheus, which flows into the Ionian Sea, and whose waters are fabled to rise up again in Sicily.

8. sinuous (sin′yo͞o·əs) **rills:** winding streams.

13. athwart a cedarn cover: crossing diagonally under a covering growth of cedar trees.

As e'er beneath a waning moon was haunted
By woman wailing for her demon-lover!
And from this chasm, with ceaseless turmoil seething,
As if this earth in fast thick pants were breathing,
A mighty fountain momently° was forced:
Amid whose swift half-intermitted burst
Huge fragments vaulted like rebounding hail,
Or chaffy grain beneath the thresher's flail:°
And 'mid these dancing rocks at once and ever
It flung up momently the sacred river.
Five miles meandering with a mazy° motion
Through wood and dale the sacred river ran,
Then reached the caverns measureless to man,
And sank in tumult to a lifeless ocean:
And 'mid this tumult Kubla heard from far
Ancestral voices prophesying war!
  The shadow of the dome of pleasure
  Floated midway on the waves;
  Where was heard the mingled measure°
  From the fountain and the caves.
It was a miracle of rare device,
A sunny pleasure-dome with caves of ice!

  A damsel with a dulcimer°
  In a vision once I saw:
  It was an Abyssinian° maid,
  And on her dulcimer she played,
  Singing of Mount Abora.°
  Could I revive within me
  Her symphony and song,
  To such a deep delight 'twould win me,
That with music loud and long,
I would build that dome in air,
That sunny dome! those caves of ice!
And all who heard should see them there,
And all should cry, Beware! Beware!
His flashing eyes, his floating hair!
Weave a circle round him thrice,
And close your eyes with holy dread,
For he on honeydew hath fed,
And drunk the milk of Paradise.

19. momently *adv.:* at each moment.

22. thresher's flail: heavy, whiplike tool used to thresh, or beat, grain in order to separate the kernels from their chaff, or husks.

25. mazy *adj.:* like a maze; having many turns.

33. measure *n.:* rhythmic sound.

37. dulcimer *n.:* musical instrument that is often played by striking the strings with small hammers.

39. Abyssinian: Ethiopian. Ethiopia is in northeast Africa.

41. Mount Abora: probably a reference to John Milton's (1608–1674) *Paradise Lost,* in which Mount Amara, in Ethiopia, is a mythical, earthly paradise.

Response and Analysis

Thinking Critically

1. In the first stanza, what **images** create pictures of the pleasure-dome that Kubla Khan decrees?
2. Why is the "deep romantic chasm" of line 12 called a "savage" place? What ominous note is introduced toward the end of the second stanza?
3. In the third stanza, what does the speaker see in a vision? What does the speaker say he wants to do?
4. The speaker in the poem has been interpreted as being an artist, perhaps a poet. Why would the "damsel with a dulcimer" be important to the speaker?
5. What could the "dome in air" which the speaker wants to create **symbolize**?
6. Many ancient cultures regarded poets as seers who had a special relationship with the gods and thus were to be treated with reverence. How might Coleridge be alluding to such beliefs in the closing lines of the last stanza?
7. How could this poem be about the creation of a poem?
8. Describe the **rhyme scheme** and **meter** of the poem. What examples of **alliteration** add to the poem's music?

Extending and Evaluating

9. The power of the imagination is often exalted in Romantic poetry. In your opinion, does "Kubla Khan" celebrate the imagination or caution against its indulgence? Support your response with evidence from the poem.

WRITING

The Stuff of Dreams

Review the Quickwrite notes you made earlier describing dreams. How do your thoughts on the way dreams work compare to the dreamlike flow of "Kubla Khan"? Use your notes to **evaluate** Coleridge's claim that the poem began as a dream. Explain whether "Kubla Khan" reads like a dream, using examples from the poem as evidence. Then, draw your own conclusion about Coleridge's claim. Do you think the poem is in fact the product of a dream?

Literary Skills Analyze alliteration.

Writing Skills Evaluate a poet's claim.

Beyond the Valley of the Kasbahs.
The Bridgeman Art Library/Getty Images.

INTERNET
Projects and Activities
Keyword: LE7 12-5

Before You Read

The Rime of the Ancient Mariner

Make the Connection

Quickwrite

Have you ever done something on impulse, knowing even while you were doing it that you would regret it later? The ancient Mariner's strange tale turns on just such an action. And the dreadful consequences of his impulsive deed are as hypnotizing to us as they are to the Mariner's spellbound listener. As you read, try to chart your responses to the Mariner's story. When do you feel sympathy for him—or sorrow or fear? When does his story seem true, and when is it hopelessly distorted by guilt?

The Mariner's tale is essentially a confession. Jot down a few of your own ideas about the act of confession. What purpose does confession have for the teller and the listener? Why do you think the act of confession plays such an important role in law and religion?

Literary Skills Understand the characteristics of a literary ballad.

Reading Skills Understand archaic words.

Literary Focus

Literary Ballad

Coleridge's **literary ballad** imitates the traditional **folk ballad** in both subject matter and form. Like the old folk ballads (see page 130), his sensational narrative blends real with supernatural events. It also uses simple language, a good deal of repetition, and strong patterns of rhythm and rhyme. Coleridge was a skilled poet, and to avoid monotony, he often varies his **meter** and **rhyme scheme.** He also uses sophisticated sound devices like **internal rhyme** ("The guests are *met*, the feast is *set*") and **assonance** ("'Tis sweeter far to me"). To give his ballad an archaic sound, he uses language that was old-fashioned for his day.

INTERNET

Vocabulary Practice

•

More About Samuel Taylor Coleridge

•

Keyword: LE7 12-5

A **literary ballad,** a songlike poem that tells a story, is written in imitation of the folk ballad, which springs from a genuine oral tradition.

For more on the Ballad, see the Handbook of Literary and Historical Terms.

Reading Skills 

Reading Archaic Words

To give his ballad an antique flavor, Coleridge used many words that were **archaic,** or out of date.

As you read, you will find the meanings of many of these words in the margin of the page. However, you may not want to interrupt the powerful rhythm of the verse to stop and check a word's meaning. If not, try reading several stanzas at once, pausing only occasionally to check words you didn't understand. Some of the words' meanings will be suggested by context clues, as in "Nor dim nor red, like God's own head, / The glorious Sun *uprist.*" Here, the prefix *up–*, in addition to your own knowledge about the sun, might lead you to guess correctly that the meaning of *uprist* is "rose." As you read, jot down any archaic words, or parts of words, that are still in use today.

Background

Coleridge wrote *The Rime of the Ancient Mariner* as part of the collaboration with Wordsworth in 1797–1798 that culminated in *Lyrical Ballads.* As Coleridge later recalled, some of the poems in this volume were intended to present ordinary people and events in a fresh and interesting way.

Others, such as *Ancient Mariner,* were to present supernatural characters and events, yet in such a way that would induce the reader to "procure for these shadows of imagination that willing suspension of disbelief for the moment, which constitutes poetic faith."

The Rime of the Ancient Mariner was the first poem in the 1798 edition of *Lyrical Ballads.* In part because of Wordsworth's discomfort with the disparity between it and the other poems in the volume, Coleridge revised the poem for later editions, modernizing many of the deliberately old-fashioned words he had used. The marginal notes were added in 1817.

It is helpful in reading this narrative to keep one or two things in mind. First, the poem gives no explanation for the killing of the albatross. The results of the act, rather than the act itself, are important. Second, all the objects and events described in the story are being seen through the eyes of the Mariner, whose frame of mind is constantly shifting. This unstable perspective makes it difficult—perhaps impossible—for the reader to tell what really happened.

Vocabulary Development

tyrannous (tir′ə•nəs) *adj.:* harsh; oppressive.

dismal (diz′məl) *adj.:* gloomy.

ghastly (gast′lē) *adj.:* dreadful; ghostly.

abated (ə•bāt′id) *v.:* lessened.

wrenched (rencht) *v.:* anguished; grief-stricken.

"With my crossbow / I shot the ALBATROSS."

The Rime of the Ancient Mariner

Samuel Taylor Coleridge

Argument

How a Ship having passed the Line was driven by storms to the cold Country toward the South Pole; and how from thence she made her course to the tropical Latitude of the Great Pacific Ocean; and of the strange things that befell; and in what manner the Ancient Mariner came back to his own Country.

Part I

An ancient Mariner meeteth three Gallants bidden to a wedding feast, and detaineth one.

It is an ancient Mariner,
And he stoppeth one of three.
"By thy long gray beard and glittering eye,
Now wherefore stopp'st thou me?

The Bridegroom's doors are opened wide,
And I am next of kin;
The guests are met, the feast is set:
May'st hear the merry din."

He holds him with his skinny hand,
"There was a ship," quoth he.
"Hold off! unhand me, gray-beard loon!"
Eftsoons° his hand dropt he.

12. eftsoons: archaic for "at once."

(Opposite) *View of a Harbour* (1815–1816) by Caspar David Friedrich. Oil on canvas.
Schloss Sanssouci, Potsdam, Germany. The Bridgeman Art Library.

He holds him with his glittering eye—
The Wedding Guest stood still,
And listens like a three years' child:
The Mariner hath his will.

The Wedding Guest is spell-bound by the eye of the old seafaring man, and constrained to hear his tale.

The Wedding Guest sat on a stone:
He cannot choose but hear;
And thus spake on that ancient man,
The bright-eyed Mariner.

"It is an ancient Mariner, And he stoppeth one of three."

"The ship was cheered, the harbor cleared,
Merrily did we drop
Below the kirk,° below the hill,
Below the lighthouse top.

23. **kirk** *n.:* church.

The Sun came up upon the left,
Out of the sea came he!
And he shone bright, and on the right
Went down into the sea.

The Mariner tells how the ship sailed southward with a good wind and fair weather, till it reached the Line.

Higher and higher every day,
Till over the mast at noon°—"
The Wedding Guest here beat his breast,
For he heard the loud bassoon.

30. **over . . . noon:** The ship has reached the equator, here called the Line.

The bride hath paced into the hall,
Red as a rose is she;
Nodding their heads before her goes
The merry minstrelsy.°

The Wedding Guest heareth the bridal music; but the Mariner continueth his tale.

36. **minstrelsy** (min′strəl·sē) *n.:* group of musicians.

The Wedding Guest he beat his breast,
Yet he cannot choose but hear;
And thus spake on that ancient man,
The bright-eyed Mariner.

"And now the STORM-BLAST came, and he
Was tyrannous and strong:
He struck with his o'ertaking wings,
And chased us south along.

The ship driven by a storm toward the South Pole.

With sloping masts and dipping prow,
As who° pursued with yell and blow
Still° treads the shadow of his foe,
And forward bends his head,
The ship drove fast, loud roared the blast,
And southward aye° we fled.

46. **who** *pron.:* one.

47. **still** *adv.:* archaic for "always."

50. **aye** *adv.:* archaic for "continually."

And now there came both mist and snow,
And it grew wondrous cold:
And ice, mast-high, came floating by,
As green as emerald.

Vocabulary

tyrannous (tir′ə•nəs) *adj.:* harsh; oppressive.

And through the drifts° the snowy cliffs°
Did send a dismal sheen:
Nor shapes of men nor beasts we ken°—
The ice was all between.

The ice was here, the ice was there,
The ice was all around:
It cracked and growled, and roared and howled,
Like noises in a swound!°

At length did cross an Albatross,
Through the fog it came;
As if it had been a Christian soul,
We hailed it in God's name.

It ate the food it ne'er had eat,
And round and round it flew.
The ice did split with a thunder fit;
The helmsman steered us through!

And a good south wind sprung up behind;
The Albatross did follow,
And every day, for food or play,
Came to the mariner's hello!

In mist or cloud, on mast or shroud,°
It perched for vespers° nine;
Whiles all the night, through fog-smoke white,
Glimmered the white Moonshine."

"God save thee, ancient Mariner!
From the fiends, that plague thee thus!—
Why look'st thou so?"—With my crossbow
I shot the ALBATROSS.

The land of ice, and of fearful sounds where no living thing was to be seen.

55. drifts *n. pl.:* windblown snow and fog. **cliffs** *n. pl.:* icebergs.

57. ken *v.:* archaic for "saw."

62. swound *n.:* swoon.

Till a great seabird, called the Albatross, came through the snow fog, and was received with great joy and hospitality.

And lo! the Albatross proveth a bird of good omen, and followeth the ship as it returned northward through fog and floating ice.

75. shroud *n.:* support rope that stretches from the top of the mast to the side of the ship.

76. vespers *n. pl:* evenings; also, evening prayers.

The ancient Mariner inhospitably killeth the pious bird of good omen.

Part II

The Sun now rose upon the right:
Out of the sea came he,
Still hid in mist, and on the left
Went down into the sea.

Vocabulary

dismal (diz′məl) *adj.:* gloomy.

And the good south wind still blew behind,
But no sweet bird did follow,
Nor any day for food or play
Came to the mariner's hello!

And I had done a hellish thing,
And it would work 'em woe:
For all averred,° I had killed the bird
That made the breeze to blow.
Ah wretch! said they, the bird to slay,
That made the breeze to blow!

His shipmates cry out against the ancient Mariner, for killing the bird of good luck.

93. averred (ə·vʉrd') *v.:* asserted; claimed.

Nor dim nor red, like God's own head,
The glorious Sun uprist:
Then all averred, I had killed the bird
That brought the fog and mist.
'Twas right, said they, such birds to slay,
That bring the fog and mist.

But when the fog cleared off, they jusified the same, and thus make themselves accomplices in the crime.

The fair breeze blew, the white foam flew,
The furrow° followed free;
We were the first that ever burst
Into that silent sea.

The fair breeze continues; the ship enters the Pacific Ocean, and sails northward, even till it reaches the Line.

104. furrow *n.:* ship's wake.

Down dropt the breeze, the sails dropt down,
'Twas sad as sad could be;
And we did speak only to break
The silence of the sea!

The ship hath been suddenly becalmed.

All in a hot and copper sky,
The bloody Sun, at noon,
Right up above the mast did stand,
No bigger than the Moon.

Day after day, day after day,
We stuck, nor breath nor motion;
As idle as a painted ship
Upon a painted ocean.

Water, water, everywhere,
And all the boards did shrink;
Water, water, everywhere,
Nor any drop to drink.

And the Albatross begins to be avenged.

The very deep did rot: O Christ!
That ever this should be!
Yea, slimy things did crawl with legs
Upon the slimy sea.

About, about, in reel and rout°
The death-fires° danced at night;
The water, like a witch's oils,
Burnt green, and blue and white.

And some in dreams assured were
Of the Spirit that plagued us so;
Nine fathom deep he had followed us
From the land of mist and snow.

And every tongue, through utter drought,
Was withered at the root;
We could not speak, no more than if
We had been choked with soot.

Ah! welladay!° what evil looks
Had I from old and young!
Instead of the cross, the Albatross
About my neck was hung.

Part III

There passed a weary time. Each throat
Was parched, and glazed each eye.
A weary time! a weary time!
How glazed each weary eye,
When looking westward, I beheld
A something in the sky.

At first it seemed a little speck,
And then it seemed a mist;
It moved and moved, and took at last
A certain shape, I wist.°

A speck, a mist, a shape, I wist!
And still it neared and neared:
As if it dodged a water sprite,
It plunged and tacked and veered.°

With throats unslaked,° with black lips baked,
We could not laugh nor wail;
Through utter drought all dumb we stood!
I bit my arm, I sucked the blood,
And cried, A sail! a sail!

A Spirit had followed them; one of the invisible inhabitants of this planet, neither departed souls nor angels; concerning whom the learned Jew, Josephus, and the Platonic Constantinopolitan, Michael Psellus, may be consulted. They are very numerous, and there is no climate or element without one or more.

127. reel and rout: violent, whirling movement.

128. death-fires *n. pl.:* firelike, luminous glow that is said to be seen over dead bodies.

The shipmates, in their sore distress, would fain throw the whole guilt on the ancient Mariner: in sign whereof they hang the dead seabird round his neck.

139. welladay *interj.:* archaic for "alas," an exclamation of sorrow.

The ancient Mariner beholdeth a sign in the element afar off.

152. wist *v.:* archaic for "knew."

156. tacked and veered: turned toward and then away from the wind.

At its nearer approach, it seemeth him to be a ship; and at a dear ransom, he freeth his speech from the bonds of thirst.

157. unslaked *v.:* unrelieved of thirst.

With throats unslaked, with black lips baked,
Agape° they heard me call:
Gramercy!° they for joy did grin,
And all at once their breath drew in,
As they were drinking all.

See! see! (I cried) she tacks no more!
Hither to work us weal;°
Without a breeze, without a tide,
She steadies with upright keel!

The western wave was all aflame.
The day was well nigh done!
Almost upon the western wave
Rested the broad bright Sun;
When that strange shape drove suddenly
Betwixt us and the Sun.

163. agape *adv.:* with mouths wide open in wonder or fear.

A flash of joy;

164. gramercy (grə·mʉr′sē) *interj.:* from Middle French *grand merci,* an exclamation of great thanks.

And horror follows. For can it be a ship that comes onward without wind or tide?

168. work us weal: do us good.

"Through utter drought all dumb we stood!"

And straight the Sun was flecked with bars,
(Heaven's Mother send us grace!)
As if through a dungeon grate he peered
With broad and burning face.

It seemeth him but the skeleton of a ship.

Alas! (thought I, and my heart beat loud)
How fast she nears and nears!
Are those *her* sails that glance in the Sun,
Like restless gossameres?°

And its ribs are seen as bars on the face of the setting Sun.

184. gossameres *n. pl.:* filmy cobwebs.

Are those *her* ribs through which the Sun
Did peer, as through a grate?
And is that Woman all her crew?
Is that a DEATH? and are there two?
Is DEATH that woman's mate?

The Specter Woman and her Deathmate, and no other on-board the skeleton ship.

Her lips were red, *her* looks were free,
Her locks were yellow as gold:
Her skin was as white as leprosy,
The Nightmare LIFE-IN-DEATH was she,
Who thicks man's blood with cold.

Like vessel, like crew!

The naked hulk alongside came,
And the twain were casting dice;
"The game is done! I've won! I've won!"
Quoth she, and whistles thrice.

Death and Life-in-Death have diced for the ship's crew, and she (the latter) winneth the ancient Mariner.

The Sun's rim dips; the stars rush out:
At one stride comes the dark;
With far-heard whisper, o'er the sea,
Off shot the specter bark.°

No twilight within the courts of the Sun.

202. specter bark: ghost ship.

We listened and looked sideways up!
Fear at my heart, as at a cup,
My lifeblood seemed to sip!
The stars were dim, and thick the night,
The steersman's face by his lamp gleamed white;
From the sails the dew did drip—
Till clomb° above the eastern bar
The hornèd° Moon, with one bright star
Within the nether tip.°

At the rising of the Moon,

209. clomb (klōm) *v.:* archaic for "climbed."
210. hornèd *adj.:* crescent.
210–211. star . . . tip: A star dogging, or following, the moon is believed by sailors to be an evil omen.

One after one, by the star-dogged Moon,
Too quick for groan or sigh,
Each turned his face with a ghastly pang,
And cursed me with his eye.

One after another,

Four times fifty living men,
(And I heard nor sigh nor groan)
With heavy thump, a lifeless lump,
They dropped down one by one.

His shipmates drop down dead.

The souls did from their bodies fly,—
They fled to bliss or woe!
And every soul, it passed me by,
Like the whizz of my crossbow!

But Life-in-Death begins her work on the ancient Mariner.

Part IV

"I fear thee, ancient Mariner!
I fear thy skinny hand!
And thou art long, and lank, and brown,
As is the ribbed sea sand.

The Wedding Guest feareth that a Spirit is talking to him;

I fear thee and thy glittering eye,
And thy skinny hand, so brown."—
Fear not, fear not, thou Wedding Guest!
This body dropt not down.

Alone, alone, all, all alone,
Alone on a wide wide sea!
And never a saint took pity on
My soul in agony.

But the ancient Mariner assureth him of his bodily life, and proceedeth to relate his horrible penance.

The many men, so beautiful!
And they all dead did lie:
And a thousand thousand slimy things
Lived on; and so did I.

He despiseth the creatures of the calm,

I looked upon the rotting sea,
And drew my eyes away;
I looked upon the rotting deck,
And there the dead men lay.

And envieth that they *should live, and so many lie dead.*

I looked to heaven, and tried to pray;
But or° ever a prayer had gusht,
A wicked whisper came, and made
My heart as dry as dust.

245. or *prep.:* before.

Vocabulary

ghastly (gast′lē) *adj.:* dreadful; ghostly.

I closed my lids, and kept them close,
And the balls like pulses beat;
For the sky and the sea, and the sea and the sky
Lay like a load on my weary eye,
And the dead were at my feet.

The cold sweat melted from their limbs,
Nor rot nor reek did they:
The look with which they looked on me
Had never passed away.

But the curse liveth for him in the eye of the dead men.

An orphan's curse would drag to hell
A spirit from on high;
But oh! more horrible than that
Is the curse in a dead man's eye!
Seven days, seven nights, I saw that curse,
And yet I could not die.

In his loneliness and fixedness he yearneth toward the journeying Moon, and the stars that still sojourn, yet still move onward; and everywhere the blue sky belongs to them, and is their appointed rest, and their native country and their own natural homes, which they enter unannounced, as lords that are certainly expected and yet there is a silent joy at their arrival.

The moving Moon went up the sky,
And nowhere did abide:
Softly she was going up,
And a star or two beside—

Her beams bemocked the sultry main,°
Like April hoarfrost° spread;
But where the ship's huge shadow lay,
The charmèd water burnt alway°
A still and awful red.

267. main *n.:* archaic for "open sea."
268. hoarfrost *n.:* frost.
270. alway *adv.:* archaic for "always."

By the light of the Moon he beholdeth God's creatures of the great calm.

Beyond the shadow of the ship,
I watched the water snakes:
They moved in tracks of shining white,
And when they reared, the elfish light
Fell off in hoary° flakes.

276. hoary *adj.:* white or gray.

Within the shadow of the ship
I watched their rich attire:
Blue, glossy green, and velvet black,
They coiled and swam; and every track
Was a flash of golden fire.

Their beauty and their happiness.

O happy, living things! no tongue
Their beauty might declare:
A spring of love gushed from my heart,
And I blessed them unaware:
Sure my kind saint took pity on me,
And I blessed them unaware.

He blesseth them in his heart.

The selfsame moment I could pray;
And from my neck so free
The Albatross fell off, and sank
Like lead into the sea.

The spell begins to break.

Part V

Oh sleep! it is a gentle thing,
Beloved from pole to pole!
To Mary Queen the praise be given!
She sent the gentle sleep from Heaven,
That slid into my soul.

The silly° buckets on the deck,
That had so long remained,
I dreamt that they were filled with dew;
And when I awoke, it rained.

297. silly *adj.:* simple; plain.

By grace of the holy Mother, the ancient Mariner is refreshed with rain.

My lips were wet, my throat was cold,
My garments all were dank;
Sure I had drunken in my dreams,
And still my body drank.

I moved, and could not feel my limbs:
I was so light—almost
I thought that I had died in sleep,
And was a blessèd ghost.

And soon I heard a roaring wind:
It did not come anear;
But with its sound it shook the sails,
That were so thin and sere.°

He heareth sounds and seeth strange sights and commotions in the sky and the element.

312. sere *adj.:* archaic for "worn."

The upper air burst into life!
And a hundred fire flags sheen,
To and fro they were hurried about!
And to and fro, and in and out,
The wan stars danced between.°

313–317. The upper . . . danced between: apparently a description of the shifting lights of an aurora, which sometimes resemble waving, luminous folds of fabric.

And the coming wind did roar more loud,
And the sails did sigh like sedge;°
And the rain poured down from one black cloud;
The Moon was at its edge.

319. sedge *n.:* reedy plants.

"I dreamt that they were filled with dew;
And when I awoke, it rained."

The thick black cloud was cleft,° and still
The Moon was at its side:
Like waters shot from some high crag,
The lightning fell with never a jag,
A river steep and wide.

The loud wind never reached the ship,
Yet now the ship moved on!
Beneath the lightning and the Moon
The dead men gave a groan.

They groaned, they stirred, they all uprose,
Nor spake, nor moved their eyes;
It had been strange, even in a dream,
To have seen those dead men rise.

The helmsman steered, the ship moved on;
Yet never a breeze up-blew;
The mariners all 'gan work the ropes,
Where they were wont° to do;
They raised their limbs like lifeless tools—
We were a ghastly crew.

The body of my brother's son
Stood by me, knee to knee:
The body and I pulled at one rope,
But he said nought to me.

322. cleft *adj.:* split.

The bodies of the ship's crew are inspired, and the ship moves on;

338. wont (wänt) *adj.:* accustomed.

"I fear thee, ancient Mariner!"
Be calm, thou Wedding Guest!
'Twas not those souls that fled in pain,
Which to their corses° came again,
But a troop of spirits blest:

But not by the souls of the men, nor by demons of earth or middle air, but by a blessed troop of angelic spirits, sent down by the invocation of the guardian saint.

348. corses *n. pl.:* archaic for "corpses."

For when it dawned—they dropt their arms,
And clustered round the mast;
Sweet sounds rose slowly through their mouths,
And from their bodies passed.

Around, around, flew each sweet sound,
Then darted to the Sun;
Slowly the sounds came back again,
Now mixed, now one by one.

Sometimes a-dropping from the sky
I heard the skylark sing;
Sometimes all little birds that are,
How they seemed to fill the sea and air
With their sweet jargoning!°

362. jargoning *n.:* archaic for "twittering."

And now 'twas like all instruments,
Now like a lonely flute;
And now it is an angel's song,
That makes the heavens be mute.

It ceased; yet still the sails made on
A pleasant noise till noon,
A noise like of a hidden brook
In the leafy month of June,
That to the sleeping woods all night
Singeth a quiet tune.

Till noon we quietly sailed on,
Yet never a breeze did breathe:
Slowly and smoothly went the ship,
Moved onward from beneath.

Under the keel nine fathom deep,
From the land of mist and snow,
The spirit slid: and it was he
That made the ship to go.
The sails at noon left off their tune,
And the ship stood still also.

The lonesome Spirit from the South Pole carries on the ship as far as the Line, in obedience to the angelic troop, but still requireth vengeance.

The Sun, right up above the mast,
Had fixed her° to the ocean:
But in a minute she 'gan stir,
With a short uneasy motion—
Backwards and forwards half her length
With a short uneasy motion.

384. fixed her: seemed to hold the ship motionless.

Then like a pawing horse let go,
She made a sudden bound:
It flung the blood into my head,
And I fell down in a swound.

How long in that same fit I lay,
I have not to declare;
But ere my living life returned,
I heard and in my soul discerned
Two voices in the air.

The Polar Spirit's fellow demons, the invisible inhabitants of the element, take part in his wrong; and two of them relate, one to the other, that penance long and heavy for the ancient Mariner hath been accorded to the Polar Spirit, who returneth southward.

"Is it he?" quoth one, "Is this the man?
By him who died on cross,
With his cruel bow he laid full low
The harmless Albatross.

The spirit who bideth by himself
In the land of mist and snow,
He loved the bird that loved the man
Who shot him with his bow."

The other was a softer voice,
As soft as honeydew:
Quoth he, "The man hath penance done,
And penance more will do."

Part VI

FIRST VOICE

"But tell me, tell me! speak again,
Thy soft response renewing—
What makes that ship drive on so fast?
What is the ocean doing?"

SECOND VOICE

"Still as a slave before his lord,
The ocean hath no blast;°
His great bright eye most silently
Up to the Moon is cast—

415. blast *n.:* wind.

If he may know which way to go;
For she guides him smooth or grim.
See, brother, see! how graciously
She looketh down on him."

The Mariner hath been cast into a trance; for the angelic power causeth the vessel to drive northward faster than human life could endure.

FIRST VOICE

"But why drives on that ship so fast,
Without or wave or wind?"°

423. without . . . wind: with neither wave nor wind.

SECOND VOICE

"The air is cut away before,
And closes from behind.

Fly, brother, fly! more high, more high!
Or we shall be belated:
For slow and slow that ship will go,
When the Mariner's trance is abated."

The supernatural motion is retarded; the Mariner awakes, and his penance begins anew.

I woke, and we were sailing on
As in a gentle weather:
'Twas night, calm night, the Moon was high;
The dead men stood together.

All stood together on the deck,
For a charnel dungeon° fitter:
All fixed on me their stony eyes,
That in the Moon did glitter.

435. charnel (chär'nəl) **dungeon:** burial vault.

The pang, the curse, with which they died,
Had never passed away:
I could not draw my eyes from theirs,
Nor turn them up to pray.

The curse is finally expiated [removed, after penance is done].

And now this spell was snapt: once more
I viewed the ocean green,
And looked far forth, yet little saw
Of what had else° been seen—

445. had else: would have otherwise.

Like one, that on a lonesome road
Doth walk in fear and dread,
And having once turned round walks on,
And turns no more his head;
Because he knows, a frightful fiend
Doth close behind him tread.

Vocabulary

abated (ə•bāt'id) *v.:* lessened.

But soon there breathed a wind on me,
Nor sound nor motion made:
Its path was not upon the sea,
In ripple or in shade.

It raised my hair, it fanned my cheek
Like a meadow gale of spring—
It mingled strangely with my fears,
Yet it felt like a welcoming.

Swiftly, swiftly flew the ship,
Yet she sailed softly too:
Sweetly, sweetly blew the breeze—
On me alone it blew.

Oh! dream of joy! is this indeed
The lighthouse top I see?
Is this the hill? is this the kirk?
Is this mine own countree?

We drifted o'er the harbor bar,
And I with sobs did pray—
O let me be awake, my God!
Or let me sleep alway.

The harbor bay was clear as glass,
So smoothly it was strewn!°
And on the bay the moonlight lay,
And the shadow of the Moon.

The rock shone bright, the kirk no less,
That stands above the rock:
The moonlight steeped in silentness
The steady weathercock.°

And the bay was white with silent light,
Till rising from the same,
Full many shapes, that shadows were,
In crimson colors came.

A little distance from the prow
Those crimson shadows were:
I turned my eyes upon the deck—
Oh, Christ! what saw I there!

"And on the bay the moonlight lay,
And the shadow of the Moon."

And the ancient Mariner beholdeth his native country.

473. strewn *v.:* stretched out; calmed.

479. weathercock *n.:* rooster-shaped weather vane.

The angelic spirits leave the dead bodies,

And appear in their own forms of light.

Each corse lay flat, lifeless and flat,
And, by the holy rood!°
A man all light, a seraph man,°
On every corse there stood.

This seraph band, each waved his hand:
It was a heavenly sight!
They stood as signals to the land,
Each one a lovely light;

This seraph band, each waved his hand,
No voice did they impart—
No voice; but oh! the silence sank
Like music on my heart.

But soon I heard the dash of oars,
I heard the Pilot's cheer;
My head was turned perforce away
And I saw a boat appear.

489. rood *n.:* crucifix.

490. seraph man: angel of the highest rank.

"Full many shapes, that shadows were,
In crimson colors came."

The Pilot and the Pilot's boy,
I heard them coming fast:
Dear Lord in Heaven! it was a joy
The dead men could not blast.

I saw a third—I heard his voice:
It is the Hermit good!
He singeth loud his godly hymns
That he makes in the wood.
He'll shrieve° my soul, he'll wash away
The Albatross's blood.

512. shrieve (shrēv) *v.:* archaic for "release from guilt after hearing confession."

Part VII

The Hermit of the Wood,

This Hermit good lives in that wood
Which slopes down to the sea.
How loudly his sweet voice he rears!
He loves to talk with marineres
That come from a far countree.

He kneels at morn, and noon, and eve—
He hath a cushion plump:
It is the moss that wholly hides
The rotted old oak stump.

The skiff boat° neared: I heard them talk,
"Why, this is strange, I trow!°
Where are those lights so many and fair,
That signal made but now?"

523. skiff boat: rowboat.
524. trow *v.:* archaic for "believe."

Approacheth the ship with wonder.

"Strange, by my faith!" the Hermit said—
"And they answered not our cheer!
The planks looked warped! and see those sails,
How thin they are and sere!
I never saw aught° like to them,
Unless perchance it were

531. aught *pron.:* anything.

Brown skeletons of leaves that lag°
My forest brook along;
When the ivy tod° is heavy with snow,
And the owlet whoops to the wolf below,
That eats the she-wolf's young."

533. lag *v.:* drift; move more slowly than the current.
535. ivy tod: clump of ivy.

"Dear Lord! it hath a fiendish look—
(The Pilot made reply)
I am afeared"—"Push on, push on!"
Said the Hermit cheerily.

The boat came closer to the ship,
But I nor spake nor stirred;
The boat came close beneath the ship,
And straight° a sound was heard.

545. straight *adv.:* straightaway; at once.

The ship suddenly sinketh.

Under the water it rumbled on,
Still louder and more dread:
It reached the ship, it split the bay;
The ship went down like lead.

The ancient Mariner is saved in the Pilot's boat.

Stunned by that loud and dreadful sound,
Which sky and ocean smote,°
Like one that hath been seven days drowned
My body lay afloat;
But swift as dreams, myself I found
Within the Pilot's boat.

551. smote *v.:* struck.

"It reached the ship, it split the bay;
The ship went down like lead."

"Upon the whirl, where sank the ship,
The boat spun round and round."

"'Ha! ha!' quoth he, 'full plain I see,
The Devil knows how to row.'"

Upon the whirl, where sank the ship,
The boat spun round and round;
And all was still, save that the hill
Was telling of the sound.

I moved my lips—the Pilot shrieked
And fell down in a fit;
The holy Hermit raised his eyes,
And prayed where he did sit.

I took the oars: the Pilot's boy,
Who now doth crazy go,
Laughed loud and long, and all the while
His eyes went to and fro.
"Ha! ha!" quoth he, "full plain I see,
The Devil knows how to row."

And now, all in my own countree,
I stood on the firm land!
The Hermit stepped forth from the boat,
And scarcely he could stand.

"O shrieve me, shrieve me, holy man!"
The Hermit crossed° his brow.
"Say quick," quoth he, "I bid thee say—
What manner of man art thou?"

Forthwith° this frame of mine was wrenched
With a woeful agony,
Which forced me to begin my tale;
And then it left me free.

Since then, at an uncertain hour,
That agony returns:
And till my ghastly tale is told,
This heart within me burns.

I pass, like night, from land to land;
I have strange power of speech;
That moment that his face I see,
I know the man that must hear me:
To him my tale I teach.

What loud uproar bursts from that door!
The wedding guests are there:
But in the garden bower the bride
And bridemaids singing are:
And hark the little vesper bell,
Which biddeth me to prayer!

O Wedding Guest! this soul hath been
Alone on a wide wide sea:
So lonely 'twas, that God himself
Scarce seemed there to be.

O sweeter than the marriage feast,
'Tis sweeter far to me,
To walk together to the kirk
With a goodly company!—

To walk together to the kirk,
And all together pray,
While each to his great Father bends,
Old men, and babes, and loving friends
And youths and maidens gay!

Vocabulary

wrenched (rencht) *v.:* anguished; grief-stricken.

The ancient Mariner earnestly entreateth the Hermit to shrieve him; and the penance of life falls on him.

575. crossed *v.:* made the sign of the cross.

578. forthwith *adv.:* at once.

And ever and anon throughout his future life an agony constraineth him to travel from land to land;

Farewell, farewell! but this I tell
To thee, thou Wedding Guest!
He prayeth well, who loveth well
Both man and bird and beast.

He prayeth best, who loveth best
All things both great and small;
For the dear God who loveth us,
He made and loveth all.

The Mariner, whose eye is bright,
Whose beard with age is hoar,
Is gone: and now the Wedding Guest
Turned from the bridegroom's door.

He went like one that hath been stunned,
And is of sense forlorn:°
A sadder and a wiser man,
He rose the morrow morn.

And to teach, by his own example, love and reverence to all things that God made and loveth.

623. forlorn *v.:* deprived.

"The Mariner, whose eye is bright,
Whose beard with age is hoar,
Is gone."

PRIMARY SOURCE / LETTER

Joseph Cottle was a close friend of Coleridge and the first publisher of Lyrical Ballads.

Coleridge Describes His Addiction

To Joseph Cottle

April 26, 1814

You have poured oil in the raw and festering wound of an old friend's conscience, Cottle! but it is *oil of vitriol!* I but barely glanced at the middle of the first page of your letter, and have seen no more of it—not from resentment, God forbid! but from the state of my bodily and mental sufferings, that scarcely permitted human fortitude to let in a new visitor of affliction.

The object of my present reply is to state the case just as it is—first, that for ten years the anguish of my spirit has been indescribable, the sense of my danger staring, but the conscience of my GUILT worse, far worse than all! I have prayed with drops of agony on my brow, trembling not only before the justice of my Maker, but even before the mercy of my Redeemer. "I gave thee so many talents. What hast thou done with them?" Secondly, overwhelmed as I am with the sense of my direful infirmity, I have never attempted to disguise or conceal the cause. On the contrary, not only to friends have I stated the whole case with tears, and the very bitterness of shame; but in two instances, I have warned young men, mere acquaintances, who had spoken of having taken laudanum, of the direful consequences, by an ample exposition of its tremendous effects on myself.

Thirdly, though before God I cannot lift up my eyelids, and only do not despair of his mercy, because to despair would be adding crime to crime, yet to my fellow men I may say, that I was seduced into the ACCURSED habit ignorantly. I had been almost bedridden for many months with swelling in the knees. In a medical journal I unhappily met with an account of a cure performed in a similar case, or what appeared to me so, by rubbing in of laudanum, at the same time taking a given dose internally. It acted like a charm, like a miracle! I recovered the use of my limbs, of my appetite, of my spirits, and this continued for near a fortnight. At length, the unusual stimulus subsided, the complaint returned—the supposed remedy was recurred to—but I cannot go through the dreary history. Suffice it to say, that effects were produced, which acted on me by terror and cowardice of PAIN and sudden death, not (so help me God!) by any temptation of pleasure, or expectation, or desire of exciting pleasurable sensations. On the very contrary, Mrs. Morgan and her sister will bear witness so far, as to say that the longer I abstained, the higher my spirits were, the keener my enjoyments—till the moment, the direful moment arrived, when my pulse began to fluctuate, my heart to palpitate, and such a dreadful falling abroad, as it were, of my whole frame, such intolerable restlessness and incipient bewilderment, that in the last of my several attempts to abandon the dire poison, I exclaimed in agony, what I now repeat in seriousness and solemnity, "I am too poor to hazard this!" Had I but a few hundred pounds, but £200, half to send to Mrs. Coleridge, and half to place myself in a private madhouse, where I could procure nothing but what a physician thought proper, and where a medical attendant could be constantly with me for two or three months (in less than that time, life or death would be determined) then there might be hope. Now there is none! O God! how willing would I place myself under Dr. Fox in his establishment; for my case is a species of madness, only that it is a derangement, an utter impotence of the volition, and not of the intellectual faculties. You bid me rouse myself: go, bid a man paralytic in both arms to rub them briskly together, and that will cure him. "Alas," he would reply, "that I cannot move my arms is my complaint and my misery."

Your affectionate, but most afflicted,

S. T. Coleridge

INFORMATIONAL TEXT

In this passage from his classic travel book, the writer Bruce Chatwin (1940–1989) tells a chilling story. Before this excerpt opens, Chatwin has said: "Albatrosses and penguins are the last birds I'd want to murder." He had been describing the penguin colony in Patagonia, on the south coast of Argentina. Now he flashes back to 1593.

from In Patagonia

Bruce Chatwin

On October 30, 1593, the ship *Desire,* of 120 tons, limping home to England, dropped anchor in the river at Port Desire, this being her fourth visit since Thomas Cavendish named the place in her, his flagship's, honor, seven years before.

The captain was now John Davis, a Devon man, the most skilled navigator of his generation. Behind him were three Arctic voyages in search of the Northwest Passage. Before him were two books of seamanship and six fatal cuts of a Japanese pirate's sword.

Davis had sailed on Cavendish's Second Voyage "intended for the South Sea." The fleet left Plymouth on August 26, 1591, the Captain-General in the galleon *Leicester;* the other ships were the *Roebuck,* the *Desire,* the *Daintie,* and the *Black Pinnace.* . . .

Cavendish was puffed up with early success, hating his officers and crew. On the coast of Brazil, he stopped to sack the town of Santos. A gale scattered the ships off the Patagonian coast, but they met up, as arranged, at Port Desire.

The fleet entered the Magellan Strait with the southern winter already begun. A sailor's frostbitten nose fell off when he blew it. Beyond Cape Froward, they ran into northwesterly gales and sheltered in a tight cove with the wind howling over their mastheads. Reluctantly, Cavendish agreed to revictual in Brazil and return the following spring.

On the night of May 20, off Port Desire, the Captain-General changed tack without warning. At dawn, the *Desire* and the *Black Pinnace* were alone on the sea. Davis made for port, thinking his commander would join him as before, but Cavendish set course for Brazil and thence to St. Helena. One day he lay down in his cabin and died, perhaps of apoplexy, cursing Davis for desertion: "This villain that hath been the death of me."

Davis disliked the man but was no traitor. The worst of the winter over, he went south again to look for the Captain-General. Gales blew the two ships in among some undiscovered islands, now known as the Falklands.

This time, they passed the Strait and out into the Pacific. In a storm off Cape Pilar, the *Desire* lost the *Pinnace,* which went down with all hands. Davis was alone at the helm, praying for a speedy end, when the sun broke through the clouds. He took bearings, fixed his position, and so regained the calmer water of the Strait.

He sailed back to Port Desire, the crew scurvied and mutinous and lice lying in their flesh, "clusters of lice as big as peason, yea, and some as big as beans." He repaired the ship as best he could. The men lived off eggs, gulls, baby seals, scurvy grass, and the fish called *pejerrey.* On this diet they were restored to health.

Ten miles down the coast, there was an island, the original Penguin Island, where the sailors clubbed twenty thousand birds to death. They had no natural enemies and were unafraid of their murderers. John Davis ordered the penguins dried and salted and stowed fourteen thousand in the hold. . . .

As they came up to the Equator, the penguins took their revenge. In them bred a "loathsome worme" about an inch long. The worms ate everything, iron only excepted—clothes, bedding, boots, hats, leather lashings, and live human flesh. The worms gnawed through the ship's side and threatened to sink her. The more worms the men killed, the more they multiplied.

Around the Tropic of Cancer, the crew came down with scurvy. Their ankles swelled and their chests, and their parts swelled so horribly that "they could neither stand nor lie nor go."

The Captain could scarcely speak for sorrow. Again he prayed for a speedy end. He asked the men to be patient; to give thanks to God and accept his chastisement. But the men were raging mad, and the ship howled with the groans and curses of the dying. Only Davis and a ship's boy were in health, of the seventy-six who left Plymouth. By the end there were five men who could move and work the ship.

And so, lost and wandering on the sea, with topsails and spritsails torn, the rotten hulk drifted, rather than sailed, into the harbor of Berehaven on Bantry Bay on June 11, 1593. The smell disgusted the people of that quiet fishing village. . . .

"The Southern Voyage of John Davis" appeared in Hakluyt's edition of 1600. Two centuries passed and another Devon man, Samuel Taylor Coleridge, set down the 625 controversial lines of *The Ancient Mariner,* with its hammering repetitions and story of crime, wandering, and expiation.

John Davis and the Mariner have these in common: a voyage to the Black South, the murder of a bird or birds, the nemesis which follows, the drift through the tropics, the rotting ship, the curses of dying men. Lines 236–239 are particularly resonant of the Elizabethan voyage:

The many men, so beautiful!
And they all dead did lie:
And a thousand thousand slimy things
Lived on; and so did I.

In *The Road to Xanadu,* the American scholar John Livingston Lowes traced the Mariner's victim to a "disconsolate Black Albitross" shot by one Hatley, the mate of Captain George Shelvocke's privateer in the eighteenth century. Wordsworth had a copy of this voyage and showed it to Coleridge when the two men tried to write the poem together. . . .

Lowes demonstrated how the voyages in Hakluyt and Purchas fueled Coleridge's imagination. "The mighty great roaring of ice" that John Davis witnessed on an earlier voyage off Greenland reappears in line 61: "It cracked and growled, and roared and howled." But he did not, apparently, consider the likelihood that Davis's voyage to the Strait gave Coleridge the backbone for his poem.

(Above) Engraving (1875) by Gustave Doré for Coleridge's *The Rime of the Ancient Mariner.*

Response and Analysis

Reading Check

1. Use a time line to summarize the **main events** of the Mariner's story. Here are the first and final events:

   The ancient Mariner stops the Wedding Guest and begins to tell his story.

   ↓

   The Wedding Guest leaves sadder and wiser.

2. Who is the **narrator** of the ballad? To whom is he telling his story?
3. In Part II, what consequences result from the Mariner's killing of the albatross?
4. In Part IV, why is the Mariner unable to pray? What happens to change this?
5. At the end of the ballad, how does the Mariner describe his current life?

Thinking Critically

6. Describe in detail the changing mental states of the Mariner in Part IV. Given the circumstances, are these changes believable?
7. Name three effects the Mariner's story has on the Wedding Guest. In your opinion, does each effect seem likely or unlikely? Explain.
8. What is the Mariner's "penance" (lines 408–409)? Does it seem fair to you that he should have to do any sort of penance? Why? (Refer to your Quickwrite notes for ideas.)
9. Explain in your own terms the Mariner's **moral** (lines 612–617). Does the story indicate that he ought to have added something to his moral conclusion? Explain.
10. This ballad is famous for its use of vivid **figurative language** and memorable sound devices. Find in the poem a striking example of each of the following: **simile, metaphor, personification, alliteration, assonance,** and **internal rhyme.**

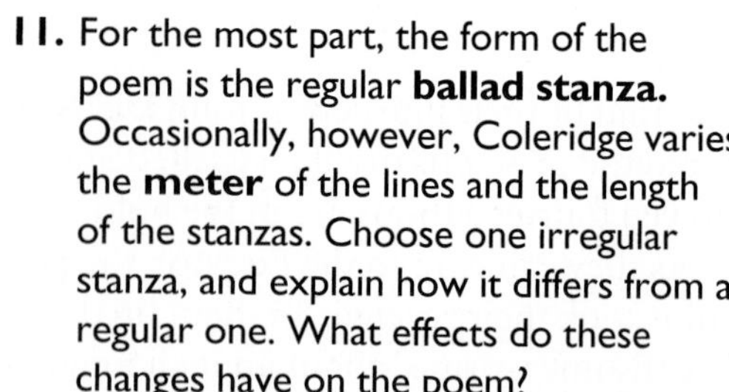

11. For the most part, the form of the poem is the regular **ballad stanza.** Occasionally, however, Coleridge varies the **meter** of the lines and the length of the stanzas. Choose one irregular stanza, and explain how it differs from a regular one. What effects do these changes have on the poem?
12. What similarities and differences do you notice between Coleridge's tale of the ancient Mariner and the story described in the excerpt from Bruce Chatwin's *In Patagonia*? (See the ***Connection*** on page 788.)
13. Compare the Mariner's experiences to those of Coleridge as described in his letter to Joseph Cottle. (See the ***Primary Source*** on page 787.) What is the source of each man's guilt? What other states of mind or body do the two men share? What similar actions do they take?
14. Sometimes the archaic meaning of a word gives us a clue to the history of a word in current use. Look at the use of the word *jargoning* in line 362, for example. What does the word *jargon* mean today? What other examples of archaic words that are still in use today can you find? You might want to consult your reading notes.
15. There was a time in American history when almost every schoolchild could recite parts of *The Rime of the Ancient Mariner.* Find some stanzas that strike you as particularly quotable. What situations in contemporary life could you apply the lines to?

Extending and Evaluating

16. What do you think of Coleridge's sidenotes to the poem? Do you think reading them alters the meaning of the poem? Should they be consulted in a careful reading of the poem? Explain why or why not.

Pages 790–791 cover

Literary Skills Analyze the characteristics of a literary ballad.

Reading Skills Analyze archaic words.

Writing Skills Write an essay analyzing a ballad.

Listening and Speaking Skills Give an oral presentation of a ballad.

Vocabulary Skills Understand word analogies.

Literary Criticism

17. Coleridge once said that he would have preferred to write *The Rime of the Ancient Mariner* as a work of "pure imagination." He believed that it had "too much" of a moral, and that the moral was stated too openly. Do you agree or disagree with Coleridge about the message in his poem? Explain.

WRITING

Left Unsaid

Like many traditional ballads, this strange story of the ancient Mariner leaves some questions unanswered. For example, how could the Mariner tell that the Wedding Guest was a fit audience for his tale? Why did the Mariner shoot the albatross? How can the Mariner's punishment be regarded as fitting his crime? In a brief **essay, analyze** these or other questions that you think are unsatisfactorily resolved in the ballad. Suggest possible reasons for Coleridge's omission of the information.

Is It an Allegory?

An **allegory** is a narrative in which the characters, settings, and actions are symbolic: that is, they have both a literal and a figurative meaning. Could Coleridge's ballad have both a literal and an allegorical meaning? If so, what do the various elements in the ballad symbolize? What meaning would the tale have on an allegorical level? In a brief **essay, analyze** the ballad as an allegory. Be sure to consider the meaning of:

- the ancient Mariner
- the wedding
- the ship
- the albatross
- the sailors
- the moral lesson

LISTENING AND SPEAKING

The Mariner Live

Prepare for an **oral presentation** of this mysterious ballad. Before you start rehearsing, you will have to determine how many speakers you will need. The ballad is long and you might want to present a shortened form of the story. If so, be careful in deciding which scenes you will omit. You will have to keep key events so that the narrative makes sense to your audience. Decide how you will place your speakers on the stage. Will each speaker stand before a podium? Or will they sit on chairs or stools?

Vocabulary Development

Analogies

tyrannous *abated*
dismal *wrenched*
ghastly

On a separate sheet of paper, write the Vocabulary word from above that best completes each analogy.

1. JOYFUL : GLAD :: ___________ : gloomy
2. LEARNED : SCHOLAR :: ___________ : dictator
3. GATHERED : COLLECTED :: ___________ : lessened
4. DEPRESSED : ECSTATIC :: ___________ : unaffected
5. HOSTILE : UNFRIENDLY :: ___________ : ghostly

Vocabulary Development

Using Context Clues

Sometimes you can determine the meaning of an unfamiliar word by looking for clues in the **context**—the surrounding words, phrases, and sentences. Below are some of the most useful types of context clues.

Restatement. A difficult word might be rephrased in more accessible language. Restatements may be signaled by specific words or phrases: *that is, or, in other words.* Look at punctuation—dashes and parentheses also serve as signals. Often a restatement will be an **appositive** set off by commas or an item in a series.

> Coleridge compares the sails on the ship to gossameres, or filmy cobwebs.

The word *gossameres* is defined in the sentence by the appositive *filmy cobwebs.*

Comparison. Compare an unfamiliar word with familiar words that surround it. Sometimes specific words and phrases may also signal a comparison context clue: *like, as, similar to.*

> And now the STORM-BLAST came, and he
> Was tyrannous and strong:
> He struck with his o'ertaking wings,
> And chased us south along.
> —from *The Rime of the Ancient Mariner*

Note all of the underlined words having to do with power. *Tyrannous* means "harsh; oppressive."

Contrast. An opposition might be set up. Certain key words and phrases signal a contrast context clue: *but, not, although, however, instead, on the other hand.*

> The sailors wanted desperately to quench their thirst; instead, they died with throats unslaked.

Unslaked, which is contrasted with "quenching thirst," means "unrelieved of thirst."

Synonym. You might find a word nearby that has the same or nearly the same meaning as the unknown word.

> The sailors averred that the Mariner had sinned, asserting that killing the albatross would bring trouble.

Assert is a synonym for *aver,* "to claim."

Example. Sometimes the text provides an example. Certain words and phrases help you spot example context clues: *such as, including, especially, namely.*

> For his sin, the ancient Mariner does not perform common acts of penance such as prayer, fasting, and giving to the poor.

Prayer, fasting, and *giving to the poor* are all examples of types of *penance*—acts done in repentance for a sin or wrongdoing.

PRACTICE

Use context clues to help you determine the meaning of each boldface word.

1. **Lugubrious** tales such as *The Rime of the Ancient Mariner* appeal to readers despite their mournful tone.
2. The Ancient Mariner and his shipmates at first believed that the Albatross was a sign of good fortune, but the bird turned out to be a **harbinger** of doom.
3. The only way the Mariner could **allay,** or relieve, his agony was to tell his tale.
4. The joy of the wedding contrasts with the Mariner's **woeful** tale.
5. After a long time at sea, sailors returning home may find their legs shaky when they first walk on **terra firma.**

SKILLS FOCUS

Vocabulary Skills
Use context clues.

George Gordon, Lord Byron

(1788–1824)

Byron, Sixth Baron (detail) (late 18th to early 19th century) by Richard Westall.

Until one fateful day in 1794, George Gordon Byron seemed destined to grow up confined by the harsh Calvinism of Scotland. On that day, Byron's cousin was killed in battle and young George became first in line to be the sixth Baron Byron of Rochdale. Byron assumed the title when he was ten years old.

Byron's literary elevation came no less suddenly. In 1812, the midpoint of the Romantic period, Byron became a celebrity with the publication of the first two cantos of a poem called *Childe Harold's Pilgrimage,* based on his recent travels to Europe and Asia Minor. Byron "awoke one morning," as he later said, "and found myself famous."

Like his father (a sea captain, a psychopath, and a spender of women's fortunes), Byron was a larger-than-life figure. He seems to have had an obsessive determination to prove himself in every way. Extraordinarily handsome, he was born with a clubfoot, and in compensation he learned swimming, boxing, and horse riding. His lifestyle aggravated a glandular problem and a tendency toward obesity, so he would periodically go on brutal diets.

The shocking aspects of Byron's private life have become legendary as a result of his literary fame, not the reverse. But they are shocking, nevertheless—and sometimes rather sad. Scandal concerning his sexual affairs (including a relationship with his half sister Augusta), his scandalous separation from his wife, and his radical, pro-French political views made life in England uncomfortable. Byron left for the Continent in 1816, never to return.

Byron's literary career had begun modestly in 1807 with a small collection of short lyric pieces that was harshly reviewed by the *Edinburgh Review.* In response, Byron wrote the satire *English Bards and Scotch Reviewers* (1809), which reveals the vein of wit that helped cast Byron as a rebellious mocker of established conventions. His target in this satire is not only the *Edinburgh Review;* he also takes on such Romantic icons as Wordsworth and Coleridge.

When Byron left England in 1816, he was drawn into contact with Percy Shelley and his wife, Mary, in Switzerland. Because of the association with Shelley, Byron's writing life now began in earnest. It intensified when he moved to Italy. The Byron we glimpse in these years, despite the debauchery and the circuslike menagerie he kept about him in Venice, is a man who works very hard at his writing. His wildness and aristocratic ease obscure what was, in fact, a period of great literary productivity.

As a poet, Byron was not a Romantic in style. His masters, in fact, were the neoclassical writers whose wit and precision he admired. Yet throughout the nineteenth century, he was regarded as the incarnation of "Romantic." His premature death seemed to reinforce this image. Byron set sail for Greece in July 1823 to support the Greek nationalists in their struggle for independence from Turkey. In a marshy town in Greece called Missolonghi, he came down with fevers that took his life only a few months after his thirty-sixth birthday.

Before You Read

She Walks in Beauty

Make the Connection

No matter how often we hear that beauty is only skin deep, we all know the undeniable allure of an extremely good-looking person. Beauty moves us. Often, we want to believe that outer appearances express inner qualities of goodness and beauty of character as well. Can a person's inward nature be accurately judged by his or her outward appearance?

Literary Focus

Simile

A **simile** is a figure of speech that makes an imaginative comparison between two seemingly unlike things by using a connective word such as *like, as, than,* or *resembles.* "He's as helpful as a doorknob on a bathtub" and "she plays flute better than the Pied Piper" are examples of similes. An **extended simile** continues the terms of the comparison as far as the writer wants to take it.

A **simile** is a figure of speech that makes a comparison between two seemingly unlike things by using a connective word such as *like, as, than,* or *resembles.*

For more on Simile, see the Handbook of Literary and Historical Terms.

Background

"She Walks in Beauty," one of Byron's most famous poems, was supposedly inspired by Lady Wilmot Horton, a beautiful woman whom Byron saw at a ball, perhaps in the spring of 1814. Lady Horton was in mourning and, in the fashion of the times, was wearing a black dress decorated with glittering spangles.

Miranda (1878) by Sir Frank Dicksee.
The Maas Gallery, London.

Literary Skills Understand simile.

She Walks in Beauty

George Gordon, Lord Byron

She walks in beauty, like the night
Of cloudless climes° and starry skies;
And all that's best of dark and bright
Meet in her aspect° and her eyes:
Thus mellowed to that tender light
Which heaven to gaudy day denies.

One shade the more, one ray the less,
Had half impaired the nameless grace
Which waves in every raven tress,
Or softly lightens o'er her face;
Where thoughts serenely sweet express
How pure, how dear their dwelling place.

And on that cheek, and o'er that brow,
So soft, so calm, yet eloquent,
The smiles that win, the tints that glow,
But tell of days in goodness spent,
A mind at peace with all below,
A heart whose love is innocent!

2. **climes** *n. pl.:* atmospheres; climates.

4. **aspect** *n.:* face; look.

Response and Analysis

Thinking Critically

1. What is the basic **simile** the speaker develops in the first stanza of the poem? What emotions does this simile evoke?
2. The words "dark and bright" in line 3 suggest a balance of opposites. How is this idea developed?
3. In line 6, what does the speaker imply about daytime when he calls it "gaudy"?
4. In stanzas 2 and 3, what conclusions does the speaker draw about the woman's character and personality?
5. What do you think the speaker means by "below" in line 17? Support your conclusion with evidence from the poem as a whole.

Extending and Evaluating

6. This poem has been criticized as sentimental and dependent on clichés. Which comparisons or conclusions might such critics have in mind? Do you agree? Why or why not?

WRITING

Only Skin Deep?

Imagine that the dark beauty described by Byron reads this poem and discovers that it was written about her. Write a letter from the woman to Byron, expressing what you think of the poem's portrayal of you. Are you flattered? embarrassed? outraged? Do you think the poem reveals the "real you"? In your response, quote specific lines from Byron's poem and respond to them. You may write your letter in the form of a poem.

Literary Skills
Analyze simile.

Writing Skills
Write a letter responding to a poem.

Before You Read

from Childe Harold's Pilgrimage

Make the Connection

A quest may have a goal, but if the journey is long enough, the traveler may discover that the prize lies in the quest itself. What is explored, all alone on a journey, is the inner self. That may be true even when the pilgrim, like Byron's Childe Harold, cuts a spirited path through exotic lands. It is especially true when the pilgrim wanders, alone, in the vastness of glorious—but heartless—nature.

Literary Focus

Apostrophe

Apostrophe (ə·päs′trə·fē) is a figure of speech in which a speaker directly addresses an absent or dead person, an abstract quality, or something nonhuman as if it were present and capable of responding. Apostrophe was a popular device among the Romantic poets. Shelley, for example, apostrophizes the west wind (see page 806); Keats apostrophizes a nightingale and a Grecian urn (see pages 831, 836); and in this poem Byron apostrophizes the ocean.

Apostrophe is a figure of speech in which a speaker directly addresses an absent or dead person, an abstract quality, or something nonhuman as if it were present and capable of responding.

For more on Apostrophe, see the Handbook of Literary and Historical Terms.

Literary Skills Understand apostrophe.

Reading Skills Understand rhyme and rhythm.

Reading Skills 

Reading Rhyme and Rhythm

In *Childe Harold's Pilgrimage,* Byron uses the **Spenserian stanza:** a tremendous undertaking of rhyme and rhythm invented by the Renaissance poet Edmund Spenser (c.1552–1599) for his epic poem *The Faerie Queene.* The Romantic poets Byron, Shelley, and Keats all employed this challenging verse form. It uses only three different end rhymes in each nine-line stanza for a rhyme scheme of *ababbcbcc.* The first eight lines of each stanza are written in **iambic pentameter,** and the ninth line adds a poetic foot to create an **alexandrine**—that is, a line of **iambic hexameter.** The alexandrine often sums up a stanza or finishes it off with a striking image. Punctuation serves as a guide for reading the poem aloud, with sentences often running over the end of a line. But each end rhyme should still be lightly emphasized to enhance the effect of the poem. As you read, watch also for the ways Byron uses the alexandrine to bring each stanza to a satisfying conclusion.

Background

In medieval times, *childe* likely meant a young noble awaiting knighthood; Byron uses it as a title, like Lord or Sir, for a youth of "gentle" birth. *Childe Harold's Pilgrimage* is a long, thinly disguised autobiographical poem about Byron's own journeys. Appearing from 1812 to 1818 in sections called cantos, it made Byron suddenly famous. The poem's pilgrim, Childe Harold, became the prototype for the moody, dashingly handsome character type who would eventually be dubbed the Byronic hero. In this excerpt from the final canto, the speaker addresses the ocean. The last two stanzas present Byron's personal conclusion to the whole poem. By this time, Byron said, he had ceased trying to separate himself from the figure of Childe Harold.

Wreckers off the Brittany Coast (1911) by Georges P. C. Maroniez.
Bonhams, London.

from Childe Harold's Pilgrimage, Canto IV

George Gordon, Lord Byron

1

There is a pleasure in the pathless woods,
There is a rapture on the lonely shore,
There is society, where none intrudes,
By the deep sea, and music in its roar:
I love not man the less, but Nature more,
From these our interviews, in which I steal°
From all I may be, or have been before,
To mingle with the Universe, and feel
What I can ne'er express, yet cannot all conceal.

6. **steal** *v.:* remove myself.

2

Roll on, thou deep and dark blue Ocean—roll!
Ten thousand fleets sweep over thee in vain;
Man marks the earth with ruin—his control
Stops with the shore; upon the watery plain
The wrecks are all thy deed, nor doth remain
A shadow of man's ravage, save his own,
When, for a moment, like a drop of rain,
He sinks into thy depths with bubbling groan,
Without a grave, unknelled,° uncoffined, and unknown.

18. unknelled (un·neld′) *v.* used as *adj.:* without the traditional ringing of a church bell to announce his death.

3

And I have loved thee, Ocean! and my joy
Of youthful sports was on thy breast to be
Borne, like thy bubbles, onward: From a boy
I wantoned° with thy breakers—they to me
Were a delight; and if the freshening° sea
Made them a terror—'twas a pleasing fear,
For I was as it were a child of thee,
And trusted to thy billows far and near,
And laid my hand upon thy mane—as I do here.

22. wantoned *v.* frolicked; played happily.

23. freshening *v.* used as *adj.:* becoming rough as the wind comes up.

4

My task is done, my song hath ceased, my theme
Has died into an echo; it is fit
The spell should break of this protracted dream.
The torch shall be extinguished which hath lit
My midnight lamp—and what is writ, is writ;
Would it were worthier! but I am not now
That which I have been—and my visions flit
Less palpably° before me—and the glow
Which in my spirit dwelt is fluttering, faint, and low.

35. palpably *adv.:* clearly.

5

Farewell! a word that must be, and hath been—
A sound which makes us linger;—yet—farewell!
Ye! who have traced the Pilgrim to the scene
Which is his last, if in your memories dwell
A thought which once was his, if on ye swell
A single recollection, not in vain
He wore his sandal shoon and scallop shell;°
Farewell! with *him* alone may rest the pain,
If such there were—with *you,* the moral of his strain.°

43. sandal shoon . . . shell: *Shoon* is archaic for "shoes." Sandals and a scallop shell worn on a hat were traditional emblems of pilgrims. The scallop shell is a symbol of Saint James, whose shrine in Spain was a great attraction to pilgrims.

45. strain *n.:* passage of poetry or song.

An Irresistible Bad Boy: The Byronic Hero

"Mad, bad, and dangerous to know."

—Lady Caroline Lamb, speaking of Byron

"A man proud, moody, cynical, with defiance on his brow, and misery in his heart, a scorner of his kind, implacable in revenge, yet capable of deep and strong affection." This model of reckless, wounded manhood described by Thomas Babington Macaulay (1800–1859) became known as the Byronic hero. Both in his life and in his poetry, George Gordon, Lord Byron (1788–1824) gave his name to a type of hero who was devastatingly attractive yet fatally flawed.

Byron's personal charms and poetic talents offset a physical disability (a clubfoot), which embarrassed him terribly, and the complicated romantic entanglements that made him a social outcast. His heroes, whom he often invited his readers to identify with himself, were also passionate yet flawed individualists: intellectually searching, incapable of compromise, forever brooding over some mysterious past sin, painfully yet defiantly alone.

Heroes for an unheroic age. The immense popularity of the Byronic hero and the Romantic-age celebration of his prototypes—Cain, Faust, Prometheus, and Napoleon—wasn't hard to understand. These were rash rebels, hailed or resurrected in reaction to a neoclassical world in which order and restraint ruled the day. Most of these daring figures, whose ambitions were doomed from the start, also embodied the deep pessimism of early nineteenth-century life.

Byron, Sixth Baron (detail) (1835) by Thomas Phillips.

By Courtesy of the National Portrait Gallery, London.

Marlon Brando in Laslo Benedek's film *The Wild One* (1954).

James Dean in Nicholas Ray's film *Rebel Without a Cause* (1955).

The failure of the French Revolution had dampened idealism throughout Europe. And the labyrinthine restrictions of state, church, and society allowed no suitable outlets for the outsized energy of creative young men like Byron and his fictional heroes.

The American heirs. The model of a sensitive rebel continues to be an engaging one for popular heroes of recent time: In post–World War II America, for example, as society settled into a bland conformity, several searching, sensitive malcontents arrested the attention of moviegoers everywhere.

One version of the Byronic bad boy was played by Marlon Brando, who popularized motorcycles, leather jackets, and a sullen demeanor in the 1954 film *The Wild One*. The leader of a motorcycle gang, Brando is asked, "What are you rebelling against?" His response: "What have you got?" The actor James Dean personified youthful rebellion in both his brief film career and his tragically short life. In *Rebel Without a Cause* (1955), Dean's portrayal of Jim Stark, an alienated character searching for the meaning of manhood, made him a cult hero.

Like all Byronic heroes, these modern characters beckon their admirers to explore personal freedoms and to reject confining conventions. Because this freedom is achieved only by questioning accepted social behavior, these heroes are invariably lonely and misunderstood. And because this freedom often compels them to perform dangerous acts, the lives of these heroes can be much too short. Lord Byron died of a fever at age thirty-six, while fighting for Greek independence. James Dean died in an automobile accident at age twenty-four.

Response and Analysis

Thinking Critically

1. Restate the meaning of stanza 1 in a single sentence. How might the stanza serve as a general comment on the Romantic view of the relationship between human beings and nature?
2. In stanza 2, what does the speaker say man does to earth? What can man do to the sea—or the sea do to him? State the **simile** that expresses the relationship between man and sea.
3. In stanza 3, what **metaphor** compares the sea to a horse? What is the effect of this comparison?
4. What single aspect of the ocean does the speaker repeatedly emphasize?
5. In spite of the ocean's destructive aspects, the speaker professes that he loves it passionately. What does this tell you about his personality?
6. In lines 44 and 45, who are "*him*" and "*you*"? Explain your reasoning.
7. What link does the speaker imply between the pilgrim and himself in the final two stanzas?
8. From this brief excerpt, what would you guess the pilgrim was seeking?
9. Byron's verse form in *Childe Harold's Pilgrimage* is the challenging **Spenserian stanza.** How closely does stanza 2 adhere to the rhythms and rhyme scheme of that form? What purpose does the alexandrine of the final line fulfill? Refer to your reading notes for help.
10. Is Byron expressing a sensibility associated solely with the Romantic period, or do people today still identify with nature and experience moments of joy in its presence? Explain.

WRITING

Speaking to Nature

In stanzas 2 and 3 of this excerpt from *Childe Harold,* the speaker uses an **apostrophe** to address the sea. Write a prose apostrophe, or address, to some element of nature—sea, wind, fire, snow, thunderstorm, hail. Use stanzas 2 and 3 as a model for your address.

Literary Skills Analyze apostrophe.

Reading Skills Analyze rhyme and rhythm.

Writing Skills Write a prose apostrophe.

The Junction of the Thames and the Medway (1807) by Joseph Mallord William Turner. Oil on canvas.

Widener Collection (1942.9.87). Image © 2007 Board of Trustees, National Gallery of Art, Washington.

Percy Bysshe Shelley

(1792–1822)

When young Percy Shelley arrived at Oxford in 1810, his father introduced him to that bookish town's most important bookseller: "My son here," he said, "has a literary turn; he's already an author . . . do pray indulge him in his printing freaks." By spring, one of those "freaks"—an unsigned pamphlet on atheism—got Percy expelled and started a lifelong quarrel with his father. It was the first of many upheavals in the short, ill-fated life of an "author" who followed his "literary turn" wherever it led.

At nineteen, already estranged from his family, Shelley embarked on a career of courting the unconventional. To "rescue" her from a tyrannical father, he eloped with sixteen-year-old Harriet Westbrook, a classmate of his sisters'. Three years later he abandoned Harriet and ran away with seventeen-year-old Mary Godwin, the daughter of two of the most important radicals of the 1790s, Mary Wollstonecraft and William Godwin. Percy's alliance with Mary also involved responsibility for Mary's fifteen-year-old stepsister, Jane Clairmont (she soon changed her name to Claire), who accompanied the pair on their elopement to Switzerland. Claire's brief affair with Byron brought Shelley and Byron together in Switzerland in 1816 in one of the age's most important literary relationships.

Shortly after their return to England after a second trip to Switzerland, Mary's older half sister, Fanny, committed suicide. Then Harriet, only twenty-one, drowned herself in a pond in London's Hyde Park. Percy was now free to wed Mary, but was denied custody of his two children with Harriet.

Shelley Composing Prometheus Unbound (detail) (1845) by Joseph Severn.

Keats-Shelley Memorial House, Rome.

Shelley and Mary fled their debts and notoriety in England and returned to the Continent. The next four years were Shelley's most productive, with one inspired work following another.

In 1822, when he was not yet even thirty, Shelley and a companion, Edward Williams, drowned when their sailing boat, the *Ariel,* sank in a storm off the northwestern coast of Italy. Almost two weeks later, Shelley's body washed ashore, a copy of Sophocles in one pocket and of Keats in the other. The body was burned in a pyre on the beach while friends (including Byron) stood by, and Shelley's ashes were buried in the Protestant cemetery in Rome.

It is said that the Italian sailors who encountered Shelley's boat in the storm on July 8, 1822, offered in vain to take Shelley and Williams on board. When this offer was refused, the sailors pleaded with the Englishmen to furl their sails. As Williams tried to do so, Shelley seized his arm and stopped him. We must certainly regret Shelley's untimely death, but at the same time, we can't help but wonder at his power to capture, and be captured by, the great dark forces that so fascinated him.

Before You Read

Ozymandias

Make the Connection

Quickwrite

All human beings and all human beauty must perish, but can't our works survive us? We pass away, but isn't what we leave behind proof that our passage through life mattered? Like the poets of another restless age, the Renaissance, the Romantic poets posed these questions. How would you answer them? Jot down some thoughts about whether—and how—human beings can achieve immortality through their words and their works.

Literary Focus

Irony

Irony is a discrepancy between expectations and reality. This poem turns on a kind of irony called **situational irony,** which is created when the opposite of an expected event or outcome occurs. Even though "Ozymandias" is a short poem, several characters appear in its lines. Which of these characters expects one thing to happen, only to find that something else comes to pass? What might this ironic outcome have to do with Shelley's poem in particular, and with works of art in general?

Literary Skills Understand irony and situational irony.

Irony occurs when what actually happens is the opposite of what is expected or appropriate.

For more on Irony, see the Handbook of Literary and Historical Terms.

INTERNET

More About Percy Bysshe Shelley

Keyword: LE7 12-5

Background

Shelley wrote relatively few sonnets, and this one is certainly among his best. It is all the more interesting because it was written as part of a friendly and informal poetry competition in 1817. The poetic topic was Egypt, inspired by some extraordinary Egyptian fragments recently displayed at the British Museum in London. Some of these fragments were from the empire of Ramses II (ruled c. 1290–1224 B.C.) who left monuments all over Egypt, including the temples of Karnak and Luxor. Ozymandias is the Greek name for Ramses II. The Great Hall at Karnak is the greatest colonnaded hall ever constructed. It was so huge that one hundred men could stand on the capital of each column.

Ozymandias

Percy Bysshe Shelley

I met a traveler from an antique land
Who said: Two vast and trunkless legs° of stone
Stand in the desert . . . Near them, on the sand,
Half sunk, a shattered visage° lies, whose frown,
And wrinkled lip, and sneer of cold command,
Tell that its sculptor well those passions read
Which yet survive, stamped on these lifeless things,
The hand that mocked them, and the heart° that fed;
And on the pedestal these words appear:
"My name is Ozymandias, king of kings,
Look on my works, ye Mighty, and despair!"
Nothing beside remains. Round the decay
Of that colossal wreck, boundless and bare
The lone and level sands stretch far away.

2. trunkless legs: that is, the legs without the rest of the body.
4. visage *n.:* face.

8. hand . . . heart: the hand of the sculptor who, with his art, derided the passions to which Ozymandias gave himself wholeheartedly.

Fragments of the Great Colossus of Memnonium, Thebes, from *Egypt and Nubia,* Vol. I (19th century) by David Roberts. Color lithograph.

Stapleton Collection, United Kingdom. The Bridgeman Art Library.

Response and Analysis

Thinking Critically

1. Even in the brief space of a sonnet, Shelley suggests a number of narrative frames. How many **speakers** do you hear in this poem? Summarize what each one says.
2. **Irony** is a discrepancy between expectations and reality. What did Ozymandias expect people to see when they looked at his "works"? What do they actually see?
3. Discuss your understanding of the poem's message about pride.
4. According to the poem, what was the sculptor's attitude toward the subject of his artwork?
5. What contemporary political figures who wield great power could this poem apply to? (Be sure to check your Quick-write notes.)

WRITING

"So long lives this . . . ?"

In a brief **essay, compare and contrast** the message of "Ozymandias" with the message of Shakespeare's Sonnet 18 (see page 313). What does each sonnet say about the lasting power of art? Which sonnet do you agree with, and why?

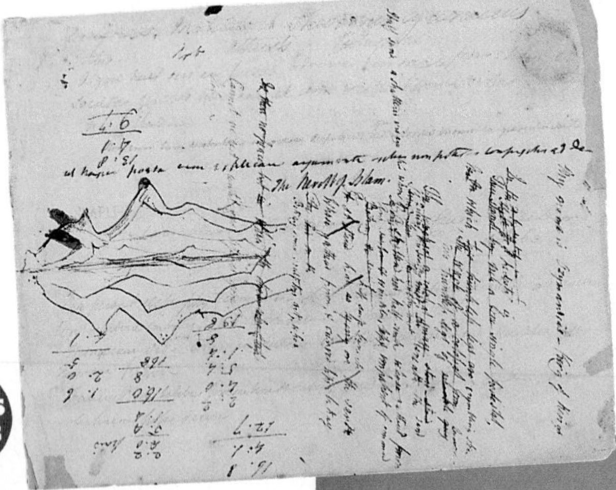

SKILLS FOCUS

Literary Skills Analyze irony and situational irony.

Writing Skills Write an essay comparing and contrasting two poems.

(Above) Manuscript page from "Ozymandias" by Percy Bysshe Shelley.

MS. Shelley e. 4, fol. 85. The Bodleian Library, Oxford.

(Right) The Colossus of Ramses II, with his daughter Benta Anta in front of his legs, from the Great Temple of Amun (c. 1320–1200 B.C.).

Karnak, Egypt. The Bridgeman Art Library.

INTERNET

Projects and Activities

Keyword: LE7 12-5

Before You Read

Ode to the West Wind

Make the Connection

Quickwrite

The faces of nature range from peaceful to terrifying, and the Romantics explored all of them. What attracted the Romantics to nature was the aspect philosophers call the sublime: the wildness, immensity, terror, and awesome grandeur of natural phenomena like the Alps or violent storms. To experience nature's power suddenly—whether by viewing Niagara Falls or by living through a hurricane—is, while terrible, also exhilarating, even transporting. Why do you think people find such displays of power so thrilling? What emotions are evoked? Jot down a few thoughts on this topic, or freewrite about a time when you experienced the sublime in nature.

Windswept Landscape (c. 1870) by Camille Corot.
The Art Archive/Galleria d'Arte Moderna, Milan/Dagli Orti (A).

Literary Focus

Ode

The **ode** was a favorite poetic form among the Romantics. A long, complex poem—usually a meditation on a serious topic—the ode provided the Romantics with a form suited to their introspective, philosophical subject matter. Like many Romantic odes, Shelley's "Ode to the West Wind" looks both outward and inward. It exalts an aspect of nature—the powerful yet invisible wind—and contemplates the movement of unseen forces in the poet's own mind and life.

An **ode** is a complex, generally long lyric poem on a serious subject.

For more on the Ode, see the Handbook of Literary and Historical Terms.

Background

This major lyric, written in late October 1819, was inspired by an oncoming storm near Florence, Italy, where Shelley was living. It marks, in his creative life, a temporary note of exaltation after a period of intense grief over the death of his three-year-old son, William. The ode demands to be read aloud.

Literary Skills
Understand the characteristics of an ode.

INTERNET

More About Percy Bysshe Shelley

Keyword: LE7 12-5

Ode to the West Wind

Percy Bysshe Shelley

I

O wild West Wind, thou breath of Autumn's being,
Thou, from whose unseen presence the leaves dead
Are driven, like ghosts from an enchanter fleeing,

Yellow, and black, and pale, and hectic° red,
Pestilence-stricken multitudes: O thou,
Who chariotest to their dark wintry bed

The winged seeds, where they lie cold and low,
Each like a corpse within its grave, until
Thine azure° sister of the Spring shall blow

Her clarion° o'er the dreaming earth, and fill
(Driving sweet buds like flocks to feed in air)
With living hues and odors plain and hill:

Wild Spirit, which art moving everywhere;
Destroyer and preserver; hear, O, hear!

II

Thou on whose stream, 'mid the steep sky's commotion,
Loose clouds like earth's decaying leaves are shed,
Shook from the tangled boughs of Heaven and Ocean,

Angels of rain and lightning: there are spread
On the blue surface of thine aery° surge,
Like the bright hair uplifted from the head

Of some fierce Maenad,° even from the dim verge
Of the horizon to the zenith's height,
The locks of the approaching storm. Thou dirge°

Of the dying year, to which this closing night
Will be the dome of a vast sepulcher,
Vaulted with all thy congregated might

Of vapors, from whose solid atmosphere
Black rain, and fire, and hail will burst: O, hear!

III

Thou who didst waken from his summer dreams
The blue Mediterranean, where he lay,
Lulled by the coil of his crystalline streams,

4. hectic *adj.:* relating to the feverish flush caused by wasting diseases such as tuberculosis.

1–14. In each of the first three sections, the speaker describes the west wind in several different ways.
? *What two words in lines 13–14 does the poet use to sum up the wind's essential nature? What does the speaker ask the west wind to do?*

9. azure *adj.:* sky-blue.
10. clarion *n.:* type of trumpet.

19. aery *adj.:* archaic for "airy"; unsubstantial; seen only in the mind.
21. Maenad (mē′nad′): in Greek mythology, a woman who performs frenzied dances in the worship of Dionysus, the god of wine.
23. dirge *n.:* slow, solemn poem or song that expresses grief or mourning.

? **28.** *In lines 14 and 28, the speaker talks directly to the wind. What is the effect of his repeated request?*

The Bard (1817) by John Martin.

Laing Art Gallery, Newcastle-upon-Tyne, England (Tyne and Wear Museums).

Beside a pumice° isle in Baiae's bay,°
And saw in sleep old palaces and towers
Quivering within the wave's intenser day,

All overgrown with azure moss and flowers
So sweet, the sense faints picturing them! Thou
For whose path the Atlantic's level powers

Cleave° themselves into chasms, while far below
The sea-blooms and the oozy woods which wear
The sapless foliage of the ocean, know

Thy voice, and suddenly grow gray with fear,
And tremble and despoil° themselves: O, hear!

IV

If I were a dead leaf thou mightest bear;
If I were a swift cloud to fly with thee;
A wave to pant beneath thy power, and share

The impulse of thy strength, only less free
Than thou, O uncontrollable! If even
I were as in my boyhood, and could be

The comrade of thy wanderings over Heaven,
As then, when to outstrip thy skiey° speed
Scarce seemed a vision; I would ne'er have striven

As thus with thee in prayer in my sore need.
Oh, lift me as a wave, a leaf, a cloud!
I fall upon the thorns of life! I bleed!

A heavy weight of hours has chained and bowed
One too like thee: tameless, and swift, and proud.

V

Make me thy lyre,° even as the forest is:
What if my leaves are falling like its own!
The tumult of thy mighty harmonies

Will take from both a deep, autumnal tone,
Sweet though in sadness. Be thou, Spirit fierce,
My spirit! Be thou me, impetuous° one!

Drive my dead thoughts over the universe
Like withered leaves to quicken a new birth!
And, by the incantation of this verse,

Scatter, as from an unextinguished hearth°
Ashes and sparks, my words among mankind!
Be through my lips to unawakened earth

The trumpet of a prophecy! O, Wind,
If Winter comes, can Spring be far behind?

32. pumice *n.:* light, porous volcanic stone. **isle in Baiae's bay:** in the Bay of Naples where pumice is found. These islands were once summer resorts for Roman nobility and, in Shelley's time, were notable for their ruins of ancient villas and monumental baths.

38. cleave *v.:* divide.

42. despoil *v.:* strip.

29–42. In sections I and II, the speaker describes the wind's powerful effect on the elements of earth and sky.
? *What third element is moved by the wind in this section?*

50. skiey *adj.:* like the sky; also, coming from the sky.

? **43–56.** *What direct request does the speaker make to the west wind? In which line is this request uttered?*

57. lyre *n.:* Aeolian (ē·ō′lē·ən) harp, a stringed instrument that emits sound when the wind blows across its strings.
62. impetuous *adj.:* forceful; rushing.
66. unextinguished hearth: from Shelley's "A Defense of Poetry": "The mind in creation is as a fading coal, which some invisible influence, like an inconstant wind, awakens to transitory brightness. . . ."

? **57–70.** *In your own words, describe what the speaker desires. How would you explain the meaning of the famous final line of the poem?*

CRITICAL COMMENT

Shelley and the Ode

INFORMATIONAL TEXT

This ode is both an expression of Shelley's sense of purpose as a public poet, and a personal meditation on the role. In what a biographer calls a moment of both "triumph and defiance," Shelley copied a Greek phrase from the dramatist Euripides in his notebook after finishing the poem: "By virtuous power, I, a mortal, vanquish thee, a mighty god."

A genuine **ode** in its overall style and arrangement, the form of this poem is special. It consists of five sonnets in **terza rima,** with each section ending, as a **Shakespearean sonnet** does, with a couplet. Each group of three lines picks up the rhyme of the second line of the preceding three lines.

Shelley's admirers have been a little embarrassed by the exaggerated self-dramatization of "I fall upon the thorns of life! I bleed!" (line 54), but the poem is full of such heightened effects. They are consistent with the manner of the ode, with its large scale—the earth, the air, and the sea—with its imagery, and with the situation of the speaker, who is striving in "sore need" in prayer with a higher power.

"Ode to the West Wind" expresses Shelley's fascination with power and with those forces—both destroyers and preservers—that inspire the same powers within the poet.

Panorama of Florence (19th century) by J.M.W. Turner.
British Museum, London.

Response and Analysis

Thinking Critically

1. What is the central **image** in each of the first three sections? What emotions does this image evoke?
2. How are sections IV and V different in tone and emphasis from the first three?
3. How can the wind be both "destroyer and preserver" (line 14)? Cite lines to support your ideas.
4. Why do you think the speaker identifies with the wind so intensely?
5. How do you explain the **paradox,** or seeming contradiction, that words are like "ashes and sparks" (line 67)?
6. What do you think lines 68–70 mean? How would you paraphrase them?
7. What lines of this **ode** can you connect with the grief of a parent who has just seen a child die? What comfort does the parent find?

Literary Criticism

8. To some, this **ode** supports an argument that poetry is created only when the poet is inspired by an outside, greater force. Explain whether you agree or disagree with this idea of poetic inspiration.

WRITING

Why the West Wind?

Review your Quickwrite notes. Then, write a brief **essay** explaining why Shelley might shout to the wind, "Be thou me!" In the first part of the essay, explain why human beings are drawn to the sublime in nature. In the second part, **draw conclusions** about Shelley's own attraction to—and identification with—the west wind.

Literary Skills Analyze the characteristics of an ode. Analyze apostrophe and terza rima rhyme scheme in sonnets.

Writing Skills Write an essay analyzing a poem.

Literary Focus

Apostrophe

An **apostrophe** is a figure of speech in which a writer directly addresses an absent or dead person, a personified inanimate object, or an abstract idea. Shelley's opening invocation, "O wild West Wind," is an apostrophe, and the device recurs repeatedly throughout the poem.

Perhaps the origins of the apostrophe lie in the repeated invocations of prayer, when the faithful call upon God to hear their prayers. Indeed, not only is the apostrophe a favorite Romantic device, but many Romantic poems are also titled or described as "hymns."

Analyzing apostrophe. The apostrophe also has an interesting connection with Romantic "empathy," or deep sympathy or identification with a person or object. In what lines of "Ode to the West Wind" does Shelley directly address the wind? Where does he ask to *become* what he apostrophizes?

Terza Rima and the Sonnet

In "Ode to the West Wind," Shelley adapts a rhyme scheme called **terza rima** to the sonnet form. Terza rima consists of sequences of three lines of interlocking rhyme.

Analyzing the ode's structure. Take Shelley's great ode apart to see how it works.

1. Identify Shelley's **rhyme scheme** in each fourteen-line section. Are the schemes all the same?
2. Each section is also a **sonnet.** Review sonnet forms (pages 311–313), and describe how Shelley has adapted them. Do Shelley's sonnets have **turns**?

Choral reading. Working in groups, prepare each section of the ode for choral reading. When you prepare your scripts, be sure to note passages that use **onomatopoeia** and **alliteration.**

Connecting to World Literature

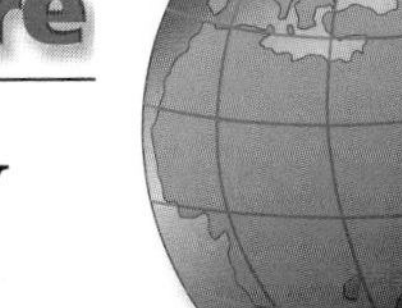

The Golden Age of Chinese Poetry

You have just read many examples of Romantic poetry. In this Comparing to World Literature feature, you will read the following poems from China:

A.D. 701–770
Li Po and Tu Fu live

c. 551–479 B.C.
Confucius teaches ethical principles known as Confucianism, recorded in his *Analects*

c. 500s B.C.
Teachings of Lao Tzu give rise to Taoism in China

c. 1500–1122 B.C.
Art of writing develops in China during the Shang dynasty

Chinese civilization as a distinct and continuous culture has existed for more than three thousand years—longer than any other world culture. The art of writing developed in China between 2000 and 1000 B.C., and with it came the birth of a literary tradition that dwarfs all others. It has been estimated that more than half the books ever written have been written in Chinese.

Harmony and Balance

All Chinese literature, including poetry, is profoundly influenced by three schools of thought, dating to the sixth and fifth centuries B.C.: **Confucianism, Taoism,** and **Buddhism** (see pages 382–396). **Confucianism** emphasizes ethical values: honesty, loyalty, respect for elders, love of learning, and moral restraint. **Taoism** reveres nature as the great teacher and urges people to seek wisdom by contemplating the simplicity and power of natural forces. **Buddhism,** imported from India, stresses the importance of ridding oneself of earthly desires and of seeking ultimate peace and enlightenment through detachment. Many Chinese still incorporate elements of all three systems of thought in their spiritual lives.

Lyrical Imagery

Chinese poetry is almost exclusively lyrical and often focuses on contemplation of nature and the search for harmony between inner and outer forces or worlds. The very essence of Chinese poetry is its exploration of passing feelings and impressions and its appreciation of the interplay of opposites. Life is seen as a process of continual change in which opposing forces balance one another. Thus, Chinese poets muse about the changing seasons and phases of the moon, and they create vivid word pictures of scenes from nature, often recalled in moods of solitude, with imagery that tends to be spare and lean. This minimalist, or simplified, approach calls upon the reader to bring to the poem an appreciation of both evocative

Pages 811–813 cover
Literary Skills
Understand Chinese poetry.
Compare and contrast Chinese poetry with Romantic poetry.

word associations and layers of meaning. So rich are such associations that Chinese poetry has inspired entire poetic movements in other cultures, such as the imagist movement of twentieth-century England and the United States.

Complex Simplicity

A further layer of complexity in Chinese poetry flows from the unique grammatical structure of the Chinese language. Classical Chinese gives no indication of pronoun gender, verb tense, or noun number, and even omits some connecting words and subjects of sentences. Since each Chinese character stands for an entire word, translators often start with a word-for-word translation, as in this literal rendering of a classical four-line poem:

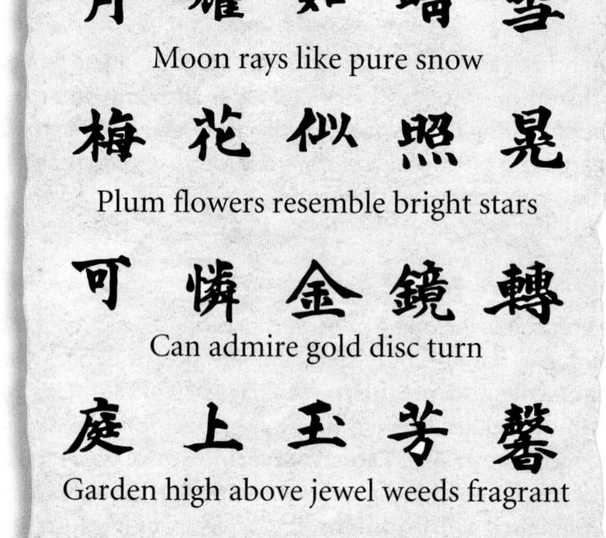

月 耀 如 晴 雪
Moon rays like pure snow
梅 花 似 照 星
Plum flowers resemble bright stars
可 憐 金 鏡 轉
Can admire gold disc turn
庭 上 玉 芳 馨
Garden high above jewel weeds fragrant

To achieve a more graceful rendering, translators must rely on clues drawn from the context and images of the poem. The American imagist poet Ezra Pound completed his translation of this poem as follows:

> The moon's snow falls on the plum tree;
> Its boughs are full of bright stars.
> We can admire the bright turning disc;
> The garden high above there, casts its pearls to our weeds.

The Golden Age of Chinese Poetry

Chinese lyrical poetry achieved its golden age during the T'ang dynasty (618–907). Although painting, sculpture, and other arts also flourished during the T'ang period, poetry was perceived as its greatest glory, and the poet Tu Fu (see page 814) is usually considered one of the greatest of all Chinese poets. His early poetry celebrates the beauty of the natural world and bemoans the passage of time, while his later work incorporates social criticism and compassion for those who suffer.

Rivaling Tu Fu as China's greatest poet is his contemporary, Li Po (see page 819). If Tu Fu represents the classical spirit of Chinese literature (somewhat like England's John Milton for Western literature), then Li Po represents its creative spirit. He is far more the romantic, both in his views of life and in his poetry. He often celebrates the joys of drinking wine and writes about friendship, solitude, the passage of time, and the glory of nature. His hallmark is brilliant freshness of expression.

Together, the poems of Li Po and the early poems of Tu Fu somewhat resemble the English Romantic poetry written one thousand years later. These poems focus on nature, they use the lyric form, and they employ simple images and language. But the voice of Chinese poetry is quieter than the voice of a Shelley or a Wordsworth. As the translator Burton Watson observes, "The Chinese poem is the voice of the poet not self-consciously addressing posterity or the world at large, but speaking quietly to a few close friends, or perhaps simply musing to himself."

Small bridge over flowing stream. Folding fan mounted as an album leaf (1733) by Shih-shu Fang. Ink, color, and mica on paper.

Arthur M. Sackler Museum, Harvard University Art Museums, USA/ The Bridgeman Art Library.

Tu Fu

(712–770)

EIGHTH-CENTURY CHINA

Yellow
KOREA
Yellow Sea
Yellow
Chang'an
CHINA
Hangzhou
East China Sea
Yangzi
TAIWAN
Xi
PACIFIC OCEAN
South China Sea

Tu Fu (dōō fōō) was born into a noble family of scholar-officials. As a youth he was confident of securing one of the imperial appointments that was the dream of every young aristocrat in the T'ang (täŋ) dynasty. So it was a bitter blow when, at the age of twenty-four, he failed the writing examinations in prose and poetry that were the means of gaining imperial positions.

Having failed the tests, Tu Fu spent most of his days wandering and moving in and out of minor government positions throughout the empire. Although he passed the imperial examinations much later in life, he did so without distinction. His failure kept him from realizing his youthful dream of becoming an advisor to the emperor.

Tu Fu's family connections and modest wealth nonetheless assured him a life of relative comfort until 755, when a violent rebellion ended the T'ang dynasty's days of glory. After that Tu Fu was often on the road, searching for a way to make a living. In 757, while Tu Fu was away seeking work, his young son died, possibly from starvation or plague. During the remaining years of his life, Tu Fu lived in hardship and poor health. He died in 770, on a houseboat on a river near Hangzhou.

The uncertain course of Tu Fu's life is reflected in his poetry, which is often marked by bitterness and melancholy. As a young man he wrote mainly about the beauty of nature and his own sorrows. As he grew older, however, Tu Fu's poems turned to more humanitarian themes. He became sensitive to people's sufferings and was the first Chinese poet to write at length about contemporary social concerns. After the bloody rebellion of 755, he wrote many poems condemning the folly of war—a common theme in Chinese poetry.

Although Tu Fu was neither well known nor especially well regarded as a poet during his own lifetime, he wrote in an elegant style that influenced Chinese poets for centuries after his death. His poetry is even more polished than that of Li Po (lē bō), the friend and fellow poet with whom he is often linked. To the Chinese, Li Po is the people's poet; Tu Fu is the poets' poet.

Portrait of Tu Fu from the Ch'ing dynasty. Rubbing from a Chinese carving, from *Travels of a Chinese Poet* by Florence Ayscough (1934).

General Research Division. New York Public Library, Astor, Lenox and Tilden Foundations.

Before You Read

Jade Flower Palace
Night Thoughts Afloat

Make the Connection

Have you ever wandered through an old, abandoned house—perhaps a ruin? Or have you ever found yourself totally apart from civilization, alone except for the whisperings of nature? If so, you may have noticed how, in the absence of human life, nature rushes in to fill the void. Animals move restlessly through shadows; weeds and trees reach upward toward the ancient, endless sky; the wind whispers like voices. The following poems by Tu Fu present a wistful view of two such encounters with places devoid of a human presence.

Literary Focus

Mood

Mood is the overall feeling or atmosphere in a work of literature. A poem's mood might be cheerful or gloomy, defiant or accepting. Writers usually establish a mood by using descriptive details and evocative language—words that call up particular images or feelings. In the traditional Chinese poetry of Tu Fu's time, a single mood usually characterized each poem. But Tu Fu broke new ground by including shifting moods within a single poem.

Mood is the overall emotion created by a work of literature.

For more on Mood, see the Handbook of Literary and Historical Terms.

Background

Perhaps the most respected of all the ancient Chinese poets, Tu Fu focused on the affairs of the world and the sufferings of his people. In stating his goal as a poet, Tu Fu once said, "If my words aren't startling, death itself has no rest."

Like many Chinese poets of his time, Tu Fu wrote in a variety of forms, but he was unequaled in his mastery of the difficult eight-line classical verse form called the *lü-shih* (lyo͞o′shə), meaning "regulated verse." This demanding form, somewhat like the Western *sonnet* (see page 311), was considered a showcase for a Chinese poet's classical technique.

The poems included here represent the poet's realistic and sometimes ironic outlook on life. As you read these poems, notice the vivid images and the concrete details that are hallmarks of Tu Fu's poetry.

Landscape (detail) (7th century) by Li Sixun. Ink and color on silk.

British Museum, London, UK/The Bridgeman Art Library.

Literary Skills
Understand mood.

A Keepsake from the Cloud Gallery (1750).

ADD Ms. 22689. By permission of the British Library, London.

Jade Flower Palace

Tu Fu

translated by **Kenneth Rexroth**

The stream swirls. The wind moans in
The pines. Gray rats scurry over
Broken tiles. What prince, long ago,
Built this palace, standing in
Ruins beside the cliffs? There are
Green ghost fires in the black rooms.
The shattered pavements are all
Washed away. Ten thousand organ
Pipes whistle and roar. The storm
Scatters the red autumn leaves.
His dancing girls are yellow dust.
Their painted cheeks have crumbled
Away. His gold chariots
And courtiers are gone. Only
A stone horse is left of his
Glory. I sit on the grass and
Start a poem, but the pathos of
It overcomes me. The future
Slips imperceptibly away.
Who can say what the years will bring?

Night Thoughts Afloat

Tu Fu

translated by **Arthur Cooper**

By bent grasses
in a gentle wind
Under straight mast
I'm alone tonight,

And the stars hang
above the broad plain
But moon's afloat
in this Great River:

Oh, where's my name
among the poets?
Official rank?
"Retired for ill health."

Drifting, drifting,
what am I more than
A single gull
between sky and earth?

Chinese landscape painting.
Private Collection/Art Resource, New York.

Response and Analysis

Jade Flower Palace
Night Thoughts Afloat

Thinking Critically

1. In "Jade Flower Palace," Tu Fu contemplates the past, the present, and the future. **Summarize** his thoughts about each one.
2. Tu Fu uses vivid verbs to describe the scene before him in "Jade Flower Palace." Choose three of these verbs, and explain how each contributes to the **mood** of the poem.
3. To what does Tu Fu compare himself in "Night Thoughts Afloat"? What emotions do you think the poet is trying to express with this comparison?
4. The first two stanzas of "Night Thoughts Afloat" describe a scene, and the last two stanzas express the poet's feelings. What is the **mood** of the first two stanzas? of the last two?

Extending and Evaluating

5. In Tu Fu's time, a poem was expected to represent only one **mood, tone,** and **setting.** Tu Fu broke with tradition and often shifted moods, tones, and images within a poem. Find at least one shift in each of the two poems you have just read. How do these shifts affect your reading of each poem? Do you think the poems would be more effective if they focused on only one mood? Explain.

Literary Skills Analyze mood. Compare and contrast Chinese poetry with Romantic poetry.

Writing Skills Write a journal entry.

Comparing Literature

6. Tu Fu's poem "Jade Flower Palace" is similar in **theme** to Shelley's "Ozymandias" (see page 803). What theme do they share? In what other ways are the poems alike or different? You may want to consider the **mood, setting,** and **imagery** of each poem.

WRITING

Journal Entry

What concerns seem to preoccupy Tu Fu in the two poems you have read? Choose one of these poems, and **paraphrase** it in the form of a **journal entry.** Include details from the poem as well as the speaker's thoughts and emotions.

Japanese silkscreen with flowers (detail) (late 19th century).

Li Po

(701–762)

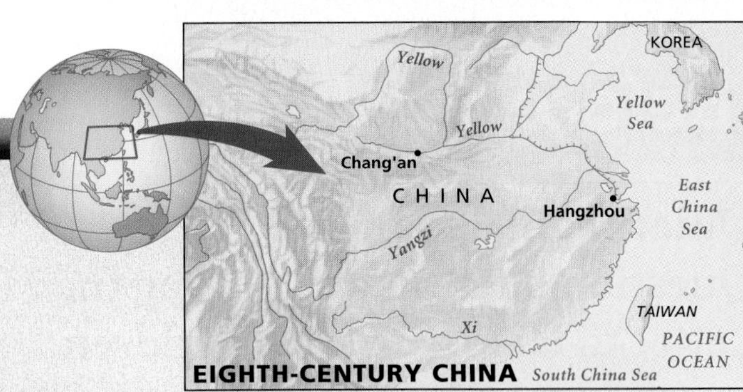

Like Tu Fu, the Chinese poet Li Po (lē bō) lived during the T'ang (täŋ) dynasty (618–907), an age of great prosperity and cultural achievement. These two poets of contrasting dispositions and styles embody the highest poetic achievements of the T'ang dynasty. Tu Fu, a melancholy wanderer, wrote innovative poetry known for its elegance, realism, and social consciousness. Li Po, a free-spirited vagabond, wrote traditional lyric poetry characterized by its sense of playfulness, fantasy, and grace.

Although Li Po was probably born in central Asia, he grew up in the province of Sichuan (sē'chwän) in southwestern China. He was a well-educated youth from a good family who chose to forgo the test for imperial service taken by many young men of the upper classes. Instead, the young Li Po lived as a hermit and served as a wandering knight, a sword-wielding avenger of wrongs against women and children. At the age of twenty-five, he became a vagabond who wandered for most of his days.

As he traveled throughout China, Li Po wrote poetry and made many friends of government officials, fellow poets, and even hermits. He also married and lived with his wife's family for a short time before resuming life as a wanderer.

Li Po's travels in China served to spread his fame as a poet. Even the emperor admired him. In fact, Li Po abandoned his nomadic life for a time to serve the emperor as an imperial court poet. There Li Po delighted in a life of unaccustomed luxuries.

Sometime afterward Li Po entered into the service of a rebel prince. When the prince's bid for power failed, however, Li Po was imprisoned and then banished, a sentence that was revoked just as he was on his way into exile. Three years later the poet died suddenly. An appropriately romantic Chinese legend tells that he drowned one night as he leaned from his boat to embrace the watery reflection of the moon.

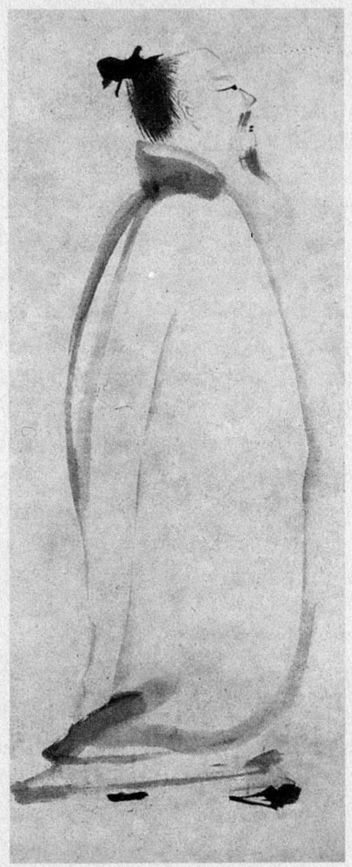

Li Po Chanting in Stroll (southern Sung dynasty, 13th century) by Liang Kai.

Tokyo National Museum.

Before You Read

Quiet Night Thoughts
Question and Answer Among the Mountains
Letter to His Two Small Children

Make the Connection

Quickwrite

In life we are often caught between two fundamental but opposing desires—to wander the world freely, experiencing all that life has to offer, and to settle into the stable security of a community and family. As you will see in the three works that follow, the Chinese poet Li Po was a restless spirit. He spent much of his life as a wanderer and a hermit, but his marriage and many friendships suggest that he also craved human connection and community. Would your ideal life emphasize solitude or fellowship—or some balance between the two? Jot down several sentences explaining your preferences.

Literary Focus

Imagery

Imagery is language that appeals to the senses—sight, hearing, smell, touch, and taste. The imagery a writer creates helps readers imagine a scene and respond emotionally to it. For example, a writer might describe an ocean as a "crashing gray tide" to build a feeling of fear, or as "rippling blue waves" to suggest tranquility. Li Po's poems rarely state an emotion directly; instead they allow the reader to extract the meaning of the poem by considering the emotional effect of the images.

Imagery is language that appeals to the senses—sight, hearing, smell, touch, and taste.

For more on Imagery, see the Handbook of Literary and Historical Terms.

Background

Like most of his contemporaries, Li Po wrote in a wide range of poetic forms. Yet according to Chinese critics, Li Po was at his best in concise four-line poems with five to seven words per line. His poem *Yeh-ssu* (ye·sə), translated here as "Quiet Night Thoughts," is a masterpiece of this form. (The English translation here has eight lines, twice as many as the original, in order to accommodate the rhythms of English verse.) A lifelong observer of nature, Li Po was renowned for creating vivid images of China's best-known mountains and streams, often recalled in a mood of solitude. The following three poems, though different in form, resonate with images of nature and the thoughts and emotions of the solitary poet.

Literary Skills Understand imagery.

Quiet Night Thoughts

Li Po

translated by **Arthur Cooper**

Before my bed
there is bright moonlight
So that it seems
like frost on the ground:

Lifting my head
I watch the bright moon,
Lowering my head
I dream that I'm home.

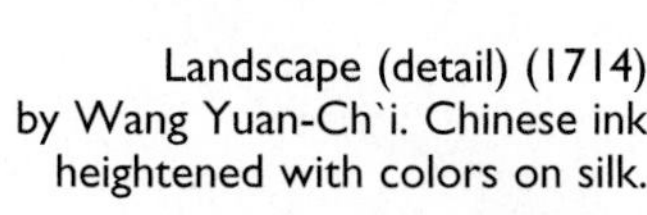

Landscape (detail) (1714) by Wang Yuan-Ch`i. Chinese ink heightened with colors on silk.

Réunion des Musées Nationaux. Art Resource, New York.

Question and Answer Among the Mountains

Li Po

translated by **Robert Kotewall** *and* **Norman L. Smith**

You ask me why I dwell in the green mountain;
I smile and make no reply for my heart is free of care.
As the peach-blossom flows down stream and is gone into
the unknown,
I have a world apart that is not among men.

Letter to His Two Small Children

Li Po

translated by **Arthur Cooper**

Here in Wu° Land mulberry leaves are green,
Silkworms in Wu have now had three sleeps:

My family, left in Eastern Lu,
Oh, to sow now Turtle-shaded fields,
Do the Spring things I can never join,
Sailing Yangtze° always on my own—

Let the South Wind blow you back my heart,
Fly and land it in the Tavern court
Where, to the East, there are sprays and leaves
Of one peach tree, sweeping the blue mist;

This is the tree I myself put in
When I left you, nearly three years past;
A peach tree now, level with the eaves,
And I sailing cannot yet turn home!

Pretty daughter, P'ing-yang is your name,
Breaking blossom, there beside my tree,
Breaking blossom, you cannot see me
And your tears flow like the running stream;

And little son, Po-ch'in you are called,
Your big sister's shoulder you must reach
When you come there underneath my peach,
Oh, to pat and pet you too, my child!

I dreamt like this till my wits went wild,
By such yearning daily burned within;
So tore some silk, wrote this distant pang
From me to you living at Wen Yang . . .

1. **Wu** (wo͞o): river in central China.

6. **Yangtze** (yaŋk'sē): the longest river in China, flowing from Tibet to the East China Sea.

A dance scene (detail), from a series of book illustrations of the Miao customs.

Réunion des Musées Nationaux. Art Resource, New York.

Response and Analysis

Quiet Night Thoughts
Question and Answer Among the Mountains
Letter to His Two Small Children

Thinking Critically

1. What is the overall **mood,** or feeling, of "Quiet Night Thoughts"? How does the poet use **imagery** to convey that mood?
2. Like many Chinese poets, Li Po uses a form of **parallelism** in which pairs of lines follow the same basic sentence structure. Point out the parallelism in the last four lines of "Quiet Night Thoughts." What two ideas are contrasted in these two pairs of lines?
3. In "Question and Answer Among the Mountains," the speaker answers a question by not answering it. Explain this **paradox,** or seeming contradiction.
4. How does the poet use **images** of nature to emphasize his solitude in "Letter to His Two Small Children"? What emotions are evoked in this poem?
5. What central nature **image** occurs in both "Letter to His Two Small Children" and "Question and Answer Among the Mountains"? What very different emotions does this image evoke in each poem?
6. Find an example of **alliteration** in each translation of Li Po's poems. How do the repeated consonant sounds add to the effect of each poem?

Extending and Evaluating

7. In these poems the speakers express their feelings by using seasonal images of nature. Do you think this is an effective way to express one's emotions? Why or why not?

Comparing Literature

8. Compare Tu Fu's "Night Thoughts Afloat" (see page 817) and Li Po's "Quiet Night Thoughts." In particular, consider the poems' **images** and descriptive **details.** Do these images and details evoke similar emotions in each speaker? Explain.
9. Li Po's poems reflect the Taoist philosophy and religion, which teach that nature contains life's essence while the conventional human world, corrupted by materialism, is not true reality. Choose one poem by Li Po and one by the English Romantic poet William Wordsworth (see pages 734–748). How does each poem express the Taoist principle described above?

WRITING

Reflecting on Solitude

Write a short **reflective essay** about solitude. What ideal balance would you strike between being alone and being with others? Can you enjoy solitude in a city or must you be in a peaceful natural setting? What are the benefits of solitude? What are its challenges? Refer to your Quickwrite notes for ideas.

Use "Writing a Reflective Essay," pages 856–863, for help with this assignment.

Literary Skills
Analyze imagery. Compare Chinese poetry with Romantic poetry.

Writing Skills
Write a reflective essay.

John Keats
(1795–1821)

John Keats by Charles Armitage Brown.
By courtesy of the National Portrait Gallery, London.

It is surprising that Keats became a poet at all, and surely a wonder that, when he died at the age of twenty-five, he had accomplished enough to become one of England's major poets.

John Keats's brief life was plagued with troubles, and he lacked most of the advantages a poet often needs to get started. His father, who ran a London stable, died when Keats was eight. His mother died of tuberculosis when he was fourteen, leaving the family finances tied up and inaccessible to the Keats children. After four years in a school where his literary interests were encouraged, he was apprenticed at the age of fifteen to learn medicine.

In 1816, not yet twenty-one, Keats completed his medical studies at Guy's Hospital in London. Before he could be legally licensed as a surgeon, he made the momentous decision to become a poet. Some harsh reviews of his first book of poetry (1817) stung him and added to the periodic doubts that made his dedication to poetry sometimes seem an awful burden. Now much of Keats's time was spent nursing his brother Tom, who was dying of tuberculosis.

After Tom's death in December 1818, Keats had a little more than two years to make what he could of his determination to lead a "literary life." Great passages and nearly perfect poems poured from him in that miraculous time. Already in failing health himself, he never knew the greatness of his achievements, which might have given him at least the consolation of literary success. He had also fallen in love—her name was Fanny Brawne—but his poor health and money problems kept him from marrying. "I am three and twenty," he wrote despairingly in March 1819, "with little knowledge and middling intellect. It is true that in the height of enthusiasm I have been cheated into some fine passages, but that is not the thing."

In the next six months, he wrote some of his most glorious poems. Yet, he lamented in a November letter to his brother George (who had immigrated to Kentucky in 1817), "Nothing could have in all circumstances fallen out worse for me than the last year has done, or could be more damping to my poetical talent." Three months later he coughed up blood. His medical training and his experience nursing Tom made the truth obvious: "That drop of blood is my death warrant." His only chance, a slim one, was to live in a warmer climate.

In late 1820, Keats and his friend Joseph Severn, an artist, travelled to Rome and settled into rooms in a house near the Spanish Steps. There Keats died in February 1821 and was buried in the Protestant cemetery—that "camp of death," as Shelley called it.

The stark sadness of Keats's life heightens our awareness of the qualities of his poems—not bleak, subdued, or heavy with resignation, but rich in sensuous detail and exciting representations of intense emotional experiences, full of courageous hope for what the imagination can seize and enjoy in life.

Before You Read

On First Looking into Chapman's Homer
When I Have Fears

Make the Connection

For all the Romantics, poetry was the true adventure. Imagination opened whole new worlds; the best poetry opened thrilling vistas of absolute newness. In the sonnet "On First Looking into Chapman's Homer," Keats addresses this theme of adventure through imagination. In the second sonnet you will read, "When I Have Fears," the young poet reflects upon the possibility that an untimely death may deny him many adventures of the mind—and the heart. How important do you think the life of the imagination is in the world today?

Literary Focus

Sonnet

Most poets who like the challenge of structure love to try the sonnet form. **Sonnets** always have fourteen lines, and they usually have two parts. The first part usually presents a problem, question, or idea that the second part resolves, answers, or emphasizes. Keats wrote "On First Looking into Chapman's Homer" in the Italian, or **Petrarchan,** form, dividing his thoughts into an octave and a sestet (see page 312). "When I Have Fears," however, uses the **Shakespearean** form—three four-line quatrains followed by a concluding couplet (see pages 312–313).

> A **sonnet** is a fourteen-line lyric poem, usually written in iambic pentameter, that has one of several rhyme schemes and structures.
>
> *For more on Sonnet, see the Handbook of Literary and Historical Terms.*

Reading Skills

Reading Inverted Syntax

Keats, like many other poets of his time, often inverts the **syntax,** or word order, of his sentences to meet the demands of meter and rhyme. The word order of a traditional English sentence is subject-verb-complement. Jot down the parts of Keats's syntax that give you trouble. Then, look for the subject and verb of each sentence.

Background

Keats wrote "On First Looking into Chapman's Homer" in 1816, just before his twenty-first birthday. The poem was inspired by an evening Keats spent with his favorite teacher, Charles Cowden Clarke. The two had stayed up all night reading a translation of Homer's *Iliad* by George Chapman, a contemporary of Shakespeare. Keats went home at dawn and by ten that morning sent Clarke this sonnet.

Keats's first Shakespearean sonnet, "When I Have Fears," was written in early 1818—a year fraught with disappointment in work and love and with the beginnings of the poet's ill health. The sonnet hauntingly anticipates Keats's ultimate doom in 1821 at the age of twenty-five.

By 1820, shortly before he died, Keats had published his new poems in "one of the richest volumes in the history of English poetry." He also hoped to nurture his "little dramatic skill" by writing a few more narrative poems to "nerve me up to the writing of a few fine plays—my greatest ambition." He longed to follow Shakespeare into "the fierce dispute / Betwixt damnation and impassioned clay."

Our wonder must be that none of the great poets who came before Keats—Chaucer, Shakespeare, Milton, Pope, or Wordsworth—would be found in this book if they had died at twenty-five.

Literary Skills
Understand the sonnet form.

Reading Skills
Understand inverted syntax.

INTERNET

More About John Keats

Keyword: LE7 12-5

On First Looking into Chapman's Homer

John Keats

Much have I traveled in the realms of gold,
And many goodly states and kingdoms seen;
Round many western islands have I been
Which bards in fealty to Apollo° hold.
Oft of one wide expanse had I been told
That deep-browed Homer ruled as his demesne;°
Yet did I never breathe its pure serene°
Till I heard Chapman speak out loud and bold:
Then felt I like some watcher of the skies
When a new planet swims into his ken;°
Or like stout Cortez° when with eagle eyes
He stared at the Pacific—and all his men
Looked at each other with a wild surmise—
Silent, upon a peak in Darien.

4. bards in fealty to Apollo: poets in loyal service (as feudal tenants to their lord) to Apollo, the Greek god of poetry.

6. demesne (di·mān′) *n.:* domain.

7. serene *n.:* archaic for "clear air."

10. ken *n.:* range of vision.

11. Cortez: sixteenth-century Spanish explorer. In this now famous mistake, Keats confuses Cortez with Balboa, another Spanish explorer. Balboa was actually the first European to see the eastern shore of the Pacific Ocean from the heights of Darien in Panama.

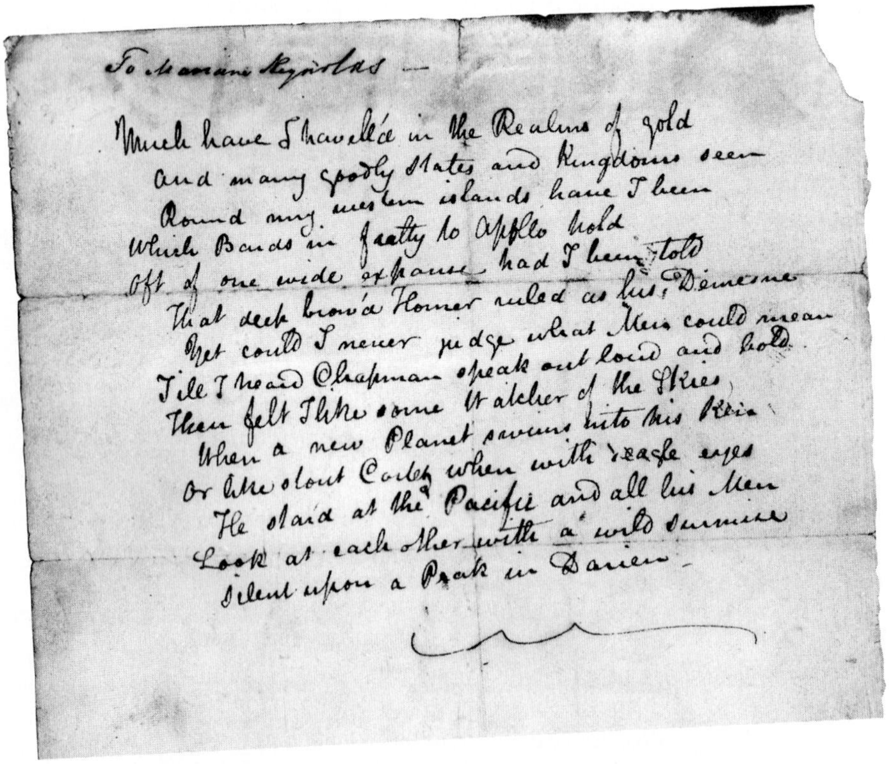

Manuscript of "On First Looking into Chapman's Homer" by John Keats.

The Poet's Theme (19th century) by John Callcott Horsley.
Sotheby's Transparency Library, London.

When I Have Fears

John Keats

When I have fears that I may cease to be
   Before my pen has gleaned my teeming brain,
Before high-pilèd books, in charact'ry,°
   Hold like rich garners the full-ripened grain;
When I behold, upon the night's starred face,
   Huge cloudy symbols of a high romance,
And think that I may never live to trace
   Their shadows, with the magic hand of chance;
And when I feel, fair creature of an hour,
   That I shall never look upon thee more,
Never have relish in the fairy° power
   Of unreflecting love!—then on the shore
Of the wide world I stand alone, and think
Till Love and Fame to nothingness do sink.

3. **charact'ry** *n.:* the characters of the alphabet.

11. **fairy** *adj.:* supernatural; unearthly.

Response and Analysis

On First Looking into Chapman's Homer
When I Have Fears

Thinking Critically

1. In "On First Looking into Chapman's Homer," what could "realms of gold" (line 1) be?
2. Keats saw something of his own country as a young man, but his only foreign travel was the desperate trip to Italy he made when he was dying. What then do you think Keats means in lines 1–4 of "On First Looking into Chapman's Homer," when he says that he has traveled much and seen many goodly states and kingdoms and western islands?
3. Keats uses two **extended similes** to describe how he felt when he read Chapman's translation of Homer. What are these two similes? What details in these similes suggest that reading Homer was like an act of discovery or exploration?
4. How would you sum up the two parts of "On First Looking into Chapman's Homer"?
5. In "When I Have Fears," what **simile** describes the books the speaker hopes to write?
6. One fear that the speaker of "When I Have Fears" expresses is that he will never be able to write the books he wishes to write. What else does he fear he will never do?
7. Whom does the speaker of "When I Have Fears" address? What line tells you this?
8. Describe the speaker's **tone** in "When I Have Fears." Do you think the tone is constant or does it change? Explain.
9. Where is the **turn** in "When I Have Fears"?

Extending and Evaluating

10. Think about the famous mistake in Keats's last simile in "On First Looking into Chapman's Homer." Does this mistake affect the power of the poem, or its quality? Explain your response.

WRITING

Keats in Your Own Words

Select one of these sonnets and **paraphrase** it, line by line, using your own words. Remember that in a paraphrase you should put inverted sentences in standard English word order. You should also rephrase figures of speech to make it clear that you understand them. Sometimes poets omit words; if that is the case in one of these sonnets, be sure to supply the missing words. Refer to your reading notes for help with any lines that give you difficulty. The first lines of "When I Have Fears" might be paraphrased like this:

> When I get worried that I might die before I have written all that is in my mind, which is teeming with ideas . . .

As you can see, a paraphrase is usually longer than the original and it is not nearly as interesting. But it forces you into the poem and sometimes challenges you to dig deep for meaning.

Literary Skills Analyze a sonnet.

Reading Skills Analyze inverted syntax.

Writing Skills Paraphrase a sonnet.

PRIMARY SOURCE / LETTER

Keats's Last Letter

Rome, 30 November 1820

My dear Brown,

'Tis the most difficult thing in the world to me to write a letter. My stomach continues so bad, that I feel it worse on opening any book, yet I am much better than I was in quarantine. Then I am afraid to encounter the proing and con-ing of anything interesting to me in England. I have an habitual feeling of my real life having passed, and that I am leading a post-humous existence. God knows how it would have been—but it appears to me—however, I will not speak of that subject. I must have been at Bedhampton nearly at the time you were writing to me from Chichester—how unfortunate—and to pass on the river too! There was my star predominant! I cannot answer anything in your letter, which followed me from Naples to Rome, because I am afraid to look it over again. I am so weak (in mind) that I cannot bear the sight of any handwriting of a friend I love so much as I do you. Yet I ride the little horse, and, at my worst, even in quarantine, summoned up more puns, in a sort of desperation, in one week than in any year of my life. There is one thought enough to kill me; I have been well, healthy, alert, etc., walking with her, and now—the knowledge of contrast, feeling for light and shade, all that information (primitive sense) necessary for a poem, are great enemies to the recovery of the stomach. There, you rogue, I put you to the torture; but you must bring your philosophy to bear, as I do mine, really, or how should I be able to live? Dr. Clark is very attentive to me; he says, there is very little the matter with my lungs, but my stomach, he says, is very bad. I am well disappointed in hearing good news from George [Keats's brother], for it runs in my head we shall all die young. I have not written to Reynolds yet, which he must think very neglectful; being anxious to send him a good account of my health, I have delayed it from week to week. If I recover, I will do all in my power to correct the mistakes made during sickness; and if I should not, all my faults shall be forgiven. Severn is very well, though he leads so dull a life with me. Remember me to all friends, and tell Haslam I should not have left London without taking leave of him, but from being so low in body and mind. Write to George as soon you receive this, and tell him how I am, as far as you can guess; and also a note to my sister—who walks about my imagination like a ghost—she is so like Tom. I can scarcely bid you goodbye, even in a letter. I always made an awkward bow.

God bless you!
John Keats

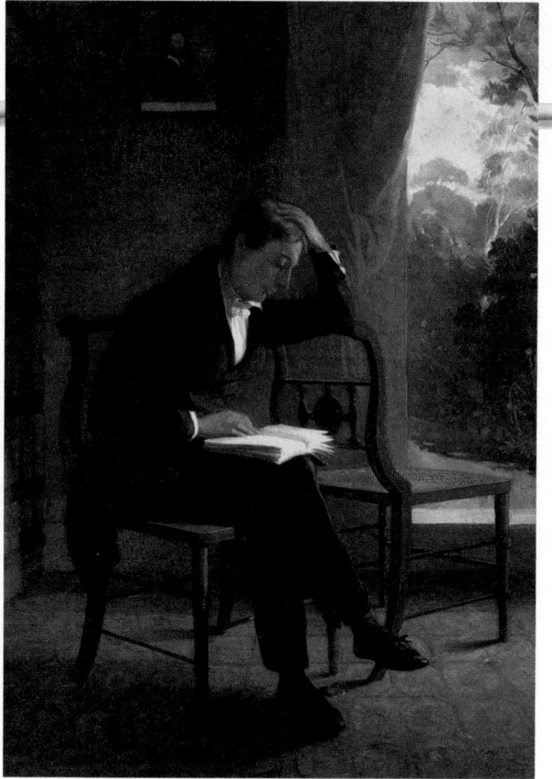

John Keats at Wentworth Place (1821–1823) by Joseph Severn. Oil.

The Granger Collection, New York.

Before You Read

Ode to a Nightingale

Make the Connection

Quickwrite

From the first lines of this poem, you realize the speaker is passing into a reverie not wholly of the waking world. He is sharing an intense experience of extremes, a searching flight of the mind at once joyful and despairing, spiritual yet startlingly concrete. If you let yourself take this daring journey with Keats (as unfamiliar as it may seem at first), you will find yourself in a mysterious realm. Keats is not afraid of the dark.

How might the act of writing—a poem, a journal entry, or a story—help someone resolve or dispel feelings of depression or gloom? Write down your thoughts.

Literary Focus

Synesthesia

In the poetic device called **synesthesia** (sin′is·thē′zhə), one sense experience (such as smell) is described as another (such as touch). For example, in "Ode to a Nightingale" the speaker remarks that he "cannot see . . . what soft incense hangs upon the boughs" (lines 41–42). Incense, usually perceived through smell, is here described as both something that might be soft to the touch and something that might be seen. By inviting the reader to use his or her senses in unexpected ways, Keats brings a startling newness to common objects.

SKILLS FOCUS

Literary Skills Understand synesthesia.

Synesthesia is a term used for descriptions of one kind of sensation in terms of another, as in describing a color as a sound or a sound as a taste.

For more on Synesthesia, see the Handbook of Literary and Historical Terms.

INTERNET

More About John Keats

Keyword: LE7 12-5

Background

When Keats was twenty-three, he spent a few months at the Hampstead home of his friend Charles Brown, who remembered:

> "In the spring of 1819 a nightingale had built her nest near my house. Keats felt a tranquil and continual joy in her song, and one morning he took his chair from the breakfast table to the grass plot under a plum tree, where he sat for two or three hours. When he came into the house, I perceived he had some scraps of paper in his hand, and these he was quietly thrusting behind the books. On inquiry, I found those scraps, four or five in number, contained his poetic feeling on the song of our nightingale."

There are no nightingales in North America. Their unearthly, sad, sweet song can only be heard in the British Isles, central and western Europe, and in Africa during the winter.

Ode to a Nightingale

John Keats

1

My heart aches, and a drowsy numbness pains
My sense, as though of hemlock° I had drunk,
Or emptied some dull opiate to the drains°
One minute past, and Lethewards° had sunk:
'Tis not through envy of thy happy lot,
But being too happy in thine happiness—
That thou, light-wingèd Dryad° of the trees,
In some melodious plot
Of beechen° green, and shadows numberless,
Singest of summer in full-throated ease.

2

O, for a draft of vintage!° that hath been
Cooled a long age in the deep-delvèd earth,
Tasting of Flora° and the country green,
Dance, and Provençal° song, and sunburnt mirth!
O for a beaker full of the warm South,
Full of the true, the blushful Hippocrene,°
With beaded bubbles winking at the brim,
And purple-stainèd mouth;
That I might drink, and leave the world unseen,
And with thee fade away into the forest dim:

3

Fade far away, dissolve, and quite forget
What thou among the leaves hast never known,
The weariness, the fever, and the fret
Here, where men sit and hear each other groan;
Where palsy° shakes a few, sad, last gray hairs,
Where youth grows pale, and specter-thin, and dies;
Where but to think is to be full of sorrow
And leaden-eyed despairs,
Where Beauty cannot keep her lustrous eyes,
Or new Love pine at them beyond tomorrow.

2. hemlock *n.:* poison.

3. drains *n. pl.:* dregs.

4. Lethewards (lē′thē·wərds): toward Lethe. In Greek and Roman mythology, Lethe is the river of forgetfulness that flows through the underworld.

7. Dryad (drī′ad′): in Greek mythology, nature goddess associated with trees.

9. beechen *adj.:* archaic for "pertaining to beech trees."

11. vintage *n.:* wine.

13. Flora: the richness of flowers. Flora is the Roman goddess of flowers.

14. Provençal (prō′vän·säl′): from Provence, a region in southern France known in the Middle Ages for its troubadors singing love songs.

16. blushful Hippocrene (hip′ō·krēn′): wine, which he would drink for inspiration. In Greek mythology, Hippocrene is the Muses' fountain, whose waters inspire the poets who drink from it.

25. palsy *n.:* a disease of the nervous system that causes partial paralysis and involuntary shaking.

Forge Valley, Scarborough (19th century) by John Atkinson Grimshaw.
Christopher Wood Gallery, London.

4

Away! away! for I will fly to thee,
Not charioted by Bacchus and his pards,°
But on the viewless wings of Poesy,°
Though the dull brain perplexes and retards:
Already with thee! tender is the night,
And haply the Queen-Moon is on her throne,
Clustered around by all her starry Fays;°
But here there is no light,
Save what from heaven is with the breezes blown
Through verdurous° glooms and winding mossy ways.

32. not . . . pards: not by getting drunk. Bacchus, the Roman god of wine, had a chariot pulled by leopards, shortened here to "pards."
33. on . . . Poesy: on the invisible wings of poetry; that is, by using his poetic imagination.
37. Fays *n. pl.:* fairies.
40. verdurous (vʉr′jər · əs) *adj.:* full of green foliage.

5

I cannot see what flowers are at my feet,
Nor what soft incense hangs upon the boughs,
But, in embalmèd° darkness, guess each sweet
Wherewith the seasonable month endows
The grass, the thicket, and the fruit tree wild;
White hawthorn, and the pastoral eglantine;°
Fast fading violets covered up in leaves;
And mid-May's eldest child,
The coming° musk rose, full of dewy wine,
The murmurous haunt of flies on summer eves.

6

Darkling° I listen; and, for many a time
I have been half in love with easeful Death,
Called him soft names in many a musèd rhyme,
To take into the air my quiet breath;
Now more than ever seems it rich to die,
To cease upon the midnight with no pain,
While thou art pouring forth thy soul abroad
In such an ecstasy!
Still wouldst thou sing, and I have ears in vain—
To thy high requiem° become a sod.°

7

Thou wast not born for death, immortal Bird!
No hungry generations tread thee down;
The voice I hear this passing night was heard
In ancient days by emperor and clown:
Perhaps the self-same song that found a path
Through the sad heart of Ruth,° when, sick for home,
She stood in tears amid the alien corn;°
The same that oft-times hath
Charmed magic casements,° opening on the foam
Of perilous seas, in fairy lands forlorn.

8

Forlorn! the very word is like a bell
To toll me back from thee to my sole self!
Adieu! the fancy° cannot cheat so well
As she is famed to do, deceiving elf.
Adieu! adieu! thy plaintive° anthem fades
Past the near meadows, over the still stream,
Up the hillside; and now 'tis buried deep
In the next valley glades:
Was it a vision, or a waking dream?
Fled is that music:—Do I wake or sleep?

43. embalmèd *adj.:* perfumed.

46. eglantine (eg'lən·tīn') *n.:* kind of rose.

49. coming *adj.:* soon to bloom.

51. darkling *adj.:* archaic for "in the dark."

60. requiem (rek'wē·əm) *n.:* Mass or song for the dead. **sod** *n.:* piece of topsoil held together by the matted roots of living grasses.

66. Ruth: in the Bible, a young widow who left her own people to go with her mother-in-law to a strange land.

67. corn *n.:* British generic term for grain.

69. casements *n. pl.:* windows. Images of open windows intrigued Keats.

73. fancy *n.:* imagination.

75. plaintive *adj.:* sad; mournful.

CRITICAL COMMENT

INFORMATIONAL TEXT

Dialogue with the Soul

Keats's completed poem is not "about" or "on" the nightingale but, as the title tells us, "to" the nightingale. The speaker seems, as the poem opens, to have already passed beyond the limit of ordinary experience and become "too happy" in the experience conveyed in the nightingale's song. The poem consists of a series of propositions, each containing its own rejection as to how the speaker might imitate the "ease" of the song he hears—wine, poetry, even death are considered. Each time, the speaker in his humanness is drawn back to his "sole self," to a preference for poetry as a celebration, not of "summer" but of human life as a process of soul making.

Response and Analysis

Reading Check

1. Describe the outward **setting** and the emotions of the speaker as they are portrayed in the first stanza.
2. According to the second stanza, what state of feeling does the speaker want to have?
3. What misfortunes does the speaker want to escape in the third stanza? What means of escape are considered in the fourth stanza?
4. What thoughts about death does the speaker have in stanza 6? How does he resolve these temptations?
5. Where does the speaker imagine the song of the nightingale has been heard in the seventh stanza?
6. What is happening in the final stanza?

Thinking Critically

7. Why do you think the speaker wants to capture the nightingale's "ease"? Why is he "too happy in [its] happiness" (stanza 1)?
8. Find an example of **synesthesia** in stanza 2 of Keats's ode. What sensory experience does it describe? What feeling or **mood** does the device help to create?
9. What differences are emphasized between the realm (or experience) of the nightingale and that of the speaker?
10. What do you think the speaker realizes by the end of the poem?
11. How is the speaker's **mood** different at the poem's end than at its beginning?
12. Keats uses many **allusions** that conjure up several different historical and mythological periods. What is the effect of all these references?

Extending and Evaluating

13. Why do you think Keats chose the nightingale as the central **image** for this poem? Was it a good choice? Explain.
14. Review your Quickwrite notes. What do you think Keats's motivation or purpose was in writing this poem? Do you think he succeeded? Use evidence from the text to support your opinions.

Literary Skills Analyze synesthesia.

Writing Skills Write an essay comparing two odes.

WRITING

Poets on Poetry

Both Keats's "Ode to a Nightingale" and Shelley's "Ode to the West Wind" (see page 806) are concerned, at least partially, with the subject of poetic inspiration. In a brief **essay,** write a **comparison** of these two odes. Focus on how each poem treats the subject of poetic inspiration.

Before You Read

Ode on a Grecian Urn

Make the Connection

This poem is a work of art about the contemplation of a work of art—a Grecian urn, or jar. That means the ode is both concrete (descriptive) and contemplative (philosophical). It moves from rich images to abstract ideas about art versus life, permanence versus change, and body versus spirit.

Literary Focus

Metaphor

In the figure of speech known as **metaphor,** two seemingly unlike things are compared without the use of a connective word such as *like* or *as*. At the beginning of "Ode on a Grecian Urn," Keats uses three metaphors to describe the urn. For example, in line 1, he refers to the urn as "Thou still unravished bride of quietness . . ." By comparing the urn to a virgin bride, the poet implies that the urn has remained untouched throughout the ages, quietly awaiting contact with the human world. As you read, look for other metaphors that describe the urn.

A **metaphor** is a figure of speech that makes a comparison between two seemingly unlike things without using a connective word such as *like, as, than,* or *resembles.*

For more on Metaphor, see the Handbook of Literary and Historical Terms.

Reading Skills

Visualizing Imagery

Poets often use **imagery**—language that appeals to the senses—to bring their subject matter to life. Most images are visual, but images can also appeal to the senses of hearing, smell, taste, and touch. To better visualize the images presented in "Ode on a Grecian Urn," try reading the poem aloud. Stop after stanzas 1–3 and then after stanza 4, and write a few sentences describing the urn's decorations as you see them. Make sketches if you like.

Background

Antique Greek vases are usually black with reddish decorative painting, often depicting mythological subjects. Many vases show gods, goddesses, heroes, and mortals entangled in adventures. Traditionally, urns have been used as containers or for burial. No one knows exactly what urn Keats had in mind when he wrote this ode. Probably it is an imaginative combination of several vases he had seen, including two in the British Museum. The urn Keats describes has a series of scenes going around it, probably something like the one pictured on page 837.

Literary Skills Understand metaphor.

Reading Skills Visualize imagery.

Side A, Greek, Attic (detail) (ca. 490 B.C.) attributed to the Berlin Painter, Amphora, Terracotta; height 16 5/16 in. (42.50 cm).

The Metropolitan Museum of Art, Fletcher Fund, 1956 (56.171.38). Photograph © 1998 The Metropolitan Museum of Art.

INTERNET

More About John Keats

Keyword: LE7 12-5

Ode on a Grecian Urn

John Keats

1

Thou still unravished bride of quietness,
Thou foster child of silence and slow time,
Sylvan° historian, who canst thus express
A flowery tale more sweetly than our rhyme:
What leaf-fringed legend haunts about thy shape
Of deities or mortals, or of both,
In Tempe or the dales of Arcady?°
What men or gods are these? What maidens loath?°
What mad pursuit? What struggle to escape?
What pipes and timbrels?° What wild ecstasy?

2

Heard melodies are sweet, but those unheard
Are sweeter; therefore, ye soft pipes, play on;
Not to the sensual ear, but, more endeared,
Pipe to the spirit ditties° of no tone:
Fair youth, beneath the trees, thou canst not leave
Thy song, nor ever can those trees be bare;
Bold Lover, never, never canst thou kiss,
Though winning near the goal—yet, do not grieve;
She cannot fade, though thou hast not thy bliss,
Forever wilt thou love, and she be fair!

3

Ah, happy, happy boughs! that cannot shed
Your leaves, nor ever bid the Spring adieu;°
And, happy melodist, unwearied,
Forever piping songs forever new;
More happy love! more happy, happy love!
Forever warm and still to be enjoyed,
Forever panting, and forever young;
All breathing human passion far above,
That leaves a heart high-sorrowful and cloyed,°
A burning forehead, and a parching tongue.

4

Who are these coming to the sacrifice?
To what green altar, O mysterious priest,
Lead'st thou that heifer lowing° at the skies,
And all her silken flanks° with garlands dressed?

3. sylvan *adj.:* of the forest. (The urn is decorated with a rural scene.)

7. Tempe (tem′pē) . . . **Arcady** (är′kə • dē): valleys in ancient Greece; ideal types of rural beauty.

8. loath *adj.:* reluctant.

10. timbrels *n. pl.:* tambourines.

14. ditties *n. pl.:* short, simple songs.

22. adieu (ȧ • dyö′): French for "goodbye."

29. cloyed (kloid) *adj.:* satiated; wearied with excess.

33. lowing *v.:* mooing.

34. flanks *n. pl.:* sides between the ribs and the hips.

What little town by river or seashore,
Or mountain-built with peaceful citadel,°
Is emptied of this folk, this pious morn?
And, little town, thy streets forevermore
Will silent be; and not a soul to tell
Why thou art desolate, can e'er return.

36. citadel (sit′ə·del′) *n.:* fortress.

5

O Attic° shape! Fair attitude!° with brede°
Of marble men and maidens overwrought,°
With forest branches and the trodden weed;
Thou, silent form, dost tease us out of thought
As doth eternity: Cold Pastoral!°
When old age shall this generation waste,
Thou shalt remain, in midst of other woe
Than ours, a friend to man, to whom thou say'st,
"Beauty is truth, truth beauty,"—that is all
Ye know on earth, and all ye need to know.

41. Attic: Athenian; classically elegant. **attitude** *n.:* disposition or feeling conveyed by the postures of the figures on the urn. **brede** *n.:* interwoven design.
42. overwrought *adj.:* decorated to excess; also, in reference to the men and maidens, overexcited.
45. Pastoral *n.:* artwork depicting idealized rural life.

Attic vase painting showing transport of amphoras.
Louvre, Paris.

CRITICAL COMMENT

The Arc of Experience

INFORMATIONAL TEXT

This poem depicts a beautiful curve of emotion and engagement that begins and ends with detachment. At its center, it abandons all restraints, including those of art itself, to live in that world which is "happy" and "forever." By itself, the third stanza seems "overwrought" (a word used in the more detached fifth stanza)—so much so that we feel that all controls have been lost. But this is precisely the nature of the speaker's experience. Bit by bit, a miniature world of human passions comes alive, only to remind us that it is as dead as the clay on which it is represented. Keats has shown us that in the midst of change, art seems to provide the only truth. Yet this is a truth that depends not on sensory experience, but on the human imagination.

Response and Analysis

Literary Skills Analyze metaphor.

Reading Skills Visualize imagery.

Writing Skills Write a response to a work of art.

INTERNET

Projects and Activities

Keyword: LE7 12-5

Reading Check

1. The urn is called a "sylvan historian" in line 3. What does the speaker say about the urn's ability to tell a tale?
2. What is suggested about the speaker's state by the last three lines of the third stanza?
3. Describe the picture on the urn according to the fourth stanza.
4. According to stanza 5, what will happen to the urn when the speaker is dead? What message does the urn give to people?

Thinking Critically

5. Describe the details represented on the urn according to the first and second stanzas. What actions are "frozen" in time on the vase? Refer to the descriptions you jotted down in your reading notes as you visualized the images.
6. Discuss your understanding of the two **metaphors** for the urn in lines 2 and 3.
7. How do you interpret lines 28–30?
8. Why do you think "unheard" melodies (lines 11–14) are "sweeter" to the speaker? How would you relate this idea to Romanticism?
9. If the urn could "tease us out of thought" (line 44), what state would we be in? In what sense would this state be superior to thought?

Literary Criticism

10. A famous textual difficulty surrounds the poem's last two lines. Based on the manuscript, some scholars enclose the entire couplet within quotation marks. Explain how this could change the meaning of the lines. (Would the sentiments expressed in the couplet be the urn's or the poet's?) Which of the two meanings makes better sense when you consider the entire poem?

WRITING

Art Inspiration

Select a work of art reproduced in this book, and like Keats in "Ode on a Grecian Urn," directly address it. In a paragraph, tell what is happening in the work, pose questions about it, and describe your feelings.

PREVIEW

Reflecting *on the* Literary Period

The Romantic Period: 1798–1832

The selections in this feature were written during the same literary period as the other selections in Collection 5, and they share many of the same ideas and concerns. The Focus Question will guide your reading and help you reflect on important aspects of the period.

A Ford on the River Arun by Sidney. Oil on canvas.

Private Collection.

Think About...

The beginning of the Romantic period in England is marked by the publication in 1798 of *Lyrical Ballads* by William Wordsworth and Samuel Taylor Coleridge (page 757). However, the literary concerns that shaped English Romanticism were evident years earlier. In the 1780s, Robert Burns was writing lyrics in Scottish dialect that grew out of the oral traditions of rural life. The strong emotions expressed in "To a Mouse" and the bond the speaker feels with the natural world bear the hallmarks of Romanticism, but the rollicking satire of "To a Louse" is more typical of eighteenth-century literature with its emphasis on reason and judgment.

In the preface to the *Lyrical Ballads,* Wordsworth announced a new subject matter and language for poetry. Central to his Romantic views was the importance of nature and experience in shaping the mind and personality. In "Ode: Intimations of Immortality," he traces the origins of joy and how our sense of joy changes as we grow up. The poetry of Percy Bysshe Shelley also focuses on the influence of nature and the poet's own emotions and subjective experience. In "To a Skylark," Shelley identifies the poet's imagination with the beauty and majesty of nature.

Focus Question

As you read each selection, keep in mind this Focus Question and take notes to help you answer it at the end of the feature:

How does Romantic poetry express the writers' beliefs in the power of nature, personal experience, emotion, and imagination to reveal the truths of human existence?

Pages 839–854 cover **Literary Skills** Evaluate the philosophical, political, religious, ethical, and social influences of a historical period.

To a Mouse
To a Louse

Meet the Writer Like Thomas Gray, **Robert Burns** (1759–1796) is often considered a pre-Romantic literary figure. Burns was born in a small village in Ayrshire in the western Lowlands of Scotland. In spite of long hours of toil on his family's farm, Burns found time to study—he would prop a book beside his place at the table and read during meals. His father encouraged him in his studies, and his mother taught him old Scottish songs and stories, many of which he later turned into poems.

A lover of Scottish folk songs, Burns collected, adapted, and wrote more than three hundred songs, including such favorites as "A Red, Red Rose" and "Auld Lang Syne." In 1786, he published his first volume of poetry, *Poems, Chiefly in the Scottish Dialect.* It contained forty-four poems and a glossary of the dialect words. The book was an immediate success: The first edition sold out in a month. In Edinburgh, Burns became a celebrity.

An acquaintance noted that Burns liked to pass himself off as an "illiterate ploughman who wrote from pure inspiration." In fact, Burns could write perfectly well in the literary English of his time as well as in a range of Scottish, from heavy dialect to a beautiful blending of folk idioms and literary language.

Upon Burns's death, the whole country joined to honor him and to contribute to the support of his family. Burns was hailed as the national poet of Scotland for using their own idiom to celebrate and exalt their lives.

Background **Dialect** is speech characteristic of a particular region or group. Burns's reputation is based chiefly on the poetry he wrote in Scots, a dialect of English spoken in Scotland during the eighteenth century.

CONNECTING TO THE
Focus Question

Burns wrote many of his poems in a language ordinary men and women could understand. As you read these poems, ask yourself: How does Burns use dialect to convey strong emotions and to create memorable images?

Burns's Cottage, Alloway (1876) by Samuel Bough. Oil on canvas.

Art Gallery and Museum, Kelvingrove, Glasgow, Scotland. © Glasgow City Council.

In this poem, the speaker addresses a mouse whose nest he has uncovered with his plow. Although he pities the mouse because her home has been destroyed, the speaker also believes the mouse is better off than he is.

To a Mouse

Robert Burns

On Turning Her Up in Her Nest,
with the Plow, November, 1785.

Wee, sleeket,° cowran, tim'rous beastie,
O, what a panic's in thy breastie!
Thou need na start awa sae hasty,
Wi' bickering brattle!°
I wad be laith° to rin an' chase thee,
Wi' murd'ring pattle!°

I'm truly sorry man's dominion
Has broken Nature's social union,
An' justifies that ill opinion,
Which makes thee startle
At me, thy poor, earth-born companion,
An' fellow mortal!

I doubt na, whyles,° but thou may thieve;
What then? poor beastie, thou maun° live!
A daimen-icker in a thrave°
'S a sma request:
I'll get a blessin wi' the lave,°
An' never miss 't!

Thy wee-bit housie, too, in ruin!
It's silly wa's° the win's are strewin!
An' naething, now, to big° a new ane,
O' foggage° green!
An' bleak December's winds ensuin,
Baith snell° an' keen!

1. sleeket: sleek.

4. bickering brattle: skirmishing, rattling sounds.

5. laith: loath; unwilling.

6. pattle: plow staff.

13. whyles: sometimes.

14. maun: must.

15. daimen-icker in a thrave: occasional ear of grain out of a bundle.

17. lave: remainder.

20. silly wa's: feeble walls.

21. big: build.

22. foggage: moss.

24. snell: bitter.

Thou saw the fields laid bare an' wast,
An' weary winter comin fast,
An' cozie here, beneath the blast,
Thou thought to dwell,
Till crash! the cruel coulter° past
Out thro' thy cell.

That wee-bit heap o' leaves an' stibble,
Has cost thee monie a weary nibble!
Now thou's turn'd out, for a' thy trouble,
But° house or hald,°
To thole° the winter's sleety dribble,
An' cranreuch° cauld!

But Mousie, thou art no thy-lane,°
In proving foresight may be vain:
The best laid schemes o' mice an' men
Gang aft agley,°
An' lea'e us nought but grief an' pain,
For promis'd joy!

Still, thou art blest, compar'd wi' me!
The present only toucheth thee:
But och! I backward cast my e'e,
On prospects drear!
An' forward, tho' I canna see,
I guess an' fear!

29. **coulter:** plow blade.

34. **but:** without. **hald:** land.

35. **thole:** endure.

36. **cranreuch:** hoarfrost.

37. **no thy-lane:** not alone.

40. **gang aft agley:** go often amiss.

Ploughing (detail) (late 19th or early 20th century) by Aldin Cecil.

In "To a Louse," the speaker addresses a louse that is crawling across a lady's expensive bonnet. At first, the speaker seems to be filled with indignation at the sight of the pest; by the end of the poem, however, his true feelings are revealed.

To a Louse

Robert Burns

On Seeing One on a Lady's Bonnet at Church.

Ha! wh'are ye gaun, ye crowlin' ferlie!°
Your impudence protects you sairly:°
I canna say but ye strunt° rarely,
    Owre gauze and lace;
Tho' faith! I fear ye dine but sparely
    On sic a place.

1. **crowlin' ferlie:** crawling wonder.
2. **sairly:** greatly; sorely.
3. **strunt:** strut.

Diana Sturt, Later Lady Milner (1800–05) by Sir Thomas Lawrence.

Kunsthistorisches Museum, Vienna, Austria.

Ye ugly, creepin', blastit wonner,°
Detested, shunn'd by saunt an' sinner!
How dare ye set your fit° upon her,
Sae fine a lady?
Gae somewhere else, and seek your dinner
On some poor body.

Swith, in some beggar's haffet squattle;°
There ye may creep, and sprawl, and sprattle°
Wi' ither kindred jumping cattle,
In shoals and nations;
Where horn nor bane° ne'er dare unsettle
Your thick plantations.

Now haud ye there,° ye're out o' sight,
Below the fatt'rels,° snug an' tight;
Na, faith ye yet! ye'll no be right
Till ye've got on it,
The very tapmost tow'ring height
O' Miss's bonnet.

My sooth! right bauld° ye set your nose out,
As plump and gray as onie grozet;°
O for some rank mercurial rozet,°
Or fell red smeddum!°
I'd gie you sic a hearty doze o't,
Wad dress your droddum!°

I wad na been surpris'd to spy
You on an auld wife's flannen toy;°
Or aiblins° some bit duddie° boy,
On's wyliecoat;°
But Miss's fine Lunardi!° fie,
How daur ye do't?

7. blastit wonner: blasted wonder.

9. fit: foot.

13. swith . . . squattle: Off! Sprawl in some beggar's temple.

14. sprattle: scramble; struggle.

17. horn nor bane (bone): materials used to make combs.

19. haud ye there: stay where you are.

20. fatt'rels: ribbon ends.

25. bauld: bold.

26. onie grozet: any gooseberry.

27. rozet: rosin, a substance derived from the resin given off by pine trees and used to make soap, varnish, and other products.

28. fell red smeddum: deadly red powder.

30. Wad dress your droddum: would put an end to you.

32. flannen toy: flannel headdress.

33. aiblins: perhaps. **bit duddie:** small ragged.

34. wyliecoat: undershirt.

35. Lunardi: a kind of bonnet, probably with winglike ribbons, named for a balloonist of the day.

O Jenny, dinna toss your head,
An' set your beauties a' abread!°
Ye little ken what cursèd speed
The blastie's makin'!
Thae winks and finger-ends,° I dread,
Are notice takin'!

O wad some Pow'r the giftie gie us
To see oursels as others see us!
It wad frae mony a blunder free us,
And foolish notion:
What airs in dress an' gait wad lea'e us,
And ev'n devotion!°

38. abread: abroad.

41. thae winks and finger-ends: Those people winking and pointing.

48. devotion: false piety.

Response and Analysis

To a Mouse
To a Louse

Thinking Critically

1. How does the speaker's **tone** change in line 37 of "To a Mouse"? What does the speaker imply in the last stanza about his own past and his prospects for the future?
2. In stanza 2 of "To a Mouse," what do the words *dominion* and *union* mean? What Romantic attitude toward people and nature does the use of these words imply?
3. What comparison between the mouse and himself does the speaker make in the last two stanzas of "To a Mouse"?
4. What is the speaker's **tone** in "To a Louse"? How does it differ from the speaker's tone in "To a Mouse"?
5. What is Burns's underlying **theme** in "To a Louse"? Is his main focus the louse or the lady? Explain.
6. Using details from the poems, respond to **Connecting to the Focus Question** on page 840.

Extending and Evaluating

7. Burns differs from most eighteenth-century poets in his use of **dialect.** What dialects are used in drama, songs, films, and fiction today? How do you feel about the use of dialect to convey realism? Cite specific examples.

Ode: Intimations of Immortality

Meet the Writer In 1807, **William Wordsworth** (1770–1850) published *Poems in Two Volumes,* which included his great ode. By then his best poetry was already behind him. The previous decade had been his greatest creative period: Wordsworth and Samuel Taylor Coleridge had collaborated on *Lyrical Ballads* (1798), the collection that laid the foundations for English Romanticism.

(For more information about William Wordsworth, see page 734.)

Background An **ode** is a complex, generally long lyric poem on a serious subject. The **epigraph**, or opening quotation, of Wordsworth's ode was taken from "My Heart Leaps Up," one of his best-loved poems.

"Ode: Intimations of Immortality" is more than two hundred lines long; only three of the eleven stanzas are reprinted here. According to Wordsworth, two years passed between the writing of the first four stanzas and the remaining seven. In the poem, Wordsworth revisits some of the themes explored in "Lines Composed a Few Miles Above Tintern Abbey" (page 736). He recalls the innocent joy of childhood, takes pleasure in the beauty of nature, and reflects on the rewards that come with maturity.

CONNECTING TO THE
Focus Question

As you read this important Romantic poem, ask yourself: How are the speaker's imagination and emotions revealed?

from Ode

Intimations of Immortality from Recollections of Early Childhood

William Wordsworth

The Child is Father of the Man;
And I could wish my days to be
Bound each to each by natural piety.

1

There was a time when meadow, grove, and stream,
The earth, and every common sight,
To me did seem
Apparelled in celestial light,
The glory and the freshness of a dream.
It is not now as it hath been of yore;—
Turn wheresoe'er I may,
By night or day,
The things which I have seen I now can see no more.

2

The Rainbow comes and goes,
And lovely is the Rose,
The Moon doth with delight
Look round her when the heavens are bare,
Waters on a starry night
Are beautiful and fair;
The sunshine is a glorious birth;
But yet I know, where'er I go,
That there hath passed away a glory from the
earth.

Age of Innocence (1788) by Sir Joshua Reynolds.

Tate Gallery, London, Great Britain.

5

Our birth is but a sleep and a forgetting:
The Soul that rises with us, our life's Star,
Hath had elsewhere its setting,
And cometh from afar:
Not in entire forgetfulness,
And not in utter nakedness,
But trailing clouds of glory do we come
From God, who is our home:
Heaven lies about us in our infancy!
Shades of the prison-house begin to close
Upon the growing Boy,
But He beholds the light, and whence it flows,
He sees it in his joy;
The Youth, who daily farther from the east
Must travel, still is Nature's Priest,
And by the vision splendid
Is on his way attended;
At length the Man perceives it die away,
And fade into the light of common day.

Response and Analysis

Thinking Critically

1. The **epigraph,** or opening quotation, presents a **paradox,** an apparent contradiction. What can childhood experiences teach us as adults?
2. In stanza 1, the speaker describes something he once had but now has lost. What is the speaker describing? What does the **image** "apparelled in celestial light" (line 4) make you see?
3. According to stanza 2, how does the speaker feel now when he looks at nature?
4. What **mood,** or feeling, do the first two stanzas create for you?
5. What does the speaker mean by "Our birth is but a sleep and a forgetting" (stanza 5)?
6. Explain how the sun is used in the **extended metaphor,** or comparison, in the fifth stanza.
7. Using details from the poem, respond to **Connecting to the Focus Question** on page 846.

Extending and Evaluating

8. Wordsworth describes growing up as "shades of the prison-house" beginning to close. Can you think of actual experiences that either support or challenge Wordsworth's view? Explain your response.

To a Skylark

Meet the Writer In his short life, **Percy Bysshe Shelley** (1792–1822) produced an astonishing range of magnificent poetry. The years 1818 and 1819 were a time of upheaval and tragedy for Shelley. Soon after he and his wife, Mary, moved to Italy, two of their children died. In spite of his grief, Shelley managed to produce some of his best works: the dramatic poem *Prometheus Unbound* and many beautiful lyrics, including "Ode to the West Wind" and "To a Skylark."

(For more information about Percy Bysshe Shelley, see page 801.)

Background Shelley wrote "To a Skylark" in 1820, when he and Mary were staying with friends near the Mediterranean coast of Italy. Mary said of the origins of this poem, "It was on a beautiful summer evening, while wandering among the lanes whose myrtle hedges were the bowers of fireflies, that we heard the caroling of the skylark which inspired one of the most beautiful of his poems."

The European skylark is known for its high-pitched musical song, which it produces while in flight. In this poem the speaker addresses a skylark, which has soared high above the earth and out of sight, and praises its natural poetry. The speaker yearns to share in the skylark's joy and natural musicality.

CONNECTING TO THE
Focus Question

In the preface to *Lyrical Ballads,* Wordsworth stated that all good poetry is based on "the spontaneous overflow of powerful feelings." As you read Shelley's poem, ask yourself: How does the poet create the impression of spontaneous emotional experience while adhering to a rigid structure and organization?

To a Skylark

Percy Bysshe Shelley

Hail to thee, blithe° Spirit!
Bird thou never wert,
That from Heaven, or near it,
Pourest thy full heart
In profuse° strains of unpremeditated° art.

Higher still and higher
From the earth thou springest
Like a cloud of fire;
The blue deep thou wingest,
And singing still dost soar, and soaring ever singest.

1. **blithe:** joyful; carefree.

5. **profuse:** abundant. **unpremeditated:** unplanned; done without forethought.

In the golden lightning
  Of the sunken sun,
O'er which clouds are bright'ning,
  Thou dost float and run;
Like an unbodied joy whose race is just begun.

The pale purple even°
  Melts around thy flight;
Like a star of Heaven,
  In the broad daylight
Thou art unseen, but yet I hear thy shrill delight,

Keen as are the arrows
  Of that silver sphere,°
Whose intense lamp narrows
  In the white dawn clear
Until we hardly see—we feel that it is there.

16. even: archaic for "evening."

22. silver sphere: "a star of Heaven" (line 18).

Nature's Glory by John Wainwright.

Fine Art of Oakham, Leicestershire, Great Britain.

All the earth and air
  With thy voice is loud,
As, when night is bare,
  From one lonely cloud
The moon rains out her beams, and Heaven is overflowed.

What thou art we know not;
  What is most like thee?
From rainbow clouds there flow not
  Drops so bright to see
As from thy presence showers a rain of melody.

Like a Poet hidden
  In the light of thought,
Singing hymns unbidden,
  Till the world is wrought
To sympathy with hopes and fears it heeded not:

Like a high-born maiden
  In a palace-tower,
Soothing her love-laden
  Soul in secret hour
With music sweet as love, which overflows her bower:°

Like a glow-worm golden
  In a dell° of dew,
Scattering unbeholden
  Its aereal hue
Among the flowers and grass, which screen it from the view!

Like a rose embowered°
  In its own green leaves,
By warm winds deflowered,
  Till the scent it gives
Makes faint with too much sweet those heavy-wingèd thieves:

Sound of vernal° showers
  On the twinkling grass,
Rain-awakened flowers,
  All that ever was
Joyous, and clear, and fresh, thy music doth surpass:

45. bower: archaic for "boudoir," a woman's bedroom, dressing room, or private sitting room.

47. dell: small valley.

51. embowered: enclosed; sheltered.

56. vernal: occurring in the spring.

Teach us, Sprite or Bird,
What sweet thoughts are thine:
I have never heard
Praise of love or wine
That panted forth a flood of rapture so divine.

Chorus Hymeneal,°
Or triumphal chant,
Matched with thine would be all
But an empty vaunt,°
A thing wherein we feel there is some hidden want.

What objects are the fountains
Of thy happy strain?°
What fields, or waves, or mountains?
What shapes of sky or plain?
What love of thine own kind? what ignorance of pain?

With thy clear keen joyance°
Languor° cannot be:
Shadow of annoyance
Never came near thee:
Thou lovest—but ne'er knew love's sad satiety.°

Waking or asleep,
Thou of death must deem
Things more true and deep
Than we mortals dream,
Or how could thy notes flow in such a crystal stream?

We look before and after,
And pine for what is not:
Our sincerest laughter
With some pain is fraught;
Our sweetest songs are those that tell of saddest thought.

Yet if we could scorn
Hate, and pride, and fear;
If we were things born
Not to shed a tear,
I know not how thy joy we ever should come near.

66. chorus Hymeneal: wedding song. *Hymeneal* is derived from Hymen, the Greek god of marriage.
69. vaunt: boast.

72. strain: melody.

76. joyance: archaic for "rejoicing."
77. languor: indifference; lack of spirit or interest.

80. satiety: feeling of weariness or disgust resulting from overindulging one's appetite or desires.

Better than all measures
  Of delightful sound,
Better than all treasures
  That in books are found,
Thy skill to poet were, thou scorner of the ground!

Teach me half the gladness
  That thy brain must know,
Such harmonious madness
  From my lips would flow
The world should listen then—as I am listening now.

Response and Analysis

Thinking Critically

1. Lines 36–55 contain four **similes.** How are the similes related, and what do you think they show about the skylark and the speaker?
2. What questions does the speaker ask the bird? What does he ask the bird to teach him?
3. According to lines 101–104, what would have to happen for "harmonious madness" to flow from the speaker of the poem?
4. How do you interpret these phrases: "unbodied joy" (line 15), "ignorance of pain" (line 75), "ne'er knew love's sad satiety" (line 80), "scorner of the ground" (line 100), and "harmonious madness" (line 103)?
5. What do you think the skylark **symbolizes** to the speaker? Which lines support your interpretation?
6. What, in your opinion, does the speaker most envy about a skylark?
7. Using details from the poem, respond to **Connecting to the Focus Question** on page 849.

Extending and Evaluating

8. Lines 86–90 are among the most frequently quoted in English poetry. Do the ideas expressed in these lines correspond with your own experiences? If so, explain how.

REVIEW

Reflecting on the Literary Period

The Romantic Period: 1798–1832

The following questions ask you to compare and analyze the selections in this feature and respond to the Focus Question. Where possible, cite passages from the selections to support your answers.

Comparing Literature

1. "To a Mouse" and "To a Louse" by Robert Burns both convey universal truths, though their subject matter is very different. What truths do you think Burns is seeking to reveal in each of these poems?
2. The Victorian writer Thomas Carlyle said: "Burns was rather the poet of feeling—Wordsworth is rather the poet of intellect." Do you agree or disagree? Support your answer with evidence from the selections.
3. Shelley's "To a Skylark" and Burns's "To a Mouse" both focus on animals and what they can teach humans. What do these poems tell you about the way Shelley and Burns view nature? How do these poets demonstrate this view in their poems?
4. Like Wordsworth's "Ode: Intimations of Immortality," Shelley's "To a Skylark" is an **ode,** a favorite poetic form among the Romantics. What aspects of the poems are characteristic of odes? Which poem do you find to be the stronger representation of this form? (To review the characteristics of an ode, see Literary Focus, page 747.)

RESPONDING TO THE

Focus Question

Review your notes and responses related to the Focus Question for this feature. Using details from the selections, write your answer to the question.

How does Romantic poetry express the writers' beliefs in the power of nature, personal experience, emotion, and imagination to reveal the truths of human existence?

SKILLS FOCUS

Pages 839–854 cover **Literary Skills** Evaluate the philosophical, political, religious, ethical, and social influences of a historical period.

READ ON: FOR INDEPENDENT READING

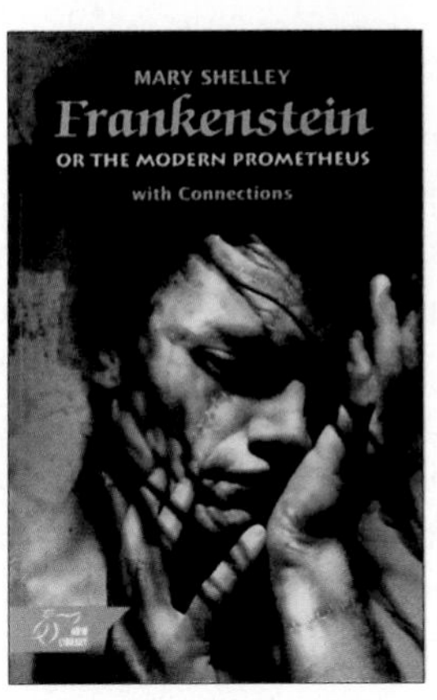

FICTION

Share the Terror

Mary Shelley said of her novel ***Frankenstein*** that she wanted to write a story that "would speak to the mysterious fears of our nature and awaken thrilling horror." She succeeded, writing an early science fiction novel as well as a vivid version of the Romantic mythology of the self.

This title is available in the HRW Library.

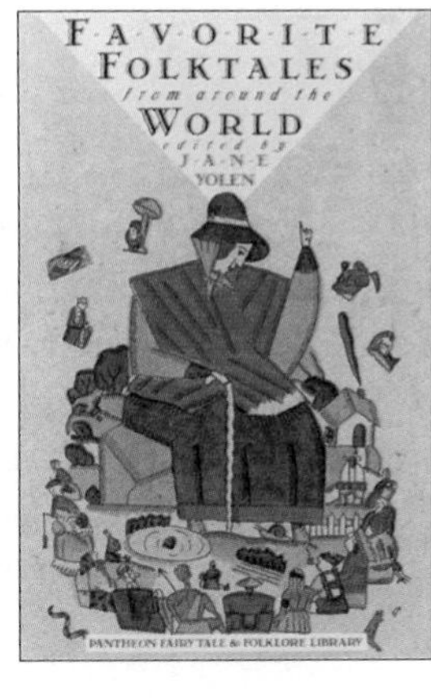

FICTION

Stories from Many Lands

The brothers Jacob and Wilhelm Grimm collected their famous fairy tales in the early part of the nineteenth century. Not everyone knows, however, that the fairy tale was a direct descendent of the folk tale—stories that were handed down orally through the ages. ***Favorite Folktales from Around the World,*** edited by Jane Yolen, features beautiful, highly readable translations of folk tales hailing from cultures as diverse as China, Africa, and Ireland.

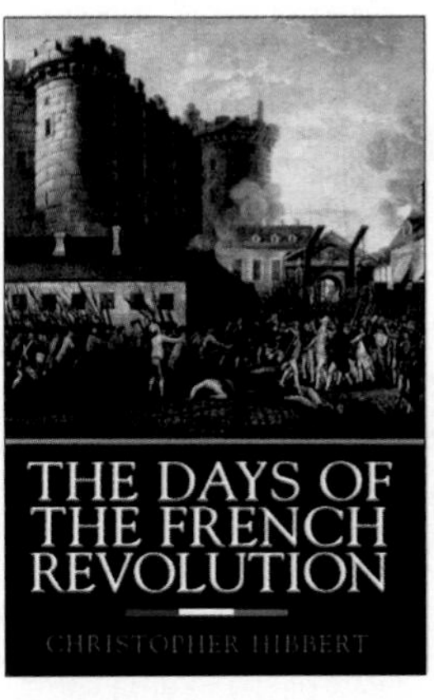

NONFICTION

Revolutionary Fever

Christopher Hibbert's ***The Days of the French Revolution*** brings all of the drama, turmoil, and bloodshed of the Reign of Terror to life. Here you will meet the principal players of the French Revolution-—everyone from Robespierre to Marie Antoinette to Napoleon—and see their stories cast in a new light, though not at the expense of truth. Swiftly plotted and gripping from start to finish, Hibbert's historical narrative reads like a good novel.

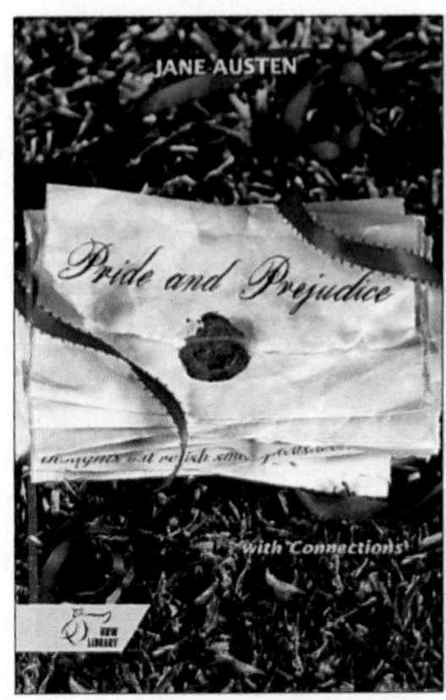

FICTION

Love and Marriage

Originally published in 1813, Jane Austen's novel ***Pride and Prejudice*** is about five husband-hunting sisters in nineteenth-century England and the delicate tangles of love and courtship they ensnare themselves in. What struck people then, and still strikes us now, is Austen's ability to make commonplace people and events interesting. The superficially trivial content is deceptive; it masks a deeper irony that exposes the manners and customs of the period.

This title is available in the HRW Library.

Writing a Reflective Essay

Writing Assignment
Write a 1,500-word reflective essay in which you explore the meaning of a personal experience.

In "Lines Composed a Few Miles Above Tintern Abbey," William Wordsworth reflects on two visits he made to the Wye River Valley and the ruins of Tintern Abbey in 1793 and 1798. Through his reflection he discovers that he has changed. On the first visit he could see only the sensory beauty in nature. Now, more mature, he sees in nature "a spirit . . . that impels / All thinking things, all objects of all thought." Thus, through writing this poem, Wordsworth explores the meaning of an experience and discovers his most significant belief about life. Writing a **reflective essay** will give you the opportunity to do the same.

Prewriting

Think About Purpose

The Write Reason Before choosing something to write about, think about your purpose for writing a reflective essay. Your **purpose** is to explore the connection between a personal experience and what it says about your life and, beyond that, what it says about the meaning of being human.

Choose an Experience

Seeking a Learning Experience To find a subject for your reflective essay, think about your most important **personal experiences,** including significant **events** you have participated in or witnessed, unusual **conditions** you have encountered, or special **concerns** you've had. The nature of the experience doesn't matter as long as it taught you something about yourself and your world.

If an experience doesn't leap immediately to mind, look through old yearbooks, photos, diaries, or journals. Also, try reading some published reflective pieces, such as poems, biographies, and essays. Remember that you will share your experience with an **audience,** so be sure the experience you select is one that is appropriate to share and one you are comfortable telling others.

Reflect on Your Subject

What's It All About? Reflective essays go beyond merely describing your personal observations and perceptions to examine abstract ideas—love, patience, courage, honor. Your examination of and reflection on your experience should lead you to a new understanding of your beliefs about life, about what it means to be human. The chart on the next page provides questions that will help you reflect on your

Writing Skills
Write a reflective essay about a personal experience.

subject. One writer, reflecting on his visit to the Vietnam Veterans Memorial in Washington, D.C., provided the sample responses.

Quick guide!

REFLECTING ON A SUBJECT

Reflection Questions	One Writer's Responses
How does (or did) the experience affect me?	Visiting the wall and meeting Joe was an emotional experience for me. I think I grew up a lot that day.
How did the experience change my attitudes or behaviors?	Before my visit, I was cynical about ideas like courage, honor, sacrifice, and duty. Now I think I understand that these are very real qualities that real people have.
What universal truth or insight into human existence did the experience teach me?	I learned that the best quality of human beings is their capacity to sacrifice themselves for others and for their beliefs.

TIP As you reflect on the significance of your experience, think not only about the **narrative**—the events that occurred—but also about the following kinds of information.

- **descriptions** of sights and sounds that contribute to your overall impression of the experience
- **explanations** of factual information that relate to an important part of your experience or to life in general
- strategies you might use to **persuade** someone of the deeper meaning of your experience

Include these kinds of information in your responses to the questions in the chart.

Gather and Record Details

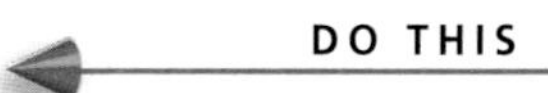

Total Recall To gather the details that will bring your experience and its significance to life for your audience, make a list of all the individual events that were an integral part of your experience. Here are some suggestions to help you recall the events.

- Visualize the entire experience, picturing each event from beginning to end.
- If someone else participated in or witnessed any of the events in your experience, ask that person to help you recall details.
- If you have any mementos of the experience—photographs, letters, journal or diary entries—use them to help jog your memory.

Now, under each event in your list, record specific details about each event to help you create **concrete images** in the minds of readers. The chart on the next page gives explanations and examples of the types of narrative and descriptive details you should include.

Writing Skills
Think about the significance of the experience. Use details to create concrete images.

NARRATIVE AND DESCRIPTIVE DETAILS

Types of Details	Examples
Narrative details	
• relate actions, thoughts, and feelings of the people involved in the events	I saw one man get on his hands and knees so that a slender teenage girl could stand on his back to reach the name she wanted to rub onto paper.
• include **dialogue**—the actual words spoken by people involved in the experience, and **interior monologue,** your thoughts during the experience	"Randy saved my life that day," Joe said. "He was quite a guy, the real deal." "Many of these people were killed when they were just my age and a little older," I thought with a chill.
Descriptive details	
• describe the way people look	My view was obstructed by an older man busily doing a pencil rubbing.
• describe settings of events	I was mesmerized by the smooth black granite panels and the thousands of names indelibly engraved into them.

TIP If you cannot remember the exact words you or someone else used, re-create them as exactly as you can in language, meaning, and spirit.

A Balancing Act Throughout your essay, **maintain a balance** in the events you are narrating. In other words, if your experience consists of three major events, don't use two thirds of your essay narrating one of the events and one third narrating the other two. Of course, if one event is more important than the others, you'll naturally spend more time narrating it. As you narrate each event, also describe your thoughts and feelings to hint at the meaning of the experience and its effect on you. In the conclusion of your essay, state the significance of the experience or its effect and explicitly connect the entire experience to more general and abstract ideas about life.

TIP A **flashback** takes readers back to an event that occurred before the story's action, while a **flash-forward** jumps ahead in time, skipping intervening events. For more on **flashbacks,** see page 1206.

Organize Your Reflective Essay

Following Orders Now decide how to organize your essay. You'll organize the events in **chronological** order, possibly varying this order by using **flashbacks** and **flash-forwards.** Within that order, though, you can also use other organizational patterns to describe people and places or to explain your ideas about the experience. For extended descriptions, you might choose to organize details **spatially.** For discussions of effects and ideas, you might use **order of importance.** The student writing about his visit to the Vietnam Veterans Memorial found that strict chronological order suited his purpose best.

SKILLS FOCUS

Writing Skills
Organize the essay's sequence of events.

PRACTICE & APPLY 1 First, choose a subject for your reflective essay. Then, reflect upon your subject, gather narrative and descriptive details, and organize your essay.

Writing

Writing a Reflective Essay

A Writer's Framework

Beginning

- Engage readers' attention.
- Provide background information necessary for understanding the experience.
- Hint at the significance or effect of the experience.

Middle

- Use narrative and descriptive details to relate the events that make up the experience.
- Effectively organize events, descriptions, and ideas.
- Continue to hint at the meaning of the experience.

End

- Bring your telling of the experience to a close.
- Reflect on the experience; explicitly reveal its significance for you or its effect on you.
- Identify the insight into life the experience gave you.

A Writer's Model

Meeting Grandfather

During spring break of 2002, I experienced the Vietnam Veterans Memorial—"the Wall"—in Washington D.C. It was there that I finally met my grandfather, who had been killed in Vietnam in 1970 when the plane he was piloting was shot down.

BEGINNING
Engaging opener
Hint at significance of experience

My grandmother has shown me pictures and told me stories about my grandfather, but somehow he never seemed real. Maybe that was because he didn't look like a grandfather in the pictures. In fact, he was only twenty-six when he died. In the photo I carried in my wallet, he looked like me and a younger version of my father combined.

Background information

I had only to walk up to the first section of the Wall to become mesmerized by the smooth black granite panels and the thousands of names engraved on them. "Many of these people were killed when they were just my age and a little older," I thought with a chill. I wandered up and down the 140 panels, staggered by the number of names, more than fifty thousand, each representing a life—a father, a son, a grandson.

MIDDLE/First event
Hint at effect of the experience
Interior monologue

I saw hundreds of people at the Wall. Some, like me, wandered up and down, looking at many panels. Others had brought flowers, photos, and other small mementos to lay at the base of a panel under a particular name. Still others took out pieces of paper and pencils and rubbed names from the Wall to their papers. I saw one man get on his hands and knees so that a slender teenage girl could stand on his back and reach the name she wanted to rub onto paper.

Narrative and descriptive details

(continued)

(continued)

Second event

Finally, realizing I wasn't just going to stumble across my grandfather's name, I got the panel and line number from the information booth. When I found the panel, my view was obstructed by an older man busily doing a pencil rubbing of one of the names on the panel. When he finished, he looked at the paper sadly, then noticing me, held it up.

Narrative and descriptive details

"The best friend I ever had," he said to me.

Dialogue

I looked at the name—Randolph C. Rogers—and back at the man.

"That's . . . that's my grandfather's name," I said. What were the odds of my running into one of my grandfather's old friends at the Wall? Astronomical! There had to be a reason.

Thoughts and feelings

Hint at effect

"You're Randy Rogers' grandkid?" the man asked.

"Yes, sir," I said, "but I never knew him."

"Well, son, you're about to. Come sit down and let ol' Joe Weiss introduce you to your grandpa," he said in his loud, friendly voice.

During the next two hours, Joe kept me spellbound with stories about my grandfather. Mixed in with many humorous tales were stories of courage and devotion to comrades and country. Joe told these stories as if they had happened the day before. My grandfather was becoming a real person to me.

Narrative and descriptive details

Hint at significance and effect of the experience

Then, in a sober, quiet voice, Joe described what was very nearly his last mission: He and Grandfather were flying on patrol and had turned for home when Joe's plane was hit by ground fire. Joe ejected over enemy territory. My grandfather kept circling Joe's position, holding off enemy ground troops who were looking for Joe until the rescue helicopter arrived and whisked Joe away.

Narrative and descriptive details

"Randy saved my life that day, no *if*'s, *and*'s, or *but*'s," Joe said, tears in his eyes. "He was quite a guy, the real deal. Three weeks later, a surface-to-air missile got him. He never knew what hit him."

END

I've thought about the Wall, Joe, and my grandfather a lot since then. I think about the cynicism I once felt about ideas like courage, honor, sacrifice, and duty—cynicism that evaporated that day. The qualities possessed by my grandfather, Joe, and thousands of others are the qualities that make human existence worthwhile.

Reflection

Effect of experience

Insight gained into life

INTERNET

More Writer's Models

Keyword: LE7 12-5

PRACTICE & APPLY 2 Using the framework on page 859 and the Writer's Model above as guides, write the first draft of your essay. Remember to maintain a balance in narrating the events.

Revising

Evaluate and Revise Your Draft

A Polished Reflection A reflective essay is a personal kind of writing. You want it to reflect your complete experience with accuracy and flair. To make sure that it does, give it at least two more careful readings before you publish it. First, use the guidelines below to evaluate and revise your essay's content and organization. Then, use the guidelines on page 862 to evaluate and revise your essay's style.

PEER REVIEW

Before you make your final revision, exchange essays with a classmate. Ask him or her for suggestions on how you could better engage readers' attention in your introduction.

First Reading: Content and Organization Using the chart below, find ways to improve your reflective essay's content and organization. As you answer the evaluation questions, think about your intended **audience** and your **purpose** for writing the essay.

Rubric: Writing a Reflective Essay

Evaluation Questions	Tips	Revision Techniques
1 Does the introduction provide necessary background information and engage readers' attention?	**Bracket** sentences that provide necessary background information. **Circle** the engaging opening.	**Add** background information. **Add** an engaging opener or **revise** existing sentences to make them more engaging.
2 Does the introduction provide a hint about the significance or effect of the experience for the writer?	**Underline** the sentence or sentences in the introduction that hint at the significance or effect of the experience.	**Add** a sentence or two to hint at the significance or effect of the experience without revealing it entirely.
3 Does the body use narrative and descriptive details to relate each event? Does it hint at the significance of the experience?	**Put a check mark** next to each narrative or descriptive passage. **Star** each hint at the significance or effect of the experience.	**Add** details or **elaborate** on events to make them clear. **Add** thoughts and feelings that hint at the significance or effect of the experience.
4 Is the essay clearly organized? Do clue words point out any shifts from strict chronological order?	**Number** events in order. **Bracket** passages not in chronological order. **Highlight** clue words within the brackets.	If necessary, **rearrange** events in strict chronological order or **add** clue words to explain shifts in organization.
5 Does the conclusion bring the narrative to a close and explicitly state the significance or effect of the experience?	**Highlight** the sentences that bring the narrative to a close. **Draw a wavy line** under the experience's significance or effect on the writer.	**Add** sentences that bring the narrative to a close. **Add** one or more sentences that explicitly state the experience's significance or effect.
6 Does the conclusion reveal the insight into life gained by the writer?	**Draw a box** around the sentences that reveal the writer's insight into life.	**Add** one or more sentences that reveal the writer's insight into life.

Second Reading: Style Now, consider your style, or the way you express yourself in writing. One way to establish a fresh **tone** and make the dialogue in your essay sound natural is to use colloquialisms. **Colloquialisms** include the common sayings and expressions found in everyday speech, such as "You said it" or "Gimme a break." Use the guidelines in the chart below to evaluate your use of colloquialisms in your essay.

Style Guidelines

Evaluation Question	Tip	Revision Technique
Does the dialogue in the reflective essay include colloquialisms that reflect natural, everyday speech?	**Bracket** all the dialogue in the essay. **Underline** colloquialisms within the dialogue.	**Add** colloquialisms to dialogue, or **replace** standard language with appropriate colloquialisms that an audience will understand.

ANALYZING THE REVISION PROCESS

Study these revisions, and answer the questions that follow.

add — "Randy saved my life that day, *no if's, and's, or but's,*" Joe said, tears in his eyes. "He was quite a guy, the real deal. Three weeks later, a surface-to-air missile got him. He never knew what hit him."

I've thought about the Wall, Joe, and my grandfather a lot since then. I think about the cynicism I once felt about ideas like courage, honor, sacrifice, and duty—cynicism that

add — evaporated that day. *The qualities possessed by my grandfather, Joe, and thousands of others are the qualities that make human existence worthwhile.*

Responding to the Revision Process

1. What does the writer achieve by adding to the first sentence?
2. Why did the writer add a new sentence to the passage?

Writing Skills
Revise for content and style.

PRACTICE & APPLY 3 Using the guidelines on page 861 and above and feedback from peers, evaluate and revise the content, organization, and style of your essay.

Publishing

Proofread and Publish Your Essay

Polish Your Reflection Your reflective essay can have it all—an engaging subject, a natural and intimate style written in an intriguing voice, and a brilliant insight into what it means to be a human being—but if it is riddled with errors in grammar, usage, and mechanics, readers will be so distracted that they will stop reading out of frustration. You can avoid this dire conclusion to your efforts by carefully proofreading your essay.

Share the Wisdom Your reflective essay tells a story only you can tell. Now it's time to share the story with others. Here are ways to share your essay with an audience.

- Give an oral presentation of your reflection to classmates or family members. For more on **presenting a reflection,** see page 864.
- Trade essays with a classmate. After reading each other's essays, discuss shared experiences, feelings, and insights.
- With classmates, create a Web page about yourselves and the experiences that have influenced you.
- Give a copy of the essay to those who shared your experience, and compare their recollections of the experience with yours.

TIP Thoroughly proofreading your paper will help you eliminate errors in the **conventions** of standard American English. As you proofread, be careful to check the punctuation of dialogue. For more on **using quotation marks,** see Quotation Marks, 13c–d, in the Language Handbook.

Reflect on Your Essay

What Did You Learn? Use the following questions to take stock of the choices you made while writing your reflective essay. Write a short response to each question, and keep your responses with your final draft in your portfolio.

- Have other experiences reinforced what you learned from the experience narrated in your essay? Explain.
- Have you had other experiences that contradicted what you learned from the experience narrated in your essay? Explain.
- What was the most difficult part of your reflection to put into words? Why do you think this part was so difficult?
- In what other kinds of writing might using narrative and descriptive details and quoting people's actual words be useful? Consider writing you might do both in this and other classes and outside of school, and explain how these strategies would enhance each type of writing.

PRACTICE & APPLY 4 Carefully proofread your essay for errors in standard American English grammar, usage, and mechanics. Then, publish your essay using one of the suggestions above. Finally, reflect on what you learned while writing your reflective essay by answering the questions above.

Writing Skills
Proofread, especially for correct use of quotation marks.

Presenting a Reflection

Speaking Assignment
Adapt your reflective essay for oral presentation to an audience.

In the reflective essay you wrote earlier in this collection, you shared a significant experience in your life and told your readers how the experience affected you and what insight into life you gained from it. In this workshop you'll adapt your reflective essay for an oral presentation, which will allow you to use your voice and body language to bring the totality of the experience to life for your listeners.

Adapt Your Reflective Essay

Punch It Up The techniques of an oral presentation are different from the techniques of a written essay in some ways, but your **purpose** is the same—to narrate an experience and to explore the connection between the experience and an insight into life in general. Here are some suggestions for adapting your essay for an oral presentation.

- **Stage your presentation. Dialogue** is an important part of any presentation that involves narration and characters. In your oral presentation, imitate the voices of the people involved in your experience to bring them life. You can also act out your **movements, facial expressions,** and **gestures** and those of other people involved in your experience. Avoid overacting and exaggerated imitations, both of which can have a negative effect on your listeners. Also consider using **visuals** and **sound effects** to heighten the effect of your presentation; however, don't overdo it. Be sure that your experience remains the center of attention.
- **Explain yourself.** You can be subtle in writing, but in your oral presentation you must provide your audience with broad hints about the significance or effect of your experience. Plan to balance those hints with the narrative and descriptive details that describe each event. At the conclusion of your presentation, make sure your explicit statements about the significance or effect of the experience and the more general insight into life that you gained are clear enough for a listening audience.
- **Use effective language.** Effective language in a reflective presentation has clarity and force, and is **aesthetic,** or artistic and tasteful. Choose **concrete images** to narrate events and to describe places. Use rhetorical questions, parallelism, figurative language, and other **rhetorical devices** to enhance the effectiveness of your language. Where appropriate, use **irony,** which is especially effective in oral presentations because it can be communicated through your tone of voice as well as through your words. For example, the student

Listening and Speaking Skills
Deliver an oral presentation of a reflective essay.

who wrote the essay that begins on page 859 used tone of voice and a pause between contrasting ideas to make clear the irony of meeting in 2002 the grandfather who died in 1970: "I met my grandfather in 2002." [Pause.] "He was killed in Vietnam in 1970."

Rehearse Your Presentation

Naturally Speaking—Almost Reading a speech word for word usually sounds stiff and unnatural. Plan to present your reflection **extemporaneously** by creating brief note cards that remind you of the important events that make up your experience. Also include notes reminding you when in your presentation to use visuals, sound effects, gestures, and dialogue.

Words and Actions Sometimes the way you say something means as much as or more than what you say. An oral presentation gives you the opportunity to use both verbal and nonverbal techniques to mesmerize your audience. Here are some techniques to consider.

DELIVERY TECHNIQUES

Verbal Techniques	Nonverbal Techniques
Language: Use **standard American English** so that everyone will understand your presentation. In dialogue, however, use **informal expressions** to capture the uniqueness of the people involved in your experience.	**Eye Contact:** Give individuals in your listening audience the impression that you are speaking directly to them by making eye contact with as many of them as you can. This gives your presentation an intimate feeling.
Tone: Change the tone of your voice to reflect the nature of the events you're narrating or the person you're describing or quoting. Humorous events require a light tone. Somber events require a serious tone.	**Gestures:** Use gestures that match the events or movements you are portraying. Gestures should appear natural and unforced. Be aware that overly dramatic gestures can detract from the content of your presentation.
Volume: Vary the volume of your voice to fit the mood you want to create, but speak loudly enough to be heard.	**Facial Expressions:** Use facial expressions to express your feelings and to characterize people involved in your experience.

Practice, Practice, Practice An effective presentation requires practice. Using your note cards, rehearse your presentation until it feels completely natural to you. Rehearse in front of a mirror to check your gestures and facial expressions. Rehearse in front of family and friends, and ask for feedback that could help you improve your presentation. If possible, videotape a rehearsal. Then, watch the tape for ways you might improve your presentation.

Listening and Speaking Skills
Rehearse your presentation. Use effective verbal and nonverbal delivery techniques.

PRACTICE & APPLY 5 Adapt your reflective essay for an oral presentation, and create note cards for rehearsal. After practicing your presentation, deliver it to an audience.

Collection 5: Skills Review

Comparing Literature

The following two poems describe cities that—from the poets' perspectives—are on the verge of social ruin. William Blake's "London" depicts the poor living conditions of England in the early nineteenth century, a time when poverty and oppressive governmental policies contributed to a fractured society. Derek Walcott's "The Virgins" describes Frederiksted, one of the oldest port cities on the U.S. Virgin Island of St. Croix. Frederiksted is now a free port where tourists can purchase goods without paying customs duties. Its economy, once based on sugar cane, is now dependent on tourism.

DIRECTIONS: Read the two poems that follow. Then, read each multiple-choice question that follows, and write the letter of the best response.

London

William Blake

I wander through each chartered° street,
Near where the chartered Thames does flow,
And mark° in every face I meet
Marks of weakness, marks of woe.

In every cry of every man,
In every infant's cry of fear,
In every voice, in every ban,°
The mind-forged manacles I hear.

How the chimney sweeper's cry
Every blackning church appalls,°
And the hapless soldier's sigh
Runs in blood down palace walls.

But most through midnight streets I hear
How the youthful harlot's curse°
Blasts the newborn infant's tear
And blights with plagues the marriage hearse.

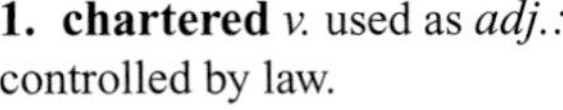

1. chartered *v.* used as *adj.:* controlled by law.

3. mark *v.:* notice.

7. ban *n.:* legal prohibition, public condemnation, or curse; also, a marriage announcement (spelled *bans*).

10. appalls *v.:* causes to lose color; also, dismays, terrifies, weakens.

14. harlot's curse: curse upon the harlot or prostitute by a hypocritical society that pushed women into prostitution and then condemned them for it; also the curse the harlot utters in return. A very real form of the "curse" is disease.

Pages 866–869 cover
Literary Skills
Compare and contrast works from different literary periods.

The Virgins

Derek Walcott

Down the dead streets of sun-stoned Frederiksted,
the first free port to die for tourism,
strolling at funeral pace, I am reminded
of life not lost to the American dream;
but my small-islander's simplicities
can't better our new empire's civilized
exchange of cameras, watches, perfumes, brandies
for the good life, so cheaply underpriced
that only the crime rate is on the rise
in streets blighted with sun, stone arches
and plazas blown dry by the hysteria
of rumor. A condominium drowns
in vacancy; its bargains are dusted,
but only a jeweled housefly drones
over the bargains. The roulettes spin
rustily to the wind—the vigorous trade
that every morning would begin afresh
by revving up green water round the pierhead
heading for where the banks of silver thresh.

---

1. In the first stanza of "London," the speaker is —
   - **A** describing how he loves London
   - **B** greeting fellow citizens of London
   - **C** noticing other people's unhappiness
   - **D** looking at the Thames

2. Which of the following is an **image** of oppression and restriction used in "London"?
   - **F** the flowing Thames
   - **G** the midnight streets
   - **H** the soldier's sigh
   - **J** the mind-forged manacles

Collection 5: Skills Review

3. In lines 11–12 of "London," the speaker suggests that —
   - **A** the country's rulers are responsible for the deaths of soldiers
   - **B** all soldiers are poorly trained for battle
   - **C** patriotism is worth the loss of lives
   - **D** soldiers are rebelling

4. The overall **tone** of Blake's poem could best be described as —
   - **F** self-pitying
   - **G** understated
   - **H** bitter
   - **J** detached

5. In lines 1–4 of "The Virgins," the speaker implies that —
   - **A** he believes in the American dream
   - **B** he is pleased by what tourism has done for his city
   - **C** he doesn't remember what life was like before his city became a "new empire"
   - **D** he thinks the American dream can be destructive

6. Which of the following literary devices does Walcott use in "The Virgins"?
   - **F** onomatopoeia
   - **G** allusion
   - **H** apostrophe
   - **J** irony

7. What do such **images** as "plazas blown dry" and "the roulettes spin rustily" suggest about the setting Walcott is describing?
   - **A** The streets are not kept clean.
   - **B** The tourists are not in the mood for gambling.
   - **C** The city is dying and decaying.
   - **D** The city is suffering from a drought.

8. Like the speaker in "London," the speaker in "The Virgins" sees the living conditions of his city as being —
   - **F** recently improved
   - **G** easily fixed
   - **H** virtually beyond hope
   - **J** a source of hope for everyone

9. Unlike Blake, Walcott focuses more on which aspect of his city's plight?
   - **A** desolation
   - **B** people's hypocrisy
   - **C** unfair treatment of women
   - **D** disease and poverty

10. What is the major difference in **tone,** or attitude, between the speakers in both poems?
    - **F** The speaker in "London" is more optimistic.
    - **G** The speaker in "London" is more focused on the solution than the problem.
    - **H** The speaker in "The Virgins" values the way his city used to be.
    - **J** The speaker in "The Virgins" is not bothered by what he sees.

Essay Question

In an essay, compare and contrast these two poems, paying particular attention to the speakers' attitudes toward their cities. How do different literary devices enhance the meaning of each poem? Be sure to consider how Blake's poem reflects some key issues and characteristics of the English Romantic period and how Walcott's poem paints a complex and challenging portrait of contemporary life. Do some of the same issues and problems appear in both time periods? Explain.

Collection 5: Skills Review

Vocabulary Skills

Test Practice

Words with Multiple Meanings

DIRECTIONS: Choose the answer in which the underlined word is used in the same way as it is used in these sentences from *The Rime of the Ancient Mariner.*

1. "The guests are met, the feast is set: / Mays't hear the merry din."
   - **A** I'll need a new set of tools.
   - **B** Infection could set in if you don't clean the cut thoroughly.
   - **C** Did you set an appointment?
   - **D** The banquet room is set.

2. "The ship drove fast, loud roared the blast, / And southward aye we fled."
   - **F** The patient was asked to fast for twenty-four hours.
   - **G** The student learned fast.
   - **H** The two athletes became fast friends after they discovered they both liked tennis.
   - **J** Rocked by his father, the toddler fell fast asleep.

3. "At length did cross an Albatross, / Through the fog it came."
   - **A** You should only cross the creek at the shallow end.
   - **B** Ben's father was extremely cross when he found out Ben had locked the keys in the car.
   - **C** If you cross her, she'll resent it and may never forgive you.
   - **D** That dog is a cross between a German shepherd and a collie.

4. "The Hermit stepped forth from the boat, / And scarcely he could stand."
   - **F** The politician decided to take a firm stand on the issue.
   - **G** After an impressive performance, audience members generally stand and applaud.
   - **H** The sculptor put two of her statues on a marble stand.
   - **J** The defendants will stand trial for their accused crimes.

5. "For the sky and the sea, and the sea and the sky / Lay like a load on my weary eye"
   - **A** Our baseball team always tries to load the bases.
   - **B** Talking to someone can help you get a load off your mind.
   - **C** We had to load new software onto our computer before we could view the files.
   - **D** Don't load those heavy boxes by yourself.

6. "Forthwith this frame of mine was wrenched / With a woeful agony"
   - **F** He likes to frame his paintings.
   - **G** I have no frame of reference to help me understand you.
   - **H** Disease made his frame seem worn and frail.
   - **J** The lawyer had to frame her argument effectively.

Vocabulary Skills
Understand words with multiple meanings.

Collection 5: Skills Review

Writing Skills

Test Practice DIRECTIONS: Read the following paragraph from a draft of a student's reflective essay. Then, answer the questions below it.

(1) The automobile collision my mother and I were involved in was an unforgettable cataclysm. (2) She was driving me home from a late soccer tournament, and we were talking sleepily, trying to keep each other awake. (3) I guess I fell asleep, but I awoke suddenly to a terrible crunching of metal and to being slammed forward violently. (4) My mother had apparently fallen asleep, too, because our car was now off the road and smashed against a fence post. (5) After realizing that I was all right, I looked over at my mother and saw her eyes closed and her forehead bleeding. (6) My screams must have brought her to consciousness, because her eyes opened and a wave of relief flooded over me.

1. To express the significance of the experience, the writer could add

- **A** My mother and I should never have gone to that tournament.
- **B** Driving is a dangerous mode of transportation.
- **C** While I ended up with only minor injuries, my mother's were major.
- **D** The wreck made me realize how important my family is to me.

2. Which sentence could the writer add to express her insight about life?

- **F** I'll always remember this experience.
- **G** I've learned that life is fragile.
- **H** I've learned that accidents do happen.
- **J** I'll never drive when I'm tired.

3. To include more narrative details, the writer could

- **A** include the dialogue that occurred before the accident
- **B** describe the accident's setting
- **C** persuade others to learn from her mother's mistake
- **D** describe the damage to the car

4. Which sentence could replace sentence 1 to maintain an informal but appropriate tone?

- **F** The automobile accident was an unfortunate occurrence.
- **G** My mom and I had such a bad wreck; you wouldn't believe it.
- **H** My mother and I were once involved in an accident.
- **J** I'll never forget the day my mother and I got into a car wreck.

5. While presenting the passage orally, the speaker could

- **A** imitate the way the people in the experience really talk
- **B** keep her hands perfectly still
- **C** use her voice to reflect a humorous tone
- **D** look at her note cards to avoid getting nervous

Writing Skills Write a reflective essay.

The Railway Station (detail) (19th century) by William Powell Frith.

Collection 6

The VICTORIAN PERIOD

1832–1901

Paradox and Progress

So many worlds, so much to do,
So little done, such things to be . . .
—Alfred, Lord Tennyson

A steam-driven threshing machine demonstrated in an open field at the Great London Exhibition (1851).

The Granger Collection, New York.

INTERNET
Collection Resources
Keyword: LE7 12-6

The Victorian Period 1832–1901

LITERARY EVENTS

1832

1837–1838 Charles Dickens publishes *Oliver Twist* in periodical form

1840 Margaret Fuller helps found *The Dial,* a U.S. Transcendentalist journal that publishes Henry David Thoreau and Ralph Waldo Emerson

1842 Nikolai Gogol draws attention to the plight of Russian serfs with his comic epic *Dead Souls*

1843 William Wordsworth becomes poet laureate

1846 Elizabeth Barrett and **Robert Browning** elope; during their courtship she writes poems included in *Sonnets from the Portuguese*

1847

1847 Charlotte Brontë publishes *Jane Eyre;* Emily Brontë publishes *Wuthering Heights*

1848 Karl Marx and Friedrich Engels publish *The Communist Manifesto*

1850 Alfred, Lord Tennyson becomes poet laureate

1850 Nathaniel Hawthorne publishes *The Scarlet Letter*

1852 Sojourner Truth delivers her "Ain't I a Woman?" speech in Akron, Ohio

1857 Mary Ann Evans publishes stories in *Blackwood's Magazine,* using her pen name, George Eliot

1859 Charles Darwin publishes *On the Origin of Species by Means of Natural Selection*

Sojourner Truth, a leader of the Underground Railroad (19th century).

© Bettmann/CORBIS.

POLITICAL AND SOCIAL EVENTS

1832

1832 First Reform Bill extends vote to men who own property worth ten pounds or more in annual rent

1836 Mexican army defeats Texans at the Alamo

1837 Victoria becomes queen of the United Kingdom of Great Britain and Ireland

1839 Reforms included in Custody Act allow divorced women legal access to their children

1842 First of what China terms "unequal treaties" makes Hong Kong a British colony

1845 Potato famine begins in Ireland; close to one million people die from starvation or famine-related diseases; massive emigration begins

Imperial state crown made for Victoria's coronation (1837).

1847

1847 Ten Hours Act limits the number of hours that women and children can work in factories

1848 In Seneca Falls, New York, women's rights convention is led by Elizabeth Cady Stanton and Lucretia Mott

1854 Japan opens trade to the West

1858 Change in laws allows Lionel de Rothschild to become first Jewish member of Parliament

1858 Medical Act closes loophole that briefly allowed women to become physicians in Great Britain

A cabin in Ballintober Bog, Roscommon, Ireland (19th century). Engraving.

The Bridgeman Art Library.

Sherlock Holmes and Dr. Watson on a train (c. 1901). Book illustration.

© Historical Picture Archive/CORBIS.

1860

1862 In France, Victor Hugo publishes *Les Misérables*

Illustration from *Alice in Wonderland* (c. 1900).

© Bettmann/CORBIS.

1865 Lewis Carroll publishes *Alice's Adventures in Wonderland*

1868–1869 Louisa May Alcott publishes *Little Women*

1869 In Russia, **Leo Tolstoy** publishes the complete text of *War and Peace*

1870

1884 Mark Twain's *Adventures of Huckleberry Finn* appears

1887 Arthur Conan Doyle introduces the world to Sherlock Holmes with *A Study in Scarlet*

1900 L. Frank Baum publishes *The Wonderful Wizard of Oz*

1860

1861 U.S. Civil War begins

1861 Russian serfs are emancipated

1863 Abraham Lincoln's Emancipation Proclamation declares slavery illegal in Confederate territories

1867 Last Japanese shogun resigns; power returns to emperor

1867 Second Reform Act gives vote to most male industrial workers, doubling the number of voters

1868 Britain ends eighty-year practice of deporting convicts to Australia

1869 Debtors' prisons are abolished in England

1869 Suez Canal is opened

1869 Mohandas K. Gandhi is born in India

1870

1879 Zulu War against British in South Africa begins

1879 Thomas Edison invents the incandescent lamp

1885 Indian National Congress is formed; begins agitating for Indian self-rule

1889 Emmeline Pankhurst forms Women's Franchise League, arguing for British women's suffrage

1893 Home Rule Bill (to create an Irish Parliament) defeated by British Parliament for second time

1898 French scientists Pierre and Marie Curie discover radium

1901 Queen Victoria dies

Mohandas Gandhi (1931).

© Hulton-Deutsch Collection/CORBIS.

Political and Social

Riots and Reforms, 1832–1848

As the Industrial Revolution put money into their pockets, members of the middle class demanded more power in the government. The Reform Bill of 1832 answered some of these demands, giving the vote to all males who owned property worth a certain amount. The growth of industry had also led to the rapid growth of cities—and of slums. Many factory workers lived poverty-stricken lives, sleeping in dirty, overcrowded rooms and working sixteen hours a day. When widespread unemployment and soaring bread prices gave way to a severe depression in the early 1840s, riots broke out. Fears of revolution spread among the upper classes. Finally, in 1845–1846, serious food shortages forced Parliament to repeal the tax on imported grains that had forced bread prices up. This measure came just in time to safeguard England from the wave of revolutions that spread across Europe in 1848.

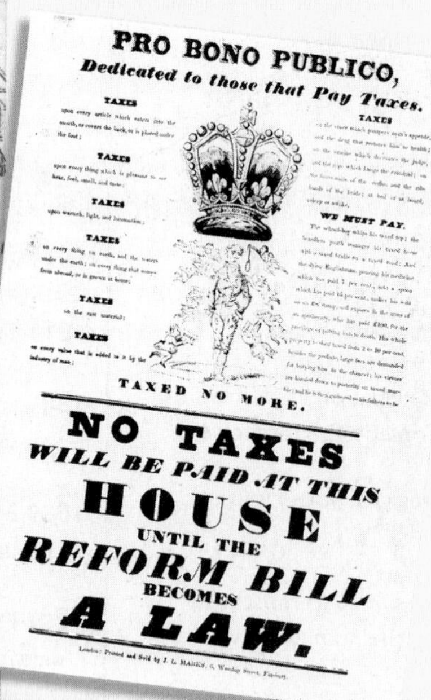

PRO BONO PUBLICO,

Dedicated to those that Pay Taxes.

WE MUST PAY.

TAXED NO MORE.

NO TAXES WILL BE PAID AT THIS HOUSE UNTIL THE REFORM BILL BECOMES A LAW.

(Above) An 1832 placard announcing passive resistance, used to promote passage of the Reform Bill.

The Granger Collection, New York.

(Left) A riot at Newport, England, November 4, 1839. Wood engraving.

The Granger Collection, New York.

The Book Stall (detail) (1874) after Edwin Austin Abbey. Colored engraving.

The Granger Collection, New York.

Milestones 1832–1901

Prosperity, 1848–1870

A new spirit of optimism lifted the nation during the middle years of the century. Reason and courage, most Victorians believed, could overcome the problems that had festered in the 1840s. A new economic policy of free trade with European nations brought financial prosperity to the aristocracy and upper classes. A series of factory acts in Parliament gradually improved the squalor of working-class lives and gave the vote to even more men. Literacy spread, and the new reading public consumed scores of novels, newspapers, and magazines. The path of progress was being paved.

A Society of Propriety

Middle-class Victorian society was characterized by its elaborate code of respectability, decorum, and morality. This code probably developed in response to the political turmoil of previous decades. The Victorians were convinced that life would be improved if it were more refined, more rationally organized, and better policed. In addition, Victorian intellectuals believed that advances in science and technology would soon overcome all social problems.

(Above) An invention for cleaning tall buildings, observing military fortifications, and performing tree surgery (c. 1856).

(Below) *Ladies and Gentlemen Playing Croquet* (detail) (19th century) by William McConnell.

The Victorian Period
1832–1901

by Donald Gray

PREVIEW

Think About . . .

The Victorian era was a time of overwhelming growth, prosperity, and progress in England. A sense of self-satisfaction characterized English society. The Victorians had unbounded confidence in progress—but this confidence led to uncomfortable questions. If progress and change are good, some Victorians wondered, should *all* things move forward and change? Should traditional values be questioned and updated? Should a government controlled by a landowning aristocracy be opened to the input of all? Much of the vast literature of this period grapples with these questions—sometimes critically, sometimes playfully, and sometimes mournfully—but always with an eye toward the paradoxes of the age.

As you read about this period, look for answers to these questions:

- What social and political factors affected life in Victorian England?
- What did Victorians value?
- How did discoveries in science affect people's religious beliefs?
- How did Victorian writers respond to issues of their time?

Collection introduction (pages 876–893) covers **Literary Skills** Evaluate the philosophical, political, religious, ethical, and social influences of a historical period.

Many Victorians thought of themselves as living in a time of great change. They were right, but the changes during Queen Victoria's long reign (1837–1901) occurred in a period of relative political and social stability, and many were the result of conditions that began before Victoria and most of her subjects were born.

Peace and Economic Growth: Britannia Rules

After Napoleon's defeat at Waterloo in 1815, Britain was not involved in a major European war until World War I began in 1914. The empire that had begun in the seventeenth and eighteenth centuries with British interests in India and North America grew steadily, until by 1900, Victoria was queen-empress of more than 200 million people living outside Great Britain.

The Opening of the Great Exhibition in Hyde Park, May 1, 1851 (detail) by Henry C. Selous. Oil on canvas. In the center are the queen, her husband, the Prince of Wales (in Highland dress), and other members of the royal family.

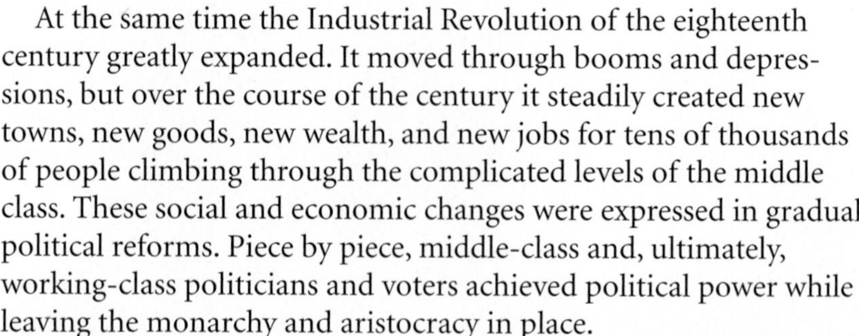

At the same time the Industrial Revolution of the eighteenth century greatly expanded. It moved through booms and depressions, but over the course of the century it steadily created new towns, new goods, new wealth, and new jobs for tens of thousands of people climbing through the complicated levels of the middle class. These social and economic changes were expressed in gradual political reforms. Piece by piece, middle-class and, ultimately, working-class politicians and voters achieved political power while leaving the monarchy and aristocracy in place.

The history of England is emphatically the history of progress.

—Thomas Babington Macaulay

The Idea of Progress

The English historian Thomas Babington Macaulay eloquently voiced the middle-class Victorian attitude toward government, history, and civilization. For Macaulay, history meant progress, and progress largely meant material improvement that could be seen and touched, counted and measured. Macaulay admired cleanliness and order. He wanted the London streets free of garbage, drained and paved, lighted at night, and patrolled by a sober police force. He wanted the city planned so that residents of respectable neighborhoods did not live next to slums and were not annoyed by beggars and peddlers. He would have the houses numbered and a population literate enough to read signs. He did not claim that his own time had entirely met these standards of material comfort and security, but his cool, almost amazed regard of the disorder and squalor of the past conveyed his sense of progress: How could those people have lived like that? How different we are; how far we have come.

Many Victorians regretted or disputed Macaulay's confident tone and materialistic standards. But in his satisfaction with the improvements that empire had brought to England, his views were typical of those of his contemporaries.

The Hungry Forties

The first decade of Victoria's reign was troubled—in fact, the period came to be known as the Hungry Forties. Victoria came to the throne in the first year of a depression that by 1842 had put 1.5 million unemployed workers and their families (in a population of 16 million in England and Wales) on some form of poverty relief.

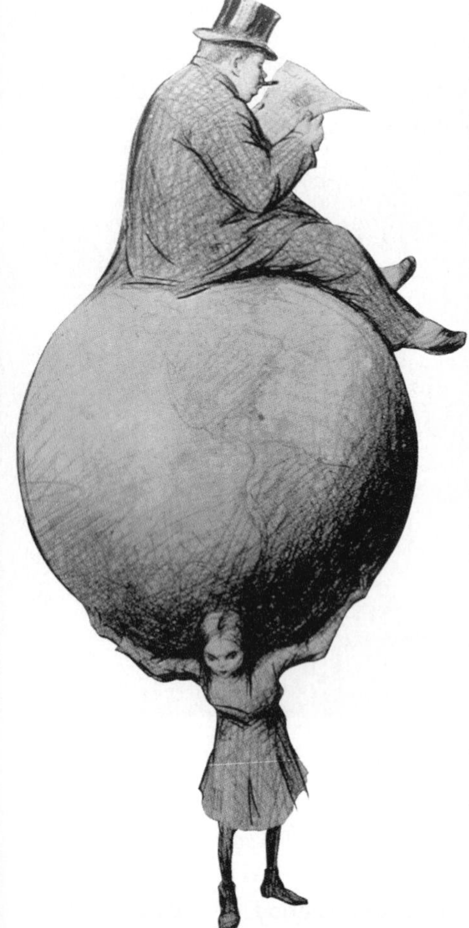

A cartoon protesting child labor (1910s) by Lewis Hines. A young girl is holding up a globe on which a capitalist is seated.

The Irish Famine (19th century) by George Frederick Watts. Oil on canvas.
Trustees of the Watts Gallery, Compton, Surrey, United Kingdom. The Bridgeman Art Library.

■ Poor Working Conditions

Government commissions investigating working conditions learned of children mangled when they fell asleep at machines at the end of a twelve-hour working day. They discovered young girls and boys hauling sledges of coal through narrow mine tunnels, working shifts so long that in winter they saw the sun only on Sundays.

■ The Potato Famine

In Ireland the potato blight (1845–1849) caused a famine that killed perhaps a million people and forced two million others—more than 25 percent of Ireland's population—to emigrate. Some went to English cities, where they lived ten or twelve to a room in slums that had two toilets for every 250 people.

■ Pollution and Filth

The rapid growth of cities often made them filthy and disorderly. Nearly two million people lived in London during the 1840s, and commercial and industrial cities such as Manchester and Liverpool expanded rapidly. In Manchester in the 1840s, 40 percent of the streets were still unpaved. The Thames River in London was

The years of the Famine [in Ireland, the 1840s], of the bad life and of the hunger, arrived and broke the spirit and strength of the community. People simply wanted to survive. Their spirit of comradeship was lost. It didn't matter what ties or relations you had; you considered that person to be your friend who gave you food to put in your mouth. Recreation and leisure ceased. Poetry, music, and dancing died. These things were lost and completely forgotten. When life improved in other ways, these pursuits never returned as they had been. The famine killed everything.

—Maire ni Grianna, from *Memories of the Famine*

polluted with sewage, industrial waste, and the drainage from graveyards, where bodies were buried in layers six or eight deep. In the 1850s, Parliament sometimes had to adjourn from its new riverside building because of the stench from the Thames.

The Movement for Reform: Food, Factories, and Optimism

Violence broke out at massive political rallies called in the 1840s to protest government policies that kept the price of bread and other food high and deprived most working men (and all women) of the vote and representation in Parliament. In 1848, a year of revolution in Europe, nervous British politicians got the army ready and armed the staffs of museums and government offices when working-class

A CLOSER LOOK: SOCIAL INFLUENCES

An Age in Need of Heroines: Reform in Victorian Britain

INFORMATIONAL TEXT

Be good, sweet maid, and let who will be
clever;
Do noble things, not dream them, all day long.
—Charles Kingsley

Great Britain was the world's first industrialized nation, and its smoky cities illustrated the dangers of "progress." Unsanitary housing and rampant disease were unremarkably common. Legal remedies addressed some of these abuses, but Victorian social reform was not merely a parliamentary process. It was also a passionate struggle to change public opinion through hard work and education.

"Do noble things." Following the Reverend Charles Kingsley's urging to "do noble things, not dream them," many women approached social reform as a moral and religious duty. The social worker Octavia Hill (1838–1912) believed that adequate housing could "make individual life noble, homes happy, and family life good," and she became an authority on housing reform. She was also a conservationist, founding the National Trust to protect historic buildings and scenic spots from industrial development. Because of Hill's efforts, the public can visit sites such as the Runnymede meadow. Thanks to the National Trust, Runnymede looks much as it did when King John accepted the Magna Carta there in 1215.

Spoiling the brutes. Perhaps the best-known Victorian reformer is Florence Nightingale (1820–1910), who transformed the public's perception of

Florence Nightingale tending the wounded during the Crimean War (19th century).

political reformers organized what they called a monster rally in London to petition Parliament and the queen.

■ Improvements in Diet

Still, most middle-class Victorians believed that things were better than in the past and that they were going to be better yet in the future. Their opinion was in part founded on a steady improvement throughout the Victorian era in the material condition of people in all social classes. The price of food dropped after midcentury, largely because of increased trade with other countries and the growing empire. Diet improved as meat, fruit, and margarine (a Victorian invention) began to appear regularly in working-class households. Factories and railroads made postage, newspapers, clothing, furniture, travel, and other goods and services cheap.

From the butchers' and greengrocers' shops the gaslights flared and flickered, wild and ghastly, over haggard groups of slipshod dirty women, bargaining for scraps of stale meat and frostbitten vegetables, wrangling about short weight and bad quality. Fish stalls and fruit stalls lined the edge of the greasy pavement, sending up odors as foul as the language of sellers and buyers. Blood and sewer water crawled from under doors and out of spouts, and reeked down the gutters among offal, animal and vegetable, in every stage of putrefaction.

—Charles Kingsley's description of London

modern nursing during the Crimean War. Two inventions—the camera and the war correspondent—made her career possible. Newspaper reports revealed that bureaucratic bungling had cost thousands of lives in the army's hospitals in Scutari, Turkey. Public indignation gave Nightingale the opportunity to become an army nurse. In Turkey she saw scores of wounded soldiers dying from diseases caused by poor hygiene, lack of medical supplies, and sheer neglect. The ordinary British soldier was thought to be, in the words of the duke of Wellington, "the scum of the earth." When Nightingale asked medical authorities for clean bedding or warm clothing, she was told: "You will spoil the brutes."

Nightingale believed British soldiers were "murdered" by incompetence, and she vowed to avenge them. With gritty tenacity, she became an authority on public health, observing that sanitation could save lives. Queen Victoria read her meticulous reports and said, "I wish we had her at the War Office." Nightingale's efforts changed hospital management and made nursing a respected career.

"We make no compromise." Reformers such as Nightingale and Hill devoted themselves to aiding the victims of Victorian "progress," agitating for better conditions and improved educational opportunities. In the name of charity, they often stepped outside the bounds of "ladylike" behavior. Josephine Butler (1828–1906) exposed the exploitation of women and girls, working to repeal acts that deprived poor women of their constitutional rights. In the name of reform, she declared that "we make no compromise; and we are ready to meet all the powers of earth and hell combined."

These reformers redefined the idea of "women's work"; in the process they set public policies that curbed many abuses and saved countless lives. As we enter the twenty-first century, we continue to benefit from these Victorian efforts to improve the quality of life.

The principle which regulates the existing social relations between the two sexes—the legal subordination of one sex to the other—is wrong in itself, and now one of the chief hindrances to human improvement.

—John Stuart Mill, from *The Subjection of Women*

■ The Reform Bills

A series of political reforms gave the vote to almost all adult males by the last decades of the century. In 1832, the First Reform Bill extended the vote to all men who owned property worth ten pounds or more in yearly rent. Continued pressure led to the Second Reform Act in 1867, which gave the right to vote to most working-class men, except for farm workers. Decades of agitation for suffrage by Victorian women succeeded only in the next century. Strengthened by their domestic contributions during the Great War, women age thirty and over won the vote in 1918. Universal adult suffrage in 1928 extended the vote to women at age twenty-one.

A series of factory acts limited child labor and reduced the usual working day to ten hours, with a half-holiday on Saturday.

A CLOSER LOOK: SOCIAL INFLUENCES

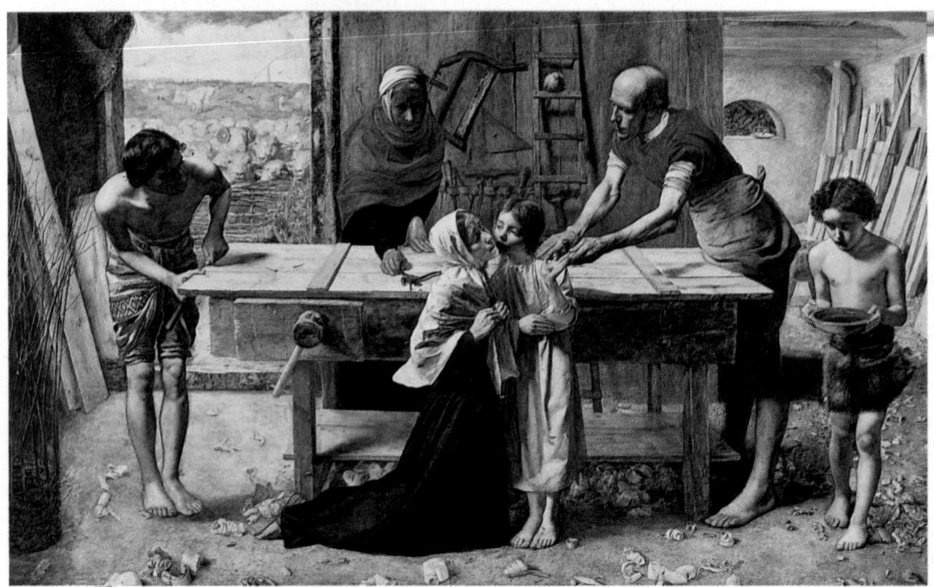

INFORMATIONAL TEXT

Christ in the House of His Parents (1850) by John Everett Millais.
Tate Gallery, London.

The Pre-Raphaelite Brotherhood: Challenging Artistic Authority

The Times called it "plainly revolting." The *Literary Gazette* found it "a nameless atrocity." Charles Dickens thought its central character "a hideous, wry-necked, blubbering, red-haired boy in a nightgown." The painting that elicited such scathing abuse was *Christ in the House of His Parents* (1850) by John Everett Millais (1829–1896). Millais shocked the art world with his innovative techniques and the treatment of his subject—he portrayed the Holy Family as ordinary people in a shavings-strewn carpentry shop.

Millais belonged to the Pre-Raphaelite Brotherhood (PRB), a group that embraced the ordinary while rejecting "conventionalities and feeble reminiscences from the Old Masters." Dissatisfied with Victorian complacency, a group of seven young men modeled their work on medieval painters—those *before* the Renaissance painter Raphael—that they believed had a more natural vision. Founded in 1848, the PRB was united in a sense, as the artist Sir Edward Burne-Jones (1833–1898) said, that "the time is out of joint."

Artistic treason. The PRB is widely known for Dante Gabriel Rossetti's sensuous portraits. A favorite model was Jane Morris,

State-supported schools were established in 1870, were made compulsory in 1880, and were made free in 1891. In the 1840s, 40 percent of the couples getting married could not write their names on their marriage certificates. By 1900, using that simple definition of literacy, more than 90 percent of the population was literate.

"Blushing Cheeks": Decorum and Prudery

Many Victorians thought of themselves as progressing morally and intellectually, as well as materially. In fact, the powerful, mostly middle-class obsession with gentility or decorum has made *prudery* almost a synonym for *Victorianism.* Book publishers and magazine editors deleted or altered words and episodes that might, in the phrase of the day, bring "a blush to the cheek" of a young person.

and her long neck and abundant, wavy hair in works such as *Proserpine* (1874) are a PRB trademark.

To members of the Royal Academy of Art, however, PRB members were artistic outlaws. Their shading techniques violated the academy's guidelines that one "principal light" should focus a painting's main elements. Their minute rendering of details seemed busy and bewildering, "a strange disorder of the mind or the eyes." PRB member William Holman Hunt (1827–1910) prided himself on botanical and geologic accuracy, laboring over his paintings' individual rocks and flowers.

Art and cultural values. The PRB disbanded in 1853, but it attracted followers, drawn by the PRB's medieval models, who had turned away from industrial Britain's materialism. The art critic John Ruskin (1819–1900) asserted that art and artists suffered from mechanization. He argued that the way art was produced could shape a culture's values.

The artist William Morris (1834–1896) applied these theories in a decorating firm that revived traditional methods of producing furniture, tapestries, and stained glass. His Kelmscott Press crafted fine books with the painstaking detail of hand-printed engravings and hand-sewn bindings. Morris, Ruskin, and former PRB members taught artisans these skills and principles at the Working Men's College, an educational experiment begun in London in 1854.

Modern viewers delight in the PRB's exuberant excess of elaborate designs and glorious medieval trappings. Yet the Pre-Raphaelites' work also made a social statement. The tensions of the Industrial Revolution bonded the brotherhood, and its rebellious movement raised difficult questions about the place of art and artists in a rapidly changing society.

Proserpine (1874) by Dante Gabriel Rossetti.
Tate Gallery, London.

The Drawing Room (late 19th or early 20th century) by Paul Gustav Fischer.

I still cling fondly to the hope that some system of female instruction will be discovered, by which the young women of England may be sent from school to the homes of their parents, habituated to be on the watch for every opportunity of doing good to others; making it the first and the last inquiry of every day, "What can I do to make my parents, my brothers, or my sisters, more happy? . . . I hope to pursue the plan to which I have been accustomed, of seeking my own happiness only in the happiness of others."

—Sarah Stickney Ellis, essayist who argued that women's education should cultivate "the heart," not the mind

In art and popular fiction, sex, birth, and death were softened by sentimental conventions, made into tender courtships, joyous motherhoods, and deathbed scenes in which old people were saints and babies angels. In the real world, people were arrested for distributing information about sexually transmitted diseases. Victorian society regarded seduced or adulterous women (but not their male partners) as "fallen" and pushed them to the margins of society.

Authoritarian Values

Victorian decorum also supported powerful ideas about authority. Many Victorians were uneasy about giving strong authority to a central government. (The fundamental conservatism of British society is revealed in the fact that its version of the 1848 European revolutions was a peaceful gathering to petition Parliament.) In Victorian private lives, however, the autocratic father of middle-class households is a vivid figure in both fact (Elizabeth Barrett Browning's father, for example) and fiction.

Women were subject to male authority. Middle-class women especially were expected to marry and make their homes a comfortable refuge for their husbands from the male domains of business, politics, and the professions. Women who did not marry had few

Applicants for Admission to a Casual Ward (1874) by Luke Fildes. Oil on canvas.
Royal Holloway and Bedford New College, University of London.

occupations open to them. Working-class women could find jobs as servants in prosperous households, while unmarried middle-class ladies could become governesses or teachers. Many middle-class women remained unmarried because men often postponed marriage until they achieved financial security. Life for these unmarried, "redundant women," as they were called, was painful, although in literature, especially literature written by men, the figure of the middle-aged maiden was often played for comedy.

The excesses, cruelties, and hypocrisies of all these repressions were obvious to many Victorians. But the codes and barriers of decorum changed slowly because they were part of the ideology of progress. Prudery and social order were intended to control the immorality and sexual excesses that Victorians associated with the violent political revolutions of the eighteenth century and with the social corruption of the regency of George IV (1811–1820).

Intellectual Progress: The March of the Mind

The intellectual advances of the Victorian period were dramatically evident to those living in it. Humans began to understand more and more about the earth, its creatures, and its natural laws. Geologists worked out the history of the earth written in rocks and fossils. Based on countless observations, Charles Darwin and other biologists theorized about the evolution of species. The industrialization of England depended on and supported science and technology, especially chemistry (in the iron and textile industries) and engineering.

Lady Bracknell. . . .
I do not approve of anything that tampers with natural ignorance. Ignorance is like a delicate exotic fruit; touch it and the bloom is gone. The whole theory of modern education is radically unsound. Fortunately in England, at any rate, education produces no effect whatsoever. If it did, it would prove a serious danger to the upper classes, and probably lead to acts of violence in Grosvenor Square.

—Oscar Wilde, from *The Importance of Being Earnest*

Thomas Huxley and the Game of Science

Those who made and used scientific and technological knowledge had a confidence of their own. Thomas Huxley, a variously accomplished scientist who wrote and lectured frequently on the necessity of scientific education, imagined science as an exhilarating, high-stakes chess game with the physical universe.

Thomas Henry Huxley (c. 1870s).

> "The chessboard is the world, the pieces are the phenomena of the universe, the rules of the game are what we call the laws of Nature. The player on the other side is hidden from us. We know that his play is always fair, just, and patient. But also we know, to our cost, that he never overlooks a mistake, or makes the smallest allowance for ignorance. To the man who plays well, the highest stakes are paid, with that sort of overflowing generosity with which the strong shows delight in strength. And one who plays ill is checkmated—without haste, but without remorse."
>
> —Thomas Huxley, from *A Liberal Education*

Huxley resembles those confident Victorians who built railways and sewers, organized markets and schools, and pushed through electoral reforms and laws regulating the conditions of work. These reformers believed that the world offered a challenging set of problems that could be understood by human intelligence and solved by science, government, and other human institutions. Huxley made the game exciting by warning that humans could lose. But so long as the game is played in the material world, Huxley and others like him saw no reason that they would not win.

Questions and Doubts

Despite the confidence of the age, the Victorian period was filled with voices asking questions and raising doubts. Speaking for many of their contemporaries, and speaking to others they thought shallow and complacent, Victorian writers asked whether material comfort fully satisfied human needs and wishes. They questioned the cost of exploiting the earth and human beings to achieve such comfort. They protested or mocked codes of decorum and authority.

In the first half of the period, some writers complained that materialist ideas of reality completely overlooked the spirit or soul that made life beautiful and just. Later in the century, writers like Thomas Hardy and A. E. Housman thought that Macaulay's and Huxley's ideas of history and nature presupposed a coherence that did not really exist. Literature in Victorian culture often reassured its readers that, rightly perceived, the universe made sense. But some writers unsettled their readers by telling them that their understanding of the universe was wrong or by asking them to consider whether human life and the natural world made as much sense as they had once hoped.

The Popular Mr. Dickens

Charles Dickens, the most popular and most important figure in Victorian literature, is a case in point. The son of a debt-ridden clerk, Dickens lived out one of the favorite myths of the age. Through his own enormous talents and energy, he rose from poverty to become a wealthy and famous man. His was a peculiarly Victorian success. It was made possible by increasing affluence and literacy, which gave him a large reading public, and by improved printing and distribution, which made book publishing a big business.

The conventional happy endings of Dickens's novels satisfied his readers', and probably his own, conviction that things usually work out well for decent people. But many of Dickens's most memorable scenes show decent people neglected, abused, and exploited. Children, especially, endure terrible suffering. The hungry Oliver Twist begs for more gruel in the workhouse; the handicapped Tiny Tim in *A Christmas Carol* cheerfully hobbles toward his possible early death; and young David Copperfield is abused by his stepfather, the cold, dark Mr. Murdstone.

In his later novels, Dickens created characters and scenes to show that even the winners in the competition for material gain had reason to be as desperate and unhappy as the losers. In *Our Mutual Friend,* his last novel, Dickens describes a dinner party at the home of a family called the Veneerings, a name that emphasizes the family's superficial qualities. (A *veneer* is a thin layer of wood applied to cheap wood to make it look

Scene from *Oliver Twist* depicting Fagin's den of child thieves and a hungry Oliver.

FAST FACTS

Political Highlights

- By the end of the century, reform bills give most adult males the right to vote.
- A series of factory acts regulates the use of child labor and improves working conditions.
- Education is made compulsory and free by the end of the century, leading to a high national literacy rate.

more costly.) The Veneerings are the "new rich," "bran-new people in a bran-new house in a bran-new quarter of London":

> "The great looking-glass above the sideboard reflects the table and the company. Reflects the new Veneering crest, in gold and eke in silver, frosted and also thawed, a camel of all work. The Herald's College found out a Crusading ancestor for Veneering who bore a camel on his shield (or might have done it if he had thought of it), and a caravan of camels take charge of the fruits and flowers and candles, and kneel down to be loaded with the salt. Reflects Veneering; forty, wavy-haired, dark, tending to corpulence, sly, mysterious, filmy. . . . Reflects Mrs. Veneering; fair, aquiline-nosed and fingered, not so much light hair as she might have, gorgeous in raiment and jewels. . . . Reflects Podsnap; prosperously feeding, two little light-colored wiry wings, one on either side of his else bald head, looking as like his hairbrushes as his hair. . . . Reflects Mrs. Podsnap; . . . quantity of bone, neck, and

A CLOSER LOOK: SOCIAL INFLUENCES

Victorian Drama: From Relief to Realism

INFORMATIONAL TEXT

Though Queen Victoria, who came to the throne in 1837, loved the theater, it was she who once remarked, "We are not amused." And certainly the theater of the early part of her reign provided little to amuse anyone. Comedy must have license to explore, to expose, to look under the bed, and to ridicule, but Victoria's England was marked by prudery, good taste, repression of natural feelings, high-mindedness, and official censorship.

Irreverent ridicule. The operettas that William S. Gilbert wrote to Arthur Sullivan's music, beginning with *Trial by Jury* (1875), provided some delightful comic relief. Though today we think of these operettas (such as *The Pirates of Penzance* and *H.M.S. Pinafore*) merely as charming, tuneful, witty entertainments, in their period they irreverently ridiculed the law, the navy, the world of aesthetes, and the aristocracy.

Intrinsic to Gilbert and Sullivan operettas was a world-turned-on-its-head view of life that would influence both Oscar Wilde and Bernard Shaw. In

Interior of Drury Lane Theater, 1808 by Thomas Rowlandson and A. Pugin.

Guildhall Library, Corporation of London.

nostrils like a rocking horse, hard features, majestic head-dress in which Podsnap has hung golden offerings. . . . Reflects . . . mature young gentleman; with too much nose in his face, too much ginger in his whiskers, too much sparkle in his studs, his eyes, his buttons, his talk, and his teeth.”

—Charles Dickens, from *Our Mutual Friend*

Attacks like Dickens's on the hollowness, glitter, superficiality, and excesses of Victorian affluence were common in Victorian literature. Dickens also raised questions about the costs of progress in his descriptions of the huddle and waste of cities and the smoke and fire of industrial landscapes. In 1871, the art historian and social critic John Ruskin noted a new phenomenon that we call smog; he called it the plague wind, or "the storm-cloud of the nineteenth century," and concluded, chillingly, ". . . [M]ere smoke would not blow to and fro in that wild way. It looks more to me as if it were made of dead men's souls."

FAST FACTS

Philosophical Views

- Victorians have confidence that all social and material problems can be solved by "progress." By the end of the century, however, the disruption and materialism of the era lead to a reevaluation of these views.
- Earlier Romantic views give way to spiritual doubt. Late Victorian intellectuals see human life as a struggle against indifferent natural forces.

Gilbert and Sullivan, "Things are seldom what they seem. / Skim milk masquerades as cream."

Moving toward realism. At the start of the era of Oscar Wilde and Bernard Shaw, drama was moving toward realism, which has remained the dominant dramatic mode for the last hundred years. In England and in Europe, fiction writers were dealing with the social realities of the time—Charles Dickens among others in England, Émile Zola in France. From Scandinavia came the revolutionary voices of Henrik Ibsen in plays such as *An Enemy of the People* (1882) and of August Strindberg in *Miss Julie* (1888).

While some playwrights were assimilating new points of view and style, theaters themselves were undergoing changes to accommodate the new plays. For years, London had been dominated by two huge theaters, Covent Garden and Drury Lane, each seating well over three thousand people—large theaters not congenial to intimate realistic drama.

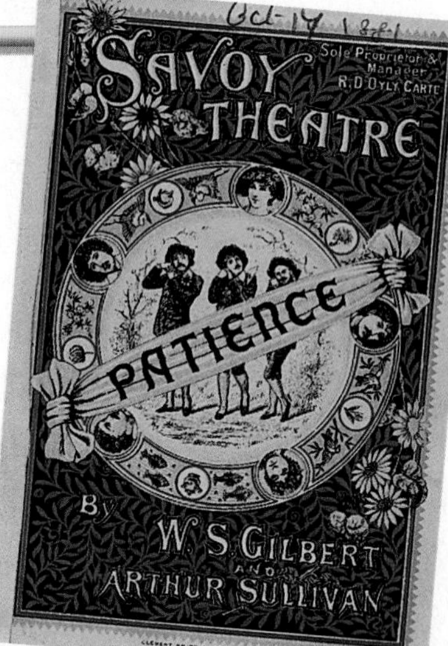

Program cover for October 17, 1881, Savoy Theatre production of *Patience* by Sir W. S. Gilbert and Sir Arthur Sullivan.
Victoria and Albert Museum, London

In the early part of the nineteenth century, new, smaller theaters were built. The forestage, or apron, was removed, and gaslight (and soon electricity) took the place of candles once used to illuminate the stage. These changes cleared the way for the staging of smaller-scale realistic dramas, which an audience might view as though through an invisible "fourth wall," allowing the audience to eavesdrop on the action. In smaller theaters, on such stages with new lighting, playwrights could now achieve an illusion of reality.

Trust in the Transcendental—and Skepticism

Trust in a transcendental power was characteristic of the early Victorian writers. They were the immediate heirs of the Romantic idea of a finite natural world surrounded by and interfused with an infinite, ideal transcendental reality. The highest purpose of a poet, of any writer, was to make readers aware of the connection between earth and heaven, body and soul, material and ideal.

Still, with some exceptions—Gerard Manley Hopkins (see page 916) is one and Christina Rossetti another—younger writers found it increasingly difficult to believe in an infinite power and order that made sense of material and human existence. Other writers at midcentury, sometimes reacting to explanations of the world that excluded the spiritual, were saddened by what seemed to them to be the withdrawal of the divine from the world. The dominant note of much mid-Victorian writing was struck by Matthew Arnold in his poem "Dover Beach" (see page 922): "The Sea of Faith," Arnold wrote, had ebbed. There was no certainty; or if there was, what was certain was that existence was not governed by a benevolent intelligence that cared for its creatures.

(Right) *Pitmen at Play* (detail) (1836) by Henry Perlee Parker. Oil on canvas.

National Coal Mining Museum for England, Wakefield, UK. The Bridgeman Art Library.

(Below) *Many Happy Returns of the Day* (19th century) by William Powell Frith.

Harrogate Museums and Art Gallery, North Yorkshire, England.

By the end of the century, this skepticism and denial had become pervasive in the works of Thomas Hardy, A. E. Housman, and others. Early and mid-Victorian novelists such as Dickens and George Eliot had dramatized a human ideal achieved through sympathy and unselfishness. They made sad or frightening examples of people like the Murdstones in *David Copperfield* and Godfrey Cass in *Silas Marner*—all hard surface and no soul. Their heroes and heroines learned to find happiness in nurturing marriages and in small communities of family and friends. But there were few such marriages and communities in the fiction and poetry of Hardy and

Housman. These late-Victorian writers told stories of lovers and friends betrayed by unfaithfulness, war, and the other troubles that humans add to the natural trials of mortal life.

Reflections of a Culture

It is important to remember that the readers of Victorian literature were living Victorian lives. Victorian literature did not exist above or outside the comfortable and often confident lives of its readers. Many of the people who read Dickens settled down with his books after dining in rooms as garishly decorated as the Veneerings'. Most of the young men and women who thrilled to Dante Gabriel Rossetti's sensualism and to Housman's tender gloom probably moved on to make proper and modestly happy marriages and to find worthy occupations. People who were making a lot of money listened to Carlyle and Ruskin telling them that they were foolish and damned. People who were disturbed by how much money was being made listened to Macaulay reminding them that a century or so before they might not have been able to afford, or even to read, his book.

Victorian literature needs to be read not just as a comment on the complexity of its culture, but also as an important part of that culture. Its writers sent their words to work in the world to alter, to reinforce, to challenge, to enlarge, or to temper the ideas and feelings with which their contemporaries managed their lives.

FAST FACTS

Social and Economic Influences

- Much of the British population moves from rural areas to the rapidly growing, industrialized cities.
- The early part of Victoria's reign, the Hungry Forties, is marked by serious economic and social problems.
- Middle-class Victorians observe strict rules of respectability and uphold authoritarian values.
- Flourishing lending libraries and the availability of cheap books and periodicals create a mass reading public.

REVIEW

Talk About . . .

Turn back to the Think About questions posed at the start of this introduction to the Victorian period (see page 878). Discuss your responses with a group of classmates.

Write About . . .

Contrasting Literary Periods

Morality, then and now. The strict social and moral codes that permeated middle-class Victorian culture were one response to the unsettling changes that threatened traditional social structures. Do you think the rapid social and technological changes in our society have caused a similar response—a renewed concern for social and moral propriety? In an essay analyze current attitudes toward morality and so-called proper behavior. Consider the causes of these attitudes and how they are similar to or different from those of middle-class Victorian society.

Alfred, Lord Tennyson
(1809–1892)

The Granger Collection, New York.

Caricature of Alfred, Lord Tennyson (1872) by Frederick Waddy.

When Alfred Tennyson learned that Lord Byron had died while helping Greek nationalist rebels, he went to the woods and carved on a piece of sandstone, "Byron is dead." Tennyson was fourteen years old. He felt sure that he would be a poet, and he was already practicing the dramatic gestures of the Romantic poets he admired.

Tennyson's father, a clergyman of good family but little money, encouraged young Alfred's interest in poetry. At Cambridge University Alfred joined a group of young intellectuals, called the Apostles, who believed that their friend was destined to become the greatest poet of their generation.

In 1831, when his father died, lack of funds forced Tennyson to leave Cambridge, and he entered a troubled period. In 1832, he published his first significant book of poems, which some reviewers mocked for its melancholy themes and weak imitations of Keats's language. The next year Tennyson was devastated by the death of his closest friend, Arthur Henry Hallam. He became engaged to marry in 1836, but the marriage was postponed for fourteen years because of his uncertain financial prospects.

During this difficult period, when both his physical and mental health suffered, Tennyson apparently never considered any career but poetry. He polished his style to develop the melodious line and rich imagery of poems like "The Lady of Shalott." Tennyson published almost nothing in his "ten years' silence" from 1832 to 1842, but the friends to whom he read his poems remained convinced of his promise.

Gradually, Tennyson began to make his way. The two-volume *Poems* (1842) was favorably reviewed, and in 1845 the government granted him an annual pension of two hundred pounds. In 1850, he published *In Memoriam*, an elegy to Hallam that was immediately successful. It tells the story of his own recovery of faith in the immortality of the soul and of the harmony of creation—despite the new, unsettling discoveries of science and his deep sense of the unfairness of Hallam's death. That year, he was named poet laureate (after Wordsworth's death), and he finally married.

In the forty years before his death in 1892, Tennyson published nearly a dozen volumes of poems. His books sold like bestselling novels and made him rich. In 1884, he was made a peer of the realm and became Alfred, Lord Tennyson.

Tennyson never lost the melancholy and sense of chaos that friends and reviewers found in his early poems. He was immensely popular with his contemporaries because he spoke in a beautiful, measured language of their sense of the fragility and sadness of life. He also assured his readers that his own experience of sadness and disorder had taught him that everything was part of a benevolent plan in which eventually all losses would be made good.

Before You Read

The Lady of Shalott

Make the Connection

Quickwrite

One of the main symbols in this dreamlike ballad is a mirror that the Lady uses as she weaves. Watch for how the mirror, with its reflected images, stands in opposition to the real world. This is only one opposition, or tension, in the world of the Lady of Shalott, of whom Tennyson said: "The newborn love for something, for someone in the wide world from which she had been so long secluded, takes her out of the region of shadows into that of realities."

What might Tennyson have meant by "the region of shadows" and the region of "realities"? Jot down a few ideas.

Literary Focus

Word Music

Ballads were originally songs, and indeed, Tennyson's ballad "The Lady of Shalott" almost begs to be sung. Its rhythms, cadences, and echoes are so strong that the ballad creates what is known as **word music.** Word music is created by the expert use of **meter** and by the regular and repetitive use of such elements as **rhyme, alliteration,** and **assonance.** Working together, these elements create an overall musical effect in a poem.

Be sure you read this poem aloud to hear the famous music of Tennyson's language. The first time you read the poem, enjoy the rhythmical power of the verse. On subsequent readings, try to identify the individual elements that contribute to the poem's musical quality.

For many years, students in both England and the United States could recite the mysterious story of the Lady of Shalott from memory. You might try to memorize the entire poem or parts of it.

Word music is created when a poet uses a variety of elements such as **meter, rhyme, alliteration,** and **assonance** to generate an overall musical quality in a work.

For more on Meter, Rhyme, Alliteration, and Assonance, see the Handbook of Literary and Historical Terms.

Reading Skills

Identifying Contrasting Images

"The Lady of Shalott" is brimming with contrasting images: the flat, flowing river and the upright, unchanging tower; the bustling lives of the villagers and the solitary life of the Lady; the weary whisper of the reaper and the robust song of Sir Lancelot. As you read the poem, be alert to such **oppositions**—the large and the small—in setting, actions, or imagery. Record the first example of each that you notice. Then, when Sir Lancelot appears in Part III, jot down at least one other contrast that he introduces.

Background

Tennyson wrote "The Lady of Shalott" in 1832 and then extensively revised it in 1842. He once commented: "I met the story first in some Italian novelle: but the web, mirror, island, etc., were my own." The symbol of Arthur's Camelot—an orderly, patriarchal kingdom in which beautiful, enchanted women languish—appealed to Tennyson, and to the Victorian imagination in general. Tennyson would return to this setting in such works as "Lancelot and Elaine" and the *Idylls of the King,* a series of twelve connected poems telling the story of King Arthur and the Knights of the Round Table.

Literary Skills Understand sound devices in poetry.

Reading Skills Understand contrasting images.

INTERNET

More About Alfred, Lord Tennyson

Keyword: LE7 12-6

The Lady of Shalott (1888) by John William Waterhouse.
Tate Gallery, London.

THE LADY OF SHALOTT

Alfred, Lord Tennyson

Part I

On either side the river lie
Long fields of barley and of rye,
That clothe the wold° and meet the sky;
And through the field the road runs by
To many-towered Camelot;°
And up and down the people go,
Gazing where the lilies blow°
Round an island there below,
The island of Shalott.

Willows whiten,° aspens quiver,
Little breezes dusk and shiver
Through the wave that runs forever
By the island in the river
Flowing down to Camelot.
Four gray walls, and four gray towers,
Overlook a space of flowers,
And the silent isle imbowers°
The Lady of Shalott.

By the margin, willow-veiled,
Slide the heavy barges trailed
By slow horses; and unhailed
The shallop° flitteth silken-sailed
Skimming down to Camelot:
But who hath seen her wave her hand?
Or at the casement seen her stand?
Or is she known in all the land,
The Lady of Shalott?

Only reapers, reaping early
In among the bearded barley,

3. **wold** *n.:* rolling plain.

5. **Camelot:** legendary city, site of King Arthur's court and Round Table.

7. **blow** *v.:* blossom.

10. **whiten** *v.:* show the white undersides of their leaves when blown by the wind.

17. **imbowers** *n. pl.:* shelters with trees, gardens, and flowers.

22. **shallop** *n.:* small, open boat.

©Manchester City Art Galleries, England.

The Lady of Shalott (c. 1886–1905) by William Holman Hunt. Oil.

Hear a song that echoes cheerly°
From the river winding clearly,
        Down to towered Camelot;
And by the moon the reaper weary,
Piling sheaves in uplands airy,
Listening, whispers "'Tis the fairy
        Lady of Shalott."

Part II

There she weaves by night and day
A magic web with colors gay.
She has heard a whisper say,
A curse is on her if she stay
        To look down to Camelot.
She knows not what the curse may be,
And so she weaveth steadily,
And little other care hath she,
        The Lady of Shalott.

And moving through a mirror clear°
That hangs before her all the year,
Shadows of the world appear.
There she sees the highway near
        Winding down to Camelot;
There the river eddy whirls,
And there the surly village churls,°
And the red cloaks of market girls,
        Pass onward from Shalott.

Sometimes a troop of damsels glad,
An abbot on an ambling pad,°
Sometimes a curly shepherd lad,
Or long-haired page in crimson clad,
        Goes by to towered Camelot;
And sometimes through the mirror blue
The knights come riding two and two:
She hath no loyal knight and true,
        The Lady of Shalott.

But in her web she still delights
To weave the mirror's magic sights,
For often through the silent nights
A funeral, with plumes and lights

30. cheerly *adv.:* archaic for "cheerily."

46. mirror clear: Weavers worked on the back of the tapestry so that they could easily knot their yarns. To see the front of their designs, weavers looked in a mirror that reflected the front of the tapestry.

52. churls *n. pl.:* peasants; country folk.

56. pad *n.:* easy-gaited horse.

And music, went to Camelot;
Or when the moon was overhead,
Came two young lovers lately wed:
"I am half sick of shadows," said
The Lady of Shalott.

Part III

A bowshot from her bower eaves,
He rode between the barley sheaves,
The sun came dazzling through the leaves,
And flamed upon the brazen greaves°
Of bold Sir Lancelot.
A red-cross knight° forever kneeled
To a lady in his shield,
That sparkled on the yellow field,
Beside remote Shalott.

The gemmy° bridle glittered free,
Like to some branch of stars we see
Hung in the golden Galaxy.°
The bridle bells rang merrily
As he rode down to Camelot;
And from his blazoned baldric° slung
A mighty silver bugle hung,
And as he rode his armor rung,
Beside remote Shalott.

All in the blue unclouded weather
Thick-jeweled shone the saddle leather,
The helmet and the helmet feather
Burned like one burning flame together,
As he rode down to Camelot;
As often through the purple night,
Below the starry clusters bright,
Some bearded meteor, trailing light,
Moves over still Shalott.

His broad clear brow in sunlight glowed;
On burnished° hooves his war horse trode;
From underneath his helmet flowed
His coal-black curls as on he rode,
As he rode down to Camelot.
From the bank and from the river
He flashed into the crystal mirror,
"Tirra lirra," by the river
Sang Sir Lancelot.

76. greaves *n. pl.:* armor for the lower legs.

78. red-cross knight: The red cross is the emblem of Saint George, England's patron saint.

82. gemmy *adj.:* set with jewels.

84. Galaxy: Milky Way.

87. blazoned baldric: richly decorated sash worn across the chest diagonally.

101. burnished *adj.:* polished.

She left the web, she left the loom,
She made three paces through the room,
She saw the waterlily bloom,
She saw the helmet and the plume,
She looked down to Camelot.
Out flew the web and floated wide;
The mirror cracked from side to side;
"The curse is come upon me," cried
The Lady of Shalott.

Part IV

In the stormy east wind straining,
The pale yellow woods were waning,
The broad stream in his banks complaining,
Heavily the low sky raining
Over towered Camelot;
Down she came and found a boat
Beneath a willow left afloat,
And round about the prow° she wrote
The Lady of Shalott.

And down the river's dim expanse
Like some bold seër° in a trance,
Seeing all his own mischance—
With a glassy countenance
Did she look to Camelot.
And at the closing of the day
She loosed the chain, and down she lay;
The broad stream bore her far away,
The Lady of Shalott.

Lying, robed in snowy white
That loosely flew to left and right—
The leaves upon her falling light—
Through the noises of the night
She floated down to Camelot;
And as the boat head wound along
The willowy hills and fields among,
They heard her singing her last song,
The Lady of Shalott.

Heard a carol, mournful, holy,
Chanted loudly, chanted lowly,
Till her blood was frozen slowly,
And her eyes were darkened wholly,
Turned to towered Camelot.

125. prow *n.:* front part of a boat.
128. seër *n.:* prophet.

The Lady of Shalott (19th century) by John William Waterhouse.

For ere she reached upon the tide
The first house by the waterside,
Singing in her song she died,
The Lady of Shalott.

Under tower and balcony,
By garden wall and gallery,
A gleaming shape she floated by,
Dead-pale between the houses high,
Silent into Camelot.
Out upon the wharfs they came,
Knight and burgher,° lord and dame,
And round the prow they read her name,
The Lady of Shalott.

Who is this? and what is here?
And in the lighted palace near
Died the sound of royal cheer;
And they crossed themselves for fear,
All the knights at Camelot:
But Lancelot mused a little space;
He said, "She has a lovely face;
God in his mercy lend her grace,
The Lady of Shalott."

160. burgher *n.:* townsperson.

CRITICAL COMMENT

INFORMATIONAL TEXT

Escaping a World of Shadows

Readers may differ in their interpretations of the meaning or moral of the simple story this richly ornamented and carefully wrought poem tells. As you learned before you read the poem, no one should disregard the clue offered by Tennyson himself: "The newborn love for something," he said of the Lady of Shalott, "for someone in the wide world from which she had been so long secluded, takes her out of the region of shadows into that of realities." He is referring particularly to the last lines of Part II when, having watched a young bride and groom in the moonlight, the Lady declares that she is "half sick of shadows."

Like the weaving that perpetually occupies the heroine—"A magic web with colors gay"—the narrative moves from scene to scene with a tapestried grace that quietly captures the romantic heart of the Age of Chivalry. The Lady is appropriately beautiful, wan, sequestered, and mysterious. Sir Lancelot, panoplied to the hilt with every object in the book of heraldry, is less a man than a vision of a man. And Camelot itself, "many-towered," exists like a little city afloat in time.

The "mirror clear" in line 46 is crucial both to the poem's narrative line and to its meaning. In the custom of weavers, the Lady has placed this mirror in a spot facing the loom from which she is able to see at a glance how her work is going. But, for the purposes of the story, the more important function of the mirror is to allow the Lady glimpses or "shadows" of the world in which she takes no part.

Response and Analysis

Reading Check

1. Describe where the Lady of Shalott lives in relation to the city of Camelot.
2. What must the Lady of Shalott do to avoid the curse?
3. After she hears Sir Lancelot singing, what does the Lady do? What is the result of this action?

Thinking Critically

4. Summarize the main events in the **plot** of this narrative poem. What moment marks the poem's **climax**?
5. Point out **images** of dazzling light associated with Sir Lancelot in Part III. Find **contrasting images** associated with the Lady. What do you think Tennyson is trying to achieve through this contrast? Refer to your reading notes.
6. Explain why lines 66–72 could **foreshadow,** or hint at, Lancelot's arrival and the Lady's actions in the second half of the poem. What yearning do you think the Lady expresses when she exclaims, "I am half sick of shadows" (line 71)?
7. How does Tennyson **contrast** the Lady's life with the lives of the villagers and court in Camelot? Do you think that Tennyson indicates a preference for any of these ways of life? Explain.
8. Scan the poem to find its **metrical form** and **rhyme scheme.** Then, locate examples of **alliteration** and **assonance** that contribute to the poem's haunting strains. How do these examples of **word music** make you feel?

Literary Skills Analyze sound devices in poetry.

Reading Skills Analyze contrasting images.

Writing Skills Write an essay analyzing a poem.

INTERNET

Projects and Activities

Keyword: LE7 12-6

Literary Criticism

9. When Tennyson published the first version of "The Lady of Shalott" in 1832, this is how the last stanza ended:

The web was woven curiously
The charm is broken utterly
Draw near and fear not—this is I,
The Lady of Shalott.

Compare this scenario to what occurs in the last stanza of the version you've just read. What do you think of Tennyson's revision? Which ending do you find more moving? Explain.

WRITING

Shadows and Reality

In a short **essay, analyze** the theme of "The Lady of Shalott" in light of Tennyson's comment about the Lady: "The newborn love for something, for someone in the wide world from which she had been so long secluded, takes her out of the region of shadows into that of realities." Before you begin, gather details for your analysis in a chart like the one that follows:

What happens in the poem	
Key words	
Key images	
Key passages	
Significance of comment (see above)	
Theme of poem	

Be sure to check your Quickwrite notes as you decide what Tennyson means by "the region of shadows" and "that of realities."

Before You Read

Ulysses

Make the Connection

Quickwrite

An old saying claims that youth is wasted on the young—that only older people have the experience and perspective to appreciate the joys of youthful health and exuberance. Stereotypes of "proper" activities for older adults often don't take into account the skills and talents developed over a lifetime of living. Tennyson's adventure-seeking Ulysses may be pursuing a young man's dream, but why should he abandon the passions of a lifetime merely because of his age?

Some famous singers, dancers, and athletes continue their careers long after their skills have peaked. What (besides money) do you think motivates them? Jot down some notes about whether you think you would behave the same way in their place.

Literary Focus

Theme

In their works of literature, most writers attempt to convey a central idea or insight about a subject. This idea is called the **theme** of a work. It is important to note that a **subject** and a theme are not the same. A subject can be summed up in a word or two—*love* or *change,* for example. A theme, however, is a complete idea that can be stated as a sentence—*True love is a mere illusion,* or *Change is painful, but can lead to growth and discovery.* As you will see, the subject of "Ulysses" is old age. While you read the poem, ask yourself what theme, or idea, Tennyson might be expressing about this subject. How might this theme represent a view on life?

A **theme** is the central idea or insight of a work of literature.

For more on Theme, see the Handbook of Literary and Historical Terms.

Background

Ulysses (*Odysseus* in Greek) is one of the Greek leaders who fought in the ten-year-long Trojan War. Homer's epic poem the *Odyssey* tells of his equally long journey home from Troy to Ithaca. In Tennyson's poem, Ulysses, now an old king, is at home with his wife and son, Telemachus (tə·lem′ə·kəs). After an exciting life of both marvels and horrors, the old king might finally rest—either thankfully or regretfully. But here, Ulysses wants to leave home yet again and embark on a final journey. He knows lost youth cannot be regained, but he seeks something else.

Tennyson said of this poem: "'Ulysses' was written soon after Arthur Hallam's death, and gave my feeling about the need of going forward, and braving the struggle of life perhaps more simply than anything in *In Memoriam.*" (*In Memoriam* is Tennyson's famous elegy to his beloved friend.)

Soldiers in battle (detail from a Greek bowl).

Alinari/Art Resource, New York.

Literary Skills Understand theme.

INTERNET

More About Alfred, Lord Tennyson

Keyword: LE7 12-6

Ulysses Deriding Polyphemus (19th century) by J.M.W. Turner.
The Tate Gallery, London.

Ulysses

Alfred, Lord Tennyson

It little profits that an idle king,
By this still hearth, among these barren crags,
Matched with an aged wife, I mete and dole°
Unequal laws unto a savage race,
That hoard, and sleep, and feed, and know not me.
I cannot rest from travel; I will drink
Life to the lees.° All times I have enjoyed
Greatly, have suffered greatly, both with those
That loved me, and alone; on shore, and when

3. **mete and dole:** measure and give out.

7. **lees** *n.:* dregs or sediment.

Through scudding drifts the rainy Hyades°
Vexed the dim sea. I am become a name;
For always roaming with a hungry heart
Much have I seen and known,—cities of men
And manners, climates, councils, governments,
Myself not least, but honored of them all,—
And drunk delight of battle with my peers,
Far on the ringing plains of windy Troy.
I am a part of all that I have met;
Yet all experience is an arch wherethrough
Gleams that untraveled world whose margin fades
Forever and forever when I move.
How dull it is to pause, to make an end,
To rust unburnished, not to shine in use!
As though to breathe were life! Life piled on life
Were all too little, and of one to me
Little remains; but every hour is saved
From that eternal silence, something more,
A bringer of new things; and vile it were
For some three suns to store and hoard myself,
And this gray spirit yearning in desire
To follow knowledge like a sinking star,
Beyond the utmost bound of human thought.
        This is my son, mine own Telemachus,
To whom I leave the scepter and the isle,°—
Well-loved of me, discerning to fulfill
This labor, by slow prudence to make mild
A rugged people, and through soft degrees
Subdue them to the useful and the good.
Most blameless is he, centered in the sphere
Of common duties, decent not to fail
In offices of tenderness, and pay
Meet° adoration to my household gods,
When I am gone. He works his work, I mine.
        There lies the port; the vessel puffs her sail;
There gloom the dark, broad seas. My mariners,
Souls that have toiled, and wrought, and thought with me,—
That ever with a frolic welcome took
The thunder and the sunshine, and opposed
Free hearts, free foreheads,—you and I are old;
Old age hath yet his honor and his toil.
Death closes all; but something ere the end,
Some work of noble note, may yet be done,
Not unbecoming men that strove with Gods.
The lights begin to twinkle from the rocks;
The long day wanes; the slow moon climbs; the deep
Moans round with many voices. Come, my friends,

10. Hyades (hī′ə·dēz′): stars that were thought to indicate rainy weather.

? **22–28.** *How does Ulysses think life should be lived?*

34. isle *n.:* Ithaca, Ulysses' island kingdom off the west coast of Greece.

? **33–43.** *What will Telemachus's work be?*

42. meet *adj.:* proper.

? **50–53.** *What can Ulysses gain in his old age?*

'Tis not too late to seek a newer world.
Push off, and sitting well in order smite
The sounding furrows;° for my purpose holds
To sail beyond the sunset, and the baths
Of all the western stars, until I die.
It may be that the gulfs will wash us down;
It may be we shall touch the Happy Isles,°
And see the great Achilles,° whom we knew.
Though much is taken, much abides; and though
We are not now that strength which in old days
Moved earth and heaven, that which we are, we are,—
One equal temper of heroic hearts,
Made weak by time and fate, but strong in will
To strive, to seek, to find, and not to yield.

58–59. smite . . . furrows: row against the waves.

63. Happy Isles: in Greek mythology, Elysium (ē·liz′ē·əm), where dead heroes lived for eternity.

64. Achilles (ə·kil′ēz′): Greek warrior and leader in the Trojan War. (See page 67.)

Response and Analysis

Literary Skills Analyze theme.

Writing Skills Write an essay analyzing theme.

INTERNET

Projects and Activities

Keyword: LE7 12-6

Thinking Critically

1. How does Ulysses contrast his past and present lives? What conclusions can you draw about his values?
2. In lines 19–21, what does Ulysses mean by his metaphor describing "all experience"?
3. Whom does Ulysses address in the second half of the poem? In the concluding lines of the poem, what qualities does he say that he shares with his mariners?
4. **Personification** is a kind of metaphor in which a nonhuman thing or quality is talked about as if it were human. Find two examples of personification in the last verse paragraph of the poem. How does this use of personification make you feel?
5. Find Ulysses' references to his wife and son. What do you think his words reveal about his feelings toward them?
6. Choose several adjectives that you feel **characterize** Ulysses. Cite evidence from the poem.

Extending and Evaluating

7. What do you think of Ulysses' decision to "sail beyond the sunset"? (It may help to review your Quickwrite notes.)

WRITING

"Not to Yield"

In an **essay, analyze** the theme of this poem—the central idea about human existence that you think it reveals. Be sure to use passages from the poem to support your statement of the theme. Before you write, gather your details in a chart like the following:

Theme	
Supporting passage	
Supporting passage	
Supporting passage	

At the end of your essay, describe your response to Ulysses' decision to leave home.

Robert Browning

(1812–1889)

Robert Browning (1858) by Michele Gordigiani. Oil on canvas (29″ × 23″).

By Courtesy of the National Portrait Gallery, London.

Robert Browning wrote of his first published book, a long poem about the spiritual development of a poet, that it was part of a "foolish plan." He intended, he said, to write in many forms and under different names. Browning eventually gave up this idea, but he held on to his ambition of dazzling the world with his range and variety.

Browning's education allowed him to indulge his wide-ranging interests in music, art, the history of medicine, drama, literature, entomology, and other oddly assorted topics. Browning attended boarding school briefly but was mainly educated at home in a London suburb by tutors and by his wide reading in his banker-father's extensive library. As a teenager, Browning was brilliant, undisciplined, and determined to be a poet like his idol, Percy Bysshe Shelley. After a term at the University of London, he published (at his family's expense) several poems, plays, and pamphlets, but not until he began writing the short dramatic monologues of the 1840s—poems like "My Last Duchess" and "Porphyria's Lover"—did Browning find his proper form. While Browning struggled to gain recognition for his writing, he lived comfortably at home, supported by his parents, until he married at thirty-four.

In 1845, Browning wrote to Elizabeth Barrett, already an established poet: "I do . . . love these books with all my heart—and I love you too." Barrett was then a semi-invalid in her father's London house, where she submitted to his sternly protective care. Four months after the two poets began their correspondence, they met and fell in love. They secretly married in 1846, and a week later eloped to Italy. Mr. Barrett estranged himself from his famous daughter for the rest of his life.

Browning's happy marriage confirmed his belief that only by acting boldly can one wrest what is good from an imperfect world. "I was ever a fighter," he wrote in "Prospice." He liked to see himself in strenuous but joyous contests with difficulties. In his dramatic poems, he also liked to emphasize the error, weakness, and even the viciousness of his characters.

Browning lived in Italy until Elizabeth's death in 1861, when he returned to England with their twelve-year-old son. During the 1860s, his fame began to grow. Gradually, readers understood that by asking them to figure out and judge wicked men like the Duke in "My Last Duchess," Browning was really challenging them to discover what is virtuous and healthy, when love nourishes, and when and why it kills. Browning believed that human beings must act by a moral standard, just as he believed that those who act bravely will be rewarded.

By the time of his death in 1889, Browning had won a place next to Tennyson as the other great Victorian poet. Like Tennyson, he was read as a kind of sage who assured his contemporaries that "This world's no blot for us, / Nor blank; it means intensely, and means good" ("Fra Lippo Lippi").

Before You Read

My Last Duchess

Make the Connection

Quickwrite

The speaker in this poem is a powerful nobleman of Renaissance Italy. The poem opens with the speaker describing a painting of a woman whom he calls his "last Duchess." By the poem's end the speaker has suggested an entire relationship, yet we are left with the uncomfortable feeling that he does not realize just how much he has revealed.

Think about a time when you wondered exactly what someone meant by something that he or she said. Did you think the person was revealing his or her innermost thoughts intentionally or unintentionally? Jot down some notes about both the experience and how it made you feel.

Literary Focus

Dramatic Monologue

"My Last Duchess" is one of Browning's earliest and most popular **dramatic monologues,** poems in which a speaker who is not the poet addresses a listener who does not speak. Instead of telling us directly what the speaker and the other characters are like, Browning allows the speaker to reveal himself, the other characters, and the situation by dropping indirect clues that we must piece together.

A **dramatic monologue** is a poem in which a character addresses one or more listeners who remain silent.

For more on Dramatic Monologue, see the Handbook of Literary and Historical Terms.

Reading Skills

Drawing Inferences from Textual Clues

As you read, jot down the names of three characters that Browning introduces, starting with the speaker (the Duke). Next to each name, write down details from the poem that give clues to that person's **character, situation,** and **motives.** After several readings, try to reconstruct the relationships among the characters and the motives for their actions by drawing **inferences,** or logical conclusions, from the clues you have recorded. Of course, another basis for your inferences will be your own experience with people.

Background

Browning identified his speaker as the Duke of Ferrara, who married three times. The Duke's first wife, a young girl, died in 1561. In the poem the Duke is negotiating to marry the daughter of a Count. He is addressing the Count's representative.

Literary Skills Understand the characteristics of dramatic monologue.

Reading Skills Draw inferences from textual clues.

Man with Glove (16th century) by Titian (Tiziano Vecellio).
Louvre, Paris.

A Lady with a Gold Chain and Earrings (1861) by Robert Braithwaite Martineau. Oil on panel (14″ × 10″).

My Last Duchess

Robert Browning

That's my last Duchess painted on the wall,
Looking as if she were alive. I call
That piece a wonder, now; Frà Pandolf's° hands
Worked busily a day, and there she stands.
Will 't please you sit and look at her? I said
"Frà Pandolf" by design, for never read
Strangers like you that pictured countenance,
The depth and passion of its earnest glance,
But to myself they turned (since none puts by

3. Frà Pandolf's: Brother Pandolf, a fictitious painter and monk.

The curtain I have drawn for you, but I)
And seemed as they would ask me, if they durst,
How such a glance came there; so, not the first
Are you to turn and ask thus. Sir, 'twas not
Her husband's presence only, called that spot
Of joy into the Duchess' cheek; perhaps
Frà Pandolf chanced to say, "Her mantle° laps
Over my lady's wrist too much," or, "Paint
Must never hope to reproduce the faint
Half flush that dies along her throat." Such stuff
Was courtesy, she thought, and cause enough
For calling up that spot of joy. She had
A heart—how shall I say?—too soon made glad,
Too easily impressed; she liked whate'er
She looked on, and her looks went everywhere.
Sir, 'twas all one! My favor° at her breast,
The dropping of the daylight in the West,
The bough of cherries some officious fool
Broke in the orchard for her, the white mule
She rode with round the terrace—all and each
Would draw from her alike the approving speech,
Or blush, at least. She thanked men—good! but thanked
Somehow—I know not how—as if she ranked
My gift of a nine-hundred-years-old name
With anybody's gift. Who'd stoop to blame
This sort of trifling? Even had you skill
In speech—(which I have not)—to make your will
Quite clear to such an one, and say, "Just this
Or that in you disgusts me; here you miss,
Or there exceed the mark"—and if she let
Herself be lessoned so, nor plainly set
Her wits to yours, forsooth,° and made excuse,
—E'en then would be some stooping; and I choose
Never to stoop. Oh sir, she smiled, no doubt,
Whene'er I passed her; but who passed without
Much the same smile? This grew; I gave commands;
Then all smiles stopped together. There she stands
As if alive. Will 't please you rise? We'll meet
The company below, then. I repeat,
The Count your master's known munificence°
Is ample warrant° that no just pretense
Of mine for dowry will be disallowed;
Though his fair daughter's self, as I avowed
At starting, is my object. Nay, we'll go
Together down, sir. Notice Neptune,° though,
Taming a seahorse, thought a rarity,
Which Claus of Innsbruck° cast in bronze for me!

? **1–13.** *Paraphrase these opening lines. What are the speaker and his guest doing? What does the guest ask the speaker?*

16. mantle *n.:* cloak.

? **13–21.** *What does the speaker think brought the "spot of joy" (line 21) to his wife's face?*

25. favor *n.:* gift; token of love.

? **21–34.** *What complaints does the speaker make against the Duchess's character in these lines? What most bothers him?*

41. forsooth *adv.:* archaic for "in truth."

? **45–47.** *How did the speaker treat his wife? What do you suspect happened to the Duchess?*

49. munificence *n.:* generosity.
50. warrant *n.:* guarantee.

54. Neptune: in Roman mythology, god of the sea.
56. Claus of Innsbruck: imaginary sculptor.

CONNECTION / NEWS FEATURE

INFORMATIONAL TEXT

Scenes from a Modern Marriage

By Julia Markus

The letter that began the most famous courtship of the 19th century opened, "I love your verses with all my heart, dear Miss Barrett." The writer, Robert Browning, a thirty-three-year-old poet respected in literary circles, was writing to a woman six years his senior, an invalid and a poet of national and international fame. Elizabeth Barrett had not long before recognized his own genius in a poem, "Lady Geraldine's Courtship," likening his poetic heart to a pomegranate "blood-tinctured" with "a veined humanity."

Cloistered in the airless bed-sitting room she never left, Elizabeth Barrett was a famous yet mysterious poet. Little could Robert know that her household on Wimpole Street was one of enforced celibacy. Her father, scion of Jamaican wealth, forbade any of his nine adult children, male or female, to marry; all were still living at home. Elizabeth's allowing Robert to visit for the first time was in its own way a dangerous act, a rebellion.

The courtship that followed—daily letters for more than twenty months, secret weekly visits while Papa Barrett was at work—is one of the most romantic and obsessively documented love stories in our tradition.

They met 150 years ago, but their successful marriage has something to say to us today. . . .

Not that any marriage is easy. Robert was disturbed by his wife's lifelong use of morphine, which she believed kept her alive, and he was skeptical of her attraction to spiritualism and furious at some of the mediums she befriended. Elizabeth also suffered four miscarriages, giving birth at the age of forty-three to one healthy son. But the birth of Pen Browning came on the day Robert's mother died in England, and his despondency drew him away from his son.

Desperate to help, Elizabeth told Robert she had once secretly written poems about him, during the courtship. She hesitantly handed him the *Sonnets from the Portuguese* as if to say, Look how love led me from despair; can I now lead you from it? "How I see the gesture, and hear the tones," he remembered years after her death, "and, for the matter of that, see the window at which I was standing, with the tall mimosa in front, and the little church court to the right."

The careers of these two poets were on different levels, which could have led to the kind of troubled celebrity marriage we read about today in the tabloids. Though they both wrote their best poetry during their marriage, Robert Browning's greatest collection, "Men and Women"—still in print—was hacked to death by the critics and sold fewer than two hundred copies. This failure added to his money worries—and, since the interest on her money supported them through most of their marriage, to his grave discomfort.

She in the meantime had written a daring novel in verse, "Aurora Leigh," which exposed the abuses against women in Victorian society and suggested, among other things, that what a female artist needed was not a husband but enough money for a garret of her own.

Elizabeth defied conventions only to find her book a best-seller that quickly went through five editions and was read and discussed everywhere. Yet while he was bitter about the critics who destroyed his hopes of critical and commercial success, "golden-hearted" Robert was thrilled by her success. He could talk of nothing else, and he always considered her the superior artist. To her sister Arabel she wrote, when people "write & talk of the 'jealousy' of authors & husbands, let them look at him!"

If this all seems too good to be true, let it be known the couple quarreled. They had very different ideas about child rearing, for one thing. Elizabeth, coming from a home in which her father's "thunder" dictated obedience and having been a child prodigy, wished for her son happy, carefree, unstructured days. Robert, who was doted on by his parents, wanted Pen to take his piano lessons seriously and learn to count. She kept Pen in long curls and velvet frocks; he wanted him to look like a real boy.

But both believed that arguments were important to the marriage. "You know I do think for myself (if the thought is right or wrong) and I do speak the truth (as I am capable of apprehending it) to my husband always," Elizabeth wrote to Arabel. "What you used to call 'our quarreling' is an element of our loving one another, & a very important element too."

—from *The New York Times*,
February 14, 1995

Response and Analysis

Thinking Critically

1. According to the Duke, what happened to his last Duchess?
2. Identify the **characters** in this poem, their **relationships,** and their **motives.** (Refer to your reading notes.)
3. What impression do you think the Duke intends to create by his remarks to the Count's emissary? Why might he choose to present himself in this way?
4. Assume that the emissary is an insightful person. What impression is the Duke unintentionally making? (Be sure to refer to your Quickwrite notes.)
5. What do you think of the Duke's description of his last Duchess? Do you question his assessments? Why or why not?

Extending and Evaluating

6. Read the last sentence of the poem (lines 54–56). Do you find it an effective conclusion? What—if anything—might the speaker intend to convey with such a comment?
7. Many people like to read autobiographical details into literature. Can you see any connection between the marriage in this poem and the Brownings' own marriage? (See the ***Connection*** on page 911.)

Literary Criticism

8. Many critics see Robert Browning as a "psychological poet," one who is more modern to us than other Victorian writers. In what sense is "My Last Duchess" an exploration of abnormal psychology and human evil? Does Browning convincingly portray the complexity of human psychology in ways that make sense to us today? Explain.

SKILLS FOCUS

Literary Skills Analyze a dramatic monologue.

Reading Skills Draw inferences from textual clues.

Writing Skills Write a dramatic monologue.

Listening and Speaking Skills Deliver a dramatic reading.

WRITING

The Duchess Talks Back

Write a **dramatic monologue,** in prose, using the voice of the Duchess. Base your monologue on an imaginary incident that could have occurred between her and the Duke—or one that the Duke himself mentions—and take into account the personality portraits of both the Duchess and the Duke.

LISTENING AND SPEAKING

Performing a Dramatic Reading

Work with a partner to prepare two dramatic readings of Browning's poem, each one conveying a different interpretation of the Duke's **tone.** (For example, his words may sound sinister if read one way, but regretful or mournful if read another way.) Use facial expressions, gestures, and tone of voice to create two distinct impressions. Be sure to pay attention to performance details, such as clarity, force, and aesthetic effect, when you perform your dramatic readings for the class.

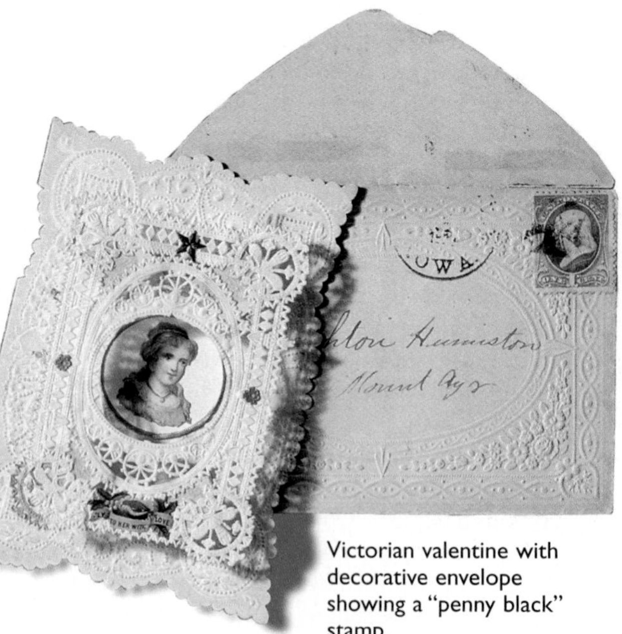

Victorian valentine with decorative envelope showing a "penny black" stamp.

Private Collection.

Elizabeth Barrett Browning

(1806–1861)

Elizabeth Barrett Browning was one of the most famous poets of her day—more successful during her lifetime than her husband, Robert Browning. She is remembered today for her *Sonnets from the Portuguese*, of which "How Do I Love Thee?" is the best known.

During her lifetime, Barrett Browning was well known as a daring, versatile poet who frequently wrote on intellectual, religious, and political matters. As a girl, she studied Greek, Latin, French, Italian, history, and philosophy—an uncommon education for a woman in nineteenth-century England. She published long narratives, a novel in verse, translations of Greek plays, and poems that dealt with the abolition of slavery, the exploitation of children in factories, religious belief, and Italian nationalism.

Through the first half of her busy literary career, Elizabeth Barrett was a semi-invalid. Her illnesses have been variously diagnosed, but it is certain that their effect was intensified by the sometimes bullying protectiveness of her father, and perhaps by the drugs routinely prescribed in those days for a "nervous collapse." She wrote to Robert Browning during their courtship, "Papa says sometimes when he comes into this room unexpectedly and convicts me of having dry toast for dinner, . . . that obstinacy and dry toast have brought me to my present condition, and if I *pleased* to have porter and beefsteaks instead, I should be as well as ever I was, in a month!"

Elizabeth Barrett Browning (1858) by Michele Gordigiani. Oil on canvas (73.7 cm × 58.4 cm).

By Courtesy of the National Portrait Gallery, London.

In 1845, she met Robert Browning, and the next year they married secretly and eloped to the Continent. Her father never forgave her for the marriage (he had forbidden all his children to marry), nor did he ever see her again. Barrett Browning flourished in Italy and bore a son when she was forty-three years old: her own "young Florentine" with "brave blue English eyes."

The Browning Readers (late 19th or early 20th century) by Sir William Rothenstein.

Bradford Galleries and Museums, London.

Before You Read

Sonnet 43

Make the Connection

Quickwrite

This poem expresses an ardent, joyful love—a truly transforming love—yet it is not a blind, infatuated love. Amid the fervor, you may find hints that love must weather more than joy. What do you think the most important emotional components of love are? Jot down your thoughts.

Literary Focus

Petrarchan Sonnet

All forty-four poems in *Sonnets from the Portuguese* are written in traditional **Petrarchan,** or Italian, **sonnet** form: an octave (eight lines) and sestet (six lines) in iambic pentameter, rhyming *abbaabba cdcdcd.* Sonnet 43 does not have the usual **turn,** or break in thought, at the sestet. Rather, the poem is broken into short units of thought.

A **Petrarchan sonnet** is a fourteen-line poem that is divided into an eight-line **octave** and a six-line **sestet.**

For more on the Sonnet, see the Handbook of Literary and Historical Terms.

Background

Elizabeth Barrett Browning wrote her sonnets before her marriage, but did not show them to her husband until two years later. Reluctant to publish the poems because they were so autobiographical, she deliberately gave them a title that suggested that they were a translation into English from an original Portuguese source.

Love Among the Ruins (1894) by Sir Edward Burne-Jones.

Wightwick Manor/National Trust Photographic Library, London.

Literary Skills Understand the Petrarchan sonnet form.

Sonnet 43

Elizabeth Barrett Browning

Angel (detail), from a tomb in the municipal cemetery of Merida, Mexico.

How do I love thee? Let me count the ways.
I love thee to the depth and breadth and height
My soul can reach, when feeling out of sight
For the ends of Being and ideal Grace.
I love thee to the level of everyday's
Most quiet need, by sun and candlelight.
I love thee freely, as men strive for Right;
I love thee purely, as they turn from Praise.
I love thee with the passion put to use
In my old griefs, and with my childhood's faith.
I love thee with a love I seemed to lose
With my lost saints°—I love thee with the breath,
Smiles, tears, of all my life!—and, if God choose,
I shall but love thee better after death.

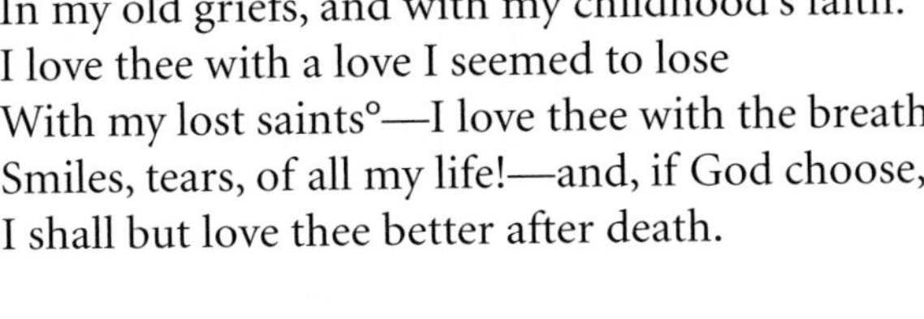

12. **lost saints:** childhood faith.

Response and Analysis

Thinking Critically

1. How many distinct ways does the speaker say that she loves her beloved?
2. What do you think the poem expresses about the speaker's religious faith?
3. How are the pauses in the last three lines different in **rhythm** from those in the rest of the poem? What is the emotional effect of this change in rhythm?
4. What examples of concrete and abstract words can you find in the poem? What different emotional effects do these different words produce?

Extending and Evaluating

5. In your opinion, has Barrett Browning described all of the important emotional aspects of love? Explain your response. (Refer to your Quickwrite notes for ideas.)

WRITING

Comparing and Contrasting Literature

In a brief **essay, compare and contrast** Sonnet 43 with Shakespeare's Sonnet 116 (see page 319). Focus on the similarities and differences in the ways in which the speakers express their love. Use passages from the poems to show how word choice and imagery work together to create a specific tone for each poem.

▶ **Use "Comparing and Contrasting Literature," pages 1002–1009, for help with this assignment.**

Literary Skills Analyze a Petrarchan sonnet.

Writing Skills Write an essay comparing and contrasting two sonnets.

Gerard Manley Hopkins

(1844–1889)

Hopkins was the eldest son of highly educated parents who were devoted to the Church of England. His father, British consul general of the Hawaiian Islands, sent the young Hopkins to Highgate, a London boarding school, where he won a poetry prize and later a scholarship to study classics at Oxford University. Hopkins intended to prepare himself for the Anglican ministry, but after much soul-searching, he converted to Roman Catholicism in 1866—a radical and shocking thing to do at the time.

In 1868, when he entered the Jesuit order, Hopkins burned almost all his poetry (a few poems remain) and "resolved to write no more, as not belonging to my profession, unless it were by the wish of my superiors." He wrote no poetry for seven years, but in 1875, he was asked to write an ode in memory of five Franciscan nuns who had drowned at sea. He sent "The Wreck of the *Deutschland*" to a Jesuit periodical. The poem's form was so eccentric that the editors "dared not print it."

Hopkins, an unusually conscientious man, was ordained as a Jesuit priest in 1877 and devoted himself to the immediate demands of the priesthood. He served in parishes in poor sections of English and Scottish cities, writing sermons and ministering to the sick. He also worked as a teacher of classics at a Jesuit seminary and later as a professor of Greek at the Roman Catholic university in Dublin. In 1889, at the age of forty-four, he died of typhoid fever in Dublin.

Hopkins published one of his poems in 1863, the year he entered college, but after that only a few insignificant poems appeared during his lifetime. He composed a small but very powerful body of poetry that he sent to his friends with careful instructions about how to understand them. In his letters, he elaborated on his ideas about using the stock of native English words for the diction of his verse. Hopkins's poems are also characterized by what he called **sprung rhythm,** and by **assonance, alliteration,** and **internal rhyme.**

Hopkins attempted in his sprung rhythm to imitate the sound of natural speech. He explained: "It consists in scanning by accents or stresses alone, . . . so that a foot may be but one strong syllable or it may be many light and one strong." In conventional metrics, a foot consists of a prescribed number of stressed and unstressed syllables (an *iamb*, for example, is an unstressed syllable followed by a stressed syllable). Sprung rhythm is not concerned with using only one kind of foot in a poem; in Hopkins's poems, a line may consist of many kinds of feet: iambs, trochees, dactyls, spondees, and so on.

For a while, literary critics regarded Hopkins as a twentieth-century poet—rather than a Victorian poet—because of his strongly individual language, compression of meaning, unconventional forms, and singular sound. But Hopkins is unmistakably rooted in the nineteenth century. In his almost ecstatic love of nature, his passionate conviction of a transcendental power, and his striving for individuality, Hopkins resembled the Romantic poets. In the "terrible sonnets" of his last four years, Hopkins expressed the doubts and spiritual anguish of many late-nineteenth-century writers.

Gerard Manley Hopkins (1880). Photograph by Forshaw and Coles.

By Courtesy of the National Portrait Gallery, London.

Before You Read

Pied Beauty

Make the Connection

Quickwrite

Perhaps not surprising from a poet as unconventional as Hopkins, "Pied Beauty" is a song of praise to God for all things that are *pied*—that is, covered with different-colored spots. Although its topic is unusual, the poem's form echoes that of a psalm—a praise song. (See page 373 for more about psalms.)

What examples of "spotted things" do you think Hopkins will include in his poem? Write down your own list of "spotted things," and include as many synonyms for *spotted* as you can think of. Then, as you read Hopkins's poem, see if he surprises you with any startling examples—or unusual synonyms.

Literary Focus

Alliteration and Assonance

In much of his poetry, Hopkins makes liberal use of two sound devices: **alliteration,** the repetition of consonant sounds, and **assonance,** the repetition of vowel sounds. In general, these devices account for the difficulty people have in reading Hopkins. (Like tongue-twisters, Hopkins's poems can prove challenging to read aloud!) In "Pied Beauty," the repeated sounds also serve a thematic purpose. Like the creatures' colorful spots, the sounds create points of connection between otherwise unlike things—"Fresh-firecoal chestnut-falls" and "finches' wings," for example, are united by the *f* sound they share. Consider the kinds of emotions these sounds conjure as you read the poem. Try reading it aloud.

Alliteration is the repetition of similar consonant sounds in words that are close to one another. **Assonance** is the repetition of similar vowel sounds in words that are close together.

For more on Alliteration and Assonance, see the Handbook of Literary and Historical Terms.

Background

Hopkins composed "Pied Beauty" in 1877, shortly before he was ordained a Roman Catholic priest. This period was also marked by Hopkins's enthusiastic return to poetry after a "seven-year silence," during which Hopkins had forsworn the craft in order to devote himself to his religious studies. However, the extensive journals he kept during those seven years provided material for much of the verse he would later write. The "Landscape plotted and pieced" in "Pied Beauty," for example, had first been viewed by Hopkins in 1872 during a vacation on the Isle of Man. There, he noted, the hillsides were "plotted and painted" with square, hedged-in fields.

Literary Skills
Understand alliteration and assonance.

Pied Beauty

Gerard Manley Hopkins

Glory be to God for dappled things—
For skies of couple-color as a brinded° cow;
For rose-moles all in stipple° upon trout that swim;
Fresh-firecoal chestnut-falls;° finches' wings;
Landscape plotted and pieced°—fold, fallow, and plow;
And áll trádes, their gear and tackle and trim.
All things counter, original, spare, strange;
Whatever is fickle, freckled (who knows how?)
With swift, slow; sweet, sour; adazzle, dim;
He fathers-forth° whose beauty is past change:
Praise him.

2. brinded *adj.:* archaic for "brindled"; streaked with a darker color.

3. stipple *n.:* random dots or spots.

4. fresh-firecoal chestnut-falls: freshly roasted chestnuts.

5. pieced *adj.:* parceled into fields.

10. fathers-forth: creates.

Evening Shadows (late 19th or early 20th century) by Viggo Christien Frederik Wilhelm Pedersen.

Response and Analysis

Thinking Critically

1. What is the purpose of Hopkins's poem? (How does the last line state the poet's purpose?)
2. What specific examples of "pied beauty" does the poet mention in lines 2–6?
3. What do you think the poet means by saying "all things counter" (line 7)?
4. How does Hopkins use **assonance** in line 5? What do these repeated sounds help you visualize and feel emotionally?
5. How does the poet combine **alliteration** with **antithesis** (opposites) in line 9?
6. In line 10, what contrast does the poet suggest between the beauty of the physical world and the beauty of God the creator?

Extending and Evaluating

7. A highly original text is always a challenge to evaluate. Is the text's newness a breakthrough to be admired, or is it merely odd (as it first seems)? Review "Pied Beauty," and find one example each of **inverted word order,** an **unusual compound,** and an **invented word.** What is the effect of Hopkins's unusual language?

WRITING

Celebrating Beauty

Hopkins catalogs a number of dappled, or pied, things whose beauty he celebrates. Starting from your Quickwrite notes, make your own list of things that are "original, spare, strange," in Hopkins's sense. Then, write a brief **praise poem** in which you catalog and describe a number of things whose beauty *you* want to celebrate.

Praise Poems

Find Psalm 8 in a Bible. In a brief **essay, compare and contrast** this psalm with Hopkins's poem. Gather details for your essay in a chart like the following one:

	Psalm	Hopkins
Purpose of poem		
Message of poem		
Images		
Key words or passages		
Tone of poem		

Use "Comparing and Contrasting Literature," pages 1002–1009, for help with this assignment.

Autumn Leaves (1856) by Sir John Everett Millais. Oil on canvas (41 1/16" × 57 1/16").

Literary Skills
Analyze alliteration and assonance.

Writing Skills
Write a praise poem. Write an essay comparing and contrasting a poem with a psalm.

INTERNET

Projects and Activities

Keyword: LE7 12-6

Matthew Arnold
(1822–1888)

Portrait of Matthew Arnold (1880) by George Frederic Watts.

Unlike the other major Victorian poets, Matthew Arnold achieved fame as both a poet and a critic. He is as famous today for his essays of literary and social criticism as he is for his poetry. His poems stand with the achievements of Tennyson and Browning, their quiet tones and carefully shaped figures of speech expressing his reflections on what Victorian society was like, what it would become, and what it had cost.

Arnold had difficulty in his youth living up to the expectations of his famous father, Dr. Thomas Arnold, one of the leading thinkers of the Victorian era and headmaster of Rugby School. An uneven student at Rugby, Arnold nevertheless won a scholarship to Oxford University in 1841. Although he was less than enthusiastic as a student, he seemed to thoroughly enjoy playing the role of a dandy. His performance at Oxford was a failure by Rugby standards, and he graduated without knowing what he wanted to do.

Arnold had won prizes for his poetry at both Rugby and Oxford. In 1849, he published his first book of poetry, *The Strayed Reveller,* to mixed reviews. Two more volumes of poetry followed in 1852 and 1853, and as a result Arnold was elected an Oxford professor of poetry in 1857.

After his marriage in 1851, Arnold became a government inspector of schools for poor children, a job he held for thirty-five years. His work was exhausting, requiring him to travel all over England and write daily reports. Though he continued to write poetry in his free time, he found it increasingly difficult. In 1853, he told a friend, "I am past thirty, and three parts iced over—and my pen, it seems to me, is even stiffer and more cramped than my feeling."

After 1860, Arnold almost completely stopped writing poetry and began a second career as a critic. His travels and his work had given him firsthand knowledge of pressing social problems, and he became an energetic essayist and lecturer on literary, political, social, and religious questions. In his essays on literature and religion, Arnold urges his readers to acquire a knowledge of history and to study "the best that has been thought and known in the world"—the Greeks, Dante, and Shakespeare—in order to judge ideas and personal conduct. Without the steadying influence of what he called culture, Arnold warns, the nineteenth century's technological and political changes would accelerate into a grossly materialistic democracy.

All through his life, Arnold knew both the excitement of trying to change the temper of his age and the loneliness of not being comfortable in his own time.

Before You Read

Dover Beach

Make the Connection

Quickwrite

Where do people look for answers in times of crisis? Do they look to science? to religion? to government? Enormous problems may seem to call for sweeping solutions. Instead of thinking big, however, what if we thought *small*? Arnold reminds people that they can also look to personal relationships to find the hope, love, and integrity that can make sense of a disordered world.

What do you think people cling to in troubled times? Write down a short list of people, places, or things you value and depend on the most when times are tough.

Literary Focus

Mood

Arnold creates a mood that shifts at certain points in the poem like the ebb and flow of the tide he describes. **Mood** is the feeling, or **atmosphere,** in a work created by the writer's choice of descriptive details, images, and sounds.

Mood is the atmosphere in a literary work.

For more on Mood, see the Handbook of Literary and Historical Terms.

At the Gallery (late 19th or early 20th century) by Paul Gustav Fischer.

Background

Arnold's first draft of "Dover Beach" dates from 1851, when he and his wife spent a night at Dover during their honeymoon trip on the English coast. Many of the beaches in the British Isles consist of round, gray pebbles, not sand. Arnold describes the sound of the sea receding over the pebbles as a "grating roar."

Literary Skills
Understand mood.

Dover Beach

Matthew Arnold

The sea is calm tonight.
The tide is full, the moon lies fair
Upon the straits°—on the French coast the light
Gleams and is gone; the cliffs of England stand,
Glimmering and vast, out in the tranquil bay.
Come to the window, sweet is the night air!
Only, from the long line of spray
Where the sea meets the moon-blanched land,
Listen! you hear the grating roar
Of pebbles which the waves draw back, and fling,
At their return, up the high strand,°
Begin, and cease, and then again begin,
With tremulous cadence slow, and bring
The eternal note of sadness in.

Sophocles° long ago
Heard it on the Aegean,° and it brought
Into his mind the turbid ebb and flow
Of human misery; we
Find also in the sound a thought,
Hearing it by this distant northern sea.

The Sea of Faith
Was once, too, at the full, and round earth's shore
Lay like the folds of a bright girdle° furled.
But now I only hear
Its melancholy, long, withdrawing roar,
Retreating, to the breath
Of the night wind, down the vast edges drear
And naked shingles° of the world.

Ah, love, let us be true
To one another! for the world, which seems
To lie before us like a land of dreams,
So various, so beautiful, so new,
Hath really neither joy, nor love, nor light,
Nor certitude, nor peace, nor help for pain;
And we are here as on a darkling plain
Swept with confused alarms of struggle and flight,
Where ignorant armies clash by night.

3. straits *n. pl.:* Strait of Dover, a body of water separating southeastern England and northwestern France.

11. strand *n.:* shore.

15. Sophocles (säf'ə·klēz') (c. 496–406 B.C.): writer of tragedies in ancient Greece.
16. Aegean (ē·jē'ən): sea between Greece and Turkey.

23. girdle *n.:* belt.

28. shingles *n. pl.:* here, beaches covered with pebbles.

(Opposite) *Pegwell Bay, Kent—A Recollection of October 5, 1858* (1859–1860) by William Dyce.
Tate Gallery, London.

CRITICAL COMMENT

INFORMATIONAL TEXT

Love Is Itself a Faith

More than any other poem written in the nineteenth century, "Dover Beach" continues to echo through the consciousness of every new generation. To say why involves matters of both technique and meaning.

Compared with the characteristic product of the Romantic or Victorian poets, "Dover Beach" is low-keyed. The speaker's tone is largely that of quiet conversation. For all its conversational tone, however, the poem is remarkably ambitious in its claim to render a universal condition.

Unlike his predecessors and contemporaries, Arnold neither reaches for the sublime nor dwells on the sentimental in this poem. Instead, he writes a love poem that, incidentally, expresses the crisis of conscience brought about by the dwindling of religion—"the Sea of Faith"—and by the rise of science. Science has transformed human life through industrialism and through the mass warfare that scientific inventions have made possible. Against these bewildering developments, Arnold poses the notion that love is itself a faith to cling to and, by implication, that individual integrity and a humanistic vision broad enough to include the tragic conclusions of Sophocles are the only defenses against a world moving toward anarchy.

Response and Analysis

Thinking Critically

1. What is the **setting** of the first stanza? Who is the speaker, and whom is he addressing?
2. What **mood** do the first six lines evoke for you? What details in these lines establish that mood?
3. What **images** in the second half of the first stanza begin to change this mood? What emotions do these images evoke?
4. What does the speaker imagine Sophocles also heard long ago? What did the sound bring to Sophocles' mind?
5. Explain the **figure of speech** used to describe faith in lines 21–23. What do you think has happened to the speaker's faith, according to lines 24–28?
6. What does the speaker urge in the last stanza, and why? (How does the speaker's resolution compare with your Quickwrite notes?)
7. Describe the speaker's view of the world as it is presented in the last stanza. Is this view still relevant to today's world? Do "ignorant armies" still "clash by night"? Explain your response to this final image.

SKILLS FOCUS

Literary Skills
Analyze mood.

Writing Skills
Write a reflective essay. Write an essay analyzing a poem.

Extending and Evaluating

8. When Arnold wrote his poem in the mid-1800s, industrialization and scientific advances had brought both improvements and problems. How does Arnold's poem express the paradox of progress felt by the Victorians? How is progress still a paradox for us today—that is, how does progress both help us and threaten or confuse us?

INTERNET

Projects and Activities

Keyword: LE7 12-6

WRITING

Dover Beach Reflections

In a personal **essay,** reflect on a line or an image from "Dover Beach" that you think has special relevance to life today. In your essay, quote the line or image exactly. Be as specific as you can in your response to the quotation.

▶ **Use "Writing a Reflective Essay," pages 856–863, for help with this assignment.**

A World of Contrasts

Arnold begins his poem with a moonlit sea and ends it with a dark plain. Write a brief **essay** in which you **analyze** the contrasting imagery in "Dover Beach." Discuss how the contrasting images reinforce the theme of the poem.

Matthew Arnold (1871), illustration published in *Vanity Fair*.

A. E. Housman
(1859–1936)

By Courtesy of the National Portrait Gallery, London.

Alfred Edward Housman (1926) by Francis Dodd. Pencil drawing (14¾″ × 10¾″).

Housman said that he was careful not to think of poetry while he was shaving, for "if a line of poetry strays into my memory, my skin bristles so that the razor ceases to act." For Housman, poetry was all feeling. The feelings produced physical effects (shivers along the spine, tears, the sensation of being pierced by a spear) that came from what Housman said was the source of his own poems, "the pit of the stomach."

Housman's poetry is more restrained than his comments suggest. His poems evoke a narrow range of subdued feelings that are controlled by simple, tight verse forms and clear language and syntax.

Alfred Edward Housman was born in Worcestershire in western England, the oldest of seven children. He was close to his mother, who died on his twelfth birthday. His father, a lawyer, allowed his practice, money, and talent to dwindle away in despondency and drink. At sixteen, Housman won a scholarship to Oxford, where he prepared for a career as a scholar and teacher of classical literature. He attended classes irregularly, though, preferring to study on his own, and in the end failed his final examinations.

In 1882, Housman entered the civil service as a clerk in the patent office, determined to prove himself as a classical scholar despite his failure at Oxford. For the next ten years, he set himself a rigorous program: writing and publishing papers on Greek and Latin literature while working as a patent clerk. In 1892, his series of scholarly papers won him an appointment as professor of Latin at London University. He stayed until 1911, when he moved to Cambridge University as professor of Latin and fellow at Trinity College. Housman spent the rest of his life as a formal and rather aloof teacher and an authority in classical scholarship.

During his lifetime, Housman published only two books of poetry containing a little more than one hundred poems. His first collection, *A Shropshire Lad* (1896), became popular because its graceful recollection of youthful pleasures and their transience fit a late-century mood of disillusionment in a world that had "much good, but much less good than ill." In "Terence, This Is Stupid Stuff," Housman acknowledged that his poems could be dismissed as self-indulgent bellyaching. The test of poetry, he believed, is not what is said but how it is said. In the refined elegance of his poems, he expressed his pessimistic vision of a cold, empty world. Unlike the major Romantic and Victorian poets who preceded him, Housman saw no hope of improvement or change, but only the possibility of enduring and making bearable the painful conditions of human existence.

For Independent Reading

The following poems by Housman are among his most popular:

- "Is My Team Ploughing"
- "Loveliest of Trees"

Before You Read

To an Athlete Dying Young

Make the Connection

Quickwrite

The strong, healthy athletes who earn fame and fortune seem to live charmed lives. But what happens when the cheering stops? When an athlete dies in the prime of life and at the peak of fame, devoted supporters discover a very sobering truth: Even these remarkable young men and women are not invincible.

At what age do you think you might be in the prime of your life—in top physical and mental condition? What do you hope to be doing at that time? Jot down a few thoughts.

Literary Focus

Couplet

"To an Athlete Dying Young" is written entirely in couplets. A **couplet** is a pair of lines, one after another, that rhyme. The lines in a couplet usually share the same meter as well. In Housman's poem, each couplet is joined with another to form a four-line stanza. The strong rhythm created by this pattern fits the poem's somber subject matter—death—and mimics the slow, mournful tempo of a funeral procession.

A **couplet** consists of two consecutive lines of poetry that rhyme.

For more on Couplets, see the Handbook of Literary and Historical Terms.

Background

"To an Athlete Dying Young" appeared in 1896 in the first edition of *A Shropshire Lad,* a volume Housman himself paid to have published. The poet scarcely made a profit from this book of sixty-three verses, which often tell stories in the voice of a young soldier or farm boy. However, Housman lived to see his poems become enormously popular during the Boer War. Soldiers fighting in South Africa identified with the homesick lad from Shropshire and heard in his voice the echo of their own melancholy.

Speed skater racing at the 1994 Winter Olympics.

Literary Skills Understand couplets.

To an Athlete Dying Young

A. E. Housman

The time you won your town the race
We chaired you through the marketplace;
Man and boy stood cheering by,
And home we brought you shoulder-high.

Today, the road all runners come,
Shoulder-high we bring you home,
And set you at your threshold down,
Townsman of a stiller town.

Smart lad, to slip betimes° away
From fields where glory does not stay
And early though the laurel° grows
It withers quicker than the rose.

Eyes the shady night has shut
Cannot see the record cut,
And silence sounds no worse than cheers
After earth has stopped the ears:

Now you will not swell the rout
Of lads that wore their honors out,
Runners whom renown outran
And the name died before the man.

So set, before its echoes fade,
The fleet foot on the sill of shade,
And hold to the low lintel° up
The still-defended challenge cup.

And round that early-laureled head
Will flock to gaze the strengthless dead,
And find unwithered on its curls
The garland briefer than a girl's.

The Scottish athlete Eric Liddell (known as the Flying Scotsman) (1902–1945) winning the 440-yard race at the Amateur Athletics Association championships in 1924.

---

9. betimes *adv.:* archaic for "early."

11. laurel *n.:* classical symbol of victory. Victorious Greek and Roman athletes were crowned with laurel wreaths.

23. lintel *n.:* top of a door frame.

Housman's poems somberly explore death. In the following excerpt, Daniel Pool explains the rituals the Victorians developed to respond to death.

Death and Other Grave Matters

INFORMATIONAL TEXT

Daniel Pool

Death—early death—was no stranger to the nineteenth-century English family, and perhaps that is why they loved to weep over the lingering demises of Dickens's small heroes and heroines. Certainly, they made a big production out of it in every other respect.

In some rural communities the ritual began even before one died, with the ringing of a "passing bell" in the parish church to signal that a member of the community lay on his or her deathbed. Characteristically, the bell tolled six times to indicate the passing of a woman, nine (the famous "nine tailors") to indicate the passing of a man, followed by a peal for each year of the dying person's life.

When a person died, a large funeral was held with everyone dressed in black (unless the deceased were a child or a young, unmarried girl, when the costume was white); mourners received black gloves and black scarfs. . . .

In most communities, funerals were an important social event, and propriety and due regard for the family's social standing necessitated that they be done right. . . . Characteristically, the undertaker would provide professional mourners, or "mutes," dressed in black to stand about and lend dignity to the affair. "There's an expression of melancholy in his face, my dear," says Mr. Sowerberry, the undertaker, to his wife when he takes on Oliver Twist as an apprentice, "which is very interesting. He would make a delightful mute, my love . . . I don't mean a regular mute to attend grown-up people, my dear, but only for children's practice. It would be very new to have a mute in proportion." When the body was actually brought to the gravesite for burial, there was often an additional tolling of the bells—the death knell—to let the parish know of the final laying to rest of the deceased. . . .

The departed were always to be mourned for specifically prescribed periods of time, which, in practice, affected mostly the clothes the survivors were permitted to wear and whether they could have fun or not. Men had it easy; they needed only to wear black armbands, a custom adopted from the military in the early years of the century. Women, however, were supposed to dress all in black. "My dear Celia," says Lady Catherine Chettam of Dorothea Casaubon [in George Eliot's novel *Middlemarch*] after her husband's death, "a widow must wear mourning at least a year." This meant an all-black wardrobe (the so-called widow's weeds), frequently of bombazine, a material especially favored because it did not gleam in light, and no jewelry or ornaments except for beads made of jet, a kind of coal. . . . A widow was expected to mourn her husband for two years, but she could moderate her funereal clothing a bit after a while to "half mourning," which consisted of pinstripe black. Parents and children were to be mourned for a year, a brother, sister, or grandparent for six months, an uncle or aunt for three months, and a first cousin got six weeks. (In-laws were mourned too, but for lesser periods of time.) Some women remained in their mourning garb for the rest of their lives. . . .

Of course, the lead in this fashionable mourning was set in part by the queen. After the death of her beloved Albert in 1861 until her own death in 1901, portraits generally show Victoria in the somber black and white attire suitable for honoring the memory of a late departed.

—from *What Jane Austen Ate and Charles Dickens Knew*

Response and Analysis

Thinking Critically

1. What parallel events are described in the first and second stanzas? What is the significance of repeating "shoulder-high"?
2. In line 9, why does the speaker call the athlete "smart"?
3. According to details in lines 13–20, what failures will the athlete miss, having died young? Do you think the speaker means what he says in lines 9–20? Explain.
4. What scene do you visualize in the last two stanzas of the poem? (Where is the athlete now?)
5. Think about the rituals described in the ***Connection*** on page 928. What emotions are the death rituals intended to express? Does "To an Athlete Dying Young" express similar sentiments or drastically different ones? Explain.
6. Poets can use **exact rhyme** (*June/moon*) or **half rhyme,** also called approximate rhyme (*moon/man*). Look at the end rhymes in Housman's poem. What pattern of rhyming sounds do you hear? Where do you hear half rhymes?
7. Housman also creates verbal music by using **alliteration,** the repetition of the same consonant sounds in words that are close together. Where do you hear alliteration in this poem?
8. The speaker suggests that it's best to die at one's peak, before glory begins to fade. Think about your Quickwrite notes, and then explain your response to this idea.

WRITING

Shakespeare's Influence

Renaissance poetry (see Collection 3) often dealt with the three timeless themes of love, death, and the ravages of time. Housman claimed that he was particularly influenced by Shakespeare's "Fear No More the Heat o' the Sun" (see page 324). In a short **essay, compare and contrast** the tone and message of Housman's poem with those of Shakespeare's song. Use details from the texts to support your comparisons.

▶ **Use "Comparing and Contrasting Literature," pages 1002–1009, for help with this assignment.**

LISTENING AND SPEAKING

Hearing Housman

Prepare this poem for a group reading. Before you read, decide how many readers you want to use. Also scan the poem before your reading to see what meter Housman uses. Where will you pause? Where will you make complete stops? How will you vary your reading so that the poem doesn't sound singsong?

Florence Griffith-Joyner (1959–1998) in action (1988).

Literary Skills
Analyze couplets.

Writing Skills
Write an essay comparing and contrasting a poem with a song.

Listening and Speaking Skills
Read a poem aloud.

INTERNET

Projects and Activities

Keyword: LE7 12-6

Rudyard Kipling

(1865–1936)

Rudyard Kipling (1899) by Philip Burne-Jones. Oil on canvas (29½" x 24½").

By courtesy of the National Portrait Gallery, London.

Rudyard Kipling was born in Bombay, India, where his father was a professor at the University of Bombay. Since it was customary for English citizens living in India (Anglo-Indians) to send their children home for their education, the six-year-old Kipling and his sister were returned to England and left in the care of foster parents in a sort of boarding house. Throughout his life, Kipling was to recall this place as "the house of desolation." Kipling recalled some of the unhappiness and rebelliousness of his school years in his novel called *Stalky & Co.* (1899).

At seventeen, Kipling returned to India to work as a journalist on a newspaper in Lahore. He quickly became popular for his stories, sketches, and poems that were published in newspapers and then collected in cheap editions sold at Indian railroad stations. His books were distributed in England as well, preparing the way for his return to England as a writer in 1889. *Barrack-Room Ballads* (1892), his first collection of poems published in England, went into three editions in its first year, and fifty more editions over the next thirty years. By the end of Queen Victoria's reign, Kipling had become the most popular British poet since Tennyson, and the most popular prose writer since Dickens. Kipling's popularity and public influence can be attributed in part to his strong endorsement of the British Empire.

Kipling's ideas about "empire" were not simple, however. He was fascinated by the ways European civilization conflicted with the ancient cultures of the places into which it intruded. This conflict is the theme of many of his Indian stories, beginning with *Plain Tales from the Hills* (1888) and continuing in *Kim* (1901), his novel about an Irish orphan submerged in the mystery of India. Kipling did not always see European culture as superior (though he nearly always presented it as such), and he knew that empires do fall. He urged readers not to trust in guns to justify their dominion over large parts of the earth. The purpose of the British Empire, he argued, was not to make the imperial nation rich, but rather to extend British efficiency, decency, and comfort throughout the world. Today, however, many readers—even as they admire Kipling's craft—view his argument as a rationalization of the often brutal practices of British imperialism.

In 1907, Kipling became the first British writer to win the Nobel Prize in literature.

For Independent Reading

You may enjoy these works by Kipling:

- *Kim* (novel)
- *Captains Courageous* (novel)
- "The Man Who Would Be King" (short story)
- "Mandalay" (poem)

Before You Read

The Mark of the Beast

Make the Connection

Many horror stories combine everyday reality with elements of the supernatural. "The Mark of the Beast" starts normally enough, with three British civil servants drinking too much at a New Year's Eve party. Then something happens on their way home, and events gradually escalate to a horrible climax. Why do we love to be scared by such stories?

Literary Focus

Conflict

Conflict is a struggle or clash between opposing characters, forces, or emotions. A conflict may be **external**—a character or group struggling against an outside character, group, or force. Or a conflict may be **internal**—a struggle between opposing needs, responsibilities, desires, or emotions within a character. As you read, be sure to note the conflict suggested by the proverb that begins the story.

> **Conflict** is a struggle or clash between opposing characters, forces, or emotions.
>
> *For more on Conflict, see the Handbook of Literary and Historical Terms.*

Reading Skills

Identifying Conflicts and Resolutions

As you read, fill in the first column of a chart like the one that follows. Write down the names of individuals, groups, and ideas that come into conflict in the story. After you have completed the story, review the conflicts and decide if there is a clear-cut victor. If you think there is, write that name in the second column. If not, write *unclear.*

Conflict	Victor?

Background

This story is set in colonial India during the late nineteenth century. As a member of the British ruling class, Kipling witnessed the conflicts that inevitably occur when two cultures are brought into contact by force. Although the battle lines between imperial Britain and colonial India seem clearly drawn in this story, the identity of the victor (if there is one) is less obvious.

The title of the story is an **allusion,** or reference, to the final book of the New Testament, Revelation. According to chapter 13 of this symbolic book, great evil will take over the world at some unknown point in the future. A beast somewhat like a leopard will rule, and the beast's followers will be branded with its mark.

Vocabulary Development

genial (jēn′yəl) *adj.:* mild-mannered; friendly.

divinity (də • vin′ə • tē) *n.:* god; sacred being.

distraught (di • strôt′) *adj.:* extremely agitated.

delusion (di • lo͞o′zhən) *n.:* false belief.

dispassionately (dis • pash′ə • nət • lē) *adv.:* without emotion; impartially.

Literary Skills
Understand internal conflict and external conflict.

Reading Skills
Identify conflicts and resolutions.

INTERNET

Vocabulary Practice

Keyword: LE7 12-6

Shrine to the monkey-god in Chamundi Hill Temple, Mysore, India.

THE MARK OF THE BEAST

Rudyard Kipling

Your Gods and my Gods—do you or I know which are the stronger?
—*Indian Proverb*

East of Suez, some hold, the direct control of Providence ceases; Man being there handed over to the power of the Gods and Devils of Asia, and the Church of England Providence only exercising an occasional and modified supervision in the case of Englishmen.

This theory accounts for some of the more unnecessary horrors of life in India; it may be stretched to explain my story.

My friend Strickland of the Police, who knows as much of natives of India as is good for any man, can bear witness to the facts of the case. Dumoise, our doctor, also saw what Strickland and I saw. The inference which he drew from the evidence was entirely incorrect. He is dead now; he died in a rather curious manner, which has been elsewhere described.

When Fleete came to India he owned a little money and some land in the Himalayas, near a place called Dharmsala. Both properties had been left him by an uncle, and he came out to finance them. He was a big, heavy, genial, and inoffensive man. His knowledge of natives was, of course, limited, and he complained of the difficulties of the language.

He rode in from his place in the hills to spend New Year in the station, and he stayed with Strickland. On New Year's Eve there was a big dinner at the club, and the night was excusably wet.[1] When men foregather from the uttermost ends of the Empire they have a right to be riotous. The Frontier had sent down a contingent o' Catch-'em-Alive-O's[2] who had not seen twenty white faces for a year, and were used to ride fifteen miles to dinner at the next Fort at the risk of a Khyberee[3] bullet where their drinks

1. **the night was excusably wet:** In other words, they drank a lot.
2. **Catch-'em-Alive-O's:** men who were forced into service as soldiers.
3. **Khyberee:** reference to the people of Khyber (kī'bər), a region now part of Pakistan and Afghanistan.

Vocabulary

genial (jēn'yəl) *adj.:* mild-mannered; friendly.

should lie. They profited by their new security, for they tried to play pool with a curled-up hedgehog found in the garden, and one of them carried the marker round the room in his teeth. Half a dozen planters had come in from the south and were talking "horse" to the Biggest Liar in Asia, who was trying to cap all their stories at once. Everybody was there, and there was a general closing up of ranks and taking stock of our losses in dead or disabled that had fallen during the past year. It was a very wet night, and I remember that we sang "Auld Lang Syne" with our feet in the Polo Championship Cup, and our heads among the stars, and swore that we were all dear friends. Then some of us went away and annexed Burma, and some tried to open up the Sudan and were opened up by Fuzzies[4] in that cruel scrub outside Suakim,[5] and some found stars and medals, and some were married, which was bad, and some did other things which were worse, and the others of us stayed in our chains and strove to make money on insufficient experiences.

Fleete began the night with sherry and bitters, drank champagne steadily up to dessert, then raw, rasping Capri with all the strength of whiskey, took benedictine with his coffee, four or five whiskeys and sodas to improve his pool strokes, beer and bones[6] at half-past two, winding up with old brandy. Consequently, when he came out, at half-past three in the morning, into fourteen degrees of frost, he was very angry with his horse for coughing, and tried to leapfrog into the saddle. The horse broke away and went to his stables; so Strickland and I formed a Guard of Dishonor to take Fleete home.

Our road lay through the bazaar, close to a little temple of Hanuman, the Monkey-god, who is a leading divinity worthy of respect. All gods have good points, just as have all priests. Personally, I attach much importance to Hanuman, and am kind to his people—the great gray apes of the hills. One never knows when one may want a friend.

There was a light in the temple, and as we passed we could hear voices of men chanting hymns. In a native temple the priests rise at all hours of the night to do honor to their god. Before we would stop him, Fleete dashed up the steps, patted two priests on the back, and was gravely grinding the ashes of his cigar butt in to the forehead of the red stone image of Hanuman. Strickland tried to drag him out, but he sat down and said solemnly:

"Shee that? Mark of the B—beasht! *I* made it. Ishn't it fine?"

In half a minute the temple was alive and noisy, and Strickland, who knew what came of polluting gods, said that things might occur. He, by virtue of his official position, long residence in the country, and weakness for going among the natives, was known to the priests and he felt unhappy. Fleete sat on the ground and refused to move. He said that "good old Hanuman" made a very soft pillow.

Then, without any warning, a Silver Man came out of a recess behind the image of the god. He was perfectly naked in that bitter, bitter cold, and his body shone like frosted silver, for he was what the Bible calls "a leper as white as snow." Also he had no face, because he was a leper of some years' standing, and his disease was heavy upon him. We two stooped to haul Fleete up, and the temple was filling and filling with folk who seemed to spring from the earth, when the Silver Man ran in under our arms,

4. **Fuzzies:** Sudanese natives. British soldiers gave them this name because of their long, frizzy hair. In the poem "Fuzzy-Wuzzy" (1890), Kipling calls the Sudanese soldier "a first-class fightin' man."
5. **Suakim:** Suakin (swä′kən), Sudan; city on the Red Sea.
6. **bones:** *n. pl.:* dice.

Vocabulary

divinity (də·vin′ə·tē) *n.:* god; sacred being.

making a noise exactly like the mewing of an otter, caught Fleete round the body and dropped his head on Fleete's breast before we could wrench him away. Then he retired to a corner and sat mewing while the crowd blocked all the doors.

The priests were very angry until the Silver Man touched Fleete. That nuzzling seemed to sober them.

At the end of a few minutes' silence one of the priests came to Strickland and said, in perfect English, "Take your friend away. He has done with Hanuman but Hanuman has not done with him." The crowd gave room and we carried Fleete into the road.

Strickland was very angry. He said that we might all three have been knifed, and that Fleete should thank his stars that he had escaped without injury.

Fleete thanked no one. He said that he wanted to go to bed. He was gorgeously drunk.

We moved on, Strickland silent and wrathful, until Fleete was taken with violent shivering fits and sweating. He said that the smells of the bazaar were overpowering, and he wondered why slaughterhouses were permitted so near English residences. "Can't you smell the blood?" said Fleete.

We put him to bed at last, just as the dawn was breaking, and Strickland invited me to have another whiskey and soda. While we were drinking he talked of the trouble in the temple, and admitted that it baffled him completely. Strickland hates being mystified by natives, because his business in life is to overmatch them with their own weapons. He has not yet succeeded in doing this, but in fifteen or twenty years he will have made some small progress.

"They should have mauled us," he said, "instead of mewing at us. I wonder what they meant. I don't like it one little bit."

I said that the Managing Committee of the temple would in all probability bring a criminal action against us for insulting their religion. There was a section of the Indian Penal Code which exactly met Fleete's offense. Strickland said he only hoped and prayed that they would do this. Before I left I looked into Fleete's room, and saw him lying on his right side, scratching his left breast. Then I went to bed cold, depressed, and unhappy, at seven o'clock in the morning.

Indian fakir with green face. A fakir is a wandering beggar who is said to perform wonders.

At one o'clock I rode over to Strickland's house to inquire after Fleete's head. I imagined that it would be a sore one. Fleete was breakfasting and seemed unwell. His temper was gone, for he was abusing the cook for not supplying him with an underdone chop. A man who can eat raw meat after a wet night is a curiosity. I told Fleete this and he laughed.

"You breed queer mosquitoes in these parts," he said. "I've been bitten to pieces, but only in one place."

"Let's have a look at the bite," said Strickland. "It may have gone down since this morning."

While the chops were being cooked, Fleete

opened his shirt and showed us, just over his left breast, a mark, the perfect double of the black rosettes—the five or six irregular blotches arranged in a circle—on a leopard's hide. Strickland looked and said, "It was only pink this morning. It's grown black now."

Fleete ran to a glass.

"By Jove!" he said, "this is nasty. What is it?"

We could not answer. Here the chops came in, all red and juicy, and Fleete bolted three in a most offensive manner. He ate on his right grinders only, and threw his head over his right shoulder as he snapped the meat. When he had finished, it struck him that he had been behaving strangely, for he said apologetically, "I don't think I ever felt so hungry in my life. I've bolted like an ostrich."

After breakfast Strickland said to me, "Don't go. Stay here, and stay for the night."

Seeing that my house was not three miles from Strickland's, this request was absurd. But Strickland insisted, and was going to say something, when Fleete interrupted him by declaring in a shamefaced way that he felt hungry again. Strickland sent a man to my house to fetch over my bedding and a horse, and we three went down to Strickland's stables to pass the hours until it was time to go out for a ride. The man who has a weakness for horses never wearies of inspecting them; and when two men are killing time in this way they gather knowledge and lies the one from the other.

A CLOSER LOOK: POLITICAL INFLUENCES

The Age of Empire

INFORMATIONAL TEXT

A breakfast table during the time of Queen Victoria's reign held many of the same items that we expect to find today: Indian tea, Kenyan coffee (more popular in the United States and Germany), perhaps Brazilian cocoa—all sweetened with Caribbean sugar.

Victorians were keenly aware that traders circled the globe to provide their morning beverages. Their knowledge came in part from writers such as Rudyard Kipling and Olive Schreiner (1855–1920), who so carefully documented the experience of Europeans abroad. (Schreiner wrote of South Africa.) Kipling's descriptions of the British presence in India capture the controversies of a period known as the Age of Empire. The nineteenth century provided European scholars with opportunities to study ancient civilizations, but the emphasis on indigenous peoples was eclipsed by the lucrative market for raw tropical materials: rubber, oil, cotton. The relationship between Europe and its colonies is summarized by the remark of an administrator, who crudely observed in 1862 that "the traffic with half-civilized peoples has risks of its own, which are generally compensated by more than ordinary profits."

European powers were in such keen competition for colonies that, between 1876 and 1914, more than a quarter of the globe's land surface was distributed as colonies among a half-dozen countries. In Victoria's reign, the British prided themselves on the fact that the sun never set on their far-flung empire.

The postcolonial legacy. As trading spread, it changed irrevocably the cultures of the colonial peoples. Ancient customs were seen as primitive, and Western models became the standards for language, education, and religion. Europeans were confident in their technological and cultural superiority; indeed, a governor of Africa's Cape Colony could tell a group of native chiefs in 1836 that British "customs and institutions are the wonder of the world." To achieve the rewards of "civilization," inhabitants of tropical climates

There were five horses in the stables, and I shall never forget the scene as we tried to look them over. They seemed to have gone mad. They reared and screamed and nearly tore up their pickets;[7] they sweated and shivered and lathered and were distraught with fear. Strickland's horses used to know him as well as his dogs; which made the matter more curious. We left the stable for fear of the brutes throwing themselves in their panic. Then Strickland turned back and called me. The horses were still frightened, but they let us "gentle" and make much of them, and put their heads in our bosoms.

"They aren't afraid of *us*," said Strickland. "D'you know, I'd give three months' pay if *Outrage* here could talk."

But *Outrage* was dumb, and could only cuddle up to his master and blow out his nostrils, as is the custom of horses when they wish to explain things but can't. Fleete came up when we were in the stalls, and as soon as the horses saw him, their fright broke out afresh. It was all that we could do to escape from the place unkicked. Strickland said, "They don't seem to love you, Fleete."

7. **pickets** *n. pl.:* hitching posts.

Vocabulary

distraught (di·strôt′) *adj.:* extremely agitated.

were fitted with heavy wool clothing, taught to prepare hearty English mutton dishes, and encouraged to enjoy the game of cricket.

Hindu servant serving tea to a European colonial woman.

Colonial empires and their international markets reaped profits for industrialized nations until the start of World War I. Most former colonies now have won independence, but these independent countries are still struggling with a past that encouraged them to abandon or to diminish their native heritage. The novelist Chinua Achebe (1930–   ) describes a clash of cultures in his novel *Things Fall Apart* (1959), when a district commissioner imposes British law on a group of Nigerian people. When the commissioner asks to settle a dispute, a tribesman says, "We cannot leave the matter in his hands because he does not understand our customs, just as we do not understand his. We say he is foolish because he does not know our ways, and perhaps he says we are foolish because we do not know his." The unexpected legacy of empire has been a redefinition of "civilized" behavior, a renewed appreciation of native customs, and an ongoing dialogue about the foolishness and arrogance of judging cultures too quickly.

The First Investiture of the Star of India (detail) (1863), after William Simpson. The star of India was a merit award given to an order of knights.

The Bridgeman Art Library.

"Nonsense," said Fleete; "my mare will follow me like a dog." He went to her; she was in a loose box;[8] but as he slipped the bars she plunged, knocked him down, and broke away into the garden. I laughed, but Strickland was not amused. He took his moustache in both fists and pulled at it till it nearly came out. Fleete, instead of going off to chase his property, yawned, saying that he felt sleepy. He went to the house to lie down, which was a foolish way of spending New Year's Day.

Strickland sat with me in the stables and asked if I had noticed anything peculiar in Fleete's manner. I said that he ate his food like a beast; but that this might have been the result of living alone in the hills out of the reach of society as refined and elevating as ours for instance. Strickland was not amused. I do not think that he listened to me, for his next sentence referred to the mark on Fleete's breast, and I said that it might have been caused by blister flies, or that it was possibly a birthmark newly born and now visible for the first time. We both agreed that it was unpleasant to look at, and Strickland found occasion to say that I was a fool.

"I can't tell you what I think now," said he, "because you would call me a madman; but you must stay with me for the next few days, if you can. I want you to watch Fleete, but don't tell me what you think till I have made up my mind."

"But I am dining out tonight," I said.

8. **loose box:** stall in which the horse is free to move about.

"So am I," said Strickland, "and so is Fleete. At least if he doesn't change his mind."

We walked about the garden smoking, but saying nothing—because we were friends, and talking spoils good tobacco—till our pipes were out. Then we went to wake up Fleete. He was wide awake and fidgeting about his room.

"I say, I want some more chops," he said. "Can I get them?"

We laughed and said, "Go and change. The ponies will be round in a minute."

"All right," said Fleete. "I'll go when I get the chops—underdone ones, mind."

He seemed to be quite in earnest. It was four o'clock, and we had had breakfast at one; still, for a long time, he demanded those underdone chops. Then he changed into riding clothes and went out into the veranda. His pony—the mare had not been caught—would not let him come near. All three horses were unmanageable—mad with fear—and finally Fleete said that he would stay at home and get something to eat. Strickland and I rode out wondering. As we passed the Temple of Hanuman the Silver Man came out and mewed at us.

"He is not one of the regular priests of the temple," said Strickland. "I think I should peculiarly like to lay my hands on him."

There was no spring in our gallop on the racecourse that evening. The horses were stale, and moved as though they had been ridden out.

"The fright after breakfast has been too much for them," said Strickland.

That was the only remark he made through the remainder of the ride. Once or twice, I think, he swore to himself; but that did not count.

We came back in the dark at seven o'clock, and saw that there was no lights in the bungalow. "Careless ruffians my servants are!" said Strickland.

My horse reared at something on the carriage drive, and Fleete stood up under its nose.

"What are you doing, groveling about the garden?" said Strickland.

But both horses bolted and nearly threw us. We dismounted by the stables and returned to Fleete, who was on his hands and knees under the orange bushes.

"What the devil's wrong with you?" said Strickland.

"Nothing, nothing in the world," said Fleete, speaking very quickly and thickly. "I've been gardening—botanizing, you know. The smell of the earth is delightful. I think I'm going for a walk—a long walk—all night."

Then I saw that there was something excessively out of order somewhere, and I said to Strickland, "I am not dining out."

"Bless you!" said Strickland. "Here, Fleete, get up. You'll catch fever there. Come in to dinner and let's have the lamps lit. We'll dine at home."

Fleete stood up unwillingly, and said, "No lamps—no lamps. It's much nicer here. Let's dine outside and have some more chops—lots of 'em and underdone—bloody ones with gristle."

Now a December evening in Northern India is bitterly cold, and Fleete's suggestion was that of a maniac.

"Come in," said Strickland sternly. "Come in at once."

Fleete came, and when the lamps were brought, we saw that he was literally plastered with dirt from head to foot. He must have been rolling in the garden. He shrank from the light and went to his room. His eyes were horrible to look at. There was a green light behind them, not in them, if you understand, and the man's lower lip hung down.

Strickland said, "There is going to be trouble—big trouble—tonight. Don't you change your riding things."

We waited and waited for Fleete's reappearance, and ordered dinner in the meantime. We could hear him moving about his own room, but there was no light there. Presently from the room came the long-drawn howl of a wolf.

People write and talk lightly of blood running

cold and hair standing up, and things of that kind. Both sensations are too horrible to be trifled with. My heart stopped as though a knife had been driven through it, and Strickland turned as white as the tablecloth.

The howl was repeated, and was answered by another howl far across the fields.

That set the gilded roof on the horror. Strickland dashed into Fleete's room. I followed, and we saw Fleete getting out of the window. He made beast noises in the back of his throat. He could not answer us when we shouted at him. He spat.

I don't quite remember what followed, but I think that Strickland must have stunned him with the long bootjack,[9] or else I should never have been able to sit on his chest. Fleete could not speak, he could only snarl, and his snarls were those of a wolf, not of a man. The human spirit must have been giving way all day and have died out with the twilight. We were dealing with a beast that had once been Fleete.

The affair was beyond any human and rational experience. I tried to say "hydrophobia,"[10] but the word wouldn't come, because I knew that I was lying.

We bound this beast with leather thongs of the punkah[11] rope, and tied its thumbs and big toes together, and gagged it with a shoehorn, which makes a very efficient gag if you know how to arrange it. Then we carried it into the dining room, and sent a man to Dumoise, the doctor, telling him to come over at once. After we had dispatched the messenger and were drawing breath, Strickland said, "It's no good. This isn't any doctor's work." I, also, knew that he spoke the truth.

The beast's head was free, and it threw it about from side to side. Anyone entering the room would have believed that we were curing a wolf's pelt. That was the most loathsome accessory of all.

Strickland sat with his chin in the heel of his fist, watching the beast as it wriggled on the ground, but saying nothing. The shirt had been torn open in the scuffle and showed the black rosette mark on the left breast. It stood out like a blister.

In the silence of the watching we heard something without mewing like a she-otter. We both rose to our feet, and, I answer for myself, not Strickland, felt sick—actually and physically sick. We told each other, as did the men in *Pinafore*,[12] that it was the cat.

Dumoise arrived, and I never saw a little man so unprofessionally shocked. He said that it was a heart-rending case of hydrophobia, and that nothing could be done. At least any palliative measures would only prolong the agony. The beast was foaming at the mouth. Fleete, as we told Dumoise, had been bitten by dogs once or twice. Any man who keeps half a dozen terriers must expect a nip now and again. Dumoise could offer no help. He could only certify that Fleete was dying of hydrophobia. The beast was then howling, for it had managed to spit out the shoehorn. Dumoise said that he would be ready to certify to the cause of death, and that the end was certain. He was a good little man, and he offered to remain with us; but Strickland refused the kindness. He did not wish to poison Dumoise's New Year. He would only ask him not to give the real cause of Fleete's death to the public.

So Dumoise left, deeply agitated; and as soon as the noise of the cart wheels had died away,

9. **bootjack** *n.:* device for pulling off boots, often made of cast iron.

10. **hydrophobia** *n.:* rabies. One of the effects of rabies is an inability to swallow water.

11. **punkah** (puŋ′kə) *n.:* swinging fan suspended from the ceiling. It is operated by pulling an attached cord or rope.

12. **Pinafore:** *H.M.S. Pinafore* (1878), a comic operetta by W. S. Gilbert and Arthur Sullivan. Lovers in the play attempt to elope. When they are discovered, the cast sings, "Why, what was that? . . . It was—it was the cat!"

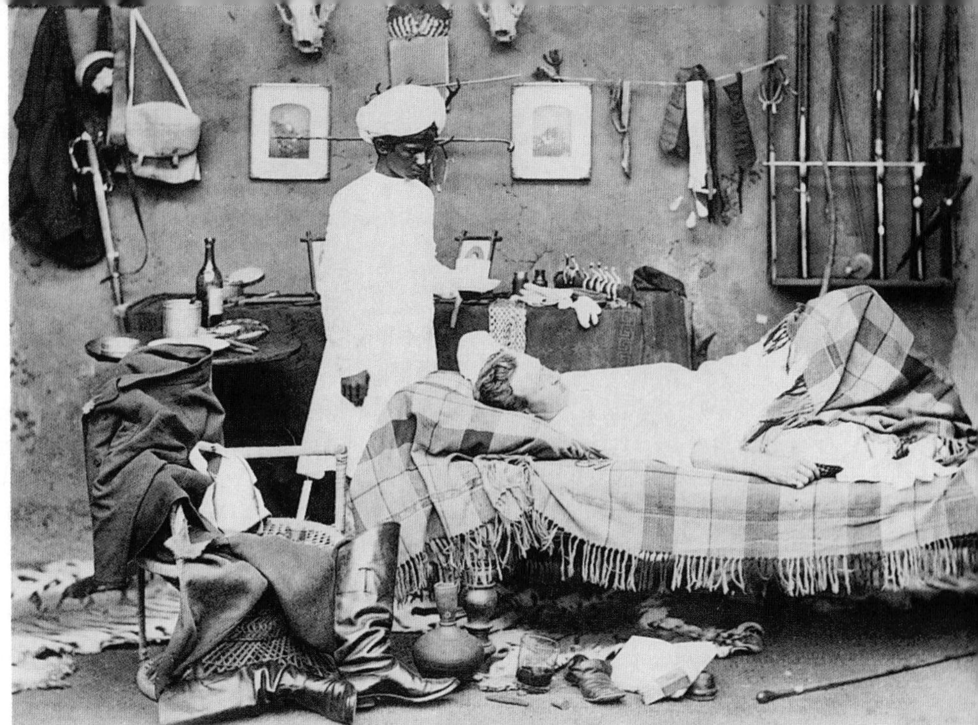

English officer attended by his Indian servant (1870s). Albumen print by Willoughby Wallace Hooper and George Western.

Strickland told me, in a whisper, his suspicions. They were so wildly improbable that he dared not say them out aloud; and I, who entertained all Strickland's beliefs, was so ashamed of owning to them that I pretended to disbelieve.

"Even if the Silver Man had bewitched Fleete for polluting the image of Hanuman, the punishment could not have fallen so quickly."

As I was whispering this the cry outside the house rose again, and the beast fell into a fresh paroxysm of struggling till we were afraid that the thongs that held it would give way.

"Watch!" said Strickland. "If this happens six times I shall take the law into my own hands. I order you to help me."

He went into his room and came out in a few minutes with the barrels of an old shotgun, a piece of fishing line, some thick cord, and his heavy wooden bedstead. I reported that the convulsions had followed the cry by two seconds in each case, and the beast seemed perceptibly weaker.

Strickland muttered, "But he can't take away the life! He can't take away the life!"

I said, though I knew that I was arguing against myself, "It may be a cat. It must be a cat. If the Silver Man is responsible, why does he dare to come here?"

Strickland arranged the wood on the hearth, put the gun barrels into the glow of the fire, spread the twine on the table, and broke a walking stick in two. There was one yard of fishing line, gut lapped with wire, such as is used for *mahseer*[13] fishing, and he tied the two ends together in a loop.

Then he said, "How can we catch him? He must be taken alive and unhurt."

I said that we must trust in Providence, and go out softly with polo sticks into the shrubbery at the front of the house. The man or animal that made the cry was evidently moving round the house as regularly as a night watchman. We could wait in the bushes till he came by and knock him over.

Strickland accepted this suggestion, and we slipped out from a bathroom window into the front veranda and then across the carriage drive into the bushes.

In the moonlight we could see the leper coming round the corner of the house. He was perfectly naked, and from time to time he mewed and stopped to dance with his shadow. It was an unattractive sight, and thinking of poor Fleete,

13. **mahseer** (mä′sir) *n.:* large Indian freshwater fish of the carp family.

Dressing the young civilian, from *Anglo Indians* (1842). Engraving by J. Bouvier after William Tayler.

Stapleton Collection, United Kingdom. The Bridgeman Art Library.

brought to such degradation by so foul a creature, I put away all my doubts and resolved to help Strickland from the heated gun barrels to the loop of twine—from the loins to the head and back again—with all tortures that might be needful.

The leper halted in the front porch for a moment and we jumped out on him with the sticks. He was wonderfully strong, and we were afraid that he might escape or be fatally injured before we caught him. We had an idea that lepers were frail creatures, but this proved to be incorrect. Strickland knocked his legs from under him and I put my foot on his neck. He mewed hideously, and even through my riding boots I could feel that his flesh was not the flesh of a clean man.

He struck at us with his hand- and feet-stumps. We looped the lash of a dog-whip round him under the armpits, and dragged him backward into the hall and so into the dining room where the beast lay. There we tied him with trunk straps. He made no attempt to escape, but mewed.

When we confronted him with the beast the scene was beyond description. The beast doubled backward into a bow as though he had been poisoned with strychnine, and moaned in the most pitiable fashion. Several other things happened also, but they cannot be put down here.

"I think I was right," said Strickland. "Now we will ask him to cure this case."

But the leper only mewed. Strickland wrapped a towel round his hand and took the gun barrels out of the fire. I put the half of the broken walking stick through the loop of fishing line and buckled the leper comfortably to Strickland's bedstead. I understood then how men and women and little children can endure to see a witch burnt alive; for the beast was moaning on the floor, and though the Silver Man had no face, you could see horrible feelings passing through the slab that took its place, exactly as waves of heat play across red-hot iron—gun barrels, for instance.

Strickland shaded his eyes with his hands for a moment and we got to work. This part is not to be printed.

The dawn was beginning to break when the leper spoke. His mewings had not been satisfactory up to that point. The beast had fainted from exhaustion and the house was very still. We unstrapped the leper and told him to take away the evil spirit. He crawled to the beast and laid his hand upon the left breast. That was all. Then he fell face down and whined, drawing in his breath as he did so.

We watched the face of the beast, and saw the soul of Fleete coming back into the eyes. Then a sweat broke out on the forehead and the eyes—they were human eyes—closed. We waited for an hour, but Fleete still slept. We carried him to his room and bade the leper go, giving him the bedstead, and the sheet on the bedstead to cover his nakedness, the gloves and the towels with which we had touched him, and the whip that had been hooked round his body. He put the sheet about him and went out into the early morning without speaking or mewing.

Strickland wiped his face and sat down. A night gong, far away in the city, made seven o'clock.

"Exactly four-and-twenty hours!" said Strickland. "And I've done enough to ensure my dismissal from the service, besides permanent quarters in a lunatic asylum. Do you believe that we are awake?"

The red-hot gun barrel had fallen on the floor and was singeing the carpet. The smell was entirely real.

That morning at eleven we two together went to wake up Fleete. We looked and saw that the black leopard rosette on his chest had disappeared. He was very drowsy and tired, but as soon as he saw us, he said, "Oh! Confound you fellows. Happy New Year to you. Never mix your liquors. I'm nearly dead."

"Thanks for your kindness, but you're over time," said Strickland. "Today is the morning of the second. You've slept the clock round with a vengeance."

The door opened, and little Dumoise put his head in. He had come on foot, and fancied that we were laying out Fleete.

"I've brought a nurse," said Dumoise. "I suppose that she can come in for . . . what is necessary."

"By all means," said Fleete cheerily, sitting up in bed. "Bring on your nurses."

Dumoise was dumb. Strickland led him out and explained that there must have been a mistake in the diagnosis. Dumoise remained dumb and left the house hastily. He considered that his professional reputation had been injured, and was inclined to make a personal matter of the recovery. Strickland went out too. When he came back, he said that he had been to call on the Temple of Hanuman to offer redress for the pollution of the god, and had been solemnly assured that no white man had ever touched the idol, and that he was an incarnation of all the virtues laboring under a delusion. "What do you think?" said Strickland.

I said, "'There are more things . . .'"[14]

But Strickland hates that quotation. He says that I have worn it threadbare.

One other curious thing happened which frightened me as much as anything in all the night's work. When Fleete was dressed he came into the dining room and sniffed. He had a quaint trick of moving his nose when he sniffed. "Horrid doggy smell, here," said he. "You should really keep those terriers of yours in better order. Try sulfur, Strick."

But Strickland did not answer. He caught hold of the back of a chair, and, without warning, went into an amazing fit of hysterics. It is terrible to see a strong man overtaken with hysteria. Then it struck me that we had fought for Fleete's soul with the Silver Man in that room, and had disgraced ourselves as Englishmen forever, and I laughed and gasped and gurgled just as shamefully as Strickland, while Fleete thought that we had both gone mad. We never told him what we had done.

Some years later, when Strickland had married and was a churchgoing member of society for his wife's sake, we reviewed the incident dispassionately, and Strickland suggested that I should put it before the public.

I cannot myself see that this step is likely to clear up the mystery; because, in the first place, no one will believe a rather unpleasant story, and, in the second, it is well known to every right-minded man that the gods of the heathen are stone and brass, and any attempt to deal with them otherwise is justly condemned. ■

14. **"There are more things":** reference to William Shakespeare's *Hamlet*, Act I, Scene 5, lines 166–167: "There are more things in heaven and earth, Horatio, than are dreamt of in your philosophy."

Vocabulary

delusion (di·lo͞o′zhən) *n.:* false belief.

dispassionately (dis·pash′ə·nət·lē) *adv.:* without emotion; impartially.

Response and Analysis

Reading Check

1. Who are the three main characters in the story?
2. On the way home from the New Year's Eve party, how does Fleete insult Hanuman, the Monkey-god? Who does what to Fleete, in response?
3. Over the course of the next day, what clues reveal that Fleete is becoming something nonhuman? What does he become?
4. How do Strickland and the narrator reverse Fleete's condition?

Thinking Critically

5. Who or what is the Silver Man? What details support your interpretation?
6. From what **point of view** is the story told? How does the point of view affect what you know about Fleete, Strickland, and the narrator?
7. Complete the chart that you filled out as you read the story. How many **conflicts**—external and internal—did you find? Which of the conflicts resulted from cultural misunderstandings?
8. What about the victors in these conflicts? Were some conflicts left unresolved?
9. Re-read the Indian proverb at the beginning of the story. How does the proverb relate to the central **conflict** and **theme** of the story?
10. Chapter 13 of the Book of Revelation reads, in part, "And the beast that I saw was like a leopard. . . . [It] seemed to have received a death-blow, . . . and yet lived. . . . Also [a second beast] causes all . . . to be marked . . . [with] the name of the [leopard-like] beast. . . ." Where does Kipling **allude** to these verses? What emotions do these allusions evoke?
11. What does this story reveal about the issues that marked the British presence in India?

Literary Skills Analyze internal conflict and external conflict.

Reading Skills Analyze conflicts and resolutions.

Writing Skills Write a multimedia report.

Vocabulary Skills Understand connotations.

INTERNET

Projects and Activities
•
Media Tutorials
•
Keyword: LE7 12-6

Extending and Evaluating

12. Do you think this story has something important to say to us today despite—or even because of—its racist elements? Cite details from the story to support your answer.

Literary Criticism

13. Critics have called this story "nasty," "poisonous," and even "sadistic." Explain why you agree or disagree with these assessments.

WRITING

The Evolution of a Myth

The werewolves in Kipling's 1890 story are far different from those we encounter in contemporary films and television programs. Prepare a **multimedia report** about werewolf stories from different periods and cultures. Show the universal and specific social concerns reflected in the stories.

Vocabulary Development

Rating Connotations

genial
delusion
divinity
dispassionately
distraught

A word's **denotation** is its dictionary definition. Some words also carry **connotations**—positive or negative emotional associations. For example, *thin* is fairly neutral in meaning, *slender* sounds positive, and *scrawny* sounds negative. List the Vocabulary words above on a separate sheet of paper. Next to each word, write *P* if the word carries a positive connotation, *N* if it is negative, and *O* if it is neutral. Then, explain the reasons for your choices.

Vocabulary Development

Analyzing Word Analogies

Reading Word Analogies. In a word analogy, the relationship between the first pair of words is the same as the relationship between the second pair of words. Three types of relationships frequently expressed in word analogies are classification, cause and effect, and characteristic.

Classification

SPARROW : BIRD :: van : automobile

[A sparrow may be classified as a bird, just as a van may be classified as an automobile.]

Cause and Effect

POLLEN : SNEEZING :: overexertion : fatigue

[Pollen can cause sneezing, just as overexertion can cause fatigue.]

Characteristic

MISER : STINGY :: comedian : funny

[Misers are characteristically stingy, just as comedians are characteristically funny.]

Solving word analogies. Use the following steps to answer an analogy question:

1. Identify the relationship between the capitalized pair of words. It is also helpful to note the part of speech of each word.
2. Look for the same relationship and the same parts of speech in the pairs of words in the answer choices. Eliminate those answers that do not have the same relationship and parts of speech.
3. Choose the pair of words whose relationship and word order match those of the capitalized pair.

PRACTICE

The following capitalized pairs include words from "The Mark of the Beast." For each numbered item, choose the pair of words that expresses a relationship that is most similar to the relationship between the pair of capitalized words. On your own paper, write the letter of your answer to each analogy and the type of relationship expressed in each analogy.

1. SWEAT : FEVER ::
   - **a.** sorrow : tragedy
   - **b.** comedy : laughing
   - **c.** illness : remedy
   - **d.** depression : elation
2. HORSE : MAMMAL ::
   - **a.** kitten : puppy
   - **b.** father : son
   - **c.** jazz : music
   - **d.** condiment : ketchup
3. CURIOUS : TODDLERS ::
   - **a.** grateful : appreciative
   - **b.** prickly : cacti
   - **c.** journalists : reporters
   - **d.** afraid : strangers
4. DROUGHT : FAMINE ::
   - **a.** fire : burn
   - **b.** calm : agitated
   - **c.** plumber : pipes
   - **d.** lawyer : courtroom
5. GLOVE : CLOTHING ::
   - **a.** ring : finger
   - **b.** teacher : student
   - **c.** sonnet : poem
   - **d.** keyboard : mouse

Vocabulary Skills
Analyze word analogies.

Connecting to World Literature

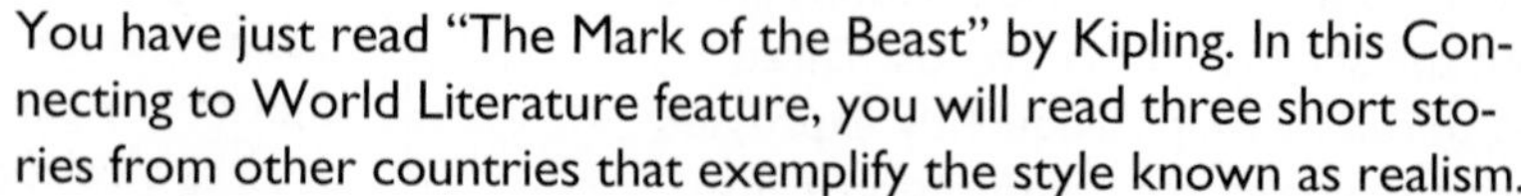

The Rise of Realism

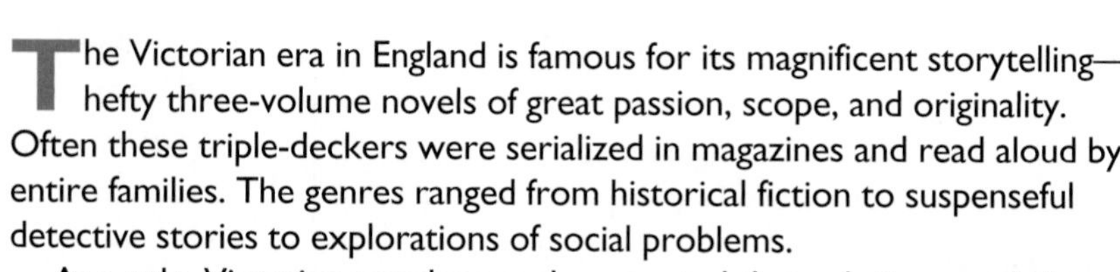

You have just read "The Mark of the Beast" by Kipling. In this Connecting to World Literature feature, you will read three short stories from other countries that exemplify the style known as realism.

The Tavern (detail) (19th century) by Édouard Manet.

Pushkin Museum of Fine Arts, Moscow. © Scala/Art Resource, New York.

SKILLS FOCUS

Pages 946–948 cover **Literary Skills** Evaluate the philosophical, political, religious, ethical, and social influences of a historical period. Compare realist works.

The Victorian era in England is famous for its magnificent storytelling—hefty three-volume novels of great passion, scope, and originality. Often these triple-deckers were serialized in magazines and read aloud by entire families. The genres ranged from historical fiction to suspenseful detective stories to explorations of social problems.

As a rule, Victorian popular novels suggested that solutions could be found to the complex social problems of the era. The novels also conveyed lessons in morality. By the latter half of the nineteenth century, however, serious writers were turning their hands to a less optimistic type of novel that expressed a literary philosophy called realism.

Realism: A Reaction to Romanticism

Realism was an attempt to produce an accurate portrayal of real life without filtering it through personal feelings or Romantic idealism. Noting that liberal reforms and the revolutions of the nineteenth century had failed to bring about an era of justice, realist writers rejected the century's earlier Romantic emotionalism, seeing it as an ineffective tool for reforming—or even describing—industrial society.

Realism concerned itself with more than just the details of daily life, however. It also sought to explain *why* ordinary people behave the way they do. Realist novelists often relied on the emerging sciences of human and animal behavior—biology, psychology, and sociology—as well as on their own insights and observations. Realists could be divided into several different camps: Some emphasized social reform, others stressed scientific objectivity, and still others leaned toward social satire.

France: Scientific Objectivity

French realists, under the leadership of the novelist Gustave Flaubert, tried to make a science of their art by eliminating all sentimentality. They aimed simply to mirror life, without judgment or distortion. Yet a novel

The Potato Eaters (1885) by Vincent van Gogh.

like Flaubert's *Madame Bovary* is admired today not so much for its objectivity as for its perfect prose and its satire of the middle class.

Naturalism, a radical offshoot of realism, arose in the 1870s. Led by Émile Zola, naturalist writers considered free will an illusion and often showed their characters as helpless victims of heredity, fate, and environment. These writers tried to abolish the boundary between scientist and artist. Relying heavily on the growing scientific disciplines of psychology and sociology, they tried to dissect human behavior with as much objectivity as a scientist would dissect a frog or a cadaver. For naturalists, human life seemed a grim, losing battle against forces beyond the individual's control. The most talented naturalists, however, could not stay within the narrow ideology of their school. Guy de Maupassant (see page 974), for example, is sometimes called a naturalist, but his work is sharpened by irony and by a gift for choosing the right details.

Russia: Ultimate Questions

Realistic Russian novels began with those of Ivan Turgenev, whose ornate, lyrical prose brimmed with sympathy and warmth. Later Russian novelists, including Leo Tolstoy (see page 949) and Fyodor Dostoevsky, wrote gigantic, sprawling novels filled with violence, love, and family crises, and

The Gross Clinic (1875) by Thomas Eakins. Oil on canvas.

Jefferson College, Philadelphia. The Bridgeman Art Library.

peopled with characters from a wide cross section of society. The novels of these writers helped foster a powerful movement that called for the liberation of the serfs (peasants) and, later, the entire society. Yet the primary aim of Russian realists was not social reform, but a desire to answer the ultimate questions of human life. In different ways, Tolstoy and Dostoevsky repeatedly asked, "How should people live?" and "What are good and evil?"

Unlike these two giants, the playwright and short-story writer Anton Chekhov (see page 965) worked on a much smaller scale. Chekhov found his subjects and themes in the common illusions and daily sufferings of unremarkable people. Like Tolstoy and Dostoevsky, however, Chekhov dealt with the meanings of life and death. His stories and plays are about people's attempts—usually frustrated—to find meaning and purpose in their lives.

The Legacy of the Nineteenth Century

The literary styles of the nineteenth century—from the effusive poetry of the Romantics to the terse prose of the realists—still influence modern writing. Powerful expressions of feeling and realistic depictions of life are both now hallmarks of literary excellence. Realistic values, such as an emphasis on unflinching factual observation of ordinary people's lives, still exert a powerful influence on literature and thought.

Leo Tolstoy

(1828–1910)

Barents Sea
FINLAND
St. Petersburg
URAL MOUNTAINS
RUSSIA
Baltic Sea
Moscow
Tula
PRUSSIA
AUSTRO-HUNGARIAN EMPIRE
Dnieper
Don
Volga
Ural
Aral Sea
Black Sea
Caspian Sea
NINETEENTH-CENTURY RUSSIA

When Count Leo Nikolayevich Tolstoy (lē′ō nē′kô·lä′ye·vich tôl′stoi′) died of pneumonia at the age of eighty-two, he may have been the most famous man in the world. His death was front-page news in England and America. In addition to being the greatest living Russian novelist, Tolstoy was also a social and religious reformer.

Tolstoy was born to wealthy aristocratic parents, both of whom had died by the time he was nine. He, his three older brothers, and his younger sister were raised by aunts on the family estate. As Tolstoy grew older, he led an aimless life—as did many young men of the Russian aristocracy.

At nineteen, Tolstoy split his inheritance with his brothers and became the master of his family's estate and its three hundred serfs. Within three years, he managed to gamble away about one fourth of his inheritance. Looking for adventure, he joined the Russian army and fought bravely during the Crimean War. The suffering that he witnessed during the war helped bring out his serious, morally questioning nature.

In 1859, Tolstoy opened a school on his estate for his serfs' children. Soon after, he married Sonya Andreyevna Bers. In addition to bearing him thirteen children, Sonya recopied her husband's illegible manuscripts and took over the management of his estate. Tolstoy was thus free to write his greatest works, *War and Peace* (1869) and *Anna Karenina* (1877)—masterpieces of realistic fiction that capped his already immense reputation.

After years of moral questioning, Tolstoy underwent a spiritual conversion. Aspiring to be holy and to do good, he found his best models in Russia's self-sufficient Christian peasants. During the last thirty years of his life, his writings became fervent attacks on private ownership, capitalism, the Orthodox Church, and Russia's czarist government.

Though Tolstoy repudiated his early works for their bourgeois focus on the aristocracy, his reputation today rests on those early novels: *War and Peace,* a monumental telling of the lives of five aristocratic families during the Napoleonic Wars, and *Anna Karenina,* the tragic story of a woman who gives up her husband and child for what she thinks is true love.

Portrait of Leo Tolstoy (1873) by Ivan Nikolayevich Kramskoy.

Before You Read

How Much Land Does a Man Need?

Make the Connection

Have you ever wanted something desperately and then gotten it? If so, perhaps you felt briefly satisfied. But how long did the satisfaction last? What feelings came afterward? In the following short story, Leo Tolstoy examines the vast difference between human wants and human needs. Getting what we *need,* Tolstoy suggests, allows us to live. Getting what we *want*—well, that can be another matter altogether.

Literary Focus

Allegory

Tolstoy's story "How Much Land Does a Man Need?" is often called a parable. A **parable** is a short, simple tale that is based on ordinary events and presents a moral lesson. Parables are related to a kind of writing called **allegory**—stories that operate on two different levels, the literal and the symbolic. The characters and events of an allegory can be understood both for what they are (the literal meaning) and for the abstract principles they represent (the symbolic meaning). As you read, try to guess what various elements of the story (such as Pahom, the Devil, and the land itself) stand for.

SKILLS FOCUS

Literary Skills Understand allegory.

An **allegory** is a story in which the characters, settings, and events stand for abstract ideas or moral concepts.

For more on Allegory, see the Handbook of Literary and Historical Terms.

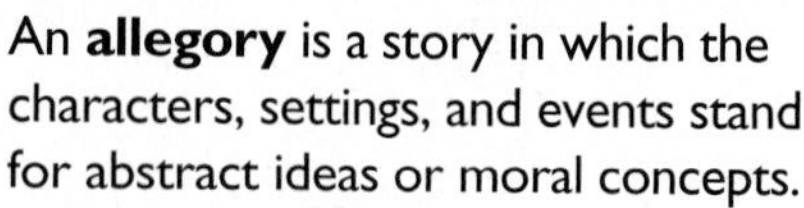

INTERNET

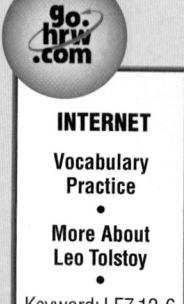

Vocabulary Practice

•

More About Leo Tolstoy

•

Keyword: LE7 12-6

Background

The nineteenth-century Russia that Leo Tolstoy describes in this story had just abandoned feudalism—a way of life dead in England since the Middle Ages. (See page 116.) Until Czar Alexander II ordered their emancipation in 1861, Russian peasants, called serfs, were virtual slaves of landowners and aristocrats: They could be bought or sold, and were not allowed to own property.

When Tolstoy wrote this story, serfs had already had twenty-five years of freedom and rights. No one, certainly not Tolstoy the reformer, would wish to see them thrust into bondage again. Yet in this parable he could wonder—with sharp, if somewhat black, humor—whether the peasants' progress had brought changes they would regret. As one character proclaims early on in the story, "Loss and gain are brothers twain."

Vocabulary Development

piqued (pēkt) *v.* used as *adj.:* provoked; resentful.

disparaged (di • spar′ijd) *v.:* belittled; spoke negatively of.

aggrieved (ə • grēvd′) *adj.:* offended.

arable (ar′ə • bəl) *adj.:* fit to be farmed or cultivated.

haggled (hag′əld) *v.:* argued about a price.

prostrate (präs′trāt′) *adj.:* lying flat.

(Opposite) *The Rainbow* by Arkhip Kuindzhi (1842–1910).

How Much Land Does a Man Need?

Leo Tolstoy

translated by Louise *and* Aylmer Maude

An elder sister came to visit her younger sister in the country. The elder was married to a tradesman in town, the younger to a peasant in the village. As the sisters sat over their tea talking, the elder began to boast of the advantages of town life: saying how comfortably they lived there, how well they dressed, what fine clothes her children wore, what good things they ate and drank, and how she went to the theater, promenades, and entertainments.

The younger sister was piqued, and in turn disparaged the life of a tradesman, and stood up for that of a peasant.

"I would not change my way of life for yours," said she. "We may live roughly, but at least we are free from anxiety. You live in better style than we do, but though you often earn more than you need, you are very likely to lose all you have. You know the proverb, 'Loss and gain are brothers twain.' It often happens that people who are wealthy one day are begging their bread the next. Our way is safer. Though a peasant's life is not a fat one, it is a long one. We shall never grow rich, but we shall always have enough to eat."

The elder sister said sneeringly:

"Enough? Yes, if you like to share with the pigs and the calves! What do you know of elegance or manners! However much your goodman may slave, you will die as you are living—on a dung heap—and your children the same."

"Well, what of that?" replied the younger. "Of course our work is rough and coarse. But, on the other hand, it is sure, and we need not bow to anyone. But you, in your towns, are surrounded by temptations; today all may be right, but tomorrow the Evil One may tempt your husband with cards, wine, or women, and all will go to ruin. Don't such things happen often enough?"

Pahom, the master of the house, was lying on the top of the stove[1] and he listened to the women's chatter.

"It is perfectly true," thought he. "Busy as we are from childhood tilling mother earth, we peasants have no time to let any nonsense settle in our heads. Our only trouble is that we haven't land enough. If I had plenty of land, I shouldn't fear the Devil himself!"

The women finished their tea, chatted a while about dress, and then cleared away the tea things and lay down to sleep.

But the Devil had been sitting behind the stove, and had heard all that was said. He was pleased that the peasant's wife had led her husband into boasting, and that he had said that if he had plenty of land he would not fear the Devil himself.

"All right," thought the Devil. "We will have a tussle. I'll give you land enough; and by means of that land I will get you into my power."

Close to the village there lived a lady, a small landowner who had an estate of about three hundred acres. She had always lived on good terms with the peasants until she engaged as her steward an old soldier, who took to burdening the people with fines. However careful Pahom tried to be, it happened again and again that now a horse of his got among the lady's oats, now a cow strayed into her garden, now his calves found their way into her meadows—and he always had to pay a fine.

Pahom paid up, but grumbled and, going home in a temper, was rough with his family. All through that summer, Pahom had much trouble because of this steward, and he was even glad when winter came and the cattle had to be stabled. Though he grudged the fodder when they could no longer graze on the pastureland, at least he was free from anxiety about them.

In the winter the news got about that the lady was going to sell her land and that the keeper of the inn on the high road was bargaining for it. When the peasants heard this they were very much alarmed.

1. **lying . . . stove:** Pahom's house is lacking in luxury if the family's oven, made of brick or tile, is used as an item of furniture.

Vocabulary

piqued (pēkt) *v.* used as *adj.:* provoked; resentful.

disparaged (di·spar′ijd) *v.:* belittled; spoke negatively of.

"Well," thought they, "if the innkeeper gets the land, he will worry us with fines worse than the lady's steward. We all depend on that estate."

So the peasants went on behalf of their Commune,[2] and asked the lady not to sell the land to the innkeeper, offering her a better price for it themselves. The lady agreed to let them have it. Then the peasants tried to arrange for the Commune to buy the whole estate, so that it might be held by them all in common. They met twice to discuss it, but could not settle the matter; the Evil One sowed discord among them and they could not agree. So they decided to buy the land individually, each according to his means; and the lady agreed to this plan as she had to the other.

Presently Pahom heard that a neighbor of his was buying fifty acres, and that the lady had consented to accept one half in cash and to wait a year for the other half. Pahom felt envious.

"Look at that," thought he, "the land is all being sold, and I shall get none of it." So he spoke to his wife.

"Other people are buying," said he, "and we must also buy twenty acres or so. Life is becoming impossible. That steward is simply crushing us with his fines."

So they put their heads together and considered how they could manage to buy it. They had one hundred rubles laid by. They sold a colt and one half of their bees, hired out one of their sons as a laborer, and took his wages in advance; borrowed the rest from a brother-in-law, and so scraped together half the purchase money.

Having done this, Pahom chose out a farm of forty acres, some of it wooded, and went to the lady to bargain for it. They came to an agreement, and he shook hands with her upon it and paid her a deposit in advance. Then they went to town and signed the deeds, he paying half the price down, and undertaking to pay the remainder within two years.

So now Pahom had land of his own. He borrowed seed, and sowed it on the land he had bought. The harvest was a good one, and within a year he had managed to pay off his debts both to the lady and to his brother-in-law. So he became a landowner, plowing and sowing his own land, making hay on his own land, cutting his own trees, and feeding his cattle on his own pasture. When he went out to plow his fields, or to look at his growing corn,[3] or at his grass meadows, his heart would fill with joy. The grass that grew and the flowers that bloomed there seemed to him unlike any that grew elsewhere. Formerly, when he had passed by that land, it had appeared the same as any other land, but now it seemed quite different.

So Pahom was well contented, and everything would have been right if the neighboring peasants would only not have trespassed on his cornfields and meadows. He appealed to them most civilly, but they still went on: Now the Communal herdsmen would let the village cows stray into his meadows, then horses from the night pasture would get among his corn. Pahom turned them out again and again, and forgave their owners, and for a long time he forbore to prosecute anyone. But at last he lost patience and complained to the District Court. He knew it was the peasants' want of land, and no evil intent on their part, that caused the trouble, but he thought:

"I cannot go on overlooking it or they will destroy all I have. They must be taught a lesson."

So he had them up, gave them one lesson, and then another, and two or three of the peasants were fined. After a time Pahom's neighbors began to bear him a grudge for this, and would now and then let their cattle on to his land on purpose. One peasant even got into Pahom's wood at night and cut down five young lime trees[4] for their bark. Pahom passing through the wood one day noticed something white. He came nearer and saw the stripped trunks lying on the ground, and close by stood the stumps where the trees had been. Pahom was furious.

---

2. **Commune** *n.:* village council.

3. **corn** *n.:* any plants producing grain, such as wheat, rye, or oats.

4. **lime trees** *n. pl.:* linden trees.

"If he had only cut one here and there it would have been bad enough," thought Pahom, "but the rascal has actually cut down a whole clump. If I could only find out who did this, I would pay him out."

He racked his brain as to who it could be. Finally he decided: "It must be Simon—no one else could have done it." So he went to Simon's homestead to have a look round, but he found nothing, and only had an angry scene. However, he now felt more certain than ever that Simon had done it, and he lodged a complaint. Simon was summoned. The case was tried, and retried, and at the end of it all Simon was acquitted, there being no evidence against him. Pahom felt still more aggrieved, and let his anger loose upon the Elder and the Judges.

"You let thieves grease your palms," said he. "If you were honest folk yourselves you would not let a thief go free."

So Pahom quarreled with the Judges and with his neighbors. Threats to burn his building began to be uttered. So though Pahom had more land, his place in the Commune was much worse than before.

About this time a rumor got about that many people were moving to new parts.

"There's no need for me to leave my land," thought Pahom. "But some of the others might leave our village and then there would be more room for us. I would take over their land myself and make my estate a bit bigger. I could then live more at ease. As it is, I am still too cramped to be comfortable."

One day Pahom was sitting at home when a peasant, passing through the village, happened to call in. He was allowed to stay the night, and supper was given him. Pahom had a talk with this peasant and asked him where he came from. The stranger answered that he came from beyond the Volga,[5] where he had been working. One word led to another, and the man went on to say that many people were settling in those parts. He told how some people from his village had settled there. They had joined the Commune, and had had twenty-five acres per man granted them. The land was so good, he said, that the rye sown on it grew as high as a horse, and so thick that five cuts of a sickle made a sheaf. One

Road in the Woods (detail) (late 19th century) by Fiodor Vasilyev.

5. **Volga:** river in western Russia flowing into the Caspian Sea.

Vocabulary

aggrieved (ə·grēvd′) *adj.:* offended.

Tretyakov Gallery, Moscow.

peasant, he said, had brought nothing with him but his bare hands, and now he had six horses and two cows of his own.

Pahom's heart kindled with desire. He thought:

"Why should I suffer in this narrow hole, if one can live so well elsewhere? I will sell my land and my homestead here, and with the money I will start afresh over there and get everything new. In this crowded place one is always having trouble. But I must first go and find out all about it myself."

Toward summer he got ready and started. He went down the Volga on a steamer to Samara,[6] then walked another three hundred miles on

6. **Samara** (su · mä′rə): city on the Volga River in southwestern Russia.

foot, and at last reached the place. It was just as the stranger had said. The peasants had plenty of land: Every man had twenty-five acres of Communal land given him for his use, and anyone who had money could buy, besides, at a ruble an acre as much good freehold land as he wanted.

Having found out all he wished to know, Pahom returned home as autumn came on, and began selling off his belongings. He sold his land at a profit, sold his homestead and all his cattle, and withdrew from membership in the Commune. He only waited till the spring, and then started with his family for the new settlement.

As soon as Pahom and his family reached their new abode, he applied for admission into the Commune of a large village. He stood treat to the Elders[7] and obtained the necessary documents. Five shares of Communal land were given him for his own and his sons' use: that is to say—125 acres (not all together, but in different fields) besides the use of the Communal pasture. Pahom put up the buildings he needed, and bought cattle. Of the Communal land alone he had three times as much as at his former home, and the land was good corn land. He was ten times better off than he had been. He had plenty of arable land and pasturage, and could keep as many head of cattle as he liked.

At first, in the bustle of building and settling down, Pahom was pleased with it all, but when he got used to it he began to think that even here he had not enough land. The first year, he sowed wheat on his share of the Communal land and had a good crop. He wanted to go on sowing wheat, but had not enough Communal land for the purpose, and what he had already used was not available; for in those parts wheat is only sown on virgin soil or on fallow land. It is sown for one or two years, and then the land lies fallow till it is again overgrown with prairie grass. There were many who wanted such land and there was not enough for all; so that people quarreled about it. Those who were better off wanted it for growing wheat, and those who were poor wanted it to let to dealers, so that they might raise money to pay their taxes. Pahom wanted to sow more wheat, so he rented land from a dealer for a year. He sowed much wheat and had a fine crop, but the land was too far from the village—the wheat had to be carted more than ten miles. After a time Pahom noticed that some peasant dealers were living on separate farms and were growing wealthy; and he thought:

"If I were to buy some freehold land and have a homestead on it, it would be a different thing altogether. Then it would all be nice and compact."

The question of buying freehold land recurred to him again and again.

He went on in the same way for three years, renting land and sowing wheat. The seasons turned out well and the crops were good, so that he began to lay money by. He might have gone on living contentedly, but he grew tired of having to rent other people's land every year, and having to scramble for it. Wherever there was good land to be had, the peasants would rush for it and it was taken up at once, so that unless you were sharp about it you got none. It happened in the third year that he and a dealer together rented a piece of pastureland from some peasants; and they had already plowed it up, when there was some dispute and the peasants went to law about it, and things fell out so that the labor was all lost.

"If it were my own land," thought Pahom, "I should be independent, and there would not be all this unpleasantness."

So Pahom began looking out for land which he could buy; and he came across a peasant who had bought thirteen hundred acres, but having got into difficulties was willing to sell again

7. **stood treat to the Elders:** provided the Elders with a meal.

Vocabulary

arable (ar′ə·bəl) *adj.:* fit to be farmed or cultivated.

cheap. Pahom bargained and haggled with him, and at last they settled the price at 1,500 rubles,[8] part in cash and part to be paid later. They had all but clinched the matter when a passing dealer happened to stop at Pahom's one day to get a feed for his horses. He drank tea with Pahom and they had a talk. The dealer said that he was just returning from the land of the Bashkirs,[9] far away, where he had bought thirteen thousand acres of land, all for 1,000 rubles. Pahom questioned him further, and the tradesman said:

"All one need do is to make friends with the chiefs. I gave away about one hundred rubles' worth of silk robes and carpets, besides a case of tea, and I gave wine to those who would drink it; and I got the land for less than a penny an acre." And he showed Pahom the title deeds, saying:

"The land lies near a river, and the whole prairie is virgin soil."

Pahom plied him with questions, and the tradesman said:

"There is more land there than you could cover if you walked a year, and it all belongs to the Bashkirs. They are as simple as sheep, and land can be got almost for nothing."

"There now," thought Pahom, "with my one thousand rubles, why should I get only thirteen hundred acres, and saddle myself with a debt besides? If I take it out there, I can get more than ten times as much for the money."

Pahom inquired how to get to the place, and as soon as the tradesman had left him, he prepared to go there himself. He left his wife to look after the homestead, and started on his journey taking his man with him. They stopped at a town on their way and bought a case of tea, some wine, and other presents, as the tradesman had advised. On and on they went until they had gone more than three hundred miles, and on the seventh day they came to a place where the Bashkirs had pitched their tents. It was all just as the tradesman had said. The people lived on the steppes, by a river, in felt-covered tents. They neither tilled the ground, nor ate bread. Their cattle and horses grazed in herds on the steppe. The colts were tethered behind the tents, and the mares were driven to them twice a day. The mares were milked, and from the milk kumiss[10] was made. It was the women who prepared kumiss, and they also made cheese. As far as the men were concerned, drinking kumiss and tea, eating mutton, and playing on their pipes, was all they cared about. They were all stout and merry, and all the summer long they never thought of doing any work. They were quite ignorant, and knew no Russian, but were good natured enough.

As soon as they saw Pahom, they came out of their tents and gathered round their visitor. An interpreter was found, and Pahom told them he had come about some land. The Bashkirs seemed very glad; they took Pahom and led him into one of the best tents, where they made him sit on some down cushions placed on a carpet, while they sat round him. They gave him some tea and kumiss, and had a sheep killed, and gave him mutton to eat. Pahom took presents out of his cart and distributed them among the Bashkirs, and divided the tea amongst them. The Bashkirs were delighted. They talked a great deal among themselves, and then told the interpreter to translate.

"They wish to tell you," said the interpreter, "that they like you, and that it is our custom to do all we can to please a guest and to repay him for his gifts. You have given us presents, now tell us which of the things we possess please you best, that we may present them to you."

8. **rubles** *n. pl.:* units of money in Russia, Ukraine, and other countries.

9. **Bashkirs** (bash·kirz'): Turkish-speaking peoples who live on the Russian steppes, or plains.

10. **kumiss** (ko͞o'mis) *n.:* fermented drink made from mare's milk.

Vocabulary

haggled (hag'əld) *v.:* argued about a price.

The Gleaners (1885–1886) by Isidore Verheyden. Oil on canvas (92 cm × 69 cm).

Collection Crédit Communal, Brussels, Belgium.

"What pleases me best here," answered Pahom, "is your land. Our land is crowded and the soil is exhausted; but you have plenty of land and it is good land. I never saw the like of it."

The interpreter translated. The Bashkirs talked among themselves for a while. Pahom could not understand what they were saying, but saw that they were much amused and that they shouted and laughed. Then they were silent and looked at Pahom while the interpreter said:

"They wish me to tell you that in return for your presents they will gladly give you as much land as you want. You have only to point it out with your hand and it is yours."

The Bashkirs talked again for a while and began to dispute. Pahom asked what they were disputing about, and the interpreter told him that some of them thought they ought to ask their chief about the land and not act in his absence, while others thought there was no need to wait for his return.

While the Bashkirs were disputing, a man in a large fox-fur cap appeared on the scene. They all became silent and rose to their feet. The interpreter said, "This is our chief himself."

Pahom immediately fetched the best dressing gown and five pounds of tea, and offered these to the chief. The chief accepted them, and seated himself in the place of honor. The Bashkirs at once began telling him something. The chief listened for a while, then made a sign with his head for them to be silent, and

addressing himself to Pahom, said in Russian:

"Well, let it be so. Choose whatever piece of land you like; we have plenty of it."

"How can I take as much as I like?" thought Pahom. "I must get a deed to make it secure, or else they may say, 'It is yours,' and afterward may take it away again."

"Thank you for your kind words," he said aloud. "You have much land, and I only want a little. But I should like to be sure which bit is mine. Could it not be measured and made over to me? Life and death are in God's hands. You good people give it to me, but your children might wish to take it away again."

"You are quite right," said the chief. "We will make it over to you."

"I heard that a dealer had been here," continued Pahom, "and that you gave him a little land, too, and signed title deeds to that effect. I should like to have it done in the same way."

The chief understood.

"Yes," replied he, "that can be done quite easily. We have a scribe, and we will go to town with you and have the deed properly sealed."

"And what will be the price?" asked Pahom.

"Our price is always the same: one thousand rubles a day."

Pahom did not understand.

"A day? What measure is that? How many acres would that be?"

"We do not know how to reckon it out," said the chief. "We sell it by the day. As much as you can go round on your feet in a day is yours, and the price is one thousand rubles a day."

Pahom was surprised.

"But in a day you can get round a large tract of land," he said.

The chief laughed.

"It will all be yours!" said he. "But there is one condition: If you don't return on the same day to the spot whence you started, your money is lost."

"But how am I to mark the way that I have gone?"

"Why, we shall go to any spot you like, and stay there. You must start from that spot and make your round, taking a spade with you. Wherever you think necessary, make a mark. At every turning, dig a hole and pile up the turf; then afterward we will go round with a plow from hole to hole. You may make as large a circuit as you please, but before the sun sets you must return to the place you started from. All the land you cover will be yours."

Pahom was delighted. It was decided to start early next morning. They talked a while, and after drinking some more kumiss and eating some more mutton, they had tea again, and then the night came on. They gave Pahom a featherbed to sleep on, and the Bashkirs dispersed for the night, promising to assemble the next morning at daybreak and ride out before sunrise to the appointed spot.

Pahom lay on the featherbed, but could not sleep. He kept thinking about the land.

"What a large tract I will mark off!" thought he. "I can easily do thirty-five miles in a day. The days are long now, and within a circuit of thirty-five miles what a lot of land there will be! I will sell the poorer land, or let it to peasants, but I'll pick out the best and farm it. I will buy two ox teams, and hire two more laborers. About a hundred and fifty acres shall be plow land, and I will pasture cattle on the rest."

Pahom lay awake all night, and dozed off only just before dawn. Hardly were his eyes closed when he had a dream. He thought he was lying in that same tent and heard somebody chuckling outside. He wondered who it could be, and rose and went out, and he saw the Bashkir chief sitting in front of the tent holding his sides and rolling about with laughter. Going nearer to the chief, Pahom asked: "What are you laughing at?" But he saw that it was no longer the chief, but the dealer who had recently stopped at his house and had told him about the land. Just as Pahom was going to ask, "Have you been here long?" he saw that it was not the dealer, but the peasant who had come up from the Volga, long ago, to Pahom's old home. Then he saw that it was not the peasant either, but the Devil himself with hoofs and horns, sitting there and chuckling,

and before him lay a man barefoot, prostrate on the ground, with only trousers and a shirt on. And Pahom dreamt that he looked more attentively to see what sort of a man it was that was lying there, and he saw that the man was dead, and that it was himself! He awoke horror-struck.

"What things one does dream," thought he.

Looking round he saw through the open door that the dawn was breaking.

"It's time to wake them up," thought he. "We ought to be starting."

He got up, roused his man (who was sleeping in his cart), bade him harness, and went to call the Bashkirs.

"It's time to go to the steppe to measure the land," he said.

The Bashkirs rose and assembled, and the chief came too. Then they began drinking kumiss again, and offered Pahom some tea, but he would not wait.

"If we are to go, let us go. It is high time," said he.

The Bashkirs got ready and they all started: some mounted on horses, and some in carts. Pahom drove in his own small cart with his servant and took a spade with him. When they reached the steppe, the morning red was beginning to kindle. They ascended a hillock (called by the Bashkirs a *shikhan*) and dismounting from their carts and their horses, gathered in one spot. The chief came up to Pahom and stretching out his arm toward the plain:

"See," said he, "all this, as far as your eye can reach, is ours. You may have any part of it you like."

Pahom's eyes glistened: It was all virgin soil, as flat as the palm of your hand, as black as the seed of a poppy, and in the hollows different kinds of grasses grew breast high.

The chief took off his fox-fur cap, placed it on the ground, and said:

"This will be the mark. Start from here, and return here again. All the land you go round shall be yours."

Pahom took out his money and put it on the cap. Then he took off his outer coat, remaining in his sleeveless undercoat. He unfastened his girdle and tied it tight below his stomach, put a little bag of bread into the breast of his coat, and tying a flask of water to his girdle, he drew up the tops of his boots, took the spade from his man, and stood ready to start. He considered for some moments which way he had better go—it was tempting everywhere.

"No matter," he concluded, "I will go toward the rising sun."

He turned his face to the east, stretched himself, and waited for the sun to appear above the rim.

"I must lose no time," he thought, "and it is easier walking while it is still cool."

The sun's rays had hardly flashed above the horizon, before Pahom, carrying the spade over his shoulder, went down into the steppe.

Pahom started walking neither slowly nor quickly. After having gone a thousand yards he stopped, dug a hole, and placed pieces of turf one on another to make it more visible. Then he went on; and now that he had walked off his stiffness he quickened his pace. After a while he dug another hole.

Pahom looked back. The hillock could be distinctly seen in the sunlight, with the people on it, and the glittering tires of the cart wheels. At a rough guess Pahom concluded that he had walked three miles. It was growing warmer; he took off his undercoat, flung it across his shoulder, and went on again. It had grown quite warm now; he looked at the sun, it was time to think of breakfast.

"The first shift is done, but there are four in a day, and it is too soon yet to turn. But I will just take off my boots," said he to himself.

He sat down, took off his boots, stuck them into his girdle, and went on. It was easy walking now.

"I will go on for another three miles," thought he, "and then turn to the left. This spot

Vocabulary

prostrate (präs′trāt′) *adj.*: lying flat.

Man in the Field by Wladimir Jegorowitsch Makowski (1846–1920).

AKG London.

is so fine, that it would be a pity to lose it. The further one goes, the better the land seems."

He went straight on for a while, and when he looked round, the hillock was scarcely visible and the people on it looked like black ants, and he could just see something glistening there in the sun.

"Ah," thought Pahom, "I have gone far enough in this direction, it is time to turn. Besides I am in a regular sweat, and very thirsty."

He stopped, dug a large hole, and heaped up pieces of turf. Next he untied his flask, had a drink, and then turned sharply to the left. He went on and on; the grass was high, and it was very hot.

Pahom began to grow tired: He looked at the sun and saw that it was noon.

"Well," he thought, "I must have a rest."

He sat down, and ate some bread and drank some water; but he did not lie down, thinking that if he did he might fall asleep. After sitting a little while, he went on again. At first he walked easily: The food had strengthened him; but it had become terribly hot and he felt sleepy, still he went on, thinking: "An hour to suffer, a lifetime to live."

He went a long way in this direction also, and was about to turn to the left again, when he perceived a damp hollow: "It would be a pity to leave that out," he thought. "Flax would do well there." So he went on past the hollow, and dug a hole on the other side of it before he turned the corner. Pahom looked toward the hillock. The heat made the air hazy: It seemed to be quivering, and through the haze the people on the hillock could scarcely be seen.

"Ah!" thought Pahom, "I have made the sides too long; I must make this one shorter." And he went along the third side, stepping faster. He looked at the sun: It was nearly halfway to the horizon, and he had not yet done two miles of the third side of the square. He was still ten miles from the goal.

"No," he thought, "though it will make my land lopsided, I must hurry back in a straight line now. I might go too far, and as it is I have a great deal of land."

So Pahom hurriedly dug a hole, and turned straight toward the hillock.

Pahom went straight toward the hillock, but he now walked with difficulty. He was done up

with the heat, his bare feet were cut and bruised, and his legs began to fail. He longed to rest, but it was impossible if he meant to get back before sunset. The sun waits for no man, and it was sinking lower and lower.

"Oh dear," he thought, "if only I have not blundered trying for too much! What if I am too late?"

He looked toward the hillock and at the sun. He was still far from his goal, and the sun was already near the rim.

Pahom walked on and on; it was very hard walking but he went quicker and quicker. He pressed on, but was still far from the place. He began running, threw away his coat, his boots, his flask, and his cap, and kept only the spade which he used as a support.

"What shall I do," he thought again. "I have grasped too much and ruined the whole affair. I can't get there before the sun sets."

And this fear made him still more breathless. Pahom went on running, his soaking shirt and trousers stuck to him, and his mouth was parched. His breast was working like a blacksmith's bellows, his heart was beating like a hammer, and his legs were giving way as if they did not belong to him. Pahom was seized with terror lest he should die of the strain.

Though afraid of death, he could not stop. "After having run all that way they will call me a fool if I stop now," thought he. And he ran on and on, and drew near and heard the Bashkirs yelling and shouting to him, and their cries inflamed his heart still more. He gathered his last strength and ran on.

The sun was close to the rim, and cloaked in mist looked large, and red as blood. Now, yes now, it was about to set! The sun was quite low, but he was also quite near his aim. Pahom could already see the people on the hillock waving their arms to hurry him up. He could see the fox-fur cap on the ground and the money on it, and the chief sitting on the ground holding his sides. And Pahom remembered his dream.

"There is plenty of land," thought he, "but will God let me live on it? I have lost my life, I have lost my life! I shall never reach that spot!"

Pahom looked at the sun, which had reached the earth: One side of it had already disappeared. With all his remaining strength he rushed on, bending his body forward so that his legs could hardly follow fast enough to keep him from falling. Just as he reached the hillock it suddenly grew dark. He looked up—the sun had already set! He gave a cry: "All my labor has been in vain," thought he, and was about to stop, but he heard the Bashkirs still shouting, and remembered that though to him, from below, the sun seemed to have set, they on the hillock could still see it. He took a long breath and ran up the hillock. It was still light there. He reached the top and saw the cap. Before it sat the chief laughing and holding his sides. Again Pahom remembered his dream, and he uttered a cry: His legs gave way beneath him, he fell forward and reached the cap with his hands.

"Ah, that's a fine fellow!" exclaimed the chief. "He has gained much land!"

Pahom's servant came running up and tried to raise him, but he saw that blood was flowing from his mouth. Pahom was dead!

The Bashkirs clicked their tongues to show their pity.

His servant picked up the spade and dug a grave long enough for Pahom to lie in, and buried him in it. Six feet from his head to his heels was all he needed. ■

Response and Analysis

Reading Check

1. What does Pahom want? What **conflicts** does he have to overcome to get it?

2. Pahom buys his first forty acres of land from an aristocrat. How does he raise the money?

3. After buying his first farm, why does Pahom quarrel with the neighboring peasants?

4. What happens when Pahom attempts to purchase land from the Bashkirs?

5. What is the **resolution** of the story's conflict?

6. According to Tolstoy, how much land does a man really need?

Thinking Critically

7. What is the central idea, or **theme,** of this story—that is, what truth does the story reveal about human life? State the theme in a sentence or two.

8. Think about the discussion between the two sisters at the beginning of the story. How does their conversation hint at, or **foreshadow,** Pahom's end? What other events foreshadow the ending of the story?

9. Contrast Pahom's attitude toward land with the attitude of the Bashkir chief. What do you think accounts for the difference in their values?

10. How does this story function as an **allegory**? Choose two elements of the story—its characters, its setting, or its events—and explain how each one can be read on both literal and symbolic levels.

11. Pahom's dreams of wealth are mocked in the story's ironic last line. Think of the stark contrast between what he wanted and "all he needed." How does Tolstoy's parable apply to our culture today?

12. In your opinion, did Pahom get what he deserved? Or did he pay too high a price for the "crime" he committed? Explain your responses to Tolstoy's moral.

Comparing Literature

13. You have seen British writers questioning the benefits of nineteenth-century industrialization and modernization. Does this questioning change in a Russian setting? In what ways does Tolstoy share or extend the British writers' debate about progress?

WRITING

Perils of Progress

"In expressing his disillusionment with private landownership, Tolstoy provides today's readers with a parable about greed and the so-called progress of materialism." In a brief **essay,** provide details from the story that support that statement.

Literary Skills Analyze allegory. Compare realist works.

Writing Skills Write an essay supporting a claim.

Vocabulary Skills Demonstrate word knowledge.

Grammar Skills Use correct pronoun and antecedent agreement.

Vocabulary Development

Summarizing the Story

piqued	*arable*
disparaged	*haggled*
aggrieved	*prostrate*

Using the Vocabulary words listed above, write a summary of "How Much Land Does a Man Need?" Not every sentence you write must contain a Vocabulary word. You may use any word more than once.

Grammar Link

Choosing the Right Reference: Pronoun and Antecedent Agreement

A **pronoun** usually refers to a noun or another pronoun. The word to which a pronoun refers is called its **antecedent.**

Pronouns should agree with their antecedents in **number** (singular or plural), **gender** (masculine, feminine, or neuter), and **person** (first person, second person, or third person).

Tolstoy tried to live the simple life he wrote about. [singular number]

Pahom wanted to own his own land. [masculine gender]

As soon as Pahom reached his new abode, he applied for admission into the Commune. [third person]

One tricky kind of pronoun and antecedent agreement involves **indefinite pronouns.** Some indefinite pronouns are always singular (*anyone, each, either, everybody, neither, nothing, one, somebody, something*); some are always plural (*both, few, many, several*); and a few can be either singular *or* plural, depending on how they are used in the sentence (*all, any, more, most, none, some*).

Each of the peasants defended his or her lifestyle. [singular]

Both of the peasants had their plows. [plural]

One of the men lost his land. [singular]

PRACTICE

The following sentences contain pronouns that do not agree with their antecedents. Rewrite each sentence to correct the error.

1. One of the sisters lives in the town with their husband, a tradesman.
2. Both of the sisters argued while drinking her tea.
3. Every man had twenty-five acres of land for their use.
4. If people want to learn about Russian peasant life, you should read Tolstoy.

Apply to Your Writing

Take out a writing assignment you are working on now or have already completed. Highlight all of the pronouns, and make sure they agree with their antecedents in number, gender, and person.

For more help, see Agreement of Pronoun and Antecedent, 2j–o, in the Language Handbook.

NINETEENTH-CENTURY RUSSIA

Anton Chekhov

(1860–1904)

Anton Pavlovich Chekhov (än′tōn pä·vlô′ vich che′kôf′), the grandson of a serf who had bought his own and his family's freedom, was born in the seaport town of Taganrog in the south of Russia. As a child, Anton spent long hours working in his father's general store.

When Chekhov was sixteen, his father went bankrupt and fled with his family to Moscow to avoid a prison sentence. Chekhov was left behind as a "hostage" to his father's creditors. He tutored the creditor's son at a cheap rate, finished school, and went to Moscow to study medicine on a scholarship. In order to support himself and his family, who were living in a Moscow slum, Chekhov began writing comic stories to sell to periodicals.

Medicine was good training for his career as a writer. Through his practice as a doctor, Chekhov came to know hundreds of ordinary people. He continued to write while practicing medicine; eventually, however, he gave up his full-time practice because it took too much of his time away from writing.

It was not until the last years of his life that Chekhov achieved some affluence and fame. At this time he settled with his parents and sister on a large country estate. Here he organized famine relief, fought cholera epidemics, and continued to examine poor patients free of charge. Although the theme of many of his works is the individual's alienation from others, Chekhov's real-life activities demonstrate that humanity, reason, and generosity were his highest values.

Chekhov's life was cut short by tuberculosis. His finest stories—those of the 1890s—and his four great plays, *The Sea Gull* (1896), *Uncle Vanya* (1897), *Three Sisters* (1901), and *The Cherry Orchard* (1904), were written while he was fatally ill. In 1901, he married the actress who played the lead role in *The Sea Gull,* but the couple spent their honeymoon in a sanitarium, or health resort. He died in Germany three years later, at the age of forty-four, at the height of his creativity.

For Independent Reading

The following stories are among Chekhov's finest. Note that titles may differ depending on the story's translator.

- "The Lady with a Dog"
- "Gooseberries"
- "The Darling"

Before You Read

The Bet

Make the Connection

Quickwrite

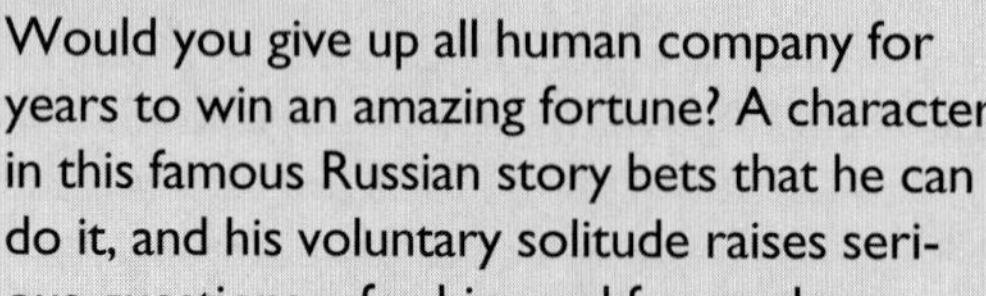

Would you give up all human company for years to win an amazing fortune? A character in this famous Russian story bets that he can do it, and his voluntary solitude raises serious questions—for him and for readers.

What motivates people to make bets? What would persuade *you* to take up a bet? Is money always the primary motivator, or are there other reasons why a person would do something on a bet? Jot down your ideas.

Literary Focus

Theme

The **theme** is the overall meaning of a work of literature that usually expresses a view or comment on life. For example, the theme of a story about growing up might be that disillusionment is part of the maturation process. Writers rarely state their theme directly; the reader must consider the complex interplay of all of the elements of the story in order to piece together the possible meanings of the work as a whole. Because each reader brings different values and experiences to the story, individual interpretations are bound to vary. Some interpretations even go beyond what the writer consciously intended the story to mean. Discerning themes always requires a tolerance for ambiguity—especially in an open-ended story like "The Bet" that raises more questions than it answers.

A **theme** is the central idea or insight of a work of literature.

For more on Theme, see the Handbook of Literary and Historical Terms.

Literary Skills Understand theme.

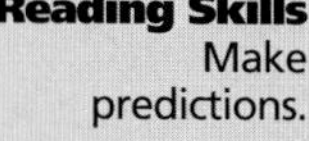

Reading Skills Make predictions.

INTERNET
Vocabulary Practice
•
More About Anton Chekhov
•
Keyword: LE7 12-6

Reading Skills

Making Predictions

A **prediction** is a special kind of **inference,** or educated guess, about what will happen later. Some predictions may turn out to be inaccurate, and adjusting or discarding them is an essential part of active reading. As you read, identify clues that suggest or foreshadow what will happen to the characters later in the story. Then, make predictions based on these clues. As you read, modify your predictions based on what actually happens in the story, and make note of the details that cause you to change your predictions.

Vocabulary Development

frivolous (friv′ə • ləs) *adj.:* light-minded; lacking seriousness.

compulsory (kəm • pul′sə • rē) *adj.:* required; enforced.

caprice (kə • prēs′) *n.:* sudden notion or desire.

zealously (zel′əs • lē) *adv.:* fervently; devotedly.

indiscriminately (in′di • skrim′i • nit • lē) *adv.:* without making careful distinctions; randomly.

ethereal (ē • thir′ē • əl) *adj.:* light and delicate; unearthly.

illusory (i • lo͞o′sə • rē) *adj.:* not real; false.

posterity (päs • ter′ə • tē) *n.:* descendants; future generations.

renounce (ri • nouns′) *v.:* formally give up; reject.

The Bet

Anton Chekhov

translated by **Constance Garnett**

1

It was a dark autumn night. The old banker was walking up and down his study and remembering how, fifteen years before, he had given a party one autumn evening. There had been many clever men there, and there had been interesting conversations. Among other things, they had talked of capital punishment. The majority of the guests, among whom were many journalists and intellectual men, disapproved of the death penalty. They considered that form of punishment out of date, immoral, and unsuitable for Christian states.[1] In the opinion of some of them, the death penalty ought to be replaced everywhere by imprisonment for life.

"I don't agree with you," said their host, the banker. "I have not tried either the death penalty or imprisonment for life, but if one may judge a priori,[2] the death penalty is more moral and more humane than imprisonment for life. Capital punishment kills a man at once, but lifelong imprisonment kills him slowly. Which executioner is the more humane, he who kills you in a few minutes or he who drags the life out of you in the course of many years?"

"Both are equally immoral," observed one of the guests, "for they both have the same object—to take away life. The state is not God. It has not the right to take away what it cannot restore when it wants to."

Among the guests was a young lawyer, a young man of five-and-twenty. When he was asked his opinion, he said: "The death sentence and the life sentence are equally immoral, but if I had to choose between the death penalty and imprisonment for life, I would certainly choose the second. To live anyhow is better than not at all."

The Verandah at Liselund (detail) (1916) by Peter Ilsted. Oil on canvas.

Courtesy of Adelson Galleries, New York.

A lively discussion arose. The banker, who was younger and more nervous in those days, was suddenly carried away by excitement; he struck the table with his fist and shouted at the young man: "It's not true! I'll bet you two million you wouldn't stay in solitary confinement for five years."

"If you mean that in earnest," said the young man, "I'll take the bet, but I would stay not five, but fifteen years."

---

1. **Christian states:** countries in which Christianity is the main religion.
2. **a priori** (ā′prī·ôr′ī) *adv.:* here, on the basis of theory rather than experience.

"Fifteen? Done!" cried the banker. "Gentlemen, I stake two million!"

"Agreed! You stake your millions and I stake my freedom!" said the young man.

And this wild, senseless bet was carried out! The banker, spoiled and frivolous, with millions beyond his reckoning, was delighted at the bet. At supper he made fun of the young man and said: "Think better of it, young man, while there is still time. To me two million is a trifle, but you are losing three or four of the best years of your life. I say three or four, because you won't stay longer. Don't forget either, you unhappy man, that voluntary confinement is a great deal harder to bear than compulsory. The thought that you have the right to step out in liberty at any moment will poison your whole existence in prison. I am sorry for you."

And now the banker, walking to and fro, remembered all this and asked himself: "What was the object of that bet? What is the good of that man's losing fifteen years of his life and my throwing away two million? Can it prove that the death penalty is better or worse than imprisonment for life? No, no. It was all nonsensical and meaningless. On my part it was the caprice of a pampered man, and on his part simple greed for money. . . ."

Then he remembered what followed that evening. It was decided that the young man should spend the years of his captivity under the strictest supervision in one of the lodges in the banker's garden. It was agreed that for fifteen years he should not be free to cross the threshold of the lodge, to see human beings, to hear the human voice, or to receive letters and newspapers. He was allowed to have a musical instrument and books and was allowed to write letters, to drink wine, and to smoke. By the terms of the agreement, the only relations he could have with the outer world were by a little window made purposely for that object. He might have anything he wanted—books, music, wine, and so on—in any quantity he desired, by writing an order, but could receive them only through the window. The agreement provided for every detail and every trifle that would make his imprisonment strictly solitary, and bound the young man to stay there *exactly* fifteen years, beginning from twelve o'clock of November 14, 1870, and ending at twelve o'clock of November 14, 1885. The slightest attempt on his part to break the conditions, if only two minutes before the end, released the banker from the obligation to pay him two million.

For the first year of his confinement, as far as one could judge from his brief notes, the prisoner suffered severely from loneliness and depression. The sounds of the piano could be heard continually day and night from his lodge. He refused wine and tobacco. Wine, he wrote, excites the desires, and desires are the worst foes of the prisoner; and besides, nothing could be more dreary than drinking good wine and seeing no one. And tobacco spoiled the air of his room. In the first year the books he sent for were principally of a light character—novels with a complicated love plot, sensational and fantastic stories, and so on.

In the second year the piano was silent in the lodge, and the prisoner asked only for the classics. In the fifth year music was audible again, and the prisoner asked for wine. Those who watched him through the window said that all that year he spent doing nothing but eating and drinking and lying on his bed, frequently yawning and talking angrily to himself. He did not read books. Sometimes at night he would sit down to write; he would spend hours writing and in the morning tear up all that he had written. More than once he could be heard crying.

In the second half of the sixth year the prisoner began zealously studying languages, philosophy, and history. He threw himself eagerly into these studies—so much so that the banker had enough to do to get him the books he

Vocabulary

frivolous (friv'ə·ləs) *adj.:* light-minded; lacking seriousness.
compulsory (kəm·pul'sə·rē) *adj.:* required; enforced.
caprice (kə·prēs') *n.:* sudden notion or desire.
zealously (zel'əs·lē) *adv.:* fervently; devotedly.

Scala/Art Resource, New York.

Portrait of the Painter Konstantin Alekseevich Korovin (1891) by Valentin Serov. Oil on canvas. Tretiakov Gallery, Moscow, Russia.

ordered. In the course of four years, some six hundred volumes were procured at his request. It was during this period that the banker received the following letter from his prisoner:

"My dear Jailer, I write you these lines in six languages. Show them to people who know the languages. Let them read them. If they find not one mistake, I implore you to fire a shot in the garden. That shot will show me that my efforts have not been thrown away. The geniuses of all ages and of all lands speak different languages, but the same flame burns in them all. Oh, if you only knew what unearthly happiness my soul feels now from being able to understand them!" The prisoner's desire was fulfilled. The banker ordered two shots to be fired in the garden.

Then, after the tenth year, the prisoner sat immovably at the table and read nothing but the Gospels. It seemed strange to the banker that a man who in four years had mastered six hundred learned volumes should waste nearly a year over one thin book easy of comprehension. Theology[3] and histories of religion followed the Gospels.

In the last two years of his confinement, the prisoner read an immense quantity of books quite indiscriminately. At one time he was busy with the natural sciences; then he would ask for Byron or Shakespeare. There were notes in which he demanded at the same time books on chemistry, and a manual of medicine, and a novel, and some treatise on philosophy or theology. His reading suggested a man swimming in the sea among the wreckage of his ship and trying to save his life by greedily clutching first at one spar[4] and then at another.

2

The old banker remembered all this and thought: "Tomorrow at twelve o'clock he will regain his freedom. By our arrangement I ought to pay him two million. If I do pay him, it is all over with me: I shall be utterly ruined."

Fifteen years before, his millions had been beyond his reckoning; now he was afraid to ask himself which were greater, his debts or his assets. Desperate gambling on the Stock Exchange, wild speculation, and the excitability which he could not get over even in advancing years had by degrees led to the decline of his fortune, and the proud, fearless, self-confident millionaire had become a banker of middling rank, trembling at every rise and fall in his investments. "Cursed bet!" muttered the old man, clutching his head in despair. "Why didn't the man die? He is only forty now. He will take my last penny from me, he will marry, will enjoy life, will gamble on the Exchange, while I shall look at him with envy like a beggar and hear from him every day the same sentence: 'I am indebted to you for the happiness of my life; let me help you!' No, it is too much! The one means of being saved from bankruptcy and disgrace is the death of that man!"

It struck three o'clock. The banker listened; everyone was asleep in the house, and nothing could be heard outside but the rustling of the chilled trees. Trying to make no noise, he took from a fireproof safe the key of the door which had not been opened for fifteen years, put on his overcoat, and went out of the house.

It was dark and cold in the garden. Rain was falling. A damp, cutting wind was racing about the garden, howling and giving the trees no rest. The banker strained his eyes but could see neither the earth nor the white statues, nor the lodge, nor the trees. Going to the spot where the lodge stood, he twice called the watchman. No answer followed. Evidently the watchman had sought shelter from the weather and was now asleep somewhere either in the kitchen or in the greenhouse.

"If I had the pluck to carry out my intention," thought the old man, "suspicion would fall first upon the watchman."

3. **Theology** (thē·äl′ə·jē) *n.:* study of religious teachings concerning God and God's relation to the world.
4. **spar** *n.:* pole that supports or extends a ship's sail.

Vocabulary

indiscriminately (in′di·skrim′i·nit·lē) *adv.:* without making careful distinctions; randomly.

He felt in the darkness for the steps and the door and went into the entry of the lodge. Then he groped his way into a little passage and lighted a match. There was not a soul there. There was a bedstead with no bedding on it, and in the corner there was a dark cast-iron stove. The seals on the door leading to the prisoner's rooms were intact.

When the match went out, the old man, trembling with emotion, peeped through the little window. A candle was burning dimly in the prisoner's room. He was sitting at the table. Nothing could be seen but his back, the hair on his head, and his hands. Open books were lying on the table, on the two easy chairs, and on the carpet near the table.

Five minutes passed and the prisoner did not once stir. Fifteen years' imprisonment had taught him to sit still. The banker tapped at the window with his finger, and the prisoner made no movement whatever in response. Then the banker cautiously broke the seals off the door and put the key in the keyhole. The rusty lock gave a grating sound and the door creaked. The banker expected to hear at once footsteps and a cry of astonishment, but three minutes passed and it was as quiet as ever in the room. He made up his mind to go in.

At the table a man unlike ordinary people was sitting motionless. He was a skeleton with the skin drawn tight over his bones, with long curls like a woman's, and a shaggy beard. His face was yellow with an earthy tint in it, his cheeks were hollow, his back long and narrow, and the hand on which his shaggy head was propped was so thin and delicate that it was dreadful to look at it. His hair was already streaked with silver, and seeing his emaciated, aged-looking face, no one would have believed that he was only forty. He was asleep. . . . In front of his bowed head there lay on the table a sheet of paper, on which there was something written in fine handwriting.

"Poor creature!" thought the banker, "he is asleep and most likely dreaming of the millions. And I have only to take this half-dead man, throw him on the bed, stifle him a little with the pillow, and the most conscientious expert would find no sign of a violent death. But let us first read what he has written here. . . ."

The banker took the page from the table and read as follows:

"Tomorrow at twelve o'clock I regain my freedom and the right to associate with other men, but before I leave this room and see the sunshine, I think it necessary to say a few words to you. With a clear conscience I tell you, as before God, who beholds me, that I despise freedom and life and health and all that in your books is called the good things of the world.

"For fifteen years I have been intently studying earthly life. It is true I have not seen the earth or men, but in your books I have drunk fragrant wine, I have sung songs, I have hunted stags and wild boars in the forests, I have loved women. . . . Beauties as ethereal as clouds, created by the magic of your poets and geniuses, have visited me at night and have whispered in my ears wonderful tales that have set my brain in a whirl. In your books I have climbed to the peaks of Elburz and Mont Blanc,[5] and from there I have seen the sun rise and have watched it at evening flood the sky, the ocean, and the mountaintops with gold and crimson. I have watched from there the lightning flashing over my head and cleaving the storm clouds. I have seen green forests, fields, rivers, lakes, towns. I have heard the singing of the sirens,[6] and the strains of the shepherds' pipes; I have touched the wings of comely devils who flew down to converse with me of God. . . . In your books I have flung myself into the bottomless pit, performed miracles, slain, burned towns, preached new religions, conquered whole kingdoms. . . .

5. **Elburz** (el·bo͝orz′) **and Mont Blanc** (mōn blän′): Elburz is a mountain range in northern Iran; Mont Blanc, in France, is the highest mountain in the Alps.
6. **sirens** *n. pl.:* in Greek mythology, partly human female creatures who lived on an island and lured sailors to their death with their beautiful singing.

Vocabulary

ethereal (ē·thir′ē·əl) *adj.:* light and delicate; unearthly.

The Verandah at Liselund (1916) by Peter Ilsted. Oil on canvas.

Courtesy of Adelson Galleries, New York.

"Your books have given me wisdom. All that the unresting thought of man has created in the ages is compressed into a small compass in my brain. I know that I am wiser than all of you.

"And I despise your books, I despise wisdom and the blessings of this world. It is all worthless, fleeting, illusory, and deceptive, like a mirage. You may be proud, wise, and fine, but death will wipe you off the face of the earth as though you were no more than mice burrowing under the floor, and your posterity, your history, your immortal geniuses will burn or freeze together with the earthly globe.

"You have lost your reason and taken the wrong path. You have taken lies for truth and hideousness for beauty. You would marvel if, owing to strange events of some sort, frogs and lizards suddenly grew on apple and orange trees instead of fruit or if roses began to smell like a sweating horse; so I marvel at you who exchange heaven for earth. I don't want to understand you.

"To prove to you in action how I despise all that you live by, I renounce the two million of which I once dreamed as of paradise and which now I despise. To deprive myself of the right to the money, I shall go out from here five minutes before the time fixed and so break the compact. . . ."

When the banker had read this, he laid the page on the table, kissed the strange man on the head, and went out of the lodge, weeping. At no other time, even when he had lost heavily on the Stock Exchange, had he felt so great a contempt for himself. When he got home, he lay on his bed, but his tears and emotion kept him for hours from sleeping.

Next morning the watchmen ran in with pale faces and told him they had seen the man who lived in the lodge climb out of the window into the garden, go to the gate, and disappear. The banker went at once with the servants to the lodge and made sure of the flight of his prisoner. To avoid arousing unnecessary talk, he took from the table the writing in which the millions were renounced and, when he got home, locked it up in the fireproof safe. ■

Vocabulary

illusory (i·lo͞o′sə·rē) *adj.:* not real; false.

posterity (päs·ter′ə·tē) *n.:* descendants; future generations.

renounce (ri·nouns′) *v.:* formally give up; reject.

Response and Analysis

Reading Check

1. What are the terms of the bet?
2. At the end of the fifteen years, how has the banker's situation changed?
3. Why does the banker go to the lodge on the last night of the lawyer's imprisonment?
4. What decision does the lawyer announce in a letter, and why?

Thinking Critically

5. The banker believes that "greed for money" was the lawyer's **motivation** for betting. Do you agree or disagree? Cite evidence in the text that supports your position. Be sure to check your Quickwrite notes.
6. For fifteen years the lawyer lives in exile. How does isolation affect him at different stages over the fifteen-year period?
7. In retrospect, the banker sees his bet as "the caprice of a pampered man." How does he feel about himself at the end of the fifteen years? What does this reveal about Chekhov's view of what is important in life?
8. At what points in your reading did you need to revise your predictions of what was to happen next? Be sure to consult your reading notes.
9. State in a full sentence what you think is the story's **theme**—the insight it provides about human experience. Discuss your theme with classmates. Can several thematic statements apply to this story?
10. Restate the philosophy revealed in the lawyer's letter, point by point, and give your reaction to each point. How could the lawyer's views provide a commentary on the state of Russian society during the last years of czarist rule?

Comparing Literature

11. Compare and contrast Chekhov's story with Leo Tolstoy's "How Much Land Does a Man Need?" (see page 951). Focus on what each story says about the pursuit of material gain, and comment on each story's ironic ending.

WRITING

Planning a Year Alone

Imagine yourself in the lawyer's place. What would you do if you were to be confined alone for a year? The rules include no human contact, no exit, no radio or television, no VCR, no telephone, no computer or Internet access. You may ask for books, hobby supplies, musical instruments, and exercise equipment. Write a brief essay, telling how you imagine you would spend one year alone.

Vocabulary Development

Sentence Sense

frivolous	ethereal
compulsory	illusory
caprice	posterity
zealously	renounce
indiscriminately	

Use each of the Vocabulary words above in an original sentence based on Chekhov's story "The Bet."

Literary Skills Analyze theme. Compare and contrast realist works.

Reading Skills Revise predictions.

Writing Skills Write an expository essay.

Vocabulary Skills Demonstrate word knowledge.

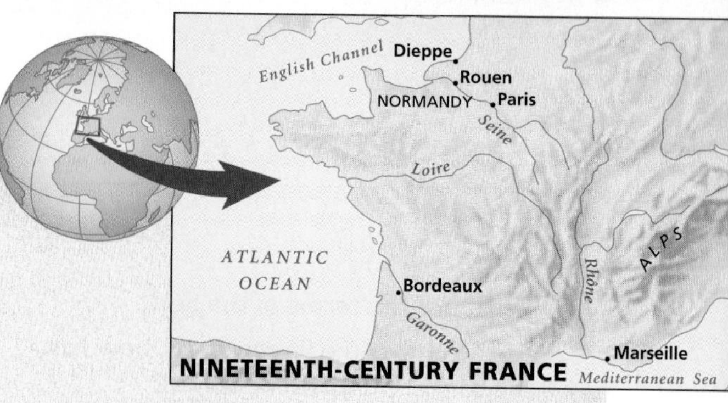

Guy de Maupassant

(1850–1893)

Guy de Maupassant (gē də mō·pä·sän′) gave new shape and direction to the short story. His works have set the standard of excellence for many writers of short fiction.

Maupassant was born into a family of merchants in rural Normandy. Among the friends of his family were many artists and writers, including the great realist novelist Gustave Flaubert (1821–1880). Maupassant was encouraged to write from an early age, especially by his mother and Flaubert.

After serving in the French army during the Franco-Prussian War, Maupassant studied law and then took a government post in Paris. There he got in touch with Flaubert, who became his mentor. Every week several great realist writers met at Flaubert's house to discuss literature. They included Émile Zola (1840–1902) and the Russian novelist Ivan Turgenev (1818–1883). Flaubert invited the young Maupassant to join the group. At that time, Maupassant was writing poems, historical dramas in verse, and horror stories. Under the influence of his new friends, he turned to realistic prose fiction.

Flaubert's influence was also helpful in getting Maupassant a better job and introductions to literary salons. Later Maupassant joined a spinoff group of younger realists, or naturalists, who met at Zola's house. The naturalists treated the older realists with respect, but they were less interested in stylistic beauty and more intent on describing social conditions objectively.

Maupassant's twenties were a period of literary apprenticeship. He did not publish his first realist story until 1879. By his thirties, however, Maupassant had become one of the best-known artists in France, earning enough to quit his government job and support himself as a writer. In 1883 alone, he turned out two novels and seventy short stories. His novels of this time are examples of realism at its most observant.

Few of his friends suspected that the strong young writer was in constant pain, nearly blind from overwork and disease. Painkilling drugs made his health worse. The end of 1891 brought a complete mental breakdown, from which Maupassant never recovered. He died in an asylum before his forty-third birthday.

For Independent Reading

You may enjoy the following stories by Maupassant:

- "The Piece of Yarn"
- "The Necklace"
- "Two Friends"

Guy de Maupassant (1876) by Francois Nicolas Augustin Feyen-Perrin. Oil on canvas.

Chateau de Versailles, France. The Bridgeman Art Library.

Before You Read

The Jewels

Make the Connection

After reading "The Jewels," you may feel as if you have just had a conversation with someone who didn't quite give you all the facts. A master of the art of suggestion, Guy de Maupassant offers the reader only the bare minimum of necessary information. From there, it's up to you—and your imagination—to figure out what's *really* going on.

Literary Focus

Theme

The **theme** of a work of literature is the insight into human experience that it expresses—or, in the case of Maupassant, that it suggests. Oftentimes, the theme of a work relates to particular issues that are relevant to the author and his or her time period. During the second half of the nineteenth century, many writers were interested in illuminating the problems of real people. As you try to formulate this story's theme, consider how Maupassant addresses real issues of the time. Also, look to Maupassant's writing style for clues. The reader is told little about the story's key character, Madame Lantin. Likewise, we learn that this character is equally unknown to her husband. As you read, ask yourself what Maupassant might be suggesting about relationships, secrecy, and how well we read the characters of even those we are closest to.

A **theme** is the insight into human experience revealed in a work of literature.

For more on Theme, see the Handbook of Literary and Historical Terms.

Reading Skills

Making Inferences

As you read "The Jewels," pay close attention to what is *not* said as well as to what *is* said. And stay alert—Maupassant often drops crucial clues in the space of one or two words. When you have finished reading, use the clues you've gathered to make **inferences,** or intelligent guesses, about what is only implied in the story. Write down one or two of your inferences, as well as any details from the story that support them.

Background

As a realist writing in the late 1800s, Guy de Maupassant helped to perfect the use of the short story to focus on the problems of real people. His stories are known for their realistic details, brisk pacing, concentration on essentials, and unexpected plot twists. You may notice as you read "The Jewels" that Maupassant uses only a few sentences to describe major events and characters. The terse style of this story, as of many others, is partly the result of the fact that many of Maupassant's stories were originally published in newspapers, which severely restricted the length of his material.

Vocabulary Development

unpretentious (ən·prē·ten′shəs) *adj.:* modest.

assuage (ə·swāj′) *v.:* ease; calm.

incurred (in·kurd′) *v.:* brought upon oneself.

surreptitiously (sur′əp·tish′əs·lē) *adv.:* sneakily or stealthily.

contemptuous (kən·temp′cho͞o·əs) *adj.:* scornful.

SKILLS FOCUS

Literary Skills Understand theme.

Reading Skills Make inferences.

INTERNET

Vocabulary Practice

Keyword: LE7 12-6

The Jewels

Guy de Maupassant

translated by **Roger Colet**

Monsieur Lantin had met the girl at a party given one evening by his office superior and love had caught him in its net.

She was the daughter of a country tax collector who had died a few years before. She had come to Paris then with her mother, who struck up acquaintance with a few middle-class families in her district in the hope of marrying her off. They were poor and decent, quiet and gentle. The girl seemed the perfect example of the virtuous woman to whom every sensible young man dreams of entrusting his life. Her simple beauty had a modest, angelic charm and the imperceptible smile which always hovered about her lips seemed to be a reflection of her heart.

Everybody sang her praises and people who knew her never tired of saying: "Happy the man who marries her. Nobody could find a better wife." (1)

> (1) The narrator gives an account of the girl's background and reputation.
>
> ? *What do you learn about the girl from this account? Does the description give you a sense of her character? Explain.*

Monsieur Lantin, who was then a senior clerk at the Ministry of the Interior with a salary of three thousand five hundred francs[1] a year, proposed to her and married her.

He was incredibly happy with her. She ran his household so skillfully and economically that they gave the impression of living in luxury. She lavished attention on her husband, spoiling and coddling him, and the charm of her person was

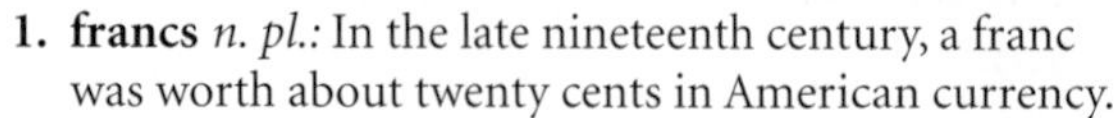

1. **francs** *n. pl.:* In the late nineteenth century, a franc was worth about twenty cents in American currency.

so great that six years after their first meeting he loved her even more than in the early days.

He found fault with only two of her tastes: her love for the theater and her passion for imitation jewelry.

Her friends (she knew the wives of a few petty officials) often obtained a box at the theater for her for popular plays, and even for first nights; and she dragged her husband along willy-nilly to these entertainments, which he found terribly tiring after a day's work at the office. He therefore begged her to go to the theater with some lady of her acquaintance who would bring her home afterwards. It was a long time before she gave in, as she thought that this arrangement was not quite respectable. But finally, just to please him, she agreed, and he was terribly grateful to her.

Now this love for the theater soon aroused in her a desire to adorn her person. True, her dresses remained very simple, always in good taste, but unpretentious; and her gentle grace, her irresistible, humble, smiling charm seemed to be enhanced by the simplicity of her gowns. But she took to wearing two big rhinestone earrings which sparkled like diamonds, and she also wore necklaces of fake pearls, bracelets of imitation gold, and combs set with colored glass cut to look like real stones. ❷

> ❷ During the nineteenth century, the theater was regarded as a place both to watch and to be watched. It was considered improper for a woman to attend the theater—and invite the gaze of others—without a companion, preferably male.
>
> ? *What might Madame Lantin's love of the theater and desire for adornment reveal about her?*

Her husband, who was rather shocked by this love of show, often used to say: "My dear, when a woman can't afford to buy real jewels, she ought to appear adorned with her beauty and grace alone: those are still the rarest of gems."

But she would smile sweetly and reply: "I can't help it. I like imitation jewelry. It's my only vice. I know you're right, but people can't change their natures. I would have loved to own some real jewels."

Then she would run the pearl necklaces through her fingers and make the cut-glass gems flash in the light, saying: "Look! Aren't they beautifully made? Anyone would swear they were real."

He would smile and say: "You have the taste of a gypsy."

Sometimes, in the evening, when they were sitting together by the fireside, she would place on the tea table the leather box in which she kept her "trash," as Monsieur Lantin called it. Then she would start examining these imitation jewels with passionate attention, as if she were enjoying some deep and secret pleasure; and she would insist on hanging a necklace around her husband's neck, laughing uproariously and crying: "How funny you look!" And then she would throw herself into his arms and kiss him passionately. ❸

> ❸ Monsieur Lantin's views of the jewels are very different from his wife's views.
>
> ? *What do you make of Madame Lantin's words and actions here?*

One night in winter when she had been to the opera, she came home shivering with cold. The next morning she had a cough, and a week later she died of pneumonia.

Lantin very nearly followed her to the grave. His despair was so terrible that his hair turned white within a month. He wept from morning to night, his heart ravaged by unbearable grief, haunted by the memory, the smile, the voice, the every charm of his dead wife.

Time did nothing to assuage his grief. Often during office hours, when his colleagues came

(Above left) Gold and silver brooch with diamonds and emeralds.

Kremlin Museums, Moscow/The Bridgeman Art Library.

(Left) *Jeanne Samary in a Scoop Neckline Dress* (detail) (19th century) by Auguste Renoir.

Pushkin Museum of Fine Arts, Moscow, Russia.

Vocabulary

unpretentious (ən·prē·ten′shəs) *adj.:* modest.

assuage (ə·swāj′) *v.:* ease; calm.

along to chat about the topics of the day, his cheeks would suddenly puff out, his nose wrinkle up, his eyes fill with tears, and with a terrible grimace he would burst out sobbing.

He had left his wife's room untouched, and every day would shut himself in it and think about her. All the furniture and even her clothes remained exactly where they had been on the day she had died.

But life soon became a struggle for him. His income, which in his wife's hands had covered all their expenses, was now no longer sufficient for him on his own; and he wondered in amazement how she had managed to provide him with excellent wines and rare delicacies which he could no longer afford on his modest salary.

He incurred a few debts and ran after money in the way people do when they are reduced to desperate shifts. Finally, one morning, finding himself without a sou[2] a whole week before the end of the month, he decided to sell something; and immediately the idea occurred to him of disposing of his wife's "trash." He still harbored a sort of secret grudge against those false gems which had irritated him in the past, and indeed the sight of them every day somewhat spoiled the memory of his beloved. ❹

> ❹ **?** *Describe the circumstances in which Lantin finds himself after his wife's death. What do you predict will happen next?*

He rummaged for a long time among the heap of gaudy trinkets she had left behind, for she had stubbornly gone on buying jewelry until the last days of her life, bringing home a new piece almost every evening. At last he decided on the large necklace which she had seemed to like best, and which, he thought, might well be worth six or seven francs, for it was beautifully made for a piece of paste.[3]

He put it in his pocket and set off for his Ministry, following the boulevards and looking for a jeweler's shop which inspired confidence.

At last he spotted one and went in, feeling a little ashamed of exposing his poverty in this way, and of trying to sell such a worthless article.

"Monsieur," he said to the jeweler, "I would like to know what you think this piece is worth."

The man took the necklace, examined it, turned it over, weighed it, inspected it with a magnifying glass, called his assistant, made a few remarks to him in an undertone, placed the necklace on the counter and looked at it from a distance to gauge the effect.

Monsieur Lantin, embarrassed by all this ritual, was opening his mouth to say: "Oh, I know perfectly well that it isn't worth anything," when the jeweler said: "Monsieur, this necklace is worth between twelve and fifteen thousand francs; but I couldn't buy it unless you told me where it came from."

> ❺ **?** *What astonishing fact does Monsieur Lantin learn from the jeweler? Did you predict this would happen?*

The widower opened his eyes wide and stood there gaping, unable to understand what the jeweler had said. Finally he stammered: "What was that you said? . . . Are you sure?" ❺

The other misunderstood his astonishment and said curtly: "You can go somewhere else and

Vocabulary

incurred (in·kʉrd′) *v.:* brought upon oneself.

Pair of Bracelets, 1815–1840. France. Gilded metal, agates.

Cooper-Hewitt, National Design Museum, Smithsonian Institution. The Decorative Arts Association Acquisitions Fund, 1994-32-3,4.

2. **sou** (so͞o) *n.:* French coin worth about two cents in American currency in the late nineteenth century.
3. **paste** *n.:* kind of glass used to make fake gems.

see if they'll offer you more. In my opinion it's worth fifteen thousand at the most. Come back and see me if you can't find a better price."

Completely dumbfounded, Monsieur Lantin took back his necklace and left the shop, in obedience to a vague desire to be alone and to think.

Once outside, however, he felt an impulse to laugh, and he thought: "The fool! Oh, the fool! But what if I'd taken him at his word? There's a jeweler who can't tell real diamonds from paste!"

And he went into another jeweler's shop at the beginning of the Rue de la Paix. As soon as he saw the necklace, the jeweler exclaimed: "Why, I know that necklace well: it was bought here."

Monsieur Lantin asked in amazement: "How much is it worth?"

"Monsieur, I sold it for twenty-five thousand. I am prepared to buy it back for eighteen thousand once you have told me, in accordance with the legal requirements, how you came to be in possession of it."

This time Monsieur Lantin was dumbfounded. He sat down and said: "But . . . but . . . examine it carefully, Monsieur. Until now I thought it was paste."

"Will you give me your name, Monsieur?" said the jeweler.

"Certainly. My name's Lantin. I'm an official at the Ministry of the Interior, and I live at No. 16, Rue des Martyrs."

The jeweler opened his books, looked for the entry, and said: "Yes, this necklace was sent to Madame Lantin's address, No. 16, Rue des Martyrs, on the 20th of July 1876."

The two men looked into each other's eyes, the clerk speechless with astonishment, the jeweler scenting a thief. Finally the latter said: "Will you leave the necklace with me for twenty-four hours? I'll give you a receipt."

"Why, certainly," stammered Monsieur Lantin. And he went out folding the piece of paper, which he put in his pocket.

Then he crossed the street, walked up it again, noticed that he was going the wrong way, went back as far as the Tuileries, crossed the Seine, realized that he had gone wrong again, and returned to the Champs-Élysées,[4] his mind a complete blank. He tried to think it out, to understand. His wife couldn't have afforded to buy something so valuable—that was certain. But in that case it was a present! A present! But a present from whom? And why was it given her?

He halted in his tracks and remained standing in the middle of the avenue. A horrible doubt crossed his mind. Her? But in that case all the other jewels were presents, too! The earth seemed to be trembling under his feet and a tree in front of him to be falling; he threw up his arms and fell to the ground unconscious. ❻

> ❻ In this paragraph, Lantin has two revelations—the first "horrible," and the second inconceivable.
>
> ? *Re-read the paragraph carefully. What realization causes Lantin to faint?*

He came to his senses in a chemist's shop into which the passersby had carried him. He took a cab home and shut himself up.

He wept bitterly until nightfall, biting on a handkerchief so as not to cry out. Then he went to bed worn out with grief and fatigue and slept like a log.

A ray of sunlight awoke him and he slowly got up to go to his Ministry. It was hard to think of working after such a series of shocks. It occurred to him that he could ask to be excused and he wrote a letter to his superior. Then he remembered that he had to go back to the jeweler's and he blushed with shame. He spent a long time thinking it over, but decided that he could not leave the necklace with that man. So he dressed and went out. ❼

> ❼ The decision Lantin makes in this paragraph seems small, but it is significant.
>
> ? *What decision does he make? What does this decision suggest about Lantin's character?*

It was a fine day and the city seemed to be smiling under the clear blue sky. People were strolling about the streets with their hands in their pockets.

4. **Champs-Élysées** (shänz ā·lē·zā′): elegant boulevard in Paris.

Watching them, Lantin said to himself: "How lucky rich people are! With money you can forget even the deepest of sorrows. You can go where you like, travel, enjoy yourself. Oh, if only I were rich!"

He began to feel hungry, for he had eaten nothing for two days, but his pocket was empty. Then he remembered the necklace. Eighteen thousand francs! Eighteen thousand francs! That was a tidy sum, and no mistake!

When he reached the Rue de la Paix he started walking up and down the pavement opposite the jeweler's shop. Eighteen thousand francs! A score of times he almost went in, but every time shame held him back.

He was hungry, though, very hungry, and he had no money at all. He quickly made up his mind, ran across the street so as not to have any time to think, and rushed into the shop.

As soon as he saw him the jeweler came forward and offered him a chair with smiling politeness. His assistants came into the shop, too, and glanced surreptitiously at Lantin with laughter in their eyes and on their lips.

"I have made inquiries, Monsieur," said the jeweler, "and if you still wish to sell the necklace, I am prepared to pay you the price I offered you."

"Why, certainly," stammered the clerk.

The jeweler took eighteen large bank notes out of a drawer, counted them and handed them to Lantin, who signed a little receipt and with a trembling hand put the money in his pocket.

Then, as he was about to leave the shop, he turned towards the jeweler, who was still smiling, and lowering his eyes said: "I have . . . I have some other jewels which have come to me from . . . from the same legacy. Would you care to buy them from me, too?"

The jeweler bowed.

"Certainly, Monsieur."

One of the assistants went out, unable to contain his laughter; another blew his nose loudly. **8**

> **8**
>
>  *What is really going on in the interaction between Lantin and the clerks at the jewelry store? Why are the clerks smiling and laughing?*

Lantin, red faced and solemn, remained unmoved.

"I will bring them to you," he said.

And he took a cab to go and fetch the jewels.

When he returned to the shop an hour later he still had had nothing to eat. The jeweler and his assistants began examining the jewels one by one, estimating the value of each piece. Almost all of them had been bought at that shop.

Lantin now began arguing about the valuations, lost his temper, insisted on seeing the sales registers, and spoke more and more loudly as the sum increased.

The large diamond earrings were worth twenty thousand francs, the bracelets thirty-five thousand, the brooches, rings, and lockets sixteen thousand, a set of emeralds and sapphires fourteen thousand, and a solitaire pendant on a gold chain forty thousand—making a total sum of one hundred and ninety-six thousand francs.

The jeweler remarked jokingly: "These obviously belonged to a lady who invested all her savings in jewelry."

Lantin replied seriously: "It's as good a way as any of investing one's money."

And he went off after arranging with the jeweler to have a second expert valuation the next day.

Out in the street he looked at the Vendôme column[5] and felt tempted to climb up it as if it were a greasy pole. He felt light enough to play leapfrog with the statue of the Emperor perched up there in the sky.

He went to Voisin's for lunch and ordered wine with his meal at twenty francs a bottle.

Then he took a cab and went for a drive in the Bois.[6] He looked at the other carriages with a

5. **Vendôme** (vän·dōm′) **column:** monument in Paris honoring Napoleon.
6. **Bois** (bwä): Bois de Bologne, a park in Paris.

Vocabulary

surreptitiously (sʉr′əp·tish′əs·lē) *adv.:* in a secret or sneaky way.

Outside the Theatre du Vaudeville by Jean Beraud (detail) (1849–1936).

slightly contemptuous air, longing to call out to the passersby: "I'm a rich man, too! I'm worth two hundred thousand francs!"

Suddenly he remembered his Ministry. He drove there at once, strode into his superior's office, and said: "Monsieur, I have come to resign my post. I have just been left three hundred thousand francs."

He shook hands with his former colleagues and told them some of his plans for the future; then he went off to dine at the Café Anglais.

Finding himself next to a distinguished-looking gentleman, he was unable to refrain from informing him, with a certain coyness, that he had just inherited four hundred thousand francs.

For the first time in his life he was not bored at the theater, and he spent the night with some prostitutes.

Six months later he married again. His second wife was a very virtuous woman, but extremely bad-tempered. She made him very unhappy. 9 ■

9

? *Describe the changes that have come over Lantin. How do you feel about him now?*

Vocabulary

contemptuous (kən·temp′cho͞o·əs) *adj.:* scornful.

Response and Analysis

Reading Check

1. In two or three sentences, describe the Lantins' married life, including the way they met, their feelings about one another, and their economic circumstances.
2. What two tastes of Madame Lantin's does Monsieur Lantin object to?
3. How does the death of his wife affect Monsieur Lantin's standard of living?

Thinking Critically

4. People who know Madame Lantin say, "Happy the man who marries her. Nobody could find a better wife." Evaluate these statements based on what you have **inferred** about Madame Lantin by the end of the story. (Consult your reading notes for help.)
5. Monsieur Lantin suffers a **conflict** about whether to accept the eighteen thousand francs the jeweler offers for the necklace. Why do you think he hesitates? Why do you think he ultimately decides to take the money?
6. Re-read the last paragraph of the story. What is **ironic** about the fact that Monsieur Lantin is unhappy with his second wife? What might this seemingly offhand detail add to the meaning of the story?
7. Maupassant and his fellow realists were intent on using fiction to examine the issues of their day. What particular social problem does "The Jewels" reveal? What cynical idea or insight—what **theme**—does Maupassant express about this social problem?

Comparing Literature

8. Compare Tolstoy's character Pahom (in "How Much Land Does a Man Need?," page 951) with Maupassant's Monsieur Lantin. How does each character's personality contribute to his changing circumstances? What does each writer seem to suggest about nineteenth-century notions of progress and self-improvement?
9. How would this story have ended if it had been written by a Romantic or by a more sentimental writer, not a realist?

Literary Skills Analyze theme. Compare and contrast realist works.

Reading Skills Analyze inferences.

Writing Skills Write a character analysis.

Vocabulary Skills Identify antonyms.

WRITING

A Close Look at Madame Lantin

We are told scarcely anything about Madame Lantin—not even her first name. However, Maupassant gives us some clues that help us to understand her personality, and we can make inferences about her motivations. Write a brief **analysis** of Madame Lantin's character. In your analysis, explain Madame Lantin's motivations, her behavior with her husband, and her seeming lack of guilt. Cite passages from the story to support your analysis.

Vocabulary Development

Antonyms

An **antonym** is a word that has the opposite or nearly the opposite meaning as another word. Choose the *best* antonym for each Vocabulary word.

1. **unpretentious:** (a) modest (b) unattractive (c) snobby
2. **assuage:** (a) upset (b) persuade (c) dismiss
3. **incurred:** (a) argued (b) avoided (c) started
4. **surreptitiously:** (a) forcefully (b) openly (c) cautiously
5. **contemptuous:** (a) tiresome (b) respectful (c) generous

PREVIEW

Reflecting *on the* Literary Period

The Victorian Period: 1832–1901

The selections in this feature were written during the same literary period as the other selections in Collection 6, and they share many of the same ideas and concerns. The Focus Question will guide your reading and help you reflect on important aspects of the period.

Autumn Scene, Leeds (1874) by John Atkinson Grimshaw. Oil on board.

Private Collection, © Bonhams, London, UK.

Think About...

Victorian poets developed a variety of styles and voices to confront the changes and challenges of their day—in particular, the new philosophies and scientific theories that seemed to threaten established religious beliefs. Alfred, Lord Tennyson's elegy *In Memoriam* recounts the crisis of faith brought on by these new theories.

Darker aspects of life pervade the work of Robert Browning. In "Porphyria's Lover," Browning creates a chilling dramatic situation that explores the sinister side of human behavior.

Although the Victorian period was a time of power and stability for Britain, writers toward the end of the century began to express growing skepticism and pessimism about the future. Thomas Hardy's "The Darkling Thrush" confronts the new century with bleak imagery, and "Ah, Are You Digging on My Grave?" undercuts sentimental illusions about love, life, and death. Similarly, A. E. Housman's "When I Was One-and-Twenty" underscores the disillusionment of youth.

Pages 983–1000 cover **Literary Skills** Evaluate the philosophical, political, religious, ethical, and social influences of a historical period.

Focus Question

As you read each selection, keep in mind this Focus Question and take notes to help you answer it at the end of the feature:

How does poetry of the Victorian period reflect beliefs in divine order and progress, as well as express spiritual doubt and pessimism about the future?

from In Memoriam A.H.H.
Crossing the Bar

Meet the Writer **Alfred, Lord Tennyson** (1809–1892) was the most popular poet of his age. Tourists hung around his house on the Isle of Wight and climbed trees to get a glimpse of him. Tennyson wrote lyrics, dramatic monologues, plays, poetic narratives, elegies, and allegories in which he evoked moods and states of mind that his Victorian readers identified with. He also had a superb mastery of the sounds and rhythms of the English language, and once remarked that he knew the metrical weight of every English word except *scissors*. The poet W. H. Auden said that Tennyson had "the finest ear, perhaps, of any English poet."

(For more information about Alfred, Lord Tennyson, see page 894.)

Background *In Memoriam* (Latin for "in memory of") is Tennyson's elegy for Arthur Henry Hallam, his closest friend at Cambridge and his sister's fiancé. In the 131 separate lyrics of this elegy, written over seventeen years, Tennyson asks and gradually answers profound questions about life and death, religion and science, and the immortality of the soul. Tennyson considered *In Memoriam* so intensely personal that he didn't plan to publish it; however, in 1850 he did finally publish what is often considered his masterpiece.

"Crossing the Bar" was not the last poem Tennyson wrote, but before his death he directed that it be printed at the end of all editions of his collected verse. Written when Tennyson was eighty, the poem is filled with echoes of his earlier work and shows that indeed his poetic powers had not diminished.

CONNECTING TO THE
Focus Question

As you read Tennyson's poems, ask yourself: What doubts, questions, and worries does Tennyson express, and how are they resolved?

from In Memoriam A.H.H.

Alfred, Lord Tennyson

55

The wish, that of the living whole
No life may fail beyond the grave,
Derives it not from what we have
The likest God within the soul?

Are God and Nature then at strife,
That Nature lends such evil dreams?
So careful of the type° she seems,
So careless of the single life,

That I, considering everywhere
Her secret meaning in her deeds,
And finding that of fifty seeds
She often brings but one to bear,

7. **type:** species.

I falter where I firmly trod,
And falling with my weight of cares
Upon the great world's altar stairs
That slope through darkness up to God,

I stretch lame hands of faith, and grope,
And gather dust and chaff, and call
To what I feel is Lord of all,
And faintly trust the larger hope.°

56

"So careful of the type?" but no.
From scarpèd° cliff and quarried stone
She° cries, "A thousand types are gone;
I care for nothing, all shall go.

"Thou makest thine appeal to me:
I bring to life, I bring to death;
The spirit does but mean the breath:
I know no more." And he, shall he,

20. larger hope: Tennyson explains this phrase in his *Memoirs:* "that the whole human race would through, perhaps, ages of suffering, be at length purified and saved."

2. scarpèd: eroded to a steep slope.
3. She: Nature.

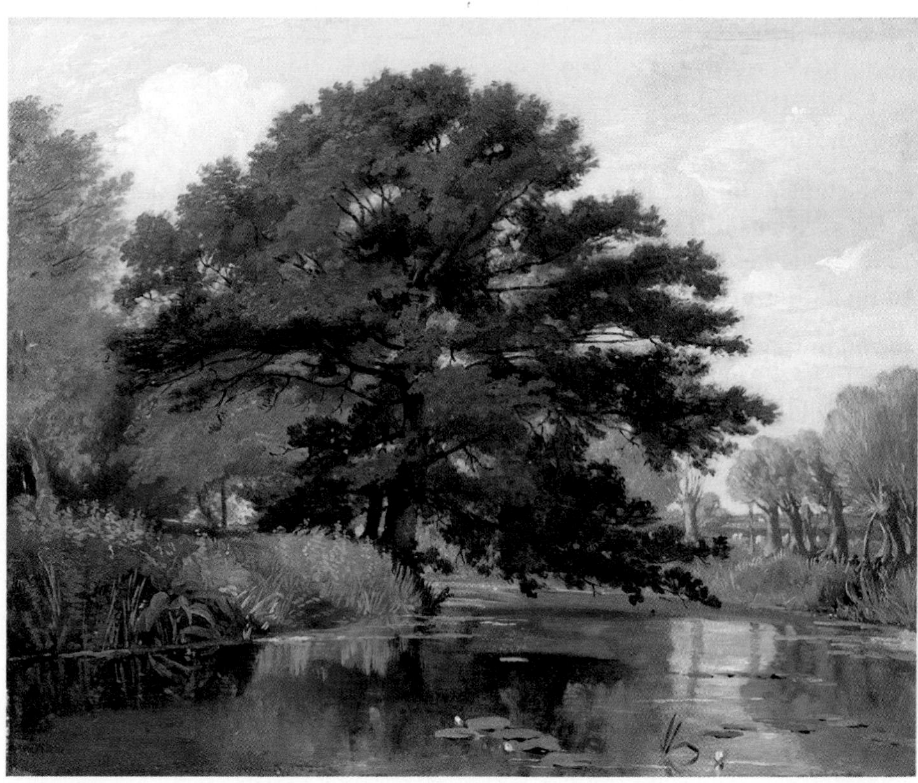

On the Isis, Waterperry, Oxfordshire (1806) by William Alfred Delamotte. Oil on panel.

Man, her last work, who seemed so fair,
    Such splendid purpose in his eyes,
    Who rolled the psalm to wintry skies,
Who built him fanes° of fruitless prayer,

Who trusted God was love indeed
    And love Creation's final law—
    Though Nature, red in tooth and claw°
With ravine, shrieked against his creed—

Who loved, who suffered countless ills,
    Who battled for the True, the Just,
    Be blown about the desert dust,
Or sealed within the iron hills?°

No more? A monster then, a dream,
    A discord. Dragons of the prime,
    That tare° each other in their slime,
Were mellow music matched with him.

O life as futile, then, as frail!
    O for thy° voice to soothe and bless!
    What hope of answer, or redress?
Behind the veil, behind the veil.°

12. fanes: temples.

15. red . . . claw: The phrase refers to the view of all life as a ruthless struggle for survival.

20. sealed . . . hills: preserved like fossils in rock.

23. tare: archaic for "tore."

26. thy: Hallam's.

28. veil: the veil of death.

95

By night we lingered on the lawn,
    For underfoot the herb was dry;
    And genial warmth; and o'er the sky
The silvery haze of summer drawn;

And calm that let the tapers° burn
    Unwavering: Not a cricket chirred;
    The brook alone far off was heard,
and on the board the fluttering urn.°

And bats went round in fragrant skies,
    And wheeled or lit the filmy shapes°
    That haunt the dusk, with ermine capes
And woolly breasts and beaded eyes;

While now we sang old songs that pealed
    From knoll to knoll, where, couched at ease,
    The white kine° glimmered, and the trees
Laid their dark arms about the field.

But when those others, one by one,
    Withdrew themselves from me and night,
    And in the house light after light
Went out, and I was all alone,

5. tapers: candles.

8. fluttering urn: teapot or coffee urn heated by a candle.
10. filmy shapes: moths.

15. kine: archaic for "cattle."

A hunger seized my heart; I read
   Of that glad year which once had been,
   In those fallen leaves which kept their green,
The noble letters of the dead.

And strangely on the silence broke
   The silent-speaking words, and strange
   Was love's dumb cry defying change
To test his worth; and strangely spoke

The faith, the vigor, bold to dwell
   On doubts that drive the coward back,
   And keen through wordy snares to track
Suggestion to her inmost cell.

So word by word, and line by line,
   The dead man touched me from the past,
   And all at once it seemed at last
The living soul° was flashed on mine,

And mine in this was wound, and whirled
   About empyreal° heights of thought,
   And came on that which is, and caught
The deep pulsations of the world,

Aeonian° music measuring out
   The steps of Time—the shocks of Chance—
   The blows of Death. At length my trance
Was canceled, stricken through with doubt.

Vague words! but ah, how hard to frame
   In matter-molded forms of speech,
   Or even for intellect to reach
Through memory that which I became;

Till now the doubtful dusk revealed
   The knolls once more where, couched at ease,
   The white kine glimmered, and the trees
Laid their dark arms about the field;

And sucked from out the distant gloom
   A breeze began to tremble o'er
   The large leaves of the sycamore,
And fluctuate all the still perfume,

And gathering freshlier overhead
   Rocked the full-foliaged elms, and swung
   The heavy-folded rose, and flung
The lilies to and fro, and said,

36. the living soul: Originally, the phrase read "his living soul." Tennyson said he changed it because he wanted the soul to be not Hallam's but the soul of "the Deity, maybe."
38. empyreal (em·pir′ē·əl): heavenly.
41. aeonian (ē·ō′nē·ən): eternal.

"The dawn, the dawn," and died away;
  And East and West, without a breath,
  Mixed their dim lights, like life and death,
To broaden into boundless day.

130

Thy° voice is on the rolling air;
  I hear thee where the waters run;
  Thou standest in the rising sun,
And in the setting thou art fair.

What art thou then? I cannot guess;
  But though I seem in star and flower
  To feel thee some diffusive power,
I do not therefore love thee less.

My love involves the love before;
  My love is vaster passion now;
  Though mixed with God and Nature thou,
I seem to love thee more and more.

Far off thou art, but ever nigh;
  I have thee still, and I rejoice;
  I prosper, circled with thy voice;
I shall not lose thee though I die.

1. **thy:** Hallam's.

Response and Analysis

Thinking Critically

1. In Lyric 55, why does the speaker envision the possibility that God and Nature may be "at strife" (line 5)? What complaint does the poem's speaker voice against Nature? How does Nature answer this complaint in Lyric 56?
2. Describe the **setting** at the beginning of Lyric 95. How does this setting contrast with the setting at the end of the poem?
3. Compare the aspects of Nature described in Lyrics 55 and 56 with those in Lyric 130. What difference is there?
4. Lyric 95 moves from a local scene to "empyreal heights of thought" (line 38) and back to the original scene. How is this movement related to the speaker's **mood** in Lyrics 55 and 56 as well as in Lyric 130?
5. Explain the **paradox,** or apparent contradiction, in line 16 of Lyric 130.
6. Using details from the poem, respond to **Connecting to the Focus Question** on page 984.

Extending and Evaluating

7. *In Memoriam* was so popular because it satisfied readers who believed poetry should deal with serious subjects, such as grieving. Do you agree or disagree with such expectations for poetry? What do you think are the proper functions of poetry?

"Crossing the Bar" has been praised as a poem in which every image can be seen to have a double meaning. The images of a sea voyage were fresh in Tennyson's mind because he penned this poem in 1889 while crossing the channel that separates the Isle of Wight from the southern coast of England.

Hove Beach (1824) by John Constable (1776–1837). Oil on paper on panel.

Crossing the Bar

Alfred, Lord Tennyson

Sunset and evening star,
    And one clear call for me!
And may there be no moaning of the bar,
    When I put out to sea,

But such a tide as moving seems asleep,
    Too full for sound and foam,
When that° which drew from out the boundless deep
    Turns again home.

Twilight and evening bell,
    And after that the dark!
And may there be no sadness of farewell,
    When I embark;

For though from out our bourne° of Time and Place
    The flood may bear me far,
I hope to see my Pilot face to face
    When I have crossed the bar.

7. **that:** the soul.

13. **bourne** (bōrn): archaic for "boundary."

Response and Analysis

Thinking Critically

1. Tennyson uses the experience of a sailor embarking on a long voyage as a **metaphor,** or comparison, for life. Use details from the poem to explain how Tennyson extends his metaphor.
2. Who might the "Pilot" in line 15 be? Why do you think the word is capitalized?
3. Paraphrase each of the speaker's wishes and hopes, and explain what they show about the speaker's feelings. Is the speaker accepting, afraid, or both?
4. What overall **mood,** or emotion, does Tennyson create in this poem?
5. Using details from the poem, respond to **Connecting to the Focus Question** on page 984.

Porphyria's Lover

Meet the Writer While he was living in Italy, **Robert Browning** (1812–1889) published *Men and Women* (1855), a collection of poetry reflecting his interest in the Italian Renaissance. In this volume, Browning uses the soliloquies in Shakespeare's plays and the poems of John Donne as models for his dramatic monologues, the form of poetry for which he is best known.

Browning's experimentation with different styles challenged the traditions of most English poetry. He uses informal diction, surprising rhymes, and harsh rhythms to expose readers to the unpredictable minds of his speakers. Browning's interest in the workings of the human mind influenced the poetry of the twentieth century.

(For more information about Robert Browning, see page 907.)

Background Like the American writer Edgar Allan Poe, Browning had a taste for morbid psychology; he once accused his wife, Elizabeth Barrett Browning, of lacking "a scientific interest in evil." In "Porphyria's Lover," he pursues that interest, exploring the complexity of human motivation.

In his **dramatic monologues,** Browning does not pass judgment on his speakers. Rather, he involves us in their desires and actions and leaves us to pass judgment on what we have experienced.

April Love (1855–1856) by Arthur Hughes (1832–1915). Oil on canvas. 88.9 × 49.5 cm.

Tate Gallery, London, Great Britain.

CONNECTING TO THE
Focus Question

As you read the following selection, ask yourself: How does "Porphyria's Lover" reflect Browning's interest in the dark side of human psychology?

Porphyria's Lover

Robert Browning

The rain set early in tonight,
The sullen wind was soon awake,
It tore the elm tops down for spite,
And did its worst to vex the lake:
I listened with heart fit to break.
When glided in Porphyria; straight
She shut the cold out and the storm,
And kneeled and made the cheerless grate
Blaze up, and all the cottage warm;
Which done, she rose, and from her form
Withdrew the dripping cloak and shawl,
And laid her soiled gloves by, untied
Her hat and let the damp hair fall,
And, last, she sat down by my side
And called me. When no voice replied,
She put my arm about her waist,
And made her smooth white shoulder bare,
And all her yellow hair displaced,
And, stooping, made my cheek lie there,
And spread, o'er all, her yellow hair,
Murmuring how she loved me—she
Too weak, for all her heart's endeavor,
To set its struggling passion free
From pride, and vainer ties dissever,°
And give herself to me forever.
But passion sometimes would prevail,
Nor could tonight's gay feast restrain
A sudden thought of one so pale
For love of her, and all in vain:
So, she was come through wind and rain.
Be sure I looked up at her eyes
Happy and proud; at last I knew
Porphyria worshipped me: Surprise
Made my heart swell, and still it grew
While I debated what to do.
That moment she was mine, mine, fair,
Perfectly pure and good: I found
A thing to do, and all her hair
In one long yellow string I wound
Three times her little throat around,
And strangled her. No pain felt she;
I am quite sure she felt no pain.

24. dissever: separate.

As a shut bud that holds a bee,
I warily oped° her lids; again
Laughed the blue eyes without a stain.
And I untightened next the tress
About her neck; her cheek once more
Blushed bright beneath my burning kiss:
I propped her head up as before,
Only, this time my shoulder bore
Her head, which droops upon it still;
The smiling rosy little head,
So glad it has its utmost will,
That all it scorned at once is fled,
And I, its love, am gained instead!
Porphyria's love: She guessed not how
Her darling one wish would be heard.
And thus we sit together now,
And all night long we have not stirred,
And yet God has not said a word!

44. oped: archaic for "opened."

April Love (detail) (1855–1856) by Arthur Hughes (1832–1915). Oil on canvas. 88.9 × 49.5 cm.

Tate Gallery, London, Great Britain.

Response and Analysis

Thinking Critically

1. What are the speaker's different **moods,** or emotions, in the poem?

2. What reasons does the speaker give for strangling Porphyria?

3. What leads the speaker to assert that Porphyria "felt no pain"? What do you think of this claim?

4. "And yet God has not said a word!" is the last line of the poem. Why does the speaker expect God to say something? What does this line tell you about the speaker's **character** and his awareness of what he has done?

5. "Porphyria's Lover" was originally published with another monologue under the title *Madhouse Cells,* a title that points to the poem's **setting.** How does knowledge of that setting affect your interpretation of the poem?

6. Using details from the poem, respond to **Connecting to the Focus Question** on page 990.

Extending and Evaluating

7. Judging from this poem, how do you think Browning might have viewed the legal plea "not guilty by reason of insanity"? What details in the poem make you think so?

The Darkling Thrush
Ah, Are You Digging on My Grave?

Meet the Writer Thomas Hardy (1840–1928) was one of the principal novelists of late-Victorian Britain, but he began and ended his literary career as a poet.

Hardy was born in a small village in Dorsetshire, an area in southwestern England, which was the setting (under its ancient name of Wessex) of many of his novels and poems. He attended the village school until he was sixteen, when he was apprenticed to an architect.

In 1862, Hardy began working as an architect in London, writing poems and stories in his free time. He tried without success to publish his poems, but by the time he returned to Dorset in 1867, he had started to publish fiction. After the publication of his fourth novel, *Far from the Madding Crowd* (1874), Hardy was able to stop working as an architect and devote himself entirely to writing.

The plots and themes of Hardy's fourteen novels express his belief in a world governed by chance and natural laws that are indifferent to what humans want and deserve. In some novels, the entire course of a character's life is determined by coincidence. To chance and the indifference of nature, humans add the misery of war, the cruelty of ingratitude and neglect, and the irrationality of laws and customs that frustrate talent and desire.

The bleakness, pessimism, and irony of Hardy's novels disturbed many readers. After *Tess of the D'Urbervilles* received unfavorable reviews in 1892 and *Jude the Obscure* was denounced in 1895, Hardy turned away from novel writing for good.

Hardy published *Wessex Poems* in 1898, when he was in his late fifties. The tone and style of Hardy's poems differs from that of earlier Victorian writers. His work reveals a late-Victorian mood of somberness, with language that has a colloquial directness. He frequently uses archaic words or homely diction in a reaction against the elaborate language of some late-Victorian verse. Hardy's verse, though deceptively simple, resounds with the voice of twentieth-century poetry.

CONNECTING TO THE
Focus Question

As you read, consider this question: What do these poems reveal about Hardy's attitudes toward nature, death, and the future of humanity?

"The Darkling Thrush" was written on December 31, 1900, the last day of the nineteenth century. As night falls, the speaker in the poem hears a thrush (a bird) singing joyfully. His thrush, like the century, is worn out and diminished—but still singing.

The Darkling Thrush

Thomas Hardy

I leant upon a coppice° gate
　　When Frost was specter-gray,
And Winter's dregs made desolate
　　The weakening eye of day.
The tangled bine-stems° scored the sky
　　Like strings of broken lyres,
And all mankind that haunted nigh
　　Had sought their household fires.

The land's sharp features seemed to be
　　The Century's corpse outleant,°
His crypt the cloudy canopy,
　　The wind his death-lament.
The ancient pulse of germ° and birth
　　Was shrunken hard and dry,
And every spirit upon earth
　　Seemed fervorless as I.

At once a voice arose among
　　The bleak twigs overhead
In a fullhearted evensong
　　Of joy illimited;
An aged thrush, frail, gaunt, and small,
　　In blast-beruffled plume,
Had chosen thus to fling his soul
　　Upon the growing gloom.

So little cause for carolings
　　Of such ecstatic sound
Was written on terrestrial things
　　Afar or nigh around,
That I could think there trembled through
　　His happy good-night air
Some blessed Hope, whereof he knew
　　And I was unaware.

1. coppice: thicket of small trees or shrubs.

5. bine-stems: climbing plants.

10. outleant: leaning out. Here, the word refers to leaning out of the crypt.

13. germ: seed or bud.

Thrushes by Fred Cuming (b. 1930). Private Collection.

Response and Analysis

Thinking Critically

1. What details in the first stanza establish the **setting** for the poem? Describe what you see.
2. At what point in the poem is the thrush introduced? How does the bird first come to the attention of the speaker?
3. Does the speaker's **mood,** or emotions, change significantly in the course of the poem? If so, how?
4. What do you think is the significance of the word *darkling* in the title? Do you think the thrush's song seems hopeful or hopeless? Explain.
5. Using details from the poem, respond to **Connecting to the Focus Question** on page 993.

Extending and Evaluating

6. The speaker in "The Darkling Thrush" seems to feel little hope that the problems of the world can ever be solved. What problems in today's society do you consider to be so large and overwhelming as to be insoluble? Explain.

"Ah, Are You Digging on My Grave?" is written in the form of a dialogue. The poem's speaker has only limited information about her situation—and she therefore receives some very unexpected answers to her repeated questions.

Ah, Are You Digging on My Grave?

Thomas Hardy

"Ah, are you digging on my grave,
　　My loved one?—planting rue?"°
—"No: Yesterday he went to wed
One of the brightest wealth has bred.
'It cannot hurt her now,' he said,
　　'That I should not be true.'"

"Then who is digging on my grave?
　　My nearest dearest kin?"
—"Ah, no: They sit and think, 'What use!
What good will planting flowers produce?
No tendance of her mound can loose
　　Her spirit from Death's gin.'"°

2. rue: yellow-flowered herb associated with grief.

12. gin: trap.

Give a Dog a Bone (1888) (board) by William Henry Hamilton Trood (1860–99).

"But some one digs upon my grave?
My enemy?—prodding sly?"
—"Nay: When she heard you had passed the Gate
That shuts on all flesh soon or late,
She thought you no more worth her hate,
And cares not where you lie."

"Then, who is digging on my grave?
Say—since I have not guessed!"
—"O it is I, my mistress dear,
Your little dog, who still lives near,
And much I hope my movements here
Have not disturbed your rest?"

"Ah, yes! *You* dig upon my grave . . .
Why flashed it not on me
That one true heart was left behind!
What feeling do we ever find
To equal among human kind
A dog's fidelity!"

"Mistress, I dug upon your grave
To bury a bone, in case
I should be hungry near this spot
When passing on my daily trot.
I am sorry, but I quite forgot
It was your resting place."

Response and Analysis

Thinking Critically

1. Where in the poem is the identity of the second speaker revealed?
2. In the first three stanzas, what information about the dead woman's life do you get from her guesses and from the dog's answers?
3. In the final stanza, how does the dog's answer combine animal traits with qualities we consider human?
4. How does Hardy use **anticlimax,** the occurrence of something trivial when something serious is expected, in each of the first three stanzas?
5. Describe the **tone** of the poem. How do you think Hardy feels about sentimental attitudes toward death?
6. Using details from the poem, respond to **Connecting to the Focus Question** on page 993.

Extending and Evaluating

7. Hardy's poem may be seen as a satire on conventional romantic attitudes toward death. What examples can you think of from literature, film, television, or music that express a similarly unsentimental, even humorous, view of death?

When I Was One-and-Twenty

Meet the Writer In his own lifetime **A. E. Housman** (1859–1936) was highly admired as a lyric poet, although his reputation was based on a slim collection of sixty-three lyrics, *A Shropshire Lad,* published in 1896. He did not publish again for twenty-six years.

Housman was a gifted classical scholar whose lyrics reveal the influence of his interest in Greek and Roman poetry. Many of these poems have a wistful, ironic tone—the theme of *A Shropshire Lad* is ***carpe diem,*** "seize the day." This philosophy advises us to enjoy life and its pleasures while we can, because death may come quickly.

(For more information about A. E. Housman, see page 925.)

Background "When I Was One-and-Twenty" is from *A Shropshire Lad.* Housman described the Shropshire lad as "an imaginary figure, with something of my own temper and view of life." This brief lyric is a good example of Housman's ability to compress much meaning into a few lines. The poem clearly shows Housman's characteristic simplicity of form, meticulous expression of emotion, directness, and melodic beauty.

CONNECTING TO THE
Focus Question

As you read, think about this question: How would you describe Housman's tone on the subjects of love and loss in this poem?

When I Was One-and-Twenty

A. E. Housman

When I was one-and-twenty
  I heard a wise man say,
"Give crowns and pounds and guineas°
  But not your heart away;
Give pearls away and rubies
  But keep your fancy free."
But I was one-and-twenty,
  No use to talk to me.

When I was one-and-twenty
  I heard him say again,
"The heart out of the bosom
  Was never given in vain;
'Tis paid with sighs a plenty
  And sold for endless rue."°
And I am two-and-twenty,
  And oh, 'tis true, 'tis true.

3. **crowns and pounds and guineas:** units of money in Great Britain.

14. **rue:** sorrow; regret.

The Sonnet (1839) by William Mulready (1786–1863).

Victoria and Albert Museum, London, Great Britain.

Response and Analysis

Thinking Critically

1. What was the speaker's first reaction to the advice he was given? How does he feel about the advice now that he is a year older?
2. What must have happened to the speaker to make him change his mind?
3. What is the effect of Housman's use of **repetition** in the last line of the poem? What other kinds of repetition do you find in the poem?
4. What do you think is the poem's **theme,** or message? Do you think Housman is being serious or humorous in his attitude toward falling in love?
5. Using details from the poem, respond to **Connecting to the Focus Question** on page 998.

Extending and Evaluating

6. Do you agree or disagree with the wise man's advice in this poem—that it is better to give away money than to give away your heart? What would you say in reply? Explain your response.

REVIEW

Reflecting on the Literary Period

The Victorian Period: 1832–1901

The following questions ask you to compare and analyze the selections in this feature and respond to the Focus Question. Where possible, cite passages from the selections to support your answers.

Comparing Literature

1. The poet T. S. Eliot said of Tennyson's *In Memoriam* that it can be considered a religious poem not "because of the quality of its faith, but because of the quality of its doubt." Considering Eliot's comment, in what way can "Crossing the Bar" also be considered a religious poem? What similarities do you see between the ideas expressed in Lyric 130 and "Crossing the Bar"?
2. Examine your reactions to the speakers in Browning's **dramatic monologues** "My Last Duchess" (page 909) and "Porphyria's Lover." How does Browning engage your interest despite the speakers' negative qualities?
3. Thomas Hardy wrote "The Darkling Thrush" and Matthew Arnold wrote "Dover Beach" (page 922) well before the onslaught of the twentieth century's two world wars. Do you think the poems are prophetic? Explain.
4. Compare the use of **irony** in Hardy's "Ah, Are You Digging on My Grave?" and in Housman's "When I Was One-and-Twenty." What similarities or differences do you see in the **tone** of each poem?

Pages 983–1000 cover **Literary Skills** Evaluate the philosophical, political, religious, ethical, and social influences of a historical period.

RESPONDING TO THE

Focus Question

Review your notes and responses related to the Focus Question for this feature. Using details from the selections, write your answer to the question.

How does poetry of the Victorian period reflect beliefs in divine order and progress, as well as express spiritual doubt and pessimism about the future?

READ ON: FOR INDEPENDENT READING

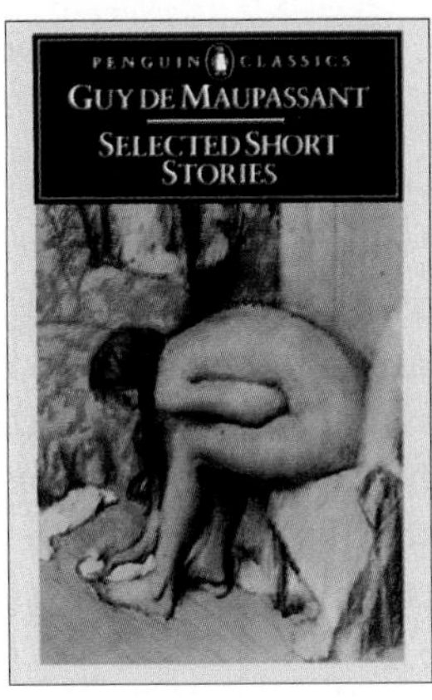

FICTION

Telling It Like It Is

Guy de Maupassant depicts all aspects of French society—from the hardships faced by the Norman peasantry to the private lives of the middle class—with unflinching clarity and accuracy. Rich in atmosphere and loaded with candor, his ***Selected Short Stories*** takes us from battlefield to parlor, featuring subjects that range from the Franco-Prussian War to domestic skirmishes, revealing a world that is still very recognizable today.

NONFICTION

A Peek at Victorian Private Lives

Welcome to nineteenth-century England! In ***What Jane Austen Ate and Charles Dickens Knew,*** Daniel Pool gives new life to the daily routines of the Victorian period. Both the nitty-gritty details (How did they keep clean?) and the posh etiquette (How did one address a duke?) of the time are covered. Find out what the Victorians ate, what they wore, how they traveled, and whom they married.

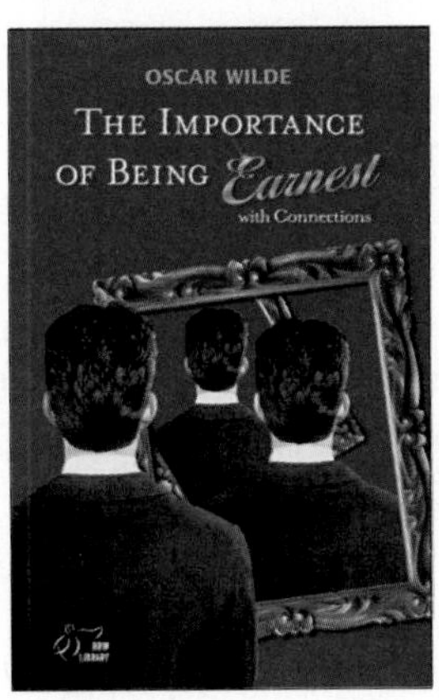

DRAMA

Found in a Handbag

Much of the satire in Oscar Wilde's play ***The Importance of Being Earnest*** is targeted at the British class system. Wilde openly defied Victorian ideas of respectability and presented his own philosophy as an alternative. The seemingly contradictory logic of the play is part of that philosophy: "The truth is rarely pure and never simple."

This title is available in the HRW Library.

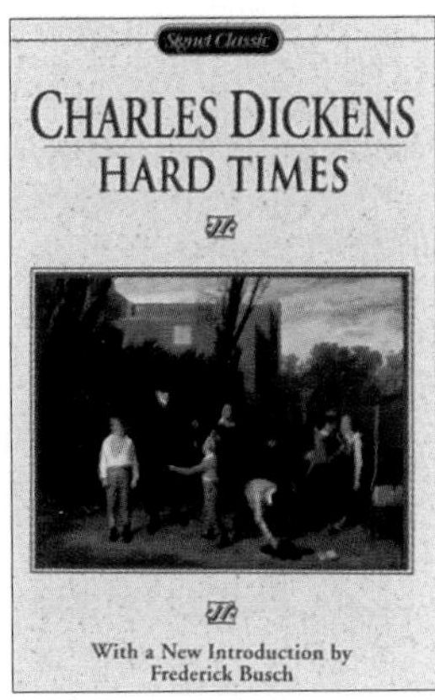

FICTION

Just the Facts

Set in Coketown, an imaginary industrial city in northern England, Charles Dickens's ***Hard Times*** is a harsh criticism of the dark side of the Industrial Revolution and of the materialist notion that concrete facts and things make up the only true reality. In this world that is populated by the likes of Professor Gradgrind and Mr. McChoakumchild, relentless lovers of facts, imagination is not tolerated. Gradgrind is forced to acknowledge the folly of his beliefs, however, as his children attempt to live up to his expectations and only make messes of their lives.

Comparing and Contrasting Literature

Writing Assignment
Write an essay of 1,500 words in which you compare and contrast two pieces of literature from the same historical period.

Now that you've just read several literary works from the Victorian period (1832–1901), you've probably discovered that one of the best ways to become familiar with a particular era in history is to read its literature. Novels, short stories, poems, essays, and plays reflect in some ways the ideas and concerns of their times. In this workshop you'll write an essay **comparing and contrasting two literary works** from the same historical period and relating them to the major issues of their era.

Prewriting

Choose Your Subjects

Variations on a Theme What period in history intrigues you? What literature of a particular era invites your curiosity—the narratives of the Anglo-Saxon period, the poetry of the Renaissance, or the stories of prerevolutionary Russia? To choose a subject for your essay, first select a historical era for study by paging through the sections in this book, scanning a history book, or asking your teacher or librarian for ideas. Then, look through literature anthologies to find two works of literature from the same genre—short stories, poems, plays, or sections of novels—that belong to that historical time period. For example, one student chose to compare and contrast Leo Tolstoy's "How Much Land Does a Man Need?" (page 951) and Anton Chekhov's "The Bet" (page 967) because the authors of the two short stories were Russian contemporaries who wrote during a fascinating period of history.

Analyze the Literature

Break It Down Carefully read the works you've selected, and take notes on the **literary elements—setting, characters, plot,** and **theme.** Then, ask yourself, "How do the literary elements relate to a major issue of the historical time period?" (If you need to do research for information about the major issues of the time period, use the usual research sources—your textbooks, the library, or the Internet.) Chart your analysis to see similarities and differences in the two pieces of literature. For example, the chart on the next page shows how one student analyzed the literary elements of two short stories and speculated on an issue behind them. Notice that his speculation is related to the theme of the two works.

Writing Skills
Write an essay comparing and contrasting two literary works.

Literary Element	"The Bet"	"How Much Land . . . ?"
Setting	The home of a wealthy Russian banker	The countryside of southern Russia
Characters	A wealthy banker and a twenty-five-year-old lawyer	Pahom, a peasant in a village
Plot	After arguing over capital punishment versus life imprisonment, the banker and the lawyer make a wager of two million dollars.	Pahom, foolishly claiming that with enough land he would not fear the devil himself, becomes obsessed with land acquisition.
Theme	The quality of human life can't be measured by money, as both the banker and lawyer learn.	Unchecked greed produces a death of the human spirit and, as Pahom learns too late, sometimes a literal death.

Issue: Both stories, written during the end of czarist Russia, address the value of human possessions and wealth—an important issue in a country with such a vast difference between serfs (who owned nothing) and aristocrats (who owned everything).

Break It Down Even Further Nothing is ever as simple as it first seems, and the same is true for literary analysis. Writers incorporate **ambiguities** (lines or words that may have more than one interpretation), **nuances** (changes in tone), and **complexities** (rich but difficult ideas) into their prose and poetry. With literary analysis, readers unwrap layers of meaning with each reading. To help you discover the many dimensions of literature, analyze the **stylistic devices** in the works you're comparing. Examine how the writers use devices such as tone, imagery, figures of speech, concrete sensory details, repetition, and irony. Ask yourself, "What effects do these devices create, and how do these effects add to the development of the literary elements?" Chart your answers. For example, the student comparing the Russian short stories noted that irony is integral to the theme in each.

Reference Note

For more on **stylistic devices,** see page 543.

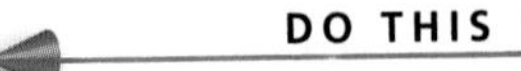

Develop a Thesis

Make a Claim Look back over your notes about the literary elements and stylistic devices. Draw a conclusion about how three or more literary elements, stylistic devices, or a combination of elements and devices develop the historical issue you've identified. This conclusion will be your preliminary **thesis statement**—a statement that shows your comprehensive understanding of the significant ideas in the works and of the historical period.

Take a look at one student's thesis statement on the next page. His thesis statement not only identifies the elements and stylistic devices that develop the issue, it also makes clear that he'll focus on the similarities of the two works.

Writing Skills
Analyze the literary works.
Develop a thesis statement.

TIP Include in your thesis statement or in your introduction the titles and authors of the works you've analyzed. Also, use the **literary present** in your discussion. For more on the **literary present tense,** see Tenses and Their Uses, 3b–c, in the Language Handbook.

> Both Chekhov's "The Bet" and Tolstoy's "How Much Land Does a Man Need?" use character, plot, and irony to bring out a similar theme—the human folly of acquiring possessions and wealth, an important issue in post-czarist Russia.

Gather Support

Proof Positive The literary elements, stylistic devices, or the combination you selected will be the key points of your essay. Develop and support these key points with accurate and detailed references to the texts. This **literary evidence** takes the form of **direct quotations** from the text, **paraphrases** of passages or scenes, and **summaries** of events. Add a page number in parentheses to document the source for each direct quotation. Although most of your literary evidence will come from the two works you're comparing and contrasting, you might consult additional sources for background information about the historical time period or for more facts about each writer. Document these additional sources also.

Reference Note

For more on **quotations, paraphrases, summaries,** and **documenting sources,** see pages 244, 245, and 247.

When you present your evidence, **elaborate** on it—tell what it means and how it proves your viewpoint. Look at the example below to see how one student elaborated on a piece of evidence.

Summary

Elaboration

> In "The Bet," a young lawyer, only twenty-five years old, accepts a two-million-dollar bet that he will not be able to endure fifteen years of willing imprisonment. His desire for money clouds his judgment and drives this sacrifice.

Organize Your Support

DO THIS

Get It in Order After you've gathered support, arrange the information so that you develop your perspective with strong organizational strategies. Make sure that the patterns and relationships of the information are clear to your readers. The two basic methods for organizing a comparison-contrast essay are the block method and the point-by-point method. In the **block method,** discuss all the key points of one literary piece, then all the key points of the other. In the **point-by-point method,** discuss each key point as it applies first to one literary piece, then the other. You may use one or the other or combine the two, but make sure you provide adequate transitions so that your readers can follow your line of reasoning.

Writing Skills
Gather and organize evidence.

PRACTICE & APPLY 1 Use the information on the previous pages to choose and analyze two literary works from the same historical era. Compare and contrast the two works; then, write a thesis statement. Gather support for your thesis, and organize it, providing transitions between your ideas.

Writing

Comparing and Contrasting Literature

A Writer's Framework

Introduction

- Provide background information for the historical period.
- Name the titles and authors of the literature.
- Use a clear thesis statement to identify the issue, key points, and your focus on similarities, differences, or both.

Body

- Develop each of the key points of your thesis.
- Use literary evidence and elaboration as support for each of your key points.
- Clarify your method of organization—block, point-by-point, or a combination.

Conclusion

- Summarize the key points about each work of literature.
- Restate your thesis.
- Close with a final, dramatic statement.

A Writer's Model

When a Man's Grasp Exceeds His Reach

INTRODUCTION
Background information

The latter part of the nineteenth century was a time of dramatic change for Russia. Millions of serfs, who until 1861 were the property of landowners, were emancipated. The country's intellectuals celebrated this reform, as well as other reforms in society, politics, and the judicial system. Therefore, the literature of this period does more than entertain; it comments on society and offers moral instruction. Anton Chekhov (1860–1904), grandson of a serf, and Leo Tolstoy (1828–1910), aristocrat, were from opposite ends of the Russian economic spectrum; yet both writers felt very deeply the ironies that life had presented them. Both Chekhov's short story "The Bet" and Tolstoy's short story "How Much Land Does a Man Need?" use character, plot, and irony to bring out a similar theme—the human folly of acquiring possessions and wealth, an important issue in czarist Russia.

Names of authors

Thesis statement
Titles of stories
Historical issue

BODY
Key point: Character
Evidence: Summary

The main characters of both stories are willing to go to great extremes to obtain the things they think will make them happy. In "The Bet," a young lawyer, only twenty-five-years old, accepts a two-million-dollar bet that he will not be able to endure fifteen years of willing imprisonment. His desire for money clouds his judgment and drives this sacrifice. In "How Much Land Does a Man Need?" an ambitious, land-hungry peasant goes to great lengths to acquire more

Elaboration
Evidence: Summary

(continued)

(continued)

land. He alienates friends, inconveniences his family, and makes move after move to satisfy his greed for a huge tract of land he can own and farm. He first journeys down the Volga River, then walks over three hundred miles only to leave and hurry over to the faraway land of the Bashkirs, hungry for their rich prairie farmland. Nothing seems ultimately to satisfy him.

Elaboration

Key point: Plot
Evidence: Summary
Evidence: Direct quotation
Elaboration
Evidence: Direct quotation
Elaboration

The developments of each story's plot intensify the inevitability of the characters' fate. The young lawyer endures years of desperate imprisonment. Searching for the life experiences he has forfeited, he reads insatiably, like "a man swimming in the sea among the wreckage of his ship and trying to save his life by greedily clutching first at one spar and then at another"(970). Yet no book can ease the young lawyer's painful life. The lawyer lives vicariously the life he has denied himself for his own greed. Similarly, Pahom in "How Much Land Does a Man Need?" desperately yearns to become a landowner, thinking that "his heart would fill with joy" (953). However, that very desire to own land and his subsequent actions put him on an inevitable course of destruction.

Key point: Irony
Evidence: Summary
Evidence: Direct quotation
Evidence: Summary
Evidence: Summary
Elaboration

The resolution in both stories reveals the sharp irony with which the authors viewed the actions of the characters. The night before he is to be released, almost having won the wager, the lawyer denounces the importance of the money, calling everything "worthless, fleeting, illusory, and deceptive, like a mirage" (972). He leaves his cell five minutes before the end of the fifteen years, forfeiting his right to the money. The peasant in Tolstoy's story, after striking a bargain for a vast amount of Bashkir land—all he can walk off in one day—pushes himself to the limits of his strength and falls dead. Ironically, all the land that Pahom now has is just the amount needed for his grave. Thus, both characters are unable to enjoy the material possessions they so passionately desired.

CONCLUSION
Summary of key points
Thesis restated
Final dramatic statement

"The Bet" and "How Much Land Does a Man Need?" both use character, plot, and irony to comment on a similiar theme. Both stories explore the destructive powers of unchecked desires for wealth. Both stories also reflect the concerns of their authors about a period of reform in Russia—concerns that still exist, making these stories and their messages just as powerful today as they were in the nineteenth century.

go.hrw.com
INTERNET
More Writer's Models
Keyword: LE7 12-6

PRACTICE & APPLY 2 Using the framework and the Writer's Model as guides, write the first draft of your essay comparing and contrasting two works of literature. Be sure to document all direct quotations.

Revising

Evaluate and Revise Your Essay

Shape It Up To turn your draft into a finished essay, commit time and effort to the revision process. Read your essay at least twice, first to evaluate content and organization and second to evaluate style.

First Reading: Content and Organization Use the questions, tips, and revision techniques in the following chart to evaluate and revise the content and organization of your essay.

PEER REVIEW

Exchange your essay with a peer. He or she may have suggestions for improving the clarity of your block or point-by-point comparisons.

editor in charge

Rubric: Comparing and Contrasting Literature

Evaluation Questions	Tips	Revision Techniques
1 Does the introduction give background information? Does it list the titles and authors of the literature?	**Bracket** any background information. **Underline** the authors' names and the works' titles. If information is missing, revise.	**Add** background information about the historical period. **Add** the titles of the works and the authors' names.
2 Does the introduction include a clear thesis statement that identifies the issue, key points, and the focus on similarities or differences?	**Highlight** the thesis statement. If you cannot find one, or if the statement is unclear, revise.	**Add** a thesis statement that identifies the issue and the key points. **Revise** an existing thesis statement to make clear the focus on similiarities, differences, or both.
3 Does the essay use literary evidence from the works to prove each key point? Does the essay use parenthetical citations for each direct quotation?	**Label** any direct quotations, paraphrases, or summaries as **DQ, P,** or **S. Circle** any parenthetical citations. If there are none for direct quotations, revise.	**Add** supporting literary evidence—direct quotations, paraphrases, and summaries—as necessary. **Add** parenthetical citations for each direct quotation.
4 Does the evidence include elaboration for the direct quotations, paraphrases, or summaries?	**Draw a wavy line** under any sentences that elaborate the quotations, paraphrases, or summaries.	**Elaborate** upon the evidence by providing a sentence or sentences to explain the meaning of each piece of evidence.
5 Is the essay clearly organized using the block method, the point-by-point, or a combination?	**Mark in the margin** if the essay uses the block method, the point-by-point method, or a combination.	**Rearrange** your key points according to one of the two methods. Be consistent in sequencing information.
6 Does the conclusion summarize the key points and restate the thesis? Is there a final, dramatic statement?	**Draw a wavy line** under the summarizing statement. **Highlight** the sentence that restates the thesis. **Circle** the dramatic statement.	**Add** a sentence that summarizes the key points. **Elaborate** with a sentence that restates the thesis. **Add** a final, dramatic statement.

Second Reading: Style When you are satisfied with the content and organization of your essay, read it again to focus on style. One way to improve style and enhance meaning is to use **parallelism**—using the same grammatical forms or structures to balance related ideas. For example, to create a natural rhythm and flow in your writing, pair an adjective with an adjective, a prepositional phrase with a prepositional phrase, a gerund with a gerund, and a noun clause with a noun clause. Use the following chart to help you ensure parallel structure in your essay.

Style Guidelines

Evaluation Question	Tip	Revision Technique
Does the essay express related ideas using the same grammatical form?	**Circle** the conjunctions *and, but,* and *or* in your essay, and **underline** the ideas they connect. If the ideas are not expressed in parallel form, revise.	**Add** words, **replace** the forms of words, or **rearrange** information to add parallel structure.

ANALYZING THE REVISION PROCESS

Study these revisions, and answer the questions that follow.

replace

, inconveniences his family, and makes move after move

He alienates friends~~, and his family is inconvenienced and he makes many moves~~ to satisfy his greed for a huge tract of land he can own and farm. He first journeys down the Volga River, then walks over three hundred miles only to leave and hurry over to the faraway land of the Bashkirs, hungry for their rich prairie farmland. *Nothing seems ultimately to satisfy him.*

add

Responding to the Revision Process

1. How did changing the form of words in the first sentence affect the style?
2. Why do you think the writer added the last sentence?

Writing Skills
Revise for content and style.

PRACTICE & APPLY 3 Use the guidelines on this page and the previous page to evaluate and revise the content, organization, and style of your essay. Review the sentences you have used. Consider using parallelism to improve the style of your essay.

Publishing

Proofread and Publish Your Essay

Put Your Best Foot Forward You've worked hard to gather, organize, and present your information, so don't diminish your essay's impact by failing to eliminate careless mistakes in your final draft. Thoroughly proofread your essay, checking for errors in grammar, usage, and mechanics. You might also work collaboratively to help edit and refine the essays of your peers.

Tell the World Consider sharing your analysis with others besides your teacher and classmates. Here are some ways you can publish your comparison-contrast essay so it can reach a wider audience.

- Share your essay with your history teacher. Ask permission to distribute your essay to one of his or her classes if the students are studying the same historical period that your essay covers.
- Enter your essay in a contest sponsored by your school, library, or other local organization.
- Put your essay together with the essays of classmates who wrote about the same historical period, and place a copy in your school's library for consultation by students interested in that period.
- Use your essay as an additional sample of your writing and include it with your applications for college. Attach a cover page explaining your interest in the subject of your essay and how the essay reflects your best work.

Reflect on Your Essay

Know Yourself Look back and think about what you've learned in the process of comparing and contrasting literature. Jot short responses to the following questions.

- How did relating the literature to the historical period in which it was written help you understand the literature better?
- How did analyzing two literary works from the same historical period help you better understand that period?
- How did comparing and contrasting the two works help you better understand and appreciate each one?
- What did you find more challenging: analyzing the works or expressing your findings in an organized way? How might you make this process easier next time?

PRACTICE & APPLY 4 Using the information on this page, first proofread your essay for errors in grammar, usage, and mechanics. Then, consider publishing your essay for a wider audience. Finally, reflect on what you've learned throughout the writing process.

TIP Careful proofreading will help ensure that you have properly used English-language **conventions.** For example, check to see that you have correctly used parallelism. For more on **using parallel structure,** see Ways to Achieve Clarity, 9c, in the Language Handbook.

COMPUTER TIP

Use computer software to create a professional-looking collection of your essays. For more on **page design** and **type,** see *Designing Your Writing* in the Writer's Handbook.

Writing Skills
Proofread, especially for correct use of parallel structure.

Collection 6: Skills Review

Comparing Literature

Test Practice

The following two nineteenth-century poems are examples of two different literary traditions. Thomas Hardy (1840–1928), an English novelist who became a poet late in life, was a realist and pessimist. Arthur Rimbaud (1854–1891) was a young French symbolist—one of a group of poets who reacted against the idealism of Romanticism and sought to express their ironic view of the world using rhythmical language and sometimes shocking imagery. "Drummer Hodge" is set in South Africa during the Boer War (1899–1902) in which the British defeated the Boers, South Africans of Dutch descent. Hardy uses some words from Afrikaans, the language spoken by the Boers. "The Sleeper of the Valley" is set in an unspecified time and place.

DIRECTIONS: Read the two poems that follow. Then, read each multiple-choice question that follows, and write the letter of the best response.

Drummer Hodge

Thomas Hardy

1

They throw in Drummer Hodge, to rest
   Uncoffined—just as found:
His landmark is a kopje°-crest
   That breaks the veldt° around;
And foreign constellations west°
   Each night above his mound.

2

Young Hodge the Drummer never knew—
   Fresh from his Wessex home—
The meaning of the broad Karoo,°
   The Bush,° the dusty loam,
And why uprose to nightly view
   Strange stars amid the gloam.

3. kopje (käp′ē) *n.:* (Afrikaans) small hill.
4. veldt (velt) *n.:* (Afrikaans) prairie.
5. west *v.:* move westward.

9. Karoo (kə·ro͞o′) *n.:* (Hottentot) dry plain.
10. Bush *n.:* uncleared, outlying area.

Pages 1010–1013 cover
Literary Skills Compare and contrast works from different literary periods.

3

Yet portion of that unknown plain
Will Hodge forever be;
His homely Northern breast and brain
Grow to some Southern tree,
And strange-eyed constellations reign
His stars eternally.

The Sleeper of the Valley

Arthur Rimbaud
translated by **Ludwig Lewisohn**

There's a green hollow where a river sings
Silvering the torn grass in its glittering flight,
And where the sun from the proud mountain flings
Fire—and the little valley brims with light.

A soldier young, with open mouth, bare head,
Sleeps with his neck in dewy watercress,
Under the sky and on the grass his bed,
Pale in the deep green and the light's excess.

He sleeps amid the iris and his smile
Is like a sick child's slumbering for a while.
Nature, in thy warm lap his chilled limbs hide!

The perfume does not thrill him from his rest.
He sleeps in sunshine, hand upon his breast,
Tranquil—with two red holes in his right side.

Collection 6: Skills Review

1. Hardy uses the word "throw" (line 1) to describe the manner in which Drummer Hodge is buried. What does this word suggest about the feelings of those burying him?
   - **A** relief
   - **B** contentment
   - **C** indifference
   - **D** grief

2. In "Drummer Hodge," which of the following words *best* describes what the landscape is to Hodge?
   - **F** cold
   - **G** alien
   - **H** beautiful
   - **J** familiar

3. According to "Drummer Hodge," what will happen to Hodge in the future?
   - **A** He will be given a formal burial.
   - **B** He will go to heaven.
   - **C** He will become a permanent part of the landscape.
   - **D** He will be remembered.

4. Hardy's use of words from Afrikaans, such as *kopje* and *veldt,* in "Drummer Hodge" serves to —
   - **F** confuse the reader
   - **G** make the reader feel at home
   - **H** establish that Hodge died in South Africa
   - **J** make the reader use a dictionary

5. What word *best* describes the landscape in which the soldier lies in "The Sleeper of the Valley"?
   - **A** tropical
   - **B** pastoral
   - **C** urban
   - **D** arid

6. In "The Sleeper of the Valley," the contrast between the beautiful language and imagery and the reality of the soldier's death is an example of —
   - **F** irony
   - **G** symbolism
   - **H** alliteration
   - **J** Romanticism

7. Which statement about both poems is *incorrect*?
   - **A** Both are patriotic.
   - **B** Both are rhymed.
   - **C** Both use irony.
   - **D** Both use imagery.

8. In "The Sleeper of the Valley," what detail *most* strongly suggests that the soldier is dead before we read the last line?
   - **F** The grass is torn.
   - **G** His limbs are chilled.
   - **H** His head is bare.
   - **J** His mouth is open.

Collection 6: Skills Review

9. In "Drummer Hodge," the setting is important because part of Drummer Hodge's tragedy is that he died in a foreign land, whereas in "The Sleeper of the Valley" the setting is —
   - **A** not significant to the poem's meaning at all
   - **B** significant because its beauty and peacefulness present an ironic contrast to the soldier's fate
   - **C** significant because it symbolizes the threatening aspects of nature
   - **D** significant because it foreshadows what will happen to the soldier

10. In both "Drummer Hodge" and "The Sleeper of the Valley," there is evidence that —
   - **F** a dead soldier is deeply mourned
   - **G** people are glad that a soldier is dead
   - **H** some people are saddened by a soldier's death and some people are happy about it
   - **J** no one seems to care about a particular soldier's death

Essay Question

Both "Drummer Hodge" and "The Sleeper of the Valley" suggest that the individual is insignificant in the larger scheme of things. Do you agree with this interpretation? If so, compare and contrast the way the two poems use diction, imagery, and irony to convey this theme. If you don't agree, what do you think the theme of the poems is? Support your response with specific details from each poem.

Collection 6: Skills Review

Vocabulary Skills

Test Practice

Analogies

DIRECTIONS: For each of the following items, choose the pair of words that expresses a relationship that is *most* similar to the relationship between the pair of capitalized words.

1. DIVINITY : ZEUS ::
   - **A** herd : cattle
   - **B** star : constellation
   - **C** science : chemistry
   - **D** skill : training

2. DISPARAGED : COMMENDED ::
   - **F** examination : doctor
   - **G** conceited : snob
   - **H** tardy : prompt
   - **J** encouraged : invited

3. ZEALOUSLY : FANATIC ::
   - **A** illegally : criminal
   - **B** heat : tropics
   - **C** forest : fern
   - **D** nervously : frantic

4. ASSUAGE : PACIFY ::
   - **F** careless : scrupulous
   - **G** inch : measurement
   - **H** equality : democracy
   - **J** embark : depart

5. COMPULSORY : MANDATORY ::
   - **A** politician : senator
   - **B** fragile : delicate
   - **C** wedding : ceremony
   - **D** funny : comedian

6. DISTRAUGHT : CALM ::
   - **F** mourner : joyful
   - **G** vessel : ocean
   - **H** wild : domesticated
   - **J** fortitude : strength

7. HAGGLED : CUSTOMER ::
   - **A** negotiated : diplomat
   - **B** model : photogenic
   - **C** determine : decide
   - **D** onion : odor

8. GENIAL : PERSONABLE ::
   - **F** secretive : public
   - **G** harsh : bitter
   - **H** dime: coin
   - **J** allow : permit

9. ARABLE : FARMLAND ::
   - **A** destructive : typhoon
   - **B** test : problems
   - **C** singer: performer
   - **D** scholar : studious

10. SURREPTITIOUSLY : OPENLY ::
    - **F** melodiously : sweetly
    - **G** bravely : timidly
    - **H** increase : reduce
    - **J** banana : fruit

Vocabulary Skills
Analyze word analogies.

Collection 6: Skills Review

Writing Skills

Test Practice

DIRECTIONS: Read the paragraph from a draft of a student's comparison-contrast essay. Then, answer the questions below it.

(1) "Ulysses" by Alfred, Lord Tennyson and "Andrea del Sarto" by Robert Browning are poems written during the Victorian period. (2) The narrators in the poems yearn for something more, yet different circumstances lead each narrator to this realization. (3) Ulysses has led an exciting life as a warrior. (4) Older and tired, he has returned home, but age and weariness have not diminished his desire to travel and learn new things. (5) The painter Andrea del Sarto, on the other hand, has not achieved the fame that many of his counterparts have. (6) Technically, his paintings are perfect but lacking spirituality. (7) Del Sarto says to his wife, "Ah, but a man's reach should exceed his grasp" (line 97). (8) Both poets use imagery in their poems as well.

1. To demonstrate an understanding of the works, which is the best sentence to add after sentence 1?

- **A** Both poems illustrate a Victorian theme—striving for improvement.
- **B** Both poems were written by popular poets of that period.
- **C** The poems have similarities and differences.
- **D** The poems are presented as dramatic monologues.

2. Which of the following sentences would support the ideas in sentence 4?

- **F** He understands that he is "a part of all that [he has] met" (line 18).
- **G** He's "become a name" (line 11).
- **H** He feels that one is never too old "to seek a newer world" (line 57).
- **J** He knows that "[d]eath closes all" (line 51).

3. Which of these could be used to elaborate sentence 7?

- **A** He knows that his technique is better than that of other artists.
- **B** He knows that he will be famous one day.
- **C** He knows that he should have expected more of himself.
- **D** His critics are too harsh.

4. To correct the parallelism, the student could replace sentence 6 with

- **F** Technically, his paintings are perfect, but they lack spirituality.
- **G** Technically, he paints perfectly, but they lack spirituality.
- **H** His paintings are technically perfect but spirituality is lacking.
- **J** Lacking spirituality, his paintings are perfect, technically.

5. Which sentence could be deleted to improve the paragraph's organization?

- **A** 2
- **B** 3
- **C** 7
- **D** 8

Writing Skills
Write an essay comparing and contrasting literary works.

Family Group (1948–1949) by Henry Moore. Bronze.

Henry Moore Foundation, Much Hadham, England. Reproduced by permission of the Henry Moore Foundation.

Collection 7

The Modern World 1900 to the Present

A Remarkable Diversity

We are sharply cut off from our predecessors. A shift in the scale . . . has shaken the fabric from top to bottom, alienated us from the past and made us perhaps too vividly conscious of the present. Every day we find ourselves doing, saying, or thinking things that would have been impossible to our fathers.

—Virginia Woolf

INTERNET

Collection Resources

Keyword: LE7 12-7

The Modern World 1900 to the Present

LITERARY EVENTS

1900 · **1911** · **1917** · **1927**

1902 Joseph Conrad's *Heart of Darkness* is published

1904 Dublin's Abbey Theatre is founded by **W. B. Yeats** and Lady Gregory to produce plays by and about the Irish

1909 Swedish writer Selma Lagerlöf is first woman awarded the Nobel Prize in literature

1913 G. B. Shaw's play *Pygmalion* is first produced; **D. H. Lawrence**'s *Sons and Lovers* is published

1915 Czech writer Franz Kafka's *The Metamorphosis* is published

1916 **James Joyce** publishes *A Portrait of the Artist as a Young Man*

1922 **Joyce**'s *Ulysses* and **T. S. Eliot**'s *The Waste Land* are published

1923 **W. B. Yeats** receives the Nobel Prize in literature

1924 E. M. Forster's *A Passage to India* is published

1926 African American writer Langston Hughes publishes his first book of verse, *The Weary Blues*

1927 **Virginia Woolf** publishes *To the Lighthouse*

1930 **W. H. Auden**'s *Poems* is published; Noel Coward's play *Private Lives* is produced

1933 Spanish writer Federico García Lorca's play *Blood Wedding* is produced

POLITICAL AND SOCIAL EVENTS

1900 · **1911** · **1917** · **1927**

1901 Queen Victoria dies and is succeeded by her son Edward VII

1909 Sigmund Freud visits United States to lecture on psychoanalysis

1910 South Africa gains independence from Britain; Union of South Africa formed; racial segregation becomes governing rule

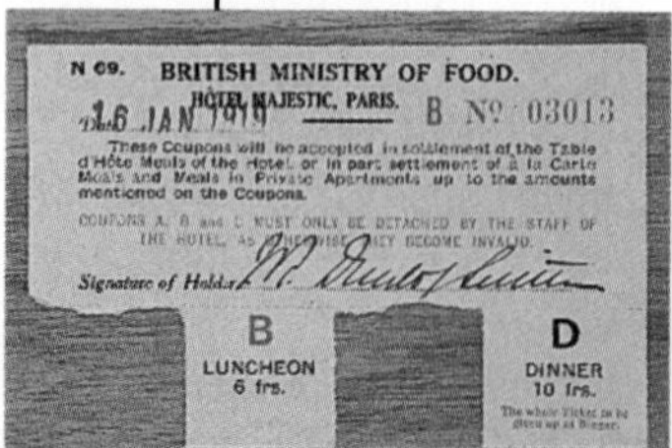
N 69. BRITISH MINISTRY OF FOOD.
HOTEL MAJESTIC, PARIS.
18 JAN 1919 B Nº 03013
These Coupons will be accepted in settlement of the Table d'Hôte Meals of the Hotel, or in part settlement of à la Carte Meals and Meals in Private Apartments up to the amounts mentioned on the Coupons.
COUPONS A, B and C MUST ONLY BE DETACHED BY THE STAFF OF THE HOTEL, AS OTHERWISE THEY BECOME INVALID.
Signature of Holder
B LUNCHEON 6 frs.
D DINNER 10 frs.

Food coupon issued by the Ministry of Food during World War I.

1913 In New York City the Armory Show introduces postimpressionism and cubism in art; in Paris the first performance of Stravinsky's *Rite of Spring* causes a riot among bewildered spectators

1914 World War I begins after the assassination of Austrian Archduke Francis Ferdinand

1915 Albert Einstein announces his general theory of relativity

1916 Easter Rebellion occurs in Dublin; uprising's leaders are executed by British

Formerly unemployed men go to work selling apples.

1917 United States enters the war in Europe; Russian Revolution begins

1918 World War I ends with nearly ten million killed; voting rights in England extended to women over age thirty

1922 Ireland is divided by treaty, with six northern counties remaining part of United Kingdom; civil war begins in Ireland

1929 United States stock market crashes, triggering worldwide depression

1933 Adolf Hitler is appointed chancellor of Germany; Germans build first concentration camp, at Dachau

1934–1938 In Russia, Stalinist purges force over ten million people into labor camps

1936–1939 Spanish Civil War is fought

1937 Pablo Picasso paints *Guernica*, protesting German firebombing of that Spanish city

1939 Germany invades Poland; World War II begins

Guernica (1937) by Pablo Picasso.

1940 — **1955**

1945 **George Orwell**'s *Animal Farm* is published; Chilean poet **Gabriela Mistral** is awarded Nobel Prize in literature

1953 **Winston Churchill** is awarded Nobel Prize in literature; Samuel Beckett's play *Waiting for Godot* is first produced in Paris

Sir Winston Churchill.

1958 Nigerian writer **Chinua Achebe**'s *Things Fall Apart* is published

1967 Colombian writer Gabriel García Márquez publishes *One Hundred Years of Solitude*

The Beatles (1964).

1988 Egyptian writer **Naguib Mahfouz** is awarded Nobel Prize in literature

1991 South African writer **Nadine Gordimer** is awarded Nobel Prize in literature

1995 Irish writer **Seamus Heaney** is awarded Nobel Prize in literature

2001 Trinidadian writer **V. S. Naipaul** is awarded Nobel Prize in literature

1940 — **1955** — **1975** — **2010**

1940 In the Battle of Britain, British Royal Air Force prevents German invasion of England

1941 United States declares war on Italy, Germany, and Japan

1945 Germany surrenders; United States drops atom bombs over Hiroshima and Nagasaki, ending World War II

1946 Development of ENIAC at the University of Pennsylvania marks first generation of modern computers

1947 Mohandas Gandhi is assassinated; State of Israel is created

1948 India gains independence from Britain; UN partitions Palestine

1949 Twenty-six of thirty-two counties in Ireland achieve full status as an independent republic

1955 Martin Luther King, Jr., leads boycott of buses in Montgomery, Alabama

1960 Nigeria wins independence from Britain

1960s British singing group the Beatles revolutionizes popular music

1969 *Apollo II* astronauts are first people to walk on the moon, as 600 million people watch live telecast

Astronaut Edwin E. Aldrin, Jr., lunar module pilot (1969).

1975 Fall of Saigon marks end of Vietnam War

1986 Nuclear disaster occurs at Chernobyl plant in Ukraine

1989 Berlin Wall is dismantled; pro-democracy protests in Tiananmen Square

1991 Soviet Union is dissolved

1994 Nelson Mandela is elected president of South Africa

1998 Peace plan for Northern Ireland is signed and ratified by referendum

2001 World Trade Towers in New York City are destroyed by terrorists

2003 U.S. and Britain go to war with Iraq

2005 Terrorists attack Britain's public transportation system

Political and Social

BRITONS

"WANTS

YOU"

JOIN YOUR COUNTRY'S ARMY!

GOD SAVE THE KING

Imperial War Museum, London.

The Great War, 1914–1918

Rising nationalism among European countries, competition for colonies, growing military forces, advances in technology—these factors, among others, created an environment ripe for conflict in the early years of the twentieth century. When the Great War (later known as World War I) broke out in 1914, Great Britain allied itself with France and Russia against the Central Powers of Germany and Austria-Hungary. Scores of young, patriotic men rushed to the front lines. By its conclusion in 1918, the war had cost Great Britain 750,000 lives. It had also cost billions of dollars, sending England into debt and severely rocking the prosperity the nation had formerly enjoyed as a major world power. The confidence and optimism of the preceding era floundered as a wave of anxiety and uncertainty washed over the nation.

Over the Top, 1st Artists' Rifles at Marcoing (detail) (December 30, 1917) by John Northcote Nash.

Imperial War Museum, London.

Milestones

World War II, 1939–1945

In the 1930s, the Great Depression sent the United States and Europe into a crushing economic slump. Mass unemployment and poverty led to despair. In a world plagued by financial and emotional crises, dictators were able to rise to power in nations such as Germany, Italy, and Russia. When Hitler's armies invaded Poland in 1939, Great Britain and France took up arms against them, thus igniting World War II. After France fell to Germany, German troops moved on England, but Britain held firm. Finally, in 1945, the Allies—Great Britain, the United States, and the Soviet Union—defeated Germany and Japan. But the horrors of this war—particularly nuclear devastation and the Nazi concentration camps—had changed the world forever.

(Opposite) Children taking refuge in trenches during air raids in southeastern England.

Crowd at Nigerian independence ceremony in Lagos (1965).

The End of the Empire: New Nations Emerge

Before World War II, countries such as Australia, Canada, and South Africa had already separated from the British Empire. The end of World War II sealed the empire's fate. During the late 1940s and the 1950s, most of Britain's remaining colonies declared independence.

As a result of the decline of Western imperial powers after World War II, dozens of newly independent states emerged in Africa and Asia, and many older nations in Europe and Latin America were politically redefined. These nations and others began to assert their own identities and reclaim territories. This process of self-determination, however, was seldom achieved without conflict. In South Africa, Northern Ireland, Eastern Europe, the Middle East, and Central America, violence is still a common experience.

BRITAIN'S PAST & PRESENT
BECKON YOU TO WEMBLEY
BRITISH EMPIRE
EXHIBITION
April to October 1924

Poster for the British Empire Exhibition (1924) by E. A. Cox.

Victoria and Albert Museum, London.

The Modern World
1900 to the Present

by John Leggett *and* David Adams Leeming

PREVIEW

Think About . . .

"The center cannot hold," wrote poet William Butler Yeats in 1919. And indeed, in the early years of the twentieth century, the prosperity and stability of the Victorian era dissolved into chaos and conflict. The Great Britain of yesterday, ruled by the principles of order, industry, and self-control, was attacked on virtually every front—intellectual, social, economic, and political. Thinkers such as Sigmund Freud scandalized Victorian self-determinists by declaring that human beings are driven by unconscious, irrational desires. The theories of German philosopher Karl Marx led to the questioning of capitalism and eventually to the transformation of Great Britain into a socialist state. Two world wars and a major economic depression eroded Great Britain's political and economic power and brought a slow, painful death upon the once-mighty empire. Disenchanted with human institutions, the artists of the age turned their backs on the world, creating wildly new, experimental forms of expression—celebrating "art for art's sake."

As you read about this period, look for answers to these questions:

- How was English society changed by the Great War—World War I?
- What were some factors that led to the outbreak of World War II?
- What were the long-term effects of the two world wars on Great Britain?
- How did social and political events in the postwar world lead to a rich diversity of world literature?

Collection introduction (pages 1020–1036) covers
Literary Skills
Evaluate the philosophical, political, religious, ethical, and social influences of a historical period.

What a story of change, of the erosion of a proud, complacent, well-ordered society, is told by the early years of the twentieth century in Great Britain!

Change on the Horizon

If we had lived in the era of Victoria, which ended with the great queen's death in 1901, or during the nine-year reign of her son Edward VII, we would have believed that Britain, with its moral and economic dominance of the world, would sail on majestically forever. But of course that is the misconception of every stable age and society—that life will go on just as it always has.

The Arrival (1923–1924) by Christopher R. W. Nevinson.

Even during this long, fairly stable period in Great Britain, though, profound changes were taking place, both externally and internally. Although the British imperial policy remained much the same throughout the Victorian era, several major colonies—Australia, South Africa, and New Zealand—gained their independence in the first decade of the twentieth century. Internally, Britain was experiencing social reforms that were to have far-reaching consequences. The rise in literacy, the growing power and influence of the Labour party, the widespread interest in socialist ideology—all would dramatically change Great Britain and the world.

Darwin, Marx, and Freud: Undermining Victorian Ideas

Many of the social and intellectual changes that were taking place in the early years of the twentieth century had their roots in the nineteenth-century work of three men: Charles Darwin (1809–1882), Karl Marx (1818–1883), and Sigmund Freud (1856–1939).

Darwin's *Origin of Species* (1859) sets forth a theory of the evolution of animal species based on natural selection: Those species that successfully adapt to their environments survive and reproduce; those that do not become extinct. This theory, which seems to contradict the Biblical account of the special creation of each species, fueled a debate that has continued from Victorian times to the present. So-called **social Darwinism,** the notion that in human society, as in nature, only the fittest should survive and flourish, was a nasty extension of Darwin's scientific theories—although Darwin had nothing to do with its formulation. Social Darwinism was used to justify unrestricted competition, rigid class distinctions, indifference to social problems, and even doctrines of racial superiority.

Karl Marx was a German philosopher and political economist who spent the last thirty years of his life in London. In *Das Kapital* (1867),

The proletarians have nothing to lose but their chains. They have a world to win. Working men of all countries, unite!

—Karl Marx and Friedrich Engels

Karl Marx.

Sigmund Freud.

The poets and philosophers before me discovered the unconscious; what I discovered was the scientific method by which the unconscious can be studied.

—Sigmund Freud

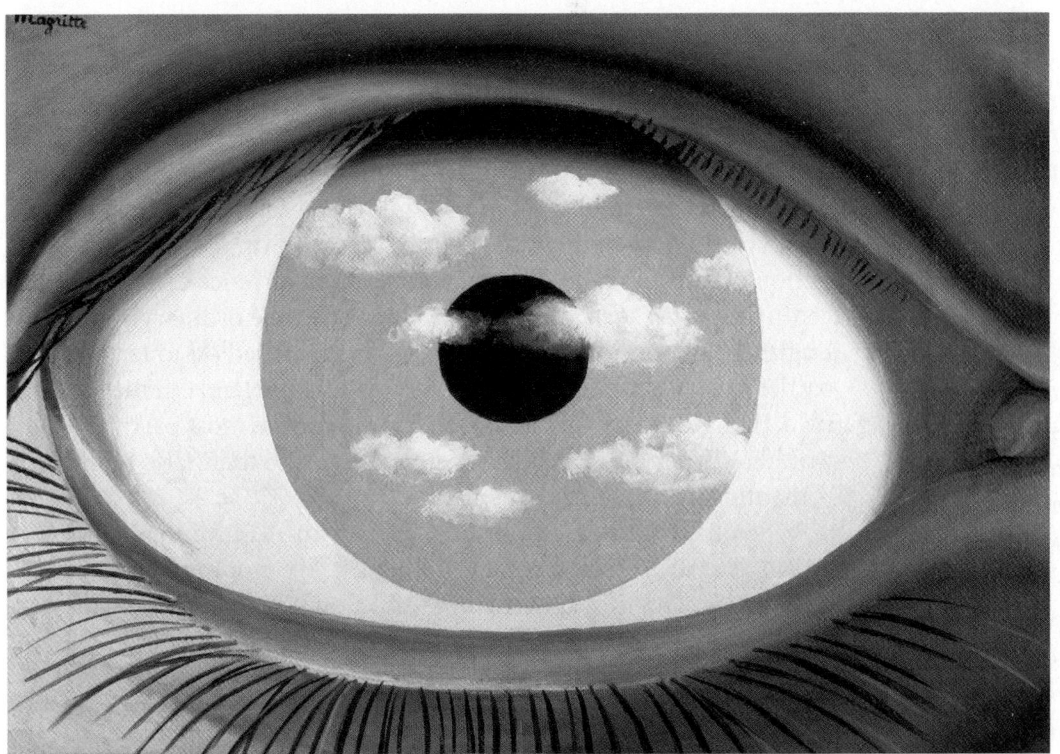

Le Faux Miroir (*The False Mirror*) (1929) by Rene Magritte. Private Collection.

he advocates doing away with private property. Marx traces economic injustices to the capitalist system of ownership, which exploits workers; he argues instead that workers should own the means of production. His theories of social and economic justice revolutionized political thought and eventually led to sweeping changes in many governments and economic systems, including those of Britain.

The psychological theories of Sigmund Freud, a doctor in Vienna, were equally revolutionary and far-reaching in their effects. In *The Interpretation of Dreams* (1900) and later works, Freud finds the motives for human behavior not in our rational, conscious minds but in the irrational and sexually driven realm of the unconscious, which is manifest mainly in our dreams. Conservative Victorians were outraged by Freud's claims that sexual drives motivated their behavior, but many artists and writers were strongly influenced by the notion of the unconscious and its mysterious, illogical workings.

The work of these three thinkers helped to undermine the political, religious, and psychological assumptions that had served as the foundation of British society and the British Empire for generations. With the calamity of the Great War and the events that followed, that foundation was largely swept away.

The Great War: "A War to End All Wars"

The truly great disaster of the first half of the century was the breakdown of the European balance of power. In 1914, Britain, France, and Russia, bound by treaties, were locked in opposition to Germany and Austria-Hungary. When the German army

To be in the trenches was to experience an unreal, unforgettable enclosure and constraint, as well as a sense of being unoriented and lost. One saw two things only: the walls of an unlocalized, undifferentiated earth and the sky above. . . . It was the sight of the sky, almost alone, that had the power to persuade a man that he was not already lost in a common grave.

—Paul Fussell

invaded Belgium, the whole of Europe was plunged into World War I—the Great War.

The Victorian writer Rudyard Kipling celebrated the British character as essentially patriotic, and he was right. When war broke out, a young Englishman felt that to be called on to defend his nation was likely to be the most glorious experience of his life. For centuries, in all sorts of wars and skirmishes, the ordinary youth of England had donned smart uniforms and marched off to faraway battlefields, just as they might go off to a sports event. On the battlefield, they would perform heroic acts, and for the most part they would return to be honored at home and to add their tales to the romantic lore of their regiments.

When Britain declared war on Germany in 1914, young Britons crowded to the recruiting stations to enlist. Six months later hordes of them lay slaughtered in the miserable, rainsoaked, vermin-infested trenches of France. Sixty thousand young British men were killed or wounded on the first day of the Battle of the Somme alone. Three hundred thousand were killed, wounded, or frozen to death at the Battle of Ypres. The generals would not stop the terrible—and, in the end, futile—carnage. Over the course of four years, an entire generation of young Englishmen was fed to the insatiable furnace of the war.

With the armistice in 1918, a new cynicism arose. The old values of national honor and glory had endorsed a war whose results were gradually recognized as negative: a weakened economy, a tottering colonial empire, and a

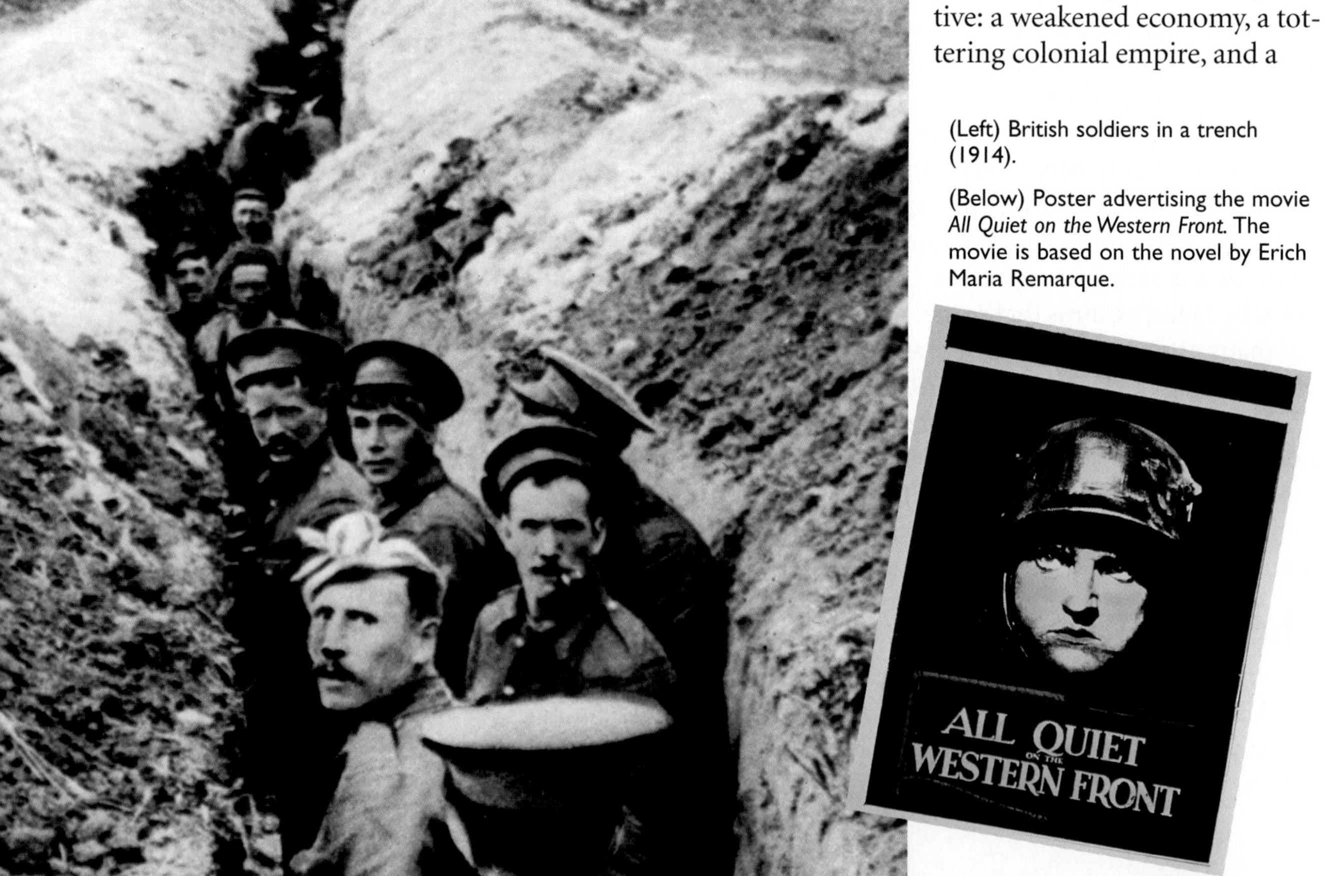

(Left) British soldiers in a trench (1914).

(Below) Poster advertising the movie *All Quiet on the Western Front.* The movie is based on the novel by Erich Maria Remarque.

loss of life equal to that caused by many plagues. Out of disillusionment came a pessimism about the state and the individual's relation to society. A new realism swept in, a response to the "romantic nonsense" of the past and, in particular, to the propaganda machine that had led a whole people into war.

Experimentation in the Arts: Shocking in Form and Content

The decade before the war had seen the beginnings of a transformation in all the arts, especially on the Continent. In Paris, Henri Matisse and other new painters exhibiting in 1905 were called *les fauves* (the wild beasts) by critics for their bold, new use of line and color. Pablo Picasso's first cubist painting, *Les Demoiselles d'Avignon,* was finished in 1907, the same year that John Millington Synge's play *The Playboy of the Western World* caused a riot at its première at Dublin's Abbey Theatre. (The audience was outraged by the suggestion that the Irish would make a hero out of a boy who claimed to have murdered his father.) In 1913, Igor Stravinsky's revolutionary music for the ballet *The Rite of Spring,* which was marked by strong, primitive (read "sexual") rhythms and dissonant harmonies, caused a riot at its première in Paris. The year after that, James Joyce's *Dubliners,* containing stories written up to a decade before, finally found an Irish publisher brave enough to publish it. All these works challenged traditional values of beauty and order and opened new avenues of expression.

Les Demoiselles d'Avignon (1907) by Pablo Picasso. Oil on canvas. 8′ × 7′8″.

The Museum of Modern Art, New York, NY, U.S.A. Acquired through the Lillie P. Bliss Bequest (333.1939).

A Revolution in Literature

The twentieth century's vision of the future might well be summed up in the final line of Joseph Conrad's *Heart of Darkness* (1902): "The offing was barred by a black bank of clouds, and the tranquil waterway leading to the uttermost ends of the earth flowed somber under an overcast sky—seemed to lead into the heart of an immense darkness."

The novelists that followed Conrad were moving from a concern with society to a focus on introspection. Virginia Woolf (see page 1104) even rejected traditional chronological order in storytelling. Experimenting with novelistic structure, with a shifting point of view, and with a style called **stream of consciousness,** Woolf probed the human mind with the delicacy of a surgeon, examining all its shifts of moods and impressions.

> *Never trust the artist. Trust the tale.*
>
> —D. H. Lawrence

> *Signatures of all things I am here to read, sea-spawn and seawrack, the nearing tide, that rusty boot. Snotgreen, bluesilver, rust: colored signs.*
>
> —James Joyce, from *Ulysses*

In his novels, D. H. Lawrence (see page 1185) was expressing his own strong resentment against British society, with its class system, industrialism, militarism, and prudery. Lawrence shocked the British with his glorification of the senses and his heated descriptions of relations between the sexes. His novel *Lady Chatterley's Lover* (1928), about an affair between an upper-class woman and her gamekeeper, is explicitly sexual, and its full publication was banned in England until 1960.

Most influential of all was the Irish poet and novelist James Joyce (see page 1173), whose novel *Ulysses* appeared to a storm of controversy in 1922. *Ulysses,* based on Homer's *Odyssey,* narrates the events of a single day in the lives of a Jewish Dubliner named Leopold Bloom and a young man named Stephen Dedalus as they unwittingly repeat the actions of Homer's Odysseus and his son, Telemachus. Joyce drew, in a wholly revolutionary way, on myth and symbol, on Freudian explorations of sexuality, and on new conceptions of time and the workings of human consciousness. Literary critics called this experimentation with form and content **modernism.**

The Rise of Dictatorships: Origins of World War II

Mussolini rallying a crowd.

The Great War, which had been called a war to end all wars, ironically led to another war. The League of Nations, the idealistic dream of U.S. president Woodrow Wilson, had no sooner been created than it was abandoned by a newly isolationist U.S. government. A worldwide economic depression that began in 1929 fostered the rise of dictators in Germany, Italy, and Russia.

In Italy and Germany the form of totalitarianism that developed was **fascism,** a type of government that is rigidly nationalistic and that relies on the rule of a single dictator whose power is absolute and backed by force. Benito Mussolini, who came to power in Italy in 1922, held control through brutality and manipulation. Adolf Hitler and the Nazi party capitalized on Germany's economic woes to convince many Germans that their problems were caused by Jews, Communists, and immigrants.

Russia's totalitarian government, based on the political theories of the economist Karl Marx, was **Communist.** Its founder, Vladimir Ilyich Lenin, had sought in the 1920s to create a society without a

Two Apprehensive Shelterers (1942) by Henry Moore.

Walter Hussey Bequest, Pallant House, Chichester, England. Reproduced by permission of the Henry Moore Foundation.

> *You cannot make a revolution with silk gloves.*
>
> —attributed to Joseph Stalin

class system, one in which the state would distribute the country's wealth equally among the people. But, in reality, the new government became as repressive as the rule of the czars had been. After Lenin's death in 1924, Joseph Stalin took power. In 1941, he became premier and continued to rule with an iron fist. Under Stalin's rule as many as fifteen million people were sent to the gulag, or system of forced-labor and detention camps.

By 1939, the Nazis were sweeping through Europe with their motorized army and superior air force. Hitler's plan for the systematic destruction of the Jews and other minorities, scapegoats on whom he blamed Germany's economic woes, resulted in the deaths of millions of innocent men, women, and children—including the six million Jews who were killed in the Holocaust. Only twenty years after the "war to end all wars," Europe had again plunged into a bloody, brutal conflict. In 1940, Germany defeated France and then prepared to invade Britain by launching devastating air attacks against London and other cities. Prime Minister Winston Churchill declared: "We shall go on to the end." The British *did* persevere, but only after the Soviet Union and the United States entered the war did Germany's defeat become inevitable. For Japan, which had allied itself with Germany and Italy, the war ended in the ultimate horror. On August 6, 1945, the entire city of Hiroshima was wiped out by a single atomic bomb dropped from an American plane. Small wonder, then, that much of the literature following the Second World War was dark and pessimistic.

> *We shall not flag or fail. We shall go on to the end, we shall fight in France, we shall fight on the seas and oceans, we shall fight with growing confidence and growing strength in the air, we shall defend our island, whatever the cost may be, we shall fight on the beaches, we shall fight on the landing grounds, we shall fight in the fields and in the streets, we shall fight in the hills; we shall never surrender.*
>
> —Sir Winston Churchill, June 4, 1940

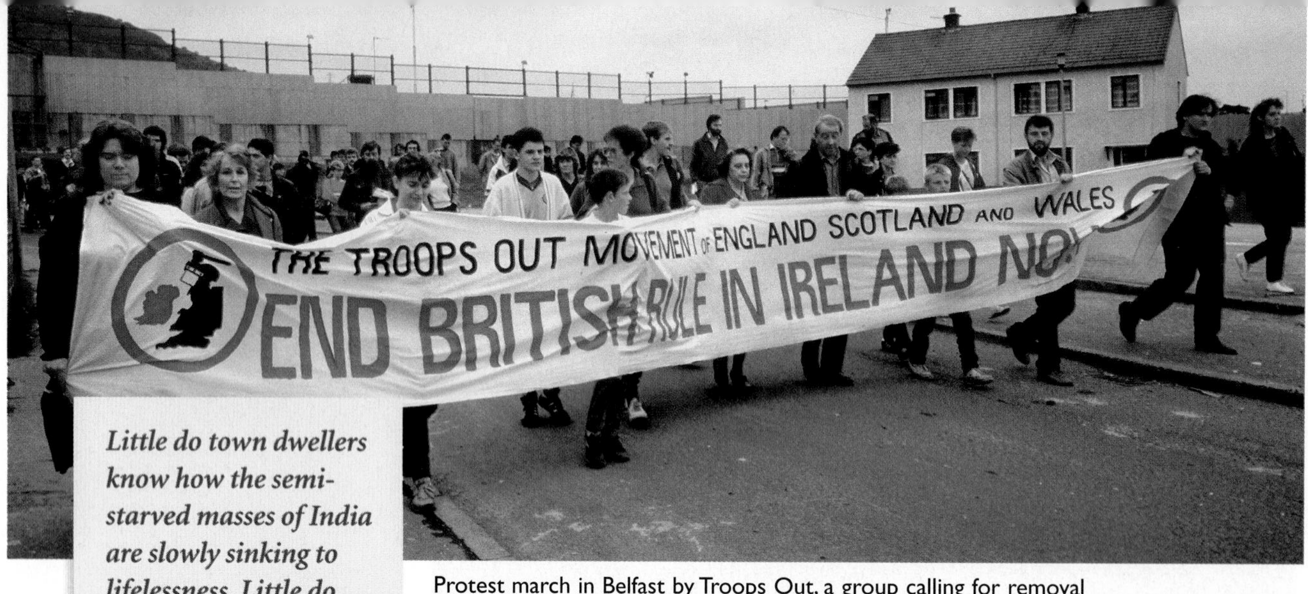

TimePix.

Protest march in Belfast by Troops Out, a group calling for removal of British troops from Northern Ireland (1986).

Little do town dwellers know how the semi-starved masses of India are slowly sinking to lifelessness. Little do they know that their miserable comfort represents the brokerage they get for the work they do for the foreign exploiter, that the profits and the brokerage are sucked from the masses. Little do they realize that the government established by law in British India is carried on for this exploitation of the masses. No sophistry, no jugglery in figures can explain away the evidence that the skeletons in many villages present to the naked eye. I have no doubt whatsoever that both England and the town dwellers of India will have to answer, if there is a God above, for this crime against humanity which is perhaps unequaled in history.

—Mohandas K. Gandhi, 1922

Britain After World War II: The Sun Sets on the Empire

After the war ended in Europe, Winston Churchill and his Conservative party were defeated by the Labour party, and Britain was transformed into a welfare state. The government assumed responsibility for providing medical care and other basic benefits for its citizens. While recovering from the war and rebuilding its own economy, Great Britain could not hold on to its many colonies. Most of them—including India, the "jewel in the crown"—became independent nations, and the sun now set nightly on the British Empire.

In the spring of 1998, an end to thirty years of violent conflict over the status of the six British-controlled counties of Northern Ireland seemed near at hand. After years of fighting in the streets of Ulster and a bombing campaign by the Irish Republican Army (IRA) that at times extended into England, representatives of the Catholics and Protestants of Northern Ireland and the prime ministers of Great Britain and Ireland hammered out a promising formula for peace. An amazing 71 percent of the population of Northern Ireland and 94 percent of the population of the Republic of Ireland voted yes in a referendum on the historic agreement on May 24, 1998.

British Writing Today

One of the most influential literary figures in England before World War II was the poet W. H. Auden (see page 1263), who had an intellectual background and a left-wing, antifascist political point of view. After the war, however, a group of younger novelists and playwrights emerged who opposed the values of the Auden group. These writers, who became known as the Angry Young Men, criticized the pretensions of intellectuals and the bland lives of the newly prosperous middle class. One of the major works of the period was Kingsley Amis's novel *Lucky Jim* (1953), a scathing satire of British university life. Much of the work written since World War II is considered **postmodernism** and often deals, either directly or indirectly, with issues of women's rights, multiculturalism, the environment, and nuclear destruction.

Nataraja (1993) by Bridget Riley. Oil on canvas (165.1 x 227.7 cm).
Tate Gallery, London.

The period since the 1960s has been marked by great variety, though it is still satire at which the British excel. Landmark novels published in Britain and Ireland from the 1960s on include the sharp and witty novels of Muriel Spark (*The Prime of Miss Jean Brodie,* 1961), the moral and linguistic experiments of Anthony Burgess (*A Clockwork Orange,* 1963), the feminist novels of Margaret Drabble (*Gates of Ivory,* 1991), the exuberant novels of Dubliner Roddy Doyle (*Paddy Clarke Ha Ha Ha,* 1993) and the multicultural explorations of Zadie Smith (*White Teeth,* 2000).

The Growth of World Literature: A Remarkable Diversity

Though our world isn't really a global village, innovations in technology and transportation have linked us in ways our ancestors couldn't have imagined. Ideas travel as fast as myriad electronic channels can carry them, and one writer may influence another living continents away. When important British, Asian, African, Middle Eastern, European, or Latin American writers publish in their native languages, translations are soon available for eager readers in other parts of the world.

Haitian village scene (20th century) by Antoine Montas.
Collection of Manu Sassoonian, New York.

Seeking Cultural Identity: Postcolonial Literature

Current world literature, more so than British literature of the past, frequently focuses on political and social problems. Literally hundreds of writers from former British colonies explore issues of personal identity and the effects of cultural domination and racism. Literary critics call their work **postcolonial literature.** These writers have seen their local cultures uprooted by colonialism or foreign influence, and they have had to ask themselves whether they are to celebrate their native traditions, imitate foreign models, or create new modes of expression. Further complicating their situation is the spread of English around the world, resulting in a kind of linguistic dominance. To reach the largest literate audience, some writers from other countries often feel obligated to write in English even if English fails to convey adequately the subtleties of their native language.

Igbo (African) mural painting depicting a cassava beetle (detail) (c. 1980s).

African Expressions

In Africa one response to colonial oppression of native cultures was a literary movement called **negritude,** which encouraged black writers to turn to precolonial African culture, art, and history as a source of inspiration and pride. Léopold Sédar Senghor, one of the movement's founders, was perhaps the source for the "black is beautiful" idea that took political form in the United States in the 1960s. Although some writers believed that negritude was a necessary response to years of imperialism, others, like the Nigerians Chinua Achebe (see page 1147) and Wole Soyinka (see page 1155), felt that negritude tended to idealize or cloak Africa's precolonial past in nostalgia or innocence. They felt that African literature must instead examine that past more critically and realistically. Soyinka quipped that "A tiger does not shout its tigritude," a witty and linguistically imaginative remark that speaks louder than volumes of postcolonial literary criticism. Though both Achebe and Soyinka write in English, Achebe has succeeded in grafting the oral tradition of Igbo storytellers and their idiom onto his novels.

Liberal white writers in Africa face another kind of identity crisis as they confront racism and social inequality. Doris Lessing (see page 1125), who grew up in Southern Rhodesia (now Zimbabwe), speaks of having "to wake up every morning with one's eyes on a fresh evidence of inhumanity." And the South African writer Nadine Gordimer (see page 1140) says, "One has an immense sense of shame." Several of Gordimer's novels are such powerful indictments of racist government policies that they have been banned in her country for being "detrimental to the security of the state."

"Two Worlds or Ten": Literature in India

In India, despite nearly one hundred years of British rule, English is only one of a diverse number of languages used by Indian writers. Two of the best known and established Indian novelists writing in English are R. K. Narayan (see page 1281) and Anita Desai (see page 1288). Narayan is perhaps India's greatest modern fiction writer. His characters often reveal a sort of pluck or stubbornness that is peculiar to India. As he said: "In spite of all its deficiencies, irritations, lack of material comforts and amenities, and general confusion, Indian life builds up inner strength." Desai, who excels at creating characters who must contend with an array of bewildering social forces vying for their attention, speaks of the chaotic patchwork that is India as "two worlds or ten." Perhaps the most startling new Indian writer is Arundhati Roy, a political activist. Her novel *The*

God of Small Things (1997), a harrowing indictment of India's caste system, won Britain's Booker Prize and sold six million copies worldwide.

Movie billboard in Madras, India.

© Hans Georg Roth/CORBIS.

Other Postcolonial Explorations

The Nobel Prize winner V. S. Naipaul (see page 1232), from Britain's former West Indies colony of Trinidad, takes an unrelentingly satirical, pessimistic view of postcolonial nations. One of his characters succinctly sums up the raw struggle for existence in a developing nation: "We lack order. Above all we lack power, and we do not understand that we lack power."

The Egyptian novelist Naguib Mahfouz (see page 1240), who writes in Arabic, helped to establish and perfect the Arabic novel. In such works as the *Cairo Trilogy,* this Nobel Prize-winning writer has used the novel form to depict the struggles of Egyptians expelling foreign invaders; he also uses his writing to criticize the social conditions, suffering, and spiritual emptiness in modern Egypt during and after British control.

Latin America and Magic Realism

In Latin America, writers have responded to their changing societies in different ways. The Chilean poet Pablo Neruda (see page 1277) was greatly influenced by the modernist movement, but his epic work, *The Heights of Machu Picchu* (*Alturas de Machu Picchu*), published in 1944, reconciles the poet to his country's ancient Indian

Our Song (1999) by Alfredo Castañeda. Oil on canvas.

Courtesy of the Mary-Anne Martin/Fine Art, New York.

heritage. The Mexican poet Octavio Paz writes about cultural questions involving the effect of history on the present in his country: "Ideas scatter / the ghosts remain: / truth of the lived and suffered." The Argentine author Jorge Luis Borges (see page 1224), one of the central figures in the Latin American literary "boom" that followed World War II, writes fiction that has stories within stories, character doubles, labyrinths, mysterious libraries filled with unreadable books, and parallel worlds that befuddle and fascinate his narrators—all in the service of exploring the nature of time and reality. Borges' works, which he called *fantástico,* foreshadowed **magic realism,** a literary style that combines realistic details with incredible events recounted in a matter-of-fact tone. For example, in the phenomenal bestseller *One Hundred Years of Solitude* (1967) by the Colombian novelist Gabriel García Márquez, the specific memory of particular mass murders is washed away by endless rain. Magic realists hope to startle readers and create doubt in their perceptions of reality—as Julio Cortázar (see page 1216) says, "A writer has to set fire to language."

Women's Voices: A "Second Sex" No More

Political concerns in postwar world literature are not the sole domain of nations and cultures; one of the strongest voices to emerge in the postwar world is that of women.

Feminist writers dramatize women's lack of power in a world controlled by men. In the influential feminist work *The Second Sex* (1949), French author Simone de Beauvoir analyzes women's secondary status in society and denounces the male middle class for perceiving women as objects; she demands an end to the "slavery of half of humanity." The Nigerian feminist Buchi Emecheta has influenced numerous women writers from various African countries and uses motherhood (but not marriage) as a symbol for artistic

FAST FACTS

Political and Economic Highlights

- World War I, the Great Depression, and World War II alter Great Britain's position as a world power and dramatically change its society.
- After World War II, most of Great Britain's colonies gain independence.
- The European Union, an alliance of European nations, is created to bring about the economic and political unification of Europe.

Philosophical Views

- The writings of Charles Darwin, Karl Marx, and Sigmund Freud cause people to question many of the social, religious, and economic beliefs of the Victorian period.
- Joseph Conrad, James Joyce, Virginia Woolf, and D. H. Lawrence experiment with form and content, changing the conventions and limits of the novel.

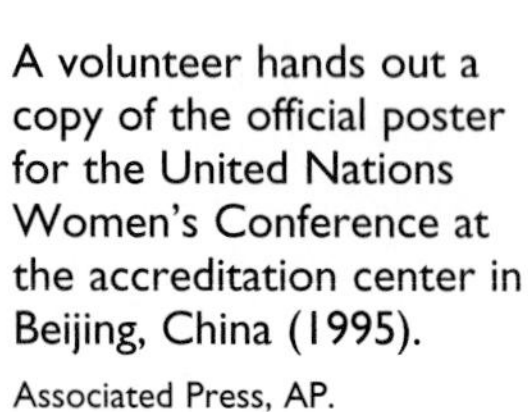

A volunteer hands out a copy of the official poster for the United Nations Women's Conference at the accreditation center in Beijing, China (1995).

Associated Press, AP.

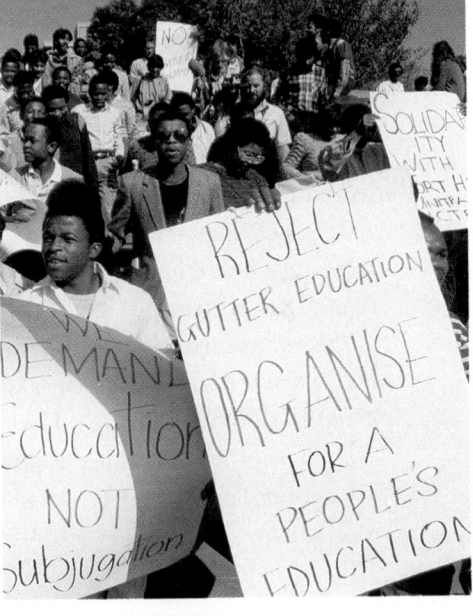

(Left) Lone protestor standing in front of tanks at Tiananmen Square (1989).

(Below) Students protesting apartheid in education, Johannesburg, South Africa.

creativity in her fiction. In *The Handmaid's Tale* (1985), the Canadian novelist Margaret Atwood (see page 1357) serves up a grim cautionary tale, warning readers of a possible future by creating a world in which a puritanical dictatorship seeks to repress and control women.

Never Forget: Responses to War and Government Repression

Since the beginning of the twentieth century, world history has been marked by periods of widespread warfare interspersed with periods of uneasy peace. Not surprisingly, then, much of modern world literature has been a direct and blistering response to war. In *All Quiet on the Western Front* (1928), the German author Erich Maria Remarque described the physical and psychological horrors of World War I with such vehemence that the novel was banned in Germany. But even this harrowing war novel paled beside the personal trauma of World War II's Holocaust as depicted by the Italian writer Primo Levi (see page 1051), interned at Auschwitz, and the Romanian writer Elie Wiesel (see page 1062), who has spent a lifetime serving as a witness to the atrocities of the Holocaust and has declared "Never shall I forget." The reclusive Polish poet Wisława Szymborska (see page 1098), winner of the 1996 Nobel Prize in literature, uses the commonplaces of everyday life to explore the most profound human truths. Few modern Japanese writers could avoid addressing World War II, and "The Silver Fifty-Sen Pieces" by Yasunari Kawabata (see page 1071) evokes the loss and pain that

FAST FACTS

Social Influences

- After World War I, in which nearly one million British soldiers die, many people in Great Britain develop a cynical attitude toward government and such values as national honor and glory.
- Writers from former British colonies and other parts of the world explore the effects of cultural domination, racism, sexism, and war.

I am cheered by a vital awareness of WORLD LITERATURE as of a single huge heart, beating out the cares and troubles of our world, albeit presented and perceived differently in each of its corners.
—Aleksandr Solzhenitsyn

civilians endured. Writers in the former Soviet Union—such as Aleksandr Solzhenitsyn, who believes that literature "becomes the living memory of the nation," and Anna Akhmatova (see page 1200), who was persecuted by the government for *not* writing on political themes (at least, the correct ones)—made an art out of defying government attempts to regulate their writing. And even though Communist China's government set out to "reeducate" its stubborn writers, some, like Ha Jin (see page 1307)—who left China after seeing the Tiananmen Square massacre in 1989—explore the troubling, unequal relationships between the state and the individual.

A "Marvelous Capacity": The Promise of World Literature

In literature as in history, many different stories can proceed at the same time. Such a variety of writing can only broaden and deepen our understanding of the human condition. As Solzhenitsyn commented in his Nobel Prize acceptance speech, "The only substitute for what we ourselves have not experienced is art and literature. They have the marvelous capacity of transmitting from one nation to another—despite differences in language, customs, and social structure—practical experience, the harsh national experience of many decades never tasted by the other nation."

REVIEW

Talk About . . .

Turn back to the Think About questions posed at the start of this introduction (page 1022). Get together with a group of classmates to discuss your views.

Write About . . .

Contrasting Literary Periods

Artistic (dis)order, then and now. Many writers of the early twentieth century struggled to express the despair they felt living in an apparently meaningless, unpredictable world. Human institutions such as government and religion had proved unreliable and ineffective. The very notion of order was itself questioned and manipulated. Writers such as Virginia Woolf and D. H. Lawrence tampered with accepted forms and boundaries, abandoning chronological order and introducing topics that were once taboo. Shock value in art was all the rage. In your opinion, are we still "shockable" today? Does art continue to challenge norms and condemn human institutions? Or does it reflect a new stability in society? As you answer these questions, consider not just literature but other contemporary art forms, such as music, film, the visual arts, and dance.

Collection 7:
The Modern World:
1900 to the Present

A World at War

Owen
Sassoon
Eliot
Levi
Duras
Wiesel
Churchill
Kawabata
Greene
Okri
Szymborska

We are all of us made by war, twisted and warped by war, but we seem to forget it.

—Doris Lessing

British soldiers at Ypres, Belgium.
Imperial War Museum, London.

Wilfred Owen

(1893–1918)

England

Wilfred Owen is one of the most poignant figures in modern literature. "The Poetry is in the pity," he said, and this famous remark could serve as his epitaph. Within the few adult years granted to him, Owen pursued a course of development that went from strength to strength. His interest in experimental techniques led him to master the use of half rhyme; this would become his most easily recognizable poetic signature. He also had a gift for lyricism that was bitterly tempered by "the truth un-told, / The pity of war, the pity war distilled." The result was a series of elegies and metrical statements as terse and stark as those carved on tombstones.

Like an apprentice determined to master his art, Owen immersed himself in the long history of English poetry. He chose for his model and mentor the poet John Keats (see page 824), whose astonishing life's work ended with his death at twenty-five (about the same age Shakespeare was when he began to write his plays). As a tutor in France for two years, Owen studied the French poets who were producing the tradition-shattering art that would become known as modernist. But all these literary influences were to become secondary to the devastating impact of a war Owen witnessed firsthand.

World War I broke out when Owen was twenty-one; he joined the British army, and the course of his life was determined. His progress in poetry was not made in the halls of an ancient university or in the country retreats where his literary forerunners were privileged to pursue their careers. His progress took place in the muddy purgatory of trench warfare and in the twilight existence of military hospitals.

In one of those hospitals, Craiglockhart, in Edinburgh, the young Owen met Siegfried Sassoon, a fellow officer and poet who had already distinguished himself for bravery in battle. Ironically, Sassoon was also the author of some of the most biting antiwar verses ever written (see page 1041). Temperamentally, the two men were far apart. Owen was an idealistic youth thwarted by circumstance; Sassoon was an aristocrat appalled by the wartime complacency of his own class. Even so, they became friends and artistic colleagues at once. After Owen's death, Sassoon became the first important British writer to herald the younger man's genius and to call attention to what he had accomplished under the most appalling conditions.

In 1918, Owen was listed among those killed in action—a mere seven days before the war ended with a joyous ringing of bells and dancing in the streets.

Before You Read

Dulce et Decorum Est

Make the Connection

Quickwrite

In trench warfare, "no man's land" is the few hundred yards that separate one army's lines from another's. But for the group of writers who became known as the Trench Poets, the war itself was a no man's land: a dehumanizing, horrific experience that made a mockery of civilization. Wilfred Owen, like many other Trench Poets, died in the muddy trenches of World War I. But his words lived on, bringing to life the evils and obscenities of war for those back home.

What is your most vivid mental image of war? Recall impressions you've absorbed from film, photographs, the nightly news, literary works, the words of veterans, or other sources. Close your eyes. Think, "War," and then record in words what you see in your mind.

Literary Focus

Figures of Speech

Many readers of Owen's poetry had never visited the front lines, nor would they ever do so. To help his readers see, understand, and feel the foreign subject of war, Owen used figures of speech to describe war's images and events.

A **figure of speech** is a word or phrase that describes one thing in terms of another. Among the most common figures of speech are **similes, metaphors,** and **symbols.** Early in Owen's poem, for instance, the poet uses a simile to describe the speaker and his fellow soldiers who lurch forward "like old beggars under sacks" (line 1). Owen also uses **oxymoron,** a figure of speech that combines apparently contradictory ideas to create a strong emphasis. The word *bittersweet,* used to describe the feeling of being happy and sad at the same time, is an example of an oxymoron. (The phrases "tough love" and "cold comfort" are other examples of oxymorons.) In literature, "darkness visible" is a famous oxymoron used by Milton in *Paradise Lost* (see page 403). Owen and other Trench Poets found oxymorons useful in describing the unimaginable slaughter of trench warfare. As you read Owen's poem, see if you can identify several different kinds of figures of speech.

> A **figure of speech** is a word or phrase that describes one thing in terms of another and is not meant to be understood on a literal level.
>
> *For more on Figures of Speech, see the Handbook of Literary and Historical Terms.*

Background

This poem's title is taken from the Latin statement *Dulce et decorum est pro patria mori,* meaning "It is sweet and honorable to die for one's country." The statement originally appeared in an ode by the ancient Roman poet Horace and has been used for centuries as a morale builder—and as an epitaph, or gravestone inscription—for soldiers. Here the motto is given a bitter twist by a soldier-poet who cannot see how the sentiment it expresses matches the reality he has experienced.

After the introduction of poison gas as a battlefield weapon during World War I, every man in the trenches was equipped with a gas mask. This poem describes the horrible consequences of not getting the mask on in time.

Literary Skills
Understand figures of speech.

Paths of Glory (1917) by Christopher R. W. Nevinson.
Imperial War Museum, London.

Dulce et Decorum Est

Wilfred Owen

Bent double, like old beggars under sacks,
Knock-kneed, coughing like hags, we cursed through sludge,
Till on the haunting flares we turned our backs
And toward our distant rest began to trudge.
Men marched asleep. Many had lost their boots
But limped on, blood-shod. All went lame; all blind;
Drunk with fatigue; deaf even to the hoots
Of tired, outstripped Five-Nines° that dropped behind.

8. Five-Nines: 5.9-caliber gas shells.

Gas! GAS! Quick, boys!—An ecstasy of fumbling,
Fitting the clumsy helmets just in time;
But someone still was yelling out and stumbling
And flound'ring like a man in fire or lime° . . .
Dim, through the misty panes and thick green light,
As under a green sea, I saw him drowning.

12. lime *n.:* powder produced from heat on limestone. It can cause severe skin irritations.

In all my dreams, before my helpless sight,
He plunges at me, guttering, choking, drowning.

If in some smothering dreams you too could pace
Behind the wagon that we flung him in,
And watch the white eyes writhing in his face,
His hanging face, like a devil's sick of sin;
If you could hear, at every jolt, the blood
Come gargling from the froth-corrupted lungs,
Obscene as cancer, bitter as the cud
Of vile, incurable sores on innocent tongues,—
My friend, you would not tell with such high zest
To children ardent for some desperate glory,
The old Lie: *Dulce et decorum est*
Pro patria mori.

In the battlefield trenches of World War I, enlisted men lived for weeks, sometimes years, in interconnected underground caverns infested by rats, with no drainage, poor ventilation, and only occasional dim shafts of natural light. In this poem, the "he" who recalls a grisly trench episode is the officer-poet, Siegfried Sassoon himself.

The Rear-Guard

Siegfried Sassoon

(Hindenburg Line,° April 1917.)

Groping along the tunnel, step by step,
He winked his prying torch° with patching glare
From side to side, and sniffed the unwholesome air.

Tins, boxes, bottles, shapes too vague to know,
A mirror smashed, the mattress from a bed;
And he, exploring fifty feet below
The rosy gloom of battle overhead.

Tripping, he grabbed the wall; saw someone lie
Humped at his feet, half-hidden by a rug,
And stooped to give the sleeper's arm a tug.
"I'm looking for headquarters." No reply.
"God blast your neck!" (For days he'd had no sleep.)

"Get up and guide me through this stinking place."
Savage, he kicked a soft, unanswering heap,
And flashed his beam across the livid face
Terribly glaring up, whose eyes yet wore
Agony dying hard ten days before;
And fists of fingers clutched a blackening wound.

Alone he staggered on until he found
Dawn's ghost that filtered down a shafted stair
To the dazed, muttering creatures underground
Who hear the boom of shells in muffled sound.
At last, with sweat of horror in his hair,
He climbed through darkness to the twilight air,
Unloading hell behind him step by step.

Hindenburg Line: German defensive barricade running across northern France. It was made of massive barbed-wire entanglements and deep trenches.
2. **torch** *n.:* flashlight.

Response and Analysis

Thinking Critically

1. What are the "misty panes" in line 13 through which the speaker glimpses the dying man?
2. An **oxymoron** is one kind of **figure of speech.** It combines apparently contradictory ideas, such as *wise fool.* What oxymorons can you find in the poem's second and last stanzas? What emotions or insights does a figure of speech that expresses contradiction evoke?
3. Who is the "you" addressed in the final stanza?
4. A **simile** is a **figure of speech** that compares two things using a word such as *like* or *as.* Explain the similes in lines 23–24. How do they relate to the **theme** of the poem?
5. What is the poem's **rhyme scheme**? Can you find any **half rhymes** (words that sound similar but do not rhyme exactly)? Describe the effect that this rhyme scheme has on the overall mood of the poem.
6. **Tone** is the attitude a writer takes toward the reader, a subject, or a character. Describe the speaker's **tone** in this poem. How does it compare with the tone of today's war stories or war movies? (Cite some examples in your answer.)

Extending and Evaluating

7. In the last lines of his poem, Owen refers to the traditional notion of an honorable death for one's country as "the old Lie." Do you agree that patriotism's high-minded idealism is a lie? Or is Owen perhaps stacking the deck by including so many gruesome battle details? In your response, relate Owen's poem to your own concepts of patriotism and warfare. Be sure to review your Quickwrite notes.

WRITING

Side-by-Side

In an **essay, analyze** the similarities and differences between Wilfred Owen's "Dulce et Decorum Est" and Siegfried Sassoon's poem "The Rear-Guard" (see the ***Connection*** on page 1041). Identify the subject of each poem, and compare and contrast the speakers' attitudes toward their subjects. Analyze how each poet uses powerful imagery and figures of speech to evoke strong emotions in the reader. How does the language of each poem reinforce the speaker's attitude? Support your ideas by citing specific words and phrases from the texts.

Literary Skills Analyze figures of speech.

Writing Skills Write an essay comparing and contrasting two poems.

Oppy Wood (1917) by John Northcote Nash.
Imperial War Museum, London.

T. S. Eliot

(1888–1965)

America / England

Unlike poets whose long, outstanding careers eventually turn them into cultural monuments, T. S. Eliot was a monument who later became known as a man. Internationally famous at an early age, Eliot was the product of an aristocratic New England family that valued privacy and regarded self-exploitation and public exposure—even fame itself—as a form of vulgarity. Consequently, millions of readers knew T. S. Eliot less as a real personality than as a presence. Eliot was remote, disciplined, and self-possessed, a man whose sparse output was nevertheless the most celebrated and influential poetry written in English over a span of three decades.

Thomas Stearns Eliot was born in 1888 in St. Louis, Missouri, where his grandfather had established Washington University. In spite of this geographical displacement, the Eliots remained New Englanders. Eliot was educated at Harvard College, after which he did graduate studies at the Sorbonne in Paris. Like many other young American writers of his generation, he found life abroad so stimulating that he decided not to return home. Settling in London before World War I, he worked in a bank, married an Englishwoman, and became an editor and a publisher. Eliot made his expatriation complete by becoming a British citizen in 1927. In 1948, he was awarded the Nobel Prize. Not long before his death in 1965, on one of his several visits to the United States, so many people wanted to see and hear Eliot read his poetry that a football stadium had to be taken over to hold the audience.

Eliot had a vast influence as a poet. His techniques, along with those of his friend and fellow American expatriate, Ezra Pound, became the hallmarks of modern poetry. For over thirty years, in classrooms and in critical studies, Eliot's was *the* voice that expressed the dislocation and despair of the twentieth century. His world-weariness and his grave, restrained, and impersonal cadences—so much like the voices he heard in New England pulpits—were widely imitated and instantly recognized.

Eliot's critical studies were also far-reaching. He argued against the commonly held view that poets were romantics who had superior powers of observation and expression. Eliot regarded poets as craftspeople who used traditional literary materials not for personal revelations but for the creation of better-made poems. The poet, according to these theories, was like those anonymous master artisans who made individual contributions to the great medieval cathedrals but who remained personally unknown. Like these humble artisans, the poet was just part of the background. What is important is the poem (or the cathedral), not the worker who made it. This point of view criticized the notion that a search through the poet's life would give clues to the meaning of the work. The work, all-important, stood apart from its creator. Submitting to Eliot's instruction, poets, students, and critics for generations studied a poem not for its messages or meaning, but for its method and structure—for its architecture.

T. S. Eliot (1907) during his first year at Harvard, age nineteen.

Before You Read

The Hollow Men

Make the Connection

In 1925, when Eliot published "The Hollow Men," he believed that humanity was plagued by a loss of will and faith. His poem reveals a world of godless despair, an empty world without religion or the promise of salvation. How would you describe the condition of humanity today? Is it a world that matches Eliot's vision, or is your sense of the state of humanity today less bleak than his?

Literary Focus

Allusion

"The Hollow Men" opens with two quotations taken from different sources. The first line after the title is an **allusion,** or reference, to Joseph Conrad's famous short novel *Heart of Darkness*. This line refers to Kurtz, the book's main character, who journeys to the center of Africa and rapidly deteriorates. The line "Mistah Kurtz—he dead." strikes a note of futility that is echoed throughout Eliot's poem. The next line—"A penny for the Old Guy"—refers to one of the most notorious incidents in British history, the Gunpowder Plot. On November 5, 1605, a band of conspirators planned to kill King James I (and others) by placing barrels of gunpowder in the cellars of Parliament. The man chosen to light the fuse was a soldier named Guy Fawkes. But the plot failed; Fawkes was arrested and, in the cruel custom of the day, was sentenced to be hanged and drawn and quartered. To commemorate this grisly event, every year on November 5 huge bonfires are set all over England. When these fires are lit, straw-filled effigies of Fawkes that look like scarecrows—the "stuffed men" of the poem—go up in flames, lighting the skies. Children join the fun by carrying a "guy" and becoming beggars who ask passersby to give them "a penny for the guy" so that they can buy fireworks.

Eliot's poem is full of other allusions, especially to works by Shakespeare and Dante. As you read, think about the associations and emotions these different allusions evoke.

Literary Skills Understand allusion.

Reading Skills Make inferences about an author's philosophical arguments.

INTERNET

More About T. S. Eliot

Keyword: LE7 12-7

An **allusion** is a reference to something in literature, history, or other subject areas that the reader should know in order to more fully understand the meaning of a work.

For more on Allusion, see the Handbook of Literary and Historical Terms.

Reading Skills

Analyzing the Author's Philosophical Arguments

In a 1923 essay, Eliot wrote of "the immense panorama of futility and anarchy which is contemporary history." As you read, make **inferences** (guesses based on evidence) about the hollow men, and analyze their character traits to show how effectively they reflect Eliot's opinion of human history. From the final four lines in the poem—among the most famous lines in modern poetry—what inferences do you think Eliot wants us to make about the fate of humanity?

City Square (*La Place*) (1948) by Albert Giacometti. Bronze. 8½″ × 25⅜″ × 17¼″. (337.1949).

The Hollow Men

T. S. Eliot

hollow men: allusion to Shakespeare's *Julius Caesar* (Act IV, Scene 2, lines 23–27): "hollow men . . . sink in the trial" (that is, fail when put to the test).

Mistah Kurtz—he dead.

A penny for the Old Guy

I

We are the hollow men
We are the stuffed men
Leaning together
Headpiece filled with straw. Alas!
Our dried voices, when
We whisper together
Are quiet and meaningless
As wind in dry grass
Or rats' feet over broken glass
In our dry cellar.

Shape without form, shade without color,
Paralyzed force, gesture without motion;

Those who have crossed
With direct eyes, to death's other Kingdom°
Remember us—if at all—not as lost
Violent souls, but only
As the hollow men
The stuffed men.

II

Eyes I dare not meet in dreams
In death's dream kingdom
These do not appear:
There, the eyes are
Sunlight on a broken column
There, is a tree swinging
And voices are
In the wind's singing
More distant and more solemn
Than a fading star.

? **1–10.** *What does having a head filled with straw (line 4) imply about the hollow men? What other words and phrases in lines 1–10 give you clues about the character of the hollow men?*

11–12. A **paradox** is an apparent contradiction that is actually true.

? *What paradoxes are listed in these lines? What do these paradoxes tell you about the hollow men?*

13–14. Those . . . Kingdom: Those with "direct eyes" have crossed from the world of the hollow men into Paradise. The allusion is to Dante's *Paradiso.*

? **17–18.** *How can the hollow men be both "hollow" and "stuffed"?*

Let me be no nearer
In death's dream kingdom
Let me also wear
Such deliberate disguises
Rat's coat, crowskin, crossed staves°
In a field
Behaving as the wind behaves
No nearer—

Not that final meeting
In the twilight kingdom

III

This is the dead land
This is cactus land
Here the stone images
Are raised, here they receive
The supplication° of a dead man's hand
Under the twinkle of a fading star.

Is it like this
In death's other kingdom
Waking alone
At the hour when we are
Trembling with tenderness
Lips that would kiss
Form prayers to broken stone.

IV

The eyes are not here
There are no eyes here
In this valley of dying stars
In this hollow valley
This broken jaw of our lost kingdoms

In this last of meeting places
We grope together
And avoid speech
Gathered on this beach of the tumid river°

Sightless, unless
The eyes reappear
As the perpetual star
Multifoliate rose°
Of death's twilight kingdom
The hope only
Of empty men.

33. staves *n. pl.:* rods or staffs; "crossed staves / in a field" form a scarecrow.

? **37–38.** *What might the "final meeting / In the twilight kingdom" be? How might this explain what the speaker is afraid of?*

43. supplication *n.:* humble plea.

? **39–44.** *What kind of* ***setting*** *is being described here? How is this setting appropriate to the nature of the hollow men?*

41–51. In line 44, the image of the star is another **allusion** to Dante, who used the symbol of a star to represent God.

? *What do "stone images" make you think of? What would "prayers to broken stone" be?*

60. tumid river: Hell's swollen river, the Acheron (ak′ər·än′), in Dante's *Inferno.* The damned must cross this river to enter the land of the dead.
64. multifoliate rose: Dante describes Paradise as a rose of many leaves (*Paradiso,* Canto 32).

V

Here we go round the prickly pear°
Prickly pear prickly pear
Here we go round the prickly pear
At five o'clock in the morning.

Between the idea
And the reality
Between the motion
And the act°
Falls the Shadow
For Thine is the Kingdom°

Between the conception
And the creation
Between the emotion
And the response
Falls the Shadow
Life is very long

Between the desire
And the spasm
Between the potency°
And the existence
Between the essence
And the descent°
Falls the Shadow
For Thine is the Kingdom

For Thine is
Life is
For Thine is the

This is the way the world ends
This is the way the world ends
This is the way the world ends
Not with a bang but a whimper.

68. prickly pear: cactus.

68–71. These lines are a parody of a children's rhyme that begins, "Here we go round the mulberry bush." The mulberry bush was traditionally a symbol of fertility. To go round and round means to never reach a destination; it is a pointless action.

? *How would you interpret going round and round a prickly pear—a type of cactus?*

74–75. between . . . act: reference to Shakespeare's *Julius Caesar:* "Between the acting of a dreadful thing / And the first motion, all the interim is / Like a phantasma or a hideous dream" (Act II, Scene1, lines 63–65).

77. For . . . Kingdom: closing lines of the Lord's Prayer: "For thine is the kingdom, and the power, and the glory, forever and ever."

86. potency *n.:* strength; power.

88–89. between. . . descent: The Greek philosopher Plato defined "the essence" as an unattainable ideal and "the descent" as its imperfect expression in material or physical reality.

95–98. These lines are a continuation of the children's singsong rhyme, parodying the original words, "This is the way we clap our hands."

? *What does it mean for the world to end with a "whimper" instead of with a "bang"?*

Response and Analysis

Thinking Critically

1. In Section I, the hollow men are compared with the effigy of Guy Fawkes and contrasted with the historical Fawkes. What does this comparison and contrast tell you about the **character** of the hollow men?
2. What **mood** or emotional effect is conveyed by **imagery** using the words *dried* and *dry* in lines 5–10? How does the imagery convey a lack of passion, emotion, or excitement in the lives of the hollow men?
3. In Section III, what **mood** or emotional effect does the **imagery** convey?
4. In Section IV, what is the hope of the hollow men? What might regaining sight **symbolize,** and why do you think they are powerless to regain sight by themselves?
5. In Section V, what do you think Eliot means by "the Shadow" that intervenes between thought and action? Why do you think the speaker is unable to complete the Lord's Prayer?
6. Eliot **parodies** a nursery rhyme in the opening and closing lines of Section V. What is the effect of parodying serious content—the end of the world—in this way?
7. The last four lines of this poem are among the most famous in modern poetry. What is the difference between ending with a "bang" (as Guy Fawkes hoped to do) and ending with a "whimper"?
8. What is **ironic** about the hollow men being able to vividly describe their particular character traits and deficiencies?
9. How would you state the **theme** of this poem? How is this theme supported by the poem's **tone**? Use specific evidence from the text in your response.

Extending and Evaluating

10. In your opinion, does Eliot's use of **allusions** reinforce the meaning of the poem and its emotional impact, or does the extensive use of allusions make it more difficult for the reader to comprehend the main ideas and theme of the poem? How would the poem have been different if Eliot had used no allusions?

Literary Criticism

11. **Philosophical approach.** Do you think Eliot effectively demonstrates his argument that contemporary history is an "immense panorama of futility and anarchy"? Are the hollow men believable representatives of a particular type of human being? Support your opinion with evidence from the poem.

WRITING

Hollow Lives

In a brief **essay, analyze** the character of the hollow men as it is revealed through their appearance, words, actions, or lack of action. Use the following questions to guide your essay:

- What are the hollow men like socially, religiously, and personally?
- What are their values?
- How are they like or unlike most people?

Based on your analysis, what can you **infer** about Eliot's attitude toward the human condition? (You may want to consult your reading notes for help.)

Literary Skills
Analyze allusion.

Reading Skills
Make inferences about an author's philosophical arguments.

Writing Skills
Write an essay analyzing characters.

Introduction Comparing Points of View

The Holocaust

Main Reading

Connected Readings

You will be reading the three selections listed above in this Comparing Points of View feature on the Holocaust. In the top corner of the pages in this feature, you'll find three stars. Smaller versions of the stars appear next to the questions on page 1057 that focus on the Holocaust. At the end of the feature (page 1065), you'll compare the various points of view expressed in the selections.

Examining the Issue: The Holocaust

After Hitler became chancellor of Germany in 1933, the Nazi Party made strong political advances. With each German conquest, more Jews and other "undesirables"—Romanies, homosexuals, political dissidents, various religious groups, and people with disabilities, to name a few—fell into Nazi hands. The Nazis secretly began transporting many of these groups to concentration camps such as Auschwitz (oush′vits′) in Poland and Buchenwald (bo͞o′kən·wôld′) in Germany. There, prisoners were shot by firing squads, executed in gas chambers, tortured in medical experiments, worked to death as slave laborers, or killed by starvation and disease. In all, about eleven million people were killed, nearly six million of them Jews.

Children behind a barbed-wire fence at Auschwitz concentration camp (c. 1945).

Getty Images.

Make the Connection

Quickwrite

The horrors of the Holocaust have been recorded in many books, movies, and television programs. Make some notes about what you most clearly remember about depictions of the Holocaust. What feelings did these facts and images evoke in you? Why might people think it so important to remember the unspeakable atrocities of the Holocaust?

SKILLS FOCUS

Pages 1050–1065 cover **Literary Skills** Analyze points of view on a topic.

Reading Skills Compare main ideas across texts.

Reading Skills

Comparing Main Ideas Across Texts

The first step in comparing texts is to identify and analyze the main idea or ideas of each text. After you have read each of the following selections, write down what you think are their main ideas. Then, compare the various points of view presented in these selections. Are these writers all saying the same things about the Holocaust?

Primo Levi

(1919–1987)

Italy

Photograph by Jerry Bauer.

Primo Levi (prē′mō lā′vē) was a university student studying chemistry at the University of Turin (Italy) when World War II erupted in Europe. After the German army occupied northern Italy, Levi, a Jew, joined a resistance group, but he was soon arrested by Italian Fascists. Levi thought that he would wait out the war in a detention center, but when the Germans took over his detention camp, all Jews were immediately deported. In February 1944, Levi and 649 others were sent to Auschwitz (oush′vits′), the infamous Nazi death camp. Levi was one of only twenty-three of the group who survived until the camp was liberated less than a year later.

After liberation, Levi returned to Italy and resumed his work as a chemist. Soon, though, he felt compelled to record his nightmarish experiences at Auschwitz. His first book, *Survival in Auschwitz* (1947), tells of his eleven months in the hell of the death camp. Levi's next book, *The Reawakening* (1963), chronicles his eight-month return journey to Italy after liberation.

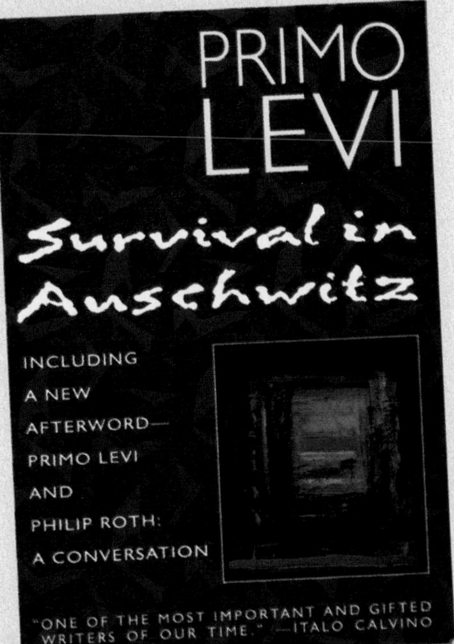

PRIMO
LEVI
Survival in
Auschwitz
INCLUDING
A NEW
AFTERWORD—
PRIMO LEVI
AND
PHILIP ROTH:
A CONVERSATION
"ONE OF THE MOST IMPORTANT AND GIFTED
WRITERS OF OUR TIME." —ITALO CALVINO

Levi did not confine his writing to Holocaust experiences. He also published poems, essays, short stories, novels, and memoirs; translated Kafka into Italian; and even dabbled in science fiction. Levi's last book, *The Drowned and the Saved* (1986), is a meditation on the meaning of the Nazi atrocities. To the critic Alexander Stille, who considered Levi's work "ultimately hopeful," this last book seemed pessimistic, causing the critic to speculate that "by the end of his life, Levi had become increasingly convinced that the lessons of the Holocaust were destined to be lost as it took a place among the routine atrocities of history."

On April 11, 1987, two days before the holiday of Passover, Levi fell to his death down the stairwell of his apartment. Some believe that the fall was an accident caused by illness and infirmity; others believe that Levi took his own life. Did Levi ultimately lose faith in humanity? That question may never be answered.

Before You Read

On the Bottom *from* Survival in Auschwitz

Points *of* View

At one time or another, most people have lost something that they treasured. But what exactly would you have to lose before you reached "rock bottom"—before your very identity was extinguished? In the following selection, Holocaust survivor Primo Levi describes his dehumanizing experience in a Nazi concentration camp in just these terms. "We had reached the bottom," Levi writes of himself and his fellow prisoners. "It is not possible to sink lower than this."

Literary Focus

Memoir

The word *memoir* comes from an Old French word meaning "memory." As this etymology suggests, a **memoir** records the memories of its author. In this way, it is a kind of autobiography, or writing about the self. Unlike an autobiography, however, a memoir usually focuses on one particular time period, often one of historical importance. The writer shares his or her experiences and gives the reader a personal glimpse into the way historical events impact people's lives.

Literary Skills
Analyze points of view on a topic. Understand the characteristics of a memoir.

Reading Skills
Evaluate historical context.

> A **memoir** is a type of autobiography that usually focuses on a single time period or historical event.
>
> *For more on Memoir, see the Handbook of Literary and Historical Terms.*

INTERNET
Vocabulary Practice
Keyword: LE7 12-7

Reading Skills

Evaluating Historical Context

As you read this excerpt from Levi's memoir, challenge yourself to think of experiences you've had or heard of or people you've known or heard about that even remotely resemble the people and events Levi writes about. Then, write responses to these questions: Is Levi describing an extreme version of what commonly happens in human history, or is he describing a singular, unforgettable atrocity? Would it be possible to understand this excerpt without knowledge of its historical context? As you read, take notes on the political, ethical, and social influences of the time that helped to shape Levi's memoir.

Background

Primo Levi wrote *Survival in Auschwitz* just after World War II ended, when the full horror of the Nazi extermination camps was not yet known to the world. The excerpt you are about to read begins after Levi and 649 other Jews have been packed into freight cars and sent to Poland with no food or water. When the doors of the boxcar finally open, the group is quickly divided into those who are able-bodied and those who are not. In Levi's convoy ninety-six men and twenty-nine women are selected to work in the labor camps of Auschwitz. All the others are murdered.

Vocabulary Development

tepid (tep′id) *adj.:* lukewarm.

taciturn (tas′ə·tʉrn′) *adj.:* not talkative.

disconcerted (dis′kən·sʉrt′id) *adj.:* frustrated; confused.

livid (liv′id) *adj.:* pale; colorless.

sordid (sôr′did) *adj.:* filthy; foul.

demolition (dem′ə·lish′ən) *n.:* destruction.

affinity (ə·fin′i·tē) *n.:* kinship; bond.

On the Bottom
from Survival in Auschwitz

Primo Levi

translated by **Stuart Woolf**

The journey did not last more than twenty minutes. Then the lorry[1] stopped, and we saw a large door, and above it a sign, brightly illuminated (its memory still strikes me in my dreams): *Arbeit Macht Frei,*[2] work gives freedom.

We climb down, they make us enter an enormous empty room that is poorly heated. We have a terrible thirst. The weak gurgle of water in the radiators makes us ferocious; we have had nothing to drink for four days. But there is also a tap—and above it a card which says that it is forbidden to drink as the water is dirty. Nonsense. It seems obvious that the card is a joke, "they" know that we are dying of thirst and they put us in a room, and there is a tap, and *Wassertrinken Verboten.*[3] I drink and I incite my companions to do likewise, but I have to spit it out, the water is tepid and sweetish, with the smell of a swamp.

This is hell. Today, in our times, hell must be like this. A huge, empty room: we are tired, standing on our feet, with a tap which drips while we cannot drink the water, and we wait for something which will certainly be terrible, and nothing happens and nothing continues to happen. What can one think about? One cannot think any more; it is like being already dead. Someone sits down on the ground. The time passes drop by drop.

We are not dead. The door is opened and an SS[4] man enters, smoking. He looks at us slowly and asks, "*Wer kann Deutsch?*"[5] One of us whom I have never seen, named Flesch, moves forward; he will be our interpreter. The SS man makes a long, calm speech; the interpreter translates. We have to form rows of five, with intervals of two yards between man and man; then we have to undress and make a bundle of the clothes in a special manner, the woolen garments on one side, all the rest on the other; we must take off

(Top) Star of David cloth patch. The Nazi government required Jews to wear such patches.

(Bottom) Gates of the Auschwitz Concentration camp.

1. **lorry** (lôr′ē) *n.:* British for "truck."
2. **Arbeit Macht Frei** (är′bīt mäkht frī).
3. **Wassertrinken Verboten** (vä′ser trink′en fer·bō′ten): German for "Drinking water is forbidden."
4. **SS:** abbreviation for *Schutzstaffel* ("elite guard"), the Nazi units in charge of the extermination camps during World War II.
5. **Wer kann Deutsch?** (ver kän doich): German for "Who knows German?"

Vocabulary

tepid (tep′id) *adj.:* lukewarm.

our shoes but pay great attention that they are not stolen.

Stolen by whom? Why should our shoes be stolen? And what about our documents, the few things we have in our pockets, our watches? We all look at the interpreter, and the interpreter asks the German, and the German smokes and looks him through and through as if he were transparent, as if no one had spoken.

I had never seen old men naked. Mr. Bergmann wore a truss[6] and asked the interpreter if he should take it off, and the interpreter hesitated. But the German understood and spoke seriously to the interpreter pointing to someone. We saw the interpreter swallow and then he said: "The officer says, take off the truss, and you will be given that of Mr. Coen." One could see the words coming bitterly out of Flesch's mouth; this was the German manner of laughing.

Now another German comes and tells us to put the shoes in a certain corner, and we put them there, because now it is all over and we feel outside this world and the only thing is to obey. Someone comes with a broom and sweeps away all the shoes, outside the door in a heap. He is crazy, he is mixing them all together, ninety-six pairs, they will be all unmatched. The outside door opens; a freezing wind enters and we are naked and cover ourselves up with our arms. The wind blows and slams the door; the German reopens it and stands watching with interest how we writhe to hide from the wind, one behind the other. Then he leaves and closes it.

Now the second act begins. Four men with razors, soapbrushes, and clippers burst in; they have trousers and jackets with stripes, with a number sewn on the front; perhaps they are the same sort as those others of this evening (this evening or yesterday evening?), but these are robust and flourishing. We ask many questions but they catch hold of us and in a moment we find ourselves shaved and sheared. What comic faces we have without hair! The four speak a language which does not seem of this world. It is certainly not German, for I understand a little German.

Finally another door is opened: here we are, locked in, naked, sheared and standing, with our feet in water—it is a shower room. We are alone. Slowly the astonishment dissolves, and we speak, and everyone asks questions and no one answers. If we are naked in a shower room, it means that we will have a shower. If we have a shower it is because they are not going to kill us yet. But why then do they keep us standing, and give us nothing to drink, while nobody explains anything, and we have no shoes or clothes, but we are all naked with our feet in the water, and we have been traveling five days and cannot even sit down.

And our women?

Mr. Levi asks me if I think that our women are like us at this moment, and where they are, and if we will be able to see them again. I say yes, because he is married and has a daughter; certainly we will see them again. But by now my belief is that all this is a game to mock and sneer at us. Clearly they will kill us, whoever thinks he is going to live is mad, it means that he has swallowed the bait, but I have not; I have understood that it will soon all be over, perhaps in this same room, when they get bored of seeing us naked, dancing from foot to foot and trying every now and again to sit down on the floor. But there are two inches of cold water and we cannot sit down.

We walk up and down without sense, and we talk, everybody talks to everybody else, we make a great noise. The door opens, and a German enters; it is the officer of before. He speaks briefly, the interpreter translates. "The officer says you must be quiet, because this is not a rabbinical[7] school." One sees the words which are not his, the bad words, twist his mouth as they come out, as if he was spitting out a foul taste. We beg him to ask what we are waiting for, how long we will stay

6. **truss** *n.:* belt with a pad, worn to support a hernia, a rupture of the intestine through the abdominal wall.

7. **rabbinical** (rə·bin′i·kəl) *adj.:* of or relating to rabbis, teachers of Jewish law.

here, about our women, everything; but he says no, that he does not want to ask. This Flesch, who is most unwilling to translate into Italian the hard, cold German phrases and refuses to turn into German our questions because he knows that it is useless, is a German Jew of about fifty, who has a large scar on his face from a wound received fighting the Italians on the Piave.[8] He is a closed, taciturn man, for whom I feel an instinctive respect as I feel that he has begun to suffer before us.

The German goes and we remain silent, although we are a little ashamed of our silence. It is still night and we wonder if the day will ever come. The door opens again, and someone else dressed in stripes comes in. He is different from the others, older, with glasses, a more civilized face, and much less robust. He speaks to us in Italian.

By now we are tired of being amazed. We seem to be watching some mad play, one of those plays in which the witches, the Holy Spirit, and the devil appear. He speaks Italian badly, with a strong foreign accent. He makes a long speech, is very polite, and tries to reply to all our questions.

We are at Monowitz, near Auschwitz, in Upper Silesia,[9] a region inhabited by both Poles and Germans. This camp is a workcamp, in German one says *Arbeitslager,*[10] all the prisoners (there are about ten thousand) work in a factory which produces a type of rubber called Buna,[11] so that the camp itself is called Buna.

We will be given shoes and clothes—no, not our own—other shoes, other clothes, like his. We are naked now because we are waiting for the shower and disinfection, which will take place immediately after the reveille,[12] because one cannot enter the camp without being disinfected.

Certainly there will be work to do; everyone must work here. But there is work and work: he, for example, acts as a doctor. He is a Hungarian doctor who studied in Italy and he is the dentist of the Lager.[13] He has been in the Lager for four and a half years (not in this one: Buna has only been open for a year and a half), but we can see that he is still quite well, not very thin. Why is he in the Lager? Is he Jewish like us? "No," he says simply, "I am a criminal."

We ask him many questions. He laughs, replies to some and not to others, and it is clear that he avoids certain subjects. He does not speak of the women: he says they are well, that we will see them again soon, but he does not say how or where. Instead he tells us other things, strange and crazy things, perhaps he too is playing with us. Perhaps he is mad—one goes mad in the Lager. He says that every Sunday there are concerts and football matches. He says that whoever boxes well can become cook. He says that whoever works well receives prize coupons with which to buy tobacco and soap. He says that the water is really not drinkable, and that instead a coffee substitute is distributed every day, but generally nobody drinks it as the soup itself is sufficiently watery to quench thirst. We beg him to find us something to drink, but he says he cannot, that he has come to see us secretly, against SS orders, as we still have to be disinfected, and that he must leave at once; he has come because he has a liking for Italians, and because, he says, he "has a little heart." We ask him if there are other Italians in the camp and he says there are some, a few, he does not know how

8. **Italians on the Piave** (pyä′vā): During World War I, Austria and Germany defeated 600,000 Italian troops in the Battle of Caporetto; the Italian forces were pushed back to the Piave River near Venice.

9. **Upper Silesia** (sī·lē′shə): region including parts of southwestern Poland, eastern Germany, and the northern Czech Republic. After World War I, Germany and Poland divided northern Silesia; southern Silesia fell under the rule of Czechoslovakia.

10. ***Arbeitslager*** (är′bīts·läg′er).

11. **Buna** (bo͞o′nə).

12. **reveille** (rev′ə·lē) *n.:* early-morning bugle call to waken military troops.

13. **Lager:** short for *Arbeitslager.*

Vocabulary

taciturn (tas′ə·turn′) *adj.:* not talkative.

many; and he at once changes the subject. Meanwhile a bell rang and he immediately hurried off and left us stunned and disconcerted. Some feel refreshed but I do not. I still think that even this dentist, this incomprehensible person, wanted to amuse himself at our expense, and I do not want to believe a word of what he said.

At the sound of the bell, we can hear the still dark camp waking up. Unexpectedly the water gushes out boiling from the showers—five minutes of bliss; but immediately after, four men (perhaps they are the barbers) burst in yelling and shoving and drive us out, wet and steaming, into the adjoining room which is freezing; here other shouting people throw at us unrecognizable rags and thrust into our hands a pair of broken-down boots with wooden soles; we have no time to understand and we already find ourselves in the open, in the blue and icy snow of dawn, barefoot and naked, with all our clothing in our hands, with a hundred yards to run to the next hut. There we are finally allowed to get dressed.

When we finish, everyone remains in his own corner and we do not dare lift our eyes to look at one another. There is nowhere to look in a mirror, but our appearance stands in front of us, reflected in a hundred livid faces, in a hundred miserable and sordid puppets. We are transformed into the phantoms glimpsed yesterday evening.[14]

Then for the first time we became aware that our language lacks words to express this offense, the demolition of a man. In a moment, with almost prophetic intuition, the reality was revealed to us: we had reached the bottom. It is not possible to sink lower than this; no human condition is more miserable than this, nor could it conceivably be so. Nothing belongs to us any more; they have taken away our clothes, our shoes, even our hair; if we speak, they will not listen to us, and if they listen, they will not understand. They will even take away our name: and if we want to keep it, we will have to find ourselves the strength to do so, to manage somehow so that behind the name something of us, of us as we were, still remains.

We know that we will have difficulty in being understood, and this is as it should be. But consider what value, what meaning is enclosed even in the smallest of our daily habits, in the hundred possessions which even the poorest beggar owns: a handkerchief, an old letter, the photo of a cherished person. These things are part of us, almost like limbs of our body; nor is it conceivable that we can be deprived of them in our world, for we immediately find others to substitute the old ones, other objects which are ours in their personification and evocation of our memories.

Imagine now a man who is deprived of everyone he loves, and at the same time of his house, his habits, his clothes, in short, of everything he possesses: he will be a hollow man, reduced to suffering and needs, forgetful of dignity and restraint, for he who loses all often easily loses himself. He will be a man whose life or death can be lightly decided with no sense of human affinity, in the most fortunate of cases, on the basis of a pure judgment of utility. It is in this way that one can understand the double sense of the term "extermination camp," and it is now clear what we seek to express with the phrase: "to lie on the bottom." ■

14. **We are transformed . . . evening:** Levi is referring to the inmates at Auschwitz whom he and the other new prisoners witnessed briefly upon arriving at the camp on the previous evening.

Vocabulary

disconcerted (dis'kən·sʉrt'id) *adj.:* frustrated; confused.
livid (liv'id) *adj.:* pale; colorless.
sordid (sôr'did) *adj.:* filthy; foul.
demolition (dem'ə·lish'ən) *n.:* destruction.
affinity (ə·fin'i·tē) *n.:* kinship; bond.

Response and Analysis

Reading Check

1. When Levi arrives in Auschwitz, what factors lead him to conclude that this is "hell"?
2. What does the SS man tell Levi and the others to do with their shoes? What happens to all their shoes later?
3. When morning comes, what do the men have to do before they can finally get dressed? After they are dressed, why do they "not dare to lift their eyes"?
4. Describe the dehumanizing process that the prisoners go through.

Thinking Critically

5. Why does Levi first think that the sign saying not to drink the water is a joke? Why do you think the prisoners were put in a room with undrinkable water?
6. Why do you think Levi uses the phrase "second act" to describe what happens to the men after they undress? Why does he later say "We seem to be watching some mad play. . . ."?
7. What does it mean to be "hollow"? Why does Levi conclude that after a man has been made "hollow" it is easy to decide if such a man lives or dies? Explain whether you think the Nazis realized this and intentionally inflicted such a state on the prisoners.
8. How would you describe Levi's **tone**? Cite passages that illustrate this tone. What effect does the tone have on your perception of Levi's experiences?
9. How do you think some people were able to survive the inhuman treatment that Levi and the others received?

Literary Criticism

10. In writing this **memoir,** is Levi primarily sharing personal experiences, or is he viewing historical events through a particular political lens? Explain how important knowledge of the political, ethical, and social influences of the historical period is to understanding this selection. Explain. (You may want to consult your reading notes for help.)

WRITING

Never Again

Like many other survivors of the Holocaust, Levi felt the need to serve as a "witness" and to tell his story so that such events would never be repeated in human history. Do you think memoirs like Levi's can help stop something similar from happening again? In a brief **essay,** explain your thoughts, citing specific examples from Levi's text.

Vocabulary Development

Synonyms and Antonyms

tepid	sordid
taciturn	demolition
disconcerted	affinity
livid	

On a separate piece of paper, use each Vocabulary word above to complete the exercise below.

1. _______ is a synonym for *pale.*
2. _______ is an antonym for *talkative.*
3. _______ is a synonym for *lukewarm.*
4. _______ is an antonym for *clean.*
5. _______ is a synonym for *connection.*
6. _______ is a synonym for *confused.*
7. _______ is an antonym for *construction.*

Literary Skills
Analyze a memoir.

Reading Skills
Evaluate historical context.

Writing Skills
Write an essay supporting an opinion.

Vocabulary Skills
Use synonyms and antonyms.

Connected Readings

The Holocaust

You have just read an excerpt from Primo Levi's memoir of the Holocaust and considered the ways in which memoirs present and interpret particular historical events. The next two selections you will read provide alternate insights into the horrors of the Holocaust. As you read, ask yourself how these insights are alike and different. After you read, you'll find questions on page 1065 that ask you to compare all three selections.

INTERNET

Interactive Reading Model

Keyword: LE7 12-7

Literary Skills Understand an author's philosophical beliefs.

Points *of* View

Before You Read

The French writer Marguerite Duras was born in Indochina (now Vietnam) in 1914, just a few weeks before the eruption of World War I. By the time World War II began in 1939, Duras had returned to her parents' homeland, France, studied law at the Sorbonne, and begun a career with the French Ministry of Colonies. She had also married poet Robert Antelme, referred to in the following excerpt as "Robert L." Antelme, a member of the French Resistance—a group that worked secretly to resist Germany's presence in France—was arrested by the Nazis in 1944. He spent two years in concentration camps, surviving by only the slimmest of margins. This excerpt, which begins shortly after the end of the war in Europe, describes Antelme's return to Paris and to Duras herself.

As you will see in this excerpt, Duras's writing is characterized by unique rhythms and by a sparse, suggestive style. As one critic puts it, "Everything she feels, she writes, stringing the syllables together as an artist strings his pearls." During her lifetime, Duras published scores of novels, a dozen plays, and several screenplays. She came to be hailed as one of France's leading feminist writers, earning the prestigious Goncourt award in 1984 for her autobiographical novel *L'Amant*, or *The Lover*. Duras died in Paris in 1996.

Reading informational materials: Implicit and explicit beliefs and assumptions. Although Duras's strong feelings about the horror of the Nazi concentration camps are unquestionable, her beliefs are not always **explicit,** or directly stated. Instead, she uses an accumulation of details to convey an **implicit,** or suggested, attitude toward her subject. Rather than directly stating how horrible the effects of a concentration camp were, Duras describes in an urgent, almost breathless style how Robert L. is taken from Dachau, what his physical condition is like, and how she and others react to the sight of him.

As you read, look for the details that reveal Duras's implicit beliefs about the horrors of the Holocaust. What techniques does Duras use to express these beliefs?

French soldier running to help a French resistance fighter who is taking aim at a German sniper (Paris, 1944).
TimePix.

MEMOIR

from The War

Marguerite Duras

translated by **Barbara Bray**

I can't remember what day it was, whether it was in April, no, it was a day in May when one morning at eleven o'clock the phone rang. It was from Germany, it was François Morland. He doesn't say hello, he's almost rough, but clear as always. "Listen carefully. Robert is alive. Now keep calm. He's in Dachau.[1] Listen very, very carefully. Robert is very weak, so weak you can't imagine. I have to tell you—it's a question of hours. He may live for another three days like that, but no more. D. and Beauchamp must start out today, this morning, for Dachau. Tell them this: they're to go straight to my office—the people there will be expecting them. They'll be given French officers' uniforms, passports, mission orders, gasoline coupons, maps, and permits. Tell them to go right away. It's the only way. If they tried to do it officially they'd arrive too late."

François Morland and Rodin were part of a mission organized by Father Riquet. They had gone to Dachau, and that was where they'd found Robert L. They had gone into the prohibited area of the camp, where the dead and the hopeless cases were kept. And there, one of the latter had distinctly uttered a name: "François." "François," and then his eyes had closed again. It took Rodin and Morland an hour to recognize Robert L. Rodin finally identified him by his teeth. They wrapped him up in a sheet, as people wrap up a dead body, and took him out of the prohibited part of the camp and laid him down by a hut in

1. **Dachau:** location of a German concentration camp that opened in 1933.

the survivors' part of the camp. They were able to do so because there were no American soldiers around. They were all in the guardroom, scared of the typhus.[2]

Beauchamp and D. left Paris the same day, early in the afternoon. It was May 12, the day of the peace. Beauchamp was wearing a colonel's uniform belonging to François Morland. D. was dressed as a lieutenant in the French army and carried his papers as a member of the Resistance,[3] made out in the name of D. Masse. They drove all night and arrived at Dachau the next morning. They spent several hours looking for Robert L.; then, as they were going past a body, they heard someone say D.'s name. It's my opinion they didn't recognize him; but Morland had warned us he was unrecognizable. They took him. And it was only afterward they must have recognized him. Under their clothes they had a third French officer's uniform. They had to hold him upright, he could no longer stand alone, but they managed to dress him. They had to prevent him from saluting outside the SS[4] huts, get him through the guard posts, see that he wasn't given any of the vaccinations that would have killed him. The American soldiers, blacks for the most part, wore gas masks against typhus, the fear was so great. Their orders were such that if they'd suspected the state Robert L. was really in, they'd have put him back immediately in the part of the camp where people were left to die. Once they got Robert L. out, the other two had to get him to walk to the Citroën II.[5] As soon as they'd stretched him out on the back seat, he fainted. They thought it was all over, but no. The journey was very difficult, very slow. They had to stop every half hour because of the dysentery.[6] As soon as they'd left Dachau behind, Robert L. spoke. He said he knew he wouldn't reach Paris alive. So he began to talk, so it should be told before he died. He didn't accuse any person, any race, any people. He accused man. Emerging from the horror, dying, delirious, Robert L. was still able not to accuse anyone except the governments that come and go in the history of nations. He wanted D. and Beauchamp to tell me after his death what he had said. They reached the French frontier that night, near Wissemburg.[7] D. phoned me: "We've reached France. We've just crossed the frontier. We'll be back tomorrow by the end of the morning. Expect the worst. You won't recognize him." They had dinner in an officers' mess. Robert L. was still talking and telling his story. When he entered the mess all the officers stood up and saluted him. He didn't see. He never had seen that sort of thing. He spoke of the German martyrdom, of the martyrdom common to all men. He told what it was like. That evening he said he'd like to eat a trout before he died. In deserted Wissemburg they found a trout for Robert L. He ate a few mouthfuls. Then he started talking again. He spoke of charity. He'd heard some rhetorical phrases of Father Riquet's, and he started to say these very obscure words: "When anyone talks to me of Christian charity, I shall say Dachau." But he didn't finish. That night they slept somewhere near Bar-sur-Aube.[8] Robert L. slept for a few hours. They reached Paris at the end of the morning. Just before they came to the rue Saint-Benoît, D. stopped to phone me again: "I'm ringing to warn you that it's more terrible than anything we've imagined . . . He's happy."

I heard stifled cries on the stairs, a stir, a clatter of feet. Then doors banging and shouts. It was them. It was them, back from Germany.

---

2. **typhus** *n.:* acute infectious fever, chiefly occurring in places where people live in unsanitary, crowded conditions.
3. **the Resistance:** underground organization that fought against Germans in occupied France during World War II.
4. **SS:** elite guard in the German military during the Nazi years.
5. **Citroën II:** model of car produced in France.
6. **dysentery** *n.:* diarrhea.
7. **Wissemburg:** town on the French side of the French-German border.
8. **Bar-sur-Aube:** town in northeast France.

I couldn't stop myself—I started to run downstairs, to escape into the street. Beauchamp and D. were supporting him under the arms. They'd stopped on the first-floor landing. He was looking up.

I can't remember exactly what happened. He must have looked at me and recognized me and smiled. I shrieked no, that I didn't want to see. I started to run again, up the stairs this time. I was shrieking, I remember that. The war emerged in my shrieks. Six years without uttering a cry. I found myself in some neighbors' apartment. They forced me to drink some rum, they poured it into my mouth. Into the shrieks.

I can't remember when I found myself back with him again, with him, Robert L. I remember hearing sobs all over the house; that the tenants stayed for a long while out on the stairs; that the doors were left open. I was told later that the concierge[9] had put decorations up in the hall to welcome him, and that as soon as he'd gone by she tore them all down and shut herself up alone in her lodge to weep.

In my memory, at a certain moment, the sounds stop and I see him. Huge. There before me. I don't recognize him. He looks at me. He smiles. Lets himself be looked at. There's a supernatural weariness in his smile, weariness from having managed to live till this moment. It's from this smile that I suddenly recognize him, but from a great distance, as if I were seeing him at the other end of a tunnel. It's a smile of embarrassment. He's apologizing for being here, reduced to such a wreck. And then the smile fades, and he becomes a stranger again. But the knowledge is still there, that this stranger is he, Robert L., totally.

He wanted to see around the apartment again. We supported him, and he toured the rooms. His cheeks creased, but didn't release his lips; it was in his eyes that we'd seen his smile. In the kitchen he saw the clafoutis[10] we'd made for him. He stopped smiling. "What is it?" We told him. What was it made with? Cherries—it was the height of the season. "May I have some?" "We don't know, we'll have to ask the doctor." He came back into the sitting room and lay down on the divan. "So I can't have any?" "Not yet." "Why?" "There have been accidents in Paris already from letting deportees eat too soon after they got back from the camps."

He stopped asking questions about what had happened while he was away. He stopped seeing us. A great, silent pain spread over his face because he was still being refused food, because it was still as it had been in the concentration camp. And, as in the camp, he accepted it in silence. He didn't see that we were weeping. Nor did he see that we could scarcely look at him or respond to what he said.

The doctor came. He stopped short with his hand on the door handle, very pale. He looked at us, and then at the form on the divan. He didn't understand. And then he realized: the form wasn't dead yet, it was hovering between life and death, and he, the doctor, had been called in to try to keep it alive. The doctor came into the room. He went over to the form and the form smiled at him. The doctor was to come several times a day for three weeks, at all hours of the day and night. Whenever we were too afraid we called him and he came. He saved Robert L. He too was caught up in the passionate desire to save Robert L. from death. He succeeded.

We smuggled the clafoutis out of the house while he slept. The next day he was feverish and didn't talk about food any more. ■

---

9. **concierge** (kän′sē·erzh′) *n.:* superintendent.

10. **clafoutis** *n.:* type of sponge cake with fruit in the center of it.

Points *of* View

Before You Read

Elie Wiesel was only fifteen years old when he and all the other Jews in his Romanian village were deported to concentration camps in Poland and Germany. Together with his father, Wiesel was taken to Auschwitz, then to camps at Buna, Gleiwitz, and Buchenwald, where his father finally died of starvation and exposure. Wiesel also lost his mother and younger sister, both victims of the gas chambers. Against the odds, Wiesel and his two older sisters survived and were later reunited.

After the war, Wiesel spent several years in a French orphanage and then studied philosophy and literature at the Sorbonne. He also worked as a journalist. In 1955, after breaking a self-imposed vow never to write about the Holocaust, Wiesel poured his memories into a nine-hundred-page volume. This work was soon condensed and republished as *Night.* The following excerpt, "Never Shall I Forget," originally appeared as a prose passage in the condensed version. It is thought by some to be one of the most powerful passages in Holocaust literature.

Wiesel now lives in the United States, where he has served as the Chairman of the President's Commission on the Holocaust and where he was awarded the Congressional Gold Medal of Achievement. In 1986, Wiesel was awarded the Nobel Peace Prize. He continues to write and to advocate for the remembrance of the Holocaust and for the end of racism, hatred, and genocide.

Study C (detail) (1995) by Samuel Bak. Oil.

Courtesy Pucker Gallery, Boston, MA, 2002.

POEM

Never Shall I Forget

Elie Wiesel

Never shall I forget that night,
the first night in the camp
which has turned my life into one long night,
seven times cursed and seven times sealed.

Never shall I forget that smoke.
Never shall I forget the little faces of the children
whose bodies I saw turned into wreaths of smoke
beneath a silent blue sky.

Never shall I forget those flames
which consumed my faith for ever.
Never shall I forget that nocturnal silence
which deprived me for all eternity of the desire to live.

Never shall I forget those moments
which murdered my God and my soul
and turned my dreams to dust.

Never shall I forget these things,
even if I am condemned to live
as long as God Himself.

Never.

Children and other prisoners liberated by the U.S. Third Army march from Buchenwald concentration camp in Germany in 1945. The freed prisoners are walking to an American-run hospital. The tall youth in line at the left, fourth from the front, is Elie Wiesel.

Associated Press.

CONNECTION/WEB PAGE

The following Web page is from the United States Holocaust Memorial Museum Web site. This Washington, D.C., museum is a memorial to the millions of people who died in the Holocaust and is devoted to the continual study of the Holocaust. The Web page below is about one night of destruction and murder inflicted on German Jews by the Nazis. This night came to be known as Kristallnacht ("Night of Broken Glass") because of all the glass storefronts that the Nazis smashed. In the end, approximately 7,500 Jewish businesses were destroyed or damaged and at least ninety-one Jews were murdered. (Pogroms are organized, government-sanctioned persecutions.)

Location: http://www.ushmm.org/kristallnacht/menu.htm

On November 9, 1938, the Nazis unleashed a wave of pogroms against Germany's Jews. In the space of a few hours, thousands of synagogues and Jewish businesses and homes were damaged or destroyed. This event came to be called Kristallnacht ("Night of Broken Glass") for the shattered store windowpanes that carpeted German streets.

The pretext for this violence was the November 7 assassination of a German diplomat in Paris, Ernst vom Rath, by Herschel Grynszpan, a Jewish teenager whose parents, along with 17,000 other Polish Jews, had been recently expelled from the Reich. Though portrayed as spontaneous outbursts of popular outrage, these pogroms were calculated acts of retaliation carried out by the SA, SS, and local Nazi party organizations.

Storm troopers killed at least 91 Jews and injured many others. For the first time, Jews were arrested on a massive scale and transported to Nazi concentration camps. About 30,000 Jews were sent to Buchenwald, Dachau, and Sachsenhausen, where hundreds died within weeks of arrival. Release came only after the prisoners arranged to emigrate and agreed to transfer their property to "Aryans."

The burning of the synagogue in Ober Ramstadt during Kristallnacht. The local fire department prevented the fire from spreading to a nearby home but made no attempt to intervene in the synagogue fire.

Trudy Isenberg Collection, Courtesy of the USHMM Archives.

Kristallnacht culminated the escalating violence against Jews that began during the incorporation of Austria into the Reich in March 1938. It also signaled the fateful transfer of responsibility for "solving" the "Jewish Question" to the SS.

Analysis Comparing Points of View

The Holocaust

The questions on this page ask you to analyze the views on the Holocaust presented in the preceding three selections:

Primo Levi . . . . *from* **Survival in Auschwitz** . . . . . (Italy)
Marguerite Duras . . . . *from* **The War** . . . . (France)
Elie Wiesel . . . . **Never Shall I Forget** . . . . (Romania)

Thinking Critically

1. The authors of the three selections in this feature were directly connected to the events of the Holocaust. As a result, each piece of writing is **subjective**—that is, it tells about actual events from a very personal point of view. Describe the similarities and differences you find in these three points of view. As a point of comparison, contrast the subjective points of view in these selections with the objective, or factual, point of view of the ***Connection*** on page 1064.
2. In your opinion, which selection could act as the most powerful deterrent against another Holocaust? Do you agree that keeping the memory of the Holocaust alive will make it less likely that such an event will occur again? (Review your Quickwrite notes on page 1050.)
3. Loss of identity is a common theme in these three works. Describe what or who stripped these writers of their identities. Was it a single person? a group of people? Or was it a broader, more subtle idea or entity? Whom or what do you think each writer would point to as the enemy?
4. Choose two of the three selections you have read in this feature, and compare the speakers of the two selections. How would you describe each speaker's **tone**? Who seems closest to the events he or she describes? Who seems furthest removed? Explain.

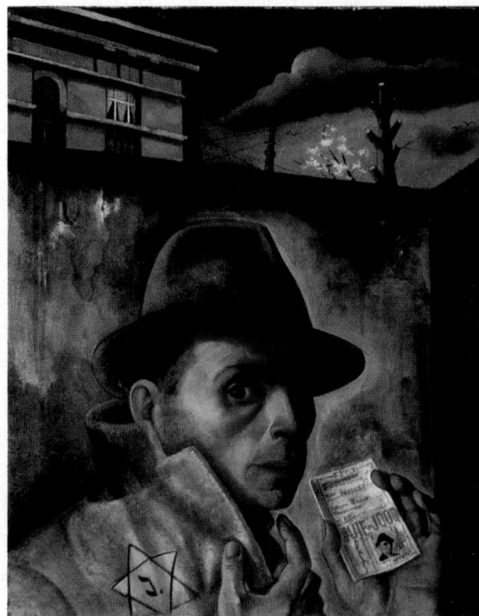

Self-portrait with Jewish Identity Card (detail) (1943) by Felix Nussbaum. Oil on canvas.

Literary Skills Analyze and compare points of view on a topic.

Reading Skills Compare main ideas across texts.

Writing Skills Write an essay analyzing political assumptions.

WRITING

Analyzing Political Assumptions

In an **essay,** unearth the political assumptions that underlie these three selections, and then evaluate how clearly these assumptions are communicated. First, summarize the claim, or the main idea, that you believe each author wants to convey. (Consult your reading notes on page 1050.) What idea *about* the Holocaust is each writer trying to express? Next, jot down specific details that help clarify this main idea. Finally, consider how all the texts work together to express a crucial idea, or assumption, about human nature and human experience. Use examples from the texts to illustrate and support your ideas.

Winston Churchill

1874–1965

England

Winston Churchill (soldier, statesman, man of letters, Nobel laureate and, in the eyes of many, savior of Britain) was born at Blenheim Palace. He was the son of Lord Randolph Churchill, a politician, and his wife Jennie Jerome. Of his early schooling, Churchill said, "I got into my bones the essential structure of the ordinary British sentence—which is a noble thing." Churchill's father, lacking confidence in his son's academic abilities, insisted that he prepare for a military career by entering Sandhurst Royal Military College.

Churchill emerged in 1895 a second lieutenant in the cavalry and volunteered to visit Cuba to observe Spain's tactics against Cuban rebels. He also went to write and send war dispatches to a British newspaper. On his return, he wrote an article about the conflict for the *Saturday Review*, and so began Churchill's simultaneous career as a writer with whatever profession—military or political—he undertook. Later, in 1897, while stationed in southern India, he joined a military action against Afghan tribesmen more than two thousand miles north at Malakand by becoming a war correspondent for the London *Daily Telegraph*. Officer casualties soon made it necessary for Churchill to drop his journalist role and take charge of troops, which he did zealously. Churchill wrote a history of the Malakand campaign, modestly mentioning himself only in a footnote.

In 1899, Churchill left the army and ran for a seat in Parliament, which he lost. The Boer War had started, and he sailed for South Africa as a war correspondent for the *Morning Post*. He was captured by the Boers but completed a daring escape that made him famous throughout Britain. He published two books on the war, one of which, *London to Ladysmith via Pretoria* (1900), was based on his press reports and sold 11,000 copies in fewer than six weeks. He was elected to Parliament in 1900.

By the time World War II began, Churchill had served in numerous government positions. For breadth of experience and energy, he had few peers when he became prime minister in 1940. He also had no equals in giving speeches that would rally the nation never to surrender, especially during the "blitz," when Germany bombed London for fifty-seven successive nights. Of the brave British fighter pilots who persevered night after night, he said, "Never in the field of human conflict has so much been owed by so many to so few." Few comments on war have been as poignant or memorable.

Following the war, Churchill published collections of his speeches and biographies and more books on military history. He was awarded the Nobel Prize for literature in 1953, when he was seventy-nine. But it was his leadership through the war that no one would forget and that prompted his daughter Mary to sum up his achievement by saying, "I owe you what every Englishman, woman and child does—Liberty itself."

Before You Read

Blood, Sweat, and Tears

Make the Connection

Quickwrite

When a country faces war or natural disaster, its citizens look to their political leaders for assurance, guidance, and inspiration. Jot down your thoughts on what you would expect to hear from a government leader in a time of crisis.

Reading Skills

Identifying and Critiquing an Author's Argument

To persuade listeners or readers to agree with their arguments, speakers and writers often try to demonstrate their credibility through **logical appeals**. They may then try to engage their audience's support with **emotional appeals.** As you read, notice how Churchill begins his speech by listing the methodical, reasonable steps he has taken to form his government. He then arouses strong feelings in his audience by using emotionally charged words like "ordeal," "struggle," and "tyranny." What exactly is Churchill's purpose? As you read, try to define his purpose, and critique his effectiveness in accomplishing it.

Background

World War II officially began with Germany's invasion of Poland on September 1, 1939. On September 3, Britain declared war on Germany and started manufacturing arms, ships, and planes for both offense and defense. By the time Churchill gave his speech to Parliament on May 13, 1940, German troops had overrun Holland and Belgium and were driving deep into France. The Battle of Britain was imminent. As newly elected prime minister, Churchill had just formed a coalition government of Labour and Liberals and knew that he had to inspire the country with an unwavering belief in its ability to survive, triumph, and endure. No one who heard Churchill's radio speeches during the war ever forgot them.

Our Heritage (1943) by Robert Austin. The poster first appeared in the London Underground.

London Transport Museum.

Vocabulary Development

rigor (rig′ər) *n.:* extreme severity.

provision (prə•vizh′ən) *n.:* arrangement or preparation beforehand.

grievous (grēv′əs) *adj.:* outrageous; horrible.

lamentable (lə•men′tə•bəl) *adj.:* regrettable; unfortunate.

buoyancy (boi′ən•sē) *n.:* lightness of spirit; cheerfulness.

Reading Skills
Identify and critique an author's argument.

INTERNET
Vocabulary Practice
Keyword: LE7 12-7

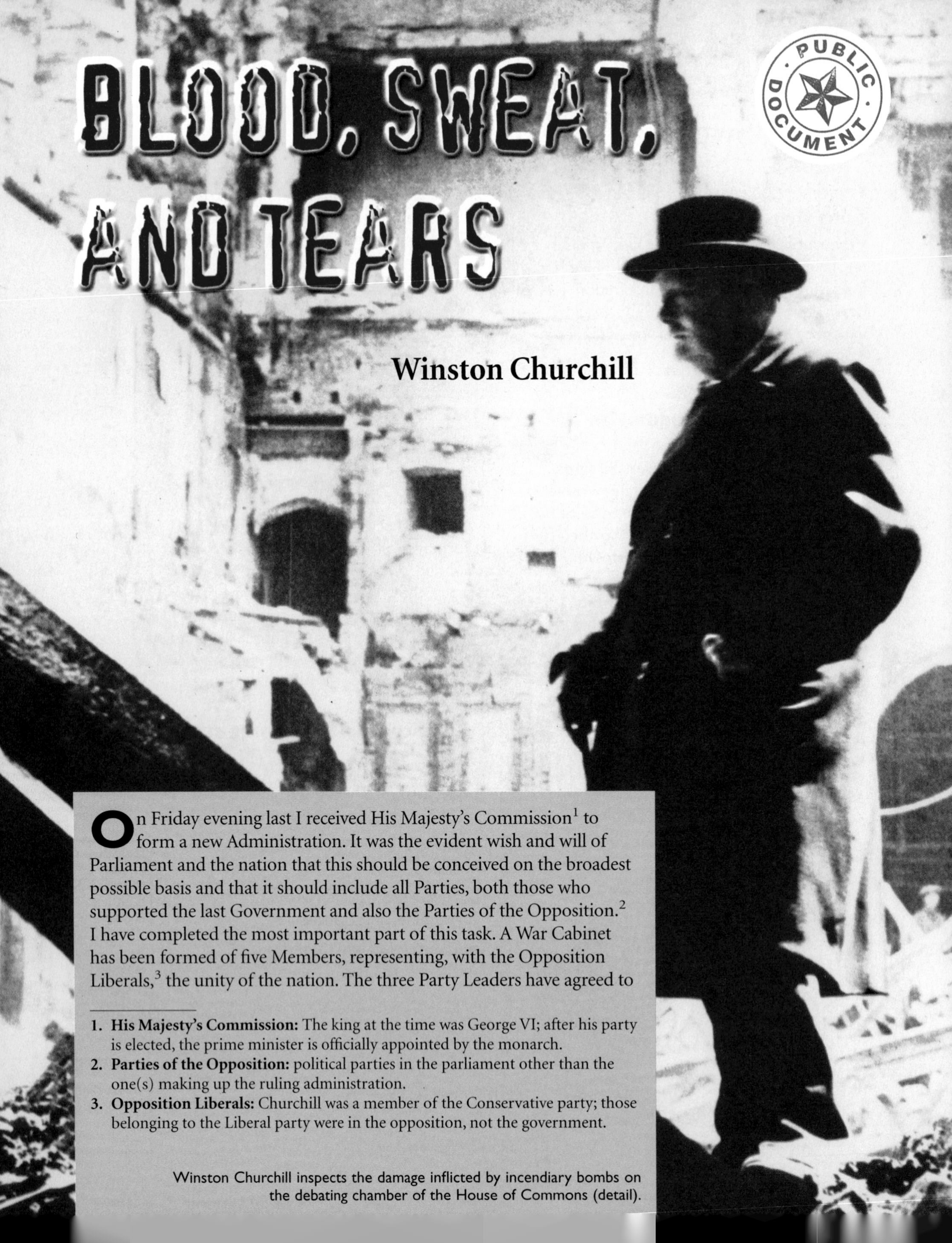

BLOOD, SWEAT, AND TEARS

Winston Churchill

On Friday evening last I received His Majesty's Commission[1] to form a new Administration. It was the evident wish and will of Parliament and the nation that this should be conceived on the broadest possible basis and that it should include all Parties, both those who supported the last Government and also the Parties of the Opposition.[2] I have completed the most important part of this task. A War Cabinet has been formed of five Members, representing, with the Opposition Liberals,[3] the unity of the nation. The three Party Leaders have agreed to

1. **His Majesty's Commission:** The king at the time was George VI; after his party is elected, the prime minister is officially appointed by the monarch.
2. **Parties of the Opposition:** political parties in the parliament other than the one(s) making up the ruling administration.
3. **Opposition Liberals:** Churchill was a member of the Conservative party; those belonging to the Liberal party were in the opposition, not the government.

Winston Churchill inspects the damage inflicted by incendiary bombs on the debating chamber of the House of Commons (detail).

serve, either in the War Cabinet or in high executive office. The three Fighting Services have been filled. It was necessary that this should be done in one single day, on account of the extreme urgency and rigor of events. A number of other key positions were filled yesterday, and I am submitting a further list to His Majesty tonight. I hope to complete the appointment of the principal Ministers during tomorrow. The appointment of the other Ministers usually takes a little longer, but I trust that, when Parliament meets again, this part of my task will be complete in all respects.

I considered it in the public interest to suggest that the House should be summoned to meet today. Mr. Speaker agreed, and took the necessary steps, in accordance with the powers conferred[4] upon him by the Resolution of the House. At the end of the proceedings today, the Adjournment of the House will be proposed until Tuesday, 21st May, with, of course, provision for earlier meeting if need be. The business to be considered during that week will be notified to Members at the earliest opportunity. I now invite the House, by the Resolution which stands in my name, to record its approval of the steps taken and to declare its confidence in the new Government.[5] ❶

> ❶ In the first two paragraphs, Churchill presents his argument by using evidence, examples, and reasons.
> ? *Is his appeal primarily to reason or to emotion? Explain.*

To form an Administration of this scale and complexity is a serious undertaking in itself, but it must be remembered that we are in the preliminary stage of one of the greatest battles in history, that we are in action at many points in Norway and in Holland, that we have to be prepared in the Mediterranean, that the air battle is continuous, and the many preparations have to be made here at home. In this crisis I hope I may be pardoned if I do not address the House at any length today. I hope that any of my friends and colleagues, or former colleagues, who are affected by the political reconstruction, will make all allowance for any lack of ceremony with which it has been necessary to act. I would say to the House, as I said to those who have joined this Government: "I have nothing to offer but blood, toil, tears, and sweat."

We have before us an ordeal of the most grievous kind. We have before us many, many long months of struggle and of suffering. You ask, What is our policy? I will say: "It is to wage war, by sea, land and air, with all our might and with all the strength that God can give us: to wage war against a monstrous tyranny, never surpassed in the dark, lamentable catalogue of human crime. That is our policy." You ask, What is our aim? I can answer in one word: Victory—victory at all costs, victory in spite of all terror, victory however long and hard the road may be; for without victory there is no survival. Let that be realized; no survival for the British Empire; no survival for all that the British Empire has stood for; no survival for the urge and impulse of the ages, that mankind will move forward towards its goal. But I take up my task with buoyancy and hope. I feel sure that our cause will not be suffered to fail among men. At this time I feel entitled to claim the aid of all, and I say, "Come, then, let us go forward together with our united strength." ❷ ❸ ■

> ❷ In this final paragraph, Churchill shifts to emotional appeals. He uses parallelism, or the repetition of and emphasis on sentence structures and key words.
> ? *What examples of parallelism can you find in this paragraph? What is the effect of this parallelism?*

> ❸ ? *In the final three sentences, how does Churchill try to uplift and inspire his listeners?*

---

4. **conferred** *v.:* granted.
5. **the new Government:** the recently elected administration led by Churchill.

Vocabulary

rigor (rig′ər) *n.:* extreme severity.
provision (prə·vizh′ən) *n.:* arrangement or preparation beforehand.
grievous (grēv′əs) *adj.:* outrageous; horrible.
lamentable (lə·men′tə·bəl) *adj.:* regrettable; unfortunate.
buoyancy (boi′ən·sē) *n.:* lightness of spirit; cheerfulness.

Response and Analysis

Reading Check

1. To whom is Churchill speaking?
2. What does he want approved?
3. What is the government's aim?

Thinking Critically

4. The credibility of a public figure is often revealed to an audience in public addresses. How would you **characterize** Churchill after reading his speech? In what ways does he convince you of his competence, credibility, and command of the situation?
5. How would you describe Churchill's **tone**—his attitude toward his audience? Find examples from the speech to support your judgment. Why do you suppose Churchill has avoided any humor or lightheartedness in his speech?
6. In the final two paragraphs, identify and analyze **rhetorical devices** that Churchill uses to arouse emotional reactions in his listeners. (Consider such techniques as emphasis, repetition, word choice, personal references, and call to action.) What is his purpose in these paragraphs? Refer to your reading notes.
7. How would you interpret Churchill's statement: "I have nothing to offer but blood, toil, tears, and sweat"? What does it reveal about Churchill and his argument?
8. Churchill knew that leaders of Germany would read his speech. What might he have been trying to convince the enemy of?

Extending and Evaluating

9. Did you find Churchill's speech persuasive and his arguments valid? Did he say the things you would expect a leader to say in a time of war? Support your responses with reasons and examples. (Be sure to consult your Quickwrite notes.)
10. Would Churchill's speech be more effective if it were longer and included more details, examples, and reasons to support his argument? Why or why not?

Reading Skills Identify and critique an author's argument.

Writing Skills Write a persuasive essay using logical, emotional, and ethical appeals.

Vocabulary Skills Complete analogies.

WRITING

Call to Action

Write a **persuasive essay** using **logical** and **emotional appeals** to convince your audience that they must take action on a particular issue affecting your school or community. To make your argument more convincing, use at least one **ethical appeal** to show that you are competent, sincere, trustworthy, fair, and knowledgeable.

For help with this assignment, see "Writing a Persuasive Essay," pages 1101–1102.

Vocabulary Development

Analogies

rigor
provision
grievous
lamentable
buoyancy

In an **analogy** the words in one pair relate to each other in the same way as the words in a second pair. On a separate sheet of paper, fill in each blank below with the Vocabulary word above that best completes the analogy.

1. ARID : DRY :: ________ : unfortunate
2. LIVELY : INACTIVE :: ______ : pleasant
3. FRIGID : COLD :: ________ : severity
4. WEALTH : POVERTY :: ________ : sadness
5. STRENGTH : VIGOR :: ________ : preparation

Yasunari Kawabata

(1899–1972)

Japan

The concern with loneliness and death that pervades the novels and short stories of Yasunari Kawabata (yä·sü′nä·re kä′wä·bä′tä) may be a result of his childhood. His father died when Kawabata was three; the following year his mother died. Within the next five years his only sister and his grandmother died. At the age of fourteen, Kawabata began to record his thoughts and feelings when he saw that his grandfather, who had raised him for about six years, was growing very ill. These writings were published after his grandfather's death as *Diary of a Sixteen-Year-Old* (1925).

Born in Osaka, Kawabata attended Tokyo Imperial University, where he studied English literature and Japanese literature. In 1924, he joined with other students to found a literary magazine that became the mouthpiece of a new avant-garde literary movement called Neosensualism, which was influenced, in part, by haiku poetry. Neosensualist writers attempted to capture intense, immediate moments in life—images, sensations, and impressions. To achieve such immediacy in his novels, Kawabata placed one psychologically charged scene right after another, with no transitions. This technique gives the effect, one critic wrote, of "a series of brief flashes in a void."

Kawabata's novels include *The Izu Dancer* (1926), *The Snow Country* (1948), *Thousand Cranes* (1952), *The Sound of the Mountain* (1952), and *The House of the Sleeping Beauties* (1961). These novels, which focus on lonely men who try to find comfort in the beauty and goodness of women, are characterized by nostalgia and sadness. Although Kawabata is best known for his novels, he also wrote what he called *tanagokoro no shosetsu,* or "palm-of-the-hand stories." In their deceptive simplicity, these stories resemble haiku poetry (see pages 749–756). Just as a haiku offers brief, vivid images that rival the richness of a longer poem, so these little stories offer images and psychological insights that rival those of longer fiction.

Kawabata died alone in his studio in 1972, about a year and a half after his friend, the novelist Yukio Mishima, had committed ritual suicide for political reasons. Kawabata also took his own life, but he left no explanation of his motives.

In 1968, Kawabata became the first Japanese writer to be awarded the Nobel Prize in literature. In his acceptance speech he remarked on an aspect of traditional Japanese ink painting that applies, with startling accuracy, to his own work and to his life: "The heart [of it] is in space, abbreviation, what is left undrawn."

For Independent Reading

You may enjoy this story by Kawabata:

- "The Jay"

Before You Read

The Silver Fifty-Sen Pieces

Make the Connection

Family members and groups of friends often cherish anecdotes about one another and embellish these stories through repeated telling. These anecdotes are often humorous and usually offer insight into the character of the person they are about. In the following story, Yasunari Kawabata describes the origins of one such family anecdote. This anecdote, as you will see, is about a small, beautiful treasure. By the story's end, however, we realize that the more striking treasure is the anecdote itself. Holding it up to the light, Kawabata shows us how a simple family story can reflect the hearts of those who share it.

Literary Focus

Theme

A **theme** is a literary work's central insight into human experience. Unlike a topic (such as *love* or *death*), a theme is a complete idea that usually takes the form of a sentence: *For a person to give love, he or she must first receive it.* As in this example, a theme does not reflect the specific content of a work. Rather, it moves beyond the work to express a general idea about life or human nature. Sometimes authors state a theme directly, but more often they imply or suggest it through the descriptive details, images, or symbols in the work itself.

> A **theme** is the central idea or insight of a work of literature.
>
> *For more on Theme, see the Handbook of Literary and Historical Terms.*

Reading Skills

Making Inferences

Some works of literature are dominated by a particular **symbol,** something that stands for itself and also for something beyond itself. This symbol can give the reader a strong clue about the **theme** of the work—that is, it can help the reader make an **inference,** or an intelligent guess, about the work's underlying message. As you read "The Silver Fifty-Sen Pieces," try to identify the story's central symbol. Then, ask yourself: What abstract idea might this symbol represent? Next, try to figure out what Kawabata wants to convey about this abstract idea. When you have determined this, you will have inferred the story's theme.

Background

The protagonist of "The Silver Fifty-Sen Pieces" is a young woman living in Tokyo, Japan, in the years prior to and during Japan's war with China and Manchuria (1937–1945) and just after World War II (1939–1945). Young women living in their parents' households often held low-level jobs for several years before "retiring" to get married by age twenty-five.

Vocabulary Development

spurned (spʉrnd) *v.:* rejected.

exquisite (eks′kwiz·it) *adj.:* beautiful; delicate.

meticulous (mə·tik′yo͞o·ləs) *adj.:* precise; extremely concerned with details.

discrimination (di·skrim′i·nā′shən) *n.:* ability to make fine distinctions.

antipathy (an·tip′ə·thē) *n.:* strong dislike; aversion.

SKILLS FOCUS

Literary Skills Understand theme.

Reading Skills Make inferences about theme.

INTERNET
Vocabulary Practice
Keyword: LE7 12-7

The Silver Fifty-Sen Pieces

Yasunari Kawabata

translated by **Lane Dunlop** *and* **J. Martin Holman**

Rain at Yotsuya Mitsuke (1930) by Takashi Henmi.

It was a custom that the two-yen allowance that she received at the start of each month, in silver fifty-sen[1] pieces, be placed in Yoshiko's purse by her mother's own hand.

At that time, the fifty-sen piece had recently been reduced in size. These silver coins, which looked light and felt heavy, seemed to Yoshiko to fill up her small red leather purse with a solid dignity. Often, careful not to waste them, she kept them in her handbag until the end of the month. It was not that Yoshiko spurned such girlish pleasures as going out to a movie theater or a coffee shop with the friends she worked with; she simply saw those diversions as being

1. **two-yen, fifty-sen:** A fifty-sen piece is half of one yen, the basic monetary unit of Japan. (One hundred sen equal one yen.) Exchange rates vary, but one yen has usually been equivalent to an amount much less than one U.S. dollar.

Vocabulary

spurned (spʉrnd) *v.:* rejected.

Harimaya-chô (1935) by Yoshinobu Sakamoto.

outside her life. She had never experienced them, and so was never tempted by them.

Once a week, on her way back from the office, she would stop off at a department store and buy, for ten sen, a loaf of the seasoned French bread she liked so much. Other than that, there was nothing she particularly wanted for herself.

One day, however, at Mitsukoshi's, in the stationery department, a glass paperweight caught her eye. Hexagonal, it had a dog carved on it in relief.[2] Charmed by the dog, Yoshiko took the paperweight in her hand. Its thrilling coolness, its unexpected weightiness, suddenly gave her pleasure. Yoshiko, who loved this kind of delicately accomplished work, was captivated despite herself. Weighing it in her palm, looking at it from every angle, she quietly and reluctantly put it back in its box. It was forty sen.

The next day, she came back. She examined the paperweight again. The day after that, she came back again and examined it anew. After ten days of this, she finally made up her mind.

"I'll take this," she said to the clerk, her heart beating fast.

When she got home, her mother and older sister laughed at her.

"Buying this sort of thing—it's like a toy."

But when each had taken it in her hand and looked at it, they said, "You're right, it *is* rather pretty," and, "It's so ingenious."

They tried holding it up against the light. The polished clear glass surface and the misty surface, like frosted glass, of the relief, harmonized curiously. In the hexagonal facets,[3] too, there was an exquisite rightness, like the meter of a poem.

2. **relief** *n.:* sculptured shape raised from a flat background surface.

3. **facets** (fas′its) *n. pl.:* A facet is one surface of a many-sided solid figure.

Vocabulary

exquisite (eks′kwiz·it) *adj.:* beautiful; delicate.

To Yoshiko, it was a lovely work of art.

Although Yoshiko hadn't hoped to be complimented on the deliberation with which she had made her purchase, taking ten days to decide that the paperweight was an object worth her possession, she was pleased to receive this recognition of her good taste from her mother and older sister.

Even if she was laughed at for her exaggerated carefulness—taking those ten days to buy something that cost a mere forty sen—Yoshiko would not have been satisfied unless she had done so. She had never had occasion to regret having bought something on the spur of the moment. It was not that the seventeen-year-old Yoshiko possessed such meticulous discrimination that she spent several days thinking about and looking at something before arriving at a decision. It was just that she had a vague dread of spending carelessly the silver fifty-sen pieces, which had sunk into her mind as an important treasure.

Years later, when the story of the paperweight came up and everybody burst out laughing, her mother said seriously, "I thought you were so lovable that time."

To each and every one of Yoshiko's possessions, an amusing anecdote of this sort was attached.

It was a pleasure to do their shopping from the top down, descending regularly from floor to floor, so first they went up to the fifth floor on the elevator. This Sunday, unusually allured by the charm of a shopping trip with her mother, Yoshiko had come to Mitsukoshi's.

Although their shopping for the day was done, when they'd descended to the first floor, her mother, as a matter of course, went on down to the bargain basement.

"But it's so crowded, Mother. I don't like it," grumbled Yoshiko, but her mother didn't hear her. Evidently the atmosphere of the bargain basement, with its competitive jockeying for position, had already absorbed her mother.

The bargain basement was a place set up for the sole purpose of making people waste their money, but perhaps her mother would find something. Thinking she'd keep an eye on her, Yoshiko followed her at a distance. It was air-conditioned so it wasn't all that hot.

Japanese fifty-sen coins (pre–World War II).
HRW photo by Sam Dudgeon.

First buying three bundles of stationery for twenty-five sen, her mother turned around and looked at Yoshiko. They smiled sweetly at each other. Lately, her mother had been pilfering Yoshiko's stationery, much to the latter's annoyance. Now we can rest easy, their looks seemed to say.

Drawn toward the counters for kitchen utensils and underwear, Yoshiko's mother was not brave enough to thrust her way through the mob of customers. Standing on tiptoe and peering over people's shoulders or putting her hand out through the small spaces between their sleeves, she looked but nevertheless didn't buy anything. At first unconvinced and then making up her mind definitely no, she headed toward the exit.

"Oh, these are just ninety-five sen? My . . ."

Just this side of the exit, her mother picked up one of the umbrellas for sale. Even after they'd burrowed through the whole heaped-up jumble, every single umbrella bore a price tag of ninety-five sen.

Apparently still surprised, her mother said, "They're so cheap, aren't they, Yoshiko? Aren't they cheap?" Her voice was suddenly lively. It was as if her vague, perplexed reluctance to leave without buying something more had found an outlet. "Well? Don't you think they're cheap?"

"They really are." Yoshiko, too, took one of the umbrellas in her hand. Her mother, holding hers alongside it, opened it up.

Vocabulary

meticulous (mə·tik′yo͞o·ləs) *adj.:* precise; extremely concerned with details.

discrimination (di·skrim′i·nā′shən) *n.:* ability to make fine distinctions.

"Just the ribs alone would be cheap at the price. The fabric—well, it's rayon, but it's so well made, don't you think?"

How was it possible to sell such a respectable item at this price? As the question flashed through Yoshiko's mind, a strange feeling of antipathy welled up in her, as if she'd been shoved by a cripple. Her mother, totally absorbed, opening up one after the other, rummaged through the pile to find an umbrella suitable to her age. Yoshiko waited a while, then said, "Mother, don't you have an umbrella at home?"

"Yes, that's so, but . . ." Glancing quickly at Yoshiko, her mother went on, "It's ten years, no, more, I've had it fifteen years. It's worn out and old-fashioned. And, Yoshiko, if I passed this on to somebody, think how happy they would be."

"That's true. It's all right if it's for a gift."

"There's nobody who wouldn't be happy."

Yoshiko smiled. Her mother seemed to be choosing an umbrella with that "somebody" in mind. But it was not anybody close to them. If it were, surely her mother would not have said "somebody."

"What about this one, Yoshiko?"

"That looks good."

Although she gave an unenthusiastic answer, Yoshiko went to her mother's side and began searching for a suitable umbrella.

Other shoppers, wearing thin summer dresses of rayon and saying, "It's cheap, it's cheap," were casually snapping up the umbrellas on their way into and out of the store.

Feeling pity for her mother, who, her face set and slightly flushed, was trying so hard to find the right umbrella, Yoshiko grew angry at her own hesitation.

As if to say, "Why not just buy one, any one, quickly?" Yoshiko turned away from her mother.

"Yoshiko, let's stop this."

"What?"

A weak smile floating at the corners of her mouth, as if to shake something off, her mother put her hand on Yoshiko's shoulder and left the counter. Now, though, it was Yoshiko who felt some indefinable reluctance. But, when she'd taken five or six steps, she felt relieved.

Taking hold of her mother's hand on her shoulder, she squeezed it hard and swung it together with her own. Pressing close to her mother so that they were shoulder to shoulder, she hurried toward the exit.

This had happened seven years ago, in the year 1939.

When the rain pounded against the fire-scorched sheet-metal roof of the shack, Yoshiko, thinking it would have been good if they had bought that umbrella, found herself wanting to make a funny story of it with her mother. Nowadays, the umbrella would have cost a hundred or two hundred yen. But her mother had died in the firebombings of their Tokyo neighborhood of Kanda.[4]

Even if they had bought the umbrella, it probably would have perished in the flames.

By chance, the glass paperweight had survived. When her husband's house in Yokohama[5] had burned down, the paperweight was among those things that she'd frantically stuffed into an emergency bag. It was her one remembrance of life in her mother's house.

From evening on, in the alley, there were the strange-sounding voices of the neighborhood girls. They were talking about how you could make a thousand yen in a single night. Taking up the forty-sen paperweight, which, when she was those girls' age, she had spent ten days thinking about before deciding to buy, Yoshiko studied the charming little dog carved in relief. Suddenly, she realized that there was not a single dog left in the whole burned-out neighborhood. The thought came as a shock to her. ■

4. **firebombings . . . Kanda:** For three years before the United States dropped atomic bombs on the Japanese cities of Hiroshima and Nagasaki in August 1945, incendiary (fire-making) bombs were used to devastate Tokyo and cripple its industry. Despite the fact that the bombs destroyed homes and landmarks and killed many people, the Japanese government would not surrender.

5. **Yokohama** (yō′kō·hä′mä): port city south of Tokyo on Tokyo Bay.

Vocabulary

antipathy (an·tip′ə·thē) *n.:* strong dislike; aversion.

Response and Analysis

Reading Check

1. How does Yoshiko usually spend her two-yen allowance?
2. Describe the special object that Yoshiko finally buys. How long does she take to make up her mind? How do her mother and sister react to her purchase?
3. What items attract Yoshiko's mother in the bargain basement? Which of these items does she buy?
4. What details at the end of the story identify the time and location in which the story takes place?

Thinking Critically

5. Jot down details from the story that **characterize** Yoshiko and her mother. What contrast between their personalities do these details suggest?
6. What conclusions can you draw about the relationship between Yoshiko and her mother from Yoshiko's thoughts and reactions in the final scene?
7. What message or **main idea** does the author convey in the umbrella episode in the department store?
8. What do you think the paperweight **symbolizes** in the story? Why, in the final scene, does it give Yoshiko a shock?
9. Summarize the **theme** or central insight that this story suggests to you. Look at your reading notes and list the clues—the details, images, or events—that helped you **infer** the theme. What does this theme suggest about life?

Extending and Evaluating

10. Do you think the title "The Silver Fifty-Sen Pieces" is appropriate? Why or why not? What other title would you give this story? Explain.

WRITING

Overtones and Echoes

In regard to one of Kawabata's novels, a critic wrote that Kawabata returns again and again to a specific moment in time, creating "circles upon circles of memory, coincidence after coincidence, innocent themes followed by their sinister, scarcely audible overtones and echoes." In a brief **essay,** use details from the story to explain how this observation applies to "The Silver Fifty-Sen Pieces." Look closely at the final scene. How does the story's conclusion give the theme "sinister" echoes?

Vocabulary Development

What's Wrong with This Picture?

Explain what's wrong with each sentence below.

1. She spurned her mother, whom she loved dearly.
2. Those giant plastic garbage bags are simply exquisite!
3. A meticulous man, Harvey rarely proofreads his writing.
4. Lisa has a fine sense of discrimination. She frequently buys damaged goods.
5. Upon seeing him, her antipathy was so great that she flung herself into his arms.

Literary Skills
Analyze theme.

Reading Skills
Make inferences about theme.

Writing Skills
Write an essay explaining a critical comment.

Vocabulary Skills
Demonstrate word knowledge.

Grammar Skills
Use parallel structure correctly.

Grammar Link

Effective Sentences: The Power of Parallelism

Good writers create **parallel structure** in a sentence by using the same grammatical form to express two or more equal, or parallel, ideas. Pairing adjectives with adjectives, prepositional phrases with prepositional phrases, and noun clauses with noun clauses emphasizes the relationship between the ideas. You can use parallel structure to link coordinate ideas, to compare or contrast ideas, and to link ideas with correlative conjunctions (such as *both ... and, either ... or*). Parallel structure can also make a passage rhythmic and memorable.

Compare the awkwardness of these examples of faulty parallelism with the clarity of phrasing in the parallel sentences from "The Silver Fifty-Sen Pieces."

FAULTY: Other shoppers, wearing thin summer dresses of rayon and who said, "It's cheap, it's cheap," were casually snapping up the umbrellas. . . . [participial phrase paired with adjective clause]

PARALLEL: Other shoppers, wearing thin summer dresses of rayon and saying, "It's cheap, it's cheap," were casually snapping up the umbrellas. . . . [participial phrase paired with participial phrase]

FAULTY: Yoshiko appreciated the paperweight both for its coolness and unexpected weightiness and because it was delicate. [prepositional phrase paired with adverb clause]

PARALLEL: Yoshiko appreciated the paperweight both for its coolness and unexpected weightiness and for its delicacy. [prepositional phrase paired with prepositional phrase]

PRACTICE

The following sentences are about Japanese literature. Rewrite each sentence to correct the nonparallel sentence structures.

1. Japanese writers have been celebrated not only for their novels, poetry, and plays but because they wrote travel journals and diaries.
2. The *Manyoshu*, an eighth-century collection of more than 4,500 poems, consists of short poems called tanka and choka, long poems of up to 150 lines.
3. The poetry anthology *Kokinshu* (*Collection from Ancient and Modern Times*), composed in A.D. 905, includes books of seasonal poems, mourning poems, and poems about love.
4. Tenth-century Japanese writer Ki Tsurayuki is well-known as a contributor to *Kokinshu* and because he wrote the first example of a "literary diary."

Apply to Your Writing

Review a writing assignment you are working on now or have already completed. Are there any nonparallel sentence structures? Revise to make them parallel sentence structures.

For more help, see Using Parallel Structure, 9c, in the Language Handbook.

Graham Greene

(1904–1991)

England

For his serious idealistic novels dealing with contemporary moral dilemmas and for his light "entertainments" and thrillers, Graham Greene has won a rare combination of popular and critical admiration. His intention in his writing was always to tell the truth, which he saw as a primary duty of the artist. In his quest for truth, Greene often wrote about life's losers—at least those whom we conventionally think of as losers.

Henry Graham Greene was born to a comfortable family in Berkhamsted, Hertfordshire. His father was the headmaster of Berkhamsted School, which Greene attended as a child. For reasons that are not clear, as Greene grew into adolescence, he became increasingly depressed and unhappy at school, which he described as his first impression of hell. After he tried to run away, he was sent to London to undergo psychoanalysis. He would later recall those six months in London as among the happiest of his life.

While he was still at Berkhamsted, Greene had a story published by a local newspaper, and he recalled feeling a sense of true literary triumph "for the first and last time." The experience convinced him to become a professional writer. He attended Oxford University, wrote a novel that failed to find a publisher, and published a book of poems in 1925, the year he graduated.

In 1926, Greene became engaged to a Roman Catholic woman, Vivien Dayrell-Browning, and agreed to take instruction in her faith. Although he had been a confirmed atheist, he became convinced of "the probable existence of something we call God." His Catholic faith would turn out to be an important factor in his writing.

Greene took a job with the London *Times* and worked there until his first novel, *The Man Within*, was published in 1929. His next books were adventure stories, which received little attention. Greene began to come into his own with the thriller *Stamboul Train* (1932; also published under the title *Orient Express*). This story of a train journey to Istanbul was the first of Greene's works that were made into movies.

Greene brought his religious concerns into his fiction with the novel *Brighton Rock* (1938), in which he explored the nature of good and evil and the inexplicable workings of divine grace. Pursuing the theme further in *The Power and the Glory* (1940), Greene revealed an unorthodox kind of Catholicism in which naturally sinful men and women, living in a fallen world, are often given a last-minute chance at redemption.

Greene's novels came out steadily, among them *The Heart of the Matter* (1948), *The End of the Affair* (1951), and *A Burnt-Out Case* (1961). In the first volume of his autobiography, *A Sort of Life* (1971), Greene revealed his motives for writing fiction as "a desire to reduce the chaos of experience to some sort of order, and a hungry curiosity. We cannot love others, so the theologians teach, unless in some degree we can love ourselves, and curiosity too begins at home."

Before You Read

The Destructors

Make the Connection

This story is set in 1954, nine years after the end of World War II. During the war, London had been regularly "blitzed" by German planes dropping firebombs, and many of its buildings were destroyed. Years after the war, Londoners still walked among the rubble. More troubling than this physical destruction, though, was what many people saw as the moral destruction of society, the collapse of hope, especially among gangs of young people who had never known a reality other than war and its aftermath.

Literary Focus

Setting

The **setting** of this story reflects both political and social influences of the historical period: a drab corner of a city still reeling from war. This setting helps establish the story's pessimistic **mood.** As the story progresses, though, the setting becomes not just a backdrop, but rather a key plot element that helps to shape the characters. Greene's characteristic use of coarse **imagery** and language creates a seedy, drab world full of shabby violence.

Literary Skills Understand setting.

Reading Skills Make inferences about character motivation.

The **setting** is the time and place of a story.

For more on Setting, see the Handbook of Literary and Historical Terms.

INTERNET

Vocabulary Practice

Keyword: LE7 12-7

Reading Skills

Inferring Motives

Each of the four numbered sections of this story gives you a bit more insight into the enigmatic main character, T. After each section, jot down how you see T., and note particular words and actions that you find most revealing. When you have finished reading the story, use these clues to make some **inferences** about the character. What do you think motivates T. to act as he does?

Background

In 1941, the London home of Graham Greene and his wife, Vivien, was blasted during an air raid. Vivien, who was devastated by the loss, later recalled "walk[ing] in tears on the edge of the front room [and] looking down at the deep frightening cavity two floors below. . . ." Graham, however, seemed less troubled. "It's sad because it was a pretty house," he wrote, "but oddly enough it leaves one very carefree." According to Vivien, Graham felt relieved of the burden of a house that had symbolized the couple's miserable marriage—and perhaps an even deeper misery in the writer himself.

Vocabulary Development

ignoble (ig·nō′bəl) *adj.:* shameful; degrading.

impromptu (im·prämp′to͞o′) *adj.:* unplanned.

exploit (eks′ploit′) *n.:* daring act.

daunted (dônt′id) *v.* used as *adj.:* intimidated.

implacable (im·plak′ə·bəl) *adj.:* inflexible; relentless; stubborn.

fickleness (fik′əl·nis) *n.:* changeableness.

altruistic (al′tro͞o·is′tik) *adj.:* unselfish.

exhilaration (eg·zil′ə·rā′shən) *n.:* excitement; high spirits.

abstain (ab·stān′) *v.:* refrain from.

stealthy (stel′thē) *adj.:* secret; sly.

THE DESTRUCTORS

Graham Greene

After the Blitz by L. S. Lowry.

1

It was on the eve of August Bank Holiday that the latest recruit became the leader of the Wormsley Common gang. No one was surprised except Mike, but Mike at the age of nine was surprised by everything. "If you don't shut your mouth," somebody once said to him, "you'll get a frog down it." After that Mike had kept his teeth tightly clamped except when the surprise was too great.

The new recruit had been with the gang since the beginning of the summer holidays, and there were possibilities about his brooding silence that all recognized. He never wasted a word even to tell his name until that was required of him by the rules. When he said "Trevor" it was a statement of fact, not as it would have been with the others a statement of shame or defiance. Nor did anyone laugh except Mike, who finding himself without support and meeting the dark gaze of the newcomer opened his mouth and was quiet again. There was every reason why T., as he was afterward referred to, should have been an object of mockery—there was his name (and they substituted the initial because otherwise they had no excuse not to laugh at it), the fact that his father, a former architect and present clerk, had "come down in the world" and that his mother considered herself better than the neighbors. What but an odd quality of danger, of the unpredictable, established him in the gang without any ignoble ceremony of initiation?

The gang met every morning in an impromptu car-park, the site of the last bomb of the first blitz. The leader, who was known as Blackie, claimed to have heard it fall, and no one was precise enough in his dates to point out that he would have been one year old and fast asleep on the down platform of Wormsley Common Underground[1] Station. On one side of the car-park leaned the first occupied house, number 3, of the shattered Northwood Terrace—literally leaned, for it had suffered from the blast of the bomb and the side walls were supported on wooden struts. A smaller bomb and some incendiaries[2] had fallen beyond, so that the house stuck up like a jagged tooth and carried on the further wall relics of its neighbor, a dado,[3] the remains of a fireplace. T., whose words were almost confined to voting "Yes" or "No" to the plan of operations proposed each day by Blackie, once startled the whole gang by saying broodingly, "Wren[4] built that house, father says."

"Who's Wren?"

"The man who built St. Paul's."[5]

"Who cares?" Blackie said. "It's only Old Misery's."

Old Misery—whose real name was Thomas—had once been a builder and decorator. He lived alone in the crippled house, doing for himself: Once a week you could see him coming back across the common with bread and vegetables, and once as the boys played in the car-park he put his head over the smashed wall of his garden and looked at them.

"Been to the loo,"[6] one of the boys said, for it was common knowledge that since the bombs fell something had gone wrong with the pipes of the house and Old Misery was too mean[7] to spend money on the property. He could do the redecorating himself at cost price, but he had never learned plumbing. The loo was a wooden shed at the bottom of the narrow garden with a star-shaped hole in the door: It had escaped the blast which had smashed the house next door and sucked out the window frames of number 3.

The next time the gang became aware of Mr. Thomas was more surprising. Blackie, Mike, and

1. **Underground** *n.:* British for "subway."

2. **incendiaries** *n.:* firebombs.
3. **dado** (dā′dō): wood paneling along the lower part of the walls of a room.
4. **Wren:** Sir Christopher Wren (1632–1723), a celebrated English architect.
5. **St. Paul's:** cathedral in London.
6. **loo:** British slang for "bathroom." *Loo* comes from the French word *lieux,* short for *les lieux d'aisances* (lā lyö de·zäns′), which means "places of convenience."
7. **mean** *adj.:* stingy.

Vocabulary

ignoble (ig·nō′bəl) *adj.:* shameful; degrading.

impromptu (im·prämp′to͞o′) *adj.:* unplanned.

Juvenile Counsel: Boys on a Doorstep (20th century) by Henry Lamb.

a thin yellow boy, who for some reason was called by his surname[8] Summers, met him on the common coming back from the market. Mr. Thomas stopped them. He said glumly, "You belong to the lot that play in the car-park?"

Mike was about to answer when Blackie stopped him. As the leader he had responsibilities. "Suppose we are?" he said ambiguously.

"I got some chocolates," Mr. Thomas said. "Don't like 'em myself. Here you are. Not enough to go round, I don't suppose. There never is," he added with somber conviction. He handed over three packets of Smarties.

The gang were puzzled and perturbed by this action and tried to explain it away. "Bet someone dropped them and he picked 'em up," somebody suggested.

"Pinched[9] 'em and then got in a bleeding funk," another thought aloud.

"It's a bribe," Summers said. "He wants us to stop bouncing balls on his wall."

"We'll show him we don't take bribes," Blackie said, and they sacrificed the whole morning to the game of bouncing that only Mike was young enough to enjoy. There was no sign from Mr. Thomas.

Next day T. astonished them all. He was late at the rendezvous, and the voting for that day's exploit took place without him. At Blackie's suggestion the gang was to disperse in pairs, take

8. **surname** *n.:* last name.

9. **pinched** *v.:* British for "stole."

Vocabulary
exploit (eks'plɔit') *n.:* daring act.

buses at random, and see how many free rides could be snatched from unwary conductors (the operation was to be carried out in pairs to avoid cheating). They were drawing lots for their companions when T. arrived.

"Where you been, T.?" Blackie asked. "You can't vote now. You know the rules."

"I've been *there*," T. said. He looked at the ground, as though he had thoughts to hide.

"Where?"

"At Old Misery's." Mike's mouth opened and then hurriedly closed again with a click. He had remembered the frog.

"At Old Misery's?" Blackie said. There was nothing in the rules against it, but he had a sensation that T. was treading on dangerous ground. He asked hopefully, "Did you break in?"

"No. I rang the bell."

"And what did you say?"

"I said I wanted to see his house."

"What did he do?"

"He showed it me."

"Pinch anything?"

"No."

"What did you do it for then?"

The gang had gathered round: It was as though an impromptu court were about to form and to try some case of deviation. T. said, "It's a beautiful house," and still watching the ground, meeting no one's eyes, he licked his lips first one way, then the other.

"What do you mean, a beautiful house?" Blackie asked with scorn.

"It's got a staircase two hundred years old like a corkscrew. Nothing holds it up."

"What do you mean, nothing holds it up. Does it float?"

"It's to do with opposite forces, Old Misery said."

"What else?"

"There's paneling."

"Like in the Blue Boar?"

"Two hundred years old."

"Is Old Misery two hundred years old?"

Mike laughed suddenly and then was quiet again. The meeting was in a serious mood. For the first time since T. had strolled into the car-park on the first day of the holidays his position was in danger. It only needed a single use of his real name and the gang would be at his heels.

"What did you do it for?" Blackie asked. He was just, he had no jealousy, he was anxious to retain T. in the gang if he could. It was the word "beautiful" that worried him—that belonged to a class world that you could still see parodied at the Wormsley Common Empire by a man wearing a top hat and a monocle,[10] with a haw-haw accent. He was tempted to say, "My dear Trevor, old chap," and unleash his hell hounds. "If you'd broken in," he said sadly—that indeed would have been an exploit worthy of the gang.

"This was better," T. said. "I found out things." He continued to stare at his feet, not meeting anybody's eye, as though he were absorbed in some dream he was unwilling—or ashamed—to share.

"What things?"

"Old Misery's going to be away all tomorrow and Bank Holiday."

Blackie said with relief, "You mean we could break in?"

"And pinch things?" somebody asked.

Blackie said, "Nobody's going to pinch things. Breaking in—that's good enough, isn't it? We don't want any court stuff."

"I don't want to pinch anything," T. said. "I've got a better idea."

"What is it?"

T. raised his eyes, as gray and disturbed as the drab August day. "We'll pull it down," he said. "We'll destroy it."

Blackie gave a single hoot of laughter and then, like Mike, fell quiet, daunted by the serious implacable gaze. "What'd the police be doing all the time?" he said.

"They'd never know. We'd do it from inside. I've found a way in." He said with a sort of

---

10. monocle *n.:* eyeglass for one eye.

Vocabulary

daunted (dônt'id) *v.* used as *adj.:* intimidated.

implacable (im·plak'ə·bəl) *adj.:* inflexible; relentless; stubborn.

intensity, "We'd be like worms, don't you see, in an apple. When we came out again there'd be nothing there, no staircase, no panels, nothing but just walls, and then we'd make the walls fall down—somehow."

"We'd go to jug,"[11] Blackie said.

"Who's to prove? And anyway we wouldn't have pinched anything." He added without the smallest flicker of glee, "There wouldn't be anything to pinch after we'd finished."

"I've never heard of going to prison for breaking things," Summers said.

"There wouldn't be time," Blackie said. "I've seen housebreakers at work."

"There are twelve of us," T. said. "We'd organize."

"None of us know how—"

"I know," T. said. He looked across at Blackie. "Have you got a better plan?"

"Today," Mike said tactlessly, "we're pinching free rides—"

"Free rides," T. said. "You can stand down, Blackie, if you'd rather. . . ."

"The gang's got to vote."

"Put it up then."

Blackie said uneasily, "It's proposed that tomorrow and Monday we destroy Old Misery's house."

"Here, here," said a fat boy called Joe.

"Who's in favor?"

T. said, "It's carried."

"How do we start?" Summers asked.

"He'll tell you," Blackie said. It was the end of his leadership. He went away to the back of the car-park and began to kick a stone, dribbling it this way and that. There was only one old Morris[12] in the park, for few cars were left there except lorries:[13] Without an attendant there was no safety. He took a flying kick at the car and scraped a little paint off the rear mudguard. Beyond, paying no more attention to him than to a stranger, the gang had gathered round T.; Blackie was dimly aware of the fickleness of favor. He thought of going home, of never returning, of letting them all discover the hollowness of T.'s leadership, but suppose after all what T. proposed was possible—nothing like it had ever been done before. The fame of the Wormsley Common car-park gang would surely reach around London. There would be headlines in the papers. Even the grown-up gangs who ran the betting at the all-in wrestling and the barrow-boys[14] would hear with respect of how Old Misery's house had been destroyed. Driven by the pure, simple, and altruistic ambition of fame for the gang, Blackie came back to where T. stood in the shadow of Misery's wall.

T. was giving his orders with decision: It was as though this plan had been with him all his life, pondered through the seasons, now in his fifteenth year crystallized with the pain of puberty. "You," he said to Mike, "bring some big nails, the biggest you can find, and a hammer. Anyone else who can better bring a hammer and a screwdriver. We'll need plenty of them. Chisels too. We can't have too many chisels. Can anybody bring a saw?"

"I can," Mike said.

"Not a child's saw," T. said. "A real saw."

Blackie realized he had raised his hand like any ordinary member of the gang.

"Right, you bring one, Blackie. But now there's a difficulty. We want a hacksaw."[15]

"What's a hacksaw?" someone asked.

---

11. **jug** *n.:* slang for "jail."
12. **Morris:** car made by the Morris firm, a British automaker.
13. **lorries** *n. pl.:* British for "trucks."
14. **barrow-boys:** boys who sold fruit or vegetables from a barrow, or cart.
15. **hacksaw** *n.:* saw made for cutting metal.

Vocabulary

fickleness (fik′əl · nis) *n.:* changeableness.
altruistic (al′tro͞o · is′tik) *adj.:* unselfish.

"You can get 'em at Woolworth's," Summers said.

The fat boy called Joe said gloomily, "I knew it would end in a collection."

"I'll get one myself," T. said. "I don't want your money. But I can't buy a sledgehammer."

Blackie said, "They are working on number fifteen. I know where they'll leave their stuff for Bank Holiday."

"Then that's all," T. said. "We meet here at nine sharp."

"I've got to go to church," Mike said.

"Come over the wall and whistle. We'll let you in."

2

On Sunday morning all were punctual except Blackie, even Mike. Mike had had a stroke of luck. His mother felt ill, his father was tired after Saturday night, and he was told to go to church alone with many warnings of what would happen if he strayed. Blackie had had difficulty in smuggling out the saw, and then in finding the sledgehammer at the back of number 15. He approached the house from a lane at the rear of the garden, for fear of the policeman's beat along the main road. The tired evergreens kept off a stormy sun: Another wet Bank Holiday was being prepared over the Atlantic, beginning in swirls of dust under the trees. Blackie climbed the wall into Misery's garden.

There was no sign of anybody anywhere. The loo stood like a tomb in a neglected graveyard. The curtains were drawn. The house slept. Blackie lumbered nearer with the saw and the sledgehammer. Perhaps after all nobody had turned up: The plan had been a wild invention: They had woken wiser. But when he came close to the back door he could hear a confusion of sound, hardly louder than a hive in swarm: a clickety-clack, a bang bang bang, a scraping, a creaking, a sudden painful crack. He thought, It's true, and whistled.

They opened the back door to him and he came in. He had at once the impression of organization, very different from the old happy-go-lucky ways under his leadership. For a while he wandered up and down stairs looking for T. Nobody addressed him: He had a sense of great urgency, and already he could begin to see the plan. The interior of the house was being carefully demolished without touching the outer walls. Summers with hammer and chisel was ripping out the skirting-boards[16] in the ground floor dining room: He had already smashed the panels of the door. In the same room Joe was heaving up the parquet[17] blocks, exposing the soft wood floorboards over the cellar. Coils of wire came out of the damaged skirting and Mike sat happily on the floor, clipping the wires.

On the curved stairs two of the gang were working hard with an inadequate child's saw on the banisters—when they saw Blackie's big saw they signaled for it wordlessly. When he next saw them a quarter of the banisters had been dropped into the hall. He found T. at last in the bathroom—he sat moodily in the least cared-for room in the house, listening to the sounds coming up from below.

"You've really done it," Blackie said with awe. "What's going to happen?"

"We've only just begun," T. said. He looked at the sledgehammer and gave his instructions. "You stay here and break the bath and the wash-basin. Don't bother about the pipes. They come later."

Mike appeared at the door. "I've finished the wire, T.," he said.

"Good. You've just got to go wandering round now. The kitchen's in the basement. Smash all the china and glass and bottles you can lay hold of. Don't turn on the taps—we don't want a flood—yet. Then go into all the rooms and turn out drawers. If they are locked get one of the others to break them open. Tear up any papers you find and smash all the ornaments. Better take a carving knife with you from the kitchen. The bedroom's opposite here. Open the pillows and tear up the sheets. That's enough for the

---

16. **skirting-boards:** baseboards; boards placed along the base of the walls of a room.
17. **parquet** (pär·kā′) *n.:* fancy wood floor made of boards arranged in geometric patterns.

moment. And you, Blackie, when you've finished in here crack the plaster in the passage up with your sledgehammer."

"What are you going to do?" Blackie asked.

"I'm looking for something special," T. said.

It was nearly lunchtime before Blackie had finished and went in search of T. Chaos had advanced. The kitchen was a shambles of broken glass and china. The dining room was stripped of parquet, the skirting was up, the door had been taken off its hinges, and the destroyers had moved up a floor. Streaks of light came in through the closed shutters where they worked with the seriousness of creators—and destruction after all is a form of creation. A kind of imagination had seen this house as it had now become.

Mike said, "I've got to go home for dinner."

"Who else?" T. asked, but all the others on one excuse or another had brought provisions with them.

They squatted in the ruins of the room and swapped unwanted sandwiches. Half an hour for lunch and they were at work again. By the time Mike returned, they were on the top floor, and by six the superficial damage was completed. The doors were all off, all the skirtings raised, the furniture pillaged and ripped and smashed—no one could have slept in the house except on a bed of broken plaster. T. gave his orders—eight o'clock next morning—and to escape notice they climbed singly over the garden wall, into the car-park. Only Blackie and T. were left; the light had nearly gone, and when they touched a switch, nothing worked—Mike had done his job thoroughly.

"Did you find anything special?" Blackie asked.

T. nodded. "Come over here," he said, "and look." Out of both pockets he drew bundles of pound notes. "Old Misery's savings," he said. "Mike ripped out the mattress, but he missed them."

"What are you going to do? Share them?"

"We aren't thieves," T. said. "Nobody's going to steal anything from this house. I kept these for you and me—a celebration." He knelt down on the floor and counted them out—there were seventy in all. "We'll burn them," he said, "one by one," and taking it in turns they held a note upward and lit the top corner, so that the flame burnt slowly toward their fingers. The gray ash floated above them and fell on their heads like age. "I'd like to see Old Misery's face when we are through," T. said.

"You hate him a lot?" Blackie asked.

"Of course I don't hate him," T. said. "There'd be no fun if I hated him." The last burning note illuminated his brooding face. "All this hate and love," he said, "it's soft, it's hooey. There's only things, Blackie," and he looked round the room crowded with the unfamiliar shadows of half things, broken things, former things. "I'll race you home, Blackie," he said.

3

Next morning the serious destruction started. Two were missing—Mike and another boy, whose parents were off to Southend and Brighton in spite of the slow warm drops that had begun to fall and the rumble of thunder in the estuary like the first guns of the old blitz. "We've got to hurry," T. said.

Summers was restive.[18] "Haven't we done enough?" he said. "I've been given a bob for slot machines.[19] This is like work."

"We've hardly started," T. said. "Why, there's all the floors left, and the stairs. We haven't taken out a single window. You voted like the others. We are going to *destroy* this house. There won't be anything left when we've finished."

They began again on the first floor picking up the top floorboards next the outer wall, leaving the joists[20] exposed. Then they sawed through the joists and retreated into the hall, as what was left of the floor heeled and sank. They had learned with practice, and the second floor collapsed more easily. By the evening an odd

18. **restive** *adj.:* impatient; nervous.
19. **a bob for slot machines:** a shilling for vending machines.
20. **joists** *n. pl.:* parallel beams that support a floor.

The Blackened Ruins, City of London (1944–1945) by Catherine Giles.
Private Collection.

exhilaration seized them as they looked down the great hollow of the house. They ran risks and made mistakes: When they thought of the windows it was too late to reach them. "Cor,"[21] Joe said, and dropped a penny down into the dry rubble-filled well. It cracked and span among the broken glass.

"Why did we start this?" Summers asked with astonishment; T. was already on the ground, digging at the rubble, clearing a space along the outer wall. "Turn on the taps," he said. "It's too dark for anyone to see now, and in the morning it won't matter." The water overtook them on the stairs and fell through the floorless rooms.

21. **cor:** British exclamation of strong surprise or irritation. *Cor* is from *Gor*, or *Gord*, an earlier regional dialect pronunciation of "God."

It was then they heard Mike's whistle at the back. "Something's wrong," Blackie said. They could hear his urgent breathing as they unlocked the door.

"The bogies?"[22] Summers asked.

"Old Misery," Mike said. "He's on his way." He put his head between his knees and retched. "Ran all the way," he said with pride.

"But why?" T. said. "He told me. . . ." He protested with the fury of the child he had never been, "It isn't fair."

"He was down at Southend," Mike said, "and he was on the train coming back. Said it

22. **bogies** (bō′gēz) *n. pl.:* slang for "police."

Vocabulary

exhilaration (eg·zil′ə·rā′shən) *n.:* excitement; high spirits.

was too cold and wet." He paused and gazed at the water. "My, you've had a storm here. Is the roof leaking?"

"How long will he be?"

"Five minutes. I gave Ma the slip and ran."

"We better clear," Summers said. "We've done enough, anyway."

"Oh, no, we haven't. Anybody could do this—" "This" was the shattered hollowed house with nothing left but the walls. Yet walls could be preserved. Façades[23] were valuable. They could build inside again more beautifully than before. This could again be a home. He said angrily, "We've got to finish. Don't move. Let me think."

"There's no time," a boy said.

"There's got to be a way," T. said. "We couldn't have got thus far . . ."

"We've done a lot," Blackie said.

"No. No, we haven't. Somebody watch the front."

"We can't do any more."

"He may come in at the back."

"Watch the back too." T. began to plead. "Just give me a minute and I'll fix it. I swear I'll fix it." But his authority had gone with his ambiguity. He was only one of the gang. "Please," he said.

"Please," Summers mimicked him, and then suddenly struck home with the fatal name. "Run along home, Trevor."

T. stood with his back to the rubble like a boxer knocked groggy against the ropes. He had no words as his dreams shook and slid. Then Blackie acted before the gang had time to laugh, pushing Summers backward. "I'll watch the front, T.," he said, and cautiously he opened the shutters of the hall. The gray wet common stretched ahead, and the lamps gleamed in the puddles. "Someone's coming, T. No, it's not him. What's your plan, T.?"

"Tell Mike to go out to the loo and hide close beside it. When he hears me whistle he's got to count ten and start to shout."

"Shout what?"

"Oh, 'Help,' anything."

"You hear, Mike," Blackie said. He was the leader again. He took a quick look between the shutters. "He's coming, T."

"Quick, Mike. The loo. Stay here, Blackie, all of you till I yell."

"Where are you going, T.?"

"Don't worry. I'll see to this. I said I would, didn't I?"

Old Misery came limping off the common. He had mud on his shoes and he stopped to scrape them on the pavement's edge. He didn't want to soil his house, which stood jagged and dark between the bomb sites, saved so narrowly, as he believed, from destruction. Even the fan-light had been left unbroken by the bomb's blast. Somewhere somebody whistled. Old Misery looked sharply round. He didn't trust whistles. A child was shouting: It seemed to come from his own garden. Then a boy ran into the road from the car-park. "Mr. Thomas," he called, "Mr. Thomas."

"What is it?"

"I'm terribly sorry, Mr. Thomas. One of us got taken short, and we thought you wouldn't mind, and now he can't get out."

"What do you mean, boy?"

"He's got stuck in your loo."

"He'd no business—Haven't I seen you before?"

"You showed me your house."

"So I did. So I did. That doesn't give you the right to—"

"Do hurry, Mr. Thomas. He'll suffocate."

"Nonsense. He can't suffocate. Wait till I put my bag in."

"I'll carry your bag."

"Oh, no, you don't. I carry my own."

"This way, Mr. Thomas."

"I can't get in the garden that way. I've got to go through the house."

"But you *can* get in the garden this way, Mr. Thomas. We often do."

"You often do?" He followed the boy with a scandalized fascination. "When? What right . . ."

"Do you see . . . ? The wall's low."

"I'm not going to climb walls into my own garden. It's absurd."

---

23. façades (fə·säds′) *n. pl.:* fronts of buildings.

"This is how we do it. One foot here, one foot there, and over." The boy's face peered down, an arm shot out, and Mr. Thomas found his bag taken and deposited on the other side of the wall.

"Give me back my bag," Mr. Thomas said. From the loo a boy yelled and yelled. "I'll call the police."

"Your bag's all right, Mr. Thomas. Look. One foot there. On your right. Now just above. To your left." Mr. Thomas climbed over his own garden wall. "Here's your bag, Mr. Thomas."

"I'll have the wall built up," Mr. Thomas said. "I'll not have you boys coming over here, using my loo." He stumbled on the path, but the boy caught his elbow and supported him. "Thank you, thank you, my boy," he murmured automatically. Somebody shouted again through the dark. "I'm coming, I'm coming," Mr. Thomas called. He said to the boy beside him, "I'm not unreasonable. Been a boy myself. As long as things are done regular. I don't mind you playing round the place Saturday mornings. Sometimes I like company. Only it's got to be regular. One of you asks leave and I say Yes. Sometimes I'll say No. Won't feel like it. And you come in at the front door and out at the back. No garden walls."

"Do get him out, Mr. Thomas."

"He won't come to any harm in my loo," Mr. Thomas said, stumbling slowly down the garden. "Oh, my rheumatics,"[24] he said. "Always get 'em on Bank Holiday. I've got to go careful. There's loose stones here. Give me your hand. Do you know what my horoscope said yesterday? 'Abstain from any dealings in first half of week. Danger of serious crash.' That might be on this path," Mr. Thomas said. "They speak in parables and double meanings." He paused at the door of the loo. "What's the matter in there?" he called. There was no reply.

"Perhaps he's fainted," the boy said.

"Not in my loo. Here, you, come out," Mr. Thomas said, and giving a great jerk at the door he nearly fell on his back when it swung easily open. A hand first supported him and then pushed him hard. His head hit the opposite wall and he sat heavily down. His bag hit his feet. A hand whipped the key out of the lock and the door slammed. "Let me out," he called, and heard the key turn in the lock. "A serious crash," he thought, and felt dithery and confused and old.

A voice spoke to him softly through the star-shaped hole in the door. "Don't worry, Mr. Thomas," it said, "we won't hurt you, not if you stay quiet."

Mr. Thomas put his head between his hands and pondered. He had noticed that there was only one lorry in the car-park, and he felt certain that the driver would not come for it before the morning. Nobody could hear him from the road in front, and the lane at the back was seldom used. Anyone who passed there would be hurrying home and would not pause for what they would certainly take to be drunken cries. And if he did call "Help," who, on a lonely Bank Holiday evening, would have the courage to investigate? Mr. Thomas sat on the loo and pondered with the wisdom of age.

After a while it seemed to him that there were sounds in the silence—they were faint and came from the direction of his house. He stood up and peered through the ventilation-hole—between the cracks in one of the shutters he saw a light, not the light of a lamp, but the wavering light that a candle might give. Then he thought he heard the sound of hammering and scraping and chipping. He thought of burglars—perhaps they had employed the boy as a scout, but why should burglars engage in what sounded more and more like a stealthy form of carpentry? Mr. Thomas let out an experimental yell, but nobody answered. The noise could not even have reached his enemies.

4

Mike had gone home to bed, but the rest stayed. The question of leadership no longer concerned the gang. With nails, chisels, screwdrivers, anything that was sharp and penetrating they

Vocabulary

abstain (ab·stān′) *v.:* refrain from.
stealthy (stel′thē) *adj.:* secret; sly.

24. **rheumatics** *n.:* type of severe arthritis.

moved around the inner walls worrying at the mortar between the bricks. They started too high, and it was Blackie who hit on the damp course[25] and realized the work could be halved if they weakened the joints immediately above. It was a long, tiring, unamusing job, but at last it was finished. The gutted house stood there balanced on a few inches of mortar between the damp course and the bricks.

There remained the most dangerous task of all, out in the open at the edge of the bomb site. Summers was sent to watch the road for passers by, and Mr. Thomas, sitting on the loo, heard clearly now the sound of sawing. It no longer came from his house, and that a little reassured him. He felt less concerned. Perhaps the other noises too had no significance.

A voice spoke to him through the hole. "Mr. Thomas."

"Let me out," Mr. Thomas said sternly.

"Here's a blanket," the voice said, and a long gray sausage was worked through the hole and fell in swathes over Mr. Thomas's head.

"There's nothing personal," the voice said. "We want you to be comfortable tonight."

"Tonight," Mr. Thomas repeated incredulously.

"Catch," the voice said. "Penny buns—we've buttered them, and sausage-rolls. We don't want you to starve, Mr. Thomas."

Mr. Thomas pleaded desperately. "A joke's a joke, boy. Let me out and I won't say a thing. I've got rheumatics. I got to sleep comfortable."

"You wouldn't be comfortable, not in your house, you wouldn't. Not now."

"What do you mean, boy?" but the footsteps receded. There was only the silence of night: no sound of sawing. Mr. Thomas tried one more yell, but he was daunted and rebuked by the silence—a long way off an owl hooted and made away again on its muffled flight through the soundless world.

At seven next morning the driver came to fetch his lorry. He climbed into the seat and tried to start the engine. He was vaguely aware of a voice shouting, but it didn't concern him. At last the engine responded and he backed the lorry until it touched the great wooden shore[26] that supported Mr. Thomas's house. That way he could drive right out and down the street without reversing. The lorry moved forward, was momentarily checked as though something were pulling it from behind, and then went on to the sound of a long rumbling crash. The driver was astonished to see bricks bouncing ahead of him, while stones hit the roof of his cab. He put on his brakes. When he climbed out the whole landscape had suddenly altered. There was no house beside the car-park, only a hill of rubble. He went round and examined the back of his car for damage, and found a rope tied there that was still twisted at the other end round part of a wooden strut.

The driver again became aware of somebody shouting. It came from the wooden erection which was the nearest thing to a house in that desolation of broken brick. The driver climbed the smashed wall and unlocked the door. Mr. Thomas came out of the loo. He was wearing a gray blanket to which flakes of pastry adhered. He gave a sobbing cry. "My house," he said. "Where's my house?"

"Search me," the driver said. His eye lit on the remains of a bath and what had once been a dresser and he began to laugh. There wasn't anything left anywhere.

"How dare you laugh," Mr. Thomas said. "It was my house. My house."

"I'm sorry," the driver said, making heroic efforts, but when he remembered the sudden check to his lorry, the crash of bricks falling, he became convulsed again. One moment the house had stood there with such dignity between the bomb sites like a man in a top hat, and then, bang, crash, there wasn't anything left—not anything. He said, "I'm sorry. I can't help it, Mr. Thomas. There's nothing personal, but you got to admit it's funny." ■

25. **damp course:** layer of waterproof material placed between two layers of brick in a house's foundation to keep moisture from rising up through the walls.

26. **shore** *n.:* beam.

Response and Analysis

Reading Check

1. Who is the gang's leader at first? Who takes over? Why?
2. What is T.'s family background?
3. Why is Mr. Thomas's house valuable?
4. Describe how the house is destroyed.

Thinking Critically

5. T.'s **motives** for destroying Old Misery's house are important. What motives can you *eliminate* based on what T. says to Mr. Thomas and what the boys do with the money?
6. What are T.'s actual motives? Support your answer with details from the story. (Your reading notes will help.)
7. A gang is a social group with a shared set of values. What are this gang's values, and from where do you think they spring?
8. Describe the **setting** of the Wormsley Common car-park and its surroundings. How does the setting contribute to the story's emotional **atmosphere**? What larger idea or concept might the setting **symbolize**?
9. When Blackie asks T. whether he hates Mr. Thomas, T. answers, "Of course I don't . . . . There'd be no fun if I hated him." How would you explain T.'s answer? In what sense does T.'s response reveal what might happen to people—even children—in the aftermath of war?

Literary Skills Analyze setting.

Reading Skills Make inferences about character motivation.

Writing Skills Write an essay analyzing imagery.

Vocabulary Skills Demonstrate word knowledge.

Extending and Evaluating

10. How do you think Greene wants his readers to see T.—as a vicious criminal who should be punished, or as a disturbed victim of society who deserves understanding? In which way do you see him? Why? Evaluate T.'s **character** in light of the political and social influences that might have shaped him. Use evidence from the story to support your opinions.

Literary Criticism

11. One critic noted that the typical Greene character lives "on the border between love and hate, good and evil, heaven and hell." Which characters in this story live "on the border"? By the end of the story, have any of them fallen completely to one side or the other? Explain.

WRITING

Rotten to the Core?

Images of hollowness—of rotting from within—appear throughout this story. In the first part of a short **essay,** identify these **images** of hollowness and discuss how they apply to the house, to Wormsley Common, and even to the story's characters. In the second part of the essay, discuss the ways in which the setting of "The Destructors" connects with images in T. S. Eliot's "The Hollow Men" (see page 1046). Explore the emotional effects of these various images on the reader.

Vocabulary Development

Sentence Sense

ignoble	fickleness
impromptu	altruistic
exploit	exhilaration
daunted	abstain
implacable	stealthy

On a separate sheet of paper, use each Vocabulary word listed above in an original sentence based on the characters and events in "The Destructors."

Ben Okri

(1959–)

Nigeria

Ben Okri grew up in the delta area of southern Nigeria. Although he later moved to London, his stories are set in Nigeria. Okri seems especially haunted by remembrances of the Nigerian Civil War (1967–1970), often called the Biafran War. This war began when the Ibo (ē′bō) people tried to secede from Nigeria and form their own state, called the Republic of Biafra. Thousands of people were killed in the civil war that ensued, and many more died of starvation. In fact, for years the very word *Biafra* conjured up images of swollen-bellied children holding up bowls and begging for food. The image of the starving child in Okri's story is a stark reminder of the horror of this war.

Okri first gained recognition in England with the publication of two novels, *Flowers and Shadows* (1980) and *The Landscapes Within* (1981), and a collection of short stories, *Incidents at the Shrine* (1986). "In the Shadow of War" is from *Stars of the New Curfew* (1988), Okri's first book to be published in the United States.

Okri's awards include the Commonwealth Writers' Prize for Africa and the *Paris Review* Aga Khan Prize for fiction. His 1991 novel, *The Famished Road*, received England's Booker Prize. *Songs of Enchantment*, a sequel to *The Famished Road*, appeared in 1993 and *Astonishing the Gods* in 1995.

Before You Read

In the Shadow of War

Make the Connection

Quickwrite

In some parts of the world, a state of war is almost constant, especially in places where ethnic and religious strife runs high. Like the author of the following story, the children of these lands struggle to come of age in a place where hostility is a given—where suspicion and paranoia infect every conversation and where random violence is common and often unprovoked.

Should children be protected from the knowledge of certain harsh realities, such as war and urban violence? What might be some of the positive and negative effects of shielding young people from harsh truths? Jot down your ideas.

Literary Focus

Point of View

Every writer tells a story from a particular **point of view,** or vantage point. Ben Okri was only eight years old when the Nigerian Civil War broke out, so it's not surprising that his main character, Omovo, is a child. Okri uses the **limited-third-person point of view** to tell the story only from Omovo's perspective. Through Omovo's eyes, we learn that war is a frightening, confusing time for children. Are the soldiers in this story good or evil? Is the veiled woman supernatural or mortal? Because Omovo's understanding is limited, the point of view from which this story is told deepens these mysteries.

Pages 1093–1094 cover
Literary Skills Understand the limited-third-person point of view.

Reading Skills Make predictions.

In **limited-third-person point of view,** the narrator is outside the story but tells the story from the vantage point of only one character.

For more on Point of View, see the Handbook of Literary and Historical Terms.

Reading Skills

Making Predictions

Instead of factual information (such as where and when the story takes place), the reader of this story is given a vivid picture of what the child, Omovo, sees and hears. Several key impressions are described early in the story—for example, Omovo's impressions of the soldiers; of his father's words and actions; and of the woman in the yellow smock. Use these details to make **predictions** about the characters you encounter—to look ahead and make educated guesses about what is likely to happen to them. Of whom should Omovo be suspicious? Which characters seem to present the most danger, and to whom? Jot down any predictions you make, and be prepared to explain why you made them. Adjust your predictions as necessary while you read.

Background

This story takes place during the Nigerian Civil War (1967–1970). After Nigeria gained its independence from Great Britain in 1960, the nation struggled to fashion a stable government. But with over 250 distinct ethnic or tribal groups in Nigeria, the task proved formidable. In 1966, one of the major groups, the Hausa-Fulani, established a military power. Another major group, the Ibo, responded by declaring their homeland to be the independent Republic of Biafra. A bitter civil war ensued, during which thousands were killed or starved to death. The Biafrans surrendered in 1970.

Vocabulary Development

stupefying (sto͞o'pə·fī'iŋ) *adj.:* dulling the mind and senses; bringing on a state of lethargy.

oppressive (ə·pres'iv) *adj.:* hard to bear.

succumbed (sə·kumd') *v.:* yielded; gave way to.

ostentatious (äs'ten·tā'shəs) *adj.:* showy.

dementedly (dē·ment'id·lē) *adv.:* madly; wildly.

At Obudu Cattle Ranch on Sonkwala Mountain, Nigeria (May 1989).

IN THE SHADOW OF WAR

Ben Okri

That afternoon three soldiers came to the village. They scattered the goats and chickens. They went to the palm-frond bar and ordered a calabash[1] of palm wine. They drank amidst the flies.

Omovo watched them from the window as he waited for his father to go out. They both listened to the radio. His father had bought the old Grundig[2] cheaply from a family that had to escape the city when the war broke out. He had covered the radio with a white cloth and made it look like a household fetish.[3] They listened to the news of bombings and air raids in the interior of the country. His father combed his hair, parted it carefully, and slapped some after-shave on his unshaven face. Then he struggled into the shabby coat that he had long outgrown.

Omovo stared out of the window, irritated with his father. At that hour, for the past seven days, a strange woman with a black veil over her head had been going past the house. She went up the village paths, crossed the Express road, and disappeared into the forest. Omovo waited for her to appear.

The main news was over. The radio announcer said an eclipse of the moon was expected that night. Omovo's father wiped the sweat off his face with his palm and said, with some bitterness:

"As if an eclipse will stop this war."

"What is an eclipse?" Omovo asked.

"That's when the world goes dark and strange things happen."

"Like what?"

His father lit a cigarette.

"The dead start to walk about and sing. So don't stay out late, eh."

Omovo nodded.

"Heclipses hate children. They eat them."

Omovo didn't believe him. His father smiled, gave Omovo his ten kobo[4] allowance, and said:

"Turn off the radio. It's bad for a child to listen to news of war."

Omovo turned it off. His father poured a libation[5] at the doorway and then prayed to his ancestors. When he had finished he picked up his briefcase and strutted out briskly. Omovo watched him as he threaded his way up the path to the bus stop at the main road. When a danfo bus[6] came, and his father went with it, Omovo turned the radio back on. He sat on the windowsill and waited for the woman. The last time he saw her she had glided past with agitated flutters of her yellow smock. The children stopped what they were doing and stared at her. They had said that she had no shadow. They had said that her feet never touched the ground.

1. **calabash** (kal′ə·bash′) *n.:* cup made from a calabash, a type of gourd.
2. **Grundig:** German brand of radio.
3. **fetish** (fet′ish) *n.:* object believed to have magical powers.
4. **kobo** (käb′ō) *n.:* Nigerian monetary unit.
5. **libation** (lī·bā′shən): liquid poured onto the ground as a sacrifice to the gods.
6. **danfo bus:** small bus. In the region surrounding Lagos, *danfo* means "in disrepair."

As she went past, the children began to throw things at her. She didn't flinch, didn't quicken her pace, and didn't look back.

The heat was stupefying. Noises dimmed and lost their edges. The villagers stumbled about their various tasks as if they were sleepwalking. The three soldiers drank palm wine and played draughts[7] beneath the sun's oppressive glare. Omovo noticed that whenever children went past the bar the soldiers called them, talked to them, and gave them some money. Omovo ran down the stairs and slowly walked past the bar. The soldiers stared at him. On his way back one of them called him.

"What's your name?" he asked.

Omovo hesitated, smiled mischievously, and said:

"Heclipse."

The soldier laughed, spraying Omovo's face with spit. He had a face crowded with veins. His companions seemed uninterested. They swiped flies and concentrated on their game. Their guns were on the table. Omovo noticed that they had numbers on them. The man said:

"Did your father give you that name because you have big lips?"

His companions looked at Omovo and laughed. Omovo nodded.

"You are a good boy," the man said. He paused. Then he asked, in a different voice:

"Have you seen that woman who covers her face with a black cloth?"

"No."

The man gave Omovo ten kobo and said:

"She is a spy. She helps our enemies. If you see her, come and tell us at once, you hear?"

Omovo refused the money and went back upstairs. He repositioned himself on the windowsill. The soldiers occasionally looked at him. The heat got to him and soon he fell asleep in a sitting position. The cocks, crowing dispiritedly, woke him up. He could feel the afternoon softening into evening. The soldiers dozed in the bar. The hourly news came on. Omovo listened without comprehension to the day's casualties. The announcer succumbed to the stupor, yawned, apologized, and gave further details of the fighting.

Omovo looked up and saw that the woman had already gone past. The men had left the bar. He saw them weaving between the eaves of the thatch houses, stumbling through the heat-mists. The woman was further up the path. Omovo ran downstairs and followed the men. One of them had taken off his uniform top. The soldier behind had buttocks so big they had begun to split his pants. Omovo followed them across the Express road. When they got into the forest the men stopped following the woman, and took a different route. They seemed to know what they were doing. Omovo hurried to keep the woman in view.

He followed her through the dense vegetation. She wore faded wrappers and a gray shawl, with the black veil covering her face. She had a red basket on her head. He completely forgot to determine if she had a shadow, or whether her feet touched the ground.

He passed unfinished estates, with their flaking, ostentatious signboards and their collapsing fences. He passed an empty cement factory: Blocks lay crumbled in heaps and the workers' sheds were deserted. He passed a baobab[8] tree, under which was the intact skeleton of a large animal. A snake dropped from a branch and slithered through the undergrowth. In the distance, over the cliff edge, he heard loud music and people singing war slogans above the noise.

He followed the woman till they came to a rough camp on the plain below. Shadowy figures moved about in the half-light of the cave. The

7. **draughts** (drafts) *n.:* British game of checkers.

8. **baobab** (bā′ō·bab′) *n.:* thick-trunked African tree; often called "upside-down tree" because its branches look like roots.

Vocabulary

stupefying (sto͞o′pə·fī′iŋ) *adj.:* dulling the mind and senses; bringing on a state of lethargy.

oppressive (ə·pres′iv) *adj.:* hard to bear.

succumbed (sə·kumd′) *v.:* yielded; gave way to.

ostentatious (äs′ten·tā′shəs) *adj.:* showy.

woman went to them. The figures surrounded her and touched her and led her into the cave. He heard their weary voices thanking her. When the woman reappeared she was without the basket. Children with kwashiorkor[9] stomachs and women wearing rags led her halfway up the hill. Then, reluctantly, touching her as if they might not see her again, they went back.

He followed her till they came to a muddied river. She moved as if an invisible force were trying to blow her away. Omovo saw capsized canoes and trailing, waterlogged clothes on the dark water. He saw floating items of sacrifice: loaves of bread in polythene[10] wrappings, gourds of food, Coca-Cola cans. When he looked at the canoes again they had changed into the shapes of swollen dead animals. He saw outdated currencies on the riverbank. He noticed the terrible smell in the air. Then he heard the sound of heavy breathing from behind him, then someone coughing and spitting. He recognized the voice of one of the soldiers urging the others to move faster. Omovo crouched in the shadow of a tree. The soldiers strode past. Not long afterward he heard a scream. The men had caught up with the woman. They crowded round her.

"Where are the others?" shouted one of them.

The woman was silent.

"You dis witch! You want to die, eh? Where are they?"

She stayed silent. Her head was bowed. One of the soldiers coughed and spat toward the river.

"Talk! Talk!" he said, slapping her.

The fat soldier tore off her veil and threw it to the ground. She bent down to pick it up and stopped in the attitude of kneeling, her head still bowed. Her head was bald, and disfigured with a deep corrugation.[11] There was a livid gash along the side of her face. The bare-chested soldier pushed her. She fell on her face and lay still. The lights changed over the forest and for the first time Omovo saw that the dead animals on the river were in fact the corpses of grown men. Their bodies were tangled with riverweed and their eyes were bloated. Before he could react, he heard another scream. The woman was getting up, with the veil in her hand. She turned to the fat soldier, drew herself to her fullest height, and spat in his face. Waving the veil in the air, she began to howl dementedly. The two other soldiers backed away. The fat soldier wiped his face and lifted the gun to the level of her stomach. A moment before Omovo heard the shot a violent beating of wings just above him scared him from his hiding place. He ran through the forest screaming. The soldiers tramped after him. He ran through a mist which seemed to have risen from the rocks. As he ran he saw an owl staring at him from a canopy of leaves. He tripped over the roots of a tree and blacked out when his head hit the ground.

When he woke up it was very dark. He waved his fingers in front of his face and saw nothing. Mistaking the darkness for blindness he screamed, thrashed around, and ran into a door. When he recovered from his shock he heard voices outside and the radio crackling on about the war. He found his way to the balcony, full of wonder that his sight had returned. But when he got there he was surprised to find his father sitting on the sunken cane chair, drinking palm wine with the three soldiers. Omovo rushed to his father and pointed frantically at the three men.

"You must thank them," his father said. "They brought you back from the forest."

Omovo, overcome with delirium, began to tell his father what he had seen. But his father, smiling apologetically at the soldiers, picked up his son and carried him off to bed. ■

---

9. **kwashiorkor** (kwä′shē·ôr′kôr′): severe disease of young children, caused by deficiency of protein and calories and marked by stunted growth and a protruding belly.

10. **polythene** (päl′i·thēn′): term used in most English-speaking countries other than the United States for *polyethylene* (päl′ē·eth′ə·lēn′), a synthetic substance used to make tough, lightweight plastics, films, and the like.

11. **corrugation** (kôr′ə·gā′shən) *n.:* groove or furrow.

Vocabulary

dementedly (dē·ment′id·lē) *adv.:* madly; wildly.

When Wisława Szymborska (vēs·wä′vä shēm·bor′skä) *was awarded the Nobel Prize in 1996, few people outside her native Poland had heard of her, but the resulting interest in Szymborska and her work has finally introduced her poetry to the world. She has been acclaimed for her ability to turn philosophical musings about subjects such as war, love, and suffering into poems that are complex yet clear. Szymborska's accessible style may be a response to the chaos and spiritual darkness she, as a twentieth-century Pole, has witnessed.*

The End and the Beginning

Wisława Szymborska

translated by **Stanislaw Baranczak** *and* **Clare Cavanagh**

After every war
someone's got to tidy up.
Things won't pick
themselves up, after all.

Someone's got to shove
the rubble to the roadsides
so the carts loaded with corpses
can get by.

Someone's got to trudge
through sludge and ashes,
through the sofa springs,
the shards of glass,
the bloody rags.

Someone's got to lug the post
to prop the wall,
someone's got to glaze the window,
set the door in its frame.

No sound bites, no photo opportunities
and it takes years.
All the cameras have gone
to other wars.

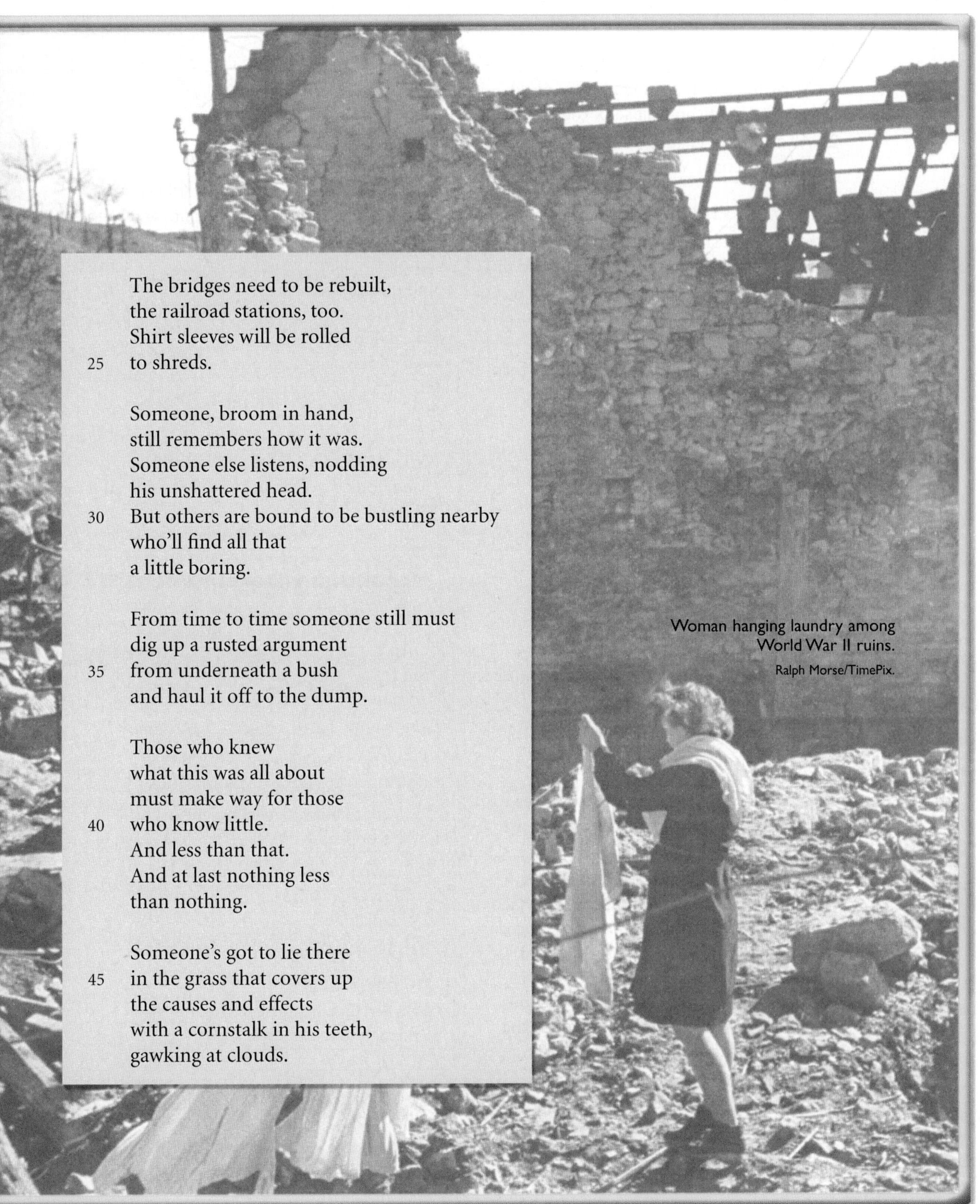

The bridges need to be rebuilt,
the railroad stations, too.
Shirt sleeves will be rolled
to shreds.

Someone, broom in hand,
still remembers how it was.
Someone else listens, nodding
his unshattered head.
But others are bound to be bustling nearby
who'll find all that
a little boring.

From time to time someone still must
dig up a rusted argument
from underneath a bush
and haul it off to the dump.

Those who knew
what this was all about
must make way for those
who know little.
And less than that.
And at last nothing less
than nothing.

Someone's got to lie there
in the grass that covers up
the causes and effects
with a cornstalk in his teeth,
gawking at clouds.

Woman hanging laundry among World War II ruins.
Ralph Morse/TimePix.

Response and Analysis

Literary Skills Analyze the limited-third-person point of view.

Reading Skills Make predictions.

Writing Skills Write an essay explaining a symbol.

Vocabulary Skills Demonstrate word knowledge.

INTERNET

Projects and Activities

Keyword: LE7 12-7

Reading Check

1. What does Omovo's father say might happen during an eclipse of the moon?
2. What do the children believe about the veiled woman? What happens to her?

Thinking Critically

3. Early in the story, what are Omovo's feelings toward the soldiers? toward the woman? What later events do these feelings help you to **predict**? (Be sure to check your reading notes.)
4. Why do you think Omovo's father tells him what he does about the eclipse? How does Omovo react?
5. What is the soldier's motive for offering Omovo money? Why do you think Omovo refuses it?
6. The story's **limited-third-person point of view** allows us to see the action and setting through a child's eyes. How do you interpret details that Omovo sees on the riverbank—the unfinished estates, the empty factory, the skeleton, and the outdated currencies? Explain how Okri uses these details to create a child's-eye view of war and to support the underlying **theme** of the story.
7. What do you think the woman takes to the people in the cave? What clues are provided?
8. Both Okri's story and Szymborska's poem "The End and the Beginning" (see the ***Connection*** on page 1098) concern war, but they are told from different **points of view.** Explain how the two points of view are different. How does Omovo feel about war? How does the speaker of the poem feel about it?
9. Re-read the final paragraph of the story. Might there be more than one explanation for the behavior of Omovo's father? (Review your Quickwrite notes.) If so, why might Okri choose to end on such an ambiguous note?

WRITING

Symbolic Object

The radio is a major **symbol** in Okri's story. Find all the references to the radio, and then write a short **essay** explaining its possible symbolic significance in the story. Here are some questions to get you started:

- Why is the brand name of the radio (a trivial detail) given?
- What is significant about the radio's being disguised as a fetish—an object believed to have magical powers?
- What does Omovo listen to on the radio?
- What is the difference between hearing a disembodied voice and actually seeing an event?

Vocabulary Development

Question and Answer

On a separate piece of paper, answer the following questions about the underlined Vocabulary words. Use complete sentences.

1. Do you ever find television stupefying? Why or why not?
2. What kind of environment might be oppressive? Why?
3. Have you ever succumbed to something and later regretted it? Explain.
4. Describe a home that you would consider ostentatious.
5. What might cause someone to laugh dementedly?

Writing a Persuasive Essay

Writing Assignment
Write a persuasive essay defending your position on an issue that is important to you.

Creators of persuasive messages use reasons, appeals, and evidence to convince others to believe or do something—as Winston Churchill did in his "Blood, Sweat, and Tears" speech (page 1068). In this workshop you'll use these tools to write a **persuasive essay** in which you develop a tightly reasoned argument for a particular audience.

Choose an Issue If you don't already have an **issue** (a topic about which reasonable people have opposing opinions) in mind for your essay, watch or listen to the news or read the newspaper for a few days. Is there an issue that inspires you to write or intrigues you? Look around you. Is there something in your school or community that you would like to see accomplished or changed? List several issues, and then use the following statements to evaluate each one. Make sure your final choice meets these criteria.

- The issue should be something you really care about.
- The issue should have clearly defined pro and con arguments.
- The issue should be narrow enough for you to argue successfully in a 1,500-word essay.

Identify Your Thesis and Call for Action Now that you have an issue, write a sentence that defines your **perspective,** or position, on that issue. This will be your **thesis statement,** sometimes called a position or opinion statement. One student created the following thesis statement, which identifies her opinion. Her thesis led her to develop her **call for action,** a sentence that tells her readers what she wants them to do.

> **Thesis:** The local animal shelter must change its euthanasia policy.
> **Call for Action:** We must write letters to our local animal shelter demanding a change in its policy of euthanizing animals.

Consider Purpose and Audience In order to succeed in your **purpose**—persuading your audience—you'll need to know something about them so that you can tailor your argument to their needs and interests. Use these questions to analyze your audience.

1. **What are their ages, interests, education levels, and values?** Use this information to determine what reasons, evidence, and language your readers will find most persuasive.
2. **What do they already know about the issue?** If your readers are not familiar with the issue, you'll need to give them enough background information to understand your argument.

Writing Skills
Write a persuasive essay. Identify the thesis statement. Determine purpose and audience.

3. **Where do they stand on the issue?** Readers who strongly disagree with your position will require much more convincing than those who share your views or who are undecided. Be prepared to address any objections they have to your proposal.

Support Your Position A tightly built argument depends on effective support. In your essay, include solid **reasons** why your readers should believe or act as you suggest in your thesis statement. Reasons may include appeals to logic, emotion, or ethics.

- **Logical appeals** engage your readers' ability to think clearly. Logical appeals should be the foundation of your essay.
- **Emotional appeals** stir readers' feelings and personalize the issue for your audience.
- **Ethical appeals** establish you as a fair and knowledgeable **speaker** and call upon your readers' sense of right and wrong.

Back up your reasons with solid **evidence,** including facts, statistics, anecdotes, expert testimony, and precise, relevant examples.

DO THIS

Create a two-column chart to help you gather support. In the first column, list three reasons that support your position on the issue you've chosen. In the second column, list at least two pieces of evidence to back up each reason. Be sure to check all facts in more than one reliable source. When you write your essay, remember to incorporate citations that refer to the sources you quote.

Reference Note

For more on **documenting sources,** see page 247.

TIP To add sophistication to the arguments in your essay, use **rhetorical devices** to enhance your ideas.

- **Analogies** give readers new ways of thinking about your issue by making a comparison between your issue and something familiar.
- **Repetition** focuses readers' attention on key terms and core ideas. Using **parallelism**—repetition of words, phrases, or sentence constructions—is especially effective.
- **Rhythm** can be used to aid the flow of ideas. Create rhythm by using rhymes, repetition, pauses, and variations in line length, and by balancing long and short words or phrases.

Organize Your Support To argue your position successfully, you'll need to **form** your argument in a coherent and focused way. Most persuasive essays are arranged by **order of importance.** To capture your audience's attention immediately, begin your essay with your strongest reason; or, to make a strong final impression, end with your strongest reason.

Writing Skills Use logical, emotional, and ethical appeals and rhetorical devices. Organize information.

PRACTICE & APPLY Use the guidelines on these two pages to choose an issue, formulate a thesis statement and a call for action, and gather and organize support. Write your persuasive essay, and share it with your intended audience.

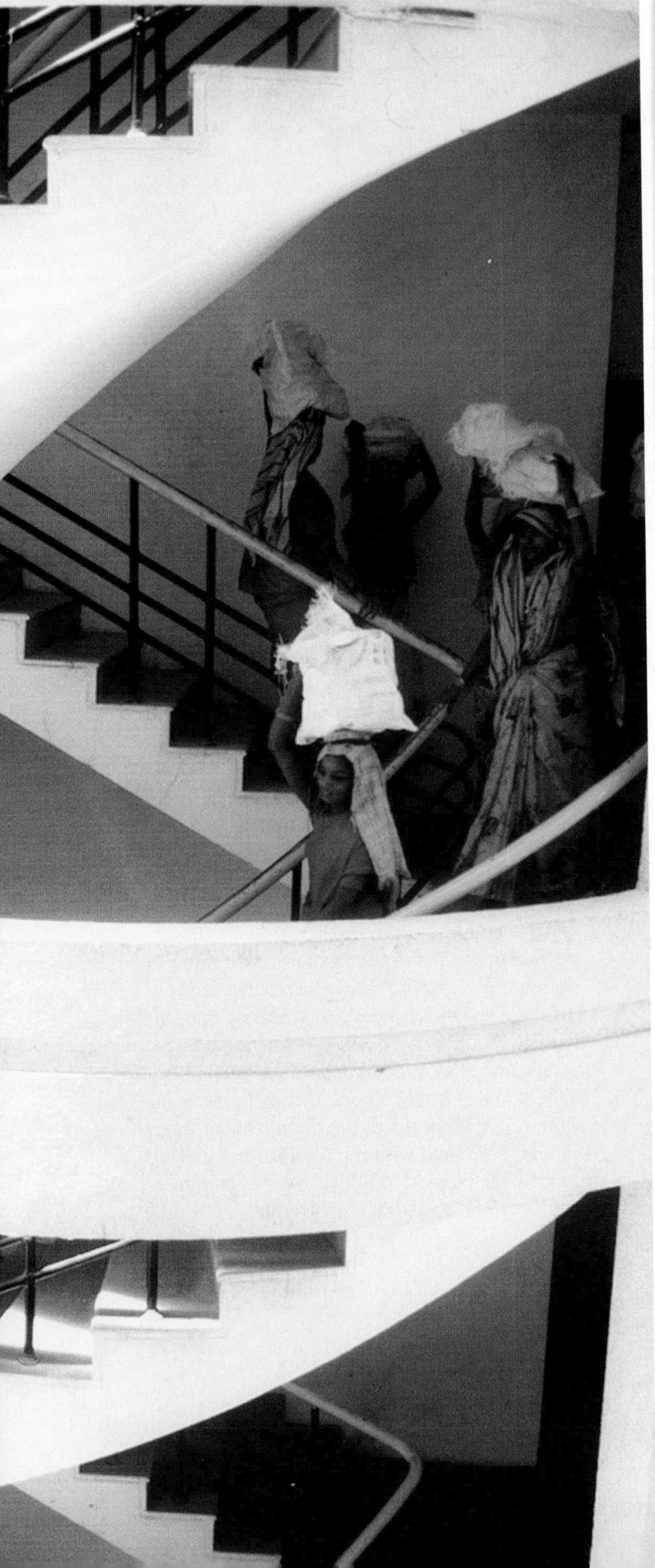

Collection 7:
The Modern World:
1900 to the Present

Clashes of Culture

Woolf
Orwell
Lessing
Chamberlain
Nehru
Gordimer
Achebe
Soyinka

As the traveler who has once been from home is wiser than he who has never left his own doorstep, so a knowledge of one other culture should sharpen our ability to scrutinize more steadily, to appreciate more lovingly, our own.

—Margaret Mead

Women carrying building supplies in Cyber Towers, a software provider in Hyderabad, India (2000).

Thomas Haley/SIPA PRESS.

Virginia Woolf

(1882–1941)

England

Virginia Woolf was born in Victorian London to the scholar and literary critic Sir Leslie Stephen and his artistic wife, Julia. In her youth, Woolf enjoyed all the advantages of a financially comfortable and intellectually challenging environment. Too frail to attend school regularly, she was privately tutored and given the luxury of access to her father's extensive library.

After her father's death in 1904, Virginia, her sister, Vanessa, and their two brothers moved to the area of London known as Bloomsbury. Soon they and their friends began to meet in what came to be called the Bloomsbury Group, an intellectual circle whose other prominent members included the writer E. M. Forster, the artist Duncan Grant, and the economist John Maynard Keynes. An informal gathering with the highest cultural standards, the Bloomsbury Group helped provide the right environment for Virginia Woolf's sensitive, experimental fiction. One member of the group was Leonard Woolf, a journalist and economist, whom Virginia married in 1912.

Woolf had been writing since she was fourteen and reviewing books since her early twenties, but it was not until she was thirty-three, in 1915, that her first novel, *The Voyage Out*, was published. The publication of *Jacob's Room* (1922) and *Mrs. Dalloway* (1925) established her position as one of the foremost writers of her time. With these novels—and with subsequent novels, such as *To the Lighthouse* (1927) and *The Waves* (1931)—Woolf pursued an experimental vision that emphasizes personal impressions over external events and focuses on the experience of life as it was being lived.

Like James Joyce, Woolf used the technique of stream of consciousness, although her version of it was somewhat different from his. For example, while *Mrs. Dalloway,* like Joyce's *Ulysses,* takes place on a single day, it covers an entire lifetime through the thoughts of its characters. Woolf was a great admirer of Joyce's *A Portrait of the Artist as a Young Man*, but she considered *Ulysses* an "illiterate, underbred book." Still, she worried that "what I am doing is probably being better done by Mr. Joyce."

Woolf also wrote a great many reviews and essays. In a number of them she explored the work of female writers, often focusing on a particular author who she felt had been neglected. In 1917, she and her husband established the Hogarth Press, which published many of the most important writers—male and female—of the day.

Troubled by sudden deaths and mental illness in her family, Woolf throughout her life suffered from bouts of depression and anxiety. These deepened with the German bombing raids over England in World War II, and in March 1941, she took her own life.

For Independent Reading

These are Woolf's two great novels:

- *Mrs. Dalloway*
- *To the Lighthouse*

Before You Read

Shakespeare's Sister

Make the Connection

Quickwrite

Gender is perhaps the most basic difference between human beings in every culture. Beyond the biological differences are the social and cultural realities: the everyday concerns that men and women have and the work they are or are not able to accomplish. Virginia Woolf scrutinized those realities in her 1929 essay collection *A Room of One's Own*, from which this essay is taken.

In your opinion, what differences exist between opportunities available to men and those available to women in our society today? Why do you think these differences exist? Write down some of your thoughts.

Literary Focus

Essay

An **essay** is a short piece of nonfiction writing that explores a particular topic. Formal essays are usually impersonal in tone, and tend to be highly organized, logical, and full of facts. An **informal essay,** on the other hand, is highly subjective, usually dominated by the author's own feelings, beliefs, and biases. Even though informal essays can be humorous and casual in tone, they often reveal deeply held principles and touch upon controversial or troubling aspects of society. The following selection by Woolf is one such essay.

An **essay** is a short piece of nonfiction writing that examines a single subject from a limited point of view.

For more on the Essay, see the Handbook of Literary and Historical Terms.

Reading Skills

Identifying the Author's Beliefs

At the top of a sheet of paper, write "Virginia Woolf believes that . . ." and write the numbers 1–5 below this heading. Then, as you read, list some of the things that Woolf believes. (You may discover more or fewer than five.) Read carefully—some of Woolf's beliefs may be stated directly while others are only hinted at. When you are finished, place a checkmark next to the belief you think is most central to the essay.

Background

A Room of One's Own is considered a pioneering work of feminist criticism. The aims of feminist criticism include exposing sexist attitudes in or toward literature, reinterpreting earlier works from a feminist perspective, uncovering neglected women writers, and analyzing how gender affects a writer's subjects, themes, and even style.

Literary Skills Understand the characteristics of an essay.

Reading Skills Identify an author's beliefs.

Vocabulary Development

servile (sʉr′vīl) *adj.:* like or characteristic of a slave; submissive; yielding.

suppressed (sə·prest′) *v.* used as *adj.:* kept from being known.

propitious (prō·pish′əs) *adj.:* favorable.

prodigious (prō·dij′əs) *adj.:* enormous.

notorious (nō·tôr′ē·əs) *adj.:* widely but unfavorably known.

formidable (fôr′mə·də·bəl) *adj.:* difficult to handle or overcome.

guffaw (gə·fô′) *n.:* loud laughter.

INTERNET

Vocabulary Practice

•

More About Virginia Woolf

Keyword: LE7 12-7

Shakespeare's Sister

from A Room of One's Own

Virginia Woolf

Here am I asking why women did not write poetry in the Elizabethan age, and I am not sure how they were educated; whether they were taught to write; whether they had sitting rooms to themselves; how many women had children before they were twenty-one; what, in short, they did from eight in the morning till eight at night. They had no money evidently; according to Professor Trevelyan[1] they were married whether they liked it or not before they were out of the nursery, at fifteen or sixteen very likely. It would have been extremely odd, even upon this showing, had one of them suddenly written the plays of Shakespeare, I concluded, and I thought of that old gentleman, who is dead now, but was a bishop, I think, who declared that it was impossible for any woman, past, present, or to come, to have the genius of Shakespeare. ❶ He wrote to the papers about it. He also told a lady who applied to him for information that cats do not as a matter of fact go to heaven, though they have, he added, souls of a sort. How much thinking those old gentlemen used to save one! How the borders of ignorance shrank back at their approach! Cats do not go to heaven. Women cannot write the plays of Shakespeare.

❶ *What facts make Woolf conclude that it would have been "extremely odd" for women in Elizabethan times to have written the plays of Shakespeare?*

Be that as it may, I could not help thinking, as I looked at the works of Shakespeare on the shelf, that the bishop was right at least in this; it would have been impossible, completely and entirely, for any woman to have written the plays of Shakespeare in the age of Shakespeare. Let me imagine, since facts are so hard to come by, what would have happened had Shakespeare had a wonderfully gifted sister, called Judith, let us say. Shakespeare himself went, very probably—his

Virginia Woolf in a Deck Chair (1912) by Vanessa Bell.

1. **Professor Trevelyan:** G. M. Trevelyan, author of *The History of England* (1926).

mother was an heiress—to the grammar school, where he may have learnt Latin—Ovid, Virgil, and Horace—and the elements of grammar and logic. He was, it is well known, a wild boy who poached rabbits, perhaps shot a deer, and had, rather sooner than he should have done, to marry a woman in the neighborhood, who bore him a child rather quicker than was right. That escapade sent him to seek his fortune in London. He had, it seemed, a taste for the theater; he began by holding horses at the stage door. Very soon he got work in the theater, became a successful actor, and lived at the hub of the universe, meeting everybody, knowing everybody, practicing his art on the boards, exercising his wits in the streets, and even getting access to the palace of the queen. Meanwhile his extraordinarily gifted sister, let us suppose, remained at home. She was as adventurous, as imaginative, as agog to see the world as he was. But she was not sent to school. She had no chance of learning grammar and logic, let alone of reading Horace and Virgil. She picked up a book now and then, one of her brother's perhaps, and read a few pages. But then her parents came in and told her to mend the stockings or mind the stew and not moon about with books and papers. They would have spoken sharply but kindly, for they were substantial people who knew the conditions of life for a woman and loved their daughter—indeed, more likely than not she was the apple of her father's eye. Perhaps she scribbled some pages up in an apple loft on the sly, but was careful to hide them or set fire to them. Soon, however, before she was out of her teens, she was to be betrothed to the son of a neighboring wool stapler.[2] She cried out that marriage was hateful to her, and for that she was severely beaten by her father. Then he ceased to scold her. He begged her instead not to hurt him, not to shame him in this matter of her marriage. He would give her a chain of beads or a fine petticoat, he said; and there were tears in his eyes. How could she disobey him? How could she break his heart? The force of her own gift alone drove her to it. She made up a small parcel of her belongings, let herself down by a rope one summer's night, and took the road to London. She was not seventeen. The birds that sang in the hedge were not more musical than she was. She had the quickest fancy, a gift like her brother's, for the tune of words. Like him, she had a taste for the theater. She stood at the stage door; she wanted to act, she said. ❷ Men laughed in her face. The manager—a fat, loose-lipped man—guffawed. He bellowed something about poodles dancing and women acting—no woman, he said, could possibly be an actress. He hinted—you can imagine what. She could get no training in her craft. Could she even seek her dinner in a tavern or roam the streets at midnight? Yet her genius was for fiction and lusted to feed abundantly upon the lives of men and women and the study of their ways. At last—for she was very young, oddly like Shakespeare the poet in her face, with the same gray eyes and rounded brows—at last Nick Greene the actor-manager took pity on her; she found herself with child by that gentleman and so—who shall measure the heat and violence of the poet's heart when caught and tangled in a woman's body?—killed herself one winter's night and lies buried at some crossroads where the omnibuses now stop outside the Elephant and Castle.[3]

> ❷
> Woolf speculates that Judith left home for a specific reason.
> **?** *What was that reason? State it in your own words.*

That, more or less, is how the story would run, I think, if a woman in Shakespeare's day had had Shakespeare's genius. But for my part, I agree with the deceased bishop, if such he was—it is unthinkable that any woman in Shakespeare's day should have had Shakespeare's genius. For genius like Shakespeare's is not born among

2. **wool stapler:** dealer in wool, a product sorted according to its fiber, or "staple."

3. **buried . . . Elephant and Castle:** Suicides, who were for years not permitted church burials, were commonly buried at a crossroad as a kind of punishment, perhaps to ensure that their souls would wander forever. The Elephant and Castle is a pub at a busy crossroads in south London.

laboring, uneducated, servile people. It was not born in England among the Saxons and the Britons. It is not born today among the working classes. How, then, could it have been born among women whose work began, according to Professor Trevelyan, almost before they were out of the nursery, who were forced to it by their parents and held to it by all the power of law and custom? Yet genius of a sort must have existed among women as it must have existed among the working classes. Now and again an Emily Brontë or a Robert Burns blazes out and proves its presence. But certainly it never got itself onto paper. When, however, one reads of a witch being ducked, of a woman possessed by devils, of a wise woman selling herbs, or even of a very remarkable man who had a mother, then I think we are on the track of a lost novelist, a suppressed poet, of some mute and inglorious[4] Jane Austen, some Emily Brontë who dashed her brains out on the moor or mopped and mowed about the highways crazed with the torture that her gift had put her to. Indeed, I would venture to guess that Anon, who wrote so many poems without signing them, was often a woman. It was a woman Edward Fitzgerald,[5] I think, suggested who made the ballads and the folk songs, crooning them to her children, beguiling her spinning with them, or the length of the winter's night.

This may be true or it may be false—who can say?—but what is true in it, so it seemed to me, reviewing the story of Shakespeare's sister as I had made it, is that any woman born with a great gift in the sixteenth century would certainly have gone crazed, shot herself, or ended her days in some lonely cottage outside the village, half witch, half wizard, feared and mocked at. For it needs little skill in psychology to be sure that a highly gifted girl who had tried to use her gift for poetry would have been so thwarted and hindered by other people, so tortured and pulled asunder by her own contrary instincts, that she must have lost her health and sanity to a certainty. ❸ No girl could have walked to London and stood at a stage door and forced her way into the presence of actor-managers without doing herself a violence and suffering an anguish which may have been irrational—for chastity may be a fetish invented by certain societies for unknown reasons—but were nonetheless inevitable. Chastity had then, it has even now, a religious importance in a woman's life, and has so wrapped itself round with nerves and instincts that to cut it free and bring it to the light of day demands courage of the rarest. To have lived a free life in London in the sixteenth century would have meant for a woman who was poet and playwright a nervous stress and dilemma which might well have killed her. Had she survived, whatever she had written would have been twisted and deformed, issuing from a strained and morbid imagination. And undoubtedly, I thought, looking at the shelf where there are no plays by women, her work would have gone unsigned. That refuge she would have sought certainly. It was the relic of the sense of chastity that dictated anonymity to women even so late as the nineteenth century. Currer Bell, George Eliot, George Sand,[6] all the victims of inner strife as their writings prove, sought ineffectively to veil themselves by using the name of a man. Thus they did homage to the convention, which if not implanted by the other sex was liberally encouraged by them (the chief glory of a

> ❸ ? *What does Woolf say is "true" in her story? How does she use this statement to advance her own persuasive argument?*

4. **mute and inglorious:** allusion to line 59 of Thomas Gray's poem "Elegy Written in a Country Churchyard."
5. **Edward Fitzgerald** (1809–1883): English translator and poet.
6. **Currer Bell, George Eliot, George Sand:** male pseudonyms for the female writers Charlotte Brontë, Mary Ann Evans, and Amantine-Aurore-Lucile Dupin.

Vocabulary

servile (sur′vīl) *adj.:* like or characteristic of a slave; submissive; yielding.

suppressed (sə·prest′) *v.* used as *adj.:* kept from being known.

A Corner of the Artist's Room, Paris (late 19th or early 20th century) by Gwen John.

Sheffield City Art Galleries, England.

woman is not to be talked of, said Pericles,[7] himself a much-talked-of man), that publicity in women is detestable. Anonymity runs in their blood. The desire to be veiled still possesses them. They are not even now as concerned about the health of their fame as men are, and, speaking generally, will pass a tombstone or a signpost without feeling an irresistible desire to cut their names on it, as Alf, Bert, or Chas. must do in obedience to their instinct, which murmurs if it sees a fine woman go by, or even a dog, *Ce chien est à moi.*[8] And, of course, it may not be a dog, I thought, remembering Parliament Square, the Sieges Allee,[9] and other avenues; it may be a piece of land or a man with curly black hair. It is one of the great advantages of being a woman that one can pass even a very fine negress without wishing to make an Englishwoman of her. ❹

❹ ? *What impulse does Woolf attribute to men but not to women? What examples of this impulse does Woolf give?*

That woman, then, who was born with a gift of poetry in the sixteenth century, was an unhappy woman, a woman at strife against herself. All the conditions of her life, all her own instincts, were hostile to the state of mind which is needed to set free whatever is in the brain. But what is the state of mind that is most propitious to the act of creation, I asked. Can one come by any notion of the state that furthers and makes possible that strange activity? Here I opened the volume containing the Tragedies of Shakespeare. What was Shakespeare's state of mind, for instance, when he wrote *Lear* and *Antony and Cleopatra*? It was certainly the state of mind most favorable to poetry that there has ever existed. But Shakespeare himself said

7. **Pericles** (c. 495–429 B.C.): Athenian legislator and general.
8. ***Ce chien est à moi*** (sə shē·en′ āt ä mwä): French for "This dog is mine."
9. **Sieges Allee** (zē′gəs ä·lā′): busy thoroughfare in Berlin. The name—more commonly written as one word, *Siegesallee*—is German for "Avenue of Victory."

Vocabulary

propitious (prō·pish′əs) *adj.:* favorable.

nothing about it. We only know casually and by chance that he "never blotted a line." Nothing indeed was ever said by the artist himself about his state of mind until the eighteenth century perhaps. Rousseau[10] perhaps began it. At any rate, by the nineteenth century self-consciousness had developed so far that it was the habit for men of letters to describe their minds in confessions and autobiographies. Their lives also were written, and their letters were printed after their deaths. Thus, though we do not know what Shakespeare went through when he wrote *Lear,* we do know what Carlyle went through when he wrote *The French Revolution;* what Flaubert went through when he wrote *Madame Bovary;* what Keats was going through when he tried to write poetry against the coming of death and the indifference of the world.

And one gathers from this enormous modern literature of confession and self-analysis that to write a work of genius is almost always a feat of prodigious difficulty. Everything is against the likelihood that it will come from the writer's mind whole and entire. Generally material circumstances are against it. Dogs will bark; people will interrupt; money must be made; health will break down. Further, accentuating all these difficulties and making them harder to bear is the world's notorious indifference. It does not ask people to write poems and novels and histories; it does not need them. It does not care whether Flaubert finds the right word or whether Carlyle scrupulously verifies this or that fact. Naturally, it will not pay for what it does not want. And so the writer, Keats, Flaubert, Carlyle, suffers, especially in the creative years of youth, every form of distraction and discouragement. A curse, a cry of agony, rises from those books of analysis and confession. "Mighty poets in their misery dead"[11]—that is the burden of their song. If anything comes through in spite of all this, it is a miracle, and probably no book is born entire and uncrippled as it was conceived. ❺

But for women, I thought, looking at the empty shelves, these difficulties were infinitely more formidable. In the first place, to have a room of her own, let alone a quiet room or a soundproof room, was out of the question, unless her parents were exceptionally rich or very noble, even up to the beginning of the nineteenth century. Since her pin money,[12] which depended on the goodwill of her father, was only enough to keep her clothed, she was debarred from such alleviations[13] as came even to Keats or Tennyson or Carlyle, all poor men, from a walking tour, a little journey to France, from the separate lodging which, even if it were miserable enough, sheltered them from the claims and tyrannies of their families. Such material difficulties were formidable; but much worse were the immaterial. The indifference of the world which Keats and Flaubert and other men of genius have found so hard to bear was in her case not indifference but hostility. The world did not say to her as it said to them, Write if you choose; it makes no difference to me. The world said with a guffaw, Write? What's the good of your writing? ❻ ■

❺ ? *What general belief about writing a "work of genius" does Woolf express here?*

❻ ? *According to Woolf, what two kinds of difficulties do all writers face? How is the difficulty women face in writing worse than that which men face?*

10. **Rousseau:** Jean-Jacques Rousseau (1712–1778), French author whose candid, autobiographical *Confessions* began a vogue in literature for confessional accounts.
11. **"Mighty poets . . . dead":** line from William Wordsworth's poem "Resolution and Independence."

12. **pin money:** small allowance for personal expenses.
13. **alleviations** (ə·lē′vē·ā′shənz): *n. pl.:* things that lighten, relieve, or make easier to bear.

Vocabulary

prodigious (prō·dij′əs) *adj.:* enormous.

notorious (nō·tôr′ē·əs) *adj.:* widely but unfavorably known; infamous.

formidable (fôr′mə·də·bəl) *adj.:* difficult to handle or overcome.

guffaw (gə·fô′) *n.:* loud laughter.

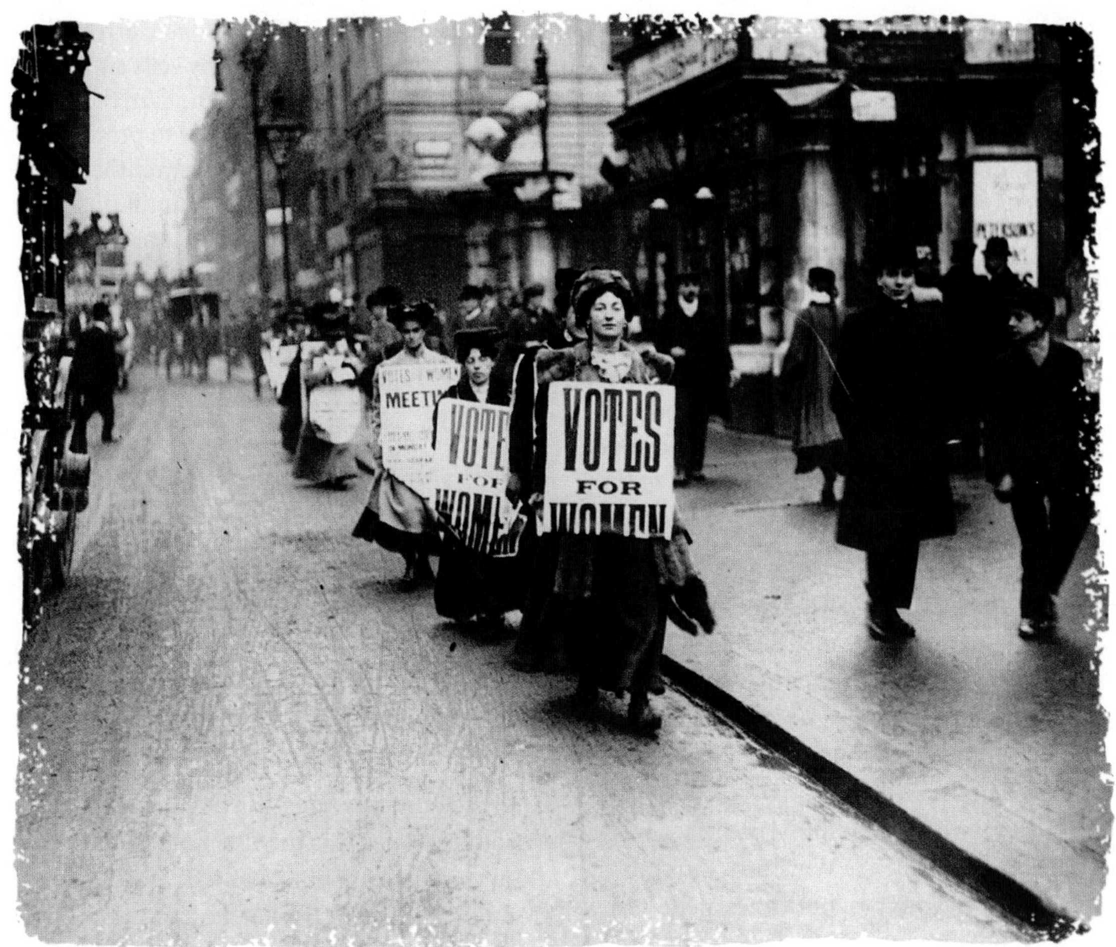

Suffragists march in London (c. 1910).

INFORMATIONAL TEXT

Votes for Women!

In December 1913, during an opera about Joan of Arc staged especially for the British royal family, three elegantly dressed women stood and addressed the king through a megaphone. The crowd was thrown into a panic as the women likened their struggle for the vote to Joan of Arc's fifteenth-century fight for liberty. When the police finally removed them, other women, hidden in the balcony, showered the audience with suffragist pamphlets. The king, of course, did not respond. But the dramatic protest joined the suffragists to Joan and other brave women's rights forerunners, just as Virginia Woolf's portrait of Shakespeare's fictional sister drew on the past to spur change in her own time.

The vote—a right not granted to British women over the age of thirty until 1918, and not granted to women over twenty-one until 1928—was the key to meaningful change for women in Woolf's day. Woolf herself was among thousands of women who joined suffrage organizations during the first decade of the century. Although she could have written articles for publications such as *The Suffragette* or *Votes for Women*, she instead lent her support in more humble ways: She sat on the platform at public meetings and folded letters for countless mailings (she later recalled spending "hours writing names like Cowgill on envelopes"). Woolf was a pacifist, and her views on the use of physical force prevented her wholehearted involvement in the increasingly combative woman suffrage movement of the early 1900s.

A new phase in an old fight. Universal suffrage was not a new idea. Women and men had campaigned for it since the mid-1800s; in fact, the philosopher John Stuart Mill had brought a suffrage bill before the British Parliament in 1867. The fight entered a new phase in 1904, when the ardent suffragist Christabel Pankhurst strode off to the Manchester Free Trade Hall to challenge Winston Churchill on the subject of voting rights for women. Churchill refused to acknowledge Pankhurst's demands, and she was howled down by the crowd, but she counted it as her first "militant" step.

Afterward, members of the Women's Social and Political Union, which Pankhurst and her mother, Emmeline, had founded in 1903, were emboldened to take other steps: They held rallies and marches, staged suffrage plays at public meetings, broke the windows of government buildings, and interrupted Parliament by shouting "Votes for women!" from their enclosed seats in the "Ladies' Gallery." (Later, several women chained themselves to the metal grille that separated this gallery from the main chamber.) From 1906 to 1914, more than a thousand British suffragists were arrested and carted off to jail. Held in tiny cells and prohibited from speaking to one another, these women still found other ways to protest, mostly through hunger strikes. In answer the government force-fed the protesters until the procedure permanently damaged many women's health. Thereafter, in what came to be called Cat and Mouse licenses, hunger strikers were released from prison only until they regained their strength—then they were rearrested.

Success at last. The sight of "respectable" women getting roughed up by hostile crowds and held for months in prison did alter public opinion: Many people came to realize how badly women wanted the right to full citizenship. Yet protests continued without results until the beginning of World War I, when the Pankhursts and others abruptly turned their energies to the war effort. Ironically, many historians now think that women's work during the war, mostly as they filled the absent soldiers' jobs, was the turning point in the suffrage movement. When the war was over, most Britishers felt that women shouldn't—indeed couldn't—be deprived of the vote any longer.

Emmeline Pankhurst (second from left) with one of her daughters at a suffragist meeting (1908).

Response and Analysis

Reading Check

1. What happens to "Judith Shakespeare" when she goes to London?
2. According to Woolf, what general conditions make works of genius difficult to produce? What special conditions do women face in creating works of genius?

Thinking Critically

3. In her essay, Woolf says of women, "Anonymity runs in their blood." According to Woolf, why do women shy away from the limelight? What do you think of the reasons she gives for women's seeking anonymity?
4. How would you describe the **tone** of this essay? Is it conversational? angry? perplexed? ironic? What purpose does this tone serve? Support your ideas with examples from the text.
5. In this essay, Woolf expresses several beliefs—some quite strongly, others more subtly. In your opinion, which belief is most central to the **theme** of the essay? (Refer to the list you created while reading.) Do you share this belief? Explain.
6. Does Woolf make any **generalizations** in this essay that you think are unsupported by historical or contemporary evidence? Explain your response, citing as examples historical and political events.

Extending and Evaluating

7. Is Woolf's use of an invented biography of Judith Shakespeare convincing to you? Why might she use such a device? Cite reasons for your answer.

WRITING

The Gender Gap

Woolf's essay contains many ideas, both explicit and implicit, about gender roles. In a brief **essay,** (a) discuss how Woolf depicts men and women; (b) evaluate the fairness of these depictions; and (c) discuss how true or relevant these depictions are for men and women today. (Your Quickwrite notes may help you.)

See "Analyzing Nonfiction," pages 1159–1160, for help with this assignment.

Vocabulary Development

What's the Difference?

Answer each of the following questions on a separate sheet of paper. (The underlined words are Vocabulary words.)

1. What's the difference between *servile* and *helpful*?
2. What's the difference between *suppressed* and *restrained*?
3. What's the difference between *propitious* and *foreboding*?
4. What's the difference between *prodigious* and *large*?
5. What's the difference between *notorious* and *famous*?
6. What's the difference between *formidable* and *unapproachable*?
7. What's the difference between *guffaw* and *laugh*?

Literary Skills Analyze an essay.

Reading Skills Evaluate an author's beliefs.

Writing Skills Write an essay analyzing a work of nonfiction.

Vocabulary Skills Clarify word meanings.

INTERNET

Project and Activities

Keyword: LE7 12-7

Introduction Comparing Points *of* View

Colonialism

You will be reading the four selections listed above in this Comparing Points of View feature on colonialism. In the top corner of the pages in this feature, you'll find three stars. Smaller versions of the stars appear next to the questions on pages 1123 and 1133 that focus on colonialism. At the end of the feature, on page 1139, you will be asked to compare the various points of view expressed in all four selections.

Examining the Issue: Colonialism

Colonialism refers to the rule of one nation over a group of people in a geographically distant land—usually for the purpose of maintaining control of that land's resources. Between the 1600s and the 1800s, Great Britain built a vast empire that included colonies in parts of Asia, Australia, Africa, and North America. Although the growth of the empire slowed significantly in the early 1800s, the rise of industrialization fueled Great Britain's need for raw materials, cheap labor, and worldwide markets. Through colonialism the British established a stronghold over millions of people, their lands, and their resources.

Make the Connection

Quickwrite

Think about impressions of British colonialism you have formed from your studies in history, from books you have read, or from movies you have seen. (Remember—the United States was once a British colony!) Make a list of some of these impressions. Then, based on your list, draw some conclusions about the ideals, principles, or beliefs behind British colonialism.

Pages 1114–1139 cover
Literary Skills Analyze points of view on a topic.
Reading Skills Compare main ideas across texts.

Reading Skills

Comparing Main Ideas Across Texts

As you read each selection, try to identify its **main idea,** or theme. Ask yourself, "How does this writer feel about the issue of colonialism?" Write a few sentences in response to this question. Then, after reading all of the selections, compare your notes. What different ideas do these writers express about their common topic?

George Orwell

(1903–1950)

England

George Orwell was born Eric Blair in Bengal, India, where his British father was a member of the Indian civil service. A few years afterward, his family returned to England. A lonely child, Orwell spent a good deal of time making up stories and poems. He later wrote that from an early age he knew he was going to be a writer.

After graduating from Eton College, a prep school, Orwell joined the Indian Imperial Police, serving in Burma (now Myanmar) from 1922 to 1927, when he resigned to devote more time to writing. Returning to Europe, he taught and took part-time, ill-paying jobs in France and England. His first book, *Down and Out in Paris and London* (1933), is based on those experiences. He based his next novel, *Burmese Days* (1934), on his life in Burma.

Although he published journalistic pieces under his real name, with the publication of his earliest books he began to use the name George Orwell, and he continued to do so until his death. After publishing three novels, Orwell was asked to write a study of conditions among industrial workers in northern England for the socialist Left Book Club. This became *The Road to Wigan Pier* (1937), a moving portrait of the difficult lives of working-class people.

Deeply disturbed by the rise of fascism in the 1930s, Orwell fought against the Nationalists (Fascists) in the Spanish Civil War and published a book based on these experiences—*Homage to Catalonia* (1938). "The Spanish war," he wrote, "turned the scale and thereafter I knew where I stood. Every line of serious work that I have written since 1936 has been written, directly or indirectly, *against* totalitarianism and *for* democratic socialism."

His two most famous novels, *Animal Farm* (1945) and *1984* (1949), illustrate this point. *Animal Farm* is a political allegory that points out the dangers of totalitarianism, whether practiced by the left or the right. And *1984* has given us an entire vocabulary for the excesses of totalitarian regimes, including such terms as *newspeak* and *Big Brother.* In this book, Orwell stresses the connections between language, thought, and power, dramatizing in fiction the ideas he earlier explored in his famous essay "Politics and the English Language" (1946)—especially the idea that corrupt language can be used to promote political oppression.

For Independent Reading

You may enjoy the following works by Orwell:

- *1984* (novel)
- "A Hanging" (essay)

George Orwell making a radio broadcast for the BBC.

Before You Read

Shooting an Elephant

Points *of* View

Wherever there were British colonies, there were British people who went there to live and to govern. No matter how long these people lived overseas, they generally remained outsiders, an alien minority holding power over a resentful people. As a police officer in British-controlled Burma (now Myanmar) in the 1920s, George Orwell did not just symbolize foreign rule—he was its agent. His awareness of being an enemy within another culture kindled enormous conflicts in him—and it propelled him to act against his conscience.

Literary Focus

Irony

The dominant literary mode in the twentieth century is **irony.** In this essay, Orwell uses several strategies to evoke a sense of irony. He uses **verbal irony**—saying one thing and meaning something else, often just the opposite. He also uses **situational irony,** in which something happens that is completely different from what we expect or what we think is appropriate.

Irony is a discrepancy between expectations and reality or between appearances and reality.

For more on Irony, see the Handbook of Literary and Historical Terms.

Reading Skills

Identifying the Author's Purpose

The purpose of an **informal essay**—such as this one by Orwell—is often to reveal the personality and opinions of its author. In the first sentence of the essay, Orwell admits that in Burma he "was hated by large numbers of people" because of the British tyranny he represented. This hatred controlled—and at times even tyrannized—Orwell himself. This ironic situation was not Orwell's alone; it was that of most British imperialists living abroad. In this essay, Orwell uses the term *imperialism* rather than *colonialism* to emphasize the tyrannical aspects of British rule. Imperialism connotes a powerful empire's control over another country's people and resources. Orwell's purpose here is twofold: to reveal his own personal dilemma and to reveal the cultural dilemma presented by colonialism itself. As you read, make note of words and phrases Orwell uses to describe these dilemmas.

Background

This essay is set in Burma, a country in Southeast Asia. After a series of wars with Great Britain during the 1800s, Burma finally came under British control in the 1880s. Although given some self-rule in 1937, Burma didn't become fully independent until 1948, after a harsh period of Japanese occupation during World War II. In 1989, the government changed the country's official name to the Union of Myanmar.

Vocabulary Development

supplant (sə·plant′) *v.:* replace; displace.

labyrinth (lab′ə·rinth′) *n.:* maze; complex or confusing arrangement.

squalid (skwäl′id) *adj.:* foul or unclean; wretched.

pretext (prē′tekst′) *n.:* excuse.

Literary Skills Analyze points of view on a topic. Understand irony.

Reading Skills Identify an author's purpose.

INTERNET

Vocabulary Practice

•

More About George Orwell

•

Keyword: LE7 12-7

Shooting an Elephant

George Orwell

Elephants carrying men and goods across a river in Nepal (c. 1910).
Getty Images.

In Moulmein, in Lower Burma, I was hated by large numbers of people—the only time in my life that I have been important enough for this to happen to me. I was subdivisional police officer of the town, and in an aimless, petty kind of way anti-European feeling was very bitter. No one had the guts to raise a riot, but if a European woman went through the bazaars alone somebody would probably spit betel juice over her dress. As a police officer I was an obvious target and was baited whenever it seemed safe to do so. When a nimble Burman tripped me up on the football field and the referee (another Burman) looked the other way, the crowd yelled with hideous laughter. This happened more than once. In the end the sneering yellow faces of young men that met me everywhere, the insults hooted after me when I was at a safe distance, got badly on my nerves. The young Buddhist priests were the worst of all. There were several thousands of them in the town and none of them seemed to have anything to do except stand on street corners and jeer at Europeans.

All this was perplexing and upsetting. For at that time I had already made up my mind that imperialism was an evil thing and the sooner I chucked up my job and got out of it the better. Theoretically—and secretly, of course—I was all for the Burmese and all against their oppressors, the British. As for the job I was doing, I hated it more bitterly than I can perhaps make clear. In a job like that you see the dirty work of Empire at close quarters. The wretched prisoners huddling in the stinking cages of the lockups, the gray, cowed faces of the long-term convicts, the scarred buttocks of the men who had been flogged with

bamboos—all these oppressed me with an intolerable sense of guilt. But I could get nothing into perspective. I was young and ill-educated and I had had to think out my problems in the utter silence that is imposed on every Englishman in the East. I did not even know that the British Empire is dying, still less did I know that it is a great deal better than the younger empires that are going to supplant it. All I knew was that I was stuck between my hatred of the empire I served and my rage against the evil-spirited little beasts who tried to make my job impossible. With one part of my mind I thought of the British Raj[1] as an unbreakable tyranny, as something clamped down, *in saecula saeculorum,*[2] upon the will of prostrate peoples; with another part I thought that the greatest joy in the world would be to drive a bayonet into a Buddhist priest's guts. Feelings like these are the normal by-products of imperialism; ask any Anglo-Indian official, if you can catch him off duty. ❶

> ❶ ? *What* ***paradox,*** *or seeming contradiction, does Orwell set up in these first two paragraphs?*

One day something happened which in a roundabout way was enlightening. It was a tiny incident in itself, but it gave me a better glimpse than I had had before of the real nature of imperialism—the real motives for which despotic governments act. ❷ Early one morning the subinspector at a police station the other end of the town rang me up on the phone and said that an elephant was ravaging the bazaar. Would I please come and do something about it? I did not know what I could do, but I wanted to see what was happening and I got on to a pony and started out. I took my rifle, an old .44 Winchester and much too small to kill an elephant, but I thought the noise might be useful *in terrorem.*[3] Various Burmans stopped me on the way and told me about the elephant's doings. It was not, of course, a wild elephant, but a tame one which had gone "must."[4] It had been chained up, as tame elephants always are when their attack of "must" is due, but on the previous night it had broken its chain and escaped. Its mahout,[5] the only person who could manage it when it was in that state, had set out in pursuit, but had taken the wrong direction and was now twelve hours' journey away, and in the morning the elephant had suddenly reappeared in the town. The Burmese population had no weapons and were quite helpless against it. It had already destroyed somebody's bamboo hut, killed a cow, and raided some fruit stalls and devoured the stock; also it had met the municipal rubbish van and, when the driver jumped out and took to his heels, had turned the van over and inflicted violences upon it. ❸

> ❷ ? *What topic does Orwell identify for the story he is about to tell—and, by extension, for the entire essay?*

> ❸ ? *Do you find Orwell's* ***tone*** *suspenseful, humorous, or both? Support your ideas with specific words and phrases from the text.*

The Burmese subinspector and some Indian constables were waiting for me in the quarter where the elephant had been seen. It was a very poor quarter, a labyrinth of squalid bamboo huts, thatched with palm leaf, winding all over a steep hillside. I remember that it was a cloudy,

---

1. **Raj** (räj): rule over India. The word is derived from *rajya,* Hindi for "kingdom."
2. ***in saecula saeculorum*** (in sē′ko͞o·lə sē′ko͞o·lôr′əm): Latin for "forever and ever" (literally, "into ages of ages").
3. ***in terrorem*** (in ter·ôr′əm): Latin for "for terror." In other words, the gun might serve to frighten the elephant.
4. **must** *n.:* state of frenzy in animals. The word comes from *mast,* Hindi for "intoxicated."
5. **mahout** (mə·hout′) *n.:* elephant keeper. The word derives from *mahaut,* Hindi for "great in measure" and, thus, "important officer."

Vocabulary

supplant (sə·plant′) *v.:* replace; displace.

labyrinth (lab′ə·rinth′) *n.:* maze; complex or confusing arrangement.

squalid (skwäl′id) *adj.:* foul or unclean; wretched.

stuffy morning at the beginning of the rains. We began questioning the people as to where the elephant had gone and, as usual, failed to get any definite information. That is invariably the case in the East; a story always sounds clear enough at a distance, but the nearer you get to the scene of events the vaguer it becomes. Some of the people said that the elephant had gone in one direction, some said that he had gone in another, some professed not even to have heard of any elephant. I had almost made up my mind that the whole story was a pack of lies, when we heard yells a little distance away. There was a loud, scandalized cry of "Go away, child! Go away this instant!" and an old woman with a switch in her hand came round the corner of the hut, violently shooing away a crowd of naked children. Some more women followed, clicking their tongues and exclaiming; evidently there was something that the children ought not to have seen. I rounded the hut and saw a man's dead body sprawling in the mud. He was an Indian, a black Dravidian coolie,[6] almost naked, and he could not have been dead many minutes. The people said that the elephant had come suddenly upon him round the corner of the hut, caught him with its trunk, put its foot on his back, and ground him into the earth. This was the rainy season and the ground was soft, and his face had scored a trench a foot deep and a couple of yards long. He was lying on his belly with arms crucified and head sharply twisted to one side. His face was coated with mud, the eyes wide open, the teeth bared and grinning with an expression of unendurable agony. (Never tell me, by the way, that the dead look peaceful. Most of the corpses I have seen looked devilish.) The friction of the great beast's foot had stripped the skin from his back as neatly as one skins a rabbit. As soon as I saw the dead man I sent an orderly to a friend's house nearby to borrow an elephant rifle. I had already sent back the pony, not wanting it to go mad with fright and throw me if it smelled the elephant. ❹

> ❹ ? *How does Orwell's description of the dead man make you feel? What purpose might such a description serve?*

The orderly came back in a few minutes with a rifle and five cartridges, and meanwhile some Burmans had arrived and told us that the elephant was in the paddy fields below, only a few hundred yards away. As I started forward practically the whole population of the quarter flocked out of the houses and followed me. They had seen the rifle and were all shouting excitedly that I was going to shoot the elephant. They had not shown much interest in the elephant when he was merely ravaging their homes, but it was different now that he was going to be shot. It was a bit of fun to them, as it would be to an English crowd; besides they wanted the meat. It made me vaguely uneasy. I had no intention of shooting the elephant—I had merely sent for the rifle to defend myself if necessary—and it is always unnerving to have a crowd following you. I marched down the hill, looking and feeling a fool, with the rifle over my shoulder and an ever-growing army of people jostling at my heels. At the bottom, when you got away from the huts, there was a metaled[7] road and beyond that a miry waste of paddy fields a thousand yards across, not yet plowed but soggy from the first rains and dotted with coarse grass. The elephant was standing eight yards from the road, his left side toward us. He took not the slightest notice of the crowd's approach. He was tearing up bunches of grass, beating them against his knees to clean them, and stuffing them into his mouth.

I had halted on the road. As soon as I saw the elephant I knew with perfect certainty that I

---

6. **Dravidian** (drə·vid′ē·ən) **coolie:** *Dravidian* denotes any of several intermixed races living chiefly in southern India and northern Sri Lanka. A coolie is an unskilled laborer. The word is derived from *quli*, Hindi for "hired servant," and has become offensive.

7. **metaled** *v.* used as *adj.:* paved with cinders, stones, or the like.

ought not to shoot him. It is a serious matter to shoot a working elephant—it is comparable to destroying a huge and costly piece of machinery—and obviously one ought not to do it if it can possibly be avoided. And at that distance, peacefully eating, the elephant looked no more dangerous than a cow. I thought then and I think now that his attack of "must" was already passing off; in which case he would merely wander harmlessly about until the mahout came back and caught him. Moreover, I did not in the least want to shoot him. I decided that I would watch him for a little while to make sure that he did not turn savage again, and then go home. 5

> 5
> ? *Once the elephant comes into view, what is Orwell's (and your) first impression of the creature? What is **ironic** about this description?*

But at that moment I glanced round at the crowd that had followed me. It was an immense crowd, two thousand at the least and growing every minute. It blocked the road for a long distance on either side. I looked at the sea of yellow faces above the garish clothes—faces all happy and excited over this bit of fun, all certain that the elephant was going to be shot. They were watching me as they would watch a conjurer about to perform a trick. They did not like me, but with the magical rifle in my hands I was momentarily worth watching. And suddenly I realized that I should have to shoot the elephant after all. The people expected it of me and I had got to do it; I could feel their two thousand wills pressing me forward, irresistibly. And it was at this moment, as I stood there with the rifle in my hands, that I first grasped the hollowness, the futility of the white man's dominion in the East. Here was I, the white man with his gun, standing in front of the unarmed native crowd—seemingly the leading actor of the piece; but in reality I was only an absurd puppet pushed to and fro by the will of those yellow faces behind. I perceived in this moment that when the white man turns tyrant it is his own freedom that he destroys. He becomes a sort of hollow, posing dummy, the conventionalized figure of a sahib.[8] For it is the condition of his rule that he shall spend his life in trying to impress the "natives," and so in every crisis he has got to do what the "natives" expect of him. He wears a mask, and his face grows to fit it. I had got to shoot the elephant. I had committed myself to doing it when I sent for the rifle. A sahib has got to act like a sahib; he has got to appear resolute, to know his own mind and do definite things. To come all that way, rifle in hand, with two thousand people marching at my heels, and then to trail feebly away, having done nothing—no, that was impossible. The crowd would laugh at me. And my whole life, every white man's life in the East, was one long struggle not to be laughed at. 6

> 6
> Orwell began his essay by remarking that a tiny incident revealed to him the nature of imperialism.
> ? *What is the link between imperialism and shooting the elephant?*

But I did not want to shoot the elephant. I watched him beating his bunch of grass against his knees, with that preoccupied grandmotherly air that elephants have. It seemed to me that it would be murder to shoot him. At that age I was not squeamish about killing animals, but I had never shot an elephant and never wanted to. (Somehow it always seems worse to kill a *large* animal.) Besides, there was the beast's owner to be considered. Alive, the elephant was worth at least a hundred pounds; dead, he would only be worth the value of his tusks, five pounds, possibly. But I had got to act quickly. I turned to some experienced-looking Burmans who had been there when we arrived, and asked them how the elephant had been behaving. They all said the same thing: He took no notice of you if

8. **sahib** (sä'ib') *n.:* master; sir. In colonial India the title was used as a sign of respect for a European gentleman.

you left him alone, but he might charge if you went too close to him.

It was perfectly clear to me what I ought to do. I ought to walk up to within, say, twenty-five yards of the elephant and test his behavior. If he charged, I could shoot; if he took no notice of me, it would be safe to leave him until the mahout came back. But also I knew that I was going to do no such thing. I was a poor shot with a rifle and the ground was soft mud into which one would sink at every step. If the elephant charged and I missed him, I should have about as much chance as a toad under a steamroller. But even then I was not thinking particularly of my own skin, only of the watchful yellow faces behind. For at that moment, with the crowd watching me, I was not afraid in the ordinary sense, as I would have been if I had been alone. A white man mustn't be frightened in front of "natives"; and so, in general, he isn't frightened. The sole thought in my mind was that if anything went wrong those two thousand Burmans would see me pursued, caught, trampled on, and reduced to a grinning corpse like that Indian up the hill. And if that happened it was quite probable that some of them would laugh. That would never do. There was only one alternative. I shoved the cartridges into the magazine and lay down on the road to get a better aim. ❼

❼ ? *Describe Orwell's inner conflict and how he deals with it.*

The crowd grew very still, and a deep, low, happy sigh, as of people who see the theater curtain go up at last, breathed from innumerable throats. They were going to have their bit of fun after all. The rifle was a beautiful German thing with cross-hair sights. I did not then know that in shooting an elephant one would shoot to cut an imaginary bar running from earhole to earhole. I ought, therefore, as the elephant was sideways on, to have aimed straight at his earhole; actually I aimed several inches in front of this, thinking the brain would be further forward.

When I pulled the trigger I did not hear the bang or feel the kick—one never does when a shot goes home—but I heard the devilish roar of glee that went up from the crowd. In that instant, in too short a time, one would have thought, even for the bullet to get there, a mysterious, terrible change had come over the

Elephants transporting munitions in Cambodia during the Indochinese War (1954).

elephant. He neither stirred nor fell, but every line of his body had altered. He looked suddenly stricken, shrunken, immensely old, as though the frightful impact of the bullet had paralyzed him without knocking him down. At last, after what seemed a long time—it might have been five seconds, I dare say—he sagged flabbily to his knees. His mouth slobbered. An enormous senility seemed to have settled upon him. One could have imagined him thousands of years old. I fired again into the same spot. At the second shot he did not collapse but climbed with desperate slowness to his feet and stood weakly upright, with legs sagging and head drooping. I fired a third time. That was the shot that did for him. You could see the agony of it jolt his whole body and knock the last remnant of strength from his legs. But in falling he seemed for a moment to rise, for as his hind legs collapsed beneath him he seemed to tower upward like a huge rock toppling, his trunk reaching skyward like a tree. He trumpeted, for the first and only time. And then down he came, his belly toward me, with a crash that seemed to shake the ground even where I lay. 8

> 8
> ? *What details in the description of the shooting seem most significant?*

I got up. The Burmans were already racing past me across the mud. It was obvious that the elephant would never rise again, but he was not dead. He was breathing very rhythmically with long rattling gasps, his great mound of a side painfully rising and falling. His mouth was wide open—I could see far down into caverns of pale pink throat. I waited a long time for him to die, but his breathing did not weaken. Finally I fired my two remaining shots into the spot where I thought his heart must be. The thick blood welled out of him like red velvet, but still he did not die. His body did not even jerk when the shots hit him, the tortured breathing continued without a pause. He was dying, very slowly and in great agony, but in some world remote from me where not even a bullet could damage him further. I felt that I had got to put an end to that dreadful noise. It seemed dreadful to see the great beast lying there, powerless to move and yet powerless to die, and not even to be able to finish him. I sent back for my small rifle and poured shot after shot into his heart and down his throat. They seemed to make no impression. The tortured gasps continued as steadily as the ticking of a clock.

In the end I could not stand it any longer and went away. I heard later that it took him half an hour to die. Burmans were bringing dahs[9] and baskets even before I left, and I was told they had stripped his body almost to the bones by the afternoon.

Afterward, of course, there were endless discussions about the shooting of the elephant. The owner was furious, but he was only an Indian and could do nothing. Besides, legally I had done the right thing, for a mad elephant has to be killed, like a mad dog, if its owner fails to control it. Among the Europeans opinion was divided. The older men said I was right, the younger men said it was a damn shame to shoot an elephant for killing a coolie, because an elephant was worth more than any damn Coringhee[10] coolie. And afterward I was very glad that the coolie had been killed; it put me legally in the right and it gave me a sufficient pretext for shooting the elephant. I often wondered whether any of the others grasped that I had done it solely to avoid looking a fool. 9 ■

> 9
> ? *What implicit, or suggested, idea about the law does Orwell express?*

9. **dahs** (däz) *n. pl.:* large carving knives.
10. **Coringhee** (kôr·iŋ′ē): port in southeastern India.

Vocabulary
pretext (prē′tekst′) *n.:* excuse.

Response and Analysis

Reading Check

1. What problem is Orwell asked to solve?
2. About how big is the crowd following Orwell? Why does he say they have come along?
3. When Orwell finds the elephant, what two reasons does he give for not wanting to shoot it?
4. How does the animal react when shot?

Thinking Critically

5. What seems to be Orwell's attitude toward the Burmese? Do you think he embodies the perspective of a colonizer? Use the details you recorded in your reading notes as well as other evidence to support your answer.
6. Explain in your own words the meaning of Orwell's **ironic** insight that tyrants destroy their own freedom. Then, identify three other ironies contained in this essay.
7. What does this **essay** reveal about Orwell's code of ethics or behavior as a young police officer in Burma? What does it reveal about the true nature of colonialism? Are these insights related? Explain.
8. There are two Orwells in this essay: the one acting and the one looking back, narrating the action. Discuss the differences between the two observers, using examples from the text. How does the older Orwell feel about the younger one?
9. The elephant has tremendous symbolic importance in this essay. What political idea or assumption might the elephant **symbolize**? In other words, what political idea was the young Orwell confronted with, confused by, and ultimately weakened by? In your own words, explain your interpretation of the elephant as a political symbol. Cite details from the text to support your interpretation.

Extending and Evaluating

10. Orwell goes to great lengths to describe the shooting and the painfully slow death of the elephant. In your opinion, is such gruesome detail necessary? Why? What does it add to or take away from the essay?

WRITING

Words to Dwell On

Review Orwell's essay, and find one passage that you think is especially important, controversial, or even upsetting. Write a brief **essay** in which you cite the passage and explain why you have chosen it. In your essay, be sure to describe your response to the passage, and state whether you think it relates to any situation in today's society.

Vocabulary Development

True or False?

Identify each of the following statements as true or false, and briefly explain your answer:

1. It is a good idea to supplant unhealthy habits with healthy ones.
2. A direct route from one place to another is sometimes called a labyrinth.
3. A room that has been thoroughly cleaned would be described as squalid.
4. A pretext is usually offered by someone who is honest.

Literary Skills Analyze points of view on a topic. Analyze irony.

Reading Skills Identify an author's purpose.

Writing Skills Write a response to an essay.

Vocabulary Skills Demonstrate word knowledge.

Vocabulary Development

The Etymology of Political Science and Historical Terms

New words and phrases are introduced into our vocabulary almost every day. George Orwell's novel *1984* gave the world a number of now familiar political phrases, such as "thought police" and "Big Brother is watching you." Words coined by Orwell include *double-think*, which means "illogical thinking that distorts the truth to make it more acceptable," and *newspeak*, which means "deliberately ambiguous and deceptive talk used by government officials."

Many political science and historical terms have been borrowed from other languages. Consider the following terms:

Term	Word origin	Meaning
apartheid	Afrikaans, "the state of being separate"	official South African policy of strict racial segregation and discrimination (c. 1948–1991)
democracy	Greek (*demokratia*)	government in which all citizens take part and limit the power of rulers
constitution	Latin (*constituere*)	document outlining the fundamental laws and principles that govern a nation
capitalism	Latin (*capitalis*)	economic system in which private individuals invest money that is earned to produce profits
governor	Latin (*gubernator*), "a pilot"	elected head of a state in the United States
imperialism	Latin (*imperialis*), "empire"	domination of a powerful nation over the political, economic, and cultural affairs of another nation or region
parliament	Medieval English from French *parler*, "to speak"	national legislative body (as in Great Britain)
laissez-faire	French, "let people do as they please"	theory that opposes government regulation of economic matters

PRACTICE

Vocabulary Skills Understand etymologies.

Use a dictionary to learn the history of the political science and historical terms listed below. Determine the language the word is borrowed from, its original meaning, and its current meaning.

coup d'état **détente** **electorate**
monarchy **veto** **fascist**

Doris Lessing

(1919–)

Zimbabwe

Doris Lessing was born in Persia (now Iran) to British parents who had fled England to escape what they saw as its narrowness and provincialism. When she was five, her father gave up his job running a bank, and the family moved to a three-thousand-acre farm in Southern Rhodesia (now Zimbabwe). The farm employed some thirty to fifty black African laborers, each of whom earned the equivalent of about $1.50 a month and who lived in mud huts with no sanitation.

In Africa, Lessing's mother was homesick for England and often ill, while her father grew increasingly eccentric. Lessing describes her own childhood as "hellishly lonely"; the nearest neighbor was miles away. Only as an adult did she appreciate that her solitude had fostered a fine education, since the lack of company allowed her to spend her time slowly reading the classics of European and American fiction.

At fourteen, Lessing left school and went to work in Salisbury, the capital of Rhodesia, first as a nursemaid and then as a stenographer and telephone operator. The city had a white population of about ten thousand and a larger black population that Lessing discovered "didn't count." When her first marriage collapsed, she entered radical politics. At twenty-six, she married a second time, but that marriage also ended in divorce.

"I can't remember a time when I didn't want to come to England," she later recalled. In 1949, she left Africa for England with her two-year-old son and the manuscript of her first novel, *The Grass Is Singing* (1950). Tracing a complex relationship between a white farmer's wife and her black servant, the book commanded attention as one of the earliest novels about Africa's racial problems. The short stories collected in Lessing's *African Stories* (1964) also take place in the Africa of her childhood.

Lessing's most widely read and discussed book is probably *The Golden Notebook* (1962), an ambitious, complexly structured work that combines fiction, parody, and factual reporting to explore Lessing's concerns with politics, mental illness, and the problems facing women in modern life. Another well-known book, *Briefing for a Descent into Hell* (1971), introduces readers to what Lessing calls "inner-space fiction," in which an individual mental breakdown is related to a wider social breakdown. Lessing also continues to write nonfiction works, and in 1994, she published *Under My Skin*, the first volume of her autobiography.

In all of Lessing's work, there is evidence of the responsibility she feels as a writer to be "an instrument of change." "It is not merely a question of preventing evil," she says, "but of strengthening a vision of a good which may defeat the evil."

For Independent Reading

The following stories by Lessing are classics:

- "A Sunrise on the Veld"
- "Through the Tunnel"

Before You Read

No Witchcraft for Sale

Points *of* View

Quickwrite

The upcoming story asks troubling, complex questions about cultural conflict. Some of its cultural clashes are obvious, some are bridged by the unifying force of deep affection, and some remain mysterious—for the people involved and perhaps for us. Do you think that some cultural differences cannot be bridged, no matter how much goodwill the parties bring to the encounter? Or do you think that with enough effort, people can truly understand and appreciate one another's grievances, beliefs, and aspirations? Write down a few of your thoughts on these questions.

Literary Focus

Theme

Stories can have many threads. A wide assortment of ideas may be conveyed through characters' attitudes, through conflicts and their outcomes, through symbols, or even through a title. Despite the variety of ideas a reader may glean from a story, one dominant, central idea, or **theme,** will unify the work.

Literary Skills Understand theme.

Reading Skills Identify historical context.

> A **theme** is the central idea, or insight, embodied in a work of literature.
>
> *For more on Theme, see the Handbook of Literary and Historical Terms.*

INTERNET

Vocabulary Practice

Keyword: LE7 12-7

Reading Skills

Identifying Historical Context

The time and place in which a writer lives often have a direct bearing on a work's themes, characters, and events—even if the work itself is set in a different time or place. This tale from Doris Lessing's *African Stories* takes place in Southern Rhodesia at a time when that South African country was still firmly under British rule. When Lessing wrote the story in 1964, however, Southern Rhodesia was demanding independence from Britain. The white minority in Southern Rhodesia was eager to establish its own government—a government that would continue the policy of denying rights to black citizens. Britain, which had come to support the voting rights of blacks in Southern Rhodesia, refused to grant independence. As you read, consider how the political climate in which Lessing wrote this story may have influenced her portrayal of the earlier time period. Record your ideas.

Background

Civil war tore apart the country of Southern Rhodesia after it declared independence from Britain in 1965. After years of fighting between black nationalists and government troops, Southern Rhodesia emerged as the republic of Zimbabwe under the leadership of a black African, Robert Mugabe (mo͞o·gäb′ē), in 1980.

Vocabulary Development

reverently (rev′ə·rənt·lē) *adv.:* with deep respect, love, or awe, as for something sacred.

inevitable (in·ev′i·tə·bəl) *adj.:* certain to happen; unavoidable.

efficacy (ef′i·kə·sē) *n.:* ability to produce a desired effect; effectiveness.

perfunctory (pər·fuŋk′tə·rē) *adj.:* halfhearted; indifferent.

annulled (ə·nuld′) *v.:* did away with; canceled.

perversely (pər·vʉrs′lē) *adv.:* disagreeably; contrarily.

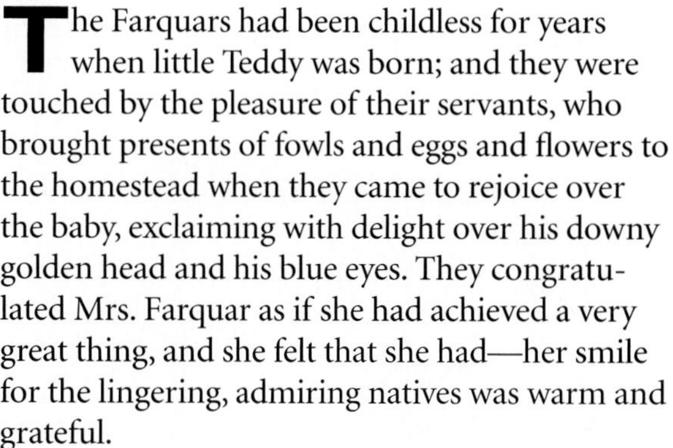

No Witchcraft for Sale

Doris Lessing

The Farquars had been childless for years when little Teddy was born; and they were touched by the pleasure of their servants, who brought presents of fowls and eggs and flowers to the homestead when they came to rejoice over the baby, exclaiming with delight over his downy golden head and his blue eyes. They congratulated Mrs. Farquar as if she had achieved a very great thing, and she felt that she had—her smile for the lingering, admiring natives was warm and grateful.

Later, when Teddy had his first haircut, Gideon the cook picked up the soft gold tufts from the ground, and held them reverently in his hand. Then he smiled at the little boy and said: "Little Yellow Head." That became the native name for the child. Gideon and Teddy were great friends from the first. When Gideon had finished his work, he would lift Teddy on his shoulders to the shade of a big tree, and play with him there, forming curious little toys from twigs and leaves and grass, or shaping animals from wetted soil. When Teddy learned to walk it was often Gideon who crouched before him, clucking encouragement, finally catching him when he fell, tossing him up in the air till they both became breathless with laughter. Mrs. Farquar was fond of the old cook because of his love for her child.

There was no second baby; and one day Gideon said: "Ah, missus, missus, the Lord above sent this one; Little Yellow Head is the most good thing we have in our house." Because of that "we" Mrs. Farquar felt a warm impulse toward her cook; and at the end of the month she raised his wages. He had been with her now for several years; he was one of the few natives who had his wife and children in the compound and never wanted to go home to his kraal,[1] which was some hundreds of miles away. Sometimes a small piccanin[2] who had been born the same time as Teddy, could be seen peering from the edge of the bush, staring in awe at the little white boy with his miraculous fair hair and Northern blue eyes. The two little children would gaze at each other with a wide, interested gaze, and once Teddy put out his hand curiously to touch the black child's cheeks and hair.

Gideon, who was watching, shook his head wonderingly, and said: "Ah, missus, these are both children, and one will grow up to be a baas,[3] and one will be a servant"; and Mrs. Farquar smiled and said sadly, "Yes, Gideon, I was thinking the same." She sighed. "It is God's will," said Gideon, who was a mission boy.[4] The Farquars were very religious people; and this shared feeling about God bound servant and masters even closer together.

Teddy was about six years old when he was given a scooter, and discovered the intoxications of speed. All day he would fly around the homestead, in and out of flowerbeds, scattering squawking chickens and irritated dogs, finishing with a wide dizzying arc into the kitchen door. There he would cry: "Gideon, look at me!" And Gideon would laugh and say: "Very clever, Little Yellow Head." Gideon's youngest son, who was

1. **kraal** (kräl): South African village.

2. **piccanin** (pik'ə·nin): black African child. Derived from *pequeno* (pā·kā'nōō), Portuguese for "small," the term is often considered offensive.
3. **baas** (bäs): Afrikaans for "master." Afrikaans, a language developed from seventeenth-century Dutch, is spoken in South Africa.
4. **mission boy:** one educated by Christian missionaries.

Vocabulary

reverently (rev'ə·rənt·lē) *adv.:* with deep respect, love, or awe, as for something sacred.

Neverdie Mushwana, a South African "witch doctor," in front of his home, with one of his snakes. Tzaneen, South Africa (March 1997).

Juhan KUUS/SIPA Press.

now a herdsboy, came especially up from the compound to see the scooter. He was afraid to come near it, but Teddy showed off in front of him. "Piccanin," shouted Teddy, "get out of my way!" And he raced in circles around the black child until he was frightened, and fled back to the bush.

"Why did you frighten him?" asked Gideon, gravely reproachful.

Teddy said defiantly: "He's only a black boy," and laughed. Then, when Gideon turned away from him without speaking, his face fell. Very soon he slipped into the house and found an orange and brought it to Gideon, saying: "This is for you." He could not bring himself to say he was sorry; but he could not bear to lose Gideon's affection either. Gideon took the orange unwillingly and sighed. "Soon you will be going away to school, Little Yellow Head," he said wonderingly, "and then you will be grown up." He shook his head gently and said, "And that is how our lives go." He seemed to be putting a distance between himself and Teddy, not because of resentment, but in the way a person accepts something inevitable. The baby had lain in his arms and smiled up into his face: The tiny boy had swung from his shoulders and played with him by the hour. Now Gideon would not let his flesh touch the flesh of the white child. He was kind, but there was a grave formality in his voice that made Teddy pout and sulk away. Also, it made him into a man: With Gideon he was polite, and carried himself formally, and if he came into the kitchen to ask for something, it was in the way a white man uses toward a servant, expecting to be obeyed.

But on the day that Teddy came staggering into the kitchen with his fists to his eyes, shrieking with pain, Gideon dropped the pot full of hot soup that he was holding, rushed to the child, and forced aside his fingers. "A snake!" he exclaimed. Teddy had been on his scooter, and had come to a rest with his foot on the side of a big tub of plants. A tree snake, hanging by its tail from the roof, had spat full into his eyes. Mrs. Farquar came running when she heard the commotion. "He'll go blind," she sobbed, holding Teddy close against her. "Gideon, he'll go blind!" Already the eyes, with perhaps half an hour's sight left in them, were swollen up to the size of fists: Teddy's small white face was distorted by great purple oozing protuberances.[5] Gideon said: "Wait a minute, missus, I'll get some medicine." He ran off into the bush.

Mrs. Farquar lifted the child into the house and bathed his eyes with permanganate.[6] She had scarcely heard Gideon's words; but when she saw that her remedies had no effect at all, and remembered how she had seen natives with no sight in their eyes, because of the spitting of a snake, she began to look for the return of her cook, remembering what she heard of the efficacy of native herbs. She stood by the window, holding the terrified, sobbing little boy in her arms, and peered helplessly into the bush. It was not more than a few minutes before she saw Gideon come bounding back, and in his hand he held a plant.

"Do not be afraid, missus," said Gideon, "this will cure Little Yellow Head's eyes." He stripped the leaves from the plant, leaving a small white fleshy root. Without even washing it, he put the root in his mouth, chewed it vigorously, and then held the spittle there while he took the child forcibly from Mrs. Farquar. He gripped Teddy down between his knees, and pressed the balls of his thumbs into the swollen eyes, so that the child screamed and Mrs. Farquar cried out in protest: "Gideon, Gideon!" But Gideon took no notice.

---

5. **protuberances** (prō·to͞o′bər·əns·iz) *n. pl.:* swellings; bulges.
6. **permanganate** (pər·maŋ′gə·nāt′) *n.:* dark purple chemical compound used as a disinfectant.

Vocabulary

inevitable (in·ev′i·tə·bəl) *adj.:* certain to happen; unavoidable.

efficacy (ef′i·kə·sē) *n.:* ability to produce a desired effect; effectiveness.

He knelt over the writhing child, pushing back the puffy lids till chinks of eyeball showed, and then he spat hard, again and again, into first one eye, and then the other. He finally lifted Teddy gently into his mother's arms, and said: "His eyes will get better." But Mrs. Farquar was weeping with terror, and she could hardly thank him: It was impossible to believe that Teddy could keep his sight. In a couple of hours the swellings were gone: The eyes were inflamed and tender but Teddy could see. Mr. and Mrs. Farquar went to Gideon in the kitchen and thanked him over and over again. They felt helpless because of their gratitude: It seemed they could do nothing to express it. They gave Gideon presents for his wife and children, and a big increase in wages, but these things could not pay for Teddy's now completely cured eyes. Mrs. Farquar said: "Gideon, God chose you as an instrument for His goodness," and Gideon said: "Yes, missus, God is very good."

Now, when such a thing happens on a farm, it cannot be long before everyone hears of it. Mr. and Mrs. Farquar told their neighbors and the story was discussed from one end of the district to the other. The bush is full of secrets. No one can live in Africa, or at least on the veld,[7] without learning very soon that there is an ancient wisdom of leaf and soil and season—and, too, perhaps most important of all, of the darker tracts of the human mind—which is the black man's heritage. Up and down the district people were telling anecdotes, reminding each other of things that had happened to them.

"But I saw it myself, I tell you. It was a puff-adder bite. The kaffir's[8] arm was swollen to the elbow, like a great shiny black bladder. He was groggy after a half a minute. He was dying. Then suddenly a kaffir walked out of the bush with his hands full of green stuff. He smeared something on the place, and next day my boy was back at work, and all you could see was two small punctures in the skin."

This was the kind of tale they told. And, as always, with a certain amount of exasperation, because while all of them knew that in the bush of Africa are waiting valuable drugs locked in bark, in simple-looking leaves, in roots, it was impossible to ever get the truth about them from the natives themselves.

The story eventually reached town; and perhaps it was at a sundowner party,[9] or some such function, that a doctor, who happened to be there, challenged it. "Nonsense," he said. "These things get exaggerated in the telling. We are always checking up on this kind of story, and we draw a blank every time."

Anyway, one morning there arrived a strange car at the homestead, and out stepped one of the workers from the laboratory in town, with cases full of test tubes and chemicals.

Mr. and Mrs. Farquar were flustered and pleased and flattered. They asked the scientist to lunch, and they told the story all over again, for the hundredth time. Little Teddy was there too, his blue eyes sparkling with health, to prove the truth of it. The scientist explained how humanity might benefit if this new drug could be offered for sale; and the Farquars were even more pleased: They were kind, simple people, who liked to think of something good coming about because of them. But when the scientist began talking of the money that might result, their manner showed discomfort. Their feelings over the miracle (that was how they thought of it) were so strong and deep and religious, that it was distasteful to them to think of money. The scientist, seeing their faces, went back to his first

7. **veld** *n.:* in South Africa, open country with very few bushes or trees; grassland. *Veld,* also spelled *veldt,* is Afrikaans for "field."

8. **kaffir's** (kaf′ərz): *Kaffir* is a contemptuous term for a black African, derived from *kāfir,* Arabic for "infidel."

9. **sundowner party:** British colloquial term for "cocktail party." The term derives from the British custom of gathering for drinks at sunset.

point, which was the advancement of humanity. He was perhaps a trifle perfunctory: It was not the first time he had come salting the tail of a fabulous bush secret.[10]

Eventually, when the meal was over, the Farquars called Gideon into their living room and explained to him that this baas, here, was a Big Doctor from the Big City, and he had come all that way to see Gideon. At this Gideon seemed afraid; he did not understand; and Mrs. Farquar explained quickly that it was because of the wonderful thing he had done with Teddy's eyes that the Big Baas had come.

Gideon looked from Mrs. Farquar to Mr. Farquar, and then at the little boy, who was showing great importance because of the occasion. At last he said grudgingly: "The Big Baas want to know what medicine I used?" He spoke incredulously, as if he could not believe his old friends could so betray him. Mr. Farquar began explaining how a useful medicine could be made out of the root, and how it could be put on sale, and how thousands of people, black and white, up and down the continent of Africa, could be saved by the medicine when that spitting snake filled their eyes with poison. Gideon listened, his eyes bent on the ground, the skin of his forehead puckering in discomfort. When Mr. Farquar had finished he did not reply. The scientist, who all this time had been leaning back in a big chair, sipping his coffee and smiling with skeptical good humor, chipped in and explained all over again, in different words, about the making of drugs and the progress of science. Also, he offered Gideon a present.

There was silence after this further explanation, and then Gideon remarked indifferently that he could not remember the root. His face was sullen and hostile, even when he looked at the Farquars, whom he usually treated like old friends. They were beginning to feel annoyed; and this feeling annulled the guilt that had been sprung into life by Gideon's accusing manner. They were beginning to feel that he was unreasonable. But it was at that moment that they all realized he would never give in. The magical drug would remain where it was, unknown and useless except for the tiny scattering of Africans who had the knowledge, natives who might be digging a ditch for the municipality in a ragged shirt and a pair of patched shorts, but who were still born to healing, hereditary healers, being the nephews or sons of the old witch doctors whose ugly masks and bits of bone and all the uncouth properties of magic were the outward signs of real power and wisdom.

The Farquars might tread on that plant fifty times a day as they passed from house to garden, from cow kraal to mealie[11] field, but they would never know it.

But they went on persuading and arguing, with all the force of their exasperation; and Gideon continued to say that he could not remember, or that there was no such root, or that it was the wrong season of the year, or that it wasn't the root itself, but the spit from his mouth that had cured Teddy's eyes. He said all these things one after another, and seemed not to care they were contradictory. He was rude and stubborn. The Farquars could hardly recognize their gentle, lovable old servant in this ignorant, perversely obstinate African, standing there in

10. **salting . . . bush secret:** allusion to the ironic advice given to children, about catching a bird by putting salt on its tail. In other words, the scientist knows his search may be futile.

11. **mealie** *n.* used as *adj.:* corn.

Vocabulary

perfunctory (pər·fuŋk'tə·rē) *adj.:* halfhearted; indifferent.

annulled (ə·nuld') *v.:* did away with; canceled.

perversely (pər·vʉrs'lē) *adv.:* disagreeably; contrarily.

front of them with lowered eyes, his hands twitching his cook's apron, repeating over and over whichever one of the stupid refusals that first entered his head.

And suddenly he appeared to give in. He lifted his head, gave a long, blank angry look at the circle of whites, who seemed to him like a circle of yelping dogs pressing around him, and said: "I will show you the root."

They walked single file away from the homestead down a kaffir path. It was a blazing December afternoon, with the sky full of hot rain clouds. Everything was hot: The sun was like a bronze tray whirling overhead, there was a heat shimmer over the fields, the soil was scorching underfoot, the dusty wind blew gritty and thick and warm in their faces. It was a terrible day, fit only for reclining on a veranda with iced drinks, which is where they would normally have been at that hour.

From time to time, remembering that on the day of the snake it had taken ten minutes to find the root, someone asked: "Is it much further, Gideon?" And Gideon would answer over his shoulder, with angry politeness: "I'm looking for the root, baas." And indeed, he would frequently bend sideways and trail his hand among the grasses with a gesture that was insulting in its perfunctoriness. He walked them through the bush along unknown paths for two hours, in that melting destroying heat, so that the sweat trickled coldly down them and their heads ached. They were all quite silent: the Farquars because they were angry, the scientist because he was being proved right again; there was no such plant. His was a tactful silence.

At last, six miles from the house, Gideon suddenly decided they had had enough; or perhaps his anger evaporated at that moment. He picked up, without an attempt at looking anything but casual, a handful of blue flowers from the grass, flowers that had been growing plentifully all down the paths they had come.

He handed them to the scientist without looking at him, and marched off by himself on the way home, leaving them to follow him if they chose.

When they got back to the house, the scientist went to the kitchen to thank Gideon: He was being very polite, even though there was an amused look in his eyes. Gideon was not there. Throwing the flowers casually into the back of his car, the eminent visitor departed on his way back to his laboratory.

Gideon was back in his kitchen in time to prepare dinner, but he was sulking. He spoke to Mr. Farquar like an unwilling servant. It was days before they liked each other again.

The Farquars made inquiries about the root from their laborers. Sometimes they were answered with distrustful stares. Sometimes the natives said: "We do not know. We have never heard of the root." One, the cattle boy, who had been with them a long time, and had grown to trust them a little, said: "Ask your boy in the kitchen. Now, there's a doctor for you. He's the son of a famous medicine man who used to be in these parts, and there's nothing he cannot cure." Then he added politely: "Of course, he's not as good as the white man's doctor, we know that, but he's good for us."

After some time, when the soreness had gone from between the Farquars and Gideon, they began to joke: "When are you going to show us the snake root, Gideon?" And he would laugh and shake his head, saying, a little uncomfortably: "But I did show you, missus, have you forgotten?"

Much later, Teddy, as a schoolboy, would come into the kitchen and say: "You old rascal, Gideon! Do you remember that time you tricked us all by making us walk miles all over the veld for nothing? It was so far my father had to carry me!"

And Gideon would double up with polite laughter. After much laughing, he would suddenly straighten himself up, wipe his old eyes, and look sadly at Teddy, who was grinning mischievously at him across the kitchen: "Ah, Little Yellow Head, how you have grown! Soon you will be grown up with a farm of your own. . . ." ■

Response and Analysis

Reading Check

1. Describe Gideon and Teddy's relationship at the beginning of the story. What incident signals a change in this relationship?
2. What crisis sets the **plot** in motion?
3. What does Gideon do for Teddy?
4. How does Teddy's relationship with Gideon change as he grows up?

Thinking Critically

5. Mrs. Farquar and Gideon share a sense of sadness about the reality of their children's future lives. What is the reality that gives these two characters—and this whole story—a feeling of sadness?
6. Why do you think Gideon refuses to share his wisdom with the Farquars? How do you feel about his refusal? (Review your Quickwrite notes about cultural differences before responding.)
7. In what ways is this story about a clash of cultures? Re-read Gideon's comment at the end of the story. What does it reveal about his understanding of the relationship between white European and black African cultures?
8. How might events in Southern Rhodesia during 1964 and 1965 have affected Lessing's portrayal of the relationship between Gideon and the Farquars? Before you respond, review your reading notes as well as the information in Reading Skills on page 1126.
9. How would you state the **theme** of this story? How does this theme make a comment on life? Use evidence from the story to support your response.

Literary Criticism

10. In her preface to *African Stories*, Lessing reveals that she holds the British responsible for much of her country's suffering. Whom does the **narrator** of the story seem to hold responsible for the suffering depicted here—the Farquars, Gideon, neither, or both? Analyze the narrator's political point of view. Use examples from the text to support your ideas.

WRITING

Between Two Worlds

The conflict that the scientist and the Farquars have with Gideon comes about because Gideon does not wish to share his knowledge. This conflict is not rooted in right and wrong or good and evil but rather in cultural differences. In an **essay, compare and contrast** Gideon's perspective with that of the Farquars and the scientist. Use details from the story to back up your opinions.

Literary Skills Analyze theme.

Reading Skills Identify historical context.

Writing Skills Write an essay comparing and contrasting different perspectives.

Vocabulary Skills Analyze context clues.

Vocabulary Development

Analyzing Context Clues

Explain why the **context clues** are wrong in each sentence below. The underlined words are Vocabulary words from the story.

1. Reverently, Tim flung his cap and mitt to the ground and stomped off.
2. Rain is inevitable; there's not a cloud in the sky.
3. Jackson was frustrated by the efficacy of the old lawn mower; he could hardly keep it running.
4. With a perfunctory yelp, the dog leapt joyfully into the cool pond.
5. The concert has been annulled and is scheduled to begin immediately.
6. The twins, who love movies, perversely agreed to attend a matinee.

INTERNET

Projects and Activities

Keyword: LE7 12-7

Connected Readings

Colonialism

Joseph Chamberlain .... **"I Believe in a British Empire"**

Jawaharlal Nehru .... **"The Noble Mansion of Free India"**

You have just read two selections that explore different kinds of conflicts that resulted from British colonialism. The next two selections you will read—by Joseph Chamberlain and Jawaharlal Nehru—are speeches that address the issue of colonialism and its sister issue, patriotism. As you read, ask yourself how the points of view presented in these speeches are both alike and different. After you read, you'll find questions on page 1139 that ask you to compare all four selections.

Points of View

Before You Read

This speech, delivered on May 15, 1903, in Birmingham, England, was part of a Conservative-party tariff-reform campaign. In it Chamberlain speaks out both as an unwavering advocate of the British Empire and as a strong isolationist. Isolationism is the "You stay on your side of the fence, and I'll stay on mine" belief that one's country should be kept free of entanglements—such as pacts and alliances—with other nations. As you will see, Chamberlain—who began his political life as a radical liberal but later became extremely conservative—felt that the British Empire should be self-reliant and should look to its own colonies—and not to foreign allies—for economic and military reinforcement. Above all, Chamberlain's speech challenges Britain's support of free trade—the tax-free exchange of goods between nations—in favor of a policy that would levy new taxes against nations outside the British Empire but would largely exempt the British colonies from those selfsame tariffs. In this way, Chamberlain reasoned, the colonies would become ever more firmly attached to—and therefore dependent on—the mother country, Great Britain.

Chamberlain's speech is a call to action, and as such it includes a full arsenal of persuasive techniques, from rhetorical questions to emotional appeals. As you read, be alert to the emotionally loaded words he uses to describe the British Empire and its "self-governing colonies." How does Chamberlain use appeals to "Imperial patriotism" to convince his listeners that the British Empire must be maintained at all costs? How must his British audience have felt as they listened to this speech?

As he opens, Chamberlain is referring to his political enemies, the Liberals who oppose tariff reform.

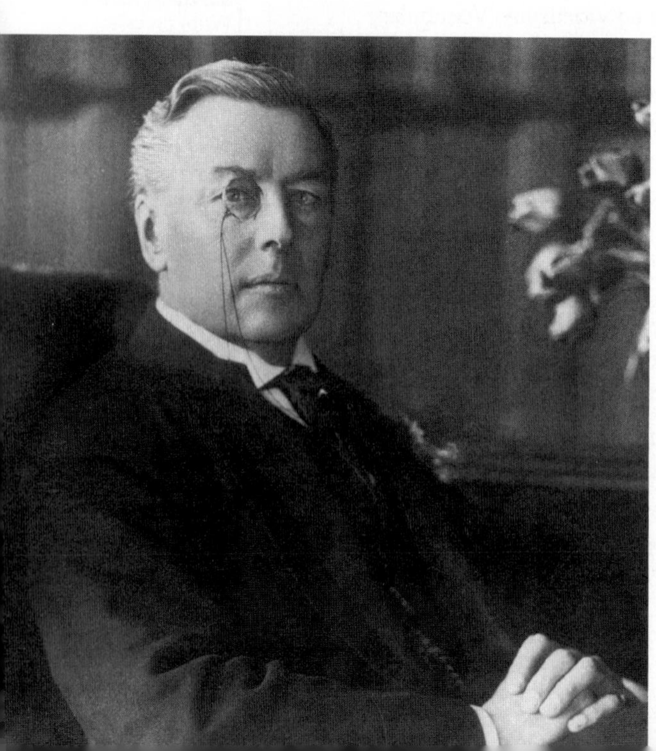

Joseph Chamberlain.

SPEECH

"I Believe in a British Empire"

Joseph Chamberlain

PUBLIC DOCUMENT

I cannot look forward without dread to handing over the security and existence of this great Empire to the hands of those who have made common cause with its enemies, who have charged their own countrymen with methods of barbarism, and who apparently have been untouched by that pervading[1] sentiment which I found everywhere where the British flag floats, and which has done so much in recent years to draw us together. I should not require to go to South Africa in order to be convinced that this feeling has obtained[2] deep hold on the minds and hearts of our children beyond the seas. It has had a hard life of it, this feeling of Imperial patriotism. It was checked for a generation by the apathy[3] and the indifference which were the characteristics of our former relations with our Colonies, but it was never extinguished. The embers were still alight, and when in the late war[4] this old country of ours showed that it was still possessed by the spirit of our ancestors, and that it was still prepared to count no sacrifice that was necessary in order to maintain the honor and the interests of the Empire, then you found a response from your children across the seas that astonished the whole world by a proof, an undeniable proof, of affection and regard. ❶

Is it to end there? Are we to sink back into the old policy of selfish isolation which went very far to dry and even to sap the loyalty of our colonial brethren? I do not think so. I think these larger issues touch the people of this country. I think they have awakened to the enormous importance of a creative time like the present, and of taking advantage of the opportunities offered in order to make permanent what has begun so well. Remember, we are a kingdom, an old country. We proceed here on settled lines. We have our quarrels and our disputes, and we pass legislation which may be good or bad; but we know that, whatever changes there may be, at all events the main stream will ultimately reach its appointed destination. That is the result of centuries of constitutional progress and freedom. ❷

But the Empire is not old. The Empire is new—the Empire is in its infancy. Now is the time when we can mold that Empire and when we and those who live with us can decide its future destinies. Just let us consider what that Empire is; I am not going tonight to speak of those hundreds of millions of our Indian and native fellow subjects for whom we have become responsible. I consider for the moment only our relations to that white British population that constitutes the majority in the great self-governing colonies of the Empire. Here in the United Kingdom there are some forty millions of us. Outside there are ten millions of men either

❶

Many British citizens were appalled by the brutal methods that were used to help win the Boer War. The "children beyond the seas" are the colonists—Canadians, Australians, New Zealanders, and even some black South Africans—who helped England fight and win the Boer War.

? *Does Chamberlain think that one can be critical of the British Empire and still be patriotic? How can you tell?*

❷

? *How does Chamberlain serve as an apologist for England here—someone who justifies and defends a belief or policy? How can you tell that he assumes his listeners agree with him?*

1. **pervading** *v.* used as *adj.:* spreading throughout. 2. **obtained** *v.:* gotten possession of. 3. **apathy** *n.:* lack of interest. 4. **the late war:** the Boer War (1899–1902) fought between Britian and the two Boer republics in South Africa. (Boers are South Africans of Dutch descent.)

directly descended from ancestors who left this country or more probably men who themselves in their youth left this country in order to find their fortunes in our possessions abroad. How long do you suppose that this proportion of population is going to endure? The development of those colonies has been delayed by many reasons—but mainly probably by a more material reason—by the fact that the United States of America has offered a greater attraction to British emigration. ❸

But that has changed. The United States, with all their vast territory, are filling up; and even now we hear of tens of thousands of emigrants leaving the United States in order to take up the fresh and rich lands of our colony in Canada. It seems to me not at all an impossible assumption that before the end of this present century we may find our fellow subjects beyond the seas as numerous as we are at home. I want you to look forward. I want you to consider the infinite importance of this not only to yourselves but to your descendants. Now is the time when you can exert influence. Do you wish that if these ten millions become forty millions they shall still be closely, intimately, affectionately united to you, or do you contemplate the possibility of their being separated, going off each in his own direction, under a separate flag? Think what it means to your power and influence as a country; think what it means to your position among the nations of the world; think what it means to your trade and commerce—I put that last. ❹

What is the meaning of an Empire? What does it mean to us? We have had a little experience. We have had a war, a war in which the majority of our children abroad had no apparent direct interest. We had no hold over them of any kind, and yet at one time during this war, by the voluntary decision of these people, at least 50,000 Colonial soldiers were standing shoulder to shoulder with British troops, displaying a gallantry equal to their own and the keenest intelligence. It is something for a beginning, and if this country were in danger, I mean if we were, as our forefathers were, face to face some day—Heaven forfend[5]—with some great coalition of hostile nations, when we had with our backs to the wall to struggle for our very lives, it is my firm conviction there is nothing within the power of these self-governing colonies they would not do to come to our aid. I believe their whole resources in men and in money would be at the disposal of the Mother Country in such an event. That is something—something which it is wonderful to have achieved, and which it is worth almost any sacrifice to maintain . . . ❺

I believe in a British Empire, in an Empire which, though it should be its first duty to cultivate friendship with all the nations of the world, should yet, even if alone, be self-sustaining and self-sufficient, able to maintain itself against the competition of all its rivals. And I do not believe in a Little England which shall be separated from all those to whom it would in the natural course look for support and affection, a Little England which would then be dependent absolutely on the mercy of those who envy its present prosperity, and who have shown they are ready to do all in their power to prevent its future union with the British races throughout the world. ❻

❸

? *What group of people is Chamberlain considering when he speaks of "the Empire"? What group does he say he is not including? How does he feel about the group he is excluding—and how can you tell? (Look for loaded words.)*

❹

? *What appeals is Chamberlain making to his audience here? Are they primarily appeals to emotion or to reason? Explain.*

❺

? *What does Chamberlain believe the "self-governing" colonies would do if England were in danger—and why would they do it? Why does Chamberlain think that the "Mother country's" relationship with the colonies is "worth almost any sacrifice to maintain"?*

5. **forfend** *v.:* prevent.

❻

? *Ultimately why does Chamberlain "believe in a British Empire"? How does he appear to view the rest of the world?*

Points *of* View

Before You Read

As a member of the Indian Congress movement, Jawaharlal Nehru (jə·wä'hər·läl nā'ro͞o) worked for Indian independence from Great Britain for twenty-eight years before he saw it become a reality, in 1947. In that year, Nehru was elected the first prime minister of the newly independent nation. He held that office until his death, in 1964.

A close friend and colleague of the great Indian leader Mohandas Gandhi, Nehru was renowned for his efforts to establish a democratic government in India. He also sought to raise the standard of living for Indians, even while opposing alliances with powerful nations and adopting a policy of nonagression.

The speech you are about to read was given by Nehru on the eve of Indian independence—August 14, 1947—to the members of the Indian Parliament.

SPEECH

"The Noble Mansion of Free India"

Jawaharlal Nehru

Jawaharlal Nehru (1961).

Long years ago we made a tryst[1] with destiny, and now the time comes when we shall redeem our pledge, not wholly or in full measure, but very substantially. At the stroke of the midnight hour, when the world sleeps, India will awake to life and freedom. A moment comes, which comes but rarely in history, when we step out from the old to the new, when an age ends, and when the soul of a nation, long suppressed, finds utterance. It is fitting that at this solemn moment we take the pledge of dedication to the service of India and her people and to the still larger cause of humanity.

At the dawn of history India started on her unending quest, and trackless centuries are filled with her striving and the grandeur of her success and her failures. Through good and ill fortune alike she has never lost sight of that quest or forgotten the ideals which gave her strength. We end today a period of ill fortune and India discovers herself again. The achievement we

1. **tryst** *n.:* rendezvous.

celebrate today is but a step, an opening of opportunity, to the greater triumphs and achievements that await us. Are we brave enough and wise enough to grasp this opportunity and accept the challenge of the future?

Freedom and power bring responsibility. The responsibility rests upon this Assembly,[2] a sovereign body representing the sovereign people of India. Before the birth of freedom we have endured all the pains of labor and our hearts are heavy with the memory of this sorrow. Some of those pains continue even now. Nevertheless, the past is over and it is the future that beckons to us now.

That future is not one of ease or resting but of incessant[3] striving so that we may fulfil the pledges we have so often taken and the one we shall take today. The service of India means the service of the millions who suffer. It means the ending of poverty and ignorance and disease and inequality of opportunity. The ambition of the greatest man of our generation[4] has been to wipe every tear from every eye. That may be beyond us, but as long as there are tears and suffering, so long our work will not be over.

And so we have to labor and to work, and work hard, to give reality to our dreams. Those dreams are for India, but they are also for the world, for all the nations and peoples are too closely knit together today for any one of them to imagine that it can live apart. Peace has been said to be indivisible;[5] so is freedom, so is prosperity now, and so also is disaster in this One World that can no longer be split into isolated fragments.

To the people of India, whose representatives we are, we make an appeal to join us with faith and confidence in this great adventure. This is no time for petty and destructive criticism, no time for ill will or blaming others. We have to build the noble mansion of free India where all her children may dwell. ●

● ? *What responsibility does the Indian government owe its people? What does the government need to do to fulfill this responsibility?*

2. **Assembly:** Indian Parliament.
3. **incessant** *adj.:* constant; never ending.
4. **greatest... generation:** Mohandas Gandhi.
5. **indivisible** *adj.:* undivided.

Analysis Comparing Points of View

Colonialism

The questions on this page ask you to analyze the views on colonialism expressed in the preceding four selections.

George Orwell ..... **Shooting An Elephant** .... (England)
Doris Lessing .... **No Witchcraft for Sale** .... (Zimbabwe)
Joseph Chamberlain .. **"I Believe in a British Empire"** .... (England)
Jawaharlal Nehru .... **"The Noble Mansion of Free India"** .. (India)

Thinking Critically

1. Based on what you have learned from these four selections, what ideals, ambitions, and prejudices do you believe led to British colonialism? (Reviewing your Quickwrite notes on page 1114 may prove helpful.) In your opinion, which selection best illustrates these ideals? Which selection best illustrates the destructive nature of colonialism? Use examples from the texts to support your ideas.
2. Imagine interviewing the author of each selection. How might each author respond to the question, "What does the word *empire* mean to you?" Using the first-person point of view (writing as "I"), write four answers to this question, each in the voice of a different author. After each response, list some words or phrases from the author's text that support the author's opinions as you have stated them.
3. Evaluate the selections you've just read for clarity and consistency. First, evaluate each piece separately. How clear is the author's argument? Jot down words and phrases that contribute to or diminish the clarity of each argument. Then, look at the texts as a whole. Among these authors, is there a prevailing opinion on the issue of colonialism? (Consult your reading notes from page 1114 for help.) Do you agree or disagree with this opinion? Why?

WRITING

Researching a Former British Colony

Choose one of the British colonies that are depicted or discussed in these selections—Burma (now Myanmar), Southern Rhodesia (now Zimbabwe), or India—and research its history. When and why did it become a British colony? What events or conditions led to its independence? What significant events occurred in the years following independence? Your research resources should include both online and print sources. After gathering your information, write a **historical research paper** giving an overview of the colony's history.

See "Reporting Literary Research," pages 240–259, for help with this assignment.

Pages 1114–1139 cover
Literary Skills Analyze and compare points of view on a topic.

Reading Skills Compare main ideas across texts.

Writing Skills Write a historical research paper.

Nadine Gordimer

(1923–)

South Africa

Nadine Gordimer was born in Springs, a small town located thirty miles from Johannesburg, on the gold-mining ridge that has brought South Africa much of its wealth. Her father was a Jewish jeweler who had emigrated from Lithuania as a teenager; her mother was a native of England. Gordimer grew up in a middle-class colonial society that imitated European conventions and values. She has said that she spent much of her childhood reading because she found that atmosphere extremely dull.

Gordimer began writing at the age of nine when, as a sickly child, she was taken out of school for a time. At fifteen she published her first story in a Johannesburg weekly. When her first internationally published short story collection, *The Soft Voice of the Serpent*, appeared in 1952, critics hailed Gordimer as a strong new voice who could draw fresh, authentic perceptions of African life. Since then, she has continued to win praise and honors, and, in 1991, she won the Nobel Prize in literature.

Gordimer is known for her ability to show, as one critic said, "the infinite variety of human character, the rich and surprising drama inherent in human personality and in the clash of personality." She has been compared to Virginia Woolf because of her talent for capturing the revealing moments in people's lives, what the critic Robert F. Haugh called "the illuminating moment, the quick perceptive glance of the author which sparkles like a gem."

Although she explores universal themes and a variety of settings, much of Gordimer's writing concerns the troubles that her own nation has experienced. She has observed that "white culture imported from Europe never had a chance in the South African context. . . . All it did was to harm black culture." Commenting on Gordimer's writing about the effects of apartheid, the enforced separation of races, on South Africa, one critic called her "one of the very few links between white and black in South Africa. She is a bearer of culture in a barbaric society. And she is a luminous symbol of at least one white person's understanding of the black man's burden."

Perhaps Gordimer's greatest achievement is her ability to treat South Africa's problems from a literary rather than a political perspective. "Here I live in a society which is fundamentally out of joint. One can't but be politically concerned," she has said, but she disclaims a political allegiance. "I don't understand politics except in terms of what politics does to influence lives," she once observed. "What interests me is the infinite variety of effects apartheid has on men and women."

Although Gordimer is respected around the world, she was a thorn in the side of her own country's government when apartheid was still in effect, and three of her novels were banned in South Africa. Nevertheless, she has always considered herself "an intensely loyal South African. I care deeply for my country. If I didn't, I wouldn't still be there."

For Independent Reading

Here are three excellent stories by Gordimer:

- "A Chip of Glass Ruby"
- "Six Feet of the Country"
- "The Train from Rhodesia"

Before You Read

Once upon a Time

Make the Connection

Isolation is one way to keep conflict at bay. Opposing parties cannot clash if they do not meet, or so the reasoning goes. The remedy has certainly been tried repeatedly throughout history and all over the world. Reservations, compounds, borders—these are all isolating walls, literal or figurative, that keep some people away from others. Even on the household level, we have today's "security systems"—a phrase to keep in mind as you read Gordimer's story.

Literary Focus

Symbol

A **symbol** is something that stands both for itself and for something beyond itself. Established symbols—sometimes known as public symbols—include the flags that stand for various states or nations, the dove as a symbol of peace, and the bald eagle as a symbol of the United States. Writers and artists often create their own personal, unique symbols, the meanings of which are revealed in the course of a poem, story, or novel.

> A **symbol** is something that stands both for itself and for something beyond itself.
>
> *For more on Symbol, see the Handbook of Literary and Historical Terms.*

Reading Skills

Identifying Language Structures

When someone begins, "Have you heard the one about . . . ," you know a joke is on the way because you recognize the language structure. Similarly, Nadine Gordimer's story title—the phrase *once upon a time*—indicates the beginning of a fairy tale. As you read Gordimer's story, jot down additional phrases that remind you of language structures typical to fairy tales. Watch also for other elements of the fairy-tale genre, such as a generic setting and characters: Fairy tales rarely supply explicit details of setting or identify characters by name.

Background

Until the 1990s, Nadine Gordimer's native land, South Africa, enforced a policy called apartheid (ə·pär′tāt′), the legal separation of races. Nonwhites experienced political and economic discrimination and were forced to live in remote areas or "townships" bordering white cities. Black South Africans could not enter white cities without "passbooks" that identified them by name, residency, and race. Decades of riots and rebellions left many black leaders in jail until finally, in 1991, the white government, headed by F. W. de Klerk—under both internal and international pressure—repealed the apartheid laws. Three years later the first all-race elections swept Nelson Mandela, a black man, former political prisoner, and leader of the African National Congress, into the office of president.

Vocabulary Development

distend (di·stend′) *v.:* expand; swell.

itinerant (ī·tin′ər·ənt) *adj.:* traveling.

audaciously (ô·dā′shəs·lē) *adv.:* boldly.

aesthetics (es·thet′iks) *n.:* principles of beauty.

serrated (ser′āt′id) *v.* used as *adj.:* having jagged, sawlike notches along the edge.

Literary Skills Understand symbols.

Reading Skills Identify language structures.

INTERNET

Vocabulary Practice

Keyword: LE7 12-7

Once upon a Time

Nadine Gordimer

Someone has written to ask me to contribute to an anthology of stories for children. I reply that I don't write children's stories; and he writes back that at a recent congress/book fair/seminar a certain novelist said every writer ought to write at least one story for children. I think of sending a postcard saying I don't accept that I "ought" to write anything.

And then last night I woke up—or rather was wakened without knowing what had roused me.

A voice in the echo chamber of the subconscious?

A sound.

A creaking of the kind made by the weight carried by one foot after another along a wooden floor. I listened. I felt the apertures of my ears distend with concentration. Again: the creaking. I was waiting for it; waiting to hear if it indicated that feet were moving from room to room, coming up the passage—to my door. I have no burglar bars, no gun under the pillow, but I have the same fears as people who do take these precautions, and my windowpanes are thin as rime,[1] could shatter like a wineglass. A woman was murdered (how do they put it) in broad daylight in a house two blocks away, last year, and the fierce dogs who guarded an old widower and his collection of antique clocks were strangled before he was knifed by a casual laborer he had dismissed without pay.

I was staring at the door, making it out in my mind rather than seeing it, in the dark. I lay quite still—a victim already—but the arrhythmia[2] of my heart was fleeing, knocking this way and that against its body-cage. How finely tuned the senses are, just out of rest, sleep! I could never listen intently as that in the distractions of the day; I

Untitled (1982) by Jannis Kounellis. Feather River travertine, cast plaster, and steel.

Collection Walker Art Center, Minneapolis. Walker Special Purchase Fund, 1987.

was reading every faintest sound, identifying and classifying its possible threat.

But I learned that I was to be neither threatened nor spared. There was no human weight pressing on the boards, the creaking was a buckling, an epicenter[3] of stress. I was in it. The house that surrounds me while I sleep is built on undermined ground; far beneath my bed, the floor, the house's foundations, the stopes[4] and passages of gold mines have hollowed the rock, and when some face trembles, detaches, and falls, three

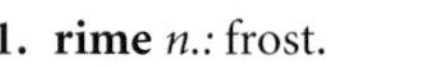

1. **rime** *n.:* frost.
2. **arrhythmia** (ə·rith′mē·ə) *n.:* irregular beating.
3. **epicenter** *n.:* central point.
4. **stopes** *n. pl.:* excavations.

Vocabulary
distend (di·stend′) *v.:* expand; swell.

thousand feet below, the whole house shifts slightly, bringing uneasy strain to the balance and counterbalance of brick, cement, wood, and glass that hold it as a structure around me. The misbeats of my heart tailed off like the last muffled flourishes on one of the wooden xylophones made by the Chopi and Tsonga[5] migrant miners who might have been down there, under me in the earth at that moment. The stope where the fall was could have been disused, dripping water from its ruptured veins; or men might now be interred there in the most profound of tombs.

I couldn't find a position in which my mind would let go of my body—release me to sleep again. So I began to tell myself a story; a bedtime story.

In a house, in a suburb, in a city, there were a man and his wife who loved each other very much and were living happily ever after. They had a little boy, and they loved him very much. They had a cat and a dog that the little boy loved very much. They had a car and a caravan trailer for holidays, and a swimming pool which was fenced so that the little boy and his playmates would not fall in and drown. They had a housemaid who was absolutely trustworthy and an itinerant gardener who was highly recommended by the neighbors. For when they began to live happily ever after they were warned, by that wise old witch, the husband's mother, not to take on anyone off the street. They were inscribed[6] in a medical benefit society, their pet dog was licensed, they were insured against fire, flood damage, and theft, and subscribed to the local Neighborhood Watch, which supplied them with a plaque for their gates lettered YOU HAVE BEEN WARNED over the silhouette of a would-be intruder. He was masked; it could not be said if he was black or white, and therefore proved the property owner was no racist.

It was not possible to insure the house, the swimming pool, or the car against riot damage. There were riots, but these were outside the city, where people of another color were quartered. These people were not allowed into the suburb except as reliable housemaids and gardeners, so there was nothing to fear, the husband told the wife. Yet she was afraid that some day such people might come up the street and tear off the plaque YOU HAVE BEEN WARNED and open the gates and stream in. . . . Nonsense, my dear, said the husband, there are police and soldiers and tear gas and guns to keep them away. But to please her—for he loved her very much and buses were being burned, cars stoned, and schoolchildren shot by the police in those quarters out of sight and hearing of the suburb—he had electronically controlled gates fitted. Anyone who pulled off the sign YOU HAVE BEEN WARNED and tried to open the gates would have to announce his intentions by pressing a button and speaking into a receiver relayed to the house. The little boy was fascinated by the device and used it as a walkie-talkie in cops and robbers play with his small friends.

The riots were suppressed, but there were many burglaries in the suburb and somebody's trusted housemaid was tied up and shut in a cupboard by thieves while she was in charge of her employers' house. The trusted housemaid of the man and wife and little boy was so upset by this misfortune befalling a friend left, as she herself often was, with responsibility for the possessions of the man and his wife and the little boy that she implored her employers to have burglar bars attached to the doors and windows of the house, and an alarm system installed. The wife said, She is right, let us take heed of her advice. So from every window and door in the house where they were living happily ever after they now saw the trees and sky through bars, and when the little boy's pet cat tried to climb in by the fanlight[7] to keep him company in his little bed at night, as it customarily had done, it set off the alarm keening[8] through the house.

5. **Chopi** (chō′pē) **and Tsonga** (tsäŋ′gä): Bantu-speaking peoples of Mozambique in southeastern Africa. Tsonga is often spelled *Thonga.*

6. **inscribed** *v.:* enrolled.

7. **fanlight** *n.:* semicircular window over a door or a larger window.

8. **keening** *n.:* wailing.

Vocabulary

itinerant (ī·tin′ər·ənt) *adj.:* traveling.

Le ciel rouge (*The Red Sky*) (1952) by Nicolas de Staël. Oil on canvas. 51½ × 64⅛ × 1½". 1954.7.

Collection of Walker Art Center, Minneapolis.
Gift of the T. B. Walker Foundation, 1954.

The alarm was often answered—it seemed—by other burglar alarms, in other houses, that had been triggered by pet cats or nibbling mice. The alarms called to one another across the gardens in shrills and bleats and wails that everyone soon became accustomed to, so that the din roused the inhabitants of the suburb no more than the croak of frogs and musical grating of cicadas'[9] legs. Under cover of the electronic harpies'[10] discourse intruders sawed the iron bars and broke into homes, taking away hi-fi equipment, television sets, cassette players, cameras and radios, jewelry and clothing, and sometimes were hungry enough to devour everything in the refrigerator or paused audaciously to drink the whiskey in the cabinets or patio bars. Insurance companies paid no compensation for single malt, a loss made keener by the property owner's knowledge that the thieves wouldn't even have been able to appreciate what it was they were drinking.

Then the time came when many of the people who were not trusted housemaids and gardeners hung about the suburb because they were unemployed. Some importuned for a job: weeding or painting a roof; anything, *baas,*[11] madam. But the man and his wife remembered the warning about taking on anyone off the street. Some drank liquor and fouled the street with discarded bottles. Some begged, waiting for the man or his wife to drive the car out of the electronically operated gates. They sat about with their feet in the gutters, under the jacaranda[12] trees that made a green tunnel of the street—for it was a beautiful suburb, spoiled only by their presence—and sometimes they fell asleep lying right before the gates in the midday sun. The wife could never see anyone go hungry. She sent the trusted housemaid out with bread and tea, but the trusted housemaid said these were loafers and *tsotsis,*[13] who would come and tie her up and shut her in a cupboard. The husband said, She's right. Take heed of her advice. You only encourage them with your bread and tea. They are looking for their chance . . . . And he brought the little boy's tricycle from the garden into the house every night, because if the house was surely secure, once locked and with the alarm set, someone might still be able to climb over the wall or the electronically closed gates into the garden.

You are right, said the wife, then the wall should be higher. And the wise old witch, the husband's mother, paid for the extra bricks as her Christmas present to her son and his wife—the little boy got a Space Man outfit and a book of fairy tales.

But every week there were more reports of intrusion: in broad daylight and the dead of night, in the early hours of the morning, and even in the lovely summer twilight—a certain family was at dinner while the bedrooms were being ransacked upstairs. The man and his wife, talking of the latest armed robbery in the suburb, were distracted by

9. **cicadas** (si·kā′dəz) *n. pl.:* Cicadas are large, flylike insects.
10. **harpies** *n. pl.:* Harpies are shrewish or grasping people. The word comes from the mythological harpies, hideous winged monsters that have the head and trunk of a woman and the tail, legs, and talons of a bird.
11. ***baas*** (bäs): Afrikaans for "master." Afrikaans, a language developed from seventeenth-century Dutch, is spoken in South Africa.
12. **jacaranda** (jak′ə·ran′də) *n.:* tropical tree with large clusters of blue or lavender flowers.
13. ***tsotsis*** (tsät′sis): colloquial expression for "flashily dressed street thugs."

Vocabulary

audaciously (ô·dā′shəs·lē) *adv.:* boldly.

the sight of the little boy's pet cat effortlessly arriving over the seven-foot wall, descending first with a rapid bracing of extended forepaws down on the sheer vertical surface, and then a graceful launch, landing with swishing tail within the property. The whitewashed wall was marked with the cat's comings and goings; and on the street side of the wall there were larger red-earth smudges that could have been made by the kind of broken running shoes, seen on the feet of unemployed loiterers, that had no innocent destination.

When the man and wife and little boy took the pet dog for its walk round the neighborhood streets they no longer paused to admire this show of roses or that perfect lawn; these were hidden behind an array of different varieties of security fences, walls, and devices. The man, wife, little boy, and dog passed a remarkable choice: There was the low-cost option of pieces of broken glass embedded in cement along the top of walls, there were iron grilles ending in lance points, there were attempts at reconciling the aesthetics of prison architecture with the Spanish Villa style (spikes painted pink) and with the plastic urns of neoclassical façades (twelve-inch pikes finned like zigzags of lightning and painted pure white). Some walls had a small board affixed, giving the name and telephone number of the firm responsible for the installation of the devices. While the little boy and the pet dog raced ahead, the husband and wife found themselves comparing the possible effectiveness of each style against its appearance; and after several weeks when they paused before this barricade or that without needing to speak, both came out with the conclusion that only one was worth considering. It was the ugliest but the most honest in its suggestion of the pure concentration-camp style, no frills, all evident efficacy. Placed the length of walls, it consisted of a continuous coil of stiff and shining metal serrated into jagged blades, so that there would be no way of climbing over it and no way through its tunnel without getting entangled in its fangs. There would be no way out, only a struggle getting bloodier and bloodier, a deeper and sharper hooking and tearing of flesh. The wife shuddered to look at it. You're right, said the husband, anyone would think twice. . . . And they took heed of the advice on a small board fixed to the wall: Consult DRAGON'S TEETH The People For Total Security.

Next day a gang of workmen came and stretched the razor-bladed coils all round the walls of the house where the husband and wife and little boy and pet dog and cat were living happily ever after. The sunlight flashed and slashed, off the serrations, the cornice of razor thorns encircled the home, shining. The husband said, Never mind. It will weather. The wife said, You're wrong. They guarantee it's rustproof. And she waited until the little boy had run off to play before she said, I hope the cat will take heed. . . . The husband said, Don't worry, my dear, cats always look before they leap. And it was true that from that day on the cat slept in the little boy's bed and kept to the garden, never risking a try at breaching security.

One evening, the mother read the little boy to sleep with a fairy story from the book the wise old witch had given him at Christmas. Next day he pretended to be the Prince who braves the terrible thicket of thorns to enter the palace and kiss the Sleeping Beauty back to life: He dragged a ladder to the wall, the shining coiled tunnel was just wide enough for his little body to creep in, and with the first fixing of its razor teeth in his knees and hands and head he screamed and struggled deeper into its tangle. The trusted housemaid and the itinerant gardener, whose "day" it was, came running, the first to see and to scream with him, and the itinerant gardener tore his hands trying to get at the little boy. Then the man and his wife burst wildly into the garden and for some reason (the cat, probably) the alarm set up wailing against the screams while the bleeding mass of the little boy was hacked out of the security coil with saws, wire cutters, choppers, and they carried it—the man, the wife, the hysterical trusted housemaid, and the weeping gardener—into the house. ■

Vocabulary

aesthetics (es·thet′iks) *n.:* principles of beauty.

serrated (ser′āt′id) *v.* used as *adj.:* having jagged, sawlike notches along the edge.

Response and Analysis

Reading Check

1. What four improvements to home security does the family make?
2. What events prompt each improvement?
3. How well does each improvement work?
4. What happens to the little boy at the end of the story?

Thinking Critically

5. Which passages in the story seem to have humorous intent? Did you find these passages funny or unsettling? Describe Gordimer's overall **tone** in this story.
6. Point out common **language structures** and other elements of the **fairy tale** genre used by Gordimer. In what sense has Gordimer created a **parody** of a fairy tale—an imitation meant to mock or amuse? How would you describe the effect of Gordimer's fairy tale parody? (Refer to your reading notes.)
7. Why do you think Gordimer uses a nonfiction introduction to her tale? How do you interpret the opening section after reading the story?
8. How can the security systems in the story—especially the wall—be seen as **symbols**? What do they symbolize?
9. **Fairy tales** often contain moral lessons. What is the moral of "Once upon a Time"? How does it contrast with the morals of traditional fairy tales you have read?
10. In your opinion, are the husband and wife in the story innocent homeowners who are merely trying to feel secure, or are they racists who cause their own tragedy? Explain your reasoning, using specific evidence from the text.

Extending and Evaluating

11. Some people might find this story to be overly brutal or violent. What do you think of this story's combination of ironic humor and a shocking ending? Why do you think Gordimer wrote her story this way? Compare your responses with those of your classmates and discuss them.

WRITING

The Great Divide

Both Gordimer's tale and George Orwell's "Shooting an Elephant" (see page 1117) carry messages about cultural clashes. Write a short **essay comparing and contrasting** the two works in terms of their themes, genres, styles, and tones.

Vocabulary Development

Analogies

distend · *aesthetics* · *itinerant* · *serrated* · *audaciously*

In an **analogy** the words in one pair relate to each other in the same way as the words in a second pair. In each item below, identify the relationship between the words in the first pair. Then, complete the second pair with the Vocabulary word from the list above that expresses the same relationship.

1. CASUALLY : INFORMALLY :: ________ : boldly
2. GRITTY : SANDPAPER :: ________ : steak knife
3. TRY : ATTEMPT :: ________ : expand
4. TRIVIAL : IMPORTANT :: ________ : stay-at-home
5. BIOLOGY : THE NATURAL WORLD :: ________ : beauty

SKILLS FOCUS

Literary Skills Analyze symbols.

Reading Skills Identify language structures.

Writing Skills Write an essay comparing and contrasting two literary works.

Vocabulary Skills Complete word analogies.

INTERNET

Projects and Activities

Keyword: LE7 12-7

Chinua Achebe

(1930–   )

Nigeria

Nigerian author Chinua Achebe (chin'wä' ä·chā'bā) planned to study medicine, but literature and his country's nationalist movement forever changed his plans. As a student, he came to realize the destructive effects of colonialism and dedicated himself to redefining Africa, to telling the true story of Africans, including their achievements and failures. In his words, the European idea that "Africa was the Primordial Void, was sheer humbug; . . . Africa had a history, a religion, a civilization."

His novels, beginning with the celebrated *Things Fall Apart* (1958), focus on the changes in Nigerian life that occurred in the twentieth century. The novels trace life in Nigeria—sometimes presented as a fictionalized nation—from the arrival of early English missionaries, through years of colonial rule, to a post-independence era rife with corruption and political turmoil. Achebe believes that "Africa's meeting with Europe must be accounted a terrible disaster in this matter of human understanding and respect," yet his African characters are not idealized. They are held responsible for their private decisions and for solving the problems that threaten their nation's future.

Achebe is himself an Ibo, born in the eastern Nigerian town of Ogidi, where his father, a Christian convert, taught at the mission school. He has chosen to write in English, which he began to learn at age eight, in order to reach a wide audience.

During Nigeria's civil war of the late 1960s, Achebe worked for the cause of the secessionist Biafrans. Since then he has concentrated on teaching and encouraging and publishing promising young authors. Through his many works of fiction, nonfiction, and poetry, he has been a catalyst for an entire younger generation of African writers.

For Independent Reading

You may enjoy the following story by Achebe:

- "Dead Men's Path"

Before You Read

Marriage Is a Private Affair

Make the Connection

Quickwrite

Like the United States, many nations are collections of diverse peoples—and when people of different backgrounds come together, conflicts tend to arise. People may focus on differences in customs, religion, and ethnic heritage and fail to notice all the things they have in common.

These cultural distinctions, however, often become less significant when people expand their horizons. They travel, they read, they watch, they listen. They go beyond "their kind." This story focuses on entrenched cultural traditions about marriage and family. Jot down similarities and differences between your generation's attitudes toward love and marriage and those of your parents' generation. What qualities about marriage do you consider important? Is there any common ground in your points of view?

Literary Focus

Verbal Irony

Verbal irony occurs when a writer or speaker says one thing but means something else—usually the opposite of what is stated. If you tell a friend that you "just love being kept waiting in the rain," you are using verbal irony. A classic example of verbal irony occurs in Jonathan Swift's essay "A Modest Proposal" (see page 582), where he suggests that the Irish solve their social problems by selling their babies to their English landlords as food.

Literary Skills Understand verbal irony.

INTERNET
Vocabulary Practice
•
More About Chinua Achebe
•
Keyword: LE7 12-7

Verbal irony occurs when a writer or speaker says one thing but means something else—usually the opposite of what is stated.

For more on Irony, see the Handbook of Literary and Historical Terms.

Background

The West African nation of Nigeria has more than 250 ethnic groups. These groups speak different languages and frequently differ in religion, customs, and traditions. Both the Ibo and the Ibibio live in southeastern Nigeria but traditionally did not intermarry. In Achebe's story a young Ibo man and a young Ibibio woman have moved from their native regions to Lagos, a large, modern city in southwestern Nigeria.

Vocabulary Development

cosmopolitan (käz′mə·päl′ə·tən) *adj.:* worldly; sophisticated.

rash (rash) *adj.:* reckless.

commiserate (kə·miz′ər·āt′) *v.:* feel sorrow or pity for; sympathize.

persevered (pʉr′sə·vird′) *v.:* continued despite difficulty or opposition; persisted.

Marriage Is a Private Affair

Chinua Achebe

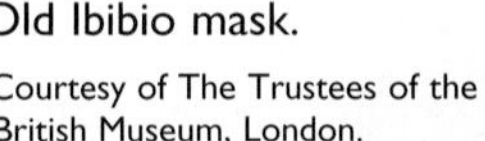

Old Ibibio mask.

Courtesy of The Trustees of the British Museum, London.

"Have you written to your dad yet?" asked Nene[1] one afternoon as she sat with Nnaemeka[2] in her room at 16 Kasanga Street, Lagos.[3]

"No. I've been thinking about it. I think it's better to tell him when I get home on leave!"

"But why? Your leave is such a long way off yet—six whole weeks. He should be let into our happiness now."

Nnaemeka was silent for a while, and then began very slowly as if he groped for his words: "I wish I were sure it would be happiness to him."

"Of course it must," replied Nene, a little surprised. "Why shouldn't it?"

"You have lived in Lagos all your life, and you know very little about people in remote parts of the country."

"That's what you always say. But I don't believe anybody will be so unlike other people that they will be unhappy when their sons are engaged to marry."

"Yes. They are most unhappy if the engagement is not arranged by them. In our case it's worse—you are not even an Ibo."[4]

This was said so seriously and so bluntly that Nene could not find speech immediately. In the cosmopolitan atmosphere of the city it had always seemed to her something of a joke that a person's tribe could determine whom he married.

At last she said, "You don't really mean that he will object to your marrying me simply on that account? I had always thought you Ibos were kindly disposed to other people."

1. **Nene** (nā'nā).
2. **Nnaemeka** ('n·nä·ā·mā'kə).
3. **Lagos** (lā'gōs'): former capital of Nigeria.
4. **Ibo** (ē'bō'): member of an African ethnic group living chiefly in southeastern Nigeria.

"So we are. But when it comes to marriage, well, it's not quite so simple. And this," he added, "is not peculiar to the Ibos. If your father were alive and lived in the heart of Ibibio-land[5] he would be exactly like my father."

"I don't know. But anyway, as your father is so fond of you, I'm sure he will forgive you soon enough. Come on then, be a good boy and send him a nice lovely letter . . ."

"It would not be wise to break the news to him by writing. A letter will bring it upon him with a shock. I'm quite sure about that."

"All right, honey, suit yourself. You know your father."

As Nnaemeka walked home that evening he turned over in his mind different ways of overcoming his father's opposition, especially now that he had gone and found a girl for him. He had thought of showing his letter to Nene but decided on second thoughts not to, at least for the moment. He read it again when he got home and couldn't help smiling to himself. He remembered Ugoye[6] quite well, an Amazon[7] of a girl who used to beat up all the boys, himself included, on the way to the stream, a complete dunce at school.

5. **Ibibio-land** (ib'ə·bē'o'land): area of southeastern Nigeria that is the traditional homeland of the Ibibio, another African ethnic group.
6. **Ugoye** (o͞o ·gō'yā).
7. **Amazon:** tall, strong, aggressive woman. The term is taken from the name for the Amazons, a race of female warriors in Greek mythology.

Vocabulary

cosmopolitan (käz'mə·päl'ə·tən) *adj.:* worldly; sophisticated.

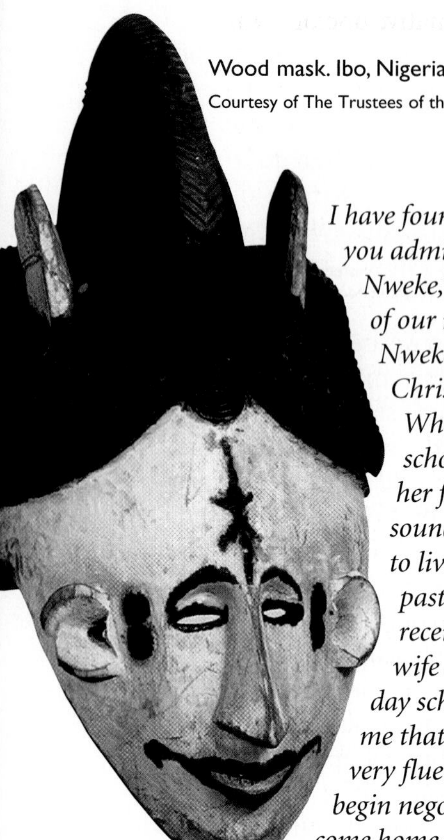

Wood mask. Ibo, Nigeria (37 cm).
Courtesy of The Trustees of the British Museum, London.

I have found a girl who will suit you admirably—Ugoye Nweke,[8] the eldest daughter of our neighbor, Jacob Nweke. She has a proper Christian upbringing. When she stopped schooling some years ago her father (a man of sound judgment) sent her to live in the house of a pastor where she has received all the training a wife could need. Her Sunday school teacher has told me that she reads her Bible very fluently. I hope we shall begin negotiations when you come home in December.

On the second evening of his return from Lagos, Nnaemeka sat with his father under a cassia tree. This was the old man's retreat where he went to read his Bible when the parching December sun had set and a fresh, reviving wind blew on the leaves.

"Father," began Nnaemeka suddenly, "I have come to ask for forgiveness."

"Forgiveness? For what, my son?" he asked in amazement.

"It's about this marriage question."

"Which marriage question?"

"I can't—we must—I mean it is impossible for me to marry Nweke's daughter."

"Impossible? Why?" asked his father.

"I don't love her."

"Nobody said you did. Why should you?" he asked.

"Marriage today is different . . ."

8. **Nweke** ('n·wā'kā).

"Look here, my son," interrupted his father, "nothing is different. What one looks for in a wife are a good character and a Christian background."

Nnaemeka saw there was no hope along the present line of argument.

"Moreover," he said, "I am engaged to marry another girl who has all of Ugoye's good qualities, and who . . ."

His father did not believe his ears. "What did you say?" he asked slowly and disconcertingly.

"She is a good Christian," his son went on, "and a teacher in a girls' school in Lagos."

"Teacher, did you say? If you consider that a qualification for a good wife I should like to point out to you, Emeka, that no Christian woman should teach. St. Paul in his letter to the Corinthians[9] says that women should keep silence." He rose slowly from his seat and paced forward and backward. This was his pet subject, and he condemned vehemently those church leaders who encouraged women to teach in their schools. After he had spent his emotion on a long homily he at last came back to his son's engagement, in a seemingly milder tone.

"Whose daughter is she, anyway?"

"She is Nene Atang."

"What!" All the mildness was gone again. "Did you say Neneataga, what does that mean?"

"Nene Atang from Calabar.[10] She is the only girl I can marry." This was a very rash reply and Nnaemeka expected the storm to burst. But it did not. His father merely walked away into his room. This was most unexpected and perplexed Nnaemeka. His father's silence was infinitely more menacing than a flood of threatening speech. That night the old man did not eat.

When he sent for Nnaemeka a day later he applied all possible ways of dissuasion. But the young man's heart was hardened, and his father eventually gave him up as lost.

9. **St. Paul . . . Corinthians:** reference to a passage in the Bible (1 Corinthians 14:34).
10. **Calabar:** seaport city in southeastern Nigeria.

Vocabulary

rash (rash) *adj.:* reckless.

"I owe it to you, my son, as a duty to show you what is right and what is wrong. Whoever put this idea into your head might as well have cut your throat. It is Satan's work." He waved his son away.

"You will change your mind, Father, when you know Nene."

"I shall never see her," was the reply. From that night the father scarcely spoke to his son. He did not, however, cease hoping that he would realize how serious was the danger he was heading for. Day and night he put him in his prayers.

Nnaemeka, for his own part, was very deeply affected by his father's grief. But he kept hoping that it would pass away. If it had occurred to him that never in the history of his people had a man married a woman who spoke a different tongue, he might have been less optimistic. "It has never been heard," was the verdict of an old man speaking a few weeks later. In that short sentence he spoke for all of his people. This man had come with others to commiserate with Okeke[11] when news went round about his son's behavior. By that time the son had gone back to Lagos.

"It has never been heard," said the old man again with a sad shake of his head.

"What did Our Lord say?" asked another gentleman. "Sons shall rise against their Fathers; it is there in the Holy Book."

"It is the beginning of the end," said another.

The discussion thus tending to become theological, Madubogwu, a highly practical man, brought it down once more to the ordinary level.

"Have you thought of consulting a native doctor about your son?" he asked Nnaemeka's father.

"He isn't sick," was the reply.

"What is he then? The boy's mind is diseased and only a good herbalist can bring him back to his right senses. The medicine he requires is *Amalile,* the same that women apply with success to recapture their husbands' straying affection."

"Madubogwu is right," said another gentleman. "This thing calls for medicine."

"I shall not call in a native doctor." Nnaemeka's father was known to be obstinately ahead of his more superstitious neighbors in these matters. "I will not be another Mrs. Ochuba. If my son wants to kill himself let him do it with his own hands. It is not for me to help him."

"But it was her fault," said Madubogwu. "She ought to have gone to an honest herbalist. She was a clever woman, nevertheless."

"She was a wicked murderess," said Jonathan, who rarely argued with his neighbors because, he often said, they were incapable of reasoning. "The medicine was prepared for her husband, it was his name they called in its preparation, and I am sure it would have been perfectly beneficial to him. It was wicked to put it into the herbalist's food, and say you were only trying it out."

Six months later, Nnaemeka was showing his young wife a short letter from his father:

> *It amazes me that you could be so unfeeling as to send me your wedding picture. I would have sent it back. But on further thought I decided just to cut off your wife and send it back to you because I have nothing to do with her. How I wish that I had nothing to do with you either.*

When Nene read through this letter and looked at the mutilated picture her eyes filled with tears, and she began to sob.

"Don't cry, my darling," said her husband. "He is essentially good-natured and will one day look more kindly on our marriage." But years passed and that one day did not come.

For eight years, Okeke would have nothing to do with his son, Nnaemeka. Only three times (when Nnaemeka asked to come home and spend his leave) did he write to him.

"I can't have you in my house," he replied on one occasion. "It can be of no interest to me where or how you spend your leave—or your life, for that matter."

Vocabulary

commiserate (kə·miz′ər·āt′) *v.:* feel sorrow or pity for; sympathize.

11. **Okeke** (ō·kā′kā).

Iknega headdress. Wood and feathers (76.1 cm).
UCLA Fowler Museum of Cultural History. Photo Richard Todd.

The prejudice against Nnaemeka's marriage was not confined to his little village. In Lagos, especially among his people who worked there, it showed itself in a different way. Their women, when they met at their village meeting, were not hostile to Nene. Rather, they paid her such excessive deference as to make her feel she was not one of them. But as time went on, Nene gradually broke through some of this prejudice and even began to make friends among them. Slowly and grudgingly they began to admit that she kept her home much better than most of them.

The story eventually got to the little village in the heart of the Ibo country that Nnaemeka and his young wife were a most happy couple. But his father was one of the few people in the village who knew nothing about this. He always displayed so much temper whenever his son's name was mentioned that everyone avoided it in his presence. By a tremendous effort of will he had succeeded in pushing his son to the back of his mind. The strain had nearly killed him but he had persevered, and won.

Then one day he received a letter from Nene, and in spite of himself he began to glance through it perfunctorily until all of a sudden the expression on his face changed and he began to read more carefully.

> *. . . Our two sons, from the day they learnt that they have a grandfather, have insisted on being taken to him. I find it impossible to tell them that you will not see them. I implore you to allow Nnaemeka to bring them home for a short time during his leave next month. I shall remain here in Lagos . . .*

The old man at once felt the resolution he had built up over so many years falling in. He was telling himself that he must not give in. He tried to steel his heart against all emotional appeals. It was a reenactment of that other struggle. He leaned against a window and looked out. The sky was overcast with heavy black clouds and a high wind began to blow, filling the air with dust and dry leaves. It was one of those rare occasions when even Nature takes a hand in a human fight. Very soon it began to rain, the first rain in the year. It came down in large sharp drops and was accompanied by the lightning and thunder which mark a change of season. Okeke was trying hard not to think of his two grandsons. But he knew he was now fighting a losing battle. He tried to hum a favorite hymn but the pattering of large raindrops on the roof broke up the tune. His mind immediately returned to the children. How could he shut his door against them? By a curious mental process he imagined them standing, sad and forsaken, under the harsh angry weather—shut out from his house.

That night he hardly slept, from remorse—and a vague fear that he might die without making it up to them. ■

Vocabulary

persevered (pʉr′sə·vird′) *v.:* continued despite difficulty or opposition; persisted.

Response and Analysis

Reading Check

1. What are Okeke's objections to his son's marriage?
2. How much time passes from the marriage to the end of the story? During that time, how does Okeke act toward his son?
3. How are Nnaemeka and his father different?
4. Why does Nene send a letter to Nnaemeka's father?

Thinking Critically

5. What makes the story's title an example of **verbal irony**? What purpose does this irony serve?
6. In his depiction of the **conflict** between Nnaemeka and his father, does the author seem to favor strongly one side or the other? Explain.
7. How would you **characterize** Okeke? Use details from the story to support your answer.
8. Why do you think Achebe included the anecdote about the herbalist? What do you think happened to the herbalist?
9. What might the rain at the end of the story **symbolize**?
10. The story's subject is a marriage that occurs against a parent's wishes, but what is the story's **theme**—its comment on human nature, as revealed by the story as a whole? On what evidence do you base your conclusion? Explain.
11. From what **point of view** is the story told? How does the point of view shape your response to the story?
12. Does Achebe's story concern only one Nigerian family, or can it also stand for conflicts over traditional values within a multicultural society like the United States? What contemporary examples of clashes in values relate to this story's plot and **theme**?

Extending and Evaluating

13. In your opinion, does Achebe make the **conflict** between Nnaemeka and his father believable? Use specific evidence from the text to support your views, and consult your Quickwrite notes about your generation's attitudes toward love and marriage as opposed to the attitudes of your parents' or guardians' generation.
14. Is Okeke's change of heart at the end of the story believable or unbelievable? Explain your reasoning.

WRITING

Old Ways, New Ways

The central conflict of this story is between old ways and new ones: rural versus urban, arranged marriages versus marriages based on love, housewives versus career women. Choose one of these conflicts, and, in a brief **essay,** discuss how it is or is not resolved by the end of the story. Include your own views on the subject.

Literary Skills Analyze verbal irony.

Writing Skills Write an essay analyzing conflict.

Vocabulary Skills Demonstrate word knowledge.

Vocabulary Development

Which Word?

cosmopolitan	*commiserate*
rash	*persevered*

On a separate sheet of paper, answer each of the following questions, using one of the Vocabulary words above.

1. Which word describes what you do when you sympathize with a friend who's had a bad day?
2. Which word might describe an impulsive decision?
3. Which word describes a sophisticated world traveler?
4. Which word would explain how the Little Engine That Could made it to the top of the hill?

INTERNET

Projects and Activities

Keyword: LE7 12-7

Grammar Link

The Wrong Place at the Wrong Time: Dangling Modifiers

What would you think if you came across the following sentence in your reading?

Having been raised in the city, marrying between tribes was perfectly acceptable.

Would you wonder who was raised in the city and who finds marrying between tribes acceptable? This sentence is confusing because it contains a **dangling modifier**—a word, phrase, or clause that does not sensibly, or reasonably, modify any word or group of words in a sentence. In the following sentence, the phrase *Having been raised in the city* now sensibly modifies *Nene:*

Having been raised in the city, Nene thought marrying between tribes was perfectly acceptable.

There are three ways to correct dangling modifiers:

DANGLING Dedicated to telling Africa's true story, Achebe's novels focus on details of twentieth-century Nigerian life. [Were Achebe's *novels* dedicated to telling Africa's true story?]

- Add a word that connects the dangling modifier to its object.

CORRECT Dedicated to telling Africa's true story, Achebe writes novels that focus on details of twentieth-century Nigerian life.

- Add words to the modifier to make its meaning clear.

CORRECT Since Achebe is dedicated to telling Africa's true story, his novels focus on details of twentieth-century Nigerian life.

- Reword the entire sentence.

CORRECT Achebe is dedicated to telling Africa's true story, so he writes novels that focus on details of twentieth-century Nigerian life.

PRACTICE

The following sentences are about Achebe and his homeland of Nigeria. Rewrite each sentence to correct the dangling modifiers.

1. One of the founders of a new Nigerian literature based on oral traditions and changing society, critics have praised his novels portraying African communal life.
2. Believing that artists should be accountable to society, Achebe's characters are depicted realistically in his works.
3. The most populous country in Africa, there are more than 250 ethnic groups in Nigeria.
4. Ruled by a military government for sixteen years, a civilian government was adopted in 1999 in Nigeria.
5. About twice the size of California, three major native languages and over one hundred dialects are spoken in Nigeria.

Apply to Your Writing

Review a writing assignment you are working on now or have already completed. Revise your sentences as necessary to correct any dangling modifiers.

For more help, see Placement of Modifiers, 5h, in the Language Handbook.

Grammar Skills
Correct dangling modifiers.

Wole Soyinka

(1934–)

Nigeria

A voice of modern Africa, Wole Soyinka in 1986 became the first African to win the Nobel Prize in literature. Soyinka's favorite African deity is Ogun, god of both war and creative fire—a fitting muse for a multitalented writer and performer whose plays, songs, novels, and poetry combine political activism, universal themes, and African traditions.

Born Akinwande Oluwole Soyinka in a village in western Nigeria, Soyinka was the son of the principal of a Christian school and a teacher. His parents both supported European-style education, but his father also retained strong ties to his heritage as a member of the Yoruba tribe. Soyinka grew up respecting both traditions; his 1981 autobiography, *Aké: The Years of Childhood*, tells of his later struggle with this dual heritage.

After attending University College at Ibadan, Nigeria, Soyinka studied English literature in England at the University of Leeds. In London in the late 1950s, he wrote plays and poetry for theater and radio. During this period of African nationalism and pressure for independence, Soyinka's themes were racism, injustice, tyranny, and corruption, all treated with satiric wit. Also concerned with the collision of ancient traditions and modern realities, he peppered his plays with vivid Yoruba masquerade ritual.

Soyinka felt brutal despotism firsthand during Nigeria's civil war of the late 1960s, when he was imprisoned for two years for the so-called crime of meeting with secessionist leaders such as the writer Chinua Achebe (see page 1147). He describes these experiences in *The Man Died: Prison Notes*, published in 1972. Since then he has continued to record and dramatize, with both passion and humor, the struggle and spirit of modern-day Africa and Africans.

Before You Read

Telephone Conversation

Make the Connection

Quickwrite

The following poem, written during Soyinka's college career in Britain in the late 1950s, records one of his own experiences with racial discrimination at a time when millions of people from former British colonies were arriving in England in search of economic and educational opportunities.

Think about the ways, both thoughtless and intentional, in which people practice discrimination. Then, jot down some examples. How might those who are discriminated against make others mindful of what they've suffered? Note any ideas that come to mind.

Literary Focus

Satire

Satire is a kind of writing that ridicules human folly, usually with the intention of bringing about awareness and possibly social reform. When writers use satire, they create an exaggerated or skewed picture of a common human vice, folly, or weakness. By making the vice appear foolish—even absurd—satirists hope to inspire people to recognize and shed the vice or to adopt the opposite behavior or attitude. In the following poem, Wole Soyinka uses satire to illustrate exactly how preposterous the human vice of racial discrimination really is.

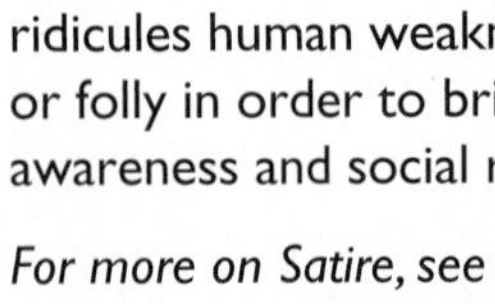

Satire is a kind of writing that ridicules human weakness, vice, or folly in order to bring about awareness and social reform.

For more on Satire, see the Handbook of Literary and Historical Terms.

Literary Skills
Understand satire.

Background

Soyinka's poem presents ideas primarily through a **dialogue.** The first speaker is talking from one of the red public telephone booths that were common in London years ago. Such phones had two buttons, A and B; pressing A put one through to the recipient of the call. In this poem the first speaker is a well-educated black African and the second a British woman who has property to rent. Soyinka's poem doesn't merely describe their exchange; it re-creates it.

Telephone Conversation

Wole Soyinka

The price seemed reasonable, location
Indifferent. The landlady swore she lived
Off premises. Nothing remained
But self-confession. "Madam," I warned,
"I hate a wasted journey—I am African."
Silence. Silenced transmission of
Pressurized good-breeding. Voice, when it came,
Lipstick coated, long gold-rolled
Cigarette-holder pipped. Caught I was, foully.

"HOW DARK?" . . . I had not misheard . . . "ARE YOU LIGHT
OR VERY DARK?" Button B. Button A. Stench
Of rancid breath of public hide-and-speak.
Red booth. Red pillar-box.° Red double-tiered
Omnibus° squelching tar. It *was* real! Shamed
By ill-mannered silence, surrender
Pushed dumbfoundment to beg simplification.
Considerate she was, varying the emphasis—

"ARE YOU DARK? OR VERY LIGHT?" Revelation came.
"You mean—like plain or milk chocolate?"
Her assent was clinical, crushing in its light
Impersonality. Rapidly, wavelength adjusted,
I chose. "West African sepia"—and as an afterthought,
"Down in my passport." Silence for spectroscopic
Flight of fancy,° till truthfulness clanged her accent
Hard on the mouthpiece. "WHAT'S THAT?" conceding,
"DON'T KNOW WHAT THAT IS." "Like brunette."

---

13. pillar-box: chiefly British for "mailbox."

13–14. double-tiered omnibus: bus with two decks, or tiers.

23–24. spectroscopic (spek′trō • skäp′ik) **. . . fancy:** wide range, or spectrum, of ideas.

"THAT'S DARK, ISN'T IT?" "Not altogether.
Facially, I am brunette, but madam, you should see
The rest of me. Palm of my hand, soles of my feet
Are a peroxide blonde. Friction, caused—
Foolishly, madam—by sitting down, has turned
My bottom raven black—One moment madam!"—sensing
Her receiver rearing on the thunderclap
About my ears—"Madam," I pleaded, "wouldn't you rather
See for yourself?"

Response and Analysis

SKILLS FOCUS

Literary Skills Analyze satire.

Writing Skills Write a character analysis.

Thinking Critically

1. Paraphrase what happens in this poem, and then state what you feel to be the poem's **theme.** How does this theme express a comment on life?
2. What might the telephone conversation itself—complete with all the inconveniences of an old-fashioned phone—**symbolize**? Explain.
3. This poem is full of colors—and not just of skin. What colors does Soyinka make his readers see in the poem? What ideas and emotions do you think he wants to communicate through these **images** of color?
4. What **irony** do you find in lines 23–26? What irony do you find in the description of the woman as an example of a well-bred person (line 7)?
5. In your opinion, which part of the poem is the most **satirical**? Quote the lines, and then explain why these lines are a good example of satire.

Extending and Evaluating

6. What do you think of the speaker's final question? What does it suggest about prejudice and discrimination?
7. Review your Quickwrite notes, and then think about whether Soyinka's poem is an effective way of making others aware of prejudice. Is it more or less effective than other ways? How so? Explain.

go.hrw.com

INTERNET

Projects and Activities

Keyword: LE7 12-7

WRITING

Judging the Landlady

What kind of person is the landlady in Soyinka's poem? Write a brief **character analysis** of her. What do you learn about her from the speaker's assumptions, judgments, and tone, and from the woman's own words? How does the fact that she is a disembodied voice add to (or detract from) her character? Cite specific details from the poem to support your analysis.

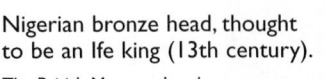

Nigerian bronze head, thought to be an Ife king (13th century). The British Museum, London.

Analyzing Nonfiction

Writing Assignment
Write an essay of at least 1,500 words in which you analyze the theme of a professional essay and support your analysis with textual evidence.

At first glance, a nonfiction selection such as George Orwell's much anthologized essay "Shooting an Elephant" (page 1117) might seem to convey only simple information about an event far removed from the experience of contemporary readers. A close analysis of the essay, however, reveals how carefully Orwell arranged the basic data of his experience to convey a **theme** that has significance beyond the essay's time and setting. In your **analysis of nonfiction,** you will examine the many layers of meaning that can make up an essay's theme, and you will share your insights with others.

Choose an Essay Find an essay whose subject matter intrigues you. You might scan the table of contents of this book for an essay you haven't yet read. You may also ask a librarian for suggestions of essay collections, or ask a teacher to recommend an essay you might enjoy.

Consider Purpose, Audience, and Tone Your **purpose** in analyzing an essay is to explain your interpretation of the essay's theme to an **audience** of your teacher or your peers. Use a serious, objective **tone** to show that you understand and respect the essay.

Gain an Overview Plan to read the essay at least twice. The first time through, read for general understanding and to note the organization of the essay. Take notes on the essay's **subject** and the author's **purpose**—informative, persuasive, expressive, or entertaining. Then, decide if the essay's **tone** is informal (personal) or formal (objective). You may need to do research to understand the context of the essay you are analyzing. Your research may include information on the author or on the topic of the essay.

Analyze the Theme To determine the **theme** of the essay, read back through the essay a second time for general statements about life or human nature, such as Orwell's declaration, "I perceived in this moment that when the white man turns tyrant it is his own freedom that he destroys" (1120). Write down any **direct quotations** that you find, along with their page numbers. You may also **paraphrase** or **summarize** from the text to help you in your notetaking. Remember that while some essays state the theme, others imply a theme. If the theme isn't stated explicitly, ask yourself, "What do all my notes imply about the essay's statements on life or human nature? In answering that question, you'll be formulating your understanding of the essay's theme.

Look for Stylistic Devices Essayists often use stylistic devices to intensify the theme of the essay. As part of your analysis, you may want to include comments about the essay's use of **concrete sensory details, figures of speech, imagery,** or **irony**—verbal, dramatic, or situational. For example, one student noted that Orwell's figure of

Writing Skills
Write an essay analyzing nonfiction. Determine purpose, audience, and tone.

speech—"If the elephant charged and I missed him, I should have about as much chance as a toad under a steamroller" (1121)—intensifies the drama of the moment and heightens Orwell's mixed feelings.

Write a Thesis Statement Sum up your ideas about the essay's theme in a sentence that will guide the rest of your analysis. The **thesis statement** should identify the theme you'll analyze and mention the stylistic device most important to the development of that theme. For example, one student's thesis statement identified the theme of Orwell's essay and hinted at the importance of irony to the development of that theme.

TIP When drafting your essay, use **standard American English** for your analysis.

In "Shooting an Elephant," George Orwell ironically describes an incident he experienced as a young police officer in colonial Burma to show that tyranny debases the oppressors as much as it debases the oppressed.

Gather Support To support your thesis statement, use three or more **key points—reasons** that readers should accept your interpretation of the theme. Then, use **evidence** you've gathered from the essay to support each of your key points. **Elaborate** by explaining how the evidence develops each key point. Here is the way one student developed a key point with evidence and elaboration.

DO THIS

Key Point: Orwell makes clear the irony of his situation in Burma: As a police officer, he was publicly required to carry out policy he did not believe in privately; privately, he despised the people who taunted him in public.

Evidence (paraphrase and direct quotation): Orwell had decided that he favored the Burmese, as much as he disliked them, but as a representative of the British Empire his job required him to see "the dirty work of Empire at close quarters" (1117).

Elaboration: As an agent of the empire, he was required to enforce a system whose aims and methods he rejected. He understood and sympathized with the Burmese people's anti-European attitude, yet their behavior infuriated him.

TIP Remember to document direct quotations with page numbers in parentheses. For more on **documenting sources,** see page 247.

Organize Your Essay Present your ideas in a logical manner—either **chronologically** or in the **order of importance.** Include background information and the author and title of the essay in your introduction. Close your essay with a restatement of thesis and a dramatic statement.

Writing Skills
Write a thesis statement. Gather support. Organize the essay.

PRACTICE & APPLY Use the instructions in this workshop to write an analysis of an essay. Share your essay with your classmates and, if possible, with a wider audience.

Collection 7:
The Modern World:
1900 to the Present

Discoveries and Transformations

Yeats
Rilke
Joyce
Lawrence
Akhmatova
Bowen
Cortázar
Borges
Naipaul
Mahfouz
Heaney

Life spends itself in the act of transformation, dissolving, bit by bit, the world as it appeared.

—Rainer Maria Rilke

Our Dream (1999) by Alfredo Castañeda. Oil on canvas.
Courtesy of Mary-Anne Martin/Fine Art, New York.

William Butler Yeats

(1865–1939)

Ireland

William Butler Yeats (detail) (20th century) by John Butler Yeats. Oil on canvas (77 cm × 64 cm).

National Gallery of Ireland, Dublin. © 2006 Artists Rights Society (ARS), New York/DACS, London.

Generally regarded as the twentieth century's greatest poet writing in English, William Butler Yeats (rhymes with *crates*) was born in Dublin, Ireland, the son of a well-known portrait painter. He arrived on the literary scene when the Pre-Raphaelite movement (see page 884) of the mid–nineteenth century was reviving.

The revival, called Art Nouveau, emphasized the mysterious and unfathomable—especially those recesses of the mind just then being scrutinized by the great pioneers in psychology, Sigmund Freud and Carl Jung. Particularly in poetry, the revival recommended suggestion above statement, symbols above facts, and musical measures above common speech. It was within this atmosphere that the young Yeats established a reputation as a lyricist of great delicacy and as a versifier of old tales drawn from Irish folklore and mythology. In a collection of his early poems, *The Wanderings of Oisin and Other Poems* (1889), Yeats was a romantic dreamer, evoking the mythic and heroic past of Ireland. At this stage of his career, he was a pioneer of the Celtic Revival, determined to make the Irish conscious of their heroic past.

In 1914, Yeats set out to create a stark, chiseled, and eloquently resonant kind of poetry. That same year, he published a volume aptly titled *Responsibilities*. The man who had once seen himself as the prophet-priest of Ireland's national destiny was now grappling with his own personal realities. For years, Yeats had idolized and yearned for Maud Gonne, the beautiful Irish political activist who rejected his hand and instead chose another, more politically radical suitor. Yeats finally accepted that rejection and in 1917, at fifty-two, married Georgie Hyde-Lees, an Englishwoman who would remain his "delight and comfort" for the next twenty-two years.

From 1922 to 1928, Yeats served as a senator of the newly formed Irish Free State. He also toured the United States, giving ritualized readings of the poems for which, in 1923, he was awarded the Nobel Prize in literature.

Yeats may be said to have carved out of English a language distinctly his own. Monumentally spare and unadorned, "cold and passionate as the dawn" in Yeats's own words, it confirms the basic definition of poetry as "heightened speech."

Yeats was also a dramatist, and in this role he helped his friend Lady Gregory establish Dublin's Abbey Theatre as a monument to Irish culture and high literary standards. Some audiences may agree with Yeats himself, who felt that some of his most memorable poems are embedded, like gems, in the scripts of his plays.

Nearly ten years after Yeats's death and burial in the south of France, his body was disinterred and sent back to Ireland. Like a primitive king, with full ceremony and military pomp, he returned on the deck of a battleship.

Before You Read

The Second Coming

Make the Connection

Quickwrite

This poem is Yeats's articulation of a feeling many of us have had—a feeling of anxiety and dread as one phase of life ends and another, more chaotic phase begins. Written after World War I, "The Second Coming" prophesies the passing of civilization from one era into the next. The change, Yeats predicts, will not be a pleasant one. Instead, it will be marked by violence, bloodshed, and the "rough beast" of totalitarianism, a form of government marked by authoritarianism and dictatorship.

Recall a major transition in your own life, especially one that you dreaded or resisted. Jot down a few sentences describing this transition. Then list four or five emotions that the transition triggered in you.

Literary Focus

Theme

The poem's title and many of its images allude to the Christian view of history—specifically, a prophecy from the Book of Revelation in the Bible. (An **allusion** is a reference to something that is known from literature, religion, politics, and so on.) In turn, the poem's **theme,** or central insight, relies upon this allusion—and turns it inside out. As you read, ask yourself why Yeats refers to this Christian idea of a just and peaceful end of time—especially in the context of the chaos just unleashed by World War I and the Russian Revolution of 1917. (Yeats wrote this poem in 1921.) What idea about the Second Coming—or about the security and comfort of Christian hope—might Yeats be attempting to express?

The **theme** of a literary work is the central idea or insight it reveals about human experience.

For more on Theme, see the Handbook of Literary and Historical Terms.

Background

In Christianity, the Second Coming refers to the belief that Jesus will one day return to earth and usher in an era of peace and justice. This Second Coming is prophesied in the Book of Revelation in the Bible. The "first coming" was the birth of Jesus in Bethlehem in Judea, just over two thousand years ago.

The poem addresses not only the Christian conception of the universe but also Yeats's personal view of history. As he explains in his book *A Vision,* Yeats saw human history as cyclical. Each cycle, known as a gyre, begins in a rational state and then gradually dissolves into chaos and irrationality. "What if the irrational returns?" Yeats asks in his poem *A Vision.* That question is repeated poetically in the work you are about to read.

Literary Skills
Understand theme.

INTERNET

More About William Butler Yeats

Keyword: LE7 12-7

The Second Coming

William Butler Yeats

Turning and turning in the widening gyre
The falcon cannot hear the falconer;
Things fall apart; the center cannot hold;
Mere anarchy is loosed upon the world,
The blood-dimmed tide is loosed, and everywhere
The ceremony of innocence is drowned;
The best lack all conviction, while the worst
Are full of passionate intensity.

Surely some revelation is at hand;
Surely the Second Coming is at hand.
The Second Coming! Hardly are those words out
When a vast image out of Spiritus Mundi°
Troubles my sight: somewhere in sands of the desert
A shape with lion body and the head of a man,
A gaze blank and pitiless as the sun,
Is moving its slow thighs, while all about it
Reel shadows of the indignant desert birds.
The darkness drops again; but now I know
That twenty centuries of stony sleep
Were vexed to nightmare by a rocking cradle,
And what rough beast, its hour come round at last,
Slouches towards Bethlehem to be born?

---

12. **Spiritus Mundi:** Latin for "the world's soul or spirit"; for Yeats, the collective reservoir of human memory from which artists draw their images.

Response and Analysis

Thinking Critically

1. The first two lines of the poem present an **image**—that of a falconer who is unable to limit the flight of his released hawk as it spirals out of control. How does this image help to convey one of the poem's central **themes**? (Consider the poem's historical context—the time during which it was written—in your response.)
2. What do you think the poet means by the word *center* in line 3? What condition is being described by the phrase "the center cannot hold"?
3. What might the "blood-dimmed tide" in line 5 refer to? What could the "ceremony of innocence" in line 6 mean?
4. What **image** of the Second Coming troubles the speaker in the second half of the poem? List some of the specific words that make this image especially vivid.
5. **Irony** is a discrepancy between what is expected and what actually happens. How does the idea of the Second Coming become **ironic** in the second stanza? In what sense is this irony frightening?
6. Comment on the poet's use of each of the following words: *mere* (line 4), *pitiless* (line 15), *indignant* (line 17), *stony* (line 19), and *slouches* (line 22). Think about the **connotations** of each word. What idea or emotion does each word help to convey? How vivid or forceful do you find each word in its particular context?
7. If you had to name one dominant emotion expressed by the speaker of this poem, what would it be? Check your Quickwrite notes for ideas before you respond.

Extending and Evaluating

8. Why might Yeats have ended the poem with a question? In your opinion, can this question be answered? Explain.

WRITING

Yesterday and Today

This poem was written after the horrors of World War I. Yeats asks, "Have we, like the falconer, lost control of the means to halt our descent into chaos?" Is Yeats's question still relevant today? In a brief **essay,** explain how "The Second Coming" reflects—or does not reflect—your own ideas about human progress and the shape of the future. Use quotations from the poem in your response.

Literary Skills
Analyze theme.

Writing Skills
Write a response to a poem.

Before You Read

The Lake Isle of Innisfree

Make the Connection

Quickwrite

Imagination can help us visualize what we want to create or accomplish—what we hope to make real. But imagination can also transport us *out* of reality, into a distant place or state of mind that renews our energy and restores our spirit. As you read this poem by Yeats, ask yourself whether the poem is more concerned with a broad vision of a life the poet wishes to create for himself than with an immediate momentary escape from the daily grind.

When your life becomes hectic or stressful, do you imagine a place or a time in which you could feel calm and free? Describe what this place is like or might be like. How does imagining this place make you feel?

Literary Focus

Assonance and Alliteration

As a young poet, Yeats inherited much of the vocabulary and poetic conventions of his nineteenth-century predecessors. Thus, some of the phrases in this poem—"veils of the morning," "midnight's all a glimmer"—are right out of the old-fashioned Victorian vocabulary. Innisfree itself is one of those impossibly idyllic, great good places that industrial-era Victorians yearned for. Nevertheless, this poem rises above its more mundane counterparts.

Yeats's lyrical skills, especially his haunting use of **assonance** and **alliteration,** create a poem whose verbal music has echoed in readers' memories for over a hundred years. The lilting rhythms of the poem and the repetition of both vowel sounds (assonance) and consonant sounds (alliteration) work together to soothe and transport the reader, much as a lullaby does a child.

Literary Skills
Understand assonance and alliteration.

INTERNET

More About William Butler Yeats

Keyword: LE7 12-7

Assonance is the repetition of similar vowel sounds in words that are close together.

Alliteration is the repetition of similar consonant sounds in words that are close together.

For more on Assonance and Alliteration, see the Handbook of Literary and Historical Terms.

Background

Innisfree is a real island in Sligo, the beautiful county in the west of Ireland where Yeats spent many summers as a child, visiting his grandparents. Yeats once said that the poem came to him when he was in London on a dreary day. He passed a store display that used dripping water in a fountain, and he thought at once of the lake island of his childhood. Yeats's father had once read Thoreau's *Walden* to him. The bean rows and cabin in this poem are straight from Thoreau's account of his life in the Walden Woods of Massachusetts.

The Lake Isle of Innisfree

William Butler Yeats

I will arise and go now, and go to Innisfree,
And a small cabin build there, of clay and wattles° made:
Nine bean-rows will I have there, a hive for the honey-bee,
And live alone in the bee-loud glade.

And I shall have some peace there, for peace comes dropping slow,
Dropping from the veils of the morning to where the cricket sings;
There midnight's all a glimmer, and noon a purple glow,
And evening full of the linnet's° wings.

I will arise and go now, for always night and day
I hear lake water lapping with low sounds by the shore;
While I stand on the roadway, or on the pavements gray,
I hear it in the deep heart's core.

2. wattles *n. pl.:* interwoven twigs or branches.

8. linnet's: A linnet is a European songbird.

Lakeside Cottages (c. 1929) by Paul Henry. Oil on canvas (16″ × 24″).
Hugh Lane Municipal Gallery of Modern Art, Dublin.

Response and Analysis

Thinking Critically

1. In the first stanza, what does the speaker say he will do? Does he do this? Explain.
2. What sounds does the speaker describe in the poem?
3. To what does the speaker compare peace?
4. How do the surroundings of the lake island contrast with the speaker's actual location?
5. Why do you think the speaker cannot find peace in the city setting?
6. How would you describe the **tone** of this poem? Do you think it could be called a Romantic poem? Explain why or why not.

Extending and Evaluating

7. The pronoun *I* is repeated seven times in this short, twelve-line poem. In your opinion, why does the speaker so often insert himself into the scene he describes? Does this intrusion make the poem more or less soothing to you, the reader? Explain.

WRITING

A Place of Peace

The first line of "The Lake Isle of Innisfree" is often quoted. Write your own **poem** or **paragraph** beginning with the words "I will arise and go now. . ." Then, go on to describe your own ideal place of peace. You should refer to your Quickwrite notes before you begin.

Literary Focus

Assonance and Alliteration

The music of this poem comes in part from Yeats's use of **assonance,** the repetition of similar vowel sounds in nearby words. The poem is also notable for a famous line (line 10) of **alliteration**—the repetition of similar consonant sounds in nearby words.

1. What vowel sounds dominate the first stanza?
2. What vowel sounds are emphasized by the rhyming words?
3. Explain how alliteration helps the reader visualize the imagery of line 10.
4. How would you describe the total effect of the vowel sounds in the poem? (How would the poem have been different if the poet had used more hard consonants, such as *k, d,* or *p*?)

Literary Skills Analyze assonance and alliteration.

Writing Skills Write a poem or a paragraph describing a place.

Lough Gill, County Sligo (20th century) by Jack Butler Yeats. Watercolor on paper.

Before You Read

The Wild Swans at Coole

Make the Connection

Quickwrite

Yeats first saw the scene described in this poem when he was thirty-two. He wrote the poem at the age of fifty-one. How might the passage of time transform a person's response to something familiar—be it a person, a place, or a thing?

Think of a familiar scene to which you have returned over the years. In a short paragraph, describe how time has affected your responses to the scene.

Literary Focus

Symbol

A **symbol** is something that can be understood literally (for what it is) and also figuratively (as a representative of something beyond itself). Yeats's swans can be regarded as symbols, but what do they represent? As you read this poem, keep in mind that symbols, by their very nature, are open-ended: Their meanings are various and open to interpretation.

> A **symbol** is a figure of speech in which a person, place, thing, or event stands both for itself and for something beyond itself.
>
> *For more on Symbol, see the Handbook of Literary and Historical Terms.*

Background

Yeats's good friend and fellow writer Lady Gregory lived on an estate known as Coole Park in Ireland's County Galway. When Yeats first visited there in 1897, he was in love with Maud Gonne, the beautiful activist for Irish independence, who was more interested in politics than in marriage. This poem, written in 1916, recalls Yeats's first view of the swans; now, nineteen years later, he realizes that "All's changed."

The swans are wild, or migratory. Like the poet, they return annually to familiar places. Yeats knew that swans are monogamous, that "lover by lover" they continue to live in a state of mated bliss denied to him. But the larger meanings of the poem lie in the relationship between memory, time, loss, and the inflexible patterns of natural life represented by the swans.

Literary Skills Understand symbols.

INTERNET

More About William Butler Yeats

Keyword: LE7 12-7

The Wild Swans at Coole

William Butler Yeats

The trees are in their autumn beauty,
The woodland paths are dry,
Under the October twilight the water
Mirrors a still sky;
Upon the brimming water among the stones
Are nine-and-fifty swans.

The nineteenth autumn has come upon me
Since I first made my count;
I saw, before I had well finished,
All suddenly mount
And scatter wheeling in great broken rings
Upon their clamorous wings.

I have looked upon those brilliant creatures,
And now my heart is sore.
All's changed since I, hearing at twilight,
The first time on this shore,
The bell-beat of their wings above my head,
Trod with a lighter tread.

Unwearied still, lover by lover,
They paddle in the cold
Companionable streams or climb the air;
Their hearts have not grown old;
Passion or conquest, wander where they will,
Attend upon them still.

But now they drift on the still water,
Mysterious, beautiful;
Among what rushes will they build,
By what lake's edge or pool
Delight men's eyes when I awake some day
To find they have flown away?

CONNECTION / POEM

The poet Rainer Maria Rilke (ri′nər mä • rē′ä ril′kə) *(1875–1926), who wrote in German, was among the most original writers of the twentieth century. One of his greatest influences was the French sculptor Auguste Rodin, with whom Rilke worked. One day, Rilke confided to Rodin that he was suffering from writer's block. Rodin suggested a cure: Go to the zoo, he said, and observe an animal until you can truly see it. Rilke took the unusual advice, concentrated on a panther, and soon after produced the first of his "thing poems"—poems that seek to communicate both the concrete outward appearance of a thing (an animal, for example) and its abstract, invisible inner vitality and spirit—its "inward nature." In "The Swan," Rilke makes an elegant extended comparison using the concrete image of a swan to explore a concept that is anything but concrete.*

The Swan

Rainer Maria Rilke

translated by Robert Bly

This clumsy living that moves lumbering
as if in ropes through what is not done
reminds us of the awkward way the swan walks.

And to die, which is a letting go
of the ground we stand on and cling to every day,
is like the swan when he nervously lets himself down

into the water, which receives him gaily
and which flows joyfully under
and after him, wave after wave,
while the swan, unmoving and marvelously calm,
is pleased to be carried, each minute more fully grown,
more like a king, composed, farther and farther on.

Response and Analysis

Thinking Critically

1. How does the speaker feel as he gazes at the swans? How did he feel nineteen years earlier when he heard the beating of their wings?
2. The second, third, and fourth stanzas offer hints about the personal experience that underlies the poem. What are those hints? Why do you think the speaker's heart is "sore" (line 14)? Reviewing your Quickwrite notes may help you understand the speaker's feeling.
3. **Paraphrase,** or state in your own words, the question the speaker asks in the last stanza.
4. What qualities of the swans do you think the speaker envies? Why? What might the swans **symbolize** to the speaker?
5. How are the time of year and the time of day in this poem appropriate to its **mood**?
6. The word *awake* in the next-to-last line is mysterious at first reading. Do you think it signifies that the poem has all been a dream? Or could it mean something else? How might this word offer a clue to the **theme** of the poem?
7. An **elegy** is a poem that mourns the death of a person or laments something that has been lost, such as beauty or times past. In what sense might this poem be thought of as an elegy? How does the poem relate in **theme, tone,** and **imagery** to any of the other famous elegies in this book (see pages 355, 927, and 1275)?

Extending and Evaluating

8. In your opinion, what is the most important word or phrase in this poem? Be sure to compare your response with the responses of other readers. Be able to defend your choice with evidence from the poem.

WRITING

Birds of a Feather

In a brief **essay, compare** "The Wild Swans at Coole" with Rilke's "The Swan" (see the ***Connection*** on page 1171). Use this graphic to collect details for your composition.

	Yeats	Rilke
Imagery		
Symbols		
Theme		

Japanese Footbridge and Water Lily Pool, Giverny (1899) by Claude Monet.

Literary Skills
Analyze symbols.

Writing Skills
Write an essay comparing two poems.

James Joyce

(1882–1941)

Ireland

James Joyce (1934) by Jacques-Émile Blanche.

James Joyce's controversial masterpiece, *Ulysses* (1922), has probably had a greater effect on twentieth-century fiction than any other work of our times. Based on Homer's *Odyssey*, Joyce's *Ulysses* describes the events of a single day in Dublin, the city where Joyce grew up. And just as Homer's epic interpreted the world of the ancient Greeks, so does Joyce's epic mirror and interpret for us our own lives in the twentieth century.

Joyce was born in Rathgar, Ireland, a Dublin suburb. One of ten children in a fairly impoverished family, he was educated at a series of Roman Catholic schools, but by the time he entered University College, Dublin, he had lost his faith. After graduating, he went to Paris and existed frugally by giving English lessons and writing book reviews.

In 1903, Joyce returned home to be at his dying mother's bedside. Afterward he lived briefly in a Martello Tower (a former military fortification) on the coast near Dublin, a site that has now become the James Joyce Museum. There he began an autobiographical novel, *Stephen Hero*, and also wrote some of the stories later published in *Dubliners* (1914).

In June 1904, Joyce met and fell in love with a Galway girl named Nora Barnacle. The date of their first walk, June 16, 1904, was later immortalized as Bloomsday, the date on which the action of *Ulysses* takes place. When Joyce's debts mounted, he persuaded Nora to leave Ireland with him; Joyce was never to live in Ireland again.

The penniless couple settled first in the Italian city of Trieste, where their two children, George and Lucia, were born. Joyce's luck began to turn after 1914, when the influential American poet Ezra Pound reviewed *Dubliners* favorably and persuaded a British magazine to serialize *A Portrait of the Artist as a Young Man*, Joyce's rewritten version of *Stephen Hero*.

When Italy entered World War I in 1915, the Joyces left Trieste for Zurich, where Joyce worked on the early chapters of *Ulysses*. Because of sizable gifts from anonymous patrons, Joyce's financial troubles had begun to ease, but his physical problems increased. Between 1917 and 1930, he endured twenty-five operations for glaucoma and cataracts. Sometimes he was totally blind, yet he continued work on *Ulysses*.

British printers found *Ulysses* so scandalous that they refused to set it in type. In 1922, however, Sylvia Beach, the American owner of a bookstore in Paris called Shakespeare & Co., agreed to put out an edition of one thousand copies. Many of the reviews were favorable, but the book was banned in both Britain and the United States. Not until 1934, after a famous court case, was *Ulysses* published in America. A British edition soon followed, and the book's fame spread rapidly worldwide.

The Joyces, who had been living in Paris, returned to Zurich in 1940, when France fell to Nazi Germany. There Joyce became increasingly ill, his eye troubles complicated by a duodenal ulcer. He died on January 13, 1941, one month short of his fifty-ninth birthday.

Before You Read

Araby

Make the Connection

When a person embarks upon a quest for the unknown—or for the deeply desired—he or she may suddenly see life in glowing terms. In place of the former, predictable routine there is a sense of endless possibilities in a fascinating world where anything can happen. Unfortunately, this "anything" is often something other than the anticipated outcome.

Literary Focus

Epiphany

Joyce called the moments of insight, or revelation, that his characters experience "epiphanies." Before Joyce used the word in this way, an **epiphany** referred solely to a religious experience, a moment during which a human being felt an intense connection with the divine or understood a spiritual truth he or she hadn't before. Although Joyce gave the word a modern, literary meaning, you will see that the main character's epiphany is described with the help of religious language and imagery.

Literary Skills Understand epiphany.

Reading Skills Compare and contrast aspects of a story.

In fiction, an **epiphany** is a moment of sudden insight or revelation experienced by a character.

For more on Epiphany, see the Handbook of Literary and Historical Terms.

INTERNET

Vocabulary Practice

•

More About James Joyce

•

Keyword: LE7 12-7

Reading Skills

Comparing and Contrasting

In "Araby" the main character has a vivid imagination that sometimes causes him to misunderstand the realities of his life. As you read the story, look for differences between the way the character imagines things to be and the way they really are. List these differences in a two-column comparison-contrast chart like the one here.

Imagination	Reality

Background

On May 14, 1894, a five-day charity bazaar came to the city of Dublin. The bazaar was called Araby, a reference to Arabia, where bazaars—markets with long rows of stalls or shops—are common. For the children of Dublin, Arabia seemed a mysterious, exotic place, very different from the streets of the dreary city in which they lived.

The house in this story is based on one in which Joyce and his family actually lived. It stood on the same blind (dead-end) street as the Christian Brothers' School Joyce attended.

Vocabulary Development

imperturbable (im′pər·tur′bə·bəl) *adj.:* calm; impassive.

somber (säm′bər) *adj.:* gloomy.

impinge (im·pinj′) *v.:* strike; touch.

annihilate (ə·nī′ə·lāt′) *v.:* destroy; make nonexistent.

monotonous (mə·nät′'n·əs) *adj.:* unvarying.

garrulous (gar′ə·ləs) *adj.:* talkative.

improvised (im′prə·vīzd′) *v.* used as *adj.:* made for the occasion from whatever is handy.

pervades (pər·vādz′) *v.:* spreads throughout.

Araby

James Joyce

North Richmond Street, being blind, was a quiet street except at the hour when the Christian Brothers' School set the boys free. An uninhabited house of two stories stood at the blind end, detached from its neighbors in a square ground. The other houses of the street, conscious of decent lives within them, gazed at one another with brown imperturbable faces.

The former tenant of our house, a priest, had died in the back drawing-room. Air, musty from having been long enclosed, hung in all the rooms, and the waste room behind the kitchen was littered with old useless papers. Among these I found a few paper-covered books, the pages of which were curled and damp: *The Abbot,* by Walter Scott, *The Devout Communicant,* and *The Memoirs of Vidocq.*[1] I liked the last best because its leaves were yellow. The wild garden behind the house contained a central apple-tree and a few straggling bushes under one of which I found the late tenant's rusty bicycle-pump. He had been a very charitable priest; in his will he had left all his money to institutions and the furniture of his house to his sister.

When the short days of winter came dusk fell before we had well eaten our dinners. When we met in the street the houses had grown somber. The space of sky above us was the color of ever-changing violet and toward it the lamps of the street lifted their feeble lanterns. The cold air stung us and we played till our bodies glowed. Our shouts echoed in the silent street. The career[2] of our play brought us through the dark muddy lanes behind the houses where we ran the gauntlet[3] of the rough tribes from the cottages, to the back doors of the dark dripping gardens where odors arose from the ashpits, to the dark odorous stables where a coachman smoothed and combed the horse or shook music from the buckled harness. When we returned to the street light from the kitchen windows had filled the areas. If my uncle was seen turning the corner we hid in the shadow until we had seen him safely housed. Or if Mangan's sister came out on the doorstep to call her brother in to his tea we watched her from our shadow peer up and down the street. We waited to see whether she would remain or go in and, if she remained, we left our shadow and walked up to Mangan's steps resignedly. She was waiting for us, her figure defined by the light from the half-opened door. Her brother always teased her before he obeyed and I stood by the railings looking at her. Her dress swung as she moved her body and the soft rope of her hair tossed from side to side.

Every morning I lay on the floor in the front parlor watching her door. The blind was pulled down to within an inch of the sash so that I could not be seen. When she came out on the doorstep my heart leaped. I ran to the hall, seized my books, and followed her. I kept her brown figure always in my eye and, when we came near the point at which our ways diverged, I quickened my pace and passed her. This happened morning after morning. I had

1. ***The Abbott . . . Vidocq*** (vē·duk′): in order, a historical romance about Mary, Queen of Scots, by Sir Walter Scott; an 1813 religious manual written by a Franciscan friar; and the memoirs (though not actually written by François Vidocq) of a French criminal who later became a detective.
2. **career** *n.:* course; path.
3. **gauntlet** (gônt′lit) *n.:* series of challenges. Derived from *gatlopp,* Swedish for "running down a lane," the term originally referred to a form of military punishment in which a wrongdoer had to run between two rows of soldiers who struck him as he passed.

Vocabulary

imperturbable (im′pər·tur′bə·bəl) *adj.:* calm; impassive.
somber (säm′bər) *adj.:* gloomy.

St Patrick's Close, Dublin by Walter Osborne.

never spoken to her, except for a few casual words, and yet her name was like a summons to all my foolish blood.

Her image accompanied me even in places the most hostile to romance. On Saturday evenings when my aunt went marketing I had to go to carry some of the parcels. We walked through the flaring streets, jostled by drunken men and bargaining women, amid the curses of laborers, the shrill litanies[4] of shop-boys who stood on guard by the barrels of pigs' cheeks, the nasal chanting of street-singers, who sang a *come-all-you* about O'Donovan Rossa,[5] or a ballad about the troubles in our native land. These noises converged in a single sensation of life for me: I imagined that I bore my chalice[6] safely through a throng of foes. Her name sprang to my lips at moments in strange prayers and praises which I myself did not understand. My eyes were often full of tears (I could not tell why) and at times a flood from my heart seemed to pour itself out into my bosom. I thought little of the future. I did not know whether I would ever speak to her or not or, if I spoke to her, how I could tell her of my confused adoration. But my body was like a harp and her words and gestures were like fingers running upon the wires.

One evening I went into the back drawing-room in which the priest had died. It was a dark rainy evening and there was no sound in the house. Through one of the broken panes I heard the rain impinge upon the earth, the fine incessant needles of water playing in the sodden beds. Some distant lamp or lighted window gleamed below me. I was thankful that I could see so little. All my senses seemed to desire to veil themselves and, feeling that I was about to slip from them, I pressed the palms of my hands together until they trembled, murmuring: *O love! O love!* many times.

At last she spoke to me. When she addressed the first words to me I was so confused that I did not know what to answer. She asked me was I going to *Araby*. I forget whether I answered yes or no. It would be a splendid bazaar, she said; she would love to go.

—And why can't you? I asked.

While she spoke she turned a silver bracelet round and round her wrist. She could not go, she said, because there would be a retreat that week in her convent.[7] Her brother and two other boys were fighting for their caps and I was alone at the railings. She held one of the spikes, bowing her head toward me. The light from the lamp opposite our door caught the white curve of her neck, lit up her hair that rested there and, falling, lit up the hand upon the railing. It fell over one side of her dress and caught the white border of a petticoat, just visible as she stood at ease.

—It's well for you,[8] she said.

—If I go, I said, I will bring you something.

What innumerable follies laid waste my waking and sleeping thoughts after that evening! I wished to annihilate the tedious intervening days. I chafed against the work of school. At night in my bedroom and by day in the classroom her image came between me and the page I strove to read. The syllables of the word *Araby* were called to me through the silence in which my soul luxuriated and cast an Eastern enchantment over me. I asked for leave to go to the bazaar on Saturday night. My aunt was surprised and hoped it was

4. **litanies** *n. pl.:* repeated sales cries. Literally, a litany is a prayer composed of a series of specific invocations and responses.
5. ***come-all-you . . .* Rossa:** A come-all-you (kum • al′yə) is a type of Irish ballad that usually begins "Come all you [young lovers, rebels, Irishmen, and so on]." O'Donovan Rossa was Jeremiah O'Donovan (1831–1915) from County Cork. He was active in Ireland's struggle against British rule in the mid–nineteenth century.
6. **chalice** (chal′is) *n.:* cup; specifically, the cup used for Holy Communion wine. Joyce's use of the term evokes the image of a young man on a sacred mission.
7. **retreat . . . convent:** temporary withdrawal from worldly life by the students and teachers at the convent school, to devote time to prayer, meditation, and studies.
8. **It's well for you:** "You're lucky" (usually said enviously).

Vocabulary

impinge (im • pinj′) *v.:* strike; touch.
annihilate (ə • nī′ə • lāt′) *v.:* destroy; make nonexistent.

not some Freemason[9] affair. I answered few questions in class. I watched my master's face pass from amiability to sternness; he hoped I was not beginning to idle. I could not call my wandering thoughts together. I had hardly any patience with the serious work of life which, now that it stood between me and my desire, seemed to me child's play, ugly monotonous child's play.

On Saturday morning I reminded my uncle that I wished to go to the bazaar in the evening. He was fussing at the hallstand, looking for the hat-brush, and answered me curtly:

—Yes, boy, I know.

As he was in the hall I could not go into the front parlor and lie at the window. I left the house in bad humor and walked slowly toward the school. The air was pitilessly raw and already my heart misgave me.

When I came home to dinner my uncle had not yet been home. Still it was early. I sat staring at the clock for some time and, when its ticking began to irritate me, I left the room. I mounted the staircase and gained the upper part of the house. The high cold empty gloomy rooms liberated me and I went from room to room singing. From the front window I saw my companions playing below in the street. Their cries reached me weakened and indistinct and, leaning my forehead against the cool glass, I looked over at the dark house where she lived. I may have stood there for an hour, seeing nothing but the brown-clad figure cast by my imagination, touched discreetly by the lamplight at the curved neck, at the hand upon the railings and at the border below the dress.

When I came downstairs again I found Mrs. Mercer sitting at the fire. She was an old garrulous woman, a pawnbroker's widow, who collected used stamps for some pious purpose. I had to endure the gossip of the tea-table. The meal was prolonged beyond an hour and still my uncle did not come. Mrs. Mercer stood up to go: She was sorry she couldn't wait any longer, but it was after eight o'clock and she did not like to be out late, as the night air was bad for her. When she had gone I began to walk up and down the room, clenching my fists. My aunt said:

—I'm afraid you may put off your bazaar for this night of Our Lord.

At nine o'clock I heard my uncle's latchkey in the halldoor. I heard him talking to himself and heard the hallstand rocking when it had received the weight of his overcoat. I could interpret these signs. When he was midway through his dinner I asked him to give me the money to go to the bazaar. He had forgotten.

—The people are in bed and after their first sleep now, he said.

I did not smile. My aunt said to him energetically:

—Can't you give him the money and let him go? You've kept him late enough as it is.

My uncle said he was very sorry he had forgotten. He said he believed in the old saying: *All work and no play makes Jack a dull boy*. He asked me where I was going and, when I had told him a second time he asked me did I know *The Arab's Farewell to his Steed.*[10] When I left the kitchen he was about to recite the opening lines of the piece to my aunt.

I held a florin[11] tightly in my hand as I strode down Buckingham Street toward the station. The sight of the streets thronged with buyers and glaring with gas recalled to me the purpose of my journey. I took my seat in a third-class carriage of a deserted train. After an intolerable delay the train moved out of the station slowly. It crept onward among ruinous houses and over the twinkling river. At Westland Row Station a crowd of people pressed to the carriage doors; but the porters moved them back, saying that it

9. **Freemason:** The Freemasons are a secret society whose practices were originally drawn from those of British medieval stonemasons' guilds; its members, almost exclusively Protestant, were often hostile to Catholics. The aunt apparently associates the exotic bazaar with the mysterious practices of Freemasonry.

10. ***The Arab's . . . Steed:*** popular sentimental poem by the English writer Caroline Norton (1808–1877).

11. **florin** *n.:* British coin worth at the time the equivalent of about fifty cents.

Vocabulary

monotonous (mə•nät′'n•əs) *adj.:* unvarying.

garrulous (gar′ə•ləs) *adj.:* talkative.

Fairground, Tottenham (1925) by Allan Gwynne-Jones. Watercolor.

Waterman Fine Art Ltd., London, UK. © Courtesy of the estate of Allan Gwynne-Jones.

was a special train for the bazaar. I remained alone in the bare carriage. In a few minutes the train drew up beside an improvised wooden platform. I passed out on to the road and saw by the lighted dial of a clock that it was ten minutes to ten. In front of me was a large building which displayed the magical name.

I could not find any sixpenny entrance and, fearing that the bazaar would be closed, I passed in quickly through a turnstile, handing a shilling to a weary-looking man. I found myself in a big hall girdled at half its height by a gallery. Nearly all the stalls were closed and the greater part of the hall was in darkness. I recognized a silence like that which pervades a church after a service. I walked into the center of the bazaar timidly. A few people were gathered about the stalls which were still open. Before a curtain, over which the words *Café Chantant*[12] were written in colored lamps, two men were counting money on a salver.[13] I listened to the fall of the coins.

Remembering with difficulty why I had come I went over to one of the stalls and examined porcelain vases and flowered tea-sets. At the door of the stall a young lady was talking and laughing with two young gentlemen. I remarked their English accents and listened vaguely to their conversation.

—O, I never said such a thing!

—O, but you did!

—O, but I didn't!

—Didn't she say that?

—Yes. I heard her.

—O, there's a . . . fib!

Observing me the young lady came over and asked me did I wish to buy anything. The tone of her voice was not encouraging; she seemed to have spoken to me out of a sense of duty. I looked humbly at the great jars that stood like eastern guards at either side of the dark entrance to the stall and murmured:

—No, thank you.

The young lady changed the position of one of the vases and went back to the two young men. They began to talk of the same subject. Once or twice the young lady glanced at me over her shoulder.

I lingered before her stall, though I knew my stay was useless, to make my interest in her wares seem the more real. Then I turned away slowly and walked down the middle of the bazaar. I allowed the two pennies to fall against the sixpence in my pocket. I heard a voice call from one end of the gallery that the light was out. The upper part of the hall was now completely dark.

Gazing up into the darkness I saw myself as a creature driven and derided by vanity; and my eyes burned with anguish and anger. ■

12. ***Café Chantant*** (kȧ·fā′shän′tän′): The name refers to a coffeehouse with musical entertainment.

13. **salver** (sal′vər) *n.:* serving tray.

Vocabulary

improvised (im′prə·vīzd′) *v.* used as *adj.:* made for the occasion from whatever is handy.

pervades (pər·vādz′) *v.:* spreads throughout.

INFORMATIONAL TEXT

The Influence of James Joyce

Joyce's influence on twentieth-century writing is hard to overstate. His impact on world literature derives from his innovations in narrative techniques.

Portraying the flow of thought. Language for Joyce had an important psychological and social element. For Joyce (following St. Thomas Aquinas, who was following Aristotle), there is nothing in the mind that does not enter through the senses. We come to know the world through our senses, and our thought processes follow a pattern of association based on what we experience through our senses. Joyce's use of point of view in his writing and his presentation of thoughts directed by association led to the best-known characteristic of his mature style, called **stream of consciousness.** This is an attempt to portray the thinking mind directly, without organizing the thoughts and without the intervention of the author.

Joyce's early novel *A Portrait of the Artist as a Young Man* (1916) contains the germ of his experiments with this technique. The method is most apparent, though, in his second novel, *Ulysses* (1922). Much of the action in this novel is presented through the thoughts of its protagonists. Here, for example, is one of the main characters, Leopold Bloom, standing in front of a Dublin tea shop, reading the labels on the cans of tea and thinking:

> His right hand once more more slowly went over his brow and hair. Then he put on his hat again, relieved: and read again: choice blend, made of the finest Ceylon brands. The far east. Lovely spot it must be: the garden of the world, big lazy leaves to float about on, cactuses, flowery meads, snaky lianas they call them. . . . Where was the chap I saw in that picture somewhere? Ah yes, in the dead sea floating on his back, reading a book with a parasol open. Couldn't sink if you tried: so thick with salt. Because of the weight of the water, no, the weight of the body in the water is equal to the weight of the what? Or is it the volume is equal to the weight? It's a law something like that. Vance in High School cracking his finger joints, teaching. The college curriculum. Cracking curriculum. What is weight really when you say the weight? Thirty-two feet per second per second. Law of falling bodies: per second per second.
>
> —James Joyce, from *Ulysses*

Bloom's mind moves by association from the tea label to the Far East to the picture he saw of a man who, he realizes, wasn't in the Far East but in the Near East, on the Dead Sea. This makes him think of the principles behind floating and falling, which reminds him of his school days and of a teacher who cracked his knuckles. Bloom's mind, as this passage demonstrates, contains a mix of personal memories, sensations, and half-remembered bits of information.

Joyce worked on his last novel, *Finnegans Wake,* for seventeen years, from 1922 to 1939. When it appeared, some critics claimed that it announced the death of the novel as a literary form. In the book, the author has completely disappeared, and the consciousness is that of a dreamer. Finnegan is a bricklayer's helper who falls from a ladder and dies on the first page of the novel.

The experiments of others. Joyce's experiments with stream of consciousness were soon adopted by Virginia Woolf (see page 1104). (Woolf detested *Ulysses,* however, calling it illiterate and underbred.) Woolf's novel *Mrs. Dalloway,* published three years after *Ulysses* in 1925, focuses on the memories, dreams, and feelings of a central character in the course of just one day in London. Like Joyce, Woolf aimed at compressing time so that she could present an entire way of life through the detailed examination of a tiny part of it.

As the book opens, Mrs. Dalloway is on her way to buy flowers for a party she will give that evening:

> Mrs. Dalloway said she would buy the flowers herself. For Lucy had her work cut out for her. The doors would be taken off their hinges; Rumpelmayer's men were coming. And then, thought Clarissa Dalloway, what a morning—fresh as if issued to children on a beach.
>
> —Virginia Woolf
> from *Mrs. Dalloway*

Stream of consciousness, as this passage shows, can place unusual demands on the reader. For example, we have to infer from the context that Lucy is one of the household servants, that the doors will be removed for the party, and that Mrs. Dalloway is leaving her house to go shopping on a glorious summer's morning in London.

The narrative method that Joyce and Woolf pioneered has grown so popular that we no longer regard it as unusual. Among its practitioners have been some of the greatest twentieth-century novelists in world literature, including William Faulkner (United States) and Samuel Beckett (Ireland). Its influence has extended even to film, in the technique of *montage,* in which images shown in rapid succession suggest a train of thought.

James Joyce with Sylvia Beach, his publisher, in Paris during the Roaring Twenties.

Response and Analysis

Reading Check

1. Who is the **narrator** of the story? Though the story is told from the **first-person point of view,** is the narrator the same age as the main character? Cite evidence to support your answer.
2. What is the **setting** at the opening of the story? Which adjectives create a gloomy **mood**?
3. What is the purpose of the narrator's quest—his journey to the bazaar? What obstacles prevent him from achieving this goal?
4. What **epiphany,** or insight, has the narrator experienced by the end of the story? What details support your answer?

Pages 1182–1184 cover
Literary Skills Analyze epiphany and irony.
Reading Skills Compare and contrast aspects of a story.
Writing Skills Write a short story. Write an essay analyzing the narrator.
Vocabulary Skills Create semantic charts.

Thinking Critically

5. What **connotations** does the word *Araby* have for the narrator? What is Araby really like?
6. Look back at the chart you made while reading, in which you compared what the narrator imagined with what was real. How could the story be seen as presenting a **conflict** between imagination—the romantic vision—and reality?
7. How often have the narrator and Mangan's sister spoken to each other? How would you describe his relationship with her?
8. In what ways are the lives of these characters narrow or restricted?
9. How does the narrator deal with intrusions of reality into his fantasy—at the market, for example? What does this tell you about the narrator?
10. How would you describe the writer's **tone**—his attitude toward the characters and what happens to them? Cite specific examples from the text.

INTERNET
Projects and Activities
Keyword: LE7 12-7

Extending and Evaluating

11. There are many religious references in this story—for example, a dead priest, a chalice, the narrator's prayerful utterances, and the bazaar's churchlike silence. In your opinion, are such references appropriate? Do they add to the significance of the narrator's quest or detract from it? Explain.
12. Evaluate the story's ending. In your opinion, is it realistic or overblown? Would any other ending have worked? Explain.

Literary Criticism

13. In a review of Joyce's *Dubliners* in *The Egoist* (July 15, 1914), the poet Ezra Pound wrote that if you could erase the local names, a few specifically local allusions, and a few historic events of the past, then substitute other names, allusions, and events, stories like "Araby" could be told about any town. Do you agree with Pound's assessment? Which details of plot and character in "Araby" would have to change if, for example, the setting was changed to your own city or neighborhood in the early twenty-first century? Would the story still work if these changes were made? Explain your response.

WRITING

A Short Story Quest

Write a **short story** about a quest or a dream that a young person sets about trying to fulfill. The quest should be one that might occur in everyday life (rather than one involving extraordinary circumstances). Your story may reflect an actual experience you have had or one that you imagine a person your age might have. In either case, use the **first-person point of view** in your story, but make the narrator older and wiser than he or she was at the time of the quest.

Use "Writing a Short Story," pages 1249–1250, for help with this assignment.

Vanity's Many Sides

At the end of the story, the narrator sees himself "driven and derided by vanity." One meaning of *vanity* is "the state of being empty, idle, valueless." Another meaning is "exaggerated self-love." Still another is "hunger for praise or admiration." In an **essay,** explain how all these definitions could apply to the narrator. Use evidence from the story to support your claims.

Vocabulary Development

Word Information Charts

imperturbable monotonous
somber garrulous
impinge improvised
annihilate pervades

The chart below organizes some basic information about the word *somber.* Using a dictionary, make similar charts for the rest of the Vocabulary words listed above.

somber
Meaning: gloomy **Origin:** Latin, "under + shade" **Synonym:** depressing **Antonym:** cheerful **Examples:** News that a relative has died makes you somber; watching a news report of a tragedy makes you somber.

Literary Focus

Irony: Things Are Not As They Seem

Here is the plot of a story: A boy has a crush on a girl. He promises to get her something from a bazaar, but he gets there late and is unable to buy anything. The story ends with him standing in the darkened hall of the bazaar.

When you consider this bare-bones plot, "Araby" doesn't seem to be much of a story. A traditional story deals with some significant action, but "Araby" deals with a simple action

National Library of Ireland, Department of Print and Drawings.

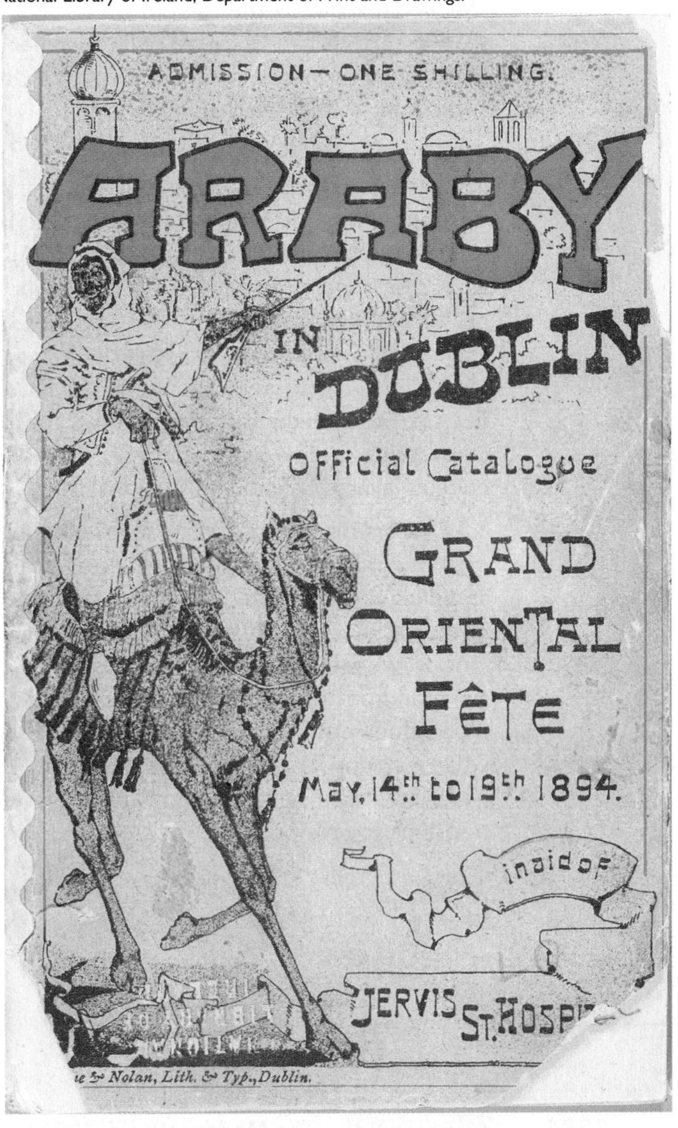

that comes to nothing. The protagonist fails to reach the goal he has been struggling to achieve, and in the end he is revealed to himself as the very opposite of the person he dreamed he was. "Araby" is ironic—both in its form and in many of its details.

In Greek comedy, an *eiron* was a character who was not what he appeared to be. From that Greek term comes *irony,* which in all its varieties also refers to things that are not what they appear to be.

1. Verbal irony. The most common form of irony is **verbal irony,** in which you say the opposite of what you really mean. We often use verbal irony in conversation. When asked how you feel after a really terrible day, you might say, for example, "I feel just great." We would know by the tone of your voice that you are being ironic—in reality, you feel anything but great. **Sarcasm** is a very broad and cutting form of verbal irony.

2. Situational irony. Another form of irony is **situational irony,** in which things turn out differently from what is expected. In its simplest form, this can involve a cartoon character laughing so hard at someone who has slipped on a banana peel that she herself walks right into an open manhole. In its most sophisticated form, as in Sophocles' *Oedipus Rex,* the hero, Oedipus, in trying to escape a curse, brings it down upon himself. Surprise endings invariably feature situational irony.

3. Dramatic irony. A third form of irony, dramatic irony, occurs when readers or an audience knows something that a character does not know. In "Little Red Riding Hood," we know the wolf has dressed in the grandmother's clothes, but Red Riding Hood does not. This discrepancy between what we know and what the characters know creates a sense of irony and a degree of dramatic tension.

4. Romance versus reality. In "Araby" almost all of the irony stems from the discrepancy between the narrator's romantic view of things and the way things really are. The boy's love for Mangan's sister is obviously overblown, an adolescent crush on someone he does not actually know. In pursuit of his love, he seeks some exotic gift from Araby, but this, too, becomes an ironic quest: In reality, he has simply taken a suburban train to a charity bazaar and returned empty-handed. In addition, through the aunt and uncle, the story shows that love in the real world—at least married love in Dublin—is not the ideal the boy imagines. It is, rather, marriage between an ineffectual woman and a man who comes home late and drunk.

But the ironies in "Araby" go still further. The hero's love and the quest he undertakes are directly associated with religion: "I imagined that I bore my chalice safely through a throng of foes. Her name sprang to my lips at moments in strange prayers and praises which I myself did not understand." Worshiping Mangan's sister is as much a religious act as an emotional one, and when his romantic dreams are shattered, his disillusion is not just with love, but with all of his spiritual values. Just as the aunt and uncle represent the reality of love, the reality of the religious part of the narrator's quest is represented by the dead priest and his rusty bicycle pump.

For Joyce, modern Ireland—its society, religion, and culture—was in a state of decay. The gap between the ideals of Ireland's past and the reality of its present was the chief source of his sense of irony.

Finding examples of irony. Illustrate the three types of irony described here with examples of your own. Your examples might be drawn from actual life, books, plays, films, personal experience, or your imagination. Do you think there is still a discrepancy between social ideals and reality today?

D. H. Lawrence

(1885–1930)

England

David Herbert Lawrence was born in the English Midlands, the frailest child of a coal miner and a former schoolteacher. An able scholar, he too chose to become a teacher, for he resented the physical and spiritual ugliness that mining had brought about in the Midlands.

While he was teaching, Lawrence began publishing poems and stories in magazines. In 1912, a year after publishing his first novel, Lawrence called on his former professor, Ernest Weekley, and became enchanted with Weekley's German-born wife, Frieda. Within weeks, Frieda Weekley had left her husband and three children and fled with Lawrence to Germany. For the next two years the couple traveled through Austria and Italy. During this short time, Lawrence finished his novel *Sons and Lovers* (1913) and began work on two others, *The Rainbow* (1915) and *Women in Love* (1920).

Reviews of *Sons and Lovers* were cautiously favorable, but the moral controversy over Lawrence's work was already heating up. While in Italy, Lawrence began to see industrialized England as corrosive and oppressive and the Victorian world he had known as overcivilized and prudish. He embraced a belief in "blood knowledge," in putting one's animal self in balance with one's intellect. Returning to England in 1914, he announced that "the source of all life and knowledge is in man and woman, and the source of all living is in the interchange and the meeting and mingling of these two." When a privately printed edition of Lawrence's novel *Women in Love* was published in 1920, one London critic judged it "a loathsome study of sex depravity leading youth to unspeakable disaster."

Around this time a wealthy American writer, Mabel Dodge Luhan, who deeply admired Lawrence's work, invited him to come to Taos, New Mexico. Lawrence found New Mexico gorgeous, but he had his doubts about Americans, calling them "a host of people who must all have a sense of inferiority complex somewhere, striving to make good over everybody else." Meanwhile, in New York, those Lawrence called "the vice people" had been trying to suppress publication of *Women in Love*. Lawrence rejoiced to learn that a magistrate had declared that his novels were not obscene and in fact made a "distinct contribution to the literature of the present day."

By now, however, Lawrence was growing used to the attacks his work provoked on each publication day. But then he learned that he had incurable tuberculosis. Knowing he had only a few years remaining, Lawrence left the United States and returned to Italy. He now wrote continually, producing *Lady Chatterley's Lover* (1928), the work for which he is best remembered. The book drew new waves of anger from the censors. U.S. customs officers seized copies as they arrived on the docks, and the novel was banned in Britain.

Giving in at last to doctors' advice, Lawrence retreated in early 1930 to a sanitarium in southern France, where he wrote every day until the end of his life. On March 2, 1930, with Frieda at his bedside, Lawrence died. He is buried at Taos.

Before You Read

The Rocking-Horse Winner

Make the Connection

Quickwrite

The old saying that "the love of money is the root of all evil" dates back to the Bible. Over the centuries, immeasurable evil—hatred, war, murder—has sprung from the desire for riches. Even on the most personal level—wife to husband, parent to child, friend to friend—the craving for wealth can have devastating effects.

Jot down some associations about money—and what people will do to get it—that come to mind.

Literary Focus

Symbol

Beginning with the title, the image of a child's rocking horse dominates this story. The horse is associated with every important development in the plot. As the story's tragedy unfolds, the horse seems to take on more than its literal meaning as a child's toy. It is slowly transformed into a **symbol,** richly suggestive of emotions, themes, and meanings for the story as a whole.

A **symbol** is a person, place, thing, or event that stands both for itself and for something beyond itself.

For more on Symbol, see the Handbook of Literary and Historical Terms.

Literary Skills
Understand symbols.

INTERNET
Vocabulary Practice
Keyword: LE7 12-7

Background

Lawrence saw men and women as torn between the promptings of their instincts (which he saw as natural and therefore good) and the demanding voices of their upbringing and education (which he saw as destructive). As you read "The Rocking-Horse Winner," which is told like a modern fable, notice which voices are most dominant in the house and what effects these voices have on the characters.

Vocabulary Development

asserted (ə•sʉrt′id) *v.:* declared.

obscure (əb•skyoor′) *adj.:* little-known.

reiterated (rē•it′ə•rāt′id) *v.:* repeated.

uncanny (un•kan′ē) *adj.:* strange; eerie; weird.

iridescent (ir′i•des′ənt) *adj.:* showing rainbowlike colors.

overwrought (ō′vər•rôt′) *adj.:* overly excited.

remonstrated (ri•män′strāt′id) *v.:* protested.

arrested (ə•rest′id) *v.* used as *adj.:* checked or halted in motion.

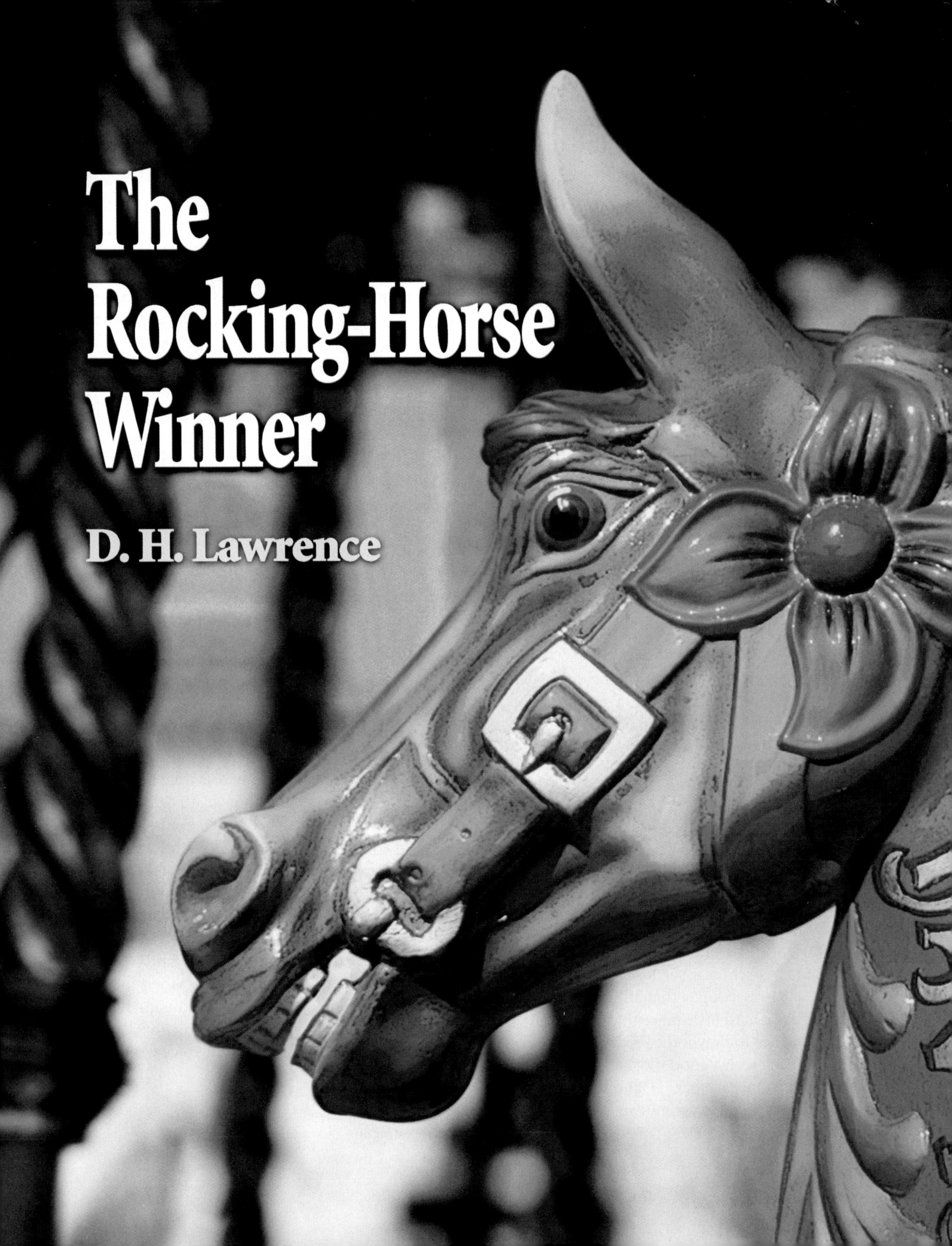
The Rocking-Horse Winner
D. H. Lawrence

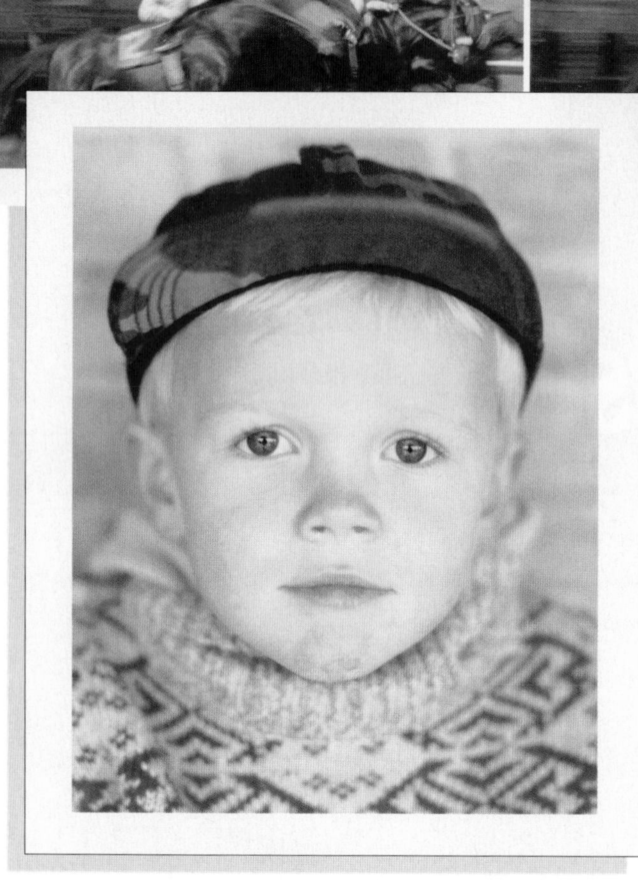

There was a woman who was beautiful, who started with all the advantages, yet she had no luck. She married for love, and the love turned to dust. She had bonny children, yet she felt they had been thrust upon her, and she could not love them. They looked at her coldly, as if they were finding fault with her. And hurriedly she felt she must cover up some fault in herself. Yet what it was that she must cover up she never knew. Nevertheless, when her children were present, she always felt the center of her heart go hard. This troubled her, and in her manner she was all the more gentle and anxious for her children, as if she loved them very much. Only she herself knew that at the center of her heart was a hard little place that could not feel love, no, not for anybody. Everybody else said of her: "She is such a good mother. She adores her children." Only she herself, and her children themselves, knew it was not so. They read it in each other's eyes.

There were a boy and two little girls. They lived in a pleasant house, with a garden, and they had discreet servants, and felt themselves superior to anyone in the neighborhood.

Although they lived in style, they felt always an anxiety in the house. There was never enough money. The mother had a small income,[1] and the father had a small income, but not nearly enough for the social position which they had to keep up. The father went into town to some office. But though he had good prospects, these prospects never materialized. There was always the grinding sense of the shortage of money, though the style was always kept up.

At last the mother said: "I will see if *I* can't make something." But she did not know where to begin. She racked her brains, and tried this thing and the other, but could not find anything successful. The failure made deep lines come into her face. Her children were growing up, they would have to go to school. There must be more money, there must be more money. The father, who was always very handsome and expensive in his tastes, seemed as if he never *would* be able to do anything worth doing. And the mother, who had a great belief in herself, did not succeed any better, and her tastes were just as expensive.

And so the house came to be haunted by the unspoken phrase: *There must be more money! There must be more money!* The children could hear it all the time, though nobody said it aloud. They heard it at Christmas, when the expensive and splendid toys filled the nursery. Behind the shining modern rocking horse, behind the smart doll's house, a voice would

1. **income** *n.:* money from an inheritance or investments—not a salary.

start whispering: "There *must* be more money! There *must* be more money!" And the children would stop playing, to listen for a moment. They would look into each other's eyes, to see if they had all heard. And each one saw in the eyes of the other two that they too had heard. "There *must* be more money! There *must* be more money!"

It came whispering from the springs of the still-swaying rocking horse, and even the horse, bending his wooden, champing head, heard it. The big doll, sitting so pink and smirking in her new pram,[2] could hear it quite plainly, and seemed to be smirking all the more self-consciously because of it. The foolish puppy, too, that took the place of the teddy bear, he was looking so extraordinarily foolish for no other reason but that he heard the secret whisper all over the house: "There *must* be more money!"

Yet nobody ever said it aloud. The whisper was everywhere, and therefore no one spoke it. Just as no one ever says: "We are breathing!" in spite of the fact that breath is coming and going all the time.

"Mother," said the boy Paul one day, "why don't we keep a car of our own? Why do we always use uncle's, or else a taxi?"

"Because we're the poor members of the family," said the mother.

"But why *are* we, mother?"

"Well—I suppose," she said slowly and bitterly, "it's because your father has no luck."

The boy was silent for some time.

"Is luck money, mother?" he asked, rather timidly.

"No, Paul. Not quite. It's what causes you to have money."

"Oh!" said Paul vaguely. "I thought when Uncle Oscar said *filthy lucker,* it meant money."

"*Filthy lucre*[3] does mean money," said the mother. "But it's lucre, not luck."

"Oh!" said the boy. "Then what is luck, mother?"

"It's what causes you to have money. If you're lucky you have money. That's why it's better to be born lucky than rich. If you're rich, you may lose your money. But if you're lucky, you will always get more money."

"Oh! Will you? And is father not lucky?"

"Very unlucky, I should say," she said bitterly.

The boy watched her with unsure eyes.

"Why?" he asked.

"I don't know. Nobody ever knows why one person is lucky and another unlucky."

"Don't they? Nobody at all? Does *nobody* know?"

"Perhaps God. But He never tells."

"He ought to, then. And aren't you lucky either, mother?"

"I can't be, if I married an unlucky husband."

"But by yourself, aren't you?"

"I used to think I was, before I married. Now I think I am very unlucky indeed."

"Why?"

"Well—never mind! Perhaps I'm not really," she said.

The child looked at her to see if she meant it. But he saw, by the lines of her mouth, that she was only trying to hide something from him.

"Well, anyhow," he said stoutly, "I'm a lucky person."

"Why?" said his mother, with a sudden laugh.

He stared at her. He didn't even know why he had said it.

---

2. **pram** *n.:* chiefly British for "baby carriage." The word is short for *perambulator.*

3. **filthy lucre** (lo͞o′kər): riches (a derogatory usage).

"God told me," he asserted, brazening it out.[4]

"I hope He did, dear!" she said, again with a laugh, but rather bitter.

"He did, mother!"

"Excellent!" said the mother, using one of her husband's exclamations.

The boy saw she did not believe him; or rather, that she paid no attention to his assertion. This angered him somewhere, and made him want to compel her attention.

He went off by himself, vaguely, in a childish way, seeking for the clue to "luck." Absorbed, taking no heed of other people, he went about with a sort of stealth, seeking inwardly for luck. He wanted luck, he wanted it, he wanted it. When the two girls were playing dolls in the nursery, he would sit on his big rocking horse, charging madly into space, with a frenzy that made the little girls peer at him uneasily. Wildly the horse careered,[5] the waving dark hair of the boy tossed, his eyes had a strange glare in them. The little girls dared not speak to him.

When he had ridden to the end of his mad little journey, he climbed down and stood in front of his rocking horse, staring fixedly into its lowered face. Its red mouth was slightly open, its big eye was wide and glassy-bright.

"Now!" he would silently command the snorting steed. "Now, take me to where there is luck! Now take me!"

And he would slash the horse on the neck with the little whip he had asked Uncle Oscar for. He *knew* the horse could take him to where there was luck, if only he forced it. So he would mount again and start on his furious ride, hoping at last to get there. He knew he could get there.

"You'll break your horse, Paul!" said the nurse.

"He's always riding like that! I wish he'd leave off!" said his elder sister Joan.

But he only glared down on them in silence. Nurse gave him up. She could make nothing of him. Anyhow, he was growing beyond her.

One day his mother and his Uncle Oscar came in when he was on one of his furious rides. He did not speak to them.

"Hallo, you young jockey! Riding a winner?" said his uncle.

"Aren't you growing too big for a rocking horse? You're not a very little boy any longer, you know," said his mother.

But Paul only gave a blue glare from his big, rather close-set eyes. He would speak to nobody when he was in full tilt. His mother watched him with an anxious expression on her face.

At last he suddenly stopped forcing his horse into the mechanical gallop and slid down.

"Well, I got there!" he announced fiercely, his blue eyes still flaring, and his sturdy long legs straddling apart.

"Where did you get to?" asked his mother.

"Where I wanted to go," he flared back at her.

"That's right, son!" said Uncle Oscar. "Don't you stop till you get there. What's the horse's name?"

"He doesn't have a name," said the boy.

"Gets on without all right?" asked the uncle.

"Well, he has different names. He was called Sansovino last week."

"Sansovino, eh? Won the Ascot.[6] How did you know this name?"

"He always talks about horse races with Bassett," said Joan.

The uncle was delighted to find that his small nephew was posted with all the racing news. Bassett, the young gardener, who had been wounded in the left foot in the war and had got his present job through Oscar Cresswell, whose batman[7] he had been, was a perfect blade of the "turf."[8] He lived in the racing events, and the small boy lived with him.

Oscar Cresswell got it all from Bassett.

"Master Paul comes and asks me, so I can't do more than tell him, sir," said Bassett, his face

4. **brazening it out:** acting boldly.
5. **careered** *v.:* rushed.

6. **Ascot:** famous horse race held annually at Ascot Heath in England. Several traditional British races are mentioned in the story.
7. **batman** *n.:* officer's personal attendant.
8. **blade of the "turf":** stylish young racing fan.

Vocabulary

asserted (ə·surt′id) *v.:* declared.

terribly serious, as if he were speaking of religious matters.

"And does he ever put anything on a horse he fancies?"

"Well—I don't want to give him away—he's a young sport, a fine sport, sir. Would you mind asking him himself? He sort of takes a pleasure in it, and perhaps he'd feel I was giving him away, sir, if you don't mind."

Bassett was serious as a church.

The uncle went back to his nephew and took him off for a ride in the car.

"Say, Paul, old man, do you ever put anything on a horse?" the uncle asked.

The boy watched the handsome man closely.

"Why, do you think I oughtn't to?" he parried.

Private Collection/The Bridgeman Art Library.

"Not a bit of it! I thought perhaps you might give me a tip for the Lincoln."

The car sped on into the country, going down to Uncle Oscar's place in Hampshire.

"Honor bright?" said the nephew.

"Honor bright, son!" said the uncle.

"Well, then, Daffodil."

"Daffodil! I doubt it, sonny. What about Mirza?"

"I only know the winner," said the boy. "That's Daffodil."

"Daffodil, eh?"

There was a pause. Daffodil was an obscure horse comparatively.

"Uncle!"

"Yes, son?"

"You won't let it go any further, will you? I promised Bassett."

"Bassett be damned, old man! What's he got to do with it?"

"We're partners. We've been partners from the first. Uncle, he lent me my first five shillings, which I lost. I promised him, honor bright, it was only between me and him; only you gave me that ten-shilling note I started winning with, so I thought you were lucky. You won't let it go any further, will you?"

The boy gazed at his uncle from those big, hot, blue eyes, set rather close together. The uncle stirred and laughed uneasily.

"Right you are, son! I'll keep your tip private. Daffodil, eh? How much are you putting on him?"

"All except twenty pounds," said the boy. "I keep that in reserve."

The uncle thought it a good joke.

"You keep twenty pounds in reserve, do you, you young romancer?[9] What are you betting, then?"

"I'm betting three hundred," said the boy gravely. "But it's between you and me, Uncle Oscar! Honor bright?"

The uncle burst into a roar of laughter.

"It's between you and me all right, you young Nat Gould,"[10] he said, laughing. "But where's your three hundred?"

"Bassett keeps it for me. We're partners."

"You are, are you! And what is Bassett putting on Daffodil?"

"He won't go quite as high as I do, I expect. Perhaps he'll go a hundred and fifty."

"What, pennies?" laughed the uncle.

"Pounds," said the child, with a surprised look at his uncle. "Bassett keeps a bigger reserve than I do."

---

9. romancer *n.:* imaginative storyteller.

10. Nat Gould: famous British authority on racing.

Vocabulary

obscure (əb•skyoor′) *adj.:* little-known.

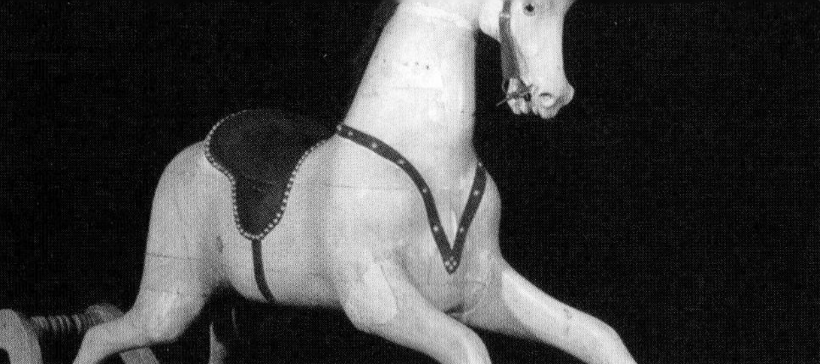

Between wonder and amusement Uncle Oscar was silent. He pursued the matter no further, but he determined to take his nephew with him to the Lincoln races.

"Now, son," he said, "I'm putting twenty on Mirza, and I'll put five on for you on any horse you fancy. What's your pick?"

"Daffodil, uncle."

"No, not the fiver on Daffodil!"

"I should if it was my own fiver," said the child.

"Good! Good! Right you are! A fiver for me and a fiver for you on Daffodil."

The child had never been to a race meeting before, and his eyes were blue fire. He pursed his mouth tight and watched. A Frenchman just in front had put his money on Lancelot. Wild with excitement, he flayed his arms up and down, yelling *"Lancelot! Lancelot!"* in his French accent.

Daffodil came in first, Lancelot second, Mirza third. The child, flushed and with eyes blazing, was curiously serene. His uncle brought him four five-pound notes, four to one.

"What am I to do with these?" he cried, waving them before the boy's eyes.

"I suppose we'll talk to Bassett," said the boy. "I expect I have fifteen hundred now; and twenty in reserve; and this twenty."

His uncle studied him for some moments.

"Look here, son!" he said. "You're not serious about Bassett and that fifteen hundred, are you?"

"Yes, I am. But it's between you and me, uncle. Honor bright?"

"Honor bright all right, son! But I must talk to Bassett."

"If you'd like to be a partner, uncle, with Bassett and me, we could all be partners. Only, you'd have to promise, honor bright, uncle, not to let it go beyond us three. Bassett and I are lucky, and you must be lucky, because it was your ten shillings I started winning with. . . ."

Uncle Oscar took both Bassett and Paul into Richmond Park for an afternoon, and there they talked.

"It's like this, you see, sir," Bassett said. "Master Paul would get me talking about racing events, spinning yarns, you know, sir. And he was always keen on knowing if I'd made or if I'd lost. It's about a year since, now, that I put five shillings on Blush of Dawn for him: And we lost. Then the luck turned, with that ten shillings he had from you: That we put on Singhalese. And since that time, it's been pretty steady, all things considering. What do you say, Master Paul?"

"We're all right when we're sure," said Paul. "It's when we're not quite sure that we go down."

"Oh, but we're careful then," said Bassett.

"But when are you *sure*?" smiled Uncle Oscar.

"It's Master Paul, sir," said Bassett in a secret, religious voice. "It's as if he had it from heaven. Like Daffodil, now, for the Lincoln. That was as sure as eggs."

"Did you put anything on Daffodil?" asked Oscar Cresswell.

"Yes, sir. I made my bit."

"And my nephew?"

Bassett was obstinately silent, looking at Paul.

"I made twelve hundred, didn't I, Bassett? I told uncle I was putting three hundred on Daffodil."

"That's right," said Bassett, nodding.

"But where's the money?" asked the uncle.

"I keep it safe locked up, sir. Master Paul he can have it any minute he likes to ask for it."

"What, fifteen hundred pounds?"

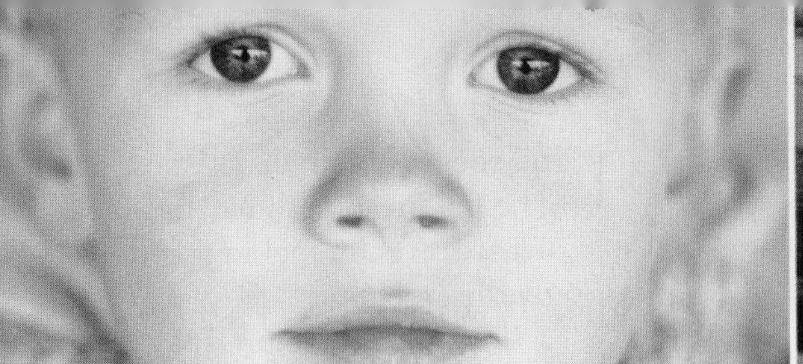

"And twenty! And *forty*, that is, with the twenty he made on the course."

"It's amazing!" said the uncle.

"If Master Paul offers you to be partners, sir, I would, if I were you: if you'll excuse me," said Bassett.

Oscar Cresswell thought about it.

"I'll see the money," he said.

They drove home again, and sure enough, Bassett came round to the garden house with fifteen hundred pounds in notes. The twenty pounds reserve was left with Joe Glee, in the Turf Commission[11] deposit.

"You see, it's all right, uncle, when I'm *sure*! Then we go strong, for all we're worth. Don't we, Bassett?"

"We do that, Master Paul."

"And when are you sure?" said the uncle, laughing.

"Oh, well, sometimes I'm *absolutely* sure, like about Daffodil," said the boy; "and sometimes I have an idea; and sometimes I haven't even an idea, have I, Bassett? Then we're careful, because we mostly go down."

"You do, do you! And when you're sure, like about Daffodil, what makes you sure, sonny?"

"Oh, well, I don't know," said the boy uneasily. "I'm sure, you know, uncle; that's all."

"It's as if he had it from heaven, sir." Bassett reiterated.

"I should say so!" said the uncle.

But he became a partner. And when the Leger was coming on Paul was "sure" about Lively Spark, which was a quite inconsiderable horse. The boy insisted on putting a thousand on the horse, Bassett went for five hundred, and Oscar Cresswell two hundred. Lively Spark came in first, and the betting had been ten to one against him. Paul had made ten thousand.

"You see," he said, "I was absolutely sure of him."

Even Oscar Cresswell had cleared two thousand.

"Look here, son," he said, "this sort of thing makes me nervous."

"It needn't, uncle! Perhaps I shan't be sure again for a long time."

"But what are you going to do with your money?" asked the uncle.

"Of course," said the boy, "I started it for mother. She said she had no luck, because father is unlucky, so I thought if *I* was lucky, it might stop whispering."

"What might stop whispering?"

"Our house. I *hate* our house for whispering."

"What does it whisper?"

"Why—why"—the boy fidgeted—"why, I don't know. But it's always short of money, you know, uncle."

"I know it, son, I know it."

"You know people send mother writs,[12] don't you, uncle?"

"I'm afraid I do," said the uncle.

"And then the house whispers, like people laughing at you behind your back. It's awful, that is! I thought if I was lucky——"

---

11. **Turf Commission:** committee of the Jockey Club, the chief governing body for horse racing. This committee operates a bank in which bettors can deposit money for future bets.

12. **writs** *n. pl.:* legal papers; here, those demanding payment.

Vocabulary

reiterated (rē•it′ə•rāt′id) *v.:* repeated.

"You might stop it," added the uncle.

The boy watched him with big blue eyes, that had an uncanny cold fire in them, and he said never a word.

"Well, then!" said the uncle. "What are we doing?"

"I shouldn't like mother to know I was lucky," said the boy.

"Why not, son?"

"She'd stop me."

"I don't think she would."

"Oh!"—and the boy writhed in an odd way—"I *don't* want her to know, uncle."

"All right, son! We'll manage it without her knowing."

They managed it very easily. Paul, at the other's suggestion, handed over five thousand pounds to his uncle, who deposited it with the family lawyer, who was then to inform Paul's mother that a relative had put five thousand pounds into his hands, which sum was to be paid out a thousand pounds at a time, on the mother's birthday, for the next five years.

"So she'll have a birthday present of a thousand pounds for five successive years," said Uncle Oscar. "I hope it won't make it all the harder for her later."

Paul's mother had her birthday in November. The house had been "whispering" worse than ever lately, and, even in spite of his luck, Paul could not bear up against it. He was very anxious to see the effect of the birthday letter, telling his mother about the thousand pounds.

When there were no visitors, Paul now took his meals with his parents, as he was beyond the nursery control. His mother went into town nearly every day. She had discovered that she had an odd knack of sketching furs and dress materials, so she worked secretly in the studio of a friend who was the chief "artist" for the leading drapers.[13] She drew the figures of ladies in furs and ladies in silk and sequins for the newspaper advertisements. This young woman artist earned several thousand pounds a year, but Paul's mother only made several hundreds, and she was again dissatisfied. She so wanted to be first in something, and she did not succeed, even in making sketches for drapery advertisements.

She was down to breakfast on the morning of her birthday. Paul watched her face as she read her letters. He knew the lawyer's letter. As his mother read it, her face hardened and became more expressionless. Then a cold, determined look came on her mouth. She hid the letter under the pile of others, and said not a word about it.

"Didn't you have anything nice in the post for your birthday, mother?" said Paul.

"Quite moderately nice," she said, her voice cold and absent.

She went away to town without saying more.

But in the afternoon Uncle Oscar appeared. He said Paul's mother had had a long interview with the lawyer, asking if the whole five thousand could not be advanced at once, as she was in debt.

"What do you think, uncle?" said the boy.

"I leave it to you, son."

"Oh, let her have it, then! We can get some more with the other," said the boy.

"A bird in the hand is worth two in the bush, laddie!" said Uncle Oscar.

"But I'm sure to *know* for the Grand National; or the Lincolnshire; or else the Derby. I'm sure to know for *one* of them," said Paul.

So Uncle Oscar signed the agreement, and Paul's mother touched the whole five thousand. Then something very curious happened. The voices in the house suddenly went mad, like a chorus of frogs on a spring evening. There were certain new furnishings, and Paul had a tutor. He was *really* going to Eton,[14] his father's school, in the following autumn. There were flowers in the winter, and a blossoming of the luxury Paul's mother had been used to. And yet the voices in the house, behind the sprays of

13. **drapers** *n. pl.:* dealers in cloth and dry goods.

14. **Eton:** Eton College, a private prep school for boys, near London.

Vocabulary

uncanny (un•kan′ē) *adj.:* strange; eerie; weird.

mimosa and almond blossom, and from under the piles of iridescent cushions, simply trilled and screamed in a sort of ecstasy: "There *must* be more money! Oh-h-h; there must be more money. Oh, now, now-w! Now-w-w—there *must* be more money!—more than ever! More than ever!"

It frightened Paul terribly. He studied away at his Latin and Greek with his tutor. But his intense hours were spent with Bassett. The Grand National had gone by: He had not "known," and had lost a hundred pounds. Summer was at hand. He was in agony for the Lincoln. But even for the Lincoln he didn't "know," and he lost fifty pounds. He became wild-eyed and strange, as if something were going to explode in him.

"Let it alone, son! Don't you bother about it!" urged Uncle Oscar. But it was as if the boy couldn't really hear what his uncle was saying.

"I've got to know for the Derby! I've got to know for the Derby!" the child reiterated, his big blue eyes blazing with a sort of madness.

His mother noticed how overwrought he was.

"You'd better go to the seaside. Wouldn't you like to go now to the seaside, instead of waiting? I think you'd better," she said, looking down at him anxiously, her heart curiously heavy because of him.

But the child lifted his uncanny blue eyes.

"I couldn't possibly go before the Derby, mother!" he said. "I couldn't possibly!"

"Why not?" she said, her voice becoming heavy when she was opposed. "Why not? You can still go from the seaside to see the Derby with your Uncle Oscar, if that's what you wish. No need for you to wait here. Besides, I think you care too much about these races. It's a bad sign. My family has been a gambling family, and you won't know till you grow up how much damage it has done. But it has done damage. I shall have to send Bassett away, and ask Uncle Oscar not to talk racing to you, unless you promise to be reasonable about it: Go away to the seaside and forget it. You're all nerves!"

"I'll do what you like, mother, so long as you don't send me away till after the Derby," the boy said.

"Send you away from where? Just from this house?"

"Yes," he said, gazing at her.

"Why, you curious child, what makes you care about this house so much, suddenly? I never knew you loved it."

He gazed at her without speaking. He had a secret within a secret, something he had not

Vocabulary

iridescent (ir′i • des′ənt) *adj.:* showing rainbowlike colors.
overwrought (ō′vər • rôt′) *adj.:* overly excited.

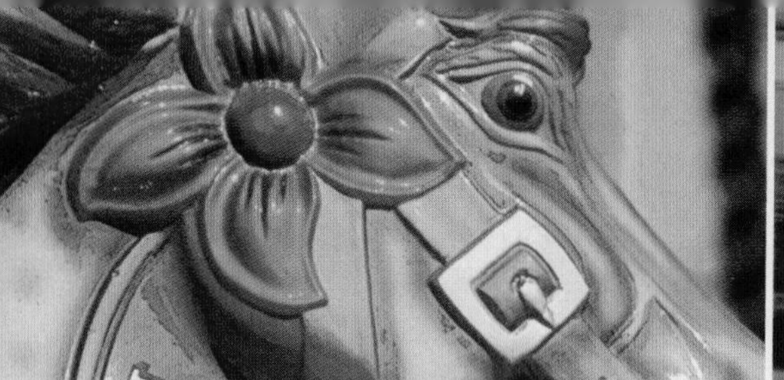

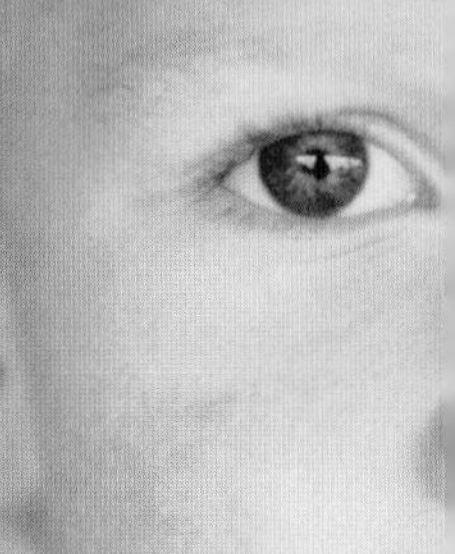

divulged, even to Bassett or to his Uncle Oscar.

But his mother, after standing undecided and a little bit sullen for some moments, said:

"Very well, then! Don't go to the seaside till after the Derby, if you don't wish it. But promise me you won't let your nerves go to pieces. Promise you won't think so much about horse racing and *events*, as you call them!"

"Oh no," said the boy casually, "I won't think much about them, mother. You needn't worry. I wouldn't worry, mother, if I were you."

"If you were me and I were you," said his mother, "I wonder what we *should* do!"

"But you know you needn't worry, mother, don't you?" the boy repeated.

"I should be awfully glad to know it," she said wearily.

"Oh, well, you *can*, you know. I mean, you *ought* to know you needn't worry," he insisted.

"Ought I? Then I'll see about it," she said.

Paul's secret of secrets was his wooden horse, that which had no name. Since he was emancipated from a nurse and a nursery-governess, he had had his rocking horse removed to his own bedroom at the top of the house.

"Surely you're too big for a rocking horse!" his mother had remonstrated.

"Well, you see, mother, till I can have a *real* horse, I like to have *some* sort of animal about," had been his quaint answer.

"Do you feel he keeps you company?" she laughed.

"Oh yes! He's very good, he always keeps me company, when I'm there," said Paul.

So the horse, rather shabby, stood in an arrested prance in the boy's bedroom.

The Derby was drawing near, and the boy grew more and more tense. He hardly heard what was spoken to him, he was very frail, and his eyes were really uncanny. His mother had sudden strange seizures of uneasiness about him. Sometimes, for half an hour, she would feel a sudden anxiety about him that was almost anguish. She wanted to rush to him at once, and know he was safe.

Two nights before the Derby, she was at a big party in town, when one of her rushes of anxiety about her boy, her firstborn, gripped her heart till she could hardly speak. She fought with the feeling, might and main, for she believed in common sense. But it was too strong. She had to leave the dance and go downstairs to telephone to the country. The children's nursery-governess was terribly surprised and startled at being rung up in the night.

"Are the children all right, Miss Wilmot?"

"Oh yes, they are quite all right."

"Master Paul? Is he all right?"

"He went to bed as right as a trivet. Shall I run up and look at him?"

"No," said Paul's mother reluctantly. "No! Don't trouble. It's all right. Don't sit up. We shall be home fairly soon." She did not want her son's privacy intruded upon.

"Very good," said the governess.

It was about one o'clock when Paul's mother and father drove up to their house. All was still. Paul's mother went to her room and slipped off her white fur cloak. She had told her maid not to wait up for her. She heard her husband downstairs, mixing a whiskey and soda.

Vocabulary

remonstrated (ri•män′strāt′id) *v.:* protested.

arrested (ə•rest′id) *v.* used as *adj.:* checked or halted in motion.

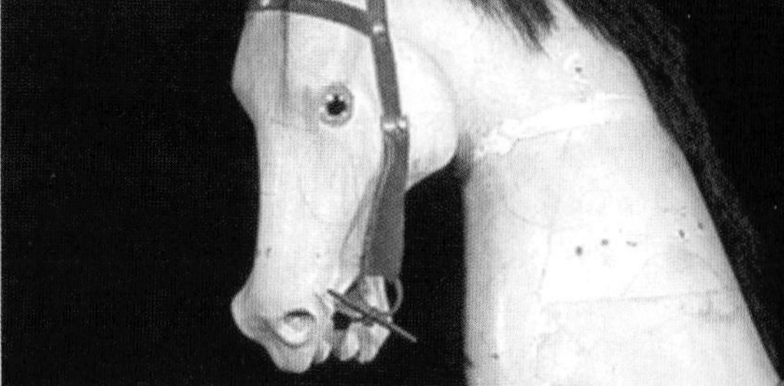

And then, because of the strange anxiety at her heart, she stole upstairs to her son's room. Noiselessly she went along the upper corridor. Was there a faint noise? What was it?

She stood, with arrested muscles, outside his door, listening. There was a strange, heavy, and yet not loud noise. Her heart stood still. It was a soundless noise, yet rushing and powerful. Something huge, in violent, hushed motion. What was it? What in God's name was it? She ought to know. She felt that she knew the noise. She knew what it was.

Yet she could not place it. She couldn't say what it was. And on and on it went, like a madness.

Softly, frozen with anxiety and fear, she turned the door handle.

The room was dark. Yet in the space near the window, she heard and saw something plunging to and fro. She gazed in fear and amazement.

Then suddenly she switched on the light, and saw her son, in his green pajamas, madly surging on the rocking horse. The blaze of light suddenly lit him up, as he urged the wooden horse, and lit her up, as she stood, blonde, in her dress of pale green and crystal, in the doorway.

"Paul!" she cried. "Whatever are you doing?"

"It's Malabar!" he screamed in a powerful, strange voice. "It's Malabar!"

His eyes blazed at her for one strange and senseless second, as he ceased urging his wooden horse. Then he fell with a crash to the ground, and she, all her tormented motherhood flooding upon her, rushed to gather him up.

But he was unconscious, and unconscious he remained, with some brain fever. He talked and tossed, and his mother sat stonily by his side.

"Malabar! It's Malabar! Bassett, Bassett, I *know*! It's Malabar!"

So the child cried, trying to get up and urge the rocking horse that gave him his inspiration.

"What does he mean by Malabar?" asked the heart-frozen mother.

"I don't know," said the father stonily.

"What does he mean by Malabar?" she asked her brother Oscar.

"It's one of the horses running for the Derby," was the answer.

And, in spite of himself, Oscar Cresswell spoke to Bassett, and himself put a thousand on Malabar: at fourteen to one.

The third day of the illness was critical: They were waiting for a change. The boy, with his rather long, curly hair, was tossing ceaselessly on the pillow. He neither slept nor regained consciousness, and his eyes were like blue stones. His mother sat, feeling her heart had gone, turned actually into a stone.

In the evening, Oscar Cresswell did not come, but Bassett sent a message, saying could he come up for one moment, just one moment? Paul's mother was very angry at the intrusion, but on second thoughts she agreed. The boy was the same. Perhaps Bassett might bring him to consciousness.

The gardener, a shortish fellow with a little brown moustache and sharp little brown eyes, tiptoed into the room, touched his imaginary cap to Paul's mother, and stole to the bedside, staring with glittering, smallish eyes at the tossing, dying child.

"Master Paul!" he whispered. "Master Paul! Malabar came in first all right, a clean win. I did as you told me. You've made over seventy thousand pounds, you have; you've got over eighty thousand. Malabar came in all right, Master Paul."

"Malabar! Malabar! Did I say Malabar, mother? Did I say Malabar? Do you think I'm lucky, mother? I knew Malabar, didn't I? Over eighty thousand pounds! I call that lucky, don't you, mother? Over eighty thousand pounds! I knew, didn't I know I knew? Malabar came in all right. If I ride my horse till I'm sure, then I tell you, Bassett, you can go as high as you like. Did you go for all you were worth, Bassett?"

"I went a thousand on it, Master Paul."

"I never told you, mother, that if I can ride my horse, and *get there,* then I'm absolutely sure—oh, absolutely! Mother, did I ever tell you? I *am* lucky!"

"No, you never did," said his mother.

But the boy died in the night.

And even as he lay dead, his mother heard her brother's voice saying to her: "My God, Hester, you're eighty-odd thousand to the good, and a poor devil of a son to the bad. But, poor devil, poor devil, he's best gone out of a life where he rides his rocking horse to find a winner." ■

PRIMARY SOURCE / LETTER

D. H. Lawrence on Money

A theme that runs through nearly all Lawrence's works is the celebration of life—the human energy and force that express the joy of existence. Opposing this natural energy is materialism, which Lawrence believed misdirects our energies and warps the soul.

Rolf Gardiner, one of Lawrence's first admirers, managed a large farm in Dorset. In 1926, Lawrence wrote to Gardiner: "And don't be too ernest—earnest—how does one spell it?—nor overburdened by a mission: neither too self-willed. One must be simple and direct, and a bit free from oneself above all."

In another letter to Gardiner, Lawrence makes a rare, brief mention of the evils of materialism.

Villa Mirenda, Scandicci
Florence
18 Dec., 1927

Dear Rolf Gardiner,

. . . If I were talking to the young, I should say only one thing to them: Don't you live just to make money, either for yourself or for anybody else. Don't look on yourself as a wage slave. Try to find out what life itself is, and live. Repudiate the money idea.

And then I'd teach 'em, if I could, to dance and sing together. The togetherness is important.

But they must first overthrow in themselves the money-fear and money-lust. . . .

Response and Analysis

Reading Check

1. The opening, written in the style of a fairy tale, tells of a woman who "had no luck." How has she been unlucky? What else does the writer tell us directly about the mother's **character**?
2. How does Paul's mother define *luck* when Paul asks her what it means? What is Paul's confusion about the word *luck*?
3. What step does Paul take to ease his mother's anxiety over the family's debts? How does she react when she learns of her birthday surprise?
4. Who is Bassett? Why does he keep Paul's secret?
5. Does Paul solve his mother's problem? Why or why not?

Thinking Critically

6. How do you explain the ever louder voices in the house? In your opinion, why do only Paul and his sisters hear and react to the voices?
7. How would you describe what happens to Paul at the end of the story?
8. What might the rocking horse **symbolize**?
9. State the **theme,** or meaning, of the story in a sentence, using the words *love* and *money*. How does this theme apply to life today? Consult your Quickwrite notes for help.
10. How would you describe the **tone** of the story?

Extending and Evaluating

11. What do you think of Lawrence's decision to end the story as he did? In what ways is the story's ending a distortion of the usual fairy-tale ending? How does this ending support Lawrence's views on money and materialism as stated in the ***Primary Source*** on page 1198?

WRITING

Keeping Up with the Joneses

"The mother's extravagance results partly from social pressure—the need to keep up appearances." Find evidence in the story to support this statement, and write a brief **essay** in which you present that evidence.

Inside His Mind

Review **stream of consciousness** as a narrative form (see pages 1180–1181), and write an **interior monologue** in which you reveal the workings of Paul's mind as he rides his rocking horse to that tragic victory. What thoughts, feelings, and associations run through his mind?

Vocabulary Development

Rating Connotations

Connotations are the feelings associated with a word—feelings that go beyond a word's strict dictionary definition, or **denotation.** Often, connotations show shades of meaning or intensity. On a separate sheet of paper, use the symbols "+," "–," or "=" to show how the words in each of the following pairs compare in intensity. Use "+" if the vocabulary word on the left seems stronger, "–" if it seems weaker, and "=" if it seems equivalent in meaning to the word on the right.

1. asserted ( )	stated
2. obscure ( )	unknown
3. reiterated ( )	repeated
4. uncanny ( )	mysterious
5. iridescent ( )	rainbowlike
6. overwrought ( )	hysterical
7. remonstrated ( )	complained
8. arrested ( )	stopped

Literary Skills
Analyze symbols.

Writing Skills
Write an essay presenting evidence to support a claim. Write an interior monologue.

Vocabulary Skills
Understand and evaluate connotations.

INTERNET
Projects and Activities
Keyword: LE7 12-7

Anna Akhmatova

(1889–1966)

Russia

When writers express political views in their work, they often run into problems with government authorities. Anna Akhmatova (ak′mät′ə·və), however, was persecuted for many years because she did *not* write on political themes. In the years following the Russian Revolution in 1917, only "socially useful" art was tolerated. Akhmatova was viciously attacked and her poems suppressed because they were too personal.

Akhmatova grew up just outside St. Petersburg in the suburb that for centuries had been the summer palace of the czars, or emperors. Here she became part of the thriving artistic community of prerevolutionary St. Petersburg. The poetry that Akhmatova began publishing in 1912 illustrates ideas of **acmeism** (ak′mē·iz′əm), a movement she and her husband, the poet Nikolai Gumilev, helped found. A reaction to French symbolism (see page 1010), which was then fashionable in Russia, acmeism rejected ambiguous symbols and the symbolists' view of the artist as mystic. For Akhmatova the poet was not a visionary but a craftsperson patiently building poems from words.

Akhmatova's early successes came to an abrupt end with the Russian Revolution in 1917. Five years later her ex-husband was shot for allegedly plotting against the new Soviet government. Although he and Akhmatova were divorced at the time, she was deemed guilty by association and her poetry was suppressed. She was not allowed to publish at all from 1922 to 1940, and in 1946 she was expelled from the Soviet Writers' Union.

Throughout the years of Stalinist terror, Akhmatova watched as friends and colleagues were arrested and sent to prison camps, many never to return. Her own son was imprisoned until Stalin's death in 1953. Akhmatova's long poem "Requiem" captures those dark days in the image of an anonymous woman standing month after month outside a St. Petersburg prison waiting for news of a loved one.

Akhmatova's home became the refuge for and meeting place of a younger generation of Russian poets. In her final years she was recognized officially again and was even allowed to travel to the West.

Before You Read

Lot's Wife
All the unburied ones
I am not one of those who left the land

Make the Connection

Quickwrite

When a comforting place—a home, a community, or a relationship—becomes a source of pain and distress, what should you do? Flee for safety, or stay and fight for change? In a time when many of her compatriots were deserting a troubled homeland, the Russian poet Anna Akhmatova made a different decision—to stay. This decision, though wrenching, yielded some remarkable poetry—poetry that later served to remind a recovering people where they had been and what they had survived.

Jot down some notes describing how you might feel if you came under intense pressure to leave your homeland because life there had become intolerable. Would you regard such a departure as an act of desertion or as a wise investment in the future? Explain.

Literary Focus

Theme

As you read the following poems, you may notice that they share a common subject—exile and its aftermath. But what *about* this subject does each poem express? What **theme,** or central insight, does each poem convey? Remember that Akhmatova's poems were shaped by the political events of her time. With whom does the poet sympathize in each poem? Whom does she seem to blame or accuse? Answering these questions as you read may help you identify each poem's central message.

Theme is the central idea or insight of a work of literature.

For more on Theme, see the Handbook of Literary and Historical Terms.

Background

The following poems express different aspects of the suffering that resulted from Akhmatova's choice to remain in totalitarian Russia. The first, "Lot's Wife," is based on the biblical incident recounted in Genesis 19. Angered by the wickedness of the city of Sodom, God sends angels to punish the inhabitants. Only one man, Lot, is looked upon favorably by God. He is told to flee Sodom with his family and to never look back. As Lot's family escapes, however, his wife disobeys the command and turns her head to gaze upon the city. She is immediately turned into a pillar of salt. Akhmatova views the story of Lot's wife, an unwilling exile, from the perspective of a modern woman who was sorely tempted by the lure of exile but who resisted.

"Lot's Wife" was written in the 1920s, shortly after Akhmatova's former husband had been executed but before the worst years of the Stalin era. It was during this time that the poet made her difficult decision to stay in Russia rather than flee. The two poems that follow "Lot's Wife" reveal a harsher, more judgmental attitude toward those who made a different decision.

Literary Skills
Understand theme.

Lot's Wife

Anna Akhmatova

translated by **Richard Wilbur**

The just man followed then his angel guide
Where he strode on the black highway, hulking and bright;
But a wild grief in his wife's bosom cried,
Look back, it is not too late for a last sight

Of the red towers of your native Sodom, the square
Where once you sang, the gardens you shall mourn,
And the tall house with empty windows where
You loved your husband and your babes were born.

She turned, and looking on the bitter view
Her eyes were welded shut by mortal pain;
Into transparent salt her body grew,
And her quick feet were rooted in the plain.

Who would waste tears upon her? Is she not
The least of our losses, this unhappy wife?
Yet in my heart she will not be forgot
Who, for a single glance, gave up her life.

Head of Akhmatova (1913) by Natan Altman.
Museum Ludwig Köln.

All the unburied ones

Anna Akhmatova

translated by **Judith Hemschemeyer**

All the unburied ones—I buried them,
I mourned for them all, but who will mourn for me?

I am not one of those who left the land

Anna Akhmatova

translated by **Stanley Kunitz**

I am not one of those who left the land
to the mercy of its enemies.
Their flattery leaves me cold,
my songs are not for them to praise.

But I pity the exile's lot.
Like a felon, like a man half-dead,
dark is your path, wanderer;
wormwood° infects your foreign bread.

But here, in the murk of conflagration,°
where scarcely a friend is left to know,
we, the survivors, do not flinch
from anything, not from a single blow.

Surely the reckoning will be made after
the passing of this cloud.
We are the people without tears,
straighter than you . . . more proud . . .

Farmwoman in a Field (1931)
by Konstantin Rozhdestvyenski.

Museum Ludwig Köln.

---

8. wormwood *n.:* herb that produces a bitter oil. The word can also refer to something that produces feelings of bitterness.

9. conflagration (kän′flə′grā′shən) *n.:* fire.

Response and Analysis

Lot's Wife
All the unburied ones
I am not one of those who left the land

Thinking Critically

1. What, in general, makes Lot's wife care about Sodom, despite its evils? What does the phrase "mortal pain" (line 10) suggest about how we should view her attitude?
2. Re-read the biography of Akhmatova on page 1200 and the Background on page 1201. Then, explain how "Lot's Wife" might have been shaped by the events of Akhmatova's life and by the political situation in Russia at the time she wrote the poem.
3. How would you state the **theme** of "Lot's Wife"? What view of life does this theme reflect, and how is this view of life shaped by historical influences?
4. What is the **tone** of "All the unburied ones"? What attitude does the speaker express, and toward whom?
5. What two groups of people are contrasted in "I am not one of those who left the land"? Paraphrase what the speaker says about each group.
6. How is the **theme** of "I am not one. . ." different from that of "Lot's Wife"? Again, consider Akhmatova's historical circumstances. What do you think accounts for the difference in the two poems?
7. Review your Quickwrite notes. Do any of Akhmatova's poems echo your feelings about leaving home during troubled times? Do any of them compel you to rethink your ideas? Explain.

SKILLS FOCUS

Literary Skills
Analyze theme.

Writing Skills
Write journal entries in response to poems.

Extending and Evaluating

8. Recall that Akhmatova helped found a poetic movement known as **acmeism.** Acmeists strove to eliminate ambiguous symbols from their work and instead emphasized the clear communication of ideas. They also organized their thoughts into **stanzas**—line groupings that followed a rhyme scheme and that often expressed a single idea. Of the three poems you have read, which do you think is the best example of acmeism? Why? Use examples from the poem to support your opinion.

WRITING

Through a Poet's Eyes

Imagine that you are Anna Akhmatova. Write three **journal entries,** each one expressing, in prose, the ideas conveyed in each of the three poems. When you are finished, swap journal entries with a classmate. How are your entries similar? How are they different?

Woman with a Rake (1928–1932) by Kasimir Malevich.

Tretyakov Gallery, Moscow.

Elizabeth Bowen

(1899–1973)

Ireland

Photograph by Robin Adler.

Elizabeth Bowen was born in Dublin and spent her early years in Ireland's County Cork, on her family's splendid country estate, Bowen's Court. As Bowen later wrote, her family strove "to live as though living gave them no trouble." An only child, Bowen was looked after by a governess, taken to the Anglican church on Sundays, and taught to dance, wear gloves, and pay attention to manners. On her mother's orders she was not taught to read until she was seven. When Bowen's father, a lawyer, was confined to a mental hospital, Elizabeth was not allowed to dwell on it. By her twelfth year her father had recovered, but her mother had contracted fatal cancer. ("Good news," her mother is reported to have remarked, with her characteristic optimism. "Now I'm going to see what Heaven's like.") Elizabeth was not allowed to attend her mother's funeral or to mourn her.

Bowen's fiction clearly bears the stamp of her early years. Much of her writing is concerned with the processes of growing up, of losing innocence, of coming to terms with reality. Her main characters are often wealthy, sensitive, and well-mannered women; yet her novels also reveal a sense that life cannot be trusted, that existence is a struggle.

At seventeen, after attending a boarding school in England, Bowen moved to London to write stories. There she attended readings at the Poetry Bookshop, where she made the first of the literary friendships that were to become the fabric of her life. Among these literary friends were Edith Sitwell and Ezra Pound.

In 1923, Bowen published her first collection of stories, *Encounters*, to little notice. She also married Alan Cameron, a teacher. For most of the next ten years, the couple lived in the university town of Oxford, where Cameron taught and his wife wrote industriously. She produced story collections regularly and wrote nearly a novel a year.

In 1935, the couple moved back to London, where Bowen became a notable hostess of the literary world. During World War II, with its nightly air raids on London, Bowen was a dedicated air-raid warden, but she also went right on giving parties. Once, while entertaining guests on her balcony, she took no notice of the magnesium flares, but when she had gathered everyone inside, she said, in a typical understatement, "I feel I should apologize for the noise." During that period, she was writing the stories published in 1945 in *The Demon Lover,* a collection she called a "diary" of her reactions to the war.

After the war, Bowen and her husband returned to Bowen's Court but had barely begun this new, serene era when Cameron died of a heart attack. Predictably, Bowen became more active than ever.

Although she had been irrepressibly healthy all her life, a persistent cough proved to be a symptom of lung cancer. She died in 1973 and is buried in an Irish churchyard.

Before You Read

The Demon Lover

Make the Connection

Ghost stories can be mesmerizing, even when they're scaring us to death. Part of why we're so drawn to them is that they make us think about which events are real and which are happening only in our imagination, or in the imagination of a character. See how well you can figure out what's real and what's not in this story. Is it a ghost story at all?

Literary Focus

Flashback

A **flashback** is a scene in a narrative or dramatic work that interrupts the present action to tell what happened at an earlier time. "The Demon Lover" uses a **flashback** to provide important background information about the main character, Mrs. Drover. To recognize where the flashback begins, look for the sudden appearance of a verb in the past perfect tense (that is, preceded by the helping verb *had*).

A **flashback** is a scene in a narrative that interrupts the present action to "flash backward" and tell what happened at an earlier time.

For more on Flashback, see the Handbook of Literary and Historical Terms.

Literary Skills Understand flashback.

Reading Skills Make and modify predictions.

Reading Skills

Modifying Your Predictions

Think about the title of this story. Then, freewrite for a few minutes, predicting what you think this story will be about. As you read, **modify,** or adjust, your predictions based on what happens in the story. Note which details lead you to modify a prediction.

go.hrw.com

INTERNET

Vocabulary Practice

Keyword: LE7 12-7

Background

"The Demon Lover" takes place in London in the early 1940s during World War II, when frequent German air raids over the city drove many Londoners to find temporary lodgings in the country.

The title of the story comes from a version of a British ballad sometimes called "The House Carpenter." In the ballad a woman's husband, who has been missing at sea for seven years, returns to take her back to "the banks of Italy." The woman, who has married a house carpenter in the meantime and had children with him, is lured by the first husband's wealth (he now owns eight ships) and goes to sea with him—only to find that he has a demon's cloven foot. The demon lover then breaks the ship in two, sinking it, so that he and his wife can go together to the place they are destined for—hell.

Vocabulary Development

prosaic (prō•zā′ik) *adj.:* ordinary; dull.

refracted (ri•frakt′id) *v.* used as *adj.:* bent by its passage from one medium to another.

assent (ə•sent′) *n.:* acceptance.

intermittent (in′tər•mit′′nt) *adj.:* starting and stopping at intervals; periodic.

precipitately (pri•sip′ə•tit•lē) *adv.:* suddenly.

emanated (em′ə•nāt′id) *v.:* flowed; came forth.

impassively (im•pas′iv•lē) *adv.:* calmly; indifferently.

aperture (ap′ər•chər) *n.:* opening.

The Demon *Lover*

Elizabeth Bowen

Toward the end of her day in London Mrs. Drover went round to her shut-up house to look for several things she wanted to take away. Some belonged to herself, some to her family, who were by now used to their country life. It was late August; it had been a steamy, showery day: At the moment the trees down the pavement glittered in an escape of humid yellow afternoon sun. Against the next batch of clouds, already piling up ink-dark, broken chimneys and parapets[1] stood out. In her once familiar street, as in any unused channel, an unfamiliar queerness had silted up; a cat wove itself in and out of railings, but no human eye watched Mrs. Drover's return. Shifting some parcels under her arm, she slowly forced round her latchkey in an unwilling lock, then gave the door, which had warped, a push with her knee. Dead air came out to meet her as she went in.

The staircase window having been boarded up, no light came down into the hall. But one door, she could just see, stood ajar, so she went quickly through into the room and unshuttered the big window in there. Now the prosaic woman, looking about her, was more perplexed than she knew by everything that she saw, by traces of her long former habit of life—the yellow smoke stain up the white marble mantelpiece, the ring left by a vase on the top of the escritoire;[2] the bruise in the wallpaper where, on the door being thrown open widely, the china handle had always hit the wall. The piano, having gone away to be stored, had left what looked like claw marks on its part of the parquet.[3] Though not much dust had seeped in, each object wore a film of another kind; and, the only ventilation being the chimney, the whole drawing room smelled of the cold hearth. Mrs. Drover put down her parcels on the escritoire and left the room to proceed upstairs; the things she wanted were in a bedroom chest.

She had been anxious to see how the house was—the part-time caretaker she shared with some neighbors was away this week on his holiday, known to be not yet back. At the best of times he did not look in often, and she was never

1. **parapets** (par′ə·pets′) *n. pl.:* low walls around rooftops.

2. **escritoire** (es′kri·twär′) *n.:* writing table.

3. **parquet** (pär·kā′) *n.:* wood floor made of boards arranged in geometric patterns.

Vocabulary

prosaic (prō·zā′ik) *adj.:* ordinary; dull.

Cat on a Pile of Blankets (1985) by Edward Bawden.
The Fine Art Society, London. © The Edward Bawden Estate.

sure that she trusted him. There were some cracks in the structure, left by the last bombing, on which she was anxious to keep an eye. Not that one could do anything—

A shaft of refracted daylight now lay across the hall. She stopped dead and stared at the hall table—on this lay a letter addressed to her.

She thought first—then the caretaker *must* be back. All the same, who, seeing the house shuttered, would have dropped a letter in at the box? It was not a circular, it was not a bill. And the post office redirected, to the address in the country, everything for her that came through the post. The caretaker (even if he *were* back) did not know she was due in London today—her call here had been planned to be a surprise—so his negligence in the manner of this letter, leaving it to wait in the dusk and the dust, annoyed her. Annoyed, she picked up the letter, which bore no stamp. But it cannot be important, or they would know . . . She took the letter rapidly upstairs with her, without a stop to look

Vocabulary

refracted (ri•frakt′id) *v.* used as *adj.:* bent by its passage from one medium to another.

at the writing till she reached what had been her bedroom, where she let in light. The room looked over the garden and other gardens: The sun had gone in; as the clouds sharpened and lowered, the trees and rank lawns seemed already to smoke with dark. Her reluctance to look again at the letter came from the fact that she felt intruded upon—and by someone contemptuous of her ways. However, in the tenseness preceding the fall of rain she read it: It was a few lines.

> Dear Kathleen: You will not have forgotten that today is our anniversary, and the day we said. The years have gone by at once slowly and fast. In view of the fact that nothing has changed, I shall rely upon you to keep your promise. I was sorry to see you leave London, but was satisfied that you would be back in time. You may expect me, therefore, at the hour arranged. Until then . . . K.

Mrs. Drover looked for the date: It was today's. She dropped the letter onto the bedsprings, then picked it up to see the writing again—her lips, beneath the remains of lipstick, beginning to go white. She felt so much the change in her own face that she went to the mirror, polished a clear patch in it, and looked at once urgently and stealthily in. She was confronted by a woman of forty-four, with eyes starting out under a hat brim that had been rather carelessly pulled down. She had not put on any more powder since she left the shop where she ate her solitary tea.[4] The pearls her husband had given her on their marriage hung loose round her now rather thinner throat, slipping in the V of the pink wool jumper her sister knitted last autumn as they sat round the fire. Mrs. Drover's most normal expression was one of controlled worry, but of assent. Since the birth of the third of her little boys, attended by a quite serious illness, she had had an intermittent muscular flicker to the left of her mouth, but in spite of this she could always sustain a manner that was at once energetic and calm.

Turning from her own face as precipitately as she had gone to meet it, she went to the chest where the things were, unlocked it, threw up the lid, and knelt to search. But as rain began to come crashing down she could not keep from looking over her shoulder at the stripped bed on which the letter lay. Behind the blanket of rain the clock of the church that still stood struck six—with rapidly heightening apprehension she counted each of the slow strokes. "The hour arranged . . . My God," she said, "*what* hour? How should I . . . ? After twenty-five years . . . "

The young girl talking to the soldier in the garden had not ever completely seen his face. It was dark; they were saying goodbye under a tree. Now and then—for it felt, from not seeing him at this intense moment, as though she had never seen him at all—she verified his presence for these few moments longer by putting out a hand, which he each time pressed, without very much kindness, and painfully, on to one of the breast buttons of his uniform. That cut of the button on the palm of her hand was, principally, what she was to carry away. This was so near the end of a leave from France that she could only wish him already gone. It was August 1916. Being not kissed, being drawn away from and looked at intimidated Kathleen till she imagined spectral glitters in the place of his eyes. Turning away and looking back up the lawn she saw, through branches of trees, the drawing-room window alight: She caught a breath for the moment when she could go running back there into the safe arms of her mother and sister, and cry: "What shall I do, what shall I do? He has gone."

Hearing her catch her breath, her fiancé said, without feeling: "Cold?"

4. **tea:** in Britain, a light, late-afternoon meal, served with tea.

Vocabulary

assent (ə•sent′) *n.:* acceptance.

intermittent (in′tər•mit′'nt) *adj.:* starting and stopping at intervals; periodic.

precipitately (pri•sip′ə•tit•lē) *adv.:* suddenly.

"You're going away such a long way."

"Not so far as you think."

"I don't understand?"

"You don't have to," he said. "You will. You know what we said."

"But that was—suppose you—I mean, suppose."

"I shall be with you," he said, "sooner or later. You won't forget that. You need do nothing but wait."

Only a little more than a minute later she was free to run up the silent lawn. Looking in through the window at her mother and sister, who did not for the moment perceive her, she already felt that unnatural promise drive down between her and the rest of all humankind. No other way of having given herself could have made her feel so apart, lost and forsworn.[5] She could not have plighted a more sinister troth.[6]

Kathleen behaved well when, some months later, her fiancé was reported missing, presumed killed. Her family not only supported her but were able to praise her courage without stint[7] because they could not regret, as a husband for her, the man they knew almost nothing about. They hoped she would, in a year or two, console herself—and had it been only a question of consolation things might have gone much straighter ahead. But her trouble, behind just a little grief, was a complete dislocation from everything. She did not reject other lovers, for these failed to appear: For years she failed to attract men—and with the approach of her thirties she became natural enough to share her family's anxiousness on this score. She began to put herself out,[8] to wonder; and at thirty-two she was very greatly relieved to find herself being courted by William Drover. She married him, and the two of them settled down in this quiet, arboreal[9] part of Kensington: In this house the years piled up, her children were born, and they all lived till they were driven out by the bombs of the next war. Her movements as Mrs. Drover were circumscribed, and she dismissed any idea that they were still watched.

As things were—dead or living the letter writer sent her only a threat. Unable, for some minutes, to go on kneeling with her back exposed to the empty room, Mrs. Drover rose from the chest to sit on an upright chair whose back was firmly against the wall. The desuetude[10] of her former bedroom, her married London home's whole air of being a cracked cup from which memory, with its reassuring power, had either evaporated or leaked away, made a crisis—and at just this crisis the letter writer had, knowledgeably, struck. The hollowness of the house this evening canceled years on years of voices, habits, and steps. Through the shut windows she only heard rain fall on the roofs around. To rally herself, she said she was in a mood—and for two or three seconds shutting her eyes, told herself that she had imagined the letter. But she opened them—there it lay on the bed.

On the supernatural side of the letter's entrance she was not permitting her mind to dwell. Who, in London, knew she meant to call at the house today? Evidently, however, this had been known. The caretaker, *had* he come back, had had no cause to expect her: He would have taken the letter in his pocket, to forward it, at his own time, through the post. There was no other sign that the caretaker had been in—but, if not? Letters dropped in at doors of deserted houses do not fly or walk to tables in halls. They do not sit on the dust of empty tables with the air of certainty that they will be found. There is needed some human hand—but nobody but the caretaker had a key. Under circumstances she did not care to consider, a house can be entered without a key. It was possible that she was not alone now. She might be being waited for, downstairs. Waited for—until when? Until "the

---

5. **forsworn** (fôr·swôrn′) *adv.:* having lied under oath; perjured.
6. **plighted . . . troth:** made a more sinister promise of marriage.
7. **stint** *n.:* limitation.
8. **put herself out:** vex or distress herself.
9. **arboreal** (är·bôr′ē·əl) *adj.:* full of trees.
10. **desuetude** (des′wi·to͞od′) *adj.:* disuse.

Rainy Weather (late 19th or early 20th century) by Vilhelm Hammershoi.

hour arranged." At least that was not six o'clock: Six has struck.

She rose from the chair and went over and locked the door.

The thing was, to get out. To fly? No, not that: She had to catch her train. As a woman whose utter dependability was the keystone of her family life she was not willing to return to the country, to her husband, her little boys, and her sister, without the objects she had come up to fetch. Resuming work at the chest she set about making up a number of parcels in a rapid, fumbling-decisive way. These, with her shopping parcels, would be too much to carry; these meant a taxi—at the thought of the taxi her heart went up and her normal breathing resumed. I will ring up the taxi now; the taxi cannot come too soon: I shall hear the taxi out there running its engine, till I walk calmly down to it through the hall. I'll ring up—But no: the telephone is cut off . . . She tugged at a knot she had tied wrong.

The idea of flight . . . He was never kind to me, not really. I don't remember him kind at all. Mother said he never considered me. He was set on me, that was what it was—not love. Not love, not meaning a person well. What did he do, to make me promise like that? I can't remember—But she found that she could.

She remembered with such dreadful acuteness that the twenty-five years since then dissolved like smoke and she instinctively looked for the weal[11] left by the button on the palm of her hand. She remembered not only all that he said and did but the complete suspension of *her* existence during that August week. I was not myself—they all told me so at the time. She remembered—but with one white burning blank as where acid has dropped on a photograph: *Under no conditions* could she remember his face.

So, wherever he may be waiting, I shall not know him. You have no time to run from a face you do not expect.

11. **weal** (wēl) *n.:* lump; welt.

The thing was to get to the taxi before any clock struck what could be the hour. She would slip down the street and round the side of the square to where the square gave on the main road. She would return in the taxi, safe, to her own door, and bring the solid driver into the house with her to pick up the parcels from room to room. The idea of the taxi driver made her decisive, bold: She unlocked her door, went to the top of the staircase, and listened down.

She heard nothing—but while she was hearing nothing the *passé*[12] air of the staircase was disturbed by a draft that traveled up to her face. It emanated from the basement: Down there a door or window was being opened by someone who chose this moment to leave the house.

The rain had stopped; the pavements steamily shone as Mrs. Drover let herself out by inches from her own front door into the empty street. The unoccupied houses opposite continued to meet her look with their damaged stare. Making toward the thoroughfare and the taxi, she tried not to keep looking behind. Indeed, the silence was so intense—one of those creeks of London silence exaggerated this summer by the damage of war—that no tread could have gained on hers unheard. Where her street debouched[13] on the square where people went on living, she grew conscious of, and checked, her unnatural pace. Across the open end of the square two buses impassively passed each other: Women, a perambulator,[14] cyclists, a man wheeling a barrow signalized, once again, the ordinary flow of life. At the square's most populous corner should be—and was—the short taxi rank. This evening, only one taxi—but this, although it

12. ***passé*** (pä·sā′) *adj.:* no longer fresh; rather old.
13. **debouched** (dē·bo͞osht′) *v.:* came out; emerged.
14. **perambulator** (pər·am′byo͞o·lāt′ər) *n.:* chiefly British for "baby carriage." The word is often shortened to *pram.*

Vocabulary

emanated (em′ə·nāt′id) *v.:* flowed; came forth.

impassively (im·pas′iv·lē) *adv.:* calmly; indifferently.

presented its blank rump, appeared already to be alertly waiting for her. Indeed, without looking round the driver started his engine as she panted up from behind and put her hand on the door. As she did so, the clock struck seven. The taxi faced the main road: To make the trip back to her house it would have to turn—she had settled back on the seat and the taxi *had* turned before she, surprised by its knowing movement, recollected that she had not "said where." She leaned forward to scratch at the glass panel that divided the driver's head from her own.

The driver braked to what was almost a stop, turned round, and slid the glass panel back: The jolt of this flung Mrs. Drover forward till her face was almost into the glass. Through the aperture driver and passenger, not six inches between them, remained for an eternity eye to eye. Mrs. Drover's mouth hung open for some seconds before she could issue her first scream. After that she continued to scream freely and to beat with her gloved hands on the glass all round as the taxi, accelerating without mercy, made off with her into the hinterland of deserted streets. ■

Vocabulary

aperture (ap′ər·chər) *n.:* opening.

Response and Analysis

Reading Check

Using the following chart, create a story map for "The Demon Lover":

Situation	
Characters	
Conflict	
Event	
Event	
Event [etc.]	
Climax	
Resolution	

Thinking Critically

1. In some stories, descriptions of the **setting** provide much more than the physical background—they also create a particular **mood.** List the **images** in the story's first paragraph that help create an unsettling mood.
2. Why has the Drover family left their London home? Cite two places in the text that make the reason clear. For what purpose has Mrs. Drover returned?
3. What details in the lovers' last meeting **foreshadow** a sinister, threatening reunion? What do we learn about Mrs. Drover's fiancé that explains why she is terrified of him?
4. The use of an **omniscient narrator** allows Bowen to give readers information about Mrs. Drover's psychological makeup that Mrs. Drover herself is not consciously aware of. Identify several such passages in the text. How do you interpret Mrs. Drover's psychological state?

Literary Skills Analyze flashback.

Reading Skills Make and modify predictions.

Writing Skills Write a character description.

Vocabulary Skills Create semantic charts.

INTERNET

Projects and Activities

Keyword: LE7 12-7

5. **Dramatic irony** occurs when a reader or an audience is aware of something that a character does not know. What is the central dramatic irony of the story? Did you predict the story would turn out the way it does? Check your reading notes.

6. The two world wars bracket this story like bookends. During each war, Mrs. Drover experiences dislocation and confusion. During each war, the demon lover is part of her life. Yet he doesn't appear during the intervening twenty-five years. Use these strands of the story—war, Mrs. Drover's inner turmoil, and the lover's appearances—to develop your understanding of the story's **theme.** What view of life does this theme suggest?

Extending and Evaluating

7. Contributing to the story's richness and depth is the interplay between present and past. Think about the **flashback** that tells what happened earlier in Mrs. Drover's life. Do you think the abrupt shift into the past is effective or merely confusing? Why?

Literary Criticism

8. Some readers believe that Mrs. Drover's experience is a hallucination: Her powers of imagination have combined with the pressures of wartime life to transform everyday reality into a waking nightmare. Other readers consider the story to be an out-and-out ghost story. Which interpretation do you favor, or do you have another? Support your interpretation with evidence from the text.

WRITING

No Prince Charming

At no time in the story are we given a description of the demon lover's face. At the end of the story, however, when Mrs. Drover is finally within six inches of his face, she begins to scream. In a few **paragraphs,** describe what you imagine Mrs. Drover sees. You might also create a drawing or painting of the demon lover.

Vocabulary Development

Word Information Charts

prosaic	intermittent	impassively
refracted	precipitately	aperture
assent	emanated	

The chart below organizes some basic information about the word *prosaic.* Using a dictionary, make similar charts for the rest of the Vocabulary words listed above.

prosaic
Meaning: ordinary; dull **Origin:** Latin, "prose" **Synonym and/or Antonym:** commonplace (synonym); exciting (antonym) **Examples:** Grocery lists are prosaic; doing laundry is prosaic.

Grammar Link

Building Coherence: Connecting Ideas

In a coherent composition, ideas are clearly connected, and every paragraph flows smoothly and sensibly from one to the next. You can connect ideas within and between paragraphs with **direct references** and **transitions.**

You use **direct references** naturally in writing—for example, using *she* to refer to Elizabeth Bowen in the sentences that follow.

> At seventeen, Elizabeth Bowen moved to London to write stories. There she became friends with other young writers.

You can improve coherence by employing direct references purposefully.

- Refer to a noun or pronoun used earlier
- Repeat a word used earlier
- Substitute a synonym for words used earlier

Transitions show *how* ideas are connected. Often these expressions show chronological or spatial relationships. They may also show relationships of cause and effect, definition, or contrast.

> During the Blitz, the German Luftwaffe targeted London. Therefore, many residents of London fled the city. [*Therefore* indicates a cause-and-effect relationship.]

Note the different purposes of the types of transitions in the chart below:

Transitions that compare ideas	again, also, and, besides, both, each of, furthermore, in addition, likewise, moreover, similarly, too
Transitions that contrast ideas	although, but, however, in spite of, instead, neither . . . nor, nevertheless, still, yet
Transitions that indicate time or position	above, afterward, before, eventually, first (second, etc.), meanwhile, nearby, next
Transitions that indicate purpose, cause, or effect	as, because, consequently, for, just as . . . so, since, so, so that, then, therefore
Transitions that indicate a summary, a conclusion, or an example	as a result, for example, for instance, in conclusion, in fact, in other words, on the whole, overall, therefore, thus

PRACTICE

Turn the sentences below into a clear paragraph by inserting direct references or effective transitions.

"The Demon Lover" by Elizabeth Bowen is set during World War II. World War II played an integral part in Elizabeth Bowen's life and writings. Many people fled to the country to escape the German air raids over London. Bowen remained in London. Bowen continued to write. Bowen incorporated her experiences in wartime England into her novels.

Apply to Your Writing

Look over a writing assignment you are working on now or have already completed. Revise your work by adding direct references and transitions to make your sentences and paragraphs flow smoothly.

For more help, see Sentence Combining, 10a–d, in the Language Handbook.

Grammar Skills
Understand and use direct references and transitions.

Julio Cortázar

(1914–1984)

Argentina

A visitor to an aquarium is transformed into a salamander; a rich Argentine woman discovers and changes places with her exact double, who is a beggar in Budapest; a man finds himself vomiting rabbits, which gradually destroy his apartment. Welcome to the world of Julio Cortázar.

For Cortázar the fantastic is not something supernatural but "something very simple, that can happen in the midst of everyday reality, during this sunny midday, now, between you and I, or on the subway. . . ." Cortázar's views of the fantastic are heavily influenced by French surrealism and the writings of Edgar Allan Poe, whose works Cortázar translated into Spanish.

Born in Belgium to Argentine parents, Julio Cortázar grew up in a suburb of Buenos Aires. Throughout his childhood he read voraciously and wrote his own imaginative tales. After high school, Cortázar qualified as a teacher of French literature, but he gave up university studies in order to take a teaching job to support his family. While he taught, he wrote stories, but he didn't publish his first collection, *Bestiary*, until 1951.

That year was a turning point in another way: Disillusioned by the regime of the Argentine dictator Juan Perón, Cortázar accepted a French government grant to study in Paris. Though he lived in exile most of his life—mainly in France, working as a freelance translator for the United Nations and for various publishers—Cortázar always considered himself a Latin American.

Cortázar once said that a writer's job is "to set fire to language," and the Argentine writer did just that in 1963, when he astounded the publishing world with *Hopscotch,* a long, structurally innovative novel whose chapters can be read in several different sequences.

Cortázar—who was influenced by jazz and classical music, Zen Buddhism, detective novels, and movies—kept the fun-loving, youthful side of his nature alive to the end of his days. "He liberated us all with a new, airy, humorous, and mysterious language, both everyday and mythical," the Mexican novelist Carlos Fuentes said in a tribute to his friend shortly after Cortázar's death from leukemia in 1984.

For Independent Reading

You may enjoy the following stories by Cortázar:

- "House Taken Over"
- "The Night Face Up"

Before You Read

Axolotl

Make the Connection

Fantastic occurrences are often the stuff of sleep. Surreal images and irrational happenings flood our dreams, yet during the day, our lives seem ordered, routine, rational. What happens when these two worlds overlap or intersect—when we can't distinguish between them?

Literary Focus

Magic Realism

The term **magic realism** (*lo real maravilloso*) was coined in 1949 by the Cuban novelist, essayist, and musicologist Alejo Carpentier. He used the term to describe a blurring of the lines that usually separate what seems real to the reader from what seems imagined or unreal to the same reader. Carpentier believed that by incorporating magic, myth, imagination, and religion into literature, we can expand our rigid concept of reality.

In "Axolotl," as in all **magic realism,** the impossible and the possible—fantasy and reality—are set in opposition. Cortázar introduces some surrealistic element or extraordinary event into an otherwise entirely realistic environment, and the two different worlds become so intertwined that neither character nor reader can separate them.

Magic realism is literature that combines incredible events with realistic details and relates them all in a matter-of-fact tone.

For more on Magic Realism, see the Handbook of Literary and Historical Terms.

Reading Skills

Identifying Point of View

As you read "Axolotl," try to determine the **point of view,** or the vantage point from which the writer tells the story. Who or what is narrating the story? Jot down clues that might reveal the identity of the narrator. Why do you think Cortázar chose this particular point of view?

Background

In Cortázar's fantastic stories—among the best of **magic realism**—daily life is often mysteriously subverted by unknown forces. This "invasion by the imaginary," as he called it, creates a tension that can both invigorate and disturb.

The creatures shown on pages 1219 and 1220 are not from a sci-fi movie. They are real axolotls (ak′sə•lät″lz)—a type of Mexican salamander.

Vocabulary Development

translucent (trans•lo͞o′sənt) *adj.:* partially transparent.

diminutive (də•min′yo͞o•tiv) *adj.:* very small.

tentative (ten′tə•tiv) *adj.:* hesitant; uncertain.

proximity (präk•sim′ə•tē) *n.:* closeness.

Literary Skills Understand the characteristics of magic realism.

Reading Skills Identify point of view.

INTERNET

Vocabulary Practice

Keyword: LE7 12-7

AXOLOTL

Julio Cortázar
translated by **Paul Blackburn**

There was a time when I thought a great deal about the axolotls. I went to see them in the aquarium at the Jardin des Plantes[1] and stayed for hours watching them, observing their immobility, their faint movements. Now I am an axolotl.

I got to them by chance one spring morning when Paris was spreading its peacock tail after a wintry Lent. I was heading down the boulevard Port-Royal, then I took Saint-Marcel and L'Hôpital and saw green among all that gray and remembered the lions. I was friend of the lions and panthers, but had never gone into the dark, humid building that was the aquarium. I left my bike against the gratings and went to look at the tulips. The lions were sad and ugly and my panther was asleep. I decided on the aquarium, looked obliquely at banal fish until, unexpectedly, I hit it off with the axolotls. I stayed watching them for an hour and left, unable to think of anything else.

In the library at Sainte-Geneviève, I consulted a dictionary and learned that axolotls are the larval stage (provided with gills) of a species of salamander of the genus *Ambystoma.* That they were Mexican I knew already by looking at them and their little pink Aztec faces and the placard at the top of the tank. I read that specimens of them had been found in Africa capable of living on dry land during the periods of drought, and continuing their life under water when the rainy season came. I found their Spanish name, *ajolote,* and the mention that they were edible, and that their oil was used (no longer used, it said) like cod-liver oil.

I didn't care to look up any of the specialized works, but the next day I went back to the Jardin des Plantes. I began to go every morning, morning and afternoon some days. The aquarium guard smiled perplexedly taking my ticket. I would lean up against the iron bar in front of the tanks and set to watching them. There's nothing strange in this, because after the first minute I knew that we were linked, that something infinitely lost and distant kept pulling us together. It had been enough to detain me that first morning in front of the sheet of glass where some bubbles rose through the water. The axolotls huddled on the wretched narrow (only I can know how narrow and wretched) floor of moss and stone in the tank. There were nine specimens, and the majority pressed their heads against the glass, looking with their eyes of gold at whoever came near them. Disconcerted, almost ashamed, I felt it a lewdness to be peering at these silent and immobile figures heaped at the bottom of the tank. Mentally I isolated one, situated on the right and somewhat apart from the others, to study it better. I saw a rosy little body, translucent (I thought of those Chinese

1. **Jardin des Plantes** (zhär·da*n*′ dā plä*n*t): Paris botanical garden, part of the French National Museum of Natural History. The name means "garden of plants" in French.

Vocabulary
translucent (trans•lo͞o′sənt) *adj.:* partially transparent.

figurines of milky glass), looking like a small lizard about six inches long, ending in a fish's tail of extraordinary delicacy, the most sensitive part of our body. Along the back ran a transparent fin which joined with the tail, but what obsessed me was the feet, of the slenderest nicety, ending in tiny fingers with minutely human nails. And then I discovered its eyes, its face. Inexpressive features, with no other trait save the eyes, two orifices, like brooches, wholly of transparent gold, lacking any life but looking, letting themselves be penetrated by my look, which seemed to travel past the golden level and lose itself in a diaphanous[2] interior mystery. A very slender black halo ringed the eye and etched it onto the pink flesh, onto the rosy stone of the head, vaguely triangular, but with curved and irregular sides which gave it a total likeness to a statuette corroded by time. The mouth was masked by the triangular plane of the face, its considerable size would be guessed only in profile; in front a delicate crevice barely slit the lifeless stone. On both sides of the head where the ears should have been, there grew three tiny sprigs red as coral, a vegetal outgrowth, the gills, I suppose. And they were the only thing quick about it; every ten or fifteen seconds the sprigs pricked up stiffly and again subsided. Once in a while a foot would barely move, I saw the diminutive toes poise mildly on the moss. It's that we don't enjoy moving a lot, and the tank is so cramped—we

2. **diaphanous** *adj.:* transparent.

Vocabulary

diminutive (də•min'yōō•tiv) *adj.:* very small.

barely move in any direction and we're hitting one of the others with our tail or our head—difficulties arise, fights, tiredness. The time feels like it's less if we stay quietly.

It was their quietness that made me lean toward them fascinated the first time I saw the axolotls. Obscurely I seemed to understand their secret will, to abolish space and time with an indifferent immobility. I knew better later; the gill contraction, the tentative reckoning of the delicate feet on the stones, the abrupt swimming (some of them swim with a simple undulation[3] of the body) proved to me that they were capable of escaping that mineral lethargy in which they spent whole hours. Above all else, their eyes obsessed me. In the standing tanks on either side of them, different fishes showed me the simple stupidity of their handsome eyes so similar to our own. The eyes of the axolotls spoke to me of the presence of a different life, of another way of seeing. Glueing my face to the glass (the guard would cough fussily once in a while), I tried to see better those diminutive golden points, that entrance to the infinitely slow and remote world of these rosy creatures. It was useless to tap with one finger on the glass directly in front of their faces; they never gave the least reaction. The golden eyes continued burning with their soft, terrible light; they continued looking at me from an unfathomable depth which made me dizzy.

And nevertheless they were close. I knew it before this, before being an axolotl. I learned it the day I came near them for the first time. The anthropomorphic[4] features of a monkey reveal the reverse of what most people believe, the distance that is traveled from them to us. The absolute lack of similarity between axolotls and human beings proved to me that my recognition was valid, that I was not propping myself up with easy analogies. Only the little hands . . . But an eft,[5] the common newt, has such hands also, and we are not at all alike. I think it was the axolotls' heads, that triangular pink shape with the tiny eyes of gold. That looked and knew. That laid the claim. They were not *animals.*

It would seem easy, almost obvious, to fall into mythology. I began seeing in the axolotls a metamorphosis which did not succeed in revoking a mysterious humanity. I imagined them aware, slaves of their bodies, condemned infinitely to the silence of the abyss, to a hopeless meditation. Their blind gaze, the diminutive gold disc without expression and nonetheless terribly shining, went through me like a message: "Save us, save us." I caught myself mumbling words of advice, conveying childish hopes. They continued to look at me, immobile; from time to time the rosy branches of the gills stiffened. In that instant I felt a muted pain; perhaps they were seeing me, attracting my strength to penetrate into the impenetrable thing of their lives. They were not human beings, but I had found in no animal such a profound relation with myself. The axolotls were like witnesses of something, and at times like horrible judges. I felt ignoble in front of them; there was such a terrifying purity in those transparent eyes. They were larvas, but larva means disguise and also phantom. Behind those Aztec faces, without expression but of an implacable cruelty, what semblance was awaiting its hour?

I was afraid of them. I think that had it not been for feeling the proximity of other visitors and the guard, I would not have been bold enough to remain alone with them. "You eat them alive with your eyes, hey," the guard said, laughing; he likely thought I was a little cracked. What he didn't notice was that it was they devouring me slowly with their eyes, in a cannibalism of gold. At any distance from the aquarium, I had only to think of them, it was as though I were being affected from a distance. It got to the point that I was going every day, and at night I thought of them immobile in the

3. **undulation** *n.:* wavelike movement.
4. **anthropomorphic** *adj.:* having human shape or characteristics; humanlike.
5. **eft** *n.:* archaic for "newt," kind of amphibious salamander.

Vocabulary

tentative (ten′tə • tiv) *adj.:* hesitant; uncertain.
proximity (präk • sim′ə • tē) *n.:* closeness.

darkness, slowly putting a hand out which immediately encountered another. Perhaps their eyes could see in the dead of night, and for them the day continued indefinitely. The eyes of axolotls have no lids.

I know now that there was nothing strange, that that had to occur. Leaning over in front of the tank each morning, the recognition was greater. They were suffering, every fiber of my body reached toward that stifled pain, that stiff torment at the bottom of the tank. They were lying in wait for something, a remote dominion destroyed, an age of liberty when the world had been that of the axolotls. Not possible that such a terrible expression which was attaining the overthrow of that forced blankness on their stone faces should carry any message other than one of pain, proof of that eternal sentence, of that liquid hell they were undergoing. Hopelessly, I wanted to prove to myself that my own sensibility was projecting a nonexistent consciousness upon the axolotls. They and I knew. So there was nothing strange in what happened. My face was pressed against the glass of the aquarium, my eyes were attempting once more to penetrate the mystery of those eyes of gold without iris, without pupil. I saw from very close up the face of an axolotl immobile next to the glass. No transition and no surprise, I saw my face against the glass, I saw it on the outside of the tank, I saw it on the other side of the glass. Then my face drew back and I understood.

Only one thing was strange: to go on thinking as usual, to know. To realize that was, for the first moment, like the horror of a man buried alive awaking to his fate. Outside, my face came close to the glass again, I saw my mouth, the lips compressed with the effort of understanding the axolotls. I was an axolotl and now I knew instantly that no understanding was possible. He was outside the aquarium, his thinking was a thinking outside the tank. Recognizing him, being him himself, I was an axolotl and in my world. The horror began—I learned in the same moment—of believing myself prisoner in the body of an axolotl, metamorphosed into him with my human mind intact, buried alive in an axolotl, condemned to move lucidly among unconscious creatures. But that stopped when a foot just grazed my face, when I moved just a little to one side and saw an axolotl next to me who was looking at me, and understood that he knew also, no communication possible, but very clearly. Or I was also in him, or all of us were thinking humanlike, incapable of expression, limited to the golden splendor of our eyes looking at the face of the man pressed against the aquarium.

He returned many times, but he comes less often now. Weeks pass without his showing up. I saw him yesterday, he looked at me for a long time and left briskly. It seemed to me that he was not so much interested in us any more, that he was coming out of habit. Since the only thing I do is think, I could think about him a lot. It occurs to me that at the beginning we continued to communicate, that he felt more than ever one with the mystery which was claiming him. But the bridges were broken between him and me, because what was his obsession is now an axolotl, alien to his human life. I think that at the beginning I was capable of returning to him in a certain way—ah, only in a certain way—and of keeping awake his desire to know us better. I am an axolotl for good now, and if I think like a man it's only because every axolotl thinks like a man inside his rosy stone semblance. I believe that all this succeeded in communicating something to him in those first days, when I was still he. And in this final solitude to which he no longer comes, I console myself by thinking that perhaps he is going to write a story about us, that, believing he's making up a story, he's going to write all this about axolotls. ■

Response and Analysis

Reading Check

1. What is an axolotl?
2. Where are the axolotls kept?
3. How does the narrator feel about axolotls?
4. What happens to the narrator?

Thinking Critically

5. Describe the **character** of the narrator as he relates his numerous trips to the aquarium. Is he well balanced psychologically? How do you know?
6. Identify at least three strong images that show how the narrator views the axolotls. How does the narrator's **imagery** describing the axolotls give the animals a surreal or otherworldly quality?
7. It is one thing to project feelings or thoughts onto an animal but quite another to become that animal and retain human consciousness. With the above sentence in mind, how would you state the **theme** or central idea of the story? What view of life does this theme represent?
8. What effect does the **point of view** have on how convincing, rational, or logical the story sounds? Refer to your reading notes.
9. As the story ends, the axolotl says, "I console myself by thinking that perhaps he is going to write a story about us. . . ." Why is this a consolation to the axolotl?
10. Describe the **tone** of the story. Is it completely serious, or is there an undercurrent of sly humor in the story? Explain.

Extending and Evaluating

11. In one of the very first sentences of the story, the narrator matter-of-factly confides, "Now I am an axolotl." As he tells his story, he alternates between the past (himself as a human fascinated by axolotls) and the present (himself as an axolotl in the tank). In your opinion, would the story have been less or more effective if it had been told in a traditional way, with the transformation into an axolotl presented as a surprise ending? In general, how do you feel about the way **magic realism** blurs the distinction between fantasy and reality in such a calm, accepting way?

WRITING

Finding Realism in the Magic

In a brief **essay, analyze** Cortázar's use of **magic realism** in "Axolotl." You may want to create a chart in which you list fantastic details on one side and realistic details on the other. As you write, keep the following questions in mind: What does magic realism allow Cortázar to express about the human condition? How does Cortázar use magic realism to comment on mundane aspects of reality?

Vocabulary Development

Analogies

translucent	*tentative*
diminutive	*proximity*

In an **analogy** the words in one pair relate to each other in the same way as the words in a second pair. On a separate sheet of paper, identify the Vocabulary word from above that completes each analogy below.

1. MOVING : STAGNANT :: __________ : opaque.
2. LAUGHTER : TEARS :: __________ : distance.
3. LAVISH : MEAGER :: __________ : certain.
4. TALL : GIRAFFE :: __________ : flea.

Literary Skills
Analyze the characteristics of magic realism.

Reading Skills
Analyze point of view.

Writing Skills
Write an essay analyzing the use of magic realism.

Vocabulary Skills
Complete word analogies.

Jorge Luis Borges

1899–1986

Argentina

When he was six years old, Jorge Luis Borges (bôr′hes) announced that he intended to become a writer. He began working at his chosen profession immediately: At the age of nine, he translated Oscar Wilde's fairy tale "The Happy Prince" into Spanish. Later in his life, Borges credited his father with inspiring his writing career: He felt that his father had made him aware of poetry—of the idea that words could be powerful and symbolic, not just a means of everyday communication.

Borges learned English at an early age from his English-born grandmother, and he devoured his father's extensive library. He loved the horror stories of Edgar Allan Poe, the adventures of Robert Louis Stevenson, and the exotic Arabic fairy tales in *The Thousand and One Nights* (see page 200). Ironically, Borges first read the great Spanish classics *El Cid* and *Don Quixote* (see page 627) in English translations. Later, when he read *Don Quixote* in its original Spanish, he said it sounded like a bad translation!

The Borges family was traveling in Europe when World War I broke out. They took refuge in neutral Switzerland, where Borges attended school and learned three more languages—French, Latin, and German. After the war the family moved first to Italy, then to Spain, and finally back to Argentina.

Borges began his career as a poet, and he always considered himself a poet first and foremost. In the 1940s, however, Borges turned to experimental prose, writing stories about transparent tigers, wizards who conjure up visions in a bowl of ink, and encyclopedias that do not record events but cause them. The stories in *The Garden of the Forking Paths* (1941) and *El Aleph* (1949) ignore plot and character and most of the usual elements of fiction. They instead blend fact and fantasy in a world of games and riddles, literary mystery, and philosophical inquiry.

It was also during the 1940s that Borges began using one of his most famous images—that of the labyrinth, or maze. Borges used the labyrinth as a metaphor for our journey through life, with all its surprising twists, turns, and dead ends.

For Independent Reading

You may enjoy the following stories by Borges:

- "Borges and Myself"
- "The Meeting"
- "A Soldier of Urbina"

Before You Read

The Book of Sand

Make the Connection

Quickwrite

We take for granted that reality is dependable—that gravity will continue to keep us from floating away, that time always moves forward, that an object can exist in only one place at a time. But what if one of our dependable realities suddenly changed? Jorge Luis Borges loved to play with puzzles and reality—and to overturn the so-called dependable realities. "The Book of Sand," like so much of his work, invites you to join in his game.

Write down at least two dependable realities of daily life—things we take for granted, that we expect will never change. Circle one, and briefly describe what you imagine the world would be like if that reality shifted slightly—or simply no longer existed.

Literary Focus

Paradox

Paradoxes—statements or situations that contain two seemingly contradictory truths—challenge the limits of our intellects and push us to conceive of reality in new and different ways. Borges was a master of paradox, partly because he placed his outrageous happenings in the context of everyday settings. In the following story, Borges drops his central paradox into the lap of a harmless book lover—much like himself—who discovers that loving a book and hating a book can be infinitely the same thing.

A **paradox** is an apparent contradiction that is actually true.

For more on Paradox, see the Handbook of Literary and Historical Terms.

Reading Skills

Making Predictions

Part of the pleasure of reading comes from making predictions about what will happen next. A **prediction** is a type of **inference,** a guess based on evidence. In a story that presents a mystery or a puzzle, we read carefully, looking for clues. We base our predictions on the characters and their situations, as well as our own experiences and knowledge about life. Typically we make initial guesses early in a work, adjusting them as the story unfolds to fit new events and information. Sometimes, despite our careful reading, a story still surprises us. Those are often the stories we remember best.

As you read "The Book of Sand," jot down any predictions you form as you read. Later, look back over your list, and identify which predictions were correct, which ones changed, and which ones were altogether inaccurate.

Vocabulary Development

pedantic (pi•dan′tik) *adj.:* showing an exaggerated concern for books, learning, and rules.

discomfiture (dis•kum′fi•chər) *n.:* frustration; embarrassment.

caste (kast) *n.:* social class.

defiled (dē•fīld′) *v.:* made unclean.

diabolic (dī′ə•bäl′ik) *adj.:* of or having to do with evil or the devil.

bibliophile (bib′lē•ə•fīl) *n.:* one who loves books.

misanthropy (mi•san′thrə•pē) *n.:* hatred for humankind.

artifice (ärt′ə•fis) *n.:* trickery; deception.

Literary Skills Understand paradox.

Reading Skills Make predictions.

INTERNET

More About Jorge Luis Borges

Keyword: LE7 12-7

The Book of Sand

Jorge Luis Borges *translated by* Andrew Hurley

. . . thy rope of sands . . .
—George Herbert (1593–1623)

The line consists of an infinite number of points; the plane, of an infinite number of lines; the volume, of an infinite number of planes; the hypervolume, of an infinite number of volumes . . . No—this, *more geometrico,*[1] is decidedly not the best way to begin my tale. To say that the story is true is by now a convention of every fantastic tale; mine, nevertheless, *is* true.

I live alone, in a fifth-floor apartment on Calle Belgrano.[2] One evening a few months ago, I heard a knock at my door. I opened it, and a stranger stepped in. He was a tall man, with blurred, vague features, or perhaps my nearsightedness made me see him that way. Everything about him spoke of honest poverty: he was dressed in gray, and carried a gray valise. I immediately sensed that he was a foreigner. At first I thought he was old; then I noticed that I had been misled by his sparse hair, which was blond, almost white, like the Scandinavians'. In the course of our conversation, which I doubt lasted more than an hour, I learned that he hailed from the Orkneys.[3]

I pointed the man to a chair. He took some time to begin talking. He gave off an air of melancholy, as I myself do now.

"I sell Bibles," he said at last.

"In this house," I replied, not without a somewhat stiff, pedantic note, "there are several English Bibles, including the first one, Wyclif's.[4] I also have Cipriano de Valera's,[5] Luther's[6] (which is, in literary terms, the worst of the lot), and a Latin copy of the Vulgate. As you see, it isn't exactly Bibles I might be needing."

After a brief silence he replied.

"It's not only Bibles I sell. I can show you a sacred book that might interest a man such as yourself. I came by it in northern India, in Bikaner."

He opened his valise and brought out the book. He laid it on the table. It was a cloth-bound octavo[7] volume that had clearly passed through many hands. I examined it; the unusual heft[8] of it surprised me. On the spine was printed *Holy Writ,* and then *Bombay.*

"Nineteenth century, I'd say," I observed.

"I don't know," was the reply. "Never did know."

I opened it at random. The characters were unfamiliar to me. The pages, which seemed worn and badly set, were printed in double columns, like a Bible. The text was cramped, and composed into versicles.[9] At the upper

1. ***more geometrico*:** in the geometrical manner.
2. **Calle Belgrano:** street in Buenos Aires.
3. **Orkneys:** group of islands off the northern coast of Scotland.

4. **Wyclif's Bible:** first English translation of the Bible. John Wycliff (c. 1330–1384) took charge of the project and perhaps did some translating.
5. **Cipriano de Valera's:** Spanish translation of the Bible; Casiodoro de Reina (1520–1594) translated the Bible, and Cipriano de Valera (1531–1602) edited it.
6. **Luther's:** German translation of the Bible. Martin Luther (1483–1546) was the German priest who set in motion the Protestant Reformation.
7. **octavo** *n.:* book, the pages of which have been made from sheets of paper that have been folded eight times.
8. **heft** *adj.:* heaviness.
9. **versicles** *n. pl.:* little verses.

(Opposite) *Head of a Man (Diego)* (1964) by Alberto Giacometti.

Vocabulary

pedantic (pi•dan′tik) *adj.:* showing an exaggerated concern for books, learning, and rules.

corner of each page were Arabic numerals. I was struck by an odd fact: the even-numbered page would carry the number 40,514, let us say, while the odd-numbered page that followed it would be 999. I turned the page; the next page bore an eight-digit number. It also bore a small illustration, like those one sees in dictionaries: an anchor drawn in pen and ink, as though by the unskilled hand of a child.

It was at that point that the stranger spoke again.

"Look at it well. You will never see it again."

There was a threat in the words, but not in the voice.

I took note of the page, and then closed the book. Immediately I opened it again. In vain I searched for the figure of the anchor, page after page. To hide my discomfiture, I tried another tack.

"This is a version of Scripture in some Hindu language, isn't that right?"

"No," he replied.

Then he lowered his voice, as though entrusting me with a secret.

"I came across this book in a village on the plain, and I traded a few rupees[10] and a Bible for it. The man who owned it didn't know how to read. I suspect he saw the Book of Books as an amulet.[11] He was of the lowest caste; people could not so much as step on his shadow without being defiled. He told me his book was called the Book of Sand because neither sand nor this book has a beginning or an end."

He suggested I try to find the first page.

I took the cover in my left hand and opened the book, my thumb and forefinger almost touching. It was impossible: several pages always lay between the cover and my hand. It was as though they grew from the very book.

"Now try to find the end."

I failed there as well.

10. **rupees** *n. pl.:* basic monetary unit of many Asian countries, including India, Pakistan, and Nepal.

11. **amulet** *n.:* ornament often inscribed with a magical incantation or symbol to protect the wearer from evil.

"This can't be," I stammered, my voice hardly recognizable as my own.

"It can't be, yet it *is*," the Bible peddler said, his voice little more than a whisper. "The number of pages in this book is literally infinite. No page is the first page; no page is the last. I don't know why they're numbered in this arbitrary way, but perhaps it's to give one to understand that the terms of an infinite series can be numbered any way whatever."

Then, as though thinking out loud, he went on.

"If space is infinite, we are anywhere, at any point in space. If time is infinite, we are at any point in time."

His musings irritated me.

"You," I said, "are a religious man, are you not?"

"Yes, I'm Presbyterian. My conscience is clear. I am certain I didn't cheat that native when I gave him the Lord's Word in exchange for his diabolic book."

I assured him he had nothing to reproach[12] himself for, and asked whether he was just passing through the country. He replied that he planned to return to his own country within a few days. It was then that I learned he was a Scot, and that his home was in the Orkneys. I told him I had great personal fondness for Scotland because of my love for Stevenson and Hume.[13]

"And Robbie Burns,"[14] he corrected.

12. **reproach** *v.:* criticize or censure.

13. **Stevenson and Hume:** Robert Louis Stevenson (1850–1894), Scottish author; David Hume (1711–1776), Scottish philosopher.

14. **Robbie Burns:** Robert Burns (1759–1796), Scottish poet.

Vocabulary

discomfiture (dis • kum′fi • chər) *n.:* frustration; embarrassment.

caste (kast) *n.:* social class.

defiled (dē • fīld′) *v.:* made unclean.

diabolic (dī′ə • bäl′ik) *adj.:* of or having to do with evil or the devil.

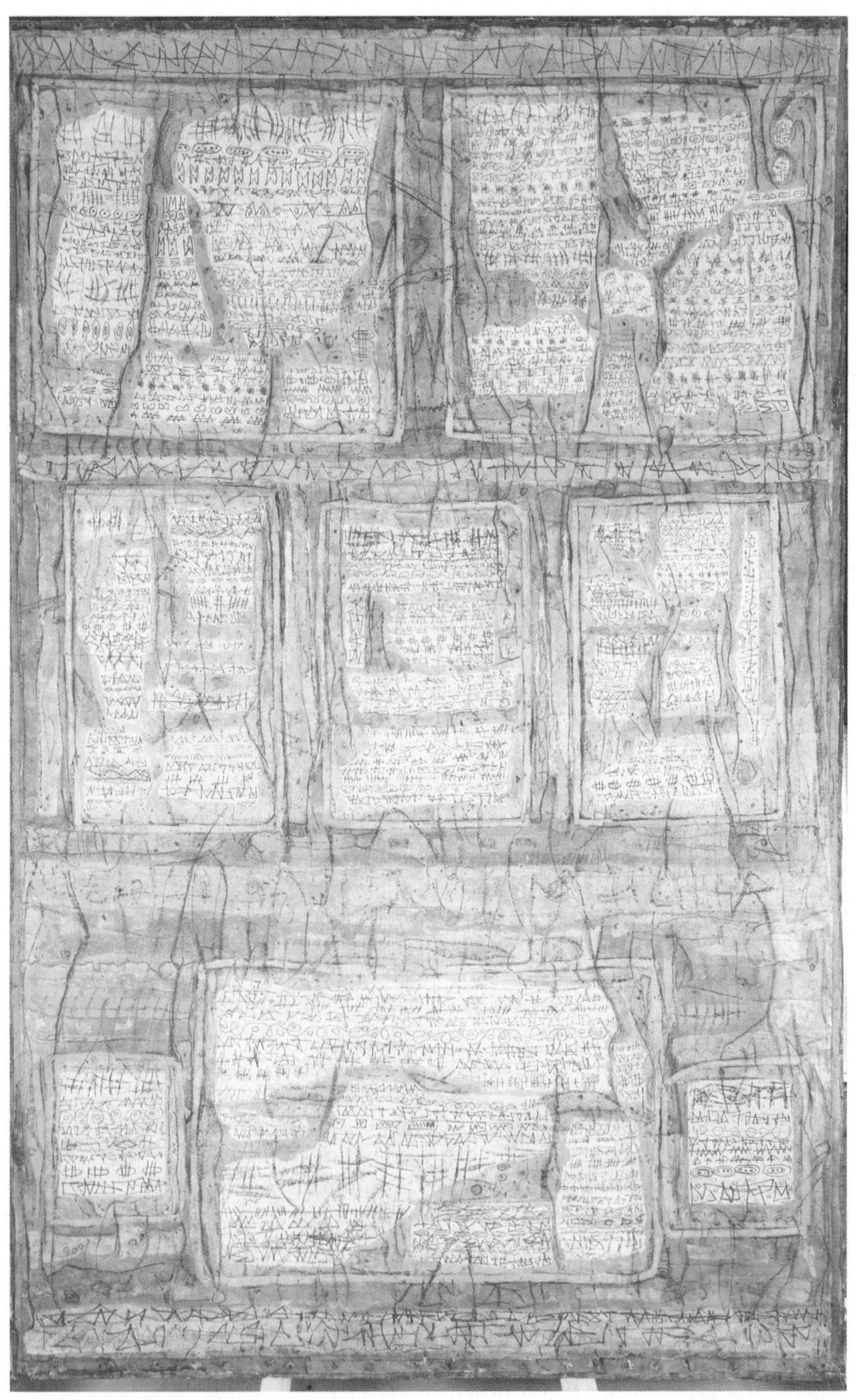

Layered Song (1980) by Clyde Connell.
Courtesy of Arthur Rogers Gallery, New Orleans.

As we talked I continued to explore the infinite book.

"Had you intended to offer this curious specimen to the British Museum, then?" I asked with feigned indifference.

"No," he replied, "I am offering it to you," and he mentioned a great sum of money.

I told him, with perfect honesty, that such an amount of money was not within my ability to pay. But my mind was working; in a few moments I had devised my plan.

"I propose a trade," I said. "You purchased the volume with a few rupees and the Holy Scripture; I will offer you the full sum of my pension, which I have just received, and Wyclif's black-letter[15] Bible. It was left to me by my parents."

"A black-letter Wyclif!" he murmured.

I went to my bedroom and brought back the money and the book. With a bibliophile's zeal he turned the pages and studied the binding.

"Done," he said.

I was astonished that he did not haggle. Only later was I to realize that he had entered my house already determined to sell the book. He did not count the money, but merely put the bills into his pocket.

We chatted about India, the Orkneys, and the Norwegian jarls[16] that had once ruled those islands. Night was falling when the man left. I have never seen him since, nor do I know his name.

I thought of putting the Book of Sand in the space left by the Wyclif, but I chose at last to hide it behind some imperfect volumes of the *Thousand and One Nights.*

I went to bed but could not sleep. At three or four in the morning I turned on the light. I took out the impossible book and turned its pages. On one, I saw an engraving of a mask. There was a number in the corner of the page—I don't remember now what it was—raised to the ninth power.

15. **black-letter** *n.:* typeset used in early printed books.

16. **jarls** *n. pl.:* Scandinavian nobles ranking directly below a king.

I showed no one my treasure. To the joy of possession was added the fear that it would be stolen from me, and to that, the suspicion that it might not be truly infinite. Those two points of anxiety aggravated my already habitual misanthropy. I had but few friends left, and those, I stopped seeing. A prisoner of the Book, I hardly left my house. I examined the worn binding and the covers with a magnifying glass, and rejected the possibility of some artifice. I found that the small illustrations were spaced at two-thousand-page intervals. I began noting them down in an alphabetized notebook, which was very soon filled. They never repeated themselves. At night, during the rare intervals spared me by insomnia,[17] I dreamed of the book.

Summer was drawing to a close, and I realized that the book was monstrous. It was cold consolation to think that I, who looked upon it with my eyes and fondled it with my ten flesh-and-bone fingers, was no less monstrous than the book. I felt it was a nightmare thing, an obscene thing, and that it defiled and corrupted reality.

I considered fire, but I feared that the burning of an infinite book might be similarly infinite, and suffocate the planet in smoke.

I remembered reading once that the best place to hide a leaf is in the forest. Before my retirement I had worked in the National Library, which contained nine hundred thousand books; I knew that to the right of the lobby a curving staircase descended into the shadows of the basement, where the maps and periodicals are kept. I took advantage of the librarians' distraction to hide the Book of Sand on one of the library's damp shelves; I tried not to notice how high up, or how far from the door.

I now feel a little better, but I refuse even to walk down the street the library's on. ■

17. **insomnia** *n.:* inability to sleep.

Vocabulary

bibliophile (bib'lē • ə • fīl) *n.:* one who loves books.
misanthropy (mi • san'thrə • pē) *n.:* hatred for humankind.
artifice (ärt'ə • fis) *n.:* trickery; deception.

Response and Analysis

Reading Check

1. You are the narrator of "The Book of Sand." Immediately after getting rid of the book, you run into an old friend. Tell him or her about your strange adventure, recounting all the **main events** of the story from beginning to end.

Thinking Critically

2. Why does the narrator come to feel that the book is "monstrous"?
3. Write two brief descriptions of the main character, one at the beginning of the story and the other at the end. What accounts for the differences in his outlook and personality? (Your response should go beyond "the book.")
4. The main character is a self-declared bibliophile, or book lover. Does he read people as skillfully as he reads books? Use evidence from the story to support your opinion.
5. A **paradox** is a seeming contradiction that nevertheless holds true. For example, the illustrations in the Book of Sand are both there and not there. How would you explain this paradox? Identify and explain another paradox in the story. Explain how these paradoxes made you feel as you read the story.
6. What dependable realities does Borges question in this story? Did the story succeed in making you think about how you take realities for granted? Why or why not? Be sure to check your Quickwrite notes.
7. Why do you think Borges gave his story the same title as the book *in* the story? Was it simply a matter of telling what the story was about? Or do the two texts share some of the same qualities? (Consider Borges' fascination with puzzles, paradoxes, and literary mystery before you respond.)

Extending and Evaluating

8. How satisfied are you with the **resolution** of the story? Why? Looking back at the **predictions** you made while reading may help you decide how you feel about the ending.

WRITING

A Never-Ending Story

Predict what happens next to the Book of Sand. Write a **story** about another adventure in the weird book's history. (Imagine, for example, what would happen if someone really did try to burn it.) Introduce new characters, a new setting, and several new events.

Vocabulary Development

Substitute Sentences

pedantic	diabolic
discomfiture	bibliophile
caste	misanthropy
defiled	artifice

Imagine that you have been assigned to read "The Book of Sand" to a group of twelve-year-olds. You're worried that Borges's vocabulary is too difficult for them, so you decide to retell the story in simpler language.

Find the sentences in the story in which the Vocabulary words listed above appear, and copy the sentences onto a sheet of paper. Then, rewrite each sentence to make it easier, substituting more commonly known words or phrases for the Vocabulary words. To locate **synonyms**—words with similar meanings—use a **thesaurus** or a **synonym finder.**

Literary Skills Analyze paradox.

Reading Skills Review predictions.

Writing Skills Write a short story.

Vocabulary Skills Identify synonyms.

V. S. Naipaul

(1932–)

Trinidad

When V. S. (Vidiadhar Surajprasad) Naipaul was born, his homeland, the Caribbean island of Trinidad, was still under the colonial rule of Britain. Like many Asian Indians, Naipaul's family had immigrated to Trinidad in the nineteenth century to work as indentured servants on the sugar plantations. With their Asian background and Hindu religion, the Naipauls felt themselves to be members of a transplanted society. As a result, from his earliest days, Naipaul felt a degree of rootlessness. He also felt—on the small island—a sense of the world as a kind of prison.

Fortunately he was an outstanding student. Scholastic honors won him a place at Trinidad's Queen's Royal College and provided him with a chance to leave the island. Granted a scholarship to England's prestigious Oxford University, Naipaul was one of only a few dark-skinned students at a university famous for educating England's privileged white upper classes.

Naipaul's father had pursued a faltering career as an island journalist, and this background inspired Naipaul to become a writer. Leaving Oxford in 1954 with no desire to return to Trinidad's narrow possibilities, he sought his identity in writing. He worked part time for the British Broadcasting Corporation (BBC) and tried his hand at writing fiction about the island life he had fled. His first short stories, which later became *Miguel Street*, went unnoticed until he was able to publish his two earlier novels set in Trinidad, *The Mystic Masseur* (1957) and *The Suffrage of Elvira* (1958).

Naipaul's first masterpiece, *A House for Mr. Biswas*, came along in 1961. The novel, which some critics compared to Dickens's comic satires, tells about a poor, ineffectual Trinidadian (much like Naipaul's father) who finds stability by marrying into an influential family. Deprived of independence, Mr. Biswas's rebellion takes shape in the desperate quest for a house of his own. The novel reveals Naipaul's special gifts as a storyteller: his unique, ironic voice; his clear vision of so-called Third World people; and his understanding of life's essentials. The book established him as a major novelist throughout the literary world.

Naipaul's search for roots has sent him traveling, first back to the West Indies and then to Africa, the Middle East, and India itself, as he pursues the meaning of his own mixed heritage. These voyages and inquiries have led Naipaul to produce more than twenty books, both fiction and nonfiction, including *A Bend in the River* (a 1979 novel set in Africa), *India: A Million Mutinies Now* (a 1991 travel book about his return to India), and *A Way in the World* (a 1994 autobiographical novel about a writer's journey toward self-understanding). All of Naipaul's works have been acclaimed for their clear and bitter yet compassionate insights into the human struggle for identity and survival.

Naipaul has won virtually all the major British literary prizes available to a prose writer, and in 2001 he was awarded the Nobel Prize in literature.

Before You Read

B. Wordsworth

Make the Connection

Quickwrite

How would you describe a poet? Would you know one if you met him or her on the street? In the story you are about to read, a young boy's encounter with a poet transforms his world into "a most exciting place." Would you agree that part of a poet's function is to suggest new angles of vision for the rest of us? Do poets really help transform the world?

Jot down four or five qualities you associate with poets. Then, as you read, see how your image of a poet corresponds with that of the poet in the story.

Literary Focus

Setting

This story's **setting** is the back streets of Port-of-Spain, the capital of Trinidad, the Caribbean island where Naipaul lived as a child. Naipaul uses **imagery** and **dialogue,** as well as factual details, to bring this setting to life. Although the time of the story is unspecified, several of its details—such as beggars asking for pennies—suggest that it takes place during the years of Naipaul's own childhood, the 1930s. These were also the years of the Great Depression, a worldwide economic crisis that was particularly devastating to the citizens of Trinidad. However, as you will see, the main characters of "B. Wordsworth"—a young boy and an old, self-proclaimed poet—seem to be set apart from their harsh surroundings. At arm's length from the story's other, more desperate characters, the pair make it their purpose to find and appreciate spots of beauty in an otherwise violent—or at best indifferent—world.

A story's **setting** is the time and place in which it occurs.

For more on Setting, see the Handbook of Literary and Historical Terms.

Background

The poet in this story is a black Trinidadian who calls himself B. Wordsworth. Before you read, review what you know of another Wordsworth, the one with the first initial W. (See page 734.) Recall, too, that William Wordsworth introduced a revolutionary new theory of poetry that glorified everyday things and everyday language. According to Wordsworth, the poet is "a man speaking to men" in "simple and unelaborated expressions," so that "ordinary things should be presented to the mind in an unusual way." As you read, ask yourself whether B. Wordsworth embodies William Wordsworth's idea of a poet.

Vocabulary Development

botanical (bə•tan′i•kəl) *adj.:* of plants or plant life; connected to the science of botany.

rite (rīt) *n.:* formal ceremony.

patronize (pā′trən•īz′) *v.:* be a customer of.

distill (di•stil′) *v.:* draw out the essence of.

Literary Skills Understand setting.

INTERNET

Vocabulary Practice

Keyword: LE7 12-7

B. Wordsworth

V. S. Naipaul

Three beggars called punctually every day at the hospitable houses in Miguel Street. At about ten an Indian came in his dhoti[1] and white jacket, and we poured a tin of rice into the sack he carried on his back. At twelve an old woman smoking a clay pipe came and she got a cent. At two a blind man led by a boy called for his penny.

Sometimes we had a rogue.[2] One day a man called and said he was hungry. We gave him a meal. He asked for a cigarette and wouldn't go until we had lit it for him. That man never came again.

The strangest caller came one afternoon at about four o'clock. I had come back from school and was in my home clothes. The man said to me, "Sonny, may I come inside your yard?"

He was a small man and he was tidily dressed. He wore a hat, a white shirt, and black trousers.

I asked, "What you want?"

He said, "I want to watch your bees."

We had four small gru-gru palm trees[3] and they were full of uninvited bees.

I ran up the steps and shouted, "Ma, it have a man outside here. He say he want to watch the bees."

My mother came out, looked at the man, and asked in an unfriendly way, "What you want?"

The man said, "I want to watch your bees."

His English was so good, it didn't sound natural, and I could see my mother was worried.

She said to me, "Stay here and watch him while he watch the bees."

The man said, "Thank you, Madam. You have done a good deed today."

He spoke very slowly and very correctly as though every word was costing him money.

We watched the bees, this man and I, for about an hour, squatting near the palm trees.

The man said, "I like watching bees. Sonny, do you like watching bees?"

I said, "I ain't have the time."

He shook his head sadly. He said, "That's what I do, I just watch. I can watch ants for days. Have you ever watched ants? And scorpions, and centipedes, and *congorees*[4]—have you watched those?"

I shook my head.

I said, "What you does do, mister?"

He got up and said, "I am a poet."

I said, "A good poet?"

He said, "The greatest in the world."

"What your name, mister?"

"B. Wordsworth."

"B for Bill?"

"Black. Black Wordsworth. White Wordsworth was my brother. We share one heart. I can watch a small flower like the morning glory and cry."

I said, "Why you does cry?"

"Why, boy? Why? You will know when you grow up. You're a poet, too, you know. And when you're a poet you can cry for everything."

I couldn't laugh.

He said, "You like your mother?"

"When she not beating me."

He pulled out a printed sheet from his hip pocket and said, "On this paper is the greatest poem about mothers and I'm going to sell it to you at a bargain price. For four cents."

---

1. **dhoti** (dō′tē) *n.:* loincloth worn by many Hindu men.
2. **rogue** (rōg) *n.:* archaic for "wandering beggar."
3. **gru-gru** (gro͞o′ gro͞o′) **palm trees:** spiny-trunked West Indian palm trees.
4. ***congorees*** (käŋ′gə·rēz′) *n. pl.:* conger eels; long, scaleless eels found in the warm waters of the West Indies.

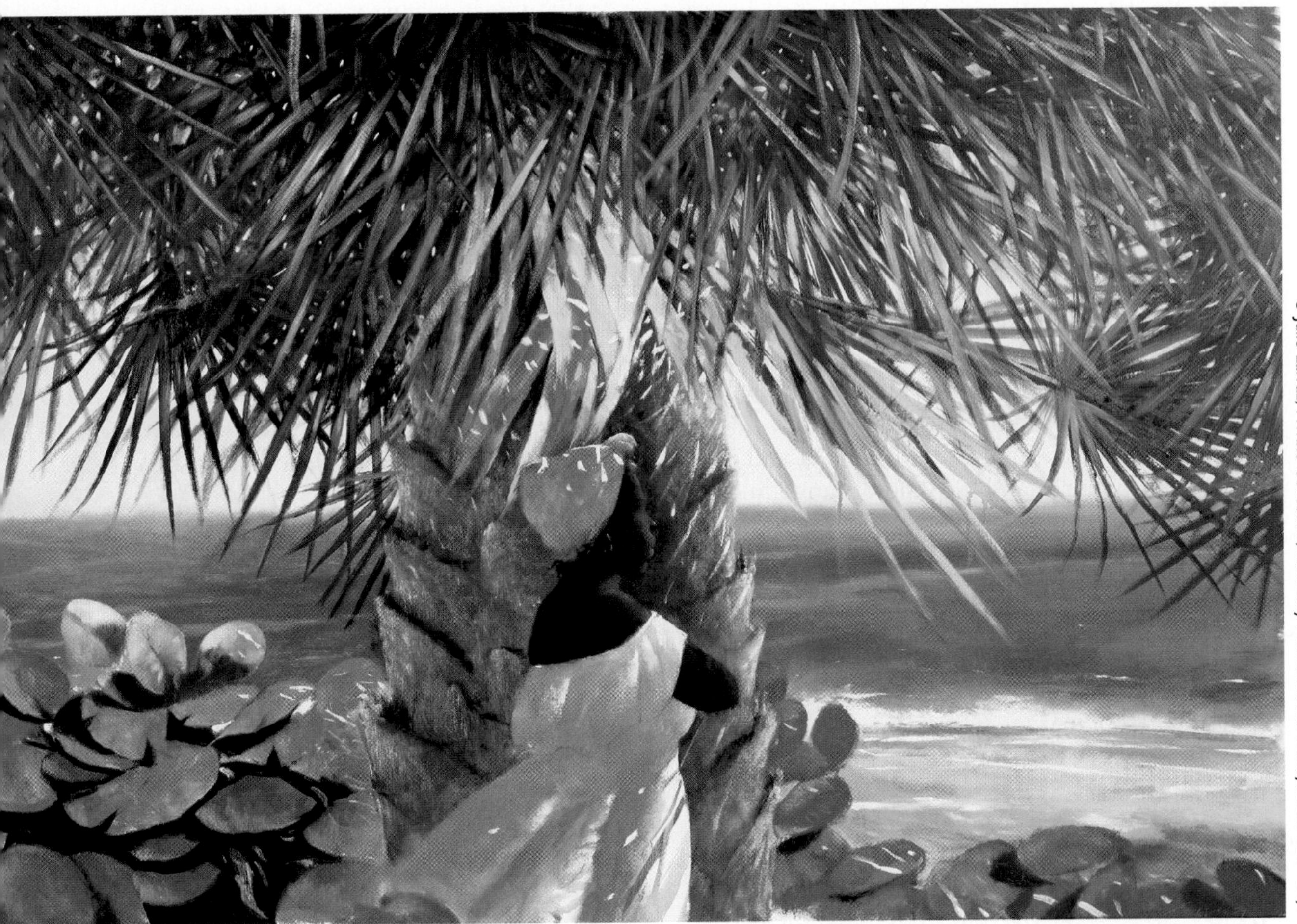

© Julio Larraz, Private Collection, Courtesy Nohra Haime Gallery, New York City.

Papiamento (1987) by Julio Larraz. Oil on canvas.

I went inside and I said, "Ma, you want to buy a poetry for four cents?"

My mother said, "Tell that blasted man to haul his tail away from my yard, you hear."

I said to B. Wordsworth, "My mother say she ain't have four cents."

B. Wordsworth said, "It is the poet's tragedy."

And he put the paper back in his pocket. He didn't seem to mind.

I said, "Is a funny way to go round selling poetry like that. Only calypsonians[5] do that sort of thing. A lot of people does buy?"

5. **calypsonians** (kə·lip′so′nē·ənz) *n. pl.:* West Indian folk musicians who traditionally perform satirical, syncopated songs that are improvised, or composed on the spot. *Calypso* possibly comes from *kaiso,* a Trinidadian dialect word meaning "town crier."

He said, "No one has yet bought a single copy."

"But why you does keep on going round, then?"

He said, "In this way I watch many things, and I always hope to meet poets."

I said, "You really think I is a poet?"

"You're as good as me," he said.

And when B. Wordsworth left, I prayed I would see him again.

About a week later, coming back from school one afternoon, I met him at the corner of Miguel Street.

He said, "I have been waiting for you for a long time."

I said, "You sell any poetry yet?"

He shook his head.

He said, "In my yard I have the best mango tree in Port-of-Spain.[6] And now the mangoes are ripe and red and very sweet and juicy. I have waited here for you to tell you this and to invite you to come and eat some of my mangoes."

He lived in Alberto Street in a one-roomed hut placed right in the center of the lot. The yard seemed all green. There was the big mango tree. There was a coconut tree and there was a plum tree. The place looked wild, as though it wasn't in the city at all. You couldn't see all the big concrete houses in the street.

He was right. The mangoes were sweet and juicy. I ate about six, and the yellow mango juice ran down my arms to my elbows and down my mouth to my chin and my shirt was stained.

My mother said when I got home, "Where you was? You think you is a man now and could go all over the place? Go cut a whip for me."

She beat me rather badly, and I ran out of the house swearing that I would never come back. I went to B. Wordsworth's house. I was so angry, my nose was bleeding.

B. Wordsworth said, "Stop crying, and we will go for a walk."

I stopped crying, but I was breathing short. We went for a walk. We walked down St. Clair Avenue to the Savannah[7] and we walked to the racecourse.

B. Wordsworth said, "Now, let us lie on the grass and look up at the sky, and I want you to think how far those stars are from us."

I did as he told me, and I saw what he meant. I felt like nothing, and at the same time I had never felt so big and great in all my life. I forgot all my anger and all my tears and all the blows.

When I said I was better, he began telling me the names of the stars, and I particularly remembered the constellation of Orion the Hunter,[8] though I don't really know why. I can spot Orion even today, but I have forgotten the rest.

Then a light was flashed into our faces, and we saw a policeman. We got up from the grass.

The policeman said, "What you doing here?"

B. Wordsworth said, "I have been asking myself the same question for forty years."

We became friends, B. Wordsworth and I. He told me, "You must never tell anybody about me and about the mango tree and the coconut tree and the plum tree. You must keep that a secret. If you tell anybody, I will know, because I am a poet."

I gave him my word and I kept it.

I liked his little room. It had no more furniture than George's front room,[9] but it looked cleaner and healthier. But it also looked lonely.

One day I asked him. "Mister Wordsworth, why you does keep all this bush in your yard? Ain't it does make the place damp?"

He said, "Listen, and I will tell you a story. Once upon a time a boy and girl met each other and they fell in love. They loved each other so much they got married. They were both poets. He loved words. She loved grass and flowers and trees. They lived happily in a single room, and then one day, the girl poet said to the boy poet, 'We are going to have another poet in the family.' But this poet was never born, because the girl died, and the young poet died with her, inside her. And the girl's husband was very sad, and he said he would never touch a thing in the girl's garden. And so the garden remained, and grew high and wild."

I looked at B. Wordsworth, and as he told me this lovely story, he seemed to grow older. I understood his story.

6. **Port-of-Spain:** seaport on the island of Trinidad; capital of Trinidad and Tobago.

7. **Savannah** (sə·van′ə): two-hundred-acre park in the center of Port-of-Spain. The racecourse is located there.

8. **Orion** (ō·rī′ən) **the Hunter:** constellation named for a hunter in Greek and Roman mythology whom Diana—the goddess of the moon and of hunting—loves but accidentally kills.

9. **George's front room:** George is a character in another story in Naipaul's book *Miguel Street.*

We went for long walks together. We went to the Botanical Gardens and the Rock Gardens. We climbed Chancellor Hill in the late afternoon and watched the darkness fall on Port-of-Spain, and watched the lights go on in the city and on the ships in the harbor.

He did everything as though he were doing it for the first time in his life. He did everything as though he were doing some church rite.

He would say to me, "Now, how about having some ice cream?"

And when I said, yes, he would grow very serious and say, "Now, which café shall we patronize?" As though it were a very important thing. He would think for some time about it, and finally say, "I think I will go and negotiate the purchase with that shop."

The world became a most exciting place. One day, when I was in his yard, he said to me, "I have a great secret which I am now going to tell you."

I said, "It really secret?"

"At the moment, yes."

I looked at him, and he looked at me. He said, "This is just between you and me, remember. I am writing a poem."

"Oh." I was disappointed.

He said, "But this is a different sort of poem. This is the greatest poem in the world."

I whistled.

He said, "I have been working on it for more than five years now. I will finish it in about twenty-two years from now, that is, if I keep on writing at the present rate."

"You does write a lot, then?"

He said, "Not any more. I just write one line a month. But I make sure it is a good line."

I asked, "What was last month's good line?"

He looked up at the sky, and said, "*The past is deep.*"

I said, "It is a beautiful line."

B. Wordsworth said, "I hope to distill the experiences of a whole month into that single line of poetry. So, in twenty-two years, I shall have written a poem that will sing to all humanity."

I was filled with wonder.

Our walks continued. We walked along the sea wall at Docksite one day, and I said, "Mr. Wordsworth, if I drop this pin in the water, you think it will float?"

He said, "This is a strange world. Drop your pin, and let us see what will happen."

The pin sank.

I said, "How is the poem this month?"

But he never told me any other line. He merely said, "Oh, it comes, you know. It comes."

Or we would sit on the sea wall and watch the liners come into the harbor.

But of the greatest poem in the world I heard no more.

I felt he was growing older.

"How you does live, Mr. Wordsworth?" I asked him one day.

He said, "You mean how I get money?"

When I nodded, he laughed in a crooked way.

He said, "I sing calypsos in the calypso season."

"And that last you the rest of the year?"

"It is enough."

"But you will be the richest man in the world when you write the greatest poem?"

He didn't reply.

One day when I went to see him in his little house, I found him lying on his little bed. He looked so old and so weak, that I found myself wanting to cry.

He said, "The poem is not going well."

He wasn't looking at me. He was looking through the window at the coconut tree, and he was speaking as though I wasn't there. He said, "When I was twenty I felt the power within

Vocabulary

botanical (bə•tan′i•kəl) *adj.:* of plants or plant life; connected to the science of botany.

rite (rīt) *n.:* formal ceremony.

patronize (pā′trən•īz′) *v.:* be a customer of.

distill (di•stil′) *v.:* draw out the essence of.

The Trial (1986) by Julio Larraz. Oil on canvas.

myself." Then, almost in front of my eyes, I could see his face growing older and more tired. He said, "But that—that was a long time ago."

And then—I felt it so keenly, it was as though I had been slapped by my mother. I could see it clearly on his face. It was there for everyone to see. Death on the shrinking face.

He looked at me, and saw my tears and sat up.

He said, "Come." I went and sat on his knees.

He looked into my eyes, and he said, "Oh, you can see it, too. I always knew you had the poet's eye."

He didn't even look sad, and that made me burst out crying loudly.

He pulled me to his thin chest, and said, "Do you want me to tell you a funny story?" and he smiled encouragingly at me.

But I couldn't reply.

He said, "When I have finished this story, I want you to promise that you will go away and never come back to see me. Do you promise?"

I nodded.

He said, "Good. Well, listen. That story I told you about the boy poet and the girl poet, do you remember that? That wasn't true. It was something I just made up. All this talk about poetry and the greatest poem in the world, that wasn't true, either. Isn't that the funniest thing you have heard?"

But his voice broke.

I left the house, and ran home crying, like a poet, for everything I saw.

I walked along Alberto Street a year later, but I could find no sign of the poet's house. It hadn't vanished, just like that. It had been pulled down, and a big, two-storied building had taken its place. The mango tree and the plum tree and the coconut tree had all been cut down, and there was brick and concrete everywhere.

It was just as though B. Wordsworth had never existed. ■

Response and Analysis

Reading Check

1. How does the boy meet B. Wordsworth?
2. Who does B. Wordsworth say he is?
3. What secret does B. Wordsworth share with the boy?
4. What does B. Wordsworth reveal to the boy at the end of the story?

Thinking Critically

5. How does the boy feel about B. Wordsworth? What does he learn from him?
6. Do you think B. Wordsworth's tragic story about the boy poet and the girl poet is true? If true, why would he deny it? If not, why did he tell it in the first place?
7. Consider what B. Wordsworth says to the policeman who asks, "What you doing here?" What deeper significance do you see in B. Wordsworth's reply? (Is that what poets also seek to know?)
8. Consider the contrast in the story between the mother's no-nonsense ways and the poetic vision of B. Wordsworth. Then, find some of B. Wordsworth's statements about poetry in the story. What might Naipaul want to express about the nature of poetry and the role of the poet in society? Consider whether you agree with these assessments. (You may want to review your Quickwrite notes for ideas.)
9. What specific pictures of the **setting** are most vivid in your mind? If you were going to illustrate the story, what **images** would you concentrate on?
10. If we think of the narrator in the story as the author's recollection of himself at that age, what does the story suggest about the influences (historical, political, cultural) that made Naipaul a writer? What does it suggest about his view of the poet's position and role in society?

Extending and Evaluating

11. In your opinion, why does Naipaul set up such a sharp contrast between the language of the two characters in the story? If both characters spoke the same dialect, would the story be stronger or weaker? Explain.

WRITING

Seeing Things Differently

Near the end of the story, the poet pays the boy the highest of compliments, saying, "I always knew you had the poet's eye." In a brief **essay,** explain what you think the poet's eye sees. How is poetic vision different from an everyday perspective? Use examples from the story to illustrate the two different kinds of vision and to support your claims.

Vocabulary Development

Question and Answer Charts

botanical *patronize*
rite *distill*

Work with a group to make up two questions about each Vocabulary word above, and organize your answers in a chart. (An example is shown below.) After you have completed charts for all the words, invite another group to answer some of your questions.

botanical	
Questions	Answers
What might you learn from a book containing botanical information?	You might learn how different plants are structured, how they grow, where they are found, and so on.

Literary Skills Analyze setting.

Writing Skills Write an essay analyzing poetic vision.

Vocabulary Skills Create semantic charts.

INTERNET

Projects and Activities

Keyword: LE7 12-7

Naguib Mahfouz

(1911–   )

Egypt

As a boy in Cairo's picturesque old quarter, Naguib Mahfouz (nä·zhēb′ mä′fo͞oz) encountered many unusual characters who would influence his life and work. Among them was the journalist El-Muwaylili, who was experimenting with new forms of fiction. At the time the novel form was virtually unknown in Arabic literature, where poetry and nonfiction were stressed. El-Muwaylili's efforts inspired Mahfouz to write full-fledged novels. Eventually Mahfouz would become the best-known fiction writer in the Arabic language and the first Arabic author to win the Nobel Prize in literature.

Interested in both philosophy and literature, Mahfouz attended Cairo University, where classes were conducted in English and French. His growing proficiency in those languages allowed him to read many European classics and to familiarize himself with the novel and short story forms. Still uncertain of his future, Mahfouz submitted a short story to a Cairo magazine. He considers the day it was accepted the most important day of his life.

The course of Mahfouz's writing career seems to recapitulate two centuries of literary movements. His early historical novels, set in the time of the pharaohs, display the idealistic nationalism of Romantic-era authors like Johann Wolfgang von Goethe. In the chaotic period leading up to World War II, Mahfouz turned to social realism in books like *New Cairo* (1946) and *Midaq Alley* (1947), which vividly evoke his boyhood neighborhood and the effects of war on the average Egyptian. Mahfouz continued in this realistic vein with his masterful Cairo trilogy—*Palace Walk* (1956), *The Palace of Desire* (1957), and *Sugar Street* (1957)—about three generations of a Cairo family who symbolize Egyptian experience in modern times. In the 1960s, Mahfouz began to experiment with stream of consciousness (see pages 1180–1181), as well as with the more indirect symbolism associated with modernism. His preoccupation with the individual facing spiritual and emotional crises was prompted in part by the growing Arab-Israeli conflict and Egypt's bitter defeat in the 1967 Six-Day War.

Before You Read

Half a Day

Make the Connection

Quickwrite

Albert Einstein theorized that time is relative. While scientists might disagree about the objective truth of this theory, most people would agree that their *perception* of time often fluctuates. Indeed, any given minute, hour, or day might seem eternal to one person but utterly fleeting to the next.

Can you recall an event or experience during which you felt that time either raced or dragged? Jot down a few sentences describing this memory. What explanation can you provide for the way you perceived time?

Literary Focus

Foreshadowing

When a writer uses **foreshadowing,** he or she provides clues that suggest what might happen later in the story. Sometimes those clues take the form of specific events that work together to create a strong sense of suspense in the story. In other cases, though, the clues are quite subtle, adding up to a certain **mood** or atmosphere that is only later revealed to have significance to the plot. As you read "Half a Day," try to determine which kind of foreshadowing Mahfouz uses.

Foreshadowing is the use of clues that hint at what will happen later in the story.

For more on Foreshadowing, see the Handbook of Literary and Historical Terms.

Background

Because so much of Egypt is desert, the majority of Egyptians have always lived on the fertile banks of the Nile River. Since World War II, more and more people from rural areas along the Nile have moved to Egypt's major cities, also located on the river. The largest of these cities is Cairo, Egypt's capital, where Mahfouz grew up and where "Half a Day" is set. Cairo's population has changed dramatically since Mahfouz was a boy, and many of the city's fields and gardens have given way to tall modern buildings, raucous crowds, and some of the world's worst traffic jams.

Vocabulary Development

unmarred (ən•märd′) *adj.:* undamaged; unspoiled.

pitiable (pit′ē•ə•bəl) *adj.:* lamentable; regrettable.

intricate (in′tri•kit) *adj.:* full of elaborate details or parts.

avail (ə•vāl′) *n.:* benefit; advantage.

refuse (ref′yo͞os) *n.:* trash.

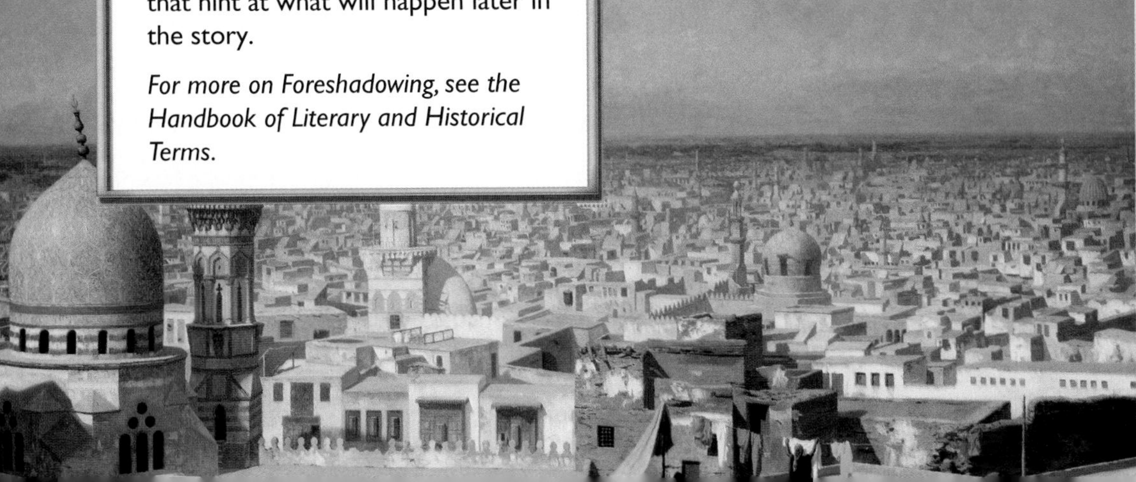

View of Cairo.

SKILLS FOCUS

Literary Skills Understand foreshadowing.

go.hrw.com

INTERNET

Vocabulary Practice

Keyword: LE7 12-7

Half a Day

Naguib Mahfouz
translated by **Denys Johnson-Davies**

I proceeded alongside my father, clutching his right hand, running to keep up with the long strides he was taking. All my clothes were new: the black shoes, the green school uniform, and the red tarboosh.[1] My delight in my new clothes, however, was not altogether unmarred, for this was no feast day[2] but the day on which I was to be cast into school for the first time.

My mother stood at the window watching our progress, and I would turn toward her from time to time, as though appealing for help. We walked along a street lined with gardens; on both sides were extensive fields planted with crops, prickly pears, henna trees, and a few date palms.

"Why school?" I challenged my father openly. "I shall never do anything to annoy you."

"I'm not punishing you," he said, laughing. "School's not a punishment. It's the factory that makes useful men out of boys. Don't you want to be like your father and brothers?"

I was not convinced. I did not believe there was really any good to be had in tearing me away from the intimacy of my home and throwing me into this building that stood at the end of the road like some huge, high-walled fortress, exceedingly stern and grim.

When we arrived at the gate we could see the courtyard, vast and crammed full of boys and girls. "Go in by yourself," said my father, "and join them. Put a smile on your face and be a good example to others."

I hesitated and clung to his hand, but he gently pushed me from him. "Be a man," he said. "Today you truly begin life. You will find me waiting for you when it's time to leave."

I took a few steps, then stopped and looked but saw nothing. Then the faces of boys and girls came into view. I did not know a single one of them, and none of them knew me. I felt I was a stranger who had lost his way. But glances of curiosity were directed toward me, and one boy approached and asked, "Who brought you?"

"My father," I whispered.

"My father's dead," he said quite simply.

I did not know what to say. The gate was closed, letting out a pitiable screech. Some of the children burst into tears. The bell rang. A lady came along, followed by a group of men. The men began sorting us into ranks. We were formed into an intricate pattern in the great courtyard surrounded on three sides by high buildings of several floors; from each floor we were overlooked by a long balcony roofed in wood.

"This is your new home," said the woman. "Here, too, there are mothers and fathers. Here there is everything that is enjoyable and beneficial to knowledge and religion. Dry your tears and face life joyfully."

We submitted to the facts, and this submission brought a sort of contentment. Living beings were drawn to other living beings, and from the first moments my heart made friends with such boys as were to be my friends and fell in love with such girls as I was to be in love with, so that it seemed my misgivings had had no basis. I had never imagined school would have this rich variety. We played all sorts of different

1. **tarboosh** (tär·bo͞osh′) *n.:* brimless cloth cap worn by Muslim men.
2. **feast day:** holiday.

Vocabulary

unmarred (ən•märd′) *adj.:* undamaged; unspoiled.
pitiable (pit′ē•ə•bəl) *adj.:* lamentable; regrettable.
intricate (in′tri•kit) *adj.:* full of elaborate details or parts.

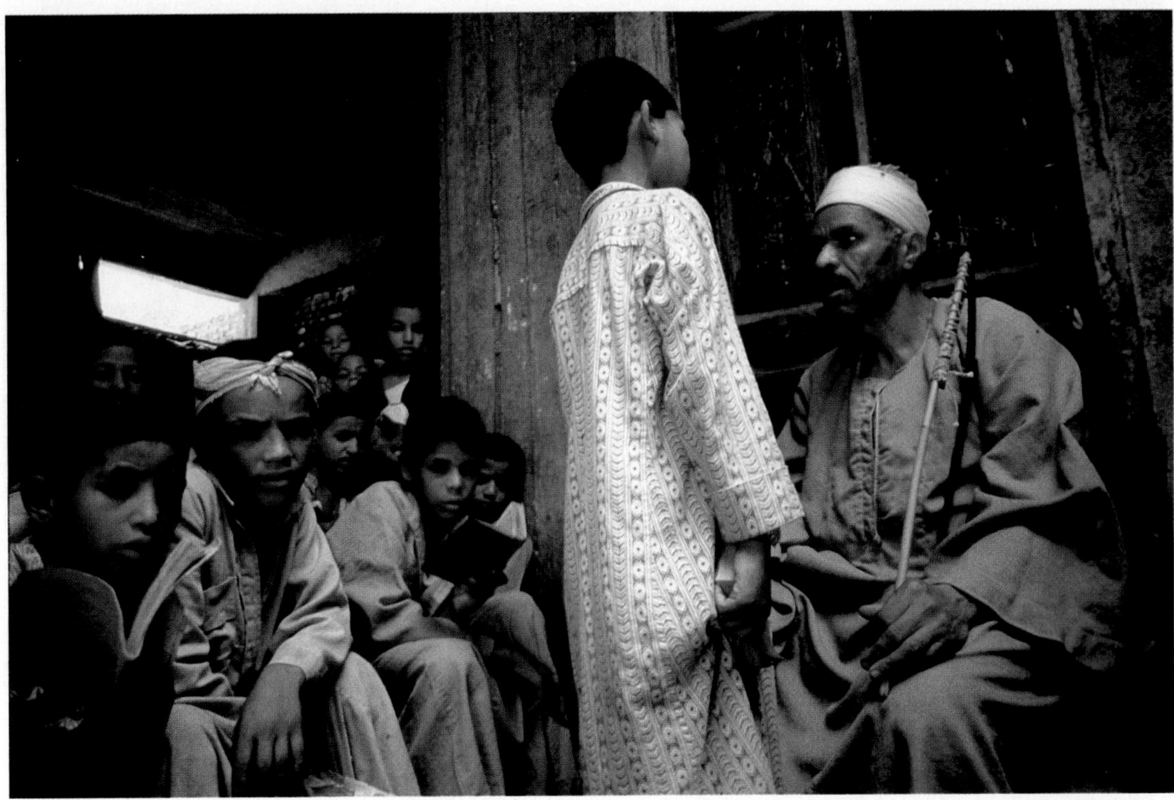

games: swings, the vaulting horse,[3] ball games. In the music room we chanted our first songs. We also had our first introduction to language. We saw a globe of the Earth, which revolved and showed the various continents and countries. We started learning the numbers. The story of the Creator of the universe was read to us, we were told of His present world and of His Hereafter, and we heard examples of what He said. We ate delicious food, took a little nap, and woke up to go on with friendship and love, play and learning.

As our path revealed itself to us, however, we did not find it as totally sweet and unclouded as we had presumed. Dust-laden winds and unexpected accidents came about suddenly, so we had to be watchful, at the ready, and very patient. It was not all a matter of playing and fooling around. Rivalries could bring about pain and hatred or give rise to fighting. And while the lady would sometimes smile, she would often scowl and scold. Even more frequently she would resort to physical punishment.

In addition, the time for changing one's mind was over and gone and there was no question of ever returning to the paradise of home. Nothing lay ahead of us but exertion, struggle, and perseverance. Those who were able took advantage of the opportunities for success and happiness that presented themselves amid the worries.

The bell rang announcing the passing of the day and the end of work. The throngs of children rushed toward the gate, which was opened again. I bade farewell to friends and sweethearts and passed through the gate. I peered around but found no trace of my father, who had promised to be there. I stepped aside to wait. When I had waited for a long time without avail, I decided to return home on my own. After I had taken a few steps, a middle-aged man passed by,

3. **vaulting horse:** that is, the horse one leaps over in gymnastics.

Vocabulary

avail (ə • vāl′) *n.:* benefit; advantage.

Cairo street scene.

and I realized at once that I knew him. He came toward me, smiling, and shook me by the hand, saying, "It's a long time since we last met—how are you?"

With a nod of my head, I agreed with him and in turn asked, "And you, how are you?"

"As you can see, not all that good, the Almighty be praised!"

Again he shook me by the hand and went off. I proceeded a few steps, then came to a startled halt. Good Lord! Where was the street lined with gardens? Where had it disappeared to? When did all these vehicles invade it? And when did all these hordes of humanity come to rest upon its surface? How did these hills of refuse come to cover its sides? And where were the fields that bordered it? High buildings had taken over, the street surged with children, and disturbing noises shook the air. At various points stood conjurers[4] showing off their tricks and making snakes appear from baskets. Then there was a band announcing the opening of a circus, with clowns and weight lifters walking in front. A line of trucks carrying central security troops crawled majestically by. The siren of a fire engine shrieked, and it was not clear how the vehicle would cleave its way to reach the blazing fire. A battle raged between a taxi driver and his passenger, while the passenger's wife called out for help and no one answered. Good God! I was in a daze. My head spun. I almost went crazy. How could all this have happened in half a day, between early morning and sunset? I would find the answer at home with my father. But where was my home? I could see only tall buildings and hordes of people. I hastened on to the crossroads between the gardens and Abu Khoda.[5] I had to cross Abu Khoda to reach my house, but the stream of cars would not let up. The fire engine's siren was shrieking at full pitch as it moved at a snail's pace, and I said to myself, "Let the fire take its pleasure in what it consumes."[6] Extremely irritated, I wondered when I would be able to cross. I stood there a long time, until the young lad employed at the ironing shop on the corner came up to me. He stretched out his arm and said gallantly, "Grandpa, let me take you across." ■

4. **conjurers** *n.:* magicians.

5. **Abu Khoda:** (ä·bo͞o′ kō′dä).

6. **Let the fire . . . consumes:** Egyptian proverb.

Vocabulary

refuse (ref′yo͞os) *n.:* trash.

Response and Analysis

Reading Check

1. As the story opens, where is the narrator's father taking him for the first time? What advice does the father give?
2. Identify four things the narrator likes about his new experience and two things he dislikes.
3. As the narrator walks home alone, what does a middle-aged man on the street do?
4. List three questions the narrator asks himself while walking home.
5. What does the "young lad" do and say at the busy intersection?

Thinking Critically

6. What surprise was revealed at the end of the story? Did you have any idea that the story might end in this way? Explain.
7. Re-read the story, and identify three details that **foreshadow** the surprise ending.
8. Describe what you thought about the narrator's identity and state of mind when you first read the story. Now, upon reviewing the story, what can you say about the narrator and his state of mind? Has Mahfouz, the writer, merely played a literary trick, or has he realistically portrayed the way a person might perceive reality? Explain.
9. What **theme** about time—and about life in general—does the ending help express? (You may want to refer to your Quickwrite notes.) How is the title of the story relevant to this theme? Support your response with examples from the text.
10. A **symbol** is a person, place, thing, or event that stands both for itself and for something beyond itself. What might the following elements in the story **symbolize**? Support your ideas with evidence from the text.
    - the father
    - the woman at the school
    - the school
    - home
    - the story's title

WRITING

What's Real?

Both Mahfouz's "Half a Day" and Cortázar's "Axolotl" (see page 1218) play with the idea of identity and self-perception. In a brief **essay, compare and contrast** these stories. How are the narrators in the two stories alike and different? How are their experiences similar and dissimilar? Use examples from both texts to support your ideas and opinions. What does each story have to say about the nature of reality?

Vocabulary Development

Analyzing Context Clues

Explain why the **context clues** in the following sentences are wrong. (The underlined words are Vocabulary words from the selection.)

1. Mia was extremely upset to learn that her new car had been unmarred by the hailstorm.
2. The most pitiable moment of the field trip was when Jackson found fifty dollars lying on the sidewalk.
3. The directions to my house are very intricate: Just walk straight for two blocks.
4. To no avail, I asked the waiter for another napkin, and within seconds he had returned with one.
5. "What a joy to see your bedroom brimming with refuse!" Mom cried.

Literary Skills Analyze foreshadowing.

Writing Skills Write an essay comparing and contrasting two stories.

Vocabulary Skills Analyze context clues.

Seamus Heaney

(1939–)

Ireland

Seamus Heaney was born to Roman Catholic parents in largely Protestant Northern Ireland. His boyhood on a farm in County Derry contributed profoundly to his identity as a poet, though Heaney never promoted himself as a rustic or regarded his work as an expression of regionalism. He earned his education as a scholarship student, first at a Catholic preparatory school and then at Queens University in Belfast, where, still in his mid-twenties, he was appointed lecturer in English.

Instead of leading him away from his roots in Irish soil, Heaney's studies—particularly those having to do with the history and psychology of myth—opened for him a way of seeing anew not only the misty grandeur of his native landscape, but also the figures in it who, unknowingly, unite the past with the present. Heaney is an acute observer of rural life and of life lived on the industrial margins of cities, and he deals with both without romanticizing them.

The American poet Robert Lowell regarded Heaney as "the best Irish poet since William Butler Yeats." In 1995, commended for his works "of lyrical beauty and ethical depth, which exalt everyday miracles and the living past," Heaney was awarded the Nobel Prize in literature. In 1999, Heaney's new translation of the Anglo-Saxon epic *Beowulf* (see page 43) accomplished what seemed to be impossible. The ancient epic beat out *Harry Potter and the Prisoner of Azkaban* for Britain's coveted Whitbread Book of the Year Award.

Before You Read

Digging

Literary Skills Understand extended metaphor.

Make the Connection

What associations, metaphorical or otherwise, do you have with the word *dig*? What are some things we might dig for—facts? roots? archeological discoveries? In this poem, Irish farmers—the poet's father and grandfather—dig two things in particular: potatoes and peat. The poet-speaker is also digging—but for what?

Literary Focus

Extended Metaphor

Up until the poem's last line, you may not realize that "Digging" contains an **extended metaphor.** In this case, the comparison between the father's work and the poet's work resonates throughout the poem. As you read, try to identify the connections between the two kinds of digging.

An **extended metaphor** is a comparison developed over a few lines or throughout an entire poem.

For more on Metaphor, see the Handbook of Literary and Historical Terms.

Digging

Seamus Heaney

Between my finger and my thumb
The squat pen rests; snug as a gun.

Under my window, a clean rasping sound
When the spade sinks into gravelly ground:
My father, digging. I look down

Till his straining rump among the flowerbeds
Bends low, comes up twenty years away
Stooping in rhythm through potato drills°
Where he was digging.

The coarse boot nestled on the lug,° the shaft
Against the inside knee was levered firmly.
He rooted out tall tops, buried the bright edge deep
To scatter new potatoes that we picked
Loving their cool hardness in our hands.

By God, the old man could handle a spade.
Just like his old man.

My grandfather cut more turf in a day
Than any other man on Toner's bog.
Once I carried him milk in a bottle
Corked sloppily with paper. He straightened up
To drink it, then fell to right away
Nicking and slicing neatly, heaving sods
Over his shoulder, going down and down
For the good turf. Digging.

The cold smell of potato mould, the squelch and slap
Of soggy peat, the curt cuts of an edge
Through living roots awaken in my head.
But I've no spade to follow men like them.

Between my finger and my thumb
The squat pen rests.
I'll dig with it.

---

8. drills *n. pl.:* furrows or rows of planted seeds.
10. lug *n.:* earlike prong or projection by which a spade is supported.

Response and Analysis

Thinking Critically

1. Describe what the speaker sees from his window.

2. Why do you think the father comes up "twenty *years* away" in line 7? (What word did you expect to find there?)

3. What different things does the speaker compare his pen to? What significance can you find in these comparisons, particularly the one in the last stanza?

4. Explain the **extended metaphor** in the poem. What kind of digging does the speaker intend to do?

5. What examples of **alliteration** (or repeated consonant sounds) and **rhyme** can you find in the poem?

6. In lines 25–27, the spade cuts through the "living roots." How might digging, either the kind done by the speaker's father or the kind done by the speaker himself, be seen as an act of violence?

7. Identify other **images** of violence or destruction in the poem. What point might the poet be making about the relationship between creation and destruction?

WRITING

Do Your Own Digging

Seamus Heaney once wrote that in "Digging" he truly found his own voice: "Finding a voice means that you can get your own feeling into your own words and that your words have the feel of you about them." Beginning with the last three lines of Heaney's poem, write your own **poem,** being careful to do your "digging" with words that suit your own voice. You might want to begin by recalling something about your parents, guardians, grandparents, or other older family members.

Portrait of Seamus Heaney (1973) by Edward McGuire. Oil on canvas (56″ × 44″).

Literary Skills Analyze extended metaphor.

Writing Skills Write a poem.

Writing a Short Story

V. S. Naipaul's B. Wordsworth lives only in the world of a short story, remembered by the narrator (and, of course, the reader) for his sad one line of poetry: "The past is deep" (page 1237). In writing s**hort stories**—short, imaginative, fictional narratives—you, too, can create a world in which characters, such as B. Wordsworth, will live and speak their memorable lines.

Writing Assignment
Write a short story of at least 1,500 words with an interesting plot and well-developed characters.

Find a Story Idea Short story topics are everywhere, if you just know where to look. One way to find an idea for a story is to remember important events in your own life and imagine what might have happened if you had made another decision. You can also observe everyday people and imagine a story about an interesting-looking person, or tell a story about a person in your family's old photo albums.

Consider Audience and Purpose As you choose a story idea, think about your purpose, audience, tone, and form. Your **purpose** for writing a short story is to develop an entertaining and interesting story for an **audience** of your classmates. To create a **tone**—serious, humorous, or ironic—use language creatively to reveal your attitude toward the subject. The usual **form** for a short story is a prose narrative; therefore, use well-formed, expressive sentences and paragraphs.

Establish the Setting Locate your story in a specific place, or **setting.** For example, in Naipaul's "B. Wordsworth," the main character lives "in a one-roomed hut placed right in the center of the lot. The yard seemed all green. There was the big mango tree. There was a coconut tree and there was a plum tree" (page 1236).

TIP Use **concrete sensory details**—the sights, sounds, and smells—to create a scene the reader won't easily forget.

Develop Characters Create one or two main characters and only one or two supporting characters. To create complex, **dynamic** main characters—characters that grow and change over the course of your story—use a combination of direct and indirect characterization techniques. Use primarily indirect characterization to allow your readers to make their own judgments about the characters.

CHARACTERIZATION TECHNIQUES

Direct characterization *tells* readers what the character is like.

Indirect characterization *shows* readers what the character is like through

- **dialogue**—what the character says and how he or she says it
- **thoughts and feelings**—what the character thinks or feels; show thoughts and feelings through **interior monologue**—telling "out loud" what the character is thinking
- **actions**—what the character does
- **reactions**—how a character responds to another character

DO THIS

Develop a Plot The things that happen in a short story—the **sequence of events**—make up the plot. Unlike the sprawl of a novel's plot, the plot for a short story has to be compressed. Follow the steps below to develop the plot of your short story.

1. Initiate the **conflict,** or the struggle between opposing forces. An **external conflict** is a conflict between two characters, between a character and an outside force, or between a character and a situation. An **internal conflict** is a conflict within a character.
2. Develop **complications,** or rising actions. These are the consequences of a character's actions or decisions.
3. Lead to a **climax,** the point at which the complications have reached their most intense moment and the conflict is resolved.
4. Resolve the conflict in the **denouement,** or falling action, that reveals the significance of the story's events for the characters.

TIP The third-person-omniscient narrator's point of view can relate a story from **shifting perspectives;** that is, the narrator can tell how two or more characters perceive the same events.

Organize the Events Most short stories are told in chronological order. However, to highlight the significance of events, use flashbacks or flash-forwards. Vary the **pace** of your story, the rate at which events occur, to show changes in time, place, or mood.

Determine Point of View The **point of view** from which you tell your story determines what your narrator—or **speaker**—in your short story can and cannot tell your audience. You can choose from three basic points of view—a first-person narrator, a third-person-limited narrator, and a third-person-omniscient narrator. Once you choose a point of view, use it consistently.

Use Stylistic Devices Writers use **style**—the creative use of language—for specific aesthetic purposes. Style distinguishes one writer's story from another's. For example, one author's use of **imagery, concrete sensory details,** and **figures of speech** is an important part of the author's particular style. Use stylistic devices in your short story.

Sometimes an author will use **irony**—the contrast between appearance and reality—for a specific purpose. **Verbal irony** occurs when a character says one thing and means another. **Situational irony** occurs when what happens is opposite of what is expected or appropriate. **Dramatic irony** occurs when the readers know something that the character does not.

Indicate the Significance Most professional short story writers do not directly express the significance, or **theme,** of their story. Instead they *show* readers the significance through the details of their short story and their style, and sometimes by writing a clever last line of the story. For example, the last line of Naipaul's "B. Wordsworth" captures the significance of the story: "It was just as though B. Wordsworth had never existed" (page 1238). Try distilling the theme of your story into one dramatic line, and use it as your last sentence.

Writing Skills
Write a short story. Determine audience and purpose. Establish setting and develop characters. Develop plot and point of view. Express the theme. Use various stylistic devices.

PRACTICE & APPLY Follow the instructions in this workshop to write a short story to share with your class.

The Caplan Collection of the Children's Museum of Indianapolis.

Collection 7:
The Modern World:
1900 to the Present

Ourselves Among Others

Mansfield
Auden
Mistral
Thomas
Neruda
Narayan
Desai
Lively
Jin
Tutu
Aung San Kyi

All paths lead to the same goal: to convey to others what we are. And we must pass through solitude and difficulty, isolation and silence, in order to reach forth to the enchanted place where we can dance our clumsy dance and sing our sorrowful song.

—Pablo Neruda

Katherine Mansfield

(1888–1923)

New Zealand

Katherine Mansfield was born Kathleen Mansfield Beauchamp in Wellington, New Zealand, the third child of an ambitious merchant. As a child she was aware of the rugged beauty of her island home, but she shared her mother's distaste for being "out here," oceans away from England, the source of their culture.

At home she was "difficult" and prone to nightmares, a lonely, resentful child who saw her father as an adversary. At school she was moody and had few friends. She had her father's talent for math and could memorize verse at sight, yet she was a careless scholar.

When Mansfield was fifteen, the Beauchamp family sailed for England to enroll their daughters in Queen's College in London. Mansfield was delighted with every aspect of her new life, and when she was summoned home to New Zealand in 1906, she closeted herself in her room and grieved for lost London.

In 1908, when she was nineteen, Mansfield's family permitted her to return to London alone. But with only the meager allowance her father granted her, Mansfield was painfully poor and frequently sick. Her first literary encouragement came in 1910, when A. R. Orage, the editor of the progressive journal *The New Age*, accepted several of her stories. These stories were collected in a volume called *In a German Pension* (1911).

About the same time an Oxford undergraduate named John Middleton Murry accepted a story and some of her poems for his new literary magazine, *Rhythm*, and the two began a long and stormy relationship.

When Mansfield's younger brother, Leslie, died in World War I, she was overcome with grief. When she at last emerged from under that cloud, she vowed to write about New Zealand from then on as "a sacred debt . . . because my brother and I were born there." She called it a "debt of love. . . . I shall tell everything, even of how the laundry basket squeaked."

As her stories were published, Mansfield became recognized as a gifted writer and an innovator of the short story. Mansfield's stories downplayed attention to plot and action; instead, she tried to illuminate moments of significance.

Despite her growing success, Mansfield's personal life continued to be troubled. In 1917, she learned that she had tuberculosis. She and Murry were married the following spring, but three weeks later they separated. As Mansfield's health worsened, her characteristic verve gave way to loneliness, anger, and morbid fears. But as she entered the final year of her life, she was reconciled to her illness. She renewed her relationship with Murry and showed a new compassion in her writing. In the brief time left to her, she also wrote some of her finest stories, many with New Zealand backgrounds, which are collected in *The Garden Party and Other Stories* (1922) and *The Dove's Nest and Other Stories* (1923).

A belief that some miracle might save her led Mansfield to an institute run by a healer and mystic named George Gurdjieff in France. The treatment did not work. There, with Murry at her side, she died in January 1923.

Before You Read

The Doll's House

Make the Connection

Quickwrite

Whenever people come together in groups, there's almost always competition for status, or high position. Some people will inevitably try to prove that they are superior to other people in the group or that their group is superior to other groups.

What gives a person so-called superior status in our society? Is status always dependent on material wealth? In what environments do you think competition for status is especially fierce? Jot down your thoughts about competition and status today.

Literary Focus

Symbol

In fiction a **symbol** is an object, a place, a person, or an animal that stands both for itself and for something beyond itself. As you read, think about what this doll's house and its little lamp symbolize in a world where wealth and social position are important—and where people of status mock the ideal of compassion for the less fortunate. Remember that the meanings of symbols are often elusive and that readers frequently disagree on their exact significance. You might want to take note of some possible meanings as they occur to you and then later compare your ideas with those of a classmate.

A **symbol** is an object, an animal, a place, or a person that stands both for itself and for something broader than itself.

For more on Symbol, see the Handbook of Literary and Historical Terms.

Background

This story is set early in the twentieth century in a small village in New Zealand. At that time, New Zealand was still a British colony, and the British colonists had brought England's rigid class system with them to their new home. Under this system, people's status in society was automatically determined by their family background. People with inherited wealth and privilege did not ordinarily associate with the poor or even with those who earn what we consider a middle-class income. In New Zealand, however, because of the shortage of schools, wealthy children were educated alongside children of different social classes.

Vocabulary Development

congealed (kən•jēld′) *v.* used as *adj.:* thickened.

conspicuous (kən•spik′yo͞o•əs) *adj.:* attracting attention.

flagged (flagd) *v.:* declined; lost strength or interest.

clambered (klam′bərd) *v.:* climbed clumsily.

Literary Skills
Understand symbols.

INTERNET
Vocabulary Practice
Keyword: LE7 12-7

THE DOLL'S HOUSE

Katherine Mansfield

The Art Archive.

When dear old Mrs. Hay went back to town after staying with the Burnells, she sent the children a doll's house. It was so big that the carter[1] and Pat carried it into the courtyard, and there it stayed, propped up on two wooden boxes beside the feed-room door. No harm could come of it; it was summer. And perhaps the smell of paint would have gone off by the time it had to be taken in. For, really, the smell of paint coming from that doll's house ("Sweet of old Mrs. Hay, of course; most sweet and generous!")—but the smell of paint was quite enough to make anyone seriously ill, in Aunt Beryl's opinion. Even before the sacking was taken off. And when it was . . .

There stood the doll's house, a dark, oily, spinach green, picked out with bright yellow. Its two solid little chimneys, glued onto the roof, were painted red and white, and the door, gleaming with yellow varnish, was like a little slab of toffee. Four windows, real windows, were divided into panes by a broad streak of green. There was actually a tiny porch, too, painted yellow, with big lumps of congealed paint hanging along the edge.

But perfect, perfect little house! Who could possibly mind the smell? It was part of the joy, part of the newness.

"Open it quickly, someone!"

The hook at the side was stuck fast. Pat pried it open with his penknife, and the whole housefront swung back, and—there you were, gazing at one and the same moment into the drawing room and dining room, the kitchen and two bedrooms. That is the way for a house to open! Why don't all houses open like that? How much more exciting than peering through the slit of a door into a mean little hall with a hatstand and two umbrellas! That is—isn't it?—what you long to know about a house when you put your hand on the knocker. Perhaps it is the way God opens houses at dead of night when He is taking a quiet turn with an angel . . .

"O-oh!" The Burnell children sounded as though they were in despair. It was too marvelous; it was too much for them. They had never seen anything like it in their lives. All the rooms were papered. There were pictures on the walls, painted on the paper, with gold frames complete. Red carpet covered all the floors except the kitchen; red plush chairs in the drawing room, green in the dining room; tables, beds with real bedclothes, a cradle, a stove, a dresser with tiny plates, and one big jug. But what Kezia liked more than anything, what she liked frightfully, was the lamp. It stood in the middle of the dining-room table, an exquisite little amber lamp with a white globe. It was even filled all ready for lighting, though, of course, you couldn't light it. But there was something inside that looked like oil, and that moved when you shook it.

The father and mother dolls, who sprawled very stiff as though they had fainted in the drawing room, and their two little children asleep upstairs, were really too big for the doll's house. They didn't look as though they belonged. But the lamp was perfect. It seemed to smile at Kezia, to say, "I live here." The lamp was real.

The Burnell children could hardly walk to school fast enough the next morning. They burned to tell everybody, to describe, to—well—to boast about their doll's house before the school bell rang.

"I'm to tell," said Isabel, "because I'm the eldest. And you two can join in after. But I'm to tell first."

There was nothing to answer. Isabel was bossy, but she was always right, and Lottie and Kezia knew too well the powers that went with being eldest. They brushed through the thick buttercups at the road edge and said nothing.

"And I'm to choose who's to come and see it first. Mother said I might."

For it had been arranged that while the doll's house stood in the courtyard they might ask the girls at school, two at a time, to come and look.

Vocabulary

congealed (kən•jēld′) *v.* used as *adj.:* thickened.

1. **carter** *n.:* delivery person.

Bonhams, London.

Girl Sitting on the Steps (late 19th or early 20th century) by Peter Vilhelm Ilsted. Colored mezzotint.

Not to stay to tea, of course, or to come traipsing[2] through the house. But just to stand quietly in the courtyard while Isabel pointed out the beauties, and Lottie and Kezia looked pleased . . .

But hurry as they might, by the time they had reached the tarred palings[3] of the boys' playground the bell had begun to jangle. They only just had time to whip off their hats and fall into line before the roll was called. Never mind. Isabel tried to make up for it by looking very important and mysterious and by whispering behind her hand to the girls near her, "Got something to tell you at playtime."

Playtime came and Isabel was surrounded. The girls of her class nearly fought to put their arms round her, to walk away with her, to beam flatteringly, to be her special friend. She held quite a court under the huge pine trees at the side of the playground. Nudging, giggling together, the little girls pressed up close. And the only two who stayed outside the ring were the two who were always outside, the little Kelveys. They knew better than to come anywhere near the Burnells.

For the fact was, the school the Burnell children went to was not at all the kind of place their parents would have chosen if there had been any choice. But there was none. It was the only school for miles. And the consequence was all the children in the neighborhood, the Judge's little girls, the doctor's daughters, the storekeeper's children, the milkman's, were forced to mix together. Not to speak of there being an equal number of rude, rough little boys as well. But the line had to be drawn somewhere. It was drawn at the Kelveys.

2. **traipsing** (trāps′iŋ) *v.* used as *adj.:* colloquial for "wandering."
3. **palings** (pāl′iŋz) *n. pl.:* fence stakes.

Many of the children, including the Burnells, were not allowed even to speak to them. They walked past the Kelveys with their heads in the air, and as they set the fashion in all matters of behavior, the Kelveys were shunned by everybody. Even the teacher had a special voice for them, and a special smile for the other children when Lil Kelvey came up to her desk with a bunch of dreadfully common-looking flowers.

They were the daughters of a spry, hardworking little washerwoman, who went about from house to house by the day. This was awful enough. But where was Mr. Kelvey? Nobody knew for certain. But everybody said he was in prison. So they were the daughters of a washerwoman and a jailbird. Very nice company for other people's children! And they looked it. Why Mrs. Kelvey made them so conspicuous was hard to understand. The truth was they were dressed in "bits" given to her by the people for whom she worked. Lil, for instance, who was a stout, plain child, with big freckles, came to school in a dress made from a green art-serge[4] tablecloth of the Burnells', with red plush sleeves from the Logans' curtains. Her hat, perched on top of her high forehead, was a grown-up woman's hat, once the property of Miss Lecky, the postmistress. It was turned up at the back and trimmed with a large scarlet quill. What a little guy[5] she looked! It was impossible not to laugh. And her little sister, our Else, wore a long white dress, rather like a nightgown, and a pair of little boy's boots. But whatever our Else wore she would have looked strange. She was a tiny wishbone of a child, with cropped hair and enormous solemn eyes—a little white owl. Nobody had ever seen her smile; she scarcely ever spoke. She went through life holding on to Lil, with a piece of Lil's skirt screwed up in her hand. Where Lil went our Else followed. In the playground, on the road going to and from school, there was Lil marching in front and our Else holding on behind. Only when she wanted anything, or when she was out of breath, our Else gave Lil a tug, a twitch, and Lil stopped and turned round. The Kelveys never failed to understand each other.

4. **art-serge** (ärt•surj): type of woven wool fabric.
5. **guy** *n.:* British for "an odd-looking person." The word comes from the name of Guy Fawkes, an English conspirator executed for taking part in the 1605 Gunpowder Plot to bomb the king and the houses of Parliament. In England, handmade likenesses of Guy Fawkes are burned annually on November 5—Guy Fawkes Day.

Now they hovered at the edge; you couldn't stop them listening. When the little girls turned round and sneered, Lil, as usual, gave her silly, shamefaced smile, but our Else only looked.

And Isabel's voice, so very proud, went on telling. The carpet made a great sensation, but so did the beds with real bedclothes, and the stove with an oven door.

When she finished Kezia broke in. "You've forgotten the lamp, Isabel."

"Oh, yes," said Isabel, "and there's a teeny little lamp, all made of yellow glass, with a white globe that stands on the dining-room table. You couldn't tell it from a real one."

"The lamp's best of all," cried Kezia. She thought Isabel wasn't making half enough of the little lamp. But nobody paid any attention. Isabel was choosing the two who were to come back with them that afternoon and see it. She chose Emmie Cole and Lena Logan. But when the others knew they were all to have a chance, they couldn't be nice enough to Isabel. One by one they put their arms round Isabel's waist and walked her off. They had something to whisper to her, a secret. "Isabel's *my* friend."

Only the little Kelveys moved away forgotten; there was nothing more for them to hear.

Days passed, and as more children saw the doll's house, the fame of it spread. It became the one subject, the rage. The one question was, "Have you seen Burnells' doll's house? Oh, ain't it lovely!" "Haven't you seen it? Oh, I say!"

Even the dinner hour was given up to talking about it. The little girls sat under the pines eating their thick mutton sandwiches and big slabs of johnny cake spread with butter. While always,

Vocabulary

conspicuous (kən•spik′yo͞o•əs) *adj.:* attracting attention.

Bethnal Green Museum, London/The Bridgeman Art Library.

as near as they could get, sat the Kelveys, our Else holding on to Lil, listening too, while they chewed their jam sandwiches out of a newspaper soaked with large red blobs . . .

"Mother," said Kezia, "can't I ask the Kelveys just once?"

"Certainly not, Kezia."

"But why not?"

"Run away, Kezia; you know quite well why not."

At last everybody had seen it except them. On that day the subject rather flagged. It was the dinner hour. The children stood together under the pine trees, and suddenly, as they looked at the Kelveys eating out of their paper, always by themselves, always listening, they wanted to be horrid to them. Emmie Cole started the whisper.

"Lil Kelvey's going to be a servant when she grows up."

"O-oh, how awful!" said Isabel Burnell, and she made eyes at Emmie.

Emmie swallowed in a very meaning way and nodded to Isabel as she'd seen her mother do on those occasions.

"It's true—it's true—it's true," she said.

Then Lena Logan's little eyes snapped. "Shall I ask her?" she whispered.

"Bet you don't," said Jessie May.

"Pooh, I'm not frightened," said Lena. Suddenly she gave a little squeal and danced in front of the other girls. "Watch! Watch me! Watch me now!" said Lena. And sliding, gliding, dragging one foot, giggling behind her hand, Lena went over to the Kelveys.

Lil looked up from her dinner. She wrapped the rest quickly away. Our Else stopped chewing. What was coming now?

"Is it true you're going to be a servant when you grow up, Lil Kelvey?" shrilled Lena.

Dead silence. But instead of answering, Lil only gave her silly, shamefaced smile. She didn't seem to mind the question at all. What a sell[6] for Lena! The girls began to titter.

Lena couldn't stand that. She put her hands on her hips; she shot forward. "Yah, yer father's in prison!" she hissed, spitefully.

This was such a marvelous thing to have said that the little girls rushed away in a body, deeply, deeply excited, wild with joy. Someone found a long rope, and they began skipping. And never did they skip so high, run in and out so fast, or do such daring things as on that morning.

In the afternoon Pat called for the Burnell children with the buggy and they drove home. There were visitors. Isabel and Lottie, who liked visitors, went upstairs to change their pinafores.[7] But Kezia thieved out at the back. Nobody was about; she began to swing on the big white gates of the courtyard. Presently, looking along the road, she saw two little dots. They grew bigger, they were coming toward her. Now she could see that one was in front and one close behind. Now she could see that they were the Kelveys. Kezia stopped swinging. She slipped off the gate as if she was going to run away. Then she hesitated. The Kelveys came nearer, and beside them walked their shadows, very long, stretching right across the road with their heads in the buttercups. Kezia clambered back on the gate; she had made up her mind; she swung out.

"Hullo," she said to the passing Kelveys.

---

6. **sell** *n.:* slang for "trick."
7. **pinafores** (pin′ə·fôrz′) *n. pl.:* sleeveless, apronlike garments that young girls wear over dresses.

Vocabulary

flagged (flagd) *v.:* declined; lost strength or interest.
clambered (klam′bərd) *v.:* climbed clumsily.

They were so astounded that they stopped. Lil gave her silly smile. Our Else stared.

"You can come and see our doll's house if you want to," said Kezia, and she dragged one toe on the ground. But at that Lil turned red and shook her head quickly.

"Why not?" asked Kezia.

Lil gasped, then she said, "Your ma told our ma you wasn't to speak to us."

"Oh, well," said Kezia. She didn't know what to reply. "It doesn't matter. You can come and see our doll's house all the same. Come on. Nobody's looking."

But Lil shook her head still harder.

"Don't you want to?" asked Kezia.

Suddenly there was a twitch, a tug at Lil's skirt. She turned round. Our Else was looking at her with big, imploring eyes; she was frowning; she wanted to go. For a moment Lil looked at our Else very doubtfully. But then our Else twitched her skirt again. She started forward. Kezia led the way. Like two little stray cats they followed across the courtyard to where the doll's house stood.

"There it is," said Kezia.

There was a pause. Lil breathed loudly, almost snorted; our Else was still as a stone.

"I'll open it for you," said Kezia kindly. She undid the hook and they looked inside.

"There's the drawing room and the dining room, and that's the—"

"Kezia!"

Oh, what a start they gave!

"Kezia!"

It was Aunt Beryl's voice. They turned round. At the back door stood Aunt Beryl, staring as if she couldn't believe what she saw.

"How dare you ask the little Kelveys into the courtyard?" said her cold, furious voice. "You know as well as I do, you're not allowed to talk to them. Run away, children, run away at once. And don't come back again," said Aunt Beryl. And she stepped into the yard and shooed them out as if they were chickens.

"Off you go immediately!" she called, cold and proud.

They did not need telling twice. Burning with shame, shrinking together, Lil huddling along

National Trust Photographic Library/Nadia Mackenzie/The Bridgeman Art Library.

like her mother, our Else dazed, somehow they crossed the big courtyard and squeezed through the white gate.

"Wicked, disobedient little girl!" said Aunt Beryl bitterly to Kezia, and she slammed the doll's house to.

The afternoon had been awful. A letter had come from Willie Brent, a terrifying, threatening letter, saying if she did not meet him that evening in Pulman's Bush, he'd come to the front door and ask the reason why! But now that she had frightened those little rats of Kelveys and given Kezia a good scolding, her heart felt lighter. That ghastly pressure was gone. She went back to the house humming.

When the Kelveys were well out of sight of Burnells', they sat down to rest on a big red drainpipe by the side of the road. Lil's cheeks were still burning; she took off the hat with the quill and held it on her knee. Dreamily they looked over the hay paddocks,[8] past the creek, to the group of wattles[9] where Logan's cows stood waiting to be milked. What were their thoughts?

Presently our Else nudged up close to her sister. But now she had forgotten the cross lady. She put out a finger and stroked her sister's quill; she smiled her rare smile.

"I seen the little lamp," she said, softly.

Then both were silent once more. ■

8. **paddocks** (pad′əks) *n. pl.:* fenced pieces of land.
9. **wattles** (wät′'lz) *n. pl.:* acacia trees.

Response and Analysis

Reading Check

1. Review the description of the doll's house. What do the furniture and the dolls themselves look like?
2. Review the descriptions of the characters in the story. Who among them appears comfortable, or truly to "belong" in the world?

Thinking Critically

3. Why does Isabel invite friends to see the doll's house? Why does Kezia invite Lil and Else to see it?
4. Describe the relationship between Lil and Else. Is it significant that Else speaks the last line of dialogue in the story? Why?
5. What do you think the doll's house might **symbolize** in the story? What in particular do you think the little lamp symbolizes? (Recall Else's comment at the end of the story—"I seen the little lamp.") In your opinion, which symbol evokes the strongest emotions in the reader? Explain.
6. How would you state this story's **theme**? What does the story reveal about cruelty, status, families, and outsiders? Use textual evidence to support your interpretation of theme.
7. How do you feel about the extraordinary meanness shown by Lil and Else's classmates? How do you account for it?
8. Look back at your Quickwrite notes about status and competition. What similarities, if any, exist between our world and the world of the story?

Extending and Evaluating

9. The narrator of "The Doll's House" enters the minds of different characters at different points in the story. Explain whether you think the narrator's **omniscient point of view** adds to the power of the story or makes the narrative confusing. Support your opinion with specific passages.

SKILLS FOCUS

Literary Skills Analyze symbols. Analyze a modern short story.

Writing Skills Write an essay comparing and contrasting two characters.

Vocabulary Skills Find context clues.

Grammar Skills Understand and identify the use of active voice and passive voice.

INTERNET

Projects and Activities

Keyword: LE7 12-7

WRITING

Burnell versus Kelvey

Choose two of the children from the story—one Burnell and one Kelvey—and write an **essay comparing and contrasting** them. In your essay, focus on one or two of each character's actions or statements. What do these actions or words reveal about the character? In your opinion, what moved the character to act or speak in such a way? Conclude by suggesting what Mansfield might have wanted her readers to realize about each of these young figures.

Vocabulary Development

Finding Context Clues

congealed	*flagged*
conspicuous	*clambered*

Go back to the text and locate each of the Vocabulary words in the list above. On a separate sheet of paper, make note of any context clues that would help you define the word (if it weren't already defined at the bottom of the page). The first word is done for you.

Word: congealed (verb used as an adjective): "thickened" (p. 1255).

Clues: The sentence says that there were "big lumps" of paint "hanging" from the edge of the porch. Thin, wet paint wouldn't hang in lumps, but thick dried globs of paint would.

Literary Focus

The Modern Short Story

People have been telling stories since the first campfire, but the short story as a distinct literary form is really an invention of the nineteenth century. A number of factors probably contributed to the rise of the short story at roughly the same time in France, Germany, and the United States. Growing literacy, the consequent popularity of magazines, and the form's flexibility and appeal to a wide variety of writers were doubtless responsible for its success.

The American critic and writer Edgar Allan Poe created the most influential theoretical foundations for the short story in his 1842 review of Nathaniel Hawthorne's *Twice-Told Tales*. In his review, Poe claimed that the story should be considered superior to the novel because, since a story could be read in one sitting, it could have a more unified aesthetic effect on the reader. To Poe, a unified effect was the most important literary goal. "A skillful artist," he wrote, "having conceived a certain *single effect* . . . then combines such events . . . as may best serve him in establishing this preconceived effect. . . . [T]here should be no word written of which the tendency, direct or indirect, is not to the one pre-established design." The effect that Poe aimed for in most of his own stories was shock or horror.

The stories of Poe and other nineteenth-century writers frequently involved people in extreme states—physical, emotional, or both. It was not unusual for characters to go mad or die at the end. Such grand events satisfied both writers' and readers' need for **closure,** or the feeling that one has reached a satisfactory conclusion. Some writers, such as Guy de Maupassant in France and O. Henry in the United States, provided this closure through the use of a surprising twist, or **trick ending.**

Realism, a literary movement that developed in the latter part of the nineteenth century, tried to portray life as it really is, not as we might wish or fear it could be. Some realists, such as the Russian Anton Chekhov, often wrote stories that had no strong beginning or end, but merely portrayed the events of daily life. These **slice-of-life** stories provided readers with snapshots of life in a variety of places and social classes. The American writer Henry James faithfully depicted his characters' perceptions and motivations in a style called **psychological realism.**

The modern story more often aims not at a sensory effect *on* the reader but at revelation *to* the reader—the revelation of some essential truth implicit in the story. The main character of the story may remain ignorant of this truth even at the end, and **dramatic irony,** the result of the reader's knowing more than the character does, is a common element in modern fiction. Though readers may clearly see dramatic irony in "The Doll's House," the story doesn't at first appear to have the unity of form that Poe championed. But closer examination reveals a coherence of language, theme, and imagery, in this case all related to the central symbol of the doll's house.

In a general sense we can say three things about the modern short story:

1. It is more likely to be concerned with explorations of character than with the construction of a fast-paced plot.
2. It is more apt to imply important facts and psychological truths than to state them directly.
3. It is more likely to move toward a revelation of truth than toward a single emotional effect.

Analyzing a modern short story. With some classmates, choose a story from a recent periodical or short story collection. Then, collaborate in writing a critique of the story for the entire class. As part of the critique, consider to what extent the story demonstrates the characteristics of the modern short story listed above.

Grammar Link

Active-Voice Verbs and Passive-Voice Verbs

Here are two ways to convey the same information:

> Katherine Mansfield uses very specific details to describe daily life in New Zealand.
>
> Very specific details are used by Katherine Mansfield to describe daily life in New Zealand.

Each sentence uses a different voice. The first sentence, which uses the **active voice,** expresses an action done *by* the subject (Katherine Mansfield). The second sentence, which uses the **passive voice,** expresses an action done *to* the subject (*very specific details*). The second sentence is awkward.

In general the active voice is preferable because it presents ideas directly and emphasizes the doer of the action. Bring your writing to life, and capture your audience's attention by using active-voice verbs whenever possible.

Use passive-voice verbs when you want to emphasize the receiver of an action rather than the performer or when you don't know the identity of the performer. Remember, however, that passive-voice verbs can be less direct and less concise than the active-voice verbs. Overusing passive-voice verbs can make it difficult for the reader to follow the action.

Doll's house nursery with toys.

Bethnal Green Museum, London/Bridgeman Art Library.

PRACTICE

Label the following sentences passive or active. Then, revise the sentences by changing passive-voice verbs to active or active-voice verbs to passive.

1. The beautiful doll house was admired by the Burnell children.
2. A description of the doll house was given by Isabel to the children.
3. Kezia invited Lil and Else into the courtyard.
4. Kezia was chastised by Aunt Beryl for inviting the Kelveys into the courtyard.
5. The symbolism of the lamp in Katherine Mansfield's "The Doll's House" is often debated by critics.

Apply to Your Writing

Take out a writing assignment you are working on now or have already completed. Highlight all the *be* verbs or verb phrases. (*Be* verbs can signal an unnecessary use of the passive voice.) If necessary, replace passive-voice verbs with active-voice verbs.

For more help, see Active Voice and Passive Voice, 3d–3e, in the Language Handbook.

W. H. Auden

(1907–1973)

England / America

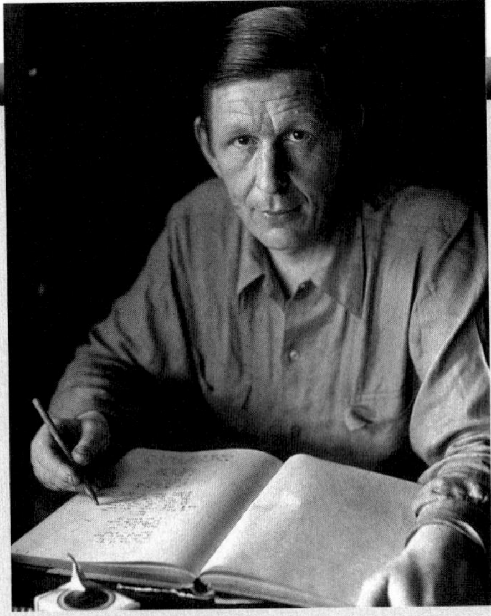

TimePix.

Wystan Hugh Auden gave a name to his times—the Age of Anxiety—and he lived to see the day when his influence was so broad and deep that, as far as poetry was concerned, that same era could have been called the Age of Auden.

Auden was born in York, a city in northern England near the city of Leeds. He was the son of a physician and a nurse who encouraged his early interest in science and engineering. But in his adolescence, Auden discovered poetry, and he studied, with an analytical eye, all its forms, from Chaucer onward. By the time he entered Oxford, he was as much a teacher as he was a student, and he quickly gathered about himself other young poets, who accepted him as their leader.

Auden as a poet was difficult to classify, and he remains so to this day. In spite of their virtuosity, uniform excellence, and formal variety, Auden's poems—lyrics, oratorios, ballads—tend to cohere as a body of work rather than to distinguish themselves as separate entities. For this reason, Auden is often regarded less as the author of certain individual poems than as the creator of a climate in which all things Audenesque thrive in an atmosphere uniquely his own.

Auden put his indelible stamp on the poetry of the 1930s, establishing his preeminence among the brilliant group of poets that included Stephen Spender, Louis MacNeice, and Cecil Day-Lewis. Auden caused his British compatriots shock and dismay when, in the critical year of 1939, as Hitler's divisions were about to march into Poland and ignite World War II, he decided to make his home in the United States. Auden had come to feel that, as the rise of fascism made war in Europe inevitable, his chances of enjoying creative freedom and of making a livelihood were greatest in America. From 1939 to 1942, he taught at the University of Michigan and various other American universities. In 1946, he became a U.S. citizen.

For the next ten years, Auden lived mostly in New York City and California. He spent his summers in Kirchstetten, Austria, in a house he bought in 1957 with profits from his extensive reading tours—the first, and last, home of his own. This retreat, not far from Vienna, provided him with much-needed privacy and the opportunity to experience firsthand the culture of central Europe.

In England, Auden's emigration to the United States was, at the time, widely regarded as a defection, if not an outright betrayal. But the British eventually welcomed him back—first by electing him professor of poetry at Oxford and later by making it possible for him to live on the campus of Christ Church College as a guest of Oxford University whenever he returned to England.

For Independent Reading

You may enjoy the following poem by Auden:

- "The Unknown Citizen"

Before You Read

Musée des Beaux Arts

Make the Connection

Quickwrite

Every generation sees imperfections and injustices in the way things are. For Auden, during what he termed the Age of Anxiety, people had grown indifferent to human suffering, and society no longer treasured the individual. Auden felt that this indifference to the plight of others and disregard for the value of individuality were symptoms of a society in need of reform.

To what extent do you think people today are indifferent to human suffering? Jot down your thoughts, and include some examples to support your viewpoint.

Literary Focus

Diction

Many of Auden's poems combine eloquent poetic language with **colloquial** words—the down-to-earth language of everyday life. This use of contrasting **diction,** or word choice, has several effects. It works to surprise the reader, who may be trained to expect only lofty, dignified language in poetry. It also creates a casual, offhand tone that unnerves the reader by mirroring the randomness of the "real world." Auden hoped that by unsettling his readers through language, he might move them to take positive action—to seek or show compassion in a seemingly indifferent world.

Diction is a writer's or speaker's choice of words.

For more on Diction, see the Handbook of Literary and Historical Terms.

The Fall of Icarus (16th century) by Pieter Bruegel the Elder.
Musées Royaux des Beaux-Arts, Brussels, Belgium.

Literary Skills
Understand diction.

The source and inspiration for this poem are found in the famous painting by the Renaissance artist Pieter Bruegel showing Icarus drowning, permanently on display in the Musée des Beaux Arts (myo͞o · zā′ dā bō zȧr′), *or Fine Arts Museum, in Brussels, Belgium. The painting depicts a dramatic moment in the Greek legend of Daedalus and his son, Icarus. According to the legend, the two were imprisoned on the island of Crete. In order to escape, Daedalus constructed wings of feathers and wax. Together they managed to take off from the island, but Icarus flew so high that the sun's heat melted the wax in his wings, causing him to fall into the sea and drown.*

According to one critic, the painting represents "the greatest conception of indifference" in the history of art. The indifference, whether it is the artist's attitude or merely a strategy of technique, lies in its unexpected focus. The painting's center of interest is not Icarus, but a peasant plowing a field. He is handsomely dressed—in medieval rather than ancient Greek costume—and the furrows he tills are richly realistic. In the lower right-hand corner of the painting, almost as an afterthought, Icarus is seen splashing into the water not far from a passing ship.

Study the painting, and find the figure of the boy falling into the sea. Then, read the poem to see how Auden interprets the painting. Has he confirmed in words what the painter expressed with paint?

Musée des Beaux Arts

W. H. Auden

About suffering they were never wrong,
The Old Masters: how well they understood
Its human position; how it takes place
While someone else is eating or opening a window or just walking dully along;
How, when the aged are reverently, passionately waiting
For the miraculous birth, there always must be
Children who did not specially want it to happen, skating
On a pond at the edge of the wood:
They never forgot
That even the dreadful martyrdom must run its course
Anyhow in a corner, some untidy spot
Where the dogs go on with their doggy life and the torturer's horse
Scratches its innocent behind on a tree.

In Bruegel's *Icarus,* for instance: how everything turns away
Quite leisurely from the disaster; the plowman may
Have heard the splash, the forsaken cry,
But for him it was not an important failure; the sun shone
As it had to on the white legs disappearing into the green
Water; and the expensive delicate ship that must have seen
Something amazing, a boy falling out of the sky,
Had somewhere to get to and sailed calmly on.

Response and Analysis

Thinking Critically

1. Who are the "Old Masters" (line 2)? What, according to the speaker, did they understand about suffering and what goes on in the presence of suffering? Do you agree that this happens? Look back at your Quickwrite notes for help.
2. Lines 5–13 describe two other paintings by Bruegel. Based on hints in these lines, what events do you think Bruegel portrays in these two paintings? How might these paintings resemble *Icarus*?
3. What theory about suffering does the speaker present in lines 1–13? What example of his theory about suffering does the speaker offer in lines 14–21?
4. What contrast in **diction** can you see between expressions such as "dreadful martyrdom" and "anyhow in a corner"? Find another example of contrasting diction, and explain its effect.
5. What **tone** is created by Auden's contrasting word choices? What emotional effect might Auden hope to create through his unsettling **diction** and tone?
6. In your own words, state the **theme** of this poem. Which lines in the poem do you think are most important to an understanding of theme?

Extending and Evaluating

7. Carefully re-read lines 14–21 of the poem, referring to the painting on page 1264 as you do so. Do you think Auden has correctly interpreted Bruegel's painting? Use evidence from both the text and the painting to support your ideas.

WRITING

Back to the Source

Read a translation or summary of Ovid's version of the myth of Daedalus and Icarus in Book 8 of the *Metamorphoses*. Then, in a brief **essay, compare** the myth to both Auden's treatment of it in his poem and to Bruegel's treatment of it in his painting. What message does the myth convey about the fall of Icarus? What messages do Bruegel's painting and Auden's poem convey?

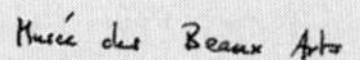

W. H. Auden's handwritten manuscript for "Musée des Beaux Arts"

Library of Congress, Washington, D.C.

SKILLS FOCUS

Literary Skills Analyze diction.

Writing Skills Write an essay comparing a poem and a painting with their myth source.

INTERNET

Projects and Activities

Keyword: LE7 12-7

Gabriela Mistral

1889–1957

Chile

Gabriela Mistral (mēs·träl′) was the first woman poet and the first Latin American to win the Nobel Prize in literature.

Mistral was born Lucila Godoy Alcayaga in the village of Vicuna, Chile, high in the Andes Mountains. The first part of her pen name refers to the archangel Gabriel and the second to the cold, dry wind known as the *mistral* that blows across southern France.

Mistral wrote much of her early poetry in response to the suicide of a man she had been engaged to marry. She received worldwide attention when Federico de Onis, a Spanish professor at Columbia University in New York, "discovered" and published her poetry.

Mistral continued to write poetry while working as a teacher and a principal, and later as an international cultural ambassador. In the 1920s she helped reorganize the rural school systems of Mexico, and in the 1930s she lectured at several American universities and was Chile's cultural representative to the League of Nations. After World War II, Mistral served as the Chilean consul in Los Angeles and Italy and was a delegate to a United Nations subcommittee on women's rights. On her frequent trips back to Chile, Mistral was often greeted by thousands of schoolchildren singing her poems. When she received the Nobel Prize in literature in 1945, she remarked, with her characteristically good-humored directness, that she must have been voted in by women and children.

Before You Read

Fear

Literary Skills Understand refrain.

Make the Connection

Quickwrite

Parents fear losing a child as the result of a violent crime or an accident, but why would they fear losing a child through good fortune, or success, or the natural cycle of growing up and leaving home? In a sentence or two, explain why a parent might fear being separated from his or her child in this way.

Literary Focus

Refrain

A **refrain** is a repeated word, phrase, line, or group of lines. Refrains are commonly used in poetry to create rhythm, build suspense, or emphasize important words or ideas. Although they usually occur at the end of a stanza, refrains can appear elsewhere. As you read "Fear," note the location of the refrain and how often it is repeated. What effect does the refrain create?

A **refrain** is a repeated word, phrase, or group of lines.

For more on Refrain, see the Handbook of Literary and Historical Terms.

INTERNET

More About Gabriela Mistral

Keyword: LE7 12-7

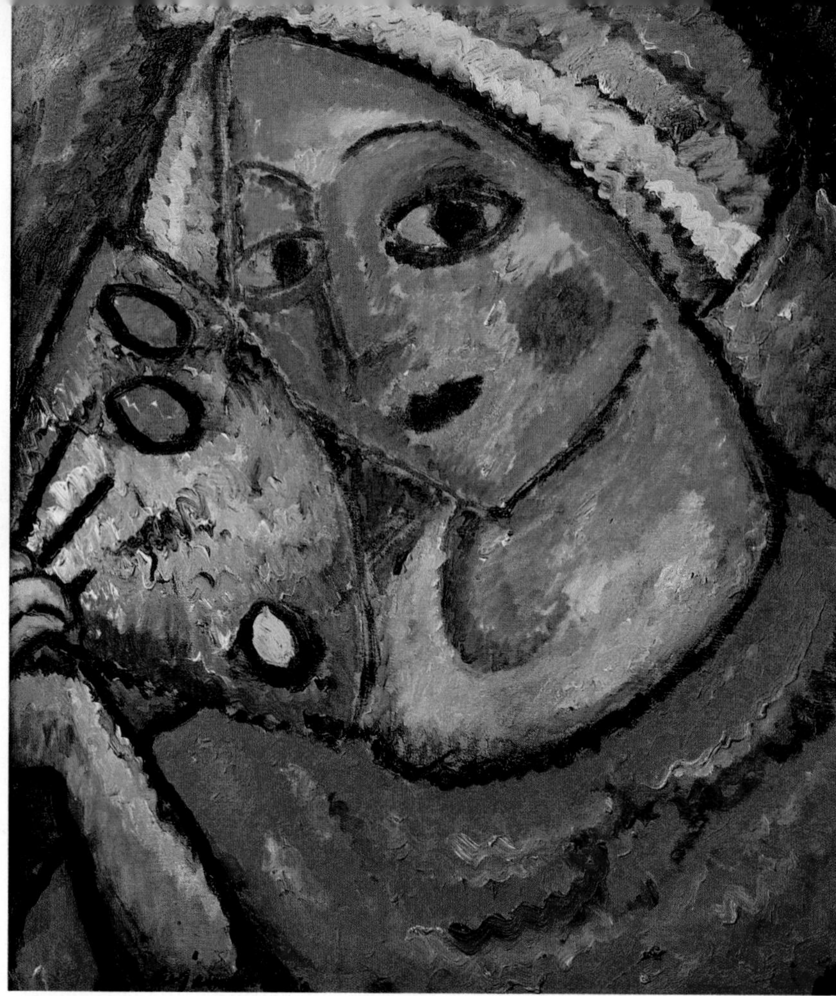

Fairy Tale Princess with Fan (1912) by Alexei von Jawlensky. Oil on cardboard.

Museum Ludwig Köln.

Fear

Gabriela Mistral
translated by **Doris Dana**

I don't want them to turn
my little girl into a swallow.
She would fly far away into the sky
and never fly again to my straw bed,
or she would nest in the eaves
where I could not comb her hair.
I don't want them to turn
my little girl into a swallow.

I don't want them to make
my little girl a princess.
In tiny golden slippers
how could she play on the meadow?
And when night came, no longer
would she sleep at my side.
I don't want them to make
my little girl a princess.

And even less do I want them
one day to make her queen.
They would put her on a throne
where I could not go to see her.
And when nighttime came
I could never rock her . . .
I don't want them to make
my little girl a queen!

Response and Analysis

Thinking Critically

1. Who is the **speaker** in this poem? What is this speaker concerned about?
2. A swallow is a bird that migrates, usually nesting in widely separated summer and winter regions. Given this information, why do you think Mistral uses the specific **image** of a swallow, rather than simply any bird?
3. What does the image of a "straw bed" tell you about the social or economic situation of the speaker? What else might that image suggest?
4. In the second stanza the speaker evokes the **image** of "tiny golden slippers" "on the meadow" as incongruous or out of place. In what other way would the slippers be incongruous for her daughter?
5. In the third stanza, why do you think the speaker fears that she could no longer see her own daughter if she were made a queen? (In your answer, consider the **connotations** of the words *queen* and *throne.*)
6. What is **ironic** about a mother fearing that her daughter will become a "queen"—someone who lives a life untouched by common cares and daily concerns?
7. In a sentence, state the **theme** of the poem. What comment on life does this theme make?
8. Explain how the **refrain** helps reveal the speaker's emotional state. What effect does it have on the **tone** of the poem?
9. Why do you think this poem is titled "Fear"? Does the poem match your idea of what a poem with this title would be about? Explain.

Extending and Evaluating

10. We are not told who the "them" of the poem are. Who do you think they are? Would the emotional impact of the poem be increased or reduced if the speaker identified "them"? Explain your response.

WRITING

Separation Anxiety

Write a brief **character analysis** of the speaker in the poem. In your analysis, consider these questions: Is she rich or poor? Why is she so fearful of being separated from her daughter—and do these fears seem justified? (Refer to your Quickwrite notes.) What seem to be the mother's values? What adjectives other than *fearful* can you use to describe her?

Mother and Child (1926) by Diego Rivera.

Literary Skills
Analyze refrain.

Writing Skills
Write a character analysis.

Dylan Thomas

(1914–1953)

Wales

Born in Swansea, Wales, Dylan Thomas was a prodigy—a supremely gifted young man who wrote some of his most famous works before he was twenty. Largely self-educated, he chose the rough-and-tumble life of a newspaper reporter over the comparative serenity of a university education. His recognition by the leading poets and critics of Britain and the United States came early, and with it came international fame. Neither was enough to prevent him from living on the edge of poverty until his death.

The only son of parents who lived by a code of "good appearances" among their neighbors, Thomas as a child was continually torn between a deep-seated wish to live up to the expectations of his schoolmaster father and an equally strong impulse to please his doting mother. At the same time, he rejected both parents' pretensions to gentility. This conflict was later intensified by a strangely childish self-indulgence that continually defeated his attempts to be a devoted husband to his wife, Caitlin, and a loving father to their three children. The temporary solace he found in alcohol led to that "insult [damage] to the brain" that caused his early and sudden death in St. Vincent's Hospital in New York City. At the time, Thomas was making his fourth visit to the United States and preparing to collaborate on an opera with the composer Igor Stravinsky.

A man of magical presence, with an endless flow of wit and a transparent hunger for affection, Thomas charmed both his British and his American contemporaries. When he first came to America in 1950, he was regarded as the most charismatic British visitor since Oscar Wilde in 1885. His first reading tour of American colleges and universities was followed by ever more extensive trips, on which he crisscrossed the continent from Florida to British Columbia. Those who attended Thomas's readings responded to his personal magnetism. But they also heard something new in modern poetry—a kind of expression combining the oratorical *hywl,* or chanting eloquence, of the Welsh chapel service with the theatrical delivery of the Victorian actors who once thrilled American audiences with thunderous recitations from Shakespeare and Marlowe. Thomas's poems are a mixture of intricate language and preacherlike eloquence, of sonorous solemnity combined with a playful use of language apparent even in his most serious works.

In his last years, Thomas found that the concentration needed to write poetry was more and more difficult to achieve. Consequently, he turned to less demanding forms of expression and produced two works that became familiar around the world: *Under Milk Wood* (1954), which he called a "play for voices," and his lyrical memoir *A Child's Christmas in Wales* (1955), now a holiday classic.

Celebrated by critics, sought after by American lecture agencies, and idolized almost like a rock star, Thomas died at the height of a fame he could neither accept nor enjoy. "Once I was lost and proud," he told a reporter from *The New York Times;* "now I'm found and humble. I prefer that other."

For Independent Reading

You may enjoy the following works by Thomas:

- "In my craft or sullen art" (poem)
- *A Child's Christmas in Wales* (memoir)

Before You Read

Fern Hill

Make the Connection

Quickwrite

Childhood is often remembered as a time of carefree innocence. Most of us have some memory of an idyllic moment from childhood, when the world was a glorious place and everything seemed just right.

Freewrite about one happy childhood memory of your own. Then, list three adjectives besides *happy* that describe the emotions you associate with this memory.

Literary Focus

Lyric Poetry

Lyric poetry focuses on expressing emotions or thoughts rather than on telling a story. In the lyric poem "Fern Hill," Dylan Thomas uses a full range of **sound effects** and **figures of speech** to convey vivid memories of a young boy's enchanted life in the Welsh countryside. Although the speaker's memories are colored by reflection and experience, it is the exuberance of his feelings, above all, that claims our attention.

> **Lyric poetry** focuses on expressing thoughts or emotions, rather than on telling a story.
>
> *For more on Lyric Poetry, see the Handbook of Literary and Historical Terms.*

Portrait of Dylan Thomas by Augustus John.

National Museum of Wales, Cardiff. © Courtesy of the Estate of Augustus John.

Background

As a child, Thomas spent his summers among relatives who worked on a farm that, in his poem, he calls Fern Hill. Set in an apple orchard, the farmhouse is made of the whitewashed stucco typical of Wales and has a number of outlying barns for livestock and hay storage. Not far from the sea, Fern Hill looks down upon enormous tidal flats, in an ever-changing seascape that provides a bountiful habitat for thousands of water birds.

"Fern Hill" is a memory of childhood joy, a vision of an earthly paradise as well as of the playground of a boy for whom every day is an enchanted adventure. Yet, typical of Thomas, joy is never unshadowed. At the end of this extended song of praise, "time" holds him not, as we might expect, "green and growing," but "green and dying." Here we have a variation on one of Thomas's persistent themes—the lurking presence of death in life, of the worm in the seed.

Literary Skills
Understand the characteristics of lyric poetry.

Fern Hill

Dylan Thomas

Now as I was young and easy under the apple boughs
About the lilting house and happy as the grass was green,
The night above the dingle° starry,
Time let me hail and climb
Golden in the heydays of his eyes,
And honored among wagons I was prince of the apple towns
And once below a time I lordly had the trees and leaves
Trail with daisies and barley
Down the rivers of the windfall light.

And as I was green and carefree, famous among the barns
About the happy yard and singing as the farm was home,
In the sun that is young once only,
Time let me play and be
Golden in the mercy of his means,
And green and golden I was huntsman and herdsman, the calves
Sang to my horn, the foxes on the hills barked clear and cold,
And the sabbath rang slowly
In the pebbles of the holy streams.

All the sun long it was running, it was lovely, the hay
Fields high as the house, the tunes from the chimneys, it was air
And playing, lovely and watery
And fire green as grass.
And nightly under the simple stars
As I rode to sleep the owls were bearing the farm away,
All the moon long I heard, blessed among stables, the nightjars°
Flying with the ricks,° and the horses
Flashing into the dark.

And then to awake, and the farm, like a wanderer white
With the dew, come back, the cock on his shoulder: it was all
Shining, it was Adam and maiden,
The sky gathered again
And the sun grew round that very day.
So it must have been after the birth of the simple light
In the first, spinning place, the spellbound horses walking warm
Out of the whinnying green stable
On to the fields of praise.

And honored among foxes and pheasants by the gay house
Under the new made clouds and happy as the heart was long,

3. dingle: little wooded valley, nestled between steep hills.

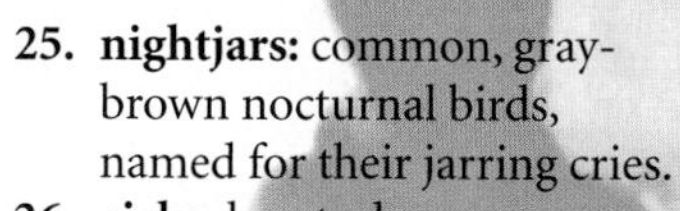

25. nightjars: common, gray-brown nocturnal birds, named for their jarring cries.

26. ricks: haystacks.

In the sun born over and over,
I ran my heedless ways,
My wishes raced through the house high hay
And nothing I cared, at my sky blue trades, that time allows
In all his tuneful turning so few and such morning songs
Before the children green and golden
Follow him out of grace,

Nothing I cared, in the lamb white days, that time would take me
Up to the swallow thronged loft by the shadow of my hand,
In the moon that is always rising,
Nor that riding to sleep
I should hear him fly with the high fields
And wake to the farm forever fled from the childless land.
Oh as I was young and easy in the mercy of his means,
Time held me green and dying
Though I sang in my chains like the sea.

Response and Analysis

Thinking Critically

1. Is the experience described in the poem a universal childhood experience? Explain. (You may want to refer to your Quickwrite notes.)
2. What details tell how the speaker felt when he was "young and easy"?
3. In what specific ways was the speaker's childhood like the life Adam and Eve led in the biblical garden of Eden? In what ways is the boy's "waking" in the last stanza like the "waking" of Adam and Eve as they left the garden?
4. Where is time **personified,** or talked about as if it were a person? Describe the different kinds of intentions that time seems to have regarding the boy.
5. How would you explain the **paradox,** or seeming contradiction, in the next-to-last line of the poem?
6. Read this entire **lyric poem** aloud, or listen to a recording of it, and try to hear the many elements that produce its music. Where does Thomas use **alliteration** and **onomatopoeia** to provide sound effects?
7. Which lines in the poem could apply to all our lives? Which line means the most to *you*?

Literary Criticism

8. Years after this poem was published, Thomas told a friend that one line continued to bother him because it was "bloody bad." The friend asked what line it was. "I ran my heedless ways," said Thomas, and he winced. Why do you think Thomas felt so strongly about a line that most people accept and even quote as part of his most celebrated poem? How do you feel about the line?

WRITING

What's It All About?

In a brief **essay,** state the **theme** of "Fern Hill," and cite the details from the poem that support that theme. At the conclusion of your essay, explain your personal response to Thomas's handling of this theme. End your essay with a comment about what relevance this theme has to your own life. Cite specific examples from your own experience.

Literary Skills
Analyze lyric poetry.

Writing Skills
Write an essay analyzing theme.

Before You Read

Do Not Go Gentle into That Good Night

Make the Connection

Quickwrite

Death may conquer every living thing in the end, but the instinct for survival remains remarkably strong. In contemporary literature, as in the *Gilgamesh* epic of four thousand years ago (see page 58), heroes often battle against death's inevitability. Literature also records the frequent, fierce refusal of the living to accept a loved one's death. Suppose you knew someone who was facing death. How would you advise that person to behave? What attitude would you want that person to have?

Throughout the ages, people have tried to dramatize the struggle against death by putting a face to death—personifying it as an actual being. How would you personify death? Would you compare it to a grim reaper? an impartial judge? Would you picture it as a fearsome, skeletal figure? Jot down some images of death.

Literary Focus

Elegy

The typical **elegy** is a poem that mourns a death that has already occurred. This poem is a bit different—it is an elegy spoken to a dying man, urging him not to surrender but to meet death in a spirit of challenge. As he often did in his poetry, here Thomas gives his own twist to a familiar subject. The poem may invite charges of irreverence, but its lyrical solemnity, not its argument, is what echoes in the reader's mind.

An **elegy** is a poem that mourns the death of someone or laments something lost.

For more on Elegy, see the Handbook of Literary and Historical Terms.

SKILLS FOCUS

Literary Skills Understand the characteristics of an elegy.

Background

Only two end-rhyme sounds occur in this poem, but both are blended into iambic pentameter with such skill that the many repetitions of similar sounds become a somber and delicate music. The use of *gentle* instead of the adverb *gently* may seem ungrammatical. But when we read the line as "Do not go, gentle, into that good night," as Thomas insisted, we gain the additional meaning of all that is gentle, including the gentle man who was Thomas's father.

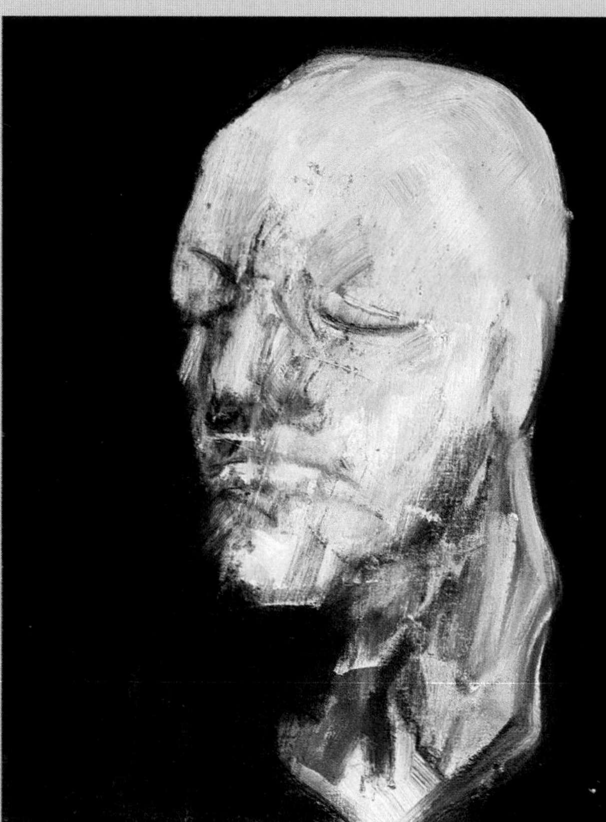

Study for Portrait V (after life mask of William Blake) (1956) by Francis Bacon.

Do Not Go Gentle into That Good Night

Dylan Thomas

Do not go gentle into that good night,
Old age should burn and rave at close of day;
Rage, rage against the dying of the light.

Though wise men at their end know dark is right,
Because their words had forked no lightning they
Do not go gentle into that good night.

Good men, the last wave by, crying how bright
Their frail deeds might have danced in a green bay,
Rage, rage against the dying of the light.

Wild men who caught and sang the sun in flight,
And learn, too late, they grieved it on its way,
Do not go gentle into that good night.

Grave men, near death, who see with blinding sight
Blind eyes could blaze like meteors and be gay,
Rage, rage against the dying of the light.

And you, my father, there on the sad height,
Curse, bless, me now with your fierce tears, I pray.
Do not go gentle into that good night.
Rage, rage against the dying of the light.

Superstock.

Comet over night sky.

Response and Analysis

Thinking Critically

1. What feelings does the speaker reveal about his father's death? Are these feelings at all contradictory? Explain.

2. What four types of people are described in stanzas 2–5? How do each of those types respond to the "dying of the light"?

3. What does the speaker pray for at the end of the poem?

4. What is the "good night"? (Explain the **pun,** or play on words, on this phrase.)

5. Given the speaker's feelings about the "good night," do you see anything contradictory in his use of the word *good?* Explain.

6. Identify at least three **metaphors** for death or dying in the poem. How do the ideas you recorded in your Quickwrite notes compare with the images that Thomas uses?

7. Why would any son beg his father to "Curse, bless, me now with your fierce tears"? What might this strange request indicate about the relationship between this father and son?

8. The **elegy** form goes back to the ancient Greeks and Romans, who used the term to refer to any serious meditation, including poems about love, war, and death. Today *elegy* is used exclusively to refer to poems of mourning. In what way does Thomas's poem fit both definitions?

Literary Criticism

9. Soon after this poem was finished, Thomas sent it to Princess Caetani in Rome, hoping she might publish it in her literary magazine. In an accompanying letter he wrote: "The only person I can't show the little enclosed poem to is, of course, my father, who doesn't know he's dying." Given the fact that the poem became one of the most famous elegies of the century, do you think Thomas's reluctance was justified? Explain why or why not. What would you have done in his situation?

Literary Skills Analyze an elegy. Analyze a villanelle.

Writing Skills Write a response to a poem.

WRITING

Facing Death

Write a **response** to the advice given by the speaker in this poem, using the voice of a very old person who is facing death. Your response might be a **poem,** an **essay,** or a **letter.** You might even try writing your response in the form of a **villanelle.** (See the Literary Focus below.)

Literary Focus

The Villanelle

Thomas has written his poem in an old form called a **villanelle,** invented by French poets. At first this term, which means "rural; countrylike," was limited to light, lyric poems about the countryside. Today villanelles are written on many topics, and as Thomas's poem illustrates, they do not require a light tone.

The villanelle is a complex form. The trick is to make it sound spontaneous and fresh yet still adhere to its strict limits:

- It should have nineteen lines divided into five three-line stanzas (tercets) and a concluding four-line stanza (quatrain).
- It can use only two end-rhyme sounds in this rhyme scheme: *aba aba aba aba aba abaa.*
- It should repeat line 1 in lines 6, 12, and 18, and it should repeat line 3 in lines 9, 15, and 19.

1. How faithfully has Thomas followed the rules for a villanelle?

2. The repeated lines in a villanelle must be significant. Has Thomas repeated ideas important to his poem? Explain.

Pablo Neruda

1904–1973

Chile

When the Chilean poet Pablo Neruda (nə·ro͞o′də) was a young boy searching for "creaturely things" behind his house, he saw a child's hand poking through a hole in a fence, offering him a toy sheep made of real wool. Thrilled, Neruda raced home to return with his most treasured possession, a fragrant pine cone, which he dropped through the same hole for the unseen friend on the other side. Neruda often related this incident. He saw poetry as a gift that he shared with the world—a gift that always brought something in return.

Neruda became a poet when he was still a teenager in Temuco, a frontier town in the south of Chile. Neruda's real name was Neftalí Ricardo Reyes Basoalto; he adopted his pen name to avoid upsetting his father, a railroad worker, who frowned on his son's poetic ambitions. A romantic, bohemian figure in black clothing and a black cape, Neruda was only twenty years old when he published *Veinte poemas de amor y una canción desesperada* (1924), a collection of love poems that eventually sold two million copies worldwide. In Latin America, lovers learned these poems by heart.

In the United States, Neruda became known primarily as a political poet. His serious involvement with politics began when he was appointed to the diplomatic service. As consul in Argentina, and later in Spain, Neruda became close friends of the Spanish poet Federico García Lorca. When fascist forces murdered García Lorca in the Spanish Civil War (1936–1939), Neruda, like many other idealists of the time, joined the Communist party and wrote letters attacking Chile's repressive, anti-Communist government. In 1946, Neruda was accused of treason and forced to flee his homeland.

Neruda returned to Chile in 1952 and began writing *Elementary Odes* (1954), poems in praise of the simple things in life—from socks to onions. In *Cien sonetos de amor,* or *One Hundred Love Sonnets* (1959), Neruda returned to his earlier themes of love and nature. "Poetry is like bread," Neruda said, "and it must be shared by everyone, the men of letters and the peasants, by everyone in our vast, incredible, extraordinary family of man." Neruda was awarded the Nobel Prize in literature in 1971.

For Independent Reading

You may enjoy the following by Neruda:

- "Ode to My Socks" (poem)
- "Ode to Walt Whitman" (poem)
- *One Hundred Love Sonnets* (collection)

Before You Read

Sonnet 79 / Soneto 79

Make the Connection

Quickwrite

Poets often declare that love unites or completes a couple so that they seem to act as one person. Jot down your thoughts on whether or not such a state is preferable to being alone or independent.

Literary Focus

Metaphor

Poets use **metaphors** to make comparisons between unlike things, to convey emotion, and to suggest more than is possible with a literal statement. For example, in the first line of this sonnet, when Neruda says "tie your heart to mine," he is comparing his lover's heart to a boat that can be moored safely or secured to his heart (the Spanish word *amarra* means "moor"). But in the English translation, *tie* can also suggest the joining of musical notes, especially in the context of the "double drum" in line 3. Readers fluent in both Spanish and English can expect a heightened emotional impact from the poem in its two versions.

Metaphor is a figure of speech that makes a comparison between two seemingly unlike things without using a connective word such as *like, as, than,* or *resembles.*

For more on Metaphor, see the Handbook of Literary and Historical Terms.

Literary Skills Understand metaphor.

INTERNET

More About Pablo Neruda

Keyword: LE7 12-7

Background

Mention the Renaissance poets, and the word *love* comes to mind almost immediately. Their sonnets resonate with the passion born of true love, but the Renaissance poets do not hold exclusive rights to this often mysterious emotion. Modern poets also write about the experience of love—in every language and culture. Sonnet 79 comes from Neruda's *One Hundred Love Sonnets,* a book that he wrote for his wife, Matilde Urrutia. In the book's dedication to her, Neruda uses the following **metaphor** to compare writing sonnets to building houses: "I built up these lumber piles of love, and with fourteen boards each I built little houses, so that your eyes, which I adore and sing to, might live in them. Now that I have declared the foundations of my love, I surrender this century to you: wooden sonnets that rise only because you gave them life." The book is divided into four parts—morning, afternoon, evening, and night—each corresponding to a different stage in a person's life. As you read Sonnet 79, try to determine which stage of life it refers to.

The Kiss (c. 1940) by Constantin Brancusi.

Musée National d'Art Moderne, Centre Georges Pompidou, Paris, France.

Sonnet 79

Pablo Neruda
translated by **Stephen Tapscott**

By night, Love, tie your heart to mine, and the two
together in their sleep will defeat the darkness
like a double drum in the forest, pounding
against the thick wall of wet leaves.

Night travel: black flame of sleep
that snips the threads of the earth's grapes,
punctual as a headlong train that would haul
shadows and cold rocks, endlessly.

Because of this, Love, tie me to a purer motion,
to the constancy that beats in your chest
with the wings of a swan underwater,

so that our sleep might answer all the sky's
starry questions with a single key,
with a single door the shadows had closed.

Los Compadres (1963) by David Alfaro Siqueiros.

Private Collection. Courtesy of Galería Arvil, Mexico City, Mexico. Reproduction authorized by: Instituto Nacional de Bellas Artes y Literatura, Mexico.

Soneto 79

De noche, amada, amarra tu corazón al mío
y que ellos en el sueño derroten las tinieblas
como un doble tambor combatiendo en el bosque
contra el espeso muro de las hojas mojadas.

Nocturna travesía, brasa negra del sueño
interceptando el hilo de las uvas terrestres
con la puntualidad de un tren descabellado
que sombra y piedras frías sin cesar arrastrara.

Por eso, amor, amárrame al movimiento puro,
a la tenacidad que en tu pecho golpea
con las alas de un cisne sumergido,

para que a las preguntas estrelladas del cielo
responda nuestro sueño con una sola llave,
con una sola puerta cerrada por la sombra.

Response and Analysis

Thinking Critically

1. The central **metaphor** of the poem is that of the lovers' hearts being tied together. What will this accomplish for the lovers?
2. Why is the speaker so fearful of "the darkness"?
3. Explain the **simile** in line 3. What feeling or emotion does it convey?
4. "Night travel" is Neruda's **image** for sleep, but to what else might it refer? What emotions or feelings does the **extended metaphor** of sleep as a "black flame . . . that snips . . ." convey?
5. Why do you think Neruda calls the "constancy that beats in your chest" (literally, his beloved's heartbeat) a "purer motion"? Interpret the remarkable visual **image** in line 11.
6. Explain what the "sky's starry questions" might mean.
7. This sonnet follows the form of the **Italian,** or **Petrarchan, sonnet** (see page 312), though it doesn't follow its traditional rhyme scheme. Neruda's nontraditional sonnet does, however, contain the abrupt turns of thought of the classic sonnet. Identify the change, or **turn,** in Sonnet 79.

Extending and Evaluating

8. Work with a classmate who speaks or reads Spanish, and evaluate the effectiveness and accuracy of the English translation. (For example, why does the translator render "brasa negra" as "black flame"?)
9. What do you think of the idea that love completes people—that it unites them so that they can be seen as one person? (Refer to your Quickwrite notes.) In what other poems in this book have you encountered this idea?

Literary Skills Analyze metaphor.

Writing Skills Write an essay comparing and contrasting two sonnets.

Literary Criticism

10. The poet and novelist Stephen Dobyns noted that by the 1960s, in Chile, Neruda's first collection of love poetry was still being "discussed, wondered over, and dreamt with. Despite having been written in the twenties, it seemed of the moment. . . . My wife and her friends felt no doubt about what the poems meant. They had no need for critics. The poems were being spoken directly to them." Does the Neruda sonnet you have just read reflect contemporary views of romantic love? Is Neruda closer in spirit to the metaphysical Renaissance poets (see page 337) or to the Romantic poets (see pages 706–717)—or does he represent a much more modern sensibility? Explain.

WRITING

What Is Love?

Review one of the Renaissance love sonnets you studied in Collection 3 and, in a brief **essay, compare and contrast** it with Neruda's sonnet. In your essay, explore these points:

- the form of each sonnet (Petrarchan or Shakespearean)
- the speaker's intention in each sonnet
- what you learn about the person to whom each sonnet is addressed
- the theme of each sonnet
- the poet's use of figures of speech
- how the views of love presented in the two sonnets differ from each other

R. K. Narayan

(1906–2001)

India

R.K. Narayan (nə·rī′yen), considered one of India's greatest writers, was born in Madras, India, into a large, middle-class family. His father was a prominent teacher, and Narayan too was groomed for a career in education, though he hated school. In spite of his dislike for academics, Narayan graduated from Maharajah's College in Mysore and served a brief stint as a village teacher. For Narayan, however, teaching proved to be a short-lived profession; he soon settled into his career as a writer.

Due to his mother's poor health and his father's itinerant career, Narayan was raised primarily by his grandmother, a strong woman sought after by neighbors for her marital advice, astrological readings, and healing remedies. She taught him traditional Indian tales and prayers and greatly fueled his interest in writing. Through her, Narayan developed an intense curiosity about the lives of so-called ordinary people.

In his first novel, *Swami and Friends* (1935), Narayan introduced the imaginary city of Malgudi, based on his hometown, Mysore, in southern India. In subsequent works, Narayan returns again and again to this fictional place and its eccentric and lovable characters. Whether writing about the timeless inhabitants of Malgudi or retelling ancient stories from the Sanskrit epics *The Mahabharata* and *The Ramayana,* Narayan based all his writings on his concept of the universality of human nature.

Narayan lived to see most of the twentieth century. He saw India dominated by political clashes, social conflicts, and historic upheavals. However, these tumultuous events did not alter his fictional world, and some critics have condemned him for seeming to ignore India's turbulent history in his writing. To such criticisms, Narayan said, "I write primarily for myself. And I write about what interests me, human beings and human relationships. . . . Only the story matters; that's all."

For Independent Reading

You may enjoy the following story by Narayan:

- "An Astrologer's Day"

Before You Read

Like the Sun

Make the Connection

Quickwrite

The expression *The truth hurts* doesn't make clear who is being hurt: the person to whom the truth is told or the truth-teller. Write down what you think might happen if, on one day each year, you told the truth no matter whose feelings were hurt.

Literary Focus

Irony

Situational irony involves a contrast between expectation and reality. In "Like the Sun," Narayan fashions a situation in which a character's obsession with telling people the truth leads to ironic consequences (people rarely want to hear the truth about themselves) and creates humor.

Situational irony occurs when what actually happens is the opposite of what is expected or appropriate.

For more on Irony, see the Handbook of Literary and Historical Terms.

Vocabulary Development

tempering (tem′pər•iŋ) *v.* used as *n.:* moderating; toning down.

resolve (ri•zälv′) *n.:* determination; firm purpose.

culinary (kul′ə•ner′ē) *adj.:* related to cooking.

wince (wins) *v.:* flinch; draw back.

shirked (shurkt) *v.:* neglected or avoided a task or duty.

inclinations (in′klə•nā′shənz) *n. pl.:* likings; tendencies.

incessantly (in•ses′ənt•lē) *adv.:* constantly; unendingly.

ingratiating (in•grā′shē•āt•iŋ) *v.* used as *adj.:* purposely trying to gain favor.

assailed (ə•sāld′) *v.:* assaulted; attacked.

sullen (sul′ən) *adj.:* resentful; gloomy.

Literary Skills Understand situational irony.

INTERNET

Vocabulary Practice

Keyword: LE7 12-7

Like the Sun

R. K. Narayan

Truth, Sekhar reflected, is like the sun. I suppose no human being can ever look it straight in the face without blinking or being dazed. He realized that, morning till night, the essence of human relationships consisted in tempering truth so that it might not shock. This day he set apart as a unique day—at least one day in the year we must give and take absolute Truth whatever may happen. Otherwise life is not worth living. The day ahead seemed to him full of possibilities. He told no one of his experiment. It was a quiet resolve, a secret pact between him and eternity.

The very first test came while his wife served him his morning meal. He showed hesitation over a tidbit, which she had thought was her culinary masterpiece. She asked, "Why, isn't it good?" At other times he would have said, considering her feelings in the matter, "I feel full up, that's all." But today he said, "It isn't good. I'm unable to swallow it." He saw her wince and said to himself, Can't be helped. Truth is like the sun.

His next trial was in the common room when one of his colleagues came up and said, "Did you hear of the death of so and so? Don't you think it a pity?" "No," Sekhar answered. "He was such a fine man—" the other began. But Sekhar cut him short with: "Far from it. He always struck me as a mean and selfish brute."

During the last period when he was teaching geography for Third Form A,[1] Sekhar received a note from the headmaster: "Please see me before you go home." Sekhar said to himself: It must be about these horrible test papers. A hundred papers in the boys' scrawls; he had shirked this work for weeks, feeling all the time as if a sword were hanging over his head.

The bell rang and the boys burst out of the class.

Sekhar paused for a moment outside the headmaster's room to button up his coat; that was another subject the headmaster always sermonized about.

He stepped in with a very polite "Good evening, sir."

1. **Third Form A:** equivalent to ninth-grade classes in the United States.

The headmaster looked up at him in a very friendly manner and asked, "Are you free this evening?"

Sekhar replied, "Just some outing which I have promised the children at home—"

"Well, you can take them out another day. Come home with me now."

"Oh . . . yes, sir, certainly . . ." And then he added timidly, "Anything special, sir?"

"Yes," replied the headmaster, smiling to himself . . . "You didn't know my weakness for music?"

"Oh, yes, sir . . ."

"I've been learning and practicing secretly, and now I want you to hear me this evening. I've engaged a drummer and a violinist to accompany me—this is the first time I'm doing it full-dress and I want your opinion. I know it will be valuable."

Sekhar's taste in music was well-known. He was one of the most dreaded music critics in the town. But he never anticipated his musical inclinations would lead him to this trial. . . . "Rather a surprise for you, isn't it?" asked the headmaster. "I've spent a fortune on it behind closed doors. . . ." They started for the headmaster's house. "God hasn't given me a child, but at least let him not deny me the consolation of music," the headmaster said, pathetically, as they walked. He incessantly chattered about music: how he began one day out of sheer boredom; how his teacher at first laughed at him, and then gave him hope; how his ambition in life was to forget himself in music.

At home the headmaster proved very ingratiating. He sat Sekhar on a red silk carpet, set before him several dishes of delicacies, and fussed over him as if he were a son-in-law of the house. He even said, "Well, you must listen with a

Vocabulary

tempering (tem′pər•iŋ) *v.* used as *n.:* moderating; toning down.

resolve (ri•zälv′) *n.:* determination; firm purpose.

culinary (kul′ə•ner′ē) *adj.:* related to cooking.

wince (wins) *v.:* flinch; draw back.

shirked (shurkt) *v.:* neglected or avoided a task or duty.

inclinations (in′klə•nā′shənz) *n. pl.:* likings; tendencies.

incessantly (in•ses′ənt•lē) *adv.:* constantly; unendingly.

ingratiating (in•grā′shē•āt•iŋ) *v.* used as *adj.:* purposely trying to gain favor.

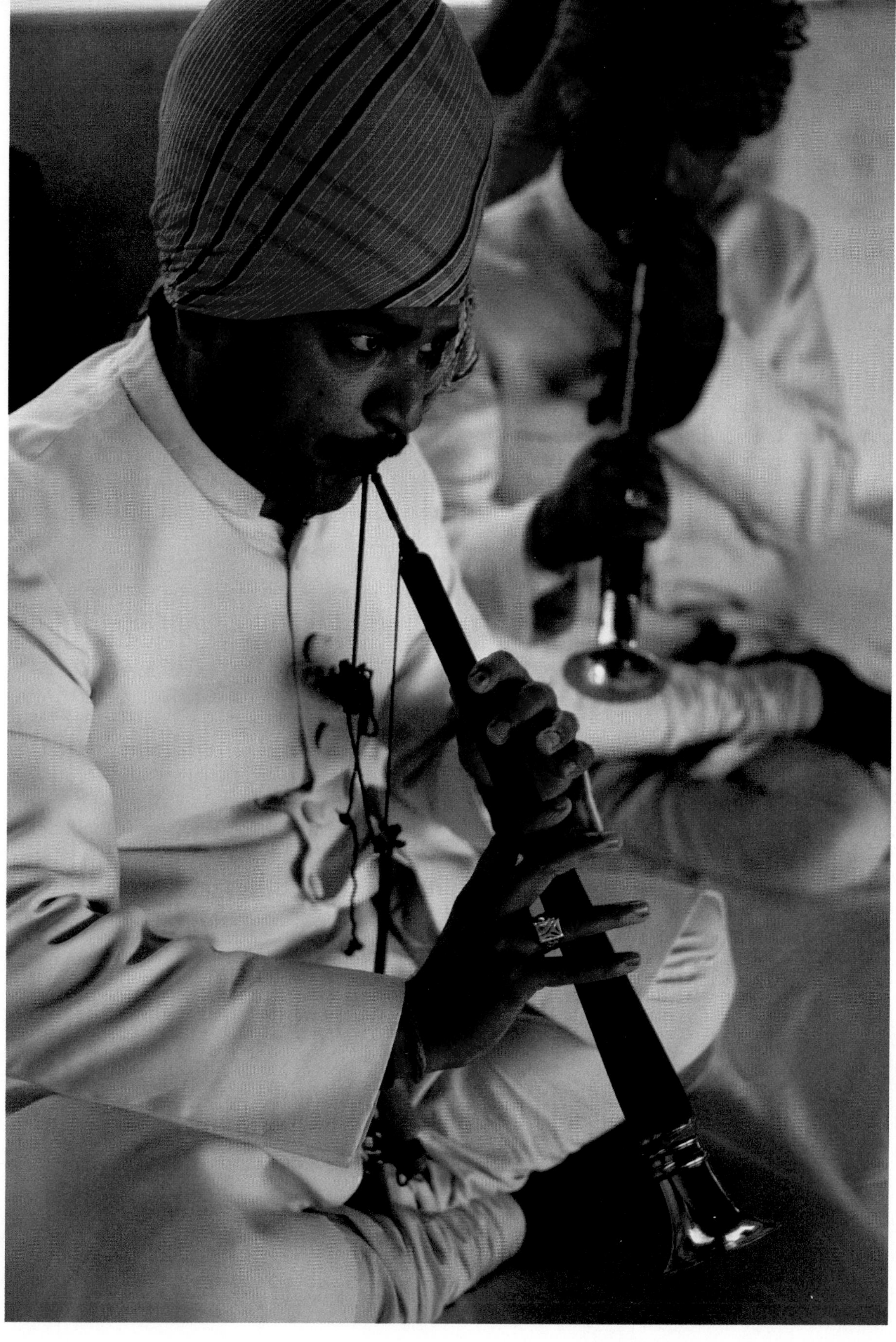

free mind. Don't worry about these test papers." He added half humorously, "I will give you a week's time."

"Make it ten days, sir," Sekhar pleaded.

"All right, granted," the headmaster said generously. Sekhar felt really relieved now—he would attack them at the rate of ten a day and get rid of the nuisance.

The headmaster lighted incense sticks. "Just to create the right atmosphere," he explained. A drummer and a violinist, already seated on a Rangoon[2] mat, were waiting for him. The headmaster sat down between them like a professional at a concert, cleared his throat, and began an alapana,[3] and paused to ask, "Isn't it good Kalyani?"[4] Sekhar pretended not to have heard the question. The headmaster went on to sing a full song composed by Thyagaraja[5] and followed it with two more. All the time the headmaster was singing, Sekhar went on commenting within himself, He croaks like a dozen frogs. He is bellowing like a buffalo. Now he sounds like loose window shutters in a storm.

The incense sticks burnt low. Sekhar's head throbbed with the medley of sounds that had assailed his eardrums for a couple of hours now. He felt half stupefied. The headmaster had gone nearly hoarse, when he paused to ask, "Shall I go on?" Sekhar replied, "Please don't, sir, I think this will do. . . ." The headmaster looked stunned. His face was beaded with perspiration. Sekhar felt the greatest pity for him. But he felt he could not help it. No judge delivering a sentence felt more pained and helpless. Sekhar noticed that the headmaster's wife peeped in from the kitchen, with eager curiosity. The drummer and the violinist put away their burdens with an air of relief. The headmaster removed his spectacles, mopped his brow, and asked, "Now, come out with your opinion."

"Can't I give it tomorrow, sir?" Sekhar asked tentatively.

"No. I want it immediately—your frank opinion. Was it good?"

"No, sir . . ." Sekhar replied.

"Oh! . . . Is there any use continuing my lessons?"

"Absolutely none, sir . . ." Sekhar said with his voice trembling. He felt very unhappy that he could not speak more soothingly. Truth, he reflected, required as much strength to give as to receive.

All the way home he felt worried. He felt that his official life was not going to be smooth sailing hereafter. There were questions of increment and confirmation and so on, all depending upon the headmaster's goodwill. All kinds of worries seemed to be in store for him. . . . Did not Harischandra[6] lose his throne, wife, child, because he would speak nothing less than the absolute Truth whatever happened?

At home his wife served him with a sullen face. He knew she was still angry with him for his remark of the morning. Two casualties for today, Sekhar said to himself. If I practice it for a week, I don't think I shall have a single friend left.

He received a call from the headmaster in his classroom next day. He went up apprehensively.

"Your suggestion was useful. I have paid off the music master. No one would tell me the truth about my music all these days. Why such antics at my age! Thank you. By the way, what about those test papers?"

"You gave me ten days, sir, for correcting them."

"Oh, I've reconsidered it. I must positively have them here tomorrow. . . ." A hundred papers in a day! That meant all night's sitting up! "Give me a couple of days, sir . . ."

"No. I must have them tomorrow morning. And remember, every paper must be thoroughly scrutinized."

"Yes, sir," Sekhar said, feeling that sitting up all night with a hundred test papers was a small price to pay for the luxury of practicing Truth. ■

2. **Rangoon:** capital of Myanmar; it is now called Yangon.
3. **alapana** *n.:* performance of Indian melody.
4. **Kalyani** *n.:* Hindustani melody.
5. **Thyagaraja:** (1767–1847) one of India's foremost composers.
6. **Harischandra:** ancient Hindu king known for his love of truth.

Vocabulary

assailed (ə•sāld′) *v.:* assaulted; attacked.
sullen (sul′ən) *adj.:* resentful; gloomy.

Response and Analysis

Reading Check

1. What does Sekhar resolve to do on the day of the story?
2. Why does Sekhar dread going to the headmaster's home?
3. What does Sekhar tell the headmaster?
4. How does the headmaster repay Sekhar for his truthfulness?

Thinking Critically

5. Describe the **character** of Sekhar and the sources of his **conflict.** What is **ironic** about such a character's resolve to tell the "absolute Truth"?
6. Why do you think Sekhar is devoting only one day to his truth-telling?
7. Explain the **situational irony** that occurs the day after Sekhar tells the headmaster that his singing is no good.
8. How can you tell that the headmaster was not entirely pleased with Sekhar's truthfulness?
9. In one sentence, state the **theme** of the story. Does the theme reinforce or contradict common ideas about truth?
10. How would you describe Narayan's attitude toward Sekhar and the subject of truth? (Consider whether Narayan is serious, admiring, slightly mocking, poking fun or ridiculing, or something else.) What point is Narayan trying to make? Explain how Narayan uses **tone** to enhance his point.
11. Humor often turns on unexpected events. How does the story's **irony** create a comic effect?

Extending and Evaluating

12. Did you find the story believable? Why or why not?

WRITING

Is Honesty the Best Policy?

Is telling the truth easy? Is it always the right thing to do? Write a brief **reflective essay** in which you share your thoughts about the expected—or unexpected—consequences of telling the truth. Use examples from your own experiences if possible. Refer to your Quickwrite notes for ideas.

See "Writing a Reflective Essay," pages 856–863, for help with this assignment.

Vocabulary Development

Analogies

tempering	inclinations
resolve	incessantly
culinary	ingratiating
wince	assailed
shirked	sullen

On a separate sheet of paper, complete each analogy below with a Vocabulary word from the list above.

1. EMPLOYED : HIRED :: _______ : neglected
2. EXCITING : DULL :: _______ : gleeful
3. EXPLOITING : USING :: ______ : moderating
4. STABILITY : SECURITY ::______ : firmness
5. BOTANICAL : PLANTS :: ______ : cooking
6. GRIEF : SADNESS :: ______ : preferences
7. QUICKLY : SWIFTLY :: _______ : constantly
8. WARY : CAUTIOUS :: ______ : charming
9. NONCHALANT : CONCERNED :: _______ : retreated
10. HARM : HURT :: ______ : flinch

Literary Skills
Analyze situational irony.

Writing Skills
Write a reflective essay.

Vocabulary Skills
Complete word analogies.

Anita Desai

(1937–   )

India

Born in Mussoorie, India, Anita Desai has been writing since the age of seven "as instinctively as I breathe." Desai's father was Bengali and her mother German, and Desai grew up hearing Hindi, English, and German spoken at home. However, it was in English that Desai learned to read and write. Educated at the University of Delhi, Desai began publishing in 1963.

Desai's fiction explores the struggles of contemporary Indian characters as they respond to cultural and social change. She sees her work as an attempt to discover "the truth that is nine-tenths of the iceberg that lies submerged beneath the one-tenth visible portion we call Reality." To evoke this "truth," Desai uses rich, sensual language and intense imagery. Because of her sensuous style and rich use of imagery and symbolism, Desai has been referred to as an "imagist-novelist."

Desai's novels often focus on the emotional and spiritual lives of wives, older women, or sisters who take responsibility for others but are unable to create satisfactory lives for themselves. Her novels include *Cry, the Peacock* (1963), *In Custody* (1984), and *Baumgartner's Bombay* (1988).

Writing in *The New Republic,* Anthony Thwaite describes Desai as "such a consummate artist that she [is able to suggest], beyond the confines of the plot and the machinations of her characters, the immensities that lie beyond them—the immensities of India."

For Independent Reading

You may enjoy the following stories by Desai:

- "A Devoted Son"
- "Studies in the Park"

Before You Read

Games at Twilight

Make the Connection

Quickwrite

Work may be the business of adults, but play is often considered the business of little children. For it is through play that children learn many of life's important lessons. They learn about rules and strategies, strengths and weaknesses. They learn about human instincts and reactions, and they learn that life is not always fair.

Take a moment or two to think about a childhood game you frequently played. How seriously did you take the game? What different feelings did you have about the game? What, in retrospect, did you learn from playing it? Write down some of your thoughts.

Literary Focus

Imagery

Imagery, or language that appeals to the five senses, is used by almost all writers of fiction to help their readers envision a given scene. Anita Desai does not simply use imagery—she drenches us in the smells, textures, sounds, and colors of a summer afternoon in India. From the bursting open of a door to the crushed silence of a defeated child, Desai enables us to experience the world through the eyes and ears of her characters.

> **Imagery** is the use of language to evoke sensory impressions.
>
> *For more on Imagery, see the Handbook of Literary and Historical Terms.*

Reading Skills 

Analyzing Details

As you read, jot down words and phrases that help you imagine the scene and share the characters' feelings and experiences. When you have finished reading, discuss the impressions created by these details. Do certain details evoke particular emotions or associations? Which single detail did you find the most striking or memorable?

Background

This story is set not long after India gained its independence from Britain in 1947. During the long British rule in India, many upper-class Indian families had adopted Western values, behaviors, and customs, including games like the one played in the story.

Vocabulary Development

maniacal (mə·nī′ə·kəl) *adj.:* crazed; wildly enthusiastic.

stridently (strīd′'nt·lē) *adv.:* harshly; sharply.

superciliously (so͞o′pər·sil′ē·əs·lē) *adv.:* disdainfully; scornfully.

temerity (tə·mer′ə·tē) *n.:* foolish or rash boldness; recklessness.

intoxicating (in·täks′i·kāt′iŋ) *v.* used as *adj.:* causing wild excitement or happiness, often to a point beyond self-control; heady.

dogged (dôg′id) *adj.:* persistent; stubborn.

lugubrious (lə·go͞o′brē·əs) *adj.:* very solemn or mournful, especially in a way that seems exaggerated or ridiculous.

ignominy (ig′nə·min′ē) *n.:* shame; dishonor.

Literary Skills Understand imagery.

Reading Skills Analyze details.

INTERNET

Vocabulary Practice

Keyword: LE7 12-7

Games at Twilight

Anita Desai

Two young girls, Rajasthan, India.

It was still too hot to play outdoors. They had had their tea, they had been washed and had their hair brushed, and after the long day of confinement in the house that was not cool but at least a protection from the sun, the children strained to get out. Their faces were red and bloated with the effort, but their mother would not open the door, everything was still curtained and shuttered in a way that stifled the children, made them feel that their lungs were stuffed with cotton wool and their noses with dust and if they didn't burst out into the light and see the sun and feel the air, they would choke.

"Please, ma, please," they begged. "We'll play in the veranda and porch—we won't go a step out of the porch."

"You will, I know you will, and then——"

"No—we won't, we won't," they wailed so horrendously that she actually let down the bolt of the front door so that they burst out like seeds from a crackling, overripe pod into the veranda, with such wild, maniacal yells that she retreated to her bath and the shower of talcum powder and the fresh sari that were to help her face the summer evening.

They faced the afternoon. It was too hot. Too bright. The white walls of the veranda glared stridently in the sun. The bougainvillea[1] hung about it, purple and magenta, in livid balloons. The garden outside was like a tray made of beaten brass, flattened out on the red gravel and the stony soil in all shades of metal—aluminum, tin, copper, and brass. No life stirred at this arid time of day—the birds still drooped, like dead fruit, in the papery tents of the trees; some squirrels lay limp on the wet earth under the garden tap. The outdoor dog lay stretched as if dead on the veranda mat, his paws and ears and tail all reaching out like dying travelers in search of water. He rolled his eyes at the children—two white marbles rolling in the purple sockets, begging for sympathy—and attempted to lift his tail in a wag but could not. It only twitched and lay still.

Then, perhaps roused by the shrieks of the children, a band of parrots suddenly fell out of the eucalyptus tree, tumbled frantically in the still, sizzling air, then sorted themselves out into battle formation and streaked away across the white sky.

The children, too, felt released. They too began tumbling, shoving, pushing against each other, frantic to start. Start what? Start their business. The business of the children's day which is—play.

"Let's play hide-and-seek."

"Who'll be It?"

"You be It."

"Why should I? You be——"

"You're the eldest——"

"That doesn't mean——"

The shoves became harder. Some kicked out. The motherly Mira intervened. She pulled the boys roughly apart. There was a tearing sound of cloth, but it was lost in the heavy panting and angry grumbling, and no one paid attention to the small sleeve hanging loosely off a shoulder.

"Make a circle, make a circle!" she shouted, firmly pulling and pushing till a kind of vague circle was formed. "Now clap!" she roared, and, clapping, they all chanted in melancholy unison: "Dip, dip, dip—my blue ship——" and every now and then one or the other saw he was safe by the way his hands fell at the crucial moment—palm on palm, or back of hand on palm—and dropped out of the circle with a yell and a jump of relief and jubilation.

Raghu was It. He started to protest, to cry "You cheated—Mira cheated—Anu cheated——" but it was too late, the others had all already streaked away. There was no one to hear when he called out, "Only in the veranda—the porch—Ma said—Ma *said* to stay in the porch!" No one had stopped to listen, all he saw were their brown legs flashing through the dusty shrubs, scrambling up brick walls, leaping over compost heaps and hedges, and then the porch stood empty in the purple shade of the bougainvillea, and the garden was as empty as before; even the limp squirrels had whisked away, leaving everything gleaming, brassy, and bare.

Only small Manu suddenly reappeared, as if he had dropped out of an invisible cloud or from a bird's claws, and stood for a moment in the center of the yellow lawn, chewing his finger and near to tears as he heard Raghu shouting, with his head pressed against the veranda wall, "Eighty-three, eighty-five, eighty-nine, ninety . . ." and then made off in a panic, half of him wanting to fly north, the other half counseling south. Raghu turned just in time to see the flash of his white shorts and the uncertain skittering of his red sandals, and charged after him with such

1. **bougainvillea** (bo͞o′gən·vil′ē·ə) *n.:* woody, tropical vine with showy, purplish leaves.

Vocabulary

maniacal (mə•nī′ə•kəl) *adj.:* crazed; wildly enthusiastic.

stridently (strīd′'nt•lē) *adv.:* harshly; sharply.

a bloodcurdling yell that Manu stumbled over the hosepipe, fell into its rubber coils, and lay there weeping, "I won't be It—you have to find them all—all—All!"

"I know I have to, idiot," Raghu said, superciliously kicking him with his toe. "You're dead," he said with satisfaction, licking the beads of perspiration off his upper lip, and then stalked off in search of worthier prey, whistling spiritedly so that the hiders should hear and tremble.

Ravi heard the whistling and picked his nose in a panic, trying to find comfort by burrowing the finger deep—deep into that soft tunnel. He felt himself too exposed, sitting on an upturned flowerpot behind the garage. Where could he burrow? He could run around the garage if he heard Raghu come—around and around and around—but he hadn't much faith in his short legs when matched against Raghu's long, hefty, hairy footballer legs. Ravi had a frightening glimpse of them as Raghu combed the hedge of crotons and hibiscus, trampling delicate ferns underfoot as he did so. Ravi looked about him desperately, swallowing a small ball of snot in his fear.

The garage was locked with a great heavy lock to which the driver had the key in his room, hanging from a nail on the wall under his workshirt. Ravi had peeped in and seen him still sprawling on his string cot in his vest and striped underpants, the hair on his chest and the hair in his nose shaking with the vibrations of his phlegm-obstructed snores. Ravi had wished he were tall enough, big enough to reach the key on the nail, but it was impossible, beyond his reach for years to come. He had sidled away and sat dejectedly on the flowerpot. That at least was cut to his own size.

But next to the garage was another shed with a big green door. Also locked. No one even knew who had the key to the lock. That shed wasn't opened more than once a year, when Ma turned out all the old broken bits of furniture and rolls of matting and leaking buckets, and the white anthills were broken and swept away and Flit sprayed into the spider webs and rat holes so that the whole operation was like the looting of a poor, ruined, and conquered city. The green leaves of the door sagged. They were nearly off their rusty hinges. The hinges were large and made a small gap between the door and the walls—only just large enough for rats, dogs, and, possibly, Ravi to slip through.

Ravi had never cared to enter such a dark and depressing mortuary of defunct household goods seething with such unspeakable and alarming animal life but, as Raghu's whistling grew angrier and sharper and his crashing and storming in the hedge wilder, Ravi suddenly slipped off the flowerpot and through the crack and was gone. He chuckled aloud with astonishment at his own temerity so that Raghu came out of the hedge, stood silent with his hands on his hips, listening, and finally shouted, "I heard you! I'm coming! *Got* you——" and came charging round the garage only to find the upturned flowerpot, the yellow dust, the crawling of white ants in a mud hill against the closed shed door—nothing. Snarling, he bent to pick up a stick and went off, whacking it against the garage and shed walls as if to beat out his prey.

Ravi shook, then shivered with delight, with self-congratulation. Also with fear. It was dark, spooky in the shed. It had a muffled smell, as of graves. Ravi had once got locked into the linen cupboard and sat there weeping for half an hour before he was rescued. But at least that had been a familiar place, and even smelled pleasantly of starch, laundry, and, reassuringly, of his mother. But the shed smelled of rats, anthills, dust, and spider webs. Also of less definable, less recognizable horrors. And it was dark. Except for the white-hot cracks along the door, there was no light. The roof was very low. Although Ravi was small, he felt as if he could reach up

Vocabulary

superciliously (so͞o′pər•sil′ē•əs•lē) *adv.:* disdainfully; scornfully.

temerity (tə•mer′ə•tē) *n.:* foolish or rash boldness; recklessness.

and touch it with his fingertips. But he didn't stretch. He hunched himself into a ball so as not to bump into anything, touch or feel anything. What might there not be to touch him and feel him as he stood there, trying to see in the dark? Something cold, or slimy—like a snake. Snakes! He leapt up as Raghu whacked the wall with his stick—then, quickly realizing what it was, felt almost relieved to hear Raghu, hear his stick. It made him feel protected.

But Raghu soon moved away. There wasn't a sound once his footsteps had gone around the garage and disappeared. Ravi stood frozen inside the shed. Then he shivered all over. Something had tickled the back of his neck. It took him a while to pick up the courage to lift his hand and explore. It was an insect—perhaps a spider—exploring *him.* He squashed it and wondered how many more creatures were watching him, waiting to reach out and touch him, the stranger.

There was nothing now. After standing in that position—his hand still on his neck, feeling the wet splodge of the squashed spider gradually dry—for minutes, hours, his legs began to tremble with the effort, the inaction. By now he could see enough in the dark to make out the large solid shapes of old wardrobes, broken buckets, and bedsteads piled on top of each other around him. He recognized an old bathtub—patches of enamel glimmered at him, and at last he lowered himself onto its edge.

He contemplated slipping out of the shed and into the fray. He wondered if it would not be better to be captured by Raghu and be returned to the milling crowd as long as he could be in the sun, the light, the free spaces of the garden, and the familiarity of his brothers, sisters, and cousins. It would be evening soon. Their games would become legitimate. The parents would sit out on the lawn on cane basket chairs and watch them as they tore around the garden or gathered in knots to share a loot of mulberries or black, teeth-splitting *jamun*[2] from the garden trees. The gardener would fix the hosepipe to the water tap, and water would fall lavishly through the air to the ground, soaking the dry yellow grass and the red gravel and arousing the sweet, the intoxicating scent of water on dry earth—that loveliest scent in the world. Ravi sniffed for a whiff of it. He half-rose from the bathtub, then heard the despairing scream of one of the girls as Raghu bore down upon her. There was the sound of a crash, and of rolling about in the bushes, the shrubs, then screams and accusing sobs of "I touched the den——" "You did not——" "I did——" "You liar, you did *not*" and then a fading away and silence again.

Ravi sat back on the harsh edge of the tub, deciding to hold out a bit longer. What fun if they were all found and caught—he alone left unconquered! He had never known that sensation. Nothing more wonderful had ever happened to him than being taken out by an uncle and bought a whole slab of chocolate all to himself, or being flung into the soda man's pony cart and driven up to the gate by the friendly driver with the red beard and pointed ears. To defeat Raghu—that hirsute,[3] hoarse-voiced football champion—and to be the winner in a circle of older, bigger, luckier children—that would be thrilling beyond imagination. He hugged his knees together and smiled to himself almost shyly at the thought of so much victory, such laurels.

There he sat smiling, knocking his heels against the bathtub, now and then getting up and going to the door to put his ear to the broad crack and listening for sounds of the game, the pursuer and the pursued, and then returning to his seat with the dogged determination of the true winner, a breaker of records, a champion.

2. ***jamun*** (jä·mən) *n.:* plumlike fruit.

3. **hirsute** (hʉr'so͞ot') *adj.:* hairy; shaggy.

Vocabulary

intoxicating (in•täks'i•kāt'iŋ) *v.* used as *adj.:* causing wild excitement or happiness, often to a point beyond self-control; heady.

dogged (dôg'id) *adj.:* persistent; stubborn.

It grew darker in the shed as the light at the door grew softer, fuzzier, turned to a kind of crumbling yellow pollen that turned to yellow fur, blue fur, gray fur. Evening. Twilight. The sound of water gushing, falling. The scent of earth receiving water, slaking its thirst in great gulps and releasing that green scent of freshness, coolness. Through the crack Ravi saw the long purple shadows of the shed and the garage lying still across the yard. Beyond that, the white walls of the house. The bougainvillea had lost its lividity, hung in dark bundles that quaked and twittered and seethed with masses of homing sparrows. The lawn was shut off from his view. Could he hear the children's voices? It seemed to him that he could. It seemed to him that he could hear them chanting, singing, laughing. But what about the game? What had happened? Could it be over? How could it when he was still not found?

It then occurred to him that he could have slipped out long ago, dashed across the yard to the veranda, and touched the "den." It was necessary to do that to win. He had forgotten. He had only remembered the part of hiding and trying to elude the seeker. He had done that so successfully, his success had occupied him so wholly, that he had quite forgotten that success had to be clinched by that final dash to victory and the ringing cry of "Den!"

With a whimper he burst through the crack, fell on his knees, got up, and stumbled on stiff, benumbed legs across the shadowy yard, crying heartily by the time he reached the veranda so that when he flung himself at the white pillar and bawled, "Den! Den! Den!" his voice broke with rage and pity at the disgrace of it all, and he felt himself flooded with tears and misery.

Out on the lawn, the children stopped chanting. They all turned to stare at him in amazement. Their faces were pale and triangular in the dusk. The trees and bushes around them stood inky and sepulchral, spilling long shadows across them. They stared, wondering at his reappearance, his passion, his wild animal howling. Their mother rose from her basket chair and came toward him, worried, annoyed, saying, "Stop it, stop it, Ravi. Don't be a baby. Have you hurt yourself?" Seeing him attended to, the children went back to clasping their hands and chanting, "The grass is green, the rose is red. . . ."

But Ravi would not let them. He tore himself out of his mother's grasp and pounded across the lawn into their midst, charging at them with his head lowered so that they scattered in surprise. "I won, I won, I won," he bawled, shaking his head so that the big tears flew. "Raghu didn't find me. I won, I won——"

It took them a minute to grasp what he was saying, even who he was. They had quite forgotten him. Raghu had found all the others long ago. There had been a fight about who was to be It next. It had been so fierce that their mother had emerged from her bath and made them change to another game. Then they had played another and another. Broken mulberries from the tree and eaten them. Helped the driver wash the car when their father returned from work. Helped the gardener water the beds till he roared at them and swore he would complain to their parents. The parents had come out, taken up their positions on the cane chairs. They had begun to play again, sing and chant. All this time no one had remembered Ravi. Having disappeared from the scene, he had disappeared from their minds. Clean.

"Don't be a fool," Raghu said roughly, pushing him aside, and even Mira said, "Stop howling, Ravi. If you want to play, you can stand at the end of the line," and she put him there very firmly.

The game proceeded. Two pairs of arms reached up and met in an arc. The children trooped under it again and again in a lugubrious circle, ducking their heads and intoning

Vocabulary

lugubrious (lə•go͞o'brē•əs) *adj.:* very solemn or mournful, especially in a way that seems exaggerated or ridiculous.

If All the World Were Paper and All the Water Sink (1962) by Jess (Burgess Franklin Collins), American (1923–2004). Oil on canvas. 38 × 56 in. (96.5 × 142.2 cm).

The Fine Arts Museums of San Francisco. Courtesy of the Odyssia Gallery, New York.

"The grass is green,
The rose is red;
Remember me
When I am dead, dead, dead, dead . . ."

And the arc of thin arms trembled in the twilight, and the heads were bowed so sadly, and their feet tramped to that melancholy refrain so mournfully, so helplessly, that Ravi could not bear it. He would not follow them, he would not be included in this funereal game. He had wanted victory and triumph—not a funeral. But he had been forgotten, left out, and he would not join them now. The ignominy of being forgotten—how could he face it? He felt his heart go heavy and ache inside him unbearably. He lay down full length on the damp grass, crushing his face into it, no longer crying, silenced by a terrible sense of his insignificance. ■

Vocabulary

ignominy (ig′nə•min′ē) *n.:* shame; dishonor.

Response and Analysis

Reading Check

1. Create a story map that outlines the important events of the story in **chronological order.**

Thinking Critically

2. What specific **details** and **images** in this story are most vivid to you? (Look over your reading notes.) If you had to draw one picture to illustrate the story, what would you draw?
3. Which **images** suggest loss and death? How do these images make you feel?
4. Why is everyone so surprised to see Ravi when he finally comes out of his hiding place?
5. What kind of game are the children playing at twilight? Why might the time of day be significant?
6. What has Ravi learned by the end of the story? Cite a passage from the text that supports your answer.
7. How would you state the **theme** of this story—that is, what truth or insight about human life does it reveal? As you think about the theme, think also about how the story's **title** reinforces its theme. (Think of the layers of meanings you can uncover in the word *games*.)
8. How do Ravi's experiences in the shed contribute to the **mood** of the story?

Literary Skills Analyze imagery.

Reading Skills Analyze details.

Writing Skills Write an essay comparing and contrasting two short stories.

Vocabulary Skills Use synonyms.

Extending and Evaluating

9. Are the children in this story—and childhood itself—realistically portrayed? (You may want to read over your Quickwrite notes before responding.) Give examples to support your view.

WRITING

Comparing Childhoods

In an **essay, compare** two unusual stories about children—"The Doll's House" (see page 1254) and "Games at Twilight." Focus on the discoveries made by the children in each story, the **theme** of each story, and the writer's **tone.** Remember that in a comparison-and-contrast essay, you are looking for both similarities and differences.

Vocabulary Development

In Other Words

Read the following sentences from the story. Then, on a separate sheet of paper, write a synonym to replace each underlined Vocabulary word.

1. ". . . [T]hey burst out like seeds from a crackling, overripe pod into the veranda, with such wild, maniacal yells. . ."
2. "The white walls of the veranda glared stridently in the sun."
3. "'I know I have to, idiot,' Raghu said, superciliously kicking him with his toe."
4. "He chuckled aloud with astonishment at his own temerity so that Raghu came out of the hedge . . ."
5. ". . . water would fall lavishly through the air to the ground . . . arousing the sweet, the intoxicating scent of water on dry earth. . . ."
6. "There he sat smiling, knocking his heels against the bathtub, now and then getting up and going to the door . . . and then returning to his seat with the dogged determination of the true winner, a breaker of records, a champion."
7. "The children trooped under [the arc of arms] again and again in a lugubrious circle. . . "
8. "The ignominy of being forgotten—how could he face it?"

Vocabulary Development

Analyzing Word Analogies

Reading word analogies. In a word analogy the relationship between the first pair of words is the same as the relationship between the second pair of words. Four types of relationships frequently expressed in word analogies are part and whole, location, action and related object, and performer and related action.

Part and Whole

CHAPTER : BOOK :: fender : car

[A *chapter* is a part of a *book*, just as a *fender* is a part of a *car*.]

Location

FISH : SEA :: deer : forest

[A *fish* can be found in a *sea*, just as a *deer* can be found in a *forest*.]

Action and Related Object

BOIL : EGG :: throw : ball

[You *boil* an *egg*, just as you *throw* a *ball*. In these types of analogies, the object always receives the action.]

Performer and Related Action

AUTHOR : WRITE :: chef : cook

[You expect an *author* to *write*, just as you expect a *chef* to *cook*.]

Solving word analogies. Use the following steps to solve an analogy question:

- Identify the relationship between the capitalized pair of words. (It is also helpful to note the part of speech of each word.)
- Look for the same relationship and the same parts of speech in the pairs of words in the answer choices.
- Eliminate choices that do not have the same relationship and parts of speech.
- Choose the pair of words whose relationship and word order match those of the capitalized pair.

PRACTICE

The following capitalized pairs include words from "Games at Twilight." For each numbered item, choose the pair of words that expresses a relationship that is most similar to the relationship between the pair of capitalized words. On your own paper, write the letter of your answer and the type of relationship expressed in each analogy.

1. KEY : LOCK ::
  a. crystal : gold
  b. crime : felony
  c. sound : solid
  d. witness : testify

2. BOUGAINVILLEA : GARDEN ::
  a. give : contributor
  b. parrot : tropics
  c. enclose : wall
  d. garden : hose

3. PURSUER : CHASE ::
  a. pilot : fly
  b. joke : insult
  c. shallow : deep
  d. instruct : teacher

4. VERANDA : HOUSE ::
  a. coast : beach
  b. steeple : church
  c. honey : sweet
  d. editor : review

5. BATHE : TUB ::
  a. choir : harmonize
  b. garden : lettuce
  c. knight : horse
  d. climb : ladder

Vocabulary Skills
Analyze word analogies.

Penelope Lively

(1933–)

England

Penelope Lively was born in Cairo, Egypt, where her father, a bank manager, and her mother left her upbringing to Lucy, her nursemaid and governess. Lively says of Lucy: "She had stern moral values—a general code of truthfulness and honesty and kindness spiced with fervent patriotism. All this rubbed off on me except the patriotism. . . ." Lucy as tutor helped Lively become a free-ranging, unrestrained, ravenous reader who was required to retell or write about everything that she read. Lively returned to England in 1945 and entered boarding school, where sports were favored over literature. Her copy of a poetry anthology was confiscated, and the school's headmistress later returned it with a rebuke: "There is no need for you to read this sort of thing in your spare time, Penelope. You will be *taught* all that." Lively then notes: "She went on to point out that my lacrosse skills were abysmally below par."

Lively survived boarding school and went on to Oxford, where she graduated "equipped both for everything and nothing." She worked briefly as a research assistant for a sociology professor, then married and raised her two children at home where, she says, "I read my way through twentieth-century literature as it were, stirring the baby food with one hand and holding a book in the other." The day her youngest child started school, Lively began writing children's fiction. Her first novel, *Astercote* (1970), has a supernatural plot, and its theme of the persistence of memory and the reality of the past as an influence on the present would pervade her later novels. She went on to write a number of successful books for children and young adults, including *The Whispering Knights* (1971), *The Driftway* (1972), and the Whitbread Award-winning *A Stitch in Time* (1976).

Lively's first novel for adults, *The Road to Lichfield* (1977), treats the complexities and difficulties of marriage, the ways that the present repeats or parallels the past, and the relationships we have with the past. In one part of the novel, a character loses her job as a history teacher because she teaches "what actually happened."

Lively believes that her thematic interest in the past influencing the present had something to do with growing up in Egypt—a place where remnants from several different eras and civilizations exist side by side, making the progression of time difficult to pinpoint.

Lively has also written numerous short stories, and in one of her unpublished lectures says, "In its very structure the short story has an eerie relationship with the processes of memory. . . . It holds up for inspection an incident, a relationship, a situation. . . ." Her comment fits "Next Term, We'll Mash You."

Before You Read

Next Term, We'll Mash You

Make the Connection

Quickwrite

Have you ever been suddenly put in a new social situation, such as enrolling in a new school, going to a camp for the first time, or moving to a different town? Jot down four or five tips that you would give someone to help him or her adjust to such a new situation and avoid problems.

Literary Focus

Theme

A **theme** is the central idea or insight in a work of literature. It is different from the subject of a work, which can be expressed in a word or two such as love, revenge, or growing up. The theme of a story is stated in a sentence as the generalization about human behavior or life that the writer is trying to dramatize or convey. Writers rarely state the theme of a story explicitly or tack it on as a moral; instead, they imply the theme by revealing it through the title, the central conflict, a symbol, or their characters' thoughts and actions. Often the key to figuring out a theme is to first understand the characters in a story—what they value and what motivates them.

Theme is the central idea or insight of a work of literature.

For more on Theme, see the Handbook of Literary and Historical Terms.

Background

Private schools in England (called public schools there) are often expensive, exclusive, highly conscious of class distinctions, and set up as boarding schools where children live and are subjected to guidance and discipline by older students. Every spring, parents take their children to visit and inspect schools where they may be enrolled in the fall. The word *mash* in the title is a colloquial term meaning "smash" or "beat up."

Vocabulary Development

subdued (səb′do͞od) *adj.:* quiet; controlled.

geniality (jē′nē·al′ə·tē) *n.:* friendliness; cordiality.

untainted (ən·tānt′id) *adj.:* untarnished; without a trace of anything offensive.

condescension (kän′di·sen′shən) *n.:* behavior that is patronizing.

indulgent (in·dul′jənt) *adj.:* lenient; permissive.

amiable (ā′mē·ə·bəl) *adj.:* friendly; likeable.

inaccessible (in·ak·ses′ə·bəl) *adj.:* not accessible; impossible to enter or reach.

haggard (hag′ərd) *adj.:* gaunt; worn and exhausted from anxiety.

SKILLS FOCUS

Literary Skills Understand theme.

INTERNET

Vocabulary Practice

Keyword: LE7 12-7

Cricket match at the Vine Cricket Ground, Kent, England.

Next Term, We'll Mash You

Penelope Lively

The photographs on pages 1300, 1303, and 1304 were taken at the five-hundredth anniversary of Eton College (1990).

Inside the car it was quiet, the noise of the engine even and subdued, the air just the right temperature, the windows tight-fitting. The boy sat on the back seat, a box of chocolates, unopened, beside him, and a comic, folded. The trim Sussex[1] landscape flowed past the windows: cows, white-fenced fields, highly priced period houses. The sunlight was glassy, remote as a colored photograph. The backs of the two heads in front of him swayed with the motion of the car.

His mother half-turned to speak to him. "Nearly there now, darling."

The father glanced downwards at his wife's wrist. "Are we all right for time?"

"Just right. Nearly twelve."

"I could do with a drink. Hope they lay something on."[2]

"I'm sure they will. The Wilcoxes say they're awfully nice people. Not really the schoolmaster-type at all, Sally says."

The man said, "He's an Oxford chap."

"Is he? You didn't say."

"Mmn."

"Of course, the fees are that much higher than the Seaford place."

"Fifty quid[3] or so. We'll have to see."

The car turned right, between white gates and high, dark, tight-clipped hedges. The whisper of the road under the tires changed to the crunch of gravel. The child, staring sideways, read black lettering on a white board: "St. Edward's Preparatory School. Please Drive Slowly." He shifted on the seat, and the leather sucked at the bare skin under his knees, stinging.

The mother said, "It's a lovely place. Those must be the playing fields. Look, darling, there are some of the boys." She clicked open her handbag, and the sun caught her mirror and flashed in the child's eyes; the comb went through her hair and he saw the grooves it left, neat as distant ploughing.

"Come on, then, Charles, out you get."

The building was red brick, early nineteenth century, spreading out long arms in which windows glittered blackly. Flowers, trapped in neat beds, were alternate red and white. They went up the steps, the man, the woman, and the child two paces behind.

The woman, the mother, smoothing down a skirt that would be ridged from sitting, thought: I like the way they've got the maid all done up properly. The little white apron and all that. She's foreign, I suppose. Au pair.[4] Very nice. If he comes here, there'll be Speech Days and that kind of thing. Sally Wilcox says it's quite dressy—she got that cream linen coat for coming down here. You can see why it costs a bomb. Great big grounds and only an hour and a half from London.

They went into a room looking out into a terrace. Beyond, dappled lawns, gently shifting trees, black and white cows grazing behind iron railings. Books, leather chairs, a table with magazines—*Country Life, The Field, The Economist.* "Please, if you would wait here. The Headmaster won't be long."

Alone, they sat, inspected. "I like the atmosphere, don't you, John?"

"Very pleasant, yes." Four hundred a term, near enough. You can tell it's a cut above the Seaford place, though, or the one at St. Albans. Bob Wilcox says quite a few City people send their boys here. One or two of the merchant bankers, those kind of people. It's the sort of contact that would do no harm at all. You meet someone, get talking at a cricket[5] match or what have you . . . Not at all a bad thing.

1. **Sussex:** county on the southeast coast of England.
2. **lay something on:** have a reception with drinks and/or snacks.
3. **quid** *n.:* slang for pounds, British monetary unit.
4. **au pair** *n.:* foreign person who does domestic work for room and board and for an opportunity to learn the language of her employers.
5. **cricket** *n.:* team sport played with balls and flat wooden bats.

Vocabulary

subdued (səb'do͞od) *adj.:* quiet; controlled.

"All right, Charles? You didn't get sick in the car, did you?"

The child had black hair, slicked down smooth to his head. His ears, too large, jutted out, transparent in the light from the window, laced with tiny, delicate veins. His clothes had the shine and crease of newness. He looked at the books, the dark brown pictures, his parents, said nothing.

"Come here, let me tidy your hair."

The door opened. The child hesitated, stood up, sat, then rose again with his father.

"Mr. and Mrs. Manders? How very nice to meet you—I'm Margaret Spokes, and will you please forgive my husband who is tied up with some wretch who broke the cricket pavilion window and will be just a few more minutes. We try to be organized but a schoolmaster's day is always just that bit unpredictable. Do please sit down and what will you have to revive you after that beastly drive? You live in Finchley,[6] is that right?"

"Hampstead,[7] really," said the mother. "Sherry would be lovely." She worked over the headmaster's wife from shoes to hairstyle, pricing and assessing. Shoes old but expensive—Russell and Bromley. Good skirt. Blouse could be Marks and Sparks—not sure. Real pearls. Super Victorian ring. She's not gone to any particular trouble—that's just what she'd wear anyway. You can be confident, with a voice like that, of course. Sally Wilcox says she knows all sorts of people.

The headmaster's wife said, "I don't know how much you know about us. Prospectuses[8] don't tell you a thing, do they? We'll look round everything in a minute, when you've had a chat with my husband. I gather you're friends of the Wilcoxes, by the way. I'm awfully fond of Simon—he's down for Winchester, of course, but I expect you know that."

The mother smiled over her sherry. Oh, I know that all right. Sally Wilcox doesn't let you forget that.

"And this is Charles? My dear, we've been forgetting all about you! In a minute I'm going to borrow Charles and take him off to meet some of the boys because after all you're choosing a school for him, aren't you, and not for you, so he ought to know what he might be letting himself in for and it shows we've got nothing to hide."

The parents laughed. The father, sherry warming his guts, thought that this was an amusing woman. Not attractive, of course, a bit homespun, but impressive all the same. Partly the voice, of course; it takes a bloody expensive education to produce a voice like that. And other things, of course. Background and all that stuff.

"I think I can hear the thud of the Fourth Form coming in from games, which means my husband is on the way, and then I shall leave you with him while I take Charles off to the common-room."

For a moment the three adults centered on the child, looking, judging. The mother said, "He looks so hideously pale, compared to those boys we saw outside."

"My dear, that's London, isn't it? You just have to get them out, to get some color into them. Ah, here's James. James—Mr. and Mrs. Manders. You remember, Bob Wilcox was mentioning at Sports Day . . ."

The headmaster reflected his wife's style, like paired cards in Happy Families. His clothes were mature rather than old, his skin well-scrubbed, his shoes clean, his geniality untainted by the least condescension. He was genuinely sorry to have kept them waiting, but in this business one lurches from one minor

6. **Finchley:** part of the London borough of Barnet.
7. **Hampstead:** part of the London borough of Camden—and a much more desirable place to live.
8. **prospectuses** *n. pl.:* advertisements.

Vocabulary

geniality (jē′nē•al′ə•tē) *n.:* friendliness; cordiality.
untainted (ən•tānt′id) *adj.:* untarnished; without a trace of anything offensive.
condescension (kän′di•sen′shən) *n.:* behavior that is patronizing.

crisis to the next . . . And this is Charles? Hello, there, Charles. His large hand rested for a moment on the child's head, quite extinguishing the thin, dark hair. It was as though he had but to clench his fingers to crush the skull. But he took his hand away and moved the parents to the window, to observe the mutilated cricket pavilion, with indulgent laughter.

And the child is borne away by the headmaster's wife. She never touches him or tells him to come, but simply bears him away like some relentless tide, down corridors and through swinging glass doors, towing him like a frail craft, not bothering to look back to see if he is following, confident in the strength of magnetism, or obedience.

And delivers him to a room where boys are scattered among inky tables and rungless chairs and sprawled on a mangy carpet. There is a scampering, and a rising, and a silence falling, as she opens the door.

"Now this is the Lower Third, Charles, who you'd be with if you come to us in September. Boys, this is Charles Manders, and I want you to tell him all about things and answer any questions he wants to ask. You can believe about half of what they say, Charles, and they will tell you the most fearful lies about the food, which is excellent."

The boys laugh and groan; amiable, exaggerated groans. They must like the headmaster's

Vocabulary

indulgent (in•dul′jənt) *adj.:* lenient; permissive.

amiable (ā′mē•ə•bəl) *adj.:* friendly; likeable.

wife: There is licensed repartee.[9] They look at her with bright eyes in open, eager faces. Someone leaps to hold the door for her, and close it behind her. She is gone.

The child stands in the center of the room, and it draws in around him. The circle of children contracts, faces are only a yard or so from him; strange faces, looking, assessing.

Asking questions. They help themselves to his name, his age, his school. Over their heads he sees beyond the window an inaccessible world of shivering trees and high racing clouds and his voice which has floated like a feather in the dusty schoolroom air dies altogether and he becomes mute, and he stands in the middle of them with shoulders humped, staring down at feet: grubby plimsolls[10] and kicked brown sandals. There is a noise in his ears like rushing water, a torrential din out of which voices boom, blotting each other out so that he cannot always hear the words. Do you? they say, and Have you? and What's your? and the faces, if he looks up, swing into one another in kaleidoscopic patterns and the floor under his feet is unsteady, lifting and falling.

And out of the noises comes one voice that is complete, that he can hear. "Next term, we'll mash you," it says. "We always mash new boys."

And a bell goes, somewhere beyond doors and down corridors, and suddenly the children are all gone, clattering away and leaving him there with the heaving floor and the walls that shift and swing, and the headmaster's wife comes back and tows him away, and he is with his parents again, and they are getting into the car, and the high hedges skim past the car windows once more, in the other direction, and the gravel under the tires changes to black tarmac.

"Well?"

"I liked it, didn't you?" The mother adjusted the car around her, closing windows, shrugging into her seat.

"Very pleasant, really. Nice chap."

9. **licensed repartee:** approved banter.
10. **plimsolls** *n. pl.:* sneakers.

"I liked him. Not quite so sure about her."

"It's pricey, of course."

"All the same . . ."

"Money well spent, though. One way and another."

"Shall we settle it, then?"

"I think so. I'll drop him a line."

The mother pitched her voice a notch higher to speak to the child in the back of the car. "Would you like to go there, Charles? Like Simon Wilcox. Did you see that lovely gym, and the swimming pool? And did the other boys tell you all about it?"

The child does not answer. He looks straight ahead of him, at the road coiling beneath the bonnet of the car. His face is haggard with anticipation. ■

Vocabulary

inaccessible (in•ak•ses′ə•bəl) *adj.:* not accessible; impossible to enter or reach.

haggard (hag′ərd) *adj.:* gaunt; worn and exhausted from anxiety.

Response and Analysis

Reading Check

1. Why are Charles and his parents going to the prep school?
2. Who takes Charles to see some of the students?
3. What do the students plan to do to Charles?
4. At the end of the story, what do Charles's parents plan to do?

Thinking Critically

5. How are Mr. and Mrs. Manders **characterized**? What is important to them, and what do you think motivates their actions? Use specific evidence from the text.
6. What does the condescending treatment of Charles by the headmistress and her husband reveal about their **characters**?
7. How does the brief description of the red brick school and its garden convey a sinister **atmosphere**?
8. How does Lively reveal Charles's **character**? In a brief paragraph, sum up his emotional **conflict**—that is, how he probably feels about his parents and the school. Use evidence from the text to support your opinion.
9. What point do you think the writer is trying to make by setting up the **ironic** contrast between the parents' approval of the school and Charles's silent dread of it?
10. What do you think is the **theme** of the story—its comment on life? Does this theme relate to the tips you listed in your Quickwrite notes? Explain.
11. Do you think Charles's parents love their son? Explain.

Extending and Evaluating

12. Do you find it believable that Charles doesn't answer his parents' questions or tell them what is going to happen to him next term? Explain your answer.

WRITING

Family Traits

Write a brief **character analysis** of the Manders family. You should show how their character is revealed through dialogue, action, and the reactions of other characters. Also, consider these questions: What adjectives will you use to describe the Manderses? What motivates them? Are they believable characters? What are their conflicts? Show how their characterization points to the theme of the story. Be sure to state the **theme** as a generalization about human behavior that goes beyond specifics of the story.

Vocabulary Development

What Do You Know About a Word?

subdued	indulgent
geniality	amiable
untainted	inaccessible
condescension	haggard

The cluster diagram below organizes some ideas about the word *subdued*. Make similar diagrams for each of the other Vocabulary words listed above.

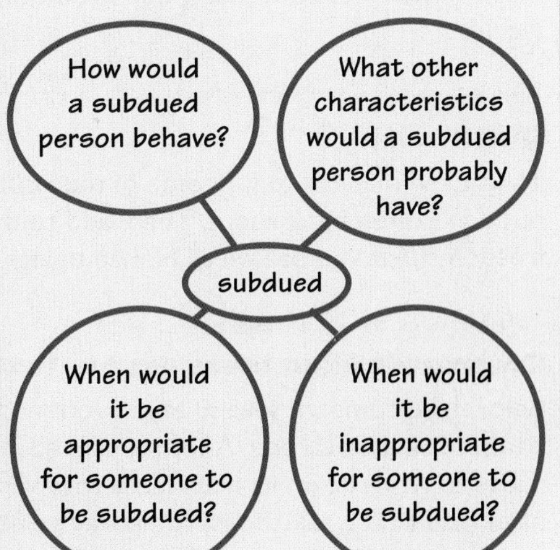
How would a subdued person behave?
What other characteristics would a subdued person probably have?
subdued
When would it be appropriate for someone to be subdued?
When would it be inappropriate for someone to be subdued?

SKILLS FOCUS

Literary Skills
Analyze theme.

Writing Skills
Write a character analysis.

Vocabulary Skills
Create semantic diagrams.

Introduction Comparing Points of View

Human Rights

Main Reading

Connected Readings

You will be reading the four selections listed above in this Comparing Points of View feature on human rights. In the top corner of the pages in this feature, you'll find three stars. Smaller versions of the stars appear next to the questions on page 1317 that focus on human rights. At the end of the feature (page 1328), you'll compare the various points of view expressed in the selections.

Examining the Issue: Human Rights

The idea of human rights has existed since the beginning of civilization. As philosophers and other thinkers have observed throughout history, human beings share an innate sense that they are entitled to certain fundamental conditions—shelter, safety, freedom from slavery, and even life itself. Tragically, these and other basic rights are often cruelly violated by those who hold or seek power. Within the last century, however, the world community—with the help of some very strong individuals—has made great strides in defining and promoting human rights throughout the world.

Make the Connection

Quickwrite

Take a few minutes to list some of the rights and freedoms that you enjoy but don't often think about. Then, add to the list any other rights and freedoms that you believe all human beings should share.

Pages 1306–1328 cover **Literary Skills** Analyze points of view on a topic.

Reading Skills Compare main ideas across texts.

Reading Skills

Comparing Main Ideas Across Texts

Before you compare several texts, you must identify and analyze the **main idea** of each one. After reading each of the following selections, pause to write down its main ideas regarding human rights. When you have read all the selections, compare the notes you have taken. Ask yourself, *What distinct perspective does each writer bring to the issue? On what points do the writers agree? On what points do they disagree?*

Ha Jin

(1956–)

China

Jin Xuefei (whose name means "golden flying snow") was born in Liaoning Province, China, where his father was an army officer. At fourteen, Jin joined the People's Liberation Army (part of China's armed forces) and for five years was stationed near the Russian border awaiting a possible invasion: "I knew there might be a war, and so we were ready and knew if we had to die, we'd die. We were quite happy . . . because everything was new: big guns and trucks. And I was young." The Cultural Revolution—the government's violent attempt at social change which included destruction of "old" art, historic buildings, and books (especially those that seemed to contradict the teachings of China's leader Mao Zedong)—had begun in 1966. Colleges were closed until 1977, when Jin entered Heilongjiang University to study English.

In 1985, Jin left China for graduate studies at Brandeis University in Massachusetts, with every intention of returning home. But after the 1989 student uprising and massacre in Tiananmen Square, Jin says, "I realized that if I wanted to be a writer, I would have to stay in the States because it would be impossible for me to write honestly in Chinese in China. So it was a painful decision, but it took a year for me to decide to write English exclusively and to stay as immigrant." He decided to use the pen name Ha Jin for the poetry and fiction books that he started publishing in 1990, barely twelve years after he formally began studying English. Jin's stories and novels dramatize life in China under a repressive government: "I guess we are compelled to write about what has hurt us most." He is a painstaking writer who revises drafts of stories and novels at least thirty times.

Jin's first novel, the comic *In the Pond* (1998), depicts an artist, who, reduced to working in a fertilizer plant, taunts his superiors with unflattering cartoons and, ironically, is promoted to a propaganda office. His second novel, *Waiting* (1999), which won the National Book Award, is about a couple who must wait eighteen years before marrying. It opens with the unforgettable sentence: "Every summer Lin Kong returned to Goose Village to divorce his wife, Shuyu."

Jin's collection of short stories, *The Bridegroom* (2000), includes "Saboteur," a story that shows how even the most tyrannized and frustrated individual can still wreak devastating revenge on a community.

Before You Read

Saboteur

Points of View

A *saboteur* is a person who commits sabotage, or purposely undermines the work of an opposing power. The word first came into use in the 1800s, when frustrated French laborers threw their wooden shoes, or *sabots,* into factory machines to protest the inhumane conditions under which they worked. Ha Jin personalizes the idea of sabotage by posing the following questions: *Is it possible to sabotage a person's humanity? If so, how would this "sabotaged" person behave?*

Literary Focus

Irony

The **irony** at work in "Saboteur" becomes apparent early on: Both the reader and the protagonist quickly learn that what *should* happen and what *will* happen are entirely different things. Ha Jin's irony, though, goes beyond the realm of fiction. It shows us that, in the real world, the discrepancy between what should and what does happen is frequently experienced as a painful injustice.

Irony is a discrepancy between expectations and reality or between appearances and reality.

For more on Irony, see the Handbook of Literary and Historical Terms.

Literary Skills Analyze points of view on a topic. Understand irony.

Reading Skills Identify political influences.

Reading Skills

Identifying Political Influences

"Saboteur" is set in contemporary China, long after the end of Mao's Cultural Revolution. However, the story critiques the oppressive conditions that continue to plague China. As you read the story, take note of symbols and characters that represent China's political heritage. What does Ha Jin seem to be saying about the fate of human rights in a society that is governed by force?

INTERNET

Vocabulary Practice

•

More About Ha Jin

•

Keyword: LE7 12-7

Background

In 1949, the Communists established the People's Republic of China under their military hero Mao Zedong (also spelled Mao Tse-tung). During Mao's Cultural Revolution, many political figures were removed from power, imprisoned, and sometimes executed. Today, China remains a communist nation, but it is gradually opening its doors to Western notions of human rights.

Vocabulary Development

coherent (kō•hir′ənt) *adj.:* logical; orderly; understandable.

propagating (präp′ə•gāt′iŋ) *v.:* publicizing; spreading.

induced (in•do͞ost′) *v.:* caused.

contemptuously (kən•temp′cho͞o•əs•lē) *adv.:* with contempt or scorn.

precedent (pres′ə•dənt) *n.:* first occurrence of something that can later be used as an example or standard.

profusely (prō•fyo͞os′lē) *adv.:* abundantly; excessively.

reactionary (rē•ak′shə•ner′ē) *adj.:* characterized by strong resistance to change or progress.

razed (rāzd) *v.:* torn down.

Saboteur

Ha Jin

Mr. Chiu and his bride were having lunch in the square before Muji Train Station.[1] On the table between them were two bottles of soda spewing out brown foam and two paper boxes of rice and sautéed cucumber and pork. "Let's eat," he said to her, and broke the connected ends of the chopsticks. He picked up a slice of streaky pork and put it into his mouth. As he was chewing, a few crinkles appeared on his thin jaw.

To his right, at another table, two railroad policemen were drinking tea and laughing; it seemed that the stout, middle-aged man was telling a joke to his young comrade, who was tall and of athletic build. Now and again they would steal a glance at Mr. Chiu's table.

The air smelled of rotten melon. A few flies kept buzzing above the couple's lunch. Hundreds of people were rushing around to get on the platform or to catch buses to downtown. Food and fruit vendors were crying for customers in lazy voices. About a dozen young women, representing the local hotels, held up placards which displayed the daily prices and words as large as a palm, like FREE MEALS, AIR-CONDITIONING, and ON THE RIVER. In the center of the square stood a concrete statue of Chairman Mao, at whose feet peasants were napping, their backs on the warm granite and their faces toward the sunny sky. A flock of pigeons perched on the Chairman's raised hand and forearm.

The rice and cucumber tasted good, and Mr. Chiu was eating unhurriedly. His sallow face showed exhaustion. He was glad that the honeymoon was finally over and that he and his bride were heading back for Harbin.[2] During the two weeks' vacation, he had been worried about his liver, because three months ago he had suffered from acute hepatitis;[3] he was afraid he might have a relapse. But he had had no severe symptoms, despite his liver being still big and tender. On the whole he was pleased with his health, which could endure even the strain of a honeymoon; indeed, he was on the course of recovery. He looked at his bride, who took off her wire glasses, kneading the root of her nose with her fingertips. Beads of sweat coated her pale cheeks.

"Are you all right, sweetheart?" he asked.

"I have a headache. I didn't sleep well last night."

"Take an aspirin, will you?"

"It's not that serious. Tomorrow is Sunday and I can sleep in. Don't worry."

As they were talking, the stout policeman at the next table stood up and threw a bowl of tea in their direction. Both Mr. Chiu's and his bride's sandals were wet instantly.

"Hooligan!" she said in a low voice.

Mr. Chiu got to his feet and said out loud, "Comrade Policeman, why did you do this?" He stretched out his right foot to show the wet sandal.

"Do what?" the stout man asked huskily, glaring at Mr. Chiu while the young fellow was whistling.

"See, you dumped tea on our feet."

"You're lying. You wet your shoes yourself."

"Comrade Policeman, your duty is to keep order, but you purposely tortured us common

---

1. **Muji Train Station:** train station in Muji City, a provincial town in central China.

2. **Harbin:** city in northeast China on the Songhua river.

3. **hepatitis** *n.:* disease marked by inflammation of the liver. It can be highly contagious.

citizens. Why violate the law you are supposed to enforce?" As Mr. Chiu was speaking, dozens of people began gathering around.

With a wave of his hand, the man said to the young fellow, "Let's get hold of him!"

They grabbed Mr. Chiu and clamped handcuffs around his wrists. He cried, "You can't do this to me. This is utterly unreasonable."

"Shut up!" The man pulled out his pistol. "You can use your tongue at our headquarters."

The young fellow added, "You're a saboteur, you know that? You're disrupting public order."

The bride was too petrified to say anything coherent. She was a recent college graduate, had majored in fine arts, and had never seen the police make an arrest. All she could say was, "Oh, please, please!"

The policemen were pulling Mr. Chiu, but he refused to go with them, holding the corner of the table and shouting, "We have a train to catch. We already bought the tickets."

The stout man punched him in the chest. "Shut up. Let your ticket expire." With the pistol butt he chopped Mr. Chiu's hands, which at once released the table. Together the two men were dragging him away to the police station.

Realizing he had to go with them, Mr. Chiu turned his head and shouted to his bride, "Don't wait for me here. Take the train. If I'm not back by tomorrow morning, send someone over to get me out."

She nodded, covering her sobbing mouth with her palm.

Vocabulary

coherent (kō•hir′ənt) *adj.:* logical; orderly; understandable.

After removing his belt, they locked Mr. Chiu into a cell in the back of the Railroad Police Station. The single window in the room was blocked by six bars; it faced a spacious yard, in which stood a few pines. Beyond the trees, two swings hung from an iron frame, swaying gently in the breeze. Somewhere in the building a cleaver was chopping rhythmically. There must be a kitchen upstairs, Mr. Chiu thought.

He was too exhausted to worry about what they would do to him, so he lay down on the narrow bed and shut his eyes. He wasn't afraid. The Cultural Revolution was over already, and recently the Party had been propagating the idea that all citizens were equal before the law. The police ought to be a law-abiding model for common people. As long as he remained cool-headed and reasoned with them, they probably wouldn't harm him.

Late in the afternoon he was taken to the Interrogation Bureau on the second floor. On his way there, in the stairwell, he ran into the middle-aged policeman who had manhandled him. The man grinned, rolling his bulgy eyes and pointing his fingers at him as if firing a pistol. Egg of a tortoise! Mr. Chiu cursed mentally.

The moment he sat down in the office, he burped, his palm shielding his mouth. In front of him, across a long desk, sat the chief of the bureau and a donkey-faced man. On the glass desktop was a folder containing information on his case. He felt it bizarre that in just a matter of hours they had accumulated a small pile of writing about him. On second thought he began to wonder whether they had kept a file on him all the time. How could this have happened? He lived and worked in Harbin, more than three hundred miles away, and this was his first time in Muji City.

The chief of the bureau was a thin, bald man who looked serene and intelligent. His slim hands handled the written pages in the folder in the manner of a lecturing scholar. To Mr. Chiu's left sat a young scribe, with a clipboard on his knee and a black fountain pen in his hand.

"Your name?" the chief asked, apparently reading out the question from a form.

"Chiu Maguang."

"Age?"

"Thirty-four."

"Profession?"

"Lecturer."

"Work unit?"

"Harbin University."

"Political status?"

"Communist Party member."

The chief put down the paper and began to speak. "Your crime is sabotage, although it hasn't induced serious consequences yet. Because you are a Party member, you should be punished more. You have failed to be a model for the masses and you—"

"Excuse me, sir," Mr. Chiu cut him off.

"What?"

"I didn't do anything. Your men are the saboteurs of our social order. They threw hot tea on my feet and on my wife's feet. Logically speaking, you should criticize them, if not punish them."

"That statement is groundless. You have no witness. Why should I believe you?" the chief said matter-of-factly.

"This is my evidence." He raised his right hand. "Your man hit my fingers with a pistol."

"That doesn't prove how your feet got wet. Besides, you could have hurt your fingers yourself."

"But I am telling the truth!" Anger flared up in Mr. Chiu. "Your police station owes me an apology. My train ticket has expired, my new leather sandals are ruined, and I am late for a conference in the provincial capital. You must compensate me for the damage and losses. Don't mistake me for a common citizen who would tremble when you sneeze. I'm a scholar, a philosopher, and an expert in dialectical

Vocabulary

propagating (präp′ə•gāt′iŋ) *v.:* publicizing; spreading.
induced (in•do͞ost′) *v.:* caused; brought about.

materialism. If necessary, we will argue about this in *The Northeastern Daily,* or we will go to the highest People's Court in Beijing. Tell me, what's your name?" He got carried away with his harangue,[4] which was by no means trivial and had worked to his advantage on numerous occasions.

"Stop bluffing us," the donkey-faced man broke in. "We have seen a lot of your kind. We can easily prove you are guilty. Here are some of the statements given by eyewitnesses." He pushed a few sheets of paper toward Mr. Chiu.

Mr. Chiu was dazed to see the different handwritings, which all stated that he had shouted in the square to attract attention and refused to obey the police. One of the witnesses had identified herself as a purchasing agent from a shipyard in Shanghai. Something stirred in Mr. Chiu's stomach, a pain rising to his rib. He gave out a faint moan.

"Now you have to admit you are guilty," the chief said. "Although it's a serious crime, we won't punish you severely, provided you write out a self-criticism and promise that you won't disrupt the public order again. In other words, your release will depend on your attitude toward this crime."

"You're daydreaming," Mr. Chiu cried. "I won't write a word, because I'm innocent. I demand that you provide me with a letter of apology so I can explain to my university why I'm late."

Both the interrogators smiled contemptuously. "Well, we've never done that," said the chief, taking a puff at his cigarette.

"Then make this a precedent."

"That's unnecessary. We are pretty certain that you will comply with our wishes." The chief blew a column of smoke toward Mr. Chiu's face.

At the tilt of the chief's head, two guards stepped forward and grabbed the criminal by the arms. Mr. Chiu meanwhile went on saying, "I shall report you to the Provincial Administration. You'll have to pay for this! You are worse than the Japanese military police."

They dragged him out of the room.

After dinner, which consisted of a bowl of millet[5] porridge, a corn bun, and a piece of pickled turnip, Mr. Chiu began to have a fever, shaking with a chill and sweating profusely. He knew that the fire of anger had gotten into his liver and that he was probably having a relapse. No medicine was available, because his briefcase had been left with his bride. At home it would have been time for him to sit in front of their color TV, drinking jasmine tea and watching the evening news. It was so lonesome in here. The orange bulb above the single bed was the only source of light, which enabled the guards to keep him under surveillance at night. A moment ago he had asked them for a newspaper or a magazine to read, but they turned him down.

Through the small opening on the door noises came in. It seemed that the police on duty were playing cards or chess in a nearby office; shouts and laughter could be heard now and then. Meanwhile, an accordion kept coughing from a remote corner in the building. Looking at the ballpoint and the letter paper left for him by the guards when they took him back from the Interrogation Bureau, Mr. Chiu remembered the old saying, "When a scholar runs into soldiers, the more he argues, the muddier his point becomes." How ridiculous this whole thing was. He ruffled his thick hair with his fingers.

4. **harangue** *n.:* ranting speech.

5. **millet** *n.* used as *adj.:* grass cultivated for its grain.

Vocabulary

contemptuously (kən•temp′cho͞o•əs•lē) *adv.:* with contempt or scorn.

precedent (pres′ə•dənt) *n.:* first occurrence of something that can later be used as an example or standard.

profusely (prō•fyo͞os′lē) *adv.:* abundantly; excessively.

He felt miserable, massaging his stomach continually. To tell the truth, he was more upset than frightened, because he would have to catch up with his work once he was back home—a paper that was due at the printers next week, and two dozen books he ought to read for the courses he was going to teach in the fall.

A human shadow flitted across the opening. Mr. Chiu rushed to the door and shouted through the hole, "Comrade Guard, Comrade Guard!"

"What do you want?" a voice rasped.

"I want you to inform your leaders that I'm very sick. I have heart disease and hepatitis. I may die here if you keep me like this without medication."

"No leader is on duty on the weekend. You have to wait till Monday."

"What? You mean I'll stay in here tomorrow?"

"Yes."

"Your station will be held responsible if anything happens to me."

"We know that. Take it easy, you won't die."

It seemed illogical that Mr. Chiu slept quite well that night, though the light above his head had been on all the time and the straw mattress was hard and infested with fleas. He was afraid of ticks, mosquitoes, cockroaches—any kind of insect but fleas and bedbugs. Once, in the countryside, where his school's faculty and staff had helped the peasants harvest crops for a week, his colleagues had joked about his flesh, which they said must have tasted nonhuman to fleas. Except for him, they were all afflicted with hundreds of bites.

More amazing now, he didn't miss his bride a lot. He even enjoyed sleeping alone, perhaps because the honeymoon had tired him out and he needed more rest.

The backyard was quiet on Sunday morning. Pale sunlight streamed through the pine branches. A few sparrows were jumping on the ground, catching caterpillars and ladybugs. Holding the steel bars, Mr. Chiu inhaled the morning air, which smelled meaty. There must have been an eatery or a cooked-meat stand nearby. He reminded himself that he should take this detention with ease. A sentence that Chairman Mao had written to a hospitalized friend rose in his mind: "Since you are already in here, you may as well stay and make the best of it."

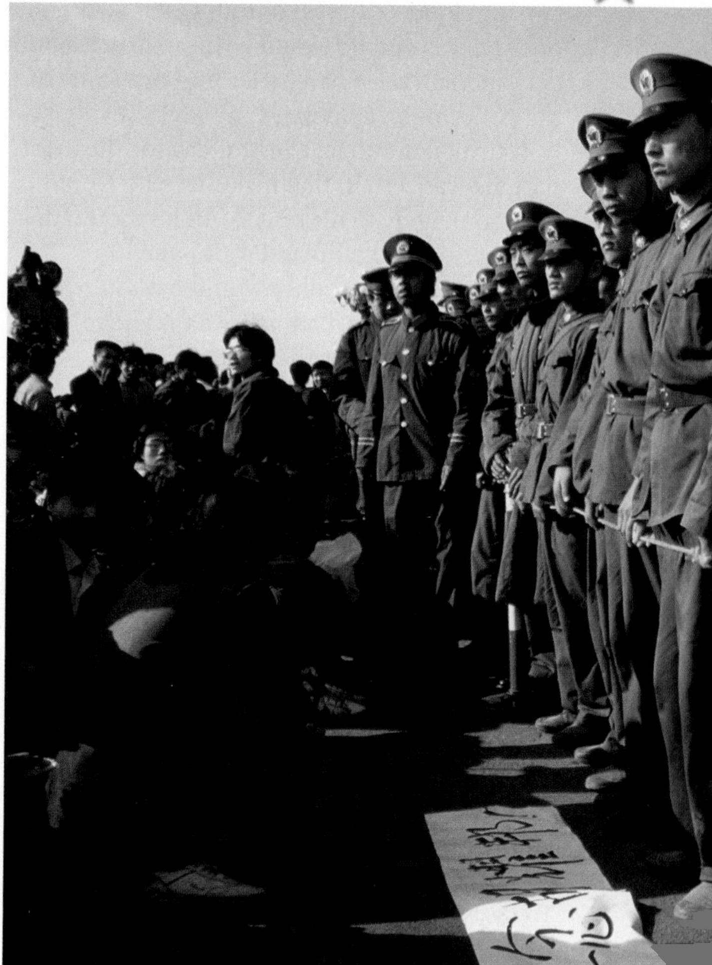

Chinese soldiers blocking student demonstrators (1989).

His desire for peace of mind originated in his fear that his hepatitis might get worse. He tried to remain unperturbed. However, he was sure that his liver was swelling up, since the fever still persisted. For a whole day he lay in bed, thinking about his paper on the nature of contradictions. Time and again he was overwhelmed by anger,

cursing aloud, "A bunch of thugs!" He swore that once he was out, he would write an article about his experience. He had better find out some of the policemen's names.

It turned out to be a restful day for the most part; he was certain that his university would send somebody to his rescue. All he should do now was remain calm and wait patiently. Sooner or later the police would have to release him, although they had no idea that he might refuse to leave unless they wrote him an apology. Damn those hoodlums, they had ordered more than they could eat!

When he woke up on Monday morning, it was already light. Somewhere a man was moaning; the sound came from the backyard. After a long yawn, and kicking off the tattered blanket, Mr. Chiu climbed out of bed and went to the window. In the middle of the yard, a young man was fastened to a pine, his wrists handcuffed around the trunk from behind. He was wriggling and swearing loudly, but there was no sight of anyone else in the yard. He looked familiar to Mr. Chiu.

Mr. Chiu squinted his eyes to see who it was. To his astonishment, he recognized the man, who was Fenjin, a recent graduate from the Law Department at Harbin University. Two years ago Mr. Chiu had taught a course in Marxist materialism, in which Fenjin had enrolled. Now, how on earth had this young devil landed here?

Then it dawned on him that Fenjin must have been sent over by his bride. What a stupid woman! A bookworm, who only knew how to read foreign novels! He had expected that she would contact the school's Security Section, which would for sure send a cadre[6] here. Fenjin held no official position; he merely worked in a private law firm that had just two lawyers; in fact, they had little business except for some detective work for men and women who suspected their spouses of having extramarital affairs. Mr. Chiu was overcome with a wave of nausea.

Should he call out to let his student know he was nearby? He decided not to, because he didn't know what had happened. Fenjin must have quarreled with the police to incur such a punishment. Yet this could never have occurred if Fenjin hadn't come to his rescue. So no matter what, Mr. Chiu had to do something. But what could he do?

It was going to be a scorcher. He could see purple steam shimmering and rising from the ground among the pines. Poor devil, he thought, as he raised a bowl of corn glue[7] to his mouth, sipped, and took a bite of a piece of salted celery.

When a guard came to collect the bowl and the chopsticks, Mr. Chiu asked him what had happened to the man in the backyard. "He called our boss 'bandit,'" the guard said. "He claimed he was a lawyer or something. An arrogant son of a rabbit."

Now it was obvious to Mr. Chiu that he had to do something to help his rescuer. Before he could figure out a way, a scream broke out in the backyard. He rushed to the window and saw a tall policeman standing before Fenjin, an iron bucket on the ground. It was the same young fellow who had arrested Mr. Chiu in the square two days before. The man pinched Fenjin's nose, then raised his hand, which stayed in the air for a few seconds, then slapped the lawyer across the face. As Fenjin was groaning, the man lifted up the bucket and poured water on his head.

"This will keep you from getting sunstroke, boy. I'll give you some more every hour," the man said loudly.

Fenjin kept his eyes shut, yet his wry face showed that he was struggling to hold back from cursing the policeman, or, more likely, that he

6. **cadre** *n.:* group of officers or personnel.

7. **corn glue:** edible paste.

was sobbing in silence. He sneezed, then raised his face and shouted, "Let me go take a piss."

"Oh yeah?" the man bawled. "Pee in your pants."

Still Mr. Chiu didn't make any noise, gripping the steel bars with both hands, his fingers white. The policeman turned and glanced at the cell's window; his pistol, partly holstered, glittered in the sun. With a snort he spat his cigarette butt to the ground and stamped it into the dust.

Then the door opened and the guards motioned Mr. Chiu to come out. Again they took him upstairs to the Interrogation Bureau.

The same men were in the office, though this time the scribe was sitting there empty-handed. At the sight of Mr. Chiu the chief said, "Ah, here you are. Please be seated."

After Mr. Chiu sat down, the chief waved a white silk fan and said to him, "You may have seen your lawyer. He's a young man without manners, so our director had him taught a crash course in the backyard."

"It's illegal to do that. Aren't you afraid to appear in a newspaper?"

"No, we are not, not even on TV. What else can you do? We are not afraid of any story you make up. We call it fiction. What we do care about is that you cooperate with us. That is to say, you must admit your crime."

"What if I refuse to cooperate?"

"Then your lawyer will continue his education in the sunshine."

A swoon swayed Mr. Chiu, and he held the arms of the chair to steady himself. A numb pain stung him in the upper stomach and nauseated him, and his head was throbbing. He was sure that the hepatitis was finally attacking him. Anger was flaming up in his chest; his throat was tight and clogged.

The chief resumed, "As a matter of fact, you don't even have to write out your self-criticism. We have your crime described clearly here. All we need is your signature."

Holding back his rage, Mr. Chiu said, "Let me look at that."

With a smirk the donkey-faced man handed him a sheet, which carried these words:

> I hereby admit that on July 13 I disrupted public order at Muji Train Station, and that I refused to listen to reason when the railroad police issued their warning. Thus I myself am responsible for my arrest. After two days' detention, I have realized the reactionary nature of my crime. From now on, I shall continue to educate myself with all my effort and shall never commit this kind of crime again.

A voice started screaming in Mr. Chiu's ears, "Lie, lie!" But he shook his head and forced the voice away. He asked the chief, "If I sign this, will you release both my lawyer and me?"

"Of course, we'll do that." The chief was drumming his fingers on the blue folder—their file on him.

Mr. Chiu signed his name and put his thumbprint under his signature.

"Now you are free to go," the chief said with a smile, and handed him a piece of paper to wipe his thumb with.

Mr. Chiu was so sick that he couldn't stand up from the chair at first try. Then he doubled his effort and rose to his feet. He staggered out of the building to meet his lawyer in the backyard, having forgotten to ask for his belt back. In his chest he felt as though there were a bomb. If he were able to, he would have razed the entire police station and eliminated all their families. Though he knew he could do nothing like that, he made up his mind to do something.

"I'm sorry about this torture, Fenjin," Mr. Chiu said when they met.

Vocabulary

reactionary (rē•ak′shə•ner′ē) *adj.:* characterized by strong resistance to change or progress.

razed (rāzd) *v.:* torn down.

"It doesn't matter. They are savages." The lawyer brushed a patch of dirt off his jacket with trembling fingers. Water was still dribbling from the bottoms of his trouser legs.

"Let's go now," the teacher said.

The moment they came out of the police station, Mr. Chiu caught sight of a tea stand. He grabbed Fenjin's arm and walked over to the old woman at the table. "Two bowls of black tea," he said and handed her a one-yuan note.

After the first bowl, they each had another one. Then they set out for the train station. But before they walked fifty yards, Mr. Chiu insisted on eating a bowl of tree-ear soup at a food stand. Fenjin agreed. He told his teacher, "You mustn't treat me like a guest."

"No, I want to eat something myself."

As if dying of hunger, Mr. Chiu dragged his lawyer from restaurant to restaurant near the police station, but at each place he ordered no more than two bowls of food. Fenjin wondered why his teacher wouldn't stay at one place and eat his fill.

Mr. Chiu bought noodles, wonton, eight-grain porridge, and chicken soup, respectively, at four restaurants. While eating, he kept saying through his teeth, "If only I could kill all the bastards!" At the last place he merely took a few sips of the soup without tasting the chicken cubes and mushrooms.

Fenjin was baffled by his teacher, who looked ferocious and muttered to himself mysteriously, and whose jaundiced[8] face was covered with dark puckers. For the first time Fenjin thought of Mr. Chiu as an ugly man.

Within a month over eight hundred people contracted acute hepatitis in Muji. Six died of the disease, including two children. Nobody knew how the epidemic had started. ■

8. **jaundiced** *adj.:* spiteful; also, yellowish pigment of the skin caused by disease, often of the liver (in this case, hepatitis).

Response and Analysis

Reading Check

1. With whom is Mr. Chiu dining in the Muji train station?
2. Describe the incident that leads to a conflict between Mr. Chiu and the nearby policemen.
3. From what ailment does Mr. Chiu suffer?
4. Why does Mr. Chiu finally sign the statement of his guilt?
5. How does Mr. Chiu exact revenge for the injustice done to him?

Thinking Critically

6. The central **irony** in this story—the difference between what should and what does happen—revolves around an injustice done to the main character. Explain what this irony is. How does the end of the story reveal yet another irony and yet another injustice?
7. Prior to the incident in the train station, do you find Mr. Chiu to be a sympathetic character? Why or why not?
8. Throughout most of his ordeal, Mr. Chiu remains optimistic that justice will prevail. Provide two or three examples of this attitude. How does Mr. Chiu's optimism help create the story's ominous **mood**?
9. What might the statue of Chairman Mao, described early in the story, represent? Might this symbol serve an **ironic** purpose in the story? Explain why or why not.
10. How, in your opinion, did the political history of China influence the plot or the characters of "Saboteur"? (Review your reading notes, the biography of Ha Jin on page 1307, and the information in the Background on page 1308 before you respond.) What message or **theme** about politics and human rights can be drawn from the story? 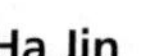

WRITING

You Can Never Go Home Again

Re-read the second-to-last paragraph of the story. Then, imagine that you are Mr. Chiu on the evening that he returns to his home and his new bride. Write a **journal entry** that describes what has happened to you and that also reflects how you have been changed by the experience.

Vocabulary Development

Synonyms and Antonyms

In items 1–4 below, choose the best **synonym** for each capitalized Vocabulary word. In items 5–8, choose the best **antonym.** Write your answers on a separate sheet of paper.

Synonyms

1. COHERENT: (a) brief (b) logical (c) disorganized (d) creative
2. PROPAGATING: (a) spreading (b) adding (c) concealing (d) beginning
3. PRECEDENT: (a) example (b) requirement (c) presentation (d) award
4. REACTIONARY: (a) influential (b) excessive (c) sudden (d) resistant

Antonyms

5. INDUCED: (a) admitted (b) caused (c) intimidated (d) halted
6. CONTEMPTUOUSLY: (a) angrily (b) sorrowfully (c) kindly (d) heartily
7. PROFUSELY: (a) loudly (b) scarcely (c) suspiciously (d) delicately
8. RAZED: (a) comforted (b) stunned (c) erected (d) interfered

Literary Skills Analyze points of view on a topic. Analyze irony.

Reading Skills Identify political influences.

Writing Skills Write a journal entry.

Vocabulary Skills Use synonyms and antonyms.

Connected Readings

United Nations Commission on Human Rights .... *from the* **Universal Declaration of Human Rights**
Desmond Tutu .... *from* **The Question of South Africa**
Aung San Suu Kyi .... *from* **Towards a True Refuge**

You have just read Ha Jin's short story "Saboteur" and considered the ways in which societies and individuals can be shaped by the denial of human rights. The next three selections you will read also make strong statements about the inherent rights of human beings—and the crucial need for respecting those rights. As you read, ask yourself how the insights presented in these selections are alike and different from Ha Jin's. After you read, you'll find questions on page 1328 asking you to compare all four selections.

Points *of* View

Before You Read

In the years following World War II, a movement to recognize and clarify the inalienable rights of human beings began to gather force. This movement was propelled by the horror people felt as they discovered the atrocities that had been committed against millions of innocent people in Nazi Germany. But who would address the issue of human rights? What group or nation could assume such a huge responsibility? With the formation of the United Nations in 1945, the creation of a universal statement of human rights became a possibility. Under the guidance of this organization—and, more specifically, of the U.S. First Lady Eleanor Roosevelt, Chairperson of the UN Commission on Human Rights—such a document was formulated, revised, and finally adopted by the UN General Assembly on December 10, 1948.

The Preamble to the United Nations' Universal Declaration of Human Rights appears on page 1319. You will notice that the Preamble consists of a series of statements beginning "Whereas. . . ." These statements provide a rationale for the declaration; that is, they say *why* such a declaration is necessary. After the Preamble comes a list (which does not appear with this selection) of thirty articles that specify the rights of all humans, in all times and in all countries. The thirty articles address such specific human rights issues as equal protection under the law, the prohibition of slavery, the right to be "presumed innocent until proved guilty," and the right to "freedom of thought, conscience, and religion," among many other rights. The document, which celebrated its fiftieth anniversary in 1998, continues to guide the leaders of nations as they envision and try to realize a world characterized by peace, justice, and unity.

United Nations, New York.

POLITICAL STATEMENT

from the Universal Declaration of Human Rights

United Nations Commission on Human Rights

Preamble

Whereas recognition of the inherent dignity and of the equal and inalienable rights of all members of the human family is the foundation of freedom, justice and peace in the world,

Whereas disregard and contempt for human rights have resulted in barbarous acts which have outraged the conscience of mankind, and the advent of a world in which human beings shall enjoy freedom of speech and belief and freedom from fear and want has been proclaimed as the highest aspiration of the common people, ❶

Whereas it is essential, if man is not to be compelled to have recourse, as a last resort, to rebellion against tyranny and oppression, that human rights should be protected by the rule of law, ❷

Whereas it is essential to promote the development of friendly relations between nations,

Whereas the people of the United Nations have in the Charter reaffirmed their faith in fundamental human rights, in the dignity and worth of the human person and in the equal rights of men and women and have determined to promote social progress and better standards of life in larger freedom, ❸

Whereas Member States° have pledged themselves to achieve, in co-operation with the United Nations, the promotion of universal respect for and observance of human rights and fundamental freedoms,

Whereas a common understanding of these rights and freedoms is of the greatest importance for the full realization of this pledge, ❹

❶ ? *What assumptions about human needs and desires underlie these two opening paragraphs? What freedoms are identified as fundamental to human rights?*

❷ ? *Why is it "essential" to protect human rights through law?*

❸ ? *What values and goals does the Charter of the United Nations set forth?*

❹ ? *What have the Member States pledged? What is identified here as most important for the "full realization" of this pledge?*

° **Member States:** When the United Nations was formed in 1945, there were fifty-one member states. As of 2000, there were 189.

Now, Therefore,
THE GENERAL ASSEMBLY
proclaims

THIS UNIVERSAL DECLARATION OF HUMAN RIGHTS as a common standard of achievement for all peoples and all nations, to the end that every individual and every organ of society, keeping this Declaration constantly in mind, shall strive by teaching and education to promote respect for these rights and freedoms and by progressive measures, national and international, to secure their universal and effective recognition and observance, both among the peoples of Member States themselves and among the peoples of territories under their jurisdiction. ❺

❺

? *According to this Declaration, how can human rights be achieved around the world?*

Points of View

Before You Read

Desmond Tutu (opposite page) is one of the best-known civil rights leaders in the world. He was born in 1931 in Klerksdorp, South Africa, not far from the South African capital of Johannesburg. Under South Africa's strict racial segregation policy, known as apartheid (ə·pär′tāt′), Tutu was educated in all-black schools. He later received a bachelor's degree in arts from the University of South Africa and, after teaching for a short while, entered the Anglican ministry. Tutu was ordained in 1961 and went on to become the first black archbishop of Capetown—the head of the Anglican Church in South Africa.

From this position of leadership, Tutu worked to end apartheid and to create a just South African government. He met with world leaders and asked them to restrict their business dealings with South Africa. These negotiations created international pressure on South Africa to abolish its unjust racial laws. Gradually and painfully, the laws of apartheid were dismantled by the end of 1991.

In 1984, in the midst of his crusade, Tutu was awarded the Nobel Peace Prize. Tutu gave the speech that begins on the next page to the United Nations Security Council shortly after receiving the prestigious award.

SPEECH

from The Question of South Africa

Desmond Tutu

I speak out of a full heart, for I am about to speak about a land that I love deeply and passionately; a beautiful land of rolling hills and gurgling streams, of clear starlit skies, of singing birds, and gamboling lambs; a land God has richly endowed with the good things of the earth, a land rich in mineral deposits of nearly every kind; a land of vast open spaces, enough to accommodate all its inhabitants comfortably; a land capable of feeding itself and other lands on the beleaguered[1] continent of Africa, a veritable breadbasket; a land that could contribute wonderfully to the material and spiritual development and prosperity of all Africa and indeed of the whole world. It is endowed with enough to satisfy the material and spiritual needs of all its peoples.

And so we would expect that such a land, veritably flowing with milk and honey, should be a land where peace and harmony and contentment reigned supreme. Alas, the opposite is the case. For my beloved country is wracked by division, by alienation, by animosity, by separation, by injustice, by avoidable pain and suffering. It is a deeply fragmented society, ridden by fear and anxiety, covered by a pall of despondency and a sense of desperation, split up into hostile, warring factions. ❶

❶ ? *How does Tutu describe the social and political conditions in South Africa? Why are these conditions "opposite" to what one might expect to find?*

It is a highly volatile[2] land, and its inhabitants sit on a powder keg with a very short fuse indeed, ready to blow us all up into kingdom come. There is endemic[3] unrest, like a festering sore that will not heal until not just the symptoms are treated but the root causes are removed.

South African society is deeply polarized. Nothing illustrates this more sharply than the events of the past week. While the black community was in the seventh heaven of delight because of the decision of that committee in Oslo, and while the world was congratulating the recipient of the Nobel Peace Prize[4], the white government and most white South Africans, very sadly, were seeking to devalue that prize. An event that should have been the occasion of uninhibited joy and thanksgiving revealed a sadly divided society. ❷

? *What event does Tutu use to show how deeply polarized South African society is?*

Before I came to this country in early September to go on sabbatical, I visited one of the trouble spots near Johannesburg. . . . In this black township, we met an old lady who told us that she was looking after her grandchildren and the children of neighbors while they were at work. On the day about which she was speaking, the police had been chasing black schoolchildren in that street, but the children had eluded the police, who then drove down the street past the old lady's house. Her wards[5] were playing in front of

1. **beleaguered** *adj.:* stressed; threatened.
2. **volatile** *adj.:* explosive.
3. **endemic** *adj.:* native.
4. **committee . . . Prize:** The committee is the Nobel Committee and the recipient is Tutu himself.
5. **wards** *n. pl.:* children who have been placed in the care of others because their parents are dead or incapable of caring for them.

the house, in the yard. She was sitting in the kitchen at the back, when her daughter burst in, calling agitatedly for her. She rushed out into the living room. A grandson had fallen just inside the door, dead. The police had shot him in the back. He was six years old. Recently, a baby, a few weeks old, became the first white casualty of the current uprisings. Every death is one too many. Those whom the black community has identified as collaborators with a system that oppresses them and denies them the most elementary human rights have met cruel death, which we deplore as much as any others. They have rejected these people operating within the system, whom they have seen as lackies[6] and stooges, despite their titles of town councilors, and so on, under an apparently new dispensation[7] extending the right of local government to the blacks. ❸

> ❸ ? What tragic examples does Tutu use here to illustrate that his nation is "a sadly divided society"? How can you tell that Tutu is fair to both sides?

Over 100,000 black students are out of school, boycotting—as they did in 1976—what they and the black community perceive as an inferior education designed deliberately for inferiority. An already highly volatile situation has been ignited several times and, as a result, over 80 persons have died. There has been industrial unrest, with the first official strike by black miners taking place, not without its toll of fatalities among the blacks.

Some may be inclined to ask: But why should all this unrest be taking place just when the South African government appears to have embarked on the road of reform? . . .

There is little freedom in this land of plenty. There is little freedom to disagree with the determinations of the authorities. There is large-scale unemployment because of the drought and the recession that has hit most of the world's economy. And it is at such a time that the authorities have increased the prices of various foodstuffs and also of rents in black townships—measures designed to hit hardest those least able to afford the additional costs. It is not surprising that all this has exacerbated an already tense and volatile situation. ❹

> ❹ ? What problems contribute to the "tense and volatile situation"?

So the unrest is continuing, in a kind of war of attrition, with the casualties not being large enough at any one time to shock the world sufficiently for it to want to take action against the system that is the root cause of all this agony. We have warned consistently that unrest will be endemic in South Africa until its root cause is removed. And the root cause is apartheid—a vicious, immoral and totally evil, and unchristian system. . . . ❺

> ❺ ? According to Tutu, why isn't the world doing anything about the situation in his country? What does he identify as the "root cause" of his country's ills?

As blacks we often run the gauntlet of roadblocks on roads leading into our townships, and these have been manned by the army in what are actually described as routine police operations. When you use the army in this fashion, who is the enemy?

The authorities have not stopped stripping blacks of their South African citizenship. Here I am, 53 years old, a bishop in the church, some would say reasonably responsible; I travel on a document that says of my nationality that it is "undeterminable at present." The South African government is turning us into aliens in the land of our birth. It continues unabated with its vicious policy of forced population removals. It is threatening to remove the people of Kwa

6. **lackies** *n. pl.:* submissive followers.
7. **dispensation** *n:* an exemption from an impediment.

Archbishop Desmond Tutu (1986).

Ngema. It treats carelessly the women in the KTC squatter camp near Cape Town[8] whose flimsy plastic coverings are destroyed every day by the authorities; and the heinous crime of those women is that they want to be with their husbands, with the fathers of their children. 6

> **6** ? *What examples does Tutu use to show that the South African government is turning its black population into "aliens" in their own country?*

White South Africans are not demons; they are ordinary human beings, scared human beings, many of them; who would not be, if they were outnumbered five to one? Through this lofty body I wish to appeal to my white fellow South Africans to share in building a new society, for blacks are not intent on driving whites into the sea but on claiming only their rightful place in the sun in the land of their birth.

We deplore all forms of violence, the violence of an oppressive and unjust society and the violence of those seeking to overthrow that society, for we believe that violence is not the answer to the crisis of our land.

We dream of a new society that will be truly nonracial, truly democratic, in which people count because they are created in the image of God. 7

> **7** ? *How can you tell that Tutu wants justice and fairness for both sides? How does he try to assure white South Africans that he is not advocating a violent overthrow of their rule?*

8. **KTC squatter camp near Cape Town:** Cape Town is a city on the southwestern coast of South Africa; the KTC squatter camp was where low-paid black South Africans, unable to afford real homes, were obliged to live in flimsy shacks. These shacks were divided by gender.

We are committed to work for justice, for peace, and for reconciliation. We ask you, please help us; urge the South African authorities to go to the conference table with the . . . representatives of all sections of our community. I appeal to this body to act. I appeal in the name of the ordinary, the little people of South Africa. I appeal in the name of the squatters in crossroads and in the KTC camp. I appeal on behalf of the father who has to live in a single-sex hostel as a migrant worker, separated from his family for 11 months of the year. I appeal on behalf of the students who have rejected this travesty of education made available only for blacks. I appeal on behalf of those who are banned arbitrarily, who are banished, who are detained without trial, those imprisoned because they have had a vision of this new South Africa. I appeal on behalf of those who have been exiled from their homes.

I say we will be free, and we ask you: Help us, that this freedom comes for all of us in South Africa, black and white, but that it comes with the least possible violence, that it comes peacefully, that it comes soon. ❽

❽

? *What is Tutu asking of the United Nations Security Council? What is his ultimate hope for his country?*

Points *of* View

Before You Read

Aung San Suu Kyi (opposite page) is the leader of the pro-democracy movement in the southeast Asian nation of Myanmar (formerly Burma). Her father, General Aung San Kyi, fought for Burmese independence from Great Britain in the 1940s and was assassinated in 1947. Like her father, Aung San Suu Kyi has been persecuted as an opponent of an established government.

After studying at Oxford University, marrying, and living in England for many years, she returned to Myanmar in 1988 and began to agitate for political reform. In that year the State Law and Order Restoration Council (SLORC), a militant, dictatorial body, seized control of the Burmese government. Since then SLORC has used force and suppression to govern and control the Burmese people.

Living conditions in Myanmar are among the worst in the world, and poverty is rampant. Four out of ten children are malnourished and according to the United Nations, the government spends only twenty-eight cents per student in public schools. The SLORC is also known to use slave labor, including children, for public projects. Many of its laws are explicitly designed to strip individuals of their rights. It is illegal, for example, for people to gather in groups larger than four or even to own a computer.

In 1990, SLORC allowed general elections, but when Aung San Suu Kyi's party won, the government refused to acknowledge the results. Aung San Suu Kyi had been placed under house arrest shortly before the election, and she remained a captive until 1995. During the years of her confinement, when she was unable to leave her home or see her family, she wrote many books and speeches promoting democracy, human rights, and world peace. She received the Nobel Peace Prize in 1991. The following excerpt is taken from a speech written by Aung San Suu Kyi during her house arrest. It was delivered by her husband at Oxford University in 1993.

SPEECH

from Towards a True Refuge

Aung San Suu Kyi

It is perfectly natural that all people should wish for a secure refuge. It is unfortunate that in spite of strong evidence to the contrary, so many still act as though security would be guaranteed if they fortified themselves with an abundance of material possessions. The greatest threats to global security today come not from the economic deficiencies of the poorest nations but from religious, racial (or tribal) and political dissensions raging in those regions where principles and practices which could reconcile the diverse instincts and aspirations of mankind have been ignored, repressed or distorted. ❶ Man-made disasters are made by dominant individuals and cliques which refuse to move beyond the autistic[1] confines of partisan[2] interest. An eminent development economist has observed that the best defense against famine is an accountable government. It makes little political or economic sense to give aid without trying to address the circumstances that render aid ineffectual. No amount of material goods and technological know-how will compensate for human irresponsibility and viciousness. ❷

> ❶ ? *What does Aung San Suu Kyi identify as the "greatest threats to global security today"?*

> ❷ ? *According to Aung San Suu Kyi, why is simply giving material aid to a nation ultimately ineffective?*

Developed and developing nations alike suffer as a result of policies removed from a framework of values which uphold minimum standards of justice and tolerance. The rapidity with which the old Soviet Union splintered into new states, many of them stamped with a fierce racial assertiveness, illustrates that decades of authoritarian rule may have achieved uniformity and obedience but could not achieve long-term harmony or stability. Nor did the material benefits enjoyed under the relatively successful post-totalitarian state of Yugoslavia succeed in dissipating the psychological impress of brooding historical experience that has now led to some of the worst religious and ethnic violence the Balkans[3] have ever witnessed. Peace, stability and unity cannot be bought or coerced; they have to be nurtured by promoting a sensitivity to human needs and respect for the rights and opinions of others. Diversity and dissent need not inhibit the emergence of strong, stable societies, but inflexibility, narrowness and unadulterated materialism can prevent healthy growth. And when attitudes have been allowed to harden to the point that otherness becomes a sufficient reason for nullifying[4] a person's claim to be treated as a fellow human being, the trappings of modern civilization crumble with frightening speed. ❸

> ❸ ? *Identify the problem that plagues both developing and developed nations. How can "peace, stability, and unity" ultimately be achieved? What can cause a civilization to "crumble"?*

In the most troubled areas of the world reserves of tolerance and compassion disappear,

1. **autistic** *adj.:* in this context, "self-centered."
2. **partisan** *adj.:* factional; biased.
3. **Balkans:** countries occupying the Balkan Peninsula in southeastern Europe.
4. **nullifying** *v.:* invalidating; canceling.

security becomes nonexistent and creature comforts are reduced to a minimum—but stockpiles of weapons abound. As a system of values this is totally mad. By the time it is accepted that the only way out of an impasse[5] of hate, bloodshed and social and economic chaos created by men is for those men to get together to find a peaceful solution through dialogue and compromise, it is usually no longer easy to restore sanity. Those who have been conditioned by systems which make a mockery of the law by legalizing injustices and which attack the very foundations of harmony by perpetuating social, political and economic imbalances cannot adjust quickly—if at all—to the concept of a fair settlement which places general well-being and justice above partisan advantage. 4

4

? *What "system of values" does Aung San Suu Kyi identify as "totally mad"? In contrast, what can you infer is her system of values?*

During the Cold War the iniquities[6] of ruthless governments and armed groups were condoned for ideological[7] reasons. The results have been far from happy. Although there is greater emphasis on justice and human rights today, there are still ardent advocates in favor of giving priority to political and economic expediency[8]—increasingly the latter. It is the old argument: achieve economic success and all else will follow. But even long-affluent[9] societies are plagued by formidable social ills which have provoked deep anxieties about the future. And newly rich nations appear to be spending a significant portion of their wealth on arms and armies. Clearly there is no inherent link between greater prosperity and greater security and peace—or even the expectation of greater peace. Both prosperity and peace are necessary for the happiness of mankind, the one to

Aung San Suu Kyi (1996).

5. **impasse** *n.:* deadlock.
6. **iniquities** *n. pl.:* sins.
7. **ideological** *adj.:* conceptual.
8. **expediency** *n.:* suitability, advantageousness.
9. **affluent** *adj.:* wealthy.

alleviate suffering, the other to promote tranquillity. Only policies that place equal importance on both will make a truly richer world, one in which men can enjoy *chantha*[10] of the body and of the mind. The drive for economic progress needs to be tempered with an awareness of the dangers of greed and selfishness which so easily lead to narrowness and inhumanity. If peoples and nations cultivate a generous spirit which welcomes the happiness of others as an enhancement of the happiness of the self, many seemingly insoluble problems would prove less intractable.[11] ❺

❺ ? *What "old argument" does Aung San Suu Kyi identify in this paragraph? What is she saying about the link between "prosperity" on one hand and "peace" on the other? In your own words, state the main idea of this paragraph.*

Those who have worked with refugees are in the best position to know that when people have been stripped of all their material supports, there only remain to sustain them the values of their cultural and spiritual inheritance. A tradition of sharing instilled by age-old beliefs in the joy of giving and the sanctity of compassion will move a homeless destitute to press a portion of his meagre ration on strangers with all the grace and delight of one who has ample riches to dispense. On the other hand, predatory traits honed by a long-established habit of yielding to "every urge of nature which made self-serving the essence of human life" will lead men to plunder fellow sufferers of their last pathetic possessions. And of course the great majority of the world's refugees are seeking sanctuary from situations rendered untenable[12] by a dearth[13] of humanity and wisdom. ❻

❻ ? *What values can sustain the impoverished and homeless—the refugees of the world? On the other hand, what attitude gives rise to "predatory traits"?*

The dream of a society ruled by lovingkindness, reason and justice is a dream as old as civilized man. Does it have to be an impossible dream? Karl Popper,[14] explaining his abiding optimism in so troubled a world as ours, said that the darkness had always been there but the light was new. Because it is new it has to be tended with care and diligence. It is true that even the smallest light cannot be extinguished by all the darkness in the world because darkness is wholly negative. It is merely an absence of light. But a small light cannot dispel acres of encircling gloom. It needs to grow stronger, to shed its brightness further and further. And people need to accustom their eyes to the light to see it as a benediction[15] rather than a pain, to learn to love it. We are so much in need of a brighter world which will offer adequate refuge to all its inhabitants. ❼

❼ ? *What is the age-old "dream" of society? In your own words, identify what you think Aung San Suu Kyi means by "light" and "darkness." How can light grow enough to overcome darkness?*

---

10. ***chantha*** *n.:* prosperity and general happiness.
11. **intractable** *adj.:* inflexible; stubborn.
12. **untenable** *adj.:* indefensible.
13. **dearth** *n.:* scarcity.
14. **Karl Popper** (1902–1994): a Viennese born philosopher who became a British subject.
15. **benediction** *n.:* blessing.

Analysis Comparing Points of View

Human Rights

The questions on this page ask you to analyze the views on human rights presented in the preceding four selections:

Ha Jin . . . . **Saboteur** . . . .(China)

United Nations Commission on Human Rights . . . . *from* **Universal Declaration of Human Rights**

Desmond Tutu . . . . *from* **The Question of South Africa** . .(South Africa)

Aung San Suu Kyi . . *from* **Towards a True Refuge** . . . .(Myanmar)

Thinking Critically

1. Review the notes you took about the main idea(s) of each text. Then, consider the political conditions or events that influenced each writer. Identify the political influences that helped to shape each story, document, or speech.
2. According to the texts you have read, what human rights do these writers believe the people of the world are entitled to? How do these rights compare with the list you made in response to the Quickwrite on page 1306?
3. What are some causes of injustice in the world, according to the texts you have read? (Consider all the selections **except** the Universal Declaration of Human Rights in your response.) How, according to each text, should we respond to injustice or restore respect for human rights? Use specific textual evidence to support your claims.
4. Review the selections, taking note of the writers' fundamental beliefs about human rights or the violation of human rights. How clear is each argument? Next, compare the notes you have taken. Explain which writers, in your view, present the clearest and most persuasive arguments. Use examples from the texts to support your ideas.

Pages 1306–1328 cover
Literary Skills Analyze and compare points of view on a topic.
Reading Skills Compare main ideas across texts.
Writing Skills Prepare a multimedia presentation.

WRITING

Message Through the Media

Identify a place in the world—or in our own nation—where the rights of human beings are being systematically violated. Do further research into this situation using a variety of reliable sources—current newspapers, magazines, Web sites, books, radio transcripts, government publications. Prepare a **multimedia presentation** in which you display your findings about the injustices being committed in the place you've chosen to focus on. In your presentation, suggest either actions or ways of thinking that might combat these injustices. If possible, include quotations from some of the selections you have read in this feature.

▶ **See "Analyzing and Using Media," pages 1344–1351, for help with this assignment.**

PREVIEW

Reflecting *on the* Literary Period

The Modern World: 1900 to the Present

The selections in this feature were written during the same literary period as the other selections in Collection 7, and they share many of the same ideas and concerns. The Focus Question will guide your reading and help you reflect on important aspects of the period.

City in Shards of Light by Carolyn Hubbard-Ford. Oil on canvas.

Private Collection.

Think About...

The years since 1900 have brought vast political and social changes that have had a profound impact on British literature. During this period, a remarkable diversity has emerged in both the issues and the writing styles explored by British writers, progressing from the more traditional to the more experimental techniques, such as absurdist and avant garde.

Rupert Brooke was one modern writer who continued to draw on traditional literary forms and ideals, as did William Butler Yeats, who at first wrote poetry based on Romantic and Pre-Raphaelite ideas. However, Yeats went on to discover his own style—a wholly new style that enabled him to craft poems he described as "cold and passionate as the dawn." Ted Hughes stands apart from the poets who came to maturity in the 1950s because of his emphasis on the ferocious side of nature rather than its idyllic and beautiful side. Likewise, the poetry of Stevie Smith does not follow any school: Her works tend to mix conventional rhythms, poetic language, even doggerel. Modern dramatists, like the modern poets, have also departed from traditional forms of writing. Harold Pinter, for example, has created a new kind of drama so unique that it is called "Pinteresque."

Pages 1329–1342 cover
Literary Skills
Evaluate the philosophical, political, religious, ethical, and social influences of a historical period.

Focus Question

As you read each selection, keep in mind this Focus Question and take notes to help you answer it at the end of the feature:

How does the writing of the modern period reflect this era's great diversity of issues and styles and demonstrate experimentation with new ideas and literary techniques?

The Soldier

Meet the Writer Rupert Brooke (1887–1915) is often identified with the Georgian poets, a literary group associated with the period of George V, who came to the throne in 1910. The Georgian poets tend to portray a golden, rural life. Brooke himself felt that his chief literary influences were the Elizabethans, John Donne, and Robert Browning.

In the years before World War I, Brooke suffered an unhappy love affair that brought him close to nervous collapse. In 1913, he toured the United States, Canada, and the Pacific, spending several months in Tahiti, where he wrote some of his most famous poems.

When war broke out, Brooke enlisted in the navy and served briefly in Belgium. During a lull in fighting toward the end of 1914, he wrote the "war sonnets" that made him famous. These five sonnets are the best-known poems expressing idealistic patriotism in the face of war. Had Brooke lived to witness the horrors of trench warfare, he might have developed a more cynical and disillusioned attitude about war; however, he died of blood poisoning en route to the Dardanelles with the British Mediterranean Expeditionary Force.

Rupert Brooke is often compared with Lord Byron (page 793). Like the earlier poet, Brooke was quite handsome and brilliant. W. B. Yeats described him as the most handsome young man in England. Brooke also died young like Byron. He was buried on the island of Skyros in the Aegean Sea, a "corner of a foreign field that is forever England."

CONNECTING TO THE
Focus Question

The poetry of Rupert Brooke represents the ideals and values of a world that was not yet shattered by war. As you read, consider this question: How does Brooke's poem reflect traditional structure and sentiments, unlike later modern works?

The Soldier

Rupert Brooke

If I should die, think only this of me;
That there's some corner of a foreign field
That is forever England. There shall be
In that rich earth a richer dust concealed;
A dust whom England bore, shaped, made aware,
Gave, once, her flowers to love, her ways to roam,
A body of England's breathing English air,
Washed by the rivers, blest by suns of home.

And think, this heart, all evil shed away,
A pulse in the eternal mind, no less
Gives somewhere back the thoughts by England given;
Her sights and sounds; dreams happy as her day;
And laughter, learnt of friends; and gentleness,
In hearts at peace, under an English heaven.

Response and Analysis

Thinking Critically

1. What are the poet's feelings toward England and the cause for which he may die? What English qualities does he stress?
2. How is the idea of immortality linked with the idea of patriotism?
3. Brooke's poem is a **sonnet.** Why might he have chosen that form?
4. How would you describe the **tone** of the poem?
5. Using details from the poem, respond to **Connecting to the Focus Question** on page 1330.

Extending and Evaluating

6. Do you think the thoughts expressed by the speaker of this poem would be felt by soldiers fighting today? Why or why not?

Sailing to Byzantium

Meet the Writer The greatest poetry of **William Butler Yeats** (1865–1939), the work that represents his major achievements, did not appear until he was middle-aged, when he was searching for a fresh tradition and an individual style. Yeats began to toughen his poetry to make it more modern both in its subject matter and style: He wanted his poetry to deal with the problems of the modern world, and he tried to incorporate the rhythms of everyday speech.

Yeats's mature style is evident in *The Tower* (1928), in which "Sailing to Byzantium" appeared. The poem is considered one of the greatest poems in the English language.

(For more information about William Butler Yeats, see page 1162.)

Background Yeats was deeply influenced by the French symbolist movement. The symbolist poets believed that emotion is indefinite and difficult to communicate. Instead of direct statements of meaning, they chose emotionally powerful symbols that suggest meaning and mood.

"Sailing to Byzantium" is a poem written by someone who is growing old, exploring the impermanence of nature and the timelessness of art. The city of Byzantium (now Istanbul in Turkey) was founded by the Greeks in the seventh century B.C. and later, as Constantinople, was the capital of the Eastern Roman Empire. For Yeats, it symbolized a unification of artistic and spiritual values.

CONNECTING TO THE
Focus Question

Yeats used both emotional and intellectual symbols. As you read, ask yourself: To what extent does the emotional power of the poem rely on symbols? How do symbols give the poem a visionary quality?

Sailing to Byzantium

William Butler Yeats

I

That is no country for old men. The young
In one another's arms, birds in the trees
—Those dying generations—at their song,
The salmon-falls, the mackerel-crowded seas,
Fish, flesh, or fowl, commend all summer long
Whatever is begotten, born, and dies.
Caught in that sensual music all neglect
Monuments of unaging intellect.

Coronation of King Roger II of Sicily (1095–1154). Byzantine mosaic.
La Martorana, Palermo, Italy.

II

An aged man is but a paltry thing,
A tattered coat upon a stick, unless
Soul clap its hands and sing, and louder sing
For every tatter in its mortal dress,
Nor is there singing school but studying
Monuments of its own magnificence;
And therefore I have sailed the seas and come
To the holy city of Byzantium.

III

O sages standing in God's holy fire
As in the gold mosaic of a wall,°
Come from the holy fire, perne in a gyre,°
And be the singing-masters of my soul.
Consume my heart away; sick with desire
And fastened to a dying animal
It knows not what it is; and gather me
Into the artifice of eternity.

17–18. sages . . . wall: Wise men and saints are depicted in gold mosaic on the walls of Byzantine churches in Ravenna, Italy, and Sicily.
19. perne in a gyre: spin in a spiraling motion. *Perne* is a spool. For Yeats, this is an image of historical cycles.

IV

Once out of nature I shall never take
My bodily form from any natural thing,
But such a form as Grecian goldsmiths make
Of hammered gold and gold enameling
To keep a drowsy Emperor awake;
Or set upon a golden bough to sing°
To lords and ladies of Byzantium
Of what is past, or passing, or to come.

29–30. a drowsy Emperor . . . sing: Yeats wrote, "I have read somewhere that in the Emperor's palace at Byzantium was a tree made of gold and silver, and artificial birds that sang."

Response and Analysis

Thinking Critically

1. What country does the speaker refer to in the first stanza? How is this country contrasted to Byzantium? What do you think Yeats means by the "Monuments of unaging intellect" (line 8)?
2. In the second stanza, what does the speaker suggest is an essential human element of the artistic monuments?
3. In the third stanza, what request does the speaker make of the sages?
4. In the last stanza, what "form" does the speaker choose as a reflection of his soul? What does his choice tell you of his feelings about old age and death?
5. Byzantium is a **symbol** in this poem. What other symbols can you find? What does each symbol represent for Yeats?
6. Using details from the poem, respond to **Connecting to the Focus Question** on page 1332.

Extending and Evaluating

7. What might Yeats be saying about the purposes of art and the motives of the artist?

The Horses

Meet the Writer Ted Hughes (1930–1998) often used violent nature imagery to symbolize the human condition. Born in West Yorkshire, Hughes was profoundly affected by the landscape of his hometown surroundings.

After serving two years in the Royal Air Force, he attended Cambridge University. In 1956, he married the American poet Sylvia Plath, who committed suicide in 1963 after the couple had separated. An intensely private person, Hughes maintained an almost complete silence about his relationship with Plath and the accusations that he was somehow responsible for her death. That silence was broken in 1998 with the publication of a collection of poems called *Birthday Letters.*

Hughes's recurring subjects are reflected in the titles of a number of his books: *The Hawk in the Rain* (1957), *Animal Poems* (1967), *Crow* (1970), *Cave Birds* (1975), and *Wolfwatching* (1989). The critic A. Alvarez called Hughes a "survivor-poet" because Hughes sees parallels between human beings and animals, creatures that will do anything to ensure survival.

Although Hughes writes about nature, he has nothing in common with the Romantics, who saw in nature a reflection of divine providence and primeval innocence. In Hughes's poems, nature represents the darkest impulses of the human heart; violence is not only an accepted fact of life, but also the impulse that links all creatures on earth. Hughes sees humans as alienated from nature, with instincts that have been diminished by reason and civilization. To see the world from the point of view of an animal, in Hughes's thinking, is to recover a power that has been lost.

In 1984, Hughes was named poet laureate of the United Kingdom, a title he held until his death.

CONNECTING TO THE
Focus Question

Hughes's poetry, which first appeared in the 1950s, was dramatically different from that of his predecessors and contemporaries. As you read "The Horses," ask yourself: How does this poem depart from earlier traditions of nature poetry?

The Horses

Ted Hughes

I climbed through woods in the hour-before-dawn dark.
Evil air, a frost-making stillness,

Not a leaf, not a bird—
A world cast in frost. I came out above the wood

Where my breath left tortuous statues in the iron light.
But the valleys were draining the darkness

Till the moorline—blackening dregs of the brightening grey—
Halved the sky ahead. And I saw the horses:

Huge in the dense grey—ten together—
Megalith-still. They breathed, making no move,°

With draped manes and tilted hind-hooves,
Making no sound.

I passed: not one snorted or jerked its head.
Grey silent fragments

Of a grey silent world.

I listened in emptiness on the moor-ridge.
The curlew's tear turned its edge on the silence.°

Slowly detail leafed from the darkness. Then the sun
Orange, red, red erupted

Silently, and splitting to its core tore and flung cloud,
Shook the gulf open, showed blue,

10. megalith: a huge stone, often used in the monuments constructed by ancient people.

17. curlew: a large brown-colored shorebird.

And the big planets hanging—.
I turned

Stumbling in the fever of a dream, down towards
The dark woods, from the kindling tops,

And came to the horses.
                    There, still they stood,
But now steaming and glistening under the flow of light,

Their draped stone manes, their tilted hind-hooves
Stirring under a thaw while all around them

The frost showed its fires. But still they made no sound.
Not one snorted or stamped,

Their hung heads patient as the horizons,
High over valleys, in the red levelling rays—

In din of the crowded streets, going among the years, the faces,
May I still meet my memory in so lonely a place

Between the streams and the red clouds, hearing curlews,
Hearing the horizons endure.

Response and Analysis

Thinking Critically

1. What kind of landscape is evoked in "The Horses"? What aspects of the scene does the poet emphasize?
2. How are the horses described? What does "Megalith-still" (line 10) suggest?
3. Why do you think Hughes emphasizes the silence of the scene?
4. Do you think "The Horses" expresses the poet's union with nature or his alienation from it? Explain.
5. Hughes does not use **end rhyme,** but he achieves subtle musical effects by using other devices. How does he use **repetition, alliteration,** and other techniques of sound?
6. Using details from the poem, respond to **Connecting to the Focus Question** on page 1334.

Extending and Evaluating

7. Hughes seems to be saying that the horses' stillness is ominous because the horses do not react the way we think they should in the presence of a stranger. What contradictions or abnormalities have you seen in nature (for example, the quiet before a storm)? How did the experience make you feel?

Not Waving but Drowning

Meet the Writer **Stevie Smith** (1902–1971) was christened Florence Margaret Smith but got the nickname "Stevie" because she was short, like the British jockey Steve Donoghue. She was born in Yorkshire but grew up in a suburb of London, raised by her mother and an aunt. Smith lived with her aunt until "Auntie Lion" died in 1968 at the age of ninety-six. She herself died only three years later.

In 1937, Smith began to publish her poems. *A Good Time Was Had by All* revealed short, matter-of-fact verses and a childishly simple but biting tone that would become characteristic of her poems. Smith's poems often deal with death, loneliness, or despair, but she is not self-pitying. Her sometimes whimsical humor adds sparkle, allowing her to distance herself from her subject. Smith herself best summed up her views when she claimed that she was "straightforward, but not simple." The poet Robert Lowell described her poetic voice as "cheerfully gruesome," and the poet-humorist Ogden Nash admired her "songs of deadly innocence."

Stevie Smith accompanied many of her poems with drawings that she called "doodles." She loved to perform her poetry. She read it on the radio and sometimes sang her verses. Since her death she has been the subject of a play by Hugh Whitemore called *Stevie,* later adapted as a film.

Background Smith said that "Not Waving but Drowning" was about "misunderstandings which may prove fatal, as in the poem I wrote about a poor fellow who got drowned. His friends thought he was waving to them but really he was asking for help."

CONNECTING TO THE
Focus Question

Stevie Smith has been called "one of the absolute originals of English literature" because her work defies classification. As you read the following selection, pay careful attention to the voices in the poem and to Smith's tone. Ask yourself: What is unusual or offbeat about the poem?

Blue and Silver-Chopping Channel (1890) by James Abbott McNeill Whistler.

Freer Gallery of Art, Smithsonian Institution, Washington, D.C.: Purchase, 1899.24ab.

Not Waving but Drowning

Stevie Smith

Nobody heard him, the dead man,
But still he lay moaning:
I was much further out than you thought
And not waving but drowning.

Poor chap, he always loved larking°
And now he's dead
It must have been too cold for him his heart gave way,
They said.

Oh, no no no, it was too cold always
(Still the dead one lay moaning)
I was much too far out all my life
And not waving but drowning.

5. **larking:** playing; having a good time.

Blue and Silver-Chopping Channel (detail) F1899.24ab (1890) by James Abbott McNeill Whistler.

Freer Gallery of Art, Smithsonian Institution, Washington, D.C.: Purchase.

Response and Analysis

Thinking Critically

1. How many different voices do you hear speaking in the poem?
2. What does the speaker mean by "it was too cold always" (line 9) and "I was much too far out all my life" (line 11)?
3. How do you explain the **title** phrase "not waving but drowning"? If Smith is not just describing a swimming disaster at the beach, what else is she describing?
4. The **tone** of this poem has been described as pessimistic, yet also humorous. Find details that support each tone.
5. Using details from the poem, respond to **Connecting to the Focus Question** on page 1337.

Extending and Evaluating

6. How could this poem be a summing up of one's whole life, or of the human condition in general?
7. Smith once said that good writing had to be "sad, true, economical, and funny." Does her poem meet these criteria? Do you agree with Smith's prescription for good writing? Explain your responses.

That's All

Meet the Writer **Harold Pinter** (1930–), an avowed disciple of Beckett and probably the most influential of the contemporary English playwrights, is on the fringe of the absurdist theater. While Beckett's absurdist drama often deals with grotesque characters and bizarre settings, Pinter most often gives us more or less real settings and identifiable characters speaking everyday language. The whole, however, is stylized in a manner that is now called Pinteresque.

Pinter was born in East London. He attended drama school briefly and later worked as an actor on television and the stage. His first play, *The Room,* appeared in 1957. His first commercial success was *The Caretaker* (1960). Five years later, his play *The Homecoming* was produced by the Royal Shakespeare Company. In addition to writing for the stage, Pinter has written many screenplays. He has adapted a number of his plays for radio and television and has directed productions of his own plays as well as those of others.

With Pinter, we are not in a storytelling theater; rather, Pinter's is a drama of ambiguities, implications, and contradictions, and there are disturbing overtones in the most ordinary situations. Pinter presents a world where the real is menacing, the pregnant pauses (all carefully indicated by Pinter) are full of terror, and the banal speech is full of mystery.

Also, unlike traditional plays, we are not dealing in Pinter's plays with the complex psychology of character. Instead, Pinter's characters are often without pasts—or they have self-contradicting pasts.

It has been noted that Pinter's recurrent themes are "time, memory, the power of the past over the present." His characters are haunted by some recollection, whether true or imaginary. The director Peter Hall has said that enigma is at the heart of Pinter's plays and that audiences must piece together the story in order to judge it.

Pinter, who has been politically active throughout his career, announced in 2005 that he would no longer write plays but would devote himself to politics and poetry. Later that year, Harold Pinter, at the age of seventy-five, won the Nobel Prize in literature.

Background Pinter's **dialogue** is the hallmark of his art. He has taken everyday speech and stylized it to the point where it becomes a kind of poetry. His dialogue is filled with repetitions and pauses, and it has been described as an evasion of communication. The language is filled with internal echoes: A detail or a bit of information appears and then is developed and woven into the drama. The following revue sketch titled *That's All* is one of five comedy sketches first presented on BBC Radio in 1964. This is the entire text.

CONNECTING TO THE
Focus Question

In Pinter's unconventional plays, the unsaid is often as important as the said. As you read *That's All,* ask yourself: What emotions and meaning lie beneath the seemingly mundane dialogue and pauses?

That's All

Harold Pinter

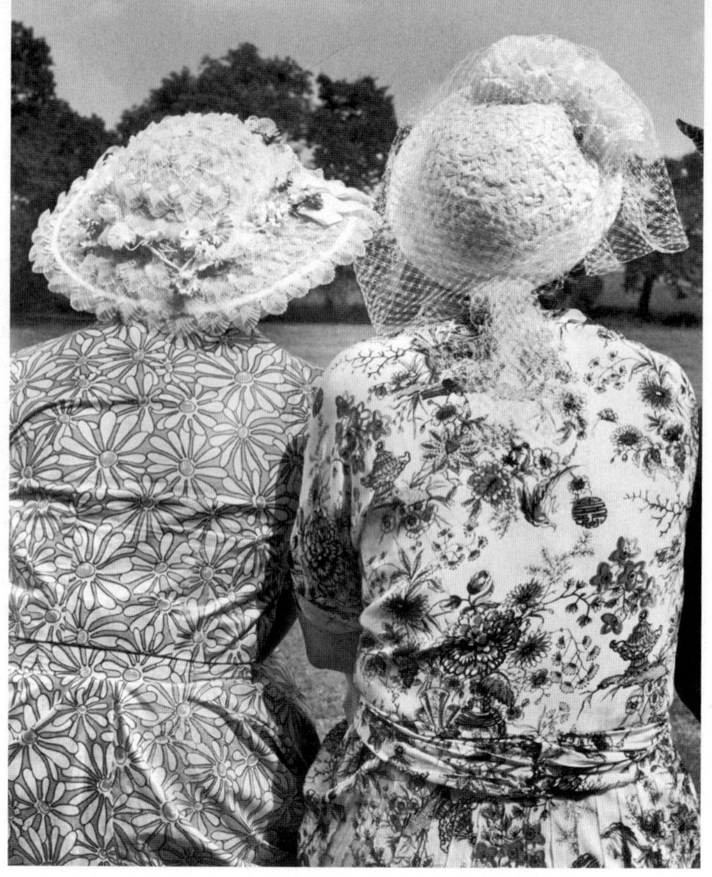

Mrs. A. I always put the kettle on about that time.
Mrs. B. Yes. *(Pause.)*
Mrs. A. Then she comes round.
Mrs. B. Yes. *(Pause.)*
Mrs. A. Only on Thursdays.
Mrs. B. Yes. *(Pause.)*
Mrs. A. On Wednesdays I used to put it on. When she used to come round. Then she changed it to Thursdays.
Mrs. B. Oh yes.
Mrs. A. After she moved. When she used to live round the corner, then she always came in on Wednesdays, but then when she moved she used to come down to the butcher's on Thursdays. She couldn't find a butcher up there.
Mrs. B. No.
Mrs. A. Anyway, she decided she'd stick to her own butcher. Well, I thought, if she can't find a butcher, that's the best thing.
Mrs. B. Yes. *(Pause.)*
Mrs. A. So she started to come down on Thursdays. I didn't know she was coming down on Thursdays until one day I met her in the butcher.
Mrs. B. Oh yes.
Mrs. A. It wasn't my day for the butcher. I don't go to the butcher on Thursday.
Mrs. B. No, I know. *(Pause.)*
Mrs. A. I go on Friday.
Mrs. B. Yes. *(Pause.)*
Mrs. A. That's where I see you.
Mrs. B. Yes. *(Pause.)*
Mrs. A. You're always in there on Fridays.
Mrs. B. Oh yes. *(Pause.)*
Mrs. A. But I happened to go in for a bit of meat, it turned out to be a Thursday. I wasn't going in for my usual weekly on Friday. I just slipped in, the day before.
Mrs. B. Yes.

Mrs. A. That was the first time I found out she couldn't find a butcher up there, so she decided to come back here, once a week, to her own butcher.

Mrs. B. Yes.

Mrs. A. She came on Thursday so she'd be able to get meat for the weekend. Lasted her till Monday, then from Monday to Thursday they'd have fish. She can always buy cold meat, if they want a change.

Mrs. B. Oh yes. *(Pause.)*

Mrs. A. So I told her to come in when she came down after she'd been to the butcher's and I'd put a kettle on. So she did. *(Pause.)*

Mrs. B. Yes. *(Pause.)*

Mrs. A. It was funny because she always used to come in Wednesdays. *(Pause.)* Still, it made a break. *(Long pause.)*

Mrs. B. She doesn't come in no more, does she? *(Pause.)*

Mrs. A. She comes in. She doesn't come in so much, but she comes in. *(Pause.)*

Mrs. B. I thought she didn't come in. *(Pause.)*

Mrs. A. She comes in. *(Pause.)* She just doesn't come in so much. That's all.

Response and Analysis

Reading Check

1. Summarize the conversation between Mrs. A and Mrs. B.

Thinking Critically

2. Are the two characters distinguished from each other by what they say? Why do you think they are identified by letters of the alphabet?
3. What is the effect of the **repetition** and **pauses** in the dialogue?
4. What do you learn about these women from their brief exchange?
5. Why do you think Pinter chose the last line of dialogue as the **title** of his play? Why is it appropriate?
6. Using details from the selection, respond to **Connecting to the Focus Question** on page 1339.

Extending and Evaluating

7. Pinter wrote this play long before cell phones could keep everyone connected on a 24/7 basis. What do you think Pinter would say about much of the chitchat that can be overheard on cell phones today?

REVIEW

Reflecting on the Literary Period

The Modern World: 1900 to the Present

The following questions ask you to compare and analyze the selections in this feature and respond to the Focus Question. Where possible, cite passages from the selections to support your answers.

Comparing Literature

1. Compare "The Soldier" with "Dulce et Decorum Est," by Wilfred Owen (page 1039), or "The Rear-Guard," by Siegfried Sassoon (page 1041). Consider the **tone** of each poem and the poet's sentiments about war.
2. Both Brooke's "The Soldier" and Smith's "Not Waving but Drowning" are concerned with death, yet the poems are dramatically different. Contrast the poems, considering **diction** (or word choice), **tone,** and **theme.**
3. In "Sailing to Byzantium" and "The Horses," Yeats and Hughes present two different views of nature. How would you describe their views? Which poet's view most closely resembles your own? Explain your answer.
4. Smith's work is characterized by a mixture of humor and seriousness. How successful is that combination in "Not Waving but Drowning"? Can you also see that combination in Pinter's *That's All*? Explain your responses.
5. British literature clearly underwent a substantial change during the period from Brooke's "The Soldier" to Pinter's *That's All.* How would you characterize that change? Cite examples to support your response.

Pages 1329–1342 cover **Literary Skills** Evaluate the philosophical, political, religious, ethical, and social influences of a historical period.

RESPONDING TO THE

Focus Question

Review your notes and responses related to the Focus Question for this feature. Using details from the selections, write your answer to the question.

How does the writing of the modern period reflect this era's great diversity of issues and styles and demonstrate experimentation with new ideas and literary techniques?

READ ON: FOR INDEPENDENT READING

NONFICTION

A Plea for Peace

Vera Brittain, born in England in 1893, grew up in an age of rich materialism and romantic idealism. But World War I suddenly and violently ended this time of comfortable isolation. After losing her fiancé and brother and serving as a volunteer nurse in France, she realized that "the world was mad and we were all victims." In her autobiography, ***Testament of Youth,*** she explores how the war affected her and her generation.

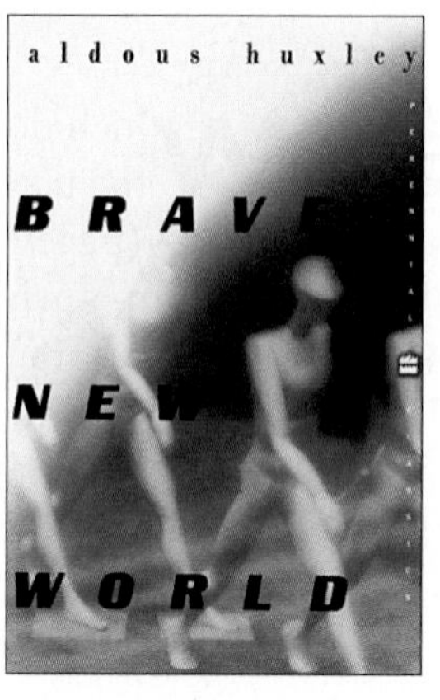

FICTION

Where Love Is Taboo

In ***Brave New World,*** Aldous Huxley presents a terrifying vision of a Utopian world gone wrong. "Community, Identity, Stability" is the motto of the future state envisioned by Huxley, and to achieve its totalitarian ideals, the government uses pleasure to subdue its citizens. It seems that everyone should be happy, yet the protagonist, Bernard Marx, feels empty and attempts to find fulfillment through love—a subversive emotion.

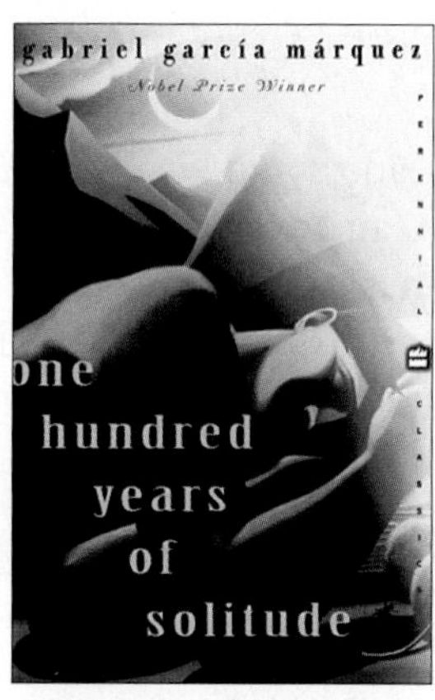

FICTION

The Magic of Realism and the Realism of Magic

Recounting one hundred years of the history of the mythical village of Macondo and its founding family, the Buendías, Gabriel García Márquez blends reality and fantasy in ***One Hundred Years of Solitude*** to explore the development of Colombia's unique culture and illuminate the wonder and strangeness of life.

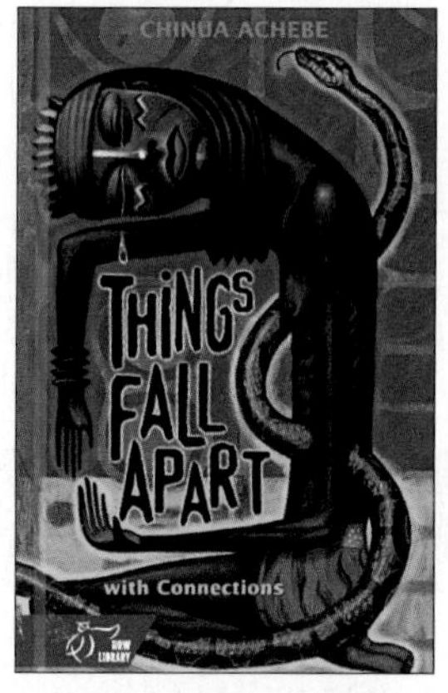

FICTION

Uniquely African

Chinua Achebe's ***Things Fall Apart*** portrays Nigerian tribal life before and after the arrival of Europeans in Africa. The novel's protagonist, Okonkwo, is a successful man who loses everything and is exiled from his tribe, yet he retains the ability to regain his former position—at least until the colonizers arrive. Losing all hope as his homeland is transformed, Okonkwo, in his downfall, becomes a poignant symbol of colonial Africa.

This title is available in the HRW Library.

Analyzing and Using Media

Assignment
Analyze media purposes, strategies, and techniques; then, create and deliver a multimedia presentation of your own.

Which do you think would have a greater impact on you: reading the text from Desmond Tutu's speech "The Question of South Africa" (page 1321) or seeing and hearing him deliver the speech? Each medium—print, film, video, radio, television, or the Internet—has distinct characteristics that shape the way you experience its message. Understanding how you are being affected by each medium and its message is an important skill to learn. In this workshop you'll first analyze how different media shape your experiences of their messages. Then, you'll also create and deliver your own **multimedia presentation,** using words, images, and sounds.

Analyzing Media

Media Sources Imagine a day with no media messages: no radio, television, or newspaper in the morning; no billboards on the way to school; and no posters in the school hallways. Obviously, receiving and decoding media messages are a part of daily life. These messages reach their intended audiences through two categories of **media sources.**

INTERNET
Media Tutorials
Keyword: LE7 12-7

- **Print media sources** include books, newspapers, magazines, pamphlets, advertising fliers, billboards, and posters.
- **Electronic media sources** include films, television, the Internet, radio, and CD-ROMs.

Media Literacy Concepts Critical readers and viewers use **media literacy concepts** to analyze, interpret, and evaluate media messages. The left column of the following chart will help you understand basic media literacy concepts. The questions in the right column will help you analyze the media messages you receive.

MEDIA LITERACY CONCEPTS

Concept	Analysis Questions
1. All media messages are created by someone. Individuals—alone or in groups—write, edit, select, illustrate, or compose every media message. They decide what to include in the message, what to omit, and how to sequence the elements.	What words, images, or sounds were used to create the message? What may have been omitted?
2. Media messages are not reality—they are *representations* of reality that reflect one point of view. Even an eyewitness news account of a flood has been edited to show only a few images and words for the nightly news.	What is the point of view or experience of the message maker? How does this message affect the way I think about this topic?

(continued)

(continued)

3. Individuals interpret media messages differently. Your interpretation of a media message is based on your knowledge of the world in which you live.	What does the message make me think of? How does the message make me feel?
4. People create media messages for many purposes— informing, persuading, entertaining, gaining power, expressing ideas, transmitting culture, and making money.	Who created this message? What is the purpose of this message? Is there more than one purpose?
5. Each mass medium has unique characteristics. Media producers shape messages according to the characteristics of the medium through which the message will be presented.	Through what medium is the message delivered? How does the form affect the message?

Media Strategies Media producers use certain strategies to achieve their purposes and to shape their messages for their intended audiences. For you to be an effective media consumer, you should be able to **interpret** and **evaluate** the use of these strategies. The chart below describes some of the most common **media strategies.**

Quick guide

MEDIA STRATEGIES

Strategy	Examples
Language is often the main strategy by which a media purpose is accomplished. It can be tailored to suit any purpose, audience, or message.	A children's educational television show might use simple, direct language to inform its young viewers. An activist's persuasive speech might use powerful, emotional language to prompt listeners to take action.
Visual representations, such as art, photographs, charts, and maps, present information that a reader or viewer can understand or respond to instantly.	A graph in a newspaper might give information about the stock market's recent performance. An advertising photo of a tropical island might elicit in the consumer a desire to travel.
Special effects, including graphics, lighting, and sound, highlight specific details and create illusions.	A film producer might use special visual effects to entertain an audience by making an actor seem to perform superhuman feats.
Stereotypes are generalized beliefs based on misinformation or insufficient evidence about an entire group of individuals.	An advertisement might use the stereotype of the overworked mother to promote a home-cleaning service.

Visual Image Makers **Visual image makers** use the media strategies shown in the chart above as well as other strategies unique to their fields to present events and communicate information. Here are the most common types of visual image makers and their strategies.

- **TV producers** and **filmmakers** use music, lighting, and camera angles to affect your attitudes and emotions.

Listening and Speaking Skills
Analyze strategies used by different forms of media.

- **Graphic artists** use computer software that alters photographs to create images that look real but aren't. In addition, software allows graphic artists to create moving, three-dimensional images.
- **Illustrators** draw or paint images, often to explain or decorate stories or texts.
- **News photographers** take pictures of current events, shaping information by deciding which images to use and by selecting the angle, distance, lighting, and composition of a shot.

Keep in mind that these media producers design their messages for specific audiences. They familiarize themselves with their intended audiences, consider what the audiences already know, and determine how they want the audiences to be affected by their messages.

Media Effects Interpreting and analyzing media messages can enhance your enjoyment and boost your understanding. Your ability to recognize the powerful, direct impact that media have on the democratic process will help you make informed decisions as a voter and as a citizen. Notice the ways media affect the democratic process at the local, state, and national levels.

- Media **influence elections** by reaching the voter directly. Politicians solicit votes and campaign donations by using TV, radio, newspaper advertisements, and direct mailings to voters' homes. Effective or ineffective use of the media can alter the outcome of elections. For example, a candidate uses direct phone calls to voters, asking them to vote—especially for himself. In a tight election, these votes could determine the final outcome.
- Media **create images of leaders,** often through campaign advertisements. For example, by showing a candidate dressed in work clothes and toiling at a community project, an advertisement portrays her as someone who works hard for a worthy cause.
- Media **shape attitudes** through the amount of attention given to an issue. The more a certain issue is covered, the more importance people begin to attach to it. For example, media coverage of the effects of pollution has inspired people to petition their representatives to support environmental protection initiatives.

PRACTICE & APPLY 1 Choose a topic that has been covered in a variety of media sources, such as employment opportunities for high school versus college graduates. Find media messages on that topic in four different media sources, including two each from both print and electronic sources. For each message, take notes on (1) its intended purpose or purposes, (2) how the message is shaped for its intended audience, and (3) how the message uses media strategies. Finally, evaluate the effectiveness of each message in a paragraph by answering the question, "How well does each message achieve its intended purpose for its intended audience?"

Listening and Speaking Skills
Analyze the impact of the media.

Create and Deliver a Multimedia Presentation

Choose a Topic With the information you've studied about analyzing and evaluating media, you're ready to affect others with your own **multimedia presentation**—a presentation that combines a spoken part with text, images, and sounds. Multimedia presentations are similar to speeches and oral presentations. A speech or an oral presentation may occasionally use text, images, or sounds to enhance the spoken part. However, multimedia presentations integrate text, images, and sounds throughout the presentation more fully, balancing the media with the spoken words.

To begin creating your presentation, choose a topic. Do that by reading and considering the contemporary literature of a country or culture that intrigues you. You may already be interested in a particular country and know of pieces of literature from that country. If not, look through this book and world literature anthologies, read magazines or newspapers, listen to radio shows, search the Internet, or ask your teacher or librarian for suggestions.

TIP Consider the **purpose** and **audience** when selecting a topic. When you know why and for whom you are writing, you should be better able to focus your thoughts and establish a direction for your presentation. In this workshop your purpose will be to inform, and your audience will be your teacher and classmates.

Research Your Topic Once you've selected a topic, you're ready to locate, access, and analyze information about the literature you've read and the country or culture of its origin. You'll use the information you collect to create the spoken part of your presentation. Use the following guidelines to help you research your topic.

- Choose one or more pieces of literature that reflect the culture or country you've chosen. One student chose an Egyptian short story—Naguib Mahfouz's "Half a Day" (page 1242).
- Analyze the literature, and decide what cultural ideas it reflects. The student who chose "Half a Day" decided that the story reflects the same ideas about change and modernization that many Egyptians might feel.
- Draw information about the culture from many sources—both print and electronic. Take careful notes on any facts, examples, or quotations that you might use in your presentation.
- Document all your sources. Your audience members can then refer to your list of documented sources for further information. You will also avoid the serious academic offense of **plagiarism**—using someone else's words, images, or sounds without giving proper credit. (For more on **documenting sources,** see page 247.)

Writing Skills
Create a multimedia presentation.

Develop a Thesis Statement Next, review the information you've gathered, and decide on what you want to say about the literature and its originating culture or country. Write a clear **thesis statement** that encompasses your ideas and presents your focus. Developing your thesis statement for your spoken content provides the blueprint for your multimedia presentation. Here is one student's thesis statement for her presentation on Egypt and Naguib Mahfouz's "Half a Day."

Reference Note

For more on **writing a thesis statement,** see page 246.

> Modernization in Egypt over the last several decades has resulted in marked cultural changes—population growth, urban expansion, and a disregard for tradition—changes lamented in Naguib Mahfouz's symbolic short story "Half a Day."

DO THIS

Select Media Choose text, images, and sounds that elaborate on the spoken content and that add to your presentation's **aesthetic appeal** and **effectiveness.** Incorporate information from a wide range of media sources, including films, newspapers, magazines, CD-ROMs, online information, television, videos, and electronic media-generated images. As you review these media sources, consider the different effects of each, and decide what type of support is appropriate for each part of your presentation and appropriate for your audience.

Use the following chart as a guide for choosing the most appealing and effective medium for each element of your presentation. The right-hand column of the chart shows examples used by the student creating a presentation on Egyptian culture.

USING MEDIA

Media	Uses	Student Examples
Text—any words that appear on a poster, the screen of a video, a computer slide, and so on	to emphasize or enhance key points or their support, and to provide captions for images	• a definition of *modernization* • quotations from "Half a Day"
Images—visual representations such as photos, illustrations, charts, video or film clips, and computer-generated animation	to provide visual impressions of people, places, and things relevant to the topic, and to appeal to the audience's emotions	• a collage of Egyptian images • a video clip from a documentary about Egypt • a map of Egypt and surrounding areas • a photograph of Naguib Mahfouz
Sounds—sound files or other recordings of music, speeches, literary readings, and sound effects	to enhance and support a key point, to create a mood, and to appeal to the audi-ence's emotions	• recordings of traditional and electronic Egyptian music • a recording of Naguib Mahfouz reading from his works

Maximize Your Impact The most appropriate text, image, or sound effect might seem ineffective and even distracting if it isn't designed properly. Pay close attention to the quality of the material you choose. Think carefully about how to incorporate it into your presentation. Use the following design principles to create the maximum impact on your audience.

- **Text** Limit the amount of text that you expect your audience to read. For each screen or slide, use a maximum of six lines, with six words per line. Write large and clearly, or, if you are using a computer program, choose a plain font and a large font size (36 to 48 points). If you decide to emphasize with color, boldface, italics, or underscoring, do so sparingly. Combining too many of these treatments distracts and confuses an audience.

COMPUTER TIP

For more on **font,** see *Designing Your Writing* in the Writer's Handbook.

- **Images** Because images should enhance, not compete with, the spoken material in your presentation, use them only when needed. Be sure images are large enough and clear enough to be seen by everyone in the room. Cue video clips so that they show only the most significant material.
- **Sounds** Adjust the sound level according to purpose. For example, a sound whose purpose is to inform, such as a recording of a speech, should be loud enough for everyone in the audience to hear. Background music or sounds that contribute to mood, however, should be soft and not intrusive.

Organize Your Presentation To help ensure that the audience finds your presentation easy to follow, plan its organization carefully. Follow the steps in the chart below to help you effectively combine the spoken content and the multimedia support you've chosen.

ORGANIZING A MULTIMEDIA PRESENTATION

1. Create **note cards** for the key points and supporting details in the spoken part of your presentation (as you would do when presenting a speech).
2. Group cards for key points and details together, and arrange the groups by **order of importance**. Begin with the most important key point and end with the least important one, or vice versa.
3. Make a note card for each piece of multimedia support you plan to use. Use a different color card from the note cards for your spoken content so that you can balance the media support you are using with your spoken content. You might even use a different color card for each type of support, such as peach for text, blue for images, and yellow for sound.
4. Insert each media card before the spoken content card that it will support.
5. Use your note cards to create an **outline** of your presentation. Check that your organization makes sense and that multimedia support is properly integrated into the presentation.

The following chart shows a portion of one student's outline for her presentation on Egyptian culture. The chart format allows her to designate clearly in the right column the media support she plans to use.

Spoken Content	Media Support
I. Introduce Egypt as a complex, developing country A. Traditional Egyptian culture B. Complex components—Arab, eastern Mediterranean, Islamic, and ancient	• play audiotape of traditional Egyptian music as background • show collage of Egyptian images • show map of Egypt and surrounding areas
II. Explain changes in Egyptian culture due to modernization A. Definition of modernization B. Cultural effects of modernization 1. Population growth 2. Urban expansion 3. Disregard for tradition	• play audiotape of modern Egyptian electronic music as background • use text definition of "modernization" • show documentary video clips to illustrate cultural changes brought by modernization
III. Explain response of contemporary literature to cultural changes A. Naguib Mahfouz as example author B. Analysis of short story "Half a Day" 1. Main character's dilemma 2. Symbols for cultural changes 3. Theme of story	• play audiotape of Naguib Mahfouz reading from his works • show photograph of Naguib Mahfouz • use quotations from the story

If you find places in your outline where you need more information to clarify the spoken content or more media to support or enhance your spoken words, locate this support, create new cards, and insert them in your stack. You can use these cards, as well as the cards you have already created, as cues during your presentation.

TIP **Transitions**—bridges between ideas—are essential to a smooth presentation. Use transitions to integrate media with your spoken content to help your presentation flow more naturally. For example, the student's multimedia presentation on Egyptian culture provided the following transition to introduce the map of the Middle East: **"Seeing this map of the Middle East** can help you to appreciate the many influences at work as a result of Egypt's geographic location."

PRACTICE & APPLY 2 Use the information that begins on page 1347 to choose and research a topic. Write a thesis statement, and select the most effective media to elaborate on and enhance your presentation's spoken content. Organize your information by creating note cards and an outline.

Practice Your Presentation Throughout the process of planning and developing your presentation, you've probably given serious consideration to the effect it will have on your intended audience. Now's the time to determine whether all of the elements truly work together as planned. Gather a group of friends or family members, and rehearse your presentation. Deliver it exactly as you would for the intended audience of your final presentation. If you need use of the school's audiovisual equipment, arrange a rehearsal before or after school.

As you rehearse, express interest in and enthusiasm about your topic. After all, your **delivery** holds the whole presentation together. Speak confidently, enunciate clearly, and avoid vocalized pauses such as *um* or *ah.* Use nonverbal behavior—eye contact, facial expressions, and gestures—to your advantage. Be familiar with your audiovisual equipment, and don't turn your back on the audience when using it.

After your rehearsal, use the questions in the chart below to ask your audience for **feedback**.

AUDIENCE FEEDBACK
Which section of the spoken part of the presentation was most memorable? Why did it succeed?
Which of the multimedia elements of the presentation were most effective? Why do you think so?
How well did I combine the spoken content of the presentation with text, images, and sounds? Explain.
What parts of the entire multimedia presentation, if any, did you find confusing? What confused you?
How did my delivery affect the presentation? Explain.

Revise the content and delivery of your presentation according to your rehearsal audience's responses. Then, practice delivering your presentation a second time to make sure all the problems have been eliminated. Check and double-check all your audiovisual equipment. The effectiveness of an excellent presentation depends on your efficient management of your equipment. Because a multimedia presentation coordinates so many different parts, anticipate any troubles you may have and be prepared for emergencies.

PRACTICE & APPLY 3 Practice your presentation for friends or family, and solicit feedback. Use the rehearsal audience's responses to improve and refine your presentation. Finally, deliver your presentation to your intended audience.

Listening and Speaking Skills
Rehearse and deliver a multimedia presentation.

Presenting and Analyzing Speeches

Speaking Assignment
Prepare a formal persuasive speech, and deliver it to an audience. Then, listen to and evaluate the persuasive speeches of others.

Multimedia presentations often have a persuasive purpose. The purpose of a **persuasive speech** is almost always obvious to listeners. In this workshop you will experience persuasion from both sides—as a speaker using the techniques of persuasion and as a listener analyzing the techniques of a persuasive speaker.

Preparing a Persuasive Speech

A Hot Topic You might already have a special topic for a persuasive speech. If not, choose a topic that is controversial, or arguable, and that you have strong feelings about. For example, if you're convinced that a controversial freeway proposed for your neighborhood will destroy the neighborhood's character, you might have a good topic for a persuasive speech. It's difficult to deliver a successful persuasive speech on a topic that isn't important to you or the audience.

TIP Keep in mind that your reasoning will be evaluated as you present your speech. Therefore, avoid faulty logic and the use of propaganda. For more on **logical fallacies** and **propaganda,** see page 1355.

Pointed Persuasion You know the general **purpose** of your persuasive speech—to convince listeners to act or think in a certain way. Now, write down your specific position or perspective on the topic you've selected as a clear **opinion statement,** like the one below.

> The proposed freeway should not be built because it would destroy the peace and safety of a family neighborhood.

Listening and Speaking Skills
Prepare a persuasive speech. Understand and identify logical fallacies and propaganda techniques. Use effective rhetorical devices.

Bull's-Eye Your next consideration should be your target **audience.** If audience members are receptive to your ideas, use your speech to reinforce those feelings and move them to action. If you think they are resistant to your ideas, anticipate and address their **counterarguments** and convince them that your perspective is a reasonable one. If you anticipate an indifferent audience, show them the importance of your topic.

INTERNET
Speeches
Keyword: LE7 12-7

Perfect Aim To convince others to accept your opinion, support your opinion statement with **reasons** that include logical, emotional, or ethical appeals.

- **Logical appeals** influence a listener's rational judgment by giving reasons supported by evidence in the form of facts, examples, statistics, or expert opinions.
- **Emotional appeals** use strong and vivid language, anecdotes, and stories to arouse feelings.

- **Ethical appeals** target a listener's sense of right and wrong. Speakers who use ethical appeals must be credible.

Logical appeals are generally preferred in more formal arguments because they are based on concrete and provable facts.

The Right Approach You want your speech to be **focused** and **coherent.** There are two classic approaches—deductive and inductive—to presenting persuasive arguments. The best method for your speech will depend upon your assessment of your audience's attitude toward your opinion statement.

- **The Deductive Approach:** Deductive reasoning moves from the general to the specific. For a neutral or favorable audience, begin with your opinion statement and then move to the particular reasons—the logical, emotional, and ethical appeals that support your opinion.
- **The Inductive Approach:** Inductive reasoning moves from specific to general. For an audience reluctant to agree with you, start with your reasons and end with your opinion statement.

TIP No matter which of these approaches you decide to take, you still have to arrange your reasons in a logical progression. **Order of importance,** usually least important to most important, is the most effective arrangement because it is often the most dramatic.

Language Power To achieve clarity, force, and an aesthetic, or artistic and tasteful, effect in your persuasive speech, use the **rhetorical devices** listed below to emphasize and enhance your appeals.

RHETORICAL DEVICES

Device	Example
Repetition is the repeated use of words, phrases, or clauses for emphasis.	The proposed freeway will destroy houses, will destroy our neighborhood, and will destroy our way of life.
Restatement is the repetition of an idea using different language.	Traffic congestion on the proposed freeway will foul our air. We will choke on the freeway pollution.
Parallelism is the rhythmic repetition of grammatical forms or parts of speech.	The proposed freeway will destroy our peace and quiet; it will foul our air; it will endanger the lives of our children; it will destroy the value of our property.
Rhetorical questions are asked for effect. They do not require a response.	Do you think the people who will use the freeway care about the peace and quiet of our neighborhood?
Argument by analogy shows a parallel between basically dissimilar events or situations.	As far as noise is concerned, building a freeway would be similar to building a jet runway through the middle of our neighborhood. Both would cause an increase in sound levels and sonic vibrations.
Irony is the contrast between expectation and reality. **Verbal irony** is most often used in speech. It is the contrast between what a speaker says and what he or she means.	Of course we believe proponents of the freeway when they tell us the freeway will be an economic boon—just ask the residents of what used to be City Heights about their so-called economic boon.

Another effective device in persuasive speaking is to frame one or more of your reasons as a syllogism. A **syllogism** presents an argument by showing that two premises—a major and a minor premise—lead to an inevitable conclusion. Here is an example.

Major Premise: The purpose of the new freeway is to help the citizens of our community.

Minor Premise: Many residents of our community will see their houses demolished in order to build the freeway.

Conclusion: The new freeway may help some, but it will also hurt many citizens of our community.

Once you set up your major and minor premises, you might find it effective to allow the audience to draw the inevitable conclusion for themselves, perhaps by putting it in the form of a rhetorical question.

Deliver Your Speech

TIP Have a friend or family member analyze your **gestures** and **movements** as you practice your speech. Make improvements to your delivery by taking into account the feedback you receive.

Formally Speaking Writing and delivering a persuasive speech on an issue that is vitally important to you requires a serious investment of time, energy, and emotion. To have your listeners take the issue as seriously as you do, deliver your speech **formally.** Adopt a serious **tone** by using formal language instead of slang, colloquialisms, and contractions. Write your speech out completely and practice it until you have it memorized so thoroughly that you are confident in your delivery. Make notes on your written speech about the tone, pitch, and volume that you intend to use at various points throughout the speech. Also, make notes to remind you to make eye contact with the audience and to pause and make appropriate gestures at particular points throughout the speech.

Listening to a Persuasive Speech

Ears Open, Mind Engaged In this age of instant communication, persuasive messages constantly bombard you. If you wish to make informed and wise decisions regarding these messages, you must become a critical listener to identify the type of persuasive message you are hearing. To decide which of the following four basic types of persuasive speech you are hearing, listen carefully to the speaker's opinion statement.

1. A **proposition of fact** is a speech that argues that an opinion can be seen as true or false. A proposition of fact has an opinion statement such as "The new pneumonia vaccine will virtually eliminate pneumonia as a serious threat to the lives of older citizens."
2. A **proposition of policy** is a speech that proposes a policy and attempts to get the audience to support a particular plan of action. A proposition of policy has an opinion statement such as "Ensuring that every schoolchild becomes computer literate should be a national priority."

Listening and Speaking Skills
Deliver a persuasive speech.
Analyze persuasive speeches.

3. A **proposition of problem** is a speech that tries to persuade an audience that a specific problem exists and is serious enough to warrant action. A proposition of problem has an opinion statement such as "The lack of an adequate water supply threatens the economic foundations of our community."
4. A **proposition of value** is a speech that argues the relative merit of a person, place, or thing. You can't prove a proposition of value; you can provide evidence to support your belief. A proposition of value has an opinion statement such as "Anyone who fails to vote has the least right to complain about governmental policies."

The first three types of persuasive speeches use the language of reason to appeal to the listener's sense of logic. Facts, statistics, expert testimony, and other hard evidence support the speaker's reasons. Propositions of value, however, often use emotional and ethical appeals more than logical appeals.

TIP It is also important to evaluate a speaker's **diction** (word choice) and **syntax** (sentence structure). If a speaker's diction and sentence structure seem to be much more complex than his or her ideas, the speaker might be trying to make an argument seem more important or impressive than it actually is.

Beware Logical Fallacies and Propaganda Critical listeners are always on the alert for fallacious reasoning and propaganda. Dishonest speakers consciously use these techniques. Honest speakers sometimes use them inadvertently. The chart below provides definitions and examples of different types of faulty logic and propaganda.

Quick guide

LOGICAL FALLACIES AND PROPAGANDA TECHNIQUES	
An **overgeneralization** is based on too little evidence or evidence that ignores exceptions.	Our music department is in a state of decline. Enrollment in the strings class dropped fifteen percent this year.
False causality wrongly assumes that one event caused another.	Because the choir teacher retired last year, this year fewer students enrolled in the class.
The **bandwagon effect** urges people to agree because everyone else does.	Vote for the new bond issue. All your neighbors support it.
A **red herring** is something that takes a listener's attention away from the real issue.	The proposed freeway is just another example of how the government of this city ignores the middle class.
An **attack *ad hominem*** criticizes a person instead of the issue itself.	Of course Mrs. Harris supports the new construction. She's never cared about the parks in this city.

Use the instructions in this section to prepare and deliver a persuasive speech. Then, evaluate the persuasive speeches of your classmates.

Collection 7: Skills Review

Comparing Literature

Test Practice

The following poems allude to two closely related legends. "The Lorelei," by the German poet Heinrich Heine (1797–1856), describes a steep, rocky cliff on the Rhine River in Germany. According to legend, the spirit of a woman sits on these rocks at night, combing her hair, singing, and luring boatmen to their deaths. The contemporary poem "Siren Song," by Canadian writer Margaret Atwood (1939–), takes its inspiration from the sirens of Greek myth—those mysterious women who tempted Odysseus and his sailors with their sweet singing.

DIRECTIONS: Read the two poems that follow. Then, read each multiple-choice question that follows, and write the letter of the best response.

The Lorelei

Heinrich Heine

translated by Louis Untermeyer

I cannot tell why this imagined
  Despair has fallen on me;
The ghost of an ancient legend
  That will not let me be:

The air is cool, and twilight
  Flows down the quiet Rhine;
A mountain alone in the high light
  Still holds the faltering shine.

The last peak rosily gleaming
  Reveals, enthroned in air,
A maiden, lost in dreaming,
  Who combs her golden hair.

Combing her hair with a golden
  Comb in her rocky bower,°
She sings the tune of an olden
  Song that has magical power.

The boatman has heard; it has bound
    him
  In throes of a strange, wild love;
Blind to the reefs that surround him,
  He sees but the vision above.

And lo, hungry waters are
    springing—
  Boat and boatman are gone. . . .
Then silence. And this, with her
    singing,
  The Lorelei has done.

---

14. bower *n.:* enclosed place or retreat, usually a lady's bedroom or private room. It can also refer to any natural enclosure.

Pages 1356–1359 cover **Literary Skills** Compare and contrast works from different literary periods.

Siren Song

Margaret Atwood

This is the one song everyone
would like to learn: the song
that is irresistible:

the song that forces men
to leap overboard in squadrons
even though they see the beached
skulls

the song nobody knows
because anyone who has heard it
is dead, and the others can't
remember.

Shall I tell you the secret
and if I do, will you get me
out of this bird suit?

I don't enjoy it here
squatting on this island
looking picturesque and mythical

with these two feathery maniacs,
I don't enjoy singing
this trio, fatal and valuable.

I will tell the secret to you,
to you, only to you.
Come closer. This song

is a cry for help: Help me!
Only you, only you can,
you are unique

at last. Alas
it is a boring song
but it works every time.

Collection 7: Skills Review

1. In lines 1–4 of "The Lorelei," the speaker —
   - **A** is pursued by a real ghost
   - **B** finds comfort in a legend
   - **C** feels love
   - **D** feels a strangely compelling connection to a legend

2. The **mood** in lines 5–8 of "The Lorelei" could *best* be described as —
   - **F** fearful
   - **G** joyful
   - **H** romantic
   - **J** reckless

3. In "The Lorelei" the song —
   - **A** has magical power
   - **B** promises the sailor money
   - **C** provides a religious experience
   - **D** makes the sailor angry

4. What has occurred in the final stanza of "The Lorelei"?
   - **F** The speaker betrays the Lorelei.
   - **G** The boatman has gone away with the woman.
   - **H** The boatman has drowned.
   - **J** The speaker envies the boatman.

5. The **tone** of "Siren Song" is —
   - **A** sarcastic
   - **B** romantic
   - **C** sorrowful
   - **D** joyful

6. What do lines 13–16 of "Siren Song" suggest about the speaker's attitude?
   - **F** She finds her situation sad.
   - **G** She does not want to be mythical.
   - **H** She is proud of her beauty.
   - **J** She does not want to find true love.

7. Who is the speaker of "Siren Song"?
   - **A** a siren
   - **B** Margaret Atwood
   - **C** a sailor
   - **D** a bird

8. What implied **theme** is contained in the last two lines of "Siren Song"?
   - **F** Help is available for those who ask.
   - **G** Women are rarely taken seriously.
   - **H** Men cannot be manipulated.
   - **J** Attraction follows a predictable pattern.

9. How does the overall **imagery** in "Siren Song" differ from that in "The Lorelei"?
   - **A** The imagery in "Siren Song" is more romantic.
   - **B** The imagery in "The Lorelei" is more violent.
   - **C** The imagery in "Siren Song" is more startling.
   - **D** The imagery in "The Lorelei" is more playful.

10. The women in both "The Lorelei" and "Siren Song" are alike in that they both —
    - **F** are mermaids
    - **G** regret their actions
    - **H** call men to their deaths
    - **J** are unattractive

Essay Question

In an **essay,** compare and contrast these two poems. Think about the way each poet uses the old legend of the women who lure sailors to the rocks. In your essay, consider these elements of each poem: **speaker, tone, imagery,** and **message.** If you take these poems as examples, how would you describe the different ways people in the nineteenth and twentieth centuries felt about the old myths and legends?

Collection 7: Skills Review

Vocabulary Skills

Test Practice

Analogies

DIRECTIONS: For each of the following items, choose the pair of words that expresses a relationship that is most similar to the relationship between the pair of capitalized words.

1. APERTURE : OPENING ::
- **A** picture : photograph
- **B** car : automobile
- **C** planet : solar system
- **D** driver : truck

2. ABSTAIN : MONK ::
- **F** repent : penitent
- **G** deny : refuse
- **H** stand : recliner
- **J** drink : water

3. REFUSE : DUMP ::
- **A** waffle : eat
- **B** garbage : recycle
- **C** laundry : hamper
- **D** socks : feet

4. PATRONIZE : CUSTOMERS ::
- **F** bore : assembly
- **G** concert : musicians
- **H** dance : ballroom
- **J** dash : sprinters

5. LABYRINTH : MAZE ::
- **A** ship : vessel
- **B** car : passenger
- **C** playground : children
- **D** tree : ocean

6. DISTEND: BALLOON ::
- **F** eat : restaurant
- **G** shower : morning
- **H** mourn : funeral
- **J** chew : gum

7. COMMISERATE : SYMPATHIZER ::
- **A** hinder : student
- **B** congratulate : critic
- **C** applaud : audience
- **D** jump : leap

8. RITE : PERFORM ::
- **F** horse : jockey
- **G** ranch : cowboy
- **H** song : sing
- **J** pediatrician : doctor

9. ANNIHILATE : BOMB ::
- **A** horse : saddle
- **B** juice : orange
- **C** imprison : jail
- **D** soak : rain

10. GUFFAW : JOKE ::
- **F** top : shelf
- **G** weep : tragedy
- **H** shout : crowd
- **J** exercise : jogging

Vocabulary Skills
Complete word analogies.

Collection 7: Skills Review

Writing Skills

Test Practice

DIRECTIONS: Read the following paragraph from a draft of a student's persuasive essay. Then, answer the questions below it.

(1) Since 1967, the Age Discrimination in Employment Act has banned age as a criterion for hiring, firing, salary decisions, and retirement. (2) However, this law still fails to offer sufficient protection for older working Americans. (3) Employed people over sixty-five still often fall victim to discrimination that their younger co-workers do not have to face. (4) Salespeople routinely ignore older people to help younger customers. (5) Also, many companies shamelessly maximize profits by routinely replacing their oldest and best-paid workers with younger, less well paid employees.

1. To convey the paragraph's perspective clearly, which of the following sentences could be added?

- **A** Lawmakers should find additional ways to stop age discrimination in the workforce.
- **B** Older Americans should not be included in the workforce.
- **C** Senior citizens contribute wisdom and love to younger generations.
- **D** Discouraging older workers from seeking employment keeps our workforce energetic.

2. What evidence could be added to support sentence 3's argument?

- **F** an anecdote about the writer's grandparents, who are enjoying a relaxing retirement
- **G** facts showing that millions of families depend on grandparents for child care
- **H** the example of Senator John Glenn, who flew aboard the space shuttle at age seventy-seven
- **J** statistics indicating that one in four older job applicants are discriminated against

3. Which rhetorical device could be used to enhance the passage's effectiveness?

- **A** explanations of the positive aspects of being a senior citizen
- **B** improved rhythm through varying the lengths of the sentences
- **C** an analogy comparing older workers to obsolete typewriters
- **D** a description of the average senior citizen's active lifestyle

4. Which sentence should be deleted to improve the coherence of the paragraph?

- **F** 1
- **G** 2
- **H** 3
- **J** 4

5. To strengthen her argument, the writer might

- **A** add photos of several retirement homes
- **B** add evidence without elaboration
- **C** issue a call to action
- **D** list her reasons in the order she thought of them

Writing Skills
Write a persuasive essay.

Resource Center

The Parisian Novels (The Yellow Books), Vincent van Gogh, 1888.

Reading Matters

When the Text Is Tough

Remember the reading you did back in first, second, and third grades? Big print. Short texts. Easy words. In high school, however, the texts you read are often filled with small print, long chapters, and complicated plots or topics. Also, you now find yourself reading a variety of material—from your driver's-ed handbook to college applications, from job applications to income-tax forms, from e-mail to e-zines, from classics to comics, from textbooks to checkbooks.

Doing something every day that you find difficult and tedious isn't much fun—and that includes reading. So this section of this book is designed for you, to show you what to do when the text gets tough. Let's begin to look at some reading matters—because after all, reading *matters.*

READING UP CLOSE: HOW TO USE THIS SECTION

- **This section is for you.** Turn to it whenever you need to remind yourself about what to do when the text gets tough. Don't wait for your teacher to assign this section for you to read. It's your handbook. Use it.
- **Read the sections that you need.** You don't have to read every word. Skim the headings, and find the information you need.
- **Use this information to help you with reading for other classes,** not just for the reading you do in this book.
- **Don't be afraid to *re-read* the information** you find in Reading Matters. The best readers constantly re-read information.
- **If you need more help, then check the index.** The index will direct you to other pages in this book with information on reading skills and strategies.

Improving Your Comprehension

Comprehension, your ability to understand what you read, is a critical part of the reading process. Your comprehension can be affected by many factors. Think about each of the following types of texts, and rate your comprehension of each from 1 (*never understand*) to 5 (*always understand*):

A. notes from friends
B. e-mail messages from friends
C. college applications
D. job applications
E. magazines
F. computer manuals
G. Internet sites
H. school textbooks
I. novels you choose
J. novels your teachers choose for you

READING UP CLOSE

Monitoring Your Comprehension

Skilled readers often pay more attention to what they don't understand than to what they do. Here are some symbols you could put on self-sticking notes and place on texts as you are reading so that you can keep up with what's confusing you. Decide how you would use each symbol.

What reading problem could each sign indicate?

You probably didn't rate yourself the same for each type of text. Factors such as your interest level and the text's vocabulary level will cause your ratings to differ from text to text. Now, go back, and look specifically at items H, I, and J. How did you rate there? If you think your comprehension of those materials is low, then you'll want to study the next few pages carefully. They are filled with tips to help you improve your comprehension.

Visualizing the text. The ability to visualize—or see in your mind—what you are reading is important for comprehension. To understand how visualizing makes a difference, try this quick test. At home, turn on a television to a program you enjoy. Then, turn your back to the television set. How long will you keep "watching" the program that way? Probably not long. Why not? Because it would be boring if you couldn't see what was happening. The same is true of reading: If you can't see in your mind what is happening on the page, then you probably will tune out quickly. You can improve your ability to visualize a text by practicing the following strategies:

1. **Read a few sentences; then pause, and describe what is happening on the page.** Forcing yourself to describe the scene will take some time at first, but doing that will help in the long run.
2. **On a sheet of paper or a stick-on note, make a graphic representation of what is happening as you are reading.** For instance, if two characters are talking, draw two stick figures with arrows pointing between them to show yourself that they are talking.
3. **Discuss a scene or a part of a chapter with a partner.** Talk about what you "saw" as you were reading.
4. **Read aloud.** You might be having trouble visualizing the text because you aren't "hearing" it. Try reading a portion of your text aloud, using good expression and phrasing. As you hear the words, you may find it easier to see the scenes.

READING UP CLOSE

▶ Visualizing What You Read

Read the following excerpt from "The Day of Destiny" (see page 216), and discuss what you "see":

> Then, on the night of Trinity Sunday, Arthur was vouchsafed a strange dream:
>
> He was appareled in gold cloth and seated in a chair which stood on a pivoted scaffold. Below him, many fathoms deep, was a dark well, and in the water swam serpents, dragons, and wild beasts. Suddenly the scaffold tilted and Arthur was flung into the water, where all the creatures struggled toward him and began tearing him limb from limb.
>
> Arthur cried out in his sleep and his squires hastened to waken him.

How's your metacognition? Your attention wanders for a moment as you are reading something, but your eyes don't quit moving from word to word. After a few minutes you realize you are several pages beyond the last point at which you can remember thinking about what you were reading. Then you know you need to back up and start over. This ability to think about your thinking—or, in this case, your lack of thinking—is called **metacognition.**

Metacognition refers to your ability to analyze what you are doing as you try to make sense of texts. A critical part of metacognition is paying attention to what you are reading. It's normal to find that your attention *sometimes* wanders while reading. If it always wanders, though, then try one of the following activities: (1) Keep paper and pen close, and jot down notes as you read; (2) read for a set amount of time (five minutes), and then stop and review what's happened since the last time you stopped. Lengthen this time as you find yourself able to focus longer. Take the following quiz to see what your metacognition level is:

READING UP CLOSE

Measuring Your Attention Quotient

The lower the score, the less you pay attention to what you are reading. The higher the score, the more you pay attention.

When I read, I

A. let my mind wander a lot

1	2	3
most of the time	sometimes	almost never

B. forget what I'm reading

1	2	3
most of the time	sometimes	almost never

C. get confused and stay confused or don't even realize I am confused

1	2	3
most of the time	sometimes	almost never

D. discover I've turned lots of pages and don't have a clue as to what I've read

1	2	3
most of the time	sometimes	almost never

E. rarely finish whatever I'm supposed to be reading

1	2	3
most of the time	sometimes	almost never

Try Think-Aloud. Comprehension problems don't appear only after you *finish* reading. Confusion occurs *as* you read. Therefore, don't wait until you complete your reading assignment to try to understand the text; instead, work on comprehending while reading by becoming an active reader.

Active readers **predict, connect, clarify, question,** and **visualize** as they read. If you don't do those things, you need to pause while you read to

- make **predictions**
- make **connections**
- **clarify** in your own thoughts what you are reading
- **question** what you don't understand
- **visualize** the text

Use the Think-Aloud strategy to practice your active-reading skills. Here is how Think-Aloud works: Read a selection of text aloud to a partner. As you read, pause to make comments and ask questions. Your partner's job is to tally your comments and classify each one according to the list at the top of this page.

READING UP CLOSE

One Student's Think-Aloud

Here's Steve's Think-Aloud for Shakespeare's Sonnet 130 (page 320):

After reading entire sonnet once: I don't get it. This is like he's saying the woman he loves is ugly. Why would he say these things? **(Question)**

After reading sonnet a second time: He isn't saying very nice things about her. At the end he still says his love is rare, so I think he does love her. **(Comment/Clarification)**

After reading sonnet a third time: You know, maybe this is a joke about love: like, it's always supposed to be perfect, you know—coral red lips and eyes like the sun—but even if she doesn't have those things, he still loves her. I think it's those last two lines that are important, you know, showing that someone you love doesn't have to be perfect. This is like realizing that even if your car isn't the coolest car in the lot, it's your car, and so you still love it. **(Connection)**

Question the text. This scenario may be familiar: You've just finished reading one of the selections in this book. Then you look at the questions that you'll be discussing tomorrow in class. You realize that you don't know the answers. In frustration you decide to give up on the questions.

While giving up is one way to approach the problem, it's not the best approach. In fact, what you need to do is focus *more* on questions—and focus on them while reading the text, not just at the end. This doesn't mean memorizing study questions before you read so that as you are reading you are thinking only about those questions. What it means is constantly asking yourself questions about characters, plot, point of view, setting, conflict, and even vocabulary while reading. You'll find that the more you question the text while reading, the more prepared you'll be to answer the questions at the end of the text.

READING UP CLOSE

Asking Questions While Reading

Here is a list of questions you can use as you read literary selections. You should recopy this list on note cards and keep it close as you read.

Character Questions

1. Who is the central character? Is this character the narrator? What are the greatest strengths and greatest weaknesses of this character? What does this character discover by the story's end? Has he or she changed?

(continued)

(continued)

2. Is the narrator telling the story while it is happening or while looking back? Can you trust this narrator? What if the narrator were a different character? How would the story change? What point of view does the narrator have—first person, limited third person, omniscient—and how does that point of view affect the narrator's authority?
3. Who are the other characters? What makes them important to the central character? What do their actions reveal about their personalities? How do your thoughts about the characters change as you read the story? Can you find specific points in the text where your feelings about characters shift? Could any character have been omitted from the story?
4. Which character do you like the best? What do you have in common with this character?

Plot, Setting, and Conflict Questions

1. What are the major events in the plot? Which events are mandatory in order for the story to reach the conclusion it does? What prior knowledge is necessary for understanding the plot?
2. How does the setting affect the story? Could you change the location or the historical context and have the same story? How does the author situate the reader in the setting? Is the setting believable?
3. What event creates the conflict? How does the central character react to the conflict? How do other characters react? How is the conflict resolved?

Re-reading and rewording. The best way to improve your comprehension is simply to **re-read.** The first time you read something, you get the basic idea of the text. The next time you read it, you revise your understanding. Try thinking of your first reading as a draft—like the first draft of an essay. As you revise your essay, you are improving your writing. As you revise your reading, you are improving your comprehension.

Sometimes, as you re-read, you find some specific sentences or even passages that you just don't understand. When that's the case, you need to spend some time closely studying those sentences. One effective way to tackle tough text is to **reword** the text:

1. On a piece of paper, write down the sentences that are confusing you.
2. Leave a few blank lines between each line that you write.
3. Then, choose the difficult words, and reword them in the space above.

While you wouldn't want to reword every line of a long text—or even a short one—this is a powerful way to help your understanding of key sentences.

READING UP CLOSE

One Student's Rewording

Thomas tried rewording some of "The Fall of Satan" (page 403, lines 1–6). Because word order is as confusing as word choice, Thomas combined reordering with rewording. Open your book to page 403, and read the original lines there. Then, see Thomas's changes below. Also, note that he has combined a Think-Aloud (see page 1366) with his rewording.

> This first part seems backwards. Look, I think he's asking this muse—what's a muse? OK, the sidenote says it's a muse of poetry; I think this is like a Greek mythology character—so I think he's asking this muse to sing—not a real song, but just to tell him something. So it really could start by saying Heavenly Muse, tell me about "man's first disobedience, and the fruit of that forbidden tree." Well, that would be in the Garden of Eden. So he's saying to the Muse,
>
> > Tell me about when man first sinned in the Garden of Eden by eating the apple that brought death to the world and all our problems because now we don't live in Eden, until Christ brings us back to that blissful—that would be like perfect—seat.

Summarizing narrative text. Understanding a long piece of text is easier if you can summarize chunks of it. If you are reading a **narrative,** or a story (including a biography or an autobiography), then use a strategy called **Somebody Wanted But So (SWBS)** for help writing a summary of what you are reading.

SWBS is a powerful way to think about the characters in a narrative and to note what each does, what conflict each faces, and what the resolution is. As you write an SWBS statement for different characters or subjects within the same narrative, you are forcing yourself to rethink the narrative from different **points of view.**

Here are the steps for writing SWBS statements:

1. Write the words *Somebody, Wanted, But,* and *So* across the top of four columns.
2. Under the "Somebody" column, write a character's name.
3. Then, under the "Wanted" column, write what that character wanted to do.
4. Next, under the "But" column, explain what happened that kept the character from doing what he or she wanted.
5. Finally, under the "So" column, explain the eventual outcome.

If you're making an SWBS chart for a long story or novel, you might need to write several SWBS statements at different points in the story.

READING UP CLOSE

One Student's SWBS Chart

Read this SWBS statement of the excerpt from *The Pilgrim's Progress* (page 420). This statement includes information up through the break on page 422. Try writing an SWBS statement from the point of view of one of the merchants at Vanity Fair.

Somebody	Wanted	But	So
Christian	did not want to buy the merchandise at Vanity Fair,	but the merchants kept pushing wares on him,	so he was taken to prison and put on trial.

Summarizing expository text. If summarizing the information in a text is difficult, try a strategy called GIST.

1. Choose three or four sections of text you want to summarize.
2. Read the first section of text.
3. Draw twenty blank lines on a sheet of paper.
4. Write a summary of the first section of text using exactly twenty words—one word for each blank.
5. Read the next section of text.
6. Now, in your next set of twenty blanks, write a new summary statement that combines your first summary with whatever you want to add from this second section of text. You still have only twenty blanks to fill in, not forty.

Repeat this process one or two more times, depending on how many more sections of text you have to read. When you are finished, you'll have a twenty-word statement that gives you the gist, or overall idea, of the entire text.

READING UP CLOSE

One Student's GIST

Study the GIST statements for the first four paragraphs of text from Desmond Tutu's speech "The Question of South Africa" found on page 1321. Then, try your hand at creating the third GIST.

GIST 1 (for the first column of text)
South Africa has enough resources to provide for its people and should be peaceful, but social unrest is dividing it.

GIST 2 (adding the second column of text)
South Africa is divided because of the repressive policies of the white government; unemployment and higher prices have worsened things.

GIST 3 (adding the first column of text on page 1322)

______ ______ ______ ______ ______ ______ ______ ______

Using question maps. Most readers at some point will struggle with a text. Some readers find reading poetry a struggle, but they can breeze through computer magazines. Others find the technical language in computer magazines difficult but read poetry easily. It's not whether you struggle with texts that matters; instead, what matters is what you *do* when you struggle.

If you are an independent reader, then you know how to find the answers on your own—independently—to whatever causes you to struggle. If you are a dependent reader, you expect others to do the explaining for you. Dependent readers often say, "I don't get it," and give up. Independent readers, by contrast, know what they don't get and then figure out how to get it.

If you think you are a dependent reader, try using a question map like the one below. As you complete the chart, you'll be mapping your way toward independent reading.

1. In the first column, **list your questions** as you are reading.
2. In the second column, **make notes about each question.** For instance, jot down what made you think about the question or what page you are on in the text.
3. In the third column, **list possibilities for finding answers.** Remember that re-reading the text is always a good idea. Other places to find answers include dictionaries (especially if you have questions about vocabulary), your own mind (sometimes the text gives you part of the information, and you must figure out the rest), or other parts of the book (especially if you are reading a science, math, or history book).
4. In the final column, **jot down answers to your questions** only after you've made notes about them and thought out where to find answers to them. If you can't answer your questions at this point, then it's time to see your teacher.

READING UP CLOSE

One Student's Question Map

Here is a part of Denise's question map for "The Mark of the Beast" (page 933):

Questions	Notes	Places to find answers	Answers
1. Why is *Providence* capitalized?	p. 933, 4th line	Ask teacher	making luck be like a person
2. Who is Hanuman?	p. 934, 2nd line	dictionary or encyclopedia	a god in Hindu mythology

Know some smart words. Sometimes you understand what you've read, but when it comes time to talk about or write about the selection, you can't find the words you want to use to discuss the plot, characters, theme, or author's writing style. Here's a list of words and phrases that can serve as a springboard to discussion. They are beginning points—you still must be able to explain why you chose those words or phrases.

Words and Phrases to Describe the Plot

Positive	Negative
realistic	unrealistic
good pace from scene to scene	plodding
suspenseful	predictable
well-developed ideas	sketchy ideas

Words and Phrases to Describe the Characters

Positive	Negative
original	stereotyped
well-rounded	flat
dynamic; able to change	static; unable to change

Words to Describe the Theme

Positive	Negative
subtle	obvious
unique	overworked
powerful	trivial

Words and Phrases to Describe the Author's Style of Writing

Positive	Negative
descriptive; filled with figurative language	boring; lacking imagery
original	filled with clichés
lively; full of action	plodding; slow-moving
poetic; lyrical	stilted

READING UP CLOSE

▶ Using Smart Words

Choose one of the stories you've read in *Elements of Literature* this semester and, using some of the words and phrases in the above list, describe the plot, characters, theme, and author's writing style. Remember to support your word choices with examples from the story.

Improving Your Reading Rate

If your reading concerns are more about getting through the words than figuring out the meaning, then this part of Reading Matters is for you.

If you think you are a slow reader, then reading can seem overwhelming. However, you can change your **reading rate**—the pace at which you read. All you have to do is practice. The point isn't to read so that you just rush over words—the I'mgoingtoreadsofastthatallthewordsruntogether approach. Instead, the goal is to find a pace that keeps you moving comfortably through the pages. Why is it important to establish a good reading rate? Let's do a little math to see why your silent-reading rate counts.

MATH PROBLEM!
If you read 40 words per minute (wpm) and there are 400 words on a page, how long will it take you to read 1 page? 5 pages? How long will it take if you read 80 wpm? 100 wpm? 200 wpm?

Words per Minute (wpm)	1 page @400 words/page	5 pages @400 words/page
40 wpm	10 minutes	50 minutes
80 wpm	5 minutes	25 minutes
100 wpm	4 minutes	20 minutes
200 wpm	2 minutes	10 minutes

Reading rate and homework. Now, assume that with literature homework, science homework, and social studies homework, you have forty pages to read in one night. If you are reading at 40 wpm, you are spending more than six *hours* just reading the information; but at 100 wpm, you spend only two hours and forty minutes. At 200 wpm, you'd finish in one hour and twenty minutes.

Figuring out your reading rate. To determine your silent-reading rate, you'll need three things: a watch or clock with a second hand, a book, and someone who will watch the time for you. Then, complete the following steps:

1. Have your friend time you as you begin reading to yourself.
2. Read at your normal rate. Don't speed just because you're being timed.
3. Stop when your friend tells you that one minute is up.
4. Count the number of words you read in that minute. Write down that number.

Example

1st minute	180 words
2nd minute	215 words
3rd minute	190 words
	585 words ÷ 3 = 195 wpm

5. Repeat this process several more times, using different passages.
6. Then, add the number of words together, and divide by the number of times you timed yourself. That's your average number of words per minute.

Reading Rate Reminders

1. **Make sure you aren't reading one word at a time with a pause between each word.** For instance, read the following rhyme. The first time you read it, pause between each word; the second time, pause only where you see the slash marks. Hear the difference the phrasing makes?

   Mary had a little lamb, / Its fleece was white as snow. / Everywhere that Mary went, / The lamb was sure to go.

   Word-at-a-time reading is much slower than phrase reading.

2. **Make sure when you are reading silently that you really are reading silently.** As you read, avoid moving your lips or reading aloud softly. Also, don't use your finger to point to words as you read. Instead, use a bookmark to stay on the correct line while you practice your phrase reading.
3. **As you practice your fluency, remember that the single best way to improve your reading rate is simply to read more.** You won't get better at what you never do. Also, always remember that your rate will vary as your purpose for reading varies. Don't rush to read fast if that means understanding less.

Vocabulary Development

Fluency, reading rate, and comprehension are all connected to how quickly you recognize words and know what they mean. No matter how many words you study in school, you can't learn all the words you'll ever encounter. So you need to understand how words work—what *prefixes, suffixes,* and *roots* mean—so that when you encounter new words, you can see their components and figure out their meanings.

LATIN AND GREEK ROOTS, PREFIXES, AND SUFFIXES

Prefixes	Meaning	Examples
ad–	to	adapt, addict, adhere, admit
amphi–	both; around	amphibian, amphitheater
an–	without	anarchy, anesthesia, anonymous, anorexia
auto–	self	autobiography, autograph, automatic, automobile
co–	together	coauthor, cognate, coincide, cooperate
de–	opposite	deactivate, deform, degrade, deplete, descend
dis–	opposite	disagree, disarm, discontinue, disgust, dishonest
for–	not	forbid, forget, forgo
il–	not	illegal, illegible, illegitimate, illiterate, illogical
im–	not	imbalance, immaculate, immature
in–	not	inaccurate, inactive, inadvertent, incognito
ir–	not	irreconcilable, irregular, irresponsible
mal–	bad	maladjusted, malaise, malevolent, malice
pro–	before	progeny, prognosis, program, prologue
pro–	forward	proceed, produce, proficient, progress
re–	again	reappear, redistribute, redo, repaint, rewrite
sub–	under	subcontract, subject, submarine, subordinate
trans–	across	transatlantic, transcend, transcribe, transfer
un–	not	unable, uncertain, uncomfortable, unhappy
Roots	**Meaning**	**Examples**
–act–	do	action, actor, enact, react, transact
–aud–	hear	audible, audience, audition, auditorium
–cred–	believe	credit, credulous, discredit, incredible
–dic–	speak	contradict, dictate, diction, predict, verdict
–graph–	write	autograph, paragraph, phonograph, photograph
–loc–	place	allocate, dislocate, locate, location

(continued)

(continued)

–man–	hand	manipulate, manual, manufacture, manuscript
–mot–	move	demote, motion, motor, promote
–ped–	foot	pedal, pedestal, pedestrian
–pop–	people	populace, popular, population
–port–	carry	export, import, portable, porter, transport
–sign–	mark	insignia, signal, signature, significant
–spec–	see	inspect, respect, spectacle, spectator, suspect
–tract–	pull; drag	attract, contract, detract, subtract, traction, tractor
–vid–	see	evidence, provide, providence, video
–volve–	roll	evolve, involve, revolution, revolve, revolver
Suffixes	**Meaning**	**Examples**
–ade	action or process	blockade, escapade, parade
–age	action or process	marriage, pilgrimage, voyage
–ant	one who	assistant, defendant, immigrant, merchant, servant
–cle	small	corpuscle, cubicle, particle
–dom	state or quality of	boredom, freedom, martyrdom, wisdom
–ent	one who	parent, resident, regent, superintendent
–ful	full of	careful, fearful, joyful, thoughtful
–ic	relating to	comic, historic, poetic, public
–less	without	ageless, careless, thoughtless, tireless
–let	small	islet, leaflet, owlet, rivulet
–ly	resembling	fatherly, helpfully, motherly, scholarly
–ly	every	daily, monthly, weekly, yearly
–ment	action or process	development, embezzlement, government
–ment	state or quality of	amazement, amusement, predicament
–ment	product or thing	fragment, instrument, ornament
–or	one who	actor, auditor, doctor, donor

Word Family Tree

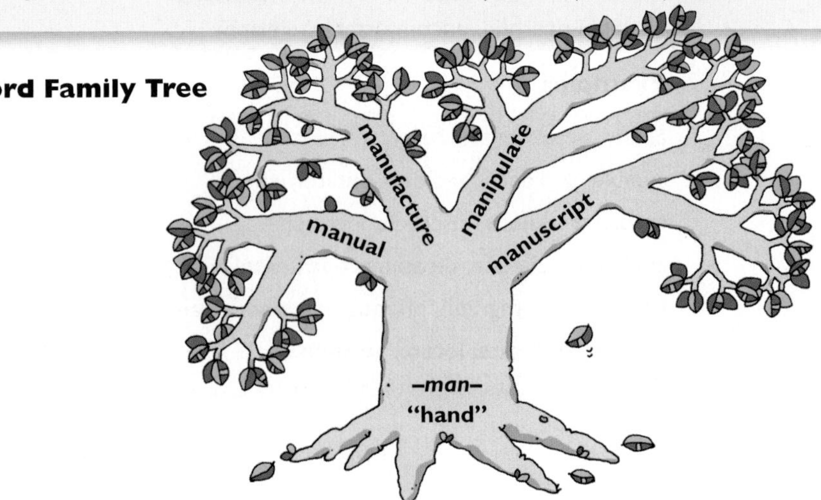

The World of Work

The ability to read critically and write effectively is your driver's license to navigating today's world. Without strong reading and writing skills, you will feel as frustrated and powerless as you do in a traffic jam. A future college student must be able to write application essays and understand scholarship guidelines. A mechanic must be able to read instruction manuals to use new equipment. A renter must understand a lease before getting an apartment. A supervisor must be able to write an effective memo to present ideas. In your life and in the world of work, you will rely on reading and writing skills to learn new information, communicate effectively, and get the results you want.

Reading

To avoid getting stranded in life and in the world of work, you will need to learn to read **informative documents** and **persuasive documents.**

Informative Documents Informative documents are like road maps: They provide facts and information. They can also be good places to check when you want to verify or clarify information from other sources. If a friend writes down directions that you're uncertain about, you consult a map to verify the directions. Likewise, if you read on a Web site an angry customer's complaint about repairs on a computer you just bought, you could review the warranty to see if the information is valid. Two kinds of common informative documents are consumer documents and workplace documents.

Consumer Documents You've probably already made thousands of buying decisions in your life. As you get older, however, buying decisions often carry bigger consequences. Should you sign a six- or a twelve-month apartment lease? Should you buy or lease a car? Being informed about the details of major purchases can help you avoid costly mistakes. This information can be found in **consumer documents,** such as warranties, contracts, product information, and instruction manuals.

- **Warranties** describe what happens if the product doesn't work properly or breaks down. Warranties note how long the product is covered for repair or replacement, which repairs the warranty does and does not cover, and how to receive repair service.

> The SureFocus digital camera is guaranteed to be free of defects in material or workmanship under normal use for a period of one (1) year from the date of purchase. Equipment covered by the warranty will be repaired by SureFocus Repair Members WITHOUT CHARGE, except for insurance, transportation, and handling charges. A copy of this warranty card and proof of purchase must be enclosed when returning equipment for warranty service. The warranty does not apply in the following cases:
>
> - the camera has been damaged through abuse
> - leaking batteries or other liquids have caused damage to the camera
> - unauthorized repair technicians have attempted to service the camera

- **Contracts** give details about an agreement that a buyer enters into with a company. A lease for an apartment or a car is a contract that defines the terms of the lease, including how long it lasts, what the responsibilities of the customer—also known as the lessee—and the landlord or car company are, how to end the lease, and what the penalties for breaking the lease are. A lease always includes a space for the customer's signature, which signifies agreement with the terms of the contract. Below is a portion of a typical apartment lease.

> This apartment lease is entered into by Althea Brown, hereinafter "Lessee," and Sun Valley Apartments.
>
> 1. **Grant of Lease:** Sun Valley Apartments does hereby lease unto Lessee Apartment #B-2, located at 101 Saguaro Drive, El Cajon, CA.
> 2. **Term of Lease:** This lease shall begin on the first day of August, 2003, and extend until the first day of August, 2004, after which the lessee can extend the lease month to month until terminated according to the terms described below.
> 3. **Rental Payments:** Lessee agrees to pay as rent the sum of $800 per month each month during the term of this lease before the fifth day of each month.

- **Product information** describes the basic features and materials of a product. A suit label would tell whether the suit is 100 percent wool or a blend of materials and would give cleaning instructions. Product information on the box of a cordless telephone would tell the frequency, number of channels, and whether it has automatic redial, memory, caller ID, voice-mail indicator light, and other features.
- **Instruction manuals** tell the owner how to set up, operate, and troubleshoot problems with a product. Instruction manuals also include safety precautions, diagrams, and descriptions of the product's features.

Workplace Documents Two common workplace documents—**procedure manuals** and **memoranda**—can tell you how to do your job and how to stay informed so you are both knowledgeable and effective.

- **Procedure manuals** are the step-by-step directions that tell employees how to serve customers, operate machinery, report problems, request vacation, or do anything that the company wants performed in a certain way. Procedure manuals are often used to train new employees and to clarify procedures for existing employees. As you read a procedure manual, pay attention to the specific instructions so you know exactly how to carry out the procedures.
- **Memoranda**—or memos—are the standard form of communication in many businesses. Memos are concise messages, generally covering only one topic. For example, an employee might send a memo to a supervisor reporting on the status of a project, or a supervisor might send a brief summary of discussions and decisions made in a meeting. To read a memo effectively, first check the subject line at the top to learn the topic of the memo. As you read, notice the pattern of organization in the body of the memo. Headings or bullets may indicate the main ideas. Pay attention to the purpose of the memo to decide whether and how to respond. Is the memo summarizing information, requesting action, or providing facts, such as dates and prices?

Persuasive Documents While informative documents are like road maps, persuasive documents are like travel brochures, trying to influence a reader's destination. Persuasive documents try to persuade readers to believe or act in a certain way. It's important for you to be able to distinguish between informative and persuasive public documents. For example, a policy statement from a county commission about recycling might quote facts, but its primary purpose is to influence citizens to support the commission's position. By critically reading persuasive public documents, you can evaluate whether you agree or disagree. Persuasive public documents include **policy statements, political platforms, speeches,** and **debates**.

- A **policy statement** outlines a person's or group's position on an issue and sometimes provides the rationale for that position. For example, the mayor might issue a policy statement explaining why she supports or opposes a tax increase for school construction. The policy statement gives the main points for the mayor's position and may provide facts or use rhetorical devices to support the position. A policy statement may also include a **call to action,** or a request for readers to take a specific action. Some organizations issue policy statements to endorse specific legislation, hoping to win the support of the voting public or of the lawmakers who can create the legislation.
- A **political platform** outlines a political candidate's position on a variety of issues so voters know where the candidate stands. It may also set forth the candidate's goals and describe the beliefs that guide his or her positions. The positions and goals are known as the *planks* of the platform. The audience for a political platform is usually friendly to the candidate, and the platform is intended to rouse support and to persuade undecided voters. Sometimes a platform will also address and rebut opposing viewpoints. Below is an excerpt from the political platform of a city council candidate about the issue of noise pollution.

> Rocky Mount is a quiet and peaceful place that does not need more intrusion from the local government to reduce noise levels. We are not close to a major airport, so we do not hear the regular drone of airplanes. Concertgoers hear Beethoven and Mozart, not the loud rock groups that play in larger cities. Noise pollution is an occasional, not regular or excessive, problem that can be handled without more city ordinances. Therefore, I do not support the development of laws to address the nonexistent issue of noise pollution.

- A **persuasive speech** is designed to change an audience's attitudes or beliefs or to move an audience to action. A speaker may make persuasive arguments and address audience counterclaims by using reasoning and rhetorical devices such as repetition. (For more on **persuasive speaking,** see page 1352.)
- A **debate** involves two teams who take turns discussing a controversial topic. The topic under discussion is called the *proposition.* One side argues for the proposition, and the other side argues against it. Each side also refutes, or argues against, its opponent's case.

Critiquing Persuasive Documents

Persuasive documents use logical, emotional, and ethical appeals to be convincing. Notice how these appeals are used to help you critique a document's validity and truthfulness.

- **Logical appeals** are based on reasons and supporting evidence. As you read, notice whether the evidence is based on reliable facts that can be confirmed through other, unbiased sources. If you are unsure, consult informative public documents, such as state laws, to verify the evidence. Notice whether the appeal makes sense and avoids fallacies, such as hasty generalizations or circular reasoning. A **hasty generalization** is a conclusion based on insufficient evidence. **Circular reasoning** occurs when the reason for an opinion is simply the opinion stated in different words.
- **Emotional appeals** rely on strong feelings to persuade readers. The writer may use examples that tug on heartstrings or arouse anger. Vivid language may make either positive or negative associations with the topic. Evaluate emotional appeals based on all of the evidence. If an argument is based primarily on emotion, the case may be weak. Watch out for signs of bias and stereotypes—including words such as *always* and *never*—that suggest the reasoning is unsound.
- **Ethical appeals** rely on the reader's sense of right and wrong. For example, a writer might persuade an audience to share a certain view by implying that the opposing position is unpatriotic or selfish.

Critique a persuasive document by seeing how fairly the writer treats the topic. Does the writer use credible evidence? Does he or she know enough about the topic to be believed?

PRACTICE & APPLY 1 Choose a persuasive public document, and critique its effectiveness and validity. Identify the appeals and the call to action, if any. Consult at least one informative public document to verify information presented in the persuasive document.

Writing

Writing is your passport to exciting places in life. A powerful résumé can win you the job of your dreams. A memo proposing cost-saving measures can earn you a promotion. A letter to your city council can lead to a new soccer field for a recreational league. Clear, effective writing is one of the best skills you can have as you enter the world of work.

Job Applications and Résumés One of the first places you will use writing beyond school will be in a job application or résumé. To fill out a **job application** completely and accurately, first read the instructions carefully. Type or write neatly in blue or black ink. Include all information requested. If a question does not apply to you, write *N/A* or *not applicable* in the blank. Proofread your completed form and neatly correct any errors. Finally, submit the form to the correct person.

A **résumé** summarizes your skills, education, achievements, and work experience. Prepare a résumé to use when you apply for a job or when you seek admission to a college or special program. Keep in mind that a résumé should be tailored to match the target audience. Select and highlight the skills and experiences that would most appeal to the employer or college reading the résumé. For a college or academic program, for example, you would highlight a strong GPA, successful class projects, and involvement in school clubs. The language would create a sophisticated, but not artificial, tone. For an employer, on the other hand, you would highlight work experience, both paid and volunteer, and the skills you learned on the job, using clear and direct language.

Here are some more tips to help you create a résumé:

- Give complete information about work experience, including job title, dates of employment, company, and location.

- Do not use *I;* instead, use short, parallel phrases that describe duties and activities.
- Proofread carefully. Mistakes on a résumé make the writer seem careless—not a positive quality for an employee.

Workplace Documents Memos are the standard form of communication in many businesses. To write a concise, easy-to-understand memo, you must first understand your main purpose for writing. Are you writing to provide information or to make a request? Memos should provide all essential information—*who, what, when, where, why,* and *how*—and get quickly to the point. If you are asking for action and information, include a deadline. Memos follow a standard format that includes the date, the recipient, the sender, and the subject at the top of the document. Notice how the following memo gets right to the point and communicates information clearly and directly.

```
Date:     February 25, 2003
To:       Sophia Cervenka
From:     Cole Hurley
Subject:  Computer Training
Training on the new software will
begin Monday, March 10, 2003.
Members of your department who are
interested in receiving training
should call me at extension 4390
by Friday, March 7, to sign up.
Training will last from 8:00
A.M.-3:00 P.M. The next training
session will be held on March 18.
```

Word-Processing Features A clear message is essential in workplace communication, but the appearance of workplace documents also counts. Learn to use word-processing features to your advantage by making documents that are easy on both the eyes and the mind.

- **Margins** are the space that surrounds the text on a page. Most word-processing programs automatically set side and top margins. You can adjust these default margins to suit your purpose.
- A **font** is a complete set of characters (including letters, numbers, and punctuation marks) in a particular size and design. For most workplace documents, use a font that is businesslike and easy to read. For more on **fonts,** see page 1392.
- **Line spacing** is the white space between lines of text. Most letters and memos are single-spaced to conserve space, but longer reports are often double-spaced to allow room for handwritten edits and comments.

Integrating Databases, Graphics, and Spreadsheets Workplace documents often integrate databases, graphics, and spreadsheets into text. For example, a pie chart or a spreadsheet can show budget expenses, or a list of customers in a specific ZIP Code might be integrated from a database into a report. Add features such as these to communicate your ideas more effectively. Place a graphic close to the related text, and explain the graphic's context. For help in integrating visuals and other components into documents, consult the Help section of your word-processing program or ask your teacher to help you.

Résumé Format Word-processing features can help you create an attractive format for your résumé. Here are some guidelines to remember:

- Make sure the résumé is not cluttered. Use wide margins for the top, bottom, and sides, and use double-spacing between sections to make the résumé easy to scan for information.
- Consider using a different font, boldface, and a larger point size for your name and for headings. Be sure all the fonts are easy to read.

The following résumé was written by a student interested in a sales job. He highlighted skills and experiences that show his interpersonal skills and initiative and used an attractive, easy-to-read format.

MIGUEL GUERRERO
1902 Greig Street
Santa Rosa, CA 95403
(707) 555-0085
E-mail: mguerrero@fhs.k12.ca.us

EDUCATION

Senior, Forsythe High School
Grade-point average: 3.3 (B)

WORK EXPERIENCE

Summer 2001–present

Waiter, Starlite Restaurant

- Serve customers quickly and efficiently
- Train new employees in effective customer service
- Twice awarded Star Employee

Summer 2000

Campaign Volunteer, Antonio Suarez Campaign for Mayor

- Assisted in door-to-door campaigns
- Collected and input data for mailing list
- Organized teen volunteers to distribute flyers

SKILLS

Communication: Telephone sales, oral presentations
Computers: Word processing, Web design

ACTIVITIES

Debate team, soccer team, student government representative

REFERENCES

Janet Matteson, Owner
Starlite Restaurant
(707) 555-0146

David Cho, Principal
Forsythe High School
(707) 555-0013

PRACTICE & APPLY 2 Create a résumé for your dream job. Think about what experiences and skills you have that would appeal to a potential employer. Present this information in a clear, concise, and eye-catching way.

Writer's Handbook

The Writing Process

Effective writing involves a process. The steps in this process, called a **recursive** process because you may repeat them several times, are like those of a spiral staircase—you must travel around and around, yet with each revolution you ascend toward your goal. While each writer's process is slightly different, most effective writers follow the steps below.

STAGES OF THE WRITING PROCESS	
Prewriting	• Identify your purpose and audience. • Choose a topic and an appropriate form. • Formulate your thesis, or main idea, about the topic. • Gather information about the topic. • Organize information in a preliminary plan.
Writing	• Draft an introduction that seizes your readers' attention and provides necessary background information. • State your thesis clearly and assertively. • Develop body paragraphs that elaborate on key ideas. • Follow an organizational plan. • Draft a conclusion that restates your thesis and leaves readers with something to think about.
Revising	• Evaluate your draft. • Revise to improve its content, organization, and style.
Publishing	• Proofread your draft, and correct errors in spelling, punctuation, grammar, and usage. • Share your final draft with readers. • Reflect on your writing experience.

Throughout the writing process, make sure you do the following:

- **Keep your ideas coherent and focused.** Keep your specific purpose in mind to help you present a tightly reasoned argument. Evaluate every idea to make sure it will focus your readers on your main point, and make that point clear in your thesis statement.

- **Share your own perspective.** You bring your own ideas to every piece you write. Share not only information you've gathered but also your viewpoint on your topic. Let your natural voice shine through to readers.
- **Keep your audience in mind.** Consider your readers' backgrounds and interests. If your form is not assigned, choose a form that will grab your readers, such as a song, editorial, screenplay, or letter.
- **Plan to publish.** Labor over every piece as though it will be published or shared with an audience. Enlist the help of a classmate when you proofread a finished piece, and use the questions in the chart below. The numbers in parentheses indicate the sections in the Language Handbook that contain instruction on each concept.

QUESTIONS FOR PROOFREADING

1. Is every sentence complete, not a fragment or run-on? (8a, 9d–e)
2. Are punctuation marks used correctly? (12a–r, 13a–o)
3. Are the first letters of sentences, proper nouns, and proper adjectives capitalized? (11a, c)
4. Does each verb agree in number with its subject? (2a) Are verb forms and tenses used correctly? (3b–c)
5. Are subject and object forms of personal pronouns used correctly? (4a–e) Does every pronoun agree with a clear antecedent in number and gender? (2j)

When revising and proofreading, use the symbols below.

SYMBOLS FOR REVISING AND PROOFREADING

Symbol	Example	Meaning of Symbol
≡	805 Linden avenue	Capitalize a lowercase letter.
/	the First of May	Lowercase a capital letter.
^	one ^of my friends	Insert a missing word, letter, or punctuation mark.
‾‾	at the beginning (onset)	Replace a word.
⌇	Give me a a number	Delete a word, letter, or punctuation mark.
∽	beleive	Change the order of letters.
¶	¶ "Yes," she answered.	Begin a new paragraph.

Paragraphs

The Parts of a Paragraph

Paragraphs can be as different as oak trees are from pines. Some paragraphs are a single word; others run several pages. Their uses differ, too: A paragraph may present a main idea, connect one idea to another, emphasize an idea, or simply give the reader's eyes a rest in a long passage.

Many paragraphs in essays and other types of nonfiction, including workplace writing, develop one main idea. A main-idea paragraph is often built from a **topic sentence, supporting sentences,** and a **clincher sentence.**

Quick guide

PARTS OF A PARAGRAPH	
Topic Sentence	• an explicit statement of the paragraph's main idea or central focus • often the first or second sentence in a paragraph, but may appear at the end to emphasize or summarize
Supporting Sentences	• provide elaboration by supporting, building, or proving the main idea • often include details of the following types: *sensory details*: information about sight, sound, taste, smell, and texture *facts*: details that can be proved true *examples*: specific instances that illustrate a general idea *anecdotes*: brief stories about people or events that illustrate a main idea *analogies*: comparisons between ideas familiar to readers and unfamiliar concepts being explained
Clincher Sentence	• may restate the topic sentence, summarize supporting details, offer a final thought, or help readers refocus on the main idea of a long paragraph

TIP Not every paragraph has, or needs, a topic sentence. In fiction, paragraphs rarely have topic sentences. Paragraphs presenting time sequences (how-to instructions or histories, for example) may also lack topic sentences—the steps or events themselves focus the reader's mind. Finally, a paragraph may imply, or suggest, its main idea without directly stating it in a topic sentence. In your school writing, however, topic sentences are a help: They keep *you* focused on each paragraph's topic.

TIP Not every paragraph needs a clincher sentence. Use one for a strong or dramatic touch or for renewing a main idea in a lengthy or complicated paragraph.

Putting the Parts Together You can clearly see the parts of a paragraph in the following example. Notice that its topic sentence expresses the paragraph's main idea and that the clincher sentence re-emphasizes it.

Topic Sentence
Supporting Sentences
Clincher Sentence

The arrival of printing in England was to be of far more importance than any of the changes of ruler during the Wars of the Roses. Up until this time books had been copied out by hand by scribes in monasteries or other workshops, a long and laborious process. As a result books were rare and very costly. Printing by machine meant that they could be cheap and plentiful. The knowledge books contained could also be spread far wider, reaching new audiences, as more people than ever before learned to read. When William Caxton set up his printing presses in the precincts of Westminster Abbey in 1476, it was to be a landmark in the history of the English language and literature, daily life, and culture.

Sir Roy Strong, *The Story of Britain*

Qualities of Paragraphs

Think about trees again. Each type is so distinct: a pine with its needles and cones, a magnolia with its glossy leaves and huge blossoms. Yet, while different, each is a pleasing whole. Paragraphs achieve this wholeness, too, through two major qualities: **unity** and **coherence.**

Unity Unity means that all of a paragraph's supporting sentences really fit the main idea—no pine cones should poke out among the magnolia blooms. In other words, all of the supporting sentences must work together and stay on the topic. Unity is achieved when

- all sentences relate to the paragraph's main idea—whether it is stated in a topic sentence or implied, or
- all sentences relate to a sequence of events

Coherence When a paragraph has coherence, the ideas are arranged in an order that makes sense so that the reader moves easily from one idea to another. The paragraph flows; it doesn't bounce readers around or befuddle them. You can create coherence in a paragraph by paying attention to

- the order you use to arrange ideas
- the connections you make between ideas to show readers how the ideas are related

To create coherence through the arrangement of your ideas, choose the type of order that best fits your purpose. The chart below explains how to use the four main types of order.

TYPES OF ORDER

Quick guide!

Order	When to Use	How It Works
Chronological	• to tell a story or relate an event • to explain a process • to show cause and effect	• presents events in the order they happen • shows how things change over time
Spatial	• to describe individual features • to create a complete visual picture	• arranges details by location in space—top to bottom, left to right, near to far, center to edge, and so on
Order of Importance	• to inform • to persuade	• arranges ideas and details from most important to least, or vice versa • places emphasis where the writer thinks it is most effective
Logical	• to inform or to persuade, often by classifying: defining, dividing a subject into parts, or comparing and contrasting	• groups ideas or details together in ways that illustrate the relationships between them; for example, as parts of a whole

TIP The types of order can overlap or can be used in combination. For example, to explain an effect, you might move **chronologically** through its causes, describing the first cause, which leads to the second cause, and so on. However, suppose that three simultaneous causes produce a single effect. You could discuss those causes in **order of importance.**

Guide readers through your clearly arranged ideas by pointing out the connections among them. Show connections by using **direct references** (repetition of ideas), **transitional expressions,** and **parallelism.** The chart on the next page details how you can use these three types of connections to add to the coherence of your writing.

CONNECTING IDEAS

Type of Connection	How to Use It
Direct References, or Repetition of Ideas	• Refer to a noun or pronoun used earlier in the paragraph. • Repeat a word used earlier. • Substitute synonyms for words used earlier.
Transitional Expressions	• Compare ideas (*also, and, another, in the same way, just, like, likewise, moreover, similarly, too*). • Contrast ideas (*although, but, however, in spite of, instead, nevertheless, on the other hand, still, yet*). • Show cause and effect (*accordingly, as a result, because, consequently, for, since, so, so that, therefore*). • Indicate time (*after, at last, before, early, eventually, first, later, next, then, thereafter, until, when, while*). • Show place (*above, across, adjacent, behind, beside, beyond, down, here, in, near, over, there*). • Show importance (*first, last, less significant, mainly, more important, to begin with*).
Parallelism	• Use the same grammatical forms or structures to balance related ideas in a sentence. • Sparingly, use the same sentence structures to show connections between related ideas in a paragraph or composition.

PRACTICE & APPLY Develop two paragraphs on a single topic that interests you. First, choose two primary methods of organizing ideas on the topic (keeping in mind that you may use a combination of orders). Then, plan a topic sentence, a variety of supporting details, and a clincher sentence for each of your two paragraphs. Finally, draft your paragraphs, clearly organizing and connecting ideas and eliminating any ideas that detract from your focus.

The Writer's Language

Revising often focuses on a piece's content and organization. However, to communicate ideas effectively, you must work just as carefully to revise a piece's **style**—how you express those ideas. When revising your style, fine-tune your writing's **sound, word choice,** and **sentence variety,** and use **rhetorical devices** to grab reader attention and make your ideas clear and interesting.

A Sound Style Keep your **audience** and **purpose** in mind to help you choose a suitable **voice, tone,** and **level of formality** for a piece of writing.

Voice In writing, voice is your unique personality on paper. Just as you recognize a friend's spoken voice, you can recognize the work of favorite writers by the unique way they express ideas. To evaluate your own writing voice, read your work out loud. If your writing doesn't sound natural, revise it to bring your personality to life.

Tone Tone reveals your attitude toward a topic and audience. Always use an appropriate tone for your audience and purpose. For example, if your purpose is to persuade readers to share your view on an important issue, your tone should be serious and respectful.

Level of Formality You wouldn't don formal wear for a beach party, and neither should you use a casual, informal style for a serious essay on a subject about which you care deeply. Match the level of formality to your subject, your audience, and your purpose. Look at these examples.

INFORMAL Some people shouldn't own pets. Period.

FORMAL Certain people should not own pets under any circumstances.

Word Choice Make sure your words express the ideas you want them to express. Every word should help create a clear, vivid picture of what you mean and communicate the connotation you want.

Precise Language Replace vague language in your writing with words that are distinct and strong. For example, you might describe a big boulder you saw on a hike as being as *huge as a car* or as *mammoth as a double-decker bus.* You could mention that the boulder *rumbled* down the hill or *squatted* by the path. Using **precise verbs, nouns,** and **adjectives** like these will make your writing clearer and more interesting.

Connotations As you choose words, notice their **connotations**—the emotional effects they create. For instance, the word *cheap* means "economical," but it also has the negative connotation of being poor in quality. The word *inexpensive* expresses the same idea as *cheap* but in a more positive way. Choose words carefully by considering their effects.

Writer's Handbook

Reference Note

For more on **revising to add variety,** see **Revising for Variety,** 9g–i, in the Language Handbook.

Sentence Variety Readers can become bored with writing that uses the same types of sentences over and over. Create variety by varying the beginnings of your sentences and mixing simple, compound, and complex sentences.

Rhetorical Devices To give your ideas a greater impact, use the rhetorical devices of **parallelism, repetition,** and **analogy.**

Parallelism Just as a train stays on its tracks because they're parallel, readers will stay on track if your written ideas are grammatically parallel.

NOT PARALLEL More lives are saved when **drivers wear seatbelts** and **motorcyclists are wearing helmets.**

PARALLEL More lives are saved when **drivers wear seatbelts** and **motorcyclists wear helmets.**

You can also use parallelism for effect by using similar sentence structures to express related ideas.

Repetition Repeating important words or phrases can create an emotional response or underscore their significance. Use this technique sparingly to make your key ideas resonate with readers.

Analogy An analogy illustrates an idea by comparing it to something with similar characteristics. For example, you could say, "The politician worked the crowd as if he were selling the Fountain of Youth."

A Stylish Model Read the following passage, noting the writer's sound, word choice, sentence variety, and rhetorical devices.

A Writer's Model

Voice/tone — Repetition — Analogy — Connotation — Precise verbs

Credit cards are a ticket to an unpleasant lesson for college freshmen. One in five college students will rack up $10,000 in credit card debt by graduation. That's right—$10,000! Some people use credit as recklessly as play money. Unfortunately, the consequences for misusing credit cards are staggering. A $5,000 credit card debt can take up to 30 years and $15,000 to pay off—three times the value of the items purchased. Credit cards only look good until the bill comes due. I encourage students to stand firm and refuse the temptations dangled before them by credit card companies.

PRACTICE & APPLY Revise the paragraph below to improve its style. Add your own ideas as appropriate.

I think students should be allowed to bring cell phones to school. What if we need to call someone? Students have rights too. I think the school staff should quit treating us like babies. This rule just isn't fair and should be changed.

Designing Your Writing

A document must be designed to convey information in a way that is easy to understand and remember. In other words, the text arrangement and appearance and any visuals must support the content. You can create effective design and visuals by hand, or you can use advanced publishing software and graphics programs to design pages and to integrate other features into your word-processed documents.

Page Design

Lay It on the Line If you want your documents to catch readers' attention, you must design them to be visually appealing and easy to read. Use the following design elements to improve readability.

- **Columns** arrange text in separate sections printed vertically side by side. Text in reference books and newspapers usually appears in columns. A **block** is a rectangle of text shorter than a page. The text in advertisements is usually set in blocks so that it may be read quickly. Blocks and columns are separated from each other by white space.
- A **bullet** (•) is a symbol used to highlight information in a text. Bullets separate information into lists like this one. Bullets attract attention and help readers remember information.
- A **heading** appears at the beginning of a section of text to tell readers what that section is about. A **subheading** indicates a smaller section within a heading. Headings and subheadings may be set off from other text in large, **boldface,** or *italic* type or in a different font.
- **White space** is any area on a page where there is little or no text or graphics. Usually, white space is limited to the margins and the spaces between words, lines, and columns. Advertisements usually have more white space than do books or articles.
- A **caption** appears under a photograph or illustration to explain its meaning and connect it to the text. Captions may appear in italics or in a smaller type size than the main text.
- **Contrast** refers to the balance of light and dark areas on a page. Dark areas contain blocks of text or graphics. Light areas have little type. A page with high contrast, or roughly balanced light and dark areas, is easier to read than a page with low contrast.
- **Emphasis** is how a page designer indicates to a reader which information on a page is most important. Because readers' eyes are drawn naturally to color, large and bold print, and graphics, these elements are commonly used to create emphasis.

Type

Letter Perfect The basic material of your document is the type. Your choice of different **cases** and **fonts** can pull the reader into the text, provide emphasis, and make your document easy to read.

Case The two cases of type are uppercase, or capital, letters and lowercase, or small, letters. You can vary case in these ways:

- **Uppercase letters** Text in all uppercase letters attracts readers' attention and may be used in headings or titles. Because text in all capital letters can be difficult to read, use all capitals only for emphasis, not for large bodies of text.
- **Small caps** Small caps are uppercase letters that are reduced in size. They are used in abbreviations of time, such as 9:00 A.M. and A.D. 1500. Small caps may be combined with capital letters for an artistic effect.

Font A font is one complete set of characters (such as letters, numbers, and punctuation marks) of a given size and design. The three types of fonts are explained in the chart below.

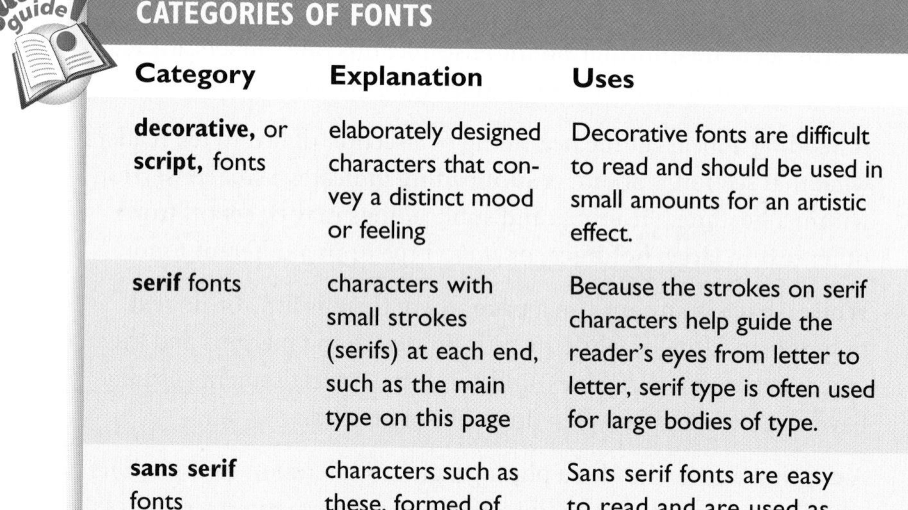

CATEGORIES OF FONTS

Category	Explanation	Uses
decorative, or **script,** fonts	elaborately designed characters that convey a distinct mood or feeling	Decorative fonts are difficult to read and should be used in small amounts for an artistic effect.
serif fonts	characters with small strokes (serifs) at each end, such as the main type on this page	Because the strokes on serif characters help guide the reader's eyes from letter to letter, serif type is often used for large bodies of type.
sans serif fonts	characters such as these, formed of straight lines with no serifs	Sans serif fonts are easy to read and are used as headings, subheadings, and captions.

- **Font size** The size of the type in a document is called the font size or point size. In general, newspapers and textbooks use type measured at 12 points. Type for headings and headlines is larger, while captions are usually smaller.
- **Font style** Most text is set in roman (not slanted) style. *Italic,* or slanted, style is used for captions or book titles. Underscored or boldface type can be used for emphasis.

Visuals

Show, Don't Tell If you wanted to tell about the weekly expenses and income from your summer lawn-care business, it would be more effective to show the information in a table than to list it in a paragraph. Visuals, or graphics, such as this must be accurate and appropriate. You can create visuals by hand or by using technology, such as advanced computer software and graphics programs. You can also add to a document's impact by integrating a database or spreadsheet into it. Here are some useful visuals.

- **Graphs** present numeric information and can show trends or changes over time or how one thing changes in relation to another. A **bar graph** can also compare quantities at a glance, or note the parts of a whole. A **line graph** can compare trends or show how two or more variables interact, as in this example.

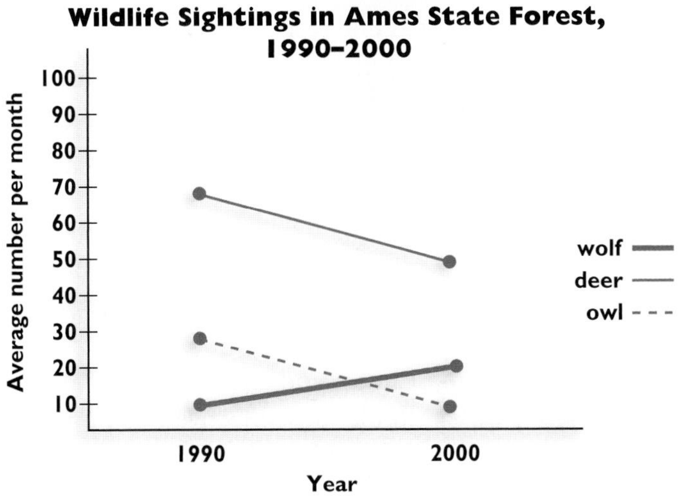

- **Tables** use rows and columns to provide detailed information arranged in an accessible way. A **spreadsheet** is a special kind of table created on a computer. The cells of a spreadsheet are associated with mathematical equations. Spreadsheets are especially useful for budgets or schedules in which the numbers are variables in an equation. In the spreadsheet below, the last column of each row calculates the average of the figures to the left of it.

First Quarter Grades

Name	Essay	Test	Speech	Project	Average
Cooper, L.	84	78	81	92	84
Nguyen, H.	90	86	88	95	90
Torres, B.	88	94	91	90	91
Watt, K.	96	90	93	88	92

TIP Consider copying and pasting information from databases into your documents. For example, if you were writing a letter to your school administration proposing a senior class trip to a national park, you could paste information from a database comparing costs and available activities at several parks in your area. (Always give credit to your sources for such data.)

- **Pictures,** such as drawings and photographs, can show how something works, what something or someone looks like, or something new, unfamiliar, or indescribable. You can scan a copyright-free picture on the computer or paste it manually into your document. Place it near the reference in the text, and include a caption.

- **Charts** show relationships among ideas or data. A **flowchart** uses geometric shapes linked by arrows to show the sequence of events in a process. A **pie chart** is a circle divided into wedges. Each wedge represents a certain percentage of the total, as in this example.

How Energy Is Used Worldwide

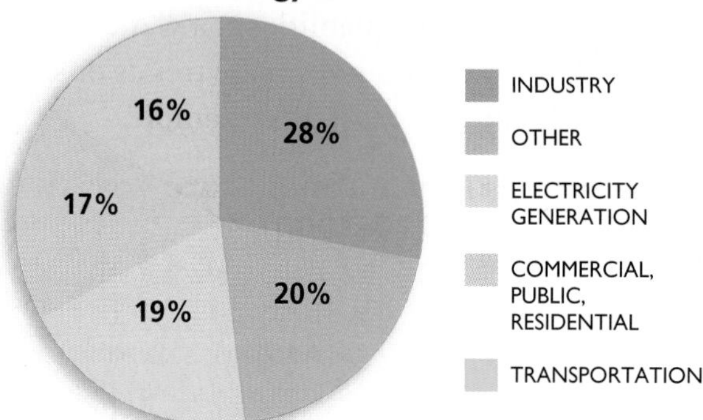

- **Time lines** identify the events that have taken place over a given period of time. (For an example of a time line, see page 2.)

PRACTICE & APPLY Choose and create the visual you think would most effectively communicate the following information using the guidelines in this section.

The estimated expenses for the Sanger High senior class trip are as follows: bus rental, $1,000; gas, $200; hotel, ten rooms at $45 per room for five days, or $2,250; food, $30 a day per person (ten people for five days), or $1,500. The total trip cost is $4,950.

Test Smarts

by Flo Ota De Lange *and* Sheri Henderson

Strategies for Taking Multiple-Choice Tests

Senior year. You're on the homestretch and on your way to—maybe you don't know yet exactly where you're headed. Whatever you do, be sure to pick up that diploma. A high school diploma will open doors whatever you choose to do, and the skills you acquire in earning your diploma are ones you'll need for lifelong learning.

To graduate, you still need to pass a lot of tests. You'll have plenty of quizzes, midterm exams, and finals to get through. You'll take the state's standardized tests, and if you plan to go on to college, you'll need to tackle the *Scholastic Assessment Test* (*SAT*) or the *American College Testing Program* (*ACT*).

The following pages can help you prepare for all your standardized tests. They are designed to help you with three goals:

- to become familiar with the different types of questions you will be asked
- to learn some strategies for approaching the questions
- to discover the kinds of questions that give you trouble

Once you have met those goals, you will want to practice answering the kinds of questions that give you trouble until you feel comfortable with them. Here are some basic strategies that will help you approach your multiple-choice tests with confidence:

Stay Calm

You have studied the material, and you know your stuff, but you're still nervous. That's OK. A little nervousness will help you focus, but so will a calm body. **Take a few deep breaths** before you begin.

Track Your Time

First, take a few minutes to estimate how much time you have for each question. Then, set checkpoints for yourself—how many questions should be completed at a quarter of the time, half of the time, and so on. That way you can **pace yourself** as you work through the test.

Master the Directions

Read the directions carefully so you know exactly what to do and how to do it. If you are supposed to fill in a bubble, fill it in carefully. Be careful to match each question's number to the number on the answer sheet.

Study the Questions

Read each question once, twice, three times—until you are absolutely certain you know what the question is asking. Watch out for words like *not* and *except:* They tell you to look for choices that are false, different, or opposite.

Anticipate Answers

Once you are sure you understand the question, **anticipate the answer** before you read the choices. If the answer you guessed is there, it is probably correct. To be sure, though, check out each choice. If you understand the question but don't know the answer, eliminate any choices you think are wrong. Then, make an educated—not a wild—guess to choose one of the remaining choices. **Avoid distracters,** answer choices that are true but don't fit the question.

Don't Give Up

If you are having a hard time with a test, take a deep breath and **keep on going.** On most tests the questions do not get more difficult as you go, and an easier question is probably coming up soon. The last question on a test is worth just as many points as the first, so give it your all—all the way to the end.

Types of Test Questions

You will feel a lot more confident if you are familiar with the kinds of questions given on a test. The following pages describe and give examples of and tips for answering the different types of multiple-choice questions you'll find on many standardized tests.

Critical-Reading Questions

The critical-reading section of a test seeks to determine how well you can think analytically about what you read. This is not news to you. That is the purpose of every reading test you have ever taken. Although challenging tests may give you long, difficult readings and complicated questions, it helps to remember that you will find everything you need—including the answers—right there on the page.

Strategies for Critical-Reading Questions

Here are some tips for answering critical-reading questions.

- **Look for main ideas.** In this kind of test, pay special attention to the **introductory and concluding paragraphs,** in which writers often state their main idea. Read all footnotes or margin notes. As you read the passage, look for **key words, phrases,** and **ideas.** If you are allowed to write on the test, circle or underline them.
- **Look for structure.** Try to determine how the logic of a passage is developed by paying attention to **transition words** and the **pattern of organization.** Does the author build an argument brick by brick, using words and phrases such as *also, and, as well as, furthermore*? Does the author instead offer an argument with contrasts, using words and phrases such as *however, although, in spite of, nevertheless*? And finally, **what is the writer's point?**
- **Eliminate obviously wrong answer choices.** If the questions are long and complicated, it often helps to translate them into plain English to be sure you understand what's being asked. Then, anticipate the possible answers. When you have eliminated the obviously wrong choices, put your finger on the choice you think is correct, and go back to the passage. **Check it.** Do not rely on memory. This is particularly important for vocabulary-in-context questions.
- **Watch out for traps.** Be wary of choices that use extreme words, like *always* and *never.* Look out for choices that are true but do not correctly answer the question—these are called *distracters.* Remember that questions using *except* or *least* or *not* are asking you to find the false answer. Trust your common sense.

We'll use the reading selection below to discuss a few of the most common kinds of critical-reading questions:

DIRECTIONS: Read the passage below. Then, read the questions that follow, and write the letter of the best answer.

***from* Acceptance and Nobel Lecture—1993**
Nelson Mandela

We speak here of the challenge of the dichotomies of war and peace, violence and nonviolence, racism and human dignity, oppression and repression and liberty and human rights, poverty and freedom from want.

We stand here today as nothing more than a representative of the millions of our people who dared to rise up against a social system whose very essence is war, violence, racism, oppression and repression, and the impoverishment of an entire people.

I am also here today as a representative of the millions of people across the globe, the antiapartheid movement, the governments and organizations that joined with us not to fight against South Africa as a country or

(continued)

(continued)

any of its peoples but to oppose an inhuman system and sue for a speedy end to the apartheid crime against humanity.

These countless human beings, both inside and outside our country, had the nobility of spirit to stand in the path of tyranny and injustice without seeking selfish gain. They recognized that an injury to one is an injury to all and therefore acted together in defense of justice and a common human decency. Because of their courage and persistence for many years, we can, today, even set the dates when all humanity will join together to celebrate one of the outstanding human victories of our century.

When that moment comes, we shall, together, rejoice in a common victory over racism.

VOCABULARY-IN-CONTEXT QUESTIONS ask you to define words within the context of the reading. If the word is fairly common, look out! A word's meaning in the reading may be an unusual or uncommon one. If it is a really tough word, read several lines above and several lines below the line in which the word is found. The meaning will be in there somewhere. Whatever you do, **always go back and check the reading** for vocabulary-in-context questions. Always.

1. The word *dichotomies* in line 2 is used to describe—

A a separation of social classes

B the establishment of groups

C an ordering of topics

D a division into opposites

E a medieval hierarchy

Answer: All the choices refer to some kind of structure. Based on the context clue of the sets of opposites that follow the word *dichotomies,* you can figure out that **D** is the correct answer. If you've taken science courses, you have another clue in the Greek prefix *di–,* which means "twice; double" in words such as *dioxide.*

PARAPHRASING or RESTATING QUESTIONS ask you to choose the best restatement of an idea, detail, or fact in the selection. You are not asked to make any judgments about the idea; instead, like an interpreter, you are simply asked to report accurately what the writer said. If the question is long and complex, put it into your own words ***before*** you read the choices. The answer is easier to find if you know what is being asked.

2. When Mandela speaks of "the apartheid crime against humanity" (lines 22–23), he is referring to how—

A a social system that injures some injures all

B like any social system, apartheid has its pros and cons

C apartheid leads to crime

D apartheid is a crime because it is illegal in South Africa

E humanity has committed crimes against apartheid

Answer: Even if you didn't know that apartheid was the South African social and legal system of segregation, the sentence tells you that it is a "crime against humanity." Only **choice A** refers to this concept. **B, C,** and **D** do not paraphrase the speaker's meaning, and **E** says the opposite of his meaning.

INFERENCE QUESTIONS ask you to read between the lines, to connect clues from the ideas in selections. You compile hints and key bits of information to arrive at the answer. Inference questions require careful reading in order to glean what is implied rather than stated outright.

3. The speaker would most likely agree that—

A South Africans alone are responsible for South Africa's problems

B apartheid could be overturned by a response from the world community

C there is a bright side to everything

D the law is the law and must be obeyed

E apartheid does not favor any one racial group over another

Answer: First, rule out any choices that are not true according to what is said in the speech. Choices **C, D,** and **E** can all be eliminated because they are contrary to what Mandela states directly. Choice **A** seems possible, and so does **B.** Re-read the speech. See that the third and fourth paragraphs make clear that the speaker believes apartheid is a world problem, not just South Africa's. Therefore, **choice B is the best answer.**

TONE or MOOD QUESTIONS ask you to infer the writer's attitude toward the subject. Pay attention to the descriptions of the subject. Are they positive, neutral, or negative? Is the writer hopeful, sad, admiring, wishy-washy, sarcastic? (A standardized test might use more difficult vocabulary words for those same words: *sanguine, melancholy, reverent, ambivalent, sardonic.*)

4. Which of the following words best describes Mandela's attitude toward his subject?

A amused

B resigned

C impassioned

D bewildered

E diplomatic

Answer: Mandela is clearly neither amused **(A),** resigned **(B),** nor bewildered **(D).** His subject is serious, and he speaks with conviction about change. Although a Nobel Peace Prize acceptance speech is an occasion that may call for diplomacy **(E),** Mandela is evidently passionate about his subject. Since *impassioned* is a synonym for *passionate,* **C is the best choice.**

MAIN-IDEA or BEST-TITLE QUESTIONS ask you to consider the big picture, much as you might do when you step back from a still-life painting to focus on the entire effect rather than zoom in on the individual fruits and objects that create that effect. Ask yourself:

- What is the subject?
- What aspect of the subject does the writer address?
- What does the writer want me to understand about this aspect?

Main ideas are often found at the beginning or end of a selection. In choosing your answers, be wary of those that may be true but are either too specific or too general to reflect the message of *this* selection.

5. Which of the following titles is best for Nelson Mandela's speech?

A "Racism Defeated"

B "Apartheid in South Africa"

C "South Africa United"

D "Millions of People Unite"

E "A Stand Against Injustice"

Answer: **The best answer is E** since Mandela talks about the stand he and millions of others have taken against the injustice of apartheid. Racism has not yet been defeated, so **A** is not right. **B** and **D** are too general. **C** is irrelevant.

EVALUATING-THE-WRITER'S-CRAFT QUESTIONS ask you to look at the selection's organization, logic, and argumentative techniques. They often look like this:

6. In his speech the speaker makes his central point primarily by—

A attacking the specific persons responsible for apartheid

B praising the efforts of many people to combat apartheid

C warning the world against future apartheids

D counting the gains of apartheid

E describing in detail crimes against humanity

Answer: **The best answer is B;** the third through fifth paragraphs praise those who fight against apartheid. Choice **A** seems possible, but the word *specific* signals that it's not the right answer—Mandela never mentions any specific persons. You can eliminate **E** because although he mentions crimes against humanity, Mandela does not describe them in detail. Choices **C** and **D** do not relate to the speech.

Vocabulary Questions

You will encounter several types of vocabulary questions on standardized tests. They all test your knowledge of word meanings, both in and out of context.

SENTENCE-COMPLETION, or FILL-IN-THE-BLANK, QUESTIONS look easy, but they require your full attention. Here's a step-by-step way to approach each question:

- **Cover up the answer choices, and read the entire sentence carefully.** Most sentences contain clues to the intended meaning and thus to the word you want. Ask yourself, "What is this blank about?" and "What else does the sentence say about the subject of the blank?"
- **Look for clue words.** Pay special attention to words that change the direction of a sentence. Look for words that **reverse** the sentence's main idea, such as *no, not, although, however, but.* Look also for words that indicate that a **synonym** is wanted: *and, also, in addition, likewise, moreover.* Finally, look for words that suggest **cause and effect:** *thus, therefore, because, since, so.*
- **Anticipate answers.** Think of words that might best fill the blank.
- **Look at the choices.** If the word you guessed is there, it is probably the correct choice. You can double-check by eliminating any choices that are obviously wrong. Then, try *each* choice in the blank, and re-read the sentence *each* time to find the best fit. Take no shortcuts on this step.

Here are four fill-in-the-blank questions:

7. Biologists say meeting a Noah's ark-like emergency today would require an ocean freighter to hold the ten million species weighing a total of one thousand tons, says Clifford Pickover in "Keys to Infinity," but successfully preserving them from extinction would still be ________ because at least fifty members of a species are required to maintain genetic health.

A feasible
B inappropriate
C abstruse
D dubious
E effortless

Answer: You are looking for a word that means "unlikely." How do you know that? Your clue lies in the part of the sentence that follows the word *because,* which tells you that it will take fifty times the two-by-two formula to keep the animals in good genetic shape. (Of course, a difficult test like the *SAT* will not give you a word as easy as *unlikely* as a choice.)

Let's imagine for a moment that those choices are all unfamiliar words, and maybe they are to you. You can still think them through. **Use what you know to eliminate incorrect answers.** You can eliminate **B** and **E**—the task described is neither inappropriate nor easy enough to be called effortless. Cross out **C** (*abstruse,* which means "difficult to understand"), because it doesn't fit the context either. **A** (*feasible,* which means "doable") and **D** (*dubious*) are the remaining choices. Choice **A** suggests the meaning that is opposite the context, so **D is the best answer.**

8. If it were possible to ________ a car body in a vat of human stomach acid, the acid would eat the car body, given enough time and assuming you could keep the vat from dissolving.

A vacillate
B vilify
C immerse
D ostracize
E refurbish

Answer: **C is the correct answer,** the only choice that makes sense in the sentence. You

Test Smarts

have a great clue in the second half of this sentence, which tells you that the car would dissolve *in* the acid. This would, of course, require the car to be *in* the acid. Thus, you would look for a word like *soak* to fill the blank, so *immerse,* which means "plunge into a liquid," is your best choice.

Two Blanks to Fill In

Some sentence-completion questions have two blanks. The trick is to find the choice that fits both blanks correctly—in the order given. **As a shortcut, determine the choices that fit *one* blank, whichever blank seems easier to you.** Cross out all the choices that don't fit. **Then, consider *only* the remaining choices when filling in the other blank.**

9. Researchers have determined that the ability to wiggle one's ears and curl one's tongue is ________, much to the disappointment of kids who have spent hours trying to ________ these skills.

A genetic, achieve

B complicated, procure

C unreliable, sustain

D inherited, flaunt

E acquired, relinquish

Answer: Before you look at the choices, make sense of the sentence. One clue lies in the word *disappointment,* which tells you that the kids are not successful in learning the skill. Another clue lies in the word *researchers,* which suggests that the blank word will be scientific. Since the kids couldn't learn the skills, the skills must be *inborn.*

Now, look at the choices. **You can immediately eliminate any first-blank choices that do not reflect the sentence's meaning**—in this case, eliminate any first-blank choices that do not mean "inborn." Strike out **E** (*acquired,* an antonym), **B** (*complicated*), and **C** (*unreliable*). Both **A** (*genetic*) and **D** (*inherited*) could fill the first blank.

Now, go on to the second blank, checking only the choices that fit the first blank—in this case, **A** and **D.** In this half of the sentence, you know you are looking for a verb that means "get; learn." **A** (*achieve*) is a possibility, but **D** (*flaunt*) doesn't work since it is not possible to flaunt what has not been acquired. Thus, **A is your best answer.**

10. Elephants, which are the largest animals walking the earth today, can ________ a number of human ________, including seasickness, colds, pneumonia, mumps, and diabetes.

A recollect, infirmities

B diagnose, junctures

C acquire, tendencies

D contract, maladies

E atrophy, ailments

Answer: You know that the second blank will mean "illnesses" because the second half of the sentence lists quite a few human illnesses. The first blank will therefore mean something akin to the word *catch.*

For this question it might be easier to begin with the second blank. Remember that you are looking for a word that means "illnesses," so you can quickly eliminate **B** and **C.** Choices **A** (*infirmities*), **D** (*maladies*), and **E** (*ailments*) all fit the second blank.

Your next step is to check the first blank for choices **A, D,** and **E,** the only choices that fit the second blank. Which of them has a first-blank choice that means "catch"? Only **choice D** (*contract*) fits the meaning you need. (Yes, *acquire* also means "catch," but you've already eliminated **C** because the second blank doesn't fit.) **D is the best answer.**

Finally, try out the sentence to make sure that both words in choice D make sense.

ANALOGY QUESTIONS require that you figure out the relationship between one pair of words and then select another pair with the same relationship. Analogies use many kinds of relationships, including **cause and effect, part and whole, performer and related object, performer and related action, person or object, quality, synonym, antonym, characteristic, degree.** (For more about analogies, see pages 596, 698, 791, 945, 1297.)

The more comprehensive your vocabulary, the better off you will be when you face an analogy question. If you are stumped, try breaking an unfamiliar word into its prefix, suffix, and root. In some tests the analogy questions get harder as you go, but don't give up. Everyone's vocabulary is different, and a word that seems difficult to others may be easy for you. Let's try one out:

11. TEACHER : STUDENTS : :

A actor : playwrights

B speaker : audience

C horse : corrals

D business owner : stocks

E enemy : airplanes

Begin by turning the first pair of words (the stem words) into a sentence that defines their relationship. Your sentence should begin with the first word in the pair and end with the second word; you fill in the middle. A sentence for item 11 might be *A teacher's job is to educate or inspire students.* Now, try each choice out within the same sentence: An actor's job is to educate or inspire playwrights? A speaker's job is to educate or inspire an audience? A horse's job is to educate or inspire corrals? (No way.) A business owner's job is to educate or inspire stocks? An enemy's job is to educate or inspire airplanes?

Answer: **B is the best answer** because it preserves the relationship and the kind of comparison being made. Both a teacher and a speaker are kinds of people. Students and audiences listen to them and—the teacher and the speaker hope—become educated or inspired as a result of what they hear. None of the other choices show the same relationship.

You may already have noticed that words in vocabulary questions are anything but commonplace. What's a student to do in the face of such *egregious, inordinate,* and *maliciously pedantic* word choices? Study them. Study them. Study them. The best way, though, to learn vocabulary words is to read. Read many different kinds of materials. Don't just skim over words you don't know: Look them up. Then, think about the meaning they add to the passage you are reading. If you follow those suggestions, you'll increase your vocabulary *exponentially,* and questions on vocabulary tests will be much less *formidable.*

In the analogy questions that follow, the first uses easy words only; the second throws in some challenging words.

12. SHEEP : FLOCK : :

A milk : water

B street : road

C car : truck

D trees : orchard

E telephone : receiver

Answer: To define the relationship in the stem words, you might make up this sentence: *Sheep are part of a group called a flock.* Then, try out that same sentence with all of the choices. You can eliminate **A, B,** and **C** because none of them make sense in your sentence. **D** makes sense: Trees are part of a group called an orchard. **E** might have made sense if the words were in reverse order (a receiver is part of a telephone)—but they're not. **So D is the correct answer.** The analogy is based on the relationship of a part to a whole.

13. LUMINOUS : GLOWING : :

A burnished : beautiful

B murky : dark

C weathered : new

D distraught : erroneous

E inane : sagacious

Answer: **The answer is B.** The relationship in this analogy is that of synonyms: *Luminous* means the same as *glowing.* You can eliminate choices **C** and **E** (the word pairs are antonyms, not synonyms) as well as **D,** in which the words seem totally unrelated. The words in **A** aren't synonyms either (*burnished* means "bright," not "beautiful"), so that leaves only **B,** whose words (*murky, dark*) are indeed synonyms.

Multiple-Choice Writing Questions

Multiple-choice writing questions are designed to test your knowledge of standard written English. Some questions ask you to spot errors in a sentence's grammar or punctuation. Some ask you to spot the best written form of a sentence. Some ask when a paragraph is (or isn't) properly developed. You will need to know the rules of punctuation and grammar. Here are some question formats you might encounter:

IDENTIFYING-SENTENCE-ERROR QUESTIONS ask you to look at underlined sections of a sentence and choose the section that includes an error. You are *not* expected to correct the error.

14. The average person knows (**A**) about 50,000 of the 150,000 words in a standard college dictionary, have learned (**B**) most of them (**C**) by high school, which means (**D**) 3,000 words per year or eight every day. No error. (**E**)

Answer: **The correct answer is B.** Replace the verb phrase *have learned* with the present participle *having learned.* The phrase *having learned most of them by high school* is a participial phrase that modifies *person.* Remember, however, that you are asked only to *find* the error, not to correct it or explain why it's wrong. By the way, have you picked up your eight words today?

IMPROVING-SENTENCES QUESTIONS ask you to correct an underlined section by choosing the best version offered. It is helpful to find the error before you look at the answer choices. Then, anticipate how it could best be corrected. The answers to questions like those are often confusing to read because they are long and very poorly written (remember that all but one of them are wrong). Take some time with such questions.

15. Over an average person's life span, his or her heart will pump about 50 million gallons, which equals enough to fill a million bathtubs or filling fifty 10-ft-deep swimming pools being as big as football fields.

A which equals enough to fill a million bathtubs or to fill fifty 10-foot-deep swimming pools as big as football fields.

B enough to fill a million bathtubs or fifty 10-foot-deep swimming pools as big as football fields.

C which means a million bathtubs or fifty 10-foot-deep swimming pools as big as football fields will be filled by it.

D enough to fill a million bathtubs with 10-foot-deep swimming pools being as big as football fields.

E which is a million bathtubs, 10-foot-deep swimming pools, and football fields.

Answer: **The best answer is B.** Your next-best choice, **A,** says the same thing but with less economy. **C** is awkward and unnecessarily switches verb tenses; **D** and **E** totally garble the information.

IMPROVING-THE-PARAGRAPH QUESTIONS present a paragraph followed by questions. You may be asked to pick a choice that combines or rewrites portions of sentences. You may be asked to decide which sentences could be added or removed from the paragraph. You may be asked which sentence could be used to strengthen the argument of the writer, or you may be asked to choose a thesis statement for the paragraph.

DIRECTIONS: Read the paragraph below. Then, find the best answer to the following questions.

(1) An initially beneficial chemical whose use had unintended consequences is DDT. (2) Beginning in 1939, this pesticide was used throughout the United States to exterminate disease-carrying and crop-eating insects. (3) This powerful chemical also helped India. (4) It helped India reduce cases of malaria from 75 million to fewer than five million. (5) In 1962, scientists began to realize that the chemical was passing through the food chain and harming some types of birds. (6) As a result of high concentrations of DDT in the birds' tissue, many species began laying thin-shelled eggs that cracked easily. (7) One result of widespread DDT spraying was the decline of some bird populations.

16. Which of the following choices represents the *best* way to combine sentences 3–4?

A This powerful chemical also helped India, it reduced cases of malaria from 75 million to fewer than five million.

B This powerful chemical also helped India by helping India to reduce cases of malaria from 75 million to fewer than five million.

C India also was helped by this powerful chemical, which had the effect of India's reducing cases of malaria from 75 million to fewer than five million.

D This powerful chemical also helped India to reduce cases of malaria from 75 million to fewer than five million.

E This powerful chemical also helped India: reduce cases of malaria from 75 million to fewer than five million.

Answer: You are looking for the sentence that contains all of the important information with the *least* amount of repetition. It takes careful reading to figure out that **the best answer is D,** which cuts the clutter and maintains the meaning. Answer **A** is a run-on sentence, so that's out. **B** is awkwardly repetitious; **C** makes the verb passive, increasing wordiness. The difference between choices **D** and **E** is slight—only a colon and the word *to.* That's enough to make **E** wrong (the rest of the sentence doesn't go with the colon) and **D** smooth, streamlined, and the only correct answer.

17. Which of the words below could *best* be inserted in sentence 5 immediately after "In 1962,"?

A also

B however

C but

D and

E because

Answer: **The best answer is B,** the only choice that makes sense in the context of the paragraph. Choice **B** (*however*) reflects the reversed direction of sentence 5, which clearly states that—unlike the information given in the preceding sentences—not everything about DDT was good.

Strategies for Taking Writing Tests

Writing a Response to Literature

When you are asked to respond to a literary passage on a writing test, the passage may be a short story, a novel excerpt, a poem, or a section of a play. No matter the type of passage, you'll need to understand not only its literal meaning, but also the deeper point the writer is making. Follow the steps below to write a response to a passage from a play. The sample responses provided are based on the prompt to the right. (The excerpt from *Macbeth* appears on page 331.)

Prompt

Macbeth follows the title character's murderous and deceitful ascent to the throne of Scotland. Macbeth gives the "Tomorrow, and tomorrow, and tomorrow" speech as his scheme begins to unravel. In an essay, explain the meaning of the speech and the deeper point you think Shakespeare is making in it.

THINKING IT THROUGH — Writing a Response to Literature

STEP 1 **Carefully read the prompt and the selection.** Be sure you can identify the task and the surface meaning of the passage.

I need to explain both what the passage means and the writer's deeper point. Macbeth is saying he thinks life is short and meaningless.

STEP 2 **Draw a conclusion about the deeper meaning of the piece, and gather support for that conclusion.** Base your conclusion on your own knowledge and on details that seem important in the selection.

It seems like Macbeth's life will be short and meaningless because of what he has done, but maybe other people's lives can be more than just one day after another if they do more important and better things than Macbeth did. Words like "petty," "fools," "poor," "idiot," and "nothing" seem to indicate how Macbeth feels about himself after realizing what he has done. In my own experience, life only seems like a series of tomorrows when you're not doing anything that matters.

STEP 3 **Develop a thesis statement for your essay based on your conclusion and your evidence.**

The "Tomorrow, and tomorrow, and tomorrow" speech from Macbeth explains how empty Macbeth's life has become, but it also points to another, better path.

STEP 4 **Write your response.** Explain how examples you use from the text relate to each other and to your thesis. Write with a serious, authoritative tone, and use precise language to explain the conclusion you have drawn. End your response by emphasizing your thesis in a memorable way. Proofread your finished response, and correct any errors in English-language conventions.

Writing a Response to Expository Text

Expository text provides information. A written **response to expository text** should demonstrate your understanding of the information provided and the organization of that information. To write a response to expository text for a test, use the steps below. The sample responses provided are based on the prompt to the right. ("Life in 999: A Grim Struggle" begins on page 40.)

Prompt

The article "Life in 999: A Grim Struggle" explains what life was like for most Europeans over 1,000 years ago. Using examples from the article, explain in an essay the main ways in which daily life then differed from life now.

THINKING IT THROUGH

Writing a Response to Expository Text

STEP 1 **Carefully read the prompt and the selection.** Make sure you understand what tasks the prompt calls for.

I need to pick out the main categories of differences between life in Europe in the year 999 and life now, and give examples of those differences.

STEP 2 **Decide on your general answer, and identify your main supporting points.** Skim the selection to identify the main points you will make to support your answer to the prompt.

The article explains what people ate, where people lived, physical problems people faced, and how time was marked.

STEP 3 **Develop a thesis statement for your essay.** Your thesis statement will sum up your main points and draw a conclusion about your topic.

Life in 999 was much different from life today, when we have better food and housing, fewer physical problems, and a clearer idea of how time passes.

STEP 4 **Gather support for your thesis.** Choose details and examples from the selection that will provide strong support, and elaborate on them.

I can compare the limited foods people ate with the selection in a typical mall food court, and I can compare the simple huts people lived in with modern housing that has electricity and running water. I can explain how much longer life expectancy is now and how crowded some cities are. Finally, I can compare the way people in 999 might not have known what month it was with all the devices people use now to identify the passage of time.

STEP 5 **Write your essay.** Begin with an attention-getter, such as a question or a surprising statement. Organize ideas clearly and logically, using transitions to show readers the links among those ideas. Then, find and correct any errors in English-language conventions in your draft.

Writing a Biographical Narrative

Writing a **biographical narrative** requires you to do more than simply retell an event from someone's life. Through vivid descriptions and explanations, you must make readers feel that they, too, witnessed the event. To give a biographical narrative meaning, share a significant conclusion about the person involved in the event. To write a biographical narrative in response to a test prompt, follow the steps below. The sample responses provided are based on the prompt to the right.

Prompt

While everyone makes mistakes, some people handle them better than others. In a narrative, relate how someone you witnessed handled making a mistake, including the consequences of the way the mistake was handled. Note what this tells you about the person and how witnessing this event affected you.

THINKING IT THROUGH

Writing a Biographical Narrative

STEP 1 **Carefully read the prompt, and choose a subject.**

I need to explain what someone I saw make a mistake did—how they handled the mistake and what the consequences were. I'll tell about when my government teacher said something negative about a political candidate during class.

STEP 2 **Identify the parts of the event you will relate.** Outline in sequence the smaller events that make up your chosen event.

A student mentioned who he planned to vote for in the upcoming election. Mrs. Jackson made a joke about the candidate that offended the student. Mrs. Jackson apologized and explained that she had strong opinions because she liked politics so much—that's why she became a government teacher—and she hoped we would also develop strong opinions, but express them more appropriately. Her apology started a great discussion.

STEP 3 **Identify important details about the people, events, and setting.** Details should be relevant and specific to bring the incident to life.

Mrs. Jackson's expressions and tone of voice are important, as are those of the student whose candidate she insulted.

STEP 4 **Draw a conclusion based on the details.** Decide why the incident is significant; this conclusion will be the basis for your narrative's thesis.

Mrs. Jackson showed what a good teacher she is by admitting her mistake and turning it into a thought-provoking lesson. I'll be careful now to back up my opinions rather than insulting someone else's position.

STEP 5 **Write your narrative.** Provide context for readers in your introduction. Make your point of view clear and consistent, and make sure every detail you include helps support your thesis or bring the event to life. Finally, correct any errors in grammar, usage, and mechanics.

Writing an Expository Composition

Expository compositions explain. You might write an expository composition to tell how to do something, define a topic, compare and contrast two things, or explain causes and effects. No matter the task, expository writing should anticipate readers' questions and clear up any potential misunderstandings or biases about the topic. Use the steps below to write an effective expository composition for a test.

Prompt

Consider an important, recent event in your community or in the larger world. In an essay, discuss what you think are the primary cause and the most important effect of the event. Support the cause and effect you identify with examples.

THINKING IT THROUGH

Writing an Expository Composition

STEP 1 Carefully read the prompt, and choose a topic you know well.

I need to explain the main cause and effect of an event. I'll pick the collapse that happened last month of the old two-lane bridge over Town Creek.

STEP 2 Identify the major parts of the topic.

The parts are one cause and one effect. There were lots of causes, including increased truck traffic and a recent flood, but the main cause is lack of funding for repairs. The main effect is increased traffic on the only other bridge over the creek.

STEP 3 Brainstorm background information and details about each part of the topic. Your essay will need to answer potential questions and clear up any misunderstandings or biases readers might have.

Voters opposed funding needed for repairs a few years ago because many thought that since the bridge had stood for so many years, the repairs were only cosmetic, not structural. Now those voters are paying the price with longer drives to cross the other bridge in heavy traffic while the old bridge is being rebuilt—at greater expense than the proposed repairs would have entailed.

STEP 4 Synthesize your ideas to plan a thesis. Draft a thesis sentence explaining the point made by all of your information about your topic.

The collapse of Old Town Creek Bridge was the result of an attempt to save money; now it is costing drivers both time and money as they are diverted to the only other bridge over the creek.

STEP 5 Write your essay. Don't just string together ideas in your draft. Instead, provide insight into your topic by thoroughly explaining your major points. Organize ideas in an easy-to-follow way, and connect them with transitional expressions to help guide readers. Finally, proofread and correct any errors in English-language conventions.

Writing a Persuasive Composition

In a **persuasive composition** written for a test, you must quickly identify a position and strong reasons and evidence that support that position. To make the most of your time, follow the steps below. The sample responses provided are based on the prompt to the right. Notice that in some cases it is faster and easier to develop a strong argument for a position that doesn't fit your views; your goal on a test is simply to write the best essay you can.

Prompt

Many states are considering enacting graduated driver's license laws, which limit such things as the time of day when teenagers may drive or the number of passengers they may carry. In an essay, explain whether you agree or disagree with such laws, and back up your position with evidence.

THINKING IT THROUGH

Writing a Persuasive Composition

STEP 1 **Carefully read the prompt, analyzing the situation and the task.**

The laws limit when teenagers can drive or how many people can ride with them. I have to decide based on evidence whether these laws are a good idea.

STEP 2 **Draft an opinion statement.** Choose the easiest position to defend.

Personally, I don't want my rights limited, but I think I can use stronger evidence if I pick the position in favor of graduated licenses. My opinion statement will be: Graduated license laws, while unpopular with teenagers, are a good idea.

STEP 3 **Identify reasons and evidence.** Use the acronym MATH (**M**oney, **A**ttitudes, **T**ime, **H**ealth/safety) to identify reasons and counterclaims.

Money: Graduated licenses will be more expensive to issue and enforce, but they might reduce expenses resulting from accidents caused by teen drivers.

Attitude: I have a friend who's a terrible driver but feels like he has the right to drive however he wants. These limits might change that attitude.

Time: Parents will waste time picking up teenagers from jobs if they have to work later than they're allowed to drive, but this is a minor problem.

Health/safety: Keeping teens from driving late at night or with a carload of friends might prevent a lot of accidents.

STEP 4 **Choose your two or three strongest reasons.** Use reasons and responses to readers' potential counterclaims that relate to the prompt.

I'll focus on the most important issues related to these laws—safety and money.

STEP 5 **Write your essay.** Write with a convincing, knowledgeable voice, and thoroughly explain your reasons and evidence. Organize your ideas in order of importance, finishing with your strongest reason to leave a lasting impression. Then, proofread your draft, and correct any errors in English-language conventions.

Writing an Analytical Composition

On a writing test, you may be asked to write an **analytical composition.** To do so, you must show insight in analyzing a statement, idea, or situation. Usually you will form a generalization and support it with evidence. Follow the steps below. The sample responses provided are based on the prompt to the right.

Prompt

Consider the following statement, and write an essay in which you analyze its meaning: "Novelty is too often mistaken for progress." Use examples from history or science as well as from your own experience to support your analysis.

THINKING IT THROUGH

Writing an Analytical Composition

STEP 1 Read the prompt, and identify your general response to it. Make sure you understand any quotations or important ideas in the prompt.

The statement means that people often see that something is different and automatically think it's better even though it may not be.

STEP 2 Identify two or three pieces of strong supporting evidence.

The Edsel was supposed to be an innovative car in the 1950s, but it turned out to have a lot of problems and was a failure.

Another example is the designated hitter rule in baseball. People thought having a designated hitter batting in place of the pitcher would make the game more exciting, but it wound up making the games longer and making pitchers less well-rounded players.

STEP 3 Synthesize your ideas to plan a thesis statement. Draft a sentence or two explaining how your examples support your analysis.

When progress takes the form of a stylish new car that runs poorly or a new sports rule that winds up hurting the game, it isn't progress at all, but only novelty.

STEP 4 Organize your support. Depending on your topic, consider using order of importance, comparison and contrast, cause and effect, chronological order, or a combination of orders.

First, I'll discuss the Edsel because its problems were so obvious. Then, I'll explain the less obvious problems with the designated hitter rule. That order can lead into a final statement about how people should consider not only obvious problems but also more subtle ones when they're deciding whether something is truly progress or only novelty.

STEP 5 Draft your essay. Clearly explain what you think quotations or important ideas in the prompt mean, and state your thesis. Connect your ideas with transitional expressions, and elaborate on those ideas with details. Conclude by restating your thesis, and close with a memorable comment. Finally, correct any errors in grammar, usage, and mechanics.

Handbook of Literary and Historical Terms

ALEXANDRINE A line of poetry made up of six iambs—that is, a line written in iambic hexameter. The following alexandrine is from Lord Byron's *Childe Harold's Pilgrimage* (Collection 5):

> Without a grave, unknelled, uncoffined, and
> unknown.

See page 796.

ALLEGORY A story in which the characters, settings, and events stand for abstract or moral concepts. Allegories thus have two meanings: a literal meaning and a symbolic meaning. Allegories were a popular literary form during the Middle Ages. The best-known English allegory is John Bunyan's *The Pilgrim's Progress* (Collection 3), which recounts the adventures of a character named Christian. The hero's journey to the Celestial City brings him up against many trials that symbolize the pitfalls facing the Christian traveling through this world toward the spiritual world.

See pages 378, 419, 950.

ALLITERATION The repetition of consonant sounds in words that are close to one another. Alliteration occurs most often at the beginning of words, as in "rough and ready." But consonants within words sometimes alliterate, as in "baby blue." The echoes that alliteration creates can increase a poem's rhythmic and musical effects and make its lines especially memorable. In this line from Shakespeare's Sonnet 30 (page 316), the *w* sounds emphasize the melancholy tone:

> And with old woes new wail my dear time's waste.

Alliteration is an essential feature of Anglo-Saxon poetry; in most lines, two or three of the four stressed syllables alliterate.

See pages 51, 316, 317, 758, 917, 1166, 1168.

"Basil, do you think the center is going to hold?"

ALLUSION A reference to a statement, person, place, event, or thing that is known from literature, history, religion, mythology, politics, sports, science, or popular culture. The concluding lines of Wilfred Owen's poem "Dulce et Decorum Est" (Collection 7) are *"Dulce et decorum est / Pro patria mori."* ("It is sweet and proper to die for one's country"). These lines allude to a line from an ode by the Latin poet Horace. The title of William Faulkner's *The Sound and the Fury* is an allusion to a line from Shakespeare's *Macbeth* (Collection 3). The cartoon above alludes to William Butler Yeats's poem "The Second Coming" (Collection 7).

See pages 415, 745, 1044.

ANALOGY A comparison of two things to show that they are alike in certain respects. Writers often make analogies to show how something unfamiliar is like something well-known or widely experienced. For example, people often draw an analogy between creating a work of art and giving birth to a child.

See pages 412, 596, 945, 1297.

ANECDOTE A brief and sometimes witty story that focuses on a single interesting incident or event, often in order to make a point or teach a moral lesson. Sometimes an anecdote reveals the character of a famous person. Taoists, Zen Buddhists, and Sufis, among others, use anecdotes to convey indirectly the teachings of their philosophies.

See pages 383, 393.

ANIMISM A belief that spirits or souls are present in all living things. This belief was at the heart of the ancient Celtic religion, and it can be found in many other ancient religions.

See page 7.

ANTAGONIST The character or force that opposes or blocks the protagonist, or main character, in a narrative. Usually the antagonist is human, like Sir Modred, the villainous rebel who destroys the Round Table in Sir Thomas Malory's *Le Morte d'Arthur* (Collection 2) or the schoolgirls who mercilessly taunt the Kelvey sisters in Katherine Mansfield's "The Doll's House" (Collection 7). Sometimes the antagonist is supernatural, like Satan, who opposes God in John Milton's *Paradise Lost* (Collection 3).

ANTICLIMAX See *Climax.*

ANTITHESIS A contrast of ideas expressed in a grammatically balanced statement. In the following line from Canto III of *The Rape of the Lock* (Collection 4), Alexander Pope balances noun against noun and verb against verb:

> And wretches hang that jurymen may dine.

See page 598.

APHORISM A concise, sometimes witty saying that expresses a principle, truth, or observation about life. Alexander Pope's poetry contains some of the most famous aphorisms in the English language, as in this example from *An Essay on Criticism* (Collection 4):

> To err is human, to forgive, divine.

APOSTROPHE A figure of speech in which a speaker directly addresses an absent or dead person, an abstract quality, or something nonhuman as if it were present and capable of responding. Apostrophe was a popular device with the Romantic poets: Wordsworth, for example, apostrophizes the river Wye in his "Tintern Abbey" (Collection 5). Among the second-generation Romantics, Shelley apostrophized the west wind; Byron apostrophized the ocean; and Keats apostrophized a nightingale and a Greek urn (all in Collection 5).

See pages 796, 810.

ARCHETYPE A pattern that appears in literature across cultures and is repeated through the ages. An archetype can be a character, a plot, an image, or a setting. All stories or myths that contain a quest, for example, share certain features, suggesting that each quest-story has been formed from a master pattern. Similarly, all epic heroes have a number of common characteristics, though each one also has culturally specific characteristics. Ignoring the culturally specific characteristics of a particular epic hero will allow you to perceive what the archetype of the epic hero is.

See pages 20, 55, 201, 206, 220, 223.

ASIDE Private words that a character in a play speaks to the audience or to another character and that are not supposed to be overheard by others onstage. Stage directions usually tell when a speech is an aside.

ASSONANCE The repetition of similar vowel sounds followed by different consonant sounds in words that are close together. Assonance differs from exact rhyme in that it does not repeat the consonant sound following the vowel. The words *face* and *base* rhyme, while the words *face* and *fade* are assonant. Like alliteration, assonance can create musical and rhythmic effects. In this line from Alfred, Lord Tennyson's "The Lady of Shalott" (Collection 6), the repetition of the short *a* sounds creates a rhythmic effect that mimics the action being described:

> An abbot on an ambling pad,

See pages 917, 1166, 1168.

ATMOSPHERE **The mood or feeling in a literary work.** Atmosphere is usually created through descriptive details and evocative language. For example, Ben Okri sets the mood of his short story "In the Shadow of War" (Collection 7) with a dreamlike description of the war-torn forest around Lagos, Nigeria.

See pages 815, 921.

AUGUSTAN **Similar to the reign of Emperor Augustus (63 B.C.–A.D. 14) or having qualities or tastes that are associated with classical Rome.** In English literary history the Augustan Age dates from the Restoration to the middle of the eighteenth century. Perhaps more than anyone else, Alexander Pope (Collection 4) exhibits Augustan literary tastes in his poetry.

See page 566.

AUTOBIOGRAPHY **A written account of the author's own life.** Unlike **diaries, journals,** and letters, autobiographies are unified narratives usually prepared for a public audience. And unlike **memoirs,** which often focus on famous events and people, autobiographies are usually quite introspective. George Orwell's "Shooting an Elephant" (Collection 7) is a well-known autobiographical essay.

See also *Memoir.*

BALLAD **A song or songlike poem that tells a story.** Most ballads have a regular pattern of **rhythm** and **rhyme,** and they use simple language with a great deal of repetition. Ballads generally have a **refrain**—lines or words that are repeated at regular intervals. They usually tell sensational stories of tragedy, adventure, betrayal, revenge, and jealousy. **Folk ballads** are composed by anonymous singers and are passed down orally from generation to generation before they are written down (often in several different versions). "Lord Randall" (Collection 2) is an example of a folk ballad. **Literary ballads,** on the other hand, are composed and written down by known poets, usually in the style of folk ballads. Samuel Taylor Coleridge's *The Rime of the Ancient Mariner* (Collection 5) is a famous literary ballad.

The typical ballad stanza is a quatrain with the rhyme scheme *abcb.* The first and third lines have four stressed syllables, and the second and fourth lines have three. The number of unstressed syllables in each line may vary, but often the meter is primarily **iambic.**

See pages 130, 133, 762.

BIOGRAPHY **An account of a person's life written by another person.** The *Life of Samuel Johnson* by James Boswell is one of the most famous biographies ever written.

BLANK VERSE **Poetry written in unrhymed iambic pentameter.** "Blank" means that the poetry is unrhymed. "Iambic pentameter" means that each line contains five iambs, or metrical feet, each consisting of an unstressed syllable followed by a stressed syllable (˘ ʹ). Blank verse is the most important metrical form used in English dramatic and epic poetry. It is the verse line used in Shakespeare's plays and John Milton's *Paradise Lost* (Collection 3). One of the reasons blank verse has been so popular, even among modern poets, is that it combines the naturalness of unrhymed verse with the structure of metrical verse. Except for **free verse,** it is the poetic form that sounds the most like natural speech. It also lends itself easily to slight variations within the basic pattern. Like most of the English Romantic poets, William Wordsworth made extensive use of blank verse, as in these lines from "Tintern Abbey" (Collection 5):

And now, with gleams of half-extinguished thought,
With many recognitions dim and faint,
And somewhat of a sad perplexity,
The picture of the mind revives again:

See pages 412, 456, 735, 748.

CADENCE **The natural rise and fall of the voice.** Poets who write in **free verse** try to imitate the natural cadences of spoken language.

See also *Rhythm.*

CAESURA **A pause or break within a line of poetry, usually indicated by the natural rhythm of the language.** A midline, or medial, caesura is a characteristic of Anglo-Saxon poetry; it divides the four-beat line in half. Later poets use the caesura less predictably, as in the following lines from Wilfred Owen's "Dulce et Decorum Est" (Collection 7). Here, the caesuras are indicated by the symbol ||.

Bent double, || like old beggars under sacks,
Knock-kneed, || coughing like hags, || we cursed
through sludge

See page 51.

CANTO A subdivision in a long poem, corresponding to a chapter in a book. Poems divided into cantos include Pope's *The Rape of the Lock* (Collection 4) and Byron's *Childe Harold's Pilgrimage* (Collection 5). Not all major subdivisions of long poems are called cantos: Milton's *Paradise Lost* (Collection 3) is divided into books, and Coleridge's *The Rime of the Ancient Mariner* (Collection 5) into parts.

The word *canto* comes from a Latin word for "song" and originally designated a section of a narrative poem that a minstrel could sing in one session.

See page 605.

CAPITALISM An economic philosophy that advocates the idea that the means of production and distribution should be owned and controlled by private individuals. Adam Smith, an eighteenth-century economist, is one of the great theorists of capitalism, a system which helped to foster the conditions that produced the Industrial Revolution in England and the technological advances of the nineteenth and twentieth centuries.

See also *Laissez Faire.*

***CARPE DIEM* A Latin phrase that literally means "seize the day"—that is, "make the most of present opportunities."** The *carpe diem* theme is common in seventeenth-century English poetry, as in this famous line from Robert Herrick's "To the Virgins, to Make Much of Time": "Gather ye rosebuds while ye may." The theme is also forcefully expressed in Andrew Marvell's "To His Coy Mistress" (both in Collection 3).

See page 299.

CHARACTER An individual in a story or play. A character always has human traits, even if the character is an animal, like the heron and the crab in "Right-Mind and Wrong-Mind" (Collection 2) or the ravens in "The Twa Corbies" (Collection 2); or a god, as in the *Iliad* (Collection 1); or a monster, as in *Beowulf* (Collection 1). A character may also be a human with superhuman powers, like Gilgamesh (Collection 1). But most characters are ordinary human beings, like Geoffrey Chaucer's colorful pilgrims in *The Canterbury Tales* (Collection 2) and the boy in James Joyce's "Araby" (Collection 7).

The process by which the writer reveals the personality of a character is called **characterization.** A writer can reveal a character in the following ways:

1. by telling us directly what the character is like: humble, ambitious, vain, easily manipulated, and so on
2. by describing how the character looks and dresses
3. by letting us hear the character speak
4. by revealing the character's private thoughts and feelings
5. by revealing the character's effect on other people—showing how other characters feel or behave toward the character
6. by showing the character's actions

The first method of revealing a character is called **direct characterization.** When a writer uses this method, we do not have to figure out what a character's personality is like—the writer tells us directly. The other five methods of revealing a character are known as **indirect characterization.** When a writer uses these methods, we have to exercise our own judgment, putting clues together to figure out what a character is like—just as we do in real life when we are getting to know someone.

Characters can be classified as static or dynamic. A **static character** is one who does not change much in the course of a story. A **dynamic character,** on the other hand, changes in some important way as a result of the story's action. Characters can also be classified as flat or round. **Flat characters** have only one or two personality traits. They are one-dimensional—they can be summed up by a single phrase. In contrast, **round characters** have more dimensions to their personalities—they are complex, solid, and multifaceted, like real people.

See pages 140, 166, 177, 327.

CHIVALRY The system of ideals and social codes governing the behavior of knights and gentlewomen in feudal times. The ideal knight was meant to be brave, honorable, and courteous; gentlewomen were meant to be chaste. The code of chivalry is reflected in medieval romance literature, particularly in Malory's *Le Morte d'Arthur* (Collection 2).

See page 122.

CLASSICISM A movement in art, literature, and music that advocates imitating the principles manifested in the art and literature of ancient ("classical") Greece and Rome. Classicism emphasizes reason, clarity, balance, harmony, restraint, order, and universal themes. Classicism is often placed in direct opposition to **Romanticism,** with its emphasis on unrestrained emotions and personal themes. However, this opposition should be approached with caution, as it is sometimes exaggerated for effect. Classicism was particularly admired in art in the eighteenth century and is exemplified in Alexander Pope's mock heroic epic, *The Rape of the Lock* (Collection 4).

See page 566.
See also *Neoclassicism, Romanticism.*

CLICHÉ An expression that was fresh and apt when it was first coined but is now so overused that it has become hackneyed and stale. "Busy as a bee" and "fresh as a daisy" are two examples. Clichés are often likened to dead metaphors—figures of speech ("leg of a chair," "mouth of a river") whose power to surprise has now been completely lost.

CLIMAX The point of greatest emotional intensity or suspense in a plot when the outcome of the conflict becomes known. In Shakespeare's plays, the climax usually occurs in the last act, just before the final scene. Following the climax, the story is **resolved,** or closed.

Some critics talk of more than one climactic moment in a long work (though usually the greatest climax occurs near the end of the plot). In drama, one such climactic moment is called the **turning point,** or **crisis.** At the turning point, something happens that seals the fate of the hero. In Shakespeare's plays, this moment usually occurs in the third act. At the turning point the hero's fortunes begin to decline or improve. All the action leading up to this turning point is **rising action,** and all the action following it is **falling action.** The turning point in Guy de Maupassant's "The Jewels" (Collection 6) occurs when Madame Lantin dies, leaving her husband alone and ravaged by grief. From that point onward, it is downhill for Monsieur Lantin—everything goes wrong, culminating in the story's climax, when Lantin, attempting to sell his wife's necklace, discovers that she has been deceptive. The sale of the jewels brings about the ironic resolution of the story: Lantin becomes wealthy and remarries, choosing a wife who is virtuous but makes him very unhappy.

In contrast, when something trivial or comical occurs at the point in a narrative when one expects something important or serious, the accompanying deflation is called an **anticlimax.** James Joyce's "Araby" (Collection 7) contains such an anticlimactic moment.

See also *Plot.*

COMEDY In general, a story that ends happily. The hero of a comedy is usually an ordinary character who overcomes a series of obstacles that block what he or she wants. Often a comedy pits two young people who wish to marry against parental blocking figures who want to prevent the marriage. The wedding that concludes these comedies suggests the formation of a new society and a renewal of life. Comedy is distinct from **tragedy,** in which a great person comes to an unhappy or disastrous end, usually through some lapse in judgment or character flaw. Comedies are often, but not always, intended to make us laugh. Two famous comedies are Oscar Wilde's play *The Importance of Being Earnest* and George Bernard Shaw's *Pygmalion.* Even though it contains some of the darker elements of tragedy, Shakespeare's *The Tempest* (Collection 3) is considered a comedy because harmony and reconciliation are achieved by the end of the play.

See also *Farce, Tragedy.*

COMMUNISM A philosophy that advocates the creation of a classless and stateless society in which economic goods are distributed equally. The most famous communist government is, of course, the now dissolved Soviet Union, a country which one could say perverted the ideals of communism, since it had a ruling class which was better off than the working class. Human nature seems to prevent people from bringing into being a perfect communist society. George Orwell's novel *Animal Farm* satirizes the ideals of communism, showing the ruination of a farm which has been taken over by radical animal reformers. Ha Jin's "Saboteur" (Collection 7) is set in communist China and focuses on issues of human rights under totalitarian regimes.

See page 1028.

CONCEIT A fanciful and elaborate figure of speech that makes a surprising connection between two seemingly dissimilar things. A conceit may be a brief metaphor, or it may form the framework of an entire poem. Two particularly important types of conceits are the **Petrarchan conceit** and the **metaphysical conceit.**

Petrarchan conceits get their name from the fourteenth-century Italian poet Petrarch, who developed their use in his influential sonnet sequence. Poets influenced by Petrarch used these conceits to describe the beauty of the lady for whom they wrote. She invariably had hair of gold, lips of cherry red, and teeth of oriental pearl. In Sonnet 130 (Collection 3), Shakespeare ridicules the use of such conceits. Petrarchan conceits were also used to describe a paradoxical state.

The metaphysical conceit is so called because it was widely used by the seventeenth-century metaphysical poets. This type of conceit is especially startling, complex, and ingenious. A famous example is John Donne's comparison of separated lovers to the legs of a compass in "A Valediction: Forbidding Mourning" (Collection 3).

See page 340.

CONFLICT **A struggle or clash between opposing characters, forces, or emotions.** In an **external conflict,** a character struggles against some outside force: another character, society as a whole, or some natural force. An **internal conflict,** on the other hand, is a struggle between opposing needs, desires, or emotions within a single character. Many works, especially longer ones, contain both internal and external conflicts. For example, in Ha Jin's "Saboteur" (Collection 7), Mr. Chiu undergoes an internal conflict between his desire to stick to his principles and his desire to be released from jail. In Doris Lessing's "No Witchcraft for Sale" (Collection 7), the conflict between Gideon and the scientist reflects larger cultural conflicts.

See page 931.
See also *Plot.*

CONNOTATIONS **All the meanings, associations, or emotions that have come to be attached to a word.** For example, an expensive restaurant might prefer to advertise its "delicious cuisine" rather than its "delicious cooking." *Cuisine* and *cooking* have the same literal meaning—"prepared food." But *cuisine* has connotations of elegance and sophistication, while *cooking* does not. The same restaurant would certainly not describe its food as "great grub."

Notice the difference between the following pairs of words: *young/immature, ambitious/cutthroat, uninhibited/shameless, lenient/lax.* We might describe ourselves using the first words but someone else using the second ones. The English philosopher Bertrand Russell once gave a classic example of the different connotations of words: "I am firm. You are obstinate. He is a pigheaded fool."

See page 595.
See also *Denotation.*

CONSONANCE **The repetition of final consonant sounds after different vowel sounds.** The words *east* and *west, dig* and *dog, turn* and *torn,* and Shakespeare's famous *"struts* and *frets"* (from *Macbeth,* in Collection 3) are examples of consonance. The term is also sometimes used to refer to repeated consonant sounds in the middle of words, as in *solemn stillness.* (Consonance, when loosely defined, can be a form of **alliteration.** Strictly speaking, however, alliteration is the repetition of initial consonant sounds.) Like **assonance,** consonance is one form of **approximate rhyme.**

See also *Alliteration, Assonance.*

COUPLET **Two consecutive lines of poetry that rhyme.** The couplet has been widely used since the Middle Ages, especially to provide a sense of closure. A couplet that presents a completed thought is called a closed couplet. Shakespeare used closed couplets to end his sonnets, as in this example from Sonnet 29 (Collection 3):

> For thy sweet love remembered such wealth
>   brings
> That then I scorn to change my state with kings.

A couplet written in **iambic pentameter** is called a **heroic couplet.** Although the heroic couplet has been used in English literature since Chaucer, it was perfected during the eighteenth century. Here is an example from Pope's *An Essay on Man* (Collection 4):

> ˘ ´ ˘ ´ ˘ ´ ˘ ´ ˘ ´
> Alike in ignorance, his reason such,
> ˘ ´ ˘ ´ ˘ ´ ˘ ´ ˘ ´
> Whether he thinks too little, or too much:

See pages 189, 314, 598, 926.

COURTLY LOVE A conventional medieval code of behavior that informed a knight of the proper way to treat his lady. The code was first developed by the troubadours (lyric poets) of southern France and extensively employed in European literature from the twelfth century throughout the medieval period.

See page 122.

DEISM The belief that God, after creating the universe, ceased to interfere with the laws of nature and society. Influenced by Newton's description of the universe as a great clock that was set in motion by the Creator, the deists of the mid-eighteenth century argued that people could only gain an understanding of the laws of nature and society by using their reason.

See page 568.

DENOTATION The literal, dictionary definition of a word. For example, a denotation, or dictionary definition, of the word *star* (as in "movie star") is an "eminent actor or actress," but the **connotation** is that of an actor or actress who is adored by fans and who leads a fascinating and glamorous life.

See also *Connotation.*

DENOUEMENT See *Plot.*

DEUS EX MACHINA **Any artificial or contrived device used at the end of a plot to resolve or untangle the complications.** The term is Latin and means "god from a machine." The phrase refers to a device used in ancient Greek and Roman drama: At the conclusion of the play, a god would be lowered onto the stage by a mechanical device so that he could save the hero and end the story happily. The term now refers to any device that resolves a plot in a forced or implausible way: An orphan finds that he has inherited a fortune just as he is being packed off to the poorhouse; a hero is saved because the villain has forgotten to load his gun. Oscar Wilde's *The Importance of Being Earnest* and Charles Dickens's *Oliver Twist* both contain examples of *deus ex machina.*

DIALECT A way of speaking that is characteristic of a particular region or group of people. A dialect may have a distinct vocabulary, pronunciation system, and grammar. In the Middle Ages, when Latin was the "literary" language of Europe, writers such as Geoffrey Chaucer (Collection 2) began writing for middle-class audiences in their own regional languages, or what are now interchangeably called **dialects** or **vernaculars.** Today one dialect usually becomes accepted as the standard for a country or culture. In the United States, the dialect used in formal writing and spoken by most TV and radio announcers is known as standard English.

Writers often use other dialects, however, to establish character or to create local color. For example, V. S. Naipaul (Collection 7) has used the dialect spoken by Trinidad's Asian Indian population in many of his works. The East London cockney dialect, and the lower-class background it betrays, are at the very heart of George Bernard Shaw's famous play *Pygmalion.* In this excerpt from the play, Henry Higgins, with his friend Colonel Pickering in attendance, begins to instruct the flower girl Eliza Doolittle in how to speak "proper" English:

Higgins. Say your alphabet.
Liza. I know my alphabet. Do you think I know nothing? I dont need to be taught like a child.
Higgins. *(thundering).* Say your alphabet.
Pickering. Say it, Miss Doolittle. You will understand presently. Do what he tells you; and let him teach you in his own way.
Liza. Oh well, if you put it like that—Ahyee, bəyee, cəyee, dəyee—
Higgins. *(with the roar of a wounded lion).* Stop. Listen to this, Pickering. . . . *(To Eliza)* Say A, B, C, D.
Liza. *(almost in tears).* But I'm saying it. Ahyee, Bəe, Cə-ee—

DIALOGUE Conversation between two or more people. Writers use dialogue to advance the action of a plot, to present an interplay of ideas and personalities, and to reveal the background, occupation, or social level of the characters through **tone** and **dialect.**

DICTION A writer's or speaker's choice of words. Speakers and writers use different types of words depending on the audience they're addressing, the subject they're discussing, and the effect they're trying to produce. For example, slang that would be suitable in a casual conversation with a friend ("He's a total nerd") would be unsuitable in a political debate. Similarly, the language that a nutritionist would use to describe a meal would be different from the language that a restaurant reviewer or a novelist would use.

Diction is an essential element of a writer's **style.** A writer's diction can be simple or flowery *(shop/boutique),* modern or old-fashioned *(pharmacy/apothecary),* general or specific *(sandwich/grilled cheese on rye).* Notice that the **connotations** of words (rather than their strict, literal meanings, or **denotations**) are an important aspect of diction.

See pages 401, 1264.

DIDACTIC LITERATURE Literary works that are meant to instruct, give advice, or convey a philosophy or moral message. Much didactic literature derives from religious teaching, as is the case with "The Parable of The Prodigal Son" (Collection 3) and the Taoist anecdotes (Collection 3). Secular works such as fables, folk tales and maxims are also didactic in intent.

See pages 382, 385, 387.
See also *Fable, Parable.*

DISSONANCE (dis′ə·nəns) **A harsh, discordant combination of sounds.** The opposite of **euphony** (yo͞o′fə·nē), a pleasant, harmonious combination of sounds, dissonance is usually created by the repetition of harsh consonant sounds. Dissonance is often used in poetry to communicate energy. Dissonance is also called **cacophony** (kə·käf′ə·nē).

DRAMATIC MONOLOGUE A poem in which a character addresses one or more listeners who remain silent or whose replies are not revealed. The occasion is usually a critical one in the speaker's life. Tennyson's "Ulysses" and Browning's "My Last Duchess" (both in Collection 6) are famous dramatic monologues.

See page 908.

DRAMATIC SONG A poem found in a play that serves to establish mood, reveal character, or advance action. The songs in Shakespeare's plays are the best songs of this kind (Collection 3). Employing a variety of techniques and forms and relying heavily on **onomatopoeia,** Shakespeare wrote songs that can be read alone, but which are best understood within the context of the plays in which they appear.

See page 322.

ELEGY A poem that mourns the death of a person or laments something lost. Elegies may lament the passing of life and beauty, or they may be meditations on the nature of death. A type of **lyric,** an elegy is usually formal in language and structure and solemn or even melancholy in tone. Much of English poetry is elegiac, from the Anglo-Saxon lyric "The Seafarer" (Collection 1) to A. E. Housman's "To an Athlete Dying Young" (Collection 6) and Dylan Thomas's "Do Not Go Gentle into That Good Night" (Collection 7).

See pages 324, 1274.

END-STOPPED LINE A line of poetry in which the meter and the meaning conclude with the end of the line. Often the end-of-line pause is marked with punctuation, though it need not be. These lines from Alexander Pope's *An Essay on Man* (Collection 4) are end-stopped:

> Know then thyself, presume not God to scan;
> The proper study of mankind is man.

See also *Run-on line.*

ENLIGHTENMENT or THE AGE OF REASON One of the names historians have applied to the eighteenth century. The period has been called the Enlightenment and the Age of Reason because at that time, people began to rely on reason and experience, rather than superstition and church authority, to gain an understanding of the world.

See page 566.

EPIC A long narrative poem that relates the great deeds of a larger-than-life hero who embodies the values of a particular society. Most epics include elements of myth, legend, folklore, and history. Their tone is serious and their language grand. Most **epic heroes** undertake quests to achieve something of tremendous value to themselves or their society. Homer's *Odyssey* and *Iliad* (Collection 1) and Virgil's *Aeneid* are the best-known epics in the Western tradition. The two most important English epics are the Anglo-Saxon poem *Beowulf* (Collection 1) and John Milton's *Paradise Lost* (Collection 3).

Many epics share standard characteristics and formulas known as **epic conventions,** which the oral poets drew upon to help them recall the stories they were recounting and which the writers of literary epics draw upon to establish the epic quality of their poems. The conventions include: an **invocation,** or formal plea for aid, to a deity or some other spiritual power; action that begins ***in medias res*** (literally "in the middle of things") and then **flashes back** to events that take place before the narrative's current time setting; **epic similes,** or elaborately extended comparisons relating heroic events to simple, everyday events; a consistently predictable **metrical structure;** and **stock epithets,** or descriptive adjectives or phrases used repeatedly with—or in place of—a noun or proper name.

See pages 20, 54, 81.
See also *Literary Epic.*

EPIGRAM A brief, clever, and usually memorable statement. Alexander Pope's writings are **epigrammatic** in style. Here is an example from his *Essay on Criticism:*

> We think our fathers fools, so wise we grow,
> Our wiser sons, no doubt, will think us so.

See pages 194, 199, 354, 602.
See also *Maxim, Proverb.*

EPIPHANY In a literary work, a moment of sudden insight or revelation that a character experiences. The word comes from the Greek and can be translated as "manifestation" or "showing forth." The term has religious meanings that have been transferred to literature by modern writers. James Joyce first gave the word its literary meaning in an early draft of *A Portrait of the Artist as a Young Man.* In Joyce's story "Araby" (Collection 7), the narrator experiences an epiphany at the end of the story when he recognizes the cheap vulgarity of the bazaar and the emptiness of his dream.

See page 1174.

EPITAPH An inscription on a tombstone or a commemorative poem written about a person who has died. Epitaphs range from the solemn to the farcical. Ben Jonson's "On My First Son" (Collection 3) contains a famously poignant epitaph.

See page 355.

EPITHET An adjective or other descriptive phrase that is regularly used to characterize a person, place, or thing. Phrases such as "Peter the Great," "Richard the Lion-Hearted," and "America the Beautiful" are epithets. Homer created so many descriptive epithets in his *Iliad* (Collection 1) and *Odyssey* that his name has been permanently associated with a type of epithet. The **Homeric epithet** consists of a compound adjective that is regularly used to modify a particular noun. Famous examples are "the wine-dark sea," "the gray-eyed goddess Athena," and the "rosy-fingered dawn."

See also *Kenning.*

ESSAY A short piece of nonfiction prose that examines a single subject from a limited point of view. There are two major types of essays. **Informal essays** (also called **personal essays**) generally reveal a great deal about the personalities and feelings of their authors. They tend to be loosely structured, conversational, sometimes even humorous, in tone; and usually highly subjective. **Formal essays** (also called **traditional essays**) are usually serious and impersonal in tone. Because they are written to inform or persuade, they are expected to be factual, logical, and tightly organized.

In the European literary tradition the essay began in France with Michel de Montaigne, who sought to test his own judgment by analyzing it in a series of short prose pieces, which he called *essais,* a common sixteenth-century spelling of the French word *assay,* which means "trial" or "attempt." Sir Francis Bacon, who published his *Essays* (see "Of Studies" Collection 3) in the late sixteenth and early seventeenth century, brought the form into England and pioneered what we now call the formal essay. Notable twentieth-century English essayists include Virginia Woolf and George Orwell (both in Collection 7).

See page 1105.

EXAGGERATION See *Hyperbole.*

FABLE A very brief story in prose or verse that teaches a moral, or a practical lesson about life. The characters in most fables are animals that behave and speak like humans. Some of the most popular fables are those attributed to Aesop, who was supposed to have been a slave in ancient Greece. Several of the pilgrims' tales in Geoffrey Chaucer's *The Canterbury Tales* (Collection 2) also contain fables. Other popular and widely influential fables include those collected in the Panchatantra, like "Right-Mind and Wrong-Mind" (Collection 2).

See page 194.
See also *Parable.*

FALLING ACTION See *Climax.*

FARCE A type of comedy in which ridiculous and often stereotyped characters are involved in far-fetched, silly situations. The humor in farce is based on crude physical action, slapstick, and clowning. Characters may slip on banana peels, get pies thrown in their faces, and knock one another on the head with ladders. The movies featuring Abbott and Costello, Laurel and Hardy, and the Marx brothers are all examples of farces.

The word *farce* comes from a Latin word for "stuffing," and in fact farces were originally used to fill in the waiting time between the acts of a serious play. Even in tragedies, farcical elements are often included to provide **comic relief,** or a break from the pervading tension. Shakespeare frequently lets his "common" characters engage in farcical actions.

FASCISM A nationalistic philosophy that advocates rule by a single charismatic dictator. Fascism properly speaking refers to the philosophy of Benito Mussolini's political party, which was founded in 1919 to oppose communism in Italy. The word, however, was soon used to describe the philosophies of similar repressive, nationalistic political parties in other countries. The German Nazis were fascists. The regimes of Francisco Franco in Spain and Juan Peron in Argentina were fascistic.

See page 1028.

FEUDALISM The economic, political, and social system of medieval Europe. This system was basically composed of three classes: the feudal lords, who were powerful landowners; vassals, who did work or military service for the feudal lords in exchange for land; and serfs, who were servants to the lords and vassals and who were bound to their masters' land.

See pages 115, 119.

FIGURE OF SPEECH A word or phrase that describes one thing in terms of another, dissimilar thing, and is not meant to be understood on a literal level. Some 250 different types of figures of speech have been identified, but the most common are the **simile** ("My love is like a red, red rose"), the **metaphor** ("The Lord is my shepherd"), and **personification** ("Death, be not proud"). These involve a comparison between unlike things, but not all figures of speech involve comparison. When one refers to the king using the word *crown,* one is not comparing the crown to the king, but associating the crown with the king.

See page 1039.
See also *Hyperbole, Metaphor, Metonymy, Oxymoron, Personification, Simile, Symbol.*

FLASHBACK A scene in a movie, play, short story, novel, or narrative poem that interrupts the present action of the plot to "flash backward" and tell what happened at an earlier time. "The Demon Lover" by Elizabeth Bowen (Collection 7) includes a flashback that describes Mrs. Drover's farewell to her fiancé twenty-five years before the main action of the story takes place.

See page 1206.

FOIL A character who sets off another character by strong contrast. This contrast emphasizes the differences between two characters, bringing out the distinctive qualities in each. In the *Epic of Gilgamesh* (Collection 1), Enkidu is a foil to Gilgamesh.

See page 57.

FORESHADOWING The use of clues to hint at what is going to happen later in the plot. Foreshadowing arouses the reader's curiosity and builds up **suspense.** Foreshadowing occurs in Elizabeth Bowen's "The Demon Lover" (Collection 7) when Mrs. Drover imagines "spectral glitters in the place of" her fiancé's eyes, and when we learn that she made an "unnatural promise" to him—that she "could not have plighted a more sinister troth."

See page 1241.
See also *Suspense.*

FRAME STORY An introductory narrative within which one or more of the characters proceed to tell individual stories. Perhaps the best-known example of stories contained in a frame story is the Persian collection called *The Thousand and One Nights* (Collection 2). In English literature, Geoffrey

Chaucer's *The Canterbury Tales* (Collection 2) uses a frame story involving a group of people on a pilgrimage; within the narrative frame, each of the pilgrims then tells his or her own story. Giovanni Boccaccio's *Decameron* (Collection 2) contains another notable example of the frame-story device.

See pages 137, 140, 191, 194, 208.

FREE VERSE **Poetry that has no regular meter or rhyme scheme.** Free verse usually relies on the natural **rhythms** of ordinary speech. Poets writing in free verse may use **alliteration, internal rhyme, onomatopoeia,** and other musical devices to achieve their effects. They may also place great emphasis on **imagery.** Matthew Arnold's "Dover Beach" (Collection 6) is an early example of free verse, and T. S. Eliot's poems, including "The Hollow Men" (Collection 7), are especially fine and famous examples.

GOTHIC **A term used to describe literary works that contain primitive, medieval, wild, mysterious, or natural elements.** Such elements were frowned upon by eighteenth-century neoclassicists but hailed by the Romantic writers of the following era. The **Gothic novel,** a genre popular in the late eighteenth and early nineteenth centuries, is chiefly characterized by gloomy settings and an atmosphere of terror and mystery. Mary Wollstonecraft Shelley's *Frankenstein* is one of the most widely known Gothic novels.

See page 714.

HAIKU **A brief, unrhymed, three-line poem developed in Japan in the 1600s.** The first and third lines of a traditional haiku have five syllables each, and the middle line has seven. Haiku generally juxtapose familiar images and present them in a compressed form, forcing the reader to make an imaginative leap to understand the connection between them.

See page 749.

HUMANISM **An intellectual movement of the Renaissance that restored the study of the classics and focused on examining human life here and now.** Though humanists were still interested in theology and religious questions, the focus of their interest expanded to include earthly matters as well. Famous humanists include Sir Thomas More and Erasmus.

See page 278.

HYPERBOLE **A figure of speech that uses exaggeration to express strong emotion or create a comic effect.** While hyperbole (also known as **overstatement**) does not express the *literal* truth, it is often used in the service of truth to capture a sense of intensity or to emphasize the essential nature of something. For instance, if you claim that it was 250 degrees in the shade, you are using hyperbole to express the truth that it was miserably hot.

See pages 307, 337.

IAMBIC PENTAMETER **A line of poetry made up of five iambs.** An **iamb** is a metrical foot, or unit of measure, consisting of an unstressed syllable followed by a stressed syllable (˘ ′). The word *suggest,* for example, is made up of one iamb. *Pentameter* derives from the Greek words *penta* (five) and *meter* (measure). Here are two lines from John Keats's "Ode to a Nightingale" (Collection 5) that are written in iambic pentameter:

> Forlorn! the very word is like a bell
> To toll me back from thee to my sole self!

Iambic pentameter is by far the most common verse line in English poetry. Shakespeare's sonnets and plays, for example, are written primarily in this meter. Many modern poets, such as W. H. Auden (Collection 7), have continued to use iambic pentameter. Other than **free verse,** it is the poetic meter that sounds the most like natural speech.

See page 314.
See also *Blank Verse.*

IMAGERY **Language that appeals to the senses.** Most images are visual—that is, they appeal to the sense of sight. But imagery can also appeal to the senses of hearing, touch, taste, or smell. While imagery is an element in all types of writing, it is especially important in poetry.

See pages 42, 166, 751, 820, 835, 1289.

INCREMENTAL REPETITION **A device widely used in ballads whereby a line or lines are repeated with slight variations from stanza to**

stanza. Each repetition advances the plot of the narrative. Incremental repetition is used in the folk ballad "Lord Randall" (Collection 2).

See page 133.

INDUSTRIAL REVOLUTION The period of social and economic change following the replacement of hand tools by machines and power tools, which allowed manufacturers to increase their production and save money. The perfection of the steam engine in the last half of the eighteenth century signaled the arrival of the age of the machine. The Industrial Revolution began on a small scale among textile manufacturers in the middle of the eighteenth century, but soon spread rapidly. Most textile products were produced by steam-engine-powered machines by the early nineteenth century. As the nineteenth century progressed, other industries began to use steam engines to produce their goods. George Eliot used the Industrial Revolution as the backdrop for *Silas Marner* (1861), and Charles Dickens satirizes its social effects in *Hard Times* (1854).

See page 711.

IN MEDIAS RES **The technique of starting a story in the middle and then using a flashback to tell what happened earlier.** *In medias res* is Latin for "in the middle of things." Epics traditionally begin *in medias res.* For example, John Milton's *Paradise Lost* (Collection 3) opens with Satan and his cohorts in Hell, after the war in Heaven and their fall, events that are recounted later in a flashback.

See page 81.

IRONY A contrast or discrepancy between expectation and reality—between what is said and what is really meant, between what is expected and what really happens, or between what appears to be true and what really is true.

Verbal irony occurs when a writer or speaker says one thing but really means something quite different—often the opposite of what he or she has said. If you tell your friend that you "just love being kept waiting in the rain," you are using verbal irony. A classic example of verbal irony is Jonathan Swift's suggestion in *A Modest Proposal* (Collection 4) that the Irish solve their poverty and overpopulation problems by selling their babies as food to their English landlords.

Situational irony occurs when what actually happens is the opposite of what is expected or appropriate. In James Joyce's story "Araby" (Collection 7), the boy hears about a bazaar called Araby and imagines that it will be a splendid, exotic place. Yet when he arrives, he finds that in reality the Araby bazaar is cheap and commonplace.

Dramatic irony occurs when the audience or the reader knows something important that a character in a play or story does not know. Dramatic irony occurs at the end of Elizabeth Bowen's "The Demon Lover" (Collection 7), when Mrs. Drover is riding in the taxi. The reader suspects that the taxi driver is the demon lover even though Mrs. Drover does not. Dramatic irony is a powerful device in William Blake's "The Chimney Sweeper" from *Songs of Innocence* (Collection 5). The speaker is a child who believes what he has been told—that "if all do their duty they need not fear harm." But the reader, who is not so innocent, realizes that this is not so.

See pages 167, 208, 580, 802, 1116, 1148, 1184, 1282, 1308.

KENNING In Anglo-Saxon poetry, a metaphorical phrase or compound word used to name a person, place, thing, or event indirectly. *Beowulf* (Collection 1) includes the kennings "whale-road" for the sea and "shepherd of evil" for Grendel.

See page 52.
See also *Epithet.*

LAISSEZ FAIRE (les′ā fer′) **An economic policy based on the idea that economic forces should be allowed to operate freely and without government regulation.**

See page 712.

LITERARY EPIC Literary epics are epics that have been composed by individual writers, often following earlier models. Unlike an **oral epic** or a **primary epic,** which is performed by generations of anonymous storytellers and modified slightly with each retelling, a literary epic is the product of a single imagination working within the epic tradition.

See page 399.
See also *Epic.*

LYRIC POETRY Poetry that focuses on expressing emotions or thoughts, rather than on telling a story. Most lyrics are short, and they usually imply rather than directly state a single strong emotion. The term *lyric* comes from the Greek. In ancient Greece, lyric poems were recited to the accompaniment of a stringed instrument called the lyre. Today, poets still try to make their lyrics melodious, but they rely only on the musical effects they can create with words (such as **rhyme, rhythm, alliteration,** and **onomatopoeia**). Samuel Taylor Coleridge's "Kubla Khan," William Wordsworth's "Tintern Abbey" (both in Collection 5), and Matthew Arnold's "Dover Beach" (Collection 6) are all lyric poems.

See page 1271.

MAGIC REALISM **A literary style that combines incredible events with realistic details and relates them all in a matter-of-fact tone.** Magic realism originated in Latin America, where writers such as Gabriel García Márquez and Julio Cortázar (Collection 7) drew on elements of surrealism and local folklore to create a style that is both timeless and innovative.

See pages 1034, 1217.

MATERIALISM **A belief that nothing exists except matter and that the operations of everything, including thought, will, and feeling, are caused by material agencies.**

MAXIM **A brief, direct statement that expresses a basic rule of human conduct or a general truth about human behavior.** "It is better to give than to receive" is an example of a well-known maxim.

See pages 391, 392.
See also *Epigram, Moral Tale, Proverb.*

MEMOIR **A type of autobiography that usually focuses on a single time period or historical event.** *Survival in Auschwitz* by Primo Levi (Collection 7) is a memoir about the author's experience at the death camp in 1944–1945.

See page 1052.

METAPHOR **A figure of speech that makes a comparison between two seemingly unlike things without using a connective word such as *like, as, than,* or *resembles.*** You are using a metaphor if you say you're "at the end of your rope" or describe two political candidates as "running neck and neck."

Some metaphors are **directly** stated, like Percy Bysshe Shelley's comparison "My soul is an enchanted boat." (If he had written, "My soul is *like* an enchanted boat," he would have been using a **simile.**) Other metaphors are **implied,** like John Suckling's line "Time shall molt away his wings." The words *molt* and *wings* imply a comparison between time and a bird shedding its feathers.

An **extended metaphor** is a metaphor that is extended, or developed, over several lines of writing or even throughout an entire poem.

A **dead metaphor** is a metaphor that has become so common that we no longer even notice that it is a figure of speech. Our everyday language is filled with dead metaphors, such as *foot of the bed, bone of contention,* and *mouth of the river.*

A **mixed metaphor** is the incongruous mixture of two or more metaphors. Mixed metaphors are usually unintentional and often conjure up ludicrous images: "If you put your money on that horse, you'll be barking up the wrong tree."

See pages 316, 377, 835, 1246, 1278.

METAPHYSICAL POETRY **A term applied to the poetry of John Donne, Andrew Marvell, and other seventeenth-century poets who wrote in a difficult and abstract style.** Metaphysical poetry is intellectual and detached. It is characterized by ingenious, obscure imagery, philosophical meditation, verbal wit, and it often uses rough-sounding meter.

See pages 337, 339.

METER **A generally regular pattern of stressed and unstressed syllables in poetry.** When we want to indicate the metrical pattern of a poem, we mark the stressed syllables with the symbol ʹ and the unstressed syllables with the symbol ˘. Indicating the metrical pattern of a poem in this way is called **scanning** the poem, or **scansion.** Here is how to scan these lines from William Blake's "The Tyger" (Collection 5):

ʹ ˘ ʹ ˘ ʹ ˘ ʹ
Tyger! Tyger! burning bright
ʹ ˘ ʹ ˘ ʹ ˘ ʹ
In the forests of the night

Meter is measured in units called feet. A **foot** usually consists of one stressed syllable and one or more unstressed syllables. The basic metrical feet used in

English poetry are the **iamb** (as in *cŏnvínce*), the **trochee** (as in *bórrŏw*), the **anapest** (as in *cŏntrădíct*), the **dactyl** (as in *áccŭratĕ*), and the **spondee** (as in *séawéed*). A poem is described as iambic, trochaic, anapestic, dactylic, or spondaic according to what kind of foot appears most often in its lines.

A complete description of a metrical line indicates both the type and number of feet the line contains. For example, a line of iambic pentameter consists of five iambs, while a line of trochaic tetrameter consists of four trochees.

See page 314.

METONYMY (mə·tän′ə·mē) **A figure of speech in which something closely related to a thing or suggested by it is substituted for the thing itself.** You are using metonymy if you call the judiciary "the bench," the king "the crown," the president (or presidential staff) "the White House," or the race track "the turf."

See also *Synecdoche*.
See page 327.

MOCK EPIC A comic narrative poem that parodies the epic by treating a trivial subject in a lofty, grand manner. A mock epic uses dignified language, elaborate figures of speech, and supernatural intervention. The style of the mock epic is called **mock heroic** (and short mock epics are often called mock heroics). Alexander Pope's *The Rape of the Lock* (Collection 4) is considered the supreme mock epic in the English language.

See page 603.

MODERNISM A broad trend in literature and other arts, from approximately 1890 to 1940, that reflected the impact of works like Sigmund Freud's writings on psychology. In general, modernist writers rejected the forms and values of the past and sought new forms to reflect the fragmentation and uncertainty that they felt characterized modern life. Many modern poets, for example, rejected traditional poetic meters and wrote **free verse.** Novelists such as James Joyce employed a technique called **stream of consciousness** to record the randomness and free associations of their characters' thoughts.

See page 1028.

MONOLOGUE A long, formal speech made by a character in a play. A monologue may be directed at another character or the audience. Shakespeare's soliloquies (Collection 3) can also be called monologues.

See page 328.
See also *Soliloquy*.

MOOD See *Atmosphere*.

MORAL TALE A tale that teaches a lesson about life. Several of the pilgrims' tales in Geoffrey Chaucer's *The Canterbury Tales* (Collection 2) are moral tales.

See pages 176, 199.

MOTIF In literature, a word, a character, an object, an image, a metaphor, or an idea that recurs in a work or in several works. The rose is a motif that runs through many love poems. *Beowulf* (Collection 1) contains many of the traditional motifs associated with heroic literature from all over the world, including a hero who does great deeds in battle or undertakes an extraordinary journey and a supernatural or fantastic being that takes part in the action. These motifs, along with others common to heroic literature, also appear in epics such as the *Iliad* (Collection 1) and Milton's *Paradise Lost* (Collection 3). A motif almost always bears an important relationship to the **theme** of a work of literature.

MOTIVATION The reasons for or forces behind the action of a character. Motivation is revealed through a combination of the character's desires and moral nature with the circumstances in which he or she is placed. In James Joyce's "Araby" (Collection 7), the narrator's crush on Mangan's sister and his romanticized view of the world combine to provide his motivation for attending the bazaar.

See also *Character*.

MYTH An anonymous traditional story, rooted in a particular society, that usually serves to explain the mysteries of nature and a society's beliefs and customs. Most myths grew out of religious rituals, and almost all of them involve the exploits of gods and heroes. Myths helped people to understand and cope with things beyond human control. Every culture has its own **mythology,** but in the Western world the most important myths have been those of ancient Greece and Rome. In twentieth-century literature, **allusions** to myths are often **ironic,** intended to reveal how diminished humanity has become in comparison with grand mythological figures.

NARRATOR One who tells, or narrates, a story. In fiction the narrator occupies any one of a variety of relations to the events described: from the center of the action to a distant, even objective, observer. A narrator may also be reliable or unreliable—if unreliable, the reader is made aware that the narrator's perceptions and interpretations of the action are different from those of the author. Such unreliable narrators can be deceitful or bumbling, but are often just naive or highly impressionable characters. The narrator at the beginning of James Joyce's "Araby" (Collection 7), for example, is an impressionable boy, and the story is, in part, about how the boy's point-of-view changes and becomes more reliable.

See page 177.
See also *Point of View.*

NEOCLASSICISM The revival of classical standards and forms during the late seventeenth and eighteenth centuries. The neoclassicists valued the classical ideals of order, reason, balance, harmony, clarity, and restraint. In particular, they studied and tried to emulate the Latin poets Horace and Virgil. Alexander Pope (Collection 4) is one of the most celebrated English neoclassical poets.

See page 566.

NOVEL A long fictional prose narrative, usually of more than fifty thousand words. In general, the novel uses the same basic literary elements as the short story: **plot, character, setting, theme,** and **point of view.** The novel's length usually permits these elements to be more fully developed than they are in the short story. However, this is not always true of the modern novel. Some modern novels are basically character studies, with only the barest plot structures. Others reveal little about their characters and concentrate instead on setting or tone or even the language of the novel itself.

Some of the greatest novels ever written are *Tom Jones* by Henry Fielding, *Pride and Prejudice* by Jane Austen, *Jane Eyre* by Charlotte Brontë, *Bleak House* and *Great Expectations* by Charles Dickens, *The Brothers Karamazov* by Fyodor Dostoyevsky, *Madame Bovary* by Gustave Flaubert, *Middlemarch* by George Eliot, *Jude the Obscure* by Thomas Hardy, *War and Peace* by Leo Tolstoy, *Lord Jim* by Joseph Conrad, *Sons and Lovers* by D. H. Lawrence, *Ulysses* by James Joyce, and *One Hundred Years of Solitude* by Gabriel García Márquez.

See page 576.

OCTAVE An eight-line stanza or poem or the first eight lines of an Italian, or Petrarchan, sonnet. The usual rhyme scheme of the octave in this type of sonnet is *abbaabba.* The octave, which is sometimes called the **octet,** is followed by a six-line **sestet** with the rhyme scheme *cdecde* or *cdcdcd.*

See page 312.
See also *Sonnet.*

ODE A complex, generally long lyric poem on a serious subject. In English poetry, there are basically two types of odes. One is highly formal and dignified in style and is generally written for ceremonial or public occasions. This type of ode derives from the choral odes of the classical Greek poet Pindar. The other type of ode derives from those written by the Latin poet Horace, and it is much more personal and reflective. In English poetry, it is exemplified by the intimate, meditative odes of such Romantic poets as Wordsworth, Keats, and Shelley (Collection 5).

See pages 747, 805.

ONOMATOPOEIA (än′ō·mat′ō·pē′ə) **The use of a word whose sound imitates or suggests its meaning.** Many familiar words, such as *clap, squish, sizzle,* and *wheeze* are onomatopoeic. In poetry, onomatopoeia can reinforce meaning while creating evocative and musical effects. The word "lapping," in the following lines from W. B. Yeats's "The Lake Isle of Innisfree" (Collection 7), is onomatopeic.

> I will arise and go now, for always night and
> day
> I hear lake water lapping with low sounds by the
> shore;

See page 322.

OTTAVA RIMA An eight-line stanza in iambic pentameter with the rhyme scheme *abababcc*. The form was developed in Italy and was popularized by the fourteenth-century Italian poet Giovanni Boccaccio (Collection 2). The most famous example of ottava rima in English poetry is Lord Byron's *Don Juan*. William Butler Yeats's "Sailing to Byzantium" is another notable example.

OXYMORON A figure of speech that combines apparently contradictory or incongruous ideas. "Bittersweet," "cruel kindness," and "eloquent silence" are oxymorons. The classic oxymoron "wise fool" is almost a literal translation of the term from the Greek—*oxys* means "sharp" or "keen," and *moros* means "foolish." A famous oxymoron in literature is John Milton's description of Hell in *Paradise Lost* (Collection 3):

> No light, but rather darkness visible. . .

See pages 411, 1039.

PARABLE A short, allegorical story that teaches a moral or religious lesson about life. The most famous parables in Western literature are those like "The Parable of the Prodigal Son" (Collection 3) told by Jesus in the Gospels of the Bible.

See pages 378, 383, 389.

PARADOX An apparent contradiction that is actually true. A paradox may be a statement or a situation; as a statement, it is a figure of speech. The metaphysical poets of the seventeenth century (Collection 3) made brilliant use of paradoxes, as in this famous example from John Donne's "Death be not proud" (Collection 3):

> One short sleep past, we wake eternally,
> And death shall be no more; Death, thou shalt die.

The speaker in the cartoon above doesn't understand the famous series of paradoxes that open *A Tale of Two Cities* by Charles Dickens.

See pages 348, 1225.

"I wish you would make up your mind, Mr. Dickens. Was it the best of times or was it the worst of times? It could scarcely have been both."

PARALLELISM The repetition of words, phrases, or sentences that have the same grammatical structure or that restate a similar idea. Parallelism is often used in literature meant to be spoken aloud, such as poetry, drama, and speeches, because it can help make lines emotional, rhythmic, and memorable. It is also one of the most important techniques used in Biblical poetry. The parallelism in the following lines from Psalm 23 (Collection 3) heightens the emotional effect and enacts a meditative tone:

> He maketh me to lie down in green pastures:
> He leadeth me beside the still waters.
> He restoreth my soul:
> He leadeth me in the paths of righteousness for
>   his name's sake.

See pages 360, 374, 396, 725.

PARODY The imitation of a work of literature, art, or music for amusement or instruction. Parodies usually use exaggeration or inappropriate subject matter to make a serious style seem ridiculous. Alexander Pope's *The Rape of the Lock* (Collection 4) is a parody of such serious and sweeping epics as the *Iliad* (Collection 1) and the *Aeneid.* Cervantes' *Don Quixote* (Collection 4) is a parody of medieval romances.

See pages 615, 626.

PASTORAL A type of literature that depicts country life in idyllic, idealized terms. The term *pastoral* comes from the Latin word for shepherd, and originally, pastorals were about shepherds, nymphs, and rural life. Today, the term has a looser meaning and refers to any literary work that portrays an idyllic rural setting or that expresses nostalgia for an age or place of lost innocence. The most famous traditional English pastoral is Christopher Marlowe's "The Passionate Shepherd to His Love," which is satirized in Sir Walter Raleigh's "The Nymph's Reply to the Shepherd" (both in Collection 3).

See page 293.

PERSONIFICATION A kind of metaphor in which a nonhuman or nonliving thing or quality is talked about as if it were human or had life. In these lines, from William Wordsworth's "The World Is Too Much with Us" (Collection 5), the sea is given human form and the wind is given a voice:

> This Sea that bares her bosom to the moon;
> The winds that will be howling at all hours,

See pages 352, 743.
See also *Apostrophe, Figure of Speech, Metaphor.*

PLOT The series of related events that make up a story or drama. The plot is the underlying structure of a story. Most plots are built on these "bare bones": A **basic situation,** or **exposition,** introduces the characters, setting, and, usually, the story's major **conflict.** Out of this basic situation, **complications** develop that intensify the conflict. **Suspense** mounts until a **climax**—the tensest or most exciting part of the plot—is reached, where something happens to determine the outcome of the conflict. Finally, all the problems or mysteries of the plot are unraveled in the **resolution,** or **denouement.**

See page 206.
See also *Climax.*

POINT OF VIEW The vantage point from which a writer tells a story. There are three main points of view: **first person, limited third person,** and **omniscient third person.**

In the **first-person point of view,** the narrator is a character in the story. Using the pronoun *I,* this narrator tells us his or her own experiences but cannot reveal the private thoughts of other characters. When we read a story told in the first person, we hear and see only what the narrator hears and sees. We may have to interpret what this narrator says because a first-person narrator may or may not be objective, honest, or perceptive. For example, in James Joyce's "Araby" (Collection 7), the narrator is a boy who is, in the beginning of the story, a youth whose point of view is romantic, and the story is about his giving up this view.

In the **limited-third-person point of view,** the narrator is outside the story—like an omniscient narrator—but tells the story from the vantage point of only one character. The narrator can enter the mind of this chosen character but cannot tell what any other characters are thinking except by observation. This narrator also can go only where the chosen character goes. For example, "In the Shadow of War" by Ben Okri (Collection 7) is told entirely from the point of view of Omovo, the main character. We experience the stupefying summer heat, the mysteriousness of the veiled woman, and the horror of the gruesome river scene through Omovo's eyes alone.

In the **omniscient** (or **"all-knowing"**) **point of view,** the person telling the story knows everything that's going on in the story. This omniscient narrator is outside the story, a godlike observer who can tell us what all the characters are thinking and feeling, as well as what is happening anywhere in the story. For example, in "The Rocking-Horse Winner" by D. H. Lawrence (Collection 7), the narrator enters into the thoughts and secrets of every character, revealing both the "hard little place" in the mother's heart and Paul's determination to "compel her attention" by being lucky.

See pages 1093, 1217.
See also *Narrator, Stream of Consciousness.*

POSTMODERNISM A trend in art and philosophy that reflects the late-twentieth-century distrust in the idea that there is a legitimate and true system of thought that can be used to understand the world and our place in it.

Postmodernists, like the modernists, see contemporary life as fragmentary, but rather than regard the fragmentary condition of our world with horror, as for instance T. S. Eliot had done in "The Hollow Men" (Collection 7), postmodernists look upon the fragments as materials that can be plundered and combined in new ways to create works of art. Postmodern writing typically experiments with nontraditional forms and allows for multiple meanings. The lines between real and imaginary worlds are often blurred, as is the boundary between fiction and nonfiction. Other characteristics of postmodern literature are cultural diversity and an often playful self-consciousness; that is, an acknowledgment that literature is not a mirror that accurately reflects the world, but a created world unto itself. Gabriel García Márquez's *One Hundred Years of Solitude,* in which reality and fantasy are blended, is an exemplary postmodern novel.

See page 1031.

PROTAGONIST The main character in fiction, drama, or narrative poetry. The protagonist is the character we focus our attention on—the person whose conflict sets the plot in motion. (The character or force that blocks the protagonist is called the **antagonist.**) In *Beowulf* (Collection 1), the title character is the protagonist and the monster Grendel his antagonist. Most protagonists are **rounded, dynamic** characters who change in some important way by the end of the story. Whatever the protagonist's weaknesses, we still usually identify with his or her conflict and care about how it is resolved.

PROVERB A short saying that expresses a common truth or experience, usually about human failings and the ways that people interact with one another. Proverbs often incorporate such literary elements as **metaphor, alliteration, parallelism,** and **rhyme.**

See page 395.
See also *Epigram, Maxim.*

PUN A play on the multiple meanings of a word or on two words that sound alike but have different meanings. Many jokes and riddles are based on puns. ("Why was Cleopatra so negative? Answer: Because she was the queen of denial.") Shakespeare was one of the greatest punsters of all time. Dylan Thomas uses a pun in his poem, "Do Not Go Gentle into That Good Night" (Collection 7):

> Do not go gentle into that good night,
> Old age should burn and rave at the close of day;
> Rage, rage against the dying of the light.

The casual farewell "good night" also means death.

QUATRAIN A four-line stanza or poem or a group of four lines unified by a rhyme scheme. The quatrain is the most common verse unit in English poetry. This quatrain from John Donne's "A Valediction: Forbidding Mourning" (Collection 3) has the rhyme scheme *abab:*

> As virtuous men pass mildly away,
> And whisper to their souls, to go,
> Whilst some of their sad friends do say,
> The breath goes now, and some say, no:

See page 314.

RATIONALISM A philosophy that advocates the idea that one should use reason rather than emotion when one is attempting to discover the truth. Rationalists believe that one must follow reason to determine what opinions are correct and what course of action one should take in any given situation. Opposed to rationalism is Romanticism, which places emphasis on the value of intuition and emotion in arriving at truth.

REALISM In literature and art, the attempt to depict people and things as they really are, without idealization. Realism as a movement developed during the mid–nineteenth century as a reaction against Romanticism. Realist writers believed that fiction should truthfully depict the harsh, gritty reality of everyday life without beautifying, sentimentalizing, or romanticizing it. The Norwegian playwright Henrik Ibsen was among the first to introduce realism to the stage. The English novelists Charles Dickens, George Eliot, Thomas Hardy, and Joseph Conrad are also considered realists.

See pages 946, 1261.
See also *Romanticism.*

REFRAIN A repeated word, phrase, line, or group of lines. While refrains are most common in poetry and songs, they are sometimes used in prose, particularly speeches. Refrains are used to create rhythm, build suspense, or emphasize important words or ideas.

See pages 130, 133, 1267.

REFORMATION The break from Catholicism and the authority of the pope that resulted in the establishment of the Protestant churches in the sixteenth century. Most scholars date the beginning of the Reformation to 1517, the year Martin Luther nailed his *Ninety-five Theses* to the door of a church in Wittenburg, Germany. The *Theses* criticized the Catholic Church's abuse of indulgences and called for reform. In response the Church leaders condemned Luther, and he was forced to break from the Catholic Church and begin his own religious movement.

See page 282.

RENAISSANCE A French word meaning "rebirth," used to designate the period in European history beginning in Italy in the fourteenth century and ending in the seventeenth century when scientific truths began to challenge long-accepted religious beliefs. The Renaissance was characterized by a renewal of interest in classical learning and a focus on the study of human life on earth, not only on God and eternity.

See page 276.

RESOLUTION See *Plot.*

RHYME The repetition of accented vowel sounds and all sounds following them in words that are close together in a poem. *Park* and *bark* rhyme, as do *sorrow* and *borrow.* The most common type of rhyme, **end rhyme,** occurs at the ends of lines. **Internal rhyme** occurs within lines. Both types are used throughout *The Rime of the Ancient Mariner* by Samuel Taylor Coleridge (Collection 5), contributing to the poem's bouncy, songlike rhythm:

> The fair breeze blew, the white foam flew,
> The furrow followed free;
> We were the first that ever burst
> Into that silent sea.

When words sound similar but do not rhyme exactly, they are called **approximate rhymes** (or **half rhymes, slant rhymes,** or **imperfect rhymes**).

The pattern of rhymed lines in a poem is called its **rhyme scheme.** A rhyme scheme is indicated by giving each new rhyme a new letter of the alphabet. For example, the rhyme scheme of Coleridge's lines is *abcb.*

See page 189.

RHYTHM The alternation of stressed and unstressed syllables in language. Rhythm occurs naturally in all forms of spoken and written language. The most obvious kind of rhythm is produced by **meter,** the regular pattern of stressed and unstressed syllables found in some poetry. Writers can also create less structured rhythms by using rhyme, repetition, pauses, and variations in line length and by balancing long and short words or phrases. (Poetry that is written without any regular meter or rhyme scheme is called **free verse.**)

See also *Free Verse, Meter.*

ROMANCE Historically, a medieval verse narrative chronicling the adventures of a brave knight or other hero who must undertake a quest and overcome great danger for love of a noble lady or high ideal. Such a heroic character is bound by the code of **chivalry,** which emphasizes loyalty to his lord and ready service to the oppressed. He also must adhere to the philosophy of **courtly love,** an idealized view of the relationship between the sexes in which a knight performs brave deeds to win the approval of his lady.

Today the term *romance* has come to mean any story that presents a world of wish-fulfillment, a world that is happier, more perfect, or more heroic than the real world. Characters in romances "live happily ever after" in a world where good always triumphs over evil. Many of today's most popular novels, movies, TV shows, and even cartoons are essentially romances. *Sir Gawain and the Green Knight* and Sir Thomas Malory's *Le Morte d'Arthur* (Collection 2) are famous English romances.

See pages 123, 215.

ROMANTICISM **A literary, artistic, and philosophical movement that developed as a reaction against neoclassicism in the late eighteenth century and dominated the early nineteenth century.** While classicism and neoclassicism emphasize reason, order, harmony, and restraint, Romanticism emphasizes emotion, imagination, intuition, freedom, personal experience, the beauty of nature, the primitive, the exotic, and even the grotesque. However, many critics feel that the traditional opposition between Romanticism and classicism is all too often forced and exaggerated.

In English literature, William Blake, Samuel Taylor Coleridge, William Wordsworth, Percy Bysshe Shelley, John Keats, Lord Byron (all in Collection 5), Mary Wollstonecraft Shelley, and Sir Walter Scott are the leading Romantic writers.

See page 713.

RUN-ON LINE **A line of poetry that does not contain a pause or conclusion at the end, but rather continues on to the next line.** Run-on lines force the reader on to the next line. Only with the next line do they form a grammatical unit and thus make complete sense. Such lines are said to exhibit **enjambment** (French for "striding over"). The following lines from Margaret Atwood's "Siren Song" (Collection 7) are run-on lines:

> This is the one song everyone
> would like to learn: the song
> that is irresistible:

See also *End-stopped Line.*

SARCASM **A kind of particularly cutting irony, in which praise is used tauntingly to indicate its opposite in meaning.** The speaker's tone of voice can be an important clue in understanding this kind of irony. When a mud-soaked, windblown friend arrives for dinner, one might say sarcastically, "Why, don't you look lovely!"

See page 1184.

SATIRE **A kind of writing that ridicules human weakness, vice, or folly in order to bring about social reform.** Satires often try to persuade the reader to do or believe something by showing the opposite view as absurd or—even more forcefully—vicious and inhumane. Among the most brilliant satirists in English literature are Geoffrey Chaucer, Alexander Pope, John Dryden, Jonathan Swift, Jane Austen, George Bernard Shaw, and Evelyn Waugh.

See pages 614, 618, 1156.

SCANSION See *Meter.*

SCOP **An Anglo-Saxon minstrel or poet.** Scops are the Anglo-Saxon equivalents to the ancient Celtic bards.

See page 14.

SESTET **A six-line stanza or poem or the last six lines of an Italian, or Petrarchan, sonnet.** The usual rhyme scheme of the sestet in an Italian sonnet is *cdecde* or *cdcdcd.* It follows an eight-line **octave** with the rhyme scheme *abbaabba.*

See page 312.

SETTING **The time and place of a story or play.** Usually the setting is established early in a story. It may be presented immediately through descriptive details, as in Anita Desai's "Games at Twilight" (Collection 7), or it may be revealed more gradually, as in Rudyard Kipling's "The Mark of the Beast" (Collection 6). Setting often contributes greatly to a story's emotional effect. The exotic setting of V. S. Naipaul's "B. Wordsworth" (Collection 7) sets the tone for its eccentric characters, while the green valley in William Wordsworth's "Tintern Abbey" (Collection 5) creates a contemplative calm. Setting may also play a role in a story's conflict, as the fortresslike suburban houses do in Nadine Gordimer's "Once upon a Time" (Collection 7). Two of the most important functions of setting are to reveal character and to suggest a theme, as the setting of blitzed London does in Graham Greene's "The Destructors" (Collection 7).

See pages 1080, 1233.
See also *Atmosphere.*

SHORT STORY A brief work of fiction. The short story generally has a simpler plot than a novel and often reveals character through significant moments, or **epiphanies,** rather than through the accretion of many incidents or detailed descriptions.

See page 1261.

SIMILE A figure of speech that makes a comparison between two seemingly unlike things by using a connective word such as *like, than,* or *resembles.* The following simile, from George Gordon, Lord Byron's "She Walks in Beauty" (Collection 5), is one of the most famous in English literary history:

> She walks in beauty, like the night
> Of cloudless climes and starry skies;

An **epic simile,** also called a **Homeric simile,** is an extended simile in which many parallels are made between two dissimilar things.

See pages 66, 81, 412, 794.
See also *Figure of Speech, Metaphor.*

SOCIAL DARWINISM The notion that, in society, only the fittest will survive. This idea is an extension of Darwin's scientific theories of natural selection—though Darwin was not involved in its development. Social Darwinism was used to justify rigid class distinctions, indifference to social ills, and doctrines of racial superiority.

See page 1024.

SOCIALISM A political movement that advocates the idea that the ownership and operation of the means of production and distribution should be owned by the community rather than by private individuals. This political movement is related to communism in that it seeks to eliminate class distinctions within society.

SOLILOQUY A long speech in which a character who is usually alone onstage expresses his or her private thoughts or feelings. The soliloquy is an old dramatic convention that was particularly popular in Shakespeare's day. Perhaps the most famous soliloquy is the "To be, or not to be" speech (Collection 3) in Shakespeare's play *Hamlet.* Another major soliloquy occurs in *Macbeth,* when Macbeth bewails his wife's death in the celebrated "Tomorrow, and tomorrow, and tomorrow" speech (Collection 3).

See page 328.
See also *Monologue.*

SONNET A fourteen-line lyric poem, usually written in iambic pentameter, that has one of several rhyme schemes. There are two major types of sonnets. The oldest sonnet form is the **Italian sonnet,** also called the **Petrarchan sonnet** (after the fourteenth-century Italian poet Petrarch, who popularized the form). The Petrarchan sonnet is divided into two parts: an eight-line **octave** with the rhyme scheme *abbaabba* and a six-line **sestet** with the rhyme scheme *cdecde* or *cdcdcd.* The octave usually presents a problem, poses a question, or expresses an idea, which the sestet then resolves, answers, or drives home. The transition from octave to sestet is known as the **turn.** Louise Labé's Sonnet 23 (Collection 3), Elizabeth Barrett Browning's Sonnet 43 (Collection 6), and John Keats's "On First Looking into Chapman's Homer" (Collection 5) are written in the Petrarchan form.

The other major sonnet form, which was widely used by Shakespeare, is called the **Shakespearean sonnet,** or the **English sonnet** (Collection 3). It has three four-line units, or **quatrains,** followed by a concluding two-line unit, or **couplet.** The organization of thought in the Shakespearean sonnet usually corresponds to this structure. The three quatrains often express related ideas or examples, while the couplet sums up the poet's conclusion or message found in the first three. The turn in the Shakespearean sonnet usually occurs during the transition from the third quatrain to the couplet. The rhyme scheme of the Shakespearean sonnet is *abab cdcd efef gg.*

A third type of sonnet, the **Spenserian sonnet,** was developed by Edmund Spenser. Like the Shakespearean sonnet, the Spenserian sonnet is divided into three quatrains and a couplet, but it uses a rhyme scheme that links the quatrains: *abab bcbc cdcd ee.*

A group of sonnets on a related theme is called a **sonnet sequence** or a **sonnet cycle.**

See pages 312, 314, 532, 747, 825, 914.

SPEAKER The imaginary voice, or persona, assumed by the author of a poem. This voice is often not identified immediately or directly. Rather, the reader gradually comes to understand that a unique voice is speaking and that this speaker's characteristics must be interpreted as they are revealed. This process is an especially important part of reading a **lyric poem.**

SPEECH A more or less formal address delivered to an audience or assembly or the written or printed copy of this address. The use of the word *speech* to designate an address to an audience seems to have entered into the English language in the sixteenth century.

Speeches are most commonly delivered by politicians, political activists, and other public figures. For an eloquent example of a twentieth-century political speech, see Desmond Tutu's "The Question of South Africa" (Collection 7).

SPENSERIAN STANZA A nine-line stanza with the rhyme scheme *ababbcbcc.* The first eight lines of the stanza are in iambic pentameter, and the ninth line is an **alexandrine**—that is, a line of iambic hexameter. The form was created by Edmund Spenser for his long poem *The Faerie Queene.* Several English Romantic poets have used the Spenserian stanza, including John Keats, Percy Bysshe Shelley, Lord Byron (all in Collection 5), and Robert Burns.

See page 796.

SPRUNG RHYTHM A term coined by Gerard Manley Hopkins (Collection 6) to designate his unconventional use of poetic meter. Instead of the regular, musical **meter** of most poetry, Hopkins uses sounds that impede smooth reading and echo the sound of Anglo-Saxon poetry, which greatly influenced him. Sprung rhythm is based on the stressed syllables in a line without regard for the number of unstressed syllables; it also makes frequent use of **alliteration** and inverted syntax.

See page 916.

STANZA A group of consecutive lines in a poem that form a single unit. A stanza in a poem is something like a paragraph in prose: It often expresses a unit of thought. A stanza may consist of only one line or of any number of lines beyond that. The word *stanza* is Italian for "stopping place" or "place to rest."

STREAM OF CONSCIOUSNESS A writing style that tries to depict the random flow of thoughts, emotions, memories, and associations running through a character's mind. The term *interior monologue* is often used interchangeably with "stream of consciousness." James Joyce and Virginia Woolf (both in Collection 7) were among the first to experiment with the stream-of-consciousness style in their novels.

See page 1027.

STYLE The manner in which writers or speakers say what they wish to say. An author's style simultaneously expresses his or her ideas and reveals his or her unique way of expressing them. Style is closely connected to **diction,** or word choice, and, depending on what the author wants to communicate, can be formal or casual, plain or ornate, abstract or concrete, as well as comic, poetic, forceful, journalistic, and so on. Sir Francis Bacon (Collection 3) and James Joyce (Collection 7) are both often studied for their styles.

See pages 401, 412.
See also *Diction.*

SUSPENSE The uncertainty or anxiety we feel about what is going to happen next in a story. Writers often create suspense by dropping hints or clues that something—especially something bad—is going to happen. In "The Demon Lover" by Elizabeth Bowen (Collection 7), we begin to feel suspense when Mrs. Drover receives a mysterious letter that makes her lips "go white"; our anxiety increases sharply when the flashback reveals that the letter writer is her old fiancé; and our suspense reaches a climax when she escapes into a taxi and we discover who the driver is.

SYMBOL A person, place, thing, or event that stands both for itself and for something beyond itself. Many symbols have become widely recognized: A lion is a symbol of power; a dove is a symbol of peace. These established symbols are sometimes called **public symbols.** But writers often invent new, personal symbols whose meaning is revealed in their work. For example, the old house in Graham Greene's "The Destructors" (Collection 7) is a symbol of civilization and beauty.

See pages 720, 1141, 1169, 1186, 1253.

SYMBOLISM A literary movement that began in France during the late nineteenth century and advocated the use of highly personal symbols to suggest ideas, emotions, and moods. The French symbolists believed that emotions are fleeting, individual, and essentially inexpressible—and that the poet is, therefore, forced to suggest meaning rather than directly express it. Many twentieth-century writers were influenced by the symbolists, including T. S. Eliot, William Butler Yeats, James Joyce, Dylan Thomas, and Virginia Woolf (all in Collection 7).

See page 1010.

SYNECDOCHE (si·nek′də·kē) **A figure of speech in which a part represents the whole.** The capital city of a nation, for example, is often spoken of as though it were the government: "Washington is claiming popular support for its position." Another example is "our daily bread" meaning food. Synecdoche is closely related to **metonymy.**

See also *Metonymy.*

SYNESTHESIA (sin′əs·thē′zhə) **In literature, a term used for descriptions of one kind of sensation in terms of another.** For example, color may be described as sound (a "loud" yellow), sound as taste (how "sweet" the sound), odor as tangible (a "sharp" smell), and so on.

See page 830.

TANKA A traditional five-line form of Japanese poetry. The tanka follows a strict form: The first and third lines have five syllables each, and the second, fourth, and fifth lines have seven syllables each.

See page 749.

TERCET A triplet, or stanza of three lines, in which each line ends with the same rhyme. It is also either of the two three-line groups forming the sestet of a **sonnet.**

TERZA RIMA An interlocking, three-line stanza form with the rhyme scheme *aba bcb cdc ded* and so on. Terza rima is an Italian verse form originally devised by Dante for *The Divine Comedy*. Among the many English poems that borrowed the form, Shelley's "Ode to the West Wind" (Collection 5) is one of the most famous.

See page 810.

THEME The central idea or insight about human experience revealed in a work of literature. A theme is not the same as the subject of a work, which can usually be expressed in a word or two: old age, ambition, love. The theme is the idea the writer wishes to convey about that subject—the writer's view of the world or revelation about human nature. For example, one theme of James Joyce's "Araby" (Collection 7) might be stated this way: One of the painful aspects of growing up is that some of our dreams turn out to be illusions.

A theme may also be different from a **moral,** which is a lesson or rule about how to live. The theme of "Araby" stated above, for example, would not make sense as a moral.

While some stories, poems, and plays have themes that are directly stated, most themes are **implied.** It is up to the reader to piece together all the clues the writer has provided about the work's total meaning.

See pages 731, 903, 966, 975, 1072, 1126, 1163, 1201, 1299.

TONE The attitude a writer takes toward the reader, a subject, or a character. Tone is conveyed through the writer's choice of words and details. For example, Jonathan Swift's *A Modest Proposal* (Collection 4) is satiric in tone, while the tone of "Pied Beauty" by Gerard Manley Hopkins (Collection 6) might be described as awed.

See pages 317, 343, 637.

TOTALITARIANISM A system of government that advocates the rule of an absolute dictator or a single political party. Totalitarian governments forbid any opposition to the government party or ruler to emerge within the state. Consequently, free speech and other liberties guaranteed in democracies are denied to those living under a totalitarian government. George Orwell's *Animal Farm* explores the consequences of a totalitarian regime.

TRAGEDY A play, novel, or other narrative depicting serious and important events, in which the main character comes to an unhappy end. In a tragedy, the main character is usually dignified, courageous, and often high ranking. This character's downfall may be caused by a **tragic flaw**—an error in judgment or a character weakness—or the downfall may result from forces beyond his or her control. The **tragic hero** usually wins some self-knowledge and wisdom, even though he or she suffers defeat, possibly even death. Tragedy is distinct from **comedy,** in which an ordinary character overcomes obstacles to get what he or she wants. *Beowulf* (Collection 1), Shakespeare's *Macbeth* (Collection 3), and John Milton's *Paradise Lost* (Collection 3) are all tragedies.

See also *Comedy.*

TURN See *Sonnet.*

UNDERSTATEMENT A figure of speech that consists of saying less than what is really meant or saying something with less force than is appropriate. Understatement is the opposite of **hyperbole** and is a form of **irony.** You are using understatement if you come in from a torrential downpour and say, "It's a bit wet out there," or if you describe a Great Dane as "not exactly a small dog." Understatement can be used to create a kind of deadpan humor, but it can also function as a sustained ironic tone throughout a work, as in Wole Soyinka's "Telephone Conversation" (Collection 7).

See also *Hyperbole, Irony.*

VERNACULAR See *Dialect.*

VILLANELLE A nineteen-line poem divided into five tercets (three-line stanzas), each with the rhyme scheme *aba,* and a final quatrain with the rhyme scheme *abaa.* Line 1 is repeated entirely to form lines 6, 12, and 18, while line 3 is repeated as lines 9, 15, and 19. Thus, there are only two rhymes in the poem, and the two lines used as **refrains** (lines 1 and 3) are paired as the final couplet. The villanelle was originally used in French pastoral poetry. Dylan Thomas's "Do Not Go Gentle into That Good Night" (Collection 7) is an example of a modern villanelle.

See page 1276.

WIT A quality of speech or writing that combines verbal cleverness with keen perception, especially of the incongruous. The definition of *wit* has undergone dramatic changes over the centuries. In the Middle Ages it meant "common sense"; in the Renaissance it meant "intelligence"; and in the seventeenth century it meant "originality of thought." The modern meaning of *wit* began to develop during the seventeenth and eighteenth centuries with the writings of John Dryden and Alexander Pope (Collection 4). In his *Essay on Criticism,* Pope said:

> True wit is Nature to advantage dressed:
> What oft was thought, but ne'er so well expressed

Perhaps the best examples of more modern wit can be found in the works of Oscar Wilde and George Bernard Shaw.

See page 575.

Language Handbook

CONTENTS

Language Handbook

I The Parts of Speech

PART OF SPEECH	DEFINITION	EXAMPLES
NOUN	Names person, place, thing, or idea	writer, Ben Okri, Anglo-Saxons, family, country, Wales, poem, "My Last Duchess," Romanticism
PRONOUN	Takes the place of one or more nouns or pronouns	
Personal	Refers to one(s) speaking (first person), spoken to (second person), spoken about (third person)	I, me, my, mine, we, us, our, ours you, your, yours he, him, his, she, her, hers, it, its, they, them, their, theirs
Reflexive	Refers to subject and directs action of verb back to subject	myself, ourselves, yourself, yourselves, himself, herself, itself, themselves
Intensive	Refers to and emphasizes noun or another pronoun	(See Reflexive.)
Demonstrative	Refers to specific one(s) of group	this, that, these, those
Interrogative	Introduces question	what, which, who, whom, whose
Relative	Introduces subordinate clause and refers to noun or pronoun outside that clause	that, which, who, whom, whose
Indefinite	Refers to one(s) not specifically named	all, any, anyone, both, each, either, everybody, many, none, nothing
ADJECTIVE	Modifies noun or pronoun by telling *what kind, which one, how many,* or *how much*	**a paperback** book, **an Anglo-Saxon** law, **this** one, **the seven brave** warriors, **less** space
VERB	Shows action or state of being	
Action	Expresses physical or mental activity	describe, travel, fight, believe, consider, remember
Linking	Connects subject with word identifying or describing it	appear, be, seem, become, feel, look, smell, sound, taste
Helping (Auxiliary)	Assists another verb in expressing time, voice, or mood	be, have, may, can, shall, must, would
ADVERB	Modifies verb, adjective, or adverb by telling *how, when, where,* or *to what extent*	walks **slowly, quite** different, **somewhat** boldly, coming **here soon**
PREPOSITION	Relates noun or pronoun to another word	about, at, by, for, from, in, on, according to, along with, because of
CONJUNCTION	Joins words or word groups	
Coordinating	Joins words or word groups used in the same way	and, but, for, nor, or, so, yet

Correlative	A pair of conjunctions that join parallel words or word groups	both . . . and, either . . . or, neither . . . nor, not only . . . but (also)
Subordinating	Begins a subordinate clause and connects it to an independent clause	although, as if, because, since, so that, unless, when, where, while
INTERJECTION	Expresses emotion	ah, wow, ugh, whew

2 Agreement

AGREEMENT OF SUBJECT AND VERB

2a. A verb should agree with its subject in number. Singular subjects take singular verbs. Plural subjects take plural verbs.

SINGULAR **He lives** in Camelot.
PLURAL **They live** in Camelot.

2b. The number of the subject is not changed by a phrase or a clause following the subject.

EXAMPLE
The **Lilliputians,** a nation of tiny people, **capture** Gulliver.

2c. Indefinite pronouns may be singular, plural, or either.

(1) The following indefinite pronouns are singular: *anybody, anyone, anything, each, either, everybody, everyone, everything, neither, nobody, no one, nothing, one, somebody, someone,* and *something.*

EXAMPLE
One of the most beautiful places in England **is** the Lake District.

(2) The following indefinite pronouns are plural: *both, few, many,* and *several.*

EXAMPLE
Both of the epics **were written** by John Milton.

(3) The indefinite pronouns *all, any, most, none,* and *some* are singular when they refer to singular words and are plural when they refer to plural words.

SINGULAR **None** of the equipment **was damaged.** [*None* refers to *equipment.*]
PLURAL **None** of the machines **were damaged.** [*None* refers to *machines.*]

2d. A *compound subject* may be singular, plural, or either.

(1) Subjects joined by *and* usually take a plural verb.

EXAMPLE
After rehearsal, **Juan, Anita,** and **Marcus are going** out to dinner.

A compound subject that names only one person or thing takes a singular verb.

EXAMPLE
His **wife** and **partner** in crime **is** Lady Macbeth.

(2) Singular subjects joined by *or* or *nor* take a singular verb.

EXAMPLE
Jill or **Jorge plans** to write a character analysis of Macduff.

(3) When a singular subject and a plural subject are joined by *or* or *nor,* the verb agrees with the subject nearer the verb.

EXAMPLE
Neither the **dancers** nor the **choreographer was** pleased with the routine.

2e. The verb agrees with its subject even when the verb precedes the subject, as in sentences beginning with *here, there,* or *where.*

SINGULAR Where **is** [*or* **where's**] **Malcolm**?
PLURAL Here **are** [*not* here's] **Malcolm** and his **brother.**

2f. A *collective noun* (such as *audience, flock,* or *team*) is singular in form but names a group of persons or things. A collective noun takes a singular verb when the noun refers to the group as a unit and takes a plural verb when the noun refers to the parts or members of the group.

SINGULAR The tour **group is** on the bus. [The group as a unit is on the bus.]

PLURAL The tour **group are talking** about their plans. [The members of the group are talking to one another.]

2g. An expression of an amount (a length of time, a statistic, or a fraction, for example) is singular when the amount is thought of as a unit or when it refers to a singular word and plural when the amount is thought of as many parts or when it refers to a plural word.

SINGULAR **Fifty years is** how long Beowulf rules Geatland. [one unit]

PLURAL **One fourth** of the seniors **are working** on a production of *Macbeth.* [The fraction refers to *seniors.*]

Expressions of measurement (length, weight, capacity, area) are usually singular.

EXAMPLE

Four and seven-tenths inches is the diameter of a compact disc.

2h. The title of a creative work (such as a book, song, film, or painting) or the name of an organization, a country, or a city (even if it is plural in form) takes a singular verb.

EXAMPLES

"Tears, Idle Tears" was written by Alfred, Lord Tennyson.

The **United Nations was formed** in 1945.

Has the **Netherlands been flooded** recently?

2i. A verb agrees with its subject, not with its predicate nominative.

SINGULAR The **subject** of the lecture **was** epic heroes.

PLURAL **Epic heroes were** the subject of the lecture.

AGREEMENT OF PRONOUN AND ANTECEDENT

A pronoun usually refers to a noun or another pronoun. The word to which a pronoun refers is called its ***antecedent***.

2j. A pronoun agrees with its antecedent in number and gender. Singular pronouns refer to singular antecedents. A few singular pronouns also indicate gender (feminine, masculine, or neuter). Plural pronouns refer to plural antecedents.

EXAMPLES

Alfred, Lord Tennyson published *Idylls of the King* after **he** became poet laureate. [singular, masculine]

Lady Macbeth helps **her** husband. [singular, feminine]

The **Lilliputians** gave **their** captive food. [plural]

2k. Indefinite pronouns may be singular, plural, or either.

(1) Singular pronouns are used to refer to the indefinite pronouns *anybody, anyone, anything, each, either, everybody, everyone, everything, neither, nobody, no one, nothing, one, somebody, someone,* and *something.* The gender of any of these pronouns is determined by the word or words that the pronoun refers to.

EXAMPLES

Each of the **boys** has learned **his** part in *Macbeth.*

One of the **girls** has injured **herself.**

If the antecedent may be either masculine or feminine, use both the masculine and feminine pronouns to refer to it.

EXAMPLE

Anyone who is going on the field trip needs to bring **his** or **her** lunch.

(2) Plural pronouns are used to refer to the indefinite pronouns *both, few, many,* and *several.*

EXAMPLE

Many of the spectators leapt from **their** seats and cheered.

(3) Singular or plural pronouns may be used to refer to the indefinite pronouns *all, any, most, none,* and *some.* These indefinite pronouns are singular when they refer to singular words and are plural when they refer to plural words.

SINGULAR **None** of the renovated theater matches **its** original beauty. [*None* refers to the singular noun *theater.*]

PLURAL **None** of the geese have left on **their** annual migration. [*None* refers to the plural noun *geese.*]

2l. A plural pronoun is used to refer to two or more singular antecedents joined by *and.*

EXAMPLE

Malcolm and Donalbain left Scotland soon after **their** father was killed.

2m. **A singular pronoun is used to refer to two or more singular antecedents joined by *or* or *nor*.**

EXAMPLE
Neither **Malcolm nor Donalbain** felt **he** was safe.

2n. **A collective noun (such as *club* or *family*) takes a singular pronoun when the noun refers to the group as a unit and takes a plural pronoun when the noun refers to the parts or members of the group.**

SINGULAR The **jury** reached **its** decision less than one hour later. [The jury decided as a unit.]

PLURAL The **jury** disagree on how much importance **they** should give to one of the defendant's statements. [The members of the jury disagree.]

2o. **The title of a creative work (such as a book, song, film, or painting) or the name of an organization, a country, or a city (even if it is plural in form) takes a singular pronoun.**

EXAMPLES
I read ***Gulliver's Travels*** and wrote a report on **it.**
The **United Arab Emirates** generates most of **its** revenue from the sale of oil.

3 Using Verbs

THE PRINCIPAL PARTS OF VERBS

Every verb has four basic forms called the ***principal parts:*** the *base form,* the *present participle,* the *past,* and the *past participle.* A verb is classified as *regular* or *irregular* depending on the way it forms its past and past participle.

3a. **A *regular verb* forms the past and past participle by adding *–d* or *–ed* to the base form. An *irregular verb* forms the past and the past participle in some other way.**

COMMON REGULAR AND IRREGULAR VERBS

The following examples include *is* and *have* in italics to show that helping verbs (forms of *be* and *have*) are used with the present participle and past participle forms.

BASE FORM	PRESENT PARTICIPLE	PAST	PAST PARTICIPLE
REGULAR			
attack	*is* attacking	attacked	*have* attacked
drown	*is* drowning	drowned	*have* drowned
occur	*is* occurring	occurred	*have* occurred
risk	*is* risking	risked	*have* risked
try	*is* trying	tried	*have* tried
use	*is* using	used	*have* used
IRREGULAR			
be	*is* being	was, were	*have* been
bring	*is* bringing	brought	*have* brought
burst	*is* bursting	burst	*have* burst
come	*is* coming	came	*have* come
eat	*is* eating	ate	*have* eaten
go	*is* going	went	*have* gone
lead	*is* leading	led	*have* led
pay	*is* paying	paid	*have* paid
see	*is* seeing	saw	*have* seen
sing	*is* singing	sang	*have* sung
steal	*is* stealing	stole	*have* stolen
take	*is* taking	took	*have* taken
throw	*is* throwing	threw	*have* thrown

NOTE If you are not sure about the principal parts of a verb, look in a dictionary. Entries for irregular verbs give the principal parts. If no principal parts are listed, the verb is a regular verb.

TENSES AND THEIR USES

3b. **The *tense* of a verb indicates the time of the action or state of being that is expressed by the verb.**

(1) The ***present tense*** is used mainly to express an action or a state of being that is occurring now.

EXAMPLE
The article **compares** Beowulf with other epic heroes.

The present tense is also used

- to show a customary or habitual action or state of being
- to convey a general truth—something that is always true
- to make a historical event seem current (such use is called the ***historical present***)
- to summarize the plot or subject matter of a literary work or to refer to an author's relationship to his or her work (such use is called the ***literary present***)
- to express future time

EXAMPLES

Every Friday, our teacher **gives** us a vocabulary quiz. [customary action]

Reptiles **are** coldblooded. [general truth]

The Greeks **establish** separate city-states, which **war** among themselves. [historical present]

In the land of the Lilliputians, Gulliver **appears** gigantic. [literary present]

The two-week seminar on Shakespeare **begins** on Monday. [future time]

(2) The ***past tense*** is used to express an action or state of being that occurred in the past but did not continue into the present.

EXAMPLE

An expert on T. S. Eliot's poetry **spoke** to our class.

(3) The ***future tense*** (*will* or *shall* + base form) is used to express an action or a state of being that will occur.

EXAMPLE

Laurie **will play** the part of Lady Macbeth.

Shall and *will* are both acceptable in forming the future tense.

(4) The ***present perfect tense*** (*have* or *has* + past participle) is used to express an action or a state of being that occurred at some indefinite time in the past.

EXAMPLE

Kenneth Branagh **has played** the roles of Henry V and of Iago.

The present perfect tense is also used to express an action or a state of being that began in the past and continues into the present.

EXAMPLE

Herot **has stood** empty for twelve years.

(5) The ***past perfect tense*** (*had* + past participle) is used to express an action or state of being completed in the past before some other past occurrence.

EXAMPLE

The kingdom **had suffered** before Beowulf arrived. [The suffering occurred before the arriving.]

Be sure to use the past perfect tense in "if" clauses that express the earlier of two past actions.

EXAMPLE

If you **had read** [*not* read *or* would have read] the article, you would have learned about Sutton Hoo.

(6) The ***future perfect tense*** (*will have* or *shall have* + past participle) is used to express an action or state of being that will be completed in the future before some other future occurrence.

EXAMPLE

By this time tomorrow, I **will** [*or* **shall**] **have memorized** "The Seafarer."

3c. Avoid unnecessary shifts in tense.

INCONSISTENT Wiglaf discovered the dragon's treasure and then brings it to Beowulf. [shift from past to present tense]

CONSISTENT Wiglaf **discovered** the dragon's treasure and then **brought** it to Beowulf. [past tense]

CONSISTENT Wiglaf **discovers** the dragon's treasure and then **brings** it to Beowulf. [present tense]

When describing events that occur at different times, use verbs in different tenses to show the order of events.

EXAMPLE

She **taught** school for several years, but now she **works** for a publishing company. [Because she taught at a specific time in the past, the past tense *taught* is correct. Because she works at the present time, the present tense *works* is correct.]

ACTIVE VOICE AND PASSIVE VOICE

3d. *Voice* is the form a transitive verb takes to indicate whether the subject of the verb performs or receives the action.

A verb is in the ***active voice*** when its subject performs the action (its object receives the action).

ACTIVE VOICE William Shakespeare **wrote** more than thirty-five plays.

A verb is in the ***passive voice*** whenever its subject receives the action (the verb has no object). A passive verb is always a verb phrase that includes a form of *be* and the past participle of an action verb.

PASSIVE VOICE More than thirty-five plays **were written** by William Shakespeare.

3e. Use the passive voice sparingly.

In general, the passive voice is less direct and less forceful than the active voice. In some cases, the passive voice also may sound awkward.

AWKWARD PASSIVE The sleeping grooms are smeared with King Duncan's blood by Lady Macbeth.

ACTIVE Lady Macbeth **smears** the sleeping grooms with King Duncan's blood.

Although you generally will want to use active voice rather than passive voice, the passive voice is not less correct than the active voice. In fact, the passive voice is useful in the following situations:

1. when you do not know the performer of the action

EXAMPLE
The Globe **was built** in 1599.

2. when you do not want to reveal the performer of the action

EXAMPLE
The actor **was criticized** for his portrayal of Macbeth.

3. when you want to emphasize the receiver of the action

EXAMPLE
King Duncan **was murdered** while he was asleep.

4 Using Pronouns

CASE

Case is the form that a noun or a pronoun takes to indicate its use in a sentence. In English, there are three cases: *nominative, objective,* and *possessive*. Most personal pronouns have a different form for each case.

The Nominative Case

4a. A subject of a verb is in the nominative case.

EXAMPLES
They built the tower near the sea as **he** had requested. [*They* is the subject of the verb *built. He* is the subject of the verb *had requested.*]

4b. A predicate nominative is in the nominative case.

EXAMPLE
The only students who auditioned for the part of King Arthur were **he** and **Carlos.** [*He* and *Carlos* are predicate nominatives that follow the linking verb *were* and identify the subject *students.*]

PERSONAL PRONOUNS			
SINGULAR			
	NOMINATIVE	OBJECTIVE	POSSESSIVE
FIRST PERSON	I	me	my, mine
SECOND PERSON	you	you	your, yours
THIRD PERSON	he, she, it	him, her, it	his, her, hers, its
PLURAL			
	NOMINATIVE	OBJECTIVE	POSSESSIVE
FIRST PERSON	we	us	our, ours
SECOND PERSON	you	you	your, yours
THIRD PERSON	they	them	their, theirs

NOTE The form of a noun is the same for both the nominative case and the objective case. A noun changes its form for the possessive case, usually by adding an apostrophe and an *s* to most singular nouns and only an apostrophe to most plural nouns.

For more information about forming possessives of nouns, see 13f.

The Objective Case

4c. An object of a verb is in the objective case.

EXAMPLES

The knight's answer pleases **her.** [*Her* is a direct object that tells *whom* the answer pleases.]

The Pardoner tells **them** a story about three greedy rioters. [*Them* is an indirect object that tells *to whom* the Pardoner tells a story.]

4d. An object of a preposition is in the objective case.

EXAMPLE

Are the Lilliputians afraid of **him**? [*Him* is the object of the preposition *of.*]

The Possessive Case

4e. A noun or a pronoun preceding a gerund is in the possessive case.

EXAMPLE

We were all thrilled by **Joetta's** [*or* **her**] scoring in the top 5 percent. [*Joetta's* or *her* modifies *scoring,* a gerund used as the object of the preposition *by.*]

Do not confuse a gerund with a present participle, which is a verb form that ends in *–ing* and may function as an adjective.

EXAMPLE

Macbeth found **them** [*not* their] standing around a caldron. [*Them* is modified by the participial phrase *standing around a caldron.*]

SPECIAL PRONOUN PROBLEMS

4f. An appositive is in the same case as the noun or pronoun to which it refers.

EXAMPLES

Duncan's sons, **Malcolm and he,** leave Scotland. [The compound appositive *Malcolm and he* refers to the subject, *sons.*]

Macduff suspects both of them, **Malcolm and him.** [The compound appositive *Malcolm and him* refers to *them,* the object of the preposition *of.*]

4g. A pronoun following *than* or *as* in an elliptical construction is in the same case as it would be if the construction were completed.

An ***elliptical construction*** is a clause from which words have been omitted.

NOMINATIVE I see him more often **than she.** [I see him more often *than she sees him. She* is the subject in the elliptical construction.]

OBJECTIVE I see him more often **than her.** [I see him more often *than I see her. Her* is the direct object in the elliptical construction.]

4h. A pronoun ending in *–self* or *–selves* should not be used in place of a personal pronoun.

EXAMPLE

Everyone except John and **me** [*not* myself] has read *Don Juan.*

4i. The pronoun *who* (*whoever*) is in the nominative case. The pronoun *whom* (*whomever*) is in the objective case.

EXAMPLES

Who wrote "Ozymandias"? [*Who* is the subject of the verb *wrote.*]

With **whom** did Wordsworth write *Lyrical Ballads*? [*Whom* is the object of the preposition *with.*]

CLEAR PRONOUN REFERENCE

The word that a pronoun stands for or refers to is called the ***antecedent*** of the pronoun.

4j. A pronoun should always refer clearly to its antecedent.

Avoid an ambiguous, a general, a weak, or an indefinite reference by

1. rephrasing the sentence, or
2. replacing the pronoun with an appropriate noun, or
3. giving the pronoun a clear antecedent.

AMBIGUOUS When the Green Knight was talking to Sir Gawain, he was holding his head in his hand. [The antecedent of *he* and *his* is unclear. Was the Green Knight holding Sir Gawain's head or his own?]

CLEAR The Green Knight was holding his head in his hand when he was talking to Sir Gawain.

GENERAL Macbeth will become king. This is one of the witches' prophecies. [*This* has no specific antecedent.]

CLEAR That Macbeth will become king is one of the witches' prophecies.

WEAK Our dog Hank is jealous of my new baby sister. To help him get over it, I try to give him extra attention. [The antecedent of *it* is not expressed.]

CLEAR To help our dog Hank get over his jealousy of my new baby sister, I try to give him extra attention.

INDEFINITE In this book it includes pictures of artifacts from the Sutton Hoo ship burial. [*It* is not necessary to the meaning of the sentence.]

CLEAR This book includes pictures of artifacts from the Sutton Hoo ship burial.

5 Using Modifiers

A ***modifier*** is a word or group of words that limits the meaning of another word or group of words. The two kinds of modifiers are *adjectives* and *adverbs.*

5a. Use an *adjective* to limit the meaning of a noun or a pronoun. Use an *adverb* to limit the meaning of a verb, an adjective, or another adverb.

COMPARISON OF MODIFIERS

5b. *Comparison* refers to the change in the form of an adjective or an adverb to show increasing or decreasing degrees in the quality the modifier expresses.

The three degrees of comparison are *positive, comparative,* and *superlative.*

1. Most one-syllable modifiers form the comparative and superlative degrees by adding *–er* and *–est.*

2. Some two-syllable modifiers form the comparative and superlative degrees by adding *–er* and *–est.* Other two-syllable modifiers form the comparative and superlative degrees by using *more* and *most.*

3. Modifiers of more than two syllables form the comparative and superlative degrees by using *more* and *most.*

4. To show a decrease in the qualities they express, all modifiers form the comparative by using *less* and the superlative by using *least.*

POSITIVE	COMPARATIVE	SUPERLATIVE
soft	softer	softest
thirsty	thirstier	thirstiest
slowly	more slowly	most slowly
skillfully	less skillfully	least skillfully

For information about adding suffixes such as *–er* and *–est* to words, see 14e–j.

5. Some modifiers form the comparative and superlative degrees in other ways.

POSITIVE	COMPARATIVE	SUPERLATIVE
bad (ill)	worse	worst
far	farther (further)	farthest (furthest)
good (well)	better	best
little	less	least
many (much)	more	most

5c. Use the comparative degree when comparing two things. Use the superlative degree when comparing more than two.

COMPARATIVE After reading *King Lear* and *The Winter's Tale,* I can understand why *King Lear* is the **more popular** play. [comparison of two plays]

SUPERLATIVE Of the three plays I saw, I think *Macbeth* was the **most powerful.** [comparison of three plays]

5d. Avoid a double comparison or a double negative. A *double comparison* is the use of two comparative forms (usually *–er* and *more* or *less*) or two superlative forms (usually *–est* and *most* or *least*) to modify the same word. A *double negative* is the use of two negative words where one is enough.

EXAMPLES

Who is the **noblest** [*not* most noblest] of King Arthur's knights?

I know **nothing** [*not* don't know nothing] about the Wars of the Roses.

5e. **Include the word *other* or *else* when comparing one member of a group with the rest of the group.**

ILLOGICAL Wiglaf is bolder than any of Beowulf's followers. [Wiglaf is one of Beowulf's followers. Logically, Wiglaf cannot be bolder than himself.]

LOGICAL Wiglaf is bolder than any of Beowulf's **other** followers.

5f. **Avoid comparing items that cannot logically be compared.**

ILLOGICAL I think Olivier's portrayal of Hamlet is more compelling than any other actor. [The sentence makes an illogical comparison between a portrayal and an actor.]

LOGICAL I think Olivier's portrayal of Hamlet is more compelling than any other actor's [portrayal]. [The sentence makes a logical comparison between portrayals.]

PLACEMENT OF MODIFIERS

5g. **Avoid using a *misplaced modifier*—a modifying word, phrase, or clause that sounds awkward because it modifies the wrong word or group of words.**

To correct a misplaced modifier, place the word, phrase, or clause as close as possible to the word or words you intend it to modify.

MISPLACED The old man told the three young rioters under a tree they would find Death. [What occurred under a tree: the telling or the finding?]

CLEAR The old man told the three young rioters they would find Death **under a tree.**

MISPLACED The anxious hunter watched the raging lion come charging at him as he readied his bow and arrow.

CLEAR **As he readied his bow and arrow,** the anxious hunter watched the raging lion come charging at him.

5h. **Avoid using a *dangling modifier*—a modifying word, phrase, or clause that does not sensibly modify any word or words in a sentence.**

You may correct a dangling modifier by

- adding a word or words that the dangling word, phrase, or clause can sensibly refer to
- adding a word or words to the dangling word, phrase, or clause
- rewording the sentence

DANGLING After becoming poet laureate, "The Charge of the Light Brigade" was written. [Who became poet laureate?]

CLEAR After becoming poet laureate, Alfred, Lord Tennyson wrote "The Charge of the Light Brigade."

CLEAR Alfred, Lord Tennyson wrote "The Charge of the Light Brigade" after he became poet laureate.

6 PHRASES

WHAT IS A PHRASE?

6a. **A *phrase* is a group of related words that is used as a single part of speech and that does not contain a verb and its subject.**

EXAMPLE

The Rime of the Ancient Mariner, **Coleridge's best-known poem, was published in 1798.** [*Coleridge's best-known poem* functions as a noun, *was published* is a verb, and *in 1798* functions as an adverb.]

THE PREPOSITIONAL PHRASE

6b. **A *prepositional phrase* begins with a preposition and ends with the *object of the preposition,* a word or word group that functions as a noun.**

EXAMPLE

From the rafters of Herot hung one **of Grendel's arms.** [The noun *rafters* is the object of the preposition *from.* The noun *Herot* is the object of the preposition *of.* The noun *arms* is the object of the preposition *of.*]

An object of a preposition may be compound.

EXAMPLE
The three men ignored the warnings **of the tavern-knave and the publican.** [Both *tavern-knave* and *publican* are objects of the preposition *of.*]

(1) An ***adjective phrase*** is a prepositional phrase that modifies a noun or a pronoun. An adjective phrase tells *what kind* or *which one.*

EXAMPLE
The three rioters found eight bushels **of gold coins.** [*Of gold coins* modifies the noun *bushels.*]

An adjective phrase usually follows the word it modifies. That word may be the object of another preposition.

EXAMPLE
They told stories on their journey **to Canterbury.** [*To Canterbury* modifies *journey,* the object of the preposition *on.*]

More than one adjective phrase may modify the same word.

EXAMPLE
Chaucer's trips **to Italy on important diplomatic missions** broadened his knowledge. [The phrases *to Italy* and *on important diplomatic missions* modify the noun *trips.*]

(2) An ***adverb phrase*** is a prepositional phrase that modifies a verb, an adjective, or an adverb. An adverb phrase tells *how, when, where, why,* or *to what extent* (*how long* or *how far*).

As you can see in the example below, more than one adverb phrase can modify the same word. The example also shows that an adverb phrase, unlike an adjective phrase, can precede the word it modifies.

EXAMPLE
In 1799, Wordsworth returned **with his sister to the Lake District.** [Each phrase modifies the verb *returned. In 1799* tells *when, with his sister* tells *how,* and *to the Lake District* tells *where.*]

VERBALS AND VERBAL PHRASES

A ***verbal*** is a form of a verb used as a noun, an adjective, or an adverb. A ***verbal phrase*** consists of a verbal and its modifiers and complements.

Participles and Participial Phrases

6c. **A *participle* is a verb form that is used as an adjective. A *participial phrase* consists of a participle and all the words related to the participle.**

The two kinds of participles are the *present participle* and the *past participle.*

(1) ***Present participles*** end in *–ing.*

EXAMPLE
Sir Gawain heard the Green Knight **sharpening his ax.** [The participial phrase modifies the noun *Green Knight.* The noun *ax* is the direct object of the present participle *sharpening.*]

(2) Most ***past participles*** end in *–d* or *–ed.* Others are irregularly formed.

EXAMPLE
Tormented by her guilt, Lady Macbeth lost her sanity. [The participial phrase modifies the noun *Lady Macbeth.* The adverb phrase *by her guilt* modifies the past participle *tormented.*]

Gerunds and Gerund Phrases

6d. **A *gerund* is a verb form ending in *–ing* that is used as a noun. A *gerund phrase* consists of a gerund and all the words related to the gerund.**

EXAMPLES
For Gulliver, **living in Brobdingnag** is quite different from **living in Lilliput.** [*Living in Brobdingnag* is the subject of the verb *is. Living in Lilliput* is the object of the preposition *from.* The adverb phrases *in Brobdingnag* and *in Lilliput* modify the gerund *living.*]
The Miller enjoys **playing the bagpipes.** [*Playing the bagpipes* is the direct object of the verb *enjoys. Bagpipes* is the direct object of the gerund *playing.*]

Infinitives and Infinitive Phrases

6e. **An *infinitive* is a verb form that can be used as a noun, an adjective, or an adverb. An infinitive usually begins with to. An *infinitive phrase* consists of an infinitive and all the words related to the infinitive.**

EXAMPLES
The three rioters vow **to kill Death.** [The infinitive phrase acts as a noun and is the direct object of the verb *vow. Death* is the direct object of the infinitive *to kill.*]
She had a great desire **to visit Stratford-on-Avon.** [The infinitive phrase acts as an adjective and modifies the noun *desire. Stratford-on-Avon* is the direct object of the infinitive *to visit.*]

Macbeth goes to the witches' haunt **to talk to them.** [The infinitive phrase acts as an adverb and modifies the verb *goes.* The adverb phrase *to them* modifies the infinitive *to talk.*]

Lady Macbeth helps her husband **become king.** [The sign of the infinitive, *to,* is omitted. The infinitive has a subject, *husband,* making the entire construction an ***infinitive clause.*** The infinitive clause acts as a noun and is the direct object of the verb *helps.*]

APPOSITIVES AND APPOSITIVE PHRASES

6f. An *appositive* is a noun or a pronoun placed beside another noun or pronoun to identify or explain it. An *appositive phrase* consists of an appositive and its modifiers.

An appositive or appositive phrase usually follows the word it identifies or explains.

EXAMPLES

Have you read Coleridge's poem **"Kubla Khan"**? [The appositive *"Kubla Khan"* identifies the noun *poem.*]

Shakespeare was born in Stratford-on-Avon, **a market town about eighty miles from London.** [The entire appositive phrase *a market town about eighty miles from London* identifies the noun *Stratford-on-Avon.*]

For emphasis, however, an appositive or an appositive phrase may precede the word that it explains or identifies.

EXAMPLE

A riot of colorful sights, intriguing aromas, and surprising noises, a Cairo bazaar is great fun to visit. [The appositive phrase explains why a Cairo bazaar is fun to visit.]

7 CLAUSES

7a. A *clause* is a group of words that contains a verb and its subject and that is used as part of a sentence. There are two kinds of clauses: the *independent clause* and the *subordinate clause.*

THE INDEPENDENT CLAUSE

7b. An *independent* (or *main*) *clause* expresses a complete thought and can stand by itself as a sentence.

EXAMPLE

SUBJECT VERB

William Shakespeare wrote more than 150 sonnets. [one independent clause]

THE SUBORDINATE CLAUSE

7c. A *subordinate* (or *dependent*) *clause* does not express a complete thought and cannot stand alone as a sentence.

EXAMPLE

SUBJECT VERB

that **Lord Byron swam** across the Hellespont

The thought expressed by a subordinate clause becomes complete when the clause is combined with an independent clause to create a complete sentence.

EXAMPLE

I read **that Lord Byron swam across the Hellespont.**

The Adjective Clause

7d. An *adjective clause* is a subordinate clause that modifies a noun or a pronoun.

An adjective clause always follows the word or words that it modifies. Usually, an adjective clause begins with a ***relative pronoun*** (such as *that, which, who, whom, whose*). A relative pronoun both relates an adjective clause to the word or words the clause modifies and performs a function within its own clause by serving as a subject, an object of a verb, an object of a preposition, or a modifier.

EXAMPLES

Mary Shelley, **who wrote *Frankenstein,*** liked reading ghost stories with her friends. [The relative pronoun *who* relates the adjective clause to the noun *Mary Shelley* and serves as the subject of the verb *wrote.*]

The knight **for whom Sir Gawain is searching** is the Knight of the Green Chapel. [The relative pronoun *whom* relates the adjective clause to the noun *knight* and serves as the object of the preposition *for.*]

An adjective clause may begin with a ***relative adverb,*** such as *when* or *where.*

EXAMPLES

My uncle Robert told us about the time **when he backpacked across the island of Luzon.** [The adjective clause modifies the noun *time.*]

Malcolm flees to England, **where he raises an army to attack Macbeth.** [The adjective clause modifies the noun *England.*]

The Noun Clause

7e. **A *noun clause* is a subordinate clause that may be used as a subject, a predicate nominative, a direct object, an indirect object, or an object of a preposition.**

Words that are commonly used to introduce noun clauses include *how, that, what, whether, who, whoever,* and *why.*

EXAMPLES

That Fleance escapes the murderers troubles Macbeth. [subject]

Power is **what Macbeth desires.** [predicate nominative]

Banquo suspected **that Macbeth had murdered Duncan.** [direct object]

The teacher will give **whoever can recite the soliloquy** ten points. [indirect object]

The teacher will give ten points to **whoever can recite the soliloquy.** [object of a preposition]

The word that introduces a noun clause may or may not have another function in the clause.

EXAMPLES

Do you know **who wrote *Don Juan***? [The word *who* introduces the noun clause and serves as the subject of the verb *wrote.*]

The witches predict **that Macbeth will become king.** [The word *that* introduces the noun clause but does not have any function within the noun clause.]

The Adverb Clause

7f. **An *adverb clause* is a subordinate clause that modifies a verb, an adjective, or an adverb.**

An adverb clause, which may come before or after the word or words it modifies, tells *how, when, where, why, to what extent,* or *under what condition.* An adverb clause is introduced by a ***subordinating conjunction***—a word or word group that relates the adverb clause to the word or words the clause modifies.

EXAMPLES

He acted **as though he had seen a ghost.** [The adverb clause modifies the verb *acted,* telling *how* he acted.]

Jane is taller **than her grandmother is.** [The adverb clause modifies the adjective *taller,* telling *to what extent* Jane is tall.]

They stayed longer **than I thought they would.** [The adverb clause modifies the adverb *longer,* telling *to what extent* their stay was longer.]

The Elliptical Clause

7g. **Part of a clause may be left out when the meaning can be understood from the context of the sentence. Such a clause is called an *elliptical clause.***

EXAMPLES

While [he was] **painting,** Rembrandt concentrated completely on his work.

Ken may ride with us **if he wants to** [ride with us].

This job took longer **than the last one** [took].

For more about using pronouns in elliptical constructions, see 4g.

8 SENTENCE STRUCTURE

SENTENCE OR FRAGMENT?

8a. **A *sentence* is a group of words that has a subject and a verb and expresses a complete thought.**

EXAMPLES

"My Last Duchess" is an example of a dramatic monologue.

For how many years was Winston Churchill the prime minister of Britain?

What an ambitious man Macbeth was!

Language Handbook

Only a sentence should begin with a capital letter and end with a period, a question mark, or an exclamation point. Do not be misled by a group of words that looks like a sentence but that either does not have a subject and a verb or does not express a complete thought. Such a word group is called a ***sentence fragment.***

FRAGMENT Awakens and finds himself surrounded by people six inches tall.

SENTENCE Gulliver awakens and finds himself surrounded by people six inches tall.

SUBJECT AND PREDICATE

8b. A sentence consists of two parts: a subject and a predicate. A *subject* tells *whom* or *what* the sentence is about. A *predicate* tells something about the subject.

In the following examples, all the words labeled *subject* make up the ***complete subject,*** and all the words labeled *predicate* make up the ***complete predicate.***

EXAMPLES

SUBJECT	PREDICATE
My sister and I	enjoyed *Gulliver's Travels.*

PREDICATE	SUBJECT	PREDICATE
For fifty years	Beowulf	ruled Geatland.

The Simple Subject

8c. A *simple subject* is the main word or group of words that tells *whom* or *what* the sentence is about.

EXAMPLE
The first **leader** of the gang was Blackie. [The complete subject is *the first leader of the gang.*]

The Simple Predicate

8d. A *simple predicate* is a verb or verb phrase that tells something about the subject.

EXAMPLE
Have you **read** "The Seafarer"? [The complete predicate is *have read "The Seafarer."*]

The Compound Subject and the Compound Verb

8e. A *compound subject* consists of two or more subjects that are joined by a conjunction—usually *and* or *or*—and that have the same verb.

EXAMPLE
A **nun** and three **priests** accompany the Prioress on the pilgrimage.

8f. A *compound verb* consists of two or more verbs that are joined by a conjunction—usually *and, but,* or *or*—and that have the same subject.

EXAMPLE
Truth **enlightens** the mind, **frees** the spirit, and **strengthens** the soul.

How to Find the Subject of a Sentence

8g. To find the subject of a sentence, ask *Who?* or *What?* before the verb.

(1) The subject of a sentence is never within a prepositional phrase.

EXAMPLES
A **group** of pilgrims gathered at the Tabard. [Who gathered? Group gathered. *Pilgrims* is the object of the preposition *of.*]
Out of the stillness came the loud **sound** of laughter. [What came? Sound came. *Stillness* is the object of the preposition *out of. Laughter* is the object of the preposition *of.*]

(2) The subject of a sentence expressing a command or a request is always understood to be *you,* although *you* may not appear in the sentence.

COMMAND Name the pilgrim accompanying the Plowman. [Who is being told to name? *You* is understood.]

The subject of a command or a request is *you* even when the sentence also contains a ***noun of direct address***—a word that names or identifies the one or ones spoken to.

REQUEST Marla, [you] please read the first stanza of "To a Skylark."

(3) The subject of a sentence expressing a question usually follows the verb or a part of the verb phrase. Turning the question into a statement will often help you find the subject.

QUESTION Have you read Lord Byron's poem "She Walks in Beauty"?

STATEMENT **You** have read Lord Byron's poem "She Walks in Beauty." [Who has read? You have read.]

QUESTION Were Shakespeare's plays popular during his own lifetime?

STATEMENT Shakespeare's **plays** were popular during his own lifetime. [What were popular? Plays were popular.]

(4) The word *there* or *here* is never the subject of a sentence.

EXAMPLES

There is **Canterbury Cathedral.** [What is there? Canterbury Cathedral is there.]

Here are my **drawings** of Chaucer's pilgrims. [What are here? Drawings are here.]

COMPLEMENTS

8h. **A *complement* is a word or a group of words that completes the meaning of a verb or a verbal. The four main kinds of complements are *direct objects, indirect objects, objective complements,* and *subject complements.***

The Direct Object and the Indirect Object

8i. **A *direct object* is a noun, a pronoun, or a word group that functions as a noun and tells *who* or *what* receives the action of a transitive verb.**

EXAMPLES

Banquo definitely suspected **him.** [Suspected whom? him]

Beethoven composed **sonatas** and **symphonies.** [Composed what? sonatas and symphonies—compound direct object]

8j. **An *indirect object* is a word or word group that comes between a transitive verb and a direct object. An indirect object, which may be a noun, a pronoun, or a word group that functions as a noun, tells *to whom, to what, for whom,* or *for what* the action of the verb is done.**

EXAMPLES

The Wife of Bath told the other **pilgrims** an interesting story. [Told to whom? pilgrims]

We should give **practicing for the concert** our full attention. [Should give our full attention to what? practicing for the concert]

The Objective Complement

8k. **An *objective complement* is a word or word group that helps complete the meaning of a transitive verb by identifying or modifying the direct object. An objective complement, which may be a noun, a pronoun, an adjective, or a word group that functions as a noun or an adjective, usually follows the direct object.**

EXAMPLES

Macduff called Malcolm **king.** [The noun *king* identifies the direct object *Malcolm.*]

He believed the money **his.** [The pronoun *his* modifies the direct object *money.*]

Everyone considered him **chivalrous.** [The adjective *chivalrous* modifies the direct object *him.*]

A ***transitive verb*** is an action verb that takes an object, which tells who or what receives the action.

The Subject Complement

8l. **A *subject complement* is a word or a word group that completes the meaning of a linking verb or a verbal and that identifies or modifies the subject. The two kinds of subject complements are *predicate nominatives* and *predicate adjectives.***

(1) A ***predicate nominative*** is a word or group of words that follows a linking verb and refers to the same person, place, thing, or idea as the subject of the verb. A predicate nominative may be a noun, a pronoun, or a word group that functions as a noun.

EXAMPLES

Of these three poets, Wordsworth was the most prolific **one.** [The pronoun *one* refers to the subject *Wordsworth.*]

The main characters are **Paul** and his **mother.** [The two nouns *Paul* and *mother* are a compound predicate nominative that refers to the subject *characters.*]

(2) A ***predicate adjective*** is an adjective that follows a linking verb and that modifies the subject of the verb.

EXAMPLES

Did King Hrothgar feel **powerless**? [The adjective *powerless* modifies the subject *King Hrothgar.*]

Iago is **sly** and **scheming.** [The two adjectives *sly* and *scheming* are a compound predicate adjective that modifies the subject *Iago.*]

For a list of linking verbs, see Part 1: The Parts of Speech.

SENTENCES CLASSIFIED ACCORDING TO STRUCTURE

8m. According to their structure, sentences are classified as *simple, compound, complex,* and *compound-complex.*

(1) A ***simple sentence*** has one independent clause and no subordinate clauses.

EXAMPLE
"Not Waving but Drowning" is one of my favorite poems.

(2) A ***compound sentence*** has two or more independent clauses but no subordinate clauses.

EXAMPLES
Othello is a great man, but his character is flawed.
Agatha Christie was a prolific writer; she wrote more than eighty books in less than sixty years.

(3) A ***complex sentence*** has one independent clause and at least one subordinate clause.

EXAMPLE
The poet who wrote "Ode on a Grecian Urn" is John Keats. [The independent clause is *the poet is John Keats.* The subordinate clause is *who wrote "Ode on a Grecian Urn."*]

(4) A ***compound-complex*** sentence has two or more independent clauses and at least one subordinate clause.

EXAMPLE
After Macbeth killed their father, Malcolm fled to England, and Donalbain escaped to Ireland. [The two independent clauses are *Malcolm fled to England* and *Donalbain escaped to Ireland.* The subordinate clause is *after Macbeth killed their father.*]

SENTENCES CLASSIFIED ACCORDING TO PURPOSE

8n. According to their purpose, sentences are classified as *declarative, interrogative, imperative,* and *exclamatory.*

(1) A ***declarative sentence*** makes a statement. It is followed by a period.

EXAMPLE
The lock on the front door is broken**.**

(2) An ***interrogative sentence*** asks a question. It is followed by a question mark.

EXAMPLE
Have you read Dylan Thomas's "Fern Hill"**?**

(3) An ***imperative sentence*** makes a request or gives a command. It is usually followed by a period. A very strong command, however, is followed by an exclamation point.

EXAMPLES
Please return this book to the library**.**
Give me the name of the warrior who succeeds Beowulf**.**
Stop making that noise**!**

(4) An ***exclamatory sentence*** expresses strong feeling or shows excitement. It is followed by an exclamation point.

EXAMPLES
What a talented writer she was**!**
We won**!**

For more information about using end marks, see 12a–e.

9 SENTENCE STYLE

WAYS TO ACHIEVE CLARITY

Coordinating Ideas

9a. To *coordinate* two or more ideas, or to give them equal emphasis, link them with a connecting word, an appropriate mark of punctuation, or both.

EXAMPLE
I read the novel *Frankenstein*, **and** then I saw the film.

Subordinating Ideas

9b. To *subordinate* an idea, or to show that one idea is related to but less important than another, use an adverb clause or an adjective clause.

EXAMPLES
Sir Gawain accepts the magic sash **because he wants it to protect him from the Green Knight.** [adverb clause]
Hrunting is the name of the sword **that Unferth gives Beowulf.** [adjective clause]

Using Parallel Structure

9c. **Use the same grammatical form (*parallel structure*) to express ideas of equal importance.**

(1) Use parallel structure when you link coordinate ideas.

EXAMPLE
In the winter I usually like **to ski** and **to skate.** [infinitive paired with infinitive]

(2) Use parallel structure when you compare or contrast ideas.

EXAMPLE
Einstein liked mathematical **research** more than laboratory **supervision.** [noun contrasted with noun]

(3) Use parallel structure when you link ideas with correlative conjunctions (*both . . . and, either . . . or, neither . . . nor,* or *not only . . . but also*).

EXAMPLE
Virginia Woolf was not only **a novelist** but also **an essayist.** [Note that the correlative conjunctions come directly before the parallel terms.]

When you revise for parallel structure, you may need to add an article, a preposition, or a pronoun before each of the parallel terms.

UNCLEAR I admire the poems of Byron more than Wordsworth.
CLEAR I admire the poems of Byron more than **those of** Wordsworth.

OBSTACLES TO CLARITY

Sentence Fragments

9d. **Avoid using a *sentence fragment*—a word or word group that either does not contain a subject and a verb or does not express a complete thought.**

For more information about sentence fragments, see 8a.

Here are two common ways to correct a sentence fragment.

1. Add words to make the thought complete.

FRAGMENT Twelve Geats around Beowulf's tower. [The verb is missing.]
SENTENCE Twelve Geats **rode** around Beowulf's tower.

2. Attach the fragment to the sentence that comes before or after it.

FRAGMENT A doctor and a gentlewoman see Lady Macbeth. Walking in her sleep. [participial phrase]
SENTENCE A doctor and a gentlewoman see Lady Macbeth **walking in her sleep.**

Sentence fragments can be effective when used in expressive and creative writing and in informal writing.

Run-on Sentences

9e. **Avoid using a *run-on sentence*—two or more complete thoughts that are run together as if they were one complete thought.**

The two kinds of run-on sentences are *fused sentences* and *comma splices.* A ***fused sentence*** has no punctuation or connecting word at all between the complete thoughts. A ***comma splice*** has just a comma between the complete thoughts.

FUSED SENTENCE Wiglaf helps Beowulf the other warriors retreat in fear.
COMMA SPLICE Wiglaf helps Beowulf, the other warriors retreat in fear.

You can correct run-on sentences in several ways.

1. Make two sentences.

EXAMPLE
Wiglaf helps Beowulf**.** The other warriors retreat in fear.

2. Use a comma and a coordinating conjunction.

EXAMPLE
Wiglaf helps Beowulf**, but** the other warriors retreat in fear.

3. Change one of the independent clauses to a subordinate clause.

EXAMPLE
Wiglaf helps Beowulf**, while the other warriors retreat in fear.**

4. Use a semicolon.

EXAMPLE
Wiglaf helps Beowulf**;** the other warriors retreat in fear.

5. Use a semicolon and a conjunctive adverb.

EXAMPLE
Wiglaf helps Beowulf**; however,** the other warriors retreat in fear.

Unnecessary Shifts in Sentences

9f. **Avoid making unnecessary shifts in subject, in tense, and in voice.**

AWKWARD Grandma goes to the farmers' market, where the freshest produce is. [shift in subject]

BETTER **Grandma** goes to the farmers' market, where **she** finds the freshest produce.

AWKWARD Macbeth sees Banquo's ghost, but no one else did. [shift in tense]

BETTER Macbeth **sees** Banquo's ghost, but no one else **does.**

AWKWARD Lyle spent four hours at the library, but no books on his research topic were found. [shift in voice]

BETTER Lyle **spent** four hours at the library, but he **found** no books on his research topic.

REVISING FOR VARIETY

9g. **Use a variety of sentence beginnings.**

Putting the subject first in a declarative sentence is not wrong, but starting every sentence with the subject can make your writing boring. To add variety to your sentences, rearrange sentence parts to vary the beginnings. The following examples show how a writer can revise sentences to avoid beginning with the subject every time.

SUBJECT FIRST Lady Macbeth is cunning and ruthless and goads her husband into committing murder.

SINGLE-WORD MODIFIERS FIRST **Cunning** and **ruthless,** Lady Macbeth goads her husband into committing murder.

SUBJECT FIRST ***In Memoriam,* which was published in 1850,** is Alfred, Lord Tennyson's elegy for his friend Arthur Hallam.

PARTICIPIAL PHRASE FIRST **Published in 1850,** *In Memoriam* is Alfred, Lord Tennyson's elegy for his friend Arthur Hallam.

APPOSITIVE PHRASE FIRST **An elegy for Alfred, Lord Tennyson's friend Arthur Hallam,** *In Memoriam* was published in 1850.

Varying Sentence Structure

9h. **Use a mix of simple, compound, complex, and compound-complex sentences in your writing.**

EXAMPLE

The three "weird sisters" greet Macbeth and Banquo with prophecies. [simple] According to the witches, Macbeth will become king, but Banquo will not, though his descendants will. [compound-complex] When Macbeth asks the witches to tell him more, they vanish. [complex] The subsequent conversation between Banquo and Macbeth lends insight into each man's character. [simple] That is, Banquo is skeptical of the witches' prophecies; however, Macbeth believes in them. [compound]

For information about the four kinds of sentence structure, see 8m.

Revising to Reduce Wordiness

9i. **Avoid using unnecessary words in your writing.**

The following guidelines suggest some ways to revise wordy sentences.

1. Take out a whole group of unnecessary words.

WORDY Grendel's mother carried Beowulf to her home where she lived.

IMPROVED Grendel's mother carried Beowulf to her home.

2. Replace pretentious words and expressions with straightforward ones.

WORDY In *Lord of the Flies,* a group of males, all of whom are under thirteen years of age, is stranded on a land mass surrounded by water and totally free of inhabitants.

IMPROVED In *Lord of the Flies,* a group of **young boys** is stranded on an **uninhabited island.**

3. Reduce a clause to a phrase.

WORDY Sir Lancelot falls in love with Queen Guinevere, who is the wife of King Arthur.

IMPROVED Sir Lancelot falls in love with Queen Guinevere, **King Arthur's wife.**

4. Reduce a phrase or a clause to one word.

WORDY At that point in time, Mr. Thomas returns.

IMPROVED **Then,** Mr. Thomas returns.

10 SENTENCE COMBINING

COMBINING BY INSERTING WORDS AND PHRASES

10a. Combine related sentences by taking a key word (or using another form of the key word) from one sentence and inserting it into another sentence.

ORIGINAL The famous magician Harry Houdini performed impossible escapes. The escapes only seemed impossible.

COMBINED The famous magician Harry Houdini performed **seemingly** impossible escapes. [The verb *seemed* becomes the adverb *seemingly.*]

10b. Combine related sentences by taking (or creating) a phrase from one sentence and inserting it into another.

ORIGINAL Have you read the poem "The Hollow Men"? It was written by T. S. Eliot.

COMBINED Have you read the poem "The Hollow Men" **by T. S. Eliot**? [prepositional phrase]

COMBINING BY COORDINATING IDEAS

10c. Combine related sentences whose ideas are equally important by using coordinating conjunctions (*and, but, or, nor, for, so, yet*) or correlative conjunctions (*both . . . and, either . . . or, neither . . . nor, not only . . . but also*).

The relationship of the ideas determines which connective will work best. When joined, the coordinate ideas form compound elements.

ORIGINAL *Paradise Lost* was written by John Milton. *Paradise Regained* was also written by him.

COMBINED *Paradise Lost* **and** *Paradise Regained* were written by John Milton. [compound subject]

ORIGINAL *Adonais* is one of Shelley's best-known poems. Many critics think that *Prometheus Unbound* is his masterpiece.

COMBINED *Adonais* is one of Shelley's best-known poems**, but** many critics think that *Prometheus Unbound* is his masterpiece. [compound sentence]

Another way to form a compound sentence is to link independent clauses with a semicolon or with a semicolon and a conjunctive adverb (such as *however, likewise,* or *therefore*) followed by a comma.

EXAMPLES

She was willing to compromise**;** he was not.

They moved to Dorsetshire**; however,** they stayed there only a few months.

COMBINING BY SUBORDINATING IDEAS

10d. Combine related sentences whose ideas are not equally important by placing the less important idea in a subordinate clause (adjective clause, adverb clause, or noun clause).

ORIGINAL I read about the life of Queen Victoria. She ruled Great Britain from 1837 to 1901.

COMBINED I read about the life of Queen Victoria, **who ruled Great Britain from 1837 to 1901.** [adjective clause]

or

COMBINED Queen Victoria, **whose life I read about,** ruled Great Britain from 1837 to 1901. [adjective clause]

ORIGINAL Grendel's mother attacks Herot. King Hrothgar once again asks Beowulf for help.

COMBINED **When Grendel's mother attacks Herot,** King Hrothgar once again asks Beowulf for help. [adverb clause]

ORIGINAL They will find Death under an oak tree. An old man tells the three rioters that this will happen.

COMBINED An old man tells the three rioters **that they will find Death under an oak tree.** [noun clause]

For more information about subordinate clauses and subordinating ideas, see 7c–g and 9b.

Language Handbook

11 Capitalization

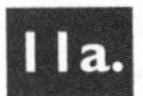

11a. Capitalize the first word in every sentence.

EXAMPLE
The warrior who succeeds Beowulf as king is Wiglaf.

(1) Capitalize the first word of a sentence following a colon.

EXAMPLE
Mrs. Kelley asked me this question: **H**ow old is Beowulf when he fights Grendel?

(2) Capitalize the first word of a direct quotation.

EXAMPLE
After winning, Brian said, "**W**e couldn't have done it without the support of the good people of Raleigh."

When quoting from another writer's work, capitalize the first word of the quotation only if the writer has capitalized it in the original work.

EXAMPLE
After winning, Brian acknowledged "the support of the good people of Raleigh."

(3) Traditionally, the first word of a line of poetry is capitalized.

EXAMPLES
If all the world and love were young,
And truth in every shepherd's tongue,
These pretty pleasures might me move
To live with thee and be thy love.
—Sir Walter Raleigh, "The Nymph's Reply to the Shepherd"

NOTE Some writers do not follow this rule. Whenever you quote from a writer's work, always use capital letters exactly as the writer uses them.

11b. Capitalize the first word in the salutation and the closing of a letter.

EXAMPLES
Dear John, **D**ear Sir or Madam: **S**incerely,

11c. Capitalize proper nouns and proper adjectives.

A ***common noun*** is a general name for a person, a place, a thing, or an idea. A ***proper noun*** names a particular person, place, thing, or idea. A ***proper adjective*** is formed from a proper noun. Common nouns are capitalized only if they begin a sentence (also, in most cases, a line of poetry), begin a direct quotation, or are part of a title.

COMMON NOUNS	PROPER NOUNS	PROPER ADJECTIVES
dramatist	**S**hakespeare	**S**hakespearean performer
country	**R**ussia	**R**ussian diplomat
mountains	the **A**lps	**A**lpine flora

In most proper nouns made up of two or more words, do not capitalize articles (*a, an, the*), short prepositions (those with fewer than five letters, such as *at, of, for, to, with*), the mark of the infinitive (*to*), and coordinating conjunctions (*and, but, for, nor, or, so, yet*).

EXAMPLES
Speaker of the **H**ouse of **R**epresentatives
American **S**ociety for the **P**revention of **C**ruelty to **A**nimals

NOTE When you're not sure whether to capitalize a word, check a dictionary.

(1) Capitalize the names of most persons and animals.

GIVEN NAMES	**V**irginia	**G**eoffrey
SURNAMES	**W**oolf	**C**haucer
ANIMALS	**L**assie	**R**ocinante

NOTE Some names contain more than one capital letter. Usage varies in the capitalization of *van, von, du, de la,* and other parts of many multiword names. Always verify the spelling of a name with the person, or check the name in a reference source.

EXAMPLES
La **F**ontaine **O'C**onnor al-**K**hansa **M**c**E**wen
Van **D**oren **I**bn **E**zra van **G**ogh de **V**ega

(2) Capitalize the names of nationalities, races, and peoples.

EXAMPLES
Japanese **C**aucasian **H**ispanic **C**elt

(3) Capitalize brand names. Notice that the noun that follows a brand name is not capitalized.

EXAMPLES
Sealtest milk **W**onder bread **C**rest toothpaste

(4) Capitalize geographical names.

TYPE OF NAME	EXAMPLES	
Towns, Cities	Stratford-on-Avon Rio de Janeiro	Dublin South Bend
Counties, Townships	Marion County Brooklyn Borough	Alexandria Township Lafayette Parish
States, Territories	Oklahoma Yucatán	North Carolina Yukon Territory
Regions	the Middle East Western Hemisphere	the Lake District the Southwest
Countries	England	Costa Rica
Continents	South America	Europe
Islands	Long Island	British Isles
Mountains	Himalayas Pikes Peak	Mount Rainier Sierra Nevada
Other Landforms and Features	Cape of Good Hope Death Valley	Isthmus of Corinth Black Forest
Bodies of Water	Indian Ocean Bering Strait	Red Sea San Francisco Bay
Parks	Hawaii Volcanoes National Park Point Reyes National Seashore	
Roads, Highways, Streets	Route 42 Interstate 75	King Avenue Thirty-fourth Street

Words such as *city, state,* and *county* are often capitalized in official documents such as proclamations. In general usage, however, these words are not capitalized.

OFFICIAL USAGE
the State of Iowa

GENERAL USAGE
the state of Iowa

Words such as *north, western,* and *southeast* are not capitalized when they indicate direction.

EXAMPLES
north of London
heading **s**outhwest

The second word in a hyphenated number begins with a small letter.

EXAMPLE
Forty-**s**econd Street

(5) Capitalize the names of organizations, teams, business firms, institutions, buildings and other structures, and government bodies.

TYPE OF NAME	EXAMPLES
Organizations	Disabled American Veterans Professional Photographers of America
Teams	River City Eastside Bombers Harlem Globetrotters
Business Firms	Aaron's Carpets National Broadcasting Corporation
Institutions	Oxford University Southern Christian Leadership Conference
Buildings and Other Structures	Lincoln Center for the Performing Arts the Great Wall of China
Government Bodies	United States Congress House of Commons

NOTE

Do not capitalize words such as *democratic, republican,* and *socialist* when they refer to principles or forms of government. Capitalize such words only when they refer to specific political parties.

EXAMPLES
The citizens demanded **d**emocratic reforms.
Who will be the **R**epublican nominee for governor?

NOTE

Do not capitalize words such as *building, hospital, theater, high school,* and *post office* unless they are part of a proper noun.

(6) Capitalize the names of historical events and periods, special events, holidays and other calendar items, and time zones.

TYPE OF NAME	EXAMPLES	
Historical Events and Periods	**M**iddle **A**ges	**R**eign of **T**error
Special Events	**S**uper **B**owl	**P**an-**A**merican **G**ames
Holidays and Other Calendar Items	**M**onday **N**ovember	**M**emorial **D**ay **N**ational **B**ook **W**eek
Time Zones	**E**astern **D**aylight **T**ime (**EDT**) **C**entral **M**ountain **T**ime (**CMT**)	

NOTE Do not capitalize the name of a season unless it is being personified or used as part of a proper noun.

EXAMPLES
We moved here last **f**all.
This month **F**all begins painting the leaves in brilliant hues.
The **F**all Festival is next week.

(7) Capitalize the names of ships, trains, aircraft, spacecraft, monuments, awards, planets and other heavenly bodies, and any other particular places and things.

TYPE OF NAME	EXAMPLES	
Ships	***M**errimac*	**U.S.S.** ***N**autilus*
Trains	***Z**ephyr*	***H**ill **C**ountry **F**lyer*
Aircraft	***E**nola **G**ay*	***S**pruce **G**oose*
Spacecraft	***C**olumbia*	***M**agellan*
Monuments	**M**ount **R**ushmore **N**ational **M**emorial **E**ffigy **M**ounds **N**ational **M**onument	
Awards	**N**obel **P**rize	**M**edal of **F**reedom
Planets and Other Heavenly Bodies	**N**eptune **B**ig **D**ipper	**P**olaris **C**assiopeia
Other Particular Places and Things	**H**urricane **A**lma **M**arshall **P**lan	**S**ilk **R**oute **U**nion **J**ack

NOTE Do not capitalize the words *sun* and *moon*. Do not capitalize the word *earth* unless it is used along with the proper names of other particular places, things, or events.

EXAMPLES
The equator is an imaginary circle around the **e**arth.
Is Mercury closer to the **s**un than **E**arth is?

For more information about the names of particular places and things, see the discussion of proper nouns in 11c.

11d. Do not capitalize the names of school subjects, except names of languages and course names followed by a number.

EXAMPLES
French art Algebra I

11e. Capitalize titles.

(1) Capitalize a title belonging to a particular person when it comes before the person's name.

EXAMPLES
General Patton **D**r. Sanchez **P**resident Clinton

In general, do not capitalize a title used alone or following a name. Some titles, however, are by tradition capitalized. If you are unsure about capitalizing a title, check in a dictionary.

EXAMPLES
Who is the **p**rime **m**inister of Britain?
When was Ann Richards **g**overnor of Texas?
The **P**rince of **W**ales met earlier today with European leaders.

A title is usually capitalized when it is used alone in direct address.

EXAMPLE
Good afternoon, **S**ir [*or* **s**ir], may I help you?

(2) Capitalize a word showing a family relationship when the word is used before or in place of a person's name, unless a possessive comes before the word.

EXAMPLES
I asked **M**om if **U**ncle Bob is named after her **u**ncle Roberto.

(3) Capitalize the first and last words and all important words in titles of books, periodicals, poems, stories, essays, speeches, plays, historical documents, movies, radio and television programs, works of art, musical compositions, and cartoons.

TYPE OF NAME	EXAMPLES	
Books	*A Tale of Two Cities*	*Gulliver's Travels*
Periodicals	*National Geographic*	*Time*
Poems	"She Walks in Beauty"	"To His Coy Mistress"
Stories	"The Rocking-Horse Winner"	"Games at Twilight"
Essays and Speeches	"A Modest Proposal"	the Gettysburg Address
Plays	*The Tragedy of Macbeth*	*Pygmalion*
Historical Documents	Magna Carta	Treaty of Versailles
Movies	*Robin Hood: Prince of Thieves*	*Clueless*
Radio and TV Programs	*Adventures in World Music*	*Nova*
Works of Art	*The Kiss*	*March of Humanity*
Musical Compositions	*War Requiem*	"Tears in Heaven"
Cartoons	*For Better or Worse*	*Jump Start*

NOTE Unimportant words in a title include articles (*a, an, the*), short prepositions (those with fewer than five letters, such as *of, to, in, for, from, with*), and coordinating conjunctions (*and, but, for, nor, or, so, yet*).

For information about which titles should be italicized and which should be enclosed in quotation marks, see 13b and 13d.

11f. Capitalize the names of religions and their followers, holy days and celebrations, holy writings, and specific deities and venerated beings.

TYPE OF NAME	EXAMPLES	
Religions and Followers	Christianity Muslim	Buddhist Judaism
Holy Days and Celebrations	Easter Passover	Ramadan Holy Week
Holy Writings	Bible Talmud	Koran I Ching
Specific Deities and Venerated Beings	Allah Dalai Lama	God Jehovah

NOTE The words *god* and *goddess* are not capitalized when they refer to mythological deities. The names of specific mythological deities are capitalized, however.

EXAMPLES
The Greek god of the sea was Poseidon.

12 PUNCTUATION

END MARKS

12a. A statement (or declarative sentence) is followed by a period.

EXAMPLE
The Ancient Mariner told an amazing tale.

12b. A question (or interrogative sentence) is followed by a question mark.

EXAMPLE
Do you know who played the leading role in the first movie version of *Hamlet*?

12c. **A request or command (or imperative sentence) is followed by either a period or an exclamation point.**

EXAMPLES
Turn the music down, please**.** [request]
Name the poet who wrote "The Lady of Shalott**.**" [mild command]
Watch out**!** [strong command]

12d. **An exclamation (or exclamatory sentence) is followed by an exclamation point.**

EXAMPLE
What an interesting story "My Oedipus Complex" is**!**

12e. **An abbreviation is usually followed by a period.**

If an abbreviation with a period ends a sentence, do not add another period. However, do add a question mark or an exclamation point if one is needed.

EXAMPLES
The store opens at 10 A.M**.**
Does the store open at 10 A.M.**?**

Some abbreviations, including those for most units of measurement, are written without periods.

EXAMPLES
AM/FM, CIA, CNN, PC, NASA, SOS,
cc, ft, lb, kw, ml, psi, rpm [*but* in. *for* inch]

TYPE OF ABBREVIATION	EXAMPLES
Personal Names	Howard G**.** Chua-Eoan W**.** H**.** Auden
Organizations, Companies	Co**.** Inc**.** Ltd**.**
Titles Used with Names	Ms**.** Sr**.** Dr**.**
Times of Day	A**.**M**.** (*or* a**.**m**.**) P**.**M**.** (*or* p**.**m**.**)
Years	B**.**C**.** (*written after the date*) A**.**D**.** (*written before the date*)
Addresses	St**.** Blvd**.** P**.** O**.** Box
States	S**.**C**.** Calif**.**

NOTE Use a two-letter state code when the ZIP Code is included. Two-letter state codes are not followed by periods, and no comma is placed between the state code and the ZIP Code.

EXAMPLE
Lexington, **KY** 40505

COMMAS

12f. **Use commas to separate items in a series.**

EXAMPLE
Virginia Woolf**,** James Joyce**,** and D. H. Lawrence are among the writers we are studying.

If all the items in a series are linked by *and, or,* or *nor,* do not use commas to separate them.

EXAMPLE
Byron **and** Shelley **and** Keats were contemporaries.

12g. **Use a comma to separate two or more adjectives preceding a noun.**

EXAMPLE
Gawain is the most gallant**,** honorable knight.

When the last adjective before a noun is thought of as part of the noun, the comma before the adjective is omitted.

EXAMPLE
I've finally found a decent, affordable used car. [*Used car* is thought of as one unit.]

12h. **Use a comma before *and, but, or, nor, for, so,* and yet when they join independent clauses.**

EXAMPLE
I read Seamus Heaney's "The Grauballe Man**,**" and now I want to read more of his poems.

You may omit the comma before *and, but, or,* or *nor* if the clauses are very short and there is no chance of misunderstanding.

12i. **Use commas to set off nonessential clauses and nonessential participial phrases.**

A ***nonessential*** clause or phrase is one that can be left out without changing the meaning of the sentence.

NONESSENTIAL CLAUSE W. H. Auden**, who was born in York, England,** became an American citizen in 1946.

NONESSENTIAL PHRASE The little blue sports car**, leaving all the others far behind,** forged into the lead.

For more information about phrases, see 6a–f. For more on clauses, see 7a–g.

An ***essential*** clause or phrase is one that cannot be left out without changing the meaning of the sentence. Essential clauses and phrases are *not* set off by commas.

ESSENTIAL CLAUSE The writer **who received the Nobel Prize in literature in 1923** was William Butler Yeats.

ESSENTIAL PHRASE The pilgrims **riding along with the Knight** are the Squire and the Yeoman.

12j. Use commas after certain introductory elements.

(1) Use a comma after a one-word adverb such as *first, next, yes,* or *no* or after any mild exclamation such as *well* or *why* at the beginning of a sentence.

EXAMPLE
Yes, I have read *Don Juan.*

(2) Use a comma after an introductory participial phrase.

EXAMPLE
Looking calm, Jill walked to the podium.

(3) Use a comma after two or more introductory prepositional phrases or after a single long one.

EXAMPLE
With the help of Wiglaf, he killed the dragon.

(4) Use a comma after an introductory adverb clause.

EXAMPLE
After I had locked the car door, I remembered that the keys were still in the ignition.

12k. Use commas to set off elements that interrupt a sentence.

(1) Appositives and appositive phrases are usually set off by commas.

EXAMPLES
George Bernard Shaw's first play**, *Widowers' Houses*,** was published in 1893.
Is that she**, the one holding the sunflowers**?

Sometimes an appositive is so closely related to the word or words near it that it should not be set off by commas. Such an appositive is called a ***restrictive appositive.***

EXAMPLE
The poet **Edmund Spenser** died suddenly in 1599.

(2) Words used in direct address are set off by commas.

EXAMPLE
Your research paper**, Dylan,** is quite interesting.

(3) Parenthetical expressions are set off by commas.

Parenthetical expressions are remarks that add incidental information or that relate ideas to each other. Some common parenthetical expressions are *for example, I think, moreover,* and *on the other hand.*

EXAMPLE
Macbeth is superstitious and sensitive; Lady Macbeth**, on the other hand,** is logical and bold.

NOTE A contrasting expression introduced by *not, rather than,* or a similar term is parenthetical. Set it off by commas.

EXAMPLE
Percy Bysshe Shelley**, not John Keats,** wrote "Ode to the West Wind."

12l. Use a comma in certain conventional situations.

(1) Use a comma to separate items in dates and addresses.

EXAMPLES
On April 23**,** 1616**,** William Shakespeare died.
My grandparents' address is 505 King Street**,** Austin**,** TX 78701.

(2) Use a comma after the salutation of a personal letter and after the closing of any letter.

EXAMPLES
Dear Alicia**,**   Yours truly**,**

(3) Use commas to set off abbreviations such as *Jr., Sr., RN, M.D., Ltd.,* or *Inc.*

EXAMPLES
Is Jorge Rivera**,** Jr.**,** in your class?
She is the owner of Flowers by Arthurine**,** Inc.

SEMICOLONS

12m. Use a semicolon between independent clauses that are closely related in thought and are not joined by *and, but, for, nor, or, so,* or *yet.*

EXAMPLE
The rain had finally stopped**;** a few rays of sunshine were pushing through breaks in the clouds.

12n. Use a semicolon between independent clauses joined by a conjunctive adverb or a transitional expression.

A ***conjunctive adverb***—such as *furthermore, however,* or *nevertheless*—or a ***transitional expression***—such as *for instance, in fact,* or *that is*—indicates the relationship of the independent clauses that it joins.

EXAMPLE
The snow made traveling difficult**;** **nevertheless,** we arrived home safely.

12o. **Use a semicolon (rather than a comma) before a coordinating conjunction to join independent clauses that contain commas.**

EXAMPLE
During the seventeenth century—the era of such distinguished prose writers as Sir Thomas Browne, John Donne, and Jeremy Taylor—the balanced compound sentence using commas and semicolons reached a high degree of perfection and popularity**;** but the tendency today is to use a fast-moving style with shorter sentences, fewer commas, and fewer semicolons. [commas within the clauses]

12p. **Use a semicolon between items in a series if the items contain commas.**

EXAMPLE
The summer reading list includes *Jude the Obscure,* by Thomas Hardy**;** *Lord Jim,* by Joseph Conrad**;** and *Lord of the Flies,* by William Golding.

COLONS

12q. **Use a colon to mean "note what follows."**

(1) Use a colon before a list of items, especially after expressions such as *as follows* and *the following.*

EXAMPLE
Collection 8 includes poems by the following authors**:** Robert Burns, William Blake, William Wordsworth, and Samuel Taylor Coleridge.

Do not use a colon before a list that directly follows a verb or a preposition.

EXAMPLES
Collection 8 includes poems by Robert Burns, William Blake, William Wordsworth, and Samuel Taylor Coleridge. [The list directly follows the preposition *by.*]
The main characters in Charles Dickens's *A Tale of Two Cities* are Dr. Manette, Lucie Manette, Charles Darnay, and Sydney Carton. [The list directly follows the verb *are.*]

(2) Use a colon before a quotation that lacks a speaker tag such as *he said* or *she remarked.*

EXAMPLE
His father's response surprised him**:** "I'm proud of you, son."

For information about punctuating quotations that do have speaker tags, see 13c.

(3) Use a colon before a long, formal statement or quotation.

EXAMPLE
When he awoke, Gulliver found himself tied down**:** "I could only look upward; the sun began to grow hot, and the light offended my eyes. I heard a confused noise about me, but in the posture I lay, could see nothing except the sky."

12r. **Use a colon in certain conventional situations.**

EXAMPLES
12**:**01 A.M. [between the hour and the minute]
Mark 3**:**10 [between chapter and verse in referring to passages from the Bible]
To Whom It May Concern**:** [after the salutation of a business letter]
"A Valediction**:** Forbidding Mourning" [between a title and a subtitle]

13 Punctuation

ITALICS

Italics are printed characters that *slant to the right like this.* To indicate italics in handwritten or typewritten work, use underlining.

13a. **Use italics (underlining) for words, letters, and symbols referred to as such and for foreign words that have not been adopted into English.**

EXAMPLES
The words *hiss* and *clang* are examples of onomatopoeia.
You typed *ie* instead of *ei.*
The motto *e pluribus unum* appears on all United States coins.

13b. **Use italics (underlining) for titles of books, plays, long poems, periodicals, newspapers, works of art, films, television series, long musical compositions, recordings, comic strips, computer software, court cases, trains, ships, aircraft, and spacecraft.**

TYPE OF NAME	EXAMPLE
Books	*The Canterbury Tales*
Plays	*The Taming of the Shrew*
Long Poems	*The Rime of the Ancient Mariner*
Periodicals	*Sports Illustrated*
Newspapers	*The Boston Globe*
Works of Art	*The Persistence of Memory*
Films	*It's a Wonderful Life*
TV Series	*American Playhouse*
Long Musical Compositions	*The Planets*
Recordings	*Unforgettable*
Comic Strips	*Doonesbury*
Computer Software	*Lotus 1-2-3*
Court Cases	*Marbury* v. *Madison*
Trains, Ships, Aircraft, and Spacecraft	*Orient Express* *Queen Elizabeth 2* *Enola Gay* *Apollo 13*

NOTE The article *the* before the title of a book, periodical, or newspaper is neither italicized nor capitalized unless it is part of the official title. The official title of a book appears on the book's title page. The official title of a periodical or newspaper is the name on its masthead, usually found on the editorial page.

EXAMPLES

What role does fate play in "The Seafarer"?

I found this information in ***The New York Times.***

My mom looks through the *Sun-Times* every morning.

For a list of titles that are enclosed in quotation marks, see 13d. For information about capitalizing titles, see 11e(3).

QUOTATION MARKS

13c. **Use quotation marks to enclose a *direct quotation*—a person's exact words.**

(1) A direct quotation usually begins with a capital letter.

EXAMPLE

Sir Francis Bacon wrote, "**K**nowledge is power."

However, when the quotation is only a part of a sentence, do not begin it with a capital letter.

EXAMPLE

In Act 1, Scene 5, Lady Macbeth describes her husband's nature as "**t**oo full o' th' milk of human kindness."

Do not use quotation marks to enclose an ***indirect quotation*** (a rewording of a direct quotation).

DIRECT QUOTATION Al said, "I'm going fishing today."

INDIRECT QUOTATION Al said that he is going fishing today.

(2) When the expression identifying the speaker divides a quoted sentence, the second part begins with a lowercase letter.

EXAMPLE

"All good moral philosophy," according to Sir Francis Bacon, "**i**s but the handmaid to religion." [Notice that each part of a divided quotation is enclosed in quotation marks.]

When the second part of a divided quotation is a new sentence, the first word begins with a capital letter.

EXAMPLE

"On his first voyage, Gulliver finds himself in Lilliput," explained Ms. Chávez. "**T**he people there are only six inches tall."

(3) When used with quotation marks, other marks of punctuation are placed according to the following rules.

- Commas and periods are always placed inside the closing quotation marks.

EXAMPLES

"Read these lines**,"** he said, "and tell me what you think they mean**."**

- Semicolons and colons are always placed outside the closing quotation marks.

EXAMPLES

Gloria promised, "I'll go to the dance with you"; however, she said that several weeks ago.

Find examples of the following figures of speech in Wordsworth's poem "I Wandered Lonely as a Cloud": personification, metaphor, and simile.

- Question marks and exclamation points are placed inside the closing quotation marks if the quotation itself is a question or an exclamation. Otherwise, they are placed outside.

EXAMPLES

Did Keats write "Ode on a Grecian Urn"?

"What an imagination you have!" exclaimed Beth.

(4) When quoting a passage that consists of more than one paragraph, put quotation marks at the beginning of each paragraph and at the end of only the last paragraph in the passage.

EXAMPLE

"At Mr. Bowyers's, a great deal of company; some I knew, others I did not. Here we stayed upon the leads and below till it was late, expecting to see the fireworks; but they were not performed tonight. Only, the City had a light like a glory round about it, with bonfires.

"At last I went to King Street; and there sent Crockford to my father's and my house to tell them I could not come home tonight, because of the dirt and a coach could not be had."

—Samuel Pepys, *The Diary of Samuel Pepys*

(5) Use single quotation marks to enclose a quotation within a quotation.

EXAMPLE

Ms. Markham asked us, "What do you think John Donne meant when he said, 'No man is an island, entire of itself'?"

(6) When writing ***dialogue*** (a conversation), begin a new paragraph every time the speaker changes, and enclose each speaker's words in quotation marks.

EXAMPLE

This frighted the fellow that attended about the work; but after some pause John Hayward, recovering himself, said, "Lord, bless us! There's somebody in the cart not quite dead!"

So another called to him and said, "Who are you?"

The fellow answered, "I am the poor piper. Where am I?"

"Where are you?" says Hayward. "Why, you are in the dead-cart, and we are going to bury you."

—Daniel Defoe, *A Journal of the Plague Year*

13d. **Use quotation marks to enclose titles of short works, such as short stories, poems, essays, articles, songs, episodes of television series, and chapters and other parts of books.**

TYPE OF NAME	EXAMPLE
Short Stories	"The Doll's House" "Games at Twilight"
Poems	"Ode to a Nightingale" "Thoughts of Hanoi"
Essays	"Shakespeare's Sister" "The Myth of Sisyphus"
Articles	"How to Improve Your Grades"
Songs	"Wind Beneath My Wings" "Frankie and Johnny"
TV Episodes	"Tony's Surprise Party" "Inside the Earth"
Chapters of a Book	"The Age of Reform" "How Ecosystems Change"

Neither italics nor quotation marks are used for the titles of major religious texts or for the titles of historical or legal documents.

EXAMPLES

the Bible
Code of Hammurabi
Bill of Rights
Monroe Doctrine

For a list of titles that are italicized, see 13b.

ELLIPSIS POINTS

13e. **Use three spaced periods called *ellipsis points* (. . .) to mark omissions from quoted material and pauses in a written passage.**

ORIGINAL At last she spoke to me. When she addressed the first words to me I was so confused that I did not know what to answer. She asked me was I going to *Araby*. I forget whether I answered yes or no. It would be a splendid bazaar, she said; she would love to go.

—James Joyce, "Araby"

(1) If the quoted material that comes before the ellipsis points is not a complete sentence, use three ellipsis points with a space before the first point.

EXAMPLE
Of his conversation with Mangan's sister, the narrator says, "When she addressed the first words to me . . . I did not know what to answer."

(2) If the quoted material that comes before the ellipsis points is a complete sentence, use an end mark before the ellipsis points.

EXAMPLE
According to Mangan's sister, "It would be a splendid bazaar. . . ."

(3) If one sentence or more is omitted, ellipsis points follow any end mark that precedes the omitted material.

EXAMPLE
The narrator recalls his encounter with Mangan's sister: "At last she spoke to me. . . . She asked me was I going to *Araby*."

(4) To show that a full line or more of poetry has been omitted, use a line of spaced periods that is as long as the line of poetry above it.

ORIGINAL It fell about the Martinmas time,
And a gay time it was then,
When our goodwife got puddings to make,
And she's boild them in the pan.
—Traditional, "Get Up and Bar the Door"

ONE LINE OMITTED It fell about the Martinmas time,
. . . .
When our goodwife got puddings to make,
And she's boild them in the pan.

APOSTROPHES

Possessive Case

13f. The *possessive case* of a noun or a pronoun indicates ownership or relationship. Use an apostrophe in forming the possessive case of nouns and indefinite pronouns.

(1) To form the possessive of a singular noun, add an apostrophe and an *s*.

EXAMPLES
Beowulf**'s** shield the principal**'s** office

When forming the possessive of a singular noun that ends in an *s* sound, add only an apostrophe if the addition of *'s* will make the noun awkward to pronounce. Otherwise, add *'s*.

EXAMPLES
Ms. Rodgers**'** class the witness**'s** testimony

(2) To form the possessive of a plural noun ending in *s*, add only the apostrophe.

EXAMPLES
the players**'** uniforms the volunteers**'** efforts

(3) Form the possessive of only the last word in a compound word, in the name of an organization or business, or in a word group showing joint possession.

EXAMPLES
brother-in-law**'s** car
Ralph Merrill and Company**'s** products
Macbeth and Lady Macbeth**'s** plan

When a possessive pronoun is part of a word group showing joint possession, each noun in the word group is also possessive.

EXAMPLE
Chen**'s,** Ramona**'s,** and **my** project

(4) Form the possessive of each noun in a word group showing individual possession of similar items.

EXAMPLE
Byron**'s,** Shelley**'s,** and Keats**'s** poems

(5) Possessive forms of words indicating time, such as *minute, day, month,* and *year,* and words indicating amounts in cents or dollars require apostrophes.

EXAMPLES
four weeks**'** vacation a dollar**'s** worth

(6) To form the possessive of an indefinite pronoun, add an apostrophe and an *s*.

EXAMPLES
no one**'s** fault somebody else**'s** jacket

Contractions

13g. Use an apostrophe to show where letters, words, or numbers have been omitted in a contraction.

EXAMPLES
let us . . . . **let's** she would . . . . . **she'd**
you will . . . . . **you'll** 1998 . . . . **'98**

The word *not* can be shortened to *–n't* and added to a verb, usually without changing the spelling of the verb.

EXAMPLES
do not . . . . **don't** should not . . . **shouldn't**
EXCEPTION
will not . . . **won't**

Plurals

13h. Use an apostrophe and an *s* to form the plurals of all lowercase letters, some uppercase letters, numerals, and some words referred to as words.

EXAMPLES

There are two **c's** and two ***m*'s** in *accommodate.*
Try not to use so many ***I*'s** in your cover letter.
[Without the apostrophe, the plural of the pronoun *I* would spell *Is.*]

NOTE You may add only an s to form the plurals of words, numerals, and capital letters if the plural forms will not cause misreading. However, it is never wrong to use an apostrophe in such cases and is usually a good idea to do so.

EXAMPLE

James I ruled England during the early **1600s** [*or* **1600's**].

HYPHENS

13i. Use a hyphen to divide a word at the end of a line.

- Do not divide a one-syllable word.

EXAMPLE

Did the Green Knight know that Sir Gawain had **kissed** [*not* kis-sed] his wife?

- Divide a word only between syllables.

EXAMPLE

First, Macbeth was killed; then he was **decapi-tated** [*not* decapita-ted].

- Divide an already hyphenated word at the hyphen.

EXAMPLE

Queen Elizabeth I was ruler of England for **forty-five** [*not* for-ty-five] years.

- Do not divide a word so that one letter stands alone.

EXAMPLE

Paradise Lost by John Milton is a famous English **epic** [*not* e-pic].

13j. Use a hyphen with compound numbers from twenty-one to ninety-nine and with fractions used as modifiers.

EXAMPLES

thirty-seven
a **three-fourths** majority [*but* **three fourths** of the voters]

DASHES

13k. Use dashes to set off abrupt breaks in thought.

EXAMPLE

The playwright handles her material**—**I should say lack of material**—**quite well.

13l. Use dashes to set off appositives or parenthetical expressions that contain commas.

EXAMPLE

Several of the British Romantic poets**—**Shelley, Keats, and Byron, for example**—**led fascinating lives.

13m. Use a dash to set off an introductory list or group of examples.

EXAMPLE

Alliteration, caesuras, and kennings**—**these are features of Anglo-Saxon poetry.

PARENTHESES

13n. Use parentheses to enclose informative or explanatory material of minor importance.

EXAMPLES

A *roman à clef* **(**literally, "novel with a key"**)** is a novel about real people to whom the novelist has assigned fictitious names.
The Globe **(s**ee the drawing on page 428**)** was built in 1599. [The *s* in *see* is lowercase because the parenthetical sentence is within a complete sentence.]
The Globe was built in 1599. **(S**ee the drawing on page 428**.)** [The *S* in *See* is capitalized and a period follows *page 428* because the parenthetical sentence is not within another sentence but instead stands on its own.]

BRACKETS

13o. Use brackets to enclose an explanation within quoted or parenthetical material.

EXAMPLE

The newspaper article stated that "at the time of that Democratic National Convention **[**in Chicago in 1968**]** there were many protest groups operating in the United States."

14 SPELLING

UNDERSTANDING WORD STRUCTURE

Many English words are made up of roots and affixes (prefixes and suffixes).

Roots

The ***root*** of a word is the part that carries the word's core meaning.

ROOT	MEANING	EXAMPLES
–fin–	end, limit	final, infinite
–gram–	write, writing	grammar, epigram
–tract–	pull, draw	tractor, extract
–vit–	life	vitamin, vital

Prefixes

A ***prefix*** is one or more letters or syllables added to the beginning of a word or word part to create a new word.

PREFIX	MEANING	EXAMPLES
contra–	against	contradict, contrast
inter–	between, among	interstate, interact
mis–	not, wrongly	misfire, misspell
re–	back, again	reflect, refinance

Suffixes

A ***suffix*** is one or more letters or syllables added to the end of a word or word part to create a new word.

SUFFIX	MEANING	EXAMPLES
–fy	make, cause	verify, pacify
–ish	suggesting, like	smallish, childish
–ist	doer, believer	artist, humanist
–ty	quality, state	cruelty, certainty

SPELLING RULES

Always keep in mind that the best way to be sure you have spelled a word correctly is to look the word up in a dictionary.

ie and *ei*

14a. Write *ie* when the sound is long e, except after *c*.

EXAMPLES
rel**ie**ve ch**ie**f f**ie**ld conc**ei**t dec**ei**ve
EXCEPTIONS
either l**ei**sure n**ei**ther s**ei**ze prot**ei**n

14b. Write *ei* when the sound is not long e.

EXAMPLES
r**ei**gn for**ei**gn th**ei**r sover**ei**gn w**ei**ght
EXCEPTIONS
anc**ie**nt v**ie**w fr**ie**nd misch**ie**f consc**ie**nce

Rules 14a and 14b apply only when the *i* and the e are in the same syllable.

–cede, –ceed, and *–sede*

14c. The only English word ending in *–sede* is *supersede*. The only words ending in *–ceed* are *exceed, proceed,* and *succeed*. Most other words with this sound end in *–cede*.

EXAMPLES
con**cede** pre**cede** re**cede** se**cede**

Adding Prefixes

14d. When adding a prefix, do not change the spelling of the original word.

EXAMPLES
over + run = **over**run mis + spell = **mis**spell

Adding Suffixes

14e. When adding the suffix *–ness* or *–ly*, do not change the spelling of the original word.

EXAMPLES
gentle + ness = gentle**ness** final + ly = final**ly**

EXCEPTIONS
For most words ending in *y*, change the *y* to *i* before adding *–ness* or *–ly*.
heavy + ness = heav**iness** ready + ly = read**ily**

One-syllable adjectives ending in *y* generally follow rule 14e.

EXAMPLES
shy + ness = shy**ness** sly + ly = sly**ly**

14f. **Drop the final silent e before a suffix beginning with a vowel.**

EXAMPLES
awake + en = awak**en** race + ing = rac**ing**
EXCEPTIONS
Keep the final silent e
- in a word ending in *ce* or *ge* before a suffix beginning with *a* or *o*
  peac**eable** courag**eous**
- in *dye* and in *singe* before *–ing*
  dy**eing** sing**eing**
- in *mile* before *–age*
  mil**eage**

When adding *–ing* to words that end in *ie*, drop the e and change the *i* to *y*.

EXAMPLES
die + ing = **dying** lie + ing = **lying**

14g. **Keep the final silent e before a suffix beginning with a consonant.**

EXAMPLES
care + less = car**eless** sure + ty = sur**ety**
EXCEPTIONS
nine + th = nin**th** judge + ment = judg**ment**
true + ly = tru**ly** wise + dom = wis**dom**

14h. **For words ending in y preceded by a consonant, change the y to *i* before any suffix that does not begin with *i*.**

EXAMPLES
heavy + est = heav**iest**
accompany + ment = accompan**iment**
verify + ing = verif**ying**

14i. **For words ending in y preceded by a vowel, keep the y when adding a suffix.**

EXAMPLES
enjoy + ing = enjo**ying** play + ed = pla**yed**
EXCEPTIONS
day + ly = da**ily** lay + ed = la**id**
pay + ed = pa**id** say + ed = sa**id**

14j. **Double the final consonant before a suffix that begins with a vowel if the word *both* (1) has only one syllable or has the accent on the last syllable *and* (2) ends in a single consonant preceded by a single vowel.**

EXAMPLES
rap + ing = ra**pping** refer + ed = refe**rred**
EXCEPTIONS
- For words ending in *w* or *x*, do not double the final consonant.
  bow + ed = bow**ed** tax + able = tax**able**
- For words ending in *c*, add *k* before the suffix instead of doubling the *c*.
  picnic + k + ing = picnic**king**

FORMING THE PLURALS OF NOUNS

14k. **Remembering the following rules will help you spell the plural forms of nouns.**

(1) For most nouns, add *–s*.

EXAMPLES
beagle**s** senator**s** taxi**s** Saxon**s**

(2) For nouns ending in *s, x, z, ch,* or *sh*, add *–es*.

EXAMPLES
glass**es** waltz**es** brush**es** Perez**es**

(3) For nouns ending in *y* preceded by a vowel, add *–s*.

EXAMPLES
journey**s** decoy**s** Saturday**s** Kelley**s**

(4) For nouns ending in *y* preceded by a consonant, change the *y* to *i* and add *–es*.

EXAMPLES
comed**ies** cavit**ies** theor**ies** sk**ies**
EXCEPTIONS
For proper nouns, add *–s*.
Gregory**s** Kimberly**s**

(5) For some nouns ending in *f* or *fe*, add *–s*. For others, change the *f* or *fe* to *v* and add *–es*.

EXAMPLES
belief**s** loa**ves** giraffe**s** wi**ves**
EXCEPTIONS
For proper nouns, add *–s*.
DeGroff**s** Rolfe**s**

(6) For nouns ending in *o* preceded by a vowel, add *–s*.

EXAMPLES
radio**s** cameo**s** shampoo**s** Matsuo**s**

(7) For nouns ending in *o* preceded by a consonant, add *–es.*

EXAMPLES
torpedo**es** echo**es** hero**es** potato**es**

For some common nouns ending in *o* preceded by a consonant, especially those referring to music, and for proper nouns, add only an *–s.*

EXAMPLES
photo**s** hairdo**s** solo**s** soprano**s** Spiro**s**

(8) The plurals of a few nouns are formed in irregular ways.

EXAMPLES
g**ee**se m**e**n child**ren** m**ice** t**ee**th

(9) For a few nouns, the singular and the plural forms are the same.

EXAMPLES
deer series Chinese Sioux

(10) For most compound nouns, form the plural of only the last word of the compound.

EXAMPLES
courthouse**s** seat belt**s** four-year-old**s**

(11) For compound nouns in which one of the words is modified by the other word or words, form the plural of the noun modified.

EXAMPLES
son**s**-in-law passer**s**by mountain goat**s**

(12) For some nouns borrowed from other languages, the plural is formed as in the original languages. In a few cases, two plural forms are acceptable.

EXAMPLES
analysis—analys**es** phenomenon—phenomen**a** *or* phenomenon**s**

(13) To form the plurals of figures, most uppercase letters, signs, and words referred to as words, add an *–s* or both an apostrophe and an *–s.*

EXAMPLES
1500**s** *or* 1500**'s** B**s** *or* B**'s**
$**s** *or* $**'s** *and***s** *or* *and***'s**

NOTE To avoid confusion, add both an apostrophe and an *–s* to form the plural of all lowercase letters, certain uppercase letters, and some words used as words.

EXAMPLES
The word *fictitious* contains three *i***'s.** [Without an apostrophe, the plural of *i* could be confused with the word *is.*]
Sebastian usually makes straight A**'s**. [Without an apostrophe, the plural of *A* could be confused with the word *As.*]
Because I mistakenly thought Evelyn Waugh was a woman, I used *her***'s** instead of *his***'s** in my paragraph. [Without an apostrophe, the plural of *her* would look like the pronoun *hers* and the plural of *his* would look like the word *hiss.*]

NOTE In names, ***diacritical marks*** (marks that show pronunciation) and capitalization are as essential to correct spelling as the letters themselves. If you're not sure about the spelling of a name, check with the person whose name it is, or consult a reference source.

EXAMPLES
Fran**ç**ois Lagerl**ö**f
Van **D**oren **v**an **G**ogh
M**á**rquez Mar**í**n
de **V**ega **a**l-**K**hansa

15 Glossary of Usage

The Glossary of Usage is an alphabetical listing of expressions with definitions, explanations, and examples. Some of the examples are labeled *standard, nonstandard, formal,* or *informal.* The label ***standard*** or ***formal*** identifies usage that is appropriate in serious writing and speaking (such as in compositions and speeches). The label ***informal*** indicates standard English that is generally used in conversation and in everyday writing such as personal letters. The label ***nonstandard*** identifies usage that does not follow the guidelines of standard English usage.

accept, except *Accept* is a verb meaning "to receive." *Except* may be a verb meaning "to leave out" or a preposition meaning "excluding."

EXAMPLES
Does Sir Gawain **accept** the challenge from the Green Knight? [verb]
Certain states **except** teachers from jury duty. [verb]
I have read all of *Macbeth* **except** the last act. [preposition]

affect, effect *Affect* is a verb meaning "to influence." *Effect* may be either a verb meaning "to bring about or to accomplish" or a noun meaning "the result [of an action]."

EXAMPLES
How did the murder of King Duncan **affect** Lady Macbeth? [verb]
In this dispute, management and labor should be able to **effect** a compromise. [verb]
What far-reaching **effects** did the *Brown* v. *Board of Education of Topeka* decision have? [noun]

all ready, already *All ready* means "all prepared." *Already* means "previously."

EXAMPLES
Are you **all ready** for the audition?
We have **already** read "The Seafarer."

all right *All right* means "satisfactory," "unhurt; safe," "correct," or, in reply to a question or to preface a remark, "yes." *Alright* is a misspelling.

EXAMPLES
Does this look **all right** [*not* alright]?
Oh, **all right** [*not* alright], you can go.

all the farther, all the faster Avoid using these expressions in formal situations. Use *as far as* or *as fast as.*

EXAMPLE
Is that **as fast as** [*not* all the faster] Chris can run?

all together, altogether *All together* means "everyone in the same place." *Altogether* means "entirely."

EXAMPLES
The knights were **all together** for the celebration.
Sir Gawain was not **altogether** honest with the Green Knight.

allusion, illusion An *allusion* is an indirect reference to something. An *illusion* is a mistaken idea or a misleading appearance.

EXAMPLES
The speaker made an **allusion** to Emily Brontë's *Wuthering Heights.*
Before selecting a career, he had to abandon some of his **illusions** about his own abilities.
The director chose certain colors to create an **illusion** of depth on the small stage.

a lot Avoid this expression in formal situations by using *many* or *much.*

EXAMPLE
Many [*not* a lot] of my friends work part time after school and on weekends.

already See **all ready, already.**

altogether See **all together, altogether.**

among See **between, among.**

and etc. *Etc.* stands for the Latin words *et cetera,* meaning "and others" or "and so forth." Always avoid using *and* before *etc.* In general, avoid using *etc.* in formal situations. Use one of its meanings instead.

EXAMPLE
We are comparing the main female characters in Shakespeare's tragedies: Lady Macbeth, Cleopatra, Juliet, **and others** [*or* **etc.** *but not* and etc.].

any one, anyone The expression *any one* specifies one member of a group. *Anyone* means "one person, no matter which."

EXAMPLES
Any one of you could win the poetry contest.
Anyone who finishes the test early may leave.

as See **like, as.**

as if See **like, as if.**

at Avoid using *at* after a construction beginning with *where.*

NONSTANDARD	Where was Beowulf at when Grendel's mother attacked?
STANDARD	**Where** was Beowulf when Grendel's mother attacked?

a while, awhile *A while* means "a period of time." *Awhile* means "for a short time."

EXAMPLES
Herot remained empty for quite **a while.**
They stayed there **awhile.**

bad, badly *Bad* is an adjective. *Badly* is an adverb. In standard English, *bad* should follow a sense verb, such as *feel, look, sound, taste,* or *smell,* or other linking verb.

EXAMPLE
The prospects for fair weather look **bad** [*not* badly].

because In formal situations, do not use the construction *reason . . . because.* Instead, use *reason . . . that.*

EXAMPLE
The **reason** Sir Gawain accepts the green sash is **that** [*not* because] he thinks it will protect him from the Green Knight.

being as, being that Avoid using either of these expressions for *since* or *because.*

EXAMPLE
Because [*not* being as *or* being that] Sir Gawain is a knight, we expect him to behave chivalrously.

beside, besides *Beside* means "by the side of" or "next to." *Besides* means "in addition to" or "other than" or "moreover."

EXAMPLES

The Geats built Beowulf's tomb **beside** the sea.

No one **besides** Wiglaf helped Beowulf battle the dragon.

I have decided that I do not want to take journalism; **besides,** I cannot fit it into my schedule.

between, among Use *between* to refer to only two items or to more than two when comparing each item individually to each of the others.

EXAMPLES

The reward money will be divided **between** Chang and Marta.

Sasha explained the difference **between** assonance, consonance, and alliteration. [Each item is compared individually to each of the others.]

Use *among* to refer to more than two items when you are not considering each item in relation to each other item individually.

EXAMPLE

The reward money will be divided **among** the four girls.

bring, take *Bring* means "to come carrying something." *Take* means "to go carrying something."

EXAMPLES

I'll **bring** my copy of *Gulliver's Travels* when I come over.

Please **take** the model of the Globe Theater to the library.

bust, busted Avoid using these words as verbs. Instead, use a form of *break* or *burst,* depending on the meaning.

EXAMPLES

The window is **broken** [*not* busted].

The water main has **burst** [*not* busted] open.

can, may Use *can* to express ability. Use *may* to express possibility.

EXAMPLES

Can you play the guitar?

It **may** rain later.

cannot (can't) help but Avoid using *but* and the infinitive form of a verb after the expression *cannot (can't) help*. Instead, use a gerund alone.

NONSTANDARD	I can't help but laugh when I look at that photograph.
STANDARD	I can't help **laughing** when I look at that photograph.

compare, contrast Used with *to, compare* means "to look for similarities between." Used with *with, compare* means "to look for both similarities and differences between." *Contrast* is always used to point out differences.

EXAMPLES

The simile at the end of the poem **compares** the eagle's fall **to** a thunderbolt.

We **compared** Shakespeare's style **with** that of Christopher Marlowe.

The tour guide also **contrasted** the two castles' provisions for defense.

could of See **of.**

double subject Avoid using an unnecessary pronoun after the subject of a sentence.

EXAMPLE

George Bernard Shaw [*not* George Bernard Shaw he] wrote *Pygmalion.*

due to Avoid using *due to* for "because of" or "owing to."

EXAMPLE

All schools were closed **because of** [*not* due to] inclement weather.

effect See **affect, effect.**

either, neither *Either* usually means "one or the other of two." In referring to more than two, use *any one* or *any* instead. *Neither* usually means "not one or the other of two." In referring to more than two, use *none* instead.

EXAMPLES

Either of the two quotations would be appropriate to use at the beginning of your speech.

You should be able to find ample information about **any one** of those four poets.

Neither of the Perez twins is in school today.

None of the seniors have voted yet.

etc. See **and etc.**

every day, everyday *Every day* means "each day." *Everyday* means "daily," "ordinary," or "usual."

EXAMPLES

Every day presents its own challenges.

The party will be casual; wear **everyday** clothes.

every one, everyone *Every one* specifies every single person or thing of those named. *Everyone* means "everybody, all of the people named."

EXAMPLES

Elizabeth Bowen wrote **every one** of these stories.

Did **everyone** read "The Demon Lover"?

except See **accept, except.**

farther, further Use *farther* to express physical distance. Use *further* to express abstract relationships of degree or quantity.

EXAMPLES
Your house is **farther** from school than mine is.
The United Nations members decided that **further** debate was unnecessary.

fewer, less Use *fewer* to modify a plural noun and *less* to modify a singular noun.

EXAMPLES
Fewer students are going out for football this year.
Now I spend **less** time watching TV.

good, well Avoid using the adjective *good* to modify an action verb. Instead, use the adverb *well,* meaning "capably" or "satisfactorily."

EXAMPLE
We did **well** [*not* good] on the exam.

Used as an adjective, *well* means "in good health" or "satisfactory in appearance or condition."

EXAMPLES
I feel **well.**
It's eight o'clock, and all is **well.**

had of See **of.**

had ought, hadn't ought Do not use *had* or *hadn't* with *ought.*

EXAMPLES
Your application **ought** [*not* had ought] to have been sent in earlier.
She **ought not** [*not* hadn't ought] to swim so soon after eating lunch.

illusion See **allusion, illusion.**

imply, infer *Imply* means "to suggest indirectly." *Infer* means "to interpret" or "to draw a conclusion."

EXAMPLES
The speaker of "To a Skylark" **implies** that the skylark is a divine being.
I **inferred** from her speech that she would support a statewide testing program.

in, in to, into *In* generally shows location. In the construction *in to, in* is an adverb followed by the preposition *to. Into* generally shows direction.

EXAMPLES
Rudyard Kipling was born **in** Bombay.
He found the treasure and turned it **in to** his king.
Sir Gawain rode **into** the wilderness to find the Green Knight.

infer See **imply, infer.**

irregardless, regardless *Irregardless* is nonstandard. Use *regardless* instead.

EXAMPLE
Regardless [*not* irregardless] of the danger, he continued his journey.

its, it's *Its* is the possessive form of *it. It's* is the contraction of *it is* or *it has.*

EXAMPLES
The community is proud of **its** school system.
It's [it is] a symbol of peace.
It's [it has] been cooler today.

kind of, sort of In formal situations, avoid using these terms for the adverb *somewhat* or *rather.*

INFORMAL Macbeth appeared to be kind of worried.
FORMAL Macbeth appeared to be **rather** [*or* **somewhat**] worried.

kind of a(n), sort of a(n) In formal situations, omit the *a*(*n*).

INFORMAL What kind of a poem is "The Passionate Shepherd to His Love"?
FORMAL What **kind of** poem is "The Passionate Shepherd to His Love"?

kind(s), sort(s), type(s) With the singular form of each of these nouns, use *this* or *that.* With the plural form, use *these* or *those.*

EXAMPLES
This type of engine performs more economically than any of **those types.**

less See **fewer, less.**

lie, lay The verb *lie* means "to rest" or "to stay, to recline, or to remain in a certain state or position." Its principal parts are *lie, lying, lay,* and *lain. Lie* never takes an object. The verb *lay* means "to put [something] in a place." Its principal parts are *lay, laying, laid,* and *laid. Lay* usually takes an object.

EXAMPLES
Gulliver was **lying** on his back and could hardly move. [no object]
The Lilliputians **laid** baskets of food near Gulliver's mouth. [*Baskets* is the object of *laid.*]

like, as In formal situations, do not use *like* for *as* to introduce a subordinate clause.

INFORMAL John looks like his father looked twenty years ago.
FORMAL John looks **as** his father looked twenty years ago.

like, as if In formal situations, avoid using the preposition *like* for the compound conjunction *as if* or *as though* to introduce a subordinate clause.

INFORMAL The heavy footsteps sounded like they were coming nearer.
FORMAL The heavy footsteps sounded **as if** [*or* **as though**] they were coming nearer.

might of, must of See **of.**

neither See **either, neither.**

nor See **or, nor.**

of *Of* is a preposition. Do not use *of* in place of *have* after verbs such as *could, should, would, might, must,* and *ought* [*to*]. Also, do not use *had of* for *had.*

EXAMPLES
If I **had** [*not* had of] known about the shortcut, I **would have** [*not* would of] been here sooner.

Avoid using *of* after other prepositions such as *inside, off,* and *outside.*

EXAMPLE
Flimnap fell **off** [*not* off of] the tightrope.

off, off of Do not use *off* or *off of* for *from.*

EXAMPLE
You can get a program **from** [*not* off of] the usher.

on to, onto In the expression *on to, on* is an adverb and *to* is a preposition. *Onto* is a preposition.

EXAMPLES
The lecturer moved **on to** her next main idea.
She walked **onto** the stage.

or, nor Use *or* with *either;* use *nor* with *neither.*

EXAMPLES
The list of authors does not include **either** James Joyce **or** [*not* nor] D. H. Lawrence.
Neither James Joyce **nor** D. H. Lawrence is on the list of authors.

ought See **had ought, hadn't ought.**

ought to of See **of.**

raise See **rise, raise.**

reason . . . because See **because.**

refer back Since the prefix *re–* in *refer* means "back," adding *back* is generally unnecessary.

EXAMPLE
The writer is **referring** [*not* referring back] to the years when he lived in Ireland.

rise, raise The verb *rise* means "to go up" or "to get up." Its principal parts are *rise, rising, rose,* and *risen. Rise* never takes an object. The verb *raise* means "to cause [something] to rise" or "to lift up." Its principal parts are *raise, raising, raised,* and *raised. Raise* usually takes an object.

EXAMPLES
Her blood pressure **rose** as she waited. [no object]
The Green Knight **raised** the ax above his head. [*Ax* is the object of *raised.*]

should of See **of.**

sit, set The verb *sit* means "to rest in an upright, seated position." Its principal parts are *sit, sitting, sat,* and *sat. Sit* seldom takes an object. The verb *set* means "to put [something] in a place." Its principal parts are *set, setting, set,* and *set. Set* usually takes an object.

EXAMPLES
Banquo's ghost **sits** in Macbeth's place. [no object]
Please **set** the groceries on the table. [*Groceries* is the object of *set.*]

some, somewhat In formal situations, avoid using *some* to mean "to some extent." Use *somewhat.*

EXAMPLE
The Wedding Guest was somewhat shaken [*not* shaken some] by the Ancient Mariner's gaze and appearance.

sort(s) See **kind(s), sort(s), type(s)** and **kind of a(n), sort of a(n).**

sort of See **kind of, sort of.**

take See **bring, take.**

than, then *Than* is a conjunction used in comparisons. *Then* is an adverb meaning "at that time" or "next."

EXAMPLES
Is King Macbeth more superstitious **than** Lady Macbeth?
First, we will read "The Lamb"; **then,** we will read "The Tyger."

that See **who, which, that.**

their, there, they're *Their* is a possessive form of *they.* As an adverb, *there* means "at that place." *There* is also used to begin a sentence. *They're* is the contraction of *they are.*

EXAMPLES
They built a tomb for **their** fallen leader.
Macduff was not **there** at the time.
There is very little time left.
They're waiting for Banquo.

theirs, there's *Theirs* is a possessive form of the pronoun *they. There's* is the contraction of *there is.*

EXAMPLES
The treasure is **theirs** now.
There's an allusion to the Bible in the poem.

them Do not use *them* as an adjective. Use *those.*

EXAMPLE
Have you seen **those** [*not* them] murals by Judith Baca at the art museum?

then See **than, then.**

there See **their, there, they're.**

there's See **theirs, there's.**

they're See **their, there, they're.**

this here, that there Avoid using *here* or *there* after *this* or *that.*

EXAMPLE
This [*not* this here] poem was written by Robert Browning.

try and, try to Use *try to,* not *try and.*

EXAMPLE
I will **try to** [*not* try and] finish reading *The Diary of Samuel Pepys* tonight.

type, type of Avoid using the noun *type* as an adjective. Add *of* after *type.*

EXAMPLE
What **type of** [*not* type] character is the knight in "The Wife of Bath's Tale"?

type(s) See **kind(s), sort(s), type(s).**

ways Use *way,* not *ways,* when referring to distance.

EXAMPLE
Is Canterbury a long **way** [*not* ways] from the Tabard Inn?

well See **good, well.**

when, where Do not use *when* or *where* to begin a definition.

NONSTANDARD A caesura is where you break or pause in a line of poetry.
STANDARD A caesura is **a break or pause in a line of poetry.**

where Do not use *where* in place of *that.*

EXAMPLE
I read **that** [*not* where] you won a scholarship.

where . . . at See **at.**

who, which, that *Who* refers to persons only. *Which* refers to things only. *That* may refer to either persons or things.

EXAMPLES
Sir Gawain was the knight **who** [*or* **that**] accepted the Green Knight's challenge.
The Globe, **which** was built in 1599, burned down in 1613.
Is this the only poem **that** Sir Walter Raleigh ever wrote?

who's, whose *Who's* is the contraction of *who is* or *who has. Whose* is the possessive form of *who.*

EXAMPLES
Well, look **who's** [who is] here!
Who's [who has] read all of the play?
Whose treasure is it?

would of See **of.**

your, you're *Your* is a possessive form of *you. You're* is the contraction of *you are.*

EXAMPLES
Is that **your** car?
I can see that **you're** tired.

Glossary

The glossary that follows is an alphabetical list of words found in the selections in this book. Use this glossary just as you would use a dictionary—to find out the meanings of unfamiliar words. (Some technical, foreign, and more obscure words in this book are not listed here but instead are defined for you in the footnotes that accompany many of the selections.)

Many words in the English language have more than one meaning. This glossary gives the meanings that apply to the words as they are used in the selections in this book. Words closely related in form and meaning are usually listed together in one entry (for instance, compassion and compassionate), and the definition is given for the first form.

The following abbreviations are used:

adj.	adjective
adv.	adverb
n.	noun
v.	verb

Each word's pronunciation is given in parentheses. A guide to the pronunciation symbols appears at the bottom of every other page. For more information about the words in this glossary or for information about words not listed here, consult a dictionary.

A

abate (ə·bāt′) *v.:* lessen.
abominable (ə·bäm′ə·nə·bəl) *adj.:* disgusting; hateful.
abrogate (ab′rə·gāt) *v.:* abolish; repeal. —**abrogated** *v.* used as *adj.*
absolve (ab·zälv′) *v.:* forgive; make free from blame.
abstain (ab·stān′) *v.:* refrain from.
accrue (ə·kro͞o′) *v.:* increase over time.
adversary (ad′vər·ser′ē) *n.:* enemy.
aesthetic (es·thet′ik) *n.:* principle of beauty.
affectation (af′ek·tā′shən) *n.:* artificial behavior designed to impress others.
affinity (ə·fin′i·tē) *n.:* kinship; bond.
affliction (ə·flik′shən) *n.:* suffering.
aggrieved (ə·grēvd′) *adj.:* offended.
agility (ə·jil′ə·tē) *n.:* ability to move quickly and easily.
allure (ə·loor′) *v.:* tempt; attract.
altruistic (al′tro͞o·is′tik) *adj.:* unselfish.
amiable (ā′mē·ə·bəl) *adj.:* friendly; likeable.
animosity (an′ə·mäs′ə·tē) *n.:* hostility; violent hatred or resentment.
annihilate (ə·nī′ə·lāt′) *v.:* destroy; make nonexistent.
annul (ə·nul′) *v.:* do away with; cancel.
antipathy (an·tip′ə·thē) *n.:* strong dislike; aversion
aperture (ap′ər·chər) *n.:* opening.
approbation (ap′rə·bā′shən) *n.:* approval.
arable (ar′ə·bəl) *adj.:* fit to be farmed or cultivated.
arbitrate (är′bə·trāt′) *v.:* settle or decide by listening to both sides of an argument.
arrest (ə·rest′) *v.:* check or halt in motion. —**arrested** *v.* used as *adj.*
artifice (ärt′ə·fis) *n.:* trickery; deception.
assail (ə·sāl′) *v.:* attack; assault.
assent (ə·sent′) *n.:* acceptance.
assert (ə·surt′) *v.:* declare.
assuage (ə·swāj′) *v.:* ease; calm.
audacious (ô·dā′shəs) *adj.:* bold. —**audaciously** *adv.*
austere (ô·stir′) *adj.:* restrained; spare; very plain.
avail (ə·vāl′) *n.:* benefit; advantage.
avarice (av′ə·ris) *n.:* too great a desire for wealth.

B

benign (bi·nīn′) *adj.:* kind; gracious.
bequest (bē·kwest′) *n.:* gift left by means of a will.
bibliophile (bib′lē·ə·fīl) *n.:* one who loves books.

at, āte, cär; ten, ēve; is, īce; gō, hôrn, look, to͞ol; oil, out; up, fur; ə *for unstressed vowels, as* a *in* ago, u *in* focus; ′ *as in* Latin (lat′n); chin; she; thin; *th*e; ŋ *as in* ring (riŋ); zh *as in* azure (azh′ər)

botanical (bə·tan′i·kəl) *adj.:* of plants or plant life; connected to the science of botany.
brandish (bran′dish) *v.:* shake in a threatening way. —**brandishing** *v.* used as *adj.*
brevity (brev′ə·tē) *n.:* being brief; shortness.
buoyancy (boi′ən·sē) *n.:* lightness of spirit; cheerfulness.

C

candor (kan′dər) *n.:* honesty; directness.
capacity (kə·pas′i·tē) *n.:* ability to absorb.
caprice (kə·prēs′) *n.:* sudden notion or desire.
caste (kast) *n.:* social class.
censure (sen′shər) *v.:* condemn.
clamber (klam′bər) *v.:* climb clumsily.
clemency (klem′ən·sē) *n.:* mercy; leniency.
coherent (kō·hir′ənt) *adj.:* logical; orderly; understandable.
commiserate (kə·miz′ər·āt′) *v.:* feel sorrow or pity for; sympathize.
compensate (käm′pən·sāt′) *v.:* repay; make up (for or to).
compulsory (kəm·pul′sə·rē) *adj.:* required; enforced.
concede (kən·sēd′) *v.:* grant.
condescension (kän′di·sen′shən) *n.:* behavior that is patronizing.
confounded (kən·foun′did) *adj.:* confused.
congeal (kən·jēl′) *v.:* thicken. —**congealed** *v.* used as *adj.*
console (kən·sōl′) *v.:* comfort.
conspicuous (kən·spik′yoo·əs) *adj.:* attracting attention.
consternation (kän′stər·nā′shən) *n.:* bewilderment; dismay.
contemptuous (kən·temp′choo·əs) *adj.:* with contempt or scorn. —**contemptuously** *adv.*
contention (kən·ten′shən) *n.:* struggle.
contortion (kən·tôr′shən) *n.:* twisted shape or motion.
contrive (kən·trīv′) *v.:* manage.
corpulent (kôr′pyoo·lənt) *adj.:* fat.
cosmopolitan (käz′mə·päl′ə·tən) *adj.:* worldly; sophisticated.
credentials (kri·den′shəlz) *n.:* evidence of a person's position.
culinary (kul′ə·ner′ē) *adj.:* related to cooking.
cursory (kur′sə·rē) *adj.:* hasty; superficial.

D

daunt (dônt) *v.:* intimidate. —**daunted** *v.* used as *adj.*
decree (dē·krē′) *v.:* order; command.
deference (def′ər·əns) *n.:* respect.
defile (dē·fīl′) *v.:* make unclean.
deject (dē·jekt′) *v.:* cast down; dispirit.
delusion (di·loo′zhən) *n.:* false belief.
demented (dē·ment′id) *adj.:* mad; wild. —**dementedly** *adv.*
demolition (dem′ə·lish′ən) *n.:* destruction.
deplore (dē·plôr′) *v.:* regret; strongly disapprove of.
desist (di·zist′) *v.:* stop.
desolation (des′ə·lā′shən) *n.:* utter misery; extreme loneliness.
diabolic (dī′ə·bäl′ik) *adj.:* of or having to do with evil or the devil.
digress (di·gres′) *v.:* wander off the subject.
diligence (dil′ə·jəns) *n.:* care; carefulness.
diminutive (də·min′yoo·tiv) *adj.:* very small.
dire (dīr) *adj.:* extreme; desperate.
discern (di·surn′) *v.:* recognize (the difference); make out clearly.
discomfiture (dis·kum′fi·chər) *n.:* frustration; embarrassment.
disconcerted (dis′kən·surt′id) *adj.:* upset; frustrated.
disconsolate (dis·kän′sə·lit) *adj.:* dejected; unhappy. —**disconsolately** *adv.*
discourse (dis′kôrs′) *n.:* speech.
discrimination (di·skrim′i·nā′shən) *n.:* ability to make fine distinctions.
dismal (diz′məl) *adj.:* gloomy.
disparage (di·spar′ij) *v.:* belittle; speak negatively of.
dispassionate (dis·pash′ə·nət) *adv.:* without emotion; impartial. —**dispassionately** *adv.*
disperse (di·spurs′) *v.:* break up.
disposition (dis′pə·zish′ən) *n.:* natural qualities of personality.
dissuade (di·swād′) *v.:* advise against.
distend (di·stend′) *v.:* expand; swell.
distill (di·stil′) *v.:* draw out the essence of.
distraught (di·strôt′) *adj.:* extremely agitated.
divinity (də·vin′ə·tē) *n.:* god; sacred being.

dogged (dôg′id) *adj.:* persistent; stubborn.
duplicity (do͞o·plis′ə·tē) *n.:* cunning; treachery.
duress (doo·res′) *n.:* pressure.

E

efficacy (ef′i·kə·sē) *n.:* ability to produce a desired effect; effectiveness.
emanate (em′ə·nāt′) *v.:* flow; come forth.
eminent (em′ə·nənt) *adj.:* high-standing; great.
endow (en·dou′) *v.:* provide with. —**endowed** *v.* used as *adj.*
enmity (en′mə·tē) *n.:* hostility.
ethereal (ē·thir′ē·əl) *adj.:* light and delicate; unearthly.
exhilaration (eg·zil′ə·rā′shən) *n.:* excitement; high spirits.
expedient (ek·spē′dē·ənt) *n.:* convenient means to an end.
exploit (eks′ploit′) *n.:* daring act.
exquisite (eks′kwiz·it) *adj.:* beautiful; delicate.
extol (ek·stōl′) *v.:* praise.
extort (eks·tôrt′) *v.:* get by threats or violence.
exult (eg·zult′) *v.:* rejoice. —**exulting** *v.* used as *adj.*

F

fastidious (fa·stid′ē·əs) *adj.:* picky; overly fussy.
fawn (fôn) *v.:* cringe and plead. —**fawning** *v.* used as *adj.*
fickleness (fik′əl·nis) *n.:* changeableness.
flaccid (flas′id) *adj.:* limp; flabby.
flag (flag) *v.:* decline; lose strength or interest.
formidable (fôr′mə·də·bəl) *adj.:* difficult to handle or overcome.
frivolous (friv′ə·ləs) *adj.:* light-minded; lacking seriousness.
frugal (fro͞o′gəl) *adj.:* thrifty; careful with money.
furl (furl) *v.:* roll up.

G

gallant (gal′ənt) *adj.:* noble; brave.
garrulous (gar′ə·ləs) *adj.:* talkative.
genial (jēn′yəl) *adj.:* mild-mannered; friendly.
geniality (jē′nē·al′ə·tē) *n.:* friendliness, cordiality.
ghastly (gast′lē) *adj.:* dreadful; ghostly.
glut (glut) *v.:* overfill. —**glutted** *v.* used as *adj.*
grievous (grēv′əs) *adj.:* outrageous; horrible.
grisly (griz′lē) *adj.:* terrifying.
grovel (gräv′əl) *v.:* crawl; humiliate oneself in front of authority. —**groveling** *v.* used as *adj.*
guffaw (gə·fô′) *n.:* loud laughter.
guile (gīl) *n.:* cunning; sly dealings; skill in deceiving.

H

haggard (hag′ərd) *adj.:* gaunt; worn and exhausted from anxiety.
haggle (hag′əl) *v.:* argue about a price.

I

ignoble (ig·nō′bəl) *adj.:* shameful; degrading.
ignominy (ig′nə·min′ē) *n.:* dishonor; disgrace; shame.
illusory (i·lo͞o′sə·rē) *adj.:* not real; false.
impassive (im·pas′iv) *adj.:* calm; indifferent. —**impassively** *adv.*
impediment (im·ped′ə·mənt) *n.:* obstacle; stumbling block.
imperturbable (im′pər·tur′bə·bəl) *adj.:* calm; impassive.
impetuous (im·pech′o͞o·əs) *adj.:* forceful; violent.
impinge (im·pinj′) *v.:* strike; touch.
implacable (im·plak′ə·bəl) *adj.:* inflexible; relentless; stubborn; unchangeable; fixed.
impromptu (im·prämp′to͞o′) *adj.:* unplanned.
improvise (im′prə·vīz′) *v.:* make for the occasion from whatever is handy. —**improvised** *v.* used as *adj.*

at, āte, cär; ten, ēve; is, īce; gō, hôrn, look, to͞ol; oil, out; up, fur; ə *for unstressed vowels, as* a *in* ago, u *in* focus; ′ *as in* Latin (lat′n); chin; she; thin; *the*; ŋ *as in* ring (riŋ); zh *as in* azure (azh′ər)

inaccessible (in·ak·ses′ə·bəl) *adj.:* not accessible; impossible to enter or reach.

incessant (in·ses′ənt) *adj.:* constant; unending. —**incessantly** *adv.*

inclination (in′klə·nā′shən) *n.:* liking; tendency.

incur (in·kur′) *v.:* bring upon oneself.

indiscriminate (in′di·skrim′i·nit) *adj.:* not making careful distinctions; random. —**indiscriminately** *adv.*

induce (in·do͞os′) *v.:* cause; bring about.

indulgent (in·dul′jənt) *adj.:* lenient; permissive.

inevitable (in·ev′i·tə·bəl) *adj.:* certain to happen; unavoidable.

infallible (in·fal′ə·bəl) *adj.:* unable to fail or be wrong.

infernal (in·fur′nəl) *adj.:* hellish; fiendish.

ingratiate (in·grā′shē·āt) *adj.:* purposely try to gain favor. —**ingratiating** *v.* used as *adj.*

initiative (i·nish′ə·tiv) *n.:* action of making the first move.

insipid (in·sip′id) *adj.:* dull; flat.

intermittent (in′tər·mit′′nt) *adj.:* starting and stopping at intervals; periodic.

intoxicate (in·täks′i·kāt′) *v.:* cause wild excitement or happiness, often to a point beyond self-control. —**intoxicating** *v.* used as *adj.*

intricate (in′tri·kit) *adj.:* full of elaborate details or parts.

iridescent (ir′i·des′ənt) *adj.:* showing rainbowlike colors.

itinerant (ī·tin′ər·ənt) *adj.:* traveling.

L

labyrinth (lab′ə·rinth′) *n.:* maze; complex or confusing arrangement.

lamentable (lə·men′tə·bəl) *adj.:* regrettable; unfortunate.

lavish (lav′ish) *adj.:* extravagant.

livid (liv′id) *adj.:* pale; colorless.

lugubrious (lə·go͞o′brē·əs) *adj.:* very solemn or mournful, especially in a way that seems exaggerated or ridiculous.

M

malice (mal′is) *n.:* ill will; evil intentions.

maniacal (mə·nī′ə·kəl) *adj.:* crazed; wildly enthusiastic.

meticulous (mə·tik′yo͞o·ləs) *adj.:* precise; extremely concerned with details.

misanthropy (mi·san′thrə·pē) *n.:* hatred for humankind.

monotonous (mə·nät′′n·əs) *adj.:* unvarying.

N

nimble (nim′bəl) *adj.:* moving in a quick, light way. —**nimbly** *adv.*

notorious (nō·tôr′ē·əs) *adj.:* widely but unfavorably known; infamous.

O

obscure (əb·skyoor′) *adj.:* little-known.

obstinate (äb′stə·nət) *adj.:* unreasonably stubborn.

oppressive (ə·pres′iv) *adj.:* hard to bear.

ostentatious (äs′ten·tā′shəs) *adj.:* showy.

overwrought (ō′vər·rôt′) *adj.:* overly excited.

P

pallor (pal′ər) *n.:* paleness.

partial (pär′shəl) *adj.:* biased.

patronize (pā′trən·īz′) *v.:* be a customer of.

pedantic (pi·dan′tik) *adj.:* showing an exaggerated concern for books, learning, and rules.

pensive (pen′siv) *adj.:* reflective; seriously thoughtful.

perfunctory (pər·fuŋk′tə·rē) *adj.:* halfhearted; indifferent.

persevere (pur′sə·vir′) *v.:* continue despite difficulty or opposition; persist.

pervade (pər·vād′) *v.:* spread throughout.

perverse (pər·vurs′) *adj.:* disagreeable; contrary. —**perversely** *adv.*

pestilence (pes′tə·ləns) *n.:* plague.

pique (pēk) *v.:* provoke. —**piqued** *v.* used as *adj.*

piteous (pit′ē·əs) *adj.:* deserving of pity.

pitiable (pit′ē·ə·bəl) *adj.:* lamentable; regrettable.

posterity (päs·ter′ə·tē) *n.:* descendants; future generations.

precedent (pres′ə·dənt) *n.:* first occurrence of something that can later be used as an example or standard.

precipitate (pri·sip′ə·tit) *adj.:* sudden. —**precipitately** *adv.*

preliminary (prē·lim′ə·ner′ē) *adj.:* preparing for the main event; introductory.
presumption (prē·zump′shən) *n.:* act of taking too much for granted.
pretext (prē′tekst′) *n.:* excuse.
prevail (prē·vāl′) *v.:* gain the desired effect.
procure (prō·kyoor′) *v.:* obtain; get.
prodigious (prō·dij′əs) *adj.:* enormous.
prodigy (präd′ə·jē) *n.:* someone gifted from childhood with an exceptional quality or talent.
profuse (prō·fyo͞os′) *adj.:* abundant; excessive. —**profusely** *adv.*
propagate (präp′ə·gāt′) *v.:* publicize; spread.
propensity (prə·pen′sə·tē) *n.:* natural inclination or tendency.
propitious (prō·pish′əs) *adj.:* favorable.
prosaic (prō·zā′ik) *adj.:* ordinary; dull.
prostrate (präs′trāt′) *adj.:* lying flat.
provision (prə·vizh′ən) *n.:* arrangement or preparation beforehand.
prowess (prou′is) *n.:* outstanding ability.
proximity (präk·sim′ə·tē) *n.:* closeness.
prudent (pro͞o′dənt) *adj.:* careful; cautious.

R

rash (rash) *adj.:* reckless.
raze (rāz) *v.:* tear down.
reactionary (rē·ak′shə·ner′ē) *adj.:* characterized by strong resistance to change or progress.
recess (rē′ses) *n.:* enclosure.
refract (ri·frakt′) *v.:* bend by passage from one medium to another. —**refracted** *v.* used as *adj.*
refuse (ref′yo͞os) *n.:* trash.
reiterate (rē·it′ə·rāt′) *v.:* repeat. —**reiterated** *v.* used as *adj.*
remonstrate (ri·män′strāt′) *v.:* protest.
renounce (ri·nouns′) *v.:* formally give up; reject.
repast (ri·past′) *n.:* meal.
reproach (ri·prōch′) *v.:* express disapproval.
reproachful (ri·prōch′fəl) *adj.:* accusing. —**reproachfully** *adv.*
reprove (ri·pro͞ov′) *v.:* disapprove of.
residue (rez′ə·do͞o′) *n.:* leftover portion; remainder.
resolute (rez′ə·lo͞ot′) *adj.:* determined.
resolve (ri·zälv′) *n.:* determination; firm purpose.
respite (res′pit) *n.:* postponement; reprieve.
reverent (rev′ə·rənt) *adj.:* having deep respect, love, or awe, as for something sacred. —**reverently** *adv.*
righteous (rī′chəs) *adj.:* morally right.
rigor (rig′ər) *n.:* extreme severity.
rite (rīt) *n.:* formal ceremony.

S

scourge (skʉrj) *n.:* means of inflicting severe punishment. Usually the word refers to a whip.
scrupulous (skro͞op′yə·ləs) *adj.:* extremely careful and precise in deciding what is right or wrong.
serrated (ser′āt′id) *adj.:* having jagged, sawlike notches along the edge.
servile (sʉr′vīl) *adj.:* like or characteristic of a slave; submissive; yielding.
shirk (shʉrk) *v.:* neglect or avoid a task or duty.
sloth (slôth) *n.:* laziness.
solicitude (sə·lis′ə·to͞od′) *n.:* care; concern.
somber (säm′bər) *adj.:* gloomy.
sordid (sôr′did) *adj.:* filthy; foul.
specious (spē′shəs) *adj.:* showy but false; lacking genuineness.
spurn (spʉrn) *v.:* reject.
squalid (skwäl′id) *adj.:* foul or unclean; wretched.
squall (skwôl) *n.:* violent storm that doesn't last very long.
stealthy (stel′thē) *adj.:* secret; sly.
strident (strīd′′nt) *adj.:* harsh; sharp. —**stridently** *adv.*
stupefying (sto͞o′pə·fī′iŋ) *adj.:* dulling the mind and senses; bringing on a state of lethargy.
subdued (səb′do͞od) *adj.:* quiet; controlled.
succor (suk′ər) *v.:* help in time of distress.
succumb (sə·kum′) *v.:* yield; give way to.
sullen (sul′ən) *adj.:* resentful; gloomy.
supercilious (so͞o′pər·sil′ē·əs) *adj.:* disdainful; scornful; haughty. —**superciliously** *adv.*
superfluity (so͞o′pər·flo͞o′ə·tē) *n.:* excess.
supplant (sə·plant′) *v.:* replace; displace.

at, āte, cär; ten, ēve; is, īce; gō, hôrn, look, to͞ol; oil, out; up, fʉr; ə *for unstressed vowels, as* a *in* ago, u *in* focus; ′ *as in* Latin (lat′′n); chin; she; thin; *the*; ŋ *as in* ring (riŋ); zh *as in* azure (azh′ər)

suppress (sə•pres′) *v.:* keep from being known. —**suppressed** *v.* used as *adj.*
surreptitious (sʉr′əp•tish′əs) *adj.:* sneaky or stealthy. —**surreptitiously** *adv.*
sustenance (sus′tə•nəns) *n.:* food or money to support life.

T

taciturn (tas′ə•tʉrn′) *adj.:* not talkative.
temerity (tə•mer′ə•tē) *n.:* foolish or rash boldness; recklessness.
temper (tem′pər) *v.:* moderate; tone down. —**tempering** *v.* used as *adj.*
temporal (tem′pə•rəl) *adj.:* limited to this world; not spiritual.
tentative (ten′tə•tiv) *adj.:* hesitant; uncertain.
tepid (tep′id) *adj.:* lukewarm.
titillate (tit″l•āt′) *v.:* excite; stimulate. —**titillating** *v.* used as *adj.*
transcend (tran•send′) *v.:* exceed; surpass.
transfigure (trans•fig′yər) *v.:* change the form of.
transgress (trans•gres′) *v.:* sin against; violate a limit.
translucent (trans•lo͞o′sənt) *adj.:* partially transparent.
tyrannous (tir′ə•nəs) *adj.:* harsh; oppressive.

U

uncanny (un•kan′ē) *adj.:* strange; eerie; weird.
unmarred (ən•märd′) *adj.:* undamaged; unspoiled.
unpretentious (ən•prē•ten′shəs) *adj.:* modest.
untainted (ən•tānt′id) *adj.:* untarnished; without a trace of anything offensive.

V

vehement (vē′ə•mənt) *adj.:* violent. —**vehemently** *adv.*
victuals (vit″lz) *n.:* provisions; pieces of food.
vigil (vij′əl) *n.:* staying watchfully awake.
vitiate (vish′ē•āt) *v.:* impair; weaken; spoil.
vivacity (vī•vas′ə•tē) *n.:* liveliness; high-spiritedness.

W

wince (wins) *v.:* flinch; draw back.
wrenched (rencht) *v.:* anguished; grief-stricken.

Z

zealous (zel′əs) *adj.:* fervent; devoted. —**zealously** *adv.*

Spanish Glossary

A

abate/reducir *v.* disminuir; aminorar; atenuar.
abominable/abominable *adj.* espantoso; detestable; horrible.
abrogate/abrogar *v.* abolir; invalidar; revocar.
absolve/absolver *v.* perdonar; indultar; dispensar.
abstain/abstenerse *v.* privarse; renunciar; callarse.
accrue/acumularse *v.* incrementar con el tiempo; crecer.
adversary/adversario *s.* enemigo; contrincante; antagonista.
aesthetic/estético *s.* artístico, fundamento de la belleza.
affectation/afectación *s.* simulación; comportamiento artificial con el fin de impresionar a los demás.
affinity/afinidad *s.* simpatía; atracción.
affliction/aflicción *s.* pesar; angustia; consternación.
aggrieved/agraviado *adj.* resentido; ofendido; maltratado.
agility/agilidad *s.* ligereza; velocidad; prontitud; presteza.
allure/atraer *v.* seducir; cautivar; conquistar.
altruistic/altruista *adj.* generoso; filántropo; sin egoísmo.
amiable/amable *adj.* afable; simpático; cordial.
animosity/animosidad *s.* antipatía; rencor; aversión; hostilidad.
annihilate/aniquilar *v.* destruir; exterminar.
annul/anular *v.* abolir; cancelar; revocar.
antipathy/antipatía *s.* hostilidad; repugnancia; aversión.
aperture/abertura *s.* rendija; grieta.
approbation/aprobación *s.* asentimiento; conformidad; adhesión.
arable/arable *adj.* cultivable; labradero.
arbitrate/arbitrar *v.* mediar; interceder; resolver; juzgar.
arrest/arrestar *v.* detener; interrumpir; demorar; retrasar; permanecer quieto.
artifice/artificio *s.* engaño; ardid; astucia.
assail/asaltar *v.* atacar; acometer un ataque; abrumar con preguntas.
assent/asentimiento *n.* afirmación; consentimiento; confirmación; aceptación.
assert/afirmar *v.* aseverar; asegurar; sostener.
assuage/aliviar *v.* mitigar; calmar; apaciguar.
audacious/audaz *adj.* atrevido; intrépido; osado.
assailant/asaltante *s.* atracador; agresor.
austere/austero *adj.* sobrio; riguroso; serio; sin adornos.
avail/servir *v.* sacar partido de; valerse de; utilizar.
avarice/avaricia *s.* codicia; egoísmo.

B

benign/benigno *adj.* favorable; sano; propicio; clemente.
bequest/legado *s.* cesión; herencia; obsequio realizado mediante un testamento.
bibliophile/bibliófilo *adj.* coleccionista de, o experto en libros; amante de los libros.
botanical/botánico *adj.* que trata de las plantas; asociado con la ciencia de la botánica.
brandish/blandir *v.* esgrimir; empuñar; aferrar.
brevity/brevedad *s.* laconismo; concisión; abreviación.
buoyancy/júbilo *s.* ligereza de espíritu; alegría; estar por las nubes.

C

candor/sinceridad *s.* franqueza; imparcialidad; candidez; ingenuidad.
capacity/capacidad *s.* facultad; volumen; aptitud.
caprice/capricho *s.* deseo repentino; extravagancia; antojo.
caste/casta *s.* clase social; casta; linaje.
censure/censurar *v.* condemnar; criticar; desaprobar.
clamber/encaramarse *v.* subir a gatas; ascender; trepar.
clemency/clemencia *s.* piedad; misericordia; compasión.

clamor/clamor s. estruendo; ruido; fragor.
coherent/coherente *adj.* lógico; claro; razonable.
commiserate/compadecer *adj.* expresar simpatía; apiadarse; conmoverse.
compensate/compensar v. indemnizar; remediar; igualar.
compulsory/obligatorio *adj.* requerido por una regla o por la ley; forzoso.
concede/conceder v. otorgar; conferir; asignar; agraciar.
condescension/condescendencia s. consentimiento; tolerancia; complacencia.
confounded/confundido *adj.* desconcertado; confuso.
congeal/congelar v. cuajar; solidificar; coagular; solidificar.
console/consolar v. tranquilizar; calmar; dar sosiego.
conspicuous/visible *adj.* obvio; llamativo; notable; patente; que llama la atención.
consternation/consternación s. abatimiento; aturdimiento tras un susto o un disgusto.
contemptuous/despreciativo *adj.* peyorativo; frío; indiferente.
contention/contienda s. disputa; controversia; discusión.
contortion/contorsión s. encogimiento; espasmo; forma o movimiento torcido.
contrive/lograr v. idear; inventar; ingeniárselas; conseguir.
corpulent/corpulento *adj.* gordo; voluminoso; enorme.
cosmopolitan/cosmopolita *adj.* internacional; vividor; mundano.
credential/credencial s. título; comprobante; justificante; cédula.
culinary/culinario *adj.* nutricio; alimenticio; asociado con la cocina.
cursory/precipitado *adj.* rápido; superficial.

D

daunt/intimidar v. desanimar; desalentar.
decree/decreto s. orden; mandato; ley.
deference/deferencia s. atención; respeto; educación.
defile/ensuciar v. manchar; contaminar; calumniar.
deject/descorazonar v. acobardar; desalentar; desmoralizar.
delusion/engaño s. error; confusión; espejismo.
demented/demente *adj.* ido; loco; tocado.
demolition/demolición s. desmoronamiento; derrumbe; destrucción.
desist/desistir v. renunciar; dimitir; ceder.
desolation/desolación s. tristeza; congoja; ruina; devastación.
diabolic/diabólico *adj.* perverso; infernal; malo; maléfico.
digress/desviarse v. apartarse del tema principal.
diligence/diligencia s. encargo; esmero; atención.
diminutive/diminuto *adj.* minúsculo; pequeño.
dire/terrible *adj.* espantoso; horrible; medida extrema o necesidad urgente.
discern/discernir v. comprender; distinguir; reconocer la diferencia.
discomfiture/desconcierto s. confusión; sorpresa; turbación.
disconcerted/desconcertado *adj.* trastornado; perturbado; alterado.
disconsolate/desconsolado *adj.* que causa tristeza o depresión; afligido; dolorido.
discourse/discurso s. alocución; oración.
discrimination/discriminación s. destreza en realizar distinciones finas.
dismal/deprimente *adj.* triste; patético; penoso.
disparage/menospreciar v. desdeñar; deslucir; rebajar.
dispassionate/desapasionado *adj.* imparcial; objetivo; falto de emoción. —**dispassionately/desapasionadamente** *adv.* imparcialmente; fríamente.
disperse/dispersar v. desordenar; desmontar.
disposition/disposición s. inclinación; carácter; tendencia.
dissuade/disuadir v. impedir; prohibir.
distend/distender v. hinchar; dilatar; alargar.
distill/destilar v. condensar; sublimar; extraer una esencia.
distraught/turbado *adj.* loco; enloquecido; trastornado.
divinity/divinidad s. Dios; deidad; ente sagrado.
dogged/tenaz *adj.* persistente; obstinado; terco.
duress/coerción s. coacción; imposición; tiranía.

E

efficacy/eficacia s. capacidad; destreza en producir el efecto deseado.
emanate/emanó v. procedió; derivó; brotó de una fuente.
eminent/eminente *adj.* ilustre; excepcional; notable.

endow/dotar *v.* hacer una donación; proporcionar; equipar; abastecer.
enmity/enemistad *s.* hostilidad; odio; antipatía.
ethereal/etéreo *adj.* celeste; sutil; impalpable; que no es de la tierra; espiritual.
exhilaration/exaltación *v.* entusiasmo; alegría; regocijo.
expedient/conveniencia *s.* utilidad; provecho.
exploit/hazaña *s.* proeza; gesta; iniciativa.
exquisite/exquisito *adj.* delicado; fino; elegante; distinguido.
extol/alabar *v.* encomiar; ensalzar; glorificar.
extort/extorsionar *v.* despojar; obtener mediante amenazas o violencia.
exult/exultar *v.* no caber en sí; gozar; exaltarse.

F

fastidious/melindroso *adj.* delicado; quisquilloso; caprichoso.
fawning/adulador *adj.* servil; lisonjero; halagador.
fickleness/inconstancia *s.* veleidad; informalidad.
flaccid/flácido *adj.* fofo; lacio; caído.
flag/flaquear *v.* aflojar; desistir.
formidable/formidable *adj.* tremendo; terrible; impresionante; que inspira la admiración de otros; que causa pavor.
frivolous/frívolo *adj.* de poco peso; mundano; trivial; de poca importancia.
frugal/frugal *adj.* sobrio; parco; abstinente.
furl/plegar *v.* aferrar las velas; poner una bandera a media asta; enrollar.

G

gallant/galante *adj.* atento; noble; rendido.
garrulous/locuaz *adj.* parlanchín; indiscreto; que habla mucho de temas poco importantes.
genial/simpático *adj.* afable; cordial.
geniality/simpatía *s.* amistad; afinidad.
ghastly/horroroso *adj.* espantoso; repulsivo; horrible.
glut/saciar *v.* inundar; hartar; saturar.
grievous/doloroso *adj.* penoso; cruel; lamentable.
grisly/horroroso *adj.* espantoso; aterrador; grotesco.
grovel/arrastrarse *v.* humillarse; someterse; mortificarse.
guffaw/carcajada *s.* risotada; carcajada; risa.
guile/engaño *s.* astucia; ardid; disimulo.

H

haggard/ojeroso *adj.* pálido; exangüe; agotado; marchito.
haggle/regatear *v.* debatir un precio.

I

ignoble/innoble *s.* vil; indigno; infame.
ignominy/ignominia *s.* infamia; deshonor; bajeza.
illusory/ilusorio *adj.* ficticio; irreal; imaginario; inexistente.
impassive/impasible *adj.* inalterable; inmutable.
impediment/impedimento *s.* obstáculo; dificultad; estorbo.
imperturbarble/imperturbable *adj.* inalterable; tranquilo; sereno.
impetuous/impetuoso *adj.* impulsivo; precipitado.
impinge/tocar *v.* tropezar con; chocar.
implacable/implacable *adj.* inclemente; severo; inflexible; que no cambia.
impromptu/improvisado *adj.* espontáneo; imprevisto; intuitivo.
improvise/improvisar *v.* crear; inventar; ingeniárselas con lo que hay.
inaccessible/inaccesible *adj.* impenetrable; cerrado; que no se puede acceder.
incessant/incesante *adj.* constante; continuo; perpetuo.
incliniation/inclinación *s.* predisposición; índole; tendencia.
incur/contraer *v.* incurrir en gastos; sufrir.
indiscriminate/indistinto *adj.* sin criterio; confuso; indeterminado.
induce/inducir *v.* persuadir; convencer; incitar.
indulgent/indulgente *adj.* tolerante; complaciente; blando.
inevitable/inevitable *adj.* necesario; irremediable; fijo.
infallible/infalible *adj.* seguro; incontestable; positivo; indudable.
infernal/infernal *adj.* diabólico; maléfico; endiablado.
ingratiating/zalamero *adj.* lisonjero; alabador.
initiative/iniciativa *s.* decisión; ingenio; atrevimiento.
insipid/insípido *adj.* soso; aburrido; incoloro.
intermittent/intermitente *adj.* esporádico; ocasional; que ocurre o aparece alternamente.
intoxicate/embriagar *v.* arrebatar; extasiar; encantar; entusiasmar.
intricate/intrincado *adj.* complejo; enrevesado; lleno de detalles espinosos.

iridescente/iridiscente *adj.* irisado; con los colores del arco iris; resplandeciente; brillante.

itinerant/itinerante *adj.* ambulante; de viaje; errante; nómada.

L

labyrinth/laberinto *s.* meandro; embrollo; enredo.

lamentable/lamentable *adj.* triste; deplorable; calamitoso.

lavish/pródigo *adj.* generoso; extravagante; profuso.

lethargy/letargo *s.* sopor; modorra; somnolencia.

livid/lívido *adj.* pálido; descolorido; exangüe; demacrado.

lugubrious/lúgubre *adj.* sombrío; tétrico; exageradamente solemne.

M

malice/malicia *s.* picardía; perfidia; deseo de hacer el mal.

maniacal/maníaco *adj.* trastornado; locamente entusiasta; desatinado; frenético

meticulous/meticuloso *adj.* minucioso; exacto; concienzudo.

misanthropy/misantropía *s.* misoginia; ascetismo; desdén por la raza humana.

monotonous/monótono *adj.* aburrido; continuo; iterativo; sin variación.

N

nimble/ágil *adj.* vivo; ligero.

notorious/célebre *adj.* famoso; popular; conocido; renombrado; un criminal notorio.

O

obscure/oscurecer *adj.* oscuro; desconocido; humilde; retirado.

obstinate/obstinado *adj.* terco; testarudo.

oppressive/opresivo *adj.* angustioso; difícil de soportar.

ostentatious/ostentoso *adj.* aparatoso; teatral; grandioso.

overwrought/sobreexcitado *adj.* emocionado; alterado; estimulado; conmovido.

P

pallor/palidez *s.* anemia; lividez.

partial/parcial *adj.* un juicio arbitrario; improcedente.

patronize/patronizar *v.* ser cliente de; favorecer; proteger.

pedantic/pedante *adj.* fatuo; afectado; que demuestra un interés desmesurado en los libros, la educación y las reglas.

pensive/pensativo *adj.* meditabundo; ensimismado; absorto.

perfunctory/negligente *adj.* descuidado; superficial; somero.

persevere/perseverar *v.* persistir; empeñarse; obstinarse.

pervade/extenderse *v.* difundirse; propagarse; esparcirse.

perverse/perverso *adj.* perjudicial; contrario; nocivo.

pestilence/pestilencia *s.* plaga; peste; epidemia.

pique/pique *s.* resentimiento; disgusto; molestia.

piteous/patético *adj.* lastimoso; lúgubre; lloroso.

pitiable/lastimoso *adj.* lamentable; deplorable; penoso.

posterity/posteridad *s.* descendencia; sucesión; porvenir; generaciones futuras.

precedent/precedente *s.* antecedente; primer ocurrencia de algo que servirá de norma en el futuro; referencia.

precipitate/precipitado *adj.* lanzado; atolondrado.

preliminary/preliminar *adj.* preparatorio; inicial; básico.

presumption/presunción *s.* engreimiento; jactancia; petulancia.

pretext/pretexto *s.* evasiva; excusa; justificación.

prevail/prevalecer *v.* triunfar; vencer.

procure/proporcionar *v.* obtener; conseguir; lograr.

prodigious/prodigioso *adj.* maravilloso; enorme; fuera de serie.

prodigy/prodigio *s.* fenómeno; niño dotado de un talento extraordinario.

profuse/profuso *adj.* abundante; pródigo; copioso.

propagate/propagar *v.* irradiar; difundir; popularizar.

propensity/propensión *s.* preferencia; inclinación; tendencia.

propitious/propicio *adj.* favorable; próspero; ventajoso.

prosaic/prosaico *adj.* insulso; mediocre; ordinario; soso.

prostrate/postrado *adj.* tumbado boca abajo; abatido; humillado.

provision/disposición *s.* arreglo; acuerdo; suministro.
proximity/proximidad *s.* cercanía; contacto; linde.
prudent/prudente *adj.* sensato; moderado; cauteloso.

R

rash/incauto *adj.* imprudente; precipitado; audaz.
raze/arrasar *v.* asolar; allanar; aplanar; talar.
reactionary/reaccionario *adj.* retrógrado; apegado; opositor de cambios y del progreso.
recess/recinto *s.* cercado; nicho; alcoba.
refract/refractar *v.* torcer pasando de un medio a otro.
refuse/basura *s.* desperdicios; desechos.
reiterate/reiterar *v.* repetir; insistir; confirmar; reincidir.
remonstrate/protestar *v.* amonestar; reprender; sermonear.
renounce/renunciar *v.* desistir; dimitir; declinar.
repast/comida *s.* colación; banquete; cena.
reproach/reprender *v.* condenar; criticar; censurar.
reproachful/reprobador *adj.* reparador; censurador.
reprove/censurar *v.* condenar; criticar; reprender.
residue/residuo *s.* resto; sobra; saldo.
resolute/resuelto *adj.* determinado; decidido; audaz; temerario.
resolve/resolución *s.* decisión; propósito; valor.
respite/respiro *s.* tregua; pausa; postergación.
reverent/reverente *adj.* respetuoso; considerado; que siente gran devoción por algo sagrado.
righteous/recto *adj.* honrado; moral.
rigor/rigor *s.* dureza; precisión; severidad.
rite/rito *s.* ceremonia; culto; acto.

S

scourge/látigo *s.* castigo; azote.
scrupulous/escrupuloso *adj.* cuidadoso; esmerado; aplicado.
serrated/serrado *adj.* dentado; apuntado.
servile/servil *adj.* bajo; esclavo; sumiso.
shirk/eludir *v.* esquivar; zafarse de un deber; rehuir.
sloth/pereza *s.* flojera; dejadez; lentitud.
solicitude/solicitud *s.* cuidado; preocupación; atención; deferencia.
somber/sombrío *adj.* oscuro; triste; lúgubre.
sordid/sórdido *adj.* mezquino; indecoroso; vil.
specious/especioso *adj.* artificioso; fingido; simulado.
spurn/despreciar *v.* rechazar; menospreciar; desfavorecer; desdeñar.
squalid/escuálido *adj.* mugrente; sucio; repugnante.
squall/ráfaga *s.* racha; borrasca; violenta tormenta de poca duración.
stealthy/cauteloso *adj.* sigiloso; secreto; disimulado.
strident/estridente *adj.* ruidoso; llamativo; chillón.
stupefying/estupefaciente *adj.* que atonta; aturdidor; soporífero; pesado.
subdued/sojuzgado *adj.* sometido; dominado; sumiso.
succor/socorro *s.* ayuda, sosiego; auxilio; refuerzo.
succumb/sucumbir *v.* ceder; rendirse; capitular.
sullen/hosco *adj.* ceñudo; resentido; huraño; arisco.
supercillious/arrogante *adj.* altanero; desdeñoso; altivo.
superfluity/superfluidad *s.* exceso; futilidad.
supplant/suplantar *v.* suplir; reemplazar; sustituir.
suppress/suprimir *v.* contener; evitar que se divulgue; reprimir; ocultar.
surreptitious/subrepticio *adj.* clandestino; disimulado.
sustenance/sustento *s.* alimento; subsistencia; nutrición.

T

taciturn/taciturno *adj.* abatido; silencioso; huraño.
temerity/temeridad *s.* imprudencia; osadía.
temper/templar *v.* suavizar; moderar; temperar.
temporal/temporal *adj.* transitorio; pasajero.
tentative/indeciso *adj.* vacilante; irresoluto; tímido.
tepid/tibio *adj.* templado; ni caliente ni frío.
titillating/excitante *adj.* apasionante; intrigante.
transcend/superar *v.* ir más allá de; exceder; rebasar; sobrepasar.
transfigure/transfigurar *v.* mudar; transformar.
transgress/transgredir *v.* infringir; desobedecer; contravenir.
translucent/translúcido *adj.* transparente; claro; diáfano.
tyrannous/tirano *s.* déspota; dictador; opresor.

U

uncanny/extraño *adj.* insólito; misterioso; raro.
unmarred/intacto *adj.* indemne; ileso; limpio; entero.

unpretentious/modesto *adj.* humilde; sencillo; moderado.

untainted/fresco *adj.* no contaminado; no corrompido.

V

vehement/vehemente *adj.* violento; apasionado; elocuente.

victuals/vituallas *s.* provisiones; víveres.

vigil/vela *s.* vigilia; vigilancia durante las horas de sueño.

vitiate/viciar *v.* corromper; invalidar; debilitar.

vivacity/vivacidad *s.* energía; vigor; brío.

W

wince/estremecerse *v.* hacer una mueca de dolor.

wrenched/angustiado *adj.* afligido; acongojado.

Z

zealous/celoso *adj.* entusiasta; apasionado.

Acknowledgments

For permission to reprint copyrighted material, grateful acknowledgment is made to the following sources:

Gillon Aitkin Associates Ltd.: "B. Wordsworth" from *Miguel Street* by V. S. Naipaul. Copyright © 1959 by V. S. Naipaul.

***Ardis Publishers*:** "Raven doth to raven fly" from *Alexander Pushkin: Collected Narrative and Lyrical Poetry,* translated by Walter Arndt. Copyright © 1984 by Walter Arndt.

***Bantam Books, a division of Random House, Inc.*:** From "The Second Teaching: Philosophy and Spiritual Decline" from *The Bhagavad-Gita,* translated by Barbara Stoler Miller. Translation copyright © 1986 by Barbara Stoler Miller. From "Give Us This Day Our Daily Bread" from *Shakespeare Alive* by Joseph Papp and Elizabeth Kirkland. Copyright © 1988 by the New York Shakespeare Festival.

***Darhansoff and Verrill Literary Agency*:** "I Am Not One of Those Who Left the Land . . ." from *Poems of Akhmatova* by Anna Akhmatova, translated by Stanley Kunitz and Max Hayward. Copyright © 1967, 1968, 1972, 1973 by Stanley Kunitz and Max Hayward.

***Anita Desai c/o Rogers, Coleridge & White Ltd., 20 Powis Mews, London W11 1JN*:** From "Games at Twilight" from *Games at Twilight and Other Stories* by Anita Desai. Copyright © 1978 by Anita Desai.

***Doubleday, a division of Random House, Inc.*:** "Marriage Is a Private Affair" from *Girls at War and Other Stories* by Chinua Achebe. Copyright © 1972, 1973 by Chinua Achebe. "A morning-glory vine" by Kobayashi Issa from *An Introduction to Haiku,* translated by Harold G. Henderson. Copyright © 1958 by Harold G. Henderson. "Half a Day" from *The Time and the Place and Other Stories* by Naguib Mahfouz, translated by Denys Johnson-Davies. Copyright © 1991 by the American University in Cairo Press.

***Dutton Signet, a division of Penguin Group (USA) Inc.*:** "Le Morte D'Arthur" (retitled "Day of Destiny") from *Le Morte D'Arthur* by Sir Thomas Malory, translated by Keith Baines. Copyright © 1962 by Keith Baines; copyright renewed © 1990 by Francesca Evans. From *Beowulf,* translated by Burton Raffel. Copyright © 1963 and renewed © 1991 by Burton Raffel. From "The Unfed Dervish," "Information and Knowledge," "The Elephant-Keeper," "Safety and Riches," and "The Fox and the Camels" from *The Way of the Sufi* by Idries Shah. Copyright © 1968 by Idries Shah.

***Faber and Faber Ltd., an affiliate of Farrar, Straus and Giroux, LLC*:** From *WIT* by Margaret Edson. Copyright © 1993, 1999 by Margaret Edson. "The Wife's Lament" from *A Choice of Anglo-Saxon Verse,* translated by Richard Hamer. Translation copyright © 1970 by Richard Hamer.

***Farrar, Straus and Giroux, LLC*:** "Once upon a Time" from *Jump and Other Stories* by Nadine Gordimer. Copyright © 1991 by Felix Licensing, B.V. "Digging" from *Selected Poems 1966–1987* by Seamus Heaney. Copyright © 1990 by Seamus Heaney. "The Horses" from *Collected Poems* by Ted Hughes. Copyright © 2003 by The Estate of Ted Hughes. "The Virgins" from *Sea Grapes* by Derek Walcott. Copyright © 1976 by Derek Walcott.

***Field Day Publications, Dublin Ireland*:** From "Memories of the Famine" by Máire Ní Grianna, translated by Emer Deane, from *The Field Day Anthology of Irish Writing,* vol. II, pp. 203–04, edited by Seamus Deane. Translation copyright © 1991 by Field Day Publications.

***The Gale Group*:** Quote by Chinua Achebe from *Contemporary Novelists, Fifth Edition,* edited by Lesley Henderson. Copyright © 1991 by Gale Group.

***General Media International, Inc.*:** From "Black Man's Burden" by Maxwell Geismar from *The Saturday Review,* March 8, 1975. Copyright © 1975 by General Media International, Inc.

***Grove/Atlantic, Inc.*:** "Next Term, We'll Mash You" from *Pack of Cards and Other Stories* by Penelope Lively. Copyright © 1978 by Penelope Lively. From "That's All" from *Complete Plays: Three by Harold Pinter.* Copyright © 1966 by H. Pinter Ltd.

***Harcourt Inc.*:** "The Hollow Men" from *Collected Poems 1909–1962* by T. S. Eliot. Copyright 1936 by Harcourt, Inc.; copyright © 1963, 1964 by T. S. Eliot. "Shooting an Elephant" from *Shooting an Elephant and Other Essays* by George Orwell. Copyright © 1936 by George Orwell. From *Mrs. Dalloway* by Virginia Woolf. Copyright © 1925 by Harcourt Inc.; copyright renewed © 1953 by Leonard Woolf. From "Shakespeare's Sister" and from page 64 from *A Room of One's Own* by Virginia Woolf. Copyright 1929 by Harcourt, Inc; copyright renewed © 1957 by Leonard Woolf.

***HarperCollins Publishers, Inc.*:** "The Swan" from *Selected Poems of Rainer Maria Rilke,* edited and translated by Robert Bly. Copyright © 1981 by Robert Bly. "# 8 The supreme good is like water" from *Tao Te Ching by Lao Tzu, A New English Version,* translated by Stephen Mitchell. Translation copyright © 1988 by Stephen Mitchell.

***Hill and Wang, a division of Farrar, Straus & Giroux, LLC*:** "Never Shall I Forget" from *Night* by Elie Wiesel, translated by Stella Rodway. Copyright © 1958 by Les Editions de Minuit; English translation copyright © 1960 by MacGibbon & Kee, renewed © 1988 by The Collins Publishing Group. All rights reserved.

***Houghton Mifflin Company*:** "Siren Song" from *Selected Poems, 1965–1975* by Margaret Atwood. Copyright © 1976 by Margaret Atwood. All rights reserved. From *Gilgamesh: A Verse Narrative* translated by Herbert Mason. Copyright © 1970 by Herbert Mason. All rights reserved. From "The Seventh Elegy" from *Duino Elegies: The Sonnets to Orpheus* by Rainer Maria Rilke, translated by Robert Hunter. Translation copyright © 1987, 1993 by Robert Hunter. All rights reserved.

***Melanie Jackson Agency, L.L.C.*:** "Telephone Conversation" by Wole Soyinka from *Reflections: Nigerian Prose and Verse,* edited by Frances Ademola. Copyright © 1962, 1990 by Wole Soyinka.

***Alfred A. Knopf, a division of Random House, Inc.*:** "The Demon Lover" from *The Collected Stories of Elizabeth Bowen.* Copyright 1946 and renewed © 1981 by Curtis Brown Ltd., Literary Executors of the Estate of Elizabeth Bowen. Excerpt (retitled "Trojan Gold") from *Gods, Graves and Scholars* by C. W. Ceram. Copyright 1951, © 1967 by Alfred A. Knopf, Inc. From *Grendel* by John Gardner. Copyright © 1971 by John Gardner. "The Doll's House" from *The Short Stories of Katherine Mansfield.* Copyright 1923 by Alfred A. Knopf, Inc., a division of Random House, Inc.; copyright renewed 1951 by John Middleton Murry.

***Edmund Morris*:** From "A Visit with Nadine Gordimer" by Edmund Morris from *The New York Times Book Review,* June 7, 1981. Copyright © 1981 by Edmund Morris.

***Navajivan Trust*:** "Speech, March 23, 1922" by Mohandas Gandhi.

***Jawaharlal Nehru Memorial Fund*:** From speech by Jawaharlal Nehru, August 14, 1947.

***New Directions Publishing Corporation*:** "Dulce et Decorum Est" and "Strange Meeting" from *The Collected Poems of Wilfred Owen.* Copyright © 1963 by Chatto & Windus, Ltd. "Do Not Go Gentle into That Good Night" and "Fern Hill" from *The Poems of Dylan Thomas.* Copyright © 1945 by The Trustees for the Copyrights of Dylan Thomas. "Jade Flower Palace" by Tu Fu from *One Hundred Poems from the Chinese,* translated by Kenneth Rexroth. Copyright © 1971 by Kenneth Rexroth. "Not Waving But Drowning" from *Collected Poems of Stevie Smith.* Copyright © 1972 by Stevie Smith.

***The New Press, (800 233-4830)*:** From *The War* by Marguerite Duras, translated by Barbara Bray. Copyright © 1986 by Barbara Bray.

***The New York Times Syndication Sales*:** From "Scenes from a Modern Marriage" by Julia Markus from *The New York Times,* February 14, 1995. Copyright © 1995 by The New York Times Co.

***The Nobel Foundation*:** From Nobel Peace Prize acceptance speech by Nelson Mandela. Copyright © 1993 by The Nobel Foundation.

***North Point Press, a division of Farrar, Straus & Giroux, LLC*:** "The Silver Fifty-Sen Pieces" from *Palm-of-the-Hand Stories* by Yasunari Kawabata, translated by Lane Dunlop and J. Martin Holman. Translation copyright © 1988 by Lane Dunlop and J. Martin Holman.

***W. W. Norton & Company, Inc.*:** "Fifth Day, Ninth Story" (retitled "Federigo's Falcon") from *The Decameron* by Giovanni Boccaccio, translated by Mark Musa and Peter Bondanella. Translation copyright © 1982 by Mark Musa and Peter Bondanella. From *Beowulf,* translated by Seamus Heaney. Copyright © 2000 by Seamus Heaney.

***Oxford University Press, Inc.*:** From "The Troglodyte World" from *The Great War and Modern Memory* by Paul Fussell. Copyright © 1975 by Oxford University Press, Inc.

***Pantheon Books, a division of Random House, Inc.*:** "A Clever Judge" by Chang Shih-nan and "Gold, Gold" by Lieh Tzu from *Chinese Fairy Tales and Fantasies,* translated and edited by Moss Roberts. Copyright © 1979 by Moss Roberts. "Axolotl" from *End of the Game and Other Stories* by Julio Cortázar, translated by Paul Blackburn. Copyright © 1963, 1967 by Random House, Inc. "Saboteur" from *The Bridegroom* by Ha Jin. Copyright © 2000 by Ha Jin.

***Peter Pauper Press, Inc.*:** From *African Proverbs,* compiled by Charlotte and Wolf Leslau. Copyright © 1962, 1985 by Peter Pauper Press. "Even stones in streams" by Uejima Onitsura from *Haiku Harvest: Japanese Haiku, Series IV,* translated by Peter Beilenson and Harry Behn. Copyright © 1962 by Peter Pauper Press, Inc.

***Penguin Books Ltd.*:** "Caedmon of Whitby" from *A History of the English Church and People* by Bede, translated by Leo Sherley-Price, revised by R. E. Latham (Penguin Classics 1955, Revised edition 1968). Translation copyright © 1955, 1968 by Leo Sherley-Price. "The Prologue," "The Pardoner's Prologue and Tale," and "The Wife of Bath's Prologue and Tale" from *The Canterbury Tales* by Geoffrey Chaucer, translated by Nevill Coghill (Penguin Classics 1951, Fourth Revised Edition 1977). Copyright © 1951, 1958, 1960, 1975, 1977 by Nevill Coghill. "Night" from *The Koran,* translated by N. J. Dawood (Penguin Classics 1956, Fifth Revised Edition 1990). Copyright © 1956, 1959, 1966, 1968, 1974, 1990 by N. J. Dawood. "The Third Voyage of Sindbad the Sailor" from *The Thousand and One Nights,* translated by N. J. Dawood (Penguin Classics 1954). Translation copyright © 1954 by N. J. Dawood. "The Jewels" from *Selected Short Stories* by Guy de Maupassant, translated by Roger Colet (Penguin Classics, 1971). Copyright © 1971 by Roger Colet. "Quiet Night Thoughts" and "Letter to His Two Small Children" by Li Po and "Night Thoughts Afloat" by Tu Fu from *Li Po and Tu Fu,* translated by Arthur Cooper (Penguin Classics, 1973). Copyright © 1973 by Arthur Cooper. "Question and answer among the mountains" by Li Po from *The Penguin Book of Chinese Verse,* translated by Robert Kotewall and Norman L. Smith (Penguin Books, 1962). Translation copyright © 1962 by N. L. Smith and R. H. Kotewall.

***Pollinger Limited and the Estate of Frieda Lawrence Ravagli*:** From "Letter to Rolf Gardiner, 18 December 1927" and from "Letter to Rolf Gardiner, 17 July 1926" from *The Letters of D. H. Lawrence,* vol. V–VI. Copyright 1932 by the Estate of D. H. Lawrence; copyright 1934 by Frieda Lawrence; copyright 1933, 1948, 1953, 1954, © 1956, 1957, 1958, 1959, 1960, 1961, 1962, 1967, 1969 by Stefano Ravagli and R. G. Seaman, executors of the Estate of Frieda Lawrence Ravagli; copyright © 1987 by the Estate of Frieda Lawrence Ravagli. Published by Cambridge University Press.

***The Random House Group Limited*:** From "William Caxton, Printer" from *The Story of Britain* by Sir Roy Strong. Copyright © 1996 by Oman Productions Ltd. Originally published by Hutchinson.

***Random House, Inc.*:** "Musée des Beaux Arts" from *W. H. Auden: Collected Poems* by W. H. Auden, edited by Edward Mendelson. Copyright 1940 and renewed © 1968 by W. H. Auden. "Sonnet 42: The spring returns, the spring wind softly blowing" from *The Sonnets of Petrarch,* translated by Joseph Auslander. Copyright © 1931 by Longmans, Green and Co., a division of Random House, Inc.

***Schocken Books, a division of Random House, Inc.*:** "Sonnet XXIII" by Louise Labé from *A Book of Women Poets from Antiquity to Now,* edited by Willis Barnstone and Aliki Barnstone. Copyright © 1980 by Schocken Books, a division of Random House, Inc.

***Scribner, an imprint of Simon & Schuster Adult Publishing Group*:** "Sailing to Byzantium" from *The Collected Works of W. B. Yeats, Volume I: The Poems, Revised,* edited by Richard J. Finneran. Copyright 1928 by The Macmillan Company; copyright renewed © 1956 by Georgie Yeats. From *In Patagonia* by Bruce Chatwin. Copyright © 1977 by Bruce Chatwin. Number 17 from *Book II,* numbers 15 and 21 from *Book VII,* and number 23 from *Book XV* from *The Analects of Confucius,* translated by Arthur Waley. Copyright © 1938 George Allen & Unwin, Ltd. "Death and Other Grave Matters" from *What Jane Austen Ate and Charles Dickens Knew* by Daniel Pool. Copyright © 1993 by Daniel Pool.

***Simon & Schuster Adult Publishing Group*:** "No Witchcraft for Sale" from *African Stories* by Doris Lessing. Copyright © 1951, 1953, 1954, 1957, 1958, 1962, 1963, 1964, 1965, 1972, 1981 by Doris Lessing. "Sailing to Byzantium" from *The Collected Works of W. B. Yeats, Volume I: The Poems, Revised,* edited by Richard J. Finneran. Copyright 1928 by the Macmillan Company; copyright renewed © 1956 by Georgie Yeats.

***Wislawa Szymborska*:** "The End and the Beginning" by Wislawa Szymborska, translated by Stanislaw Baranczak and Clare Cavanagh from *The New Republic,* January 18, 1993. Copyright © 1993 by Wislawa Szymborska.

***Anthony Thwaite*:** "I waited and I" by Princess Nukada, "The end of my journey" by Oshikochi Mitsune, "Now, I cannot tell" by Ki Tsurayuki, "How helpless my heart!" by Ono Komachi, and "Every single thing" by Priest Saigyo from *The Penguin Book of Japanese Verse,* translated by Geoffrey Bownas and Anthony Thwaite (Penguin Classics, 1964). Translation copyright © 1964 by Geoffrey Bownas and Anthony Thwaite.

***Time Inc.*:** From "Life in 999: A Grim Struggle" by Howard G. Chua-Eoan from *Time,* vol. 140, no. 27, October 15, 1992. Copyright © 1992 by Time Inc.

***Charles E. Tuttle Co., Inc., Boston, MA, and Tokyo, Japan*:** "The First Principle," "The Gates of Paradise," "The Moon Cannot Be Stolen," and "Temper" from *Zen Flesh, Zen Bones: A Collection of Zen and Pre-Zen Writings,* compiled by Paul Reps. Copyright © 1957 by Charles E. Tuttle Co., Inc.

***United Nations Publication Board*:** Preamble to the *Universal Declaration of Human Rights,* United Nations, December 10, 1948. Copyright © 1948 by United Nations. From "The Question of South Africa" by Desmond Tutu from a speech to the United Nations Security Council, October 23, 1984. Copyright © 1984 by United Nations.

***United States Holocaust Memorial Museum*:** From "Historic Overview" from *U. S. Holocaust Memorial Museum – Kristallnacht* Web site, accessed November 15, 2001, at http://www.ushmm.org/kristallnacht/frame.htm. Copyright © by United States Holocaust Memorial Museum.

***University of California Press*:** Excerpts (retitled "The First Day of the Great Fire of London") from *The Diary of Samuel Pepys,* vol. VII, edited by Robert Latham and William Matthews. Copyright © 1972 by the University of California Press.

***The University of Chicago Press*:** From "Sir Gawain and the Green Knight" from *The Complete Works of the Gawain-Poet,* translated by John Gardner. Copyright © 1965 by The University of Chicago. From *The Panchatantra,* translated from the Sanskrit by Arthur William Ryder. Copyright 1925 by the University of Chicago Press.

***University of Texas Press and Agencia Literaria Carmen Balcells*:** "Sonnet 79/Soneto 79" from *100 Love Sonnets/Cien sonetos* *de amor* by Pablo Neruda, translated by Stephen Tapscott. Copyright © 1959 by Pablo Neruda and Fundación Pablo Neruda; translation copyright © 1986 by University of Texas Press.

Laurence S. Untermeyer on behalf of The Estate of Louis Untermeyer, Norma Anchin Untermeyer c/o Professional Publishing Services Company: "The Lorelei" from *Heinrich Heine: Paradox and Poet* by Louis Untermeyer. Copyright 1937 by Louis Untermeyer.

Viking Penguin, a division of Penguin Group (USA) Inc.: From "The Book of Sand" from *Collected Fictions* by Jorges Luis Borges, translated by Andrew Hurley. Copyright © 1998 by Maria Kodama; translation copyright © 1998 by Penguin Putnam Inc. "Top of the Food Chain" from *Without A Hero* by T. Coraghessan Boyle. Copyright © 1993 by T. Coraghessan Boyle. From *Don Quixote* by Miguel de Cervantes Saavedra, translated by Samuel Putnam. Copyright 1949 by The Viking Press, Inc. "The Destructors" from *Collected Stories of Graham Greene.* Copyright © 1955, 1983 by Graham Greene. "The Death of Hector" and "The Rage of Achilles" from *The Iliad* by Homer, translated by Robert Fagles. Copyright © 1990 by Robert Fagles. "The Rocking-Horse Winner" from *Complete Short Stories of D. H. Lawrence.* Copyright 1933 by the Estate of D. H. Lawrence; copyright renewed © 1961 by Angelo Ravagli and C.M. Weekley, Executors of the Estate of Frieda Lawrence Ravagli. "On the Bottom" from *If This Is a Man (Survival in Auschwitz)* by Primo Levi, translated by Stuart Woolf. Copyright © 1958 by Guilio Einaudi editore S.P.A.; copyright © 1959 by Orion Press, Inc. "Like the Sun" from *Under the Banyan Tree* by R. K. Narayan. Copyright © 1985 by R. K. Narayan. "In the Shadow of War" from *Stars of the New Curfew* by Ben Okri. Copyright © 1988 by Ben Okri. From "Towards a True Refuge" from *Freedom from Fear and Other Writings, Revised Edition* by Aung San Suu Kyi, foreword by Vaclav Havel, translated by Michael Aris. Copyright © 1991, 1995 by Aung San Suu Kyi and Michael Aris.

Wiley Publishing, Inc.: Symbols from Pronunciation Key from *Webster's New World™ College Dictionary, Fourth Edition.* Copyright © 1999, 2000 by Wiley Publishing, Inc. All rights reserved.

Writer's House, Inc., as agents for the proprietors: "Fear" from *Selected Poems of Gabriela Mistral: A Bilingual Edition,* translated by Doris Dana. Copyright © 1961, 1964, 1970, 1971 by Doris Dana. Published by The Johns Hopkins University Press, Baltimore, 1971.

Yale University Press: "The Seafarer" and from "The Wanderer" from *Poems and Prose from the Old English,* translated by Burton Raffel. Copyright © 1960, 1964, 1998 by Burton Raffel.

Zephyr Press: From "All the Unburied Ones . . ." from *The Complete Poems of Anna Akhmatova,* vol. II, translated by Judith Hemschemeyer, edited by Roberta Reeder. Translation copyright © 1983, 1984, 1985, 1986, 1987, 1988, 1989 by Judith Hemschemeyer.

Sources Cited:

From "Marguerite Duras, The unspeakable, she said . . ." by Jean-Louis Arnaud from *Label France,* no. 24, June 1996, Web site accessed June 27, 2001, at http://www.france.diplomatie.fr/label_france/ENGLISH/LETTRES/DURAS/duras.html.

Program Staff Credits: Kristen Azzara, Julie Beckman-Key, Tom Browne, Matt Bucher, Susan Cakars, Kimberly Cammerata, Melissa Ciano, Gail Coupland, Grant Davidson, Nina Degollado, Scott Deneroff, Christine Devall, Liz Dickson, Lydia Doty, Amy Fleming, Emily Force, Betty Gabriel, Jeff Galvez, Mikki Gibson, Guy Guidici, Leora Harris, Sally Hartin-Young, Anne Heausler, Sean Henry, Eric Higgerson, Julie Hill, Julie Hoover, Julia Hu, Liz Huckestein, Rodney Jester, Stephanie Jones, Dolores Keller, Marcia Kelley, Juliana Koenig, Karen Kolar, Jane Kominek, Cathy Kuhles, Elizabeth LaManna, Jamie Lane, Carolyn Logan, Belinda Lopez, Mary Malone, Kris Marshall, Carol Marunas, Pat McCambridge, Mark McDonald, Dick Metzger, Betty Mintz, Mary Monaco, Laura Mongello, Victoria Moreland, Cynthia Muñoz, Michael Neibergall, Steve Oelenberger, Karen Peterfreund, Marie Price, Jeff Raun, Amber Rigney, Mike Rinella, Kathryn Rogers, Beth Sample, Susan Sato, Annette Saunders, Peter Sawchuk, Kathleen Scheiner, Gloria Shahan, Mary Shaw, Dakota Smith, Emily R. Stern, Jeff Streber, Ralph Tachuk, Jennifer Tench, Carol Trammel, Lisa Vecchione, Katie Vignery, Ken Whiteside, Tamesa Williams, Evan Wilson, Sari Wilson, Richard Wright, Michael Zakhar, Sara Zettner

Picture Credits

The illustrations and/or photographs on the Contents pages are picked up from pages in the textbook. Credits for those works can be found either on the textbook page on which they appear or in the list below.

Page A20: *Le Faux Miroir (The False Mirror)* (1929) by Rene Magritte. Private Collection © 2005 C. Herscovici, Brussels/Artists Rights Society (ARS), New York, Herscovici/Art Resource, NY; **Page xx:** Art Resource, NY; **3:** (bottom left) © Justin Kerr Photography; (bottom right) The Pierpont Morgan Library, NY/Art Resource, NY; **4–5:** (bottom) Bridgeman Art Library; **7:** © David Parker/ Science Photo Library/Photo Researchers, Inc.; **9:** Bridgeman Art Library; **10:** © Michael Holford; **11:** © Erich Lessing/Art Resource, NY; **13:** © Werner Forman/Art Resource, NY; **16:** Art Resource, NY; **17:** Bridgeman Art Library; **18:** © Michael Holford; **20:** © Werner Forman/Art Resource, NY; **22:** Bridgeman Art Library; **29:** Bridgeman Art Library; **30:** Bridgeman Art Library; **32:** © Werner Forman/Art Resource, NY; **33:** © Michael Holford; **34:** © Werner Forman/Art Resource, NY; **35:** Boltin Picture Library; **42:** Courtesy of Ted Spiegel; **43:** (background) British Library, London, UK/The Art Archive; **44:** (background) detail, © Werner Forman/Art Resource, NY; **49:** © Werner Forman/Art Resource, NY; **53:** © Erich Lessing/Art Resource, NY; **58:** © Giraudon/Art Resource, NY; **59, 60, 61, 62, 63:** (bottom borders) Bildarchiv Steffens/ Bridgeman Art Library; **62, 64:** Bildarchiv Steffens; **83:** © The British Museum/Topham-HIP/The Image Works; **85:** Bridgeman Art Library; **87:** ©AAAC/Topham/The Image Works; **90:** © Jon Sparks/ CORBIS; **91:** Bridgeman Art Library; **92:** Réunion des Musées Nationaux/Art Resource, NY; **93:** Scala/Art Resource, NY; **95:** (top left) Cover from *The Hobbit* and *The Lord of the Rings* by J.R.R. Tolkien. Copyright © 1982 by Christopher R. Tolkien, Michael H. R. Tolkien, John F. R. Tolkien and Priscilla M.A.R. Tolkien. Cover art by Michael Herring. Used by permission of Ballantine Books, a division of Random House, Inc.; (top right) Cover from *Grendel* by John Gardner. Copyright © 1971 by John Gardner. Cover illustration by Mark Penbenhy. Used by permission of Vintage Books, a division of Random House, Inc.; (bottom left) Cover from *Mythology: The Voyage of the Hero* by David Adams Leeming. Copyright © 1998 by David Adams Leeming. Used by permission of Oxford University Press; (bottom right) Cover painting courtesy Professor Donal Cruise O'Brien; **111:** Bibliothèque Nationale de France; **112:** (top left) © Giraudon/Art Resource, NY; (bottom right) Bridgeman Art Library, London/New York; **113:** (top) © Giraudon/Art Resource, NY; (bottom left) Bibliothèque Nationale/AKG London; (bottom right) Photograph by Schecter Lee/Photo © 1986 The Metropolitan Museum of Art; **115:** (top and bottom) The Bridgeman Art Library; **119:** Robert Harding Picture Library; **121:** Art Resource, NY; **129:** The Bridgeman Art Library; **132:** Photo AKG London; **134:** The Bridgeman Art Library; **137, 138** (bottom): SuperStock; **143:** Bridgeman Art Library, London/New York; **144, 145, 146, 148, 151, 152, 153, 154, 156, 157, 158, 160, 161, 165, 168:** SuperStock; **171:** Photograph © 1991 The Metropolitan Museum of Art; **178:** SuperStock; **180:** G. Dagli Orti/The Art Archive; **183:** © Bettmann/CORBIS; **187:** Bridgeman Art Library, London/New York; **189:** G. Dagli Orti/The Art Archive; **190:** The Bridgeman Art Library; **207:** © Scala/Art Resource, NY; **211:** © Giraudon/Art Resource, NY; **218–219, 222:** Bridgeman Art Library; **230:** Bridgeman Art Library; **234–235:** Snark/Art Resource, NY; **237:** Art Resource, NY; **239:** (top left) Cover from *The Arabian Nights,* translated by Hussain Haddaway. Based on the text edited by Muhsin Mahdi. Cover illustration by Dia Azzawi. Copyright © 1990 by W. W. Norton & Company; (top right) *Life in a Medieval Castle* by Joseph and Frances Gies. Copyright © 1974 by Joseph and Frances Gies. HarperCollins Publishers; (bottom left) From *The Hitchhiker's Guide to the Galaxy* by Douglas Adams, copyright © 1979 by Douglas Adams. Used by permission of Harmony Books, a division of Random House, Inc.; (bottom right) Cover (Ace Edition) from *The Once and Future King* by T. H. White, © 1938, 1939, 1940, © 1958 by T. H. White, renewed. Used by permission of G. P. Putnam's Sons, a division of Penguin Group (USA), Inc.; **270:** (top) Bridgeman Art Library, London/New York; (center) Bridgeman Art Library; (bottom) © Bettmann/CORBIS; **271:** (top) © Erich Lessing/ Art Resource, NY; (bottom left) Photo AKG London; (bottom right) Bridgeman Art Library, London/New York; **272:** (left) © Scala/Art Resource, NY; **276** (bottom): Bridgeman Art Library, London/New York; **280** (right): © Erich Lessing/Art Resource, NY; **285, 291, 292, 297:** Bridgeman Art Library, London/New York; **299:** (left) Erica Lansner/Black Star Publishing/PictureQuest; (right) Bridgeman Art Library; **301:** Christie's, London/Art Resource, NY; **305:** Bridgeman Art Library, London/New York; **306:** Sotheby's Transparency Library, London; **310:** Martha Swope/© Time, Inc.; **311:** Bridgeman Art Library, London/New York; **316:** David Young-Wolff/PhotoEdit; **318:** © 1985 Jose Azel/AURORA/PictureQuest; **326:** Pictor International, Ltd./PictureQuest; **328:** Collections/Julian Nieman; **333, 334:** © Michal Daniel; **336, 338:** Bridgeman Art Library, London/New York; **339:** James P. Blair/Words & Pictures/ PictureQuest; **340:** Art Resource, NY; **342:** Bridgeman Art Library, London/New York; **344:** © Woodmansterne Limited Watford; **346:** Pictor International, Ltd./PictureQuest; **352:** Photograph © 1979 The Metropolitan Museum of Art; **355:** Bridgeman Art Library, London/New York; **356:** © Getty Images; **357, 359:** Bridgeman Art Library, London/New York; **362, 363:** G. Dagli Orti/The Art Archive; **365:** Collections/Alain Le Garsmeur; **367:** © Ted Spiegel; **372, 373:** Art Resource, NY; **375:** Foto Marburg/Art Resource, NY; **379:** © SCALA/Art Resource, NY; **380:** © SCALA/Art Resource, NY; **386:** Photograph © 1989 The Metropolitan Museum of Art; **390:** © Ben Simmons/CORBIS/The Stock Market; **409:** Art Resource, NY; **415:** Dennis MacDonald/PhotoEdit/PictureQuest; **425:** TopFoto.co.uk/The Image Works; **427:** © Lebrecht Music & Arts/The Image Works; **430:** Bridgeman Art Library; **437:** (bottom) Bridgeman Art Library; **506:** Bridgeman Art Library; **521:** Photowrap/TopFoto.co.uk/The Image Works; **531:** Bridgeman Art Library; **533:** Bridgeman Art Library; **534:** Art Resource, NY; **536:** Bridgeman Art Library; **538:** Art Resource, NY; **541:** (top left) *The Enlightened Mind* by Stephen Mitchell. Cover design © 1992 by David Bullen. HarperCollins Publishers; (top right) Used by permission of William Morrow & Company; (bottom left) From *Shakespeare Alive!* (jacket cover) by Joseph Papp and Elizabeth Kirkland. Used by permission of Bantam Books, a division of Random House, Inc.; (bottom right) *The Tragedy of Macbeth* by William Shakespeare. Cover, © HRW. Cover art by Joe Melomo; **558:** Bridgeman Art Library, London/New York; **560:** (right) Bolton Picture Library; (bottom left) Mansell/© Time, Inc.; **561:** (right) © Photothèque des Musées de la Ville de Paris; (bottom left) Bridgeman Art Library, London/New York; **562** (left): Bolton Museum and Art Gallery, Lancashire, UK/Bridgeman Art Library; **563:** (left middle) Victoria and Albert

Museum, London, UK/Bridgeman Art Library; (bottom middle) Mary Evans Picture Library; **565:** Derby Museum and Art Gallery, Derbyshire, UK/Bridgeman Art Library; **567, 568:** Bridgeman Art Library, London/New York; **569** (top): © Bettmann/CORBIS; **571:** Culver Pictures, Inc.; **572** (top), **573:** Bridgeman Art Library, London/New York; **574:** Max A. Polster Archive; **575:** Bridgeman Art Library, London/New York; **576:** Roger-Viollet, Paris/Bridgeman Art Library; **577:** North Wind Picture Archives; **578:** Bridgeman Art Library, London/New York; **582, 583:** The Illustrated London News Picture Library; **597:** Bridgeman Art Library, London/New York; **598:** Yale Center for British Art, Paul Mellon Collection, USA/Bridgeman Art Library; **600:** Bridgeman Art Library, London/New York; **604:** Hermitage, St. Petersburg/Bridgeman Art Library; **608:** Robert Halsband Collection; **617:** North Wind Picture Archives; **619, 622, 623:** © Martha Swope/TimePix; **625:** Bridgeman Art Library; **627:** Collection Kharbine-Tapabor, Paris, France/Bridgeman Art Library; **638–639:** Victoria and Albert Museum, London, UK/Bridgeman Art Library; **643:** National Gallery, London, UK/Bridgeman Art Library; **646:** Eric Kamp/Index Stock Imagery/PictureQuest; **648:** National Gallery, London, UK/Bridgeman Art Library; **651:** Bridgeman Art Library; **652:** one interior illustration, From GULLIVER'S TRAVELS IN LILLIPUT by Ann Keay Beneduce, illustrated by Gennady Spirin, copyright © 1993 by Gennady Spirin. Used by permission of Philomel, A Division of Penguin Young Readers Group, A Member of Penguin Group (USA) Inc., 345 Hudson Street, New York, NY 10014. All rights reserved.; **654:** © Mary Evans Picture Library/The Image Works; **661:** © Mary Evans Picture Library/The Image Works; **671:** © Michael Nicholson/CORBIS; **672:** Bridgeman Art Library; **674:** Culver Pictures; **683:** (top left) *The Misanthrope and Tartuffe* by Molière. Cover illustration by Mark English. Used by permission of Harcourt Publishers; (top right) From *Robinson Crusoe* by Daniel Defoe. Used by permission of Bantam Books, a division of Random House, Inc.; (bottom left) *Isaac Newton and the Scientific Revolution* by Gale E. Christianson. © 1996 by Gale E. Christianson. Cover used courtesy of Oxford University Press; (bottom right) *Animal Farm* by George Orwell. Cover © HRW, art by Fred Lynch; **701:** © Getty Images; **702:** (left) © Bettmann/CORBIS; **707:** Bridgeman Art Library, London/New York; **708:** Photo Bulloz, Paris; **709:** © Giraudon/Art Resource, NY; **710:** Bridgeman Art Library, London/New York; **711:** (top) © Getty Images; (bottom) Fine Art Photographic Library Ltd.; **712** (top): Mary Evans Picture Library; **717** (detail): The Bridgeman Art Library; **720:** Art Resource, NY; **721:** Bridgeman Art Library, London/New York; **722:** Tate Gallery, London/Art Resource, NY; **723:** Bridgeman Art Library; **725:** © Getty Images; **731:** Larry Lefever from Grant Heilman Photography, Inc.; **732:** Bridgeman Art Library, London/New York; **733:** The Pierpont Morgan Library, New York/Art Resource, NY; **737, 738–739:** Bridgeman Art Library, London/New York; **742:** © Michael Jenner/Robert Harding Picture Library; **744:** Sotheby's Transparency Library, London; **745:** © Erich Lessing/Art Resource, NY; **765:** © W. Perry Conway/CORBIS; **793:** Sotheby's Transparency Library, London; **794, 797:** Bridgeman Art Library, London/New York; **799** (center): © Getty Images; **800:** Photo by Richard Carafelli; **801:** Robert Harding Picture Library; **812** (background): © Frank Lane Picture Agency/CORBIS; **814:** Photographer: Robert Rubic; **819:** Bridgeman Art Library, London/New York; **826:** The Pierpont Morgan Library/Art Resource, NY; **827:** Sotheby's Transparency Library, London; **830:** © Eric and David Hosking/CORBIS; **832:** Bridgeman Art Library, London/New York; **837:** © Scala/Art Resource, NY; **839:** Bridgeman Art Library; **840:** Bridgeman Art Library; **842:** Sotheby's Picture Library, London; **843:** Bridgeman Art Library; **847:** Tate Gallery, London/Art Resource, NY; **850:** Fine Art Photographic Library, London/Art Resource, NY; **855:** (top left) *Frankenstein, Or the Modern Prometheus* by Mary Shelley. Cover © HRW, illustration by Cliff Nielsen; (top right) Cover illustration © Philippe Weisbecker. Used by permission of Riley Illustration; (bottom left) Used by permission of William Morrow & Company, an imprint of HarperCollins Publishers; (bottom right) From *Pride and Prejudice* by Jane Austen. Used by permission of Bantam Books, a division of Random House, Inc.; **872:** Fine Art Photographic Library Ltd.; **874 (center):** Ashmolean Museum, Oxford; **882:** © Getty Images; **884, 885:** Art Resource, NY; **886:** Fine Art Photographic Library Ltd.; **887** (top), **890:** Bridgeman Art Library, London/New York; **891:** Victoria and Albert Museum, London/Art Resource, NY; **892:** Bridgeman Art Library; **893** (detail), **896–897:** Art Resource, NY; **900:** Mary Evans Picture Library; **904–905, 908:** © Erich Lessing/Art Resource, NY; **912:** The Art Archive; **913** (bottom): Bridgeman Art Library, London/New York; **914:** Photo by Derrick E. Witty; **915:** © Pablo Corral Vega/CORBIS; **917:** © Getty Images; **918:** © Fine Art Photographic Library, London/Art Resource, NY; **921:** Sotheby's Transparency Library, London; **922–923:** © Tate Gallery, London/Art Resource, NY; **923** (top): © Getty Images; **924:** Mary Evans Picture Library; **926:** © Karl Weatherly/CORBIS; **927:** © Getty Images; **932:** © Bernard-Pierre Wolf/Magnum Photos; **935:** © Lindsay Hebberd/Woodfin Camp & Associates; **949** (bottom): © Getty Images; **951, 954–955:** © Scala/Art Resource, NY; **964** (detail): AKG London; **965:** Sovfoto/Eastfoto; **969:** © Scala/Art Resource, NY; **981:** The Bridgeman Art Library; **983:** Bridgeman Art Library; **985:** Bridgeman Art Library; **989:** Bridgeman Art Library; **990:** Tate Gallery, London/Art Resource, NY; **992:** Tate Gallery, London/Art Resource, NY; **993:** © Clive Druett; Papilio/CORBIS; **995:** Bridgeman Art Library; **996:** Bridgeman Art Library; **999:** Victoria and Albert Museum, London/Art Resource, NY; **1001:** (top left) Cover from *Selected Short Stories* by Guy de Maupassant. Cover art: *After the Bath* by Edgar Degas (1834–1917). Pastel on cardboard. Photo: Jean Schormans. Musée d'Orsay, Paris, France. © Réunion des Musées Nationaux/Art Resource, NY; (top right) Reprinted with permission of Simon & Schuster from *What Jane Austen Ate and Charles Dickens Knew: From Fox Hunting to Whist—The Facts of Daily Life in 19th-Century England* by Daniel Pool. Copyright © 1993 by Daniel Pool; (bottom left) *The Importance of Being Earnest* by Oscar Wilde. Cover © HRW, photo by Scott Van Osdol; (bottom right) Cover from *Hard Times* by Charles Dickens. Cover art: *The Fight Interrupted,* 1815-1816, by William Mulready (1786–1863). © Victoria & Albert Museum, London/Art Resource, NY; **1017:** © Michael Hart/Getty Images; **1018:** (bottom left) Bridgeman Art Library, London/New York; (center right) © Bettmann/CORBIS; **1019:** (top) © Erich Lessing/Art Resource, NY; (center left) © Max Nauta/Bettmann/CORBIS; (center right) The Kobal Collection/United Artists; (bottom) NASA; **1020:** (bottom left) Bridgeman Art Library; (right) © Topham/The Image Works; **1021:** (bottom right) Bridgeman Art Library; (top) © Marilyn Silverstone/Magnum Photos, Inc.; **1023:** Tate Gallery, London/Art Resource, NY; **1024:** (left) © Bettmann/CORBIS; (right) Culver Pictures, Inc.; **1025:** Herscovici/Art Resources, NY; **1026:** (left) © Getty Images; (right) The Kobal Collection/Universal; **1027:** Digital Image © The Museum of Modern Art/Licensed by SCALA/Art Resource, NY; **1028:** © Bettmann/CORBIS; **1029:** Bridgeman Art Library; **1030:** © Bill Pierce/TimePix; **1031:** (bottom) Manu Sassoonian/Art Resource, NY; (top) Tate Gallery, London/Art Resource. © Bridget Riley; **1032:** © Margaret Courtney-Clark/CORBIS; **1033** (top): © Hans Georg Roth/CORBIS; **1034:** AP/Wide World Photos; **1035:** (left) © Charlie Cole/SIPA Press; (right) © Paul Velasco; Gallo Images/CORBIS; **1036:** (bottom) © Tate Gallery/Art Resource, NY; (top) © Bettmann/CORBIS; **1038:** © Getty Images; **1040:** Bridgeman Art Library, London/New York; **1041:** © Getty Images; **1044–1045:** Digital Image © The Museum of Modern Art/Licensed by SCALA/Art Resource, NY; **1050:** © Getty Images; **1051:** (bottom) Courtesy of Touchstone Book, Published by Simon & Schuster. Cover painting *Just,* oil on canvas by Mindy Weisel, 1989; (top) © Jerry Bauer; **1053:** (bottom) © Ira Nowinski/CORBIS; (top) Private Collection/Bridgeman Art

Library; **1058:** © Ralph Morse/TimePix; **1059:** © Mascolo Jean/CORBIS Sygma; **1063:** (bottom right) AP/Wide World Photos; **1066:** AP/Wide World Photos; **1068:** AP/Wide World Photos; **1071:** Kyodo News International Inc.; **1075, 1077:** Sam Dudgeon; **1078:** Detail of *Rain at Yotsuya Mitsuke,* 1930, Takashi Henmi. Courtesy of the Trustees of the British Museum, London; **1079:** © Bettmann/CORBIS; **1083, 1085:** Bridgeman Art Library, London/New York; **1088:** The Fine Arts Society, London, UK/Bridgeman Art Library; **1093:** © Syndicated Features Ltd/The Image Works; **1094:** © Bruce Paton/Panos Pictures; **1096, 1097:** © CORBIS; **1098–1099:** © Ralph Morse/TimePix; **1103:** © Thomas Haley/SIPA Press; **1104:** AP/Wide World Photos; **1106:** Permission of Angelica Garnett/Sotheby's Transparency Library, London; **1109:** Bridgeman Art Library, London/New York; **1111:** © Getty Images; **1112:** © Hulton-Deutsch Collection/CORBIS; **1115:** Globe Photos, Inc.; **1117:** © Getty Images; **1121:** SIPA Press; **1126:** © Bettmann/CORBIS; **1127:** © Hans Reinhard/Bruce Coleman, Inc.; **1128:** © Juhan Kuus/SIPA Press; **1131:** © Hans Reinhard/Bruce Coleman, Inc.; **1134:** © Michael Nicholson/CORBIS; **1137:** AP/Wide World Photos; **1138:** © Bill Ellzey/National Geographic Image Collection; **1140, 1147:** AP/Wide World Photos; **1155:** © Wyman Ira/CORBIS Sygma; **1156–1157:** © Masa Uemura/Getty Images; **1158:** © Werner Forman Archive/Art Resource, NY; **1164:** © Steve Vidler/Estock Photo; **1169:** © Clive Druett; Papilio/CORBIS; **1170:** © George Lepp/CORBIS; **1170–1171:** © Jon Sparks/CORBIS; **1172:** © Philadelphia Museum of Art/CORBIS; **1179:** Bridgeman Art Library, London/New York; **1181, 1185:** © Bettmann/CORBIS; **1187:** © Derek P. Redfearn/Getty Images; **1188:** (left center) © Anna Palma/CORBIS; (top) AP/Wide World Photos; **1189:** AP/Wide World Photos; **1191:** Private Collection/Bridgeman Art Library; **1192:** (top, center) Private Collection/Bridgeman Art Library; (top right, left) AP/Wide World Photos; **1193:** (top center) © Anna Palma/CORBIS; (top right, left) AP/Wide World Photos; **1195:** AP/Wide World Photos; **1196:** (top center) AP/Wide World Photos; (top left) Private Collection/Bridgeman Art Library, (top right) © Anna Palma/CORBIS; **1197:** (top center) AP/Wide World Photos; (top left) © Anna Palma/CORBIS; (top right) Private Collection/Bridgeman Art Library; **1200:** © Topham Picturepoint/The Image Works; **1202:** © Rheinisches Bildarchiv/Stadt Köln; **1203:** © Rheinisches Bildarchiv/Stadt Köln; **1204:** Bridgeman Art Library, London/New York; **1205:** © Syndicated Features Ltd/The Images Works; **1208:** Bridgeman Art Library, London/New York; **1211:** Sotheby's Transparency Library, London; **1216:** © Bettmann/CORBIS; **1219:** Jane Burton/Bruce Coleman, Inc.; **1220:** © Stephen Dalton/Photo Researchers, Inc.; **1224:** © Nancy Crampton; **1229:** Neil Johnson Photo, Shreveport, LA; **1232:** © Bettmann/CORBIS; **1240:** AP/Wide World Photos; **1241:** © Christie's Images/CORBIS; **1243:** © SIPA Press; **1244:** © Gary John Norman/Panos Pictures; **1246:** © Smith Richard Frank/CORBIS Sygma; **1247:** © Nicholas Devore III/Bruce Coleman, Inc.; **1252:** © Liaison Agency/Getty Images; **1253, 1254:** The Art Archive; **1256:** Bridgeman Art Library, London/New York; **1258:** Bethnal Green Museum, London/Bridgeman Art Library; **1259:** Nadia Mackenzie/National Trust Photographic Library/Bridgeman Art Library; **1262:** Bethnal Green Museum, London/Bridgeman Art Library; **1263:** © Rollie McKenna; **1264:** © Scala/Art Resource, NY; **1268:** © Rheinisches Bildarchiv/Stadt Köln; **1269:** Photo: © Art Resource, NY. © 2003 Banco de Mexico Diego Rivera & Frida Khalo Museums Trust, Av. Cinco de Mayo No. 2, Col. Centro, Del. Cuauhtemoc 06059, Mexico. D.F.; **1271:** Bridgeman Art Library; **1272:** © Hulton Archive/Getty Images; **1274:** The Bridgeman Art Library; **1275:** © Rollie McKenna; **1277:** © Bettmann/CORBIS; **1278:** CNAC/MNAM/Dist. Réunion des Musées Nationaux/Art Resource, NY; **1281:** AP/Wide World Photos; **1282:** © Michael S. Yamashita/CORBIS; **1283:** © Ron Miller/Photonica; **1283:** (background) © Ron Miller/Getty; (inset) © Michael Freeman/CORBIS; **1285:** © Michael Boys/CORBIS; **1288:** © Timothy Greenfield-Sanders/CORBIS OUTLINE; **1290:** © Jon Hicks/Estock Photo; **1295:** Museum purchase, Roscoe and Margaret Oaks Income Fund, Museum Society Auxiliary, Mr. and Mrs. John N. Rosekrans, Jr., Walters H. and Phyllis J. Shorestein Foundation Fund, Mrs. Paul L. Wattis, Bobbie and Mike Wilsey, Mr. and Mrs. Steven McGregor Read, Mr. and Mrs. Gorham B. Knowles, Mrs. Edward T. Harrison, Mrs. Nan Tucker McEvoy, Harry and Ellen Parker in honor of Steven Nash, Katherine Doyle Spann, Mr. and Mrs. William E. Steen, Mr. and Mrs. Leonard E. Kingsley, George Hopper Fitch, Princess Ranieri de San Faustino, Mr. and Mrs. Richard Madden (1994.31); **1298:** © Miriam Berkley; **1299:** © Michael Busselle/CORBIS; **1300, 1303, 1304:** Graham Tim/CORBIS Sygma; **1307:** AP/Wide World Photos; **1310:** © Dean Conger/CORBIS; **1313:** © Peter Turnley/CORBIS; **1316:** © Dermot Tatlow/Panos Pictures; **1318:** © Joseph Sohm; ChromoSohm Inc./CORBIS; **1323:** © David Turnley/CORBIS; **1326:** AP/Wide World Photos; **1329:** Bridgeman Art Library; **1330:** © Michael Busselle/Stone/Getty Images; **1331:** © Craig Aurness/CORBIS; **1332:** Scala/Art Resource, NY; **1335:** PhotoLink/Getty Images; **1339:** © Robert Holmes/CORBIS; **1340:** © Cornell Capa C/Magnum Photos; **1343:** (top left) "Logo & Design" from *Testament of Youth* by Vera Brittain, © 1933 by Vera Brittain. Used by permission of Penguin, a division of Penguin Group (USA), Inc.; (top right) *Brave New World* by Aldous Huxley. Copyright © 1932, 1946 by Aldous Huxley. Cover design © Marc Cohen. Cover photo © Jeffery Zaruba/Photonica; (bottom left) *One Hundred Years of Solitude* by Gabriel Garcia Márquez. Cover design © 1998 by Marc Cohen. Cover painting © Cathleen Toelke. HarperCollins Publishers; (bottom right) *Things Fall Apart* by Chinua Achebe. Cover, © HRW, art by Earl Keleny; **1362:** © Christie's Images/CORBIS.

Illustrations

Costello, Chris, A7, 215, 216

Sawchuk, Peter, 603, 605, 609, 1166

Maps

Index of Skills

The boldface page numbers indicate an extensive treatment of the topic.

LITERARY SKILLS

VOCABULARY SKILLS

READING SKILLS

WRITING SKILLS

LANGUAGE (GRAMMAR, USAGE, AND MECHANICS) SKILLS

LISTENING AND SPEAKING SKILLS

INDEPENDENT READING

Index of Art

Index of Authors and Titles

Page numbers in italic type refer to the pages on which author biographies appear.